# THE SCHOTTENSTEIN EDITION

ספר

# THE BOOK OF MITZVOS

החינוך

**THE JAN CZUKER FAMILY ELUCIDATION OF THE TORAH'S COMMANDMENTS**

The ArtScroll Series™

Rabbi Nosson Scherman / Rabbi Meir Zlotowitz
General Editors

A PROJECT OF THE

# Mesorah Heritage Foundation

## BOARD OF TRUSTEES

**RABBI DAVID FEINSTEIN**
*Rosh HaYeshivah, Mesivtha Tifereth Jerusalem*

**ABRAHAM BIDERMAN**
*Chairman,*
*Eagle Advisers LLC*

**JOEL L. FLEISHMAN**
*Director, Sam & Ronnie Heyman Center on Ethics,*
*Public Policy, and the Professions, Duke University*

**RABBI NOSSON SCHERMAN**
*General Editor, ArtScroll Series*

**JUDAH I. SEPTIMUS**
*Pres., Atlantic Land Title & Abstract, Ltd.*

**JOSEPH C. SHENKER**
*Chairman, Sullivan & Cromwell*

**JAMES S. TISCH**
*President, Loews Corp.*

**RABBI MEIR ZLOTOWITZ**
*Chairman*

## AUDIT COMMITTEE

**SAMUEL ASTROF**
*CFO, The Jewish Federations of*
*North America*

**JOEL L. FLEISHMAN**
*Director, Sam & Ronnie Heyman Center on Ethics,*
*Public Policy, and the Professions, Duke University*

**JUDAH I. SEPTIMUS**
*Pres., Atlantic Land Title & Abstract, Ltd.*

**JOSEPH C. SHENKER**
*Chairman, Sullivan & Cromwell*

**JAMES S. TISCH**
*President, Loews Corp.*

## INTERNATIONAL BOARD OF GOVERNORS

**JAY SCHOTTENSTEIN** *(Columbus, OH)*
*Chairman*

| | |
|---|---|
| STEVEN ADELSBERG | ANDREW J. NEFF |
| HOWARD BALTER | BARRY M. RAY *(Chicago)* |
| MOSHE BEINHORN | ZVI RYZMAN *(Los Angeles)* |
| RABBI RAPHAEL B. BUTLER | A. GEORGE SAKS |
| EDWARD MENDEL CZUKER *(Los Angeles)* | JOSEPH A. SCHOTTENSTEIN |
| YOSEF DAVIS *(Chicago)* | JONATHAN R. SCHOTTENSTEIN |
| REUVEN D. DESSLER *(Cleveland)* | JEFFREY A. SCHOTTENSTEIN |
| BENJAMIN C. FISHOFF | FRED SCHULMAN |
| HOWARD TZVI FRIEDMAN *(Baltimore)* | ELLIOT SCHWARTZ |
| YITZCHOK GANGER | AUBREY SHARFMAN *(Los Angeles)* |
| JACOB M.M. GRAFF *(Los Angeles)* | HERBERT E. SEIF *(Englewood, NJ)* |
| HASHI HERZKA | NATHAN B. SILBERMAN |
| JACOB HERZOG *(Toronto)* | SOLI SPIRA *(Jerusalem / Antwerp)* |
| SHIMMIE HORN | A. JOSEPH STERN *(Edison, NJ)* |
| AMIR JAFFA *(Cleveland)* | JACQUES STERN *(Sao Paulo)* |
| LLOYD F. KEILSON | ELLIOT TANNENBAUM |
| LESTER KLAUS | SOL TEICHMAN *(Encino, CA)* |
| MENACHEM KLEIN *(Los Angeles)* | THOMAS J. TISCH |
| MOTTY KLEIN | GARY TORGOW *(Detroit)* |
| ELLY KLEINMAN | STANLEY WASSERMAN *(New Rochelle)* |
| IRA A. LIPMAN | JOSEPH H. WEISS |
| EZRA MARCOS *(Geneve)* | STEVEN WEISZ |
| RABBI MEYER H. MAY *(Los Angeles)* | SHLOMO WERDIGER |
| ASHER D. MILSTEIN | LESLIE M. WESTREICH |

# MITZVOS

**THE JAN CZUKER FAMILY ELUCIDATION
OF THE TORAH'S COMMANDMENTS**

VOLUME II
MITZVOS 66-130

The ArtScroll Series®

Published by

*Mesorah Publications, ltd*

# THE SCHOTTENSTEIN EDITION

## ספר החינוך
## THE BOOK OF

TRANSLATED AND ANNOTATED,
WITH HALACHIC AND AGGADIC INSIGHTS

by a team of Torah Scholars
under the General Editorship of
**Rabbi Eliezer Herzka**
**Rabbi Yosaif Asher Weiss**

Originated by
**Rabbi Shmuel Kirzner**

Reviewed and commented on by
**Rabbi Eliyahu Meir Klugman**
**Rabbi Nosson Klugman**
**Rabbi Chaim Zev Malinowitz**
**Rabbi Avrohom Forman**

Newly vowelized Hebrew,
based on the
Machon Yerushalayim text

Project Coordinator
**Rabbi Mordechai Sonnenschein**

Designed by
**Rabbi Sheah Brander**

FIRST EDITION
*First Impression ... September 2012*

*Published and Distributed by*
**MESORAH PUBLICATIONS, Ltd.**
4401 Second Avenue
Brooklyn, New York 11232

*Distributed in Europe by*
**LEHMANNS**
Unit E, Viking Business Park
Rolling Mill Road
Jarrow, Tyne & Wear NE32 3DP
England

*Distributed in Australia & New Zealand by*
**GOLDS WORLD OF JUDAICA**
3-13 William Street
Balaclava, Melbourne 3183
Victoria Australia

*Distributed in Israel by*
**SIFRIATI / A. GITLER — BOOKS**
6 Hayarkon Street
Bnei Brak 51127, Israel

*Distributed in South Africa by*
**KOLLEL BOOKSHOP**
Northfield Centre, 17 Northfield Avenue
Glenhazel 2192, Johannesburg, South Africa

---

ARTSCROLL SERIES® / THE SCHOTTENSTEIN EDITION
**SEFER HACHINUCH / BOOK OF MITZVOS**
VOL. 2 — MITZVOS 66-130

© *Copyright 2012 by* MESORAH PUBLICATIONS, Ltd.
4401 Second Avenue / Brooklyn, N.Y. 11232 / (718) 921-9000 / FAX (718) 680-1875 / www.artscroll.com

---

**ALL RIGHTS RESERVED.** *The texts of the Sefer HaChinuch have been edited, corrected, and newly set;
the English translation and commentary — including introductory material, notes, and insights —
as well as the vowelization, typographic layout and cover artwork, have been written,
designed, edited and/or revised as to content, form and style.
Additionally, new fonts have been designed for the texts and commentaries.
All of the above are fully protected under this international copyright.*

> No part of this volume may be reproduced
> IN ANY FORM — PHOTOCOPY, ELECTRONIC, DIGITAL MEDIA, OR OTHERWISE
> — EVEN FOR PERSONAL, STUDY GROUP, OR CLASSROOM USE —
> without WRITTEN permission from the copyright holder,
> except by a reviewer who wishes to quote brief passages in connection
> with a review written for inclusion in magazines or newspapers.

NOTICE IS HEREBY GIVEN THAT THE PUBLICATION OF THIS WORK
INVOLVED EXTENSIVE RESEARCH AND COSTS,
AND THE RIGHTS OF THE COPYRIGHT HOLDER WILL BE STRICTLY ENFORCED

ISBN 10: 1-4226-1313-5
ISBN 13: 978-1-4226-1313-9

*Typography by CompuScribe at ArtScroll Studios, Ltd.*
*4401 Second Avenue / Brooklyn, N.Y. 11232 / (718) 921-9000*

Printed in the United States of America by Noble Book Press
Bound by Sefercraft, Quality Bookbinders, Ltd. Brooklyn, N.Y.

## Dedication of THIS VOLUME

This volume is dedicated in memory of our parents

ר' מנחם מענדל ב"ר יעקב ז"ל
ומרת מינדל בת ר' אריה ליב ע"ה
**Milton and Minnie Tepper** ז"ל

ר' ראובן ב"ר נחמיה ז"ל
ומרת עטיל בת ר' ישראל נתן נטע ע"ה
**Rubin and Etta Gralla** ז"ל

Their memory is a link to the eternity of the Jewish people.
They were loyal to the mitzvos of the Torah
even in difficult circumstances.
Therefore, we are privileged beyond words
that thousands of our fellow Jews
will achieve knowledge and understanding of the mitzvos,
in their merit, through this volume.

Their dedication to the present and future of Torah life,
their profound gemilus chessed and tzedakah,
and their sensitive concern for others are the road map for us
and our children, grandchildren, and great-grandchildren.

They were magnificent bearers of a great legacy.
Their devotion to family, their sterling character,
and uncompromising integrity made them beloved and respected
by the countless people whose lives they touched.

They fulfilled the mission of Avraham Avinu —
למען אשר יצוה את בניו ואת ביתו אחריו ושמרו דרך ה'
They instructed us and our posterity
to follow the path of Hashem.

תנצב"ה

**David and Joan Tepper
and family**

## Dedication of
## The Jan Czuker Family Elucidation of the Torah's Commandments

The **Jan Czuker Family Elucidation of the Torah's Commandments** in the **Sefer HaChinuch / Book of Mitzvos** is dedicated in loving memory of our beloved father,

**Jan Czuker** ז"ל
ר' יוסף ב"ר מנחם מענדל ז"ל
נפ' פסח שני תש"ע

Our father survived the Holocaust, but his faith and spirit remained intact.
His determination to rebuild not only his own life and family but also those of others made him a generous supporter of many Jewish institutions and individuals in the community.
His good cheer and charisma drew others to him.
He was a loyal friend, always ready to help.
He was a blessing to all who crossed his path.

Torah education, chessed, and ahavas Yisrael were all precious to him. A devoted father and grandfather, in words and deeds he instilled Jewish values in his children and grandchildren.

And in honor of our beloved mother,

**Mrs. Susanne Czuker** שתחי'

She is the quintessential Eishes Chayil. Accomplished in her own right, her steady guidance and encouragement enabled our father to achieve all that he did. The love she has for her children and grandchildren lights up all of our lives.
May Hashem bless her with many years of good health and the nachas of seeing that her offspring live up to her hopes and example.

Together, our parents laid the foundation for us to carry on their Torah values and ideals, and fulfill their dreams.

**Edward Mendel and Elissa Czuker
and Family**

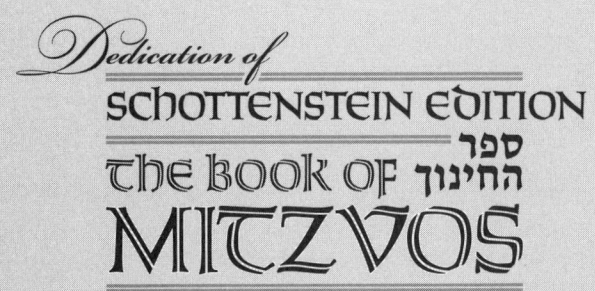

*Dedication of*
## SCHOTTENSTEIN EDITION
## ספר THE BOOK OF החינוך
## MITZVOS

**S**efer HaChinuch / Book of Mitzvos symbolizes the chain of learning and service that unites generations and embraces the entire world. It is fitting, therefore, that we dedicate it to our children and grandchildren,

### Joseph Aaron and Lindsay Brooke
Jacob Meir, Jonah Philip, and Emma Blake
### Jonathan Richard, and Jeffrey Adam

**W**e are proud that our children are forging new links in the chain that we inherited from our parents and grandparents.

We pray that they will continue to grow in their concern for others, loyalty to community, support of Torah education, and allegiance to our eternal tradition.

The Book of Mitzvos was written for the author's own son, so that he would use it as his guide in life, and we dedicate it to our family in the same spirit.

May this classic work be a beacon to them and all those who share our conviction that Torah and its commandments are the cornerstone of our existence.

### Jay and Jeanie Schottenstein

# PATRONS OF THE SEFER HACHINUCH / BOOK OF MITZVOS

With generosity, vision, and devotion to the perpetuation of Torah study,
the following patrons have dedicated individual volumes of The Sefer HaChinuch

## ☙ Yaakov and Chaya Willinger
**Racheli   Malka   Tamar   Adina**

dedicated to the memory of our dear mother

דבורה יהודית בת משה יששכר ע״ה — Dorothy Willinger ע״ה
נפטרה ט׳ ניסן תשס״ח

And יבלח״ט it is dedicated in tribute to our beloved parents שיחיו
Emerich (Yisroel Isser) Willinger עמו״ש
Mrs and Mrs. Binyomin and Toba (Jacobs) Jakubovic עמו״ש

## ☙ David and Joan Tepper and family

dedicated in memory of our parents

ר׳ מנחם מענדל ב״ר יעקב ז״ל — Milton Tepper ז״ל
מינדל בת ר׳ אריה ליב ע״ה — Minnie Tepper ע״ה
ר׳ ראובן ב״ר נחמיה ז״ל — Rubin Gralla ז״ל
עטיל בת ר׳ ישראל נתן נטע ע״ה — Etta Gralla ע״ה

## ☙ Adam and Suri Sokol
**Ari   Yehuda   Akiva   Aaron**

in honor of our parents and grandparents
Mendy and Susan Sokol
Rabbi Mordechai and Edna Besser

and in honor of our grandmothers and great grandmothers
Bernice Scharaga, Tzila Besser and Zena Sales Neuhaus

In loving memory of our grandparents and great grandparents

צבי אריה בן ר׳ יעקב מנחם ז״ל — Harry Sokol ז״ל
רחל בת יצחק ע״ה — Dolly Sokol ע״ה
צבי בן יצחק מאיר הכהן ז״ל — Harry Scharaga ז״ל
עקיבא בן נפתלי ז״ל — Akiva Besser ז״ל
יהודה בן אליעזר ליבר ז״ל — Leon Sales ז״ל

## ☙ Avrum and D'vorah Weinfeld (Chicago)
**Flora   Efriam Mordechai   Ariella   Faige Ita   Shoshana Hinda**

in memory of

הרב שלמה ברוך ב״ר אברהם קדיש ז״ל — Rabbi Shlomie Pomerantz ז״ל
נפטר י׳ שבט תשע״ב

## Mitzvah Associates

A fellowship of benefactors dedicated to
the dissemination of Sefer HaChinuch

❖

Yitzchok Menachem and Gittel Raizel Haas

## In Memoriam — לזכר נשמת

Dedicated by the Mitzvah Associates
to those who forged eternal links

❖

| | |
|---|---|
| חנצא בת מרדכי ע"ה | מרדכי בן משה ז"ל |
| בלימא בת שמואל אליהו ע"ה | שמואל פישל בן אברהם ז"ל |

# Publisher's Preface

**W**e are proud to present this second volume in an unprecedented multi-volume English elucidation of a 700-year-old classic. Sefer HaChinuch has been a staple of Torah scholarship and the subject of many commentaries over the centuries. It is our privilege, therefore, to make it available to the public with all the clarity and accuracy that two generations of readers have come to expect from the exceptional team of scholars who have done so much to bring Torah to our people, through the agency of ArtScroll/Mesorah.

We are gratified that JAY AND JEANIE SCHOTTENSTEIN and their children, JOSEPH AND LINDSAY, JONATHAN, and JEFFREY, have chosen to dedicate this historic project, and to add it to their long list of momentous contributions to Klal Yisrael. The Schottenstein name will go down in history as the family that brought intensive Torah study to tens of thousands of people in ways never before imagined.

To evaluate what the Schottenstein family has accomplished, one need only go back one generation. There was no Schottenstein Edition of the Babylonian Talmud in English or Hebrew; no Schottenstein Interlinear Series of the Siddur, Machzor, liturgy, or Chumash; no Perek Shirah; no Schottenstein Edition of Talmud Yerushalmi in English or Hebrew; no Schottenstein Edition of Sefer HaChinuch/Book of Mitzvos. How much poorer our world would have been without them!

It began with the foresight and generosity of the unforgettable Jerome Schottenstein ע"ה and has been carried on and brought to new heights by Jay and Jeanie. Now, their children have joined in their multiple endeavors, so that one of Jewry's proudest family traditions is being carried into the future by two generations. Our people is fortunate indeed, that, thanks to this family, there is a renaissance of Torah study throughout the world.

The Elucidation of the Torah's Commandments portion of the Chinuch has been dedicated by EDWARD MENDEL AND ELISSA CZUKER of Los Angeles in memory of their beloved father Mr. Jan Czuker ז"ל. Modest people who resist honors, their generosity will be rewarded in the most meaningful way: the increased study and understanding of countless people who will benefit from their vision.

*Sefer HaChinuch has been a staple of Torah scholarship and the subject of many commentaries over the centuries.*

*The Schottenstein name will go down in history as the family that brought intensive Torah study to tens of thousands of people.*

*How much poorer our world would have been without them!*

*Now, their children have joined in their multiple endeavors.*

*Edward Mendel and Elissa Czuker will be rewarded by the increased study and understanding of countless people.*

This volume is dedicated by our dear, personal friends, MR. AND MRS. DAVID TEPPER. The Teppers are unusually gracious and loyal people, who never seek honors. Wherever they lived, Dave and Joan Tepper were always instrumental in strengthening synagogue life and making shuls more hospitable to young people. Many families are strong cogs in today's Torah world thanks to their vision, energy, and generosity.

Written in the thirteenth century, Sefer HaChinuch is a compendium of the 613 commandments. It lists them, explains them, suggests underlying purposes, or "roots," of each commandment, and provides a brief summary of the major laws. This ArtScroll treatment elucidates every phrase of the Chinuch, in the same manner that has been so universally accepted and admired in the Schottenstein Editions of the Talmud Bavli and Yerushalmi, the Kleinman Edition of the Midrash, and the Sapirstein Edition of Rashi. In addition, this treatment includes scores of beautifully presented "Insights," which present scholarly, ethical, and homiletical lessons based on the text. The sum total is truly a masterpiece that will appeal to scholar and layman alike, as they broaden the message of the text. We are confident that the Jewish public will derive great benefit from this project and that it will be a much appreciated and widely used addition to the growing ArtScroll library of Torah classics.

Sefer HaChinuch is a remarkable work, not only for its content, but for the humility of its author. He wrote it anonymously and to this day his exact identity is unknown, although scholars have narrowed it down over the years. The author writes in his introductory letter that the reader should not be deceived into thinking that the work was written by a great scholar with encyclopedic knowledge. To the contrary, he insists he merely assembled the teachings of his great predecessors, and did so only so that his son and other youngsters could make constructive use their free time on the Sabbath. True, the Talmud teaches that although the Torah forbids falsehood, a scholar has a right to avoid praise by denying that he possesses knowledge. Nevertheless, although the author successfully concealed his identity, he fails to convince any reader that he is not a Torah authority of the highest order. His manuscript and the verdict of history prove otherwise.

The concept of this elucidation was introduced to us by Rabbi Shmuel Kirzner, at the suggestion of his father, Rabbi Yisroel Meir Kirzner, a distinguished *talmid chacham* and Rav. R' Shmuel composed the sample draft that became the basis of the final format. He brings credit to his distinguished lineage, and, as a member of the editorial staff of this project, adds luster to the exemplary team of scholars who create the manuscript.

We are grateful to all those who have a part in bringing this project to fruition; they are named below in the Acknowledgments.

There are no adequate words to express our gratitude to Hashem for the enormous privilege of making His Torah accessible to His people for the last thirty-six years. We pray that, with His help and the support of the friends of our work, we can continue to serve Him and Klal Yisrael for many more years.

# ACKNOWLEDGMENTS

We are deeply grateful to those who have been instrumental in creating this volume of the SCHOTTENSTEIN EDITION of the SEFER HACHINUCH/BOOK OF MITZVOS.

HAGAON HARAV DAVID FEINSTEIN שליט״א, the Rosh Yeshivah of Mesivtha Tifereth Jerusalem and one of the world's leading *poskim*, and a Founding Trustee of the Foundation, has been a guide and counselor from the inception of Mesorah Publications thirty-six years ago. He recognized the importance of this project and provided invaluable guidance and counsel.

The General Editors of this project are RABBI ELIEZER HERZKA, Rav of Khal Me'or Chaim, Lakewood, N.J., who also serves as one of the Editorial Directors of the SCHOTTENSTEIN EDITION OF TALMUD YERUSHALMI, and RABBI YOSAIF ASHER WEISS, Rosh Yeshivas Ohr Hadaas, Staten Island, N.Y., who also serves as the General Editor of the KLEINMAN EDITION DAILY DOSE OF TORAH – LIMUD YOMI series. Both have been instrumental in editing many ArtScroll projects, including the SCHOTTENSTEIN EDITION OF TALMUD BAVLI and the KLEINMAN EDITION OF KITZUR SHULCHAN ARUCH.

RABBI SHMUEL KIRZNER introduced the format of this project and authored a large part of this volume. The final product is a credit to his skill.

RABBI MORDECHAI SONNENSCHEIN undertook the difficult task of coordinating the various elements of this project and simultaneously serving as an author and editor, with his hallmark intelligence, competence, and unassuming manner.

RABBI DOVID ARYEH KAUFMAN, a primary editor of the SCHOTTENSTEIN EDITION OF TALMUD BAVLI and YERUSHALMI, as well as the KLEINMAN EDITION OF THE KITZUR SHULCHAN ARUCH, served with distinction as one of the primary editors of this volume. We thank RABBIS YOSEF DAVIS and AVROHOM GREENWALD, contributing editors of the SCHOTTENSTEIN EDITIONS OF TALMUD BAVLI and YERUSHALMI, for their important editorial contributions to this volume.

We are grateful to the outstanding Torah scholars who contributed to the writing of this volume: RABBIS MOSHE ARIEFF, DOVID HOLLANDER, YOSEF KAMENETSKY, AVROHOM YESHAYA MORGENSTERN, GIDON MOSKOVITZ, BERYL SCHIFF, and YISROEL DOV WEISS. We also thank RABBI DORON BECKERMAN for his valuable writing contribution.

We are fortunate to have had the assistance of four distinguished Torah scholars to review this volume: RABBI AVROHOM FORMAN of Jerusalem, Rosh Kollel of Aix-les-Bains; ELIYAHU MEIR KLUGMAN, a Rosh Yeshivah of Yeshiva Neveh Zion and Rav of Beis Midrash L'Torah u'Tefillah, Ramat Eshkol, Jerusalem; RABBI NOSSON KLUGMAN, a noted *talmid chacham* with

wide-ranging Torah knowledge and the gift of painstaking thoroughness; and RABBI CHAIM MALINOWITZ, one of the primary editors of the SCHOTTENSTEIN EDITIONS OF TALMUD BAVLI and YERUSHALMI, and a Rav in Beit Shemesh. They each reviewed and commented upon the manuscript, improving the final product immeasurably with their efforts.

We are very grateful to RABBI MOSHE BUXBAUM of Machon Yerushalayim for graciously permitting us to use their text of Sefer HaChinuch. Our very few variations are explained in the notes.

We thank RABBI MOSHE ROSENBLUM for reviewing and correcting the *nikud* of this volume.

MRS. AHUVA WEISS read the entire volume and provided skilled literary editing, as well as many insightful comments; MRS. CHUMIE LIPSCHITZ paginated the volume with her customary typographic expertise, superbly assisted by MRS. SURY ENGLARD; MRS. ESTIE DICKER, MRS. ESTHER FEIERSTEIN, MRS. TOBY GOLDZWEIG, and MRS. RACHEL GROSSMAN of Jerusalem provided editorial expertise; MRS. MINDY STERN read the manuscript for accuracy with exceptional dedication and made many important suggestions; MRS. JUDI DICK and MRS. FRIMY EISNER assisted in the reading with diligence.

Our dear friend and colleague RABBI SHEAH BRANDER has set the standard for graphics beauty for over thirty years. The clarity of the page design for this work is further testimony to his expertise and vision. ELI KROEN designed the sculpted embossed cover with his customary imagination and good taste.

RABBI GEDALIAH ZLOTOWITZ, a key member of the Artscroll administration, encouraged this project from the start.

The stellar staff members mentioned above, as well as the publishers, are grateful to the people who coordinate the production of, and facilitate the communication between, staff members on two continents. SHMUEL BLITZ, director of our Jerusalem office, is an indispensable colleague who, as per the popular saying, uncomplicates problems; AVROHOM BIDERMAN and MENDY HERZBERG oversee the often complex task of keeping the workflow smooth and efficient.

We are profoundly grateful to all the staff members who enable Artscroll/Mesorah to carry out its mission of maintaining the highest possible standard of quality in bringing Torah classics to the English-speaking public with clarity and accuracy.

We express our appreciation to the Trustees and Governors of the MESORAH HERITAGE FOUNDATION. They are all accomplished, busy men who contribute time and expertise to the cause of Torah literacy.

Finally, we thank Hashem Yisbarach for the indescribable privilege of bringing His word to His people. May He bless all those who take part in this work with good health, and the ability to continue to serve Him.

Rabbi Nosson Scherman / Rabbi Meir Zlotowitz

*Tishrei, 5773 / September, 2012*

# Table of Contents

## General Introduction — xxii

## אִם כֶּסֶף — Im Kesef (Mishpatim II) — 1

66. מִצְוַת הַלְוָאָה לֶעָנִי — The Obligation to Lend Money to the Poor — 3
67. שֶׁלֹּא נִתְבַּע חוֹב מֵעָנִי שֶׁאֵין לוֹ בַּמֶּה לְפָרֵעַ — The Prohibition to Demand Payment of a Debt From a Poor Person Who Does Not Have the Means to Repay — 9
68. שֶׁלֹּא נַשִּׁית יָד בֵּין לֹוֶה לְמַלְוֶה בְּרִבִּית — The Prohibition to Be Involved in an Interest-Based Loan — 13
69. שֶׁלֹּא לְקַלֵּל הַדַּיָּן — The Prohibition to Curse a Judge — 19
70. לָאו דְּבִרְכַּת הַשֵּׁם — The Prohibition of "Blessing" Hashem [Blasphemy] — 27
71. שֶׁלֹּא לְקַלֵּל הַנָּשִׂיא — The Prohibition to Curse the *Nasi* — 35
72. שֶׁלֹּא לְהַקְדִּים חֻקֵּי הַתְּבוּאוֹת — The Prohibition to Give Improper Precedence to the Produce-Obligations — 40
73. שֶׁלֹּא לֶאֱכֹל טְרֵפָה — The Prohibition to Eat *Tereifah* — 47
74. שֶׁלֹּא לִשְׁמֹעַ טַעֲנַת בַּעַל דִּין שֶׁלֹּא בִּפְנֵי בַּעַל דִּינוֹ — The Prohibition [for a Judge] to Listen to One Litigant's Claim When the Other Litigant Is Not Present — 67
75. שֶׁלֹּא יָעִיד בַּעַל עֲבֵרָה — The Prohibition to Allow a Sinner to Testify — 74
76. שֶׁלֹּא לִנְטוֹת אַחֲרֵי רַבִּים בְּדִינֵי נְפָשׁוֹת בִּשְׁבִיל אֶחָד — The Prohibition to Follow a Majority of One in Capital Cases — 82
77. שֶׁלֹּא יְלַמֵּד חוֹבָה מִי שֶׁלִּמֵּד זְכוּת תְּחִלָּה בְּדִינֵי נְפָשׁוֹת — The Prohibition [Upon a Judge] to Argue for Conviction in Capital Cases After Having First Argued for Acquittal — 86
78. מִצְוַת הַטָּיָה אַחֲרֵי רַבִּים — The Obligation to Follow the Majority — 99
79. שֶׁלֹּא לְרַחֵם עַל עָנִי בַּדִּין — The Prohibition [Upon a Judge] to Have Mercy on a Poor Person in Litigation — 108
80. מִצְוַת פְּרוּק מַשָּׂא — The Obligation to Help Remove a Burden [From a Faltering Animal] — 111
81. שֶׁלֹּא לְהַטּוֹת מִשְׁפַּט חוֹטֵא מִפְּנֵי רִשְׁעוֹ — The Prohibition to Bend the Judgment of a Sinner Because of his Wickedness — 118
82. שֶׁלֹּא לַחְתֹּךְ הַדִּין בְּאֹמֶד הַדַּעַת — The Prohibition to Render Judgment Based Upon Assumptions — 121
83. שֶׁלֹּא לִקַּח שֹׁחַד — The Prohibition [Upon a Judge] to Accept Bribery — 129
85. מִצְוַת שְׁבִיתָה בְּשַׁבָּת — The Obligation to Rest on the Sabbath — 151
86. שֶׁלֹּא לְהַשְׁבִּיעַ בַּעֲבוֹדָה זָרָה — The Prohibition to Swear in the Name of an *Avodah Zarah* — 154
87. שֶׁלֹּא לְהַדִּיחַ בְּנֵי יִשְׂרָאֵל אַחַר עֲבוֹדָה זָרָה — The Prohibition to Subvert Jewish People to Idolatry — 160
88. מִצְוַת חֲגִיגָה בָּרְגָלִים — The Obligation to Celebrate the Pilgrimage Festivals — 166
89. שֶׁלֹּא נִשְׁחַט שֶׂה הַפֶּסַח בְּאַרְבָּעָה עָשָׂר בְּנִיסָן בְּעוֹד שֶׁהֶחָמֵץ בִּרְשׁוּתֵנוּ — The Prohibition to Slaughter the *Pesach* Offering on the Fourteenth of Nissan While *Chametz* Is Still in Our Possession — 174

| | | |
|---|---|---|
| 90. | שֶׁלֹּא נַנִּיחַ אֵמוּרֵי הַפֶּסַח לְפָסֵל בְּלִינָה — The Prohibition to Leave the Sacrificial Parts of the *Pesach* Offering Overnight | 180 |
| 91. | מִצְוַת הֲבָאַת בִּכּוּרִים — The Obligation to Bring *Bikkurim* [to the Temple] | 186 |
| 92. | שֶׁלֹּא לְבַשֵּׁל בָּשָׂר בְּחָלָב — The Prohibition to Cook Meat With Milk | 194 |
| 93. | שֶׁלֹּא לִכְרֹת בְּרִית לְשִׁבְעָה עֲמָמִים וְכֵן לְכָל עוֹבֵד עֲבוֹדָה זָרָה — The Prohibition to Seal a Covenant With Any of the Seven Canaanite Nations, or With Any Worshipers of *Avodah Zarah* | 200 |
| 94. | שֶׁלֹּא לְהוֹשִׁיב עוֹבֵד עֲבוֹדָה זָרָה בְּאַרְצֵנוּ — The Prohibition to Settle a Worshiper of *Avodah Zarah* in Our Land | 205 |

## וְיִקְחוּ לִי תְּרוּמָה — Terumah   211

| | | |
|---|---|---|
| 95. | מִצְוַת בִּנְיַן בֵּית הַבְּחִירָה — The Obligation to Build the Holy Temple | 212 |
| 96. | שֶׁלֹּא לְהוֹצִיא בַּדֵּי הָאָרוֹן מִמֶּנּוּ — The Prohibition to Remove the Poles From the Ark of the Covenant | 233 |
| 97. | מִצְוַת סִדּוּר לֶחֶם הַפָּנִים וּלְבוֹנָה — The Obligation to Arrange the *Lechem HaPanim* and the *Levonah* | 237 |

## וְאַתָּה תְּצַוֶּה — Tetzaveh   245

| | | |
|---|---|---|
| 98. | מִצְוַת עֲרִיכַת נֵרוֹת הַמִּקְדָּשׁ — The Obligation to Arrange the Lamps of [the Menorah in] the Temple | 246 |
| 99. | מִצְוַת לְבִישַׁת בִּגְדֵי הַכֹּהֲנִים — The Obligation [for Kohanim] to Don the Priestly Garments | 254 |
| 100. | שֶׁלֹּא יִזַּח הַחֹשֶׁן מֵעַל הָאֵפוֹד — The Prohibition to Detach the *Choshen* From the *Ephod* | 265 |
| 101. | שֶׁלֹּא לִקְרֹעַ הַמְּעִיל שֶׁל כֹּהֲנִים — The Prohibition to Tear the *Me'il* of the Kohen Gadol | 270 |
| 102. | מִצְוַת אֲכִילַת בְּשַׂר חַטָּאת וְאָשָׁם — The Obligation [Upon the Kohanim] to Eat the Meat of the *Chatas* and *Asham* Offerings | 273 |
| 103. | מִצְוַת הַקְטָרַת קְטֹרֶת — The Obligation [Upon the Kohanim] to Offer the Incense | 281 |
| 104. | שֶׁלֹּא לְהַקְטִיר וּלְהַקְרִיב עַל מִזְבַּח הַזָּהָב — The Prohibition to Burn or Offer [Anything but the Incense] on the Golden Altar | 289 |

## כִּי תִשָּׂא — Ki Sisa

| | | |
|---|---|---|
| 105. | מִצְוַת נְתִינַת מַחֲצִית הַשֶּׁקֶל בְּשָׁנָה — The Obligation to Give the Half-*Shekel* Annually | 296 |
| 106. | מִצְוַת קִדּוּשׁ יָדַיִם וְרַגְלַיִם בִּשְׁעַת עֲבוֹדָה — The Obligation [Upon Kohanim] to Sanctify Their Hands and Feet When Serving [in the Temple] | 305 |
| 107. | מִצְוַת מְשִׁיחַת כֹּהֲנִים גְּדוֹלִים וּמְלָכִים בְּשֶׁמֶן הַמִּשְׁחָה — The Obligation of Anointing Kohanim Gedolim and Kings With the Anointment Oil | 314 |
| 108. | שֶׁלֹּא יָסוּךְ זָר בְּשֶׁמֶן הַמִּשְׁחָה — The Prohibition to Anoint an Outsider With the Anointment Oil | 321 |
| 109. | שֶׁלֹּא לַעֲשׂוֹת בְּמַתְכֹּנֶת שֶׁמֶן הַמִּשְׁחָה — The Prohibition to Replicate the Anointment Oil | 328 |
| 110. | שֶׁלֹּא לַעֲשׂוֹת בְּמַתְכֹּנֶת הַקְּטֹרֶת — The Prohibition to Replicate the Incense | 332 |
| 111. | שֶׁלֹּא לֶאֱכֹל וְלִשְׁתּוֹת תִּקְרֹבֶת עֲבוֹדָה זָרָה — The Prohibition to Consume Idolatrous Offerings | 337 |

| | | |
|---|---|---|
| 112. | מִצְוַת שְׁבִיתַת הָאָרֶץ בִּשְׁנַת הַשְּׁמִטָּה — The Obligation to Rest the Land During the *Shemittah* Year | 354 |
| 113. | שֶׁלֹּא לֶאֱכֹל בָּשָׂר בְּחָלָב — The Prohibition to Eat a Mixture of Meat and Milk | 357 |

## ☙ וַיַּקְהֵל — *Vayakhel*

| | | |
|---|---|---|
| 114. | שֶׁלֹּא יַעֲשׂוּ בֵּית דִּין מִשְׁפַּט מָוֶת בְּשַׁבָּת — The Prohibition Upon Beis Din to Carry Out Capital Punishment on the Sabbath | 372 |

## ☙ וַיִּקְרָא — *Vayikra*

| | | |
|---|---|---|
| 115. | מִצְוַת מַעֲשֵׂה הָעוֹלָה — The Obligation Regarding the Process of the *Olah* Offering | 383 |
| 116. | מִצְוַת קָרְבַּן מִנְחָה — The Obligation Regarding the *Minchah* Offering | 390 |
| 117. | שֶׁלֹּא לְהַקְרִיב שְׂאוֹר אוֹ דְּבַשׁ — The Prohibition to Bring Leaven or Honey as an Offering | 401 |
| 118. | שֶׁלֹּא לְהַקְרִיב קָרְבָּן בְּלֹא מֶלַח — The Prohibition to Bring Up an Offering Without Salt | 412 |
| 119. | מִצְוַת מְלִיחַת הַקָּרְבָּן — The Obligation to Salt the Offering | 417 |
| 120. | מִצְוַת קָרְבַּן בֵּית דִּין אִם טָעוּ בְּהוֹרָאָה — The Obligation Upon *Beis Din* to Bring an Offering for an Erroneous Ruling | 422 |
| 121. | מִצְוַת קָרְבַּן חַטָּאת לְיָחִיד בְּמִצְוָה לֹא תַעֲשֶׂה שֶׁחַיָּבִין עָלֶיהָ כָּרֵת — The Obligation Upon an Individual Who Inadvertently Committed a *Kares*-Bearing Prohibition to Bring a *Chatas* Offering | 430 |
| 122. | מִצְוַת עֵדוּת — The Obligation Regarding Testimony | 436 |
| 123. | מִצְוַת קָרְבַּן עוֹלֶה וְיוֹרֵד — The Obligation of the *Oleh V'Yoreid* Offering | 447 |
| 124. | שֶׁלֹּא לְהַבְדִּיל הָרֹאשׁ בְּחַטַּאת הָעוֹף — The Prohibition to Sever the Head of a Bird *Chatas* Offering | 463 |
| 125. | שֶׁלֹּא לִתֵּן שֶׁמֶן זַיִת בְּמִנְחַת חוֹטֵא — The Prohibition to Place Olive Oil Upon a Sinner's *Minchah* Offering | 470 |
| 126. | שֶׁלֹּא לִתֵּן לְבוֹנָה בְּמִנְחַת חוֹטֵא — The Prohibition to Place *Levonah* Upon a Sinner's *Minchah* Offering | 475 |
| 127. | מִצְוַת תּוֹסֶפֶת חֹמֶשׁ לָאוֹכֵל מִן הַהֶקְדֵּשׁ אוֹ מוֹעֵל בּוֹ — The Obligation to Add a Fifth [to the Payment] for [Improper] Consumption of Temple Property or Its Misappropriation | 476 |
| 128. | מִצְוַת קָרְבַּן אָשָׁם תָּלוּי — The Obligation of the Pending-*Asham* Offering | 485 |
| 129. | מִצְוַת קָרְבַּן אָשָׁם וַדַּאי — The Obligation of the Definite-*Asham* Offering | 491 |
| 130. | מִצְוַת הֲשָׁבַת גָּזֵל — The Obligation to Return a Stolen Item | 506 |

# Sefer HaChinuch / The Book of Mitzvos
# General Introduction

Rambam opens his Introduction to *Mishneh Torah,* his classic halachic Code that encompasses the requirements of all the Torah's commandments, by citing the verse (*Psalms* 119:6): אָז לֹא אֵבוֹשׁ בְּהַבִּיטִי אֶל כָּל מִצְוֹתֶיךָ, *Then, I will not be ashamed, when I gaze at all Your commandments.* The implication is clear: It is important for a Jew to be knowledgeable in *all* the commandments that Hashem has given us, not only those that apply to him in his daily life, but even those that he might never have the opportunity to fulfill. Why is this knowledge crucial? One reason is that studying Torah is a mitzvah unto itself (Mitzvah 419), and that mitzvah obligates us to learn and master the Torah in its entirety, both the Written Torah and the Oral Torah, as every detail in each of its commandments is the Word of God (*Smag,* Introduction). But there is another reason.

## I. Studying the 613 Mitzvos

The Sages of the Talmud teach that God dictated 613 commandments to Moses at Sinai, of which 365 are Prohibitions, corresponding to the days of the solar year, and 248 are Obligations, corresponding to the number of parts in the human body (*Makkos* 23b). The commentators explain that each mitzvah is related to a different day of the year or to another one of a person's limbs. When a mitzvah is observed, the corresponding day or limb is spiritually elevated, such that observance of all the 613 mitzvos sanctifies man's entire corporeal existence and every moment of his time (see the Overview for elaboration of this theme).

A review of the 613 mitzvos, however, reveals that no single Jew can possibly fulfill all of them. Some pertain only to Kohanim and others only to non-Kohanim; some specifically to a king and others specifically to commoners. How, then, does any one individual attain the full range of sanctity inherent in the performance of *all* the mitzvos?

Early commentators explain that there are two methods. One way is to encourage and assist others in the performance of the obligations that apply to them, and likewise, to help others overcome any temptation to transgress the prohibitions that apply to them. In this manner, one becomes a partner in the observance of those mitzvos and shares in the credit for their fulfillment. Since each Jew is responsible for his brethren's observance of the Torah (*Sotah* 37b), by facilitating the observance of the mitzvos that he himself cannot physically observe, he becomes, in a very real sense, a participant in the fulfillment of all 613 mitzvos.

This approach, however, does not fully solve the problem. A large number of the 613 mitzvos are applicable only when the *Beis HaMikdash* — the Holy Temple — is standing, but not nowadays. How is one to attain the benefit of comprehensive observance of the Torah's commandments in our times? For this, the second method is necessary: If one studies the Torah and delves into its teachings, and is thereby inspired to accept upon himself to fulfill every mitzvah that he possibly can, then even if he is prevented from performing some of them by circumstances beyond his control, he is considered as though he has actually fulfilled them. As our Sages teach (*Menachos* 109a), based on Scripture, *Anyone who delves into the laws of a chatas* (sin) *offering is considered as though he has brought a chatas offering.* The Talmud goes on to say that the same holds true for the other offerings. Thus, in any situation where one is unable to perform a specific mitzvah, the in-depth study of its laws is comparable to actual performance of that mitzvah. In this manner, one is able to infuse *all* 248 parts of his body and 365 days of the year with the sanctity inherent in the full body of 613 mitzvos contained in the Torah (*Kiryas Sefer,* Introduction, Ch. 7; see also *Smak,* Introduction).

## II. Is the Number 613 Exclusive?

The Vilna Gaon addresses a fundamental question: According to the Sages' teaching that the Torah contains 613 mitzvos, it emerges that many of its passages do not contain any mitzvos. Indeed, the entire Book of *Genesis* contains only three of the 613 mitzvos. Can it be that the remaining passages are merely a collection of historical facts? [Why, the very name "Torah" means *"to teach,"* for תּוֹרָה is from the same root as הוֹרָאָה, *teaching,* and מוֹרֶה, *teacher.*] How can it possibly contain passages that do not include lessons of life? Rather, says the Vilna Gaon, each and every verse in the Torah is a "mitzvah" in that it teaches some moral or halachic lesson, and it behooves us to observe every one of those teachings, for they are all the Word of God. When the Sages state that there are 613 Mitzvos, they mean that this is the number of *categories* into which the laws of the Torah are divided. In reality, each of these categories contains a myriad of details, and the observance of every single detail is a mitzvah unto itself (Vilna Gaon, cited at the beginning of *Sefer Maalos HaTorah*).[1]

To cite but one example, Chinuch counts as Mitzvah 58: The Obligation Upon *Beis Din* to Adjudge Cases of Civil Litigation. In his discussion of this mitzvah, Chinuch lists more than sixty laws, but actually, the guidelines of this mitzvah comprise nearly all of the *Choshen Mishpat* section of *Shulchan Aruch,* encompassing many thousands of individual rulings. Similarly, each of the other mitzvos has many laws, and we are commanded to observe all of them. Thus, the Vilna Gaon explains, an astute and learned person can, if he sets his mind to it, fulfill a mitzvah with his every action and every word, each moment of his life. No number can be assigned to these virtuous deeds and expressions, but they were given to us in distinct categories, and those are the 613 Mitzvos.

## III. Early Works on the 613 Mitzvos

The early authorities of the post-Talmudic era invested considerable effort in identifying which Biblical passages and verses are reckoned as the 613 commandments and which laws are subsumed in those primary categories.[2] From the times of the Geonim, great authorities such

---

NOTES

1. Chinuch expresses a similar thought in his Author's Introduction (see note 114 there).

2. This question is not only a matter of accurate reckoning; the identification of a law as one of the 613 mitzvos

as *Halachos Gedolos, R' Saadiah Gaon,* and *R' Eliyahu HaZaken,* followed by *R' Shlomo ibn Gabirol,* composed lists of the 613 Mitzvos, sometimes in the form of liturgical poems known as *Azharos* (directives).[3]

*Rambam* was the first to publish an entire tome on the subject, which he titled *Sefer HaMitzvos* (Book of the Mitzvos), and which he prefaced with a discussion of fourteen *shorashim* (principles) by which he determines whether a law of the Torah is to be counted among the 613 Mitzvos or not. In this work, *Rambam* disputes the positions of many of the earlier authorities on this subject. In time, the *Sefer HaMitzvos* became accepted as the most authoritative enumeration of the mitzvos. Nearly a century later, *Ramban* wrote Glosses (*Hasagos*) to the *Sefer HaMitzvos,* in which he challenges both the *shorashim* of *Rambam* and his count of the mitzvos, and defends the position of earlier authorities such as *Halachos Gedolos.*[4]

Other Rishonim who authored works on the Mitzvos are the Tosafists, R' Eliezer of Metz (*Sefer Yerei'im*), R' Moshe of Coucy (*Sefer Mitzvos Gadol,* or *Smag*), and R' Yitzchak of Corbeil (*Sefer Mitzvos Katan,* or *Smak*).

## IV. The Sefer HaChinuch

The Sefer HaChinuch was authored some time after *Ramban* published his glosses to *Sefer HaMitzvos,* and is actually based on *Rambam's Sefer HaMitzvos* together with *Ramban's* glosses. [See Section VII below regarding the authorship of Sefer HaChinuch.] At the beginning of his Order and Count of the Mitzvos (below), Chinuch states that he based this work on *Rambam's* reckoning of the 613 Mitzvos. This is not to say that Chinuch always agrees with *Rambam's* count. In his opening Missive to this work, Chinuch notes that he relied also on *Ramban's* glosses to *Sefer HaMitzvos,* which Chinuch does not refer to as "glosses" but as "a highly esteemed book." In cases where *Ramban* disagrees with *Rambam* regarding the listing of a particular mitzvah, Chinuch almost invariably cites *Ramban's* view as well in the course of explaining the mitzvah, often quoting *Ramban* at length. Moreover, there are several instances in which he states explicitly that he prefers *Ramban's* opinion over that of *Rambam* (see, for example, Mitzvos 138 and 153). Nevertheless, as he states in Mitzvah 138, in this work he did not veer from the reckoning of the mitzvos established by *Rambam,* because "he is truly our impetus for this labor, and it is through him that we merited engaging in it."

The Sefer HaChinuch has been, for many centuries since its publication, perhaps the most popular composition on the 613 Mitzvos. While not written primarily as a halachic work, Chinuch's opinion is often cited authoritatively by great halachic authorities who followed him.[5] Moreover, many prominent Acharonim wrote commentaries on Chinuch. Luminaries such as *Mishneh LaMelech* and *R' Yeshayah Pik* wrote Glosses, and in later times, a large number

---

NOTES

has practical ramifications as well. For discussion of these ramifications, see below, Mitzvah 7 with notes 17-19; Introduction to *R' Y. F. Perla's* Commentary to *Sefer HaMitzvos* of *R' Saadiah Gaon*; and Introduction to *Mitzvas HaMelech* Vols. I and III.

3. The *Azharos* are often cited by Rishonim (see *Rashi, Exodus* 24:12; *Tosafos, Yoma* 8a ד"ה דכולי and *Makkos* 3b ד"ה איכא), and numerous commentaries have been written on them. In many communities, it is customary to study some of these *Azharos* on Shavuos or to recite them during the day's *Mussaf* service; some versions of them are therefore included in the *Machzor* for Shavuos.

4. This, in turn, induced a number of later scholars to compose responses in defense of *Rambam's* views. The most well-known of these, and other works on the 613 Mitzvos, are listed below, at the end of this General Introduction.

5. For example, see *Shach, Yoreh Deah* 25:2, 70:33.

of full-length commentaries were authored.[6] Among the most famous works composed on Chinuch is the *Minchas Chinuch,* by R' Yosef Babad of Tarnipol (Lemberg 5629/1869), which is renowned for its thorough halachic analyses.

Chinuch's popularity derives primarily from two features unique among the early works on the mitzvos. The first is that whereas other Rishonim arranged the mitzvos topically, Chinuch arranges them according to the *Parashiyos* (weekly readings) of the Torah, and within each *Parashah,* in the order that the Torah records them.[7] As he states in his Introduction, this was done for the express purpose that the mitzvos be studied in conjunction with the *Parashah* of the week.

The second innovative feature is that, for each mitzvah, Chinuch offers a שׁוֹרֶשׁ, *underlying purpose* (literally, *root*). This is a moral lesson contained in the mitzvah, that may be internalized through observance of the mitzvah. Chinuch declares in his Introduction that these are mere "glimpses," and that he puts them forward only as his own suggestions. Moreover, he stresses that what he writes is in each case only one of *many* purposes of the mitzvah, for no mortal can claim to have fathomed the full purpose of any of God's commandments. In his discussion of Mitzvah 117, Chinuch adds that the underlying purposes he provided are very basic thoughts, intended to give the uneducated "youngsters" for whom he composed this work an appreciation of some of the benefits of mitzvah observance.[8] Nevertheless, the lessons that Chinuch teaches have become the basis of subsequent discussion of the mitzvos and their purposes. The scope, depth, and eloquence of this work belie the author's repeated protestations of inadequacy, and history has given Chinuch a position of prominence among the great works of the Rishonim.

## V. The Format of Sefer HaChinuch

Chinuch's presentation of each mitzvah is generally divided into four or five parts.

1. *Description of the Mitzvah.* Chinuch begins each mitzvah by presenting its Scriptural source, as well as a brief description of what it entails.
2. *Underlying Purpose of the Mitzvah.* As explained above, this is a moral lesson we are supposed to glean from the mitzvah.
3. *Laws of the Mitzvah.* In this section, Chinuch gives the reader a general sense of the main laws of the mitzvah, both Biblical and Rabbinic, including a description of how the mitzvah is fulfilled.[9] Chinuch typically closes this section with a reference to where the mitzvah is discussed in the Talmud.

---

### NOTES

6. The most prominent among these are listed below, at the end of this General Introduction.

7. The author arranged the Obligations and Prohibitions separately within each *Parashah,* first presenting all the Obligations and then all the Prohibitions. This arrangement was preserved in the earliest printed editions of Chinuch. In the 18th century, however, the format was changed, and since then the Chinuch has been printed with the Obligations and Prohibitions intermingled, in the order of their verses in the Torah. Our edition conforms to this format, which by now has become the standard one. For this reason, in instances where Chinuch refers to another mitzvah in his work, his own numbering differs from that of contemporary editions, including ours. In all such instances, we have preserved Chinuch's wording but have added the references appropriate for contemporary editions.

8. See Mitzvah 545, where Chinuch discusses at length the concept of providing logical "reasons" for God's commandments. See also note 119 to the Author's Introduction for further discussion regarding this matter.

9. It should be noted that when citing laws, Chinuch does not focus exclusively on the specific mitzvah he is discussing. Often, he includes laws that are only marginally related to that mitzvah, but actually fall under the province of other, related mitzvos. For example,

4. *Applicability of the Mitzvah.* In this section Chinuch sets forth: (a) at which times the mitzvah applies; (b) in which locations it applies; (c) to which people the mitzvah applies; and (d) what penalty (if any) its violation carries. In order to fully understand this typically terse section of the mitzvah, it is important to clarify some of the background regarding these four factors in the applicability of the mitzvah. This is provided in the following section of this Introduction.

5. *Dispute Regarding the Mitzvah.* In the instances where *Ramban* disagrees with *Rambam* as to whether something should be counted as one of the 613 Mitzvos, Chinuch addresses the dispute, sometimes analyzing each view at length.

## VI. Applicability of the Mitzvos

Mitzvos vary widely in their applicability with respect to time, location, and people, and with respect to the penalties for transgression. The following are some, but not all, of the distinctions:

**Time** Many mitzvos can be performed at any time, but some apply only in the daytime and others only at night. There are mitzvos that are limited to special occasions, such as the Sabbath or Festivals. Additionally, some mitzvos apply constantly, while others become applicable only in specific circumstances (see Author's Introduction with notes 103-106).

Aside from the above, there are some mitzvos that apply only when the *Beis HaMikdash* is standing, and many that apply even nowadays when it is not. With regard to those mitzvos that are not limited to the Temple period, Chinuch writes simply: נוֹהֶגֶת בְּכָל זְמַן, *it applies in all times.*

**Location** Most mitzvos apply everywhere, but many are relevant only in Eretz Yisrael or only in the *Beis HaMikdash*. Among the mitzvos that are specific to Eretz Yisrael, some pertain only when the majority of the Jewish people reside there (see notes 99-100 to the Author's Introduction). When Chinuch describes the mitzvos that apply even outside Eretz Yisrael, he writes simply: נוֹהֶגֶת בְּכָל מָקוֹם, *it applies in every location.*

**People** As Chinuch explains in his Introduction, not all the mitzvos are equally applicable to all people.

(a) Kohanim, Leviim, and Yisraelim: Some mitzvos are incumbent only upon Kohanim, some only upon Leviim, and some only upon Yisraelim (see notes 94-102 ibid.).

(b) Men and Women: Men and women are equally subject to the requirement of observing the Torah's Prohibitions [מִצְוֹת לֹא תַעֲשֶׂה], except for a few that are relevant to only one of the genders.[10] With respect to the Obligations [מִצְוֹת עֲשֵׂה], however, there is a distinction. Men are required to fulfill all the Obligations, while women are generally required to fulfill those Obligations that are not time-specific (e.g., affixing a mezuzah to one's doorpost; Mitzvah 423). For the most part, women are exempt from Obligations that must be fulfilled at specific times [מִצְוֹת עֲשֵׂה שֶׁהַזְמַן גְּרָמָא], though there are

---

NOTES

in Mitzvah 26, which is the first of numerous Prohibitions and Obligations in the Torah pertaining to idolatry, Chinuch lists laws that, strictly speaking, fall under some of those other mitzvos (see note 11 there).

In our elucidation of the Chinuch, we generally present the background for the laws cited by Chinuch and refer the reader to where they are discussed by the halachic authorities. While every effort was made to ensure that all citations are accurate, the reader is cautioned that this elucidation was not written for halachic purposes and should not be relied upon for any halachic application.

10. See, for example, Mitzvos 251-252.

some notable exceptions (e.g., reciting *Kiddush* on the Sabbath [Mitzvah 31], and eating matzah on the first night of Pesach [Mitzvah 10]).[11] Nevertheless, a woman may commit herself to performing time-specific mitzvos, and she is rewarded for fulfilling them.[12]

(c) Individuals: There are mitzvos that are incumbent only upon specific individuals, such as a monarch or the Kohen Gadol (see note 97 to the Author's Introduction).

(d) Community: Some mitzvos apply only to the community as a whole, rather than to each person on his own (see note 98 ibid.).

(e) Noahides: Although most of the mitzvos are limited to Jews, several of the most fundamental commandments are incumbent upon Noahides as well. Chinuch generally points these out (see note 44 ibid.).

**Penalties** The Torah sets various penalties for those who intentionally violate its laws. As Chinuch writes (Mitzvah 594), the Jewish people are God's children, and, in order that they repent and merit the World to Come, He decreed that they be punished for their violations in this world.

For failure to observe an Obligation, the Torah does not specify any particular punishment.[13] For the transgression of a Prohibition, a punishment is usually imposed.

The standard penalty imposed by *beis din* in earlier times for violation of a Prohibition was *malkus* (lashes). This punishment is discussed in Mitzvah 594.[14]

In certain cases involving severe transgressions, the Torah imposes the death penalty. There are four methods of execution and, in each case of a capital offense, *beis din* is commanded to execute the offender, should he be found guilty, with a specific form of execution. These forms are described in Mitzvos 47, 50, 261 and 555.

In order for a *beis din* to impose either *malkus* or capital punishment, it must be composed of judges who have received *semichah* (ordination) according to the procedure Chinuch sets forth in Mitzvah 491. Nowadays, when we lack judges who have been ordained in this manner, no *beis din* can impose these penalties.

Chinuch explains in Mitzvah 82 that neither *malkus* nor capital punishment may be imposed except on the basis of direct eyewitness testimony of two valid witnesses; circumstantial evidence does not suffice. In Mitzvah 32, he explains further that there must be absolute certainty

---

NOTES

11. Rishonim explain that the Torah releases women from having to fulfill most of the time-specific Obligations, because their time is often curtailed by the obligations of tending to their families. [This does not, however, provide license to disregard any of the Obligations that the Torah did impose on women] (see *Abudraham, Seder Tefillos Shel Chol,* p. 25 in Jerusalem, 1963 ed.; *Kol Bo* §73).

12. According to many authorities, a woman may even recite the appropriate blessings for the time-specific mitzvos, including the text אֲשֶׁר קִדְּשָׁנוּ בְּמִצְוֹתָיו וְצִוָּנוּ, *Who has sanctified us with His commandments and has commanded us* ... For discussion of this matter, see *Rama, Orach Chaim* 17:2, with *Mishnah Berurah* §2, and *Shulchan Aruch, Orach Chaim* 589:6 with *Rama*.

13. The exceptions to this rule are the Obligation of circumcision (Mitzvah 2) and the Obligation to bring the *pesach* offering (Mitzvah 5), for whose willful neglect the Torah prescribes the penalty of *kares* (see note 17).

14. There are numerous exceptions to the rule of *malkus*. Some of the categories excluded from *malkus* are:

(1) לָאו שֶׁאֵין בּוֹ מַעֲשֶׂה, *A prohibition that does not involve action,* such as keeping *chametz* in one's possession over Pesach (Mitzvos 11 and 20).

(2) לָאו הַנִּתָּק לַעֲשֵׂה, *A prohibition that can be remedied through [fulfillment of] an obligation,* meaning that the Torah has prescribed an act that rectifies the sin. For example, one who violated the prohibition of taking a mother bird together with its eggs or fledglings (Mitzvah 544) does not incur *malkus,* because he can rectify the sin by fulfilling the mitzvah of sending the mother bird away (Mitzvah 545).

(3) לָאו הַנִּיתָּן לְתַשְׁלוּמִין, *A prohibition that is subject to repayment,* such as the prohibition of stealing (Mitzvah 229), which can be rectified by return of the stolen property (Mitzvah 130).

that the violator sinned deliberately. Thus, in order for *beis din* to punish him, the witnesses must warn him before he commits the crime that what he is about to do is forbidden, they must specify the punishment that it carries, and he must acknowledge the warning and commit the crime nonetheless (see note 38 there).[15]

An additional punishment that was sometimes imposed is the Rabbinic penalty known as מַכַּת מַרְדּוּת, *makkas mardus,* i.e., lashes of discipline.[16] This was a less severe form of punishment than the Biblical lashes of *malkus,* either because less lashes were meted out (*R' Saadiah Gaon,* cited in *Otzar HaGeonim, Nazir* 23a), or because the strap used was less painful (*Ran* to *Kesubos,* fol. 16b in *Rif*).

In some instances, the Torah declares that a transgressor is liable to the Heavenly punishments of מִיתָה בִּידֵי שָׁמַיִם, *death at the hands of Heaven,* or כָּרֵת, *kares* (excision).[17]

The preceding pertains to intentional sinners. There also are instances in which an unintentional transgressor must bring an offering for atonement, when the *Beis HaMikdash* is standing. Chinuch explains regarding each mitzvah which, if any, of these consequences it has.

## VII. Authorship of the Sefer HaChinuch

The authorship of the Sefer HaChinuch is unknown. Wishing to remain anonymous, the author, toward the end of his Introduction (see note 116 there), identifies himself simply as "a Jewish man from the House of Levi of Barcelona." However, a remark in the body of the work itself, near the beginning of Mitzvah 95, was understood by many as alluding that the author's name was Aharon, giving rise to the suggestion that the author was *R' Aharon HaLevi* (*Re'ah*), a disciple of *Ramban.* This suggestion was accepted by major Acharonim, including *Shach* (see *Yoreh Deah* 25:2, 70:33), *Pri Megadim* (Introduction to *Mishbetzos Zahav*), *R' Akiva Eiger* (*Teshuvos,* §129, 169), and *Yad Malachi* (*Kelalei Shaar HaMechaberim VeHamefarshim* §23), among others. However, *Chida,* in his work *Shem HaGedolim* (ע' רבינו אהרן הלוי), points out a number of difficulties with this identification, including numerous contradictions between Chinuch and writings of *Re'ah*. For thorough discussion of this matter, see the essays of R' C. D. Chavel (*Sefer HaChinuch,* Mossad HaRav Kook ed., pp. 797-806), R' M. Leiter (Introduction to *Sefer HaHashlamah* on *Minchas Chinuch*), and R' D. Metzger (Introduction to Machon Yerushalayim ed. of *Minchas Chinuch*). In the final analysis, the author succeeded in concealing his identity, as it remains a mystery until this day.

---

NOTES

15. In capital cases, additional precautions are put in place to prevent the execution of an innocent person. The *beis din* must consist of no fewer than twenty-three judges, who thoroughly cross-examine the witnesses on every detail. The judges are required to make every endeavor to acquit the violator, either by disqualifying the testimony of the witnesses or by otherwise calling his culpability into question. This is discussed in Mitzvah 409. See further, introduction to Mitzvah 47.

As a result of these measures, execution was an extremely rare occurrence. The Mishnah (*Makkos* 7a) states that if a *beis din* imposed the death sentence more than once in seven years (or, according to some Sages, once in seventy years), it was called a "barbaric court."

16. This translation follows *Rav Hai Gaon,* cited in *Otzar HaGeonim, Nazir* 23a, and is based on *Targum Onkelos, Leviticus* 26:18. See also Rashi to *Shabbos* 40b ד״ה מרדות, and *Chullin* 141b ד״ה מכת מרדות, who relates the word מַרְדּוּת to רְדִיי, *dominance. Aruch* v. מרד, however, understands the term מַרְדּוּת as *rebelliousness,* related to מֶרֶד, *rebellion.* These lashes are given as a punishment for the person's rebellion against the law of the Sages. [In certain instances, they are given as punishment for violation of a Biblical law (*Rambam, Hil. Sanhedrin* 18:5).]

17. "Death at the hands of Heaven" means that the sinner dies prematurely. *Kares* (literally, *cutting off* or *excision*) may entail the premature death of the sinner as well as the loss of his future generations (see *Rashi* to *Genesis* 17:14 et al.; see, however, *Tosafos* to *Shabbos* 25a ד״ה כרת, *Ramban* to *Leviticus* 18:29 and in *Shaar HaGemul* ד״ה והכרת). In some instances of *kares,* the soul of the sinner is cut off from the next world, should he fail to repent (*Ramban* ibid.; see, however, *Rambam, Hil. Teshuvah* 8:1, and *Tiferes Yisrael, Sanhedrin* Ch. 9 §53).

At the beginning of this Introduction, it was mentioned that one who learns diligently about a particular mitzvah is considered as though he has fulfilled it. The study of the 248 positive obligations sanctifies each of the corresponding 248 parts of the body, and the study of the 365 prohibitions sanctifies each of the corresponding 365 days of the solar year. It is our hope that through reading, reviewing, and studying this work, we will accrue the merits of all the 613 mitzvos, thus elevating our entire corporeal existence and every moment of our time. In this merit, may we witness the arrival of Mashiach, when the *Beis HaMikdash* will be rebuilt and the Jewish people will return to Eretz Yisrael, making it possible for our people to again observe all the 613 mitzvos in practice.

## ⌒ Works on the 613 Mitzvos ⌒

Aside from Chinuch, a great number of works have been written on the mitzvos, from the days of the Geonim until our time. The following is a list of some of the best-known of these *sefarim*. It includes works written directly on the mitzvos, as well as those written as commentaries to earlier *sefarim*. This list includes numerous works that are cited regularly in the notes or Insights of this edition of Chinuch.

**Halachos Gedolos.** The list of 613 mitzvos presented as an introduction to this work is the earliest known compilation on mitzvos. While it is known that *Halachos Gedolos* was composed in the Geonic era, its precise authorship is a matter of question. *Rambam* (*Sefer HaMitzvos, Shoresh* 10) attributes authorship to *R' Shimon Kaira*, who lived in the 8th century. *Tosafos* (*Succah* 38b ד״ה שמע et al.), however, attribute it to *R' Yehudai Gaon*, of the same era. The author is generally referred to as *Baal Halachos* (author of the *Halachos*), and sometimes by the acronym בה״ג, *Bahag*, i.e., *Baal Halachos Gedolos*.

**Sefer HaMitzvos, R' Saadiah Gaon** (4642-4702/882-942). Born in Egypt, *R' Saadiah* was eventually appointed to head the great Academy of Sura in Babylon. He defended the validity of the Oral Torah from those who challenged it, and, in the words of *Rambam* (*Iggeres Teiman*), "the law of God would almost have become lost without him." He authored his list of the Mitzvos in the form of a poem. He also authored a poem that shows how all the 613 mitzvos are contained in the Ten Commandments.

**Azharos R' Eliyahu HaZakein.** The author, who was a brother-in-law of *R' Hai Gaon*, lived during the latter portion of the 10th century. Little else is known about him, but his *Azharos* were widely incorporated into the Shavuos liturgy and appear in most current *machzorim*, in the *chazzan's* repetition of the *Mussaf* prayer.

**Azharos R' Shlomo ibn Gabirol** (4782-4819/1021-1058). The author of this compilation of the mitzvos lived in the first half of the 11th century. In his work, he adhered to the count of the *Halachos Gedolos*. He composed his work in the form of a poem, and in many communities it was customary to include it in the prayers of the Shavuos festival.

**Sefer Yerei'im, R' Eliezer of Metz (Re'eim)** (circa 4874-4957/1114-1197). Cited by *Tosafos* numerous times, *Sefer Yerei'im* follows the reckoning of *Halachos Gedolos* in his arrangement of the mitzvos. He divided the mitzvos into seven categories, which are further divided into *simanim*, with each *siman* often including more than one mitzvah. Although portions of this *sefer* were published in the 16th century, the *sefer* was not published in its entirety until 5652/1892, when it appeared in print with the commentary **Toafos Re'eim** by *R' Abba Schiff*.

***Sefer HaMitzvos*, Rambam (*R' Moshe ben Maimon*)** (4898-4964/1138-1204). *Rambam* wrote this work in Arabic, as an introduction to his *Mishneh Torah*. The actual enumeration of the mitzvos is preceded by fourteen *shorashim* (principles; sing. *shoresh*), which, *Rambam* asserts, are to be used to determine whether a law of the Torah should be counted among the 613 mitzvos. Based on these *shorashim,* he challenges the count of the earlier authorities, and establishes his own reckoning of the mitzvos of the Torah. This work has become accepted as the most authoritative enumeration of the mitzvos. The *Sefer HaMitzvos* was translated into Hebrew by *R' Moshe ibn Tibbon*, and was first published in 1510. In recent times it was retranslated from the Arabic by *R' Chaim Heller*, who published his latest version in 1946.

Many commentaries have been wrtten to *Rambam's Sefer HaMitzvos*. The most famous of these, which are generally included in contemporary editions of *Sefer HaMitzvos,* are: **Megillas Esther** (*R' Yitzchak Leon*; pub. 1592); **Lev Same'ach** (*R' Avraham Alegri*; pub. 1652); **Kinas Soferim** (*R' Chananyah Kazis*; pub. 1680); **Margenisa Tava** (*R' Aryeh Leib Horowitz*; pub. 1756).

**Hasagos HaRamban — Glosses of Ramban (*R' Moshe ben Nachman*)** (4954-5030/1194-1270). *Ramban* wrote Glosses to *Rambam's Sefer HaMitzvos,* in which he challenged both the *shorashim* and *Rambam's* actual count of the mitzvos. In this way, *Ramban* defended the earlier authorities (primarily *Halachos Gedolos*), whose count *Rambam* had rejected. Although composed in the form of Glosses, *Ramban's* comments are encyclopedic, and Chinuch, in his opening Missive, refers to these Glosses as "a highly esteemed book."

[The Commentary to *Song of Songs* that is attributed to *Ramban* also contains an enumeration of the mitzvos; however, because this enumeration is largely inconsistent with *Ramban's* positions in his Glosses, *Shem HaGedolim* concludes that the attribution to *Ramban* is erroneous.]

***Sefer Mitzvos Gadol* (*Smag*), *R' Moshe of Coucy*** (circa 4960-5020/1200-1260). This work does not merely enumerate the mitzvos, but also cites the halachic conclusions of the Talmud regarding many laws of the mitzvos. Hence, it was widely accepted as a halachic text. For this reason, *Ein Mishpat* (printed in the margin of *Talmud Bavli*), which provides references throughout the Talmud to *Rambam* and *Tur,* also provides references to *Smag*.

A number of commentaries were written to *Smag*. These include, among others: **Beur of *R' Eizik Stein*** (d. 5256/1496); **Dina D'Chayei** (*R' Chaim Benveniste,* author of *Knesses HaGedolah*, 5360-5434/1600-1674); **Megillas Sefer** (*R' Binyamin Kazis,* pub. 5500/1740). In addition, Glosses were written by early authorities including *R' Eliyahu Mizrachi* (5210-5286/1450-1526), *R' Shlomo Luria* (*Maharshal*, 5270-5333/1519-1573), and others.

***Sefer Mitzvos Katan* (*Smak*), *R' Yitzchak of Corbeil*** (circa 4970-5030/1210-1270). This work discusses only mitzvos that apply in our time, and was composed for use by laymen. *Smak* divided the mitzvos into seven categories corresponding to the days of the week, and urged that his work be reviewed on a weekly basis. Although *Smak* includes only limited discussion of the laws of the mitzvos, such that the author advises those seeking a more comprehensive treatment to study *Smag,* the rulings contained in *Smak* are cited frequently by later halachic authorities.

A disciple of the author, *R' Peretz of Corbeil* (author of *Tosefos R' Peretz* to the Talmud), composed a brief commentary to his teacher's work. These Glosses, known as **Hagahos Smak,** are quoted extensively in later halachic literature.

***Zohar HaRakia*, *R' Shimon ben Tzemach Duran* (*Tashbatz*)** (5121-5204/1361-1444). This work is a commentary on the *Azharos* of *R' Shlomo ibn Gabirol*. In it, *Tashbatz* clarifies some of the disagreements between *Rambam* and *Ramban* in their counting of the mitzvos, often defending *Rambam* from *Ramban's* challenges.

***Metzudas David*, R' David ben Zimra (Radvaz)** (5240-5333/1479-1573). In this work, *Radvaz* follows *Rambam's* enumeration, and suggests both simple and Kabbalistic reasons for the mitzvos.

***Sefer Chareidim*, R' Elazar Azkari** (5293-5360/1533-1600). This work discusses only the mitzvos that apply in our time. It is arranged in chapters listing the mitzvos done with different parts of the body. R' Avraham Danzig (author of the *Chayei Adam*) published a condensed version of this work, known as **Kitzur Sefer Chareidim.** *Mishnah Berurah* (156:4) urges the study of works on the mitzvos, and mentions especially *Sefer Chareidim*.

***Sh'nei Luchos HaBris* (Sh'lah), R' Yeshaya HaLevi Horowitz** (5325-5390/1565-1630). *Sh'lah* sets forth some of the Kabbalistic aspects of the mitzvos, and explains how man's character becomes refined through mitzvah observance.

***Poel Tzedek*, R' Shabsai Kohen (Shach)** (5381-5422/1621-1662). This is a concise list of the mitzvos, consisting of the verses from which each mitzvah is derived. *Shach* urged that his work be reviewed on a daily or weekly basis so that the mitzvos not be forgotten.

***Derech Mitzvosecha*, R' Yehudah Rozanis (Mishneh LaMelech)** (5417-5487/1657-1727). This work discusses the discrepancies between the counts of the various earlier authorities, as well as some differences in their interpretations of the mitzvos. The final section of this *sefer* contains Glosses on the Sefer HaChinuch, which are cited often in the notes in this edition.

***Maayan HaChachmah*, R' Noach Chaim Zvi Berlin** (5494-5562/1734-1802). In this fascinating work, the author sets forth the mitzvos in the form of a poem, which is comprised almost entirely of Scriptural verses, and is arranged according to the letters of the *aleph-beis*. Alongside the poem, he discusses the Talmudic background of the mitzvos at length. This work is quoted in many of the later *sefarim* on the mitzvos.

***Minchas Chinuch*, R' Yosef Babad** (5561-5634/1801-1874). While based on the Chinuch, this work quickly acquired independent recognition. It contains stimulating analyses of a broad array of aspects of the laws of the mitzvos, and, since its publication, has become very popular and has evoked widespread study.

***Maharam Schik*, R' Moshe Schik** (5567-5639/1807-1879). The manuscript of this *sefer* was prepared many years prior to its publication. Upon publication of *Minchas Chinuch*, the author recognized that his work would seem redundant if published as it was; he thus subjected it to a thorough review, removing much of the material it originally contained. The final version was published posthumously.

***Commentary to Sefer HaMitzvos of R' Saadiah Gaon*, R' Yerucham Fishel Perla** (5606-5694/1846-1934). This extensive work interprets and develops the concise words of *R' Saadiah Gaon*, and articulates his position regarding which Torah obligations are counted as mitzvos. R' Perla's discussion of each mitzvah has remarkable scope, and testifies to the author's encyclopedic knowledge of the Talmud and its commentaries.

***Me'il HaEphod*, R' Dovid Pipano** (5611-5685/1851-1925). This work, published in Jerusalem in 5758, nearly seventy-five years after its author's passing, is based on the Sefer HaChinuch, and contains discussion regarding the Scriptural sources of the mitzvos and their laws.

***Minchas Yitzchak*, R' Yizchak Aronovski** (Vilna, 1908). This work is written as a commentary to the Sefer HaChinuch and is a valuable aid in studying the Chinuch. It explains difficult passages, provides sources for many of the laws cited by Chinuch, and suggests resolutions for difficulties with Chinuch's positions.

***Imrei David, R' Dovid Schlissel*** (5624-5699/1864-1939). This work consists of two sections: *Imrei David* and *Keser Torah*. *Imrei David* contains analytical discussion of the mitzvos; *Keser Torah* focuses on various practical questions regarding the laws of the mitzvos, and refers the reader to earlier sources related to these discussions.

***Minchah Chadashah, R' Yosef Papersz*** (pub. 5694/1934 and 5698/1938). The author of this work was a grandson of *R' Yosef Babad,* author of the *Minchas Chinuch*, and often discusses topics included in that classic work. The *sefer* addresses mitzvos 1-114.

***Minchas Soless, R' Dovid Zvi Zehman*** (pub. 5694-5699/1934-1939). This analytical work on the laws of the mitzvos and their sources covers the mitzvos from Parashas *Bereishis* until Parashas *Kedoshim* (1-261). It consists of three volumes; the first and second volumes were published by the author, in 5694/1934 and 5697/1937, respectively, and the third volume was printed from manuscript approximately half a century later, by a grandson of the author.

In addition to the above works, Glosses were written to the Chinuch by great Torah scholars, and these are often cited in the notes to the current edition. They include:

***R' Yehudah Rozanis*** in *Derech Mitzvosecha*; see above.

***R' Yeshaya Pik*** (5479-5559/1719-1799). Known for his Glosses to the Talmud, *R' Pik* also wrote Glosses to the Chinuch, first published in the Vienna, 5587/1827, edition of the Chinuch.

***Tzava Rav, R' Zvi Hersh Berlin*** (5481-5560/1721-1800). These Glosses first appeared in part in the Torah journal *Megged Yerachim* (Lemberg, 5617-1857). They were later published in their entirety from a manuscript, in the Machon Yerushalayim edition of *Minchas Chinuch* (Jerusalem, 5748/1988).

ספר החינוך

# THE BOOK OF MITZVOS

# פרשת אם כסף
# Parashas Im Kesef

Chinuch follows the custom of his community, which would divide *Parashas Mishpatim* into two portions and begin a separate *parashah* (weekly portion) with the verse in *Exodus* 22:24: אִם כֶּסֶף תַּלְוֶה אֶת עַמִּי, *When you lend money to My people* (*Im kesef*). This custom, cited in *Orchos Chaim,* by R' Aharon HaKohen of Lunil (*Hil. Krias Sefer Torah* 1:63), is based on the following:

Typically, in a Jewish leap year (when an additional month of Adar is added), there are 28 Sabbaths between Succos and Pesach. However — depending on the day of the week with which the year begins — a leap year may have 29 Sabbaths during that period. In order to maintain consistency with the usual schedule of Torah readings, some communities would divide *Parashas Mishpatim* into two weekly portions. In ordinary years, as well as leap years with 28 weeks between Succos and Pesach, the entire *Parashas Mishpatim* (i.e., both portions) would be read on a single Sabbath. But in those leap years that had an extra Sabbath between Succos and Pesach, the two portions would be read on separate Sabbaths, and the second week's reading would begin with the verse אִם כֶּסֶף תַּלְוֶה אֶת עַמִּי. Hence, Chinuch calls the remainder of *Parashas Mishpatim* (*Exodus* 22:24-24:18) *"Parashas Im Kesef."*

Nowadays, the prevalent custom is as follows: In an ordinary leap year, *Parashas Metzora* is read on the last Sabbath before Pesach (for the reason, see *Beur Halachah* 428:4 ד"ה צו קודם פסח), and *Parashas Acharei Mos* is read after Pesach, but in a leap year with 29 Sabbaths between Succos and Pesach, we read *Parashas Acharei Mos* before Pesach. See *Shulchan Aruch, Orach Chaim* 428:4. See also the additional sources cited in the Machon Yerushalayim ed. of *Minchas Chinuch,* beginning of Mitzvah 66.

---

אִם כֶּסֶף יֵשׁ בָּהּ שֶׁבַע מִצְווֹת עֲשֵׂה
וְעֶשְׂרִים וּשְׁתַּיִם מִצְווֹת לֹא תַעֲשֶׂה

*Parashas Im Kesef* contains seven Mitzvah-Obligations
and twenty-two Mitzvah-Prohibitions.

---

### CONTAINS TWENTY NINE MITZVOS:
### MITZVOS 66-94

66. מִצְוַת הַלְוָאָה לֶעָנִי — **The Obligation to Lend Money to the Poor**
67. שֶׁלֹּא נִתְבַּע חוֹב מֵעָנִי שֶׁאֵין לוֹ בְּמָה לִפְרֹעַ — **The Prohibition to Demand Payment of a Debt From a Poor Person Who Does Not Have the Means to Repay**
68. שֶׁלֹּא נָשִׂית יָד בֵּין לֹוֶה לְמַלְוֶה בְּרִבִּית — **The Prohibition to Be Involved in an Interest-Based Loan**
69. שֶׁלֹּא לְקַלֵּל הַדַּיָּן — **The Prohibition to Curse a Judge**

70. לָאו דְּבִרְכַּת הַשֵּׁם – The Prohibition of "Blessing" Hashem [Blasphemy]
71. שֶׁלֹּא לְקַלֵּל הַנָּשִׂיא – The Prohibition to Curse the *Nasi*
72. שֶׁלֹּא לְהַקְדִּים חֻקֵּי הַתְּבוּאוֹת – The Prohibition to Give Improper Precedence to the Produce-Obligations
73. שֶׁלֹּא לֶאֱכֹל טְרֵפָה – The Prohibition to Eat *Tereifah*
74. שֶׁלֹּא לִשְׁמוֹעַ טַעֲנַת בַּעַל דִּין בִּפְנֵי שֶׁלֹּא בַּעַל דִּינוֹ – The Prohibition [for a Judge] to Listen to One Litigant's Claim When the Other Litigant Is Not Present
75. שֶׁלֹּא יָעִיד בַּעַל עֲבֵרָה – The Prohibition to Allow a Sinner to Testify
76. שֶׁלֹּא לִנְטוֹת אַחֲרֵי רַבִּים בְּדִינֵי נְפָשׁוֹת בִּשְׁבִיל אֶחָד – The Prohibition to Follow a Majority of One in Capital Cases
77. שֶׁלֹּא יְלַמֵּד חוֹבָה מִי שֶׁלִּמֵּד תְּחִלָּה זְכוּת בְּדִינֵי נְפָשׁוֹת – The Prohibition [Upon a Judge] to Argue for Conviction in Capital Cases After Having First Argued for Acquittal
78. מִצְוַת הַטִּיָּה אַחֲרֵי רַבִּים – The Obligation to Follow the Majority
79. שֶׁלֹּא לְרַחֵם עַל עָנִי בַּדִּין – The Prohibition [Upon a Judge] to Have Mercy on a Poor Person in Litigation
80. מִצְוַת פָּרוֹק מַשָּׂא – The Obligation to Help Remove a Burden [From a Faltering Animal]
81. שֶׁלֹּא לְהַטּוֹת מִשְׁפַּט חוֹטֵא מִפְּנֵי רִשְׁעוֹ – The Prohibition to Bend the Judgment of a Sinner Because of his Wickedness
82. שֶׁלֹּא לַחְתּוֹךְ הַדִּין בְּאוֹמֶד הַדַּעַת – The Prohibition to Render Judgment Based Upon Assumptions
83. שֶׁלֹּא לִקַּח שֹׁחַד – The Prohibition [Upon a Judge] to Accept Bribery
85. מִצְוַת שְׁבִיתָה בְּשַׁבָּת – The Obligation to Rest on the Sabbath
86. שֶׁלֹּא לִשָּׁבַע בַּעֲבוֹדָה זָרָה – The Prohibition to Swear in the Name of an *Avodah Zarah*
87. שֶׁלֹּא לְהַדִּיחַ בְּנֵי יִשְׂרָאֵל אַחַר עֲבוֹדָה זָרָה – The Prohibition to Subvert Jewish People to Idolatry
88. מִצְוַת חֲגִיגָה בָּרְגָלִים – The Obligation to Celebrate the Pilgrimage Festivals
89. שֶׁלֹּא נִשְׁחַט שֶׂה הַפֶּסַח בְּאַרְבָּעָה עָשָׂר בְּנִיסָן בְּעוֹד שֶׁהֶחָמֵץ בִּרְשׁוּתֵנוּ – The Prohibition to Slaughter the *Pesach* Offering on the Fourteenth of Nissan While *Chametz* Is Still in Our Possession
90. שֶׁלֹּא נַנִּיחַ אֵמוּרֵי הַפֶּסַח לִפָּסֵל בְּלִינָה – The Prohibition to Leave the Sacrificial Parts of the *Pesach* Offering Overnight
91. מִצְוַת הֲבָאַת בִּכּוּרִים – The Obligation to Bring *Bikkurim* [to the Temple]
92. שֶׁלֹּא לְבַשֵּׁל בָּשָׂר בְּחָלָב – The Prohibition to Cook Meat With Milk
93. שֶׁלֹּא לִכְרוֹת בְּרִית לְשִׁבְעָה עֲמָמִים וְכֵן לְכָל עוֹבֵד עֲבוֹדָה זָרָה – The Prohibition to Seal a Covenant With Any of the Seven Canaanite Nations, or With Any Worshipers of *Avodah Zarah*
94. שֶׁלֹּא לְהוֹשִׁיב עוֹבֵד עֲבוֹדָה זָרָה בְּאַרְצֵנוּ – The Prohibition to Settle a Worshiper of *Avodah Zarah* in Our Land

# MISHPATIM / MITZVAH 66: THE OBLIGATION TO LEND MONEY TO THE POOR

## מִצְוָה סו: מִצְוַת הַלְוָאָה לֶעָנִי

לְהַלְווֹת לֶעָנִי¹, כְּהַשָּׂגַת הַיָּד כְּפִי מַה שֶּׁצָּרִיךְ לוֹ², לְמַעַן הַרְחִיב לוֹ וּלְהָקֵל מֵעָלָיו אַנְחָתוֹ. וְזֹאת הַמִּצְוָה שֶׁל הַלְוָאָה הִיא יוֹתֵר חֲזָקָה וּמְחֻיֶּבֶת מִמִּצְוַת נְתִינַת הַצְּדָקָה³, שֶׁמִּי שֶׁנִּתְגַּלָּה וְנוֹדַע דָּחֳקוֹ בֵּין בְּנֵי אָדָם וְגִלָּה פָּנָיו לִשְׁאֹל מֵהֶן, אֵין דָּחֳקוֹ וַאֲפֵלָתוֹ כְּמִי שֶׁעֲדַיִן לֹא בָא לְאוֹתָהּ בּוּשָׁה וְיָרֵא מֵהִכָּנֵס בָּהּ⁴, וְאִם יִהְיֶה לוֹ מְעַט סַעַד שֶׁל הַלְוָאָה, בַּמֶּה שֶּׁיְּרַוַּח מְעַט⁵ אוּלַי לֹא יִצְטָרֵךְ לָבֹא לִשְׁאֵלָה לְעוֹלָם, וּכְשֶׁיְּרַחֲמֶנּוּ הָאֵל בְּרֶוַח, יְשַׁלֵּם נִשְׁיוֹ וְיִחְיֶה בַּנּוֹתָר.

---

## Mitzvah 66

## The Obligation to Lend Money to the Poor

אִם כֶּסֶף תַּלְוֶה אֶת עַמִּי אֶת הֶעָנִי עִמָּךְ לֹא תִהְיֶה לוֹ כְּנֹשֶׁה לֹא תְשִׂימוּן עָלָיו נֶשֶׁךְ
*When you lend money to My people, to the poor person who is with you, do not act toward him as a creditor; do not lay interest upon him* (Exodus 22:24).

לְהַלְווֹת לֶעָנִי — **We are commanded to lend** money **to a poor person,**[1] כְּהַשָּׂגַת הַיָּד — **to the extent of our means** כְּפִי מַה שֶּׁצָּרִיךְ לוֹ — **and according to [the borrower's] needs,**[2] לְמַעַן הַרְחִיב לוֹ וּלְהָקֵל מֵעָלָיו אַנְחָתוֹ — **in order to afford him relief and alleviate his stress.**

A person is also required to give charity to the poor (see below, Mitzvah 479). Chinuch contrasts the requirement to give charity to a poor person with the requirement of this mitzvah — lending to the needy: וְזֹאת הַמִּצְוָה שֶׁל הַלְוָאָה הִיא יוֹתֵר חֲזָקָה וּמְחֻיֶּבֶת מִמִּצְוַת נְתִינַת — **This mitzvah of extending a loan** הַצְּדָקָה — **is of greater magnitude and obligation than the mitzvah of giving charity.**[3] שֶׁמִּי שֶׁנִּתְגַּלָּה וְנוֹדַע דָּחֳקוֹ בֵּין בְּנֵי אָדָם — **For someone whose** financial **distress has been publicized and has become common knowledge among people,** וְגִלָּה פָּנָיו לִשְׁאֹל מֵהֶן — **and who has** already **faced the embarrassment of requesting** support **from them,** אֵין דָּחֳקוֹ וַאֲפֵלָתוֹ כְּמִי שֶׁעֲדַיִן לֹא בָא לְאוֹתָהּ בּוּשָׁה — **his strain and gloom are not comparable to** those of **someone who has not yet experienced that shame,** וְיָרֵא מֵהִכָּנֵס בָּהּ — **and who is apprehensive about submitting to it.**[4] וְאִם יִהְיֶה לוֹ מְעַט סַעַד שֶׁל הַלְוָאָה — **Now, if [the latter] would have the slight support of a loan,** בַּמֶּה שֶּׁיְּרַוַּח מְעַט אוּלַי לֹא יִצְטָרֵךְ לָבֹא לִשְׁאֵלָה לְעוֹלָם — **perhaps, through the slight easing** of his financial situation,[5] **he will be spared from ever having to beg,** וּכְשֶׁיְּרַחֲמֶנּוּ הָאֵל בְּרֶוַח, יְשַׁלֵּם נִשְׁיוֹ וְיִחְיֶה בַּנּוֹתָר — **and,** it can be anticipated that **when the Almighty will mercifully allow him a profit** from the borrowed funds, **he will** be able to **repay his creditors and earn a livelihood**

---

### NOTES

1. See Insight regarding an obligation to lend to a wealthy person.

2. While the Torah obligates lending to the needy, the amount that one must lend to fulfill the mitzvah is not specified. *Chafetz Chaim* (*Ahavas Chesed* I, 1:4-6,5:5), based on these words of Chinuch, provides the practical parameters of this obligation: One is obligated to lend *to the extent of one's means*, but no more. Even if one has funds at hand, if he needs them for his own business purposes he is not required to lend them to another. Likewise, if one can afford to extend a loan only for a brief term, that is all he is required to do. On the other hand, if he has the means to do so, this mitzvah obligates him to lend "according to [the borrower's] needs."

3. As Chinuch proceeds to explain, extending a loan to someone who has never resorted to begging, but who now needs a loan, often accomplishes more than giving charity to someone who is accustomed to begging. Some understand this to mean that lending money to the former takes priority over giving it away to the latter. For discussion, see *Taz, Choshen Mishpat* §97 ד"ה בטור, מצות עשה להלוות, and *Pischei Choshen, Dinei Halvaah*, Ch. 1 note 2.

4. Thus, if the loan is not extended and as a result the latter must resort to begging, his distress will be far greater than that of the former, who is already accustomed to it.

5. Some editions of Chinuch read בַּמֶּה שֶּׁיַּרְוִיחַ מְעַט, *by making a small profit.*

וְעַל כֵּן הִזְהִירַתְנוּ תּוֹרָתֵנוּ הַשְּׁלֵמָה עַל זֶה לִסְעֹד הַמָּךְ בְּהַלְוָאָה טֶרֶם יִצְטָרֵךְ לָבוֹא אֶל הַשְּׁאֵלָה, שֶׁנֶּאֱמַר (שמות כ״ב, כ״ד) אִם כֶּסֶף תַּלְוֶה אֶת עַמִּי, וְאָמְרוּ זִכְרוֹנָם לִבְרָכָה בַּמְּכִילְתָּא [כָּאן] כָּל אִם וְאִם שֶׁבַּתּוֹרָה רְשׁוּת חוּץ מִשְּׁלֹשָׁה שֶׁהֵם[6] חוֹבָה, וְזֶה אֶחָד מֵהֶם[7], וְיַכְרִיחוּ הַדָּבָר מִדִּכְתִיב בְּמָקוֹם אַחֵר בַּתּוֹרָה דֶּרֶךְ צַוָּאָה וְהַעֲבֵט תַּעֲבִיטֶנּוּ (דברים ט׳, ח׳).

שֹׁרֶשׁ הַמִּצְוָה, שֶׁרָצָה הָאֵל לִהְיוֹת בְּרוּאָיו מְלֻמָּדִים וּמֻרְגָּלִים בְּמִדַּת הַחֶסֶד וְהָרַחֲמִים, כִּי הִיא מִדָּה מְשֻׁבַּחַת, וּמִתּוֹךְ הֶכְשֵׁר גּוּפָם בַּמִּדּוֹת הַטּוֹבוֹת יִהְיוּ רְאוּיִים לְקַבָּלַת הַטּוֹבָה[8], כְּמוֹ שֶׁאָמַרְנוּ שֶׁחָלוֹת הַטּוֹב וְהַבְּרָכָה לְעוֹלָם עַל הַטּוֹב לֹא בְּהִפּוּכוֹ, וּבְהֵיטִיב הַשֵּׁם יִתְבָּרַךְ לַטּוֹבִים, יֻשְׁלַם חֶפְצוֹ, שֶׁחָפֵץ לְהֵיטִיב לָעוֹלָם[9].

---

**from the remainder.** Thus, by extending him a loan, one may spare him the anguish of ever having to submit to begging.

וְעַל כֵּן הִזְהִירַתְנוּ תּוֹרָתֵנוּ הַשְּׁלֵמָה עַל זֶה — **Therefore, our perfect Torah cautions us about this,** טֶרֶם יִצְטָרֵךְ לִסְעֹד הַמָּךְ בְּהַלְוָאָה — **and commands us to sustain a destitute person with a loan** לָבוֹא אֶל הַשְּׁאֵלָה — **before he needs to resort to begging,** שֶׁנֶּאֱמַר — **as it is stated** (Exodus 22:24): ״אִם כֶּסֶף תַּלְוֶה אֶת עַמִּי״ — **When you lend money to My people,** to the poor person who is with you ... וְאָמְרוּ זִכְרוֹנָם לִבְרָכָה בַּמְּכִילְתָּא [כָּאן] — **Although the verse begins with the word** *"im"* which usually mean *if* and thus would seem to indicate that lending money is optional, rather than obligatory, **[our Sages], of blessed memory, have said in** *Mechilta* (to this verse), כָּל אִם וְאִם שֶׁבַּתּוֹרָה רְשׁוּת — **"Each and every** *'im'* **in the Torah means** *if* **and denotes a matter that is optional,** חוּץ מִשְּׁלֹשָׁה שֶׁהֵם חוֹבָה — **except for three, which** mean *when*[6] and **are obligatory,"** וְזֶה אֶחָד מֵהֶם — **and this is one of those** exceptions.[7] וְיַכְרִיחוּ הַדָּבָר מִדִּכְתִיב בְּמָקוֹם אַחֵר בַּתּוֹרָה דֶּרֶךְ צַוָּאָה — **[The Sages] prove this matter** (that the verse is *obligating* one to lend money to the needy) from that which is stated elsewhere in the Torah (Deuteronomy 15:8) **in the form of a command:** ״וְהַעֲבֵט תַּעֲבִיטֶנּוּ״ — *you shall open your hand to him;* **you shall lend him** his requirement, whatever is lacking to him. That verse, which treats lending to the needy as an obligation, serves as an indication that our verse, too, is to be understood as an obligatory statement.

### ~ Underlying Purpose of the Mitzvah ~

שֹׁרֶשׁ הַמִּצְוָה — **The underlying purpose of the mitzvah** is שֶׁרָצָה הָאֵל לִהְיוֹת בְּרוּאָיו מְלֻמָּדִים וּמֻרְגָּלִים בְּמִדַּת הַחֶסֶד וְהָרַחֲמִים — **that the Almighty willed that those whom He created be trained and accustomed in the trait of kindliness and compassion,** כִּי הִיא מִדָּה מְשֻׁבַּחַת — **for it is a laudable trait.** וּמִתּוֹךְ הֶכְשֵׁר גּוּפָם בַּמִּדּוֹת הַטּוֹבוֹת — **Moreover, by conditioning their physical selves with virtuous traits** יִהְיוּ רְאוּיִים לְקַבָּלַת הַטּוֹבָה — **they will become worthy of receiving His goodness,**[8] כְּמוֹ שֶׁאָמַרְנוּ — **as we have stated** (above, Mitzvos 42 and 63) שֶׁחָלוֹת הַטּוֹב וְהַבְּרָכָה לְעוֹלָם עַל הַטּוֹב לֹא בְּהִפּוּכוֹ — **that** Hashem's **goodness and blessing are invariably manifested upon the good, not on the opposite [of good].** וּבְהֵיטִיב הַשֵּׁם יִתְבָּרַךְ לַטּוֹבִים — **This** results in the fulfillment of Hashem's ultimate Will, **for when Hashem, blessed be He, bestows goodness upon those who are** themselves **good,** יֻשְׁלַם חֶפְצוֹ, שֶׁחָפֵץ לְהֵיטִיב לָעוֹלָם — **His desire is fulfilled, for He always desires to bestow goodness** upon His creations.[9]

---

NOTES

6. *Rashi, Exodus* 20:22.

7. For the reason why, in fact, the word אם (which usually means *if*) is used here, when the requirement is actually obligatory, see *Sma, Choshen Mishpat* 97:1 and *Ahavas Chesed, Nesiv HaChesed* I, 1:2; see also *Ibn Ezra, Sforno,* and *Ohr HaChaim* to this verse.

8. By performing good deeds, one's essence is changed for the better, and he is thus fit to serve as a receptacle for Hashem's goodness. This is a recurring theme in Sefer HaChinuch: Only those whose essence is good, and who have thus cultivated in themselves Hashem's Attributes, are suitable to receive His beneficence. This was mentioned in Mitzvos 42 and 63, and will be developed further in Mitzvos 74, 95, and 611, among others.

9. Hashem's ultimate will in Creation is to bestow kindness upon mankind. Since only those who themselves

## 5 ☐ MISHPATIM / MITZVAH 66: THE OBLIGATION TO LEND MONEY TO THE POOR

וְאִם לָאו מִצַּד שֹׁרֶשׁ זֶה, הֲלֹא הוּא בָּרוּךְ הוּא יַסְפִּיק לֶעָנִי דֵּי מַחְסוֹרוֹ זוּלָתֵנוּ, אֶלָּא שֶׁהָיָה מֵחַסְדּוֹ בָּרוּךְ הוּא שֶׁנַּעֲשֵׂינוּ שְׁלוּחִים לוֹ לְזַכּוֹתֵנוּ. וְעוֹד טַעַם אַחֵר בַּדָּבָר, שֶׁרָצָה הָאֵל בָּרוּךְ הוּא לְפַרְנֵס הֶעָנִי עַל יְדֵי בְּנֵי אָדָם מִגֹּדֶל חֶטְאוֹ[10], כְּדֵי שֶׁיְּוֻכַּח בְּמַכְאוֹב בִּשְׁנֵי פָּנִים, בְּקַבָּלַת הַבֹּשֶׁת מֵאֲשֶׁר כְּגִילוֹ וּבְצִמְצוּם מְזוֹנוֹ. וּכְעִנְיָן זֶה שֶׁאָמַרְנוּ כְּדֵי לְזַכּוֹתֵנוּ, הֵשִׁיב חָכָם מֵחֲכָמֵינוּ לְמִין אֶחָד שֶׁשְּׁאָלוֹ, אִם אֱלֹהִים אוֹהֵב עֲנִיִּים שֶׁהֲרֵי צִוָּה עֲלֵיהֶם, לָמָה אֵינוֹ מְפַרְנְסָן וְכוּ׳, כְּמוֹ שֶׁבָּא בַּמַּסֶּכֶת (עבודה זרה) (בבא בתרא דף י׳ ע״א)[11].

---

Chinuch proceeds to prove that this must be the purpose of the mitzvah:

וְאִם לָאו מִצַּד שֹׁרֶשׁ זֶה — **Were it not for this underlying purpose** of having us perform benevolent acts, הֲלֹא הוּא בָּרוּךְ הוּא יַסְפִּיק לֶעָנִי דֵּי מַחְסוֹרוֹ זוּלָתֵנוּ — **then certainly [Hashem], blessed is He, would provide the poor person whatever he is lacking, without us!** אֶלָּא שֶׁהָיָה מֵחַסְדּוֹ בָּרוּךְ הוּא — **Rather,** it is clear that the reason He does not do so is **that it is** an aspect **of His kindness, blessed is He,** שֶׁנַּעֲשֵׂינוּ שְׁלוּחִים לוֹ לְזַכּוֹתֵנוּ — **that** *we* **be delegated as His agents** to support the poor, **to allow us to attain virtue,** as explained above.

Another reason why God may choose to have a poor person supported by others:

וְעוֹד טַעַם אַחֵר בַּדָּבָר — **Sometimes** there may **also** be **another reason for** this **matter,** which is שֶׁרָצָה הָאֵל בָּרוּךְ הוּא לְפַרְנֵס הֶעָנִי עַל יְדֵי בְּנֵי אָדָם מִגֹּדֶל חֶטְאוֹ — **that the Almighty, blessed is He, wishes to sustain the poor person** only through the generosity of other **human beings, due to the severity of his sin,**[10] כְּדֵי שֶׁיְּוֻכַּח בְּמַכְאוֹב בִּשְׁנֵי פָּנִים — **in order that he be chastised by two dimensions of pain:** בְּקַבָּלַת הַבֹּשֶׁת מֵאֲשֶׁר כְּגִילוֹ — **first, by enduring the shame of** dependency on **his peers,** וּבְצִמְצוּם מְזוֹנוֹ — **and** second, **by the limitation of his sustenance.**

Chinuch concludes:

וּכְעִנְיָן זֶה שֶׁאָמַרְנוּ — **Indeed, in accordance with** the first explanation that **we stated** above, כְּדֵי לְזַכּוֹתֵנוּ — that we are granted the opportunity to support the poor **in order to enable us to attain virtue,** הֵשִׁיב חָכָם מֵחֲכָמֵינוּ לְמִין אֶחָד שֶׁשְּׁאָלוֹ — **one of our Sages responded to a heretic, who posed the** following **question to him:** אִם אֱלֹהִים אוֹהֵב עֲנִיִּים שֶׁהֲרֵי צִוָּה עֲלֵיהֶם — **If God loves poor people,** as is evident from the fact **that He has commanded** that acts of charity be performed **on their behalf,** לָמָה אֵינוֹ מְפַרְנְסָן וְכוּ׳ — **why does He not provide for them** Himself?, **etc.,** כְּמוֹ שֶׁבָּא בַּמַּסֶּכֶת — **as is related in Tractate** *Bava Basra* **(10a).**[11]

---

### NOTES

are good are fit to be recipients of the good that God wishes to bestow, He gives people the opportunity to act benevolently and kindly to those in need, so that by acting in this manner, they will merit to benefit fully from His goodness (see further, Mitzvah 95, at notes 17-19).

10. That is, at times, due to one's sins, one may not be deserving of directly receiving his livelihood in an honorable manner. God will therefore arrange that he receive his livelihood through others; see further in Chinuch. [Obviously, Chinuch does not mean that this is the case as a rule, for, throughout the generations, many righteous people were subject to a life of poverty and destitution, having to resort to accepting assistance from others in order to live (see Author's Introduction to Sefer HaChinuch, Vol. I, pp. 17-22). Rather, his intention is that at times this *may* be the reason for the poor person's lack of means.]

This thought is expressed also by *Ohr HaChaim* (*Exodus* 22:24), who notes further that when one sees that he has attained riches beyond what is necessary for his personal needs, he must realize that the purpose of his wealth is for the benefit of those who were not fortunate enough to receive their livelihood directly from God in an honorable manner. He is thus charged with the task of serving as a custodian, whose responsibility is to distribute the funds to the rightful beneficiaries.

11. The Gemara there states that the Roman official, Turanus Rufus, posed this question to R' Akiva. R' Akiva replied that God causes people to be needy in order that, through our performance of charitable deeds, we may be saved from the judgment of Gehinnom. [Elaborating further, *R' Chaim Shmulevitz* (*Sichos Mussar* 5764 ed., §94) explains that this in fact brings great merit to the poor person himself, for it is through him that people are spared from the judgment of Gehinnom.]

דִּינֵי הַמִּצְוָה, כְּגוֹן אֵיזֶה עָנִי קוֹדֵם בְּמִצְוָה זוֹ,[12] וְהָאַזְהָרוֹת הַרְבֵּה שֶׁהִזְהִירוּנוּ זִכְרוֹנָם לִבְרָכָה עָלֶיהָ,[13] שֶׁאָמְרוּ (כתובות דף ס"ח ע"א) שֶׁהָאָדָם מֻרְחָק וְנִמְאָס וְנִתְעָב וְנֶאֱלָח וּמְשֻׁקָּץ עַד שֶׁקָּרוֹב לִהְיוֹת מָאוּס כְּמָאוּס עֲבוֹדָה זָרָה, אִם יֵשׁ לוֹ וּמוֹשֵׁךְ יָדוֹ מִמִּצְוָה זוֹ,[14] וְכַמָּה נֶחְמָד וְנֶאֱהָב וּמְרֻחָם וּמִתְבָּרֵךְ בְּכַמָּה בְּרָכוֹת הַמַּחֲזִיק בָּהּ, הַכֹּל מְבֹאָר בִּמְקוֹמוֹת מִכְּתֻבּוֹת (דף ס"ז ע"א), וּבְבָתְרָא (דף ח' ע"א ואילך), וּבִמְקוֹמוֹת רַבִּים מִן הַתַּלְמוּד.[15]

## ⁓ Laws of the Mitzvah ⁓

דִּינֵי הַמִּצְוָה — **The laws pertaining to this mitzvah** of lending money to the needy include, כְּגוֹן אֵיזֶה עָנִי קוֹדֵם בְּמִצְוָה זוֹ — **for example, which poor person takes precedence with regard to this mitzvah.**[12]

Chinuch discusses matters pertaining to the severity of neglecting to perform this mitzvah:

וְהָאַזְהָרוֹת הַרְבֵּה שֶׁהִזְהִירוּנוּ לִבְרָכָה עָלֶיהָ — **In addition,** there are **the many admonitions with which [the Sages], of blessed memory, have cautioned us regarding** the fulfillment of this mitzvah,[13] including שֶׁאָמְרוּ — **that which [the Sages] have stated** (*Kesubos* 68a) שֶׁהָאָדָם מֻרְחָק וְנִמְאָס וְנִתְעָב וְנֶאֱלָח וּמְשֻׁקָּץ — **that a person is distanced** from God, **repulsive, despicable, depraved, and abominable,** עַד שֶׁקָּרוֹב לִהְיוֹת מָאוּס כְּמָאוּס עֲבוֹדָה זָרָה — **to the extent that his repulsiveness is nearly** as great **as the repulsiveness of idolatry,** אִם יֵשׁ לוֹ וּמוֹשֵׁךְ יָדוֹ מִמִּצְוָה זוֹ — **if one has** the wherewithal to provide assistance to the poor, **yet he draws his hand back from** performing **this mitzvah;**[14] וְכַמָּה נֶחְמָד וְנֶאֱהָב וּמְרֻחָם — **and,** on the other hand, **how cherished, beloved, and subject to** God's mercy, וּמִתְבָּרֵךְ בְּכַמָּה בְּרָכוֹת הַמַּחֲזִיק בָּהּ — **and blessed with a number of blessings, is one who embraces [this mitzvah].**

הַכֹּל מְבֹאָר בִּמְקוֹמוֹת מִכְּתֻבּוֹת וּבְבָתְרָא — These and other laws and admonitions **are all detailed in** various **places in** Tractate ***Kesubos*** (67a-68a) and Tractate *Bava Basra* (8a-11a), וּבִמְקוֹמוֹת רַבִּים מִן הַתַּלְמוּד — **and in numerous places throughout the Talmud.**[15]

---

### NOTES

12. For example, extending loans to members of one's own family and to residents of one's own city takes precedence over lending to others (*Bava Metzia* 71a; see also *Choshen Mishpat* 97:1 and *Ahavas Chesed* I, Ch. 6).

13. The admonitions that will be cited by Chinuch apply to the requirement of lending money to those in need as well as to the general mitzvah of performing acts of charity (see *Minchas Yitzchak*).

14. *Maharsha* (*Chidushei Aggados, Bava Basra* 9a ד"ה שקולה) explains that one who performs acts of charity with his money is assured that Hashem will repay him. A person who refuses to perform acts of charity denies that there is One Who will repay him, putting his faith instead in "idols" of gold and silver [i.e., his wealth]. Along similar lines, R' Elchonon Wasserman (*Kovetz Shiurim, Bava Basra* §51) explains that one who worships idols believes that the idols are capable of effecting good or bad. So too, one who refuses to part with his money believes that his success or failure is dependent upon his money, when, in reality, his money plays no role in his destiny. In fact, at times one who is destined to suffer a financial loss may actually avert the loss by giving money to charity (see *Bava Basra* 9a).

15. The obligation to lend money to the needy is codified in *Rambam, Hil. Malveh VeLoveh* 1:1, 5:7 and *Shulchan Aruch, Choshen Mishpat* 97:1. [See also below, Mitzvah 479, The Obligation of *Tzedakah* (charity).] In addition, *Chafetz Chaim* devotes the first six chapters of his work, *Ahavas Chesed,* to the laws of this mitzvah.

At this point in the discussion of each mitzvah, Chinuch usually addresses the applicability of the mitzvah and the consequences for its transgression; here, however, he does not. The parameters here are the same as those of the mitzvah of *tzedakah* (Mitzvah 479), which applies in Eretz Yisrael and the Diaspora, and whether the *Beis HaMikdash* is standing or not, to both men and women. [With regard to the extent of the obligation of a married woman to extend a loan, see *Ahavas Chesed* I, 2:2, with *Nesiv HaChesed*.] One who neglects to perform the mitzvah when he is capable of fulfilling it has violated a mitzvah-obligation.

# MISHPATIM / MITZVAH 66: THE OBLIGATION TO LEND MONEY TO THE POOR

### ⁗§ Insight: Lending to the Wealthy

From both the title and Chinuch's presentation of this mitzvah, it is evident that the mitzvah to lend money is limited to lending to a poor person, and does not include lending to one who is wealthy and needs funds for business or personal needs (for example, due to a lack of liquidity of his assets). This position is taken also by *Rambam* (*Sefer HaMitzvos*, Asei 197; *Hil. Malveh VeLoveh* 1:1), *Smag* (Asei 93), *Smak* (Asei 197), and others.

*Tur* and *Shulchan Aruch* (see *Choshen Mishpat* 97:1, with *Sma* §1), however, write that there is a mitzvah to lend money even to a wealthy person who is pressed for funds. Similarly, *Rosh* (*Teshuvos HaRosh* 90:11) writes that there is a mitzvah to lend money whenever someone needs funds to purchase merchandise, implying that the mitzvah applies to lending to a wealthy person, as well.

*R' Y. F. Perla* (*Sefer HaMitzvos* of *Rav Saadia Gaon*, Asei 25; Vol. I, p. 329 מ"ה ומד) explains that these two positions are not contradictory. For while Chinuch says that *this* mitzvah specifically requires one to lend money to a poor person, lending money to a wealthy person who is in need *also* constitutes an act of kindness, which one should perform even though not required to do so by our mitzvah. In fact, a careful reading of the words of *Tur* and *Shulchan Aruch* cited earlier would indicate that the "mitzvah" of lending money to a wealthy person who is pressed for funds is not an *actual* mitzvah-obligation. Rather, they use the term "mitzvah" in a broader sense, as a reference to an act that is fitting and proper to be performed, as it is Hashem's will that we should assist, encourage, and advise even a wealthy person who is in need of assistance (see *Tur* and *Shulchan Aruch* there; cf. *Sma* there §1; see also Chinuch below, Mitzvah 479).

*Chafetz Chaim* (see preface to *Ahavas Chesed*, note 9, and *Nesiv HaChesed* I, 6:3) has a similar understanding of this matter, but adds that — in some circumstances — our mitzvah, too, which obligates one to lend money to a poor person, obligates one to lend money to a wealthy person as well. This applies in a situation where the wealthy person is affected by his need for a significant amount of money to the same extent that a poor person is affected by his need for a smaller amount. In such a case, *our* mitzvah, which requires one to lend money to one who is in need, requires one to grant a short-term loan to a wealthy person, just as it requires one to lend money to a poor person. Nevertheless, *this* mitzvah applies only to a wealthy person who is in severe distress. If his needs are not as great, there is no obligation under our mitzvah to extend him a loan — though this is certainly a virtuous act of kindness.

Now, in actuality, the Torah enjoins us to perform acts of kindness and emulate Hashem's ways in all our dealings with others (see Mitzvos 243, 479, and 611; see also *Rambam, Sefer HaMitzvos, Shoresh* §2, and *Hil. Aveil* 14:1). Thus, one who performs acts of kindness would be presumably fulfilling a mitzvah-obligation as well. Nevertheless, performance of an act of kindness that is not specified by the Torah, while it constitutes fulfillment of the general Torah requirement to act with kindness to another person, does not constitute performance of a mitzvah on the level of the mitzvah-obligations that are specified by the Torah (for further explanation, see *Haamek She'eilah, Parashas Mattos* 137:2). Whether performance of granting a loan to a wealthy person is on the level of a mitzvah-obligation or only an act of kindness has a number of practical ramifications, as follows:

The law is that a pledge to perform a mitzvah creates an obligation on the level of an oath (*Nedarim* 8a, with *Ran*; *Shulchan Aruch, Yoreh Deah* 213:2). Thus, if one pledges to lend money to a poor person, he is required to fulfill his pledge. One who pledges to lend an *item* to a poor person (for temporary use by the poor person), however, is not bound by his pledge, and — while it may be improper to do so — he may legally renege on the agreement before the borrower actually takes the item (see *Bava Metzia* 99a). This is because this specific mitzvah (to lend to a poor person) pertains to money, not items, as stated (*Exodus* 22:24), "When you lend *money* to My people" (*Panim Yafos* to the verse; see *Minchah Chadashah* §4 and *Ahavas Chesed* I, 1:2-3 for discussion). Although lending an *item* is certainly an act of kindness, since it is not specifically mandated by the Torah, a pledge in its regard is not binding as an oath. It follows that whether a pledge to lend money to a wealthy person is binding or not is dependent upon the question at hand. If the specific mitzvah to lend money encompasses even lending to a wealthy person, the pledge is binding, but if lending money

to a wealthy person is "merely" an act of kindness, it is not binding (see *Ahavas Chesed* I, 1:11, with *Nesiv HaChesed* §18).

Another ramification concerns the general principle that one who is engaged in a mitzvah is exempt from performing another mitzvah [עוֹסֵק בְּמִצְוָה פָּטוּר מִן הַמִּצְוָה] (*Succah* 25a). Based on this principle, one who is engaged in taking care of a lost object is not obligated to give charity to a poor person who requests alms at that moment (*Bava Kamma* 56b; *Bava Metzia* 29a). The same applies to one who is occupied with extending a loan to a poor person. Since he is engaged in a specific mitzvah-obligation, he is exempt from performing another mitzvah. Thus, if the mitzvah to lend encompasses even lending to a wealthy person, one engaged in extending a loan to a wealthy person is exempt from performing another mitzvah at that time. If, however, one who lends money to a wealthy person is fulfilling only the general mitzvah to perform acts of kindness, one engaged in lending money to a wealthy person is not exempt from performing another mitzvah (see *Ahavas Chesed* ibid., *Nesiv HaChesed* §7; see also *Beur Halachah* 72:4 ד"ה אם).

# MISHPATIM / MITZVAH 67: NOT TO DEMAND PAYMENT FROM A POOR PERSON

## 🙠 מִצְוָה סז: שֶׁלֹּא נִתְבַּע חוֹב מֵעָנִי שֶׁאֵין לוֹ בַּמֶּה לִפְרֹעַ 🙠

שֶׁנִּמְנַעְנוּ מִלִּתְבֹּעַ הַחוֹב מִן הַלֹּוֶה בְּעֵת שֶׁנֵּדַע שֶׁאֵינוֹ יָכוֹל לִפְרֹעַ לוֹ חוֹבוֹ לְפִי שֶׁאֵין לוֹ, שֶׁנֶּאֱמַר (שמות כ״ב, כ״ד): לֹא תִהְיֶה לוֹ כְּנֹשֶׁה[1]. וְדַע כִּי זֹאת הַמְּנִיעָה תִּכְלֹל גַּם כֵּן שֶׁלֹּא לְהַלְווֹת בְּרִבִּית לְיִשְׂרָאֵל[2].

מִשָּׁרְשֵׁי הַמִּצְוָה, לִקְנוֹת לָנוּ מִדַּת הַחֶסֶד וְהַחֲנִינָה וְהַחֶמְלָה, וּכְשֶׁיִּהְיוּ קְבוּעוֹת לָנוּ אָז נִהְיֶה רְאוּיִין לְקַבָּלַת הַטּוֹבָה[3] וְיֻשְׁלַם חֵפֶץ הַשֵּׁם יִתְבָּרַךְ בָּנוּ, שֶׁחָפֵץ הַשֵּׁם יִתְבָּרַךְ לְהֵטִיב בָּעוֹלָם הַזֶּה וּבָעוֹלָם הַבָּא[4].

---

## 🙠 Mitzvah 67 🙠
## The Prohibition to Demand Payment of a Debt From a Poor Person Who Does Not Have the Means to Repay

אִם כֶּסֶף תַּלְוֶה אֶת עַמִּי אֶת הֶעָנִי עִמָּךְ לֹא תִהְיֶה לוֹ כְּנֹשֶׁה לֹא תְשִׂימוּן עָלָיו נֶשֶׁךְ
*When you lend money to My people, to the poor person who is with you, do not act toward him as a creditor; do not lay interest upon him (Exodus 22:24).*

**שֶׁנִּמְנַעְנוּ מִלִּתְבֹּעַ הַחוֹב מִן הַלֹּוֶה** — We are enjoined against demanding payment of **a debt from a borrower** **בְּעֵת שֶׁנֵּדַע שֶׁאֵינוֹ יָכוֹל לִפְרֹעַ לוֹ חוֹבוֹ לְפִי שֶׁאֵין לוֹ** — when we know that he is unable to repay his debt because he does not have the means to pay, **שֶׁנֶּאֱמַר** — as it is stated (*Exodus* 22:24): **"לֹא תִהְיֶה לוֹ כְּנֹשֶׁה"** — *do not act toward him as a creditor.*[1] **תִּכְלֹל גַּם כֵּן שֶׁלֹּא לְהַלְווֹת בְּרִבִּית** **וְדַע כִּי זֹאת הַמְּנִיעָה** — Also, be aware that this injunction **לְיִשְׂרָאֵל** — includes not lending at interest to a Jew as well.[2]

### 🙠 Underlying Purpose of the Mitzvah 🙠

**מִשָּׁרְשֵׁי הַמִּצְוָה** — Among the underlying purposes of this mitzvah **לִקְנוֹת לָנוּ מִדַּת הַחֶסֶד וְהַחֲנִינָה וְהַחֶמְלָה** — is so that we should acquire for ourselves the traits of kindness, generosity, and compassion. **וּכְשֶׁיִּהְיוּ קְבוּעוֹת לָנוּ** — When those traits will be ingrained in us, **אָז נִהְיֶה** **רְאוּיִין לְקַבָּלַת הַטּוֹבָה** — we will then be worthy of receiving the goodness of Hashem,[3] **וְיֻשְׁלַם** **חֵפֶץ הַשֵּׁם יִתְבָּרַךְ בָּנוּ** — and the Will of Hashem, blessed be He, will be fulfilled through us, **שֶׁחָפֵץ הַשֵּׁם יִתְבָּרַךְ לְהֵטִיב בָּעוֹלָם הַזֶּה וּבָעוֹלָם הַבָּא** — for Hashem, blessed be He, desires to bestow goodness upon us in this world and in the World to Come.[4]

---

### NOTES

1. The term נֹשֶׁה refers to a demanding creditor, who is insensitive to the debtor's situation and pressures him to pay when he is unable.

2. Lending at interest constitutes a violation of the prohibition of "acting as a creditor," because this practice is typical of aggressive moneylenders, who refuse to extend loans unless the borrower agrees to pay interest. The borrower is thus automatically pressured to pay, due to the constant accrual of interest (see *Maggid Mishneh, Hil. Malveh VeLoveh* 4:2 and *Maharam Schif, Bava Metzia* 75b; *R' Y. F. Perla, Sefer HaMitzvos* of *Rav Saadiah Gaon, Lo Saaseh* 123-124, Vol. 2, p. 301). For further discussion of the various prohibitions pertaining to a loan taken with interest, see Mitzvah 68.

[This explanation is consistent with Chinuch's implication that *lending* at interest is in itself considered *acting as a creditor*. However, it would appear that *Rashi* (*Bava Metzia* 75b ד״ה מלוה עובר בכולן) disagrees, and maintains that one who lends money at interest transgresses the prohibition of acting as a demanding creditor only when he presses the borrower for payment (see *Maharam Schif* ibid. and *Tos. Yom Tov, Bava Metzia* 5:11 ד״ה המלוה). See also *Rambam, Sefer HaMitzvos, Lo Saaseh* 334, and *Ramban* and *Ralbag* (ד״ה התועלת החמישי) to this verse. See further in the Insight.]

3. See Mitzvah 66 note 8.

4. See Mitzvah 66 note 9.

## 10 □ משפטים / מצוה סז: שלא נתבע חוב מעני שאין לו במה לפרע

מִדִּינֵי הַמִּצְוָה, מַה שֶּׁאָמְרוּ זִכְרוֹנָם לִבְרָכָה (בבא מציעא דף ע״ה ע״ב) מִנַּיִן לְנוֹשֶׁה בַּחֲבֵרוֹ מָנֶה[5] וְיוֹדֵעַ שֶׁאֵין לוֹ שֶׁאָסוּר לַעֲבֹר לְפָנָיו, שֶׁנֶּאֱמַר לֹא תִהְיֶה לוֹ כְּנֹשֶׁה[6], וּמַה שֶּׁאָמְרוּ גַם כֵּן בַּמְּכִילְתָּא (כאן), לֹא תִהְיֶה לוֹ כְּנֹשֶׁה, שֶׁלֹּא יֵרָאֶה לוֹ בְּכָל זְמָן[7], וּדְבָרִים אֲחֵרִים הַנֶּאֱמָרִים בָּעִנְיָן הַזֶּה במציעא (שם) וּבִמְקוֹמוֹת בַּתַּלְמוּד[8].

וְנוֹהֶגֶת בִּזְכָרִים וּנְקֵבוֹת, בְּכָל מָקוֹם וּבְכָל זְמָן[9].

וְהָעוֹבֵר עָלֶיהָ וְתָבַע הַלְוָאָתוֹ לַחֲבֵרוֹ[10], וְיוֹדֵעַ שֶׁאֵין לוֹ וְתוֹבְעוֹ כְּדֵי לְצַעֲרוֹ,[11]

---

### ⸙ Laws of the Mitzvah ⸙

**מִדִּינֵי הַמִּצְוָה** — Among the laws of this mitzvah [the Sages], of blessed memory, have stated (Bava Metzia 75b): **מַה שֶּׁאָמְרוּ זִכְרוֹנָם לִבְרָכָה** — is that which **מִנַּיִן לְנוֹשֶׁה בַּחֲבֵרוֹ מָנֶה וְיוֹדֵעַ שֶׁאֵין לוֹ** — From where in Scripture is it known with regard to one who is owed a maneh (i.e., 100 zuz) by his fellow,[5] but knows that [the borrower] does not have the means to pay, **שֶׁאָסוּר לַעֲבֹר לְפָנָיו** — that he is forbidden to pass before him even without demanding payment? **שֶׁנֶּאֱמַר ״לֹא תִהְיֶה לוֹ כְּנֹשֶׁה״** — It is from that which is stated: *Do not act toward him as a creditor*.[6] **וּמַה שֶּׁאָמְרוּ גַם כֵּן בַּמְּכִילְתָּא [כאן]** — These laws also include that which is stated in Mechilta in explanation of this verse: **״לֹא תִהְיֶה לוֹ כְּנֹשֶׁה״** — The words *do not act toward him as a creditor* teach **שֶׁלֹּא יֵרָאֶה לוֹ בְּכָל זְמָן** — that [the lender] may not constantly make himself visible to [the borrower].[7] **וּדְבָרִים אֲחֵרִים הַנֶּאֱמָרִים בָּעִנְיָן הַזֶּה במציעא וּבִמְקוֹמוֹת בַּתַּלְמוּד** — Other matters that are stated regarding this topic can be found in Tractate Bava Metzia (75b) and other places in the Talmud.[8]

### ⸙ Applicability of the Mitzvah ⸙

**וְנוֹהֶגֶת בִּזְכָרִים וּנְקֵבוֹת, בְּכָל מָקוֹם וּבְכָל זְמָן** — This prohibition applies to men and women, in every location and in all times.[9]

**וְהָעוֹבֵר עָלֶיהָ וְתָבַע הַלְוָאָתוֹ לַחֲבֵרוֹ** — One who transgresses [this mitzvah] by demanding payment of his loan from his fellow[10] **וְיוֹדֵעַ שֶׁאֵין לוֹ** — when he knows that [the borrower] lacks the ability to repay, **וְתוֹבְעוֹ כְּדֵי לְצַעֲרוֹ** — yet he demands payment from him nonetheless, in order

---

### NOTES

5. [Literally, *one who is demanding [payment of] a maneh from his fellow*.] This amount is taken as an example; the law applies regardless of the amount of the loan (see *Rambam, Hil, Malveh VeLoveh* 1:3 and *Shulchan Aruch, Choshen Mishpat* 97:2).

6. The verse is being interpreted as saying: *Do not give the appearance as though you are coming to collect that debt*, causing the debtor concern and embarrassment (see *Rashi, Bava Metzia* 75b).

7. Merely seeing one's creditor will cause the debtor embarrassment when he knows that he cannot pay his debt (see *Tur* and *Shulchan Aruch, Choshen Mishpat* 97:2). [Chinuch seems to understand that the previous law, cited from the Gemara, and this law, cited from Mechilta, are addressing two distinct matters. The Gemara teaches that one may not pass in a manner that would cause the debtor to be concerned that the creditor is coming to demand payment. *Mechilta* teaches that even if no impression is given that he is coming to demand payment, he may nevertheless not make himself conspicuous to the borrower in a constant manner, for this too causes the borrower shame (see, however, *Rambam, Hil. Malveh VeLoveh* 1:3).]

8. The laws governing collection of a debt are codified in *Rambam, Hilchos Malveh VeLoveh* (Chs. 1-2), and *Shulchan Aruch, Choshen Mishpat* §97.

9. I.e., in Eretz Yisrael and the Diaspora, and whether the *Beis HaMikdash* is standing or not.

Men and women are equally bound by this mitzvah, in accordance with the general rule pertaining to mitzvah-prohibitions.

10. In actuality, as Chinuch cited earlier, even passing before an indigent borrower without actually demanding payment is prohibited. Nevertheless, as *Lechem Mishneh* (in explanation of *Rambam, Hil. Malveh VeLoveh* 1:2-3) states, although the distress caused to the borrower by the lender's mere presence is forbidden, it is not a violation of the Biblical prohibition. [The Scriptural phrases cited in the passages from *Bava Metzia* and *Mechilta* are thus instances of *asmachta*, a Scriptural phrase that is used as an allusion to a Rabbinic law, but does not constitute the actual interpretation of the verse.]

# 11 ☐ MISHPATIM / MITZVAH 67: NOT TO DEMAND PAYMENT FROM A POOR PERSON

עוֹבֵר עַל לָאו זֶה,[12] וְהוּא כְּעוֹבֵר עַל מִצְוַת מֶלֶךְ[13].

**וְהוּא כְּעוֹבֵר** עוֹבֵר עַל לָאו זֶה — **is in violation of this prohibition.**[12] **to cause him distress,**[11] עַל מִצְוַת מֶלֶךְ — **He is considered as one who transgresses a decree of the King.**[13]

---

## NOTES

11. The implication of the words וְיוֹדֵעַ שֶׁאֵין לוֹ (when he knows that he lacks the ability to repay), which originate from Bava Metzia 75b, is that the prohibition of demanding payment applies only when the lender specifically knows that the borrower does not have the means to repay the loan; if he is unsure of the borrower's financial status, he is permitted to ask for payment. Rambam (Hil. Malveh VeLoveh 1:2-3) and Shulchan Aruch (Choshen Mishpat 97:2) also frame the prohibition in this manner.

Minchas Chinuch, however, raises an issue with the ruling of Shulchan Aruch, for normally one must deal stringently in doubtful cases of Scriptural prohibitions (see below, Mitzvah 246). Thus, if one is unsure whether the borrower is capable of paying, he should seemingly be required to refrain from demanding payment, in order to avoid the possibility of transgressing the Biblical prohibition! Minchas Chinuch therefore suggests that the Torah prohibits demanding payment only when one knows with certainty that the borrower is incapable of paying. The prohibition does not apply at all when the borrower's status is unknown. This is because the lender cannot know whether the borrower possesses concealed assets. Therefore, the Torah does not require a lender to be certain that the borrower is capable of paying before attempting to collect the debt, as such a requirement could stand in the way of collecting any debt.

Others, however, point out that according to Chinuch, Minchas Chinuch's question would not seem to present a difficulty at all. Chinuch states clearly that the prohibition applies only if one demands payment from a indigent borrower in order to distress him. It follows that the lender may certainly request repayment when there is a possibility that the borrower can repay. Even if the borrower is actually unable to repay the loan, no prohibition has been violated, since the lender has no intention of causing the borrower distress, and is approaching the borrower only because he believes that there is a possibility that the borrower has the means to repay (Shevet HaLevi Vol. V, Kuntres HaMitzvos §29; see also Minchah Chadashah and Minchas Soless). [Nevertheless, if one knows that the borrower has no money, it is certainly prohibited — if only on a Rabbinic level — to request payment even if he has no intent to cause him distress. For, as Chinuch has stated earlier, in such a case, it is prohibited for the lender to even pass before the borrower.]

12. See below, Mitzvah 476, where Chinuch writes that according to Ramban, one who demands payment of a debt when the borrower is unable to pay has also transgressed a mitzvah-obligation.

13. That is, malkus (lashes) are not administered for transgressing this prohibition (see next paragraph). Nonetheless, one who violates this prohibition defies his Creator's command and thus subjects himself to Divine retribution (see above, end of Mitzvah 38).

[Malkus, which is the standard penalty for one who transgresses a prohibition, is administered only upon transgression of prohibitions that are performed through action, and does not generally apply to prohibitions that are transgressed through speech alone (see above, Mitzvah 63 and below, Mitzvah 351).]

---

> **⸻§ Insight: Interest-Bearing Loans and Acting as a Creditor**
>
> Chinuch here cites the law that one who extends an interest-based loan, in violation of Mitzvah 343, also violates the current prohibition of acting toward the borrower "as a creditor." [In Mitzvah 68, Chinuch notes that the lender actually violates a total of six prohibitions; they are listed in note 7 there.] The commentators offer various explanations as to the connection between lending at interest and acting as a creditor.
>
> As noted above (see note 2), the implication of Chinuch's words is that one who lends at interest violates the prohibition of acting as a creditor even though he never actually pressures the borrower for repayment (see also Maggid Mishneh, Hilchos Malveh VeLoveh 4:2). Some suggest that this is due to the fact that interest-bearing loans always contain an element of pressure upon the borrower, as the constant accrual of interest itself "presses" the lender to repay the principal. That is, with every passing day he owes more money, and he is therefore pressured to repay the loan. However, he currently lacks the funds to be able to repay the principal [or else he would ostensibly not allow the interest to continue to accrue]; thus, this "pressure" is a violation of the current mitzvah (R' Y. F. Perla to Sefer HaMitzvos of Rav Saadiah Gaon, Lo Saaseh 123-124, Vol. 2, p. 301 ד"ה ומה; Tiferes Yisrael, Bava Metzia 5:11, second explanation; see Zohar HaRakia, Lavin 39).
>
> R' Moshe Feinstein (Igros Moshe, Yoreh Deah III §161.22) offers a different explanation of the

connection between lending at interest and acting as a creditor. As Chinuch notes, the prohibition of acting as a creditor is classically violated when one pressures a poor borrower, who does not have the means to repay the debt. Applying pressure to such a borrower is in violation of the current mitzvah, because his lack of funds puts him in a situation of being unable to make the payment demanded of him. R' Feinstein points out that the same can be said with regard to any situation in which a lender requests payment of the stipulated interest — even in a situation of a rich person who borrowed at interest. This is because paying interest is in itself a violation of multiple Biblical prohibitions (Mitzvos 232 and 572; see Mitzvah 68 note 8), and thus the borrower is actually "unable" (by dint of these Torah precepts) to make such payments — irrespective of his financial status. In this regard, demanding payment of the principal of a non-interest bearing loan from a destitute borrower and demanding payment of interest from even a wealthy borrower are essentially alike, in that, in both cases, the borrower is simply unable to meet the lender's demands. Thus, the very attempt to collect the interest on an interest-bearing loan inevitably involves "acting as a creditor," whether the borrower has the means to make the payment or not.

Others, however, take an entirely different approach to this matter, and explain (unlike Chinuch) that one who lends with interest does not violate the prohibition of acting as a creditor unless he literally presses for repayment (*Rashi, Bava Metzia* 75b ד"ה מלוה עובר בכולן). While interest-bearing loans are thus no different from other loans, as there, too, one violates the prohibition of "acting as a creditor" when he presses the borrower, the Mishnah nevertheless associates this prohibition specifically with one who lends at interest. This is due to the fact that, generally, such lenders are more motivated to press for repayment, since their clientele is usually composed of those of meager means whose desperate financial situation leaves them with little other choice for obtaining funds other than taking an interest-bearing loan. The lender, fearing the loss of his principal, will often apply pressure to these poor borrowers to repay the loan, and thereby violate the current mitzvah (*Tiferes Yisrael* ibid.; see also *Maharam Schif, Bava Metzia* 75b ד"ה גמרא).

# MISHPATIM / MITZVAH 68: NOT TO BE INVOLVED IN AN INTEREST-BASED LOAN

## מִצְוָה סח: שֶׁלֹּא נָשִׂית יָד בֵּין לֹוֶה לְמַלְוֶה בְּרִבִּית

שֶׁלֹּא נִתְעַסֵּק בְּמִלְוַת רִבִּית בֵּין הַלֹּוֶה וְהַמַּלְוֶה, כְּלוֹמַר שֶׁלֹּא נַעֲשֶׂה לָהֶם עֲרֵבוּת[2] וְלֹא נָעִיד אֲלֵיהֶם[3] וְלֹא נִכְתֹּב בֵּינֵיהֶם שְׁטָר שֶׁיֵּשׁ בּוֹ הַזְכָּרַת רִבִּית[4], שֶׁנֶּאֱמַר (שמות כ״ב, כ״ד)

---

## ← Mitzvah 68 →
## The Prohibition to Be Involved in an Interest-Based Loan

אִם כֶּסֶף תַּלְוֶה אֶת עַמִּי אֶת הֶעָנִי עִמָּךְ לֹא תִהְיֶה לוֹ כְּנֹשֶׁה לֹא תְשִׂימוּן עָלָיו נֶשֶׁךְ

*If you lend money to My people, to the poor person who is with you, you shall not act toward him as a creditor; you shall not lay interest upon him* (Exodus 22:24)

In *Leviticus* 25:37 (Mitzvah 343), the Torah prohibits a lender to extend a loan to another Jew at interest. The prohibition in our verse is not specific to the lender. The Midrash (*Shemos Rabbah* 31:6) notes that while the first injunction in the verse, לֹא תִהְיֶה לוֹ כְּנֹשֶׁה, *you shall not act toward him as a creditor,* is written in the singular form, addressing specifically the lender, the next injunction, לֹא תְשִׂימוּן עָלָיו נֶשֶׁךְ, *you shall not lay interest upon him,* is written in the plural form.[1] The injunction against "laying interest" upon the borrower thus applies to *all* who participate in formalizing his obligation to pay interest, including the guarantor of the loan, the witnesses, and the scribe who draws up the loan document. It should be noted that "laying interest" does not refer to *collecting* an interest payment, but to *creating an obligation* to pay interest. Even if the interest is never collected, those who participate in creating the obligation transgress this prohibition.

שֶׁלֹּא נִתְעַסֵּק בְּמִלְוַת רִבִּית בֵּין הַלֹּוֶה וְהַמַּלְוֶה — We are commanded **not to collaborate in** effecting **an interest-based loan between a borrower and a lender.** כְּלוֹמַר שֶׁלֹּא נַעֲשֶׂה לָהֶם עֲרֵבוּת — **That is to say, we may not guarantee** the loan **on their behalf,**[2] וְלֹא נָעִיד אֲלֵיהֶם — **nor may we serve as witnesses for them,**[3] וְלֹא נִכְתֹּב בֵּינֵיהֶם שְׁטָר שֶׁיֵּשׁ בּוֹ הַזְכָּרַת רִבִּית — **nor may we compose a document** of an agreement **between them containing a record of** an obligation to pay **interest.**[4] שֶׁנֶּאֱמַר — Collaborating in any of these ways is prohibited, **as it is stated** (*Exodus* 22:24):

---

### NOTES

1. The phrase לֹא תִהְיֶה is second-person singular (*you* [singular] *shall not act* ...), whereas the phrase לֹא תְשִׂימוּן is second-person plural (*you* [plural] *shall not lay* ...).

2. By making a commitment to pay the principal and interest if the lender is unable to recoup those amounts from the borrower, the guarantor is complicit in the lender's imposition of forbidden interest charges on the borrower (see *Shulchan Aruch HaRav, Hilchos Ribbis* §3). Even if the guarantor is never called upon to make good on his promise, and he never pays anything to the lender or collects anything from the borrower, by merely participating in formalizing an agreement under which the borrower will owe interest the guarantor transgresses the prohibition of "laying an interest obligation" upon the borrower (see Mishnah, *Bava Metzia* 75b, and Gemara there, 62a, with *Rashi* ד״ה אלא לאו; see further, note 15).

3. Since the lender extends credit to the borrower with reliance upon the witnesses, by acting as witnesses in an interest-based loan they participate in laying the interest obligation upon the borrower. [See the Insight for discussion of whether the guarantor and witnesses transgress this prohibition only by affixing their signatures to a loan document, or even by guaranteeing or witnessing an undocumented loan.]

4. Even preparing the loan document that mandates the payment of interest is considered to be a form of "laying" the interest obligation upon the borrower.

[This is actually a matter of dispute in the Mishnah, *Bava Metzia* 75b. The Tanna Kamma does not hold the scribe liable for "laying interest," but the Sages do hold him liable. Chinuch follows *Rambam* (*Hil. Malveh VeLoveh* 4:2), who rules in accordance with the Sages. *Smag* (*Lo Saaseh* 193), as well as *Tur* and *Shulchan Aruch* (*Yoreh Deah* 160:1), omit mention of the scribe, from which some infer that they disagree and exempt the scribe (*Meleches Shlomo* to Mishnah *Bava Metzia* 5:11). See, however, *Shach* 160:1, who asserts that there is no disagreement regarding this matter; see also *Igros*

לֹא תְשִׂימוּן עָלָיו נֶשֶׁךְ, וּבָא הַפֵּרוּשׁ בִּמְצִיעָא (דף ע״ה ע״ב) שֶׁהַלָּאו הַזֶּה נֶאֱמַר עַל הַמִּתְעַסְּקִים בָּעִנְיָן כְּגוֹן עָרֵב וְעֵדִים וְסוֹפֵר.[5] וְשָׁם נֶאֱמַר גַּם כֵּן שֶׁהַמַּלְוֶה נִכְלָל עִמָּהֶם בְּלָאו זֶה[6] מִלְּבַד הַלָּאוִין הָאֲחֵרִים שֶׁמְּיֻחָדִין בּוֹ. וּכְלַל הָעִנְיָן שֶׁאָמַר אַבַּיֵי שָׁם, שֶׁהַמַּלְוֶה עוֹבֵר עַל שִׁשָּׁה לָאוִין,[7]

**וּבָא הַפֵּרוּשׁ בִּמְצִיעָא** — The explanation of this Scriptural phrase, **"לֹא תְשִׂימוּן עָלָיו נֶשֶׁךְ"** — *you shall not lay interest upon him,* **as transmitted** by the Sages in Tractate *Bava Metzia* (75b), is **שֶׁהַלָּאו הַזֶּה נֶאֱמַר עַל הַמִּתְעַסְּקִים בָּעִנְיָן** — that this prohibition refers to those who collaborate in the matter of imposing interest charges upon a borrower, **כְּגוֹן עָרֵב וְעֵדִים וְסוֹפֵר** — such as the guarantor of such a loan, the witnesses to the transaction, and the scribe who draws up the loan document.[5] **וְשָׁם נֶאֱמַר גַּם כֵּן שֶׁהַמַּלְוֶה נִכְלָל עִמָּהֶם בְּלָאו זֶה** — It is also stated there, in *Bava Metzia* (ibid.), that the lender himself is also included in this prohibition,[6] **מִלְּבַד הַלָּאוִין הָאֲחֵרִים שֶׁמְּיֻחָדִין בּוֹ** — in addition to the other prohibitions regarding interest-based loans that are specific to him and are not applicable to the guarantor, witnesses, or scribe. **וּכְלַל הָעִנְיָן שֶׁאָמַר אַבַּיֵי שָׁם** — The summary of the matter, which the Talmudic sage Abaye states there, in *Bava Metzia* (ibid.), is **שֶׁהַמַּלְוֶה עוֹבֵר עַל שִׁשָּׁה לָאוִין** — that the lender who extends a loan at interest transgresses six prohibitions,[7]

---

NOTES

Moshe, *Choshen Mishpat* I §93. For discussion of the circumstances in which the scribe is considered liable, see *Minchah Chadashah*.]

5. As mentioned in the introduction to the mitzvah, this interpretation is based on the fact that the phrase לֹא תְשִׂימוּן עָלָיו נֶשֶׁךְ, *you shall not lay interest upon him*, is written in the second-person *plural*, unlike the earlier phrase in the verse.

It is important to note that this prohibition is distinct from the prohibition of (*Leviticus* 19:14): וְלִפְנֵי עִוֵּר לֹא תִתֵּן מִכְשֹׁל, *you shall not place a stumbling block before the blind,* which forbids causing another person to commit a sin (see Mitzvah 232). *Tosafos* (*Bava Metzia* 75b ד״ה ערב) explain that the prohibition to "place a stumbling block" applies only when the person would not have sinned without the facilitator's help, but the prohibition to "lay interest" applies in all cases. Thus, if a lender would have extended credit without a guarantor or witnesses, one who agrees to guarantee or to witness the loan does not transgress the prohibition of *you shall not place a stumbling block,* since the loan would have taken place even without his involvement. Nevertheless, he transgresses the prohibition of *you shall not lay interest,* since he participates in the "laying" of an interest obligation. If, on the other hand, the lender would have denied credit unless someone agreed to guarantee the loan, or unless there were witnesses, then the guarantor or witnesses in that case will transgress the prohibition of "placing a stumbling block," *in addition* to the prohibition of "laying interest."

*Rambam* (Hil. *Malveh VeLoveh* 4:2) points out another distinction: The prohibition to "place a stumbling block" applies to *anyone* who abets the sinner [by providing critical assistance], including a broker who sets up the interest-based loan, or an adviser who facilitates its implementation. The prohibition against "laying interest," however, applies specifically to those involved in the transaction — i.e., the guarantor, witnesses, and scribe — for although they have only a supportive role, they participate in actually placing the interest obligation upon the borrower. [See *Lechem Mishneh* to *Rambam* ibid., who maintains that *Rambam* and *Tosafos* are in agreement regarding both of the preceding points. See further, *Minchas Chinuch* §1.]

6. For he, too, "lays interest" upon the borrower. [*Chinuch* implies that the borrower (upon whom interest charges are imposed) is not included in this prohibition, although borrowing at interest does involve other violations, as we shall immediately see. There are, however, authorities who suggest that the borrower, too, transgresses the prohibition of "laying interest" by formalizing an interest-based loan. See *Teshuvos Toras Emes* (R' Aharon Sasson, Venice, 5386) §162 ד״ה באופן; *Ketzos HaChoshen* 38:1 ד״ה ועיין בפרק איזהו נשך שמכל; *Tos. R' Akiva Eiger* to Mishnah *Sanhedrin* 3:3.]

7. These prohibitions are:

(1) אֶת כַּסְפְּךָ לֹא תִתֵּן לוֹ בְּנֶשֶׁךְ, *you shall not give him your money for interest* (*Leviticus* 25:37; see Mitzvah 343).

(2) וּבְמַרְבִּית לֹא תִתֵּן אָכְלֶךָ, *and you shall not give your food for increase* (ibid.). [Each of these injunctions applies equally to interest-based loans of cash or food commodities (*Bava Metzia*, 60b-61a; see also Mitzvah 343).]

(3) אַל תִּקַּח מֵאִתּוֹ נֶשֶׁךְ וְתַרְבִּית, *you shall not take from him interest and increase* (ibid., v. 36; see Mitzvah 343).

(4) לֹא תִהְיֶה לוֹ כְּנֹשֶׁה, *you shall not act as a creditor toward him* (*Exodus* 22:24; see Mitzvah 67 with Insight).

(5) לֹא תְשִׂימוּן עָלָיו נֶשֶׁךְ, *you shall not lay interest upon him* (this mitzvah).

(6) וְלִפְנֵי עִוֵּר לֹא תִתֵּן מִכְשֹׁל, *you shall not place a stumbling block before the blind* (*Leviticus* 19:14; see Mitzvah 232). [The lender violates this prohibition by causing the borrower to transgress the prohibition that pertains to *him,* as set forth in the following note.]

*Chinuch's* reference to six injunctions does not mean that all these Scriptural phrases are enumerated

## 15 □ MISHPATIM / MITZVAH 68: NOT TO BE INVOLVED IN AN INTEREST-BASED LOAN

וְהַלּוֶה בִּשְׁנַיִם,⁸ וְהַמִּתְעַסְּקִין בְּאֶחָד.⁹

מִשָּׁרְשֵׁי הַמִּצְוָה, כִּי הָאֵל הַטּוֹב חָפֵץ בְּיִשּׁוּב עַמּוֹ אֲשֶׁר בָּחַר, וְעַל כֵּן צִוָּה לְהָסִיר
מִכְשׁוֹל מִדַּרְכָּם לְבַל יִבְלַע הָאֶחָד חֵיל חֲבֵרוֹ מִבְּלִי שֶׁיַּרְגִּישׁ בְּעַצְמוֹ עַד שֶׁיִּמָּצֵא
בֵּיתוֹ רֵיקָן מִכָּל טוֹב,¹⁰ כִּי כֵן דַּרְכּוֹ שֶׁל רִבִּית, יָדוּעַ הַדָּבָר, וּמִפְּנֵי זֶה נִקְרָא נֶשֶׁךְ.¹¹

---

וְהַלּוֶה בִּשְׁנַיִם – the borrower **transgresses two** prohibitions,[8] וְהַמִּתְעַסְּקִין בְּאֶחָד – **and those who collaborate** in imposing interest charges transgress this **one** prohibition.[9]

### ⌒ Underlying Purpose of the Mitzvah ⌒

Chinuch prefaces his discussion of the purpose of this mitzvah by explaining an underlying purpose of *all* of Scripture's prohibitions against interest-based lending, including the prohibition to lend money to a Jew at interest (Mitzvah 343) and the prohibition upon a borrower to pay interest to a Jewish lender (Mitzvah 572):

מִשָּׁרְשֵׁי הַמִּצְוָה – **Among the underlying purposes of this mitzvah,** as well as the other mitzvos prohibiting interest, is the following principle: כִּי הָאֵל הַטּוֹב חָפֵץ בְּיִשּׁוּב עַמּוֹ אֲשֶׁר בָּחַר – **The Almighty, Who is beneficent, desires that His Chosen People form a settled society.** וְעַל כֵּן צִוָּה לְהָסִיר מִכְשׁוֹל מִדַּרְכָּם – **Therefore, He has commanded** His people **to remove** the **pitfall** of interest **from their path,** לְבַל יִבְלַע הָאֶחָד חֵיל חֲבֵרוֹ – thereby ensuring **that one** member of His nation **shall not swallow up his fellow's resources** מִבְּלִי שֶׁיַּרְגִּישׁ בְּעַצְמוֹ עַד שֶׁיִּמָּצֵא בֵּיתוֹ רֵיקָן מִכָּל טוֹב – **without [the latter] realizing his situation until he finds his home bereft of all goodness.**[10] כִּי כֵן דַּרְכּוֹ שֶׁל רִבִּית – **For such is the normal effect of interest,** יָדוּעַ הַדָּבָר – as indeed **the matter is** well **known;** וּמִפְּנֵי זֶה נִקְרָא נֶשֶׁךְ – **and** it is **for this reason** that [interest] **is termed *neshech*** — literally, *bite* — in Scripture (*Exodus* 22:24, *Leviticus* 25:36-37, *Deuteronomy* 23:20, et al.).[11]

---

### NOTES

separately among the 613 Mitzvos. Actually, the first three injunctions cited constitute repeated exhortations against lending at interest, which express its severity, but do not constitute distinct mitzvos (Chinuch in Mitzvah 343; see *Sefer HaMitzvos, Shoresh* 9). See Mitzvah 573, where Chinuch mentions another mitzvah that the lender may violate, according to some opinions.

8. These prohibitions are:
(1) לֹא תַשִּׁיךְ לְאָחִיךָ, *You shall not pay interest to your brother* (*Deuteronomy* 23:20; see Mitzvah 572). [This prohibition is reiterated in the next verse, but both verses count as a single prohibition (*Teshuvos Radvaz* Vol. 5 §1676; *Mirkeves HaMishneh, Hil. Avadim* 8:11; cf. *Maggid Mishneh* and *Lechem Mishneh, Hil. Malveh VeLoveh* 4:2).]
(2) וְלִפְנֵי עִוֵּר לֹא תִתֵּן מִכְשֹׁל, *you shall not place a stumbling block before the blind* (*Leviticus* 19:14; Mitzvah 232). [The borrower violates this prohibition by causing the lender to transgress the prohibitions that pertain to *him*.]

9. The guarantor, the witnesses, and the scribe who help formalize an interest-based loan violate only the injunction that is the subject of the current mitzvah: לֹא תְשִׂימוּן עָלָיו נֶשֶׁךְ, *you shall not lay interest upon him.* [This means that they *surely* transgress this prohibition. In *some* instances, they also transgress the prohibition of "placing a stumbling block," as explained in note 5.]

10. The practice of interest-based lending and borrowing is a slippery slope that can easily result in depletion of the borrower's resources (see the following note). Since God intends for His People to exemplify a high degree of societal perfection and enjoy a tranquil, prosperous existence, He has forbidden them to engage in this practice with each other. Accordingly, both lending and borrowing at interest are Scripturally prohibited (as explained above, notes 7 and 8).

*R' S. R. Hirsch* explains further that lending at interest guarantees a profit to the lender at the expense of the borrower and escalates financial inequality, which in turn undermines social stability. By prohibiting this practice, the Torah forces a person of means, who wishes to profit from his capital, to *invest* it in a business venture — thus creating opportunities for people of lesser means to also profit by laboring in those ventures. In this manner, the prohibition of interest-based loans ensures the establishment of a commercial environment that is beneficial to all (*R' Hirsch Commentary* to *Exodus* 22:24 and *Leviticus* 25:36).

*Ramban* (*Deuteronomy* 23:20) explains that the prohibition is limited to loans between Jewish people because, since both parties agree to the terms of the loan, there is nothing inherently immoral about the interest charge. God, however, demands of His Chosen People that they treat their brethren with a *superior measure* of kindness and benevolence, such that they must extend credit to a fellow Jew in need without expecting anything in return.

11. Chinuch refers to a commonplace phenomenon: A borrower may, in his mind, dismiss interest charges as

16 ☐ משפטים / מצוה סח: שלא נשית יד בין לוה למלוה ברבית

וּבְהִמָּנַע מִן הַמַּעֲשֶׂה הַזֶּה עָרֵב וְסוֹפֵר וְעֵדִים, יִמָּנְעוּ בְּנֵי אָדָם מִמֶּנּוּ.
וְיֶתֶר פְּרָטֶיהָ מְבֹאָרִים בְּמְצִיעָא (דף ע״ה ע״ב).[12]
וְנוֹהֶגֶת בְּכָל מָקוֹם וּבְכָל זְמַן,[13] בִּזְכָרִים וּנְקֵבוֹת.[14]
וְהָעוֹבֵר עַל זֶה וְנַעֲשָׂה סוֹפֵר אוֹ עָרֵב אוֹ עֵד בְּמִלְוָה, עָבַר עַל לָאו זֶה,[15] אֲבָל
אֵין לוֹקִין עָלָיו,[16] שֶׁאֲפִלּוּ הַמַּלְוֶה אֵינוֹ בְּמַלְקוּת שֶׁהֲרֵי נִתָּן לְהִשָּׁבוֹן,[17] וְאֵינוֹ בְּדִין

Chinuch proceeds to provide an explanation of the purpose of this mitzvah in particular:

וּבְהִמָּנַע מִן הַמַּעֲשֶׂה הַזֶּה עָרֵב וְסוֹפֵר וְעֵדִים — **By virtue of** the fact that those who would act as **a guarantor, a scribe, or witnesses will,** on account of our prohibition, **refrain from** aiding **this practice** of lending and borrowing at interest, יִמָּנְעוּ בְּנֵי אָדָם מִמֶּנּוּ — all **people** who lend and borrow **will** have no choice but to **refrain from it** as well, assuring that one member of God's Chosen People will not have his resources depleted by another.

### ～ Laws of the Mitzvah ～

Chinuch has already mentioned the basic laws above — viz., that one may not act as a guarantor, a witness, or a scribe for an interest-based loan — so here he simply concludes:

וְיֶתֶר פְּרָטֶיהָ מְבֹאָרִים בְּמְצִיעָא — **The additional details of [this mitzvah] are elaborated in** *Bava Metzia* (62a, 75b).[12]

### ～ Applicability of the Mitzvah ～

בִּזְכָרִים וְנוֹהֶגֶת בְּכָל מָקוֹם וּבְכָל זְמַן — **[This mitzvah] applies in every location and in all times,**[13] וּנְקֵבוֹת — **to both men and women.**[14] וְהָעוֹבֵר עַל זֶה — **One who transgresses this** mitzvah וְנַעֲשָׂה סוֹפֵר אוֹ עָרֵב אוֹ עֵד בְּמִלְוָה — **by acting as a scribe, or as a guarantor, or as a witness, to** an interest-based **loan** עָבַר עַל לָאו זֶה — **has violated this prohibition.**[15] אֲבָל אֵין לוֹקִין עָלָיו — **However, one does not receive** *malkus* (lashes) **for [its violation].**[16] שֶׁאֲפִלּוּ הַמַּלְוֶה אֵינוֹ בְּמַלְקוּת — **This is so because even the lender** himself **is not subject to** *malkus,* שֶׁהֲרֵי נִתָּן לְהִשָּׁבוֹן — **since [interest wrongfully collected] is subject to restitution;**[17] וְאֵינוֹ בְּדִין — **and since the lender is exempt from** *malkus,* **it would not be reasonable**

---

NOTES

a small price to pay for access to the funds he requires. All too often, however, it proves impossible for him to repay the loan in a timely fashion. As a result, he is forced to continue paying interest, which eventually adds up to a staggering sum. Scarcely realizing it, the borrower has brought financial ruin upon himself.

It is because the harm caused by interest is so insidious that Scripture depicts it as a *snake-bite* (נֶשֶׁךְ): A man whose foot is bitten by a snake barely senses the tiny wound and remains unaware of his mortal danger until the snake's venom has coursed through his entire body (*Shemos Rabbah* 31:6, *Rashi* to *Exodus* 22:24).

12. The laws of this mitzvah are codified in *Rambam, Hil. Malveh VeLoveh* 4:2-3, and *Shulchan Aruch, Yoreh Deah* 160:1.

13. I.e., in Eretz Yisrael and the Diaspora, and whether the *Beis HaMikdash* is standing or not.

14. In accordance with the general rule pertaining to mitzvah-prohibitions, which apply equally to men and women (see General Introduction).

15. These collaborators transgress this prohibition as soon as they participate in formalizing the loan; merely laying an interest obligation upon the borrower is forbidden, even if no interest payments are ultimately collected (see *Bava Metzia* 62a with *Rashi* ד״ה אלא לאו, *Tosafos* ד״ה לא, and *Pnei Yehoshua* there ד״ה משום שומא; ibid. 75b with *Rashi* ד״ה מלוה עובר בכולן; בגמרא אלא לאו; see also *Teshuvos Toras Emes* cited in note 6).

As Chinuch mentioned earlier, the lender also violates this prohibition, in addition to other prohibitions.

16. This ruling reflects the view of *Rambam,* who, in his list of violations that carry the penalty of *malkus* (found in *Hil. Sanhedrin* 19:4), does not mention collaboration in an interest-based loan (*Mishneh LaMelech, Hil. Malveh VeLoveh* 4:6; *Pnei Yehoshua* ibid.; *Minchas Chinuch* §3; see also *Kesef Mishneh, Hil. Eidus* 10:4; cf. *Lechem Mishneh, Hil. Malveh VeLoveh* 4:3, and *Gidulei Terumah* 46:2:1). This is also the view of *Meiri* (*Bava Metzia* 62a ד״ה כבר ביארנו) and *Shiltei HaGibborim* (to *Rif, Bava Metzia* fol. 45b). Others disagree, as shall be explained in note 18.

17. By Torah law, the lender is required to return to the borrower any Biblically forbidden interest he may have collected, and *beis din* can actually force him to return

## MISHPATIM / MITZVAH 68: NOT TO BE INVOLVED IN AN INTEREST-BASED LOAN

דְּהָנֵי דַאֲתוּ מֵחֲמָתֵיהּ יִתְחַיְּבוּ בְּמַלְקוּת.[18]

דְּהָנֵי דַאֲתוּ מֵחֲמָתֵיהּ יִתְחַיְּבוּ בְּמַלְקוּת — **for those** secondary participants **who are included** in this prohibition **on his account** — namely, the scribe, the guarantor, and the witnesses — **to be liable to malkus.**[18]

### NOTES

it (see *Bava Metzia* 61b-62a; *Rambam, Hil. Malveh VeLoveh* 4:3; see *Shulchan Aruch, Yoreh Deah* 161:5 for the definition of "Biblically forbidden interest"). Hence, this transgression falls under the category of לָאו הַנִּיתָּן לְתַשְׁלוּמִין, *a prohibition that is subject to repayment*, which is excluded from the penalty of *malkus* (*Makkos* 16a; *Rambam, Hil. Sanhedrin* 18:2; see *Rambam, Hil. Malveh VeLoveh* 4:3; see also note 14 to the General Introduction).

[The prohibition *you shall not place a stumbling block before the blind* — which the lender also violates (as detailed in note 7, above) — is not rectified by repayment. However, Chinuch writes in Mitzvah 232 that *malkus* are never administered for transgression of this prohibition because it is considered to be לָאו שֶׁאֵין בּוֹ מַעֲשֶׂה, *a prohibition that does not entail action* (see note 14 to the General Introduction).]

18. Chinuch states a novel rationale: Since the lender, who is the primary offender in this transgression, is exempt from *malkus* because he is charged with making restitution instead, it follows that the secondary participants — such as the scribe, guarantor, and witnesses — are not liable to *malkus* either. Although the *reason* that exempts the lender does not apply to them, for their sin does not involve taking money and thus is not subject to restitution, they cannot have greater liability than the primary offender.

One might wonder, though: Granted that by making restitution the lender rectifies his transgression of *taking* interest (i.e., Mitzvah 343; see note 7), but he does not rectify his transgression of *laying* interest, which is committed as soon as the loan is formalized. Let him *and* the other perpetrators incur *malkus* for *this* violation!? *Meiri* (ibid.) explains that the prohibition of laying interest is ancillary to the prohibition of taking interest, and once the primary violation has been rectified, the ancillary violation is considered rectified as well.

It should be noted, though, that there is an opinion that the lender is exempt from *malkus* only for his violation of *taking* interest, but he actually is liable to *malkus* for his violation of *laying* interest (*Smag, Lo Saaseh* 193, based on *Tosafos* to *Bava Metzia* 62a ד"ה לא). According to this view, it follows that the guarantor, the witnesses, and the scribe also are liable to *malkus*.

Moreover, some reject Chinuch's reasoning, and maintain that even if the lender is completely exempted from *malkus* by making restitution, the witnesses [and other collaborators] are liable to *malkus* (*Gidulei Terumah* 46:2:1, cited by *Mishneh LaMelech, Hil. Malveh VeLoveh* 4:6 ד"ה והנה כל מ"ש). For additional sources that the witnesses incur *malkus*, see *Shemos Rabbah* 31:6 (but see *Eitz Yosef* there); *Nimukei Yosef* to *Bava Metzia* 72a, fol. 42b in *Rif* ד"ה ת"ר שטר שיש בו רבית; *Ramban* there; and *Ketzos HaChoshen* 38:1 ד"ה ועיין.

See the Insight for further discussion of Chinuch's reasoning.

---

### ◆§ Insight: The Exemption From Malkus

Chinuch, at the end of the Mitzvah, offers a novel rationale for why those who transgress the prohibition of "laying interest" on the borrower are exempt from *malkus*: The lender does not incur *malkus* because he is instead required to make restitution of the illegally obtained interest payment, and since the primary offender is exempt, the secondary participants must also be exempt.

*Mishneh LaMelech* (*Hil. Malveh VeLoveh* 4:6) wonders why Chinuch resorts to this explanation. There is a principle, often quoted by Chinuch, that לָאו שֶׁאֵין בּוֹ מַעֲשֶׂה אֵין לוֹקִין עָלָיו, *one does not incur malkus for [violating] a prohibition that does not involve action* (see above, note 17). Since the guarantor and the witnesses to a loan do not perform any action, as the guarantor merely *promises* to pay in the event of a default, and the witnesses merely *observe* the transaction, it should be obvious that they are exempt from *malkus*! One might respond that this holds true only in the case of an undocumented loan. But in the case of a documented loan, where the guarantor and witnesses sign the note, they perform an action and *would* theoretically incur *malkus*; thus, Chinuch must explain that since the lender is exempt they are also exempt. This explanation, however, does not suffice, for the following reason.

The Rishonim disagree about the scope of the principle that a prohibition that does not involve action is excluded from *malkus*. Chinuch, throughout this work, takes the position that any prohibition

that *can* be transgressed without action is completely excluded from *malkus* — even if one commits the transgression by means of an action. For example, Chinuch writes in Mitzvah 241 that since one can violate the prohibition of taking revenge without resorting to action (e.g., by refusing to help someone who had previously refused to help him), even one who takes revenge through action does not incur *malkus* (see also Mitzvos 94, 113, 344-346, et al.). [For a very different understanding of the principle, see *Maggid Mishneh, Hil. Sechirus* 13:2, and *Noda BiYehudah* II, *Orach Chaim* §76.] According to Chinuch's view, it should be obvious that *malkus* are not incurred for the transgression of *you shall not lay interest upon him*. Since this prohibition *can* be violated without action, by verbally guaranteeing or witnessing an undocumented loan, the participants should be exempt from *malkus* even if they commit the transgression through action, by writing or signing a loan document. Why does Chinuch need to provide another rationale for their exemption?

Because of this difficulty, *Mishneh LaMelech* suggests that Chinuch understands the prohibition of "laying interest" to apply *only* in a case where the interest-based loan is recorded in a note. It is specifically where the interest obligation is backed by a legal document, which provides strong assurance that the lender will be able to enforce payment, that the participants are considered to have "laid an interest obligation" upon the borrower. Accordingly, the guarantor and the witnesses are able to transgress this prohibition *only* through the action of signing the note, and they would theoretically be liable to *malkus* — were it not for the reasoning that they cannot bear more liability than the lender himself.

Many authorities, however, maintain that the prohibition of "laying interest" is violated even by guaranteeing or witnessing an undocumented loan (see *Shiltei HaGibborim* to *Rif, Bava Metzia* fol. 45b; *Teshuvos Toras Emes* [R' Aharon Sasson, Venice, 5386] §162 ד"ה באופן and ד"ה והנה משטחיות; *Knesses HaGedolah, Choshen Mishpat* §52 to *Beis Yosef* §3). It is noteworthy that *Rambam* (*Hil. Malveh VeLoveh* 4:2), as well as *Tur* and *Shulchan Aruch* (*Yoreh Deah* 160:1), state unequivocally that the guarantor and witnesses to an interest-based loan transgress *you shall not lay interest upon him*, and they do not qualify this as applying to the case of a documented loan. Indeed, *Mishneh LaMelech* seems to concede that his explanation of Chinuch's view is a novel one. [For further discussion, see *Mishneh LaMelech* at length, *Ketzos HaChoshen* 52:1, and *Minchas Chinuch* §3.]

If one is to assume (unlike *Mishneh LaMelech*) that Chinuch agrees with those who rule that the prohibition of "laying interest" applies to an undocumented loan, the question returns: Why did he not simply state that there are no *malkus* here because this violation does not necessitate action? The following resolution is possible: Although Chinuch consistently maintains that any prohibition that *can* be violated without action is completely excluded from *malkus*, some explain that this refers only to the specific *situation* in which it can be violated without action (e.g., he has the opportunity to take revenge passively but chooses to do so actively). Since in the context of the person's violation, his action is superfluous, for he could just as well have committed the violation without action, his action does not make him liable to *malkus*. If, however, there is a situation in which the violation cannot be committed without action, then the one who commits the action in that situation incurs *malkus* for his transgression, even though in *different* circumstances it would have been possible to commit the transgression without action (see *Shaar HaMelech, Hil. Chametz U'Matzah* 1:3 ד"ה איברא שעיקר דברי הרב, cited above, Mitzvah 11 Insight B; see also below, Mitzvah 75 note 37). According to this approach, in a case where the lender refuses to extend credit unless a document is drawn up — such that the guarantor and witnesses cannot possibly "lay interest" *in this situation* without signing the document — they would be liable to *malkus* for signing it. Chinuch therefore needs to explain that they are exempt because they cannot bear greater liability than the lender himself.

## מִצְוָה סט: שֶׁלֹּא לְקַלֵּל הַדַּיָּן

שֶׁלֹּא לְקַלֵּל הַדַּיָּנִים, שֶׁנֶּאֱמַר (שמות כ״ב, כ״ז) אֱלֹהִים לֹא תְקַלֵּל, וּפֵרוּשׁוֹ לַדַּיָּנִים כְּמוֹ (שם כ״ב, ח׳) אֲשֶׁר יַרְשִׁיעֻן אֱלֹהִים.[1] וְהוֹצִיאָן הַכָּתוּב בִּלְשׁוֹן אֱלֹהִים כְּדֵי שֶׁיְּהֵא נִכְלָל עִם הַלָּאו הַזֶּה לָאו אַחֵר, וְהוּא לָאו דְּבִרְכַּת הַשֵּׁם יִתְבָּרַךְ,[2] כְּמוֹ שֶׁאָמְרוּ זִכְרוֹנָם לִבְרָכָה בַּמְּכִילְתָּא וּבַסִּפְרֵי:[3]

## Mitzvah 69
### The Prohibition to Curse a Judge

אֱלֹהִים לֹא תְקַלֵּל
*You shall not revile Elohim (Exodus 22:27)*

The term *Elohim* appears most often in Scripture as a reference to God, but sometimes it appears as a reference to the judges of *beis din* (e.g., *Exodus* 21:6, 22:7-8). In the above verse, *Elohim* has both connotations. Hence, the phrase *You shall not revile Elohim* is the source of two distinct mitzvah-prohibitions: Mitzvah 69, The Prohibition to Curse a Judge; and Mitzvah 70, The Prohibition of "Blessing" Hashem (i.e., blaspheming His Name).

Chinuch has a unique format here, as he combines the two prohibitions contained in this single phrase into one chapter. He begins by introducing both prohibitions, and then proceeds to present the underlying purposes, laws, and applicability of each of them. In most of the recent editions of the Chinuch, however, these mitzvos have been separated into two chapters, one called "Mitzvah 69" and another called "Mitzvah 70." For the sake of simplicity and clarity, we have followed that format, but it should be noted that some aspects of the latter prohibition are discussed in "Mitzvah 69."

It is important to note also that the Torah prohibits cursing *any* Jew (Mitzvah 231). Chinuch explains below that the prohibition against cursing a judge, stated here, exists in addition to the general prohibition against cursing any Jew, such that one who curses a judge has violated *two* prohibitions.

שֶׁלֹּא לְקַלֵּל הַדַּיָּנִים — We are commanded **not to curse the judges** of *beis din,* שֶׁנֶּאֱמַר "אֱלֹהִים לֹא תְקַלֵּל" — **as it is stated** (*Exodus* 22:27): *You shall not revile Elohim;* וּפֵרוּשׁוֹ לַדַּיָּנִים — **and the meaning of [***Elohim***], in this context, is that it refers to judges,** כְּמוֹ "אֲשֶׁר יַרְשִׁיעֻן אֱלֹהִים" — **as in** the verse (ibid. 22:8), *whomever the Elohim find guilty* shall pay, where *"Elohim"* obviously refers to the judges of a *beis din.*[1] וְהוֹצִיאָן הַכָּתוּב בִּלְשׁוֹן אֱלֹהִים — **The verse expresses** the prohibition against cursing **[judges] with the term "***Elohim***"** (rather than the more literal שׁוֹפֵט, *shofeit*) כְּדֵי שֶׁיְּהֵא נִכְלָל עִם הַלָּאו הַזֶּה לָאו אַחֵר — **so as to include, along with this prohibition, an additional prohibition,** וְהוּא לָאו דְּבִרְכַּת הַשֵּׁם יִתְבָּרַךְ — **namely, the prohibition of "blessing" Hashem, blessed be He,** i.e., committing blasphemy.[2] כְּמוֹ שֶׁאָמְרוּ זִכְרוֹנָם לִבְרָכָה בַּמְּכִילְתָּא וּבַסִּפְרֵי — **As our Sages, of blessed memory, have stated in** *Mechilta* (to our verse) **and** *Sifrei:*[3]

---

### NOTES

1. Chinuch's explanation here is based on *Mechilta* to our verse, which he cites below. See the Insight for further discussion of which type of judge is protected by our prohibition.

2. That is, although in this context *Elohim* refers to judges (see *Rashbam* and *Chizkuni* to the verse, and *Shaarei Teshuvah* 3:46), it is also understood as a reference to God. Since the verse could have used the word שׁוֹפֵט (*shofeit*), which refers specifically to a *judge,* and it chose instead to use the term *Elohim,* which usually refers to God, we additionally derive from this verse the prohibition to "bless" His Name (*Tosafos, Sanhedrin* 66a ד״ה גמר). Moreover, the expression *You shall not revile* could have been written as לֹא תקל, with one *lamed*. By stating לֹא תְקַלֵּל with two *lameds,* the verse indicates that its prohibition applies to *both* subjects that are described as *Elohim* (see Gemara ibid. 66a-b). See further, note 4.

3. Our versions of *Sifrei* do not contain this reference (*Minchas Yitzchak* §1), but it does appear in *Sanhedrin* 66a.

אַזְהָרָה לִבְרְכַּת הַשֵּׁם מִדְּכְתִיב אֱלֹהִים לֹא תְקַלֵּל[5,4], וּמַה שֶּׁכָּתוּב בְּמָקוֹם אַחֵר (ויקרא כ״ד, ט״ז) וְנֹקֵב שֵׁם ה' מוֹת יוּמָת, זֶהוּ הָעֹנֶשׁ, אֲבָל הָאַזְהָרָה הִיא מִכָּאן, כִּי לֹא יַסְפִּיק לָנוּ הַזְכָּרַת הָעֹנֶשׁ בַּמִּצְוָה מִבְּלִי אַזְהָרָה. וְזֶהוּ שֶׁיֹּאמְרוּ רַבּוֹתֵינוּ ז״ל תָּמִיד עֹנֶשׁ שָׁמַעְנוּ אַזְהָרָה מִנַּיִן, וְהָעִנְיָן הוּא מִפְּנֵי שֶׁאִם לֹא תָּבוֹא לָנוּ בַּדָּבָר מְנִיעַת הָאֵל, אֶלָּא שֶׁיֹּאמַר עוֹשֶׂה דָּבָר פְּלוֹנִי יֵעָנֵשׁ בְּכָךְ, הָיָה בְּמַשְׁמָע שֶׁיִּהְיֶה רְשׁוּת בְּיַד כָּל הָרוֹצֶה לְקַבֵּל הָעֹנֶשׁ וְלֹא יָחוּשׁ לְצַעֲרוֹ לַעֲבֹר עַל הַמִּצְוָה וְלֹא יָבוֹא בָּזֶה כְּנֶגֶד חֵפֶץ הַשֵּׁם יִתְבָּרַךְ וּמִצְוָתוֹ[6],

---

**אַזְהָרָה לְבִרְכַּת הַשֵּׁם מִדִּכְתִיב "אֱלֹהִים לֹא תְקַלֵּל"** — The Scriptural warning against "blessing" Hashem is derived from that which is written, *You shall not revile Elohim.* Effectively, then, the word *Elohim* is interpreted in accordance with both of its meanings — referring to both "judges" and "God" — and the verse prohibits reviling either of them.[4] These count as two distinct mitzvah-prohibitions.[5]

Chinuch now cites another verse that discusses blasphemy, and explains why both verses are necessary:

**וּמַה שֶּׁכָּתוּב בְּמָקוֹם אַחֵר** — Now, with regard to **that which is written elsewhere** (*Leviticus* 24:16): **"וְנֹקֵב שֵׁם ה' מוֹת יוּמָת"** — *One who blasphemously pronounces the Name of* Hashem *shall be put to death,* the entire assembly shall surely stone him, **זֶהוּ הָעֹנֶשׁ** — **that is** a reference to **the penalty** for one who commits blasphemy; **אֲבָל הָאַזְהָרָה הִיא מִכָּאן** — but the Scriptural warning against committing blasphemy in the first place **is from here,** i.e., our verse, *You shall not revile Elohim.* **כִּי לֹא יַסְפִּיק לָנוּ הַזְכָּרַת הָעֹנֶשׁ בַּמִּצְוָה מִבְּלִי אַזְהָרָה** — Both of these verses are necessary, **as it is insufficient** for the Torah **to mention** just **the penalty for** violating **the commandment, without** providing **a warning** against it (as shall be explained shortly). **וְזֶהוּ שֶׁיֹּאמְרוּ רַבּוֹתֵינוּ ז״ל תָּמִיד** — **This is what our Sages, of blessed memory,** mean when they **state repeatedly** in the Talmud (*Sanhedrin* 54a, et al.): **עֹנֶשׁ שָׁמַעְנוּ אַזְהָרָה מִנַּיִן** — **We have heard the punishment, but where is the Scriptural warning?** That is, in any case where the Torah has spelled out a punishment for a certain misdeed but there is no obvious prohibition against that deed, the Sages will search the Torah for a verse containing the prohibition, because invariably, the Torah specifically prohibits the acts for which it imposes punishment.

Chinuch proceeds to explain why the Torah does this, rather than relying on the specification of a punishment to indicate that the act is prohibited:

**וְהָעִנְיָן הוּא** — **The reason** why it is necessary to have a prohibition stated in addition to the penalty is **מִפְּנֵי שֶׁאִם לֹא תָּבוֹא לָנוּ בַּדָּבָר מְנִיעַת הָאֵל** — **because if we would not receive the Almighty's injunction against this** particular **matter, אֶלָּא שֶׁיֹּאמַר עוֹשֶׂה דָּבָר פְּלוֹנִי יֵעָנֵשׁ בְּכָךְ** — **but rather, [the Torah] would** simply **state** that **one who does such-and-such a thing will be punished with such**-and-such a penalty, **הָיָה בְּמַשְׁמָע** — **it would give the** false **impression that** — **שֶׁיִּהְיֶה רְשׁוּת בְּיַד כָּל הָרוֹצֶה לְקַבֵּל הָעֹנֶשׁ וְלֹא יָחוּשׁ לְצַעֲרוֹ לַעֲבֹר עַל הַמִּצְוָה it is up to the discretion of anyone who is willing to accept the penalty, and who is unconcerned for his own pain** that such a penalty would invariably cause, **to proceed to violate the mitzvah; וְלֹא יָבוֹא בָּזֶה כְּנֶגֶד חֵפֶץ הַשֵּׁם יִתְבָּרַךְ וּמִצְוָתוֹ** — **and** the implication would be that such an act simply bears an unpleasant consequence, but **[the one who does it] does not thereby come in** direct **conflict with the Will of Hashem, blessed be He, and His command.**[6]

---

NOTES

4. The Gemara (*Sanhedrin* 66a) cites a Tannaic dispute whether, in its simple meaning, the verse refers to judges or to Hashem. All Tannaim agree, however, that the verse is to be expounded as referring to both judges and Hashem, and as containing a prohibition regarding each of them. Chinuch follows the view that the simple meaning of the verse refers to judges, and the reference to Hashem is included through exposition; see also *Targum Onkelos* to the verse (*Me'il HaEphod*).

5. Although both prohibitions are contained in the very same phrase, since they refer to distinct subjects for which the Torah explicitly set forth distinct punishments (one who curses a judge is liable to *malkus,* whereas one who blasphemes the Name is liable to death by *sekilah* [*stoning*], as Chinuch will state), they count as separate prohibitions in the count of the 613 Mitzvos (see *Rambam, Sefer HaMitzvos, Lo Saaseh* 60 and 315).

6. Although it would be obvious that Hashem does not

## 21 ❑ MISHPATIM / MITZVAH 69: THE PROHIBITION TO CURSE A JUDGE

וְיַחֲזֹר דְּבַר הַמִּצְוָה כְּעֵין מִקָּח וּמִמְכָּר, כְּלוֹמַר הָרוֹצֶה לַעֲשׂוֹת דָּבָר פְּלוֹנִי יִתֵּן כָּךְ וְכָךְ וְיַעֲשֵׂהוּ אוֹ יִתֵּן שִׁכְמוֹ לִסְבֹּל כָּךְ וְיַעֲשֵׂהוּ, וְאֵין הַכַּוָּנָה עַל הַמִּצְווֹת בְּכָךְ, אֶלָּא שֶׁהָאֵל לְטוֹבָתֵנוּ מְנָעָנוּ בִּדְבָרִים וְהוֹדִיעָנוּ בְּמִקְצָתָן הָעֹנֶשׁ הַמַּגִּיעַ לָנוּ מִיָּד מִלְּבַד הַעֲבָרַת רְצוֹנוֹ שֶׁהִיא קָשָׁה מִן הַכֹּל.[7] וְזֶהוּ אָמְרָם ז״ל בְּכָל מָקוֹם לֹא עָנַשׁ אֶלָּא אִם כֵּן הִזְהִיר, כְּלוֹמַר לֹא יוֹדִיעַ הָאֵל הָעֹנֶשׁ הַבָּא עָלֵינוּ עַל הַעֲבָרַת הַמִּצְוָה אֶלָּא אִם כֵּן[8] הוֹדִיעָנוּ תְּחִלָּה שֶׁרְצוֹנוֹ הוּא שֶׁלֹּא נַעֲשֶׂה אוֹתוֹ הַדָּבָר שֶׁהָעֹנֶשׁ בָּא עָלָיו.[9]

---

וְיַחֲזֹר דְּבַר הַמִּצְוָה כְּעֵין מִקָּח וּמִמְכָּר — **The matter of the mitzvah would then become similar to a financial transaction,** כְּלוֹמַר הָרוֹצֶה לַעֲשׂוֹת דָּבָר פְּלוֹנִי יִתֵּן כָּךְ וְכָךְ וְיַעֲשֵׂהוּ — **as if to say, "Anyone who wishes to do such-and-such an act must give such-and-such** as payment, **and he may then do it";** אוֹ יִתֵּן שִׁכְמוֹ לִסְבֹּל כָּךְ וְיַעֲשֵׂהוּ — **or,** alternatively, as if to say, **"Let him put forth his shoulder to bear** the burden of **such**-and-such a consequence, **and he may then do [the act]."** וְאֵין הַכַּוָּנָה עַל הַמִּצְווֹת בְּכָךְ — **This,** however, **is not the intention of** the Torah **with regard to the mitzvos.** Mitzvah observance is not optional, nor do we refrain from violating prohibitions simply to avoid the consequences. אֶלָּא שֶׁהָאֵל לְטוֹבָתֵנוּ מְנָעָנוּ בִּדְבָרִים — **Rather, the Almighty restricted us from** certain **things for our own good,** וְהוֹדִיעָנוּ בְּמִקְצָתָן הָעֹנֶשׁ הַמַּגִּיעַ לָנוּ מִיָּד — **and, in regard to some of them, He** further **informed us of the punishment that will befall us immediately,** in this world, if we transgress His Word. These punitive consequences, however, are not the ultimate reason that we desist from such acts. They may act as deterrents, but actually are secondary consequences, מִלְּבַד הַעֲבָרַת רְצוֹנוֹ שֶׁהִיא קָשָׁה מִן הַכֹּל — as they exist **aside from** the overriding issue of **defying His Will, which is** itself **the most severe of all** the aspects that such violations entail. Therefore, even when a punishment for a specific act is stated, the Torah will invariably inform us, in addition, that the act is *prohibited*.[7] וְזֶהוּ אָמְרָם ז״ל בְּכָל מָקוֹם — **This is what [our Sages], of blessed memory,** refer to when they **state throughout** the Talmud (*Yoma* 81a, et al.): לֹא עָנַשׁ אֶלָּא אִם כֵּן הִזְהִיר — **[The Torah] did not punish unless it** also **warned that the act is prohibited.** כְּלוֹמַר — **That is to say,** לֹא יוֹדִיעַ הָאֵל הָעֹנֶשׁ הַבָּא עָלֵינוּ עַל הַעֲבָרַת הַמִּצְוָה — **the Almighty will not inform us of a penalty that we incur for violating a mitzvah,** אֶלָּא אִם כֵּן הוֹדִיעָנוּ תְּחִלָּה — **unless He first**[8] **informs us** שֶׁרְצוֹנוֹ הוּא שֶׁלֹּא נַעֲשֶׂה אוֹתוֹ הַדָּבָר שֶׁהָעֹנֶשׁ בָּא עָלָיו — **that it is His Will** *that we shall not do* **that matter that bears this penalty.** Had He not stated the prohibition, we might mistakenly have thought that such acts are permitted as long as one is willing to "pay the price" for them, as has been explained.[9]

---

### NOTES

desire such an act, one might think that He merely *discouraged* it by imposing a negative consequence for it, but did not actually *prohibit* it.

7. Thus, the violation of a prohibition is to be avoided not merely because of the penalties involved, but more importantly, because it is in direct conflict with Hashem's stated Will. The disregarding of His command is the most egregious aspect of such a violation. As R' Moshe Chaim Luzzatto puts it (*Mesillas Yesharim* Ch. 1; *Derech Hashem* 1:4:6,11): We were placed in this world so as to have the opportunity to attain closeness to Hashem through obeying His Word; thus, the true purpose of fulfilling mitzvos is to draw us near to Him, that we may ultimately bask in His Light, and the purpose of refraining from sin is to avoid that which distances us from Him.

8. This means that *conceptually* every punishment is "preceded" by a prohibition, such that the one who incurs punishment was directly prohibited, somewhere in the Torah, from performing the misdeed. It does not mean that the prohibition must appear earlier in the Torah than the punishment.

9. *Minchas Chinuch* (§1) questions Chinuch's reasoning here: The Gemara (*Sanhedrin* 56a, *Temurah* 3b-4a) states that the Scriptural injunction that leads to a punishment must always be stated in the language of a *prohibition* (i.e., *you shall not ...*); an injunction in the positive language of a *commandment* (e.g., *you shall fear ...*) is insufficient. If, as Chinuch states, the purpose of the injunction is merely to teach that one does not have the option of doing the act and incurring the punishment, why should the phraseology make a difference? *Minchas Chinuch* therefore explains that the requirement of a Scriptural injunction was received by the Sages through Oral Tradition, and Chinuch does not mean to provide the *basis* of the law, but merely to give some explanation of its rationale. For another approach, see *Minchas Yitzchak* §4.

[Actually, as a rule, the Torah prescribes punishment only for the transgression of a mitzvah-*prohibition*,

## 22 □ משפטים / מצוה סט: שלא לקלל הדין

מִשָּׁרְשֵׁי הַמִּצְוָה, לְהָסִיר מֵעַל הַדַּיָּנִין יִרְאַת הַנָּדוֹן וְקִלְלָתוֹ,[10] כְּדֵי שֶׁיּוֹצִיאוּ הַדִּין לַאֲמִתּוֹ, וְעוֹד הִזְהִיר עַל זֶה גַּם כֵּן בְּמָקוֹם אַחֵר בַּתּוֹרָה.[11] וְעוֹד[12] נִמְצָא תּוֹעֶלֶת אַחֵר בַּמִּצְוָה, כִּי בְּקִלְלַת הַדַּיָּן תַּקָּלוֹת רַבּוֹת, כִּי הֲמוֹן הָעָם בְּסִכְלוּתָם שׂוֹנְאִים אוֹתוֹ,[13] וְאִם לֹא יִזָּהֲרוּ עַל קִלְלָתוֹ אוּלַי יְקַלְלוּהוּ וְיִתְעוֹרְרוּ מִתּוֹךְ כָּךְ לָקוּם עָלָיו, כְּמוֹ שֶׁאָמַר הֶחָכָם לַמֶּלֶךְ עַל הֲמוֹן הָעָם, הִזָּהֵר שֶׁלֹּא יֹאמְרוּ, שֶׁאִם יֹאמְרוּ יַעֲשׂוּ,[14] וְיִהְיֶה בָּזֶה רָעָה רַבָּה, כִּי הוּא בְּמִשְׁפָּט יַעֲמִיד אָרֶץ.[16,15]

---

### ◆ Underlying Purpose of the Mitzvah ◆

Chinuch has established that the verse *You shall not revile Elohim* serves to prohibit two distinct things — cursing a judge, and "blessing" Hashem — and that these count as separate mitzvos (Mitzvos 69 and 70). He now proceeds to explain the underlying purpose, the laws, and the applicability, of the prohibition to curse a judge.

מִשָּׁרְשֵׁי הַמִּצְוָה — **Among the underlying purposes of the mitzvah** that prohibits cursing a judge is לְהָסִיר מֵעַל הַדַּיָּנִין יִרְאַת הַנָּדוֹן וְקִלְלָתוֹ — **to remove from judges** any **fear** they might otherwise have **of the litigant and his curse,**[10] כְּדֵי שֶׁיּוֹצִיאוּ הַדִּין לַאֲמִתּוֹ — **in order that they may bring out the truth of the** matter **of judgment** and issue a ruling unaffected by intimidation. וְעוֹד הִזְהִיר עַל זֶה גַּם כֵּן בְּמָקוֹם אַחֵר בַּתּוֹרָה — **Indeed, [the Torah],** in its desire to preclude rulings tainted by intimidation, **additionally warns** judges **regarding this** matter **elsewhere in the Torah,** by stating (*Deuteronomy* 1:17): *you shall not tremble before any man* (see Mitzvah 415).[11]

Chinuch offers an additional rationale for this mitzvah:[12]

וְעוֹד נִמְצָא תּוֹעֶלֶת אַחֵר בַּמִּצְוָה — **There is yet another benefit of the mitzvah** not to curse a judge, כִּי בְּקִלְלַת הַדַּיָּן תַּקָּלוֹת רַבּוֹת — **inasmuch as the cursing of a judge entails many** potentially larger **pitfalls.** כִּי הֲמוֹן הָעָם בְּסִכְלוּתָם שׂוֹנְאִים אוֹתוֹ — **For the masses, in their foolishness, hate [the judge],**[13] וְאִם לֹא יִזָּהֲרוּ עַל קִלְלָתוֹ — **and if they were not warned against cursing him,** אוּלַי יְקַלְלוּהוּ — it is **quite possible** that **they** actually **would curse him,** וְיִתְעוֹרְרוּ מִתּוֹךְ כָּךְ לָקוּם עָלָיו — **and as a result** of this disparagement **they** might further **be instigated to** violently **rise up against him;** כְּמוֹ שֶׁאָמַר הֶחָכָם לַמֶּלֶךְ עַל הֲמוֹן הָעָם — **as the wise man told the king regarding the masses of the people,** הִזָּהֵר שֶׁלֹּא יֹאמְרוּ — **"Beware that they not say** anything inflammatory against you, **for if they say** such things, **they will** eventually **do** them."[14] וְיִהְיֶה בָּזֶה רָעָה רַבָּה — **Terrible things would result from such** an uprising against those of authority, כִּי הוּא בְּמִשְׁפָּט יַעֲמִיד אָרֶץ — **for it is through justice that He establishes the land,**[15] and without respect for institutions of justice society cannot exist.[16]

---

### NOTES

but not for the transgression of a mitzvah-*obligation*. Hence, it is necessary that the injunction be phrased as a prohibition in order that it conform to that general rule (see *Rambam, Sefer HaMitzvos,* Introduction to *Asei* 1).]

10. In Mitzvah 231, the prohibition to curse any Jew, Chinuch addresses the power of the spoken word, and notes that a curse can in fact work in a metaphysical way to harm its subject. In this vein, he quotes the statement of our Sages (*Moed Katan* 18a) that "a covenant has been made with the lips" — i.e., a man's words have power (see also *Ohr HaChaim, Numbers* 23:8). However, Chinuch notes there that *Rambam* (*Sefer HaMitzvos, Lo Saaseh* 317) seems to disagree and maintains that curses have no real effect upon their subject. Rather, they are forbidden primarily because of the negative traits of anger and vengeance that curses tend to encourage (see also *R' S. R. Hirsch, Leviticus* 19:14; *Igros Moshe, Orach Chaim* III §78 (ד"ה ולכן אמינא). In line with his own approach there, Chinuch explains

that one of the purposes of our mitzvah is to protect judges from the danger of a litigant's curse.

11. According to this explanation of our mitzvah, the Torah provides two separate prohibitions to ensure that judicial rulings are untainted by intimidation: the current mitzvah addressed to the litigants, and Mitzvah 415 addressed to the judges.

12. The following is based on *Ramban, Leviticus* 19:14.

13. That is, they hate a judge who rules against them (*Ramban* ibid.), for they automatically assume such a ruling to be unfair and mistaken (*Sforno, Exodus* 22:27; see also *Rashbam* there).

14. Chinuch seems to refer here to some specific incident involving such a conversation between a king and his adviser. Possibly, though, he is speaking hypothetically to bring out his point.

15. Stylistic paraphrase of *Proverbs* 29:4.

16. Chinuch has stated numerous times (e.g., Mitzvah 49)

# 23 ❏ MISHPATIM / MITZVAH 69: THE PROHIBITION TO CURSE A JUDGE

מִדִּינֵי הַמִּצְוָה בְּדַיָּנִין, מַה שֶּׁאָמְרוּ שֶׁאֵין חִיּוּב הַלָּאו אֶלָּא עַל הַמְקַלֵּל הַדַּיָּן בְּשֵׁם מִשְּׁמוֹת הַשֵּׁם יִתְבָּרַךְ,[17] כְּגוֹן יָ־הּ אוֹ שַׁדַּ־י וֵאלֹקִים וְכַיּוֹצֵא בָּהֶן,[18] אוֹ בְּכִנּוּי, כְּגוֹן חַנּוּן קַנָּא וְכַיּוֹצֵא בָּהֶן,[19] אֲבָל בְּלֹא שֵׁם וְכִנּוּי כְּגוֹן אָרוּר פְּלוֹנִי אוֹ אַל יְהִי בָּרוּךְ, אֵין בּוֹ חִיּוּב לָאו[20] אֲבָל אָסוּר הוּא.[21]

---

## ⟿ Laws of the Mitzvah ⟾

מַה שֶּׁאָמְרוּ is — מִדִּינֵי הַמִּצְוָה בְּדַיָּנִין — **Among the laws of the mitzvah regarding** cursing **judges that which [our Sages] have said** (Mishnah, *Shevuos* 35a), שֶׁאֵין חִיּוּב הַלָּאו אֶלָּא עַל הַמְקַלֵּל הַדַּיָּן בְּשֵׁם מִשְּׁמוֹת הַשֵּׁם יִתְבָּרַךְ — **that liability for** a transgression of **the prohibition** (i.e., the penalty of *malkus* — lashes) **is** imposed **only on one who curses the judge with one of the** proper **Names of Hashem, blessed be He,**[17] כְּגוֹן יָ־הּ אוֹ שַׁדַּ־י וֵאלֹקִים וְכַיּוֹצֵא בָּהֶן — **such as** the Name *YAH,* the Name *SHADDAI,* the Name *ELOKIM,* and the like,[18] אוֹ בְּכִנּוּי — **or,** he curses the judge **with a descriptive term** for Hashem, כְּגוֹן חַנּוּן קַנָּא וְכַיּוֹצֵא בָּהֶן — **such as,** *the Gracious One, the Jealous One,* **and the like.**[19] אֲבָל בְּלֹא שֵׁם וְכִנּוּי — **However,** if one curses a judge **without** using either a proper **Name or a descriptive term** for Hashem, כְּגוֹן אָרוּר פְּלוֹנִי — **for example,** by saying merely, **"Accursed be So-and-so,"** אוֹ אַל יְהִי בָּרוּךְ — **or,** if one curses through inference, such as by saying, **"Let [So-and-so] not be blessed,"** אֵין בּוֹ חִיּוּב לָאו — **there is no liability** to *malkus* **for** violating the **prohibition** against cursing.[20] אֲבָל אָסוּר הוּא — **Nevertheless, it is forbidden** to utter even such curses.[21]

---

NOTES

that law and order are the basis of a flourishing society. An uprising that undermines this system surely would jeopardize the underpinnings of society. See Mitzvah 71, where Chinuch explains similarly the purpose of the prohibition to curse a *Nasi*.

17. Such as by saying to the judge, *May* [a Name of God] *smite you* (Mishnah, *Shevuos* 35a, with *Rambam* Commentary).

18. This category includes any proper Name for Hashem Himself, as opposed to attributes and adjectives with which He is described. Additional proper Names are the Tetragrammaton (Four-Letter Name, spelled *Yud, Hei, Vav, Hei*), as well as *Adonai, El, Eloha, Eheyeh,* and *Tzevaos* (*Rambam, Hilchos Yesodei HaTorah* 6:2).

19. Descriptive terms [כִּינּוּיִים] are those adjectives and attributes with which Hashem is described. Other examples of descriptive terms would be רַחוּם, *the Merciful One*; הַגָּדוֹל, *the Great One*; הַגִּבּוֹר, *the Mighty One*; הַנּוֹרָא, *the Awesome One*; הַנֶּאֱמָן, *the Trustworthy One,* and others like these (*Rambam* ibid. 6:5).

Chinuch here follows *Rambam* (*Hil. Sanhedrin* 26:3), who rules that one incurs *malkus* for cursing whether he employs a proper Name of God or a descriptive term for Him (see also Tractate *Soferim* 4:9). *Raavad* (ad loc.; based on *Yerushalmi Shevuos* 4:10) disagrees and rules that, although the prohibition against cursing a judge applies in all these cases, one incurs *malkus* only if he employs the Distinct Name of God — i.e., *Adonai,* or the Tetragrammaton (see Mitzvah 70 note 4), but not if he uses any other name, be it proper or descriptive (see also *Raavad's* glosses to *Rif, Shevuos,* end of Ch. 4 [printed after *Mordechai,* in Vilna ed.]). For further discussion, see *Kesef Mishneh* and *Radvaz* to *Hil. Sanhedrin* ibid., *Minchas Chinuch* §2, and *Me'il HaEphod*

§4. See also *Shulchan Aruch, Choshen Mishpat* 27:1.

20. In the latter case, where one curses only by inference, he is exempt even if he uses a Name, such as by saying "Let God not bless So-and-so" (*Rambam, Hil. Sanhedrin* 26:4, based on Mishnah, *Shevuos* 35a; *Minchas Chinuch* §3). Although one from whom God withholds His Countenance and blessing is effectively cursed (*Sma, Choshen Mishpat* 27:7), there is no liability for this curse insofar as it is not explicit.

21. *Tur* (*Choshen Mishpat* 27:2) similarly states that such non-punishable curses are nevertheless forbidden (see also the language of *Rambam* ibid.; cf. *Minchas Chinuch* §4). As for the basis of the prohibition, *Minchas Chinuch* (§3-4) notes that "inference" is deemed a valid means of expression in various areas of Torah law (see *Shevuos* 36a-b), so it is logical that cursing through inference is prohibited (see also *Bedek HaBayis, Choshen Mishpat* 27:2). *Minchas Chinuch* wonders, however, on what basis Chinuch and *Tur* rule that cursing without using a Name of God is prohibited.

Some explain that the simple understanding of the verse *You shall not revile Elohim* is that it forbids *all* curses of a judge, with or without use of God's Name. Thus, although the Sages (through Scriptural exposition) limit the penalty of *malkus* to those curses that employ a Name of God, the prohibition applies to all cases (*Chazon Ish, Sanhedrin* 20:7; see *R' Y. F. Perla, Sefer HaMitzvos* of *Rav Saadiah Gaon, Lo Saaseh* 47 [Vol. II, p. 84-85 ד"ה אלא] for a list of Rishonim who concur). Others suggest that cursing a judge (or any Jew) without invoking a Name of God is not forbidden under our prohibition, but is a transgression of Mitzvah 243 (*Leviticus* 19:18): וְאָהַבְתָּ לְרֵעֲךָ כָּמוֹךָ, *you shall love your fellow as yourself* (*Minchas Yitzchak* §5).

24 ❑ משפטים / מצוה סט: שלא לקלל הדין

וּמַה שֶּׁפֵּרְשׁוּ ז״ל גַּם כֵּן בְּעִנְיָן זֶה שֶׁהַחִיּוּב אֵינוֹ בְּמִקַלְלוֹ בִּלְשׁוֹן הַקֹּדֶשׁ דַּוְקָא אֶלָּא אֲפִלּוּ בְּכָל לָשׁוֹן,²² וְכִי צָרִיךְ עֵדִים וְהַתְרָאָה בָּזֶה בְּכָל חַיָּבֵי לָאוִין,²³ וְיֶתֶר פְּרָטֶיהָ, מְבֹאָרִין בְּסַנְהֶדְרִין (דף ס״ו ע״א)²⁴.

וְנוֹהֶגֶת בְּכָל מָקוֹם וּבְכָל זְמַן²⁵ (בִּזְכָרִים וּנְקֵבוֹת).²⁶
וְעוֹבֵר עָלֶיהָ וְקִלֵּל הַדַּיָּן בְּשֵׁם אוֹ בְכִנּוּי, לוֹקֶה שְׁתֵּי מַלְקֻיּוֹת, אַחַת לְפִי שֶׁהוּא כְּכָל אֶחָד

וּמַה שֶּׁפֵּרְשׁוּ ז״ל גַּם כֵּן בְּעִנְיָן זֶה — **Also** included in the laws of this mitzvah is **that which [our Sages], of blessed memory, explained in this regard** (see *Sanhedrin* 60a), שֶׁהַחִיּוּב אֵינוֹ בְּמִקַלְלוֹ בִּלְשׁוֹן הַקֹּדֶשׁ דַּוְקָא — **that liability** to *malkus* for violating this prohibition **is** incurred **not** only **for cursing [a judge] specifically in the Holy Tongue,** אֶלָּא אֲפִלּוּ בְּכָל לָשׁוֹן — **but even** for cursing him **in any** other **language.**[22]

וְכִי צָרִיךְ עֵדִים וְהַתְרָאָה בָּזֶה — **Also** included is the law that in order for one to incur *malkus* for violating this [prohibition], it is necessary that there be valid witnesses who hear the curse, and that the violator receive forewarning as to the consequences his transgression will carry, בְּכָל חַיָּבֵי לָאוִין — as is the case with regard to incurring liability for violating any prohibition.[23]

וְיֶתֶר פְּרָטֶיהָ — These laws, and the additional details of [this mitzvah], מְבֹאָרִין בְּסַנְהֶדְרִין — are set forth in Tractate *Sanhedrin* (66a).[24]

## ✧ Applicability of the Mitzvah ✧

וְנוֹהֶגֶת בְּכָל מָקוֹם וּבְכָל זְמַן — [The prohibition to curse a judge] applies in every location and in all times,[25] בִּזְכָרִים וּנְקֵבוֹת — to both men and women.[26]

וְעוֹבֵר עָלֶיהָ — One who transgresses [this mitzvah] וְקִלֵּל הַדַּיָּן בְּשֵׁם אוֹ בְכִנּוּי — and curses a judge with either a proper Name of God or a descriptive term for Him לוֹקֶה שְׁתֵּי מַלְקֻיּוֹת — incurs two sets of *malkus*, because he actually has violated two prohibitions. אַחַת לְפִי שֶׁהוּא בְּכָל אֶחָד מִיִּשְׂרָאֵל הַכְּשֵׁרִים — One set of *malkus* is incurred because [the judge] is like any other

---

### NOTES

22. Chinuch again follows *Rambam* (*Hil. Sanhedrin* 26:3), who writes that since one is liable for cursing even if he simply incorporates a כינוי (*descriptive term*) in his curse, he also is liable when he incorporates a reference to Hashem in a language other than the Holy Tongue, [such as the English term "God"]. This is because a Name in a foreign language is equivalent to a "descriptive term." The Gemara (*Sanhedrin* 60a) in fact uses the term כינוי in describing non-Hebrew references to Hashem (see *Beur HaGra, Choshen Mishpat* 27:2). *Raavad* (cited in note 19) disagrees with this ruling as well.

[The preceding laws apply also to the prohibition of cursing any Jew; see Mitzvah 71 note 7 and Mitzvah 231.]

23. The requirement for witnesses and forewarning as preconditions for liability is well known (see General Introduction, Sec. VI), and, as Chinuch notes here, applies to all other prohibitions as well. One might therefore wonder why Chinuch, as well as *Rambam* (*Hil. Sanhedrin* 26:4), needed to spell this out here. *Kesef Mishneh* (to *Rambam* ibid.) gives two explanations.

(1) One might have thought that the prohibition against cursing a judge is excluded from the general requirement of forewarning, because it is in any event an exceptional prohibition, inasmuch as one incurs *malkus* for a violation even though it does not involve physical action (see note 28 below). Thus, just as action is not required to incur liability (in contrast to almost all other punishable prohibitions), perhaps forewarning is also unnecessary. (2) One might have thought this prohibition to be excluded from the forewarning requirement because, by its very nature as stemming from one's unchecked anger, a curse will generally be uttered hastily, before there is opportunity to provide forewarning. To counter these arguments, *Rambam* and Chinuch specify that forewarning is indeed necessary.

24. The laws are codified in *Rambam, Hil. Sanhedrin* 26:1-6, and in *Shulchan Aruch, Choshen Mishpat* §27.

25. I.e., in Eretz Yisrael and the Diaspora, whether the *Beis HaMikdash* is standing or not. See the Insight for discussion of the applicability of this prohibition in our times.

26. In accordance with the general rule pertaining to mitzvah-prohibitions.

## MISHPATIM / MITZVAH 69: THE PROHIBITION TO CURSE A JUDGE

מִיִּשְׂרָאֵל הַכְּשֵׁרִים שֶׁהֵם בִּכְלָל אִסּוּר זֶה, כְּמוֹ שֶׁנִּכְתֹּב בְּסֵדֶר קְדֹשִׁים תִּהְיוּ,[27] וְאַחַת מִפְּנֵי שֶׁהוּא דַיָּן.[28]

**upstanding Jew,** שֶׁהֵם בִּכְלָל אִסּוּר זֶה — all of **whom are included in this prohibition,** meaning that one is prohibited to curse any of them, כְּמוֹ שֶׁנִּכְתֹּב בְּסֵדֶר קְדֹשִׁים תִּהְיוּ — **as we will write in *Parashas Kedoshim*** (Mitzvah 231);[27] וְאַחַת מִפְּנֵי שֶׁהוּא דַיָּן — **and one** additional set of *malkus* **because he is a judge,** whom one is specifically forbidden to curse under the current prohibition.[28]

---

### NOTES

27. Mitzvah 231 prohibits cursing any Jew, as long as he is not a wicked person whose behavior is outside the norms of his people (*Mechilta* to our verse; *Sanhedrin* 85a).

28. Since the judges referred to by the current mitzvah are also upstanding Jews, one who curses them has violated two separate prohibitions and therefore receives two sets of *malkus* (Rambam, *Hil. Sanhedrin* 26:2; cf. *Tur, Choshen Mishpat* 27:1, as understood by *Taz* 27:1 and *Sma* 27:5; see *Shaarei Teshuvah* 3:46 regarding a corrupt judge).

Although, generally speaking, the penalty of *malkus* is reserved for transgressions that involve action, and not merely speech alone, the prohibitions against cursing are an exception to this rule (see *Temurah* 3a-4a, where this is derived from Scripture). [For further discussion of the *malkus* penalty in this case, see Rambam, *Sefer HaMitzvos, Lo Saaseh* 60; *Maharsha, Sanhedrin* 66a ד"ה אם כן; *Urim VeTumim* 27:2; see also *Lechem Mishneh, Hil. Mamrim* 5:4.]

---

### ✎§ Insight: Which Judges Are One Prohibited to Curse?

The Torah phrases the prohibition to curse a judge as אֱלֹהִים לֹא תְקַלֵּל, *You shall not revile Elohim* (*Exodus* 22:27). Rambam states (*Hil. Sanhedrin* 4:4) that, as a rule, when the Torah refers to judges with the term אֱלֹהִים, *Elohim*, it refers specifically to judges ordained with the special form of *semichah* that existed in earlier times. This ordination was conferred in Eretz Yisrael by a sage whose own ordination could be traced back through an unbroken chain of sages all the way to Moses (as described in Mitzvah 491). Some therefore explain that our prohibition applies only to such judges. Accordingly, it emerges that nowadays, when we have no judges who have been ordained in that manner, this prohibition is not in force (*Urim VeTumim* 27:2, *Minchas Chinuch* §5). However, Rambam (*Hil. Sanhedrin* 4:11) does suggest a means through which *semichah* can be reinstituted nowadays (see there). Based on that, this prohibition could theoretically be applicable even in our times (*Minchas Chinuch* ibid.).

*Minchas Chinuch* and others note, however, that this approach does not fit well with Chinuch's words. Chinuch states (at notes 1-2) that in our verse the Torah refers to a judge with the term *Elohim* (rather than the more literal שׁוֹפֵט, *shofeit*) in order to include in the same expression the additional prohibition against blaspheming the Divine Name. If in fact the prohibition against cursing a judge pertains specifically to one who received the special *semichah*, then that itself explains why the term *Elohim* is used, and there is no basis to additionally include a prohibition against blasphemy (see *Minchas Chinuch* ibid., *Minchas Soless* §69, and *Shevet HaLevi, Kuntres HaMitzvos* §30). Moreover, Chinuch states at the end of the mitzvah that the prohibition applies in every location and in all times — and he does not add any qualification about the need for the now-lapsed *semichah*. By contrast, in Mitzvah 71, the Prohibition to Curse a *Nasi*, Chinuch does qualify it as applying only when the position of *Nasi* exists. Since he omits any such qualification here, we may infer that the prohibition against cursing a judge *literally* applies in our times, even though the judges lack *semichah*.

Indeed, numerous authorities draw the same inference from *Shulchan Aruch* (*Choshen Mishpat* 27:1), who sets down the prohibition to curse a judge without any qualification, even though *Shulchan Aruch* customarily cites only laws that apply in our times. These authorities therefore rule that the prohibition to curse a judge applies to anyone who holds an official position as a judge, even nowadays. This prohibition does not, however, apply to a person who is not an official judge but was chosen by litigants to adjudicate their case. Such a person is covered only by the prohibition to curse any upstanding Jew, i.e., Mitzvah 231 (*Birkei Yosef, Choshen Mishpat* 27:4; *Aruch HaShulchan* 27:1; see

also *Teshuvos HaRivash* §79 ד"ה ולכן and §80 ד"ה לך ודע; and *Nesivos HaMishpat* 27:3). Although the Torah uses the term *Elohim* here, that is because it wishes to include the additional prohibition of blasphemy in the same verse, not because it wishes to limit the prohibition to the cursing of a judge ordained with the special *semichah* (*Minchas Soless* ibid., *Shevet HaLevi* ibid.; see also *Minchah Chadashah* 71:2).

Some suggest further that the prohibition not to revile *Elohim* encompasses not only a judge, but any person appointed to a position of authority over a community (*Teshuvos Raanach* §111 שהוא ועוד ד"ה ממונה, cited by *Ketzos HaChoshen* 27:1; see *Minchas Soless*). For an application of this principle, see Mitzvah 71 note 9.

## 27 ☐ MISHPATIM / MITZVAH 70: THE PROHIBITION OF BLASPHEMY

### ~ מִצְוָה ע: לָאו דְּבִרְכַּת הַשֵּׁם ~

וּמִשָּׁרְשֵׁי הַמִּצְוָה בְּבִרְכַּת הַשֵּׁם, לְפִי שֶׁמִּתְרוֹקֵן הָאָדָם בַּמַּאֲמָר הָרַע הַהוּא מִכָּל טוֹבָה, וְכָל הוֹד נַפְשׁוֹ נֶהְפָּךְ לְמַשְׁחִית,[1] וְהִנֵּה הוּא נֶחְשָׁב כַּבְּהֵמוֹת, כִּי בְּאוֹתוֹ דָּבָר מַמָּשׁ שֶׁהִבְדִּילוֹ הַשֵּׁם יִתְבָּרַךְ לְטוֹבָה וּבוֹ נַעֲשָׂה אָדָם, וְהוּא הַדִּבּוּר שֶׁנִּבְדַּל בּוֹ מִמִּינֵי הַבְּהֵמוֹת, מַבְדִּיל הוּא אֶת עַצְמוֹ לְרָעָה[2] וּמוֹצִיא עַצְמוֹ לְגַמְרֵי מִכָּל גֶּדֶר הַדַּעַת,

---

## ~ Mitzvah 70 ~
## The Prohibition of "Blessing" Hashem [Blasphemy]

אֱלֹהִים לֹא תְקַלֵּל
*You shall not revile Elohim* (Exodus 22:27)

Chinuch explained at the beginning of Mitzvah 69 that the verse *You shall not revile Elohim* has a dual interpretation: It prohibits cursing a judge (Mitzvah 69), and it also prohibits "blessing" Hashem (Mitzvah 70). In his discussion there, Chinuch demonstrated that the Torah intended for both of these interpretations, such that this single phrase encompasses two distinct mitzvah-prohibitions. Chinuch also explained why it is necessary for a verse to specifically prohibit blasphemy, when we already know from another verse that a blasphemer is liable to execution. Having previously established the basis for the prohibition of blasphemy, Chinuch focuses here on the underlying purpose, the laws, and the applicability of this mitzvah. As was explained in our introduction to Mitzvah 69, Chinuch originally wrote these two mitzvos as one chapter, but in recent editions they are commonly divided into separate chapters. Hence, Chinuch's words here are a direct continuation of what he wrote in Mitzvah 69.

### ~ Underlying Purpose of the Mitzvah ~

Chinuch addresses the unspoken question of why God, Who is clearly impervious to any curse, forbids us from uttering one against Him:

וּמִשָּׁרְשֵׁי הַמִּצְוָה בְּבִרְכַּת הַשֵּׁם – **And, among the underlying purposes of the mitzvah, with regard to "blessing" Hashem,** לְפִי שֶׁמִּתְרוֹקֵן הָאָדָם בַּמַּאֲמָר הָרַע הַהוּא מִכָּל טוֹבָה – is that it is for-bidden **because by way of this evil utterance, a person becomes emptied of all goodness,** וְכָל הוֹד נַפְשׁוֹ נֶהְפָּךְ לְמַשְׁחִית – **and** the faculty of speech, which is **the very glory of his soul, is** thereby **transformed** from glory **to destructiveness.**[1] וְהִנֵּה הוּא נֶחְשָׁב כַּבְּהֵמוֹת – **Indeed,** on account of the blasphemer's corrupted speech, **he is considered comparable to animals;** כִּי בְּאוֹתוֹ דָּבָר מַמָּשׁ שֶׁהִבְדִּילוֹ הַשֵּׁם יִתְבָּרַךְ לְטוֹבָה – **because with that very thing through which Hashem, blessed be He, distinguished him for goodness,** וּבוֹ נַעֲשָׂה אָדָם – **and by which he becomes** uniquely **human,** וְהוּא הַדִּבּוּר שֶׁנִּבְדַּל בּוֹ מִמִּינֵי הַבְּהֵמוֹת – **namely, the** faculty of **speech through which he is distinguished from the** various **species of animals,** מַבְדִּיל הוּא אֶת עַצְמוֹ לְרָעָה – with that very faculty **he distinguishes himself for evil!**[2] וּמוֹצִיא עַצְמוֹ לְגַמְרֵי מִכָּל גֶּדֶר הַדַּעַת – **Moreover,**

---

### NOTES

1. [I.e., although the blasphemy is ineffective, it destroys the person's character.] It would seem that Chinuch bases his approach here on the Gemara (*Kereisos* 7b), which compares the word מְגַדֵּף (*blasphemer*) to the similar word מְגָרֵד (*to shovel* or *empty out*). [The letter *dalet* is exegetically interchangeable with the letter *reish* (*Rashi* ad loc.).] This linguistic similarity, which points to a relationship between blasphemy and emptying out, is explained there by way of a simile whereby a blasphemer is viewed as one who has "emptied the plate and even diminished it." Chinuch apparently understands this "plate" to refer to the person's character, which through blasphemy becomes emptied of goodness and diminished — or, in the words of Chinuch (paraphrasing *Daniel* 10:8), "transformed to destructiveness." See *Rashi* to *Kereisos* loc. cit. for another explanation.

2. The capacity for intelligent speech is the hallmark of our distinctly human essence, and is therefore referred

## 28 ❑ משפטים / מצוה ע: לאו דברכת השם

וְנַעֲשָׂה כְּשֶׁרֶץ נִמְאָס וְנֶאֱלָח וּלְמַטָּה מִמֶּנּוּ, וְעַל כֵּן הִזְהִירַתְנוּ הַתּוֹרָה עַל זֶה, כִּי הָאֵל הַטּוֹב יַחְפֹּץ בְּטוֹבָתֵנוּ, וְכָל דִּבּוּר וְדִבּוּר הַגּוֹרֵם מְנִיעַת הַטּוֹבָה מִמֶּנּוּ יָבוֹא כְּנֶגֶד חֶפְצוֹ בָּרוּךְ הוּא[3].

מִדִּינֵי הַמִּצְוָה, כְּגוֹן מַה שֶּׁפֵּרְשׁוּ שֶׁאֵין הַחִיּוּב עַד שֶׁיְּפָרֵשׁ אֶת הַשֵּׁם הַמְיֻחָד שֶׁהוּא יוּ"ד הֵ"א וָי"ו הֵ"א, אוֹ שֶׁל אָלֶ"ף דָּלֶ"ת נוּ"ן יוּ"ד כְּדַעַת קְצָת מְפָרְשִׁים[4].

---

with such abominable speech **he completely removes himself from any framework of intelligence,** וְנַעֲשָׂה כְּשֶׁרֶץ נִמְאָס וְנֶאֱלָח — and thereby **becomes comparable to a loathsome and detestable vermin,** וּלְמַטָּה מִמֶּנּוּ — and even **lower than that.** וְעַל כֵּן הִזְהִירַתְנוּ הַתּוֹרָה עַל זֶה — **Therefore, the Torah warns us against [such speech];** for — כִּי הָאֵל הַטּוֹב יַחְפֹּץ בְּטוֹבָתֵנוּ **the Almighty, Who is Good, desires** only **our benefit,** וְכָל דִּבּוּר וְדִבּוּר הַגּוֹרֵם מְנִיעַת הַטּוֹבָה מִמֶּנּוּ — **and each and every** evil **utterance that brings about the withholding of benefit from us** יָבוֹא כְּנֶגֶד חֶפְצוֹ בָּרוּךְ הוּא — **comes in conflict with His desire, blessed is He.**[3]

### ✑ Laws of the Mitzvah ✑

מִדִּינֵי הַמִּצְוָה — **Among the laws of the mitzvah** (i.e., the prohibition of "blessing" Hashem) is, כְּגוֹן מַה שֶּׁפֵּרְשׁוּ — **for example, that which [our Sages] explained** (*Sanhedrin* 56a), שֶׁאֵין הַחִיּוּב עַד שֶׁיְּפָרֵשׁ אֶת הַשֵּׁם הַמְיֻחָד — **that** although (as we shall see) a violator is liable to the death penalty, one does **not incur liability** to death **unless he explicitly pronounces the Distinct Name** of Hashem, שֶׁהוּא יוּ"ד הֵ"א וָי"ו הֵ"א — **which is** the Name spelled *Yud, Hei, Vav, Hei* (i.e., the Tetragrammaton), and he pronounces it according to that written form, אוֹ שֶׁל אָלֶ"ף דָּלֶ"ת נוּ"ן יוּ"ד כְּדַעַת קְצָת מְפָרְשִׁים — **or, according to some commentators,** if he pronounces the Name in accordance with the spelling of *Aleph, Dalet, Nun, Yud* (i.e., *Adonai*), and "blesses" either of those Names.[4]

---

NOTES

to by Chinuch as the "glory of our soul." This relationship between speech and our very essence is borne out by *Targum Onkelos* to the verse (*Genesis* 2:7): וַיְהִי הָאָדָם לְנֶפֶשׁ חַיָּה — literally, *and man became a living being* — which *Onkelos* renders, *and man became a speaking spirit,* thus underscoring that speech is the distinguishing feature of a human being. Hence, one who abuses his faculty of speech is comparable to a beast.

3. Chinuch states repeatedly throughout this work that Hashem bestows His blessing upon those who are worthy, namely, those with good character traits who emulate His ways (see, for example, Mitzvah 66, at notes 7-8). One who stoops to blasphemy acts in a subhuman manner and obviously renders himself unworthy of Hashem's blessing. The prohibition of such speech thus protects us from forfeiting His blessing of goodness.

[It should be noted also that one who speaks blasphemously against Hashem is viewed as being כּוֹפֵר בְּעִיקָר, *denying the fundamental basis [of Judaism],* since such speech encompasses a rejection of belief in His omnipotence (see *Sanhedrin* 45b). The prohibition protects against this moral collapse as well.]

4. The Torah states (*Leviticus* 24:16): וְנֹקֵב שֵׁם ה' מוֹת יוּמָת, *One who blasphemously pronounces the Name of* HASHEM *shall be put to death.* Since in this verse the Name is written *Yud, Hei, Vav, Hei,* the Sages derive that, in order for a blasphemer to be liable to the death penalty, the Name that he targets with his "blessing" must be the Distinct Name (see *Sanhedrin* 56a).

Now, although this Name is written as *Yud, Hei, Vav, Hei,* it is ordinarily not pronounced that way. The common pronunciation is *Adonai* — as though it were written *Aleph, Dalet, Nun, Yud* [אֲדֹנָי]. This is because the Torah states (*Exodus* 3:15): זֶה שְׁמִי לְעֹלָם וְזֶה זִכְרִי לְדֹר דֹּר, *This is My Name forever, and this is My remembrance from generation to generation,* which teaches that "not as My Name is written shall it be pronounced" (*Pesachim* 50a). Some authorities maintain that, since *Adonai* is a correct pronunciation of the Distinct Name, one is liable to death for "blessing" the Name if he pronounces it in that manner (*Rambam, Hil. Avodah Zarah* 2:7; *Shach, Yoreh Deah* 340:53; see also *Tosafos, Shevuos* 35a ד"ה בפר"ח גרס). Others, however, rule that one is not liable to death for blasphemy unless he pronounces the Distinct Name according to its written form of *Yud, Hei, Vav, Hei* (*Yad Ramah, Sanhedrin* 60a ד"ה אמר ר' יהושע; *Igros Ramah* §13, cited by *Kesef Mishneh* to *Rambam* ibid.).

The preceding pertains to incurring the death penalty in *beis din* for blaspheming the Name; since the verse that spells out the death penalty states the Distinct Name, only one who "blesses" that Name incurs that penalty. The *prohibition* of blasphemy, however, states: *You shall not revile "Elohim."* Hence, it is prohibited to "bless" even one of the secondary Names of God, and even one of the descriptive terms for Him, including the Name in a foreign language (*Sanhedrin* 56a; for elaboration, see Mitzvah 69 notes 18-19 and note 22). [One who does so incurs *malkus* (*Meiri* to *Sanhedrin* ibid.; see below, end of note 25).]

Moreover, according to some Rishonim, although one

# 29 ☐ MISHPATIM / MITZVAH 70: THE PROHIBITION OF BLASPHEMY

וּמַה שֶּׁאָמְרוּ שֶׁבְּכָל יוֹם וָיוֹם שׁוֹאֲלִין אֶת הָעֵדִים בְּכִנּוּיֵי[5], יַכֶּה יוֹסֵי אֶת יוֹסֵי[6], נִגְמַר הַדִּין מוֹצִיאִין כָּל הָאָדָם לַחוּץ[7] וְשׁוֹאֲלִין אֶת הַגָּדוֹל שֶׁבָּעֵדִים וְאוֹמְרִין לוֹ אֱמֹר מַה שֶּׁשָּׁמַעְתָּ בְּפִיךָ[8], וְהוּא אוֹמֵר[9], וְהַדַּיָּנִין עוֹמְדִין עַל רַגְלֵיהֶם וְקוֹרְעִין[10] וְלֹא מְאַחִין[11],

---

Chinuch now delineates laws related to the court proceedings for the blasphemer:

וּמַה שֶּׁאָמְרוּ — The laws include **also that which [our Sages] said** (Mishnah, *Sanhedrin* 56a) with regard to the court proceedings, שֶׁבְּכָל יוֹם וָיוֹם שׁוֹאֲלִין אֶת הָעֵדִים בְּכִנּוּיֵי — **that on each day** over which those proceedings take place and the witnesses must testify, **[the judges] interrogate the witnesses** by using **a pseudonym** for God's Name,[5] so as to avoid having them explicitly repeat the blasphemy. Instead of asking the witnesses to report the actual utterance that they allegedly heard, יַכֶּה יוֹסֵי אֶת יוֹסֵי — the judges have them use a euphemistic utterance such as, **"May Yose strike Yose."**[6] נִגְמַר הַדִּין — However, when **the case is** about to be **completed,** מוֹצִיאִין כָּל הָאָדָם לַחוּץ — **they send** **everyone** other than the witnesses **out** of the courtroom,[7] וְשׁוֹאֲלִין אֶת הַגָּדוֹל שֶׁבָּעֵדִים — **and they ask the more eminent of the** two **witnesses** to repeat his testimony without use of any pseudonym, וְאוֹמְרִין לוֹ אֱמֹר מַה שֶּׁשָּׁמַעְתָּ בְּפִיךָ — **saying to him, "State** explicitly **with your** own **mouth what you heard** the blasphemer say."[8] וְהוּא אוֹמֵר — **He** then **says** what he heard,[9] וְהַדַּיָּנִין עוֹמְדִין עַל רַגְלֵיהֶם וְקוֹרְעִין — **and the judges stand on their feet and rend** their garments,[10] וְלֹא מְאַחִין —

---

## NOTES

who "blesses" a secondary Name is exempt from the death penalty in *beis din,* he is liable to *kares* (excision). This is because Scripture states (*Leviticus* 24:15): אִישׁ אִישׁ כִּי יְקַלֵּל אֱלֹהָיו וְנָשָׂא חֶטְאוֹ, *Any man who will blaspheme his God shall bear his sin.* This verse does not mention the Distinct Name, and when it states that the man shall "bear his sin" it refers to *kares* (*Rashi, Sanhedrin* 56a ד"ה וחכ"א and *Tosafos* there ד"ה ועל הכינויים; cf. *Rambam, Hil. Avodah Zarah* 2:7, as explained by *Pri Chadash,* cited in *Sefer HaLikkutim* in Frankel ed.).

5. The term כִּנּוּי, translated here as "pseudonym," should not be confused with the same term used in the preceding mitzvah (at note 19) to indicate the "descriptive terms" for God. Rather, it refers to the court's substitution of another name in place of the Name of God that the perpetrator had actually used, as if the curse were directed at some entity other than God (*Rashi, Sanhedrin* 56a ד"ה בכל יום).

6. The name יוֹסֵי (Yose) was chosen as the pseudonym for Hashem because it shares the same number of letters as the Tetragrammaton — i.e., the Name that one must employ in his curse (either as it is written or as it is read) in order to be liable. Furthermore, the *gematria* (numeric equivalent) of the name יוֹסֵי is 86, the same as one of the other Names of God — the Name אֱלֹהִים (*Rashi* ibid.; cf. *Yad Ramah* there).

The expression "May Yose strike Yose" reflects the law that a blasphemer is not liable unless His blasphemy employs a *double* usage of Hashem's Name and, so to speak, turns the Name against itself. Thus, in order to incur the death penalty, he must say "May [a Name] strike [a Name]," or "May [a Name] curse [a Name]." Since the witnesses substitute "Yose" for the Name of Hashem, when testifying about blasphemy they would say that the perpetrator uttered a curse with the formula of "May Yose strike Yose" (*Sanhedrin* ibid. with *Rashi* ד"ה שם בשם). This will be additionally clarified below, in note 16.

7. The spectators are sent out because before the judges issue a verdict they must hear explicit testimony about the blasphemy, and it is disrespectful for this to occur in public (*Rashi* ibid. ד"ה אלא מוציאין).

8. The judges may not sentence the accused to death based on testimony that employs only the euphemistic curse, "May Yose strike Yose," for a curse that is literally phrased in such a manner is not blasphemy, and surely not punishable. Rather, the testimony must be explicit in order for *beis din* to issue a guilty verdict against the accused (*Rashi* ibid. ד"ה נגמר הדין; see also *Meiri* there).

9. Some argue that he does not actually repeat the curse, for then he himself would be uttering blasphemy. Rather, he explicitly says the Name and then states that it was this actual Name that the accused person blasphemed with the formula of "May Yose strike Yose" (*Kesef Mishneh, Hil. Avodah Zarah* 2:8, citing *Yerushalmi Sanhedrin* 7:8). Others explain, however, that the witness does repeat the blasphemy word for word, and since this is a requirement of the judicial process it is not deemed a sinful utterance (*Meiri, Sanhedrin* 56a, and *Tos. Yom Tov, Sanhedrin* 7:5, based on the plain language of the Mishnah there, and *Talmud Bavli's* omission of any qualification of the Mishnah's words; for further discussion, see *Mishnas Chachamim, Yavin Shemuah* 13:3; see also *Minchas Chinuch* §10).

10. The rending requirement is derived from an incident recorded in *II Kings* (18:37), in which the officers of King Hezekiah rent their garments upon hearing blasphemy uttered by Rabshakeh, an emissary of the Assyrian king Sennaherib (*Sanhedrin* 60a; see Chinuch below, at note 18). [This is a Rabbinic obligation (*Minchas Chinuch* §10; *Pischei Teshuvah, Yoreh Deah* 340:18).]

The rending of garments as a display of mourning is

## 30 ❏ משפטים / מצוה ע: לאו דברכת השם

וְהָעֵד הַשֵּׁנִי אוֹמֵר אַף אֲנִי כָּמוֹהוּ שָׁמַעְתִּי, וְאִם הָיוּ עֵדִים רַבִּים, כֻּלָּם אוֹמְרִין כֵּן.[12] וּמַה שֶּׁאָמְרוּ זִכְרוֹנָם לִבְרָכָה שֶׁמְּגַדֵּף אַף עַל פִּי שֶׁחָזַר תּוֹךְ כְּדֵי דִבּוּר נִסְקָל,[13] וּמִי שֶׁגִּדֵּף הַשֵּׁם בְּשֵׁם מֵעֲבוֹדָה זָרָה,[14] קַנָּאִין פּוֹגְעִין בּוֹ,[15] וְאִם לֹא פָּגְעוּ בּוֹ וּבָא לְבֵית דִּין, אֵינוֹ נִסְקָל

וְהָעֵד הַשֵּׁנִי אוֹמֵר אַף אֲנִי כָּמוֹהוּ שָׁמַעְתִּי — The **and do not** ever **repair** those rent garments.[11] **second witness** does not explicitly repeat the blasphemy, but merely **says, "I too heard the same as he";** כֻּלָּם אוֹמְרִין כֵּן — **they all** וְאִם הָיוּ עֵדִים רַבִּים — **and if there were multiple witnesses, say this** — i.e., that they heard the same as the first witness.[12]

Chinuch now turns to other laws of blasphemy:

וּמַה שֶּׁאָמְרוּ זִכְרוֹנָם לִבְרָכָה — **Also** included is **that which [our Sages], of blessed memory, said** (Nedarim 87a), שֶׁמְּגַדֵּף אַף עַל פִּי שֶׁחָזַר תּוֹךְ כְּדֵי דִבּוּר נִסְקָל — **that the blasphemer is subject to** sekilah (stoning) for his blasphemy **even if he retracts** it **within "the time of an utterance."**[13]

וּמִי שֶׁגִּדֵּף הַשֵּׁם בְּשֵׁם מֵעֲבוֹדָה זָרָה — **Also,** the law that **if one blasphemed the Name** of God **with a name of an** avodah zarah,[14] קַנָּאִין פּוֹגְעִין בּוֹ — **zealots could assault him.**[15] וְאִם לֹא פָּגְעוּ בּוֹ וּבָא לְבֵית דִּין — **If,** however, **they did not assault him** at the time of his sin **and he was brought to** beis din to be tried for his blasphemy, אֵינוֹ נִסְקָל — **he is not subject to** sekilah,

### NOTES

always done while standing (Moed Katan 20b), and the rending for blasphemy is no different. Furthermore, even before hearing the testimony, the judges were required to rise in deference to the Divine Name that the witness was about to pronounce (see Sanhedrin 60a and Minchas Chinuch ibid.).

11. This stands in contrast to the law of one who rends his clothing for a departed relative (other than a parent), where the tear may be mended after thirty days (see Rambam, Hil. Aveil 9:1-2). The rending done upon hearing blasphemy is considered more severe and may never be mended (see Sanhedrin ibid.).

12. In general, whenever a second (or third, etc.) witness states that he heard or witnessed what the first witness had, that is sufficient to count as valid testimony on the Biblical level. Ordinarily, the Sages did not rely on this, and they required the latter witness (or witnesses) to explicitly repeat the testimony. In the case of the blasphemer, however, they did not do so, out of respect for the Divine Name (Sanhedrin 60a with Rashi).

13. The "time of an utterance" is the length of time it takes for a student to greet his teacher by saying: שָׁלוֹם עָלֶיךָ רַבִּי, Shalom alecha Rebbi ["Peace unto you, my teacher"] (see Makkos 6a and Bava Kamma 73b; Rambam, Hil. Shevuos 2:17; Mishnah Berurah 206:12 with Shaar HaTziyun §10). In almost every area of Torah law (e.g., commerce, testimony), if one makes a transaction or a statement and then retracts it within "the time of an utterance," his retraction is valid and his transaction or statement is void. In the case of blasphemy, however, no such grace period is given. The reason a statement can generally be retracted within "the time of an utterance" is that people sometimes say or do things without proper contemplation,

relying on the assumption that they will be afforded the opportunity to retract if they recognize their error immediately. This dispensation does not apply in the case of blasphemy, for it is a matter of such gravity that no one would utter it without premeditation (Ran, Nedarim 87a ד"ה והלכתא; for other explanations, see Rashbam, Bava Basra 129b ד"ה לבר and Tosafos there ד"ה חוץ).

[The same applies to idolatry (and for the same reason): If one accepts an idol upon himself as his god and then retracts immediately, within "the time of an utterance," he is nevertheless liable to the death penalty for idolatry (Chinuch above, Mitzvah 26; see notes 19-21 there, and see there for an additional context in which this law applies; see also Mitzvah 30 with note 35).]

14. For example, he said, "May Pe'or (the name of an idol) strike 'Yose' [i.e., the Distinct Name]" (Rambam, Commentary to the Mishnah, Sanhedrin 81b, and Hil. Avodah Zarah 2:9; cf. Rashi, Sanhedrin 81b ד"ה יכה קוסם את קוסמו; see also Yad Ramah and Meiri there).

15. In this case, he is not liable to execution through beis din, as Chinuch will explain. Nevertheless, God-fearing and zealous individuals who heard such an utterance were (in earlier times) authorized to assault him and put him to death. Since the blasphemer publicly acted with blatant audacity before God, Halachah LeMoshe MiSinai (the Law transmitted Orally to Moses at Sinai) authorized "zealots" — i.e., righteous individuals who were justly provoked by the affront to God, to avenge His dishonor — to kill him [see Chinuch further]. However, this authorization pertained only at the moment of his sin, not afterward (Mishnah, Sanhedrin 81b with Rashi).

# 31 ☐ MISHPATIM / MITZVAH 70: THE PROHIBITION OF BLASPHEMY

עַד שֶׁיְּבָרֵךְ בְּשֵׁם מִן הַשֵּׁמוֹת הַמְיֻחָדִין[16], וְהַטַּעַם שֶׁאֵינוֹ נִסְקָל לְפִי שֶׁהוּא מַכִּיר בְּעַצְמוֹ מַכִּיר אֲפִלּוּ בְּעֵת הַכַּעַס שֶׁאֵין דְּבָרָיו אֶלָּא שְׁטוּת גָּמוּר, וּמִכָּל מָקוֹם פּוֹגְעִין בּוֹ קַנָּאִין אַחַר שֶׁהִשְׁחִית וְהִתְעִיב וְהֵעֵז פָּנָיו לְדַבֵּר דְּבָרִים רָעִים כָּאֵלֶּה.[17] וּמַה שֶּׁאָמְרוּ שֶׁכָּל הַשּׁוֹמֵעַ בִּרְכַּת הַשֵּׁם מִפִּי יִשְׂרָאֵל חַיָּב לִקְרֹעַ, אֲבָל הַשּׁוֹמֵעַ מִן הַגּוֹי אֵינוֹ חַיָּב לִקְרֹעַ, וְלֹא קָרְעוּ אֶלְיָקִים וְשֶׁבְנָא אֶלָּא מִפְּנֵי שֶׁרַבְשָׁקֵה מוּמָר הָיָה.[18] וְכָל הָעֵדִים וְהַדַּיָּנִין סוֹמְכִין יְדֵיהֶם אֶחָד אֶחָד עַל רֹאשׁ הַמְגַדֵּף

---

עַד שֶׁיְּבָרֵךְ בְּשֵׁם מִן הַשֵּׁמוֹת הַמְיֻחָדִין — **for one does not incur** *sekilah* **unless he "blesses" the Distinct Name with a Name from among the specific Names** of God.[16] וְהַטַּעַם שֶׁאֵינוֹ נִסְקָל — **The reason he is not subject to** *sekilah* for "blessing" Hashem via the name of an *avodah zarah* is לְפִי שֶׁהוּא בְּעַצְמוֹ מַכִּיר אֲפִלּוּ בְּעֵת הַכַּעַס — **because he himself recognizes, even in his time of anger** when he pronounces the "blessing," שֶׁאֵין דְּבָרָיו אֶלָּא שְׁטוּת גָּמוּר — **that his words are nothing more than utter foolishness,** since the *avodah zarah* is powerless. וּמִכָּל מָקוֹם פּוֹגְעִין בּוֹ קַנָּאִין — **Nevertheless,** notwithstanding the utter foolishness of his statement, **zealots may assault him,** אַחַר שֶׁהִשְׁחִית וְהִתְעִיב וְהֵעֵז פָּנָיו — **insofar as he acted perversely, despicably, and brazenly** לְדַבֵּר דְּבָרִים רָעִים כָּאֵלֶּה — **in expressing evil utterances such as these.**[17]

Chinuch discusses a law pertaining to those who hear blasphemy:

וּמַה שֶּׁאָמְרוּ — **Also** included is **that which [our Sages] said** (*Sanhedrin* 60a), שֶׁכָּל הַשּׁוֹמֵעַ בִּרְכַּת הַשֵּׁם מִפִּי יִשְׂרָאֵל חַיָּב לִקְרֹעַ — **that anyone who hears a "blessing" of the Name from a Jew is obligated to rend** his garments, אֲבָל הַשּׁוֹמֵעַ מִן הַגּוֹי אֵינוֹ חַיָּב לִקְרֹעַ — **but one who hears it from an idolater is not obligated to rend** his garments. And although Scripture (*II Kings* 18:17-37) relates that when Rabshakeh, an emissary of the Assyrian king Sennaherib, stood at the gates of Jerusalem and blasphemed the Name, King Hezekiah's officers who heard the blasphemy — namely, Elyakim ben Hilkiah, Shevna the Scribe, and Yoach ben Assaf — rent their garments, this is not a difficulty; וְלֹא קָרְעוּ אֶלְיָקִים וְשֶׁבְנָא אֶלָּא מִפְּנֵי שֶׁרַבְשָׁקֵה מוּמָר הָיָה — **Elyakim and Shevna** (and Yoach) **rent** their garments **only because Rabshakeh,** who had uttered the blasphemy, **was not an idolater but an apostate** Jew, as the Gemara (ibid.) notes.[18]

Chinuch turns to a unique law pertaining to the execution of a blasphemer:

וְכָל הָעֵדִים וְהַדַּיָּנִין סוֹמְכִין יְדֵיהֶם אֶחָד אֶחָד עַל רֹאשׁ הַמְגַדֵּף — **If one is found guilty of blasphemy and sentenced to death, then before his execution, all the witnesses and the judges lean their hands,**

---

### NOTES

16. That is, he employs the formula of "May [a Name] strike [the Name]," which has been referred to as "May Yose strike Yose" (see note 6). This rule is derived from the repetitive expression in the verse (*Leviticus* 24:16): *one who blasphemously pronounces the Name of* HASHEM *shall be put to death ... when he blasphemes the Name*. The double reference to "blaspheming the Name" teaches that one is liable to death only if he *uses the Name Itself* to "bless" the Name (*Sanhedrin* 56a with *Rashi*; cf. *Kesef Mishneh, Hil. Avodah Zarah* 2:7).

There is disagreement whether the Name *with which* one "blesses" must be the Distinct Name of God, or it may be another of His Names. *Rambam* (*Hil. Avodah Zarah* 2:7) rules that only the blasphemed Name needs to be the Distinct Name, but the Name with which one "blesses" it can be any one of the specific Names that one is forbidden to erase. [In addition to the Tetragrammaton and *Adonai*, these Names include *El, Eloka, Elokim, Eheyeh, Shaddai, Tzevaos* (*Rambam, Hil. Yesodei HaTorah* 6:2; see Mitzvah 69 note 18).] Others maintain that *both* the Name that one "blesses" *and* the Name with which he "blesses" it must be the Distinct Name of God, i.e., the Tetragrammaton (*Igros Ramah* §13, cited by *Kesef Mishneh* ibid.). [Chinuch's ruling here is a direct quotation of *Rambam, Hil. Avodah Zarah* 2:9, indicating that he concurs with *Rambam's* view (see *Minchas Chinuch* §5).]

If no Name at all is used to "bless" the distinct Name (e.g., one simply says, "May 'Yose' be cursed"), then the perpetrator is not liable to death. Presumably, the law that Chinuch stated in Mitzvah 69 in the context of cursing a judge — that the utterance is forbidden though not punishable — applies here as well [see note 21 there] (*Minchas Chinuch* §2,4; cf. *Chidushei HaRan, Sanhedrin* 56a, who states that the perpetrator is liable to *malkus*).

17. See note 15 above. [Others explain that the blasphemer's death is authorized because his "blessing" God in the name of an idol implies a heretic belief that the idol has the power to impact God (*Yad Ramah, Sanhedrin* 81b ד״ה מתני; see Gemara there, end of 82b).]

18. See the Insight below for further discussion.

## 32 □ משפטים / מצוה ע: לאו דברכת השם

וְאוֹמְרִים לוֹ דָּמְךָ בְּרֹאשְׁךָ שֶׁאַתָּה גָּרַמְתָּ לָךְ, וְאֵין בְּכָל הֲרוּגֵי בֵּית דִּין מִי שֶׁסּוֹמְכִין עָלָיו אֶלָּא מְגַדֵּף בִּלְבַד[19], שֶׁנֶּאֱמַר (ויקרא כ״ד, י״ד) וְסָמְכוּ כָל הַשֹּׁמְעִים אֶת יְדֵיהֶם עַל רֹאשׁוֹ[20], וְיֶתֶר פְּרָטֶיהָ, מְבֹאָרִים בְּסַנְהֶדְרִין פֶּרֶק ז' (דף נ״ה ע״ב)[21].

וְנוֹהֵג אִסּוּר זֶה בְּכָל מָקוֹם וּבְכָל זְמַן[22]. וְהָעוֹבֵר עַל זֶה וּבֵרַךְ הַשֵּׁם בָּעִנְיָן שֶׁאָמַרְנוּ, נִסְקָל בָּאָרֶץ עַל פִּי סְמוּכִין[23]. וְעַכְשָׁו בְּחוּצָה לָאָרֶץ שֶׁאֵין לָנוּ סְמוּכִין[24],

---

**וְאוֹמְרִים לוֹ** — and they say to him, each one individually, upon the head of the blasphemer, **דָּמְךָ בְּרֹאשְׁךָ שֶׁאַתָּה גָּרַמְתָּ לָךְ** — "Your blood is upon your own head, for you caused this fate to come upon yourself." **וְאֵין בְּכָל הֲרוּגֵי בֵּית דִּין מִי שֶׁסּוֹמְכִין עָלָיו** — There is no one else among all those who are executed by beis din upon whom they lean their hands before the execution, **אֶלָּא מְגַדֵּף בִּלְבַד** — other than the blasphemer alone.[19] **שֶׁנֶּאֱמַר** — This requirement in regard to a blasphemer is explicit in Scripture, **as it is stated** (Leviticus 24:14): "וְסָמְכוּ כָל הַשֹּׁמְעִים אֶת יְדֵיהֶם עַל רֹאשׁוֹ" — and all those who heard shall lean their hands upon his head.[20] **וְיֶתֶר פְּרָטֶיהָ** — These laws, and the additional details of [this mitzvah], **מְבֹאָרִים בְּסַנְהֶדְרִין פֶּרֶק ז'** — are set forth in Tractate Sanhedrin, Chapter 7 (55b-57a, 60a, 63a).[21]

### ⌘ Applicability of the Mitzvah ⌘

**וְנוֹהֵג אִסּוּר זֶה בְּכָל מָקוֹם וּבְכָל זְמַן** — This prohibition of "blessing" Hashem applies in every location and in all times.[22]

**וְהָעוֹבֵר עַל זֶה וּבֵרַךְ הַשֵּׁם בָּעִנְיָן שֶׁאָמַרְנוּ** — One who violates this [prohibition] and "blesses" the Name in the manner that we mentioned above, i.e., by employing the formula of "May Yose strike Yose," **נִסְקָל בָּאָרֶץ עַל פִּי סְמוּכִין** — is subject to sekilah (stoning), in Eretz Yisrael, when the punishment can be administered under the jurisdiction of ordained [judges].[23] **וְעַכְשָׁו בְּחוּצָה לָאָרֶץ שֶׁאֵין לָנוּ סְמוּכִין** — But nowadays, in the Diaspora, where we lack properly ordained judges, since the institution of semichah ordination long ago ceased to exist, so we do not administer capital penalties,[24]

---

### NOTES

19. Some suggest that the blasphemer is subject to this procedure because he sinned not only with his initial utterance, but also caused the blasphemy to be repeated in court. The witnesses who were forced to utter the blasphemy, and the judges who were forced to hear it, declare that *this* sin is not theirs, but rests upon the blasphemer's head, in addition to the sin of his original utterance (*Rosh*, *Chizkuni* and *Malbim* to Leviticus 24:14).

20. The word הַשֹּׁמְעִים, *those who heard*, refers to the witnesses who heard the original blasphemy; and the additional word כָּל, *all*, comes to include the judges, who heard it repeated by the witnesses. The phrase עַל רֹאשׁוֹ, *upon his head*, in addition to teaching literally that they lean their hands upon his head, is understood as alluding that they declare to him that his blood is "upon his own head" — i.e., he alone is responsible for his imminent demise (*Sifra* to the verse; see *Rambam*, *Hil. Avodah Zarah* 2:10 with *Kesef Mishneh*).

21. The laws of a blasphemer are codified in *Rambam*, *Hilchos Avodah Zarah* 2:6-10. The laws for rending garments upon hearing blasphemy are found there and in *Shulchan Aruch*, *Yoreh Deah* 340:37.

22. I.e., in Eretz Yisrael and the Diaspora, whether the *Beis HaMikdash* is standing or not.

Furthermore, it applies to both men and women, in accordance with the general rule pertaining to mitzvah-prohibitions. It also applies to Noahides, as this is one of the Seven Noahide Laws (*Sanhedrin* 56a-b; *Rambam*, *Hil. Melachim* 9:1,3). [*Chinuch* uncharacteristically omits this point (*Minchas Chinuch* §6; see there for discussion).]

23. The penalty of *sekilah* is stated explicitly in Leviticus 24:16. The stipulation that it can be administered only by "ordained" judges is consistent with the general rule that capital cases may be tried only by judges who received the special *semichah* (ordination) that was conferred in Eretz Yisrael in earlier times (see *Rambam*, *Hil. Sanhedrin* 14:14). [See Mitzvah 491 for a description of this *semichah* and how it was conferred.] *Chinuch*'s reference to administering the punishment in Eretz Yisrael, though, is unclear. The law is that as long as the Great Sanhedrin sat in the Chamber of Hewn Stone [לִשְׁכַּת הַגָּזִית] in the *Beis HaMikdash* and tried capital cases, such cases could be tried even in the Diaspora by judges who had received *semichah* in Eretz Yisrael (*Rambam* ibid. 14:11,14; *Minchas Chinuch* §12). Perhaps this is actually *Chinuch*'s intention — that a blasphemer may be tried, and executed, only by a *beis din* that received the special ordination in Eretz Yisrael (for further discussion, see above, Mitzvah 47 note 16).

24. Actually, even if we would have ordained judges, they would not be authorized to judge capital cases,

# 33 ☐ MISHPATIM / MITZVAH 70: THE PROHIBITION OF BLASPHEMY

מַרְחִיקִין כָּל יִשְׂרָאֵל מִמֶּנּוּ וּמַחֲרִימִין אוֹתוֹ.[25]

מַרְחִיקִין כָּל יִשְׂרָאֵל מִמֶּנּוּ — all Jews distance themselves from [the blasphemer] וּמַחֲרִימִין אוֹתוֹ — and we excommunicate him.[25]

## NOTES

since the Sanhedrin no longer exists (*Tzava Rav*; see previous note).

25. Excommunication (*cheirem*) triggers various injunctions that are directed at the excommunicated individual, including restrictions on dining or even sitting with him, doing business with him, learning Torah with him, counting him toward a *minyan* or *zimun*, and more (see *Shulchan Aruch, Yoreh Deah* §334, for details).

*Rambam* (*Hil. Talmud Torah* 6:14) and *Shulchan Aruch* (*Yoreh Deah* 334:43) list 24 offenders who are subject to excommunication by *beis din*. The list does not include a blasphemer [because by law the blasphemer is liable to *sekilah*]. It does, however, include one who pronounces the Name of Hashem in vain, and a blasphemer obviously has pronounced the Name in vain (see *Temurah* 3b). Moreover, in times when *beis din* cannot administer capital punishment, in order to deter sinners they are authorized by Biblical law to punish *all* capital offenders with any means that are at their disposal under the law of the land [which would presumably include excommunication] (*Tur, Choshen Mishpat* 425:1, citing *Rav Natronai Gaon*). See above, Mitzvah 49 (at note 33), for another instance in which excommunication is imposed. See also *Teshuvos Ha-Rosh* 17:8, cited by *Darchei Moshe, Choshen Mishpat* 425:1, regarding the treatment of a blasphemer.

[*Chinuch* does not mention the penalty of *malkus* (lashes) for one who blasphemes a secondary Name of God. As mentioned in note 4, however, *Meiri* states that he is liable to *malkus*. For discussion of this subject, see *Chikrei Lev* (*Chazan*) to *Shevuos* 4a ד"ה ויש לחקור.]

> ### ❧ Insight: Rending Garments Upon Hearing Blasphemy
>
> Chinuch (at note 18) cites the incident recorded in Scripture in which Sennaherib's emissary Rabshakeh stood at the gates of Jerusalem and blasphemed the Name, and King Hezekiah's officers rent their garments. Chinuch explains that one is not obligated to rend his garments upon hearing blasphemy by an idolater, but Rabshakeh was actually an apostate Jew. Now, Scripture relates that Rabshakeh deliberately uttered his blasphemy in the Holy Tongue so that the Jews assembled there should understand it (see *II Kings* 18:26 ff.). Based on Chinuch's explanation that rending was required only because he was a Jew, it emerges that the exemption from rending one's garments over an *idolater's* blasphemy applies even if the idolater pronounces the Name and "blesses" it in the Holy Tongue.
>
> This is actually a matter of Talmudic dispute in *Sanhedrin* 60a. According to one opinion, the Sages instituted the requirement of rending garments only for blasphemy uttered by a Jew, not for blasphemy uttered by an idolater [who presumably does not believe in God]. Thus, whether the idolater pronounces the Name as it is written in the Holy Tongue or in another language, one who hears his blasphemy need not rend his garments. To explain the rending by King Hezekiah's officers, we must say (as Chinuch does) that Rabshakeh was actually an apostate Jew.
>
> According to a second opinion, by right one ought to rend his garment even upon hearing blasphemy from an idolater, and in fact that is how the Sages initially instituted the law. Hence, it is possible that Rabshakeh was an idolater, and those who heard him blaspheme were nevertheless obligated to rend their garments (*Yerushalmi Sanhedrin* 7:8). Nowadays, however, when there is no Sanhedrin that can punish blasphemers, blasphemy by idolaters has become so commonplace that rending our garments upon each occurrence would cause them to be reduced to tatters. The Sages therefore suspended the rending requirement in regard to blasphemy by idolaters.
>
> While Chinuch follows *Rambam* (*Hil. Avodah Zarah* 2:10, as understood by *Kesef Mishneh*; cf. *Bach, Yoreh Deah* 340:37), who rules in accordance with the first opinion, *Rif* (*Sanhedrin* fol. 16a) and *Rosh* (*Sanhedrin* 7:2) rule in accordance with the second opinion.
>
> *Rosh* states further that, according to the second opinion, the exemption applies only to a case where the idolater pronounces the Name in his language (in which case it has the status of a כִּנּוּי, *descriptive term*; see Mitzvah 69 note 22), or he actually pronounces a descriptive term in the Holy Tongue and "blesses" it. Since it is indeed common for idolaters to blaspheme the Name in

their own language, with which they are familiar, the Sages were forced to suspend the rending of garments for such blasphemy. It is very uncommon, however, for an idolater to blaspheme the Distinct Name in the Holy Tongue, since he is not familiar with that pronunciation of the Name; therefore, in the rare instance in which he does commit such blasphemy, one who hears it *is* required to rend his garment, even nowadays (see also *Tur, Yoreh Deah* 340:37).

It emerges that according to *Rambam* and Chinuch, one is *never* required to rend his garments on account of blasphemy by an idolater. According to *Rosh,* one is exempt from rending his garment only when the idolater who blasphemes pronounces the Name in a foreign language, or he uses a descriptive term for God, but if he blasphemes the Distinct Name in the Holy Tongue, one is required to rend his garments. For the halachah, see *Shulchan Aruch, Yoreh Deah* 340:37, with *Shach* §53.

*Yad Ramah* (*Sanhedrin* 60a) has yet another opinion. He maintains that the Sages suspended the rending of garments only in regard to those idolaters who have demonstrated a tendency to blaspheme, such that the concern for reducing one's garments to tatters is realistic. Hence, he rules that even nowadays, the first time that an idolater is heard to blaspheme, those who hear it must rend their garments, and the exemption applies only from the second time onward.

For blasphemy by a Jew, one would need to rend his garments even if the Jew pronounced only a descriptive term for God, or the Name in a foreign language (*Shulchan Aruch* ibid.). With regard to blasphemy by an apostate Jew nowadays, see *Rama, Yoreh Deah* loc. cit. with *Shach* §54, and *Bach* ibid.

## מִצְוָה עא: שֶׁלֹּא לְקַלֵּל הַנָּשִׂיא

שֶׁלֹּא לְקַלֵּל אֶת הַנָּשִׂיא, שֶׁנֶּאֱמַר (שמות כ"ב, כ"ז) וְנָשִׂיא בְעַמְּךָ לֹא תָאֹר, וּבָא הַפֵּרוּשׁ שֶׁהַנָּשִׂיא זֶה הַמֶּלֶךְ[1], וְאָמְנָם זֶה הַלָּאו כּוֹלֵל כְּמוֹ כֵן הַנָּשִׂיא שֶׁבְּיִשְׂרָאֵל, וְהוּא רֹאשׁ סַנְהֶדְרֵי גְדוֹלָה שֶׁנִּקְרָא נָשִׂיא גַּם כֵּן[2], לְפִי שֶׁכַּוָּנַת הַכָּתוּב לְהַזְהִירֵנוּ עַל כָּל מִי שֶׁהוּא רֹאשׁ שְׂרָרָה עַל יִשְׂרָאֵל בֵּין מֶמְשֶׁלֶת מַלְכוּת בֵּין מֶמְשֶׁלֶת תּוֹרָה[3].

---

# Mitzvah 71
## The Prohibition to Curse the Nasi

וְנָשִׂיא בְעַמְּךָ לֹא תָאֹר
*And you shall not curse a Nasi among your people (Exodus 22:27).*

Having described in Mitzvos 69 and 70 the prohibitions that emerge from the first half of this verse — *You shall not revile Elohim,* which prohibits reviling either a judge or Hashem — Chinuch proceeds to explain the mitzvah that emerges from the second half of the verse: *and you shall not curse a Nasi among your people.*

שֶׁנֶּאֱמַר "וְנָשִׂיא בְעַמְּךָ לֹא — שֶׁלֹּא לְקַלֵּל אֶת הַנָּשִׂיא — We are commanded **not to curse the Nasi,** תָאֹר" — **as it is stated** (*Exodus 22:27*): **and you shall not curse a Nasi among your people.** וּבָא הַפֵּרוּשׁ — **The explanation** of this, **as transmitted** to us by the Sages (Mishnah, *Horayos* 10a) **is** שֶׁהַנָּשִׂיא זֶה הַמֶּלֶךְ — **that the** term *Nasi* **refers to the king** of the Jewish people.[1] וְאָמְנָם זֶה הַלָּאו כּוֹלֵל כְּמוֹ כֵן הַנָּשִׂיא שֶׁבְּיִשְׂרָאֵל — **However, this prohibition includes the** non-royal *Nasi* **of the Jewish people, as well,** וְהוּא רֹאשׁ סַנְהֶדְרֵי גְדוֹלָה שֶׁנִּקְרָא נָשִׂיא גַּם כֵּן — **namely, the head of the Great Sanhedrin, who is also called "Nasi."**[2] לְפִי שֶׁכַּוָּנַת הַכָּתוּב לְהַזְהִירֵנוּ — **The latter is** included in the prohibition **because the intention of the Torah is to caution us** עַל כָּל מִי שֶׁהוּא רֹאשׁ שְׂרָרָה עַל יִשְׂרָאֵל — **with regard to** cursing **anyone who is a leader with dominion over the Jewish people,** בֵּין מֶמְשֶׁלֶת מַלְכוּת בֵּין מֶמְשֶׁלֶת תּוֹרָה — **whether** that leader has **governmental authority or Torah authority.**[3]

---

### NOTES

1. The word נָשִׂיא, *Nasi,* is from the same root as וִישָּׂא, *elevated,* and thus, נָשִׂיא בְעַמְּךָ, *a Nasi among your people,* refers to the one who is elevated above all the other people — i.e., the king (*Ramban, Exodus 22:27*).

This definition of *Nasi* is stated by the Sages in a different context. The Torah (*Leviticus* 4:22-26) requires a *"Nasi"* who has sinned to bring a he-goat as his *chatas* (sin) offering [as opposed to a commoner, who brings a she-goat as his *chatas*]. Based on verses in that passage, the Mishnah (*Horayos* 10a) teaches that the special offering is brought only by the person who answers to no authority other than God Himself — i.e., the king (see Gemara ibid. 11a-b). Chinuch explains that here, similarly, the term *Nasi* refers to a king (see also *Rambam, Sefer HaMitzvos, Lo Saaseh* 316). [We will see, however, that in our context it is not limited to a king.]

For much of the First Temple Era, Eretz Yisrael was divided into two separate regions — the southern region (Judea), which was ruled by a scion of the House of David, and the northern region (Samaria), which was ruled by an Israelite king. With regard to the *chatas* offering, the term *Nasi* includes both of these kings, since neither of them answered to a higher human authority (Gemara ibid. 11b). It would seem to follow that cursing either one was forbidden under the current prohibition. Possibly, though, since the Torah forbids cursing נָשִׂיא בְעַמְּךָ, *a Nasi among your people,* the prohibition pertains only to one who is the king over *all* the people (see *Minchas Soless;* see also *Radvaz, Hil. Sanhedrin* 26:6).

[For discussion of whether the prohibition applies to a king who seized power by force, see *Minchas Chinuch* §4.]

2. The Great Sanhedrin consisted of seventy eminent sages, headed by a seventy-first sage who was the preeminent halachic authority of Israel, and who had the title *Nasi.* The greatest of the remaining seventy sages was given the title *Av Beis Din* ("Father of the Court") and was the *Nasi's* second-in-command (*Rambam, Hil. Sanhedrin* 1:3). See following note.

3. As explained in note 1, the term *"Nasi"* refers to one who is elevated above the other people of the land.

מִשָּׁרְשֵׁי הַמִּצְוָה, לְפִי שֶׁאִי אֶפְשָׁר לְיִשּׁוּב בְּנֵי אָדָם מִבְּלִי שֶׁיַּעֲשׂוּ אֶחָד מִבֵּינֵיהֶם רֹאשׁ עַל הָאֲחֵרִים לַעֲשׂוֹת מִצְוָתוֹ וּלְקַיֵּם גְּזֵרוֹתָיו, מִפְּנֵי שֶׁדֵּעוֹת בְּנֵי אָדָם חֲלוּקִין זֶה מִזֶּה וְלֹא יַסְכִּימוּ כֻּלָּם לְעוֹלָם לְדַעַת אַחַת לַעֲשׂוֹת דָּבָר מִכָּל הַדְּבָרִים, וּמִתּוֹךְ כָּךְ יֵצֵא מִבֵּינֵיהֶם הַבִּטּוּל [וְהָאֲסִיפָה] (וההפיסה)[4] בַּפְּעֻלּוֹת, וְעַל כֵּן צְרִיכִין לְקַבֵּל דַּעַת אֶחָד מֵהֶם אִם טוֹב וְאִם רַע, לְמַעַן יִצְלְחוּ וְיַעַסְקוּ בְּעִסְקוֹ שֶׁל עוֹלָם, פַּעַם יִמְצָא בַּעֲצָתוֹ וְחֶפְצוֹ תּוֹעֶלֶת רַב וּפַעַם הַהֵפֶךְ, וְכָל זֶה טוֹב מִן הַמַּחֲלֹקֶת שֶׁגּוֹרֵם בִּטּוּל גָּמוּר. וּמֵאַחַר שֶׁהַמְמֻנֶּה לְרֹאשׁ סִבָּה אֶל הַתּוֹעֶלֶת שֶׁאָמַרְנוּ,

## ⸺ Underlying Purpose of the Mitzvah ⸺

מִשָּׁרְשֵׁי הַמִּצְוָה — **Among the underlying purposes of this mitzvah is that it is imperative to pro**hibit cursing a national leader, לְפִי שֶׁאִי אֶפְשָׁר לְיִשּׁוּב בְּנֵי אָדָם — **because it is impossible for a** functioning **society of people to exist** מִבְּלִי שֶׁיַּעֲשׂוּ אֶחָד מִבֵּינֵיהֶם רֹאשׁ עַל הָאֲחֵרִים — **unless they appoint one from among them** to be the **head over** all **the others,** לַעֲשׂוֹת מִצְוָתוֹ וּלְקַיֵּם גְּזֵרוֹתָיו — such that they are obligated **to carry out his command and fulfill his decrees.** מִפְּנֵי שֶׁדֵּעוֹת בְּנֵי אָדָם חֲלוּקִין זֶה מִזֶּה — **The reason such an authority is needed is because the perspectives of people differ one from the other,** וְלֹא יַסְכִּימוּ כֻּלָּם לְעוֹלָם לְדַעַת אַחַת — **and** without leadership **they will never all agree on one viewpoint** לַעֲשׂוֹת דָּבָר מִכָּל הַדְּבָרִים — **that would allow them to do any of the things** that they need to do as a society, וּמִתּוֹךְ כָּךְ יֵצֵא מִבֵּינֵיהֶם הַבִּטּוּל [וְהָאֲסִיפָה] (וההפיסה)[4] בַּפְּעֻלּוֹת — **and consequently,** what **will emerge from them** is the **negation and cessation of** all productive **activity.** וְעַל כֵּן צְרִיכִין לְקַבֵּל דַּעַת אֶחָד מֵהֶם אִם טוֹב וְאִם רַע — **Therefore, they need to accept the viewpoint of one** individual **from among themselves** as authoritative, **whether** that perspective is actually **good or bad** in any particular instance, לְמַעַן יִצְלְחוּ וְיַעַסְקוּ בְּעִסְקוֹ שֶׁל עוֹלָם — **so that** overall **they may prosper and** productively **engage in the endeavors of the world.** פַּעַם יִמְצָא בַּעֲצָתוֹ וְחֶפְצוֹ תּוֹעֶלֶת רַב וּפַעַם הַהֵפֶךְ — **At times** what **will emerge from [the leader's] counsel and ambition** is **great benefit, and at times** what will emerge is **the opposite,** for his decisions will sometimes be poor and have a negative impact, וְכָל זֶה טוֹב מִן הַמַּחֲלֹקֶת שֶׁגּוֹרֵם בִּטּוּל גָּמוּר — **but nevertheless, all this is better than discord, which leads to a complete negation** of progress. וּמֵאַחַר שֶׁהַמְמֻנֶּה לְרֹאשׁ סִבָּה אֶל הַתּוֹעֶלֶת שֶׁאָמַרְנוּ — **Now, insofar as the one appointed as head**

### NOTES

This includes not only the one who has administrative authority over the land — i.e., the king — but also the one who has halachic authority — i.e., the head of the Sanhedrin (Rambam in Sefer HaMitzvos, Lo Saaseh 316, and Hil. Sanhedrin 26:1; Ramban ibid.). Indeed, the king is often referred to as "Nasi" in Scripture [e.g., Ezekiel 45:7,9,16-17], and the head of the Sanhedrin is consistently referred to as "Nasi" in the Talmud (Sefer HaMitzvos ibid.).

It is of note that in the event the Nasi of the Sanhedrin committed a transgression, he would bring the chatas offering of a commoner, not that of a king (see Horayos 11b). That is because (as mentioned in note 1) the Torah indicates that the special chatas is brought only by the person who answers to no ruler other than God Himself. This includes specifically a king, and excludes the head of the Sanhedrin, who is a subject of the king. In the context of the prohibition against cursing a Nasi, however, no such qualification is stated, so the term "Nasi" includes one who has authority over Israel in any field, whether administrative authority or halachic authority (Kesef Mishneh, Hil. Sanhedrin 26:1; see, however, Lechem Yehudah there).

The Torah also refers to the leader of each of the twelve tribes as a Nasi (see Numbers 1:4 ff., 2:3 ff., 7:18 ff.). Minchas Chinuch (§1) wonders why, then, Rambam (ibid.) and Chinuch mention only the king and the head of the Sanhedrin as subjects of our prohibition. Some suggest that it is because, as mentioned in note 1, the prohibition applies to נָשִׂיא בְעַמְּךָ, a Nasi among your people, which is understood as referring to one who has dominion over all the people of Israel, and not merely over one tribe (Maharam Schik; see also Chidushei HaGriz to Parashas Vayeilech). Others point out that Scripture consistently (Numbers 2:3 ff.; 7:18 ff.) refers to the head of each tribe as the Nasi of his tribe, but never as "Nasi" unqualified. The prohibition to curse a "Nasi" refers to one who has this title without any qualification, and that includes only the king and the head of the Sanhedrin, each of whom was the leader of all of Israel in his particular domain (Minchas Yitzchak).

4. Emendation follows numerous printed editions of Chinuch.

# 37 ☐ MISHPATIM / MITZVAH 71: THE PROHIBITION TO CURSE THE NASI

הֵן שֶׁהוּא גָּדוֹל לְהַדְרִיכֵנוּ בְּדַרְכֵי הַדָּת אוֹ גָּדוֹל בַּמַּלְכוּת לִשְׁמֹר אִישׁ מֵרֵעֵהוּ שֶׁתַּקִּיף מִמֶּנּוּ,[5] רָאוּי הַדָּבָר וְכָשֵׁר שֶׁלֹּא נָקֵל בִּכְבוֹדוֹ, וְגַם שֶׁלֹּא לְקַלְּלוֹ אֲפִלּוּ שֶׁלֹּא בְּפָנָיו, וְכָל שֶׁכֵּן בִּפְנֵי עֵדִים, כְּדֵי שֶׁלֹּא נָבוֹא מִתּוֹךְ כָּךְ לַחֲלֹק עִמּוֹ, לְפִי שֶׁהַהֶרְגֵּל הָרַע שֶׁאָדָם מַרְגִּיל עַצְמוֹ בֵּינוֹ לְבֵין עַצְמוֹ הוּא סוֹף מַעֲשֵׂהוּ, וְהַמַּחֲלֹקֶת עָלָיו כְּבָר אָמַרְנוּ הַהֶפְסֵד הַנִּמְצָא בִּשְׁבִילוֹ.[6]

מִדִּינֵי הַמִּצְוָה, מַה שֶּׁאָמְרוּ זִכְרוֹנָם לִבְרָכָה שֶׁאֵין חַיָּב עָלָיו אֶלָּא הַמְקַלְלוֹ בְּשֵׁם אוֹ בְּכִנּוּי,[7] וְשֶׁהַמְקַלְלוֹ לוֹקֶה שָׁלֹשׁ מַלְקִיּוֹת, מִשּׁוּם אֱלֹהִים לֹא תְקַלֵּל,[8] וּמִשּׁוּם וְנָשִׂיא בְעַמְּךָ לֹא תָאֹר,[9]

---

הֵן שֶׁהוּא גָּדוֹל לְהַדְרִיכֵנוּ of the people **is the source of the benefit that we have mentioned,** בְּדַרְכֵי הַדָּת — **whether he is** the **preeminent** scholar who is charged **to guide us in the ways of** our **religion** (i.e., the head of the Great Sanhedrin), אוֹ גָּדוֹל בַּמַּלְכוּת לִשְׁמֹר אִישׁ מֵרֵעֵהוּ שֶׁתַּקִּיף מִמֶּנּוּ — **or he is the preeminent governmental authority** who is charged **to protect each man from his more powerful fellow** (i.e., the king),[5] רָאוּי הַדָּבָר וְכָשֵׁר שֶׁלֹּא נָקֵל בִּכְבוֹדוֹ — **it is appropriate and fitting that we not be irreverent with his honor** by cursing him. וְגַם שֶׁלֹּא לְקַלְּלוֹ אֲפִלּוּ שֶׁלֹּא בְּפָנָיו — It is in fact **appropriate that we not curse him even** in private, when **not in his presence,** such that the affront to his honor is minimal, וְכָל שֶׁכֵּן בִּפְנֵי עֵדִים — **and all the more so** that we not curse him **before witnesses,** whose presence magnifies the slight to his honor, כְּדֵי שֶׁלֹּא נָבוֹא מִתּוֹךְ כָּךְ לַחֲלֹק עִמּוֹ — **so that we should not thereby come to defy him** and reject his leadership. לְפִי שֶׁהַהֶרְגֵּל הָרַע שֶׁאָדָם מַרְגִּיל עַצְמוֹ בֵּינוֹ לְבֵין עַצְמוֹ — This is a likely outcome of being irreverent to the leader and cursing him, **because a bad habit to which a person accustoms himself in private** הוּא סוֹף מַעֲשֵׂהוּ — **will ultimately manifest** itself **in his actions.** וְהַמַּחֲלֹקֶת עָלָיו — **And,** with regard to **defying [a leader],** כְּבָר אָמַרְנוּ הַהֶפְסֵד הַנִּמְצָא בִּשְׁבִילוֹ — **we have already mentioned** (in Mitzvah 69) **the detrimental [consequences] that result from it.**[6]

### ☙ Laws of the Mitzvah ☙

מִדִּינֵי הַמִּצְוָה — **Among the laws of this mitzvah** are מַה שֶּׁאָמְרוּ זִכְרוֹנָם לִבְרָכָה — **that which [our Sages], of blessed memory, have stated** (see Mishnah, *Shevuos* 35a, and Gemara there 36a), שֶׁאֵין חַיָּב עָלָיו אֶלָּא הַמְקַלְלוֹ בְּשֵׁם אוֹ בְּכִנּוּי — **that one is liable** to punishment **for** violating **[this prohibition] only if he curses [the *Nasi*] with a** proper **Name of God or with a descriptive term for Him.**[7] וְשֶׁהַמְקַלְלוֹ לוֹקֶה שָׁלֹשׁ מַלְקִיּוֹת — **Also, that one who curses [the *Nasi*] incurs three** sets of *malkus* (lashes).[8] מִשּׁוּם אֱלֹהִים לֹא תְקַלֵּל — **He is liable** (1) **for** violating (*Exodus* 22:27): ***You shall not revile Elohim*** (Mitzvah 69),[9] וּמִשּׁוּם וְנָשִׂיא בְעַמְּךָ לֹא תָאֹר — (2) **for** violating (ibid.):

---

### NOTES

5. Protection of the weak is a function of the government, and by extension, of the head of government, as the Mishnah states (*Avos* 3:2): *Pray for the welfare of the government, because if [people] did not fear it, each person would swallow his fellow alive* (see *Tehillim* 72:2-4). By imposing the rules of law and order, the king protects the populace from the wicked designs of those who would seek to victimize them (*Ralbag* and *Metzudas David*, *Proverbs* 29:4).

6. In Mitzvah 69 (at notes 13-16), and elsewhere (e.g., Mitzvah 49), Chinuch discusses the importance of law and order, based on the verse (*Proverbs* 29:4): מֶלֶךְ בְּמִשְׁפָּט יַעֲמִיד אָרֶץ, *through justice a king establishes a land*. The verse teaches that the very foundation of a flourishing society is the existence of systems of justice and equity through which the land is governed.

7. This is the same as the law that applies to cursing a judge. For elaboration of what is considered a "proper Name" and what is a "descriptive term," see Mitzvah 69, with notes 18-19. [There, Chinuch adds that one is liable also for cursing in a language other than the Holy Tongue. As mentioned there in notes 19 and 22, these rulings reflect the opinion of *Rambam*, but *Raavad* disagrees on both counts.]

Cursing the *Nasi* without invoking a Name of God is not punishable, but is nevertheless forbidden, just as with regard to cursing a judge (see Mitzvah 69 at notes 20-21), and with regard to cursing any Jew (see Mitzvah 231; *Shulchan Aruch, Choshen Mishpat* 27:2).

8. Even though he utters only one curse, since it is directed at the *Nasi*, the speaker violates three distinct prohibitions, and is therefore liable to three sets of *malkus* [and sometimes even four, as Chinuch will explain below] (*Mechilta* to *Exodus* 22:27; *Rambam, Hil. Sanhedrin* 26:2, and *Sefer HaMitzvos, Lo Saaseh* 317; cf. *Ramban* there to *Lo Saaseh* 318).

9. This is the prohibition to curse a judge. One who curses the *Nasi* who presides over the Sanhedrin has clearly

## 38 □ משפטים / מצוה עא: שלא לקלל הנשיא

וּמִשּׁוּם לֹא תְקַלֵּל חֵרֵשׁ (ויקרא י״ט, י״ד), שֶׁהוּא לָאו כּוֹלֵל כָּל יִשְׂרָאֵל[10], וְיֶתֶר פְּרָטֶיהָ, מְבֹאָרִין בְּסַנְהֶדְרִין (דף ס״ו ע״א)[11].

וְנוֹהֶגֶת בִּזְכָרִים וּנְקֵבוֹת[12], בָּאָרֶץ וּבְכָל מָקוֹם שֶׁנִּהְיֶה עִם מַלְכֵּנוּ אוֹ עִם רֹאשׁ סַנְהֶדְרֵי גְדוֹלָה[13].

וְעוֹבֵר עָלֶיהָ וְקִלְּלוֹ בְּשֵׁם אוֹ בְּכִנּוּי[14], לוֹקֶה שָׁלֹשׁ מַלְקִיּוֹת. וְאִם בֶּן הַנָּשִׂיא קִלְּלוֹ לוֹקֶה אַרְבַּע, שָׁלֹשׁ שֶׁאָמַרְנוּ וְאֶחָד מִשּׁוּם מְקַלֵּל אָבִיו (שמות כ״א, י״ז)[15].

---

**וּמִשּׁוּם לֹא תְקַלֵּל חֵרֵשׁ** — and and you shall not curse a Nasi among your people (i.e., this mitzvah), finally, (3) **for** violating (*Leviticus* 19:14): *You shall not curse the deaf* (Mitzvah 231), **שֶׁהוּא לָאו כּוֹלֵל כָּל יִשְׂרָאֵל** — which is a prohibition that encompasses cursing **any Jew**.[10] **מְבֹאָרִין בְּסַנְהֶדְרִין וְיֶתֶר פְּרָטֶיהָ** — These laws, **and the additional details of [this mitzvah] are set forth in** Tractate *Sanhedrin* (66a).[11]

### ~ Applicability of the Mitzvah ~

**בָּאָרֶץ וּבְכָל מָקוֹם — וְנוֹהֶגֶת בִּזְכָרִים וּנְקֵבוֹת** — [This mitzvah] applies to both men and women,[12] **שֶׁנִּהְיֶה עִם מַלְכֵּנוּ אוֹ עִם רֹאשׁ סַנְהֶדְרֵי גְדוֹלָה** — in Eretz Yisrael, as well as any other place where we might be together with our king or the head of the Great Sanhedrin.[13] **וְעוֹבֵר עָלֶיהָ וְקִלְּלוֹ בְּשֵׁם אוֹ בְּכִנּוּי** — One who transgresses [this prohibition] and curses [the *Nasi*] with a proper Name of God or a descriptive term for Him **לוֹקֶה שָׁלֹשׁ מַלְקִיּוֹת** — receives three sets of *malkus*, as enumerated above.[14] **וְאִם בֶּן הַנָּשִׂיא קִלְּלוֹ לוֹקֶה אַרְבַּע** — Moreover, if the son of the *Nasi* curses [the *Nasi*], he receives four sets of *malkus*: **שָׁלֹשׁ שֶׁאָמַרְנוּ וְאֶחָד מִשּׁוּם מְקַלֵּל אָבִיו** — the three that we mentioned above, and one additional set for violating the prohibition against cursing his father (Mitzvah 260).[15]

---

### NOTES

violated this prohibition. As for one who curses the king, *Minchas Chinuch* (§2) explains that this prohibition is violated in a case where the king is a scholar who was ordained through *semichah* to be a judge. [For discussion of the possibility of a king receiving this ordination, see *Minchas Chinuch, Minchah Chadashah,* and *Shevet HaLevi* Vol. 5, *Kuntres HaMitzvos* §30.] Others explain that this prohibition is violated even if the king is not a judge, because the term *Elohim* encompasses not only a judge, but also anyone else who has been appointed to a position of authority over the community (*Teshuvos Raanach* §111 ד״ה ועוד שהוא ממונה, cited by *Ketzos HaChoshen* 27:1; *Minchas Soless, Mitzvah* 69; see also *Shevet HaLevi* ibid.). [For further discussion of the scope of the term *Elohim*, see Insight to Mitzvah 69.]

10. Although the verse specifies the deaf, all Jews are included. The verse is understood as though it says, *You shall not curse "even" the deaf,* i.e., even those who do not hear your curse and are therefore not pained by it. Surely, it is forbidden to curse others who can hear the curse (*Rambam* ibid. 26:1; *Tur Choshen Mishpat* 27:1; see Mitzvah 231; cf. *Ramban* to *Sefer HaMitzvos, Lo Saaseh* 318). See the Insight for further discussion.

11. The laws are codified by *Rambam* in *Hilchos Sanhedrin* 26:1-6.

12. In accordance with the general rule pertaining to mitzvah-prohibitions.

13. Chinuch does not discuss the *times* in which this prohibition applies, but obviously, it is in effect whenever there is a *Nasi*. After the destruction of the *Beis HaMikdash,* there was no monarchy in Israel, but for many generations thereafter the Jews had a monarchical leader in Babylonia known as the *Reish Galusa,* or Exilarch. These leaders were descendants of King David who enjoyed semi-autonomy and, among the Jewish people, had the status of a king with regard to imposing justice (*Rambam, Hil. Sanhedrin* 4:13; see *Sanhedrin* 5a and *Horayos* 11b). The office of *Nasi* of the Sanhedrin, too, lasted many centuries into our current exile, even after the Great Sanhedrin ceased to sit in the Chamber of Hewn Stone [לִשְׁכַּת הַגָּזִית] on the Temple Mount (see *Sanhedrin* and *Horayos* ibid.; *Rambam, Hil. Kiddush HaChodesh* 5:2-3; *Chidushei HaGrach al HaShas* בענין קידוש החודש). As long as these positions existed, the prohibition to curse a *Nasi* applied with respect to these leaders. Nowadays, since neither the monarchy nor either of these positions exists, this mitzvah is not applicable (see *Radvaz, Hil. Sanhedrin* 26:6; see also *Minchah Chadashah* §2).

14. See Mitzvah 69 note 28, regarding the imposition of *malkus* here even though the transgression does not involve action.

15. See the Insight below for discussion of this point.

## MISHPATIM / MITZVAH 71: THE PROHIBITION TO CURSE THE NASI

### ❧ Insight: How Many Malkus Penalties Can a Curser Incur?

Chinuch states at the end of the Mitzvah that one who curses a *Nasi* receives three sets of *malkus*, and if the one who utters the curse is the *Nasi's* son, then he receives an additional set of *malkus* on account of having cursed his father. This statement is based on *Mechilta* (to *Exodus* 22:27) and *Rambam* (*Hil. Sanhedrin* 26:2, and *Sefer HaMitzvos, Lo Saaseh* 317). *Ramban* (to *Sefer HaMitzvos, Lo Saaseh* 318), however, questions the notion that one who curses his father incurs *malkus*, for the Torah explicitly states that he is subject to the death penalty, and this precludes *malkus* (see *Exodus* 21:17 and *Leviticus* 20:9).

Some explain that there are situations in which the death penalty is not incurred, and in those cases the violator would receive *malkus* instead. First, the death penalty is incurred only for cursing a parent with the Distinct Name of Hashem [i.e., the Tetragrammaton, or *Adonai*; see Mitzvah 70 note 4], but if one curses a parent with one of the other Names [such as *Elokim*; see ibid.], he is liable to *malkus* (*Rambam, Hil. Mamrim* 5:2; Chinuch, Mitzvah 260; see *Lechem Mishneh, Hil. Mamrim* 5:4; cf. *Lechem Yehudah, Hil. Sanhedrin* 26:1). Additionally, as in all cases, a transgressor is subject to execution only if he was forewarned by witnesses that this would be the consequence of his transgression (see General Introduction). Hence, if a son was not warned about the death penalty, but was instead told that he would incur *malkus* for cursing his father, he does receive *malkus* for that transgression, in addition to the *malkus* for each of the other transgressions (see *Ramban* and *Megillas Esther* to *Sefer HaMitzvos* ibid.; see also *Minchas Chinuch* 260:4). [*Ramban* objects to this answer, based on the rule that a prohibition that carries a potential death penalty (לאו שניתן לאזהרת מיתת בית דין) is not punishable with *malkus*. For a resolution of this objection, see *Lechem Mishneh* ibid.]

Some, however, raise another difficulty. There is no specific verse that states the prohibition for cursing a father. Rather, this prohibition may be derived from (*Leviticus* 19:14): *You shall not curse the deaf*, which some understand as a prohibition to curse *any* Jew (see above, note 10). Alternatively, it is derived from the combination of that prohibition and the prohibition to curse a judge and the *Nasi*; i.e., since the Torah forbids cursing the most prominent people (a judge and a *Nasi*) and the least prominent (a deaf person), it follows that all who fall between them are included (*Mechilta* to *Exodus* 21:17, cited by Chinuch, Mitzvah 260). Accordingly, if one's father is the *Nasi*, how can he receive a fourth set of *malkus* for cursing him, when the prohibition for cursing a father is actually derived from one of the other prohibitions against cursing, and he is already receiving *malkus* for each of those prohibitions? (*Lechem Mishneh* ibid.).

Due to this difficulty, some explain that *Mechilta* and *Rambam* do not mean that the person actually receives a fourth set of *malkus*, but rather, that he has committed an additional violation that *potentially* carries the penalty of *malkus*. The practical ramification is that if the violator was not forewarned that he would incur *malkus* on account of the other violations, but he was forewarned that he would incur *malkus* on account of cursing his father, the *malkus* could be meted out as punishment for that transgression. Surely, though, he cannot receive *malkus* for cursing his father *and* for the other three transgressions. Indeed, a careful reading of *Mechilta* and *Rambam* leads to this interpretation (*Knesses HaGedolah* to *Hil. Sanhedrin* 26:2, cited in *Sefer HaLikkutim* [Frankel] there; see also *Ohr Same'ach* there). Chinuch's assertion that the person can actually receive *four* sets of *malkus* requires further study. [For other explanations of *Mechilta* and *Rambam*, see *Meiri* to *Sanhedrin* 66a, and *Kesef Mishneh, Hil. Mamrim* 5:4. See further below, Mitzvah 260.]

It should be noted that although Chinuch writes that one incurs *malkus* for cursing the *Nasi*, and, as we have learned, the term *Nasi* includes the king, there is actually a more severe penalty for this infraction. Cursing a king is an act of sedition against him, and the king is authorized to punish the offender with death (*Yerushalmi Sanhedrin* 2:3; *Rambam, Hil. Melachim* 3:8; see Chinuch below, Mitzvah 497). Nevertheless, even if the king pardons the offender for his sedition, he incurs *malkus*, since he has in any event transgressed the prohibition of *and you shall not curse a Nasi among your people*. [Similarly, in any case where a person who was cursed forgives the one who cursed him, the offender receives *malkus* nonetheless for transgressing the Biblical prohibition against cursing a Jew (see *Rambam, Hil. Sanhedrin* 26:6).] For further discussion of the *malkus* penalty for cursing a king, see *Minchas Soless*.

## מִצְוָה עב: שֶׁלֹּא לְהַקְדִּים חֻקֵּי הַתְּבוּאוֹת[1]

שֶׁלֹּא נַקְדִּים חֻקֵּי הַתְּבוּאָה קְצָתָם עַל קְצָתָם, אֶלָּא שֶׁנּוֹצִיאֵם בְּסֵדֶר. וּבֵאוּר עִנְיָן זֶה הוּא, שֶׁהַחִטָּה כְּשֶׁתּוּדַשׁ וְתִנָּקֶה הִיא טֶבֶל, וּפֵרוּשׁ טֶבֶל הִיא תְּבוּאָה שֶׁלֹּא הִתְרְמָה[2], וְהַחִיּוּב עָלֵינוּ בָּהּ לְהוֹצִיא מִמֶּנָּה תְּחִלָּה תְּרוּמָה גְּדוֹלָה[3], וּמִן הַתּוֹרָה

---

## ⸺ Mitzvah 72 ⸺
# The Prohibition to Give Improper Precedence to the Produce-Obligations

מְלֵאָתְךָ וְדִמְעֲךָ לֹא תְאַחֵר בְּכוֹר בָּנֶיךָ תִּתֶּן לִי

*Do not delay your grain or your fluid (i.e., wine and oil) produce-obligations; the firstborn of your sons shall you present to Me (Exodus 22:28).*

Before partaking of produce that has been harvested in Eretz Yisrael, the Torah requires that various tributes be set aside. These include *terumah*, *maaser rishon* (the "first tithe"), and *maaser sheni* (the "second tithe"), as well as others, some of which Chinuch will presently describe. While the Torah sets forth each of these obligations in a separate mitzvah, this verse contains a general prohibition, which pertains to all the tributes — to refrain from separating these tributes in any order other than the one set forth in the Torah.[1]

שֶׁלֹּא נַקְדִּים חֻקֵּי הַתְּבוּאָה קְצָתָם עַל קְצָתָם — We are commanded **not to give** improper **precedence to some produce-obligations before others,** אֶלָּא שֶׁנּוֹצִיאֵם בְּסֵדֶר — **but rather, to set them aside in** their proper **order.**

Chinuch prefaces his description of the mitzvah by introducing some of the produce-obligations and the order in which they must be separated, and by describing some laws of these separated portions:

וּבֵאוּר עִנְיָן זֶה הוּא — **The explanation of this matter is** as follows: שֶׁהַחִטָּה כְּשֶׁתּוּדַשׁ וְתִנָּקֶה הִיא — **After** a crop of **wheat has been threshed and made clean** of chaff, **it is** known as ***tevel***. וּפֵרוּשׁ טֶבֶל — **The meaning of *tevel*,** הִיא תְּבוּאָה שֶׁלֹּא הִתְרְמָה — **is produce from which *terumah* and *maaser* have not been set aside.**[2] וְהַחִיּוּב עָלֵינוּ בָּהּ לְהוֹצִיא מִמֶּנָּה תְּחִלָּה תְּרוּמָה גְּדוֹלָה — **Our obligation pertaining to [*tevel*] is to first set aside from it** a portion as ***terumah gedolah*** (i.e., *terumah*).[3] וּמִן הַתּוֹרָה — **According to Biblical law,** there is no fixed amount that must be set

---

### NOTES

1. According to Biblical law, the produce-obligations largely pertain only to grains such as wheat and barley, and to wine and oil. Thus, when the verse refers to these obligations, it employs the phrase מְלֵאָתְךָ וְדִמְעֲךָ, which is explained as "grains and fluids." For explanation of how this phrase connotes grains and fluids, see *Ramban's* commentary to this verse. [Chinuch will later cite an alternative interpretation of this phrase from *Mechilta*, based on which additional laws of the mitzvah are derived. See notes 18 and 19.]

2. Produce is considered *tevel* once the final tasks of its harvesting have been completed. In Chinuch's example, the harvesting of wheat is deemed complete once the kernels have been separated from the stalks and the chaff, and have been placed in finished piles. The same is true of the other grains as well. The harvesting of wine-grapes is complete once they have been pressed

and their juice has been poured into barrels, and the harvesting of olives used for oil is concluded when their oil flows into the vat at the base of the press (*Rambam, Hil. Maaser* 3:1, 13-15; see also Mitzvah 395).

According to Biblical law, the produce-obligations apply only once the produce becomes *tevel*, i.e., when its harvesting is completed, as just described. Moreover, from that time, one is prohibited to partake of the produce in any manner, until all the applicable obligations have been addressed. This prohibition is set forth in Mitzvah 284. [There is an additional tribute that must be set aside, known as *bikkurim*, whose obligation begins even before the harvest of the produce is completed. Chinuch will later explain that our mitzvah applies with regard to that obligation as well.]

3. The standard *terumah* is known as *terumah gedolah* (the major *terumah*), in contrast to *terumas maaser*,

# 41 □ MISHPATIM / MITZVAH 72: NOT TO CHANGE THE ORDER OF THE PRODUCE-OBLIGATIONS

אֲפִלּוּ חִטָּה אַחַת פּוֹטֶרֶת הַכְּרִי, אֲבָל חֲכָמִים אָמְרוּ שֶׁהִיא חֵלֶק אֶחָד מֵחֲמִשִּׁים,[4] וְאַחַר כָּךְ מִמַּה שֶּׁנִּשְׁאַר הַחִיּוּב עָלֵינוּ לְהוֹצִיא מִמֶּנָּה מַעֲשֵׂר וְהוּא נִקְרָא מַעֲשֵׂר רִאשׁוֹן,[5] וְאַחַר כָּךְ מִמַּה שֶּׁנִּשְׁאַר יֵשׁ לָנוּ לְהוֹצִיא מַעֲשֵׂר אַחֵר וְהוּא מַעֲשֵׂר שֵׁנִי,[6] וְנִתָּן תְּרוּמָה לַכֹּהֵן,[7] וּמַעֲשֵׂר רִאשׁוֹן לַלֵּוִי,[8] וּמַעֲשֵׂר שֵׁנִי יֹאכְלוּהוּ בְעָלָיו בִּירוּשָׁלַיִם.[9] וְעַל זֶה הַסֵּדֶר אָנוּ חַיָּבִים שֶׁנַּפְרִישׁ מִן הַתְּבוּאָה חֲלָקִים אֵלֶּה,[10] וּבָאָה לָנוּ הַמְּנִיעָה בָּזֶה שֶׁלֹּא נַקְדִּים מִזֶּה מַה

---

אֲפִלּוּ חִטָּה אַחַת פּוֹטֶרֶת הַכְּרִי — and even designating **a single wheat** kernel as aside as *terumah*, **discharges the** obligation of an entire **heap.** אֲבָל חֲכָמִים אָמְרוּ שֶׁהִיא חֵלֶק אֶחָד מֵחֲמִשִּׁים — **But the Sages stated** (Mishnah, *Terumos* 4:3) **that it** should generally **be one part in fifty.**[4] וְאַחַר כָּךְ — **After this** procedure of setting aside *terumah*, מִמַּה שֶּׁנִּשְׁאַר — **from what remains,** הַחִיּוּב עָלֵינוּ לְהוֹצִיא מִמֶּנָּה מַעֲשֵׂר — **there is an obligation upon us to set one-tenth of it aside;** וְהוּא נִקְרָא מַעֲשֵׂר רִאשׁוֹן — **and that** tribute **is known as** *maaser rishon* (the first tithe).[5] וְאַחַר כָּךְ — **And after that,** מִמַּה שֶּׁנִּשְׁאַר יֵשׁ לָנוּ לְהוֹצִיא מַעֲשֵׂר אַחֵר — **we are to set aside yet another tenth from what remains,** וְהוּא מַעֲשֵׂר שֵׁנִי — **and that is** known as *maaser sheni* (the second tithe).[6]

Chinuch explains what must be done with these portions once they have been set aside:

וְנִתָּן תְּרוּמָה לַכֹּהֵן — **The terumah is given to a Kohen,**[7] וּמַעֲשֵׂר רִאשׁוֹן לַלֵּוִי — **and the maaser rishon to a Levi.**[8] וּמַעֲשֵׂר שֵׁנִי יֹאכְלוּהוּ בְעָלָיו בִּירוּשָׁלַיִם — **As for the maaser sheni, its owner eats it in Jerusalem.**[9]

Chinuch proceeds to discuss the mitzvah at hand:

וְעַל זֶה הַסֵּדֶר אָנוּ חַיָּבִים שֶׁנַּפְרִישׁ מִן הַתְּבוּאָה חֲלָקִים אֵלֶּה — **It is in accordance with [the above] sequence that we are obligated to set aside these portions from the produce.**[10] וּבָאָה לָנוּ הַמְּנִיעָה בָּזֶה שֶׁלֹּא נַקְדִּים מִזֶּה מַה — **And in this [regard] an injunction was transmitted to us,**

---

## NOTES

which is described in note 8.

4. The Torah does not specify an amount for *terumah*, but states only (*Deuteronomy* 18:4) that *the first* part of the produce be set aside. Accordingly, the Biblical *terumah* obligation can be fulfilled with any portion, regardless of its size. The Sages, however, instituted that the normative amount designated as *terumah* should be one part in fifty. One who wishes to give liberally should set aside ¹⁄₄₀ of the crop to be *terumah,* and one who wishes to give sparingly should give ¹⁄₆₀ (Mishnah, *Terumos* 4:3; *Yerushalmi* ad loc.). [In Mitzvah 507, the mitzvah to set aside *terumah,* Chinuch provides a rationale for why Biblical law allows any amount to be given yet the Sages established a designated amount.]

5. The mitzvah of *maaser rishon* appears in Chinuch in Mitzvah 395.

6. The mitzvah of *maaser sheni* appears in Mitzvah 473. See further, note 9.

7. *Terumah* may be eaten only by Kohanim or by the members of their households, and only while they are ritually pure (*tahor*). [The regulations pertaining to eating *terumah* are set forth in Mitzvos 279-283.]

8. As will be explained in Mitzvah 396, the Leviim are required to further tithe the *maaser rishon* portions that they receive, and to give the portion that they set aside to a Kohen. This portion is known as *terumas maaser* (see below, note 10). Thereafter, they may partake of the *maaser* without any restrictions.

9. That is, one is required to bring the produce to Jerusalem and to eat it while in a state of ritual purity. Alternatively, produce that is outside of Jerusalem may be redeemed, and its sanctity transferred onto money. The money is then brought to Jerusalem, and must be used to purchase food that will then be eaten in accordance with the rules of *maaser sheni*. [Mitzvos 442-444, Mitzvah 473, and Mitzvos 608-610, all pertain to the consumption of *maaser sheni*. See also *Ramban,* Glosses to *Sefer HaMitzvos, Additional Asei* 1.]

[The obligation of *maaser sheni* applies during the first and second years of the seven-year *Shemittah* cycle (see below, Mitzvah 84), and again during the fourth and fifth years. During the third and sixth years, however, the second tithe is known as *maasar ani,* tithe of the pauper. As its name indicates, this tithe is given to the poor. This mitzvah is discussed in Mitzvah 474.]

10. The Mishnah (*Terumos* 3:7) determines the proper order of the produce-obligations on the basis of the following. It notes that the Torah refers to *terumah* as רֵאשִׁית, *the first,* of the harvest (for example, see *Numbers* 18:12 and *Deuteronomy* 18:4). This teaches that *terumah* is the first obligation that must be set aside. For a similar reason, *maaser rishon* must precede *maaser sheni*. For, as mentioned in note 8, the Levi is required to give a portion of his *maaser* to the Kohen, and since the Torah refers to this portion as *terumah* (i.e., *terumas maaser*), it too is considered a "first"

## 42 □ משפטים / מצוה עב: שלא להקדים חקי התבואות

שֶׁרָאוּי לְאַחֵר, וְלֹא לְאַחֵר מַה שֶּׁרָאוּי לְהַקְדִּים, שֶׁנֶּאֱמַר (שמות כ״ב, כ״ח) מְלֵאָתְךָ וְדִמְעֲךָ לֹא תְאַחֵר, וְהוּא כְאִלּוּ אָמַר מִמְּלֵאָתְךָ וְדִמְעֲךָ לֹא תְאַחֵר מַה שֶּׁרָאוּי לְהַקְדִּימוֹ.[11]

מִשָּׁרְשֵׁי הַמִּצְוָה, כִּי בְּהֵעָשׂוֹת הַדְּבָרִים עַל סִדְרָן לֹא יָבוֹא בָּהֶם הָעִרְבּוּב וְהַטָּעוּת, וּכְשֶׁאֵינָן נַעֲשִׂים כֵּן יִהְיֶה הַטָּעוּת נִמְצָא בָּהֶן תָּמִיד, וּבִהְיוֹת הַתְּרוּמוֹת וְהַמַּעַשְׂרוֹת דָּבָר גָּדוֹל בְּקִיּוּם הַדָּת, כְּמוֹ שֶׁנְּפָרֵשׁ בְּעֶזְרַת הַשֵּׁם בְּסֵדֶר רְאֵה וְשׁוֹפְטִים, צִוָּנוּ הַשֵּׁם יִתְבָּרַךְ לְהִזָּהֵר בָּהֶם הַרְבֵּה שֶׁלֹּא לָבֹא בְּחֶשְׁבּוֹנָן לִידֵי טָעוּת לְעוֹלָם.[12] וּבְשָׁמְעֵנוּ טוֹב מִזֶּה מִן הַמְקֻבָּלִים נְקַבֵּל.[13]

---

שֶׁרָאוּי לְאַחֵר וְלֹא לְאַחֵר מַה שֶּׁרָאוּי לְהַקְדִּים — **that we not give precedence to what ought to be delayed, nor delay what ought to have precedence;** שֶׁנֶּאֱמַר ״מְלֵאָתְךָ וְדִמְעֲךָ לֹא תְאַחֵר״ — **as it is stated** (*Exodus 22:28*): ***Do not delay your grain or your fluid produce-obligations.*** וְהוּא כְאִלּוּ אָמַר מִמְּלֵאָתְךָ וְדִמְעֲךָ לֹא תְאַחֵר מַה שֶּׁרָאוּי לְהַקְדִּימוֹ — **[This verse] is to be understood as though it states: *Among the produce-obligations* that you set aside from *your grain and your fluid, do not postpone those which ought to have precedence.***[11]

### ~ Underlying Purpose of the Mitzvah ~

מִשָּׁרְשֵׁי הַמִּצְוָה — **Among the underlying purposes of this mitzvah is** the concept כִּי בְּהֵעָשׂוֹת הַדְּבָרִים עַל סִדְרָן לֹא יָבוֹא בָּהֶם — **that when matters are performed in their** proper **order** הָעִרְבּוּב וְהַטָּעוּת — **confusion and error will not occur in them;** וּכְשֶׁאֵינָן נַעֲשִׂים כֵּן — **but when they are not performed thus,** i.e., in order, יִהְיֶה הַטָּעוּת נִמְצָא בָּהֶן תָּמִיד — **error will be ever-present in** the execution of **[these matters].** וּבִהְיוֹת הַתְּרוּמוֹת וְהַמַּעַשְׂרוֹת דָּבָר גָּדוֹל בְּקִיּוּם הַדָּת — **Now, since *terumos* and *maasros* are of great importance in** ensuring the **endurance of our faith,** כְּמוֹ שֶׁנְּפָרֵשׁ בְּעֶזְרַת הַשֵּׁם בְּסֵדֶר רְאֵה וְשׁוֹפְטִים — **as we shall explain, with the help of Hashem, in *Parashas Re'eh*** (Mitzvah 450, 473) **and *Parashas Shoftim*** (Mitzvah 507), צִוָּנוּ הַשֵּׁם יִתְבָּרַךְ לְהִזָּהֵר בָּהֶם הַרְבֵּה — **Hashem, blessed be He, commanded us to be exceedingly careful with regard to them,** שֶׁלֹּא לָבֹא בְּחֶשְׁבּוֹנָן לִידֵי טָעוּת לְעוֹלָם — **so that we never arrive at an error when calculating them.**[12]

וּבְשָׁמְעֵנוּ טוֹב מִזֶּה מִן הַמְקֻבָּלִים נְקַבֵּל — **Upon hearing a better** explanation of the purpose of this mitzvah **from those who are learned in Kabbalah, we shall accept it.**[13]

---

### NOTES

portion. Accordingly, since *maaser rishon* contains the latent *terumas maaser*, it must be set aside before *maaser sheni* or *maasar ani*. [Obviously, the names *maaser rishon* and *maaser sheni* are reflections of the sequence in which these tithes are to be set aside.]

11. *Yerushalmi* (*Terumos* 3:3) cites an opinion that this verse actually prohibits *delaying* to give the produce-obligations beyond the required time, as is set forth in Mitzvah 607. Chinuch, however, follows the opinion of the Mishnah (*Terumos* 3:6) and *Mechilta* to the verse, which interpret this verse as a prohibition against *changing the sequence* of the produce-obligations. That is, one should not delay fulfilling an obligation that has precedence over the others. See also *Rambam, Sefer HaMitzvos, Lo Saaseh* 154.

12. In Mitzvos 450, 473, and 507 (see also Mitzvah 360), Chinuch explains that the purpose of the mitzvah of *terumah* is so that man bear in mind God's sovereignty over all aspects of the universe; the purpose of *maaser rishon* is to ensure that the tribe of Levi be able to remain dedicated to studying and teaching God's ways and laws without becoming preoccupied with providing for its own sustenance; and the purpose of *maaser sheni* is so that even the common folk among the Jews visit the *Beis HaMikdash* regularly and thus become imbued with knowledge of the Torah. Since these objectives are essential to the continuity of Judaism, the Torah insisted that one set aside his *terumos* and *maasros* in a meticulous manner, without deviating from their proper order.

13. The purpose that Chinuch offered for this mitzvah explains only why it is necessary to follow the sequence that was established for the produce-obligations, but does not explain the sequence itself. Chinuch thus acknowledges that there is need for Kabbalistic insight into the essence of the mitzvah.

## 43 ☐ MISHPATIM / MITZVAH 72: NOT TO CHANGE THE ORDER OF THE PRODUCE-OBLIGATIONS

מִדִּינֵי הַמִּצְוָה, מַה שֶּׁאָמְרוּ זִכְרוֹנָם לִבְרָכָה (תרומות פ״ג מ״ו) שֶׁאִם עָבַר וְהִקְדִּים בְּעִנְיָן זֶה מַה שֶּׁאֵינוֹ רָאוּי לְהַקְדִּים, מַה שֶּׁעָשָׂה עָשׂוּי, וְלֹא נְחַיְּבֶנּוּ לַחֲזֹר וּלְעָרֵב הַכֹּל וְיַפְרִישֵׁם פַּעַם שְׁנִיָּה[14]. וְכֵן[15] מַה שֶּׁדָּרְשׁוּ בְּמַסֶּכֶת תְּמוּרָה[16] וּבַמְּכִילְתָּא (כאן), "מְלֵאָתְךָ", אֵלּוּ הַבִּכּוּרִים הַנִּטָּלִין מִן הַמָּלֵא, כְּלוֹמַר קֹדֶם שֶׁנִּטַּל מִן הַדָּבָר כְּלוּם, וְזֶהוּ לְשׁוֹן מָלֵא כְּלוֹמַר שֶׁהוּא כְּדָבָר שָׁלֵם לְגַמְרֵי[17], "וְדִמְעֲךָ" זוֹ תְּרוּמָה[18], "לֹא תְאַחֵר", שֶׁלֹּא תַקְדִּים תְּרוּמָה לַבִּכּוּרִים וְכוּ'[19],

---

### ⌘ Laws of the Mitzvah ⌘

**מִדִּינֵי הַמִּצְוָה — Among the laws of this mitzvah** מַה שֶּׁאָמְרוּ זִכְרוֹנָם לִבְרָכָה **— is that which [the Sages], of blessed memory, have stated** (*Terumos* 3:6), שֶׁאִם עָבַר וְהִקְדִּים בְּעִנְיָן זֶה מַה שֶּׁאֵינוֹ רָאוּי לְהַקְדִּים **— that if one transgressed, and, among the [produce-obligations], gave precedence to one that ought not have precedence,** מַה שֶּׁעָשָׂה עָשׂוּי **— what he did is nevertheless effective.** וְלֹא נְחַיְּבֶנּוּ לַחֲזֹר וּלְעָרֵב הַכֹּל **— That is, we do not obligate him to go back and mix everything together** וְיַפְרִישֵׁם פַּעַם שְׁנִיָּה **— and to then set aside [the *terumos* and *maasros*] a second time.**[14]

There is an additional tribute that must be set aside from the produce, known as *bikkurim*, which Chinuch did not describe above. Nonetheless, Chinuch explains that the Sages interpret the verse of our mitzvah in a manner that applies to *bikkurim* as well:[15]

וְכֵן מַה שֶּׁדָּרְשׁוּ בְּמַסֶּכֶת תְּמוּרָה[16] וּבַמְּכִילְתָּא **— Also among the laws of the mitzvah is that which [the Sages] expounded, in Tractate *Temurah* (4a) and in *Mechilta* (to our verse):** "מְלֵאָתְךָ" **— When the verse describing our mitzvah mentions *melei'ascha*, which literally means "your fullness,"** אֵלּוּ הַבִּכּוּרִים הַנִּטָּלִין מִן הַמָּלֵא **— this is a reference to the *bikkurim*, which are taken from the "fullness" of the crop,** כְּלוֹמַר קֹדֶם שֶׁנִּטַּל מִן הַדָּבָר כְּלוּם **— that is to say, before anything else is taken from it.** וְזֶהוּ לְשׁוֹן מָלֵא **— For that is the connotation of the term *fullness*;** כְּלוֹמַר שֶׁהוּא כְּדָבָר שָׁלֵם לְגַמְרֵי **— it means to say that [the crop] is entirely complete,** as no part has been removed from it.[17] "וְדִמְעֲךָ" **— And when the verse mentions *vedim'acha*,** זוֹ תְּרוּמָה **— this is a reference to *terumah*.**[18] "לֹא תְאַחֵר" שֶׁלֹּא תַקְדִּים תְּרוּמָה לַבִּכּוּרִים וְכוּ' **— And the verse states regarding these, *you may not delay*, which teaches that you may not give precedence to *terumah* over *bikkurim*.**[19]

---

### NOTES

14. Although our mitzvah prohibits deviation from the sequence in which the produce-obligations must be fulfilled, that is not to say that *terumah* or *maaser* that had been set aside without the proper sequence is invalid. [See further, note 24.]

15. The mitzvah of *bikkurim* applies to the fruits of the Seven Species (i.e., wheat, barley, grapes, figs, pomegranates, olives, and dates), and requires that one bring the first fruit of each year's crop to the *Beis HaMikdash* and give it to the Kohen. Chinuch discusses this obligation in Mitzvah 95.

16. In most editions, the text reads מַסֶּכֶת תְּרוּמָה, *Tractate Terumah*. Our text (here, and later in this mitzvah) is corrected according to the emendation of *Maharam Schik*.

17. Unlike the other produce-obligations, the obligation of *bikkurim* begins even before the harvesting of the crop is completed. For example, whereas the *terumah* and *maaser* obligations of a wine-grape crop set in only once the grapes have been pressed, one is required to bring *bikkurim* from the grapes themselves. In this sense the term מְלֵאָתְךָ (*melei'ascha*), *your fullness*, refers to *bikkurim*, as it is taken from the produce before any of the other produce-obligations are set aside.

18. The literal meaning of the term וְדִמְעֲךָ (*vedim'acha*) is *and your drippings*, which implies that it refers to the produce-obligations that pertain to fluids such as wine and oil. [This is in contrast to the *bikkurim* obligation, which applies to whole fruit, and which is thus referred to as מְלֵאָתְךָ, *your fullness*.] The Sages understand *your drippings* as a reference to the *terumah* obligation, which applies to fluids (*Tosafos, Temurah* 4a ד״ה מלאתך). [According to the simple explanation of the phrase מְלֵאָתְךָ וְדִמְעֲךָ, it means *your grains and fluids,* and refers to all the various obligations of the harvested crop, i.e., *terumah* and *maasros* (see above, note 1). According to the current exposition, the meaning of the verse is expanded to include even *bikkurim* (see *Ramban* to the verse).]

19. According to this exposition of *your fullness* as referring to *bikkurim* and *your drippings* as referring to *terumah*, the verse means to specify that one not delay the separation of *bikkurim*, meaning that one may not give precedence to *terumah* (whose obligation comes after the crop is harvested) over *bikkurim* (whose obligation comes before the harvesting). By the same token, as was explained in note 10, one may not give precedence to *maaser rishon* over *terumah*, nor to *maaser sheni* over *maaser rishon* (see *Mechilta* with *Malbim*).

# 44 □ משפטים / מצוה עב: שלא להקדים חקי התבואות

וְיֶתֶר פְּרָטֶיהָ, בְּמַסֶּכֶת תְּמוּרָה[20] (שם).

וְנוֹהֶגֶת בִּזְכָרִים וּנְקֵבוֹת[21], בְּאֶרֶץ יִשְׂרָאֵל[22], וּבִזְמַן שֶׁיִּשְׂרָאֵל שָׁם, כְּדַעַת הָרַמְבַּ״ם זִכְרוֹנוֹ לִבְרָכָה, שֶׁכָּתַב (פ״א מתרומות הכ״ו) שֶׁמִּצְוַת תְּרוּמָה וּמַעְשְׂרוֹת מִן הַתּוֹרָה אֵינָה אֶלָּא בִּזְמַן שֶׁאֶרֶץ יִשְׂרָאֵל בְּיִשּׁוּבָהּ[23].

וְהָעוֹבֵר עָלֶיהָ וְהִקְדִּים דְּבָרִים אֵלּוּ זוֹ לָזוֹ, דִּינוֹ כְּעוֹבֵר עַל מִצְוַת מֶלֶךְ, אֲבָל אֵין לוֹקִין עָלָיו, שֶׁכָּךְ נִתְבָּאֵר שָׁם בִּתְמוּרָה[24] שֶׁאֵין בָּזֶה הַלָּאו מַלְקוּת[25].

---

וְיֶתֶר פְּרָטֶיהָ בְּמַסֶּכֶת תְּמוּרָה — These laws, **and the additional details of [this mitzvah],** are set forth **in** Tractate *Temurah*.[20]

## ☙ Applicability of the Mitzvah ❧

בְּאֶרֶץ יִשְׂרָאֵל — **[This prohibition] applies to** both **men and women;**[21] וְנוֹהֶגֶת בִּזְכָרִים וּנְקֵבוֹת — **but only in Eretz Yisrael,**[22] וּבִזְמַן שֶׁיִּשְׂרָאֵל שָׁם — **and only in a time when** the **Jewish people are settled there.** כְּדַעַת הָרַמְבַּ״ם זִכְרוֹנוֹ לִבְרָכָה — This is **in accordance with the opinion of** *Rambam*, **of blessed memory** (Hil. Terumos 1:26), שֶׁכָּתַב שֶׁמִּצְוַת תְּרוּמָה וּמַעְשְׂרוֹת מִן הַתּוֹרָה אֵינָה אֶלָּא בִּזְמַן שֶׁאֶרֶץ יִשְׂרָאֵל בְּיִשּׁוּבָהּ — **who wrote that the Biblical obligation of** *terumah* **and** *maasros* **are** applicable **only when Eretz Yisrael is** properly **settled.**[23] וְהָעוֹבֵר עָלֶיהָ וְהִקְדִּים דְּבָרִים אֵלּוּ זוֹ לָזוֹ — **One who violates [this prohibition] and gives precedence to** some **of these items over others** in a manner that is not in accordance with their proper sequence דִּינוֹ כְּעוֹבֵר עַל מִצְוַת מֶלֶךְ — **is considered as one who has violated the command of the King (God).** אֲבָל אֵין לוֹקִין עָלָיו — **Nevertheless, one does not incur** *malkus* **(lashes)** for [this transgression], שֶׁכָּךְ נִתְבָּאֵר שָׁם בִּתְמוּרָה — **for thus has** the matter **been clarified there, in** Tractate *Temurah* (4a-4b),[24] שֶׁאֵין בָּזֶה הַלָּאו מַלְקוּת — **that this prohibition does not bear a** *malkus* **penalty.**[25]

---

## NOTES

20. See *Temurah* 4a-5b. See also *Terumos* 3:6-7. The laws of this mitzvah are codified in *Rambam, Hil. Terumos* 3:23, and *Shulchan Aruch, Yoreh Deah* 331:19, 27. [See note 16 regarding the reading of the text.]

21. In accordance with the standard rule that pertains to mitzvah-prohibitions.

22. Produce-obligations generally apply only in Eretz Yisrael (*Kiddushin* 36b). [See, however, Mitzvah 284 and *Minchas Chinuch* there §18-20.]

23. According to *Rambam*, nowadays the obligation to separate *terumah* and *maasros* is Rabbinic. See Mitzvah 507, where Chinuch elaborates on *Rambam's* position, and where he also cites the position of other Rishonim regarding this matter.

24. See note 16 regarding the reading of the text.

25. Although one who violates this prohibition does not incur any penalty in *beis din*, he is subject to Divine retribution as one who defies his Creator's command.

The commentators offer two reasons for why this prohibition does not bear *malkus*, based on various points mentioned in the Gemara in *Temurah* that Chinuch cites. Some explain that our prohibition is considered לָאו הַנִּיתָּק לַעֲשֵׂה, *a prohibition that is remedied through [fulfillment of] a mitzvah-obligation* (see General Introduction, note 14). That is, the Torah specifically reiterates the *terumah* obligation for one who has violated our prohibition, indicating that the violation does not carry any penalty, but is remedied by the separation of *terumah*. Now, since the initial separation was valid (as Chinuch stated above, at note 14), there is no point in doing it again. Rather, the intention is that the transgression is automatically "remedied" by the fact that the *terumah* separation is valid even though it was done in the improper order. [This is different from the typical case of לָאו הַנִּיתָּק לַעֲשֵׂה, in which a specific act must be performed *after* the transgression in order to remedy it; here, the remedy is automatic] (*Radvaz, Hil. Terumos* 3:23; *Derech Emunah* there, in *Beur HaHalachah* ד״ה ומנין; see also *Mahari Korkos* there; see, however, *Rashi, Temurah* 4b ד״ה לאו הניתק לעשה, as elaborated by *Radvaz* ibid.).

Others explain that our prohibition is considered לָאו שֶׁאֵין בּוֹ מַעֲשֶׂה, *a prohibition that does not entail an action*, as the separation of *terumos* and *maasros* can be accomplished through verbal designation and does not require physical action. [See Insight.] As Chinuch frequently mentions (see, for example, end of Mitzvah 74), such prohibitions are not subject to *malkus* (*Imrei Binah, Dinei Terumos U'Maasros,* §21; *Maadanei Eretz, Hil. Terumos* 3:23 §1).

## MISHPATIM / MITZVAH 72: NOT TO CHANGE THE ORDER OF THE PRODUCE-OBLIGATIONS

**◈§ Insight: Annulment of a Terumah Designation**

As with the designation of an animal as an offering, which is done through verbal consecration, *terumah* and *maaser* are designated orally. Even if one merely states that a specified portion of his crop should be *terumah*, but does not physically set it aside, his statement is effective. In this sense, since the designation of *terumah* is accomplished verbally, it is considered a form of a vow. The Gemara therefore explains (*Nedarim* 59a; see *Ran* ad loc. ד"ה והרי תרומה) that just as one can annul a vow through the procedure of הַתָּרַת נְדָרִים, *annulment of vows*, that is set forth in Mitzvah 406, so can he annul his designation of *terumah*. In the same vein, *Rambam* (*Hil. Terumos* 4:17; see however *Meiri*, *Shabbos* 127b) explains that one can annul his designation of *maaser*.

The law that one can annul his designation of *terumah* has several implications with regard to our mitzvah.

*Teshuvos Beis Yitzchak* (by R' Yitzchak Yehudah Shmelkis; *Yoreh Deah* II §138) raises the following question: As Chinuch explains in Mitzvah 406, the essence of the annulment of vows, and similarly, the annulment of a *terumah* designation, is to identify some oversight that occurred at the time of the vow, and on that basis to declare that the vow was made in error. For this reason, the annulment of a vow works retroactively: it is as though the vow was never taken. Now, if one set aside *terumah* and *maaser* in the proper sequence, but he then annuls his designation of *terumah*, it will emerge that he violated our mitzvah, for since his annulment of the *terumah* designation works retroactively, it turns out that he designated *maaser* before *terumah*! How can we permit him to annul his designation of *terumah* if the result will be that he violated a prohibition? Must we assume that it is permitted to annul a *terumah* designation only if one has not yet designated *maaser*, or if one annuls the *maaser* designation at the same time?

*Beis Yitzchak* suggests that this is not the case. He argues that our mitzvah prohibits only *proactively* changing the sequence of the produce-obligations, by actually designating them in the wrong order. In the case of one who annuls his *terumah* designation, since he did not proactively change the sequence in which he addressed his obligations, but it only *turned out retroactively* that their sequence was changed, he is not considered to have violated the prohibition.

*Beis Yitzchak* cites a parallel to this from *Turei Even* (*Rosh Hashanah* 28b ד"ה הרי הוא), pertaining to the prohibition against slaughtering an animal of *chullin* (i.e., one that had not been consecrated as an offering) in the *Beis HaMikdash*. *Turei Even* explains that in certain cases it is permitted to annul the consecration of an offering even after it has been slaughtered. Although it then turns out that he slaughtered *chullin* in the *Beis HaMikdash*, since at the time that he actually slaughtered the animal it was not *chullin*, and it only *turned out* to be *chullin* because he later annulled the consecration, it is not considered a violation of that prohibition. Similarly, says *Beis Yitzchak*, although it is prohibited to proactively alter the sequence of the produce-obligations, it is permitted to annul a *terumah* designation even though the result will be that the order of the obligations has been reversed. Since at the time that he designated the *maaser* it was preceded by his *terumah* designation, he never actually gave precedence to the *maaser* over the *terumah*.

[For another approach to this matter, see *Pardes Yosef* (R' Yosef Patzanovski) to the verse of our mitzvah (*Exodus* 22:28).]

A related question is raised regarding annulment of a *terumah* designation: Since one recites a blessing at the time that he designates *terumah* (see Mishnah, *Terumos* 1:2, with *Rav*), when the designation is retroactively annulled, it turns out that the blessing was recited in vain. How can one annul his designation of *terumah* if that will cause him to retroactively violate the prohibition against reciting a blessing in vain? *Chasam Sofer* (*Teshuvos*, *Yoreh Deah* §320) explains that the blessing actually will not have been recited in vain. The mitzvah of designating *terumah* itself dictates that one has the prerogative to annul his designation after the fact, if he discovers an error in it. Now, the blessing, "… *Who has sanctified us with His commandments and commanded us to separate terumah,"* means that God has given us this commandment *with all its stipulations* — including the privilege of annulment. If it should occur that one has occasion to take advantage of that privilege, he is abiding by the laws of the mitzvah itself, and thus, his blessing over the mitzvah remains valid despite the fact that the actual designation was annulled. [Cf. *HaDerash VeHaIyun*, *Vayishlach* §165; *Pardes Yosef* ibid.; see also *Pardes Yosef* to *Exodus* 23:7.]

*Minchas Chinuch* (§4) points out that the ability to annul the *terumah* and *maaser* designations

has an additional ramification with regard to our mitzvah. He suggests that one who violated our prohibition has the ability to undo his transgression, through annulment. If he improperly set aside *terumah* before *bikkurim,* he can simply annul the *terumah* designation, and similarly, if he set aside *maaser* before *terumah* he can annul his *maaser* designation. Indeed, *Minchas Chinuch* urges that one who violated this prohibition should be encouraged to annul his first designation, as by so doing he completely undoes his transgression!

[It seems, however, that according to the approach of *Beis Yitzchak* cited above, annulling the designation would not undo the transgression. Since at the time that the person made the respective designations, he *proactively* changed the sequence of the produce-obligations and gave precedence to the wrong one, even if it later turns out through annulment that the matter was rectified, he still has violated the prohibition. This matter requires further study.]

## MISHPATIM / MITZVAH 73: THE PROHIBITION TO EAT TEREIFAH

### מִצְוָה עג: שֶׁלֹּא לֶאֱכֹל טְרֵפָה

שֶׁלֹּא לֶאֱכֹל מִן הַטְּרֵפָה, שֶׁנֶּאֱמַר (שמות כ״ב, ל׳) "וּבָשָׂר בַּשָּׂדֶה טְרֵפָה לֹא תֹאכֵלוּ, וּמַשְׁמָעוּת הַגְּלֻיָּה בַּכָּתוּב זֶה הוּא לְהַזְהִירֵנוּ עַל בְּהֵמָה שֶׁטְּרָפָהּ זְאֵב אוֹ אֲרִי בַּשָּׂדֶה, וְשֶׁטְּרָפָהּ בְּעִנְיָן שֶׁהִיא נְטוּיָה לָמוּת בַּטֶּרֶף הַהוּא, דְּוַדַּאי אֵין בְּמַשְׁמָע שֶׁאִם נָגַע בְּרֹאשׁ אָזְנָהּ אוֹ תָּלַשׁ מִצַּמְרָהּ שֶׁתִּקָּרֵא טְרֵפָה בְּכָךְ, אֶלָּא וַדַּאי הַמַּשְׁמָעוּת הַנָּכוֹן,

---

## Mitzvah 73
# The Prohibition to Eat Tereifah

> וְאַנְשֵׁי קֹדֶשׁ תִּהְיוּן לִי וּבָשָׂר בַּשָּׂדֶה טְרֵפָה לֹא תֹאכֵלוּ לַכֶּלֶב תַּשְׁלִכוּן אֹתוֹ
> People of holiness shall you be to Me; flesh [of a creature] torn in the field you shall not eat; to the dog shall you throw it (Exodus 22:30).

Two mitzvah-prohibitions deal with the consumption of animals and birds of the kosher species: the prohibitions to eat meat that is either *neveilah* or *tereifah*. *Neveilah* [נְבֵלָה, literally, *carcass*] is meat from an animal or bird that was not properly slaughtered through the procedure of *shechitah* (ritual slaughter; see Mitzvah 451). An animal killed in a manner other than a proper *shechitah*, or one that dies naturally, is known as *neveilah* and is forbidden for consumption. In addition to being forbidden for consumption, a *neveilah* is a source of *tumah* (impurity). The prohibition of its consumption is the topic of Mitzvah 472; its being a source of *tumah* is the topic of Mitzvah 161.

A *tereifah* [טְרֵפָה, literally, *torn*] is, generally speaking, an animal or bird that is afflicted with a fatal defect involving a critical organ. It makes no difference whether the defect arises from an external injury, such as attack by a predator [from which the name *tereifah* (torn) derives], from an illness, or from a birth defect. In any event, the animal or bird suffering from the fatal defect is included in the category of *tereifah*. When the Torah forbids the consumption of meat of a *tereifah,* it cannot be referring to a case where the animal or bird died of its injury, since then it would in any event be prohibited as *neveilah*. Rather, the Torah refers to a case where the animal or bird was properly slaughtered, and it nevertheless declares the meat prohibited. This is the subject of our mitzvah.[1]

שֶׁלֹּא לֶאֱכֹל מִן הַטְּרֵפָה — **We are commanded not to eat of a *tereifah*,** שֶׁנֶּאֱמַר — **as it is stated** (*Exodus* 22:30): "וּבָשָׂר בַּשָּׂדֶה טְרֵפָה לֹא תֹאכֵלוּ — ***flesh* of a creature *torn in the field you shall not eat*.** וּמַשְׁמָעוּת הַגְּלֻיָּה בַּכָּתוּב זֶה הוּא — **The evident,** simple **meaning of this verse is** לְהַזְהִירֵנוּ — **to warn us against** eating עַל בְּהֵמָה שֶׁטְּרָפָהּ זְאֵב אוֹ אֲרִי בַּשָּׂדֶה — **an animal that a wolf or lion mauled in the field,** וְשֶׁטְּרָפָהּ בְּעִנְיָן שֶׁהִיא נְטוּיָה לָמוּת בַּטֶּרֶף הַהוּא — **and,** more specifically, **that it mauled [the animal] in** such **a manner that it is inclined to die** as a result **of that mauling.**[2] דְּוַדַּאי אֵין בְּמַשְׁמָע שֶׁאִם נָגַע בְּרֹאשׁ אָזְנָהּ — **For surely it is not the meaning** of the verse **that if [the predator]** merely **nicked the tip of [the animal's] ear,** אוֹ תָּלַשׁ מִצַּמְרָהּ — **or plucked out** some **of its wool,** שֶׁתִּקָּרֵא טְרֵפָה בְּכָךְ — **it should be considered "torn"** (and hence, prohibited) **on that account.** אֶלָּא וַדַּאי הַמַּשְׁמָעוּת הַנָּכוֹן — **Rather, certainly the sound** and logical **meaning** of the verse,

---

### NOTES

1. The prohibitions of *neveilah* and *tereifah* are related. If one eats a *kezayis* (olive's volume) of *neveilah* and *tereifah* combined, he incurs *malkus* (lashes). This is an exception to the general rule that one must eat a *kezayis* of a *single* prohibited food to incur punishment (see below, Mitzvah 368). The reason for this exception is that "*tereifah* is the beginning of *neveilah*"; i.e., a mortal defect causing the animal to be rendered *tereifah* is the onset of the animal's death, which will result in its becoming *neveilah* (*Rambam, Hil. Maachalos Asuros* 4:17).

2. Obviously the animal is still alive. If it had been killed by its predator then it would be a *neveilah*, and we would not need to resort to the prohibition of *tereifah* (*Rambam, Hil. Maachalos Asuros* 4:6). Chinuch emphasizes, though, that the mauled animal suffered a fatal wound.

## 48 □ משפטים / מצוה עג: שלא לאכל טרפה

וְהַקַּבָּלָה מְסַיַּעַת בְּכָךְ הוּא, שֶׁנִּטְרְפָה בִּכְדֵי שֶׁתָּמוּת לְשָׁעָה אוֹ לִזְמַן קָרוֹב בִּשְׁבִיל הַטֶּרֶף הַהוּא[3], וְאָמְרוּ זִכְרוֹנָם לִבְרָכָה (חולין דף נ״ז ע״ב) שֶׁזְּמַן זֶה הוּא שָׁנָה אַחַת. וְעוֹד יֵשׁ לְהָבִין לְכָל מֵבִין כִּי לֹא תַקְפִּיד הַתּוֹרָה כְּשֶׁהִגִּיעַ לָהּ טַרְפוּת זֶה עַל יְדֵי זְאֵב אוֹ אֲרִי אוֹ דֹב, אֶלָּא שֶׁתֵּאָסֵר כָּל בְּהֵמָה הַמַּכָּה מַכָּה הַמְבִיאָה אוֹתָהּ לִידֵי מָוֶת עַל כָּל פָּנִים, וְהֵם הַמַּכּוֹת שֶׁמָּנוּ אוֹתָן חֲכָמִים שֶׁהֵם מְמִיתוֹת, וּכְמוֹ שֶׁבָּא בַּמִּשְׁנָה (שם דף מ״ב ע״א) זֶה הַכְּלָל כָּל שֶׁאֵין כָּמוֹהָ חַיָּה טְרֵפָה[4], וְזֶה שֶׁאָמַר הַכָּתוּב בַּשָּׂדֶה לָאו דַּוְקָא, אֶלָּא שֶׁדֶּרֶךְ הַכָּתוּב לְדַבֵּר לְעוֹלָם בַּהֹוֶה, וּבַשָּׂדוֹת דֶּרֶךְ בְּהֵמוֹת לִטְרֹף[5]. וְכֵן הוּא בַּמְּכִילְתָּא (כאן) דִּבֶּר הַכָּתוּב בַּהֹוֶה.

---

שֶׁנִּטְרְפָה וְהַקַּבָּלָה מְסַיַּעַת בְּכָךְ הוּא — which, additionally, is supported by the Oral Tradition, is בִּכְדֵי שֶׁתָּמוּת לְשָׁעָה אוֹ לִזְמַן קָרוֹב בִּשְׁבִיל הַטֶּרֶף הַהוּא — that [the animal] was mauled to the extent that it will die momentarily, or in a relatively short time, as a result of that mauling.[3] שֶׁזְּמַן זֶה הוּא שָׁנָה) וְאָמְרוּ זִכְרוֹנָם לִבְרָכָה — [The Sages,] of blessed memory, said (*Chullin* 57b) אַחַת — that this short amount of time is one year. Thus, the verse is teaching that if an animal is mauled and suffers a wound that will cause its death within a year, then even if the animal is slaughtered through a proper *shechitah*, its meat is prohibited.

Having clarified that when the verse states "torn" it means that the animal suffered a fatal wound, Chinuch focuses on the circumstances of the mauling, and the meaning of the verse's words, "in the field": וְעוֹד יֵשׁ לְהָבִין לְכָל מֵבִין — Furthermore, it is clearly to be understood by every discerning [person] כִּי לֹא תַקְפִּיד הַתּוֹרָה כְּשֶׁהִגִּיעַ לָהּ טַרְפוּת זֶה עַל יְדֵי זְאֵב אוֹ אֲרִי אוֹ דֹב — that the Torah does not mean to be particular and to limit the prohibition of *tereifah* to the specific case where this fatal defect was brought upon [the animal] through mauling by a wild animal such as a wolf, lion, or bear in the field. אֶלָּא שֶׁתֵּאָסֵר כָּל בְּהֵמָה הַמַּכָּה מַכָּה הַמְבִיאָה אוֹתָהּ לִידֵי מָוֶת עַל כָּל פָּנִים — Rather, [the Torah] mentions "torn in the field" as a prototype of *tereifah*, but actually means to prohibit any animal that suffered a type of wound that will deliver it to its death in any event (i.e., a fatal wound), regardless of the circumstances through which this wound came about; וְהֵם הַמַּכּוֹת שֶׁמָּנוּ אוֹתָן חֲכָמִים שֶׁהֵם מְמִיתוֹת — and this includes all the wounds and defects that the Sages (*Chullin* 42a-54a) listed as fatal, וּכְמוֹ שֶׁבָּא בַּמִּשְׁנָה — following the basic principle of *tereifah* law, as transmitted to us in the Mishnah (ibid. 42a): זֶה הַכְּלָל כָּל שֶׁאֵין כָּמוֹהָ חַיָּה טְרֵפָה — "This is the general rule: Any slaughtered [animal] possessing a defect because of which [a living animal] similarly affected would not live more than twelve months is a *tereifah*."[4] וְזֶה שֶׁאָמַר הַכָּתוּב "בַּשָּׂדֶה" לָאו דַּוְקָא — And as for that which the verse states, *in the field*, it does not mean to prohibit specifically the meat of an animal that was mauled in the wild; אֶלָּא שֶׁדֶּרֶךְ הַכָּתוּב לְדַבֵּר לְעוֹלָם בַּהֹוֶה — rather, it is the way of Scripture to always speak of that which is common, וּבַשָּׂדוֹת דֶּרֶךְ בְּהֵמוֹת לִטְרֹף — and out in the fields it is the norm for wild beasts to maul other animals. Realistically, though, an animal that possesses one of the fatal defects that the Sages listed is deemed *tereifah* wherever and however it contracted its defect — and even if it was born with the defect.[5] וְכֵן הוּא בַּמְּכִילְתָּא — Thus is it stated in *Mechilta* (ad loc.): דִּבֶּר הַכָּתוּב בַּהֹוֶה — The verse merely

---

### NOTES

3. *Rambam* (ibid. 4:7) notes that the verse itself indicates as much, for it concludes that the *tereifah* meat shall be thrown to the dog — indicating that the reference is to an animal that has been torn to the extent that it is already fit food for canines. [See *Beitzah* 6a.]

4. As explained above, the meat of a *tereifah* is forbidden even if it is slaughtered through a proper *shechitah*. The Mishnah is discussing such a case of an animal that has already been slaughtered. Thus, the Mishnah does not state simply that the animal is *tereifah* if it cannot survive. Instead it states that if a living animal with a similar defect would not survive, then this slaughtered animal is *tereifah* (*Tosafos, Chullin* 32a ד״ה ורמינהו; see also *Rambam* ibid. 4:7-8).

5. As *Rambam* (ibid.) puts it: There is no difference whether a wild animal mauled and crushed it, or it fell from the roof and broke its bones, or someone shot it with an arrow and punctured its heart or lung, or it contracted an illness that caused a puncture of its heart or lung, or anything of the like occurred. Since it suffered a fatal injury, whether through an act of God or an act of man, it is *tereifah*. [Indeed, the animal is *tereifah* even if it was born with one of these defects (see Mishnah, *Chullin* 72b).]

## MISHPATIM / MITZVAH 73: THE PROHIBITION TO EAT TEREIFAH

וְגַם כֵּן נִצְרַךְ לִכְתֹּב בַּשָּׂדֶה כְּדֵי לְלַמֵּד בּוֹ עוֹד דְּבָרִים אֲחֵרִים רַבִּים, כִּי דִּבְרֵי הַתּוֹרָה נִדְרָשִׁים לְכַמָּה פָנִים, יִתְלַבְּשׁוּ מִבַּחוּץ לְבוּשׁ מַלְכוּת שֵׁשׁ וָמֶשִׁי וְרִקְמָה טְהוֹרִים, וּמִבִּפְנִים יֵשׁ זָהָב וְרֹב פְּנִינִים,[6] וּלְבוּשׁ זֶה הַפָּסוּק הַנִּגְלֶה וְהַנִּרְאֶה בּוֹ יוֹתֵר בִּתְחִלַּת הָעִיּוּן הוּא לְלַמֵּד עַל הַטְּרֵפָה לְבַד, כְּמוֹ שֶׁכְּתַבְנוּ, וְעַל בָּשָׂר מִן הַחַי שֶׁבִּכְלַל טְרֵפָה הוּא,[7] וּמַה שֶּׁבִּפְנִים בּוֹ הוּא, שֶׁמְּלַמֵּד עַל כָּל בָּשָׂר שֶׁיָּצָא חוּץ מִמְּחִצָתוֹ שֶׁאָסוּר וְנַעֲשָׂה כִּטְרֵפָה, כְּגוֹן בְּשַׂר [קָדְשֵׁי] קָדָשִׁים שֶׁיָּצָא חוּץ לָעֲזָרָה,[8] וּבְשַׂר קָדָשִׁים קַלִּים שֶׁיָּצָא חוּץ לַחוֹמָה,[9]

---

**speaks of that which is common;** it does not mean that the law of *tereifah* hinges on the animal being "torn in the field."

Having explained that, in its simple sense, *in the field* is merely describing a common situation of *tereifah*, Chinuch proceeds to add a deeper meaning to this expression. He begins poetically: וְגַם כֵּן נִצְרַךְ לִכְתֹּב "בַּשָּׂדֶה" כְּדֵי לְלַמֵּד בּוֹ עוֹד דְּבָרִים — **It was also necessary to write *in the field***, אֲחֵרִים רַבִּים — **in order to teach us numerous additional things through it,** כִּי דִּבְרֵי הַתּוֹרָה נִדְרָשִׁים לְכַמָּה פָנִים — **for the words of the Torah are expounded to** bring to light **many facets of** meaning; יִתְלַבְּשׁוּ מִבַּחוּץ לְבוּשׁ מַלְכוּת שֵׁשׁ וָמֶשִׁי וְרִקְמָה טְהוֹרִים — it is as if **[the Torah's words] are clothed on** their **outside in royal garments of linen, silk, and embroidered finery,** וּמִבִּפְנִים יֵשׁ זָהָב וְרֹב פְּנִינִים — **and within** these garments **is** a concealed treasure of **gold and a multitude of pearls.**[6]

וּלְבוּשׁ זֶה הַפָּסוּק — **The "garment" of this verse,** הַנִּגְלֶה וְהַנִּרְאֶה בּוֹ יוֹתֵר בִּתְחִלַּת הָעִיּוּן — i.e., that **which is revealed and easily visible in it at first glance,** הוּא לְלַמֵּד עַל הַטְּרֵפָה לְבַד כְּמוֹ שֶׁכְּתַבְנוּ — **is** that it means **merely to teach about the** law of *tereifah*, **as we have written,** וְעַל בָּשָׂר מִן הַחַי שֶׁבִּכְלַל טְרֵפָה הוּא — **and** additionally, to teach **about** the prohibition of **flesh from a living animal, which is included in the prohibition of *tereifah*.**[7] וּמַה שֶּׁבִּפְנִים בּוֹ הוּא — **What is within [this "garment"],** i.e., the deeper meaning of the verse, **is** שֶׁמְּלַמֵּד עַל כָּל בָּשָׂר שֶׁיָּצָא חוּץ מִמְּחִצָתוֹ — **that it teaches, regarding any meat that has gone outside of its** halachically defined **boundary,** שֶׁאָסוּר וְנַעֲשָׂה כִּטְרֵפָה — **that it is forbidden and becomes like** meat that is *tereifah*.

Before explaining how this is implied by the verse, Chinuch provides illustrations of this principle: כְּגוֹן בְּשַׂר [קָדְשֵׁי] קָדָשִׁים שֶׁיָּצָא חוּץ לָעֲזָרָה — **This means, for example, that meat of *kodshei kodashim* offerings that has gone out of the Temple Courtyard is** prohibited;[8] וּבְשַׂר קָדָשִׁים קַלִּים שֶׁיָּצָא חוּץ לַחוֹמָה — **meat of *kodashim kalim* offerings that has gone out of the** city **walls** of Jerusalem is

---

### NOTES

6. The relationship of a verse's simple meaning to its deeper meaning is like that of a beautiful garment that cloaks a treasure of gold and precious stones. While the surface is meaningful in its own right, one should not be satisfied with merely glimpsing the verse's "clothing," but should endeavor to uncover the great treasures contained within. Cf. *Ibn Ezra's* introduction to *Lamentations*.

7. If one cuts flesh from a living animal, that flesh is prohibited as *tereifah* (*Chullin* 102b). As Rambam explains (*Hil. Maachalos Asuros* 4:10): "This flesh is from an animal that was neither ritually slaughtered nor died naturally; there is no difference whether a beast mauled the animal or a human cut it with a knife, nor is there any difference whether the entire animal was torn or a part of it was torn ... once the animal has been rendered *flesh torn in the field*, it is *tereifah*." [Cf. *Rashi*, *Chullin* 102b ד"ה ובשר בשדה.]

It should be noted that, in many instances, flesh detached from a live animal is forbidden as אֵבֶר מִן הַחַי, *a limb from a living creature*. See Mitzvah 452, where Chinuch discusses when the prohibition of *tereifah* applies and when the prohibition of *a limb from a living creature* applies. See also *Minchas Chinuch* here §2.

8. *Kodshei kodashim* are the "most holy" offerings, including the *olah, chatas, asham,* and communal *shelamim* offerings. Parts of these offerings (other than the *olah*) are eaten by the Kohanim, and the Torah stipulates that they be eaten only within the confines of the Temple Courtyard (*Leviticus* 6:9,19,7:6; see Mitzvah 102). The law is that if the meat was taken outside of the Courtyard, it becomes disqualified, and even if it is subsequently brought back into the Courtyard, it may not be eaten, because it has gone outside its legal boundaries (*Zevachim* 82b, *Chullin* 68b; *Rambam, Hil. Maaseh HaKorbanos* 11:6).

וּבְשַׂר הַפֶּסַח שֶׁיָּצָא חוּץ לַחֲבוּרָה,[10] וְכֵן הָעֻבָּר שֶׁיָּצָא חוּץ לִמְעֵי אִמּוֹ,[11] וּמַשְׁמָעוּתוֹ שֶׁל מִקְרָא יָבוֹא כֵן, כְּאִלּוּ אָמַר וּבָשָׂר בַּשָּׂדֶה טְרֵפָה הוּא, כְּלוֹמַר בָּשָׂר שֶׁיָּצָא חוּץ לִמְחִצָּתוֹ, שֶׁזֶּהוּ לְשׁוֹן שָׂדֶה שֶׁאֵין לוֹ מְחִצּוֹת, טְרֵפָה הוּא.[12] וְכָל אֵלֶּה שֶׁזָּכַרְנוּ יָצְאוּ חוּץ לִמְחִצָּתָן, וְדִינָן כִּטְרֵפָה, וּמִי שֶׁאָכַל מֵהֶן כַּזַּיִת לוֹקֶה.[13]

---

prohibited;[9] וּבְשַׂר הַפֶּסַח שֶׁיָּצָא חוּץ לַחֲבוּרָה — **meat of the *pesach* offering that has gone out** of the location **of its group** is prohibited;[10] וְכֵן הָעֻבָּר שֶׁיָּצָא חוּץ לִמְעֵי אִמּוֹ — **and likewise, if an [animal] fetus put forth** a limb **from its mother's womb**, that limb becomes prohibited.[11] All these laws are encompassed by the principle that meat that has gone out of its boundary is considered like *tereifah*.

Chinuch now explains how this principle is derived from the verse:

וּמַשְׁמָעוּתוֹ שֶׁל מִקְרָא יָבוֹא כֵן — **The inner meaning of the verse emerges to** yield **this** principle, כְּאִלּוּ אָמַר — **for the verse is understood as if it is saying:** וּבָשָׂר בַּשָּׂדֶה — **And flesh that is in the field** (an unbounded area) טְרֵפָה הוּא — **is** pronounced *tereifah* (unfit for consumption). כְּלוֹמַר שֶׁזֶּהוּ — **That is to say,** any **flesh that has gone outside its boundary** — בָּשָׂר שֶׁיָּצָא חוּץ לִמְחִצָּתוֹ לְשׁוֹן שָׂדֶה שֶׁאֵין לוֹ מְחִצּוֹת — **for this is** implied by **the term "field,"** which is an area that **has no barriers** around it — טְרֵפָה הוּא — **is** pronounced ***tereifah***.[12] And, as the verse concludes, it may not be eaten. וְכָל אֵלֶּה שֶׁזָּכַרְנוּ יָצְאוּ חוּץ לִמְחִצָּתָן — **Now, all these** things **that we mentioned have gone outside their** respective halachically defined **boundaries,** וְדִינָן כִּטְרֵפָה — **so** on the basis of the interpretation of the verse as *And flesh that is in the field is [pronounced] tereifah*, **their status is the same as *tereifah*,** וּמִי שֶׁאָכַל מֵהֶן כַּזַּיִת לוֹקֶה — **and one who eats a *kezayis*** (olive's volume) **of them incurs *malkus*** (lashes) for violating the prohibition of "*tereifah*."[13]

---

NOTES

9. *Kodashim kalim* are the offerings of "lesser holiness," including the *shelamim, todah, bechor,* and *maaser* offerings. Scripture indicates (see *Zevachim* 55a) that these offerings must be eaten within the city walls of Jerusalem. Thus, these walls are their legal boundaries, and if they go beyond those boundaries they may no longer be eaten, even if subsequently returned (*Zevachim* 82b; *Rambam* ibid.).

10. The Torah (*Exodus* 12:46) expressly forbids removing the *pesach* meat from the house in which it is eaten. Furthermore, the Gemara (*Pesachim* 85b) infers from Scripture that if two groups are eating their offerings in the same house, it is forbidden to take the meat from the place where one group is eating to the place where the other group is eating (see above, Mitzvah 15 note 8). Since the Torah prohibits the removal of the *pesach* meat from its group's location, the legal boundary of the meat is the location of that group. If it was removed from its group's location, even temporarily, the meat becomes prohibited for consumption (*Pesachim* 85a; *Rambam*, *Hil. Korban Pesach* 9:2; see above, Mitzvah 15 note 7).

11. This refers to a case where an animal was slaughtered and a fetus was found in its womb. The fetus is permitted for consumption on the basis of its mother's *shechitah* and need not be slaughtered itself. If, however, the fetus thrust a limb out of the womb before the mother's slaughter, then even if it pulled back the limb before the slaughter, that limb is prohibited. This is because the mother's womb serves as a legal "boundary" for the fetus, inasmuch as the mother's *shechitah* permits consumption of the fetus that is inside it. A limb that was thrust out of the womb has "gone outside its boundary" and is forbidden (*Chullin* 68a with *Rashi* ד"ה ובשר בשדה; *Rambam*, *Hil. Maachalos Asuros* 5:9).

[This means only that the limb cannot be eaten on the basis of the *mother's shechitah*, for it had a "boundary" in that regard only. If, however, the fetus is born before the mother is slaughtered, even the limb can be rendered permissible through the newborn's own *shechitah*, since it had no boundary in this regard (*Beis Yosef* and *Rama*, *Yoreh Deah* 14:2).]

12. Just as a field is an area unbounded by barriers, so too are various items that leave the confines assigned to them by the Torah considered to be "in the field" [i.e., lacking boundaries] and prohibited for consumption like *tereifah* (*Rashi* ibid. and to *Makkos* 18a ד"ה כיון שיצא בשר; see further, *Chiddushei HaGriz* to *Rambam*, *Hil. Pesulei HaMukdashin*, p. 43b).

13. To summarize, the verse has two interpretations, and thus is understood as incorporating two subjects into the prohibition of "*tereifah*." According to its simple meaning, טְרֵפָה (*tereifah*) means "torn," and the phrase וּבָשָׂר בַּשָּׂדֶה טְרֵפָה לֹא תֹאכֵלוּ means, *and flesh torn in the field you shall not eat*. This is the basic prohibition of an animal that possesses a fatal defect. According to its deeper meaning, the phrase וּבָשָׂר בַּשָּׂדֶה טְרֵפָה לֹא תֹאכֵלוּ means, *and flesh that is "in the field" is tereifah* [i.e., unfit]; *you shall not eat it*. This prohibits any flesh that has been removed from its prescribed boundary. For an explanation of the connection between these two seemingly disparate interpretations, see *R' S. R. Hirsch* to the verse.

## MISHPATIM / MITZVAH 73: THE PROHIBITION TO EAT TEREIFAH

מִשָּׁרְשֵׁי מִצְוָה זוֹ, לְפִי שֶׁהַגּוּף כְּלִי לַנֶּפֶשׁ וּבוֹ תַעֲשֶׂה פְּעֻלָּתָהּ, וְזוּלָתוֹ לֹא תַשְׁלִם מְלַאכְתָּהּ לְעוֹלָם, וְעַל כֵּן בָּאָה בְצִלּוֹ[14] וְלֹא לְרָעָתָהּ[15], בֶּאֱמֶת כִּי הָאֵל לֹא יָרִיעַ אֲבָל יֵיטִיב לַכֹּל[16], נִמְצָא כִּי הַגּוּף בֵּין יָדֶיהָ כְּמוֹ הַצְּבָת בְּיַד הַנַּפָּח אֲשֶׁר עִמּוֹ יוֹצִיא כְּלִי לְמַעֲשֵׂהוּ[17], וּבֶאֱמֶת כִּי בִּהְיוֹת הַצְּבָת חֲזָק וּמְכֻוָּן לֶאֱחֹז בּוֹ הַכֵּלִים, יַעֲשֶׂה הָאֻמָּן טוֹבִים, וְאִם לֹא יִהְיֶה הַצְּבָת טוֹב לֹא יָבוֹאוּ לְעוֹלָם הַכֵּלִים מְכֻוָּנִים וְנָאִים, וּכְמוֹ כֵן בִּהְיוֹת בַּגּוּף שׁוּם הֶפְסֵד מֵאֵי זֶה עִנְיָן שֶׁיִּהְיֶה, תִּתְבַּטֵּל פְּעֻלַּת הַשֵּׂכֶל[18] כְּפִי אוֹתוֹ הֶפְסֵד, וְעַל כֵּן הִרְחִיקַתְנוּ תּוֹרָתֵנוּ הַשְּׁלֵמָה מִכָּל דָּבָר הַגּוֹרֵם בּוֹ הֶפְסֵד[19]. וְעַל הַדֶּרֶךְ הַזֶּה לְפִי הַפְּשָׁט נֹאמַר שֶׁבָּא לָנוּ הָאִסּוּר בַּתּוֹרָה בְּכָל מַאֲכָלוֹת הָאֲסוּרוֹת, וְאִם יֵשׁ מֵהֶם שֶׁאֵין נוֹדָע לָנוּ וְלֹא לְחַכְמֵי הָרְפוּאָה נִזְקָן,

### ⸺ Underlying Purpose of the Mitzvah ⸺

מִשָּׁרְשֵׁי מִצְוָה זוֹ — **Among the underlying purposes of this mitzvah** is the following: לְפִי שֶׁהַגּוּף — **Considering that the body is the instrument of the soul,** וּבוֹ תַעֲשֶׂה פְּעֻלָּתָהּ — **through which [the soul] carries out its assignment** in this world, וְזוּלָתוֹ לֹא תַשְׁלִם מְלַאכְתָּהּ לְעוֹלָם — **and without which [the soul] would never** be able to **complete its mission,** וְעַל כֵּן בָּאָה — **and it is for this purpose** that **[the soul] comes** to reside **"in [the body's] shadow,"**[14] וְלֹא לְרָעָתָהּ — such that this arrangement is to the benefit of the soul **and not to its detriment,**[15] בֶּאֱמֶת כִּי הָאֵל לֹא יָרִיעַ אֲבָל יֵיטִיב לַכֹּל — **for indeed, God does not do bad, but rather, He does only good for all;**[16] נִמְצָא כִּי הַגּוּף בֵּין יָדֶיהָ — considering this, **it emerges that the body is, in "the hands" of [the soul],** כְּמוֹ הַצְּבָת בְּיַד הַנַּפָּח אֲשֶׁר עִמּוֹ יוֹצִיא כְּלִי לְמַעֲשֵׂהוּ — **like a** set of **tongs in the hands of the smith, through which he can produce a vessel** fashioned **to its function.**[17] וּבֶאֱמֶת כִּי בִּהְיוֹת הַצְּבָת חֲזָק וּמְכֻוָּן לֶאֱחֹז בּוֹ הַכֵּלִים — **Now,** it is **a fact that when the tongs are strong and properly adjusted for grasping vessels,** יַעֲשֶׂה הָאֻמָּן טוֹבִים — **the craftsman** who uses those tongs **will be able to produce [vessels] of fine quality,** וְאִם לֹא יִהְיֶה הַצְּבָת טוֹב — **but if the tongs are not in good** condition, לֹא יָבוֹאוּ לְעוֹלָם הַכֵּלִים מְכֻוָּנִים וְנָאִים — **the vessels** produced with them **will never come out precise and attractive.** וּכְמוֹ כֵן בִּהְיוֹת בַּגּוּף שׁוּם הֶפְסֵד מֵאֵי זֶה עִנְיָן שֶׁיִּהְיֶה — **Likewise,** since the body is like a set of tongs through which the intelligent soul functions, **if the body should have any impairment, of any sort,** תִּתְבַּטֵּל פְּעֻלַּת הַשֵּׂכֶל כְּפִי אוֹתוֹ הֶפְסֵד — **the achievements of the soul**[18] **will be reduced commensurate to that impairment.** וְעַל כֵּן הִרְחִיקַתְנוּ תּוֹרָתֵנוּ הַשְּׁלֵמָה מִכָּל דָּבָר הַגּוֹרֵם בּוֹ הֶפְסֵד — **Therefore, our perfect Torah distanced us from anything that** might **cause impairment** to the body, such as flesh of an animal or bird that has a fatal defect.[19]

Chinuch expands this thesis, applying it to other mitzvos as well:

וְעַל הַדֶּרֶךְ הַזֶּה לְפִי הַפְּשָׁט נֹאמַר — **Following this approach, we can** further **say, according to the simple understanding** of matters, שֶׁבָּא לָנוּ הָאִסּוּר בַּתּוֹרָה בְּכָל מַאֲכָלוֹת הָאֲסוּרוֹת — **that** this is the reason why the various **prohibitions against all the forbidden foods were transmitted to us in the Torah;** it is to protect us from the harmful effects of those foods, so that our bodies should be able to function properly in the service of our souls. וְאִם יֵשׁ מֵהֶם שֶׁאֵין נוֹדָע לָנוּ וְלֹא לְחַכְמֵי הָרְפוּאָה נִזְקָן — **And**

---

NOTES

14. Stylistic paraphrase of *Genesis* 19:8.
15. Some manuscripts read explicitly לְטוֹבָתָהּ וְלֹא לְרָעָתָהּ, *to its benefit and not to its detriment*.
16. Superficially, it would seem that the spiritual soul's descent to this terrestrial world is a demotion for it. Chinuch counters that this cannot be so, for God would not create an arrangement that is detrimental to the soul. Rather, it must be that the soul is sent down to this world and made to reside in the physical body for its own benefit. This benefit is the opportunity to carry out its mission and perform the Will of God, which can be done only in *this* world. [See *Daas Tevunos* of *R' Moshe Chaim Luzzatto* §71 ff., for a fuller explanation of the benefit provided to the soul by its descent to this world.]
17. Stylistic paraphrase of *Isaiah* 54:16.
18. Literally: *intellect*. [Chinuch frequently uses the term שֵׂכֶל, *intellect,* to refer to the soul. See similarly Mitzvah 95 note 28.]
19. Chinuch will shortly explain why such meat is detrimental to one's health. See next note for the opinion of other commentators regarding the underlying purpose of the *tereifah* prohibition.

## משפטים / מצוה עג: שלא לאכל טרפה

אַל תִּתְמַהּ עֲלֵיהֶן, כִּי הָרוֹפֵא הַנֶּאֱמָן שֶׁהִזְהִירָנוּ בָּהֶן חָכָם יוֹתֵר מִמְּךָ וּמֵהֶם, וְכַמָּה נִסְכָּל וְנִבְהָל מִי שֶׁחָשַׁב שֶׁאֵין לַדְּבָרִים נֶזֶק אוֹ תּוֹעֶלֶת אֶלָּא בְּמַה שֶּׁהִשִּׂיג הוּא[20]. וְיֵשׁ לְךָ לָדַעַת כִּי לְתוֹעַלְתֵּנוּ לֹא נִתְגַּלָּה סִבָּתָן וְנִזְקָן, פֶּן יָקוּמוּ אֲנָשִׁים מַחֲזִיקִים עַצְמָן כַּחֲכָמִים גְּדוֹלִים וְיִתְחַכְּמוּ לוֹמַר נֶזֶק פְּלוֹנִי שֶׁאָמְרָה הַתּוֹרָה שֶׁיֵּשׁ בְּדָבָר פְּלוֹנִי אֵינֶנּוּ כִּי אִם בְּמָקוֹם פְּלוֹנִי שֶׁטִּבְעוֹ כֵּן אוֹ בְּאִישׁ פְּלוֹנִי שֶׁטִּבְעוֹ כֵּן וְכֵן, וּפֶן יִתְפַּתֶּה לְדִבְרֵיהֶם אֶחָד מִן הַפְּתָאִים, עַל כֵּן לֹא נִתְגַּלָּה טַעֲמָן לְהוֹעִיל לָנוּ מִן הַמִּכְשׁוֹל הַזֶּה. וְיָדוּעַ הַדָּבָר מִדַּרְכֵי הָרְפוּאָה שֶׁבְּשַׂר כָּל הַטְּרֵפוֹת הָאֲסוּרוֹת לָנוּ מוֹלִיד הֶפְסֵד אֶל גּוּף אוֹכְלוֹ, מֵחֲמַת שֶׁהַטְּרֵפוּת מוֹרָה חֹלִי בַּבְּהֵמָה. וְאַל תַּקְשֶׁה עָלֶיךָ וְתֹאמַר מַה הֶפְסֵד אֶפְשָׁר לִהְיוֹת בַּבְּהֵמָה שֶׁנִּטְרְפָה מִיָּד וְנִשְׁחֲטָה, כִּי לֹא מֵחָכְמָה תַּקְשֶׁה עַל זֶה[21], הֲלֹא יָדַעְתָּ כִּי לְכָל דָּבָר יֵשׁ הַתְחָלָה,

**if among** [the prohibited foods] **there are** some **whose harmful effects are not known to us, nor to those wise in** the ways of **healing,** אַל תִּתְמַהּ עֲלֵיהֶן – **do not wonder about** the prohibitions pertaining **to them,** כִּי הָרוֹפֵא הַנֶּאֱמָן שֶׁהִזְהִירָנוּ בָּהֶן חָכָם יוֹתֵר מִמְּךָ וּמֵהֶם – **for the Trustworthy Doctor Who warned us against** consuming **them is wiser than you and [the wise healers];** וְכַמָּה נִסְכָּל וְנִבְהָל מִי שֶׁחָשַׁב שֶׁאֵין לַדְּבָרִים נֶזֶק אוֹ תּוֹעֶלֶת אֶלָּא בְּמַה שֶּׁהִשִּׂיג הוּא – indeed, **how foolish and precipitous is one who thinks that there is no harm or benefit in anything other than what he himself has comprehended!**[20]

Chinuch explains why, if the prohibited foods are indeed harmful, the Torah did not spell out their ill effects:

וְיֵשׁ לְךָ לָדַעַת כִּי לְתוֹעַלְתֵּנוּ לֹא נִתְגַּלָּה סִבָּתָן וְנִזְקָן – **You should know that** it is **for our benefit** that **the consequences and harmful effects of** eating **[these foods] were not revealed** to us. פֶּן יָקוּמוּ אֲנָשִׁים מַחֲזִיקִים עַצְמָן כַּחֲכָמִים גְּדוֹלִים וְיִתְחַכְּמוּ לוֹמַר – **For had they been revealed, there would be a concern lest people who consider themselves great scholars arise and cunningly say,** נֶזֶק פְּלוֹנִי שֶׁאָמְרָה הַתּוֹרָה שֶׁיֵּשׁ בְּדָבָר פְּלוֹנִי – **"Such-and-such harm that the Torah said is** contained **within such-and-such an article** of food אֵינֶנּוּ כִּי אִם בְּמָקוֹם פְּלוֹנִי שֶׁטִּבְעוֹ כֵּן – **is** to be feared **only in such-and-such a place, where its nature is so";** אוֹ בְּאִישׁ פְּלוֹנִי שֶׁטִּבְעוֹ כֵּן וְכֵן – **or** they might say, "This food is harmful only **to such-and-such a person, whose nature is so-and-so,"** but in other places or for other people they are not harmful; וּפֶן יִתְפַּתֶּה לְדִבְרֵיהֶם אֶחָד מִן הַפְּתָאִים – **and lest one of the simpletons be lured by their words** and come to eat the prohibited foods. עַל כֵּן לֹא נִתְגַּלָּה טַעֲמָן – **Therefore, the reasons for [the prohibitions]** of those foods **were not revealed,** לְהוֹעִיל לָנוּ מִן הַמִּכְשׁוֹל הַזֶּה – in order **to safeguard us from this pitfall.**

Chinuch now explains why the flesh of an animal that possesses a *tereifah* defect is in fact harmful:

וְיָדוּעַ הַדָּבָר מִדַּרְכֵי הָרְפוּאָה – **It is a known matter in the ways of medicine** שֶׁבְּשַׂר כָּל הַטְּרֵפוֹת הָאֲסוּרוֹת לָנוּ מוֹלִיד הֶפְסֵד אֶל גּוּף אוֹכְלוֹ – **that the flesh of all the *tereifos* that are forbidden to us** (i.e., the flesh of an animal with any of the various *tereifah* defects that will be discussed below) **causes harm to the body of the one who eats it,** מֵחֲמַת שֶׁהַטְּרֵפוּת מוֹרָה חֹלִי – **because the *tereifah* defect indicates that sickness is present** בַּבְּהֵמָה – **in the animal.** וְאַל תַּקְשֶׁה עָלֶיךָ וְתֹאמַר מַה הֶפְסֵד אֶפְשָׁר לִהְיוֹת בַּבְּהֵמָה שֶׁנִּטְרְפָה מִיָּד וְנִשְׁחֲטָה – **Now do not ask yourself and say, "What harm can there be in eating an animal that was wounded and** then **immediately slaughtered?"** Surely sickness could not have developed in the animal in such a short time! כִּי לֹא מֵחָכְמָה תַּקְשֶׁה עַל זֶה – Do not ask this, **for it is not a question prompted by wisdom.**[21] הֲלֹא יָדַעְתָּ כִּי לְכָל דָּבָר יֵשׁ הַתְחָלָה – **Surely, you know that everything has an onset,**

---

### NOTES

20. It should be noted that other commentators disagree with Chinuch's explanation and maintain that the reason certain foods are prohibited is because they generate spiritual harm, not physical harm. For further discussion, see the Insight.

21. Stylistic paraphrase of *Ecclesiastes* 7:10.

# 53 □ MISHPATIM / MITZVAH 73: THE PROHIBITION TO EAT TEREIFAH

וְאִם תּוֹדֶה אֵלַי כִּי בְּאֹרֶךְ הַזְּמַן יִמָּצֵא הַהֶפְסֵד בָּהּ מֵחֲמַת הַטְּרֵפוּת, תִּתְחַיֵּב לְהוֹדוֹת כִּי בְּרֶגַע הָרִאשׁוֹן הִתְחַל הַהֶפְסֵד אֶלָּא שֶׁהוּא מוּעָט בַּהַתְחָלָה, וְאֵין סָפֵק כִּי מִן הַנֶּזֶק רַע אֲפִלּוּ מְעוּטוֹ, וְעוֹד שֶׁכָּל דִּינֵי תּוֹרָה וְכָל דָּבָר שֶׁיֵּשׁ לוֹ קְיָמָא, בִּגְדַר כָּזֶה יִתְחַיֵּב לִהְיוֹת, שֶׁאִם תִּתֵּן דְּבָרֶיךָ לְשִׁעוּרִין לֹא יִתְקַיֵּם דָּבָר בְּיָדְךָ לְעוֹלָם.

דִּינֵי הַמִּצְוָה, כְּגוֹן הַטְּרֵפִיּוֹת שֶׁנִּמְסְרוּ לוֹ לְמֹשֶׁה בְּסִינַי,[22] וְהֵן שְׁמוֹנָה אָבוֹת, דְּרוּסָה, נְקוּבָה, חֲסֵרָה, נְטוּלָה, פְּסוּקָה, קְרוּעָה, נְפוּלָה, שְׁבוּרָה.[23]

---

וְאִם תּוֹדֶה אֵלַי כִּי בְּאֹרֶךְ הַזְּמַן יִמָּצֵא הַהֶפְסֵד בָּהּ מֵחֲמַת הַטְּרֵפוּת — **and if you admit to me that over a lengthy** period of **time** some **noxiousness will be found in [the animal] as a result of the defect,** תִּתְחַיֵּב לְהוֹדוֹת כִּי בְּרֶגַע הָרִאשׁוֹן הִתְחַל הַהֶפְסֵד — **then you must** also **admit that the noxiousness began from the first moment,** אֶלָּא שֶׁהוּא מוּעָט בַּהַתְחָלָה — **though it is** present only to a **minor** degree **at its onset.** וְאֵין סָפֵק כִּי מִן הַנֶּזֶק רַע אֲפִלּוּ מְעוּטוֹ — **And, there is no doubt that even a minor** degree of **harm is** somewhat **bad** for a person. Thus, from the moment an animal suffers a fatal injury that renders it *tereifah,* even if it is slaughtered immediately, eating its flesh will be *somewhat* detrimental. וְעוֹד — **Furthermore,** a *tereifah* must be forbidden from the first moment for another reason. שֶׁכָּל דִּינֵי תּוֹרָה וְכָל דָּבָר שֶׁיֵּשׁ לוֹ קְיָמָא — **It is because all the laws of the Torah, and** likewise **any** other **matter that is to endure,** בִּגְדַר כָּזֶה יִתְחַיֵּב לִהְיוֹת — **must be** established **with** concrete **parameters such as these,** in which exceptions are not made on the basis of deadlines that cannot be clearly defined; שֶׁאִם תִּתֵּן דְּבָרֶיךָ לְשִׁעוּרִין לֹא יִתְקַיֵּם דָּבָר בְּיָדְךָ לְעוֹלָם — **for if you subject your rules to** constant **evaluation, nothing will ever endure for you.** Therefore, the flesh of a *tereifah* is prohibited even if one could manage to slaughter it before it is harmful at all.

## ☞ Laws of the Mitzvah ☜

הַטְּרֵפִיּוֹת שֶׁנִּמְסְרוּ לוֹ — **The laws of this mitzvah** include, כְּגוֹן — **for example,** דִּינֵי הַמִּצְוָה — **the descriptions of the various *tereifah*-defects that were** orally **transmitted to Moses at Sinai.**[22] וְהֵן שְׁמוֹנָה אָבוֹת — **These consist of eight primary categories** (literally: *fathers*), which the Gemara (*Chullin* 43a) lists as follows: **(1)** דְּרוּסָה — **clawed, (2)** נְקוּבָה — **punctured, (3)** חֲסֵרָה — **deficient, (4)** נְטוּלָה — **removed, (5)** פְּסוּקָה — **severed, (6)** קְרוּעָה — **torn, (7)** נְפוּלָה — **fallen,** and **(8)** שְׁבוּרָה — **fractured.**[23]

---

## NOTES

22. The Written Torah states simply that we shall not eat flesh of a *tereifah,* which is understood in the general sense as referring to an animal (or bird) that suffered a mortal wound. God transmitted orally to Moses at Sinai [i.e., through *Halachah LeMoshe MiSinai*] the categories of wounds that are legally defined as *tereifah*-defects (*Maggid Mishneh, Hil. Maachalos Asuros* 4:6; see *Rambam, Hil. Shechitah* 5:2). No animal is classified as *tereifah* unless it possesses a defect in one of these categories. An animal that is dying of debilitation resulting from age or the like — or from an external cause not in any of these categories, such as a snakebite — is not a *tereifah* (Mishnah and Gemara, *Chullin* 37a; Mishnah ibid. 58b; *Rambam, Hil. Maachalos Asuros* 4:11-12; see there regarding the propriety of eating meat of such animals).

23. The Gemara states that these categories of *tereifah*-defects were transmitted orally to Moses at Sinai. They encompass the numerous *tereifah* defects listed in the opening Mishnah of *Chullin* Chapter 3 (42a), and in the Gemara throughout that chapter, for as Chinuch notes below, each of these is a general category that includes other, similar defects.

(1) "Clawed" refers to an animal that was mauled by a predator. This is the case of *tereifah* addressed by the verse (*Rambam, Hil. Shechitah* 5:1-4). [The mauled animal is *tereifah* even if no internal organ was punctured (*Tosafos, Chullin* 42a ד"ה דרוסת הנץ ב׳), because the predator's claws leave behind "venom" that eventually permeates the body and causes death (*Chullin* 53a). Some explain this "venom" as a reference to bacteria (see *Michtav MeEliyahu,* Vol. IV, pp. 355-6, and *Sichas Chullin,* pp. 344-5).]

(2) "Punctured" refers to an animal that suffered a puncture of a vital organ, such as the esophagus, membrane of the brain, heart, intestines, or lung (*Rambam* ibid. 6:1).

(3) "Deficient" refers to an animal missing a critical part of its lung or hind leg (ibid. 8:1,11). [Chinuch will discuss below the case of a "deficient" lung.]

(4) "Removed" refers to an animal whose entire liver

וְהַדְּרוּסָה הִיא הַטְּרֵפוּת הֶחָמוּר בְּכֻלָּן, לְפִי שֶׁהוּא מְפֹרָשׁ בַּתּוֹרָה, לְפִיכָךְ אָמְרוּ זִכְרוֹנָם לִבְרָכָה שֶׁכָּל סָפֵק הַבָּא לָנוּ עָלָיו אָסוּר, וּבִשְׁאָר הַטְּרֵפוּת יֵשׁ בָּהֶן סְפֵקִין מַתִּירִין.[24] וְכָל אֶחָד וְאֶחָד מֵאֵלּוּ הָאָבוֹת יֵשׁ לוֹ כַּמָּה וְכַמָּה תּוֹלָדוֹת כְּמוֹ שֶׁבָּא פְּרָטָן בַּגְּמָרָא[25] (חולין דף מ"ב ע"א ואילך), וְחֶשְׁבּוֹן כְּלָל הַטְּרֵפִיּוֹת שֶׁאֶפְשָׁר שֶׁיִּמָּצְאוּ בִּבְהֵמָה וְחַיָּה[26] וָעוֹף הָעוֹלֶה בְּיָדֵינוּ בִּפְרָטָן לְפִי הַדּוֹמֶה מִדִּבְרֵי הַגְּמָרָא הֵם ע"ב עִם טְרֵפוּת אֶחָד שֶׁיֵּשׁ יֶתֶר בָּעוֹף עַל הַבְּהֵמָה,[27]

---

Chinuch notes a distinction between these categories:

וְהַדְּרוּסָה הִיא הַטְּרֵפוּת הֶחָמוּר בְּכֻלָּן — "Clawed" is the *tereifah*-category that is most severe of all of them, לְפִי שֶׁהוּא מְפֹרָשׁ בַּתּוֹרָה — because it is mentioned explicitly in the Torah, which speaks of an animal "torn in the field." לְפִיכָךְ אָמְרוּ זִכְרוֹנָם לִבְרָכָה — Therefore [the Sages], of blessed memory, said, שֶׁכָּל סָפֵק הַבָּא לָנוּ עָלָיו אָסוּר — that in any case of uncertainty that comes to us regarding whether an animal suffered a wound in [this category], the animal is prohibited, וּבִשְׁאָר הַטְּרֵפוּת — whereas, concerning the other *tereifah*-categories, יֵשׁ בָּהֶן סְפֵקִין מַתִּירִין — there are some cases of uncertainty regarding them in which the animal is permitted.[24]

Chinuch now discusses how many *tereifah*-defects there are in total:

וְכָל אֶחָד וְאֶחָד מֵאֵלּוּ הָאָבוֹת יֵשׁ לוֹ כַּמָּה וְכַמָּה תּוֹלָדוֹת — Each and every one of these primary categories has many subcategories (literally, *offspring*), כְּמוֹ שֶׁבָּא פְּרָטָן בַּגְּמָרָא — which are detailed in the Gemara (*Chullin* Ch. 3, 42a-58b; Ch. 4, 76a-77a).[25] וְחֶשְׁבּוֹן כְּלָל הַטְּרֵפִיּוֹת שֶׁאֶפְשָׁר שֶׁיִּמָּצְאוּ בִּבְהֵמָה וְחַיָּה וָעוֹף — The sum total of all the different types of *tereifah*-defects that can possibly be found among domestic animals, nondomestic animals,[26] and fowl, הָעוֹלֶה בְּיָדֵינוּ בִּפְרָטָן לְפִי הַדּוֹמֶה מִדִּבְרֵי הַגְּמָרָא — according to the count we have arrived at, based on what seems correct to us, from the words of the Gemara, הֵם ע"ב — are seventy-two, עִם טְרֵפוּת אֶחָד שֶׁיֵּשׁ יֶתֶר בָּעוֹף עַל הַבְּהֵמָה — including one type of *tereifah*-defect that exists only among birds, in excess of those that exist among animals, which total only seventy-one.[27]

---

NOTES

was removed (ibid. 8:21), or if certain other organs were removed (ibid. 6:20, 8:23-24).

(5) "Severed" refers to an animal whose spinal cord or trachea was severed (ibid. 9:1; *Kesef Mishneh, Hil. Shechitah* 3:23).

(6) "Torn" refers to an animal that suffered a tear of the abdominal wall (*Rambam* ibid. 9:5).

(7) "Fallen" refers to an animal that fell from a roof (Mishnah ibid.). [It is deemed *tereifah* because of the presumption that the fall caused רִסּוּק אֵבָרִים, *a concussion of the limbs* — i.e., a fatal loosening of the vertebrae and joints (*Rashi, Chullin* 42a ד"ה נפלה מן הגג; cf. *Rambam* ibid. 9:8; see further, *Shulchan Aruch, Yoreh Deah* §58).]

(8) "Fractured" refers to an animal that suffered the breakage of most of its ribs (*Rambam* ibid. 10:1-2).

24. This distinction between "clawed" (which is explicit in Scripture) and the other seven categories of *tereifah* (which are הֲלָכָה לְמֹשֶׁה מִסִּינַי, an Oral Tradition from Sinai) is stated by *Rambam, Hil. Shechitah* 5:3. Others question the validity of this distinction, since any law received via the Oral Tradition has the same status as a law that is explicit in the Written Torah — both are Biblical Law. Regardless of whether a law was transmitted to us in Scripture or by Oral Tradition from Sinai, the rule is that סָפֵק דְּאוֹרַיְיתָא לְחוּמְרָא, *a doubt regarding Biblical Law is treated stringently*. Why, then, should they be treated differently here? (*Maggid Mishneh, Hil. Shechitah* loc. cit.; *Teshuvos Rivash* §163; see also *Ramban* to *Sefer HaMitzvos, Shoresh* 1 [p. 22 in Frankel ed.] and *Shoresh* 2 [p. 52 ibid.]). For possible resolutions of *Rambam's* opinion, see *Maggid Mishneh* ibid. and *Lev Same'ach* to *Sefer HaMitzvos, Shoresh* 2 [pp. 84-85 in Frankel ed.].

Numerous other Rishonim do *not* distinguish between "clawed" and other *tereifah*-categories regarding cases of uncertainty; see *Tosafos, Chullin* 43b ד"ה קסבר; *Rashba, Chullin* 46b, et al.

25. The Gemara discusses many *tereifah*-defects in addition to those listed above, but does not categorize them. *Kesef Mishneh, Hil. Shechitah* 10:9, lists all the subcategories of *tereifah* under their primary categories.

26. There are numerous species of nondomestic animals that are kosher (and thus subject to the prohibition of *tereifah*), such as deer.

27. *Rambam* (*Hil. Shechitah* 10:9-11) lists *seventy* defects that pertain to animals and another *two* that pertain to birds. *Minchas Yitzchak* explains that Chinuch follows the opinion of *Raavad* (ibid. 10:11), who maintains that one of the two additional *tereifah*-defects that *Rambam* assigns to fowl can exist in animals as well, so the number of *tereifah*-defects pertaining to animals is seventy-one, and only a single additional defect pertains solely to fowl. [*Shulchan Aruch* (*Yoreh Deah* 52:7)

## 55 □ MISHPATIM / MITZVAH 73: THE PROHIBITION TO EAT TEREIFAH

וַעֲלֵיהֶן אֵין לְהוֹסִיף וּמֵהֶן אֵין לִגְרֹעַ, לְפִי שֶׁכָּל מַכָּה שֶׁתֶּאֱרַע לִבְהֵמָה אוֹ לְחַיָּה אוֹ לְעוֹף חוּץ מֵאֵלוּ שֶׁמָּנוּ חֲכָמִים בַּדּוֹרוֹת הָרִאשׁוֹנִים וְהִסְכִּימוּ עֲלֵיהֶם בָּתֵּי דִינֵי יִשְׂרָאֵל אֶפְשָׁר שֶׁתִּחְיֶה, וַאֲפִלּוּ נוֹדַע לָנוּ מִדֶּרֶךְ הָרְפוּאָה שֶׁאֵין סוֹפָהּ לִחְיוֹת[28], וְכָל אֵלּוּ הַמַּכּוֹת שֶׁמָּנוּ וְאָמְרוּ שֶׁהֵן טְרֵפוֹת, אַף עַל פִּי שֶׁנִּרְאֶה בְּדַרְכֵי הָרְפוּאָה שֶׁבְּיָדֵינוּ שֶׁמִּקְצָתָן אֵין מְמִיתִין וְאֶפְשָׁר שֶׁתִּחְיֶה מֵהֶן, אֵין לְךָ אֶלָּא מַה שֶׁמָּנוּ חֲכָמִים, שֶׁנֶּאֱמַר (דברים י״ז, י״א) "עַל פִּי הַתּוֹרָה"[29]. וְכָל אֶחָד מִן הָע״ב טְרֵפִיּוֹת שֶׁאָמַרְנוּ מְפֹרָשׁ בַּאֲרֻכָּה עִם כָּל תְּנָאָיו בְּמַסֶּכֶת חֻלִּין (דף מ״ב ע״א ואילך).

---

The seventy-two *tereifah*-defects that emerge from the Gemara (ibid.) are listed by *Rambam* (*Hilchos Shechitah* 10:9-11). Chinuch now quotes *Rambam's* explanation (ibid. §12-13) of the significance of this list:

וַעֲלֵיהֶן אֵין לְהוֹסִיף — **To these we are not to add,** וּמֵהֶן אֵין לִגְרֹעַ — **and from these we are not to detract.** No defect omitted from the list can *ever* be considered *tereifah,* and conversely, every defect included in the list must *always* be considered *tereifah.* לְפִי שֶׁכָּל מַכָּה שֶׁתֶּאֱרַע לִבְהֵמָה אוֹ לְחַיָּה אוֹ לְעוֹף — We are not to add additional defects to the list of *tereifos,* **because any wound that may be inflicted upon** either **a domestic animal, or a nondomestic animal, or a bird,** חוּץ מֵאֵלוּ שֶׁמָּנוּ חֲכָמִים בַּדּוֹרוֹת הָרִאשׁוֹנִים וְהִסְכִּימוּ עֲלֵיהֶם בָּתֵּי דִינֵי יִשְׂרָאֵל — **other than those listed by the Sages of early generations, which were agreed upon by the** Rabbinic **courts of Israel** of early times as being considered *tereifah,* אֶפְשָׁר שֶׁתִּחְיֶה — **is not deemed fatal, and [the animal or bird that suffered the wound] can survive** for longer than twelve months. וַאֲפִלּוּ נוֹדַע לָנוּ מִדֶּרֶךְ הָרְפוּאָה שֶׁאֵין סוֹפָהּ לִחְיוֹת — This holds true **even** if it is **known to us, based on** current **medical knowledge, that [the animal or bird] will not survive.** Since the Oral Tradition handed down to us does not list the wound as a *tereifah*-defect, it is deemed a survivable wound even if nowadays the animal will surely perish from it.[28] וְכָל אֵלּוּ הַמַּכּוֹת שֶׁמָּנוּ וְאָמְרוּ שֶׁהֵן טְרֵפוֹת — Conversely, with respect to **all the wounds that [the Sages] listed and pronounced to be *tereifah*-defects,** אַף עַל פִּי שֶׁנִּרְאֶה בְּדַרְכֵי הָרְפוּאָה שֶׁבְּיָדֵינוּ שֶׁמִּקְצָתָן אֵין מְמִיתִין — **even though it seems, based on the medical knowledge we possess** today, **that some of them are not fatal,** וְאֶפְשָׁר שֶׁתִּחְיֶה מֵהֶן — **and [the animal] can survive them,** the law established by the early Sages remains in effect. אֵין לְךָ אֶלָּא מַה שֶׁמָּנוּ חֲכָמִים — **You have no** basis for determining the law of *tereifah* other than abiding by **that which the Sages enumerated** and considering every wound on their list as a *tereifah*-defect, שֶׁנֶּאֱמַר — in accordance **with what is stated** (Deuteronomy 17:11): "עַל פִּי הַתּוֹרָה" — **According to the teaching** that they (the Sages) *will teach you ... shall you do; you shall not deviate from the word that they will tell you, right or left.*[29]

Chinuch concludes this part of his discussion:

וְכָל אֶחָד מִן הָע״ב טְרֵפִיּוֹת שֶׁאָמַרְנוּ — **Each one of the seventy-two *tereifah*-defects that we mentioned** מְפֹרָשׁ בַּאֲרֻכָּה עִם כָּל תְּנָאָיו בְּמַסֶּכֶת חֻלִּין — **is explained at length with all its variables in Tractate *Chullin*** (ibid.).

---

NOTES

rules in accordance with *Rambam,* but *Rama* (ad loc.) rules in accordance with *Raavad.*]

28. *Rambam, Hil. Shechitah* 10:12. Even if there is no means of saving the animal under current medical knowledge, the animal is not considered *tereifah,* because the Sages surely knew through the Oral Tradition that there *is* some way of saving it, though nowadays we may be ignorant of the method (*Kesef Mishneh* to *Rambam* loc. cit., based on *Chullin* 54a; see the following note).

29. *Rambam* ibid. 10:13. [This statement is perplexing. Since, as stated above, a *tereifah* is defined as an animal that has suffered a fatal wound, why should the animal be considered a *tereifah* simply because the early Sages deemed it as such, when nowadays its wound is not fatal? *Tzafnas Pane'ach* (to *Rambam* ibid.) explains that the animal's inability to survive a wound is not the *reason* it is considered *tereifah.* Rather, the true determinant is the Oral Tradition transmitted from Sinai that a particular type of wound renders *tereifah.* The inability to survive is merely a *sign* provided by the Sages that this is a type of wound to which the Torah referred when it prohibited a "*tereifah.*" The advancement of medical knowledge may have diminished the accuracy of the sign, but it has no bearing on the *law,* which is based on the Oral Tradition. For other explanations, see *Yad Yehudah* 30:3, and *Chazon Ish, Yoreh Deah* 5:3.]

## משפטים / מצוה עג: שלא לאכל טרפה

וְכָל טַרְפִיּוֹת אֵלּוּ שֶׁמָּנוּ חֲכָמִים בַּבְּהֵמָה וּבָעוֹף אֵין אָדָם צָרִיךְ לַחֲזֹר אַחֲרֵיהֶן וְלִבְדֹּק אוֹתָם טֶרֶם שֶׁיֹּאכַל בְּשַׂר הַבְּהֵמָה וְהָעוֹף מִפְּנֵי שֶׁחֶזְקָתָן[30] שֶׁכְּשֵׁרִים הֵם, כִּי רֹב בַּעֲלֵי חַיִּים בְּחֶזְקַת בְּרִיאִים אָנוּ מַחֲזִיקִים אוֹתָן,[31] זוּלָתִי בְּאַחַת מֵהֶן שֶׁהִצְרִיכוּ חֲכָמִים לִבְדֹּק טֶרֶם שֶׁנֹּאכַל הַבָּשָׂר מִפְּנֵי שֶׁזֶּה הַטַּרְפוּת מָצוּי הַרְבֵּה,[32] וְהוּא טַרְפוּת הָרֵאָה שֶׁמְּצוּיִין בָּהּ רִירִין הַנִּקְרָאִין סִרְכוֹת,[33] וְיֵשׁ לָחוּשׁ בָּהֶן שֶׁלֹּא יִמְשְׁכוּ קְרוּם הָרֵאָה וְיִנְקָבוּהוּ. לְפִיכָךְ צָרִיךְ אָדָם לִרְאוֹת לְעוֹלָם בְּאֵי זֶה צַד יִהְיוּ אוֹתָן רִירִין בָּרֵאָה טֶרֶם שֶׁיֹּאכַל מִן הַבְּהֵמָה,

---

Having informed us that there are seventy-two different types of *tereifah*-defects, Chinuch discusses how they are dealt with on a practical level:

וְכָל טַרְפִיּוֹת אֵלּוּ שֶׁמָּנוּ חֲכָמִים בַּבְּהֵמָה וּבָעוֹף — **Concerning all these** different types of possible ***tereifah*-defects that the Sages listed for animals and birds,** אֵין אָדָם צָרִיךְ לַחֲזֹר אַחֲרֵיהֶן וְלִבְדֹּק אוֹתָם — **a person is not obligated to seek after them and inspect** the slaughtered animal or bird for **them** טֶרֶם שֶׁיֹּאכַל בְּשַׂר הַבְּהֵמָה וְהָעוֹף — **before he eats the meat of an animal or a bird.** מִפְּנֵי שֶׁחֶזְקָתָן שֶׁכְּשֵׁרִים הֵם — **This is because their *chazakah*[30] is that they are kosher,** כִּי רֹב בַּעֲלֵי חַיִּים בְּחֶזְקַת בְּרִיאִים אָנוּ מַחֲזִיקִים אוֹתָן — **for the majority of living creatures are presumed by us to be in an unchanged state of good health** from the moment of their birth. Thus, unless there is reason to suspect otherwise, we assume that a slaughtered animal is healthy and does not have any of the defects listed.[31] זוּלָתִי בְּאַחַת מֵהֶן — **This applies to all the possible *tereifah*-defects except one of them,** שֶׁהִצְרִיכוּ חֲכָמִים לִבְדֹּק טֶרֶם שֶׁנֹּאכַל הַבָּשָׂר — **for which the Sages required us to check before we may eat the meat,** מִפְּנֵי שֶׁזֶּה הַטַּרְפוּת מָצוּי הַרְבֵּה — **because this type of *tereifah*-defect is very common.** וְהוּא טַרְפוּת הָרֵאָה — **This is the** unique ***tereifah*-defect found in the lung.**[32]

Chinuch provides a general description of this defect:

שֶׁמְּצוּיִין בָּהּ רִירִין הַנִּקְרָאִין סִרְכוֹת — **It is common for fibrous adhesions called *sirchos*** (sing. *sircha*) **to be found on [the lung],** and these *sirchos* also adhere to other surfaces within the chest cavity (e.g., other lobes of the lung, the ribs, the flesh of the chest walls), attaching the lung to them,[33] וְיֵשׁ לָחוּשׁ בָּהֶן שֶׁלֹּא יִמְשְׁכוּ קְרוּם הָרֵאָה וְיִנְקָבוּהוּ — **and there is** thus **a concern that** when the animal moves about (while it is alive) **they might tug at the membrane of the lung** to which they are adhered **and perforate it,** thus rendering the animal *tereifah* on account of a puncture of the lung. לְפִיכָךְ צָרִיךְ אָדָם לִרְאוֹת לְעוֹלָם בְּאֵי זֶה צַד יִהְיוּ אוֹתָן רִירִין בָּרֵאָה — **Therefore,** after slaughtering an animal, **a person must always examine** its lungs, to determine whether, and **in what circumstances, these fibrous adhesions are present on the lung,** טֶרֶם שֶׁיֹּאכַל מִן הַבְּהֵמָה — **before he eats of the animal.**

---

NOTES

30. *"Chazakah"* in this context refers to a *presumed status*. The principle of *chazakah* states that, barring evidence to the contrary, a given legal state (e.g., being free of a defect, being permitted for consumption) is presumed to continue unchanged. The presumed state of an animal is that it is healthy, for the majority of animals are not born *tereifah*.

31. If, however, something occurred to create a suspicion that a defect exists, for example, an animal or bird was shot with an arrow that *may* have punctured an internal organ, it must be examined for the defect in question before it may be eaten (*Rambam* ibid. 11:3,4).

32. This pertains to animals only, not birds. The defect itself (which will immediately be described) would render even a bird *tereifah*, but the concern that prompted the Sages to require examination in every instance, and not rely on *chazakah*, exists only for animals (*Rambam* ibid. 11:12; *Pri Megadim, Sifsei Daas*, end of §38).

[There is some question whether the examination of an animal's lungs is a Rabbinic *requirement* or merely a *custom*. *Rambam* (ibid. 11:6-12) states clearly that unless there is some reason to suspect the existence of a *tereifah*-defect in the lung, there is no requirement to examine the lungs, but it is nevertheless *customary in all communities* to examine the lungs of every slaughtered animal. This is also implicit in *Rashi, Chullin* 12a ד"ה מאי and 50b ד"ה פסח. *Ramban* (*Chullin* 12a), however, maintains that examination of the lungs is a Rabbinic *requirement*. This issue is discussed at length by *Teshuvos Rivash* (§163) and *Tashbetz* (Vol. 1 §67), both of whom side with *Ramban*. As evidence, they cite *Midrash Tanchuma, Shemini* §8, which mentions examination of the lungs as a standard procedure before eating the meat of a slaughtered animal. Chinuch, too, clearly adopts this view. See also *Shulchan Aruch, Yoreh Deah* 39:1 with *Beur HaGra* §2.]

33. See *Maggid Mishneh, Hil. Shechitah* 11:15, and *Shulchan Aruch, Yoreh Deah* 39:7.

## MISHPATIM / MITZVAH 73: THE PROHIBITION TO EAT TEREIFAH

וְאִם יִמָּצֵא אוֹתָן בְּעִנְיָן שֶׁאֶפְשָׁר כִּי בִּתְנוּעָתָם יִנָּקְבוּ הָרֵאָה, טְרֵפָה, שֶׁאָנוּ אוֹמְרִין כָּל הָעוֹמֵד לִנָּקֵב עַל כָּל פָּנִים כְּנָקוּב חָשְׁבִינַן לֵיהּ וּכְאִלּוּ מֵתָה הִיא, אַחַר שֶׁאִי אֶפְשָׁר לָהּ לְהִנָּצֵל מִן הַמָּוֶת, וְיָדוּעַ הוּא כִּי אוֹתוֹ הַחֳלִי הַגּוֹמֵל אוֹתָן רִירִין בִּמְקוֹמוֹת הָעֲתִידִין לִנָּקֵב הַתְחָלַת חֳלִי הַמֵּבִיא לִידֵי מָוֶת הוּא, אַחַר שֶׁבְּבוֹאָתָן מְקוֹמוֹת נַעֲשׂוּ הָרִירִין.[34] וְאֵלּוּ[35]

---

וְאִם יִמָּצֵא אוֹתָן בְּעִנְיָן שֶׁאֶפְשָׁר כִּי בִּתְנוּעָתָם יִנָּקְבוּ הָרֵאָה — **If he finds [such adhesions] situated in a manner by which it is possible that through their movement they could** theoretically **have punctured the lung** while the animal was alive, טְרֵפָה — **it is** deemed **tereifah**. This law applies even if the lung is not actually punctured, שֶׁאָנוּ אוֹמְרִין — **for we say:** כָּל הָעוֹמֵד לִנָּקֵב עַל כָּל פָּנִים — **"Whatever was eventually bound to be punctured,** כְּנָקוּב חָשְׁבִינַן לֵיהּ — **is considered as if** it is already **punctured,"** וּכְאִלּוּ מֵתָה הִיא אַחַר שֶׁאִי אֶפְשָׁר לָהּ לְהִנָּצֵל מִן הַמָּוֶת — **and** conceptually, **it is as if [the animal] was** already **dead** (i.e., mortally wounded) during its lifetime on account of that adhesion, **since it cannot escape death.** That is, since the animal during its lifetime had a condition that was bound to result in its death, it is considered tereifah, even though the existing condition had not yet created an actual wound that would precipitate its death. וְיָדוּעַ הוּא כִּי אוֹתוֹ הַחֳלִי הַגּוֹמֵל אוֹתָן רִירִין בִּמְקוֹמוֹת הָעֲתִידִין לִנָּקֵב — Moreover, **it is known that the illness that produces those fibrous adhesions in spots** on the lung **that are destined to become punctured** through them הַתְחָלַת חֳלִי הַמֵּבִיא לִידֵי מָוֶת הוּא — **is** itself **the beginning of a fatal disease.** אַחַר שֶׁבְּבוֹאָתָן מְקוֹמוֹת נַעֲשׂוּ הָרִירִין — **Thus, the animal is automatically considered tereifah once the fibrous adhesions have formed in those spots,** even before they actually create a perforation in the lung.[34]

The lobes of the lung are divided by halachah into three types called *uma*, *una* (pl. *unos*), and *in-unita d'varda* (known in modern terms as the caudal lobe, cranial lobes, and intermediate lobe).[35]

---

### NOTES

34. Chinuch's explanation of why a *sircha* renders the animal *tereifah* follows the approach of *Tosafos*, *Chullin* 46b-47a ד"ה היינו רביתייהו, and numerous other Rishonim there, but with a slight difference. *Tosafos* explain that when part of the lung becomes joined through a *sircha* (adhesion) to a surface to which it is normally not joined, the animal is *tereifah* because the two attached surfaces will eventually work their way apart, tearing away the *sircha* and the underlying membrane in the process, and thereby puncturing the lung. Since a puncture will *inevitably* occur, the animal is deemed to be *tereifah* immediately. Chinuch adds, however, that a healthy lung does not form *sirchos* that cause punctures, so the existence of such a *sircha* is itself a sign of a fatal illness (see *Mateh Yehonasan* to *Yoreh Deah* 40:3). [This is consistent with Chinuch's explanation above that an underlying reason for the *tereifah* prohibition is the fact that every *tereifah*-defect signifies the existence of sickness in the animal. Accordingly, it is insufficient to explain merely that the *sircha* was *destined* to cause a perforation of the lung through tugging at it; Chinuch must add that the *sircha* is *already* a sign of disease.]

*Rashi* (*Chullin* 46b) has an entirely different approach, according to which a *sircha* is presumed to *result* from a hole in the lung from which viscous fluids leaked, forming a scab over the spot of the puncture that eventually adhered to some other surface in the vicinity. Hence, the animal is *tereifah* because its lung *was* already punctured. For discussion of both approaches, see *Aruch HaShulchan, Yoreh Deah* 39:18-27.

[As is well known, there is a common assumption, adopted by some prominent Acharonim, that the anonymous author of the *Sefer HaChinuch* is R' Aharon HaLevi (*Re'ah*), a disciple of *Ramban* (see above, Mitzvah 95 note 7). There are, however, contradictions between the Chinuch and other works of *Re'ah*, which has caused many scholars to conclude that the *Sefer HaChinuch* was not authored by *Re'ah* (see the General Introduction to this work, in Vol. I, p. xliii). The explanation given here by Chinuch is an example of such a contradiction, for *Re'ah* in *Bedek HaBayis* (33b ff. in Josefov edition of *Toras Habayis*) and in *Chidushei Re'ah* to *Chullin* (ibid.) follows *Rashi's* understanding of *sirchos*, whereas Chinuch follows the approach of *Tosafos* (*Tzava Rav*, cited in footnote 16 in Mechon Yerushalayim edition of *Minchas Chinuch*; *Rosh Ephraim, Kuntres HaRaayos* 39:3). Within this mitzvah, there are additional contradictions of this sort, as will be pointed out below, in notes 53, 55, 57, and 59.]

35. A basic understanding of the structure of animal lungs is necessary for study of the following section in Chinuch. The lungs have two major subdivisions — the right lung and the left lung. Each lung consists of a main lower (caudal) lobe and several upper (cranial) lobes. As Chinuch states below, the right lung has three cranial lobes, whereas the left lung has two. On the underside of the lung [i.e., the part facing the animal's stomach] there is sometimes found yet another, smaller (intermediate) lobe. The Gemara (*Chullin*

הֵן הַמְּקוֹמוֹת שֶׁהֲרֵירִין טוֹרְפִין לְפִי הַכְּלָל הָעוֹלֶה בְּיָדֵינוּ מִדִּבְרֵי הַגְּמָרָא (שם דף מ"ו ע"ב ואילך) עִם הַפֵּרוּשִׁים הַטּוֹבִים,[36] כָּל מָקוֹם בָּעוֹלָם שֶׁהָאֻמָּה סְרוּכָה,[37] טְרֵפָה וְאֵינָהּ נִתֶּרֶת בִּבְדִיקָה,[38] זוּלָתִי בְּעִנְיָן אֶחָד אִם סְרוּכָה לַדֹּפֶן וְיֵשׁ מַכָּה בַּדֹּפֶן וְהַסִּרְכָא כֻּלָּהּ יוֹצֵאת מִמְּקוֹם הַמַּכָּה,

Chinuch explains the laws of *sirchos* pertaining to each type of lobe, beginning with the *uma* (caudal lobe):

וְאֵלּוּ הֵן הַמְּקוֹמוֹת שֶׁהֲרֵירִין טוֹרְפִין — **These are the places where fibrous adhesions** found there **render** the animal ***tereifah***, לְפִי הַכְּלָל הָעוֹלֶה בְּיָדֵינוּ מִדִּבְרֵי הַגְּמָרָא עִם הַפֵּרוּשִׁים הַטּוֹבִים — **according to the rules we have arrived at from** analyzing **the words of the Gemara** (46b ff.) together **with the finest commentaries:**[36] כָּל מָקוֹם בָּעוֹלָם שֶׁהָאֻמָּה סְרוּכָה — **If the *uma* is** discovered to have **adhered to any place whatsoever** within the chest cavity,[37] טְרֵפָה — the animal is ***tereifah***, וְאֵינָהּ נִתֶּרֶת בִּבְדִיקָה — **and it cannot be permitted through examination** and declared kosher,[38] זוּלָתִי בְּעִנְיָן אֶחָד — **except in one case.** אִם סְרוּכָה לַדֹּפֶן — **The exception is the case where [the *uma*] is adhered to the wall** of the chest cavity, וְיֵשׁ מַכָּה בַּדֹּפֶן — **and there is an injury in** that **wall**, וְהַסִּרְכָא כֻּלָּהּ יוֹצֵאת מִמְּקוֹם הַמַּכָּה — **and the entire *sircha*** (adhesion) **stems from the area of the wound,**

---

### NOTES

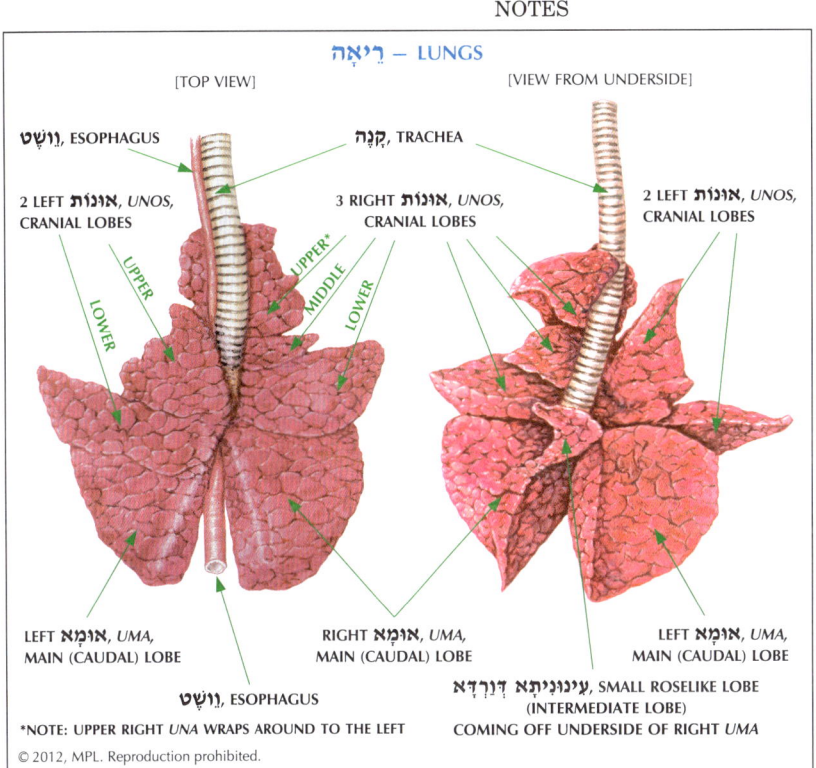

47a) refers to each of the five cranial lobes as an אוּנָא, *una* (earlike lobe), and to the intermediate lobe as עִינוּנִיתָא דְוַרְדָּא, *inunita d'varda* (the small roselike lobe) [perhaps because of its reddish color and floral shape]. In the Gemara we do not find any particular name for the main lobe; however, in post-Talmudic literature (and in *Tikkunei Zohar* §25) each of the main lower lobes is called an אוּמָּא, *uma* (lit., mother).

36. It should be noted that the laws of *sirchos* are among the most complex subjects in the entire field of halachah, and an enormous body of Rabbinic literature exists regarding them. The notes in the following section are limited to explaining Chinuch's view, and are far from a complete treatment of the subject matter. Moreover, one must bear in mind that Chinuch's view is not always the one recognized as the final halachah by *Shulchan Aruch* and *Rama*. Hence, what follows should be viewed as an *introduction* to the subject of *sirchos*, not as halachically conclusive.

37. E.g., the trachea, or another lobe of the lung, or the fat surrounding the heart, or the abdominal wall (see *Yoreh Deah* 39:7 for additional examples).

38. As shall be explained in the following note, it is sometimes possible to perform an examination to determine that a *sircha* is not of the type that would cause a perforation of the lung. When the *sircha* is on the *uma*, it is generally assumed to be a problematic *sircha*, so there is no basis for examination.

## 59 ☐ MISHPATIM / MITZVAH 73: THE PROHIBITION TO EAT TEREIFAH

שֶׁבָּזוֹ נֹאמַר תִּבָּדֵק[39], וְיֵשׁ מַתִּירִין בְּלֹא בְדִיקָה[40]. וְיֵשׁ מוֹצִיאִין מִכְּלָל זֶה אִם סְרוּכָה לְאוּנָה שֶׁבְּצִדָּהּ[41] מֵחִתּוּךְ לְחִתּוּךְ[42], וְכֵן מִנְהֲגֵנוּ הַיּוֹם לְהֶתֵּר[43].

כָּל מָקוֹם שֶׁבָּעוֹלָם שֶׁהָעִינוּנִיתָא דְוַרְדָּא שֶׁהִיא מִצַּד יָמִין[44] סְרוּכָה, טְרֵפָה[45], וְאוּנוֹת הָרֵאָה הֵם חָמֵשׁ מִלְּבַד הָעִינוּנִיתָא, וְיֵשׁ מֵהֶן שְׁלֹשָׁה מִצַּד יָמִין הַבּוֹדֵק בְּשָׁעָה

---

שֶׁבָּזוֹ נֹאמַר תִּבָּדֵק — **for in this** case **we say** that **[the lung] should be examined,** and if it is not punctured, the animal is declared kosher.[39] וְיֵשׁ מַתִּירִין בְּלֹא בְדִיקָה — **And there are** some authorities **who** rule even more leniently and **permit** the animal in this instance even **without examination.**[40] וְיֵשׁ מוֹצִיאִין מִכְּלָל זֶה — **Additionally, there are** some authorities **who exclude from this rule** (that any *sircha* found on the *uma* renders the animal *tereifah*) אִם סְרוּכָה לְאוּנָה שֶׁבְּצִדָּהּ מֵחִתּוּךְ לְחִתּוּךְ — a case **where [the *uma*]** (caudal lobe) **is adhered to the *una*** (cranial lobe) **adjacent to it,**[41] with the *sircha* extending **from the "cut"** of the *uma* **to the** immediately adjacent **"cut"** of the *una*, against which it lies.[42] וְכֵן מִנְהֲגֵנוּ הַיּוֹם לְהֶתֵּר — **Indeed, it is our custom nowadays to permit** this type of *sircha*.[43]

The law pertaining to the *inunita d'varda* (intermediate lobe):

כָּל מָקוֹם שֶׁבָּעוֹלָם שֶׁהָעִינוּנִיתָא דְוַרְדָּא שֶׁהִיא מִצַּד יָמִין סְרוּכָה — **If the *inunita d'varda*, which is on the** animal's **right side,**[44] is discovered to have **adhered to any place whatsoever** within the chest cavity, טְרֵפָה — the animal is ***tereifah*.**[45]

The laws pertaining to the *una* (cranial lobe):

וְאוּנוֹת הָרֵאָה הֵם חָמֵשׁ מִלְּבַד הָעִינוּנִיתָא — **The *unos* of the lung are five** in number, **aside from the *inunita d'varda*.** The animal's right lung contains three *unos*, and its left lung contains two *unos*. Thus, from the perspective of an observer who examines the lungs for *sirchos*, וְיֵשׁ מֵהֶן שְׁלֹשָׁה מִצַּד יָמִין הַבּוֹדֵק — **three of [the *unos*] are on the examiner's right side** as he faces the animal, בְּשָׁעָה

---

### NOTES

39. The examination consists of immersing the lung in a basin of lukewarm water and inflating it in order to see if the water bubbles. If it does bubble, then we know that the outer membrane of the lung has been punctured, and the animal is *tereifah* (*Chullin* 46b, 48a). If the water does not bubble, we permit this type of *sircha*. Although Chinuch has explained that a *sircha* renders the animal *tereifah* even before it actually punctures the lung (see note 34), that is only where it is inevitable that such a puncture will occur. In a case where the *sircha* originates from a wound on the chest wall, it is less firmly attached to the lung, and a separation of the *sircha* will not necessarily cause a puncture of the lung. Accordingly, the animal can be declared kosher — provided that an examination proves that the lung is not *already* punctured (*Ran* to *Rif, Chullin* fol. 12a-b). If, however, there is no injury to the chest wall, then the *sircha* originated from the lung. In such a case, even if an examination was performed and it indicated that there is no puncture of the lung, the animal is *tereifah*, for the *sircha* that is stuck to the chest wall would have tugged at the lung and eventually torn its outer membrane. [See *Ran* there for explanation of this law according to *Rashi's* understanding of *sirchos*, cited in note 34.]

40. See *Ran* ibid. and *Baal HaMaor* there; see also *Beur HaGra, Yoreh Deah* 39:37.

41. I.e., the *uma* (caudal lobe) is adhered to the rearmost *una* (cranial lobe), which is the one abutting it; see diagram at note 35.

42. The "cut" refers to the part of the lobe that actually lies flush against the adjacent lobe, i.e., the section where the lobes appear as if they are separated by no more than an incision — as opposed to the parts of the lobes that naturally have a gap between them (see *Yoreh Deah* 39:4 and *Aruch HaShulchan* 39:33). See the diagram at note 35.

According to Chinuch (who follows *Tosafos'* understanding of *sirchos*, cited in note 34), the basis for leniency in this case is that since the *sircha* is attaching two parts of the lung that naturally lie flush against each other, it will not necessarily tear on account of the animal's movement, and thus, no puncture is destined to occur (*Tosafos* ibid.). [*Rashi* (*Chullin* 46b ד"ה היינו רביתייהו) discusses this case at length and also rules leniently. For discussion of the basis for leniency according to *Rashi's* understanding of *sirchos* (cited in note 34), see *Ran* ibid. fol. 11a, and Schottenstein edition of *Chullin*, 46b note 30 and 48a note 32; see also there, 43a note 29.]

43. For the actual halachah, see *Yoreh Deah* 39:4 with *Rama*.

44. This lobe comes off the underside of the right lung. See diagram at note 35.

45. Since the *inunita d'varda* is situated by itself and does not naturally lie against any other surface, any *sircha* on it will cause it to eventually tear (*Rashi* ibid.; see *Yoreh Deah* 39:6).

שֶׁהַבְּהֵמָה תְּלוּיָה בְּרַגְלֶיהָ הָאַחֲרוֹנִים כְּדֶרֶךְ שֶׁתּוֹלִין אוֹתָהּ הַטַּבָּחִים, וּשְׁתַּיִם מִצַּד שְׂמֹאל[46], אִם סְרוּכוֹת אוֹ סְמוּכוֹת זוֹ אֵצֶל זוֹ[47] וְהַסִּרְכָא יוֹצֵאת מֵחִתּוּךְ לְחִתּוּךְ[48], וְכֵן אִם סְרוּכוֹת אֶל צַלְעוֹת הַבְּהֵמָה שֶׁהֵן רְבוּצוֹת בְּתוֹכָן, וְהַסִּרְכָא יוֹצֵאת מִגַּב הָאוּנוֹת אֶל הַצְּלָעוֹת וְתוֹפֶשֶׂת בַּצְּלָעוֹת וּבַבָּשָׂר שֶׁבֵּין הַצְּלָעוֹת, וְכָל שֶׁכֵּן בַּבָּשָׂר לְבַד, כָּל זֶה דָּנִין אוֹתוֹ לְהֶתֵּר[49]. אֲבָל אִם הַסִּרְכָא יוֹצֵאת בֵּינֵיהֶן מֵחִתּוּךְ הָאוּנָה לְגַב חֲבֶרְתָּהּ[50]

---

שֶׁהַבְּהֵמָה תְּלוּיָה בְּרַגְלֶיהָ הָאַחֲרוֹנִים כְּדֶרֶךְ שֶׁתּוֹלִין אוֹתָהּ הַטַּבָּחִים — **when the animal is hanging from its hind legs, in the manner that butchers hang it,** וּשְׁתַּיִם מִצַּד שְׂמֹאל — **and two** of the *unos* **are on** his **left side.**[46] Should he find a *sircha*, the law is as follows: אִם סְרוּכוֹת אוֹ סְמוּכוֹת זוֹ אֵצֶל זוֹ וְהַסִּרְכָא יוֹצֵאת מֵחִתּוּךְ לְחִתּוּךְ — **If** two of **[the** *unos***] are adhered or attached to each other,**[47] **and the** *sircha* **extends from the "cut"** of one lobe **to the "cut"** of the adjacent lobe that lies against it,[48] וְכֵן אִם סְרוּכוֹת אֶל צַלְעוֹת הַבְּהֵמָה שֶׁהֵן רְבוּצוֹת בְּתוֹכָן — **and likewise, if [the** *unos***] are adhered to the animal's ribcage in which they** naturally **lie,** וְהַסִּרְכָא יוֹצֵאת מִגַּב הָאוּנוֹת אֶל הַצְּלָעוֹת — **and the** *sircha* **extends from the back** (i.e., dorsal side) **of the** *unos* **to the ribcage,** וְתוֹפֶשֶׂת בַּצְּלָעוֹת וּבַבָּשָׂר שֶׁבֵּין הַצְּלָעוֹת — **and is attached to** both **the ribs and the flesh that is between the ribs,** וְכָל שֶׁכֵּן בַּבָּשָׂר לְבַד — **and certainly** if it is attached **only to the flesh** but not to the ribs, כָּל זֶה דָּנִין אוֹתוֹ לְהֶתֵּר — **in all these** cases **we rule [the animal] permitted.**[49] אֲבָל אִם הַסִּרְכָא יוֹצֵאת בֵּינֵיהֶן — **However, if the** *sircha* **develops between [the** *unos***],** adhering them together, מֵחִתּוּךְ הָאוּנָה לְגַב חֲבֶרְתָּהּ — in a way that it extends **from the "cut"** of one *una* **to the outer part of the**

---

### NOTES

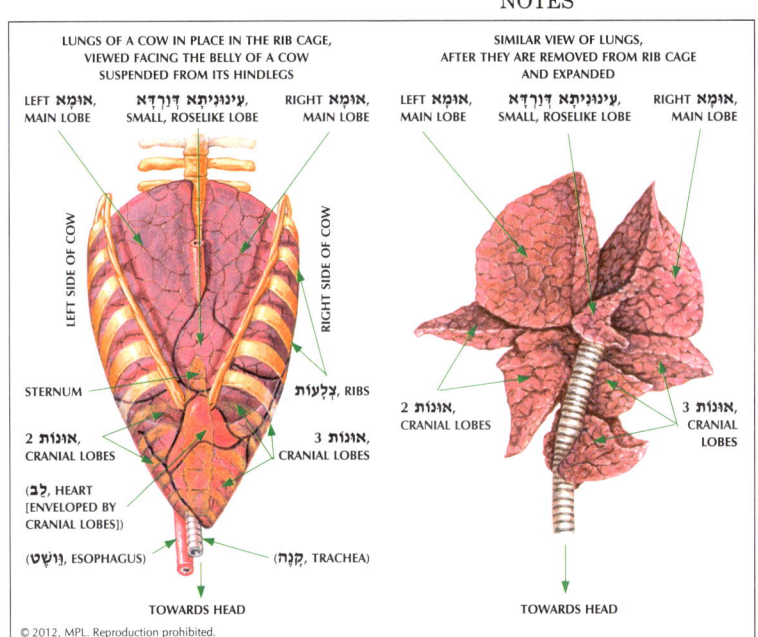

11a, and *Yoreh Deah* 39:4 with *Beur HaGra* §9).

48. This is essentially the same as the case discussed above, at note 42, except that there the "cut" of an *uma* was attached to the "cut" of an adjacent *una*, and here the "cuts" of two adjacent *unos* are attached to each other (see *Chullin* 46b with *Rashi* ד"ה היינו רביתייהו). The reason the animal is permitted in this case (as Chinuch shall rule) is the same as above; see note 42.

49. The *unos* lie in the narrow, forward part of the chest, near the neck, and therefore remain at all times naturally flush against the soft flesh of the chest wall. Hence, even if an *una* would become perforated on account of a *sircha*, as long as the *sircha* is on the side that faces the chest wall, the fibrous tissue of the *sircha* together with the flesh of the chest wall would form an effective seal, preventing the animal from becoming *tereifah* (see *Chullin* 48a with *Rashi* ד"ה התם במקום רביתא).

Chinuch maintains that this applies not only when the *una* is adhered exclusively to the flesh of the chest, but even when it is adhered partially to the flesh and partially to the bone. Although the bone is stiff and does not form an effective seal, since the part of the *una* attached to the flesh will heal, the remainder will

---

46. A butcher generally opens the abdomen of the slaughtered animal by suspending the carcass from its hind legs and slitting open the animal's underside. As he faces the animal's exposed insides, the animal's right side is to the butcher's right, and its left side is to his left. Viewing the underside of the lungs from this position, he sees three *unos* on his right, and two *unos* on his left.

47. "Adhered" means that they are connected by a *sircha* in one spot. "Attached" means that their entire adjacent surfaces are attached by a large *sircha* (see *Ran* ibid. fol.

# 61 □ MISHPATIM / MITZVAH 73: THE PROHIBITION TO EAT TEREIFAH

אוֹ מִגַּב לְגַב, וְכֵן אִם יוֹצֵאת מִן הָאוּנוֹת אֶל הַצְּלָעוֹת וְאֵינָהּ תּוֹפֶשֶׂת כִּי אִם בַּעֲצָמוֹת לְבַד, וְכֵן כָּל מָקוֹם אַחֵר בָּעוֹלָם שֶׁבַּבְּהֵמָה שֶׁתִּהְיֶינָה הָאוּנוֹת סְרוּכוֹת שָׁם אוֹ סְמוּכוֹת, דָּנִין אוֹתוֹ לְאִסּוּר.[51] וְהָרַמְבַּ"ם זִכְרוֹנוֹ לִבְרָכָה הוֹצִיא מִכְּלָל זֶה כָּל זְמַן שֶׁסְּרוּכוֹת לֶחָזֶה וּלְשַׁמְנוּנִית דְּחָזֶה וְדָן לְהֶתֵּר,[52] וְלֹא כֵן אָנוּ נוֹהֲגִין.[53] סִרְכָא הַתְּלוּיָה בְּכָל מָקוֹם בֵּין בָּאוּנוֹת בֵּין בָּאֻמָּה,[54] כְּשֵׁרָה, וְיֵשׁ שֶׁטּוֹרְפָהּ, וְאָנוּ נוֹהֲגִין בָּהּ הֶתֵּר.[55]

---

**adjacent** *una*,[50] אוֹ מִגַּב לְגַב – **or** it extends **from** the **outer part** of one *una* **to** the **outer part** of another *una*, וְכֵן אִם יוֹצֵאת מִן הָאוּנוֹת אֶל הַצְּלָעוֹת – **and likewise, if it stems from the** *unos* and is adhered **to the ribcage,** וְאֵינָהּ תּוֹפֶשֶׂת כִּי אִם בַּעֲצָמוֹת לְבַד – **but it is fastened only to the bones** of the ribcage, and not to any flesh, וְכֵן כָּל מָקוֹם אַחֵר בָּעוֹלָם שֶׁבַּבְּהֵמָה שֶׁתִּהְיֶינָה הָאוּנוֹת סְרוּכוֹת שָׁם אוֹ סְמוּכוֹת – **and likewise,** if there is **any other place whatsoever in the animal to which the** *unos* **are adhered or attached,** דָּנִין אוֹתוֹ לְאִסּוּר – in all these cases **we rule [the animal] prohibited.**[51]

וְהָרַמְבַּ"ם זִכְרוֹנוֹ לִבְרָכָה הוֹצִיא מִכְּלָל זֶה – *Rambam* (*Hil. Shechitah* 11:7), **of blessed memory, excluded from this rule** כָּל זְמַן שֶׁסְּרוּכוֹת לֶחָזֶה וּלְשַׁמְנוּנִית דְּחָזֶה – **all instances in which [the** *unos***] are adhered to** the flesh of **the chest or the fat of the chest,** וְדָן לְהֶתֵּר – **and he ruled them permitted.**[52] וְלֹא כֵן אָנוּ נוֹהֲגִין – **However, our custom is not in accordance with this lenient ruling.**[53]

Chinuch concludes the discussion of *sirchos* with a ruling that pertains to all the lobes:

סִרְכָא הַתְּלוּיָה בְּכָל מָקוֹם – **A** *sircha* **that** is not fastened to any surrounding tissue, but merely **hangs from any place** on the lungs, בֵּין בָּאוּנוֹת בֵּין בָּאֻמָּה – **whether from the** *unos* **or from the** *uma* on either side,[54] כְּשֵׁרָה – **is** deemed **kosher.** וְיֵשׁ שֶׁטּוֹרְפָהּ – **There is** actually an opinion **that deems it** *tereifah*, וְאָנוּ נוֹהֲגִין בָּהּ הֶתֵּר – **but our custom is to permit it.**[55]

---

## NOTES

eventually also heal (see *Ran* ibid. fol. 12b ד"ה והוא; *Shulchan Aruch, Yoreh Deah* 39:18; and *Aruch HaShulchan* 39:71; see, however, *Rama* 39:18).

50. I.e., the part of the lobe that is not flush against this adjacent lobe.

51. In all these cases, the lung will inevitably become punctured and will not be able to be effectively sealed. This is because the adhesion is stuck at its other end to a place that does not naturally lie flush against the affected location of the lung. Similarly, in the case where the *sircha* is attached to the rib bone only, but not to its flesh, the stiff rib bone will not be able to lie snugly against the affected spot in the lung. Thus, it will not effectively seal a puncture that develops there (see *Ran* ibid., fol. 11a, 12b).

52. *Rambam* maintains that the flesh of the chest and its fat have the same status as the flesh of the ribs.

53. This custom is recorded by *Rashba* in *Toras HaBayis* 2:3 (Josefov ed., p. 36a), and *Teshuvos HaRashba* Vol. I §161; see also *Shulchan Aruch* ibid. [Interestingly, *Chidushei Re'ah* to *Chullin* 48a, and in his halachic rulings at end of Ch. 3 §42, concurs with *Rambam*. Here, too, the view of *Re'ah* is inconsistent with that of Chinuch (see above, note 34).]

54. Or from the *inunita d'varda* (see *Rosh, Chullin* 3:14).

55. According to Chinuch's explanation of the reason that a *sircha* renders the animal *tereifah* — namely, because when the *sircha* is pulled by the animal's movement the lung will become punctured (see note 34) — it is obvious that when the *sircha* is not attached to any other surface there is no basis for concern, so this *sircha* does not render the animal *tereifah*.

The dissenting opinion that Chinuch cites is that of *Re'ah* (*Chidushei Re'ah* to *Chullin* 47b ד"ה אמר רב יוסף and at end of Ch. 3 §31; *Bedek HaBayis* to *Toras HaBayis* ibid., p. 34b) who states that אֵין סִירְכָא בְּלֹא נֶקֶב, *there is no sircha without a puncture*. This is apparently based on *Rashi's* understanding of the reason that a *sircha* renders the animal *tereifah* — because the adhesion indicates that there *already is* a perforation beneath it (see note 34). Hence, even a "hanging" *sircha* is an indication of *tereifah*. [Here, again, the position of *Re'ah* is at odds with that of Chinuch.]

However, numerous Rishonim maintain that even according to *Rashi* a "hanging" *sircha* is permitted, because only a *sircha* formed of a thick, tacky secretion, which causes the lung to adhere to another surface, is indicative of a perforation in the lung, since this type of secretion must have come from within the lung. A *sircha* formed of a loose substance that merely is attached to the surface of a lung, but does not adhere to anything else, is not a sign of a perforation in the lung, since it might result from moisture on the exterior of the lung (*Rosh*

נִמְצְאוּ[56] הָאוּנוֹת שֶׁלֹּא כַּסֵּדֶר הַזֶּה אוֹ חֲסֵרוֹת מֵחֶשְׁבּוֹן זֶה, טְרֵפָה, וְהָעֵינוּנִיתָא דְוַרְדָּא מַשְׁלֶמֶת חֶסְרוֹן אֶחָד[57]. וְאִם נִמְצְאוּ יְתֵרוֹת מֵחֶשְׁבּוֹן זֶה הַרְבֵּה, אֵין בְּכָךְ כְּלוּם, וּבִלְבַד שֶׁלֹּא יִמָּצֵא הַיִּתְרוֹן מִצַּד גַּבָּן[58], דְּאִלּוּ מִצַּד גַּבָּן אֵלּוּ אַחַת קְטַנָּה כַּעֲלֵה הֲדַס אוֹ יוֹתֵר קְטַנָּה אוֹסֶרֶת, וְיֵשׁ מַתִּירִין כְּשֶׁהִיא קְטַנָּה יוֹתֵר מֵעֲלֵה הֲדַס[59].

---

Having discussed the laws of *sirchos*, Chinuch turns to another possible *tereifah* defect of the lung:[56] נִמְצְאוּ הָאוּנוֹת שֶׁלֹּא כַּסֵּדֶר הַזֶּה — **If the *unos* are found not to be in this order** described above, e.g., instead of three on the right side and two on the left, there are two on the right and three on the left, אוֹ חֲסֵרוֹת מֵחֶשְׁבּוֹן זֶה — **or if they are lacking from this number**, i.e., there are only four *una* lobes in total, טְרֵפָה — **[the animal] is** considered ***tereifah*** on account of its having a deficient lung. וְהָעֵינוּנִיתָא דְוַרְדָּא מַשְׁלֶמֶת חֶסְרוֹן אֶחָד — **However, the *inunita d'varda* lobe compensates for a deficiency of one** *una*, so if this lobe is present, then even if there are only four *unos*, the animal is kosher.[57]

וְאִם נִמְצְאוּ יְתֵרוֹת מֵחֶשְׁבּוֹן זֶה הַרְבֵּה — **If more [*unos*] than this number** of five **are found**, (i.e., the cranial lobes are divided into more than five sections), even if there are **many** more sections than five, וּבִלְבַד שֶׁלֹּא יִמָּצֵא הַיִּתְרוֹן — **this is of no consequence** and the animal is kosher, מִצַּד גַּבָּן — **provided that the additional** lobe section **is not** emanating **from the rear side** of the lungs.[58] דְּאִלּוּ מִצַּד גַּבָּן — **For if** the additional lobe emanates **from the rear side of [the lungs]**, אֲפִילּוּ אַחַת קְטַנָּה כַּעֲלֵה הֲדַס — then **even if** it is **a single** lobe **as small as** the size of **a myrtle leaf**, אוֹ יוֹתֵר קְטַנָּה — **or even smaller**, אוֹסֶרֶת — **it renders** the animal **prohibited**. וְיֵשׁ מַתִּירִין כְּשֶׁהִיא קְטַנָּה יוֹתֵר מֵעֲלֵה הֲדַס — **There are**, however, some **who permit** the animal when **[the additional lobe] is smaller than a myrtle leaf**.[59]

---

### NOTES

ibid.; *Maggid Mishneh, Hilchos Shechitah* 11:15; see also *Kesef Mishneh* there and *Shach, Yoreh Deah* 39:25).

56. *Sirchos* are a subcategory of the "punctured" category of *tereifos*. The following discussion pertains to a subcategory of the "deficient" category. See above, note 23.

57. As explained in note 35, not every animal has the *inunita d'varda* (intermediate) lobe. Hence, its presence can compensate for the deficiency of another lobe.

Chinuch does not distinguish between a case in which the missing lobe is on the right side and one in which it is on the left. Some Rishonim maintain that, since the *inunita d'varda* is attached to the *right* lung (see note 44), it can compensate only for the deficiency of an *una* lobe on the right side. Yet others disagree with the entire premise that the *inunita d'varda* can compensate for a missing *una* (see Rashi, *Chullin* 47a ד״ה אפילו כטרפא; *Shulchan Aruch, Yoreh Deah* 35:7; and *Shach* ad loc. §41-42).

[*Chidushei Re'ah* (47a, and end of Ch. 3, ruling §28) adopts the middle view — that the *inunita d'varda* can compensate for a missing *una*, but only on the right side. Here, again, we find *Re'ah* to be in disagreement with Chinuch.]

58. The cranial lobes are joined at their back (dorsal) side, facing the spine, and are divided at their front (ventral) side, facing the belly. [See diagram.] If the divisions create more than five sections of lobes at the front, the animal is kosher because this is a common phenomenon. If there is an extra lobe section at the back, however, it is an abnormality and the animal is deemed *tereifah*. This defect falls under the category of "deficient," because there is a rule that "anything extra is like something removed" (כָּל יָתֵר כְּנָטוּל דָּמֵי); i.e., an extra organ has the same law as a missing organ (see *Chullin* 47a and 58b).

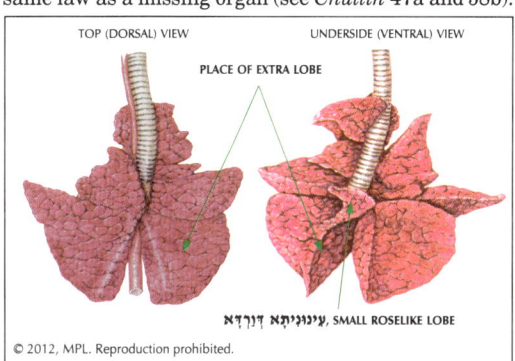

59. The two opinions disagree as to the meaning of the Gemara's phrase (*Chullin* 47b): "But if the extra lobe is on the rear side of the lung, then even if it is as small as a myrtle leaf, the animal is *tereifah*." The first opinion maintains that "even as small as a myrtle leaf" is not a specific size, but is merely an example of something very small. Therefore, even if the extra lobe is smaller than a myrtle leaf, the animal is *tereifah* (*Rashba* ad loc.). The second opinion maintains that this is a precise measurement; therefore, if the extra lobe is smaller than a myrtle leaf, the animal is kosher (*Re'ah* there, 47a; *Rambam* ibid. 8:4). [Here, again, we find *Re'ah* disagreeing with the view adopted by Chinuch.]

## MISHPATIM / MITZVAH 73: THE PROHIBITION TO EAT TEREIFAH

וְיֶתֶר רָבֵּי פְּרָטֵי מִצְוָה זוֹ מְבֹאָרִים בְּפֶרֶק ג' מֵחֻלִּין (דף מ״ב ע״א ואילך),[60] וּבְפֶרֶק זֶה בְּעַצְמוֹ כְּמוֹ כֵן וּבְפֶרֶק אַחֲרוֹן מִמַּכּוֹת (דף י״ח ע״א) וְרִאשׁוֹן מִבְּכוֹרוֹת יִתְבָּאֲרוּ דִּינֵי שְׁאָר הָאִסּוּרִין שֶׁכְּתַבְנוּ לְמַעְלָה שֶׁנִּשְׁמָעִין בִּלְשׁוֹן הַכָּתוּב בִּפְנִים שֶׁלּוֹ.[61]

וְנִכְפְּלָה אַזְהָרָה זוֹ בַּנְּבִיאִים בְּסֵפֶר יְחֶזְקֵאל (מ״ד, ל״א), בַּכֹּהֲנִים לְבַד, שֶׁכָּתוּב עֲלֵיהֶם, כָּל נְבֵלָה וּטְרֵפָה [וְגוֹ'] לֹא יֹאכְלוּ הַכֹּהֲנִים, וְהוֹדִיעוּנוּ חֲכָמִים (מנחות דף מ״ה ע״א) שֶׁמִּפְּנֵי זֶה נִכְפְּלָה בָּהֶן, לְפִי שֶׁהַכָּתוּב צִוָּה לֶאֱכֹל חַטַּאת הָעוֹף בִּמְלִיקָה,[62] וְאַף עַל פִּי שֶׁאֲסוּרָה לְיִשְׂרָאֵל כִּנְבֵלָה,[63] וְאוּלַי תַּחְשֹׁב מִתּוֹךְ כֵּן שֶׁיֻּתַּר לָהֶם אֲפִלּוּ בְּחֻלִּין מְלִיקָה

---

וְיֶתֶר רָבֵּי פְּרָטֵי מִצְוָה זוֹ מְבֹאָרִים בְּפֶרֶק ג' מֵחֻלִּין — **These laws and the many additional details of this mitzvah are elaborated in the third chapter of** Tractate **Chullin** (42a-58b).[60] וּבְפֶרֶק זֶה בְּעַצְמוֹ כְּמוֹ כֵן — **Likewise, in that chapter itself,** וּבְפֶרֶק אַחֲרוֹן מִמַּכּוֹת וְרִאשׁוֹן מִבְּכוֹרוֹת — **and in the last chapter of** Tractate **Makkos and the first** chapter of Tractate **Bechoros,** יִתְבָּאֲרוּ דִּינֵי שְׁאָר הָאִסּוּרִין שֶׁכְּתַבְנוּ לְמַעְלָה — **are elaborated the laws of the other prohibitions that we have recorded above,** שֶׁנִּשְׁמָעִין בִּלְשׁוֹן הַכָּתוּב בִּפְנִים שֶׁלּוֹ — **which are understood from the language of the verse in its deeper sense.**[61]

### ⌐ Applicability of the Mitzvah ⌐

Like all mitzvos pertaining to non-sacred foods, the prohibition to eat *tereifah* applies to all Jews, whether Kohanim, Leviim, or Israelites. Considering this point to be obvious, Chinuch discusses a verse in *Ezekiel* that seems to limit the applicability of this mitzvah:

וְנִכְפְּלָה אַזְהָרָה זוֹ בַּנְּבִיאִים בְּסֵפֶר יְחֶזְקֵאל בַּכֹּהֲנִים לְבַד — **This prohibition is repeated in the Prophets, in the Book of** *Ezekiel* (44:31), **but only concerning Kohanim,** שֶׁכָּתוּב עֲלֵיהֶם — **as it is written** there **concerning them:** "כָּל נְבֵלָה וּטְרֵפָה [וְגוֹ'] לֹא יֹאכְלוּ הַכֹּהֲנִים" — ***Any neveilah*** (carcass) **or *tereifah* etc.** *[of fowl or livestock],* **the Kohanim may not eat.** This is problematic, for the verse would seem to imply that the prohibitions of *neveilah* and *tereifah* apply only to Kohanim. וְהוֹדִיעוּנוּ חֲכָמִים — **The Sages** (*Menachos* 45a) **informed us,** however, that this is not so. These prohibitions certainly apply to all Jews, שֶׁמִּפְּנֵי זֶה נִכְפְּלָה בָּהֶן — **but it was** necessary, **due to this** following reason, for [the prohibition] **to be repeated** by Ezekiel specifically **concerning [the Kohanim]:** לְפִי שֶׁהַכָּתוּב צִוָּה לֶאֱכֹל חַטַּאת הָעוֹף בִּמְלִיקָה — **Since Scripture commanded [the Kohanim] to eat** the flesh of a **bird-*chatas* offering,** which is slaughtered **through** the process of ***melikah*,**[62] וְאַף עַל פִּי שֶׁאֲסוּרָה לְיִשְׂרָאֵל כִּנְבֵלָה — **even though [the bird] is forbidden to an Israelite** or a Levite **as *neveilah*,**[63] וְאוּלַי תַּחְשֹׁב מִתּוֹךְ כֵּן שֶׁיֻּתַּר לָהֶם אֲפִלּוּ בְּחֻלִּין מְלִיקָה — **you might therefore suppose**

---

### NOTES

60. The laws are codified in *Rambam, Hil. Shechitah* Chs. 5-11, and *Hil. Maachalos Asuros* 4:6-12; and in *Shulchan Aruch, Yoreh Deah* §29-60. [As mentioned in note 36, these laws are extremely complex, and the brief discussions contained in our notes are intended merely to provide an outline of Chinuch's view regarding the specific cases he mentions, not to represent the final halachah.]

61. This refers to the laws of flesh that went "outside its boundary," as described above, at notes 8-11. [These laws are actually discussed in *Chullin* Ch. 4 (68a-69b, 74a-75b); *Makkos* Ch. 3 (18a); *Zevachim* 82b, and *Pesachim* 85a. Chinuch's references to *Chullin* Ch. 3 and *Bechoros* Ch. 1 are perplexing. *Rambam*, at the end of *Lo Saaseh* 181, which deals with *tereifah*, cites these sources regarding a different context, and perhaps they were transcribed here in error (see footnote 26 to Mechon Yerushalayim ed. of *Minchas Chinuch*).]

62. The Torah (*Leviticus* 1:15, 5:8) prescribes a distinct slaughtering procedure for bird-offerings, called *melikah*, which is different from the standard process of *shechitah* through which birds and animals are ordinarily slaughtered. *Melikah* consists of a Kohen piercing the back of the bird's neck with his right thumbnail, cutting the nape and spinal cord (without severing the majority of the neck's flesh), and then piercing deeper until he cuts most of either the trachea or esophagus in the case of the bird-*chatas* offering, or both in the case of the bird-*olah* offering (see *Zevachim* 64b-66a). Thus, *melikah*-slaughter differs from *shechitah*-slaughter in two ways: (1) The cutting is done with the Kohen's thumbnail rather than a knife; (2) the neck is cut from the back rather than the front.

63. In order for a bird to be permitted for consumption,

אוֹ שְׁחִיטָה נִפְסֶדֶת[64], שֶׁלֹּא תַקְפִּיד תּוֹרָה בָּהֶן, דְּמִכֵּיוָן שֶׁיָּצְאוּ מִן הַגֶּדֶר בְּדָבָר אֶחָד, יָצְאוּ לְגַמְרֵי בְּכָל עִנְיַן הַשְּׁחִיטָה[65], וּלְפִיכָךְ הִזְהִיר הַנָּבִיא בָּהֶם בְּפֵרוּשׁ לְהוֹדִיעֵנוּ שֶׁלֹּא הִתִּירוּ רַק בִּמְלִיקָה לְבַד בְּקָרְבָּן, אֲבָל בְּחֻלִּין נִשְׁאָרִים הֵם בְּאִסּוּרָן כְּמוֹ יִשְׂרְאֵלִים[66].
וְנוֹהֶגֶת מִצְוָה זוֹ בְּכָל מָקוֹם וּבְכָל זְמַן, בִּזְכָרִים וּנְקֵבוֹת[67].
וְהָעוֹבֵר עָלֶיהָ וְאָכַל כַּזַּיִת מִן הַטְּרֵפָה[68], וּמִכָּל אֵלּוּ שֶׁנִּשְׁמָעִים בְּפֵרוּשׁ הַכָּתוּב שֶׁיָּצְאוּ חוּץ לִמְחִצָּתָן[69], לוֹקֶה.

---

שֶׁלֹּא תַקְפִּיד אוֹ שְׁחִיטָה נִפְסֶדֶת — that it is permitted for [Kohanim] to consume even an unconsecrated bird that was slaughtered through *melikah* — or through an improper *shechitah*,[64] תּוֹרָה בָּהֶן — since you might reason that the Torah is not particular about this matter in regard to [Kohanim], דְּמִכֵּיוָן שֶׁיָּצְאוּ מִן הַגֶּדֶר בְּדָבָר אֶחָד יָצְאוּ לְגַמְרֵי בְּכָל עִנְיַן הַשְּׁחִיטָה — for since they are removed from the confines of the prohibition to eat *neveilah* concerning one matter (viz., eating the bird-*chatas* offering), perhaps they are entirely removed from the matter of *shechitah*, and may eat birds or even animals that are killed in any manner.[65] וּלְפִיכָךְ הִזְהִיר הַנָּבִיא בָּהֶם בְּפֵרוּשׁ — The prophet therefore gave an explicit warning about *neveilah* concerning [the Kohanim], לְהוֹדִיעֵנוּ שֶׁלֹּא הִתִּירוּ רַק בִּמְלִיקָה לְבַד בְּקָרְבָּן — to inform us that they were granted permission only to consume flesh slaughtered specifically through *melikah*, and that this permit applies only in the case of a bird-*chatas* offering, אֲבָל בְּחֻלִּין נִשְׁאָרִים הֵם בְּאִסּוּרָן כְּמוֹ יִשְׂרְאֵלִים — but in regard to unconsecrated fowl, and certainly livestock, they remain within the confines of the prohibition of *neveilah*, just like Israelites.[66]

Having explained the verse in *Ezekiel*, Chinuch addresses the applicability of the mitzvah in his usual style:

וְנוֹהֶגֶת מִצְוָה זוֹ בְּכָל מָקוֹם וּבְכָל זְמַן — This mitzvah applies in every location and in all times, בִּזְכָרִים וּנְקֵבוֹת — to both men and women.[67] וְאָכַל כַּזַּיִת מִן הַטְּרֵפָה — and eats a *kezayis* (olive's volume) of flesh from a *tereifah* animal,[68] וְהָעוֹבֵר עָלֶיהָ — One who transgresses [this mitzvah] וּמִכָּל אֵלּוּ שֶׁנִּשְׁמָעִים בְּפֵרוּשׁ הַכָּתוּב שֶׁיָּצְאוּ חוּץ לִמְחִצָּתָן — or from any of those animals whose prohibition is implied by the verse's deeper interpretation, namely, those that went out of their respective halachic boundaries, as elaborated above,[69] לוֹקֶה — incurs the penalty of *malkus* (lashes).

---

NOTES

it must be slaughtered through the process of *shechitah*. If it is killed in any other way, including *melikah*, it is prohibited as *neveilah* (Mitzvah 472). Indeed, if an Israelite or a Levite eats of a bird offering, he transgresses the prohibition of *neveilah* (see *Yevamos* 32b and *Asvan DeOraisa* §1). Nevertheless, the Torah permits the flesh of a bird-*chatas* to Kohanim, and in fact commands them to eat it.

64. See Chinuch Mitzvah 451 for the specifications of a proper *shechitah*.

65. I.e., one might think that the requirement of *shechitah* and the related prohibition of *neveilah* do not apply to Kohanim at all. [Cf. *Rashi* to *Shabbos* 13b ד"ה דרש, who explains that one might think merely that *melikah* is a valid means of slaughter for Kohanim in cases other than a bird offering as well.]

66. Chinuch mentions only *neveilah* in the supposition of what might be permitted to Kohanim, but the verse in *Ezekiel* actually warns against both *neveilah* and *tereifah*. The Gemara (*Menachos* 45a) states explicitly that, due to the permit involving *melikah*, one might have thought that Kohanim are permitted to eat both *neveilah* and *tereifah*. This is because a bird killed through *melikah* is actually *tereifah* as well as *neveilah*. When the Kohen severs the bird's spinal cord with his thumbnail, he renders it *tereifah*, and when he subsequently severs its trachea and esophagus, he renders it *neveilah* (*Rashi* to *Ezekiel* 44:31; see *Tosafos*, *Chullin* 20a ד"ה לא, and *Cheshek Shlomo*, *Menachos* 45a).

67. It applies in Eretz Yisrael and the Diaspora, and whether the *Beis HaMikdash* is standing or not. It also applies to women, as to men, in accordance with the general rule pertaining to mitzvah-prohibitions (see General Introduction).

68. This includes both the meat of an animal with a *tereifah*-defect that was slaughtered, and flesh that was torn from a live animal (which is included in the term "*tereifah*"; see note 7).

69. At notes 8-11.

# 65 □ MISHPATIM / MITZVAH 73: THE PROHIBITION TO EAT TEREIFAH

וְאַל יַקְשֶׁה עָלֶיךָ וְאֵיךְ לוֹקֶה, וְהָא קַיְמָא לָן (פסחים דף כ״ד ע״א) אֵין לוֹקִין עַל לַאו שֶׁבִּכְלָלוֹת,[70] וַהֲרֵי זֶה שֶׁכָּלַל כַּמָּה דְּבָרִים כְּמוֹ שֶׁאָמַרְנוּ, כִּי פֵּרוּשׁ עִנְיָן זֶה כְּבָר בֵּאֲרוּהוּ בְּסֵפֶר הַמִּצְוֹת בָּעִקָּר הַתְּשִׁיעִי שְׁנֵי גְּדוֹלֵי הַדּוֹר,[71] וְהֵם הָרַמְבַּ״ם זִכְרוֹנוֹ לִבְרָכָה וְהָרַמְבַּ״ן זִכְרוֹנוֹ לִבְרָכָה, וְהִרְחִיבוּ שָׁם פֵּרוּשֵׁיהֶם וּרְאָיוֹתֵיהֶם בָּזֶה לְבָרֵר הַדָּבָר יָפֶה, וְיַאֲרִיךְ הָעִנְיָן, עַל כֵּן הִנַּחְתִּיו כְּפִי מִנְהָגַי בַּסֵּפֶר,[72] וּמִכָּל מָקוֹם יֵשׁ לְךָ לָדַעַת כִּי הָעוֹלֶה מִדִּבְרֵי שְׁנֵיהֶם, שֶׁאֵין זֶה מִכְּלָל לַאו שֶׁבִּכְלָלוֹת.

---

Chinuch addresses an apparent difficulty with the imposition of *malkus* for these transgressions: וְאַל יַקְשֶׁה עָלֶיךָ — **Do not let** the following **disturb you:** וְאֵיךְ לוֹקֶה — **How can [the transgressor] incur *malkus*?** וְהָא קַיְמָא לָן — **But we have** an **established rule** (*Pesachim* 24a) that אֵין לוֹקִין עַל לַאו שֶׁבִּכְלָלוֹת — **one does not incur *malkus* for** transgressing **a generalized prohibition,**[70] וַהֲרֵי זֶה שֶׁכָּלַל כַּמָּה דְּבָרִים כְּמוֹ שֶׁאָמַרְנוּ — **and this** verse would **indeed** seem to be a "generalized prohibition," **for it includes many** diverse **things, as we said above!?** כִּי פֵּרוּשׁ עִנְיָן זֶה כְּבָר בֵּאֲרוּהוּ בְּסֵפֶר הַמִּצְוֹת בָּעִקָּר הַתְּשִׁיעִי שְׁנֵי גְּדוֹלֵי הַדּוֹר — **This should not disturb you, for the explanation of this matter has already been elucidated in the *Sefer HaMitzvos*, in *Shoresh* (Introductory Rule) Nine, by two greats of the generation,**[71] וְהֵם הָרַמְבַּ״ם זִכְרוֹנוֹ לִבְרָכָה וְהָרַמְבַּ״ן זִכְרוֹנוֹ לִבְרָכָה — **namely, *Rambam*, of blessed memory, and *Ramban*, of blessed memory.** וְהִרְחִיבוּ שָׁם פֵּרוּשֵׁיהֶם וּרְאָיוֹתֵיהֶם בָּזֶה לְבָרֵר הַדָּבָר יָפֶה — **They expanded there with their commentaries and proofs regarding this** matter, **thoroughly clarifying the issue.** וְיַאֲרִיךְ הָעִנְיָן — **The subject would be too lengthy** for me to elucidate here, עַל כֵּן הִנַּחְתִּיו כְּפִי מִנְהָגַי בַּסֵּפֶר — **therefore, I have left it aside, as it is my custom in** this **book** to omit lengthy digressions.[72] וּמִכָּל מָקוֹם יֵשׁ לְךָ לָדַעַת — **In any event, you should know** כִּי הָעוֹלֶה מִדִּבְרֵי שְׁנֵיהֶם — **that what emerges from the words of both of them is** שֶׁאֵין זֶה מִכְּלָל לַאו שֶׁבִּכְלָלוֹת — **that this** mitzvah-prohibition **is not** considered **a generalized prohibition,** and therefore, one who transgresses it in any of its details does incur *malkus*.

---

NOTES

70. A *generalized prohibition* is an umbrella injunction that prohibits several different things.

71. These two great men (*Rambam* and *Ramban*) actually lived about a century apart, but each of them was a "great one" of his generation.

72. The discussion there is likewise beyond the scope of these notes.

---

> ◆§ **Insight: The Reasons for Prohibitions on Certain Foods**
>
> Chinuch writes at length that the underlying purpose of the *tereifah* prohibition, as well as all the other prohibitions in the Torah against consuming certain foods, is to keep us away from any food that might have a detrimental effect on the body. As he explains, keeping the body whole is vital in the service of Hashem, since the body is the "tool" through which the soul carries out its mission in this world and any weakening of the body is liable to diminish the accomplishments of the soul. This thought is also expressed by *Recanati* to *Leviticus* 11:2 (see similarly, *Rambam, Hilchos Dei'os* 3:3). Following this approach, Chinuch introduces the novel thought that every *tereifah*-defect is indicative of a degree of illness in the animal that has such a defect; and even if the defect results from an externally inflicted wound, since the wound is fatal it surely brought on the beginnings of illness from the moment that it occurred. [See also above, note 34.] Chinuch reiterates and expands this concept below, in Mitzvos 147 and 154.
>
> Other authorities, however, disagree with Chinuch's approach to this matter.
>
> *Ramban* (*Exodus* 22:30) notes that the verse containing the prohibition of *tereifah* prefaces this prohibition with the declaration: וְאַנְשֵׁי קֹדֶשׁ תִּהְיוּן לִי, *People of holiness shall you be to Me*. This indicates that the purpose of the *tereifah* prohibition is to preserve *holiness of the soul*, rather than robustness of the body. *Ramban* therefore explains that in fact *all* the prohibitions pertaining to foods are means of perpetuating purity of the soul, for the foods that the Torah prohibits have *spiritual* ill effects.

*Rabbeinu Bachya* and *Recanati* (ad loc.) offer Kabbalistic explanations of the spiritual negativity of a *tereifah*. *R' S. R. Hirsch*, however, provides a moral explanation accessible to all: An animal or bird that suffers a fatal wound has lost its ability to live independently and has been relegated to eventually (when it dies) serving as nourishment for other creatures of the wild, or for plants. Thus, the Torah (*Exodus* 30:22) identifies it as בָּשָׂר בַּשָּׂדֶה, *meat in the field* — i.e., food of the wild. As אַנְשֵׁי קֹדֶשׁ, *people of holiness*, whose lives are dedicated to the service of the Most High, it behooves us to refrain from partaking of the same foods as beasts of the wild, so that we may remember our higher calling and avoid equating ourselves with creatures whose existence is purely corporeal (*R' Hirsch Commentary*, *Exodus* 22:20 and *Leviticus* 11:4).

*Ramban*, following the approach he established here in the context of *tereifah*, explains elsewhere (*Leviticus* 11:13) that when the Torah prohibits consumption of certain birds and animals, it is also on account of their spiritual ill effects. The birds that the Torah prohibits are birds of prey, and the animals that it prohibits are beasts of prey — and eating their meat could cause a person to acquire some of their vicious nature and thus suffer spiritually. See also *Abarbanel* there, who elaborates on this concept at length.

Interestingly, Chinuch in Mitzvah 148 offers a similar explanation for the prohibition of consuming blood. His primary approach to the subject of forbidden foods, however, is that the spiritual benefit emerges from preserving the body's health and thereby enabling the soul to reach its full potential.

The concept that the food one ingests can have a negative spiritual impact finds expression in an interesting halachah. *Rama* (*Yoreh Deah* 81:7) rules that one should prevent even little children from eating anything nonkosher because the ill effects of consuming such foods in their youth will emerge when they are older. Moreover, he rules that a nursing mother must avoid all nonkosher foods. *Shach* (ad loc.) wonders why the latter ruling had to be said; surely, a nursing mother is subject to the same prohibitions against nonkosher foods as all others! *Shach* therefore explains that *Rama* refers to a case where the mother's life is endangered, and what he means is the following: Obviously, if the mother needs a nonkosher food in order to survive, she may eat it, for saving her life overrides the prohibition of consuming the food. Nevertheless, she should not nurse her child soon afterward, for if she does then the child will have been nourished by milk that is a product of nonkosher food. Even the "secondhand" ingestion of something nonkosher can have a detrimental effect on the baby (see *Pri Megadim* ad loc.).

*R' Chaim Kanievski* (*Orchos Yosher*, Ch. 13; *Derech Sichah*, *Shemini*) notes that the mother herself will not be negatively impacted by the nonkosher food, for she is permitted — and indeed, commanded — to eat it in order to save her life, and the merit of the mitzvah of preserving her life protects her from any spiritual ill effects of the food. Nevertheless, the child that she nurses will be negatively impacted, since there is no lifesaving necessity for the child to nurse at this time, as it can survive on other foods or liquids. [For another application of this concept, see *Meshech Chochmah* and *Haamek Davar* to *Deuteronomy* 6:10-11.]

*R' Moshe Feinstein* (*Darash Moshe*, *Leviticus* 20:25), however, cautions that one must always remember that the primary reason not to consume that which is forbidden by the Torah is *because God has so commanded*, and not because of any ill effects such consumption may have. Indeed, *Rashi* (*Genesis* 26:5) states that the prohibition of pork is in the category of חֻקִּים, *[God's] decrees*; i.e., mitzvos whose reasons we are unable to fathom. [Although Chinuch and others have provided some rationale, the ultimate reasons for the mitzvos are beyond our comprehension, as Chinuch himself points out in his Author's Introduction (see Vol. I, pp. 31-33, with note 119).] *R' Moshe* posits that it is to emphasize this very point that the Torah repeats at the end of *Parashas Kedoshim* (*Leviticus* 20:25): וְהִבְדַּלְתֶּם בֵּין הַבְּהֵמָה הַטְּהֹרָה לַטְּמֵאָה, *And you shall distinguish between the clean animal and the unclean*. Even were it to be proven that nonkosher meat is not harmful, or that it is actually healthful, we are still bidden to distance ourselves from it because God has declared it "unclean." [See similarly *Rashi* to *Leviticus* 20:26.]

## MISHPATIM / MITZVAH 74: LISTENING TO ONE LITIGANT WITHOUT THE OTHER

### מִצְוָה עד: שֶׁלֹּא לִשְׁמֹעַ טַעֲנַת בַּעַל דִּין שֶׁלֹּא בִּפְנֵי בַּעַל דִּינוֹ

שֶׁלֹּא יִשְׁמַע הַדַּיָּן טַעֲנַת הָאֶחָד שֶׁלֹּא בִּפְנֵי בַּעַל דִּינוֹ[1], שֶׁנֶּאֱמַר (שמות כ״ג, א׳) לֹא תִשָּׂא שֵׁמַע שָׁוְא, וְהַטַּעַם לְפִי שֶׁבְּנֵי אָדָם יְדַבְּרוּ דִּבְרֵי שָׁוְא שֶׁלֹּא בִּפְנֵי בַּעַל דִּינָם[2], וְצִוָּה הַדַּיָּן עַל זֶה כְּדֵי שֶׁלֹּא יַכְנִיס בְּנַפְשׁוֹ כְּזָבָיו שֶׁל אֶחָד מֵהֶם[3], וְכֵן בָּא בַּמְּכִילְתָּא (דרשב״י כאן) שֶׁאַזְהָרָה זוֹ שֶׁל לֹא תִשָּׂא וְגוֹ׳ עַל זֶה נֶאֶמְרָה. וְעוֹד אָמְרוּ שָׁם שֶׁהִיא אַזְהָרָה גַם לְבַעַל הַדִּין שֶׁלֹּא יִטְעַן גַּם הוּא טַעֲנוֹתָיו לַדַּיָּן שֶׁלֹּא בִּפְנֵי בַּעַל דִּינוֹ, וַאֲפִלּוּ יִרְצֶה לִשְׁמֹעַ אוֹתָן הַדַּיָּן[4],

## ⇒ Mitzvah 74 ⇒

# The Prohibition [for a Judge] to Listen to One Litigant's Claim When the Other Litigant Is Not Present

לֹא תִשָּׂא שֵׁמַע שָׁוְא
*Do not accept a false report (Exodus 23:1).*

שֶׁלֹּא יִשְׁמַע הַדַּיָּן טַעֲנַת הָאֶחָד — **We are commanded that a judge shall not hear the claim of one litigant** שֶׁלֹּא בִּפְנֵי בַּעַל דִּינוֹ — **while not in the presence of [the litigant's] adversary** as well;[1] שֶׁנֶּאֱמַר — **as it is stated** (*Exodus* 23:1): "לֹא תִשָּׂא שֵׁמַע שָׁוְא" — "*Do not accept a false report.*"

Chinuch explains why a claim registered in such fashion is called "a false report":

וְהַטַּעַם — **The reason** that listening to a litigant's claim in private is called "accepting a false report" is לְפִי שֶׁבְּנֵי אָדָם יְדַבְּרוּ דִּבְרֵי שָׁוְא שֶׁלֹּא בִּפְנֵי בַּעַל דִּינָם — **because people** in litigation have a tendency to **speak false words when they are not in the presence of their adversaries,** as they are not embarrassed to lie when no one is there to challenge them;[2] וְצִוָּה הַדַּיָּן עַל זֶה — **the judge is therefore commanded regarding this issue,** namely, not to listen to one litigant when the other is absent, כְּדֵי שֶׁלֹּא יַכְנִיס בְּנַפְשׁוֹ כְּזָבָיו שֶׁל אֶחָד מֵהֶם — **so that he should not allow into his consciousness the lies of one of [the litigants].**[3] וְכֵן בָּא בַּמְּכִילְתָּא — **And so has** the explanation of this verse **been transmitted** to us by our Sages, **in** *Mechilta* (*Exodus* 23:1), שֶׁאַזְהָרָה זוֹ שֶׁל "לֹא תִשָּׂא וְגוֹ׳" עַל זֶה נֶאֶמְרָה — **that this prohibition of** *do not accept* a *false report* was stated in regard to this law.

Chinuch explains further that this prohibition is a multifaceted one:

וְעוֹד אָמְרוּ שָׁם — **In addition, [the Sages] stated there** (*Mechilta* ibid.) שֶׁהִיא אַזְהָרָה גַם לְבַעַל הַדִּין — **that [this verse] also serves as a Scriptural injunction upon a litigant,** שֶׁלֹּא יִטְעַן גַּם הוּא טַעֲנוֹתָיו לַדַּיָּן שֶׁלֹּא בִּפְנֵי בַּעַל דִּינוֹ — **teaching that he, likewise, may not present his claims to a judge while not in the presence of his adversary,** וַאֲפִלּוּ יִרְצֶה לִשְׁמֹעַ אוֹתָן הַדַּיָּן — **even if the judge** should indicate that he **desires to hear [the claims]** while the adversary is absent.[4]

---

### NOTES

1. Both litigants must be present when the judge hears each claim (*Sanhedrin* 7b; *Shevuos* 31a; *Rambam, Sefer HaMitzvos, Lo Saaseh* 281, and *Hil. Sanhedrin* 21:7 with *Kesef Mishneh*).

2. *Rashi, Shevuos* 31a ד״ה שמע שוא.

3. Even if the other litigant later disputes this one's claim, once the first litigant has embellished his claim before the judge without opposition, the judge may be prejudiced by what he has heard, and his mind will be closed to the other litigant's rebuttal (*Rashi, Sanhedrin* 7b). [Some explain that there is a concern even if the first litigant does not deliberately lie, since people tend to believe the side of the story that they have heard first, unless there is an immediate response (*Beis Yosef* and *Perishah, Choshen Mishpat* 17:5, citing *Proverbs* 18:17).]

4. The verse of לֹא תשא, upon which our mitzvah is based, may be read two different ways. According to the traditional Masoretic reading, it states לֹא תִשָּׂא, *Do not "accept" a false report.* However, it also can be vowelized as לֹא תַשִּׂא, *Do not "issue" a false report.* This dual reading allows the verse to serve both as a prohibition upon

## 68 □ משפטים / מצוה עד: שלא לשמע טענת בעל דין שלא בפני בעל דינו

וְעַל זֶה נֶאֱמַר גַּם כֵּן (כאן, ז) מִדְּבַר שֶׁקֶר תִּרְחָק[5]. וְעוֹד אָמְרוּ זִכְרוֹנָם לִבְרָכָה (מכות דף כ"ג ע"א) שֶׁזֶּהוּ הַלָּאו כּוֹלֵל מְסַפֵּר לְשׁוֹן הָרָע וּמְקַבְּלוֹ[6] וּמֵעִיד עֵדוּת שֶׁקֶר[7].

שֹׁרֶשׁ הַמִּצְוָה יָדוּעַ, כִּי הַשֶּׁקֶר נִתְעָב וְנֶאֱלָח[8] בְּעֵינֵי הַכֹּל, אֵין דָּבָר מָאוּס מִמֶּנּוּ, וְהַמְאֵרָה וְהַקְּלָלוֹת בְּבֵית כָּל אוֹהֲבָיו, מִפְּנֵי שֶׁהַשֵּׁם יִתְבָּרַךְ אֵל אֱמֶת[9] וְכָל אֲשֶׁר אִתּוֹ אֱמֶת, וְאֵין הַבְּרָכָה מְצוּיָה וְחָלָה אֶלָּא בַּמִּתְדַּמִּים אֵלָיו בְּמַעֲשֵׂיהֶם, לִהְיוֹתָם אֲמִתִּיִּים כְּמוֹ שֶׁהוּא אֵל אֱמֶת, וְלִהְיוֹתָם מְרַחֲמִים כְּמוֹ שֶׁיָּדוּעַ שֶׁהוּא רַחוּם, וְלִהְיוֹתָם גּוֹמְלֵי חֲסָדִים כְּמוֹ שֶׁהוּא רַב הַחֶסֶד[10], אֲבָל כָּל מִי שֶׁמַּעֲשָׂיו בְּהֵפֶךְ מִדּוֹתָיו הַטּוֹבוֹת,

---

"מִדְּבַר שֶׁקֶר" — Chinuch adds another source for prohibiting this practice: וְעַל זֶה נֶאֱמַר גַּם כֵּן — **In regard to this** matter, **it is also stated** (*Exodus* 23:7): "תִּרְחָק" — **Distance yourself from a false word.**[5]

Chinuch explains that our verse serves to prohibit other activities as well: שֶׁזֶּהוּ — וְעוֹד אָמְרוּ זִכְרוֹנָם לִבְרָכָה — **[The Sages], of blessed memory, state further** (*Makkos* 23a) הַלָּאו כּוֹלֵל מְסַפֵּר לְשׁוֹן הָרָע — **that this prohibitory verse,** *Do not issue/accept a false report*, **includes** also a prohibition upon **one who speaks *lashon hara*** (disparaging speech), וּמְקַבְּלוֹ — **as well as** a prohibition upon **one who** listens to and **accepts** [*lashon hara*];[6] וּמֵעִיד עֵדוּת שֶׁקֶר — **and** it further includes a prohibition upon **one who presents false testimony.**[7]

### ⁓ Underlying Purpose of the Mitzvah ⁓

שֹׁרֶשׁ הַמִּצְוָה יָדוּעַ — **The underlying purpose of this mitzvah is** well **known,** כִּי הַשֶּׁקֶר נִתְעָב וְנֶאֱלָח בְּעֵינֵי הַכֹּל — **for falsehood is** inherently **loathsome and detestable**[8] **in the eyes of all;** אֵין דָּבָר מָאוּס מִמֶּנּוּ — **there is nothing more repugnant than it.** וְהַמְאֵרָה וְהַקְּלָלוֹת בְּבֵית כָּל אוֹהֲבָיו — **Moreover, malediction and curses** reside **in the homes of all who love [falsehood].** מִפְּנֵי שֶׁהַשֵּׁם יִתְבָּרַךְ אֵל אֱמֶת — **This is because Hashem, blessed be He, is the God of Truth,**[9] וְכָל אֲשֶׁר אִתּוֹ אֱמֶת — **and all that is with Him is Truth;** וְאֵין הַבְּרָכָה מְצוּיָה וְחָלָה אֶלָּא בַּמִּתְדַּמִּים אֵלָיו בְּמַעֲשֵׂיהֶם — **and blessing is not found, nor will it take hold, except among those who model themselves after Him with their deeds,** לִהְיוֹתָם אֲמִתִּיִּים כְּמוֹ שֶׁהוּא אֵל אֱמֶת — meaning that they strive **to be truthful, just as He is the God of Truth,** וְלִהְיוֹתָם מְרַחֲמִים כְּמוֹ שֶׁיָּדוּעַ שֶׁהוּא רַחוּם — **to be merciful, just as it is known that He is Merciful,** וְלִהְיוֹתָם גּוֹמְלֵי חֲסָדִים כְּמוֹ שֶׁהוּא רַב הַחֶסֶד — **and to perform acts of kindness, just as He is Abundant in Kindness.**[10] אֲבָל כָּל מִי שֶׁמַּעֲשָׂיו בְּהֵפֶךְ מִדּוֹתָיו הַטּוֹבוֹת — **But anyone whose deeds**

---

### NOTES

the judge to *listen* to one litigant's claim when the other is absent, and a prohibition upon the litigant to *present* his claim in that situation (*Sanhedrin* 7b; *Shevuos* 31a with *Rashi*; see also *Rambam, Hil. Sanhedrin* 21:7 with *Kesef Mishneh*; cf. *Rashbam, Pesachim* 118a ד"ה וקרי).

5. This applies to both the litigant and the judge; each of them must "distance himself from a false word" by neither presenting nor listening to the claim unless the opposing party is present (*Shevuos* ibid.).

The Gemara (*Sanhedrin* ibid.) adds that the verse (*Deuteronomy* 1:16), שָׁמֹעַ בֵּין אֲחֵיכֶם וּשְׁפַטְתֶּם צֶדֶק, *hear among your brethren and judge righteously*, also teaches that the judge must hear the litigants' claims only when he is "among your brethren" — i.e., in the presence of both parties.

6. *Lashon hara* may not be spoken or accepted even if the report is true (see Mitzvah 236). For the explanation

of why it is called a "false report," see the Insight. [The prohibition in this verse is in addition to the explicit prohibition against *lashon hara* (*Leviticus* 19:16; Mitzvah 236).]

7. This is in addition to the explicit prohibition in the Ten Commandments against testifying falsely (*Exodus* 20:13; Mitzvah 37).

8. Stylistic citation of *Job* 15:16.

9. See *Jeremiah* 10:10 and *Psalms* 31:6; see also *Devarim Rabbah* 1:10.

10. We are commanded to emulate God and follow in His good ways (Mitzvah 611; see *Shabbos* 133b, *Sotah* 14a, and *Rambam, Hil. Dei'os* 1:6). Throughout this work, Chinuch states repeatedly that only by emulating Him [and thus meriting His Presence] do we become worthy of receiving His blessing. See, for example, above, Mitzvah 66, and below, Mitzvah 611.

# MISHPATIM / MITZVAH 74: LISTENING TO ONE LITIGANT WITHOUT THE OTHER

וְהֵם בַּעֲלֵי הַשֶּׁקֶר שֶׁהֵם בְּהֵפֶךְ מִדּוֹתָיו מַמָּשׁ,[11] כְּמוֹ כֵן תָּנוּחַ עֲלֵיהֶם לְעוֹלָם מַה שֶּׁהוּא הֵפֶךְ מִדּוֹתָיו, וְהֵפֶךְ מִדַּת הַבְּרָכָה שֶׁהִיא בּוֹ הִיא הַמְּאֵרָה וְהַקְּלָלָה, וְהֵפֶךְ שִׂמְחָה וְהַשָּׁלוֹם וְהַתַּעֲנוּג שֶׁהֵם אִתּוֹ הוּא הַדְּאָגָה וְהַקְּטָטָה וְהַצַּעַר, כָּל אֵלֶה חֵלֶק אָדָם רָשָׁע מֵאֱלֹהִים,[12] וְעַל כֵּן הִזְהִירָתְנוּ הַתּוֹרָה לְהַרְחִיק מִן הַשֶּׁקֶר הַרְבֵּה, כְּמוֹ שֶׁכָּתוּב מִדְּבַר שֶׁקֶר תִּרְחָק, וְהִנֵּה הִזְכִּירָה בּוֹ לְשׁוֹן רִחוּק לְרֹב מִאוּסוֹ מַה שֶּׁלֹּא הִזְכִּירָה כֵּן בְּכָל שְׁאָר הָאַזְהָרוֹת,[13] וּמִצַּד הָרִחוּק הִזְהִירָתְנוּ שֶׁלֹּא נַטֶּה אָזְנֵנוּ כְּלָל לְשׁוּם דָּבָר שֶׁנַּחְשׁוֹב שֶׁהוּא שֶׁקֶר, וְאַף עַל פִּי שֶׁאֵין אָנוּ יוֹדְעִין בִּבְרִיאָה[14] שֶׁיְּהֵא אוֹתוֹ הַדָּבָר שֶׁקֶר,[15] וּכְעֵין מַה שֶּׁאָמְרוּ זִכְרוֹנָם לִבְרָכָה (חולין דף מ״ד ע״ב) הַרְחֵק מִן הַכִּעוּר וּמִן הַדּוֹמֶה לוֹ.[16]

וְהֵם בַּעֲלֵי הַשֶּׁקֶר — **that is, people who adopt falsehood, reflect the opposite of [God's] Good Attributes,** שֶׁהֵם בְּהֵפֶךְ מִדּוֹתָיו מַמָּשׁ — **and who thus act in a manner that is completely antithetical to [God's] Attributes,**[11] כְּמוֹ כֵן תָּנוּחַ עֲלֵיהֶם לְעוֹלָם מַה שֶּׁהוּא הֵפֶךְ מִדּוֹתָיו — **upon them will, similarly, rest forever that which is the opposite of His Attributes.** וְהֵפֶךְ מִדַּת הַבְּרָכָה שֶׁהִיא בּוֹ — **Now, the opposite of the Attribute of Blessing** (i.e., beneficence), **which is** to be found **in [God],** הִיא הַמְּאֵרָה וְהַקְּלָלָה — **is the pervasion of malediction and curses;** וְהֵפֶךְ שִׂמְחָה וְהַשָּׁלוֹם וְהַתַּעֲנוּג שֶׁהֵם אִתּוֹ — **and** likewise, **the opposites of happiness, peace, and gratification, which are** all to be found **with Him,** הוּא הַדְּאָגָה וְהַקְּטָטָה וְהַצַּעַר — **are worry, strife, and suffering.** כָּל אֵלֶה חֵלֶק אָדָם רָשָׁע מֵאֱלֹהִים — **All these** consequences **are "the wicked man's portion from God."**[12]

Chinuch notes that, due to the repugnance of falsehood, Scripture warns us about it more strongly than about other things, and this serves to explain our mitzvah:

וְעַל כֵּן הִזְהִירָתְנוּ הַתּוֹרָה לְהַרְחִיק מִן הַשֶּׁקֶר הַרְבֵּה — **Therefore, the Torah commands us to distance ourselves exceedingly from falsehood,** כְּמוֹ שֶׁכָּתוּב מִדְּבַר שֶׁקֶר תִּרְחָק — **as it is written** (Exodus 23:7): *Distance yourself from a false word.* וְהִנֵּה הִזְכִּירָה בּוֹ לְשׁוֹן רִחוּק לְרֹב מִאוּסוֹ — **Behold! Due to the extreme repugnance of [falsehood], [the Torah] employs the term** "*distancing*" **regarding it,** מַה שֶּׁלֹּא הִזְכִּירָה כֵּן בְּכָל שְׁאָר הָאַזְהָרוֹת — **which** is an expression that **[the Torah] does not employ in regard to any other injunction.**[13] וּמִצַּד הָרִחוּק — **It is because of this** requirement of *distancing* from falsehood הִזְהִירָתְנוּ שֶׁלֹּא נַטֶּה אָזְנֵנוּ כְּלָל לְשׁוּם דָּבָר שֶׁנַּחְשׁוֹב שֶׁהוּא שֶׁקֶר — **that [the Torah] admonishes us** in the current mitzvah **not to tilt our ears at all to anything that we** *think* **may be false,** וְאַף עַל פִּי שֶׁאֵין אָנוּ יוֹדְעִין (בבירור) [בִּבְרִיאָה][14] שֶׁיְּהֵא אוֹתוֹ הַדָּבָר שֶׁקֶר — **even though we do not know with certainty that it is false.**[15] וּכְעֵין מַה שֶּׁאָמְרוּ זִכְרוֹנָם לִבְרָכָה — **This concept, that we are required to maintain a distance from not only what is clearly false, but even what we suspect may be false, is similar to that which [the Sages], of blessed memory, have stated** (Avos DeRabbi Nassan 2:2, Chullin 44b): הַרְחֵק מִן הַכִּעוּר וּמִן הַדּוֹמֶה לוֹ — **Distance yourself from unseemliness, and from anything resembling it.**[16]

---

### NOTES

11. Scripture states (Psalms 101:7): דֹּבֵר שְׁקָרִים לֹא יִכּוֹן לְנֶגֶד עֵינָי, *one who tells lies shall not be established before My eyes,* which the Gemara (Sanhedrin 102b,103a) understands to mean that liars are in a class of sinners who do not merit to stand before the Divine Presence in the Afterlife.

12. Stylistic citation of Job 20:29. [Actually, as Chinuch has explained, these are the wicked man's portion because he has moved *away* from God.]

13. The Torah generally prohibits things by stating simply "You shall not [do such-and-such]." The only thing from which it commands us to *distance* ourselves is falsehood.

14. Emendation follows numerous manuscript and printed editions; see footnote 5 in the Mechon Yerushalayim edition.

15. This includes, in regard to a judge, listening to the claim of one litigant when his adversary is not present; and in regard to any person, listening to a report of *lashon hara* (see the Insight).

16. The Sages use this expression to teach that one should avoid doing something that is *suggestive* of impropriety, for even if it is technically permissible, people may suspect him of sinning. Chinuch expands it to mean that one should avoid something that *may contain a tinge* of impropriety.

# 70 ❑ משפטים / מצוה עד: שלא לשמע טענת בעל דין שלא בפני בעל דינו

וּבְאָמְרִי[17] מִדּוֹת בְּהַקָּדוֹשׁ בָּרוּךְ הוּא יִתְעַלֶּה, אֲנִי נִמְשָׁךְ בַּדָּבָר אַחַר דִּבְרֵי רַבּוֹתֵינוּ זִכְרוֹנָם לִבְרָכָה שֶׁיִּחֲסוּ אֵלָיו בָּרוּךְ הוּא שֵׁם מִדּוֹת עַל צַד הַמְקַבְּלִים[18], אֲבָל הוּא בָּרוּךְ הוּא לְגָדְלוֹ וְיִחוּדוֹ מִצַּד עַצְמוֹ אֵין לְיַחֵס אֵלָיו מִדּוֹת, כִּי הוּא וְחָכְמָתוֹ וְחֶפְצוֹ וִיכָלְתּוֹ וּמִדּוֹתָיו אֶחָד בְּלִי שׁוּם שִׁתּוּף וּפֵרוּד בָּעוֹלָם[19].

מִדִּינֵי הַמִּצְוָה, מַה שֶּׁאָמְרוּ זִכְרוֹנָם לִבְרָכָה (שבועות דף ל׳ ע״ב) שֶׁכָּל דַּיָּן שֶׁיּוֹדֵעַ בְּדִין שֶׁהוּא מְרֻמֶּה[20] שֶׁחַיָּב לְהִסְתַּלֵּק מִמֶּנּוּ[21], וְלֹא יֹאמַר אֶחְתְּכֶנּוּ וִיהֵא קוֹלָר תָּלוּי בַּצַּוָּאר

---

Having mentioned above the "Attributes" of God, Chinuch digresses to discuss the appropriateness of ascribing human attributes to Him:[17] וּבְאָמְרִי מִדּוֹת בְּהַקָּדוֹשׁ בָּרוּךְ הוּא יִתְעַלֶּה — **When I ascribe "Attributes,"** such as Truth, Mercifulness, and Kindness, **to the Holy One, blessed is He, may He be exalted,** אֲנִי נִמְשָׁךְ בַּדָּבָר אַחַר דִּבְרֵי רַבּוֹתֵינוּ זִכְרוֹנָם לִבְרָכָה — **I am drawn in this matter after the words of our Sages, of blessed memory,** שֶׁיִּחֲסוּ אֵלָיו בָּרוּךְ הוּא שֵׁם מִדּוֹת — **who have ascribed to Him, blessed is He, the designation of Attributes,** עַל צַד הַמְקַבְּלִים — **in accordance with the perspective of the perceivers** of these matters, i.e., human beings who perceive the effects of God's actions.[18] אֲבָל הוּא בָּרוּךְ הוּא לְגָדְלוֹ וְיִחוּדוֹ מִצַּד עַצְמוֹ — **However, with respect to [God], blessed is He, Himself — due to His greatness and His singularity —** אֵין לְיַחֵס אֵלָיו מִדּוֹת — **we cannot ascribe** any **attributes to Him,** כִּי הוּא וְחָכְמָתוֹ וְחֶפְצוֹ וִיכָלְתּוֹ וּמִדּוֹתָיו אֶחָד — **because He, His Wisdom, His Will, His Power, and His Attributes are One,** בְּלִי שׁוּם שִׁתּוּף וּפֵרוּד בָּעוֹלָם — **without any "combination" or "separation" whatsoever.**[19]

## ~ Laws of the Mitzvah ~

מִדִּינֵי הַמִּצְוָה — **The laws of this mitzvah include** מַה שֶּׁאָמְרוּ זִכְרוֹנָם לִבְרָכָה — **what [the Sages], of blessed memory, have said** (*Shevuos* 30b): שֶׁכָּל דַּיָּן שֶׁיּוֹדֵעַ בְּדִין שֶׁהוּא מְרֻמֶּה — **that any judge who is aware that the proceedings** before him **are fraudulent**[20] שֶׁחַיָּב לְהִסְתַּלֵּק מִמֶּנּוּ — **is obligated to withdraw from [the proceedings],**[21] וְלֹא יֹאמַר אֶחְתְּכֶנּוּ וִיהֵא קוֹלָר תָּלוּי בַּצַּוָּאר

---

### NOTES

17. The subject matter discussed by Chinuch in the coming paragraph is extremely profound. *Rambam* (*Hil. Yesodei HaTorah* 2:12) writes in regard to such topics: *These are very deep issues; not all can bear their contemplation.* As such, we will adhere to the most basic explanation of Chinuch's words.

18. When Scripture or the Sages use human attributes to describe Hashem, it is merely to provide a frame of reference through which human beings may comprehend His actions. For example, when Hashem chooses to punish one who is deserving of punishment, it is said that He is a Vengeful God (*Exodus* 20:5, et al.), because that is how we humans perceive His actions. Since we recognize these actions as something *we* would do out of a feeling of vengefulness, we use the term "Vengeful" to describe His attitude in this situation. It does not at all mean that He has, or is motivated by, "feelings" of vengefulness.

19. Attributes, such as kindness and vengefulness, are diverse aspects of the human personality. A human being is composed of many distinct elements and attributes, which combine to form his character and personality, and each of these attributes can be isolated from the others to govern his actions at a given moment. [Thus, he is a product of "combination" and "separation."]

God, however, is not corporeal. It would be sacrilege to impute to Him actual "feelings" such as kindness and vengefulness, for that would imply that He is governed by such feelings and is somehow subject to change based on their influence, which is patently untrue. God is the essence of Oneness; He is absolute and unchanging, and not subject to any of the conflicting emotions of human beings. Rather, any assignment of Attributes to Him is merely an allegorical device to describe His behavior toward the world in language understandable by humans. [See similarly, above, Mitzvah 30 at notes 61-72, and below, Mitzvah 611. For further discussion of this subject, see *Rambam, Hil. Yesodei HaTorah* 1:7-12; and *Chovos HaLevavos, Shaar HaYichud.*]

20. I.e., he discerns from the testimony of the witnesses that they are not being completely truthful, although he cannot prove that this is so (*Rashi, Shevuos* 30b ד״ה שהוא מרומה). See next note.

21. If, even after meticulously examining the witnesses, he is unable to prove that they have lied, yet he believes that they have, or he feels for other reasons that the proceedings are moving forward in an untruthful direction, he must withdraw from judging the case (*Rambam, Hil. Sanhedrin* 24:3).

## 71 ❑ MISHPATIM / MITZVAH 74: LISTENING TO ONE LITIGANT WITHOUT THE OTHER

הָעֵדִים,[22] וְהַשְּׁבָחִים הַגְּדוֹלִים שֶׁמְּשַׁבְּחִים חֲכָמִים בְּבַקָּשַׁת הָאֱמֶת וְהַרְחָקַת הַשֶּׁקֶר בַּדִּין, וְיֶתֶר רֻבֵּי הַפְּרָטִים, מְבֹאָרִים בְּסַנְהֶדְרִין וּבַמִּדְרָשִׁים כְּמוֹ כֵן.[23]

וְנוֹהֶגֶת בְּכָל מָקוֹם וּבְכָל זְמָן,[24] בִּזְכָרִים אֲבָל לֹא בִּנְקֵבוֹת לְפִי שֶׁאֵינָן דָּנוֹת,[25] וּלְכָךְ אֵינָן בִּכְלַל אַזְהָרָה זוֹ שֶׁלֹּא לְקַבֵּל טַעֲנַת בַּעַל דִּין אֶחָד שֶׁלֹּא בִּפְנֵי בַּעַל דִּינוֹ, אֲבָל מִכָּל מָקוֹם בִּכְלַל לָאו זֶה הֵן שֶׁלֹּא יַטְעִימוּ טַעֲנוֹתָן לַדַּיָּן שֶׁלֹּא בִּפְנֵי בַּעַל הַדִּין, וְכֵן מֻזְהָרוֹת לְהַרְחִיק מִכָּל שֶׁקֶר כְּמוֹ הָאֲנָשִׁים.

וְעוֹבֵר עָלֶיהָ הֲרֵי הוּא כְּעוֹבֵר עַל מִצְוַת מֶלֶךְ, אֲבָל אֵין לוֹקִין עַל לָאו זֶה לְפִי שֶׁאֵין בּוֹ מַעֲשֶׂה.[26]

---

הָעֵדִים — **and he may not say,** "Since witnesses have testified to the matter, **I will decide [the case]** in accordance with their testimony, **and the chain** of iniquity **will hang from the necks of the witnesses.**"[22] וְהַשְּׁבָחִים הַגְּדוֹלִים שֶׁמְּשַׁבְּחִים חֲכָמִים — **The great praises with which the Sages praise** בְּבַקָּשַׁת הָאֱמֶת וְהַרְחָקַת הַשֶּׁקֶר בַּדִּין — **the pursuit of truth and the distancing from falsehood in** matters of **justice,** וְיֶתֶר רֻבֵּי הַפְּרָטִים — **as well as the many additional details** of this mitzvah, מְבֹאָרִים בְּסַנְהֶדְרִין וּבַמִּדְרָשִׁים כְּמוֹ כֵן — **are set forth in** Tractate *Sanhedrin*, **as well as in** various **Midrashim.**[23]

### ☞ Applicability of the Mitzvah ☜

בִּזְכָרִים — וְנוֹהֶגֶת בְּכָל מָקוֹם וּבְכָל זְמָן — [This mitzvah] applies in every location and in all times,[24] אֲבָל לֹא בִּנְקֵבוֹת לְפִי שֶׁאֵינָן דָּנוֹת — **to men, but not to women, because** [women] **are not** eligible **to judge.**[25] וּלְכָךְ אֵינָן בִּכְלַל אַזְהָרָה זוֹ — **Hence, [women] are not included in this injunction** שֶׁלֹּא לְקַבֵּל טַעֲנַת בַּעַל דִּין אֶחָד שֶׁלֹּא בִּפְנֵי בַּעַל דִּינוֹ — inasmuch as it relates **to not accepting the claim of one litigant without the presence of his adversary.** אֲבָל מִכָּל מָקוֹם בִּכְלַל לָאו זֶה הֵן — **Nevertheless, [women] are included in this prohibition** שֶׁלֹּא יַטְעִימוּ טַעֲנוֹתָן לַדַּיָּן שֶׁלֹּא בִּפְנֵי בַּעַל הַדִּין — with respect to the law **that they may not present their claims to a judge without the presence of their adversary,** וְכֵן מֻזְהָרוֹת לְהַרְחִיק מִכָּל שֶׁקֶר כְּמוֹ הָאֲנָשִׁים — **and, similarly, they are enjoined to distance themselves from all** matters of **falsehood, just as men** are.

וְעוֹבֵר עָלֶיהָ — **One who transgresses [this mitzvah]** הֲרֵי הוּא כְּעוֹבֵר עַל מִצְוַת מֶלֶךְ — **is considered as one who has violated a command of the King,** אֲבָל אֵין לוֹקִין עַל לָאו זֶה — **but one does not incur *malkus*** (lashes) **for** the violation of **this prohibition,** לְפִי שֶׁאֵין בּוֹ מַעֲשֶׂה — **because it does not involve action.**[26]

---

### NOTES

22. A judge might reason, "Even if it is as I suspect and the witnesses have testified falsely, it is not my concern, as *they* will bear the responsibility for the false judgment" (*Rashi* to *Shevuos* 31a ד"ה קולר). He may not say this; rather, since he suspects that the testimony is tainted, he must withdraw from the case and let another judge — assuming that he is confident in the veracity of the testimony — decide it (*Rambam* ibid.). This is an application of the commandment *Distance yourself from a false word,* which, as Chinuch has explained, obligates us to turn away even from something that we *suspect* is false (*Shevuos* 30b-31a).

23. See *Sanhedrin* 7a-8a; *Devarim Rabbah* 5:1-7; *Tanchuma, Parashas Shoftim* 1-7. The laws are codified in *Rambam, Hil. Sanhedrin* 21:7-11, 23:6-10, 24:3; and *Shulchan Aruch, Choshen Mishpat* 15:3-5, 17:5-9.

24. I.e., in Eretz Yisrael and the Diaspora, and whether the *Beis HaMikdash* is standing or not.

25. See Mitzvah 77, at note 40.

26. See General Introduction, note 14; see also above, end of Mitzvah 9.

---

### ◆§ Insight: Accepting a Report of Lashon Hara

Chinuch states (at note 6) that the prohibition of לֹא תִשָּׂא שֵׁמַע שָׁוְא, *do not issue/accept a false report,* includes an injunction against speaking or accepting *lashon hara* (disparaging speech). In fact, according to some, the prohibition to accept *lashon hara* is the main focus of this verse,

while the prohibition for a judge to hear the claim of one litigant without the other's presence is a secondary derivation (*Smag, Lo Saaseh* 10; see *Mechilta, Mishpatim* §20). It is absolutely clear, though, that even truthful disparaging speech is forbidden as *lashon hara* (*Chafetz Chaim, Hil. Lashon Hara* 1:1). Why, then, is this prohibition phrased specifically in terms of a "false" report, when even an accurate one is considered *lashon hara*?

Some explain that any speech that is forbidden is, by definition, despicable and loathsome, even if it happens to be factually correct. Such dialogue is termed שָׁוְא, *vain*, and שֶׁקֶר, *false*, because of its spiritual repugnance; it is void of any authentic value. Indeed, the word שָׁוְא, translated as "false" in the verse above, can also be translated as "evil" (see *Psalms* 26:4). Such talk is evil, for the Torah forbids us from engaging in it, and from accepting it. It is thus, necessarily, שֵׁמַע שָׁוְא, *a vain* — or *evil* — *report* (*Yad HaKetanah, Hilchos Dei'os* 9:8).

On a simpler level, *Chafetz Chaim* notes that, in reality, most *lashon hara* contains inaccurate information. The Torah, in its understanding of the human psyche, recognizes that when the other party — the alleged wrongdoer — is not present, it is practically impossible that some partial falsehood not be mixed into this report about him. Just as Chinuch writes above that a litigant is likely to speak falsely when his adversary is not present, as he is not embarrassed to lie, so too is it with one who speaks negatively about another. In fact, in the case of *lashon hara*, where the other party is *never* given the opportunity to rebut, the speaker is all the more likely to add falsehoods. Nothing deters him from unabashedly embellishing his story, so as to make it more appealing to his listener (*Chafetz Chaim, Pesichah, Lavin* 2, with *Be'er Mayim Chaim*). The listener must therefore not be naive. He is required to recognize this basic truism and continue to judge the subject of the *lashon hara* favorably. In so doing, he avoids accepting the disparaging report. And additionally, he fulfills the dictum of דָּן לְכַף זְכוּת, *judging one's fellow to the side of merit* [Mitzvah 235] (*Chafetz Chaim, Hil. Lashon Hara* 6:7-8).

It should be noted, however, that this refers to *accepting* the disparaging report, i.e., *believing* it fully. One is categorically prohibited to accept *lashon hara* as true; one must, in his mind, always question the veracity of the report, or at least retain an open mind as to the possibility that there were mitigating circumstances (*Chafetz Chaim* ibid. 6:1, 6:7-8; see also below, Mitzvah 75 note 1). With respect to *listening* to *lashon hara*, the prohibition is qualified. To be sure, the verse *Do not accept a false report* prohibits a judge even to *listen* to one litigant without the presence of the other, because this may lead him to believe the person's lies (see note 3) — and likewise, it is prohibited for anyone to even listen to a disparaging report about another (*Chafetz Chaim* ibid. 6:2). There is, however, a permit to listen to the report if one anticipates that it will contain information that may prove useful to him, as long as he does not fully *believe* the disparaging information, but merely adopts a cautious attitude. For example, one who is considering entering a business partnership with another is allowed to inquire about that person's integrity, and one who is contemplating marriage may inquire about the prospective spouse's character. Any negative information that one hears, however, may not be accepted as *definitely* true, and may be relied upon merely to protect oneself (ibid. 6:3).

Refusing to consider even the possibility that a report is true is sometimes not only foolhardy but halachically wrong. A classic example of this is recorded in *Jeremiah*, Chapters 40-41. After the destruction of the First Temple, the king of Babylonia appointed a righteous Jew, Gedaliah ben Ahikam, governor of the remnant Jews who had not been exiled from Eretz Yisrael. Scripture relates that an assassination plot was hatched against Gedaliah by certain prominent people, and he was alerted to the plot by one of his confidants. Deeming this report to be *lashon hara*, Gedaliah told the speaker (ibid. 40:16): *you are speaking falsely!* — and he neglected to protect himself. The report, however, proved to be true, and the plot was successfully carried out, resulting in the death of Gedaliah and many others. This, in turn, led to the extinguishing of the last vestige of Jewish life in Eretz Yisrael, which is why we observe the Fast of Gedaliah on the third day of Tishrei, the anniversary of Gedaliah's assasination (*Rambam, Hil. Taaniyos* 5:2). Remarkably, our Sages (*Niddah* 61a) lay the blame for all those deaths on Gedaliah himself, for failing to consider even the *possibility* that the report of a plot against him was true. As the Gemara (ibid.) states, although one is prohibited to *accept* — i.e., fully believe — a disparaging report, one is required to harbor a healthy wariness about it, to the extent that this enables him to protect himself or others from harm (see *Tosafos* there ד"ה אטמרינכו).

Nevertheless, even when adopting a wary and self-protective attitude, one must be careful to

continue to confer upon the subject of the *lashon hara* the same esteem, and behave with him in the same fashion, as he was required to do before having heard the report. The alleged wrongdoer has in no way lost his חֶזְקַת כַּשְׁרוּת, *presumption of innocence,* and therefore (appropriate wariness aside), he must be afforded the same rights and dignity that were his due all along (*Chafetz Chaim* ibid. 6:10). The information is, after all, hearsay, and as explained above, has the very real chance of being nothing more than a "false report."

## מִצְוָה עה: שֶׁלֹּא יָעִיד בַּעַל עֲבֵרָה

שֶׁלֹּא נְקַבֵּל עֵדוּת אִישׁ חוֹטֵא וְלֹא נַעֲשֶׂה בִּשְׁבִיל עֵדוּתוֹ שׁוּם דָּבָר[1], שֶׁנֶּאֱמַר (שמות כ״ג, א׳) אַל תָּשֶׁת יָדְךָ עִם רָשָׁע לִהְיוֹת עֵד חָמָס, וּבָא הַפֵּרוּשׁ אַל תָּשֶׁת רָשָׁע עֵד, אַל תָּשֶׁת חָמָס עֵד, כְּלוֹמַר בַּעַל חָמָס[2], לְהוֹצִיא אֶת הַחַמְסָנִין וְאֶת הַגַּזְלָנִין[3] שֶׁהֵם פְּסוּלִין לְעֵדוּת,

## ~ Mitzvah 75 ~
## The Prohibition to Allow a Sinner to Testify

אַל תָּשֶׁת יָדְךָ עִם רָשָׁע לִהְיוֹת עֵד חָמָס
*Do not place your hand with the wicked to be a corrupt witness (Exodus 23:1).*

שֶׁלֹּא נְקַבֵּל עֵדוּת אִישׁ חוֹטֵא — **We are commanded that we** (i.e., *beis din*) **shall not accept the testimony of a man who is a sinner** וְלֹא נַעֲשֶׂה בִּשְׁבִיל עֵדוּתוֹ שׁוּם דָּבָר — **and shall not take any action whatsoever on account of his testimony,**[1] שֶׁנֶּאֱמַר — **as it is stated** (*Exodus* 23:1): "אַל תָּשֶׁת יָדְךָ עִם רָשָׁע לִהְיוֹת עֵד חָמָס" — *Do not place your hand with the wicked to be a corrupt witness.*

Chinuch explains how this prohibition is derived from the verse:

וּבָא הַפֵּרוּשׁ — **The explanation** of this verse, **as transmitted** to us by the Sages (*Mechilta* to the verse) is that it instructs us: אַל תָּשֶׁת רָשָׁע עֵד — **Do not place a wicked person as a witness** אַל תָּשֶׁת חָמָס עֵד — **that is to say, a corrupt individual.**[2] לְהוֹצִיא אֶת הַחַמְסָנִין וְאֶת הַגַּזְלָנִין — **The verse comes to exclude extortionists and robbers** from testifying,[3] שֶׁהֵם פְּסוּלִין לְעֵדוּת — meaning **that they are** *disqualified* from

---

### NOTES

1. "Accepting" a sinner's testimony refers to believing it and acting on it. Thus, the prohibition here is for *beis din* to issue a ruling that has been impacted by the testimony of a sinner (*Minchas Yitzchak* §10; see similarly, *Chafetz Chaim, Hil. Lashon Hara* 6:1, cited in the Insight to Mitzvah 74). It is quite clear from Chinuch's language at the end of this mitzvah (at note 33) that *beis din* transgresses only by acting (i.e., issuing a ruling) on the testimony of a sinner, not by merely *listening* to him. This is also evident from Chinuch below, in Mitzvah 589 (the prohibition to allow a relative of a litigant to testify). [*Rambam*, in setting down this law (*Hil. Eidus* 10:1), states simply that a sinner is *disqualified* from testifying, which means that his testimony is inadmissible in *beis din* and cannot be relied upon.]

2. The verse could have been understood as a warning against lending one's hand *to* a wicked person by testifying falsely on his behalf (see *Onkelos* ad loc.). *Mechilta* teaches that this is not the verse's intention. [Testifying falsely is prohibited under Mitzvah 37.] Rather, the verse means to warn *beis din* not to validate testimony *by* a wicked person or a corrupt person (*Malbim* ad loc.). [The verse is understood as saying two things: (1) Do not place your hand with a wicked person, and (2) do not place your hand with a corrupt witness (see *Yad Ramah, Sanhedrin* 27a ד״ה מתיבי).] By accepting testimony from either of these people, *beis din* "places its hand" (i.e., collaborates) with them in carrying out an injustice.]

In this context, a "wicked" person is an individual who has intentionally transgressed any Biblical prohibition that carries the penalty of *malkus* [e.g., eating nonkosher food] or the penalty of death [e.g., desecrating the Sabbath] (see *Sanhedrin* 27a; *Rambam* ibid. §3). The rationale for this person's disqualification will be discussed in note 5.

A "corrupt" individual refers to one who is guilty of financial wrongdoing; he is disqualified even though his crime does not carry corporal punishment. [The word חָמָס, which we have translated as *corruption,* refers to obtaining property through illicit means, whether outright robbery, or extortion, or coercion (see Mitzvah 38).] Anyone who has committed a crime of חָמָס, meaning that he has gained money through corrupt means, is disqualified from testifying. His testimony is deemed unreliable, for since he has demonstrated a tendency to transgress for monetary gain, he might also testify falsely for profit (see *Sanhedrin* 27a; *Rambam, Hil. Eidus* 10:4; *Minchas Chinuch* §2 ד״ה רשעים).

In sum, the verse disqualifies two categories of sinners from testifying in *beis din*: (1) A "wicked" person, referring to a transgressor of a Biblical prohibition, as above; and (2) a "corrupt" person, referring to one who has obtained money through illicit means (*Rambam* ibid. 10:2-5).

3. *Gra* emends the text of *Mechilta* to read אֶת לְהוֹצִיא הָרְשָׁעִים וְאֶת הַחַמְסָנִין, *to exclude wicked and corrupt individuals.* This fits with *Mechilta's* initial exposition of the verse as prohibiting us from placing either a רָשָׁע, *wicked individual,* or a בַּעַל חָמָס, *corrupt individual,* as a witness.

## 75 □ MISHPATIM / MITZVAH 75: THE PROHIBITION TO ALLOW A SINNER TO TESTIFY

שֶׁנֶּאֱמַר (דברים י״ט, ט״ז) (לֹא) [כִּי] יָקוּם עֵד חָמָס בְּאִישׁ.[4]

שֹׁרֶשׁ מִצְוָה זוֹ נִגְלֶה, שֶׁכָּל מִי שֶׁעַל עַצְמוֹ לֹא חָס וְלֹא יָחוּשׁ עַל מַעֲשָׂיו הָרָעִים, לֹא יָחוּשׁ עַל אֲחֵרִים, וְעַל כֵּן אֵין רָאוּי לְהַאֲמִינוֹ בַּדָּבָר.[5]

מִדִּינֵי הַמִּצְוָה, מַה שֶּׁאָמְרוּ זִכְרוֹנָם לִבְרָכָה שֶׁעֲשָׂרָה הֵם הַפְּסוּלִין לְעֵדוּת מִן הַתּוֹרָה, וְאֵלּוּ הֵן,[6] נָשִׁים וַעֲבָדִים וּקְטַנִּים[7] חֵרְשִׁים[8] שׁוֹטִים סוּמִים[9] רְשָׁעִים[10] וַאֲנָשִׁים

---

serving **as witnesses.** שֶׁנֶּאֱמַר — This emerges also from another verse, **as it is stated** (*Deuteronomy* 19:16): (לֹא) [כִּי] יָקוּם עֵד חָמָס בְּאִישׁ — **If a corrupt witness stands against a man** to testify spuriously against him.[4]

### ☞ Underlying Purpose of the Mitzvah ☜

שֹׁרֶשׁ מִצְוָה זוֹ נִגְלֶה — **The underlying purpose of this mitzvah is obvious,** שֶׁכָּל מִי שֶׁעַל עַצְמוֹ לֹא חָס — **for anyone who does not care about his own well-being,** וְלֹא יָחוּשׁ עַל מַעֲשָׂיו הָרָעִים — **and** therefore **does not concern himself regarding his evil deeds,** לֹא יָחוּשׁ עַל אֲחֵרִים — **will** certainly **not concern himself with** the well-being **of others,** וְעַל כֵּן אֵין רָאוּי לְהַאֲמִינוֹ בַּדָּבָר — **and it is therefore inappropriate** for us **to trust him regarding anything** of consequence.[5]

### ☞ Laws of the Mitzvah ☜

מִדִּינֵי הַמִּצְוָה — **Among the laws of the mitzvah** מַה שֶּׁאָמְרוּ זִכְרוֹנָם לִבְרָכָה — **is that which [the Sages], of blessed memory, have stated** (see *Rambam, Hil. Eidus* 9:1), שֶׁעֲשָׂרָה הֵם הַפְּסוּלִין לְעֵדוּת מִן הַתּוֹרָה — **that there are ten** individuals **who are disqualified from testifying under Biblical law,** וְאֵלּוּ הֵן — **and they are the following:**[6] נָשִׁים וַעֲבָדִים וּקְטַנִּים — (1) **Women,** (2) **Canaanite slaves, and** (3) **minors,**[7] חֵרְשִׁים — (4) **deaf or mute individuals,**[8] שׁוֹטִים — (5) **mentally**

---

### NOTES

4. This verse states clearly that an עֵד חָמָס, *corrupt witness*, is a type of person who would testify spuriously against his fellow. As mentioned, this refers to one who is guilty of financial wrongdoing. See *Shevus Yehudah* to *Mechilta* for further discussion.

5. With this explanation, Chinuch provides the rationale for disqualifying all types of evildoers, whether they are guilty of financial wrongdoing or of transgressing a general prohibition. Their disqualification is rooted in the cavalier attitude that is evidenced by their misdeeds, so the particular *type* of misdeed is of no moment.

It emerges from Chinuch's explanation that *all* sinners are disqualified because they are deemed untrustworthy (see also *Urim VeTumim, Urim* 28:3, and *Imrei Binah, Eidus* §31). Others maintain that only "corrupt" individuals — i.e., those whose misdeeds are of a financial nature — are disqualified on account of suspicion. "Wicked" individuals — i.e., those who committed sins of a general nature — are not suspect to testify falsely, since they may have sinned for personal gratification and not for monetary gain. Nevertheless, the Torah has decreed that they be disqualified (see *Tosafos, Bechoros* 36a ד״ה אימר; *Ketzos HaChoshen* 46:17; *Gevuras Ari, Makkos* 5b ד״ה אף ג׳; *Minchas Chinuch* §2 ד״ה רשעים, and above, 37:16; for further discussion, see *Maharam Schik* above, 37:5-6).

6. While the specific topic of this mitzvah is the prohibition to accept the testimony of a sinner, Chinuch utilizes this opportunity to discuss all the individuals who are disqualified from testifying. Indeed, one of the categories listed by Chinuch here, namely that of relatives, is the subject of an independent prohibition (Mitzvah 589). *Rambam* lists these ten individuals in *Hil. Eidus* 9:1 and elaborates the details of these disqualifications in Chapters 9-16 there.

[Regarding Chinuch's statement that all ten individuals he will list are disqualified under *Biblical* law, see note 11.]

7. Women and minors are excluded by the verse (*Deuteronomy* 19:17): וְעָמְדוּ שְׁנֵי הָאֲנָשִׁים, *The two **men** shall stand*, etc. (*Shevuos* 30a, *Bava Basra* 155b). The disqualification of a Canaanite slave is derived through exegesis (see *Bava Kamma* 88a; see further *Minchas Chinuch* §2).

[Women certainly have the *credibility* to serve as witnesses, even regarding matters that involve a potential death penalty. Their testimony is accepted regarding אִסּוּרִים (matters of ritual law), such as *niddah*, the kosher or nonkosher status of a food, or that a man has died and his wife may remarry (see below, Mitzvah 523; *Rambam, Hil. Geirushin* 12:15; *Tosafos, Gittin* 2b ד״ה עד אחד). See Mitzvah 37, with note 17 there, for explanation of why the Torah excludes them from testifying in monetary or criminal cases.]

8. Although the term חֵרֵשׁ generally refers to one who is deaf *and* mute, in the context of this mitzvah it refers

## משפטים / מצוה עה: שלא יעיד בעל עברה

הַבְּזוּיִין בְּיוֹתֵר[11] וּקְרוֹבִים[12] וְנוֹגְעִים בָּעֵדוּת, הֲרֵי אֵלּוּ עֲשָׂרָה. וְטֻמְטוּם וְאַנְדְּרוֹגִינוֹס[13] בִּכְלַל נָשִׁים[14], וּמִי שֶׁחֶצְיוֹ עֶבֶד[15] בִּכְלַל עֲבָדִים[16], הַנִּכְפֶּה בְּעֵת כְּפִיָּתוֹ בִּכְלַל שׁוֹטֶה, וְגַם שֶׁלֹּא בְּעֵת כְּפִיָּתוֹ צָרִיךְ הַדַּיָּן לְהִתְיַשֵּׁב בַּדָּבָר אִם דַּעְתּוֹ מְבֻלְבֶּלֶת מִצַּד הַחֹלִי[17], וְכֵן הַפְּתָאִים בְּיוֹתֵר

**רְשָׁעִים** — (7) **wicked individuals,**[10] **סוּמִים** — (6) **blind individuals,**[9] **deficient individuals, וַאֲנָשִׁים הַבְּזוּיִין בְּיוֹתֵר** — (8) **exceedingly lowly individuals,**[11] **וּקְרוֹבִים** — (9) **relatives** of the litigants,[12] **וְנוֹגְעִים בָּעֵדוּת** — (10) **and those who have** a personal **interest in the** matter for which they seek to give **testimony. הֲרֵי אֵלּוּ עֲשָׂרָה** — **These are** a total of **ten** categories of disqualified individuals.

Chinuch elaborates, expanding on some of these categories: **וְטֻמְטוּם וְאַנְדְּרוֹגִינוֹס** — **A** *tumtum* **and an** *androginos*[13] **בִּכְלַל נָשִׁים** — **are included in the category of women** in regard to this disqualification.[14] **וּמִי שֶׁחֶצְיוֹ עֶבֶד** — **One who is half slave and half freeman**[15] **בִּכְלַל עֲבָדִים** — **is included in the category of slaves.**[16] **הַנִּכְפֶּה בְּעֵת כְּפִיָּתוֹ** — **An epileptic, while experiencing a seizure, בִּכְלַל שׁוֹטֶה** — **is included in the category of the mentally deficient; וְגַם שֶׁלֹּא בְּעֵת כְּפִיָּתוֹ** — **and even if he testifies when he is not experiencing a seizure, צָרִיךְ הַדַּיָּן לְהִתְיַשֵּׁב בַּדָּבָר** — **the judge is required to analyze the situation,** in order to ascertain **אִם דַּעְתּוֹ מְבֻלְבֶּלֶת מִצַּד הַחֹלִי** — **whether he is confused as a result of his condition** and is therefore an unreliable witness, or he is of sound mind and thus credible.[17] **וְכֵן הַפְּתָאִים בְּיוֹתֵר** — **Similarly, those who are exceedingly dimwitted,**

---

### NOTES

to anyone who is deaf *or* mute. A mute person is unfit because a witness must be fit to testify orally (not in writing), and a deaf person is unfit because the witness must be fit to hear the judges' interrogation and their warnings against testifying falsely (*Rambam, Hil. Eidus* 9:11; for discussion, see *Minchas Chinuch* §2 ד"ה החרש).

9. A blind person is disqualified from testifying even on the basis of voice recognition, because the Torah (*Leviticus* 5:1) indicates that only one who is able to see may serve as a witness (*Rambam* ibid. 9:12).

10. The disqualification of a wicked person is the focus of our mitzvah. As explained in note 2, there are two types of individuals included in this category: (1) anyone guilty of transgressing a Biblical prohibition that carries the penalty of *malkus* or death; (2) anyone guilty of financial wrongdoing.

11. Such as one who eats before the entire public as he walks in the marketplace, or one who engages in filthy work outdoors while unclothed, for such actions indicate that the person has no shame. The Sages disqualified this type of individual from testifying because he obviously lacks the sense of personal dignity that provides a natural barrier against perjury (*Rambam* ibid. 11:5; *Rashi, Kiddushin* 40b ד"ה ופסול לעדות).

*Minchas Chinuch* §1 notes that there is a difficulty with Chinuch's statement above that the ten individuals listed here are disqualified under *Biblical* law, for "exceedingly lowly individuals" are disqualified only by Rabbinic decree [as Chinuch himself states explicitly in Mitzvah 122 (at note 32)]. It seems, however, from Chinuch's presentation of this law in Mitzvah 122, that these "exceedingly lowly" individuals are not a completely new category of disqualified people, but are actually likened by Rabbinic decree to "sinners," inasmuch as they demonstrate a dearth of scruples. See *Minchas Soless* §2 for another explanation.

12. [Or, witnesses who are related to one another, or to one of the judges (*Shulchan Aruch, Choshen Mishpat* 33:17).] It should be noted that relatives are disqualified not because they are suspect of lying on behalf of their kin, but by Scriptural decree. Hence, one may not testify even *against* his relative (*Rambam* ibid. 13:15). This is the subject of Mitzvah 589.

13. A *tumtum* is one whose gender cannot be ascertained. An *androginos* (hermaphrodite) is a person that possesses signs of both genders. Both of these individuals are halachically deemed to be of indeterminate gender (see *Bikkurim* Ch. 4).

14. Since there is a possibility that they have the halachic status of women, their testimony is of questionable validity. Thus, *beis din* cannot exact money from a litigant, or punish an accused, on the basis of their testimony (*Rambam* ibid. 9:3; see, however, *Minchas Chinuch* §2 ד"ה טומטום וד"ה ומה).

15. E.g., a Canaanite slave was initially owned by two partners and *one* of them emancipated his share. Hence, the other partner still owns half of him, but the remaining half is free (*Rashi* to *Gittin* 41a).

16. Since the half of him that is enslaved is unfit to testify, he cannot testify at all (*Rambam* ibid. 9:5 with *Kesef Mishneh*; see *Minchas Chinuch* §2 ד"ה ומי שחציו עבד).

17. *Rambam* ibid. 9:9.

## MISHPATIM / MITZVAH 75: THE PROHIBITION TO ALLOW A SINNER TO TESTIFY

שֶׁאֵינָם מְבִינִין דְּבָרִים הַסּוֹתְרִין זֶה אֶת זֶה, וְכֵן אֲנָשִׁים מְבֹהָלִים וְנֶחְפָּזִים בְּדַעְתָּן וּמִשְׁתַּגְּעִין בְּיוֹתֵר, כָּל אֵלּוּ בִּכְלַל שׁוֹטִים[18]. וְכֵן מַה שֶּׁאָמְרוּ זִכְרוֹנָם לִבְרָכָה (סנהדרין דף כ״ד ע״ב) אֵי זֶהוּ הַנִּקְרָא רָשָׁע שֶׁפָּסוּל מִן הַתּוֹרָה, וְאֵי זֶהוּ רָשָׁע שֶׁפָּסוּל מִדִּבְרֵיהֶם, כְּגוֹן הָעוֹבֵר עַל גֶּזֶל שֶׁל דִּבְרֵיהֶם[19], שֶׁהוּא פָּסוּל מִדִּבְרֵיהֶם[20], וּמִכְּלָלָם הוּא מְשַׂחֵק בְּקֻבְיָא שֶׁאֵין לוֹ אֻמָּנוּת אֶלָּא הוּא[21], וּמַפְרִיחֵי יוֹנִים בְּיִשּׁוּב[22], וּמְגַדְּלֵי בְהֵמָה דַקָּה[23].

---

שֶׁאֵינָם מְבִינִין דְּבָרִים הַסּוֹתְרִין זֶה אֶת זֶה — **such that they are unable to discern issues that contradict each other**, וְכֵן אֲנָשִׁים מְבֹהָלִים וְנֶחְפָּזִים בְּדַעְתָּן — **as well as those who have a neurotic or reckless nature**, וּמִשְׁתַּגְּעִין בְּיוֹתֵר — **and those who act** in an **exceedingly foolish** manner, כָּל אֵלּוּ בִּכְלַל שׁוֹטִים — **all of these are included in** the category of **the mentally deficient**.[18]

Chinuch notes that aside from those disqualified from testifying by Biblical law, some individuals are disqualified by Rabbinic decree:

וְכֵן מַה שֶּׁאָמְרוּ זִכְרוֹנָם לִבְרָכָה — **Also** included in the laws of this mitzvah **is that which [the Sages]**, of blessed memory, said (*Sanhedrin* 25b; *Rambam* ibid. 10:3-4) when they described for us אֵי זֶהוּ הַנִּקְרָא רָשָׁע שֶׁפָּסוּל מִן הַתּוֹרָה — **which** individual **is the one who is classified as a "wicked person" who is disqualified** from testifying **Biblically**, וְאֵי זֶהוּ רָשָׁע שֶׁפָּסוּל מִדִּבְרֵיהֶם — **and which** is the one who is classified as a **"wicked person" who is disqualified by decree of [the Sages]**. כְּגוֹן — An **example** of the latter is הָעוֹבֵר עַל גֶּזֶל שֶׁל דִּבְרֵיהֶם — **one who transgresses a Rabbinic** prohibition of **theft**, i.e., he commits an act that is not prohibited Biblically but is considered theft under Rabbinic law,[19] שֶׁהוּא פָּסוּל מִדִּבְרֵיהֶם — **such that he is disqualified** from testifying **by [Rabbinic] decree**.[20] וּמִכְּלָלָם הוּא — **Among those also included in [this group] are:** מְשַׂחֵק בְּקֻבְיָא — **One who plays with dice**, שֶׁאֵין לוֹ אֻמָּנוּת אֶלָּא הוּא — **provided that he has no occupation other than this**;[21] וּמַפְרִיחֵי יוֹנִים בְּיִשּׁוּב — **those who engage in pigeon-flying in a settled area**;[22] וּמְגַדְּלֵי בְהֵמָה דַקָּה — **and those who raise small domestic animals**.[23]

---

### NOTES

18. *Rambam* (ibid. 9:10) writes in regard to this last group (exceedingly dimwitted, etc.) that their fitness to testify is up to the discretion of the judge, who must decide on a case-by-case basis who is of sufficiently sound mind to be a credible witness, and who is not. It is impossible to establish precise guidelines for such a matter.

19. For example, he seizes an object from a minor who found it. The minor cannot acquire legal ownership of an abandoned object under Biblical law, but the Sages considered the one who grabs it from him as a robber (*Sanhedrin* 25b).

20. Since his passion for profit has led him to transgress Rabbinic law, the Sages consider him suspect to testify falsely for pay (*Rashi, Sanhedrin* 25b סוף ד״ה סוף ו(ד״ה פסלינהו).

21. One who bets on dice or engages in other forms of gambling keeps winnings that may not have been willingly surrendered to him (since the loser, when agreeing to the wager, might not have seriously considered the possibility that he would lose). There is therefore an element of theft involved in keeping these winnings, and the gambler is considered a thief by Rabbinic law (see *Sanhedrin* 24b with *Rashi* ד״ה אסמכתא; *Rambam*, *Hil. Gezeilah VaAveidah* 6:10).

Since gambling for money involves Rabbinic theft, one who engages in this practice is automatically disqualified by Rabbinic decree from testifying. If, however, the person is not known to gamble for *money*, but is known to spend time playing games such as dice that *often* involve taking winnings from others, then his law varies: If he has another occupation that provides him income, then (until we know otherwise) we assume that he plays merely for entertainment, and he remains fit to testify. But if he has no other occupation, then we assume he is gambling for profit, and he is disqualified from testifying (*Rambam, Hil. Eidus* 10:4, as explained by *Kesef Mishneh*; for other explanations, see *Lechem Mishneh* there and *Chasdei David* to *Tosefta Sanhedrin* 5:2).

22. This refers to a pigeon-decoyer who, by various methods, lures pigeons into his own cote. It is permissible to do this in the wild, but when performed in a settled neighborhood it involves an element of theft, since pigeons from neighboring cotes might be lured into one's own. This practice does not constitute Biblically prohibited theft, because nobody truly "owns" free-flying pigeons (see *Aruch HaShulchan, Choshen Mishpat* 370:2). Once they settled in another's cote, however, taking them is forbidden by Rabbinic decree, so a pigeon-decoyer is Rabbinically disqualified from testifying (*Sanhedrin* 25a; *Rambam* ibid., as explained by *Kesef Mishneh*).

23. Those who raise small animals such as sheep and goats are disqualified because these animals often escape their enclosures and graze in fields that belong

וְהַחִלּוּק שֶׁהוּא בֵּין פָּסוּל מִדְּאוֹרַיְתָא לְפָסוּל מִדִּבְרֵיהֶם, שֶׁבַּפָּסוּל מִן הַתּוֹרָה אָמְרוּ זִכְרוֹנָם לִבְרָכָה (שם דף כ"ו ע"ב) הֵעִיד, עֵדוּתוֹ בְּטֵלָה אֲפִלּוּ קֹדֶם שֶׁהִכְרִיזוּ עָלָיו,[24] וְהַפָּסוּל דְּרַבָּנָן עֵדוּתוֹ קַיֶּמֶת עַד שֶׁיַּכְרִיזוּ עָלָיו.[25] וְאֵי זוֹ תְּשׁוּבָה מַחֲזִירוֹ לְכַשְׁרוּתוֹ, וְהוּא כְּמוֹ שֶׁאָמַר רַב אִידִי בְּפֶרֶק זֶה בּוֹרֵר (שם דף כ"ה ע"א) דְּאָמַר רַב אִידִי בֶּן אָבִין, הֶחָשׁוּד עַל הַטְּרֵפוֹת[26] אֵינוֹ יוֹצֵא מֵחֶזְקָתוֹ עַד שֶׁיֵּלֵךְ לְמָקוֹם שֶׁאֵין מַכִּירִין אוֹתוֹ וְיַחֲזִיר אֲבֵדָה בְּדָבָר חָשׁוּב

---

Chinuch notes a difference in law between those disqualified from testifying Biblically and those disqualified Rabbinically:

וְהַחִלּוּק שֶׁהוּא בֵּין פָּסוּל מִדְּאוֹרַיְתָא לְפָסוּל מִדִּבְרֵיהֶם — **Also** included in these laws **is the** halachic **difference that exists between one who is disqualified** from testifying **by Biblical law and one who is disqualified by Rabbinic law.** What is this difference? שֶׁבַּפָּסוּל מִן הַתּוֹרָה אָמְרוּ זִכְרוֹנָם לִבְרָכָה — **In regard to one who is disqualified by Biblical law, [the Sages], of blessed memory, have said** (Sanhedrin 26b) הֵעִיד עֵדוּתוֹ בְּטֵלָה — that if **he testified** after committing the act for which he became disqualified, **his testimony is deemed null** and void אֲפִלּוּ קֹדֶם שֶׁהִכְרִיזוּ עָלָיו — **even** if he submitted the testimony **before [beis din] issued a proclamation about him** having been disqualified.[24] וְהַפָּסוּל דְּרַבָּנָן — **However,** in regard to **one who is disqualified by Rabbinic law,** if he testified after committing the disqualifying act but before his disqualification was publicized, עֵדוּתוֹ קַיֶּמֶת עַד שֶׁיַּכְרִיזוּ עָלָיו — **his testimony stands,** for he remains fit to testify **until such time as [beis din] issues a proclamation about him** having been disqualified.[25]

Chinuch discusses how an individual disqualified on account of wrongdoing can regain his qualification:

וְאֵי זוֹ תְּשׁוּבָה מַחֲזִירוֹ לְכַשְׁרוּתוֹ — **Also** included are the details as to **what form of repentance restores [the sinner] to his** original status of **being qualified** to act as a witness. וְהוּא כְּמוֹ שֶׁאָמַר רַב אִידִי בְּפֶרֶק זֶה בּוֹרֵר — **In this, the law is as stated by Rav Idi in** Tractate Sanhedrin, **Chapter Zeh Borer** (Ch. 3; 25a), דְּאָמַר רַב אִידִי בֶּן אָבִין — **for Rav Idi ben Avin said:** הֶחָשׁוּד עַל הַטְּרֵפוֹת — **One who is suspect of** dispensing meat of tereifah [animals] under the guise of kosher meat, and who is thus disqualified from testifying,[26] אֵינוֹ יוֹצֵא מֵחֶזְקָתוֹ — **does not lose his** chazakah (i.e., established status) of being presumed a sinner עַד שֶׁיֵּלֵךְ לְמָקוֹם שֶׁאֵין מַכִּירִין אוֹתוֹ — **until he travels to a locale where no one recognizes him,** וְיַחֲזִיר אֲבֵדָה בְּדָבָר חָשׁוּב — **and,** when the

---

NOTES

to others (Sanhedrin 25b with Rashi ד"ה מגדלין אתמר). Rambam (ibid.) explains that this disqualification pertains specifically to one who raises small animals in the settled areas of Eretz Yisrael. Since the person does not intentionally send them to graze in others' fields, Biblically he is not considered a thief. However, the Sages prohibited raising these animals in settled parts of Eretz Yisrael (Mishnah, Bava Kamma 79b; Rambam, Hil. Nizkei Mamon 5:2). One who violates this Rabbinic decree, and thus flouts Rabbinic law for profit, is disqualified from testifying. If one knowingly lets his animals graze in others' fields, he is disqualified in any event — whether they are small beasts or large ones, and whether he does this in Eretz Yisrael or elsewhere (Sanhedrin ibid., Rambam, Hil. Eidus ibid.).

24. When one is found to be disqualified from giving testimony, beis din issues a proclamation to this effect, so that people should not unwittingly rely on him to witness transactions (see Sanhedrin 26b). If the disqualification stems from a violation of Biblical law, the disqualified individual's testimony is deemed worthless retroactive to the time of the transgression that caused him to be disqualified — regardless of whether a proclamation to this effect was issued or not (Rambam ibid. 10:4, 11:6).

25. Although the Sages decreed that certain violators of Rabbinic law be disqualified, they were concerned about causing losses to people who, unaware of these violators' misdeeds, had unwittingly relied on them to witness transactions. The Sages therefore stated that the Rabbinic disqualifications do not take effect until they have been publicized by beis din, and any testimony that the violator submits prior to the proclamation remains valid (Rambam ibid.).

For another difference between the Biblical disqualifications and the Rabbinic ones, see the Insight.

26. A tereifah is an animal or bird possessing one of a defined group of fatal defects; the Torah forbids consumption of its meat (see Mitzvah 73). A person who sells tereifah meat to unsuspecting Jews under the guise of kosher meat has, by causing others to sin, violated Biblical law for profit, and is deemed untrustworthy (Sma, Choshen Mishpat 34:16; see Kesef Mishneh, Hil. Eidus 12:9).

## 79 ☐ MISHPATIM / MITZVAH 75: THE PROHIBITION TO ALLOW A SINNER TO TESTIFY

אוֹ יוֹצִיא טְרֵפָה מִתַּחַת יָדוֹ בְּדָבָר חָשׁוּב וּמְשֶׁלּוֹ[27], וּכְמוֹ כֵן נֹאמַר בֶּחָשׁוּד עַל עֲבֵרָה אַחֶרֶת לְפִי הַדּוּמֶה[28], וְיֶתֶר פְּרָטֶיהָ מְבֹאָרִים שָׁם בְּסַנְהֶדְרִין[29].

וְנוֹהֶגֶת מִצְוָה זוֹ בְּכָל מָקוֹם וּבְכָל זְמַן[30], בִּזְכָרִים אֲבָל לֹא בְּנָשִׁים, שֶׁאֵין דָּנוֹת[31] שֶׁיִּצְטָרְכוּ לְקַבֵּל עֵדוּת[32].

וְעוֹבֵר עָלֶיהָ וְקִבֵּל עֵדוּת אִישׁ רָשָׁע וְעָשָׂה דָבָר בִּשְׁבִיל עֵדוּתוֹ[33], עָבַר עַל לָאו[34],

opportunity presents itself, **returns a lost object of considerable value** to its owner, **אוֹ יוֹצִיא טְרֵפָה מִתַּחַת יָדוֹ בְּדָבָר חָשׁוּב וּמְשֶׁלּוֹ** — **or,** alternatively, **he is found to discard his own** *tereifah* **meat of considerable value,** thereby voluntarily suffering financial loss to avoid a transgression.[27] **וּכְמוֹ כֵן נֹאמַר בֶּחָשׁוּד עַל עֲבֵרָה אַחֶרֶת לְפִי הַדּוּמֶה** — **We apply similar** guidelines **regarding one who is suspect of** any **other transgression, as seems** appropriate for each situation.[28] **וְיֶתֶר פְּרָטֶיהָ מְבֹאָרִים שָׁם בְּסַנְהֶדְרִין** — **The additional details of [this mitzvah] are elaborated in** *Sanhedrin* ibid. (Ch. 3; 24b-27b).[29]

### ⁍ Applicability of the Mitzvah ⁌

**וְנוֹהֶגֶת מִצְוָה זוֹ בְּכָל מָקוֹם וּבְכָל זְמַן** — **[This mitzvah] applies in every location and in all times,**[30] **בִּזְכָרִים אֲבָל לֹא בְּנָשִׁים** — and is applicable **to men, but not to women, שֶׁאֵין דָּנוֹת שֶׁיִּצְטָרְכוּ לְקַבֵּל עֵדוּת** — as [women] are not eligible **to judge,**[31] so it will not occur **that they should** ever **need to accept testimony.**[32] **וְעוֹבֵר עָלֶיהָ** — **[A judge] who transgresses [this mitzvah] וְקִבֵּל עֵדוּת אִישׁ רָשָׁע** — **and accepts the testimony of an individual who is a sinner וְעָשָׂה דָבָר בִּשְׁבִיל עֵדוּתוֹ** — **and takes action** (i.e., issues a ruling) **on the basis of his testimony**[33] **עָבַר עַל לָאו** — **has violated a** mitzvah-**prohibition.**[34]

---

NOTES

27. By demonstrating a willingness to suffer financial loss in order to avoid transgressing, he indicates that he has repented and no longer will allow his desire for money to lead him astray. Doing this in his hometown does not suffice, since he might be trying to deceive his neighbors into thinking that he is reformed. But when he does this in a new locale where people are not acquainted with his past history, it can be assumed that his actions are sincere (*Rashi, Sanhedrin* 25b ד"ה ויחזיר אבידה and ד"ה שאין מכירין).

28. In each case, one who became disqualified on account of a specific sin will regain his trustworthiness upon proving that he has repented from that sin. For example, one who lends with interest can again become qualified to testify if he returns any interest that he collected, tears up his interest-based loan documents, and refrains from lending with interest even to idolaters (*Sanhedrin* 25b; *Rambam, Hil. Eidus* 12:4-5; see §6-10 there for further examples).

29. The laws regarding the disqualification of a "wicked person" are codified in *Rambam, Hil. Eidus* Chs. 10-12, and *Shulchan Aruch, Choshen Mishpat* §34. The laws regarding *all* disqualifications are found in *Rambam* ibid. Chs. 9-16 and *Choshen Mishpat* §33-37.

30. I.e., in Eretz Yisrael and the Diaspora, and whether the *Beis HaMikdash* is standing or not.

31. See Mitzvah 77, at note 42; see, similarly, Mitzvah 81 note 5 and Mitzvah 83 note 18.

32. Since women are never in a position to accept testimony, they are not subject to the prohibition against accepting it from a sinner. *Minchas Chinuch* §4 posits that there actually can be a situation in which a woman is subject to this mitzvah. As we will learn in Mitzvah 77 (at note 49), litigants can by mutual consent choose any person to be their judge, and they are subsequently bound to abide by that judge's decision (see *Choshen Mishpat* 22:1). Should they choose a woman to judge their case, she would presumably be prohibited to accept a sinner's testimony.

33. See above, note 1. [That is, a *beis din* rules on the basis of a sinner's testimony, such that each of the judges has transgressed.]

34. *Rambam* (ibid. 10:1) states that there is also a case in which a witness violates this prohibition. If a disqualified witness testifies before a *beis din* that is unaware of his disqualification, and a valid witness who is aware of it joins together with the disqualified witness to testify — thus creating testimony of a "pair" of witnesses, and causing the court to accept the testimony of the disqualified witness — the valid witness has violated this prohibition. Even if the testimony is true, the witness has transgressed *Do not place you hand with the wicked*, etc. (see *Mechilta DeRashbi* to our verse). [For discussion of whether the disqualified witness himself also violates this prohibition, see *Teshuvos Chavos Yair* §15 ד"ה האמנם and *Urim VeTumim* §28, *Urim* §3.]

וְאֵין לוֹקִין עַל לַאו זֶה לְפִי שֶׁאֵין בּוֹ מַעֲשֶׂה,[35] וַאֲפִלּוּ עָשָׂה בּוֹ מַעֲשֶׂה,[36] בְּכָל דָּבָר שֶׁבְּמָמוֹן לְפִי שֶׁנִּתָּן לְהִשָּׁבוֹן אֵין לוֹקִין עָלָיו.[37]

וְאֵין לוֹקִין עַל לַאו זֶה — **However, one does not incur** *malkus* (lashes) **on account of** violating **this prohibition,** לְפִי שֶׁאֵין בּוֹ מַעֲשֶׂה — **because** the violation of **[this prohibition] does not involve action.**[35] וַאֲפִלּוּ עָשָׂה בּוֹ מַעֲשֶׂה — **And even if one did perform an action in** violating **[this prohibition],**[36] there is another reason to exempt him, בְּכָל דָּבָר שֶׁבְּמָמוֹן — **for regarding any monetary manner,** the rule is that לְפִי שֶׁנִּתָּן לְהִשָּׁבוֹן — **since [any money]** wrongly extracted from one litigant and given to another **is subject to restitution,** אֵין לוֹקִין עָלָיו — **one does not incur** *malkus* on account of [the transgression].[37]

---

NOTES

35. It is a principle, oft mentioned in Chinuch (e.g., end of Mitzvah 9), that לַאו שֶׁאֵין בּוֹ מַעֲשֶׂה אֵין לוֹקִין עָלָיו, *One does not incur malkus for [violating] a prohibition that does not involve action.* See General Introduction, note 14.

36. For example, judges issued a ruling based on a sinner's testimony and then physically took funds from the losing litigant and gave them to the winning litigant.

37. Since the transgression can be rectified through return of the funds, the penalty of *malkus* does not apply (see Mitzvah 68 note 17, and General Introduction note 14).

*Mishneh LaMelech* (glosses here) wonders why Chinuch needs to resort to this explanation. In many instances throughout this work, Chinuch takes the position that that any prohibition that *can* be transgressed without action is completely excluded from *malkus* — even if one commits the transgression by means of an action. [See, for example, Mitzvos 94, 113, 241, 344-346.] It should thus be obvious that *malkus* are never meted out for a violation of this prohibition! For a possible resolution of this matter, see *Maharam Schik* and *Minchas Yitzchak.* See also Insight to Mitzvah 68.

---

> **◆§ Insight: Situations in Which a Disqualified Person's Testimony May Be Admissible**
>
> Chinuch has listed numerous people who are deemed unfit to testify by Rabbinic decree. *Minchas Chinuch* (§2 par. 8, and below, 122:9) notes, however, that while people disqualified Biblically are unfit to testify before *beis din* in any case, those disqualified Rabbinically are sometimes fit — and even required — to testify. In this, he distinguishes between monetary cases and corporal or capital cases.
>
> By way of introduction, a basic question must be addressed: Let us assume that a witness who is Rabbinically disqualified comes before *beis din* to testify in a litigant's favor. Under Biblical law, this witness' testimony is valid and the litigant that it supports deserves to win the case; due to the Rabbinic disqualification, however, his testimony must be rejected and that litigant will lose. How can the Sages actually require the court to reject his testimony and rule against the litigant that it supports, when by doing so they are contradicting Biblical law? Conversely, if such a witness testifies against a person who was sued, then under Biblical law that person is liable; how can the court reject the damaging testimony and exonerate him at the expense of the one who sued him?
>
> To answer these questions, we must analyze a basic difference between monetary law and criminal law. In monetary matters, there is a principle, derived from Scripture (see *Yevamos* 89b), that הֶפְקֵר בֵּית דִּין הֶפְקֵר, *Something declared ownerless by beis din is ownerless.* This means that the court has the right to vacate a person's rights to specific property, when circumstances demand it. On the basis of this authority, the court is, in monetary cases, empowered to completely reject the testimony of those who are Rabbinically disqualified. Even if a litigant would have won his case on the basis of testimony by a certain individual, and he loses it because the Sages invalidated that person's testimony, the verdict does not contradict Biblical law. To the contrary — Biblical law recognizes the authority of the Sages to strip the litigant of his property rights when there is a valid reason to do so. It follows that people whom the Sages considered suspect, and therefore disqualified, are *completely* excluded from testifying in monetary cases — whether their exclusion causes the court to find a litigant liable and extract money from him, or causes them to exempt him of liability and dismiss the suit.
>
> In corporal and capital cases, however, there is no such overriding principle. Thus, the Sages'

## MISHPATIM / MITZVAH 75: THE PROHIBITION TO ALLOW A SINNER TO TESTIFY

disqualification of a witness must operate within the guidelines of Biblical judicial law, and is subject to certain strictures. If Rabbinically-suspect witnesses testify that someone committed an offense for which he should be liable to *malkus* or the death penalty, the court may reject the testimony of these witnesses and exonerate the defendant. The fact that he will not receive a punishment that he would have incurred under Biblical law need not concern us, since the Sages consider the damaging testimony suspect and unworthy of acceptance. If, on the other hand, *valid* witnesses testify that someone committed an offense for which he should be liable to *malkus* or the death penalty, and then Rabbinically-suspect witnesses contradict them and say that he is innocent, the court cannot simply reject the latter testimony and declare him guilty. Since under Biblical law there is contradictory testimony, which means that the defendant must be *acquitted,* the Sages are not empowered to impose punishment on him. Although they consider the latter testimony suspect, they do not *know* that it is false; hence, they must give consideration to the fact that under Biblical law it is valid. In this case, therefore, the court has no choice but to allow the testimony of the latter witnesses to stand, leaving the guilt of the defendant in doubt, and allowing him to go free.

Since the testimony of Rabbinically-disqualified witnesses is effective in this case, it follows that if such witnesses have knowledge that will acquit a defendant, they are *obligated* to present it in *beis din*. Regarding this situation, these witnesses are no different from valid witnesses, whom the Torah obligates to present their testimony in every case, as stated in Mitzvah 122 (*Minchas Chinuch* ibid.; see also *Turei Even, Rosh Hashanah* 22a ד"ה זה הכלל; *Teshuvos R' Akiva Eiger* §99 ד"ה ואיני כדאי).

For application of these guidelines to another context, see *Minchas Chinuch* §2 par. 1 ד"ה טומטום and ד"ה ומה.

## מִצְוָה עו: שֶׁלֹּא לִנְטוֹת אַחֲרֵי רַבִּים בְּדִינֵי נְפָשׁוֹת בִּשְׁבִיל אֶחָד [2,1]

שֶׁלֹּא יֵלֵךְ הַדַּיָּן אַחַר דַּעַת הָרֹב בְּדִינֵי נְפָשׁוֹת כְּשֶׁיִּהְיֶה הַתּוֹסֶפֶת אִישׁ אֶחָד לְבַד, וּבֵאוּר זֶה כִּי כְּשֶׁתִּהְיֶה מַחֲלֹקֶת בֵּין הַדַּיָּנִין בְּדִין אָדָם אֶחָד וְיֹאמְרוּ קְצָתָם שֶׁהוּא חַיָּב מִיתָה וּקְצָתָם שֶׁאֵינוֹ חַיָּב, וְהָיוּ הַמְחַיְּבִין יוֹתֵר עַל הַמְזַכִּין אֶחָד, שֶׁלֹּא יַעֲשֶׂה הַדַּיָּן בַּחוֹטֵא כְּדִבְרֵי הַמְחַיְּבִין, שֶׁנֶּאֱמַר (שמות כ"ג, ב') לֹא תִהְיֶה אַחֲרֵי רַבִּים לְרָעֹת,[3]

# Mitzvah 76

## The Prohibition to Follow a Majority of One in Capital Cases

לֹא תִהְיֶה אַחֲרֵי רַבִּים לְרָעֹת
*Do not follow a majority to harm (Exodus 23:2).*

A Jewish court (*beis din*) that tries monetary cases is generally composed of three judges; a *beis din* that tries capital cases is composed of twenty-three judges.[1] In Mitzvah 78, Chinuch sets forth the mitzvah upon *beis din* to follow a majority in reaching its verdicts. In this mitzvah, Chinuch sets out how the precept of majority decision is applied in capital cases.[2]

According to its simple meaning, the above verse teaches that although a majority decides the law, one may not follow the majority when it is clear that justice is being perverted (*Rashi* to verse). However, the Sages understood from this verse an additional reference to a prohibition to convict on the basis of a simple majority (i.e., a majority of one) in capital cases, as Chinuch shall explain.

שֶׁלֹּא יֵלֵךְ הַדַּיָּן אַחַר דַּעַת הָרֹב בְּדִינֵי נְפָשׁוֹת — We are commanded **that a judge shall not follow the opinion of the majority** of the judges of the court **in a capital case** כְּשֶׁיִּהְיֶה הַתּוֹסֶפֶת אִישׁ אֶחָד לְבַד — **when** the majority **exceeds** the opposing minority **by the vote of only one person.** וּבֵאוּר זֶה — **The explanation of this is** as follows: כִּי כְּשֶׁתִּהְיֶה מַחֲלֹקֶת בֵּין הַדַּיָּנִין בְּדִין אָדָם אֶחָד — In a case **where there is a disagreement between the judges regarding** how to rule on **the case of an individual** being tried for a capital offense, וְיֹאמְרוּ קְצָתָם שֶׁהוּא חַיָּב מִיתָה — **and some** of the judges **say that [the defendant] is liable to execution** וּקְצָתָם שֶׁאֵינוֹ חַיָּב — **and some** say **that he is not liable,** וְהָיוּ הַמְחַיְּבִין יוֹתֵר עַל הַמְזַכִּין אֶחָד — **and those who hold [the defendant] liable** to execution **outnumber those who hold him innocent by** a count of **one,** שֶׁלֹּא יַעֲשֶׂה הַדַּיָּן בַּחוֹטֵא כְּדִבְרֵי הַמְחַיְּבִין — in this case we are commanded **that the judge may not implement** the sentence **of the sinner following the opinion of [the judges] who say that he is liable.**[3] שֶׁנֶּאֱמַר — **We are so commanded, as the verse states** (*Exodus* 23:2): "לֹא תִהְיֶה אַחֲרֵי רַבִּים לְרָעֹת":

---

### NOTES

1. Nowadays, when we no longer have judges who have received *semichah* (ordination according to the procedure set forth by Chinuch in Mitzvah 491), *beis din* no longer has the authority to impose capital punishment.

2. Note that according to the author's original arrangement, all the mitzvah-obligations (מִצְוֹת עֲשֵׂה) of each *Parashah* appeared before the mitzvah-prohibitions (מִצְוֹת לֹא תַעֲשֶׂה) of that *Parashah* (see General Introduction, note 7). Thus, Mitzvah 78, the obligation to decide cases by a majority, appeared before this mitzvah, which is a specific application of that rule.

3. In a standard capital court of twenty-three (see the introduction to this mitzvah), if eleven judges vote for conviction and twelve for acquittal, the accused is acquitted; if eleven vote for acquittal and twelve for conviction, the accused may not be convicted based on that vote. In that case, two judges are added to the court so that the verdict can be reached either for acquittal by a vote of at least one, or conviction by a vote of at least two.

If the expanded court remains split on the matter, additional judges are added, in pairs, until there are seventy-one judges on the court. If at that point the split court cannot reach a verdict of acquittal by one or conviction by two, the accused is acquitted (*Sanhedrin* 40a,42a; see *Rambam, Hil. Sanhedrin* 9:2).

## MISHPATIM / MITZVAH 76: NOT TO FOLLOW A MAJORITY OF ONE IN CAPITAL CASES

כְּלוֹמַר לֹא תֵלֵךְ אַחַר הָרֹב שֶׁיִזְדַּמֵּן לַחְתֹּךְ מִשְׁפָּט מָוֶת,[4] וְזֶהוּ לְשׁוֹן הַכָּתוּב שֶׁאָמַר לְרָעֹת, כְּלוֹמַר לְחִיּוּב מִיתָה, וְזֶה כְּשֶׁיִּהְיֶה רֹב מֵעַצְמָם, כְּלוֹמַר שֶׁהַהֶכְרֵעַ אֵינוֹ אֶלָּא מֵחֲמַת אִישׁ אֶחָד, אֲבָל כְּשֶׁיִהְיֶה הַהֶכְרֵעַ בִּשְׁנַיִם אֲפִלּוּ לְרָעוֹת, מַטִּין עַל פִּיהֶם, וּבַמְּכִילְתָּא הַטָּיָתְךָ לְטוֹבָה עַל פִּי (עֵד)[5] אֶחָד, וּלְרָעָה עַל פִּי שְׁנַיִם.

מִשָּׁרְשֵׁי מִצְוָה זוֹ, לְפִי שֶׁנִּצְטַוִּינוּ לְהִדַּמּוֹת בְּמַעֲשֵׂינוּ לְמִדּוֹת הַשֵּׁם בָּרוּךְ הוּא, וּמִמִּדּוֹתָיו שֶׁהוּא רַב חֶסֶד, כְּלוֹמַר שֶׁעוֹשֶׂה עִם בְּנֵי אָדָם לִפְנִים מִשּׁוּרַת הַדִּין, וְגַם אֲנַחְנוּ נִצְטַוִּינוּ בְּכָךְ

---

*Do not follow a majority for harm*; בְּלֹא תֵלֵךְ אַחַר הָרֹב שֶׁיִזְדַּמֵּן לַחְתֹּךְ מִשְׁפָּט מָוֶת — that is to say, **do not follow a majority that happens to occur** (i.e., a mere majority of one), **to rule in favor of a death sentence.**[4] וְזֶהוּ לְשׁוֹן הַכָּתוּב שֶׁאָמַר "לְרָעֹת" — **This** meaning **is** expressed in the **language of the verse, "for harm,"** כְּלוֹמַר לְחִיּוּב מִיתָה — for the phrase **means to say,** regarding a ruling of **liability to execution.**

Chinuch explains that when the verse prohibits following "*a majority*" to convict in capital cases, it clearly does not preclude *ever* following a majority to convict in capital cases, but prohibits only following a certain kind of majority:

וְזֶה כְּשֶׁיִּהְיֶה רֹב מֵעַצְמָם — **This** prohibition applies only **when there is a limited majority,** כְּלוֹמַר שֶׁהַהֶכְרֵעַ אֵינוֹ אֶלָּא מֵחֲמַת אִישׁ אֶחָד — **that is, when the ascendancy** of one side over the other **is only due to** the vote of **one person.** אֲבָל כְּשֶׁיִהְיֶה הַהֶכְרֵעַ בִּשְׁנַיִם — **However, when the ascendancy** of the majority over the minority **is by** a vote of **two people,** אֲפִלּוּ לְרָעוֹת — then **even** if the majority votes **for harm,** i.e., in favor of conviction for capital punishment, מַטִּין עַל פִּיהֶם — **we do decide in accordance with their position.**

Chinuch cites an exposition from *Mechilta*, where this law is derived from a study of the two clauses in the above verse. The beginning of the verse, "*Do not follow a majority for harm*," indicates that there is a majority that we are not to follow, whereas the end of the verse, "... *according to the majority [the matter] shall be decided*," indicates that there is a majority that should be followed even "for harm." *Mechilta* explains that there are two kinds of majorities:

וּבַמְּכִילְתָּא הַטָּיָתְךָ לְטוֹבָה עַל פִּי (עֵד)[5] אֶחָד — **In** *Mechilta* (*Mechilta DeRashbi* to *Exodus* 23:2), the ruling is cited as follows: **Your deciding a case for good,** i.e., for acquittal, **shall be** even **by** a majority **of one;** וּלְרָעָה עַל פִּי שְׁנַיִם — **but for harm,** i.e., to convict in a capital case, it must be **by** a majority of at least **two.**

### ⸿ Underlying Purpose of the Mitzvah ⸀

In Mitzvah 611, Chinuch explains at length that a person is obligated to try to emulate the ways of God in all of his actions. For example, just as God is referred to as "the Compassionate One," people too should be compassionate in their actions. Here, Chinuch points to another of God's Attributes as the underlying concept behind this mitzvah:

מִשָּׁרְשֵׁי מִצְוָה זוֹ — **Among the underlying purposes of the mitzvah is,** לְפִי שֶׁנִּצְטַוִּינוּ לְהִדַּמּוֹת בְּמַעֲשֵׂינוּ לְמִדּוֹת הַשֵּׁם בָּרוּךְ הוּא — **since we are commanded** (Mitzvah 611) **to emulate with our deeds the Attributes of Hashem, blessed is He;** וּמִמִּדּוֹתָיו שֶׁהוּא רַב חֶסֶד — **and among** **[Hashem's] Attributes is that He is "Abundant in Kindness"** (*Exodus* 34:6), כְּלוֹמַר שֶׁעוֹשֶׂה עִם בְּנֵי אָדָם לִפְנִים מִשּׁוּרַת הַדִּין — **that is to say, He deals with people beyond the boundaries of strict judgment;** וְגַם אֲנַחְנוּ נִצְטַוִּינוּ בְּכָךְ — **we are** therefore **also commanded** to judge **in this** way,

---

NOTES

4. That is, the words "*Do not follow a majority*" mean that a judge may not follow every kind of majority that may occur; rather there are certain majorities that one may follow and certain majorities that one may not, as Chinuch explains below.

5. Emendation following Brünn ed., 1799, and *Mechilta*; see also *Tosefta, Sanhedrin* 3:4.

## משפטים / מצוה עו: שלא לנטות אחרי רבים בדיני נפשות בשביל אחד

שֶׁיִּהְיֶה הַזְּכוּת בְּדִינֵי נְפָשׁוֹת יוֹתֵר עַל הַחִיּוּב[6], לְפִי שֶׁהוּא דָּבָר שֶׁאֵין לוֹ תַּשְׁלוּמִין[7]. וּמִשְׁפְּטֵי הַמִּצְוָה בְּפֶרֶק ד׳ מִסַּנְהֶדְרִין, כְּמוֹ שֶׁכָּתַבְתִּי לְמַעְלָה בְּמִצְוַת עֲשֵׂה שֶׁל אַחֲרֵי רַבִּים לְהַטֹּת[8].

וְהָעוֹבֵר עָלֶיהָ וְחִיֵּב בְּרֹב הַמַּכְרִיעַ בְּאֶחָד, עָבַר עַל מִצְוַת מֶלֶךְ[9], וְעָנְשׁוֹ גָּדוֹל מְאֹד, שֶׁגָּרַם לְאַבֵּד נֶפֶשׁ שֶׁלֹּא כַּדִּין.

---

שֶׁיִּהְיֶה הַזְּכוּת בְּדִינֵי נְפָשׁוֹת יוֹתֵר עַל הַחִיּוּב — **that is,** to see to it **that the** possibility of **acquittal in capital cases should be greater than the** possibility of **conviction.**[6] לְפִי שֶׁהוּא דָּבָר שֶׁאֵין לוֹ תַּשְׁלוּמִין — This law applies to capital cases only **because,** unlike other forms of punishment, if one is wrongly executed, **there is no** possibility **of rectifying** the error.[7]

### ~ Laws of the Mitzvah ~

וּמִשְׁפְּטֵי הַמִּצְוָה בְּפֶרֶק ד׳ מִסַּנְהֶדְרִין — **The laws of this mitzvah** may be found **in the fourth chapter of** *Sanhedrin*, כְּמוֹ שֶׁכָּתַבְתִּי לְמַעְלָה בְּמִצְוַת עֲשֵׂה שֶׁל אַחֲרֵי רַבִּים לְהַטֹּת — **as I have written above, in the mitzvah-obligation of** "According to the Majority Shall [the matter] be Decided" (Mitzvah 78).[8]

### ~ Applicability of the Mitzvah ~

וְהָעוֹבֵר עָלֶיהָ — **One who transgresses [this mitzvah],** וְחִיֵּב בְּרֹב הַמַּכְרִיעַ בְּאֶחָד — **and convicts** an accused in a capital case **based on a majority of one,** עָבַר עַל מִצְוַת מֶלֶךְ — **has violated the command of the King** (God);[9] וְעָנְשׁוֹ גָּדוֹל מְאֹד שֶׁגָּרַם לְאַבֵּד נֶפֶשׁ שֶׁלֹּא כַּדִּין — **and his punishment is exceedingly great, for he has caused an unlawful loss of life.**

---

### NOTES

6. See *Rosh Hashanah* 17a and *Rambam, Hil. Teshuvah* 3:5).

7. See also below, Mitzvah 78, where Chinuch discusses other laws that are unique to capital cases, and how the proceedings of capital cases are constructed to lean toward acquittal (see also Mitzvah 77 and Mitzvah 409).

8. In Mitzvah 78, Chinuch cites some laws relating to this mitzvah as well. [Chinuch refers to Mitzvah 78 as "above" since, as explained above (in note 2), in the author's arrangement, Mitzvah 78 appeared before this mitzvah.]

The laws of this mitzvah are codified in *Rambam, Hil. Sanhedrin*, Chapters 8-9.

9. I.e., he receives no penalty in *beis din*, but he has violated a command of God and is deserving of Heavenly retribution.

---

### ❧ Insight: When Conviction Is Unanimous

As was explained in this mitzvah, a majority of two is needed — and is sufficient — to convict in capital cases. There is, however, one instance where there is a much greater majority to convict, yet the defendant cannot be held liable by the *beis din*. The Gemara states (*Sanhedrin* 17a; cited by Chinuch, Mitzvah 77) that when the entire court is *unanimous* in their opinion to convict, the defendant is exempt from the death penalty. The Gemara explains the reason for this law as follows: A court may not issue a death sentence on the same day that the case was initiated, so that the judges will have time to consider the matter further and perhaps find a basis upon which to acquit (Mishnah ibid. 40a). Where all the judges are of the opinion that the defendant is guilty, however, such an overnight delay would be meaningless, as no arguments for acquittal have been left open for consideration at that time. Since delaying the verdict to the next day would serve no purpose, and handing it down that day is not allowed, the case cannot be brought to a conclusion by this *beis din*.

In a way, this rule seems counterintuitive: if the case is so clear-cut as to generate a unanimous ruling from the *beis din*, surely the defendant is guilty! How may we understand the fact that the very clarity of his guilt leads to his acquittal?

Many Acharonim explain that in this case, the lack of deliberation in favor of the defendant is a

## 85 ❑ MISHPATIM / MITZVAH 76: NOT TO FOLLOW A MAJORITY OF ONE IN CAPITAL CASES

sign of a critically deficient judicial process. In other judicial systems, the responsibility for presenting the case for the defense rests on the defendant himself or on an advocate for the defendant. In a Sanhedrin (i.e., a *beis din* assigned judgment of a capital case), however, the judges of the court serve in this capacity, as the court is charged with raising every possible reason or circumstance that could lead to acquittal (see Mitzvah 77 at length). The phenomenon of not even one of the twenty-three judges finding any argument to acquit the defendant may indicate a lack of sufficient astuteness or patience on the part of the judges to adequately represent the defense. Alternatively, it may be a sign that the court is somehow tainted with a bias to convict. Either way, when the court is so unanimous that there is not one sustained argument for the defense, there is reason for concern that this vital function is not being properly conducted, and the case must therefore be closed (see *Maharatz Chayes, Sanhedrin* 17a; *Milchemes Mitzvah*, Peterkov ed. 5670, p. 20). [Indeed, according to some Acharonim, in this case the defendant is subsequently tried in another court. It is only when a unanimous conviction occurs before the Great Sanhedrin (of seventy-one judges), after whose judgment no court can rule, that the defendant is absolved of the death penalty (see *Ohr Same'ach, Hil. Sanhedrin* 9:1).]

For further discussion in a similar vein, see *Sefer Chassidim* §411 and *Maharal, Be'er HaGolah, Be'er* §2 ד"ה פרק קמא; for other reasons and sources for this law, see *Pardes Yosef, Parashas Masei* §98.

*Ohr HaChaim* (*Exodus* 23:2) offers an intriguing insight into the source verse of the current mitzvah, based on the above law. He notes that a judge who is fully aware of this procedure may be tempted to manipulate it to arrive at what he feels to be the appropriate outcome. For example, if a judge sees that all of his colleagues have ruled that the defendant is guilty, but he himself feels that the defendant is innocent, he may calculate as follows: If he states his true opinion, the court will no longer be unanimous in its conviction. His vote for acquittal will then serve as the one vote necessary to, in his opinion, wrongly send the defendant to his death! Thus, it would be better for him to vote for conviction, making the vote unanimous and thereby setting the accused free!

It is this circumstance that the verse refers to with the words לֹא תִהְיֶה אַחֲרֵי רַבִּים לְרָעֹת, *do not follow the majority to harm*. The verse enjoins the judges that when they do not agree with the majority to convict, they may not follow that majority in their vote to convict (interpreting לְרָעֹת — literally, *to harm* — as *to convict*), even if their intention is to effect an acquittal.

*Ohr HaChaim* continues that the second part of the verse addresses the converse situation: Where a judge agrees with all of his colleagues as to the guilt of the accused, he may wish to refrain from voting his opinion since, as the last vote in a unanimous judgment, his vote would result in the defendant being acquitted. Instead, he may wish to put forward a vote for acquittal, thus ensuring "justice" to the guilty party!

To preclude such manipulation, the verse writes וְלֹא תַעֲנֶה עַל רִב לִנְטֹת אַחֲרֵי רַבִּים, *do not declare regarding a grievance (i.e., an accusation) by yielding to the majority*. That is, do not vote (to acquit) only so *its result* will be in accord with the ruling of the majority (which votes to convict). To vote this way would be לִנְטֹת, *turning away*, from your true opinion regarding the case, for the sole purpose of ensuring a different result.

In summary, the Torah commands judges to be forthright with their true opinion and let the judgment fall as it may, even if by so doing, the outcome will be the opposite of the judge's view. A judge must honestly perform his responsibilities as judge, leaving the determination of a just outcome to God, the ultimate Arbiter of Truth.

[For s similar discussion regarding a judge's responsibility to vote his opinion, not the outcome, see *Pischei Teshuvah, Choshen Mishpat* 18:4.]

## מִצְוָה עז:
### שֶׁלֹּא יְלַמֵּד חוֹבָה מִי שֶׁלִּמֵּד זְכוּת תְּחִלָּה בְּדִינֵי נְפָשׁוֹת[1]

שֶׁלֹּא יֵלֵךְ אֶחָד מִן הַדַּיָּנִין אַחַר דַּעַת דַּיָּן אֶחָד גָּדוֹל, אוֹ אֲפִלּוּ אַחַר דַּעַת הָרֹב, עַל צַד שֶׁיַּאֲמִינֵהוּ לְחִיּוּב אוֹ לִזְכוּי מִבְּלִי שֶׁיִּהְיֶה הַדָּבָר מוּבָן אֶצְלוֹ בְּשִׂכְלוֹ[2], וְאִם הוּא דִין הַתָּלוּי

---

## Mitzvah 77
### The Prohibition [Upon a Judge] to Argue for Conviction in Capital Cases After Having First Argued for Acquittal

וְלֹא תַעֲנֶה עַל רִב לִנְטֹת

*Do not declare [your judicial opinion] upon a grievance by veering [to convict]* (Exodus 23:2).

In this mitzvah, Chinuch lists four separate judicial actions that are prohibited, each derived exegetically from the words of the verse cited above, and each included in the general prohibition of this mitzvah. The title of the mitzvah highlights only one of these actions — the prohibition upon a judge to argue for conviction after having previously argued for acquittal — and the translation of the verse presented above follows the interpretation that forbids that particular action. The interpretations that yield each of the other actions are explained in the course of this mitzvah.[1]

All four of the forbidden actions that Chinuch lists share the central theme that, in capital cases, the judges must exercise great care in their deliberations, and the judicial procedures must generally be weighted toward acquittal.

Chinuch explains the first forbidden action included in this verse:

שֶׁלֹּא יֵלֵךְ אֶחָד מִן הַדַּיָּנִין אַחַר דַּעַת דַּיָּן אֶחָד גָּדוֹל — **We are commanded that one of the judges** serving on a capital case **may not,** in casting his vote on the case, simply **follow the view of** another **great judge** on the court, אוֹ אֲפִלּוּ אַחַר דַּעַת הָרֹב — **or even follow the view of the majority** עַל צַד שֶׁיַּאֲמִינֵהוּ — **based** solely **on his trust of [the other judge]** or of the majority. לְחִיּוּב אוֹ לִזְכוּי — **The** judge may not follow another, whether it is **to convict or to acquit** the defendant by his vote, מִבְּלִי שֶׁיִּהְיֶה הַדָּבָר מוּבָן אֶצְלוֹ בְּשִׂכְלוֹ — **unless the matter** of conviction or acquittal **is understood by him with his own understanding.**[2] וְאִם הוּא דִין הַתָּלוּי בִּגְזֵרַת הַכָּתוּב — **And if the decision** in this case **hinges,** not upon a logical argument, but **upon** the interpretation of a law based on **a Scriptural**

---

### NOTES

1. [Below, Chinuch discusses the unique nature of Scriptural exegesis wherein many separate prohibitions can be derived from a single phrase of the Torah.] All the interpretations discussed fall under the category of *derush*, Scriptural exegesis. On the level of *p'shat* (plain meaning), however, the cited words of our verse are explained differently, and in fact do not even stand on their own as an independent phrase. The full verse, according to the *p'shat*, is an admonition to the judge not to follow the majority where it is clear that the majority is perverting justice. The verse thus reads as follows: לֹא תִהְיֶה אַחֲרֵי רַבִּים לְרָעֹת — *Do not follow the majority for evil*; וְלֹא תַעֲנֶה עַל רִב לִנְטֹת אַחֲרֵי רַבִּים לְהַטֹּת — *and (when asked your opinion) do not respond regarding a dispute in a manner that follows the [evil] majority in turning [the judgment away from the truth]* (Rashi to verse).

As Chinuch discusses in this mitzvah, the exegetical interpretation is equally as authoritative as the plain meaning, as both make up a part of the multifaceted interpretations of the Torah.

2. That is, if he is truly convinced by the arguments of the other judges, then he may vote according to that which he now understands to be the true judgment. However, without truly understanding and agreeing with that position, he may not cast his vote following that opinion (see Insight for further discussion).

## MISHPATIM / MITZVAH 77: NOT TO ARGUE FOR CONVICTION IN CAPITAL CASES

בִּגְזֵרַת הַכָּתוּב אוֹ מִצַּד גְּזֵרָה שָׁוָה[3] אוֹ הֶקֵּשׁ[4] שֶׁיְּהֵא יוֹדֵעַ אוֹתוֹ הוּא, וְלֹא יִסְמֹךְ וְיִבְטַח עַל אֶחָד מִן הַדַּיָּנִין, וְלֹא עַל הָרֹב, שֶׁנֶּאֱמַר (שמות כ"ג, ב') וְלֹא תַעֲנֶה עַל רִב לִנְטֹת,[5] רוֹצֶה לוֹמַר, לֹא תֹאמַר עַל הָרִיב דָּבָר לִנְטוֹת, כְּלוֹמַר מִצַּד הַנְּטִיָּה לְבַד, אַחַר דִּבְרֵי דַּיָּן אֶחָד גָּדוֹל אוֹ אַחַר הָרֹב וְלֹא מִצַּד הֲבָנָתְךָ, אוֹ שֶׁתִּרְצֶה לְהַחֲרִישׁ מִמַּה שֶּׁבְּלִבְּךָ עַל הַדִּין וּלְהַטּוֹת אַחַר דִּבְרֵיהֶם, לֹא תַעֲשֶׂה כֵן.[6] וּלְשׁוֹן[7] מְכִילְתָּא לֹא תַעֲנֶה עַל רִיב לִנְטוֹת, שֶׁלֹּא תֹאמַר דַּיִּי שֶׁאֶהְיֶה כְּרַב פְּלוֹנִי אֶלָּא אֱמֹר מַה שֶּׁלְּפָנֶיךָ,[8] יָכוֹל אַף דִּינֵי מָמוֹנוֹת כֵּן,

---

**אוֹ מִצַּד גְּזֵרָה שָׁוָה אוֹ הֶקֵּשׁ** — **or** a law **derived by way of** an exegetical principle such as **a *gezeirah shavah*,**[3] **or a *hekeish*,**[4] **שֶׁיְּהֵא יוֹדֵעַ אוֹתוֹ הוּא** — it is required **that [the judge] himself know it, וְלֹא יִסְמֹךְ וְיִבְטַח עַל אֶחָד מִן הַדַּיָּנִין וְלֹא עַל הָרֹב** — **and not rely upon, nor trust, one of the judges or** even **the majority** of the court. **שֶׁנֶּאֱמַר** — We are so commanded, **as it is stated** (*Exodus* 23:2): **"וְלֹא תַעֲנֶה עַל רִב לִנְטֹת"** — *do not declare with regard to a grievance by following*;[5] **רוֹצֶה לוֹמַר** — **meaning to say, לֹא תֹאמַר עַל הָרִיב דָּבָר לִנְטוֹת** — **you** (the judge) **shall not declare** your position **regarding a grievance,** i.e., a judicial case, by stating **something that is "following," כְּלוֹמַר מִצַּד הַנְּטִיָּה לְבַד** — **that is to say,** something **that is based solely upon following** the opinion of another, **אַחַר דִּבְרֵי דַּיָּן אֶחָד גָּדוֹל אוֹ אַחַר הָרֹב** — whether **following the words of a great judge** on the court, **or the** opinion of the **majority** of the judges, **וְלֹא מִצַּד הֲבָנָתְךָ** — **when it is not a result of your own understanding. אוֹ שֶׁתִּרְצֶה לְהַחֲרִישׁ מִמַּה שֶּׁבְּלִבְּךָ עַל הַדִּין** — **Or,** in the event that you do have a clear opinion based on your own understanding, but **you wish to remain silent regarding what is in your heart with respect to the case וּלְהַטּוֹת אַחַר דִּבְרֵיהֶם** — **and** instead **to follow the words of [the others], לֹא תַעֲשֶׂה כֵן** — **you may not do so.**[6]

Chinuch cites *Mechilta*, which arrives at this same law through a slightly different derivation based on the unusual spelling of the word רִב, *grievance*, in this verse. In all other places in the Torah, the word is spelled with a *yud* (רִיב), but here it is spelled without a *yud* (רִב). Since the written text of the Torah does not contain vowels, this spelling lends itself to another interpretation, and *Mechilta* explains it as alluding to the word רַב, *Torah teacher* (Rabbi):[7]

**וּלְשׁוֹן מְכִילְתָּא** — **In the words of *Mechilta*** (*Mechilta DeRashbi* to this verse): **לֹא תַעֲנֶה עַל רַב לִנְטוֹת** — In the verse, ***do not declare upon* "רב"** *to follow*, the word רב is spelled without a *yud*, so it can be read as *"rav"* — a Torah teacher. **שֶׁלֹּא תֹאמַר דַּיִּי שֶׁאֶהְיֶה כְּרַב פְּלוֹנִי** — This teaches that **you** (the judge) **may not say, "It is sufficient for me to be like So-and-so the Rabbi,** i.e., I need not vote my own decision, for I can fulfill my responsibility as a judge by reiterating the decision of my fellow judge who is a great Torah scholar." You may not say this; **אֶלָּא אֱמֹר מַה שֶּׁלְּפָנֶיךָ** — **rather, you must state** your own opinion **in accordance with what** you see **before you.**[8]

*Mechilta* continues:

**יָכוֹל אַף דִּינֵי מָמוֹנוֹת כֵּן** — **It might be** thought that **this** applies **even to cases of monetary law;**

---

### NOTES

3. A *gezeirah shavah* is a method of exegesis whereby laws may be derived from one context to another by means of a common word found in Biblical verses in each context. Such linkage must be established by tradition.

4. A *hekeish* is a Scriptural analogy whereby two subjects that are juxtaposed in the Torah are compared to each other, allowing for derivation of laws from one subject to the other.

5. This translation differs from the translation in the heading of this mitzvah, and reflects the law discussed by Chinuch here, as Chinuch explains.

6. Thus, when a judge has no personal opinion regarding the case, he may not issue a ruling that simply follows the opinion of other judges; and even if he does have his own opinion, he may not squelch it and rule in accordance with the other judges' opinion.

7. Chinuch discusses this type of derivation below as well, in the fourth action prohibited by the verse.

8. According to this interpretation, the verse is understood as saying, לֹא תַעֲנֶה עַל רַב לִנְטֹת, *do not declare [your opinion relying] upon a [greater] rabbi, [merely] following [his view]*.

## משפטים / מצוה עז: שלא ילמד חובה מי שלמד זכות בדיני נפשות

תַּלְמוּד לוֹמַר אַחֲרֵי רַבִּים לְהַטֹּת[9]. וּבָזֶה הַלָּאו בְּעַצְמוֹ נִכְלָל שֶׁהַמְלַמֵּד זְכוּת בְּדִינֵי נְפָשׁוֹת לֹא יַחֲזֹר וִילַמֵּד חוֹבָה[10], בַּמֶּה שֶׁאָמַר לֹא תַעֲנֶה עַל רִב לִנְטֹת[11], כְּלוֹמַר לֹא יִהְיֶה דְּבָרְךָ לְהַטּוֹת אוֹתוֹ לְחוֹבָה[12]. וּכְמוֹ כֵן נִכְלָל בּוֹ אֵין פּוֹתְחִין בְּדִינֵי נְפָשׁוֹת לְחוֹבָה[13], וְיָבוֹא הַפֵּרוּשׁ כֵּן, לֹא תַעֲנֶה עַל רִב לִנְטֹת, כְּלוֹמַר לֹא יִהְיֶה פֶּתַח דְּבָרֶיךָ לְהַטּוֹת אוֹתוֹ לְחוֹבָה[14], כִּי עַל כָּרְחֵנוּ בִּתְחִלַּת הַדִּין יֵשׁ

---

תַּלְמוּד לוֹמַר "אַחֲרֵי רַבִּים לְהַטֹּת" — **the** end of the **verse** therefore **teaches** us, *you shall follow the majority.* That is, there are times that one may follow the view of others. It is logical to conclude that the prohibition applies to the more severe situation of capital cases and the permit applies to the less severe situation of monetary cases.[9]

Chinuch lists the second of the four judicial actions prohibited by this verse:

שֶׁהַמְלַמֵּד זְכוּת בְּדִינֵי וּבָזֶה הַלָּאו בְּעַצְמוֹ נִכְלָל — **Also included in this very** mitzvah-**prohibition** נְפָשׁוֹת לֹא יַחֲזֹר — **is that [a judge] who advances an argument for acquittal in a capital case** וִילַמֵּד חוֹבָה — **may not change** his argument **and advance an argument for conviction.**[10] בַּמֶּה שֶׁאָמַר "לֹא תַעֲנֶה עַל רִב לִנְטֹת" — This law may be seen **in [the verse's] statement: "Do not declare upon a grievance by turning"**;[11] כְּלוֹמַר לֹא יִהְיֶה דְּבָרְךָ לְהַטּוֹת אוֹתוֹ לְחוֹבָה — **that is to say, your words shall not** change in an attempt **to turn him** (i.e., the defendant) **from acquittal to conviction.**[12]

Chinuch now lists the third judicial action forbidden by the verse:

אֵין פּוֹתְחִין בְּדִינֵי נְפָשׁוֹת לְחוֹבָה וּכְמוֹ כֵן נִכְלָל בּוֹ — **Similarly included in [this prohibition]** — is the law that **we do not open** the deliberations **in capital cases** with arguments **for conviction.**[13] וְיָבוֹא הַפֵּרוּשׁ כֵּן — **The explanation** of the verse that results in this law **emerges as follows:** "לֹא תַעֲנֶה עַל רִב לִנְטֹת" — *Do not declare [your words] upon the grievance by turning;* כְּלוֹמַר לֹא יִהְיֶה פֶּתַח דְּבָרֶיךָ לְהַטּוֹת אוֹתוֹ לְחוֹבָה — **that is, your opening words** of argument **should not be to "turn" the defendant toward conviction.**[14] כִּי עַל כָּרְחֵנוּ בִּתְחִלַּת הַדִּין יֵשׁ

---

### NOTES

9. That is, in monetary cases it is permitted for a judge to simply reiterate the ruling of another judge on the court whose opinion he deems reliable. Below, Chinuch elaborates on the reasons for this distinction. See note 26.

10. A judge, who, during deliberations, advances an argument for acquittal must stand by his position for the duration of the deliberations, so that he will argue strenuously in support of it and perhaps arrive at convincing arguments for acquittal (*Rashi, Sanhedrin* 32a ד"ה אינו חוזר). At the time of the final verdict, however, he may change his position, as Chinuch notes below.

11. In this derivation, the word לִנְטֹת is not translated as "to follow" but as "to turn" or "by turning."

12. [The verse does not indicate which "turning" is prohibited, whether it is a turn toward conviction or a turn toward acquittal. Nevertheless, there is an overarching principle in capital cases that the court must do its utmost to acquit the defendant from the death penalty. The source of this principle is the verse וְהִצִּילוּ הָעֵדָה, *and the congregation [i.e., the court] shall rescue* (see *Sanhedrin* 69a, *Pesachim* 12a). It is thus understood that when the Torah instructs that the judge may not "turn," it means that he may not turn from acquittal toward conviction (see *Radvaz* to *Hil. Sanhedrin* 10:2 in a slightly different context).]

13. Some understand Chinuch to mean that at the opening of deliberations, it is incumbent upon each judge to find an argument for acquittal (*Minchas Yitzchak*). *Minchas Chinuch* (§3) notes, however, that if this were so, then each judge who has done so would automatically become disqualified from offering any argument for conviction, since the previous law stated that once a judge argues for acquittal he can no longer argue for conviction. It would then be nearly impossible to ever convict anyone! Rather, *Minchas Chinuch* explains (based on the Gemara, *Sanhedrin* 32b), the requirement is merely that the court as a whole must begin its deliberations with some type of statement in favor of acquittal (see also *Rambam, Hil. Sanhedrin* 10:7). [That is, at least one judge must make an opening argument for acquittal, and if no such argument can readily be found, then the court makes a statement that raises the possibility of acquittal, such as telling the defendant, "If you are innocent, you have nothing to fear" (Gemara ibid., as explained by *Yad Ramah*). In the case where a judge is able to open with an argument for acquittal, that judge is then barred from arguing for conviction for the remainder of the deliberations, as Chinuch points out at the end of Mitzvah 78. See further below, note 28.]

14. Here too, the "turning" is interpreted to mean turning toward conviction (not toward acquittal), as explained in note 12.

## 89 ☐ MISHPATIM / MITZVAH 77: NOT TO ARGUE FOR CONVICTION IN CAPITAL CASES

לָנוּ לְפָרֵשׁ אוֹתוֹ, שֶׁאִי אֶפְשָׁר לוֹמַר שֶׁבְּכָל הַדִּין יַזְהִיר שֶׁלֹּא תַעֲנֶה בּוֹ לְחוֹבָה, שֶׁאִם כֵּן לֹא יִהְיֶה שׁוּם אָדָם נִדּוֹן לְעוֹלָם.

וּכְמוֹ כֵן שָׁמַעְנוּ מִזֶּה הַלָּאו שֶׁאֵין מַתְחִילִין בְּדִינֵי נְפָשׁוֹת מִן הַגָּדוֹל, אֶלָּא שֶׁלְּמַטָּה הֵימֶנּוּ יַגִּיד תְּחִלָּה דַעְתּוֹ[15], וְזֶה לֹא תַעֲנֶה עַל רַב, כְּמוֹ עַל רַב, כִּי בְּלֹא יוֹ"ד הוּא נִכְתָּב, כְּלוֹמַר לֹא תַעֲנֶה עַל גָּדוֹל אֶלָּא הוּא יַעֲנֶה אֵלֶיךָ, שֶׁאַתָּה תְּדַבֵּר תְּחִלָּה, וְהָעִנְיָן הוּא כְּדֵי שֶׁלֹּא יִסָּמְכוּ עַל דִּבְרֵי הַגָּדוֹל.[16]

---

לָנוּ לְפָרֵשׁ אוֹתוֹ — **The verse is explained in this manner, because we must perforce explain [this prohibition] as referring to the beginning of** the deliberations regarding **the case,** שֶׁאִי אֶפְשָׁר לוֹמַר שֶׁבְּכָל הַדִּין יַזְהִיר שֶׁלֹּא תַעֲנֶה בּוֹ לְחוֹבָה — **since it is impossible to say that [the verse] forbids declaring an argument for conviction at any point during the case,** שֶׁאִם כֵּן לֹא יִהְיֶה שׁוּם אָדָם נִדּוֹן לְעוֹלָם — **for if it were so** then **no person would ever be convicted.** That is, although the verse does not indicate that it forbids such argument only at the beginning of deliberations, it must be so understood, for a blanket prohibition on advancing arguments for conviction would result in no person ever being convicted.

Chinuch presents the fourth judicial action forbidden by the verse:

שֶׁאֵין מַתְחִילִין בְּדִינֵי נְפָשׁוֹת וּכְמוֹ כֵן שָׁמַעְנוּ מִזֶּה הַלָּאו — **We likewise learn from this prohibition** מִן הַגָּדוֹל — **that we are not to begin** deliberations **in capital cases with** the words of **the preeminent** judge, אֶלָּא שֶׁלְּמַטָּה הֵימֶנּוּ יַגִּיד תְּחִלָּה דַעְתּוֹ — **rather, a less eminent** judge **than him should state his view first.**[15]

Chinuch explains how this prohibition is derived from the verse. It should be noted that above, the word תַעֲנֶה was translated as "*declare*," but according to the following exposition, the word is translated as "*respond.*"

וְזֶה "לֹא תַעֲנֶה עַל רִב" — **In this** derivation, the words *you shall not respond upon a grievance* (רִב) כְּמוֹ עַל רַב — are to be understood **as** if they said *you shall not respond to a master* (רַב). כִּי בְּלֹא יוֹ"ד הוּא נִכְתָּב — **The indication to interpret the verse thus is because [the word *riv*, רב]**, which according to the plain meaning of the verse connotes *grievance*, **is written** in its incomplete form, **lacking the letter *yud*;** this indicates that we are to expound it as reading *rav* — *a master.* כְּלוֹמַר לֹא תַעֲנֶה עַל גָּדוֹל אֶלָּא הוּא יַעֲנֶה אֵלֶיךָ — **According to this interpretation, the intention of the verse is to say: you** (the judge) **shall not respond to** the argument of **the preeminent** judge, who is the "master"; **rather, he shall respond to you,** שֶׁאַתָּה תְּדַבֵּר תְּחִלָּה — **for you,** i.e., one of the lesser judges, **shall speak first** in the deliberations. וְהָעִנְיָן הוּא כְּדֵי שֶׁלֹּא יִסָּמְכוּ עַל דִּבְרֵי הַגָּדוֹל — **The reason** for this prohibition **is so that [the other judges] should not rely upon the preeminent judge** when issuing their opinions.[16]

In summary, four prohibitions regarding capital cases are included in this verse: (1) A judge may not simply repeat the opinion of another judge that he respects, or of the majority, but must render his own considered decision. (2) A judge who advanced an argument for acquittal may not reverse himself during the deliberations and advance an argument for conviction. (3) The deliberations may not begin with an argument for conviction, but must begin with an argument for acquittal. (4) The preeminent judge may not be the first to voice his opinion.

Having explained the four things prohibited by this verse, Chinuch digresses to explain the phenomenon of so many disparate concepts being derived from a single verse:

---

### NOTES

15. According to another view, the *least* eminent judge must speak first; see *Tos. Yom Tov, Sanhedrin* 4:2; *Rama, Choshen Mishpat* 18:1.

16. This is out of concern that the preeminent judge may advance an argument for conviction, and the other judges will be unwilling to challenge his position, instead relying on the opinion of the preeminent judge (see *Minchas Chinuch* §10; *Lechem Mishneh, Hil. Sanhedrin* 10:6).

# משפטים / מצוה עז: שלא ילמד חובה מי שלמד זכות בדיני נפשות

כָּל אֵלֶּה הַדְּבָרִים לָמַדְנוּ מִלֹּא תַעֲנֶה עַל רִב לִנְטֹת, וְעִנְיָן זֶה מִכֹּחַ חָכְמַת הַתּוֹרָה שֶׁיֵּשׁ לְהָבִין מִדָּבָר אֶחָד מִמֶּנָּה כַּמָּה דְבָרִים, זֶהוּ שֶׁאָמְרוּ זִכְרוֹנָם לִבְרָכָה (במדבר רבה י״ג, ט״ז) שִׁבְעִים פָּנִים יֵשׁ לַתּוֹרָה[17], וּלְפִי שֶׁיּוֹדֵעַ אֱלֹהִים כִּי הָעָם מְקַבְּלֵי הַתּוֹרָה בְּהִתְנַהֲגָם עַל הַדֶּרֶךְ שֶׁנִּצְטַוּוּ בָהּ, יִהְיוּ נְכוֹנִים אֶל הַחָכְמָה וְאֶל הַתְּבוּנָה וְיָבִינוּ בָהּ כָּל הַצָּרִיךְ לָהֶם אֶל הַנְהָגַת הָעוֹלָם[18], סָתַם לָהֶם הַדְּבָרִים בִּמְקוֹמוֹת, וּמָסַר לָהֶם הַפֵּרוּשׁ עַל יַד הַסַּרְסוּר הַגָּדוֹל אֲשֶׁר בֵּינֵיהֶם וּבֵינוֹ[19], וְלֹא[20] נָתְנָה בְּמִלּוֹת רְחָבוֹת יוֹתֵר לְפִי שֶׁכָּל מִלּוֹתֶיהָ גְּזוּרוֹת וּמְחֻיָּבוֹת בְּחֶשְׁבּוֹנָן וּבְצוּרָתָן לִהְיוֹת כָּכָה[21], כִּי מִלְּבַד מַשְׁמָעוּת מִצְוֹתֶיהָ הַיְקָרוֹת שֶׁאָנוּ מְבִינִין בָּהּ,

כָּל אֵלֶּה הַדְּבָרִים לָמַדְנוּ מִ"לֹּא תַעֲנֶה עַל רִב לִנְטֹת" — **All these matters are derived from** the single verse, *You shall not declare upon a grievance by turning.* וְעִנְיָן זֶה מִכֹּחַ חָכְמַת הַתּוֹרָה — **This matter is** possible **by dint of the** Divine **wisdom of the Torah,** שֶׁיֵּשׁ לְהָבִין מִדָּבָר אֶחָד מִמֶּנָּה כַּמָּה דְבָרִים — **on account of which it is possible to understand from one of its words many things.** זֶהוּ שֶׁאָמְרוּ זִכְרוֹנָם לִבְרָכָה — **This** concept is expressed by **that which [the Sages], of blessed memory, have stated** (*Bamidbar Rabbah* 13:16): שִׁבְעִים פָּנִים יֵשׁ לַתּוֹרָה — **There are seventy facets to the Torah,** i.e., the words of the Torah are multifaceted, and contain numerous meanings.[17]

Chinuch explains how God knew that the Jewish people would be able to plumb the depths of this wisdom, and derive these many concepts from the limited number of words:

וּלְפִי שֶׁיּוֹדֵעַ אֱלֹהִים כִּי הָעָם מְקַבְּלֵי הַתּוֹרָה — **And because God knows that the nation that has accepted the Torah,** i.e., the Jewish people, בְּהִתְנַהֲגָם עַל הַדֶּרֶךְ שֶׁנִּצְטַוּוּ בָהּ — **by virtue of their following the path they have been commanded** to follow, i.e., the way of the Torah, יִהְיוּ נְכוֹנִים אֶל הַחָכְמָה וְאֶל הַתְּבוּנָה — **would be qualified to** receive **wisdom and understanding** — וְיָבִינוּ בָהּ כָּל הַצָּרִיךְ לָהֶם אֶל הַנְהָגַת הָעוֹלָם — **and,** as a result of this understanding, **would perceive in [the Torah] all that is required for the proper administration of** all that is necessary for them in **the world** —[18] סָתַם לָהֶם הַדְּבָרִים בִּמְקוֹמוֹת — **He left matters veiled in** various **places** in Scripture, leaving only allusions to these laws, וּמָסַר לָהֶם הַפֵּרוּשׁ — **and He transmitted the explanation** of these things **to them** orally, עַל יַד הַסַּרְסוּר הַגָּדוֹל אֲשֶׁר בֵּינֵיהֶם וּבֵינוֹ — **by way of the great "intermediary" who was between [the nation] and Himself,** i.e., Moses. Together with the Written Law, in which many matters were not stated explicitly, God gave Moses the Oral Law, which contains the complete explanation of all the laws of the Torah.[19]

Chinuch explains why God did not simply expand upon all these laws in the Written portion of the Torah:[20]

וְלֹא נָתְנָה בְּמִלּוֹת רְחָבוֹת יוֹתֵר — **[God] did not set out [the laws of the Torah] with more expansive phraseology,** לְפִי שֶׁכָּל מִלּוֹתֶיהָ גְּזוּרוֹת וּמְחֻיָּבוֹת בְּחֶשְׁבּוֹנָן וּבְצוּרָתָן לִהְיוֹת כָּכָה — **because all of [the Torah's] words are fixed, and it is essential for them to be in their count and form** exactly **as they are.**[21] כִּי מִלְּבַד מַשְׁמָעוּת מִצְוֹתֶיהָ הַיְקָרוֹת שֶׁאָנוּ מְבִינִין בָּהּ — **For aside from the** direct

---

## NOTES

17. For a discussion of the nature of Torah wisdom and how it can contain so many levels of wisdom within each word, see *Kad HaKemach* (*Rabbeinu Bachya*) ערך סוכה.

18. Following the ways of the Torah molds the nation to be a wise and understanding one, as the Torah writes: *You shall safeguard and perform [the decrees and ordinances of the Torah], for it is your wisdom and discernment in the eyes of the peoples, who shall hear all these decrees and who shall say, "Surely a wise and discerning people is this great nation!"* (Deuteronomy 4:6).

19. *Rashi, Leviticus* 25:1. All the laws of the Torah in all their detail were orally transmitted to Moses, but God placed allusions to many of these oral laws within the written verses, such that much of the Oral Torah can also be derived from the Written Torah (see *Rambam,* Introduction to his *Commentary to the Mishnah*; see also *Ohr HaChaim, Leviticus* 13:37). As Chinuch has explained, such is the case with the derivations of the prohibitions included in this mitzvah.

20. For example, God could have recorded every facet of this mitzvah in its own, distinct verse. Instead, in His wisdom, He chose to include all of them in the few words of this one verse, and to transmit to us the knowledge required for their derivation by way of the Oral Law.

21. The form and construct of the Torah is precise; every single letter, as well as the order of the letters

## 91 □ MISHPATIM / MITZVAH 77: NOT TO ARGUE FOR CONVICTION IN CAPITAL CASES

נִכְלְלוּ בָהּ חָכְמוֹת גְּדוֹלוֹת וּמְפֹאָרוֹת,[22] עַד שֶׁהֶעֱלוּ רַבּוֹתֵינוּ זִכְרוֹנָם לִבְרָכָה גֹּדֶל הַחָכְמָה שֶׁהִנִּיחַ הָאֵל בָּרוּךְ הוּא בְּתוֹכָהּ, שֶׁאָמְרוּ עָלֶיהָ (בראשית רבה פר׳ א׳, א׳) שֶׁהִבִּיט הַקָּדוֹשׁ בָּרוּךְ הוּא בָּהּ וּבָרָא אֶת הָעוֹלָם.[23]

מִשָּׁרְשֵׁי מִצְוָה זוֹ, כְּמוֹ שֶׁאָמַרְנוּ תְּחִלָּה שֶׁלֹּא יֵלֵךְ אֶחָד מִן הַדַּיָּנִין אַחַר חֲבֵרוֹ אֶלָּא יָבִין הַדְּבָרִים מֵעַצְמוֹ, הַטַּעַם מִפְּנֵי שֶׁאֶפְשָׁר שֶׁמִּתּוֹךְ כָּךְ יָבוֹא הַדִּין כֻּלּוֹ לִפְעָמִים עַל דַּעַת אֶחָד מֵהֶם, הָבֵן הַדָּבָר כִּי כֵן הוּא, וְלֹא רָצָה הַשֵּׁם יִתְבָּרַךְ לִמְסֹר דִּין נֶפֶשׁ לְדַעַת אֶחָד,

---

**implications of its precious commandments,** which we understand from a simple reading of **it,** נִכְלְלוּ בָהּ חָכְמוֹת גְּדוֹלוֹת וּמְפֹאָרוֹת — **there is** also **included in [the words of the Torah] great and glorious wisdom** beyond the plain meaning of the words.[22] עַד שֶׁהֶעֱלוּ רַבּוֹתֵינוּ זִכְרוֹנָם לִבְרָכָה גֹּדֶל הַחָכְמָה שֶׁהִנִּיחַ הָאֵל בָּרוּךְ הוּא בְּתוֹכָהּ — This is so, **to the extent that our Sages, of blessed memory, so highly valued the greatness of the wisdom that the Almighty, blessed is He, placed in [the Torah],** שֶׁאָמְרוּ עָלֶיהָ — **that they stated regarding it** (*Bereishis Rabbah* 1:1) שֶׁהִבִּיט הַקָּדוֹשׁ בָּרוּךְ הוּא בָּהּ וּבָרָא אֶת הָעוֹלָם — **that the Holy One, blessed is He, looked into [the Torah] and created the world.**[23]

### ∽ Underlying Purpose of the Mitzvah ∽

Chinuch begins his discussion of the underlying purpose of the mitzvah with the first of the four judicial actions prohibited by this mitzvah:

מִשָּׁרְשֵׁי מִצְוָה זוֹ — **Among the underlying purposes of this mitzvah** are the following: כְּמוֹ שֶׁאָמַרְנוּ תְּחִלָּה — With respect to the first facet of the prohibition, **as we have stated** it **at the outset of this mitzvah,** שֶׁלֹּא יֵלֵךְ אֶחָד מִן הַדַּיָּנִין אַחַר חֲבֵרוֹ — i.e., **that one of the judges may not follow the view of his fellow** judge, אֶלָּא יָבִין הַדְּבָרִים מֵעַצְמוֹ — **but rather, he must understand the matters** pertaining to the case and reach a decision **independently,** הַטַּעַם — **the reason** for this prohibition is מִפְּנֵי שֶׁאֶפְשָׁר שֶׁמִּתּוֹךְ כָּךְ יָבוֹא הַדִּין כֻּלּוֹ לִפְעָמִים עַל דַּעַת אֶחָד מֵהֶם — **because,** if it would be permitted for one judge to follow the opinion of another judge, **it is possible that, as a result, an entire case would sometimes be decided on the basis of the opinion of** only **one of [the judges];** הָבֵן הַדָּבָר כִּי כֵן הוּא — **consider the matter** and you will see **that it is so.** וְלֹא רָצָה הַשֵּׁם יִתְבָּרַךְ לִמְסֹר דִּין נֶפֶשׁ לְדַעַת אֶחָד — **And Hashem, blessed be He, did not wish to submit the judgment regarding a life to the opinion of one** man.

Chinuch above cited *Mechilta,* which excludes monetary cases from this prohibition. Here Chinuch explains why that should be so:

---

### NOTES

and words, is Divinely ordained. Indeed, a *Sefer Torah* containing a single misspelled word is invalid — even if the error does not change the meaning of the word (see *Rambam, Hil. Sefer Torah* 7:11).

22. *Ramban,* in his introduction to his Commentary on the Torah, explains at length that all the wisdom of the world, from the physical to the spiritual, is to be found in the words of the Torah. Aside from the direct meanings of the words, from which we can derive great wisdom, the Torah contains many secrets within the words themselves. Some of the ways that this wisdom is contained are through the shapes of the letters, their order, various configurations of the spaces of the Torah (where words and sentences can be formed by spacing the letters in different configurations), and the numerical values of the letters. See there for a fuller discussion of these concepts. See also *Derashos Chasam Sofer,* last *Derush* on 8 *Teves* ד״ה כתיב במגילת קינות.

23. God, as it were, used His Torah, which preceded the world (*Shabbos* 88b), as the blueprint for Creation. While we cannot perceive this information in a simple reading of the text, all the knowledge, wisdom, and understanding that went into the creation of the universe is contained within the precise construct of the Torah, just as we received it from Moses.

## משפטים / מצוה עז: שלא ילמד חובה מי שלמד זכות בדיני נפשות

אֲבָל בְּדִין מָמוֹן שֶׁנִּתַּן לְהִשָּׁבוֹן אֵין חוֹשְׁשִׁין לְכָל זֶה,[24] וַאֲפִלּוּ לִשְׁלֹשָׁה מוֹסְרִין אוֹתוֹ לְכַתְּחִלָּה עַל סְמָךְ דְּאִי אֶפְשָׁר דְּלֵיכָּא בְּהוּ חַד דְּגָמִיר.[25,26] וּשְׁאָר הַדְּבָרִים שֶׁנִּלְמְדוּ מִמֶּנּוּ, כְּגוֹן מְלַמֵּד זְכוּת שֶׁלֹּא יְלַמֵּד חוֹבָה, וְשֶׁאֵין פּוֹתְחִין לְחוֹבָה, וְאֵין מַתְחִילִין מִן הַגָּדוֹל, כָּל זֶה לְחֶמְלַת הַשֵּׁם יִתְבָּרַךְ עַל בְּרִיּוֹתָיו כְּאָדָם הַחוֹמֵל עַל בָּנָיו, דֶּרֶךְ מָשָׁל, כְּמוֹ שֶׁכָּתוּב (דברים י״ד, א׳) בָּנִים אַתֶּם לַה׳ אֱלֹהֵיכֶם וְגוֹ׳. וְהַגַּע עַצְמְךָ עַל דֶּרֶךְ מָשָׁל, אִם יוֹלִיד אִישׁ מֵאָה[27] וּבָנָה לָהֶם עִיר וְהוֹשִׁיבָם שָׁם, וְרָאָה שֶׁלֹּא יִתְקַיְּמוּ בַּיִּשּׁוּב אֶלָּא אִם כֵּן יִגְזֹר עֲלֵיהֶם שֶׁכָּל הַמַּכֶּה רֵעֵהוּ יֵעָנֵשׁ בְּמָמוֹנוֹ, וְאִם יְמִיתֵהוּ יוּמָת, וְקָם הָאֶחָד וְעָבַר עַל גְּזֵרָתוֹ,

---

אֲבָל בְּדִין מָמוֹן שֶׁנִּתַּן לְהִשָּׁבוֹן — **However, with regard to monetary law, where** errors in judgment are **subject to** redress by way of **repayment,** אֵין חוֹשְׁשִׁין לְכָל זֶה — **we are not concerned with all these** issues.[24] וַאֲפִלּוּ לִשְׁלֹשָׁה מוֹסְרִין אוֹתוֹ לְכַתְּחִלָּה — Indeed, **even** the fact that **we initially submit [monetary cases] to** a court comprised of **three** judges עַל סְמָךְ דְּאִי אֶפְשָׁר דְּלֵיכָּא בְּהוּ חַד דְּגָמִיר — **is based upon** the premise **that it is impossible that** at least **one of the judges is not proficient** in monetary law.[25] Since essentially only one learned judge is required, there is no reason to prohibit the other judges from following the opinion of the most learned judge among them.[26]

Chinuch discusses the underlying purpose of the other facets of the mitzvah:

וּשְׁאָר הַדְּבָרִים שֶׁנִּלְמְדוּ מִמֶּנּוּ — **As to the rest of the laws that are learned from [this verse],** כְּגוֹן מְלַמֵּד זְכוּת שֶׁלֹּא יְלַמֵּד חוֹבָה — **such as** the law **that** a judge **who advances an argument for acquittal may not** subsequently **advance an argument for conviction,** וְשֶׁאֵין פּוֹתְחִין לְחוֹבָה — **and** the law **that we do not open** deliberations in capital cases with arguments **for conviction,** וְאֵין מַתְחִילִין מִן הַגָּדוֹל — **and** the law **that we do not begin** the deliberations **with the** words of the **preeminent** judge, כָּל זֶה לְחֶמְלַת הַשֵּׁם יִתְבָּרַךְ עַל בְּרִיּוֹתָיו — **all these** laws are expressions **of the compassion that Hashem, blessed be He, has for His creations,** כְּאָדָם הַחוֹמֵל עַל בָּנָיו דֶּרֶךְ מָשָׁל — **as, by way of analogy, a person has compassion for his children;** כְּמוֹ שֶׁכָּתוּב ״בָּנִים — **as it is written** regarding the relationship of God to the Jewish people, **You are children to Hashem, your God, etc.** (Deuteronomy 14:1). All these laws distance the possibility of conviction in capital cases, and serve to make acquittal from capital punishment more likely.

Chinuch presents a parable to explain the paradox that God sets the death penalty for certain violations, yet seeks to distance its use:

וְהַגַּע עַצְמְךָ עַל דֶּרֶךְ מָשָׁל — **Reflect** upon this matter **yourself, by way of** the following **analogy:** אִם יוֹלִיד אִישׁ מֵאָה — **If a man should father one hundred** children,[27] וּבָנָה לָהֶם עִיר וְהוֹשִׁיבָם שָׁם — **and build for them a city and settle them there,** וְרָאָה שֶׁלֹּא יִתְקַיְּמוּ בַּיִּשּׁוּב — **and [the** man] **perceives that they will not endure as a society** אֶלָּא אִם כֵּן יִגְזֹר עֲלֵיהֶם — **unless he decrees upon them** שֶׁכָּל הַמַּכֶּה רֵעֵהוּ יֵעָנֵשׁ בְּמָמוֹנוֹ — **that anyone who strikes his fellow shall be punished with a monetary fine,** וְאִם יְמִיתֵהוּ יוּמָת — **and, if one should kill [his fellow], he shall be executed,** וְקָם הָאֶחָד וְעָבַר עַל גְּזֵרָתוֹ — **and** then, after the father has so decreed, **one** of the children **should arise and violate [the father's] decree** and murder one of his brethren;

---

NOTES

24. Monetary cases are not subject to any of the prohibitions of this verse. [However, cases involving sentencing a litigant to *malkus* (lashes), or *galus* (the term of exile for one convicted of inadvertent murder) are, with regard to these prohibitions, the same as capital cases (*Rambam, Hil. Sanhedrin* 11:4; see *Kesef Mishneh* ad loc.).]

25. According to Biblical law, one judge is sufficient to preside on monetary cases. The Sages, however, require three judges to ensure that there would be at least one judge on the panel who is proficient in monetary law (*Sanhedrin* 3a). [*Minchas Chinuch* §1 notes, however, that there are certain kinds of monetary law that require three judges by Biblical law as well; see Insight.]

26. *Minchas Chinuch* (§1) finds great difficulty with the position that a judge may vote following the opinion of another judge in monetary cases; see Insight for further discussion. [Even according to Chinuch, a judge may not rely upon a fellow judge who is *less* learned than he, even in monetary cases.]

27. Stylistic citation of *Ecclesiastes* 6:3.

## 93 ☐ MISHPATIM / MITZVAH 77: NOT TO ARGUE FOR CONVICTION IN CAPITAL CASES

אִם יִמְחַל לוֹ הֲרֵי הַיִּשׁוּב בָּטֵל, שֶׁלֹּא תִשָּׁאֵר מוֹרָא עַל הַנִּשְׁאָרִים, מַה יֵּשׁ לוֹ לַעֲשׂוֹת וְאַל יִרְאֶה בְּמוֹת בְּנוֹ הַשֵּׁנִי, יַחֲזֹר עַל כָּל פָּנִים בְּכָל צַד שֶׁיּוּכַל לְפָטְרוֹ מִן הַדִּין, אִם יוּכַל מוּטָב, וְאִם אִי אֶפְשָׁר בְּשׁוּם צַד, יְצַוֶּה לַהֲמִיתוֹ כְּדֵי לְקַיֵּם יִשּׁוּב הָאֲחֵרִים, וְכֵן הַדָּבָר הַזֶּה, וַהֲבִינֵהוּ.

מִדִּינֵי הַמִּצְוָה, מַה שֶּׁאָמְרוּ זִכְרוֹנָם לִבְרָכָה (סנהדרין דף י״ז ע״א) שֶׁאִם פָּתְחוּ כֻלָּם לְחוֹבָה שֶׁפָּטוּר[28], וְאִם הַמְחַיְּבִים וְהַמְזַכִּים שָׁוִים שֶׁמּוֹסִיפִין עֲלֵיהֶם[29], וְעַד כַּמָּה מוֹסִיפִין[30],

---

אִם יִמְחַל לוֹ — clearly, **if [the father] would pardon [the murderer]** and not carry out the decreed punishment, הֲרֵי הַיִּשּׁוּב בָּטֵל — **the result would be** that civil **society would fail** and be reduced to anarchy, שֶׁלֹּא תִשָּׁאֵר מוֹרָא עַל הַנִּשְׁאָרִים — **for no fear** of punishment **would remain upon the rest** of the populace. מַה יֵּשׁ לוֹ לַעֲשׂוֹת וְאַל יִרְאֶה בְּמוֹת בְּנוֹ הַשֵּׁנִי — **What,** then, **is [the father] to do so that he shall not see the death of a second** of his children, i.e., the perpetrator? יַחֲזֹר עַל כָּל פָּנִים בְּכָל צַד שֶׁיּוּכַל לְפָטְרוֹ מִן הַדִּין — **He will at least examine every** possible **means of acquitting [the accused] in accordance with the law.** אִם יוּכַל מוּטָב — **If he is able** to spare him while maintaining the integrity of the law, **it is good.** וְאִם אִי אֶפְשָׁר בְּשׁוּם צַד — **If, however, it is impossible** to spare him **by any** legal **means,** יְצַוֶּה לַהֲמִיתוֹ כְּדֵי לְקַיֵּם יִשּׁוּב הָאֲחֵרִים — then **[the father] will give the order to put [the perpetrator] to death, in order to maintain the society** for the benefit **of all the others** of his children who remain. וְכֵן הַדָּבָר הַזֶּה וַהֲבִינֵהוּ — **So, too, is this matter** regarding the Torah laws that favor acquittal in capital cases — **reflect upon it!**

### ☙ Laws of the Mitzvah ❧

Chinuch begins by citing laws that pertain to general judicial procedures of deliberation and voting: מִדִּינֵי הַמִּצְוָה — **Among the laws of this mitzvah** מַה שֶּׁאָמְרוּ זִכְרוֹנָם לִבְרָכָה — **is that which [the Sages], of blessed memory, have stated** (*Sanhedrin* 17a), שֶׁאִם פָּתְחוּ כֻלָּם לְחוֹבָה שֶׁפָּטוּר — **that if all [the judges]** on a capital case **opened** with opinions **for conviction, then [the defendant] must be acquitted.**[28] וְאִם הַמְחַיְּבִים וְהַמְזַכִּים שָׁוִים — **Further laws pertaining to the mitzvah are that if the** number of **[judges] who vote to convict and** the number of **those who vote to acquit are equal,** שֶׁמּוֹסִיפִין עֲלֵיהֶם — **then we** are to **add** additional judges **to [the judges]** already on the court, so that a decision may be reached;[29] וְעַד כַּמָּה מוֹסִיפִין — **and** the law regarding **up to what**

---

### NOTES

28. The Gemara (*Sanhedrin* 17a) explains the reason for this unusual law as follows: There is a requirement in capital cases that the court may not issue a verdict for conviction on the day on which the case began, so that those judges who are of a mind to convict will have time to reconsider their positions. However, since the purpose of this mandatory delay is to give time for additional consideration of the arguments for acquittal, in the case where the judges are unanimous in their position of conviction, delay is purposeless because the case for acquittal will not be considered at all. Since delay is pointless, but the law precludes a same-day decision, the case is aborted. [For further discussion regarding this rule, see Insight to Mitzvah 76.]

One might wonder, however: We learned above that the deliberations are supposed to begin with an argument for acquittal, and if no judge is able to find any such argument, it suffices for the court to issue a general statement that raises the possibility of acquittal, such as "If you are innocent, you have nothing to fear" (see note 13). Does the current rule mean that if the court neglected to make such a statement, this causes the defendant to be acquitted?

*Minchas Chinuch* (§4) explains that this is not the intention at all. What the current rule means is that if *at the end of the first day* of deliberations the judges are unanimous for conviction, the defendant is acquitted, for the reason just explained. The expression "all the judges *opened* for conviction" reflects the fact that the judgment is opened on one day and not sealed until the next day. See also *Aruch HaShulchan, Choshen Mishpat* 18:7. See further, *Minchas Soless* ד״ה והנה הרמב״ם.

29. Capital cases require a court of twenty-three judges; thus when all the judges are voting, a numerically split vote is not possible. Chinuch refers here to a case where one of the judges was unable to come to a decision, so the judges who actually voted were an equal number. Alternatively, he refers to a case where eleven judges vote to acquit and twelve vote to convict. Since in capital cases a majority of at least two is necessary to convict (see

# 94 □ משפטים / מצוה עז: שלא ילמד חובה מי שלמד זכות בדיני נפשות

וְאִם אוֹמֵר אֶחָד אֵינִי יוֹדֵעַ מַה יְהֵא בְּכָךְ[31] (שם דף ל״ד ע״א), וּמַה שֶּׁאָמְרוּ שֶׁהַמְלַמֵּד זְכוּת אֵינוֹ חוֹזֵר וּמְלַמֵּד חוֹבָה דַּוְקָא בִּשְׁעַת מַשָּׂא וּמַתָּן נֶאֱמַר, אֲבָל בִּגְמַר דִּין חוֹזֵר לְהִמָּנוֹת עִם הַמְחַיְּבִין, וְאִם פָּתַח וְאָמַר אֶחָד יֶשׁ לִי לְלַמֵּד זְכוּת[32] וְנִשְׁתַּתֵּק אוֹ מֵת, שֶׁהוּא כְּמִי שֶׁאֵינוֹ[33], וְהַמְזַכֶּה וּמֵת רוֹאִין אוֹתוֹ בִּגְמַר דִּין כְּאִלּוּ הוּא בִּמְקוֹמוֹ[34],

---

**number** of judges **we continue to add to the court;**[30] וְאִם אוֹמֵר אֶחָד אֵינִי יוֹדֵעַ מַה יְהֵא בְּכָךְ **— and if one** of the judges **says, "I do not know"** how the law should be decided," and therefore abstains from the vote, **what is to be with that** case.[31]

Chinuch cites laws relating to the prohibition to retract an argument for acquittal, and how an argument is counted if the judge could not offer a final vote:

וּמַה שֶּׁאָמְרוּ — **Also** included in the laws of the mitzvah is **that which [the Sages] have stated** (*Sanhedrin* 34a), שֶׁהַמְלַמֵּד זְכוּת אֵינוֹ חוֹזֵר וּמְלַמֵּד חוֹבָה — that the prohibition **that [a judge] who has advanced an argument for acquittal may not retract and advance an argument for conviction** דַּוְקָא בִּשְׁעַת מַשָּׂא וּמַתָּן נֶאֱמַר — **applies only during the deliberations.** אֲבָל בִּגְמַר דִּין חוֹזֵר לְהִמָּנוֹת עִם הַמְחַיְּבִין — **However, at the time the final verdict** is decided, **[the judge] may retract and be counted among** those **who vote to convict.**

וְאִם פָּתַח וְאָמַר אֶחָד יֶשׁ לִי לְלַמֵּד זְכוּת — **Also, if one** of the assembled[32] **opens** his arguments **by saying "I have an argument for** the defendant's **acquittal,"** וְנִשְׁתַּתֵּק אוֹ מֵת — and then, before he actually states his position, **he is struck dumb or dies,** שֶׁהוּא כְּמִי שֶׁאֵינוֹ — **it is as if he is not present** and his opinion is not counted.[33] וְהַמְזַכֶּה וּמֵת — **However, if there is one who** actually **advanced an argument for acquittal,** explained his reasoning, **and then died,** רוֹאִין אוֹתוֹ בִּגְמַר דִּין — **at** the time of **the final verdict we consider** his vote כְּאִלּוּ הוּא בִּמְקוֹמוֹ — **as if he is present in his position** on the court.[34]

When capital cases were in session, there were three rows of disciples, each with twenty-three members, seated on the floor before the court so that, should the need arise, judges could be appointed to the court from their ranks (Mishnah, *Sanhedrin* 37a). Chinuch discusses the procedure in the event that one of these disciples wishes to put forth an argument regarding the case:

---

NOTES

previous mitzvah), this is considered a split decision and judges are added to the court (*Minchas Chinuch* §11).

Judges are always added two at a time (Mishnah, *Sanhedrin* 40a), to allow for the possibility that with the additional judges the court can reach a decision of either conviction or acquittal. If only one judge were added to an evenly divided court, no conviction could result; and if one judge were added to a court that voted eleven for acquittal and twelve for conviction, no clear verdict of acquittal could result (see *Dinah DeChayei, Lavin* 195-196).

30. Even after two judges are added, it is possible that the two judges will split their decision, so that the court is in the same position of conviction by a majority of one. In that case, pairs of judges are added until a decisive vote is obtained, or until the court reaches a total of seventy-one judges. If, at that point, the split court cannot reach a verdict of acquittal by one or conviction by two, the accused is acquitted (*Sanhedrin* 40a, 42a; see *Rambam, Hil. Sanhedrin* 9:2).

31. When a judge abstains from voting because he does not know how to decide, he is no longer counted as a member of the court. Thus, even if the opinion of that judge could not have affected the outcome of the case, such as when a large majority already exists and only one judge abstains, the court cannot issue a verdict, because its required quorum of twenty-three judges is now deficient. The court must therefore add judges and take a new vote (Mishnah, *Sanhedrin* 40a with *Rashi* ד״ה שנים עשר).

32. This law applies not only to the judges but even to the disciples who are assembled before the court. [As we shall see below, these disciples are allowed to voice their opinions, and sometimes are elevated to join the court and have their votes counted] (*Rambam, Hil. Sanhedrin* 10:3-4).

33. Since he never articulated his reasoning, and he is not present at the final ruling, his position is not recognized.

34. Since his opinion has been articulated and explained, it is recognized even though the one who presented it is no longer there.

In the case where one presented an argument for *conviction* and then died or was struck mute, his position is not recognized even if he already articulated his argument (*Minchas Chinuch* §6).

# 95 □ MISHPATIM / MITZVAH 77: NOT TO ARGUE FOR CONVICTION IN CAPITAL CASES

וְתַלְמִיד הַבָּא לְלַמֵּד חוֹבָה מְשַׁתְּקִין אוֹתוֹ, וְאִם אָמַר לְלַמֵּד זְכוּת מַעֲלִין אוֹתוֹ עִם סַנְהֶדְרִין, וְאִם יֵשׁ מַמָּשׁ בִּדְבָרָיו שׁוֹמְעִין לוֹ[35] וְאֵינוֹ יוֹרֵד מִשָּׁם לְעוֹלָם[36], וְאִם אֵין מַמָּשׁ בִּדְבָרָיו אֵינוֹ יוֹרֵד מִשָּׁם כָּל אוֹתוֹ הַיּוֹם דֶּרֶךְ מוּסָר[37], וְהַנִּדּוֹן בְּעַצְמוֹ שֶׁאָמַר יֵשׁ לִי לְלַמֵּד עַל עַצְמִי זְכוּת שׁוֹמְעִין לוֹ, וְהוּא שֶׁיֵּשׁ מַמָּשׁ בִּדְבָרָיו[38], וְיֶתֶר פְּרָטֶיהָ, מְבֹאָרִים בְּפֶרֶק (ז') (רביעי) מִסַּנְהֶדְרִין (דף ל״ב ואילך)[39].

וְנוֹהֶגֶת מִצְוָה זוֹ בִּזְכָרִים, אֲבָל לֹא בְּנָשִׁים, שֶׁאֵינָן דָּנוֹת כְּמוֹ שֶׁאָמַרְנוּ לְמַעְלָה בְּהַרְבֵּה מְקוֹמוֹת[40]. וְלֹא[41] יִקְשֶׁה בְּעֵינֶיךָ מַה שֶּׁכָּתוּב בִּדְבוֹרָה הַנְּבִיאָה (שופטים ד׳, ד׳) (ו)״הִיא שֹׁפְטָה

וְתַלְמִיד הַבָּא לְלַמֵּד חוֹבָה מְשַׁתְּקִין אוֹתוֹ — **A disciple who wishes to advance an argument for conviction, we silence him,** and his argument is not heard. וְאִם אָמַר לְלַמֵּד זְכוּת — **If,** however, he states that he wishes **to advance an argument for acquittal,** מַעֲלִין אוֹתוֹ עִם סַנְהֶדְרִין — we **elevate him** to sit **among** the other members of **the Sanhedrin** (court); וְאִם יֵשׁ מַמָּשׁ בִּדְבָרָיו שׁוֹמְעִין לוֹ — **if his words have substance, we listen to him,**[35] וְאֵינוֹ יוֹרֵד מִשָּׁם לְעוֹלָם — **and he never descends from [this position].**[36] וְאִם אֵין מַמָּשׁ בִּדְבָרָיו — **If,** however, **there is no substance to his words,** אֵינוֹ יוֹרֵד מִשָּׁם כָּל אוֹתוֹ הַיּוֹם דֶּרֶךְ מוּסָר — although his view is not taken into account, **he does not descend from this position** on the court **that entire day, out of propriety.**[37] וְהַנִּדּוֹן בְּעַצְמוֹ שֶׁאָמַר יֵשׁ לִי לְלַמֵּד עַל עַצְמִי זְכוּת — **As for a case** where **the defendant himself states, "I have** grounds **to advance an argument for acquittal on my own behalf,"** שׁוֹמְעִין לוֹ וְהוּא שֶׁיֵּשׁ מַמָּשׁ בִּדְבָרָיו — **we listen to him, but only when there is substance to his words.**[38] וְיֶתֶר פְּרָטֶיהָ — These laws, **and the additional details of this mitzvah,** מְבֹאָרִים בְּפֶרֶק רְבִיעִי מִסַּנְהֶדְרִין — **are set forth in the fourth chapter of** Tractate *Sanhedrin* (32a-34a).[39]

## ⸺ Applicability of the Mitzvah ⸺

וְנוֹהֶגֶת מִצְוָה זוֹ בִּזְכָרִים — **This mitzvah applies to men,** אֲבָל לֹא בְּנָשִׁים שֶׁאֵינָן דָּנוֹת — **but not to women, because they are not eligible to serve as judges,** כְּמוֹ שֶׁאָמַרְנוּ לְמַעְלָה בְּהַרְבֵּה מְקוֹמוֹת — **as we have stated previously in many places.**[40]

Having stated his opinion that women are ineligible to serve as judges, Chinuch digresses to discuss this topic at length, citing differing opinions on the matter, and explaining how he reached this conclusion. Chinuch begins by raising the case of one of the earliest leaders of the Jewish people, Deborah the Prophetess, who, Scripture indicates, served as a judge for the Jewish people:[41]

וְלֹא יִקְשֶׁה בְּעֵינֶיךָ — **Let not be difficult in your eyes** מַה שֶּׁכָּתוּב בִּדְבוֹרָה הַנְּבִיאָה (ו) ״הִיא שֹׁפְטָה

## NOTES

35. According to some Rishonim (see *Ramban, Sanhedrin* 32a and *Ran* ibid. 32a), the disciple's position is counted as a vote in the verdict; see *Ran* there for the exact circumstances in which the disciple's vote is counted.

36. I.e., he maintains his position on the court. *Meiri* (*Sanhedrin* 42a) notes that this does not mean that he remains an actual, permanent member of the court; rather, he remains on the court for the duration of this particular case — however long that may be. According to *Tos. Yom Tov* (*Sanhedrin* 5:4), the Mishnah means that the disciple always remains elevated from his position on the ground among the rows of disciples to a position on the benches among the judges; he does not, however, retain the actual position of judge.

37. Removing him publicly in the middle of the day would cause him embarrassment.

38. According to most Rishonim, the view of the defendant is listened to by the court to see if there is value to his argument, but it is certainly not counted in the final vote of the court (*Ramban, Sanhedrin* 32a; *Ran* ibid. 33b; *Yad Ramah* ibid. 42a). [Some maintain, however, that there are limited circumstances where the view of the defendant himself *is* counted as a vote (see *Meiri* ibid. 42a; *Mirkeves HaMishneh* to *Rambam, Hil. Sanhedrin* 10:8, and *Chazon Yechezkel, Sanhedrin* 7:2).]

39. See also *Sanhedrin* 40a, 42a. These laws are codified in *Rambam, Hil. Sanhedrin,* Chapters 9-11.

40. See, for example, Mitzvos 49, 53, 74, and 75.

41. Deborah was the third of the "Judges," i.e., the leaders who guided the Jewish people after the death of Joshua; she held this position for forty years (see *Judges*, Chapters 4-5).

## 96 □ משפטים / מצוה עז: שלא ילמד חובה מי שלמד זכות בדיני נפשות

אֶת יִשְׂרָאֵל, שֶׁאֶפְשָׁר לָנוּ לְתָרֵץ שֶׁלֹּא הָיָה הַדִּין נֶחְתָּךְ עַל פִּיהָ אֲבָל הָיְתָה אִשָּׁה חֲכָמָה וּנְבִיאָה וְהָיוּ נוֹשְׂאִים וְנוֹתְנִים עִמָּהּ אֲפִלּוּ בִּדְבָרִים שֶׁל אִסוּר וְהֶתֵּר וְדִינִין גַּם כֵּן, וְלָכֵן כָּתוּב עָלֶיהָ (ו)"הִיא שֹׁפְטָה אֶת יִשְׂרָאֵל",[42] אוֹ נֹאמַר שֶׁקִּבְּלוּהָ לָדוּן עֲלֵיהֶם רָאשֵׁי יִשְׂרָאֵל וְאַחֲרֵיהֶן כָּל אָדָם יָדוֹן עַל פִּיהָ, דְּבְקַבָּלָה וַדַּאי הַכֹּל כְּשֵׁרִים, דְּכָל תְּנַאי שֶׁבְּמָמוֹן קַיָּם. וּמִכָּל מָקוֹם כָּל זֶה שֶׁאָמַרְנוּ שֶׁאֵינָן דָּנוֹת הוּא כְּדַעַת קְצָת הַמְפָרְשִׁים וּכְדַעַת הַיְרוּשַׁלְמִי (שבועות פ"ד ה"א, סנהדרין פ"ג ה"ט), שֶׁכֵּן נִמְצָא שָׁם מְפֹרָשׁ, אֲבָל לְדַעַת קְצָת מִן הַמְפָרְשִׁים כְּשֵׁרוֹת הֵן לָדוּן, וְאָמְרוּ כִּי מִקְרָא מָלֵא הוּא שֶׁנֶּאֱמַר (ו)"הִיא שֹׁפְטָה", וּמַה שֶׁאָמְרוּ בְּסַנְהֶדְרִין (דף ל"ד ע"ב) דְּכָל שֶׁאֵינוֹ כָּשֵׁר לְהָעִיד אֵינוֹ כָּשֵׁר לָדוּן, וְנָשִׁים וַדַּאי אֵינָן כְּשֵׁרוֹת לְהָעִיד כִּדְמוּכָח שָׁם (ב"ק דף פ"ח ע"א, שבועות דף ל' ע"א),[43] אֶפְשָׁר שֶׁיֹּאמְרוּ לְפִי דַעְתָּם זֶה לְפִי שֶׁאֵין לְמֵדִין מִן הַכְּלָלוֹת (עירובין דף כ"ז ע"א).[44]

---

אֶת יִשְׂרָאֵל — that which is stated regarding Deborah the Prophetess, *She judged Israel* (*Judges* 4:4), which implies that a woman may serve as a judge, שֶׁאֶפְשָׁר לָנוּ לְתָרֵץ שֶׁלֹּא הָיָה הַדִּין נֶחְתָּךְ עַל פִּיהָ — because we can answer that judicial cases were not actually decided by her. אֲבָל הָיְתָה אִשָּׁה חֲכָמָה וּנְבִיאָה — Rather, the verse means that **she was a wise woman and a prophetess,** וְהָיוּ נוֹשְׂאִים וְנוֹתְנִים עִמָּהּ — and [the other leaders] of the nation would **consult and discuss** all matters **with her,** אֲפִלּוּ בִּדְבָרִים שֶׁל אִסוּר וְהֶתֵּר וְדִינִין גַּם כֵּן — even halachic **matters relating to that which is forbidden and that which is permissible, and** matters of **judicial law as well,** וְלָכֵן כָּתוּב עָלֶיהָ (ו)"הִיא שֹׁפְטָה אֶת יִשְׂרָאֵל" — **and therefore,** with regard to this advisory function, **it is written** that *she judged Israel*.[42]

אוֹ נֹאמַר — **Alternatively, we may say** to explain the verse, שֶׁקִּבְּלוּהָ לָדוּן עֲלֵיהֶם רָאשֵׁי יִשְׂרָאֵל — **that the leaders of Israel accepted her upon themselves as a judge** וְאַחֲרֵיהֶן כָּל אָדָם יָדוֹן עַל פִּיהָ — **and following them, all individuals** also accepted **to be judged by her.** דְּבְקַבָּלָה וַדַּאי הַכֹּל — **Because certainly, when** the litigants **accept** someone to be a judge, כְּשֵׁרִים — **anyone is fit** to serve, דְּכָל תְּנַאי שֶׁבְּמָמוֹן קַיָּם — **for any stipulation** made between two parties **concerning monetary matters is binding.**

Chinuch now introduces and explains the opinion of the Rishonim who maintain that a woman may serve as a judge:

וּמִכָּל מָקוֹם כָּל זֶה שֶׁאָמַרְנוּ שֶׁאֵינָן דָּנוֹת — **Nevertheless, all that we have stated, that [women] are not eligible to judge,** הוּא כְּדַעַת קְצָת הַמְפָרְשִׁים וּכְדַעַת הַיְרוּשַׁלְמִי — **is in accordance with some of the commentators, and in accordance with the view of** Talmud *Yerushalmi* (*Shevuos* 4:1; *Sanhedrin* 3:9), אֲבָל לְדַעַת קְצָת — שֶׁכֵּן נִמְצָא שָׁם מְפֹרָשׁ — **for this** view **is stated there explicitly.** מִן הַמְפָרְשִׁים כְּשֵׁרוֹת הֵן לָדוּן — **However, according to the view of some commentators, [women] are eligible to judge.** וְאָמְרוּ כִּי מִקְרָא מָלֵא הוּא — **[These commentators] say that [this position] is expressed by an unqualified verse,** which we cited above, שֶׁנֶּאֱמַר (ו)"הִיא שֹׁפְטָה" — **as it is stated, *She** (Deborah) *judged Israel*.

Chinuch resolves a possible difficulty with this position:

וּמַה שֶׁאָמְרוּ בְּסַנְהֶדְרִין דְּכָל שֶׁאֵינוֹ כָּשֵׁר — **As to what** [the Sages] **have said in** *Sanhedrin* (34b), לְהָעִיד אֵינוֹ כָּשֵׁר לָדוּן — **that anyone who is ineligible to give testimony is** likewise **ineligible to judge,** וְנָשִׁים וַדַּאי אֵינָן כְּשֵׁרוֹת לְהָעִיד כִּדְמוּכָח שָׁם — **and women are certainly ineligible to give testimony, as is clear from there** (*Bava Kamma* 88a; *Shevuos* 30a),[43] אֶפְשָׁר שֶׁיֹּאמְרוּ לְפִי דַעְתָּם זֶה — **perhaps [these authorities] will say, according to this opinion of theirs,** לְפִי שֶׁאֵין לְמֵדִין מִן הַכְּלָלוֹת — **that this is not a difficulty because we do not derive** categorical rulings **from general rules** (*Eruvin* 27a).[44]

---

### NOTES

42. See also *Tosafos*, *Gittin* 88b ד"ה ולא, for a similar explanation.

43. See below, Mitzvah 122 note 38.

44. Often the rules stated by the Sages have exceptions (see also *Tosafos*, *Bava Kamma* 15a). Thus, the rule that "whoever is ineligible to give testimony is ineligible to judge" may have an exception with regard to women.

## MISHPATIM / MITZVAH 77: NOT TO ARGUE FOR CONVICTION IN CAPITAL CASES

וְהַנִּרְאֶה מִן הַדְּבָרִים וּמִן הַסְּבָרָא שֶׁאֵינָן בְּתוֹרַת דִּין, כִּדְאִיתָא בִּירוּשַׁלְמִי וְכִדְמַשְׁמַע לְפִי גְמָרִין דֶּרֶךְ פְּשִׁיטוּת.

וְנוֹהֶגֶת מִצְוָה זוֹ בְּאֶרֶץ יִשְׂרָאֵל בִּלְבַד, שֶׁאֵין דָּנִין דִּינֵי נְפָשׁוֹת אֶלָּא שָׁם.[45]

וְהָעוֹבֵר עַל זֶה וְלֹא רָצָה לְלַמֵּד בַּדִּין מַה שֶּׁרוֹאֶה בְּדַעְתּוֹ וְסוֹמֵךְ עַל חֲבֵרָיו, אוֹ שֶׁפָּתַח לְחוֹבָה, אוֹ שֶׁחָזַר וְלִמֵּד חוֹבָה אַחַר הַזְּכוּת, אוֹ גָּדוֹל שֶׁפָּתַח תְּחִלָּה, עָבְרוּ עַל לָאו. וְאֵין לוֹקִין עָלָיו לְפִי שֶׁאֵין בּוֹ מַעֲשֶׂה.[46]

---

Chinuch concludes:

וְהַנִּרְאֶה מִן הַדְּבָרִים וּמִן הַסְּבָרָא שֶׁאֵינָן בְּתוֹרַת דִּין — **However, it appears, from** what is written regarding the subject **matter as well as from reason, that [women] are not included in the laws of judging,** כִּדְאִיתָא בִּירוּשַׁלְמִי וְכִדְמַשְׁמַע לְפִי גְמָרִין דֶּרֶךְ פְּשִׁיטוּת — **as it is stated in** *Yerushalmi* (ibid.), **and as is indicated by the simple understanding of our Talmud,** i.e., the Babylonian Talmud, *Sanhedrin*, ibid.

Chinuch returns to the application of this mitzvah.

וְנוֹהֶגֶת מִצְוָה זוֹ בְּאֶרֶץ יִשְׂרָאֵל בִּלְבַד — **This mitzvah applies only in Eretz Yisrael,** שֶׁאֵין דָּנִין דִּינֵי נְפָשׁוֹת אֶלָּא שָׁם — **because it is only there that we judge capital cases.**[45]

וְהָעוֹבֵר עַל זֶה וְלֹא רָצָה — **One who violates this** prohibition with regard to any of its four aspects, לְלַמֵּד בַּדִּין מַה שֶּׁרוֹאֶה בְּדַעְתּוֹ — **and he** either (1) **does not wish to express judgment of a case in accordance with what he sees in his own opinion,** וְסוֹמֵךְ עַל חֲבֵרָיו — **and** instead **relies upon his fellow** judges, אוֹ שֶׁפָּתַח לְחוֹבָה — **or** (2) **opens the deliberations** of a capital case with an argument **for conviction,** אוֹ שֶׁחָזַר וְלִמֵּד חוֹבָה אַחַר הַזְּכוּת — **or** (3) **advances an argument for conviction after** having already advanced **an argument for acquittal,** אוֹ גָּדוֹל שֶׁפָּתַח תְּחִלָּה — **or** (4) he is the **preeminent** judge **who voices his opinion first** during deliberations, עָבְרוּ עַל לָאו — in all of these instances, **[the violators] transgress** this prohibition. וְאֵין לוֹקִין עָלָיו לְפִי שֶׁאֵין בּוֹ מַעֲשֶׂה — However, **they are not liable to** *malkus* (lashes) **because** transgression of this prohibition **does not involve action.**[46]

---

### NOTES

45. Capital cases are tried only when the *Beis HaMikdash* is standing, and the Great Sanhedrin is sitting in its chamber on the Temple Mount (i.e., the לִשְׁכַּת הַגָּזִית, *Chamber of Hewn Stone*). When these conditions are in effect, however, capital cases may be tried outside of Eretz Yisrael as well, with a *beis din* of judges who were ordained in Eretz Yisrael (*Rambam, Hil. Sanhedrin* 14:11,14). Chinuch's statement that capital cases are tried only in Eretz Yisrael must be taken to mean that capital cases are tried in all places when the Great Sanhedrin judges in Eretz Yisrael (see *Minchas Chinuch* §9; for further discussion, see above, Mitzvah 47 note 16; see also below, Mitzvah 87 note 14).

46. This follows the principle that לָאו שֶׁאֵין בּוֹ מַעֲשֶׂה אֵין לוֹקִין עָלָיו, *one does not incur malkus for [violating] a prohibition that does not involve action*. See General Introduction, note 14.

---

> ### ☙ Insight: Reaching an Opinion
>
> Chinuch writes that the prohibition to rely on another judge's opinion or on the opinion of the majority applies only in capital cases, but in monetary cases a judge may base his vote on the opinion of other judges on the case. As mentioned above, in note 26, *Minchas Chinuch* (§1) finds great difficulty with this position. Even without this specific prohibition, *Minchas Chinuch* writes, a judge is obligated to assess the matters of the case from all angles and to deliver his own opinion on the matter — this is the basic definition of what it means to be a judge on any Torah court. To do any less, that is, to decide a case based on anything other than the facts before him and his own halachic opinion, is to pervert justice and abdicate his basic judicial responsibility! And although Chinuch mentions that monetary cases can essentially be decided by one judge, *Minchas Chinuch* points out that this is true only regarding certain kinds of monetary cases; in many other monetary cases

(such as torts), three judges are required by Biblical law.

*Minchas Chinuch* therefore maintains that, in fact, even in monetary cases it is prohibited for a judge to base his vote on the opinion of any of the other judges. The difference between monetary and capital cases is that with regard to capital cases, due to their severity, if one bases his vote on that of another judge he violates two prohibitions — one, the specific prohibition of this mitzvah, and another, the prohibition against perverting judgment — whereas if a judge does this in monetary cases he violates only the general prohibition against perverting judgment.

Nevertheless, *Minchas Chinuch* himself acknowledges that the language of *Mechilta* cited by Chinuch does indicate that in monetary cases a judge may rely on the opinion of other judges. Various solutions have therefore been proposed by the Acharonim to resolve the apparently intractable difficulty raised by *Minchas Chinuch*.

Some explain that when *Mechilta* permits a judge to rely on the opinion of others in monetary cases, it refers only to a situation where the opinion of that judge cannot affect the outcome of the case. For example, on a standard monetary court of three, if two judges are split, the third judge may certainly not rely on the opinion of one of the others to render his judgment, since this vote, in effect, decides the case. However, if two judges both agree, the vote of the third judge can have no effect on the outcome of the case; therefore, he may render his judgment based on the position of another judge. In a capital case, however, even if the majority lean one way and the vote of one particular judge will make no difference, he may not rely on the opinion of another judge (*Mishnas Yaavetz* [R' Betzalel Zolty], *Choshen Mishpat* 5:6; see *Minchas Soless* for another suggestion along these lines).

Other Acharonim take an entirely different approach to this question, one that reexamines what we mean when we speak of an "opinion" of a judge. According to this approach, Chinuch agrees that a judge who does not know how to rule is never allowed to simply parrot the opinion of another judge; to do this is not to judge at all. The case under discussion here is where the judge did in fact reach his own opinion, but nevertheless, the opinion might not be considered entirely his — as shall be explained.

Imagine two judges who disagree regarding a case, where one of the judges is on a completely different level of competence, knowledge, and understanding than the other. If we were to ask the lesser judge his final opinion on the matter, he would respond as follows: I myself would think one way about this case, but I know quite clearly that the other judge is unequivocally wiser than myself. Knowing as I do that his view is more likely to be the truth, I must therefore conclude that my view is mistaken, and embrace the view of the greater judge.

According to *Minchas Yitzchak*, this is the case to which Chinuch refers. In monetary cases, the lesser judge may rule according to what he believes to be the truth — that is, he may rule in accordance with the opinion of the more eminent judge, whom he knows to be so much greater than himself. In capital cases, however, the Torah forbids a judge to do this. There, the lesser judge is obligated to state his own view, even when he knows that those much greater than him have concluded otherwise. [See a related view of *R' Hai Gaon*, cited by *Ramban*, *Sanhedrin* 32a.]

*Minchah Chadashah* suggests another possibility. *Mechilta* is referring to a case where the judge reached his own opinion on the matter, and is actually voting according to his own opinion, but the judge did not arrive at this opinion by his own research and reflection. Instead, before deciding the case for himself, he listened to the analysis of a judge greater than himself, and found that he agreed fully with that analysis. In monetary cases, there is nothing wrong with a judge deciding a case after hearing what he believes to be a correct dissertation of the merits. In capital cases, however, we demand that every judge arrive at his opinion through his own research and independent study. To vote after hearing another's understanding of the case, even if he finds that he agrees with that approach, is unacceptable when a life is at stake (see also *Aruch HaShulchan*, *Choshen Mishpat* 18:9 and *Maharam Schik* to this mitzvah).

## מִצְוָה עח: מִצְוַת הַטָיָה אַחֲרֵי רַבִּים

לִנְטוֹת אַחֲרֵי רַבִּים, וְהוּא כְּשֶׁיִּפֹּל מַחֲלֹקֶת בֵּין הַחֲכָמִים בְּדִין מִדִּינֵי הַתּוֹרָה כֻּלָּהּ,[1] וּכְמוֹ כֵן בְּדִין פְּרָטִי, כְּלוֹמַר, בְּדִין שֶׁיְּהֵא בֵּין רְאוּבֵן וְשִׁמְעוֹן עַל דֶּרֶךְ מָשָׁל, כְּשֶׁתִּהְיֶה הַמַּחֲלֹקֶת בֵּין דַּיָּנֵי עִירָם שֶׁקְּצָתָם דָּנִין לְחִיּוּב וּקְצָתָם לִפְטוֹר, לִנְטוֹת אַחַר הָרֹב לְעוֹלָם,[2] שֶׁנֶּאֱמַר (שמות כ"ג, ב') אַחֲרֵי רַבִּים לְהַטֹּת,[3] וּבְבֵאוּר אָמְרוּ זִכְרוֹנָם לִבְרָכָה (חולין דף י"א ע"א) רֻבָּא דְאוֹרַיְתָא.[4,5]

## ⁓ Mitzvah 78 ⁓
## The Obligation to Follow the Majority

אַחֲרֵי רַבִּים לְהַטֹּת

*According to the majority shall [the matter] be decided (Exodus 23:2).*

לִנְטוֹת אַחֲרֵי רַבִּים — **We are commanded to follow** the opinion of **the majority.**

Chinuch explains that this mitzvah has two distinct applications.

וְהוּא כְּשֶׁיִּפֹּל מַחֲלֹקֶת בֵּין הַחֲכָמִים — (1) **This** law **applies when a disagreement occurs between the Sages** בְּדִין מִדִּינֵי הַתּוֹרָה כֻּלָּהּ — **regarding** the proper interpretation of **any law of the laws of the entire Torah;** in this case we are enjoined by this mitzvah to follow the majority opinion.[1]

וּכְמוֹ כֵן בְּדִין פְּרָטִי — (2) **Likewise,** this mitzvah applies **to** the procedure for deciding **a specific** court **case;** כְּלוֹמַר, בְּדִין שֶׁיְּהֵא בֵּין רְאוּבֵן וְשִׁמְעוֹן עַל דֶּרֶךְ מָשָׁל — **that is to say, in a litigation between two individuals — Reuven and Shimon, for example —** כְּשֶׁתִּהְיֶה הַמַּחֲלֹקֶת בֵּין דַּיָּנֵי עִירָם — **if there is disagreement between the judges of** the court of **their city** regarding the correct ruling on their case, שֶׁקְּצָתָם דָּנִין לְחִיּוּב וּקְצָתָם לִפְטוֹר — **where some of them argue** that one of the parties **is liable, while some of them** argue **that he is exempt** from liability, לִנְטוֹת אַחַר הָרֹב לְעוֹלָם — we are commanded **to always follow the majority opinion.**[2]

שֶׁנֶּאֱמַר "אַחֲרֵי רַבִּים לְהַטֹּת" — **We are so commanded as it is stated** (Exodus 23:2): ***According to the majority shall [the matter] be decided.***[3] וּבְבֵאוּר אָמְרוּ זִכְרוֹנָם לִבְרָכָה — Indeed, **[the Sages], of blessed memory, state explicitly** (Bava Basra 24a): רֻבָּא דְאוֹרַיְתָא — **The principle of following the majority is Biblical** in origin.[4] And elsewhere (Chullin 11a), the Sages state that the principle of following the majority can be derived from this verse.[5]

---

### NOTES

1. That is, in a question pertaining to any aspect of Jewish law, one must follow the opinion of the majority of Torah scholars regarding that law. Various qualifications to this general rule are discussed by the halachic authorities; see, for example, *Rama, Choshen Mishpat* 25:2 with commentaries; and *Chazon Ish, Yoreh Deah* 150:8. See also Chinuch below.

2. That is, we follow the opinion of the majority of judges sitting on the case. In this application, only the votes of the judges on the court are taken into account, not the opinions of any other Torah scholars. See Chinuch further.

3. According to the simple meaning, the verse, of which the cited phrase is a part, enjoins a judge *not* to follow the majority when the majority is clearly perverting justice (see *Rashi* to verse for how the words of the verse are understood following this interpretation). The translation here follows the exegetical approach of the Sages (*Sanhedrin* 2b, *Chullin* 11a), according to which this part of the verse teaches that we are to follow a simple majority in most cases of halachic or judicial dispute.

4. Since the simple meaning of the verse does not expressly indicate a mitzvah to follow the majority (see previous note), Chinuch cites this source to show that indeed the mitzvah to follow the majority is Biblical in origin (see *R' Y. F. Perla, Sefer HaMitzvos* of Rav Saadiah Gaon, *Asei* 96, Volume I, p. 651).

5. In addition to the obligation to follow the majority in the two situations mentioned by Chinuch (regarding a dispute in halachah, and in the context of a court case), there are other applications of this principle as well, as set out in the Insight.

וּבְחִירַת רֹב זֶה לְפִי הַדּוֹמֶה הוּא בִּשְׁנֵי הַכִּתּוֹת הַחוֹלְקוֹת יוֹדְעוֹת בְּחָכְמַת הַתּוֹרָה בְּשָׁוֶה, שֶׁאֵין לוֹמַר שֶׁכַּת חֲכָמִים מוּעֶטֶת לֹא תַכְרִיעַ כַּת בּוּרִים מְרֻבָּה וַאֲפִלּוּ כְּיוֹצְאֵי מִצְרַיִם[6], אֲבָל בְּהִשְׁתַּוּוֹת הַחָכְמָה אוֹ בְּקֵרוּב הוֹדִיעָתְנוּ הַתּוֹרָה שֶׁרִבּוּי הַדֵּעוֹת יַסְכִּימוּ לְעוֹלָם אֶל הָאֱמֶת יוֹתֵר מִן הַמִּעוּט, וּבֵין שֶׁיַּסְכִּימוּ לָאֱמֶת אוֹ לֹא יַסְכִּימוּ לְפִי דַעַת הַשּׁוֹמֵעַ, הַדִּין נוֹתֵן שֶׁלֹּא נָסוּר מִדֶּרֶךְ הָרֹב[7]. וּמַה שֶּׁאֲנִי אוֹמֵר כִּי בְּחִירַת הָרֹב הוּא לְעוֹלָם בִּשְׁנֵי הַכִּתּוֹת הַחוֹלְקִין שָׁוּוֹת בְּחָכְמַת הָאֱמֶת[8], כִּי כֵן נֶאֱמַר בְּכָל מָקוֹם חוּץ מִן הַסַּנְהֶדְרִין[9], שֶׁבָּהֶם לֹא נְדַקְדֵּק בִּהְיוֹתָם חוֹלְקִים אֵי זוֹ כַת יוֹדַעַת יוֹתֵר, אֶלָּא לְעוֹלָם נַעֲשֶׂה כְּדִבְרֵי הָרֹב מֵהֶם,

---

Chinuch qualifies the general guideline of following the majority in cases of disagreement in Torah law: וּבְחִירַת רֹב זֶה לְפִי הַדּוֹמֶה הוּא — This obligation of **choosing** the side of **the majority, it would seem, applies** only בִּשְׁנֵי הַכִּתּוֹת הַחוֹלְקוֹת יוֹדְעוֹת בְּחָכְמַת הַתּוֹרָה בְּשָׁוֶה — **when the two disagreeing groups are equally knowledgeable in Torah wisdom.** שֶׁאֵין לוֹמַר שֶׁכַּת חֲכָמִים מוּעֶטֶת לֹא תַכְרִיעַ כַּת בּוּרִים מְרֻבָּה — **This distinction must be made, for one cannot say** that the principle of following the majority dictates **that a small group of wise men should not outweigh** the opinions of **a large group of ignoramuses;** surely the opinion of the wise men should be given greater weight, וַאֲפִלּוּ כְּיוֹצְאֵי מִצְרַיִם — **even** if the group of ignoramuses is as numerous **as those who left Egypt!**[6] אֲבָל בְּהִשְׁתַּוּוֹת הַחָכְמָה אוֹ בְּקֵרוּב — **However, when** the two groups are **equal in wisdom, or** at least **close** to being equal, הוֹדִיעָתְנוּ הַתּוֹרָה שֶׁרִבּוּי הַדֵּעוֹת יַסְכִּימוּ לְעוֹלָם אֶל הָאֱמֶת יוֹתֵר מִן הַמִּעוּט — the **Torah informs us,** regarding that case, **that the majority of minds will, as a rule, arrive at the truth** with **greater** frequency **than the minority.** וּבֵין שֶׁיַּסְכִּימוּ לָאֱמֶת אוֹ לֹא יַסְכִּימוּ לְפִי דַעַת הַשּׁוֹמֵעַ — Furthermore, regardless of **whether [the majority] does or does not arrive at the truth according to the opinion of the individual who hears their** decision, הַדִּין נוֹתֵן שֶׁלֹּא נָסוּר מִדֶּרֶךְ הָרֹב — **logic dictates that we may not diverge from the path set out by the majority.**[7]

Chinuch notes that although the relative wisdom of the parties must be taken into account, this is not a universal rule:

וּמַה שֶּׁאֲנִי אוֹמֵר כִּי בְּחִירַת הָרֹב הוּא לְעוֹלָם בִּשְׁנֵי הַכִּתּוֹת הַחוֹלְקִין שָׁוּוֹת — **This that I have said,** בְּחָכְמַת הָאֱמֶת — **that** the principle of **choosing the majority applies only when the two differing groups are equal in the true wisdom** (i.e., Torah knowledge and wisdom),[8] כִּי כֵן נֶאֱמַר בְּכָל מָקוֹם — surely we say this rule **in all areas** of dispute **with the exception of** disagreements between the judges of **the Sanhedrin** (High Court),[9] שֶׁבָּהֶם לֹא נְדַקְדֵּק בִּהְיוֹתָם חוֹלְקִים אֵי זוֹ כַת יוֹדַעַת יוֹתֵר — **with regard to whom we are not particular, when they disagree,** about **which group is more knowledgeable;** אֶלָּא לְעוֹלָם נַעֲשֶׂה כְּדִבְרֵי הָרֹב מֵהֶם — **rather, we always act in accordance with the** opinion of the **majority of [judges]** irrespective of the relative knowledge and

---

NOTES

6. This is an expression for an exceedingly large number. Six hundred thousand men left Egypt, aside from women and children (*Exodus* 12:37).

7. Chinuch elaborates on this point further, below, explaining why any other approach to settling halachic disputes is untenable.

[Although Chinuch seems to present the above qualification regarding the relative wisdom of the two groups as an independent logical argument (introducing it with the words, לְפִי הַדּוֹמֶה, *it seems*), *Minchas Chinuch* §1 notes that there is a clear source for this distinction in the Gemara (*Yevamos* 14a).]

8. [It may be that the word "בְּחָכְמַת" in this sentence is a result of a copyist's error, and should actually read "בְּחָכְמָה". In that case, the sentences would read as follows: בִּשְׁנֵי הַכִּתּוֹת הַחוֹלְקִין שָׁוּוֹת בְּחָכְמָה, הָאֱמֶת כִּי כֵן נֶאֱמַר בְּכָל מָקוֹם ..., *when the two differing groups are equal in wisdom, in truth we say this in all areas...*]

9. There were two tiers of Sanhedrin in the times of the *Beis HaMikdash*. The Great Sanhedrin was made up of seventy-one of the greatest sages of the Jewish nation, who were seated in a special chamber on the Temple Mount; it was the highest court in the judicial system. In addition, there were smaller sanhedrins made up of twenty-three sages each, which operated throughout the cities of Eretz Yisrael (see Mitzvah 491 where Chinuch elaborates on the organization and laws of these institutions). See further, below, note 12.

# 101 ◻ MISHPATIM / MITZVAH 78: THE OBLIGATION TO FOLLOW THE MAJORITY

וְהַטַּעַם לְפִי שֶׁהֵם הָיוּ בְּחֶשְׁבּוֹן מְחֻיָּב מִן הַתּוֹרָה,[10] וְהוּא כְּאִלּוּ צִוְּתָה הַתּוֹרָה בְּפֵרוּשׁ, אַחַר רֹב שֶׁל אֵלּוּ תַּעֲשׂוּ כָּל עִנְיְנֵיכֶם,[11] וְעוֹד שֶׁהֵם כֻּלָּם הָיוּ חֲכָמִים גְּדוֹלִים.[12]

וּמִשָּׁרְשֵׁי מִצְוָה זוֹ, שֶׁנִּצְטַוֵּינוּ בָּזֶה לְחַזֵּק קִיּוּם דָּתֵנוּ, שֶׁאִלּוּ נִצְטַוֵּינוּ קַיְּמוּ הַתּוֹרָה כַּאֲשֶׁר תּוּכְלוּ לְהַשִּׂיג כַּוָּנַת אֲמִתָּתָהּ, כָּל אֶחָד וְאֶחָד מִיִּשְׂרָאֵל יֹאמַר דַּעְתִּי נוֹתֶנֶת שֶׁאֲמִתַּת עִנְיַן פְּלוֹנִי כֵּן הוּא, וַאֲפִלּוּ כָּל הָעוֹלָם יֹאמְרוּ בְּהֶפְכּוֹ לֹא יִהְיֶה לוֹ רְשׁוּת לַעֲשׂוֹת הָעִנְיָן בְּהֵפֶךְ הָאֱמֶת לְפִי דַעְתּוֹ, וְיֵצֵא מִזֶּה חֻרְבָּן שֶׁתֵּעָשֶׂה הַתּוֹרָה כְּכַמָּה תוֹרוֹת,

---

wisdom of the differing parties. וְהַטַּעַם לְפִי שֶׁהֵם הָיוּ בְּחֶשְׁבּוֹן מְחֻיָּב מִן הַתּוֹרָה – **The reason** for this difference **is, because [the judges]** of the Sanhedrin **are of a fixed number designated by the Torah,**[10] וְהוּא כְּאִלּוּ צִוְּתָה הַתּוֹרָה בְּפֵרוּשׁ – **and** therefore, by directing us to follow the majority of the Sanhedrin in judicial cases, **it is as if the Torah has expressly commanded:** אַחַר רֹב שֶׁל אֵלּוּ תַּעֲשׂוּ כָּל עִנְיְנֵיכֶם – **"Following the majority of these** specific Sages who compose the Sanhedrin **shall you conduct all your issues."**[11] וְעוֹד שֶׁהֵם כֻּלָּם הָיוּ חֲכָמִים גְּדוֹלִים – **Furthermore, all [the judges of the Sanhedrin] were Sages of great stature,** and therefore there would generally not be a great discrepancy in the relative wisdom of those judges.[12]

## ⌒ Underlying Purpose of the Mitzvah ⌒

וּמִשָּׁרְשֵׁי מִצְוָה זוֹ – **Among the underlying purposes of this mitzvah** שֶׁנִּצְטַוֵּינוּ בָּזֶה לְחַזֵּק קִיּוּם דָּתֵנוּ – **is that we are commanded regarding this** matter of following the majority opinion in order **to strengthen the** continued **existence of our law,** i.e., the Torah.

Chinuch explains why this mitzvah is essential to the continuity of Torah law and observance:

שֶׁאִלּוּ נִצְטַוֵּינוּ – **For if we** were not commanded to follow the majority, but instead **had been commanded:** קַיְּמוּ הַתּוֹרָה כַּאֲשֶׁר תּוּכְלוּ לְהַשִּׂיג כַּוָּנַת אֲמִתָּתָהּ – **"Fulfill** the dictates of **the Torah following** the best of **your ability to comprehend its true intent,"** כָּל אֶחָד וְאֶחָד מִיִּשְׂרָאֵל יֹאמַר – **each individual member of Israel would say,** דַּעְתִּי נוֹתֶנֶת שֶׁאֲמִתַּת עִנְיַן פְּלוֹנִי כֵּן הוּא – **"My understanding is that the truth of such-and-such matter** (i.e., a particular law) **is such."** Each individual would have his own opinion on matters of Torah law, and would be obligated to follow his own judgment. וַאֲפִלּוּ כָּל הָעוֹלָם יֹאמְרוּ בְּהֶפְכּוֹ – **And, even if the entire world would state the opposite [of his opinion]** לֹא יִהְיֶה לוֹ רְשׁוּת לַעֲשׂוֹת הָעִנְיָן בְּהֵפֶךְ הָאֱמֶת לְפִי דַעְתּוֹ – **he would not have the right to act** in regard to **that matter in a way that is incompatible with the truth according to his** own **view.** וְיֵצֵא מִזֶּה חֻרְבָּן שֶׁתֵּעָשֶׂה הַתּוֹרָה כְּכַמָּה תוֹרוֹת – **This** system would

---

### NOTES

10. The number of Sages on the Sanhedrin is designated by Torah law (see *Sanhedrin* 2a).

11. When there is a general disagreement among scholars regarding Torah law, the number and identification of the participants in the disagreement is not defined. It is therefore logical in that case to say that we look only at scholars of basically equal stature when judging a majority. However, when dealing with a dispute that is adjudicated by the Sanhedrin, the number of judges is set by the Torah. Therefore, the imperative to follow the majority refers to the majority of the specific Sages sitting on that court, regardless of their comparative wisdom.

12. See Mitzvah 491, where Chinuch describes at length the high caliber of wisdom and character that was required to be a member of the Sanhedrin.

In this section, Chinuch apparently refers to both levels of Sanhedrin, the Great Sanhedrin, and the lower courts of twenty-three (see above, note 9; see *Minchas Yitzchak*, Mitzvah 77 §1). Regarding courts of three judges, which preside on monetary cases, Chinuch seems to indicate that the majority is followed only when the judges are of equal stature. Although a similar opinion is recorded by *Ramban* (*Sanhedrin* 32a in the name of *Rav Hai Gaon*), *Ramban* himself (ibid.) disputes this view and maintains that with regard to judges sitting on a court, the majority is always followed regardless of the comparative wisdom of the individual judges. [In fact, following Chinuch's reasoning above, that we do not follow comparative wisdom where the Torah ordained a specific number of judges, there should be no difference between a court of twenty-three and a court of three. It may be suggested that when Chinuch speaks of "Sanhedrin" in this context, he actually refers to all judicial proceedings including monetary courts of three, and Chinuch's primary point is only to distinguish in a general sense between non-judicial halachic disputes and dissenting votes in any court case.]

## 102 ❑ משפטים / מצוה עח: מצות הטיה אחרי רבים

כִּי כָל אֶחָד יָדִין כְּפִי עֲנִיּוּת דַּעְתּוֹ. אֲבָל עַכְשָׁו שֶׁבַּפֵּרוּשׁ נִצְטַוִּינוּ לְקַבֵּל בָּהּ דַּעַת רֹב הַחֲכָמִים, יֵשׁ תּוֹרָה אַחַת לְכֻלָּנוּ[13] וְהוּא קִיּוּמֵנוּ גָּדוֹל בָּהּ, וְאֵין לָנוּ לָזוּז מִדַּעְתָּם וִיהִי מָה, וּבְכֵן בַּעֲשׂוֹתֵנוּ מִצְוָתָם אָנוּ מַשְׁלִימִין מִצְוַת הָאֵל, וַאֲפִלּוּ אִם לֹא יְכַוְּנוּ לִפְעָמִים הַחֲכָמִים אֶל הָאֱמֶת חָלִילָה, עֲלֵיהֶם יִהְיֶה הַחַטָּאת וְלֹא עָלֵינוּ[14]. וְזֶהוּ הָעִנְיָן שֶׁאָמְרוּ זִכְרוֹנָם לִבְרָכָה בְּהוֹרָיוֹת (דף ב' ע"א) שֶׁבֵּית דִּין שֶׁטָּעוּ בְּהוֹרָאָה וְעָשָׂה הַיָּחִיד עַל פִּיהֶם, שֶׁהֵם בְּחִיּוּב הַקָּרְבָּן[15] לֹא הַיָּחִיד כְּלָל[16], זוּלָתִי בִּצְדָדִים מְפֹרָשִׁים שָׁם[17].

---

**result in a destruction** of the Torah system, **for the Torah would become as if** it were comprised of **many** divergent, individual **Torahs,** as every person would practice a markedly different set of laws, כִּי כָל אֶחָד יָדִין כְּפִי עֲנִיּוּת דַּעְתּוֹ — **because each individual would judge** how the Torah's laws are to be interpreted **in accordance with the limitations of his own intellect.**

אֲבָל עַכְשָׁו שֶׁבַּפֵּרוּשׁ נִצְטַוִּינוּ לְקַבֵּל בָּהּ דַּעַת רֹב הַחֲכָמִים — **Now, however, that we have been expressly commanded** by this mitzvah **to accept, with regard to [Torah law], the opinion of the majority of the Sages** as the authoritative interpretation of the Law, יֵשׁ תּוֹרָה אַחַת לְכֻלָּנוּ — **we** have only **one** version of **Torah** law that applies **to us all.**[13] וְהוּא קִיּוּמֵנוּ גָּדוֹל בָּהּ — Thus, **this will cause our continued endurance** in observing **[the Torah] to be great.** וְאֵין לָנוּ לָזוּז מִדַּעְתָּם וִיהִי מָה — **We are** therefore **not to deviate from the views [of the Sages], come what may;** וּבְכֵן בַּעֲשׂוֹתֵנוּ מִצְוָתָם אָנוּ מַשְׁלִימִין מִצְוַת הָאֵל — **and it follows** that **when we perform the commandment of [the Sages]** (i.e., we abide by their interpretation of Torah law), **we are** actually **fulfilling the commandment of the Almighty** Himself. וַאֲפִלּוּ אִם לֹא יְכַוְּנוּ לִפְעָמִים הַחֲכָמִים אֶל הָאֱמֶת חָלִילָה — **And even if, on occasion, the Sages do not arrive at the truth** regarding a Torah law, **[God] forbid,** עֲלֵיהֶם יִהְיֶה הַחַטָּאת וְלֹא עָלֵינוּ — we must still follow their dictates, and the burden of **the sin** committed as a result of the erroneous decision **will be upon them and not upon us.**[14]

Chinuch illustrates that the individual is not liable when following the dictates of the Sages, by citing a law relating to atonement offerings. When a person mistakenly violates certain severe Torah prohibitions, he is obligated to offer a *chatas* (sin) offering (see Mitzvah 121). Chinuch explains how this obligation is affected when one was following the ruling of the Sages:

וְזֶהוּ הָעִנְיָן שֶׁאָמְרוּ זִכְרוֹנָם לִבְרָכָה בְּהוֹרָיוֹת — **This** idea **is the** underlying **concept of that which [the Sages], of blessed memory, have stated in** Tractate *Horayos* (2a), שֶׁבֵּית דִּין שֶׁטָּעוּ בְּהוֹרָאָה — **that when beis din** (i.e., the Great Sanhedrin) **erred in their ruling,** declaring an action permitted when in fact it violates a prohibition for which a *chatas* offering would be required, וְעָשָׂה הַיָּחִיד עַל פִּיהֶם — **and an individual acted according to their [ruling],** שֶׁהֵם בְּחִיּוּב הַקָּרְבָּן — the law is **that,** when the ruling is later discovered to be erroneous, it is **[the judges] who are obligated to** bring **the offering,**[15] לֹא הַיָּחִיד כְּלָל — **and the individual** who committed the sin has **no** liability **whatsoever,**[16] זוּלָתִי בִּצְדָדִים מְפֹרָשִׁים שָׁם — **with the exception of certain cases delineated there** (Tractate *Horayos*).[17]

---

### NOTES

13. We learn from this mitzvah that each individual is not obligated to search for the "truth" of how the Torah is to be followed, relying on his own final decision; rather, the entire nation is charged with following the Torah laws according to the interpretation of the majority of the Torah Sages, even if it is not "true" according to one's own opinion.

14. Since the Torah commands us to accept the decisions of the Sages, we are not held accountable for any wrongdoing committed when following their rulings. In this case it is the Sages who bear the responsibility for issuing a faulty ruling.

For further discussion, see Mitzvah 496, where Chinuch elaborates on the necessity for a system where the Torah has one deciding body for all to follow, despite the remote possibility of a mistaken ruling on occasion.

15. That is, there is an obligation upon the Sanhedrin to offer a special sacrifice to atone for this error. This offering is called the פַּר הֶעְלֵם דָּבָר, *bull for the communal error* (see Mitzvah 120).

16. When the *bull for the communal error* is brought, all individuals who acted upon the ruling of the Sanhedrin are not liable to bring their own *chatas* offerings for their violations.

17. In Mitzvah 120, Chinuch mentions some of the criteria for the obligatory *bull for the communal error* to be brought. [When those criteria are not met, the individual does indeed bring a *chatas*.]

## MISHPATIM / MITZVAH 78: THE OBLIGATION TO FOLLOW THE MAJORITY

דִּינֵי הַמִּצְוָה, כְּגוֹן הַחִלּוּקִים שֶׁיֵּשׁ בָּרֹב זֶה בֵּין דִּינֵי מָמוֹנוֹת לְדִינֵי נְפָשׁוֹת, שֶׁבְּדִינֵי נְפָשׁוֹת צָרִיךְ שֶׁיְּהֵא הָרֹב יוֹתֵר נִכָּר,[18] וְכַמָּה אֲנָשִׁים צְרִיכִים לְדִינֵי נְפָשׁוֹת מֵחֲמַת שֶׁאָנוּ מְצֻוִּין לַעֲשׂוֹת כְּדִבְרֵי הָרֹב וְאֵין רָאוּי לְהָמִית אִישׁ אֶחָד בִּשְׁנֵי דַיָּנִין שֶׁהֵם רֹב כְּנֶגֶד אֶחָד,[19] וְכֵן מַה שֶּׁאָמְרוּ זִכְרוֹנָם לִבְרָכָה (סנהדרין דף ל״ז ע״א) שֶׁצְּרִיכִין גַּם כֵּן אֵלּוּ הָעוֹשִׂים רֹב בְּדִינֵי נְפָשׁוֹת לִהְיוֹת סְמוּכִין,[20] וְהַסְּמִיכָה עֵדוּת לָהֶם שֶׁהֵם חֲכָמִים וּנְבוֹנִים וּשְׁלֵמִים שֶׁרְאוּיִים לַעֲשׂוֹת כָּל דָּבָר עַל יָדָם,[21] וְלֹא נָמִית אֲנָשִׁים עַל פִּי אֲנָשִׁים חַסְרֵי חָכְמָה

---

### ~ Laws of the Mitzvah ~

דִּינֵי הַמִּצְוָה — **The laws of the mitzvah** include כְּגוֹן הַחִלּוּקִים שֶׁיֵּשׁ בָּרֹב זֶה בֵּין דִּינֵי מָמוֹנוֹת לְדִינֵי נְפָשׁוֹת — **for example, the differences regarding this** requirement to follow the **majority between** judgments of **monetary cases and** judgments of **capital cases.** שֶׁבְּדִינֵי נְפָשׁוֹת צָרִיךְ שֶׁיְּהֵא הָרֹב יוֹתֵר נִכָּר — **The difference is that in capital cases the** convicting **majority must be more distinct** than in monetary cases, i.e., there must be a majority of at least two judges in order to convict in capital cases.[18]

Chinuch discusses a ramification of the preceding law:

וְכַמָּה אֲנָשִׁים צְרִיכִים לְדִינֵי נְפָשׁוֹת — **And,** also included is the law as to **how many men are required to** compose a Sanhedrin that can judge **capital cases.** This law is impacted by our mitzvah, מֵחֲמַת שֶׁאָנוּ מְצֻוִּין לַעֲשׂוֹת כְּדִבְרֵי הָרֹב — **due to the fact that we are commanded** by our mitzvah **to follow the majority,** וְאֵין רָאוּי לְהָמִית אִישׁ אֶחָד בִּשְׁנֵי דַיָּנִין שֶׁהֵם רֹב כְּנֶגֶד אֶחָד — **and it would not be appropriate to execute a person on the basis of** a simple majority of **two judges against one,** i.e., the court may not execute a person based on a majority of one, as mentioned above. Since a majority of at least two is required for conviction, additional judges are required for capital cases.[19]

Chinuch widens his discussion to include laws pertaining to the court procedures of capital cases and the qualification of its judges. These laws derive from the extreme caution that must be taken, even when following a majority, when a life is at stake:

וְכֵן מַה שֶּׁאָמְרוּ זִכְרוֹנָם לִבְרָכָה — **Also** included in these laws is **that which [the Sages], of blessed memory, have stated** (*Sanhedrin* 37a), שֶׁצְּרִיכִין גַּם כֵּן אֵלּוּ הָעוֹשִׂים רֹב בְּדִינֵי נְפָשׁוֹת לִהְיוֹת סְמוּכִין — **that the [judges] that constitute the majority in capital cases must be ordained with** *semichah*,[20] וְהַסְּמִיכָה עֵדוּת לָהֶם — **and the** *semichah* **serves as testimony regarding them** שֶׁהֵם חֲכָמִים וּנְבוֹנִים וּשְׁלֵמִים — **that they are wise, understanding, and of complete** character, i.e., not deficient in any refined character trait, שֶׁרְאוּיִים לַעֲשׂוֹת כָּל דָּבָר עַל יָדָם — **through whom it is befitting that all acts** of significance **be performed.**[21] וְלֹא נָמִית אֲנָשִׁים עַל פִּי אֲנָשִׁים חַסְרֵי חָכְמָה — The Torah requires this **so that we shall not put people to death based on the words of**

---

### NOTES

18. In monetary cases, a simple majority is always followed. In capital cases, however, while a simple majority is sufficient to acquit, a two-judge majority is required to convict. Chinuch elaborated on this requirement above, in Mitzvah 76.

19. A court that tries capital cases must consist of at least twenty-three judges. The Mishnah (*Sanhedrin* 2a-b) deduces this number as follows: In describing a capital case, the Torah indicates that there must be enough judges on the court for it to be possible that at least ten judges will vote for conviction and ten for acquittal. This gives us a minimum of twenty judges. Since a two-judge majority is required in order to convict, we must have an additional two judges on the court, to allow a possibility of superseding the ten votes for acquittal by two (a vote of twelve to ten). This brings us to twenty-two judges. Finally, since a court cannot consist of an even number of judges, as that would allow for a split decision, we add another judge, bringing the total to twenty-three judges. Thus, the necessity for a two-judge majority for conviction in capital cases causes us to increase the number of judges required to try such cases (see *Minchas Chinuch* §4).

20. *Semichah* refers to a special ordination, which is conferred only in Eretz Yisrael, by a sage whose own ordination can be traced back through a line of sages all the way to Moses. See Mitzvah 491 for a discussion of the *semichah* ordination. [Today, the chain of sages ordained with *semichah* has been broken and, consequently, we no longer have judges qualified to judge capital cases.]

21. See Mitzvah 491 for other requirements regarding the stature of judges who sit on capital cases.

## משפטים / מצוה עח: מצות הטיה אחרי רבים / 104

פֶּן יִטְעוּ בַדִּין, וּלְמִיתָה אֵין תַּשְׁלוּמִין, וְשֶׁבְּדִינֵי נְפָשׁוֹת הַמְלַמְּדִים זְכוּת אֵין חוֹזְרִין וּמְלַמְּדִין חוֹבָה[22], וּבְדִינֵי מָמוֹנוֹת אֵינוֹ כֵן[23], וְשֶׁפּוֹתְחִין בְּזָכוּת בְּדִינֵי נְפָשׁוֹת[24], וְהִנֵּה נִסְתַּלֵּק הַפּוֹתֵחַ בְּכָךְ מִכַּת הַמְחַיֶּבֶת[25], וְשֶׁהַכֹּל מְלַמְּדִין זְכוּת[26], בֵּין רַב בֵּין תַּלְמִיד, וְיֶתֶר פְּרָטֶיהָ, מְבֹאָרִין בְּסוֹף סַנְהֶדְרִין[27].

וְנוֹהֶגֶת בְּכָל מָקוֹם וּבְכָל זְמַן[28], בִּזְכָרִים וּנְקֵבוֹת.

---

וּלְמִיתָה אֵין תַּשְׁלוּמִין — **lest they err in judgment.** פֶּן יִטְעוּ בַדִּין — **people lacking in wisdom,** — This is a particular concern with regard to capital cases **for,** unlike other cases, **there is no redress for** an erroneous **death** sentence.

Chinuch cites laws relating to the deliberation process in capital cases:

וְשֶׁבְּדִינֵי נְפָשׁוֹת הַמְלַמְּדִים זְכוּת אֵין חוֹזְרִין וּמְלַמְּדִין חוֹבָה — Also included in these laws is that in capital cases, **those [judges] who have advanced arguments for acquittal may not subsequently advance arguments for conviction.**[22] וּבְדִינֵי מָמוֹנוֹת אֵינוֹ כֵן — **In monetary cases, this** restriction **does not apply.**[23] וְשֶׁפּוֹתְחִין בְּזָכוּת בְּדִינֵי נְפָשׁוֹת — In addition, **we open** the deliberations **in capital cases by** advancing arguments that are in favor of **acquittal;**[24] וְהִנֵּה נִסְתַּלֵּק הַפּוֹתֵחַ בְּכָךְ מִכַּת הַמְחַיֶּבֶת — **and [the judge] who began** with arguments for acquittal **is thereby removed from the group** of judges who can advance arguments **for conviction,** as above.[25]

וְשֶׁהַכֹּל מְלַמְּדִין זְכוּת — **All** present **may advance arguments for acquittal,** בֵּין רַב בֵּין תַּלְמִיד — **both a teacher,** i.e., a judge, **and** any attending **disciple.**[26] וְיֶתֶר פְּרָטֶיהָ — These laws, **and the additional details of this mitzvah,** מְבֹאָרִין בְּסוֹף סַנְהֶדְרִין — **are delineated at the end of** Tractate *Sanhedrin* (beginning with Chapter 4).[27]

### ⸺ Applicability of the Mitzvah ⸺

בִּזְכָרִים וְנוֹהֶגֶת בְּכָל מָקוֹם וּבְכָל זְמַן — **[This mitzvah] applies in every location and in all times,**[28] וּנְקֵבוֹת — **to both men and women.**

---

### NOTES

22. That is, a judge who put forth an argument to acquit the defendant may not later in the deliberations present arguments for conviction (although at the final decision he may vote for conviction). *Rashi* (*Sanhedrin* 32a ד"ה אינו חוזר) explains that this is in keeping with the Torah's injunction of (*Numbers* 35:25) וְהִצִּילוּ הָעֵדָה, *The congregation shall save,* which obligates judges to seek to acquit the defendant. By barring a judge who advanced an argument for acquittal from changing his position throughout the deliberations, the judge will be induced to seek reasons to uphold his initial position, and in so doing, he may possibly hit upon a decisive argument for acquittal. This prohibition is actually one of the subjects of the previous mitzvah; see there for further discussion.

23. During the deliberation of a monetary case, a judge who began by arguing the side of one litigant may then change his position and put forth arguments against him.

24. See above, Mitzvah 77 note 13, where this requirement is discussed.]

25. That is, since he advanced an argument for acquittal he may no longer advance an argument for conviction, as Chinuch noted in the previous law. He is thus removed from the deliberative process with regard to conviction. (He may, however, reverse his position in the final stage of the proceedings, as explained in the previous mitzvah.)

For further discussion of this sentence of Chinuch, (see *Minchas Chinuch* §6, and glosses of *Tzava Rav* and *R' Yeshayah Pik* to Chinuch.

26. This refers to the three rows of disciples seated before the Sanhedrin. These laws are discussed at length in the previous mitzvah.

27. These laws are codified in *Rambam, Hil. Sanhedrin,* Chapters 8-12. See also *Rama, Choshen Mishpat* 25:2 for laws relating to following the majority with regard to a dispute about a Torah law.

28. I.e., in Eretz Yisrael and the Diaspora, and whether the *Beis HaMikdash* is standing or not. [The mitzvah to follow the majority in capital cases is not applicable today, since capital cases are no longer tried by a Sanhedrin. Chinuch refers to the other aspects of the mitzvah: following the majority in other court cases and in situations of halachic dispute between sages.]

# MISHPATIM / MITZVAH 78: THE OBLIGATION TO FOLLOW THE MAJORITY

וְעוֹבֵר עָלֶיהָ וְלֹא נָטָה אַחֲרֵיהֶם, בִּטֵּל עֲשֵׂה,[29] וְעָנְשׁוֹ גָּדוֹל מְאֹד, שֶׁהוּא הָעַמּוּד שֶׁהַתּוֹרָה נִסְמֶכֶת בּוֹ[30].

וְעוֹבֵר עָלֶיהָ וְלֹא נָטָה אַחֲרֵיהֶם — **One who transgresses [this mitzvah] and does not follow** the ruling of **[the majority],** whether in a specific court case or in regard to a dispute concerning Torah law, בִּטֵּל עֲשֵׂה — **has violated a** mitzvah-**obligation,**[29] וְעָנְשׁוֹ גָּדוֹל מְאֹד — **and his punishment will be very great,** שֶׁהוּא הָעַמּוּד שֶׁהַתּוֹרָה נִסְמֶכֶת בּוֹ — **for [this mitzvah] is the pillar upon which the Torah is supported.**[30]

### NOTES

29. *Minchas Chinuch* §8 writes that when there is a dispute regarding Torah law, and the majority rules leniently, one who acts stringently violates this mitzvah-obligation (see *Pischei Teshuvah*, *Yoreh Deah* 116:10 regarding abstaining from food that is ruled permissible by halachah; see also *Ritva*, *Yevamos* 14a).

30. As Chinuch explained above, no standard of observance of the Torah's laws would be possible without adherence to this mitzvah.

### ❧ Insight: The Broad Application of the Principle of Following the Majority

Although Chinuch discusses the principle of following the majority only in the context of the halachic decision-making process, this principle carries a far-broader influence. It applies in numerous types of circumstances, including, for example, where the reality of a situation needs to be ascertained, or the halachic status of a mixture must be determined.

A classic application of the principle of רוֹב, *majority*, is that if an item is found somewhere, removed from its original place where it was identifiable as permitted or forbidden, and we do not know where it came from, we can assume that it came from the majority. As the Gemara states: כָּל דְּפָרִישׁ מֵרוּבָּא פָּרִישׁ, *whatever departs [is assumed to have] departed from the majority* (see *Berachos* 28a, et al.). For instance, someone finds meat in the street and is unable to determine whether it is kosher or not. If that area has ten stores that sell that type of meat, nine of them kosher and one nonkosher, under Biblical law he may assume that the meat came from one of the kosher stores (see *Yoreh Deah* 110:3 for the practical halachah).

Another field of halachah where the principle of following the majority plays a significant role concerns mixtures of permitted and forbidden foods. Under Biblical law, whenever two foods, one kosher and the other nonkosher, are mixed together so that they cannot be identified, and the kosher food forms the majority of the mixture, the smaller amount of nonkosher food becomes "nullified"; that is, it loses its separate identity, and is viewed as no longer present in the mixture. This concept is known as בָּטֵל בְּרֹב, *nullification in the majority*. [The laws regarding such nullification are extremely complex, with numerous distinctions based on whether the mixture consists of liquids or solids, and what types of food are involved. In many cases, a simple majority does not suffice, and nullification occurs only when the mixture contains sixty parts kosher food for one part nonkosher food. These laws are addressed in *Shulchan Aruch*, *Yoreh Deah* §98-111. Chinuch touches on these laws in Mitzvah 111.]

### ❧ Majorities of Defined and Undefined Groups

The Gemara (*Chullin* 11a) divides majorities into two categories: a majority that is "in front of us" [רוּבָּא דְּאִיתָא קַמָּן] and a majority that is "not in front of us" [רוּבָּא דְּלֵיתֵיהּ קַמָּן]. The first category refers to majorities of actual, defined groups, such as those discussed above — the majority of votes among the judges in *Beis Din*, or the majority of stores that sell meat in a particular locale. In these cases, determining the majority is simply a matter of counting the votes or the stores. The second category refers to majorities of undefined groups. These majorities cannot be ascertained through a direct count; rather, they reflect theoretical assumptions based on statistical evidence or pure logic. An example of this type of majority appears in the laws of *tereifos* — animals that are prohibited because they carry certain fatal defects. As we learned in Mitzvah 73 (at notes 30-31), although *tereifah*-defects can occur in many different organs, the halachah does not require us to examine all of the organs

of a slaughtered animal to ascertain that they are free of defects. We check only the lungs of an animal, in which such defects are very common (see note 32 there). With respect to the other organs, we rely on the principle of majority, which, in this case, states that since the statistical majority of animals do not have fatal defects, the animal is not a *tereifah* and its meat may be eaten. In this instance, we cannot point to any group of animals and assert with certainty that most of them are free of *tereifah*-defects. In fact, it is theoretically possible for all the animals currently alive to be *tereifos*. Nevertheless, we rely on the statistical premise that in the ordinary course of events most animals have their organs intact. [For discussion about the strengths and weaknesses of the two types of majority, see *Teshuvos Chasam Sofer, Even HaEzer* II §147 ד"ה והנה; *Chidushei R' Akiva Eiger* to *Kesubos* 13b; and *Shaarei Yosher* 3:1,4.]

The Gemara (ibid.) assumes that the two types of majorities are essentially different. It therefore asks: Since the verse in *Exodus* 23:2, אַחֲרֵי רַבִּים לְהַטֹּת, *according to the majority shall it be decided*) speaks about relying upon a majority of judges, which is the majority of a *defined* group ("in front of us"), what is the basis for relying upon the other type of majority — one that is "not in front of us"? The Gemara (ibid. 11a-12a) puts forth various Scriptural sources, but does not conclusively settle the matter, leading *Rashi* (12a ד"ה פסח) to suggest that the source actually is *Halachah LeMoshe MiSinai* (a law transmitted orally to Moses at Sinai). Alternatively, *Rashi* suggests that the verse אַחֲרֵי רַבִּים לְהַטֹּת encompasses both types of majorities, for in the final analysis both are founded on the same principle. For yet another approach, see *Rashi* ibid. 50b ד"ה מאי.

### ☙ The Majority Is Tantamount to the Entirety (רֻבּוֹ כְּכֻלּוֹ):

The principle of רֹב, *majority,* has yet another application, which is that in certain circumstances the majority of a single object is halachically equivalent to the entire object. An example of this concept, which is termed רֻבּוֹ כְּכֻלּוֹ (literally, *its majority is like its entirety*), involves the laws of *shechitah*. The proper *shechitah* of an animal requires severing its trachea and esophagus. However, based on the aforementioned principle, it is not necessary to cut all the way through these organs; rather, even if one cut *most* of the way through them, the *shechitah* is still valid because they are halachically perceived as though they have been severed in their entirety (see *Yoreh Deah* 21:1). Another example pertains to the requirement to drink four cups of wine at the Pesach Seder. Although it is preferable to drink each cup in its entirety, one can discharge his obligation by drinking the majority of each cup, since "its majority is tantamount to its entirety" (see *Orach Chaim* 472:9 and *Bach* there §6).

Some suggest that this law is not derived from the verse אַחֲרֵי רַבִּים לְהַטֹּת, for it represents a different concept entirely. The verse refers to a situation in which something is unknown or unidentified, such as the correct verdict of an accused person brought before *beis din*, or the origin of a piece of meat found in the street. Regarding such instances, the Torah teaches here that the determination of the verdict, or of the meat's identity, shall be based on the concept of majority. In the above cases of *shechitah* or cups of wine, however, nothing is unknown, nor are two things intermingled. It is evident that a portion of the organs is severed and a portion is intact, or that part of the cup has been drunk and part remains, and these portions are clearly distinguished. Here, the law must tell us that severing the majority of the organs or drinking the majority of the cup is *tantamount* to severing or drinking their entirety. In other words, the law must state that the halachic *status* of an object is determined by the status of its majority. This cannot be derived from the verse that discusses *beis din*, and must be derived from another verse. Indeed, the Gemara, *Nazir* 42a, offers a different source for this law (*Kehillos Yaakov, Succah* 1:2).

*R' Chaim Soloveitchik* (*Chidushei HaGrach Al HaShas* to *Bava Kamma* 27a-b), however, explains that the principle that *its majority is tantamount to its entirety* can also be derived from the verse אַחֲרֵי רַבִּים לְהַטֹּת. On a simple level, this verse, which is stated in the context of *beis din*, teaches that the halachic truth lies with the majority of judges; their opinion is considered the authoritative one and therefore determines the verdict. But there is another dimension to the law: In every case brought before a *beis din*, a specific number of judges is required to render a decision; for example, capital cases require 23 judges. If the majority of the court would issue a verdict without the participation of the minority, their decision would have no legal standing, since it would not have been issued by 23 judges. In order for the verdict to be valid, it must be issued by the *entire* court of 23 judges. Accordingly, the question must be asked: When several of the judges disagree with the majority

opinion, how is the court's decision valid? The answer must be that רֻבּוֹ כְּכֻלּוֹ, *the majority of [the court] is tantamount to its entirety*. That is, once the votes are taken and the opinion of the majority is determined, this is considered to be the opinion of the *beis din* as a *whole*. The verdict that is put forth thus emerges from the *entirety* of the court (see *Tosafos, Bava Kamma* 27b ד"ה קמ"ל). It follows that in regard to *shechitah* (and similar cases) as well, once the majority of the trachea and esophagus have been severed, the halachah considers the entirety of these organs as severed.

*Shaarei Yosher* (3:4) also raises the question as to how a verdict issued by the mere majority of a *beis din* can be valid, but he answers somewhat differently. In his view, the matter is based on the principle of בִּטּוּל בְּרוֹב, *nullification in the majority*. The difference of opinion among the judges results in a "mixture" of opinions within the court. By commanding us to follow the majority, the Torah in effect teaches that the minority opinion is "nullified" by the majority opinion, with the result that the *entire* court issues the verdict espoused by the majority. Thus, this verse serves as the source for the concept of nullification by majority. Indeed, *Rashi* (*Beitzah* 3b ד"ה אפילו; *Gittin* 54b ד"ה לא יעלו; *Chullin* 98b ד"ה דמדאורייתא) states that this concept is derived from the verse of אַחֲרֵי רַבִּים לְהַטֹּת.

## מִצְוָה עט: שֶׁלֹּא לְרַחֵם עַל עָנִי בַּדִּין

שֶׁלֹּא יַחְמֹל הַדַּיָּן עַל הַחַלָּשׁ וְהַדַּל בִּשְׁעַת הַדִּין אֶלָּא שֶׁיָּדִין דִּינוֹ לַאֲמִתּוֹ, לֹא עַל צַד הַחֶמְלָה עָלָיו, אֲבָל יַשְׁוֶה בֵּין הֶעָשִׁיר וְהַדַּל לְהַכְרִיחוֹ לִפְרֹעַ מַה שֶּׁהוּא חַיָּב, שֶׁנֶּאֱמַר (שמות כ״ג, ג׳) וְדָל לֹא תֶהְדַּר בְּרִיבוֹ.[1] וְנִכְפַּל זֶה הָעִנְיָן בְּמָקוֹם אַחֵר, שֶׁנֶּאֱמַר (ויקרא י״ט, ט״ו) לֹא תִשָּׂא פְנֵי דָל. וּלְשׁוֹן[2] סִפְרָא (קדושים פ״ד, ב׳) שֶׁלֹּא תֹּאמַר עָנִי הוּא זֶה, וַאֲנִי וְהֶעָשִׁיר חַיָּבִים לְפַרְנְסוֹ,[3] אֲזַכֶּנּוּ וְנִמְצָא מִתְפַּרְנֵס בִּנְקִיּוּת, תַּלְמוּד לוֹמַר לֹא תִשָּׂא פְנֵי דָל.

# Mitzvah 79
## The Prohibition [Upon a Judge] to Have Mercy on a Poor Person in Litigation

וְדָל לֹא תֶהְדַּר בְּרִיבוֹ
*Do not honor a destitute person in his grievance (Exodus 23:3).*

שֶׁלֹּא יַחְמֹל הַדַּיָּן עַל הַחַלָּשׁ וְהַדַּל בִּשְׁעַת הַדִּין — **We are commanded that a judge not take pity on the weak or the destitute during litigation** to bend the law in his favor; אֶלָּא שֶׁיָּדִין דִּינוֹ לַאֲמִתּוֹ — **rather, he must adjudicate his case based on its true** merits, לֹא עַל צַד הַחֶמְלָה עָלָיו — **not based on any compassion** that the judge has **for him.** אֲבָל יַשְׁוֶה בֵּין הֶעָשִׁיר וְהַדַּל — **Instead** of basing his judgment on compassion, **[the judge] must equate** his treatment of **the rich and the poor** לְהַכְרִיחוֹ לִפְרֹעַ מַה שֶּׁהוּא חַיָּב — and, regardless of the litigant's status, **he must compel [the liable party] to pay what he is obligated.** שֶׁנֶּאֱמַר ״וְדָל לֹא תֶהְדַּר בְּרִיבוֹ״ — **We are so commanded, as the verse states** (Exodus 23:3): ***Do not honor a destitute person in his grievance.***[1] שֶׁנֶּאֱמַר ״לֹא וְנִכְפַּל זֶה הָעִנְיָן בְּמָקוֹם אַחֵר — **This concept is repeated elsewhere** in the Torah, תִשָּׂא פְנֵי דָל״ — **as** the verse **states** (Leviticus 19:15): *You shall not commit a perversion of justice;* **you shall not favor the poor,** etc.

Chinuch cites *Sifra* in explanation of the verse in *Leviticus*, which clarifies why it is necessary for the verse to warn specifically against bending the law for a poor person, when the beginning of this verse already warned against *all* perversions of justice. *Sifra* explains why a judge might reason that bending the law for the poor is not actually a perversion of justice:[2]

וּלְשׁוֹן סִפְרָא — **The words of *Sifra*** (ad loc.) in explanation of this verse are as follows: שֶׁלֹּא תֹּאמַר עָנִי הוּא זֶה וַאֲנִי וְהֶעָשִׁיר חַיָּבִים לְפַרְנְסוֹ — **So that you** (the judge) **shall not say, "This litigant is poor, and I and the rich adversary are obligated to support him;**[3] אֲזַכֶּנּוּ וְנִמְצָא מִתְפַּרְנֵס בִּנְקִיּוּת — **I will rule in his favor, and, as a result, he will be supported in a dignified fashion."** One might suppose that arranging for the rich person to fulfill his obligation and support his poor adversary is not considered a perversion of justice. תַּלְמוּד לוֹמַר ״לֹא תִשָּׂא פְנֵי דָל״ — **To counter this supposition *[the Torah]* teaches: *You shall not favor the poor;*** every case must be judged on its merits alone, unaffected by any external factors.

---

NOTES

1. In Mitzvah 235, the judge is commanded to adjudicate all cases with complete equity between the two litigants; here the Torah adds a specific prohibition regarding favoring one of the litigants on account of compassion (see *Minchas Chinuch* §3).

2. *Gur Aryeh* to the verse; see also *Maharam Shick* to this mitzvah.

3. This refers to the mitzvah of *tzedakah*, charity (Mitzvah 479), which obligates every person to support the poor.

# MISHPATIM / MITZVAH 79: NOT TO HAVE MERCY ON A POOR PERSON IN LITIGATION

וְשֹׁרֶשׁ הַמִּצְוָה יָדוּעַ, שֶׁהַשֵּׂכֶל מֵעִיד בְּהַשְׁוָיַת הַדִּין שֶׁדָּבָר רָאוּי וְכָשֵׁר הוּא.[4]
וְנוֹהֶגֶת בְּכָל מָקוֹם וּבְכָל זְמַן,[5] בִּזְכָרִים.
וְעוֹבֵר עָלֶיהָ וְהִטָּה הַדִּין לְחֶמְלָתוֹ עַל הַדַּל, עָבַר עַל מִצְוַת מֶלֶךְ. וְאֵין בָּהּ מַלְקוּת, שֶׁאֵין בָּהּ מַעֲשֶׂה.[6]

## ☞ Underlying Purpose of the Mitzvah ☜

שֶׁהַשֵּׂכֶל מֵעִיד וְשֹׁרֶשׁ הַמִּצְוָה יָדוּעַ — **The underlying purpose of this mitzvah is well known,** בְּהַשְׁוָיַת הַדִּין שֶׁדָּבָר רָאוּי וְכָשֵׁר הוּא — **for logic dictates that equality in judgment is a fitting and proper thing.**[4]

## ☞ Applicability of the Mitzvah ☜

וְנוֹהֶגֶת בְּכָל מָקוֹם וּבְכָל זְמַן — **[This mitzvah] applies in all places and in all times,**[5] בִּזְכָרִים — **and applies only to men,** who serve as judges (see Mitzvah 77). וְעוֹבֵר עָלֶיהָ — **One who transgresses [this mitzvah]** וְהִטָּה הַדִּין לְחֶמְלָתוֹ עַל הַדַּל — **and bends the law out of his compassion for the destitute** litigant עָבַר עַל מִצְוַת מֶלֶךְ — **violates the command of the King,** i.e., God; וְאֵין בָּהּ מַלְקוּת שֶׁאֵין בָּהּ מַעֲשֶׂה — **however, [this transgression] does not carry the punishment of** *malkus* (lashes), **because it does not involve an action.**[6]

---

NOTES

4. See Insight.
5. I.e., in Eretz Yisrael and the Diaspora, and whether the *Beis HaMikdash* is standing or not.
6. A violation that does not necessarily involve an action (לָאו שֶׁאֵין בּוֹ מַעֲשֶׂה) is not subject to *malkus*; see General Introduction, note 14.

---

**◆§ Insight: "Honoring" the Destitute**

The verse upon which this prohibition is based, *do not honor a destitute person in his grievance* (*Exodus* 23:3), can be understood as prohibiting a judge from showing honor to the destitute person when he is a party in judicial proceedings. In his treatment of this mitzvah, however, Chinuch does not mention a separate prohibition against giving deferential treatment to the poor in court. Rather, Chinuch reads the verse as does *Rashi* (*Exodus* ibid.): "do not accord him honor *by ruling in his favor*." *Targum Onkelos*, too, translates our verse, לָא תְרַחֵם בְּדִינֵהּ, *Do not show compassion in judgment*.

Some Rishonim (*Yerei'im* §185; *Smag, Lo Saaseh* 204), however, do follow the simple reading of the verse, and explain that aside from the prohibition against bending the law in favor of the poor, there is an additional prohibition upon a judge to *show honor* to a destitute litigant while he is in court. A judge may feel that, owing to the pauper's predicament, it is appropriate to speak to him with greater respect, and therefore favor him over his adversary with the use of gentler words. Against such acts of consideration, our verse emphatically states: *Do not honor a destitute person in his grievance*. Even an outward show of honor to one party over his adversary is expressly forbidden, as it upsets the perfect balance that is required in judicial proceedings (see *Minchas Soless* for why Chinuch does not recognize this as a separate prohibition).

The inclination of a judge to apply mercy in deciding a pauper's case is certainly understandable and in any other context is, indeed, commendable. Our Sages tell us that compassion is at the very core of the Jewish ethos (*Yevamos* 79a). However, this mitzvah cautions us that using compassion is inappropriate in deciding court cases. *Rambam* writes (*Moreh Nevuchim* 3:35) that when true justice is not carried out in all cases, injustice will continue unabated, and those who plot wrongdoing will never be stopped. Relaxing the obligations of justice for the poor is not an act of mercy, as some might suppose, but rather an act of great callousness, as it ultimately leads to social disorder and lawlessness. True mercy in this case is manifested by following God's command to set up proper institutions of justice, as per the obligation (*Deuteronomy* 16:18): שֹׁפְטִים וְשֹׁטְרִים תִּתֶּן לְךָ בְּכָל שְׁעָרֶיךָ,

*Judges and officers shall you appoint in all your cities* (Mitzvah 491; see also *Orchos Tzaddikim, Shaar* 7).

Not only is bending the final ruling forbidden, but any show of honor during the court case is also inappropriate (and according to the Rishonim mentioned above, forbidden by this verse). It must be emphasized that when not in court, according esteem and honor to such a destitute individual is nothing short of a great mitzvah. [This is especially so according to those who explain that the destitute man referred to in the verse is one who at one time was an affluent and honored person, who has since fallen on hard times (see *R' S. R. Hirsch, Exodus* 23:3).] According honor at his time of need communicates to him that our respect toward him does not fluctuate based on his degree of affluence. However, while compassion is a great value, it has no place in the courtroom.

The mutual exclusivity of justice and compassion is the basis of a question posed by the Gemara (*Sanhedrin* 6b) regarding a verse describing King David's rule: *David administered justice and kindness to his entire people* (*II Samuel* 8:15). The Gemara wonders: If King David administered "justice," there should have been no room for kindness, and if he administered "kindness," there should have been no room for justice! How could he possibly have administered both of these contradictory approaches?

The Gemara answers that, when approached for litigation, David would first attempt to bring the quarreling parties to a compromise solution, rather than going down the path of straightforward judgment. Compromise, in effect, is a harmonious balance between justice and kindness, and is therefore the preferable method of dealing with monetary grievances (see Mitzvah 233; *Rambam, Hil. Sanhedrin* 22:4; *Shulchan Aruch, Choshen Mishpat* 12:2).

There is, however, an opinion in the Gemara that the courts do not have the prerogative to offer compromise, as they are the arena for strict unadulterated justice. According to this view, the Gemara explains the verse to mean that David found a way to fulfill the seemingly competing values of justice and kindness without one coming at the expense of the other. When serving as a judge (as kings of the Davidic dynasty were allowed to do; see *Sanhedrin* 19a), King David would never allow mercy for the poor to cloud his judgment (or, as explained above, to influence his treatment of litigants during the case). However, if justice called for him to rule in favor of the poor man's opponent, then, after the litigants had left the courtroom, King David would supply the pauper with monies from his own treasury to help him pay his debt. In so doing, King David displayed the trait of mercy that is at the core of the Jew's character, while at the same time upholding the value of justice, the foundation upon which society is built.

# 111 ❑ MISHPATIM / MITZVAH 80: THE OBLIGATION TO HELP REMOVE A BURDEN

## מִצְוָה פ: מִצְוַת פְּרוֹק מַשָּׂא[1]

לְהָסִיר הַמַּשָּׂא מֵעַל הַבְּהֵמָה[2] שֶׁיָּגְעָה בְּמַשָּׂאָהּ בַּדֶּרֶךְ[3], שֶׁנֶּאֱמַר (שמות כ״ג, ה׳) "כִּי תִרְאֶה חֲמוֹר שֹׂנַאֲךָ וְגוֹ'"[4].

## ⸺ Mitzvah 80 ⸺
## The Obligation to Help Remove a Burden
## [From a Faltering Animal]

כִּי תִרְאֶה חֲמוֹר שֹׂנַאֲךָ רֹבֵץ תַּחַת מַשָּׂאוֹ וְחָדַלְתָּ מֵעֲזֹב לוֹ עָזֹב תַּעֲזֹב עִמּוֹ

*If you see the donkey of someone you hate crouching beneath its burden, would you refrain from helping him? — you shall help repeatedly with him* (Exodus 23:5).

There are three mitzvos that relate to one who encounters a load-bearing animal that is in distress. The first of the three, this mitzvah, requires that one assist a traveler in removing the load that is weighing down his animal, causing it to falter. This is known as *perikah*, unloading. Mitzvah 541 requires that one further assist the owner in reloading the animal, allowing the owner to proceed to his destination. That is known as the mitzvah of *te'inah*, loading. In the mitzvah immediately preceding that one (Mitzvah 540), the Torah prohibits ignoring the plight of one whose animal has faltered on the way.[1] **לְהָסִיר הַמַּשָּׂא מֵעַל הַבְּהֵמָה שֶׁיָּגְעָה בְּמַשָּׂאָהּ בַּדֶּרֶךְ** — We are commanded **to remove the burden from upon an animal**[2] **that has faltered with its load** while **on the road,**[3] **שֶׁנֶּאֱמַר** — as it is stated (Exodus 23:5): **״כִּי תִרְאֶה חֲמוֹר שֹׂנַאֲךָ וְגוֹ׳״** — *If you see the donkey of someone you hate* etc. *crouching beneath its burden ... you shall help repeatedly with him*.[4]

---

### NOTES

1. The last two mitzvos are expressed in the verse (*Deuteronomy* 22:4): לֹא תִרְאֶה אֶת חֲמוֹר אָחִיךָ אוֹ שׁוֹרוֹ נֹפְלִים בַּדֶּרֶךְ וְהִתְעַלַּמְתָּ מֵהֶם הָקֵם תָּקִים עִמּוֹ, *You shall not see the donkey of your brother or his ox falling on the road and hide yourself from them; you shall surely stand them up with him*. The clause *You shall not see ...* expresses a prohibition against ignoring the situation when the animal is in distress, and the clause *you shall surely stand them up ...* indicates a mitzvah-obligation to assist with reloading it (i.e., *te'inah*).

Below, in Mitzvos 540 and 541, Chinuch indicates that he has elaborated on the particulars of those mitzvos in the discussion of our mitzvah. The elucidation of our mitzvah will accordingly include discussion of all three mitzvos.

2. *Rambam* (introductory list of mitzvos to *Mishneh Torah, Asei* 202) writes that included in this mitzvah is a requirement to relieve a *person* who is in distress due to the weight of the burden he *himself* is carrying. Chinuch himself follows this position in Mitzvos 540 and 541, and presumably maintains this position with regard to our mitzvah as well. [This is in fact implicit in Chinuch's discussion, below, of the underlying purpose of the mitzvah] (see *Minchas Chinuch* §1; see, however, *Minchas Soless*).

3. When expressing the prohibition against ignoring the plight of one's fellow whose animal has faltered (Mitzvah 540), the Torah discusses an animal that is falling "on the road" (see above, note 1). Accordingly, this prohibition [and presumably, the related mitzvah-obligations as well] applies only when the animal is away from home. *Netziv* (*Emek HaNetziv* to *Sifrei, Ki Seitzei*, Piska 9) explains that the concern here is limited to a wayfarer, as he can easily become overwhelmed by his predicament, and the essence of this mitzvah is to help him in such a situation. However, when the owner of the animal is close to home, the mitzvah does not apply, since he is not likely to be overwhelmed in such a case. [Presumably, even in this situation, the mitzvah to relieve an animal of its suffering applies (see below, note 10), as does the general mitzvah to protect the possessions of a fellow Jew from loss (Mitzvah 243). Nevertheless, the specific mitzvos of *perikah* and *te'inah* ("unloading" and "loading") do not apply. See the Insight for a practical difference between these obligations.]

4. If, after the burden is unloaded and then reloaded, the burden shifts, causing the animal to experience further distress, one is not permitted to forsake it. Rather, one is required to repeatedly adjust the burden until it is positioned in a manner that allows the animal to proceed to its destination. In addition, as Chinuch will write below (at note 19), one is required to accompany the owner of the animal for a distance as

וְהַשׂוֹנֵא זֶה פֵּרוּשׁוֹ יִשְׂרָאֵל⁵, וְאַף עַל פִּי שֶׁכָּתוּב (ויקרא י״ט, י״ז) לֹא תִשְׂנָא אֶת אָחִיךָ בִּלְבָבֶךָ, דְּהַיְנוּ יִשְׂרָאֵל, אָמְרוּ חֲכָמִים (פסחים דף קי״ג ע״ב) שֶׁעִנְיָן זֶה הוּא כְּגוֹן שֶׁרָאָהוּ עוֹבֵר עֲבֵרָה בְּיָחִיד וְהִתְרָה בּוֹ וְלֹא חָזַר, שֶׁזֶּה מֻתָּר לְשׂנְאָתוֹ⁶. וּמַה שֶּׁאָמַר חֲמוֹר, לָאו דַּוְקָא חֲמוֹר אֶלָּא כָּל בְּהֵמָה, אֶלָּא שֶׁדִּבֵּר הַכָּתוּב בַּהֹוֶה, שֶׁהַחֲמוֹרִים לְמַשָּׂא⁷.

---

Chinuch explains various particulars of the verse, beginning with the term שֹׂנַאֲךָ, *someone you hate*: וְאַף עַל פִּי – **The enemy that is referred to** in this verse **is a Jew.**[5] וְהַשׂוֹנֵא זֶה פֵּרוּשׁוֹ יִשְׂרָאֵל – שֶׁכָּתוּב "לֹא תִשְׂנָא אֶת אָחִיךָ בִּלְבָבֶךָ" – **Now, although** one may normally not hate his fellow Jew, for **it is written** (*Leviticus* 19:17), ***You shall not hate your brother in your heart,*** דְּהַיְנוּ יִשְׂרָאֵל – **which is referring to a Jew,** אָמְרוּ חֲכָמִים – **the Sages stated** (*Pesachim* 113b) שֶׁעִנְיָן זֶה הוּא – **that this situation** (i.e., where one may harbor animosity toward his fellow Jew) **is possible,** כְּגוֹן שֶׁרָאָהוּ עוֹבֵר עֲבֵרָה בְּיָחִיד – **in a case where one saw [the owner of the animal] commit a transgression in private,** וְהִתְרָה בּוֹ וְלֹא חָזַר – **and he warned him** not to sin, **yet he did not desist;** שֶׁזֶּה מֻתָּר לְשׂנְאָתוֹ – **one is permitted to hate this [person],** because he is a deliberate sinner.[6]

Chinuch proceeds to discuss the term חֲמוֹר, *donkey*: וּמַה שֶּׁאָמַר חֲמוֹר – **And that which [the verse] states "donkey,"** לָאו דַּוְקָא חֲמוֹר – **is not** to indicate that this mitzvah pertains **specifically** to **a donkey;** אֶלָּא כָּל בְּהֵמָה – **rather,** it applies **to any animal.** אֶלָּא שֶׁדִּבֵּר הַכָּתוּב בַּהֹוֶה – **The Torah merely spoke of the common situation,** שֶׁהַחֲמוֹרִים לְמַשָּׂא – **as donkeys** serve **for the purpose of carrying burdens.**[7]

---

## NOTES

he embarks once more on his journey, in case further assistance is necessary.

It should be noted that the mitzvos of *perikah* and *te'inah* apply even when the animal has been loaded with an exceptionally heavy burden, which it is able to carry only with great effort (*Bava Metzia* 32b; *Rambam, Hil. Rotze'ach U'Shemiras HaNefesh* 13:1). Nevertheless, if the burden is so heavy that it is not realistically feasible for the animal to carry it at all, one is required to reload only the portion of its load that it can carry (*Ralbag*, after *Exodus* 23:9, ד״ה השרש השני).

It should further be noted that the mitzvah of *perikah* pertains to an animal that is רֹבֵץ תַּחַת מַשָּׂאוֹ, *crouching beneath its burden,* or as Chinuch puts it, one that "has faltered" with its load. The mitzvah does not require one to help his fellow unload a beast of burden that is standing upright with its load, even if the animal is weary (*Bava Metzia* 33a; *Rama, Choshen Mishpat* 272:1). Nevertheless, the obligation to relieve an animal of its suffering applies even in this case [see note 10 and the Insight] (*Beis Yosef* 272:1; *Beur HaGra* 272:1).

5. This is derived from the word אָחִיךָ, *your brother,* which appears in the verse [cited in note 1] that sets forth the mitzvah of *te'inah* (*Levush, Choshen Mishpat* 272:8).

6. Since it is generally forbidden to hate any Jew, the verse would not be addressing the situation of one who hates his fellow for personal reasons, as that is prohibited. Rather, the verse must be discussing one who hates a person because he has intentionally sinned, in which case — in certain situations — it is permitted to hate him. However, the implication of the term שֹׂנַאֲךָ, *someone "you" hate,* is that other people are on friendly terms with him. Now, if he is a known sinner, *all* Jews will bear animosity toward him. What, then, is the situation in which only the person being addressed by the verse is permitted to hate the sinner and not others? The Gemara (*Pesachim* 113b) explains that the verse speaks of one who personally witnessed the transgressor sinning when no one else was present. The witness may not relay this information to others, and is even prohibited to inform *beis din* of the matter, because he alone witnessed it, and, as a *single* witness, his testimony will not be accepted [and indeed is considered *lashon hara*] (see *Chofetz Chaim* 4:4 with *Be'er Mayim Chaim* for further particulars of this law). Nevertheless, until the transgressor repents, the witness himself may harbor animosity toward the sinner, since he himself witnessed him blatantly sinning (*Rambam* ibid. 13:14). [However, as Chinuch (and *Rambam* ibid.) writes, the transgressor must have been forewarned before performing the act; otherwise, it may be assumed that the transgressor was unaware that his action was prohibited (see *Chofetz Chaim, Be'er Mayim Chaim* 4:14; see also below, Mitzvah 238).]

Although it is permissible to hate this sinner, there is still a mitzvah to provide him with the assistance that he needs. *Rambam* (ibid.) explains that this requirement applies despite the fact that he is a sinner, since our failure to help him may cause him to tarry on the road, which can ultimately pose a risk to his life. Since even the life of a sinner is valuable, as God prefers that he live and repent from his evil ways, rather than be subject to Divine retribution for his sins, it is a mitzvah to assist him.

7. See *Bava Kamma* 54b.

# 113 ☐ MISHPATIM / MITZVAH 80: THE OBLIGATION TO HELP REMOVE A BURDEN

וּכְתִיב⁸ עָזֹב תַּעֲזֹב עִמּוֹ, כְּלוֹמַר עָזְרֵהוּ, מִלְּשׁוֹן וַיַּעַזְבוּ יְרוּשָׁלַיִם (נחמיה ג׳, ח׳), שֶׁהוּא לְשׁוֹן חֹזֶק.⁹

מִשָּׁרְשֵׁי הַמִּצְוָה, לְלַמֵּד נַפְשֵׁנוּ בְּמִדַּת הַחֶמְלָה שֶׁהִיא מִדָּה מְשֻׁבַּחַת, וְאֵין צָרִיךְ לוֹמַר שֶׁחוֹבָה עָלֵינוּ לַחְמֹל עַל הָאִישׁ הַמִּצְטַעֵר בְּגוּפוֹ, אֶלָּא אֲפִלּוּ הַמִּצְטַעֵר בַּאֲבֵדַת מָמוֹנוֹ מִצְוָה עָלֵינוּ לַחְמֹל עָלָיו וּלְהַצִּילוֹ.

דִּינֵי הַמִּצְוָה, כְּגוֹן אִם הַבְּהֵמָה שֶׁל גּוֹי וּמַשָּׂאוֹי שֶׁל יִשְׂרָאֵל אוֹ בְּהֶפֶךְ,¹⁰

---

Chinuch discusses the meaning of the final words of the verse, עָזֹב תַּעֲזֹב עִמּוֹ, *you shall help repeatedly with him*:[8]

כְּלוֹמַר עָזְרֵהוּ — **And it is written** *azov taazov imo*, — **which means to say "help him."** מִלְּשׁוֹן וַיַּעַזְבוּ יְרוּשָׁלַיִם שֶׁהוּא לְשׁוֹן חֹזֶק — **The term** *azov* **is from the same root as the term** (*Nehemiah* 3:8) *"vayaazvu" Yerushalayim* (and they fortified Jerusalem), **in which the root** [עזב] **denotes fortification.**[9]

### ~ Underlying Purpose of the Mitzvah ~

מִשָּׁרְשֵׁי הַמִּצְוָה — **Among the underlying purposes of the mitzvah** לְלַמֵּד נַפְשֵׁנוּ בְּמִדַּת הַחֶמְלָה — **is to train ourselves in the trait of compassion,** שֶׁהִיא מִדָּה מְשֻׁבַּחַת — **which is a praiseworthy trait.** In teaching this, the Torah does not focus on a situation where the obligation to be compassionate is obvious, but on one in which some might have overlooked it. וְאֵין צָרִיךְ לוֹמַר שֶׁחוֹבָה עָלֵינוּ לַחְמֹל עַל הָאִישׁ הַמִּצְטַעֵר בְּגוּפוֹ — **It goes without saying that it is incumbent upon us to have compassion for a person who is in physical pain,** so this requirement is not mentioned explicitly. אֶלָּא אֲפִלּוּ הַמִּצְטַעֵר בַּאֲבֵדַת מָמוֹנוֹ — **Rather,** the Torah teaches here that **even when someone is in distress over a** potential **monetary loss,** מִצְוָה עָלֵינוּ לַחְמֹל עָלָיו וּלְהַצִּילוֹ — **it is a mitzvah upon us to have compassion on him and save him** from his plight.

### ~ Laws of the Mitzvah ~

דִּינֵי הַמִּצְוָה — **The laws of the mitzvah** include several details pertaining to ownership of the animal and its burden: כְּגוֹן אִם הַבְּהֵמָה שֶׁל גּוֹי וּמַשָּׂאוֹי שֶׁל יִשְׂרָאֵל אוֹ בְּהֶפֶךְ — **For example,** the law that applies **if the animal belongs to an idolater and the burden belongs to a Jew, or vice versa;**[10]

---

### NOTES

8. Throughout Scripture, the term עָזֹב generally means *to abandon*. Here, however, the Torah is certainly not instructing us to abandon the owner of the distressed animal! Chinuch explores the source of the translation of the words in this verse.

9. Another resolution to this issue can be found in *Targum Onkelos* and *Targum Yonasan,* who interpret the words עָזֹב תַּעֲזֹב in a manner that is consistent with the usual meaning, *to abandon*. As Chinuch explained, the mitzvah of *perikah* requires that one come to the assistance of the animal's owner even when one has contempt for him. Thus, they explain that this phrase indeed means to abandon: One is required to abandon the feelings of enmity he has toward the owner of the animal, and instead assist him with unloading his animal. See also *Ibn Ezra, Chizkuni,* and *Rav Saadiah Gaon* to the verse.

10. The mitzvos of *perikah* and *te'inah* (unloading and loading) apply to "your brother" (see note 5) and not to an idolater. Thus, if the animal is owned and accompanied by an idolater, there is no obligation under *these* mitzvos to provide assistance when it stumbles. Even if the animal is transporting a load that belongs to a Jew, the mitzvos of *perikah* and *te'inah* apply only when the Jew who owns the burden is accompanying the animal (*Rambam* ibid. 13:9).

Nevertheless, there is an additional obligation that requires one to alleviate an animal's suffering (*tzaar baalei chaim*), discussed below in Mitzvos 451 and 550, and that obligation applies even if the animal belongs to an idolater (see *Rama, Choshen Mishpat* 272:9 and *Sma* there §15; cf. *Beur HaGra* there). [See the Insight for a practical difference between these obligations.] Moreover, if refraining from providing assistance to an idolater might engender ill will, one is surely required to assist him (see *Shulchan Aruch, Choshen Mishpat* ibid.).

וְדִין הַפּוֹגֵעַ בְּאוֹהֲבוֹ יִשְׂרָאֵל וּבְשׂוֹנְאוֹ שֶׁמִּצְוָה לְכֹף הַיֵּצֶר, וַאֲפִלּוּ אוֹהֵב לִפְרֹק וְשׂוֹנֵא לִטְעֹן[11]. וְשׂוֹנֵא זֶה אֵינוֹ כַּשּׂוֹנֵא שֶׁזְּכַרְנוּ מֵחֲמַת עֲבֵרָה, אֶלָּא שֶׁאֵין לִבּוֹ שָׁלֵם עִמּוֹ[12]. וּפֵרוּשׁ כִּי תִרְאֶה, מֵאֵימָתַי הוּא הַחִיּוּב[13], וְשִׁעֲרוּ חֲכָמִים (בבא מציעא דף ל״ג ע״א) שֶׁהוּא אֶחָד מִשִּׁבְעָה וּמֶחֱצָה בְּמִיל וְזֶהוּ רִיס[14], אֲבָל רָחוֹק מִזֶּה הַשִּׁעוּר אֵין חַיָּב לְהַטּוֹת הַדֶּרֶךְ אֵלָיו, וְהָעוֹשֶׂה לִפְנִים מִן הַשּׁוּרָה תָּבֹא עָלָיו בְּרָכָה[15], וְדִין זָקֵן אוֹ נִכְבָּד

וְדִין הַפּוֹגֵעַ בְּאוֹהֲבוֹ יִשְׂרָאֵל וּבְשׂוֹנְאוֹ — **and the law of one who encounters his Jewish friend and his Jewish enemy** who each require assistance at the same time. שֶׁמִּצְוָה בְּשׂוֹנֵא לְכֹף הַיֵּצֶר — In the latter case, the law is **that it is a mitzvah** to give precedence **to the enemy,** and assist him, **so as to subdue** one's Evil **Inclination,** וַאֲפִלּוּ אוֹהֵב לִפְרֹק וְשׂוֹנֵא לִטְעֹן — **and this applies even if the friend** requires assistance **to unload** his animal **and the enemy** requires assistance **to load** his animal.[11] וְשׂוֹנֵא זֶה אֵינוֹ כַּשּׂוֹנֵא שֶׁזְּכַרְנוּ מֵחֲמַת עֲבֵרָה — One should note, **however,** that this **"enemy"** mentioned here **is not the same as the enemy that we mentioned** above, where one hates the person **on account of** his having committed a **sin.** In that situation, it is appropriate to harbor animosity toward the sinner, and one should not seek to curtail that animosity by awarding the sinner precedence. אֶלָּא שֶׁאֵין לִבּוֹ שָׁלֵם עִמּוֹ — **Rather,** here we speak of a person **with whom "one's heart is not complete"** (i.e., toward whom one bears a grudge) for personal reasons.[12]

Chinuch cites a number of limitations to the extent of one's obligation under this mitzvah: וּפֵרוּשׁ "כִּי תִרְאֶה" — **The laws of the mitzvah also** include how **to define** the words of the verse, **If you see;** מֵאֵימָתַי הוּא הַחִיּוּב — that is, **from when** (i.e., within what distance) **does the obligation** begin.[13] וְשִׁעֲרוּ חֲכָמִים שֶׁהוּא אֶחָד מִשִּׁבְעָה וּמֶחֱצָה בְּמִיל — **The Sages** (Bava Metzia 33a) **determined this amount to be one in seven and one-half parts of a mil,** וְזֶהוּ רִיס — **which is** the distance known as **a ris.**[14] If one is within that distance of the animal in distress he must come and help. אֲבָל רָחוֹק מִזֶּה הַשִּׁעוּר — **However,** if he is **further than this distance,** אֵין חַיָּב לְהַטּוֹת הַדֶּרֶךְ אֵלָיו — **he is not obligated to veer** from **his path so as to** reach it. וְהָעוֹשֶׂה לִפְנִים מִן הַשּׁוּרָה תָּבֹא עָלָיו בְּרָכָה — **Nevertheless, one who does beyond what is required** by law, and goes to even greater lengths to assist one who is in need, merits that **blessing shall come upon him.**[15] וְדִין זָקֵן אוֹ נִכְבָּד — Also included is **the law of an elderly or dignified** individual,

---

NOTES

11. Normally, if one encounters two people stranded on the road, one who needs assistance unloading the burden from his animal and the other who needs assistance reloading his animal, the person is required to first assist with the unloading, in order to alleviate the suffering of the animal struggling with its burden. However, if one of the owners is his enemy, one should give precedence to assisting his enemy, even if the other animal is suffering. By resisting the urge to ignore his enemy's plight, he will learn to foster a love for all, regardless of his personal feelings. [For a discussion of why tzaar baalei chaim (see previous note) is not taken into consideration here, see the Insight.]

12. Although the verse does not speak of this situation (as explained in note 6), the law mentioned here refers to a situation where one bears ill will toward the owner of the animal due to a personal grievance. Since such a grievance is prohibited, one is required to overcome it by giving precedence to assisting this person (see Ramban, Bava Metzia 32b; see also Tosafos there ד״ה לכוף; cf. Tosafos, Pesachim 113b ד״ה שראה).

13. The Gemara (Bava Metzia 33a) notes the juxtaposition of our mitzvah, regarding which it is stated (Exodus 23:4), If you "see" an animal crouching beneath its burden, and the verse that immediately precedes it, which states If you will "encounter" an animal that has strayed and has become lost to its owner. This teaches that the mitzvah of perikah does not apply in every instance in which one sees an animal struggling with its load; rather, it applies only when one sees the animal from such proximity that it could be called an encounter. See further in Chinuch.

14. I.e., ⅖₁₅ of a mil. [A mil is equivalent to 2,000 amos, which according to many authorities is a distance equal to approximately 3750 ft. (1143 meters). A ris is thus 266 ⅔ amos, which is somewhat less than a tenth of a mile (approximately 500 feet/152 meters).]

15. Although there is no obligation to come to the assistance of a stricken animal that is beyond this distance, it is nevertheless meritorious to do so.

Minchas Chinuch (§1) notes that while the Gemara does state in connection with other exemptions from the mitzvah of perikah that it is meritorious to perform the mitzvah despite the exemption, there is no source to suggest that this pertains also to where the animal is too far for the mitzvah to apply. On this basis, he

## 115 ☐ MISHPATIM / MITZVAH 80: THE OBLIGATION TO HELP REMOVE A BURDEN

וְאֵינָה לְפִי כְבוֹדוֹ[16], שֶׁהַכֹּל נָדוֹן לְפִי מַה שֶׁיִּהְיֶה עוֹשֶׂה בְּשֶׁלּוֹ[17], וְדִין פְּרִיקָה בְּחִנָּם וּטְעִינָה בְּשָׂכָר[18], וְשֶׁמְּדַדֶּה עִמּוֹ עַד פַּרְסָה[19], וְנוֹטֵל שָׂכָר עַל הַלְוָיָה[20], כְּמוֹ שֶׁמְּבֹאָר הַכֹּל בְּפֶרֶק שֵׁנִי

וְאֵינָה לְפִי כְבוֹדוֹ — **for whom it is not in accordance with his dignity** to assist with unloading or loading an animal;[16] שֶׁהַכֹּל נָדוֹן לְפִי מַה שֶׁיִּהְיֶה עוֹשֶׂה בְּשֶׁלּוֹ — **the rule is that** his obligation in this mitzvah **is determined entirely by what he would do with his own** property.[17]

Chinuch concludes the laws of the mitzvah:

וְדִין פְּרִיקָה בְּחִנָּם וּטְעִינָה בְּשָׂכָר — **Also** included is **the law that unloading** must be performed **free of charge, but loading** may be done **for compensation;**[18] וְשֶׁמְּדַדֶּה עִמּוֹ עַד פַּרְסָה — **and** the law **that one must walk along with [the person that he assisted with loading] for** the distance of **a parsah**[19] in case the animal will falter a second time, וְנוֹטֵל שָׂכָר עַל הַלְוָיָה — **and** that **he** is entitled to **take compensation for accompanying** him.[20] כְּמוֹ שֶׁמְּבֹאָר הַכֹּל בְּפֶרֶק שֵׁנִי

---

NOTES

suggests that there is an error in our text of Chinuch, and that this sentence should be placed after the next law that Chinuch cites (see, however, *Minchas Yitzchak* §9). See note 17.

16. *Rashi* to this verse explains that the words וְחָדַלְתָּ מֵעֲזֹב לוֹ (which are rendered here as *would you refrain from helping him?*) can also be understood to be saying "you *may* (i.e., you are permitted to) refrain from helping him." This implies that there are situations where one is indeed not obligated, and may refrain from providing assistance (see also *Bava Metzia* 30a-b). This is expounded to teach that an elderly or distinguished individual, for whom it would be demeaning to assist with unloading or loading an animal, is not required to suffer indignity in order to assist his fellow. [For discussion of the extent of this exemption, see Insight.]

17. That is, the determination of whether assisting the owner of the animal compromises the dignity of the elderly or distinguished individual is determined by judging how this individual would conduct himself if the stricken animal were his own. If, had the animal been his own, he would toil to assist it, he cannot claim that doing so for his fellow is beneath his dignity! He is thus obligated to assist the owner of the animal. If, however, he would abandon even his own animal rather than demean himself to save it, he is not required to assist with his fellow's animal (see *Bava Mezia* 30b).

The Gemara (ibid.) adds that it is nevertheless meritorious to go beyond what is required, and to forgo one's honor in order to assist his fellow. [As stated in note 15, *Minchas Chinuch* suggests that it is in connection with this law that Chinuch wrote above that it is meritorious to go beyond the letter of the law.]

*Tur* (*Choshen Mishpat* 272:3) cites a disagreement among Rishonim regarding whether a *Torah scholar* may forgo his honor in order to assist with his fellow's animal: *Rosh* (*Bava Metzia* 2:21) maintains that the honor that is due a Torah scholar is not his own, but is rather due the Torah itself. He is therefore not permitted to forgo his honor to assist with his fellow's animal. Instead, a Torah scholar who wishes to go beyond the requirement of the law should hire workers to provide the necessary assistance. *Rambam* (ibid. 13:4), however, maintains that it is actually desirable for even a Torah scholar to *personally* assist with unloading and loading the animal, and that doing so does not compromise the honor of the Torah. To the contrary, it is considered an honor to the Torah, since he would not do so for his own animal and is only doing so because it is a mitzvah (*Beis Yosef, Choshen Mishpat* 263:3).

18. The Gemara (*Bava Metzia* 32a) derives this law through the following reasoning: Why must the Torah instruct the mitzvah of *perikah* (unloading) in addition to the mitzvah of *te'inah* (loading)? If there is a mitzvah to assist with reloading, in which case the (unloaded) animal is not suffering, certainly there is an obligation to assist with unloading in order to relieve its suffering! It must be that the mitzvah of *perikah* imposes a greater obligation than the mitzvah of *te'inah,* namely, that while one who assists with unloading (*perikah*) cannot demand compensation, one who assists with reloading an animal (*te'inah*) is entitled to compensation for the service rendered. [Nevertheless, even in a situation of *perikah*, one is entitled to a certain amount of compensation for loss of income incurred while providing assistance (see *Shulchan Aruch, Choshen Mishpat* 272:6; see ibid. 265:1 with *Rama* and *Shach* for details). Beyond this amount, however, one is forbidden to accept monetary compensation for performing the mitzvah even if the owner of the animal offers it (*Sma, Choshen Mishpat* 272:17).]

19. One *parsah* is equivalent to four *mil* (about 2.8 miles [4.6 km]; see above, note 14). [There is disagreement among the authorities whether the obligation to accompany the animal is of Biblical or Rabbinic origin. For discussion, see *Minchas Chinuch* §15; *Minchas Soless,* end of this mitzvah; *Chazon Yechezkel* to *Tosefta, Bava Metzia* 2:10.]

20. Although unloading must be performed free of charge, one is entitled to compensation for the service of *accompanying* the animal's owner, even if there is concern that help might be needed to unload the animal. If he will end up assisting with unloading the animal, he is entitled to compensation only for accompanying him, not for the actual unloading.

מִמְּצִיעָא[21] (דף ל"ב ע"א ואילך)•.
וְנוֹהֶגֶת בְּכָל מָקוֹם וּבְכָל זְמַן[22], בִּזְכָרִים וּנְקֵבוֹת[23].
וְעוֹבֵר עָלֶיהָ בִּטֵּל עֲשֵׂה[24], וּמַרְאֶה בְּעַצְמוֹ מִדַּת הָאַכְזָרִיּוּת שֶׁהִיא מִדָּה מְכֹעֶרֶת, וְכָל שֶׁאֵינוֹ מְרַחֵם אֵין מְרַחֲמִין עָלָיו מִן הַשָּׁמַיִם, שֶׁאֵין רָאוּי גּוּפוֹ לְקַבֵּל הָרַחֲמָנוּת[25].

---

מִמְּצִיעָא — **All** these laws **are set forth in the second chapter of** *Bava Metzia*.[21]

## ～ Applicability of the Mitzvah ～

וְנוֹהֶגֶת בְּכָל מָקוֹם וּבְכָל זְמַן — **[This mitzvah] applies in every location and in all times,**[22] בִּזְכָרִים וּנְקֵבוֹת — **and is incumbent upon both men and women.**[23] וְעוֹבֵר עָלֶיהָ בִּטֵּל עֲשֵׂה — **One who transgresses [this mitzvah] has violated a mitzvah-obligation,**[24] וּמַרְאֶה בְּעַצְמוֹ מִדַּת הָאַכְזָרִיּוּת — **and has displayed in himself the trait of cruelty,** שֶׁהִיא מִדָּה מְכֹעֶרֶת — **which is a repugnant trait.** וְכָל שֶׁאֵינוֹ מְרַחֵם אֵין מְרַחֲמִין עָלָיו מִן הַשָּׁמַיִם — With regard to such a person, the Sages have stated (*Shabbos* 151b): **Whoever is not compassionate** toward God's creatures **is not shown compassion by Heaven,** שֶׁאֵין רָאוּי גּוּפוֹ לְקַבֵּל הָרַחֲמָנוּת — **for his physical being is not worthy of receiving compassion.**[25]

---

### NOTES

21. See *Bava Metzia* 30b and 32a-33a. The laws of this mitzvah are codified in *Rambam, Hil. Rotze'ach U'Shemiras HaNefesh,* Ch. 13, and *Shulchan Aruch, Choshen Mishpat* §272.

22. I.e., the mitzvah applies in Eretz Yisrael and in the Diaspora, whether or not the *Beis HaMikdash* is standing.
    *Aruch HaShulchan* (*Choshen Mishpat* 272:8) applies the mitzvos of *perikah* and *te'inah* to a situation of one who sees an animal struggling to pull a wagon that is stuck in mud, requiring him to assist in unloading the wagon, repositioning the animal and wagon on dry land, and then reloading the wagon. Similarly, if the wheel or axle of the wagon broke, one is required to assist the owner, and then to accompany him for a short distance in case he should need further assistance; see also *She'arim Metzuyanim BaHalachah* 189:1. See further there, and *Yad HaLevi* to *Rambam, Sefer HaMitzvos, Asei* 203, end of §2, regarding the obligation to assist a person whose automobile has become disabled on the road.

23. In accordance with the general rule that applies to mitzvah-obligations that are not time-specific (see General Introduction).

24. One who fails to fulfill this mitzvah also transgresses the prohibition expressed in the verse (*Deuteronomy* 22:4): לֹא תִרְאֶה אֶת חֲמוֹר אָחִיךָ אוֹ שׁוֹרוֹ נֹפְלִים בַּדֶּרֶךְ וְהִתְעַלַּמְתָּ מֵהֶם, *You shall not see the donkey of your brother or his ox falling on the road and hide yourself from them* (see below, Mitzvah 540).

25. As *Chinuch* explains in Mitzvah 66, man is worthy of receiving God's goodness only to the extent that he himself possesses the refined Attributes of God. One who fails to display compassion for God's creations is thus not worthy of receiving His mercy.

---

> ◈§ **Insight: Man's Needs vs. Tzaar Baalei Chaim (Pain of Living Creatures)**
>
> In establishing the mitzvah to assist a fellow in unloading his animal, the Torah (*Exodus* 23:5) states: עָזֹב תַּעֲזֹב עִמּוֹ, *you shall help repeatedly with him.* The phrase *with him* teaches that the mitzvah of *perikah* (unloading) requires one to assist with unloading a distressed animal only if the owner is also participating in the effort. If, however, the owner is present and capable of helping, yet unwilling to participate, the mitzvah does not apply (see *Mishnah, Bava Metzia* 32a, and *Rambam, Hil. Rotze'ach U'Shemiras HaNefesh* 13:8). Nevertheless, there is a separate obligation to relieve *tzaar baalei chaim,* the pain of living creatures, regarding which no such limitation is stated, and which therefore applies even if the owner does not participate (see above, note 10). The difference between these obligations is that whereas one may not accept payment for performing the mitzvah of *perikah* (see end of note 18), he is permitted to accept payment for relieving *tzaar baalei chaim* (see *Rama, Choshen Mishpat* 272:9 with *Sma* §17). Hence, if the owner refuses to participate, one must nevertheless unload the animal to relieve its suffering, but he may accept payment for it.
>
> *Rishonim,* however, raise a difficulty with this matter: We have learned (see *Chinuch* at notes 16-17) that an elderly or dignified individual who would not lower himself to unload his own animal

is exempt from assisting with unloading his fellow's distressed animal. This exemption is derived from the verse pertaining to the mitzvah of *perikah* (see above, note 16). But why does the elderly or dignified individual not remain obligated to unload the animal under the requirement to relieve *tzaar baalei chaim*?

*Ramban* (*Bava Metzia* 33a, cited by *Nimukei Yosef* there fol. 17b) explains that the exemption of an "elderly or dignified individual" refers only to a Torah scholar, whom it is a mitzvah to honor (Mitzvah 257). The mitzvah to honor a Torah scholar is greater than the mitzvah to relieve *tzaar baalei chaim*, and a Torah scholar is therefore permitted to preserve his dignity even in a situation where an animal is enduring pain. *Ran*, however, argues that [as Chinuch stated at note 17] the exemption of an "elderly or dignified individual" is not limited to a Torah scholar, but applies in any situation where, due to his status, the individual would not assist the animal if it were his own (*Chidushei HaRan* to *Bava Metzia* 33a, cited by *Nimukei Yosef* ibid.; see also *Chidushei HaRan* [previously attributed to *Ritva*] to *Shabbos* 154b). The question thus returns: Why is there no obligation to relieve *tzaar baalei chaim* in such a situation?

*Ran* therefore explains that although there is an obligation to relieve *tzaar baalei chaim*, the needs of an animal do not take precedence over the needs of man. Man is permitted to use an animal for plowing and similar heavy labor even though such exertion certainly causes distress to the animal; and he is permitted even to slaughter an animal, either for personal or for commercial purposes (see Mitzvah 551). Certainly, then, the Torah would not require a person to suffer indignity for the sake of an animal! Thus, in any situation where assisting with unloading the animal would compromise a person's dignity, for which reason the mitzvah of *perikah* does not apply, the obligation to relieve *tzaar baalei chaim* also does not apply. Rather, the obligation to relieve *tzaar baalei chaim* requires one only to refrain from inflicting pain on an animal without need, and to relieve an animal from pain in a situation where the person's dignity will not be compromised.

This idea, that the needs of an animal are secondary to the needs of man, can help us understand another law of our mitzvah as well. Chinuch (at note 11) mentioned that if one encounters two people who are both in a situation in which they require help with an animal at the same time, one a friend and the other an enemy, he is required to give precedence to helping the animal of his enemy. Even if his friend's animal is suffering under a heavy burden and waiting to be *unloaded*, he is required to give precedence to *loading* the enemy's animal in order to suppress his hatred. But why does the law of *tzaar baalei chaim* not demand the opposite? *Minchas Chinuch* (§8) explains that this matter can be understood based on the above premise: Man's need to refine his character, and to purge feelings of hatred toward another Jew from his heart, are no less important than his physical needs, which are given priority over the needs of an animal. Therefore, he is required to give precedence to his enemy's animal in order to suppress his hatred, even if his friend's animal is in pain, for here too, his own needs have a greater priority than the needs of the animal.

## מִצְוָה פּא: שֶׁלֹּא לְהַטּוֹת מִשְׁפַּט חוֹטֵא מִפְּנֵי רִשְׁעוֹ

שֶׁלֹּא לְהַטּוֹת הַדִּין עַל אֶחָד מִבַּעֲלֵי הַדִּין כְּשֶׁיֵּדַע שֶׁהוּא רָשָׁע בַּעַל עֲבֵרוֹת, שֶׁנֶּאֱמַר (שמות כ״ג, ו׳) לֹא תַטֶּה מִשְׁפַּט אֶבְיֹנְךָ בְּרִיבוֹ. וּפֵרוּשׁוֹ שֶׁהוּא אֶבְיוֹן בַּמִּצְוֹת, שֶׁאֵין בְּמַשְׁמָע שֶׁיְּהֵא אֶבְיוֹן בַּמָּמוֹן, שֶׁאֵין צָרִיךְ לוֹמַר שֶׁלֹּא יַטּוּ עָלָיו הַדִּין לִגְזֹל מִמֶּנּוּ בְּעָנְיוֹ,[1] אֶלָּא נִצְטַוֵּינוּ שֶׁאַף עַל פִּי שֶׁהוּא רָשָׁע לֹא יֹאמַר הַדַּיָּן הוֹאִיל וְרָשָׁע הוּא אַטֶּה עָלָיו אֶת הַדִּין,[2] כִּי הַמִּשְׁפָּט בָּרְשָׁעִים לֵאלֹהִים הוּא וְלֹא לוֹ. וְכֵן הוּא בַּמְּכִילְתָּא (כאן) רָשָׁע וְכָשֵׁר עוֹמְדִין לְפָנֶיךָ בַּדִּין, שֶׁמָּא תֹּאמַר וְכוּ׳.[3]

# Mitzvah 81

## The Prohibition to Bend the Judgment of a Sinner Because of his Wickedness

לֹא תַטֶּה מִשְׁפַּט אֶבְיֹנְךָ בְּרִיבוֹ
*Do not bend the judgment of your destitute person in his grievance (Exodus 23:6).*

Although the plain meaning of the above verse seems to refer to bending the judgment of the *poor*, the Sages taught that the term אֶבְיוֹן, *destitute*, is actually a reference to a wicked person, who is destitute of all good deeds, as Chinuch states below. This mitzvah, instructing a judge not to tilt the judgment of a wicked person against him due to his wickedness, is one of several mitzvos regarding the importance of treating all litigants equally, no matter their status (see Mitzvos 79, 234, 235).

שֶׁלֹּא לְהַטּוֹת הַדִּין עַל אֶחָד מִבַּעֲלֵי הַדִּין — We (i.e., judges) are commanded **not to tilt the judgment against one of the litigants** — כְּשֶׁיֵּדַע שֶׁהוּא רָשָׁע בַּעַל עֲבֵרוֹת — even **when he,** i.e., the judge, **knows that he is a wicked, sinful person,** — שֶׁנֶּאֱמַר ״לֹא תַטֶּה מִשְׁפַּט אֶבְיֹנְךָ בְּרִיבוֹ״ — **as it is stated** (*Exodus* 23:6): *Do not bend the judgment of your destitute person in his grievance;* וּפֵרוּשׁוֹ שֶׁהוּא אֶבְיוֹן בַּמִּצְוֹת — **and the meaning of** the word אֶבְיוֹן in this verse is a *sinful person,* **who is destitute of good deeds.**

Chinuch explains why the Sages understood this verse as referring to a wicked person, and not literally a financially destitute person:

שֶׁאֵין בְּמַשְׁמָע שֶׁיְּהֵא אֶבְיוֹן בַּמָּמוֹן — This is **because it is not sensible** to say **that [the "destitute person"] of the verse is one who is destitute of money,** — שֶׁאֵין צָרִיךְ לוֹמַר שֶׁלֹּא יַטּוּ עָלָיו הַדִּין — **for it is not necessary** for the Torah to **say that [the judges] may not tilt the judgment against him,** לִגְזֹל מִמֶּנּוּ בְּעָנְיוֹ — **to rob him in his poverty.**[1] אֶלָּא נִצְטַוֵּינוּ — **Rather,** the meaning of this verse is that **we were commanded** שֶׁאַף עַל פִּי שֶׁהוּא רָשָׁע — **that even though [this litigant] is** known to be **a wicked person,** לֹא יֹאמַר הַדַּיָּן — **the judge may not say,** הוֹאִיל וְרָשָׁע הוּא אַטֶּה עָלָיו אֶת הַדִּין — **"Since [this litigant] is a wicked person, I will tilt the judgment against him,** to punish him for his wickedness";[2] כִּי הַמִּשְׁפָּט בָּרְשָׁעִים לֵאלֹהִים הוּא וְלֹא לוֹ — **for judgment of the wicked is** reserved **for God, and** is not the prerogative **of [the judge]** to carry out at his discretion. וְכֵן הוּא בַּמְּכִילְתָּא — **So, too, is [the verse]** explained **in** *Mechilta* (ad loc.): רָשָׁע וְכָשֵׁר עוֹמְדִין לְפָנֶיךָ בַּדִּין — **If a wicked person and an upright person are standing before you for judgment,** שֶׁמָּא תֹּאמַר וְכוּ׳ — **lest you say, etc.**[3]

---

### NOTES

1. Having warned in general against bending justice (Mitzvah 233), the Torah adds specific prohibitions only for cases where a judge might find some moral justification to tilt the verdict one way or another, as in Mitzvah 79, where the Torah warns a judge not to bend the verdict *in favor* of a poor person. It is, however, unnecessary to have a special prohibition regarding turning the verdict *against* the poor person, since that is something for which no judge could find justification.

2. This explanation follows *Rambam, Sefer HaMitzvos, Lo Saaseh* 278. See Insight.

3. *Mechilta* concludes: *Lest you say, "Since he is a*

# 119 ◻ MISHPATIM / MITZVAH 81: THE PROHIBITION TO BEND THE JUDGMENT OF A SINNER

שֹׁרֶשׁ הַשְׁוָיַת הַדִּין בְּכָל אָדָם, דָּבָר מֻשְׂכָּל הוּא.
וְנוֹהֶגֶת בְּכָל מָקוֹם וּבְכָל זְמַן[4], בִּזְכָרִים, אֲבָל לֹא בִּנְקֵבוֹת, שֶׁאֵינָן דָּנוֹת[5].
וְעוֹבֵר אוֹתָהּ וְהִטָּה הַדִּין עַל הָרָשָׁע, עָבַר עַל מִצְוַת מֶלֶךְ[6].

## ☙ Underlying Purpose of the Mitzvah ☙

שֹׁרֶשׁ הַשְׁוָיַת הַדִּין בְּכָל אָדָם — The underlying purpose of providing equality of judgment to all people  דָּבָר מֻשְׂכָּל הוּא — is a self-understood, logical matter.

## ☙ Applicability of the Mitzvah ☙

וְנוֹהֶגֶת בְּכָל מָקוֹם וּבְכָל זְמַן — [This mitzvah] applies in every location, and in all times,[4] בִּזְכָרִים — to men, אֲבָל לֹא בִּנְקֵבוֹת שֶׁאֵינָן דָּנוֹת — but not to women, for they do not judge.[5] וְעוֹבֵר אוֹתָהּ וְהִטָּה הַדִּין עַל הָרָשָׁע — [A judge] who transgresses [this mitzvah] and tilts the judgment against a wicked person עָבַר עַל מִצְוַת מֶלֶךְ — has transgressed the King's command.[6]

---

### NOTES

wicked person, I will bend the judgment against him," the Torah teaches, "Do not bend the judgment of your destitute person in his grievance"; this refers to one who is destitute of mitzvos [i.e., a wicked person].

4. I.e., in Eretz Yisrael and the Diaspora, and whether the Beis HaMikdash is standing or not.

5. See Mitzvah 77 for further discussion. [Minchas Chinuch (§2) notes that in the cases where a woman can preside over cases (such as in monetary cases where she was accepted by the litigants; see Mitzvah 77, at note 42), she would presumably be included in prohibitions such as this one relating to a judge. See similarly above, Mitzvah 75 note 32, and below, Mitzvah 83 note 18.]

6. The punishment for this sin is in the hands of God, for no punishment is given by the courts. This prohibition is not punishable by malkus (lashes) as it is לָאו שֶׁאֵין בּוֹ מַעֲשֶׂה, a prohibition that does not involve an action; see General Introduction, note 14.

---

### ⁘§ Insight: Equal Before the Law

Chinuch explains that, were it not for the specific prohibition to bend the judgment against the wicked, a judge might have supposed that he may rule against a wicked person in order to punish him, even though that person is actually free of liability in the particular case before the judge. This is also indicated by Mechilta cited by Chinuch, and is stated clearly by Rambam in Sefer HaMitzvos when discussing this prohibition: The Torah prohibits us from imposing [the wicked person's] punishment by bending his judgment (Lo Saaseh 278).

Minchas Yitzchak explains that this does not mean that a judge would have been able to indiscriminately convict a person because he had sinned in the past. Rather, it refers to a situation where two people come before the court, and the court knows one of them to be deserving of a monetary fine due to serious sins that he had previously committed. In this case, the judge might have attempted to force the wicked person to lose the money that he has justly forfeited due to those sins. This prohibition states that, nevertheless, the court is forbidden to convict based on anything but the merits of this specific case — even if there is no other way to force payment from the wicked individual for his previous sins. As Chinuch states: Judgment of the wicked is reserved for God, and not [the judge]. [The prohibition of this verse is thus the converse of the prohibition against favoring a destitute person in court (Mitzvah 79), which forbids a judge to force a wealthy person to give money to the poor through a judgment, even though in other circumstances the wealthy person is indeed obligated to give him the money as charity.]

There is another source, however, which puts the prohibition of this verse in an entirely different light. Mechilta DeRashbi (Exodus 23:6), in explaining this prohibition, writes as follows: So you should not say, "This [litigant] is a wicked person, and it can be assumed that he is lying, while this [other litigant] is assumed not to be lying; I will therefore rule against [the wicked]," the Torah teaches, Do not bend the judgment.

According to Mechilta DeRashbi, the Torah does not address a judge who believes the wicked

person exempt in this case but wishes to rule against him punitively. Rather, the Torah refers to a case where the judge wishes to take the wickedness of one of the litigants as a clear indication of his guilt *in the very case upon which he is presiding*. The Torah warns that such generalities may not be made. *Shulchan Aruch* (*Choshen Mishpat* 17:10), in citing this law, concludes: *Rather, both litigants should be assumed wicked* (i.e., suspect of lying) *in your eyes*. Regardless of any previous experience the judge has had with the litigants, both must appear equally suspect before him in adjudicating the case currently before him (see Mishnah, *Avos* 1:8).

*Be'er Eliyahu* (*Choshen Mishpat* 17:18) writes that this does not mean that the judge must entirely ignore the litigant's past. A judge is required to assess each case using all the information at his disposal (*Choshen Mishpat* 15:5), and, if the record of one of the litigants adds to the judge's perception that he is lying, he surely may take that into account. What is forbidden is for the judge to make a sweeping assumption that the wicked person is lying and that the other litigant must surely be telling the truth in this case. Such generalities are unfair and cannot be used in judging cases.

For further discussion, and for some practical differences between these two approaches to the mitzvah, see *Minchas Chinuch* §1, *Minchas Yitzchak*, and *Be'er Eliyahu* ibid.

## מִצְוָה פב: שֶׁלֹּא לַחְתֹּךְ הַדִּין בְּאֹמֶד הַדַּעַת.[2,1]

שֶׁלֹּא יַהַרְגוּ בֵּית דִּין הַנִּדּוֹן כִּי אִם בְּעֵדִים מְעִידִין עַל אוֹתוֹ עִנְיָן שֶׁהוּא נֶהֱרָג עָלָיו שֶׁרָאוּהוּ שֶׁעָשָׂה אוֹתוֹ בְּעֵינֵיהֶם מַמָּשׁ, [לֹא] שֶׁיָּעִידוּ עָלָיו מִצַּד אוֹתוֹת חֲזָקוֹת[3], וְעַל זֶה נֶאֱמַר (שמות כ״ג, ז׳) וְנָקִי וְצַדִּיק אַל תַּהֲרֹג, כְּלוֹמַר הִזָּהֵר עַד מְאֹד לְבַל תַּהֲרֹג אָדָם שֶׁיְּהֵא בְּאֶפְשָׁרוּת שֶׁלֹּא עָשָׂה מַה שֶּׁאָמְרוּ עָלָיו שֶׁעָשָׂה.[4] וְכֵן הוּא מְפֹרָשׁ בַּמְּכִילְתָּא,

# Mitzvah 82
## The Prohibition to Render Judgment Based Upon Assumptions

וְנָקִי וְצַדִּיק אַל תַּהֲרֹג כִּי לֹא אַצְדִּיק רָשָׁע

*The blameless or the innocent you shall not slay, for I shall not exonerate the guilty (Exodus 23:7).*

The injunction of this verse, that *beis din* not execute the innocent, is certainly unnecessary with regard to one who was completely exonerated of his alleged crime. Rather, as Chinuch shall explain, the verse refers to specific instances in which one might have supposed that the accused should be found guilty by the court and executed, and regarding these cases, the Torah warns that the defendant *cannot* be considered definitely guilty and therefore may not be executed by the court.[1]

Chinuch cites two situations where this applies: The first pertains to all manner of circumstantial evidence. The second deals with certain types of testimony, where there is a lack of "unity of testimony" of the two witnesses, as shall be explained below.

Regarding all these cases, the verse concludes: *for I* [Hashem] *shall not exonerate the guilty*. The verse assures us that we need not fear that as a result of these acquittals we will be exonerating one who is in fact guilty of the crime. God is the true Judge and He will ensure that the guilty are appropriately punished and justice is served.[2]

שֶׁלֹּא יַהַרְגוּ בֵּית דִּין הַנִּדּוֹן — We are commanded **that *beis din* shall not execute the defendant** in a capital case כִּי אִם בְּעֵדִים מְעִידִין עַל אוֹתוֹ עִנְיָן שֶׁהוּא נֶהֱרָג עָלָיו — **unless there are witnesses testifying regarding the matter for which he is to be executed** שֶׁרָאוּהוּ שֶׁעָשָׂה אוֹתוֹ בְּעֵינֵיהֶם מַמָּשׁ — that they actually saw him commit [the act] with their eyes, [לֹא] שֶׁיָּעִידוּ עָלָיו מִצַּד — **that they actually saw him commit [the act] with their eyes,** אוֹתוֹת חֲזָקוֹת — **but not when they testify against him on the basis of** even **powerful circumstantial evidence.**[3] וְעַל זֶה נֶאֱמַר "וְנָקִי וְצַדִּיק אַל תַּהֲרֹג" — **Regarding this, the verse states** (*Exodus* 23:7): *The blameless or the innocent you shall not slay;* כְּלוֹמַר — **that is to say,** הִזָּהֵר שֶׁיְּהֵא עַד מְאֹד לְבַל תַּהֲרֹג אָדָם — **take exceedingly great caution not to execute an individual** בְּאֶפְשָׁרוּת שֶׁלֹּא עָשָׂה מַה שֶּׁאָמְרוּ עָלָיו שֶׁעָשָׂה — **when it is possible that he did not do that which they said he did.**[4]

Chinuch cites *Mechilta*, which explains the verse as just stated and provides an example of the sort of powerful circumstantial evidence that is the subject of this prohibition:

וְכֵן הוּא מְפֹרָשׁ בַּמְּכִילְתָּא — **That is how [the prohibition] is explained in *Mechilta*** (to this verse),

---

NOTES

1. *Mechilta DeRashbi* to *Exodus* 23:7.

2. See also end of this mitzvah, where Chinuch presents another consideration to counter the concern that due to these laws a guilty party will be exonerated.

3. Literally, *powerful signs*.

4. The verse certainly does not refer to one against whom there is no evidence at all, for in that case the prohibition would be superfluous (see Introduction to this mitzvah). See *Ramban*, Glosses to *Sefer HaMitzvos*, *Lo Saaseh* §290, for further explanation of this derivation.

## משפטים / מצוה פב: שלא לחתוך הדין באמד הדעת

שֶׁאָמְרוּ שָׁם, רָאוּהוּ רוֹדֵף אַחַר חֲבֵרוֹ לְהָרְגוֹ וְהִתְרוּ בוֹ יִשְׂרָאֵל הוּא, בֶּן בְּרִית הוּא, אִם הֲרַגְתָּ אוֹתוֹ תֵּהָרֵג, וְהֶעֱלִימוּ עֵינֵיהֶם שֶׁלֹּא רָאוּ בְּהַכּוֹתוֹ אוֹתוֹ, וּמְצָאוּהוּ מִיָּד הָרוּג וּמְפַרְפֵּר וְהַסַּיִף מְנַטֵּף דָּם מִיַּד הַהוֹרֵג, שׁוֹמֵעַ אֲנִי יְהֵא חַיָּב, תַּלְמוּד לוֹמַר וְנָקִי וְצַדִּיק אַל תַּהֲרֹג. הֲרֵי שֶׁמִּפְּנֵי שֶׁהֶעֱלִימוּ עֵינֵיהֶם בְּעֵת הַהַכָּאָה נִפְטָר זֶה. וְכָשֵׁר הַדָּבָר וְרָאוּי לִהְיוֹת כֵּן, שֶׁאִלּוּ הִתִּירָה הַתּוֹרָה לְהָקִים גְּבוּלֵי הָעֹנֶשׁ בְּאֶפְשָׁרוּת הַקָּרוֹב, יֵצֵא מִן הָעִנְיָן לִפְעָמִים לְהָקִים גְּבוּלֵי הָעֹנֶשׁ בְּאֶפְשָׁרוּת רָחוֹק עַד שֶׁנָּמִית בְּנֵי אָדָם לִפְעָמִים עַל מַה שֶּׁלֹּא עָשׂוּ, כִּי יֵשׁ לָאֶפְשָׁרוּת רֹחַב גָּדוֹל. וְדַע זֶה וַהֲבִינֵהוּ כִּי דָבָר בָּרוּר הוּא, וּלְפִיכָךְ סָגַר יִתְעַלֶּה זֶה הַשַּׁעַר וְצִוָּה אוֹתָנוּ עַל זֶה,

שֶׁאָמְרוּ שָׁם – as [the Sages] state there: רָאוּהוּ רוֹדֵף אַחַר חֲבֵרוֹ לְהָרְגוֹ – If [witnesses] saw one chasing his fellow to kill him, וְהִתְרוּ בוֹ יִשְׂרָאֵל הוּא בֶּן בְּרִית הוּא – and they warned [the aggressor], "[Your intended victim] is an Israelite! He is a member of the covenant! אִם הֲרַגְתָּ אוֹתוֹ תֵּהָרֵג – If you kill him, you yourself will be executed by *beis din*!"[5] וְהֶעֱלִימוּ עֵינֵיהֶם שֶׁלֹּא רָאוּ בְּהַכּוֹתוֹ אוֹתוֹ – And, subsequently, [the witnesses] averted their eyes, so they did not see [the aggressor] actually strike [the victim],[6] וּמְצָאוּהוּ מִיָּד הָרוּג וּמְפַרְפֵּר – but [the witnesses] immediately afterward found [the victim] murdered, i.e., mortally wounded, in his death throes, וְהַסַּיִף מְנַטֵּף דָּם מִיַּד הַהוֹרֵג – and the sword was dripping blood from the hands of the alleged murderer, שׁוֹמֵעַ אֲנִי יְהֵא חַיָּב – I might have understood that in such a case, where there is such compelling circumstantial evidence, [the alleged murderer] should be judged guilty; תַּלְמוּד לוֹמַר וְנָקִי וְצַדִּיק אַל תַּהֲרֹג – [the Torah] therefore teaches us: *The blameless or the innocent you shall not slay*. הֲרֵי שֶׁמִּפְּנֵי שֶׁהֶעֱלִימוּ עֵינֵיהֶם בְּעֵת הַהַכָּאָה נִפְטָר זֶה – Thus, we see from *Mechilta* that because [the witnesses] averted their eyes at the moment of the blow, and did not witness the actual act of murder, [the defendant] is acquitted – despite the overwhelming circumstantial evidence pointing to his guilt.

Chinuch explains why the Torah prohibits the judging of a capital case based upon even extremely compelling circumstantial evidence (such as the preceding case), where it is almost certain that the accused is guilty of the murder:

וְכָשֵׁר הַדָּבָר וְרָאוּי לִהְיוֹת כֵּן – This matter is indeed proper, and it is appropriate for the law to be so. שֶׁאִלּוּ הִתִּירָה הַתּוֹרָה לְהָקִים גְּבוּלֵי הָעֹנֶשׁ בְּאֶפְשָׁרוּת הַקָּרוֹב – For if the Torah would permit the establishment of the guidelines of capital punishment to be based upon a high probability of guilt, יֵצֵא מִן הָעִנְיָן לִפְעָמִים לְהָקִים גְּבוּלֵי הָעֹנֶשׁ בְּאֶפְשָׁרוּת רָחוֹק – this practice would at times result in the guidelines of capital punishment being based upon even a low probability of guilt, עַד שֶׁנָּמִית בְּנֵי אָדָם לִפְעָמִים עַל מַה שֶּׁלֹּא עָשׂוּ – until, at times, we might execute an individual for something that he did not do, כִּי יֵשׁ לָאֶפְשָׁרוּת רֹחַב גָּדוֹל – for the spectrum of what may or may not be considered "possible" is very broad.[7] וְדַע זֶה וַהֲבִינֵהוּ כִּי דָבָר בָּרוּר הוּא – Know this and understand it well, because it is clearly so.[8] וּלְפִיכָךְ סָגַר יִתְעַלֶּה זֶה הַשַּׁעַר וְצִוָּה אוֹתָנוּ עַל זֶה – Therefore, because of this risk, [Hashem], may He be exalted, "closed this gate," i.e., excluded any possibility of relying on such testimony, and commanded us regarding this issue, stating that we may not convict a defendant in a capital case except on the basis of eyewitness testimony.[9]

---

### NOTES

5. One cannot be sentenced to any corporal punishment by *beis din* (execution or *malkus*), unless, immediately prior to committing the crime, the accused was warned of the prohibited nature of his intended act and the punishment to which he will be liable should he commit it (see *Rambam, Hil. Sanhedrin* 12:1-2 and above, Mitzvah 32, note 38).

6. This does not mean that they *intentionally* looked away; rather, for whatever reason, the witnesses did not actually see the act of murder with their own eyes (e.g., the "murderer" chased the victim into a house and the witnesses immediately entered the house and found him dead; see *Sanhedrin* 37b).

7. That is, once we allow circumstantial evidence, even of the most compelling nature, we open up the possibility of a court allowing such evidence when it is less compelling as well, with the result that the court might execute a person for something that he did not actually do.

8. See *Sefer HaMitzvos, Lo Saaseh* §290, where *Rambam* details this argument at length.

9. *Rambam* (*Sefer HaMitzvos* ibid.) concludes this

# 123 ☐ MISHPATIM / MITZVAH 82: NOT TO RENDER JUDGMENT BASED UPON ASSUMPTIONS

וְכָל פִּקּוּדֵי הַשֵּׁם יִתְבָּרַךְ יְשָׁרִים.[10]

וְעוֹד נִכְלַל בִּכְלָל לָאו זֶה, מִי שֶׁהֵעִידוּ עָלָיו שְׁנֵי עֵדִים שֶׁרָאוּהוּ שֶׁעָבַר עֲבֵרָה אַחַת, כְּגוֹן שֶׁהָאֶחָד מֵעִיד עָלָיו שֶׁעָשָׂה מְלָאכָה בַּשַּׁבָּת וְהָאֶחָד שֶׁעָבַד עֲבוֹדָה זָרָה, שֶׁזֶּה אֵינוֹ נִדּוֹן בְּעֵדוּתָם, שֶׁנֶּאֱמַר וְנָקִי וְצַדִּיק אַל תַּהֲרֹג.[11] וְכֵן אָמְרוּ זִכְרוֹנָם לִבְרָכָה (מכילתא כאן) הָיָה אֶחָד מְעִידוֹ שֶׁרָאָהוּ עוֹבֵד לַחַמָּה וְאֶחָד לַלְּבָנָה, שׁוֹמֵעַ אֲנִי יִצְטָרְפוּ, תַּלְמוּד לוֹמַר וְנָקִי וְצַדִּיק אַל תַּהֲרֹג.[12]

שֹׁרֶשׁ הַמִּצְוָה נִגְלֶה הוּא כְּמוֹ שֶׁאָמַרְנוּ.[13]

---

**וְכָל פִּקּוּדֵי הַשֵּׁם יִתְבָּרַךְ יְשָׁרִים** — **All the precepts of Hashem, blessed be He, are upright.**[10]

Chinuch now introduces the second facet of this mitzvah. A defendant can be executed for a capital crime only based upon the testimony of at least two acceptable witnesses who saw the crime being committed. Here Chinch discusses the association that the two testimonies must have with each other in order for them to be considered a valid "unit" of testimony:

**וְעוֹד נִכְלַל בִּכְלָל לָאו זֶה** — **Also included in this prohibition** is **מִי שֶׁהֵעִידוּ עָלָיו שְׁנֵי עֵדִים** — the law regarding **one about whom two witnesses testified** **שֶׁרָאוּהוּ שֶׁעָבַר עֲבֵרָה אַחַת** — **that they** each **saw him violate a certain prohibition,** but the two of them did not see the same act. **כְּגוֹן** — **For example,** **שֶׁהָאֶחָד מֵעִיד עָלָיו שֶׁעָשָׂה מְלָאכָה בַּשַּׁבָּת** — **one** witness **testified against [the defendant] that he performed** *melachah* (forbidden activity) **on the Sabbath, וְהָאֶחָד** **שֶׁעָבַד עֲבוֹדָה זָרָה** — **and** the **other one** testified **that he worshiped** *avodah zarah* (an idol). Although each of these acts is a capital offense, so each witness testified that the accused commited a crime for which he is liable to be executed, **שֶׁזֶּה אֵינוֹ נִדּוֹן בְּעֵדוּתָם** — this mitzvah teaches **that this [defendant] cannot be punished on the basis of their testimony,** **שֶׁנֶּאֱמַר "וְנָקִי וְצַדִּיק אַל תַּהֲרֹג"** — **as it is stated:** *The blameless or the innocent you shall not slay.*[11] **וְכֵן אָמְרוּ זִכְרוֹנָם לִבְרָכָה** — **[The Sages], of blessed memory, similarly state** (*Mechilta* to this verse): **הָיָה אֶחָד** **מְעִידוֹ שֶׁרָאָהוּ עוֹבֵד לַחַמָּה וְאֶחָד לַלְּבָנָה** — **If one [witness] testifies against [the accused] that he saw him worship the sun, and one** witness testifies that he saw him worship **the moon, שׁוֹמֵעַ אֲנִי יִצְטָרְפוּ** — **I might have understood that their testimony could combine,** and it could be considered as two testimonies that the defendant is liable to death for idolatry; **תַּלְמוּד לוֹמַר "וְנָקִי** **וְצַדִּיק אַל תַּהֲרֹג"** — **[the Torah] therefore teaches** us: *The blameless or the innocent you shall not slay.*[12]

## ⁓ Underlying Purpose of the Mitzvah ⁓

**שֹׁרֶשׁ הַמִּצְוָה נִגְלֶה הוּא כְּמוֹ שֶׁאָמַרְנוּ** — **The underlying purpose of the mitzvah is clear, as we have stated** previously.[13]

---

### NOTES

discussion with the statement that even if, due to this prohibition, a thousand guilty people would be free of punishment, that is better than running the risk of having one person who is actually innocent wrongly executed.

10. Stylistic citation of *Psalms* 19:9.

11. Without this verse, one might have supposed that it is sufficient to have two witnesses who each testify that the defendant is liable to the death penalty, even though they are not testifying about the same action. We learn from the verse that we must take advantage of any possible way to find a defendant innocent in a capital case. Included in this is the disqualification of such testimony, since we do not have two witnesses testifying to the very same action (see *Rambam, Hil. Sanhedrin* 20:1; see also *Ramban,* Glosses to *Sefer HaMitzvos, Lo Saaseh* §290).

12. We shall see further that even if both witnesses testify about the very same act, but they did not observe it together, the accused also cannot be found guilty.

13. See Mitzvah 77, where Chinuch explains that God, in His compassion, commanded us to go to great lengths to avoid finding one liable to capital punishment.

# 124 □ משפטים / מצוה פב: שלא לחתך הדין באמד הדעת

דִּינֶיהָ, כְּגוֹן מַה שֶּׁאָמְרוּ זִכְרוֹנָם לִבְרָכָה (מכות דף ו' ע"ב), שֶׁאֵין עֵדוּתָן מִצְטָרֶפֶת אֲפִלּוּ מְעִידִים בַּעֲבֵרָה אַחַת עַד שֶׁיִּרְאוּ שְׁנֵיהֶם כְּאֶחָד,[14] וְעוֹד שֶׁיְּהוּ רוֹאִין זֶה אֶת זֶה בִּשְׁעַת הַמַּעֲשֶׂה, לְהוֹצִיא אִם הָאֶחָד רָאָהוּ מֵחַלּוֹן זֶה וְהָאַחֵר מֵחַלּוֹן אַחֵר וְאֵין יְכוֹלִין לִרְאוֹת זֶה אֶת זֶה,[15] וְשֶׁהַמַּתְרֶה מְצָרְפָן אִם רָאָה שְׁנֵיהֶם,[16],[17] וְיֶתֶר פְּרָטֶיהָ, בְּסַנְהֶדְרִין (דף ל"ז ע"ב).[18] וְנוֹהֶגֶת בְּאֶרֶץ יִשְׂרָאֵל,[19] בִּזְכָרִים כְּמוֹ שֶׁאָמַרְנוּ לְפִי שֶׁבָּהֶם הַמִּשְׁפָּט, כְּמוֹ שֶׁאָמַרְנוּ

---

## ~ Laws of the Mitzvah ~

In capital cases there is a requirement that both witnesses be joined as a *set of witnesses*, i.e., they cannot simply be two individuals who both testify to the same criminal act; rather, their testimony must be joint testimony. When the witnesses are not seen as a set of witnesses, their testimony is considered עֵדוּת מְיֻחֶדֶת, the testimony of *isolated witnesses*, and is inadmissible (*Makkos* 6b). Chinuch cites three laws pertaining to the requirement in capital cases that the testimony to the guilt of the defendant derive from a joint set of witnesses:

דִּינֶיהָ — **The laws of [this mitzvah] include**, כְּגוֹן מַה שֶּׁאָמְרוּ זִכְרוֹנָם לִבְרָכָה — **for example, that which [the Sages], of blessed memory, have said** (*Makkos* 6b), שֶׁאֵין עֵדוּתָן מִצְטָרֶפֶת אֲפִלּוּ מְעִידִים בַּעֲבֵרָה אַחַת — **that the testimonies of** two independent witnesses **do not combine** to form valid *joint testimony*, **even if they** both **testify that** the defendant committed **the same sinful act,** עַד שֶׁיִּרְאוּ שְׁנֵיהֶם כְּאֶחָד — **until the two** witnesses **see the act simultaneously.**[14] וְעוֹד שֶׁיְּהוּ רוֹאִין זֶה אֶת זֶה בִּשְׁעַת הַמַּעֲשֶׂה — **Furthermore,** the law is **that the [two witnesses] must see each other at the time of the action** as well, לְהוֹצִיא אִם הָאֶחָד רָאָהוּ מֵחַלּוֹן זֶה וְהָאַחֵר מֵחַלּוֹן אַחֵר — **to the exclusion** of a case **where one** witness **sees [the perpetrator] from one window** as he commits the crime, **while** at the very same moment **the other** witness sees him **from a different window,** וְאֵין יְכוֹלִין לִרְאוֹת זֶה אֶת זֶה — **but [the two witnesses] cannot see each other.**[15] וְשֶׁהַמַּתְרֶה מְצָרְפָן אִם רָאָה שְׁנֵיהֶם — **But** the law is **that the one who warns** the perpetrator[16] **can "join"** the two isolated witnesses together so that they form a set of witnesses, **if he sees both of [the witnesses].**[17] וְיֶתֶר פְּרָטֶיהָ בְּסַנְהֶדְרִין — These, **and the additional details** of this mitzvah, **are** discussed **in** Tractate *Sanhedrin* (37b).[18]

## ~ Applicability of the Mitzvah ~

וְנוֹהֶגֶת בְּאֶרֶץ יִשְׂרָאֵל — **[This mitzvah] applies in Eretz Yisrael.**[19] בִּזְכָרִים כְּמוֹ שֶׁאָמַרְנוּ לְפִי שֶׁבָּהֶם הַמִּשְׁפָּט — It applies **to men, as we have stated** (Mitzvah 77), **for judging is their** charge כְּמוֹ שֶׁאָמַרְנוּ

---

### NOTES

14. For example, one witness looked out of a window and saw an individual committing a capital crime (e.g., idol worship), and then, afterward, a second witness looked out the window and he too saw the perpetrator still engaged in the same forbidden act. These two witnesses cannot together form a *set of witnesses* to render the defendant liable, because they did not both see the violation at the same time. Instead, they are considered two separate individuals who each *independently* witnessed a crime.

15. In this case, too, since the witnesses cannot see each other at the time of the crime (e.g., they are looking out of adjacent windows in two separate rooms) they are also considered עֵדוּת מְיֻחֶדֶת, *isolated witnesses,* and their testimony is inadmissible.

16. See note 5.

17. That is, even if the two witnesses looking out of windows do not see each other, they can be joined as a set of witnesses if the one who warned the perpetrator was standing with him in the street and he can see both witnesses (*Makkos* 6b). The Gemara (ibid.) adds that another way to join the two separate witnesses is if the witnesses themselves both see the one who warned the perpetrator (even if he does not see them). *Rambam* (*Hil. Eidus* 4:1) rules that *both* of these factors are required: the one who gave the warning must see the witnesses, *and* both of the witnesses must see the one who gave the warning (see *Minchas Chinuch* §4).

18. The concept of circumstantial evidence is discussed in *Sanhedrin*. The concept of *isolated witnesses* is discussed in *Makkos* 6b. *Rambam* codifies these laws in *Hil. Sanhedrin* 20:1 and *Hil. Eidus* 4:1.

19. Chinuch consistently states that capital cases are tried only in Eretz Yisrael. See above, Mitzvah 77 note 45, regarding the meaning of this statement.

## MISHPATIM / MITZVAH 82: NOT TO RENDER JUDGMENT BASED UPON ASSUMPTIONS

כַּמָּה פְּעָמִים[20], אֲבָל לֹא בִּנְקֵבוֹת לְפִי שֶׁאֵינָן דָּנוֹת[21]. וְהָעוֹבֵר עָלֶיהָ וְדָן עַל פִּי עֵדוּת שֶׁאֵינָהּ מְכֻוֶּנֶת כְּמוֹ שֶׁאָמַרְנוּ, עָבַר עַל מִצְוַת מֶלֶךְ, וְעָנְשׁוֹ גָּדוֹל מְאֹד, שֶׁגּוֹרֵם לַהֲרֹג נְפָשׁוֹת שֶׁלֹּא כַדִּין.

וְהָרַמְבַּ"ן זִכְרוֹנוֹ לִבְרָכָה (בהשגותיו למצוה זו) חָשַׁב זֶה הַמִּקְרָא בִּשְׁנֵי לָאוִין וּלְעִנְיָן אַחֵר, וְהוּא שֶׁנִּפְטָר בְּדִינֵי נְפָשׁוֹת בִּצְדָדִין שֶׁנִּתְחַיֵּב בְּדִינֵי מָמוֹנוֹת[22], וְסָמַךְ עַל מַה שֶּׁאָמְרוּ בִּגְמָרַת סַנְהֶדְרִין (דף ל"ג ע"ב), תָּנוּ רַבָּנָן, מִנַּיִן לַיּוֹצֵא מִבֵּית דִּין חַיָּב וְאָמַר אֶחָד יֵשׁ לִי לְלַמֵּד עָלָיו זְכוּת שֶׁמַּחֲזִירִין אוֹתוֹ, שֶׁנֶּאֱמַר וְנָקִי וְצַדִּיק אַל תַּהֲרֹג,

---

כַּמָּה פְּעָמִים — **as we have** already **stated several times;**[20] אֲבָל לֹא בִּנְקֵבוֹת לְפִי שֶׁאֵינָן דָּנוֹת — **but** it does **not** apply **to women, because they do not judge.**[21] וְהָעוֹבֵר עָלֶיהָ — **One who violates [this mitzvah],** וְדָן עַל פִּי עֵדוּת שֶׁאֵינָהּ מְכֻוֶּנֶת — **and issues a ruling** in a capital case **based upon testimony that is not** in **precise** accordance with the requirements of the law, כְּמוֹ שֶׁאָמַרְנוּ — such **as** the cases that **we mentioned** above, עָבַר עַל מִצְוַת מֶלֶךְ — **has transgressed a commandment of the King** (God) וְעָנְשׁוֹ גָּדוֹל מְאֹד — **and his punishment will be exceedingly great,** שֶׁגּוֹרֵם לַהֲרֹג נְפָשׁוֹת שֶׁלֹּא כַדִּין — **because he causes the unlawful execution of people.**

### ☙ Dispute Regarding the Mitzvah ☙

וְהָרַמְבַּ"ן זִכְרוֹנוֹ לִבְרָכָה — **Ramban, of blessed memory** (Glosses to *Sefer HaMitzvos, Lo Saaseh* §290), חָשַׁב זֶה הַמִּקְרָא בִּשְׁנֵי לָאוִין — **reckons this verse** (*the blameless or the innocent you shall not slay*) as presenting **two** distinct **prohibitions,** וּלְעִנְיָן אַחֵר — **and** he maintains that the verse speaks of **a different topic** than that presented above. וְהוּא שֶׁנִּפְטָר בְּדִינֵי נְפָשׁוֹת בִּצְדָדִין שֶׁנִּתְחַיֵּב בְּדִינֵי מָמוֹנוֹת — According to *Ramban*, the meaning of **this** verse **is that we must acquit** the defendant in **capital cases in** certain **situations where we would find** him **liable in monetary cases,** as will be explained below.[22] וְסָמַךְ עַל מַה שֶּׁאָמְרוּ בִּגְמָרַת סַנְהֶדְרִין — *Ramban* **relies** in this position **upon that which [the Sages] have stated in Tractate** *Sanhedrin* (33b), as we shall immediately cite.

The Mishnah (*Sanhedrin* 32a) lists a number of procedural differences between capital cases and monetary cases. Among them is the rule that, in monetary cases, if after the judges issue a ruling they realize that they erred, they are able to reverse their ruling, whether to exonerate a defendant that they had ruled liable, or to impose liability on a defendant that they had exonerated. In capital cases, however, they may reverse only a ruling of guilt in order to correctly acquit the defendant, but they can never reverse an acquittal, even if it was wrong. The Gemara there (33b) cites a Baraisa that derives two applications of this rule from the verse וְנָקִי וְצַדִּיק אַל תַּהֲרֹג, *the blameless or the innocent you shall not slay*. The Baraisa explains that *"the blameless"* and *"the innocent"* refer to two situations, where, although the defendant was sentenced to death, he may not be executed. *Ramban* (ibid.) quotes this Baraisa to support his understanding of the verse:

תָּנוּ רַבָּנָן — **The Sages taught in a Baraisa:** מִנַּיִן לַיּוֹצֵא מִבֵּית דִּין חַיָּב — **From where** do we derive **that if one left the court convicted** of the charge against him, וְאָמַר אֶחָד יֵשׁ לִי לְלַמֵּד עָלָיו זְכוּת — **and,** as he was being taken to be executed, **someone said, "I have an argument to advance in favor of his acquittal,"** שֶׁמַּחֲזִירִין אוֹתוֹ — **that we return [the defendant]** to court to consider this new argument in his favor? שֶׁנֶּאֱמַר "וְנָקִי וְצַדִּיק אַל תַּהֲרֹג" — **We are in fact so commanded,**

---

### NOTES

20. Mitzvos 49, 53, 74, and 75.

21. See Mitzvah 77, where Chinuch deals with this topic at length, and discusses exceptions.

22. *Ramban* maintains that this verse commands us to acquit the defendant of execution by any means, even those that would not acquit a defendant in monetary cases. *Ramban* finds difficulty with *Rambam's* approach that the verse forbids accepting circumstantial evidence, since such evidence is unacceptable in monetary cases as well. [*Ramban*, however, does list as a separate mitzvah-prohibition the prohibition to accept isolated witnesses in capital cases; see *Ramban's* list of "Mitzvos that *Rambam* Omitted."] See Insight for further discussion.

## 126 □ משפטים / מצוה פב: שלא לחתך הדין באמד הדעת

בִּכְלוֹמַר וְזֶה נָקִי הוּא, דְּשֶׁמָּא זֶה יְלַמֵּד שֶׁהוּא נָקִי, וּמִנַּיִן יוֹצֵא מִבֵּית דִּין זַכַּאי וְאָמַר אֶחָד יֵשׁ לִי לְלַמֵּד עָלָיו חוֹבָה שֶׁאֵין מַחֲזִירִין אוֹתוֹ, תַּלְמוּד לוֹמַר וְצַדִּיק אַל תַּהֲרֹג, וְזֶה צַדִּיק הוּא, שֶׁכְּבָר יָצָא צַדִּיק. הִנֵּה יְדַקְדְּקוּ הַמִּקְרָא לִשְׁנֵי לָאוִין.[23] וְכָל עִנְיָנִים אֵלֶה מִן הַשֹּׁרֶשׁ שֶׁכָּתַבְתִּי, שֶׁרָצָה הָאֵל שֶׁנְּהַפֵּךְ בְּכָל זְכוּת הַנִּדּוֹן שֶׁמָּא עָשָׂה תְּשׁוּבָה וְנִחַם עַל רָעָתוֹ שֶׁעָשָׂה, וְיִהְיֶה עֲדַיִן מִמְיַשְּׁבֵי עוֹלָם, וְהוּא בָּרוּךְ הוּא חָפֵץ בְּיִשּׁוּבוֹ.[24]

---

**בִּכְלוֹמַר וְזֶה נָקִי הוּא** — **for the verse states:** *The blameless or the innocent you shall not slay;* **דְּשֶׁמָּא** that is **to say, this [individual]** may not be executed, for perhaps he **is** actually **blameless, זֶה יְלַמֵּד שֶׁהוּא נָקִי** — **since perhaps this** person who is now advancing a new argument on the defendant's behalf **will** successfully **teach** us that **[the defendant] is blameless** of his accused crime.

The Baraisa continues with another case:

**וּמִנַּיִן יוֹצֵא מִבֵּית דִּין זַכַּאי** — **And from where** do we derive **that if one left the court acquitted** of the charge against him, **וְאָמַר אֶחָד יֵשׁ לִי לְלַמֵּד עָלָיו חוֹבָה** — **and someone says, "I have an argument to advance for his conviction," שֶׁאֵין מַחֲזִירִין אוֹתוֹ** that **we do** *not* **return [the defendant]** to court to consider this new argument? **תַּלְמוּד לוֹמַר "וְצַדִּיק אַל תַּהֲרֹג"** — **[The Torah] teaches:** *the innocent you shall not slay;* **וְזֶה צַדִּיק הוּא** — **this [defendant] is** classified as **"innocent," שֶׁכְּבָר יָצָא צַדִּיק** — **since he has already emerged** from the court having been declared **innocent.**

**הִנֵּה יְדַקְדְּקוּ הַמִּקְרָא לִשְׁנֵי לָאוִין** — **Thus [the Sages] infer from this verse two** distinct **prohibitions.**[23]

**וְכָל עִנְיָנִים אֵלֶה מִן הַשֹּׁרֶשׁ שֶׁכָּתַבְתִּי** — **All these matters** can be understood as **based on the underlying purpose I have written** above, **שֶׁרָצָה הָאֵל שֶׁנְּהַפֵּךְ בְּכָל זְכוּת הַנִּדּוֹן** — **that it is the Will of the Almighty that we explore any reason for acquitting the defendant, שֶׁמָּא עָשָׂה תְּשׁוּבָה וְנִחַם עַל רָעָתוֹ שֶׁעָשָׂה** — for even if he in fact committed the crime of which he is accused, **perhaps he has repented and regrets the evil that he committed, וְיִהְיֶה עֲדַיִן מִמְיַשְּׁבֵי עוֹלָם** — **and he can still be among those who settle the world** productively; **וְהוּא בָּרוּךְ הוּא חָפֵץ בְּיִשּׁוּבוֹ** — **and [God], blessed is He, desires the** productive **settlement of [the world].**[24]

---

### NOTES

23. One is the prohibition to execute a defendant who has been found guilty, if an argument for acquittal was subsequently raised; and the other is the prohibition to execute a defendant who has been found innocent, even if an argument for conviction was subsequently raised. With regard to monetary law, however, the final ruling may be reconsidered in all cases (*Rambam, Hil. Sanhedrin* 11:1).

According to *Ramban*, the prohibitions derived from the verse in the above Baraisa represent the primary meaning of this verse, while those outlined in *Mechilta* (cited by Chinuch above) are merely *asmachtas*, i.e., Scriptural allusions to the laws that *Mechilta* mentions (*Ramban*, Glosses ibid.). *Rambam* takes the opposite approach, maintaining that *Mechilta's* interpretation is primary, while the prohibitions derived by the Baraisa are mere *asmachtas* (*Megillas Esther* to *Sefer HaMitzvos, Lo Saaseh* §290).

24. See above, Mitzvah 34, where Chinuch explains that the prescribed execution for those who commit the most heinous crimes is necessary because God wishes the world to be productively settled, and those evil people destroy this productive settlement. Accordingly, Chinuch writes here that even if one actually committed a terrible crime, he might subsequently repent and prove to be a person who contributes to the beneficial settlement of the world — and it might not be the Will of God that this particular person be put to death. For this reason, we acquit the defendant even in the case mentioned by the Baraisa, where an argument for conviction was advanced subsequent to his acquittal. Once the accused emerged from court with a verdict of innocence, we must consider the possibility that God actually desires that he be exonerated, even if he actually committed the crime of which he is accused.

[It seems that Chinuch's source for this concept is *Mechilta DeRashbi* to the conclusion of the above verse. On the words כִּי לֹא אַצְדִּיק רָשָׁע, *for I* (God) *shall not exonerate the guilty*, *Mechilta* writes: *I shall exonerate him with repentance.* One who sincerely repents is no longer considered "guilty." God, Who alone knows whether the defendant sincerely repented from his sins, will see to it that he is acquitted of his crime, even if he actually did commit it.]

## 127 ☐ MISHPATIM / MITZVAH 82: NOT TO RENDER JUDGMENT BASED UPON ASSUMPTIONS

◈§ **Insight: Circumstantial Evidence in Monetary Cases**

Chinuch, following *Rambam* (*Sefer HaMitzvos, Lo Saaseh* 290), explains that this mitzvah prohibits executing a person based on circumstantial evidence. Now, the verse explicitly states this restriction with regard to capital cases, which, as Chinuch explains, is due to the Torah's great concern that basing a verdict on such evidence might result in the wrongful loss of life. Since the verse teaches that such evidence is inadmissible specifically in capital cases, it apparently means that with regard to other cases, such as monetary matters, such evidence is admissible. However, as *Ramban* points out (Glosses to *Sefer HaMitzvos* ibid.), in actuality this is not true, for circumstantial evidence is not accepted in monetary cases either, as is evident from the following law: The Gemara (*Sanhedrin* 37b) discusses a case where one camel in a group was in a wild state and another camel was found dead beside it, such that it seems apparent that the wild one killed it. Can *beis din* obligate the owner of the wild animal to pay the owner of the dead animal for his loss, or is he exempt because there are no eyewitnesses to the actual event? The halachah is that despite all signs indicating that the wild animal was the killer, *beis din* may not rule based upon that assumption, since there is no credible testimony to that effect (see *Rambam, Hil. Nizkei Mamon* 8:14).

The question thus arises: Why was it necessary for the Torah to prohibit judging capital cases based on circumstantial evidence, if such evidence is inadmissible even in civil cases? Indeed, this is one of the reasons why *Ramban* explains the prohibition expressed in this verse differently, as Chinuch noted at the end of the mitzvah (see above, note 22). How do Chinuch and *Rambam* resolve this difficulty?

*R' Elchanan Wasserman* (*Kovetz Shiurim* II §38 ד"ה ומה שכתב; see also *Minchas Chinuch* §1) suggests that although circumstantial evidence is indeed disqualified even in civil cases, in regard to capital cases the Torah here expresses a *special prohibition* upon *beis din* not to base judgment on circumstantial evidence. In civil cases, judges who accept such evidence are guilty of not following the Torah's guidelines for justice, and have violated the mitzvos that demand the fair administration of justice in accordance with those guidelines (Mitzvos 233 and 235). They have not, however, transgressed *this* prohibition, which applies only to capital judgments.

R' Elchanan notes, though, that *Rambam* does apparently differentiate between capital cases and civil cases in regard to the type of evidence required. *Rambam* writes (*Hil. Sanhedrin* 24:1) that judges are granted wide latitude in deciding monetary cases, and may issue judgment based on their own conviction, or based on information provided by someone that they implicitly trust — even if that person is not qualified to serve as a witness in the case (for another example of this latitude, see *Be'er Eliyahu* cited in Insight to Mitzvah 81). *Rambam* concludes that the Torah requires that a judge rule based on testimony from two witnesses in civil cases only when the judge has no personal conviction regarding the matter. But when he is convinced of the facts, he may rule on that basis alone. [However, *Rambam* (ibid. §2) goes on to state that the courts of later times agreed not to determine even civil cases on the basis of the judges' discretion.] This latitude is obviously not granted in capital cases. There, no judgment may be issued except on the basis of eyewitness testimony from two valid witnesses.

It remains unclear, though, in regard to civil cases, why circumstantial evidence such as in the example of the camel is ruled inadmissible, when the evidence does seem compelling if judges have the discretion to issue judgment even without having heard eyewitness testimony.

*Avi Ezri* (*Tinyana, Hil. Sanhedrin* 20:1) offers a novel explanation of this matter. In his view, when the Gemara discusses whether the owner of the wild camel can be made to pay for the animal found dead beside his camel, the question is whether the Sages established that this is *definitely* a sufficient basis for liability, such that the court would *have to* hold him liable. Regarding this question, the answer is that they did not; the fact that one camel is in a wild state does not automatically *prove* — as an equivalent to two eyewitnesses — that it is the one that did the killing. Thus, the court is not *compelled* to hold the owner of the wild camel liable, and may consider exonerating him. The Sages did not, however, mean to rule out using such evidence in a discretionary manner. Thus, if in a particular instance, the judges would feel, based on their analysis of the situation, that the evidence is sufficiently compelling to hold the owner of the wild camel liable, they would

be authorized to do so, based on their personal conviction that his camel was the one that caused the damage.

*Avi Ezri* concludes that, according to *Rambam* (and Chinuch), it is this manner of determining a case — that is, through the judges' discretion — that our mitzvah comes to forbid with regard to capital cases. When a life is at stake, even if the court is convinced beyond any doubt that the accused is guilty, he may not be executed unless there are two valid eyewitnesses to the act.

## MISHPATIM / MITZVAH 83: THE PROHIBITION TO ACCEPT BRIBERY

### מִצְוָה פג: שֶׁלֹּא לָקַח שֹׁחַד

שֶׁלֹּא יִקַּח הַדַּיָּן שֹׁחַד מִבַּעֲלֵי הַדִּין אֲפִלּוּ לָדוּן דִּין אֱמֶת, שֶׁנֶּאֱמַר¹ (שמות כ״ג, ח׳) וְשֹׁחַד לֹא תִקָּח², וְנִכְפַּל הַלָאו בַּתּוֹרָה בְּזֶה הָעִנְיָן בְּמָקוֹם אַחֵר (דברים ט״ז, י״ט)³, וְכֵן אָמְרוּ בְּסִפְרִי (שם) [וְ]לֹא תִקַּח שֹׁחַד, אֲפִלּוּ לְזַכּוֹת זַכַּאי וּלְחַיֵּב חַיָּב.

מִשָּׁרְשֵׁי הַמִּצְוָה, שֶׁנֶּאֱסַר עָלֵינוּ לָקַח הַשֹּׁחַד אֲפִלּוּ לָדוּן אֶת הַדִּין לַאֲמִתּוֹ⁴,

---

## Mitzvah 83

# The Prohibition [Upon a Judge] to Accept Bribery

וְשֹׁחַד לֹא תִקָּח כִּי הַשֹּׁחַד יְעַוֵּר פִּקְחִים וִיסַלֵּף דִּבְרֵי צַדִּיקִים

*Do not accept a bribe, for the bribe will blind those who see and corrupt words that are just* (Exodus 23:8).

In addition to the prohibitions against unfair judgment (Mitzvos 79,81; also Mitzvah 233), there is a specific prohibition for a judge to accept bribery, regardless of any perversion of justice that may or may not occur as a result.

**שֶׁלֹּא יִקַּח הַדַּיָּן שֹׁחַד מִבַּעֲלֵי הַדִּין** — We are commanded **that a judge may not accept a bribe from the litigants,** **אֲפִלּוּ לָדוּן דִּין אֱמֶת** — **even** if it is accepted with the intention **to judge the case truthfully,**[1] **שֶׁנֶּאֱמַר** — **as it is stated** (Exodus 23:8): **"וְשֹׁחַד לֹא תִקָּח"** — *Do not accept a bribe.*[2] **וְנִכְפַּל הַלָאו בַּתּוֹרָה בְּזֶה הָעִנְיָן בְּמָקוֹם אַחֵר** — **The prohibition to this effect** (i.e., against accepting a bribe even to judge truthfully) **is repeated elsewhere in the Torah** (Deuteronomy 16:19).[3] **וְכֵן אָמְרוּ בַּסִפְרִי** — **So it is stated in** *Sifrei* on that verse: **"[וְ]לֹא תִקַּח שֹׁחַד"** — when Scripture says, *You shall not accept a bribe,* **אֲפִלּוּ לְזַכּוֹת זַכַּאי וּלְחַיֵּב חַיָּב** — it prohibits the acceptance of a bribe **even** if it is with the intention **to exonerate the one who is** truly **innocent and to impose liability on the one who is** truly **liable.**

### Underlying Purpose of the Mitzvah

**מִשָּׁרְשֵׁי הַמִּצְוָה** — **Among the underlying purposes of the mitzvah,** **שֶׁנֶּאֱסַר עָלֵינוּ לָקַח הַשֹּׁחַד** **אֲפִלּוּ לָדוּן אֶת הַדִּין לַאֲמִתּוֹ** — in which we are **prohibited from accepting bribery even** with

---

### NOTES

1. That is, a litigant — believing that he is in the right — pays the judge to research the case thoroughly and issue a decisive ruling instead of opting to impose a compromise [under certain conditions, a judge may nullify a dispute by mediating a compromise between the parties; see *Rambam, Hil. Sanhedrin* 22:4 and Insight to Mitzvah 79] (*Tosafos, Bechoros* 29a ד״ה מה אני, as explained by *Igros Moshe, Choshen Mishpat* II 26:4; see *Rashi, Kesubos* 105a ד״ה בתורת שוחדא). The Torah calls this a "bribe" because it influences the manner in which the judge adjudicates the case, even if it appears to promote justice (see below for why the Torah prohibited this type of bribe).

The judge may not accept such a bribe from either one or both litigants (*Derishah, Choshen Mishpat* 9:1, based on *Kesubos* ibid.; for discussion, see *Igros Moshe* ibid.).

2. This verse clearly prohibits acceptance of *any* bribe — even to judge truthfully — since taking a bribe to judge *dishonestly* is perversion of justice, and Scripture has already said (*Exodus* 23:6 and *Deuteronomy* 16:19): *You shall not pervert judgment* (*Kesubos* ibid.). [Needless to say, our mitzvah *does* include the corrupt form of bribery; the Gemara means merely that the mitzvah is not limited to it.]

3. The verse there states: וְלֹא תִקַּח שֹׁחַד כִּי הַשֹּׁחַד יְעַוֵּר עֵינֵי חֲכָמִים וִיסַלֵּף דִּבְרֵי צַדִּיקִים, *You shall not accept a bribe, for the bribe will blind the eyes of the wise, and corrupt words that are just.* [Translation follows *Rashi;* for another translation, see Insight. For explanation as to why the Torah repeats this prohibition, see *Minchas Soless.*]

כְּדֵי לְהָסִיר מִבֵּינֵינוּ הַהֶרְגֵּל הָרַע פֶּן נָבוֹא מִתּוֹךְ כָּךְ לָדוּן בְּשֹׁחַד דִּינֵי שֶׁקֶר,[5] וְדָבָר בָּרוּר הוּא, אֵין צָרִיךְ מוֹפֵת.

מִדִּינֵי הַמִּצְוָה, מַה שֶּׁאָמְרוּ זִכְרוֹנָם לִבְרָכָה[6] שֶׁהַנּוֹתֵן וְהַמְקַבֵּל עוֹבְרִין בְּלָאו, הַנּוֹתֵן מִשּׁוּם וְלִפְנֵי עִוֵּר לֹא תִתֵּן מִכְשֹׁל[7] (ויקרא י״ט, י״ד), וְאִם קִבְּלוּ שֶׁהוּא בִּכְלַל אָרוּר[8], וְחַיָּב לְהַחֲזִירוֹ,[9]

---

intention **to judge the case truthfully,**[4] כְּדֵי לְהָסִיר מִבֵּינֵינוּ הַהֶרְגֵּל הָרַע — is in order **to remove the evil habit** of bribery **from our midst;** פֶּן נָבוֹא מִתּוֹךְ כָּךְ לָדוּן בְּשֹׁחַד דִּינֵי שֶׁקֶר — **lest we come, through** accustoming ourselves to **this** habit of accepting bribery — even for innocuous purposes — **to issue false judgments due to** the influence of **bribery.**[5] וְדָבָר בָּרוּר הוּא אֵין צָרִיךְ מוֹפֵת — **This is a clear** and obvious **matter,** which **requires no proof.**

## ～ Laws of the Mitzvah ～

מִדִּינֵי הַמִּצְוָה — **Among the laws of the mitzvah** מַה שֶּׁאָמְרוּ זִכְרוֹנָם לִבְרָכָה — is that which **[the Sages] have said,**[6] שֶׁהַנּוֹתֵן וְהַמְקַבֵּל עוֹבְרִין בְּלָאו — that both **the one giving** the bribe **and the one receiving** it **transgress a** mitzvah-**prohibition:** הַנּוֹתֵן מִשּׁוּם "וְלִפְנֵי עִוֵּר לֹא תִתֵּן מִכְשֹׁל" — the one receiving it transgresses the prohibition to accept a bribe, as stated above, while **the** transgression of the **one giving** the bribe is **on account of** the verse (Leviticus 19:14): **You shall not place a stumbling block before the blind.**[7]

וְאִם קִבְּלוּ — **If [the judge]** violated this prohibition and **accepted [the bribe],** שֶׁהוּא בִּכְלַל "אָרוּר" — **he is in the category of the "accursed"**; i.e., he is subject to the curse expressed by Scripture in the verse (Deuteronomy 27:25): Accursed is one who takes a bribe.[8] וְחַיָּב לְהַחֲזִירוֹ — **He is also obligated**

---

### NOTES

4. If it were prohibited only to accept bribes with intent to deliver a corrupt ruling, no explanation would be needed. As Chinuch states in Mitzvah 49, with regard to the mitzvos that enjoin us to have a fair justice system: "I need not toil to find the underlying reason, as it is sensible and easily understood … for it is impossible for the world to survive without justice." However, having established that the prohibition applies also to a bribe that ostensibly promotes justice (see note 1), Chinuch seeks to explain its underlying purpose.

5. The Gemara in Kesubos (105b) explains that it is prohibited to accept a bribe to judge truthfully because the very acceptance of a bribe engenders in the judge a strong bias toward the giver of the bribe, which will inevitably tilt the judgment in the giver's favor. This is indicated in the word שׁוֹחַד (bribery), which is a combination of two words, שֶׁהוּא (for he) and חַד (one), alluding that through bribery the donor and the recipient become united as one. [Rashi to Deuteronomy 16:19 reads this reasoning in the verse itself: You shall not accept a bribe, "for the bribe will blind the eyes of the wise"; even if the judge intends to be honest, the power of a bribe is such that it will blind him to the truth. See Insight for another interpretation of the verse.]

Chinuch suggests that, in addition to the Gemara's reasoning, the Torah wanted to distance us from taking bribes altogether — even innocuous ones — so that we do not end up taking bribes in a corrupt fashion. Perhaps, this explanation is necessary because the Gemara's reason would explain only why it is forbidden to accept a bribe from one litigant; as indicated in note 1, however, the prohibition applies even if the judge accepted payment from both litigants, in which case the judge is not prone to this bias (see Sma, Choshen Mishpat 9:2; Pnei Yehoshua to Kesubos 105a ד״ה והיכי; cf. Meiri to Kesubos ibid. ד״ה עקר טעם; Haamek She'eilah, Shoftim 149:3).

6. The reference to the Sages is not to an explicit statement regarding bribery, but rather to a passage in Bava Metzia (75b) discussing the transgressions of those who participate in an interest-based loan (see Mitzvah 68 with notes 5,7-8). Chinuch (following Rambam, Hil. Sanhedrin 23:2) applies the law to bribery as well (see Beur HaGra, Choshen Mishpat 9:3).

7. This is a prohibition to influence another to commit a sin [thus placing a spiritual "stumbling block" before him] (Mitzvah 232). Since the one giving the bribe facilitates commission of a sin by the judge, he violates this prohibition. [For explanation as to why the Torah did not specifically prohibit the giving of a bribe, as it forbade its acceptance, see Teshuvos Chavos Yair §136.]

8. Rambam ibid §1. Chinuch's assertion – that a judge adjudicating a monetary case who had accepted a bribe to judge truthfully is subject to this curse – requires study, since the verse, Accursed is one who takes a bribe "to kill a person of innocent blood," suggests that it applies only to a judge who takes a bribe to pervert justice – and only in a capital case (Minchas Chinuch §6; R' Y. F. Perla, Sefer HaMitzvos of Rav Saadiah Gaon, Lo Saaseh 84, Vol II, p. 100a; see also Minchas Yitzchak).

[The Torah imposed a curse on one who accepts bribery because it is an act ordinarily performed in secrecy, and thus not subject to penalty through the justice system (Rashbam to Deuteronomy 27:15).]

# 131 ☐ MISHPATIM / MITZVAH 83: THE PROHIBITION TO ACCEPT BRIBERY

וְשֶׁאָסוּר לַדַּיָּן לְהַגְדִּיל מַעֲלָתוֹ לְכַוָּנָה כְּדֵי לְהַרְבּוֹת שָׂכָר לְסוֹפְרָיו,[10] וְשֶׁאֲפִלּוּ שֹׁחַד דְּבָרִים אָסוּר לִקַּח,[11] אֶלָּא יַרְאֶה עַצְמוֹ כְּאִלּוּ אֵינוֹ מֵשִׂים לִבּוֹ כְּלָל אֶל הַדְּבָרִים אִם אוּלַי יְכַבְּדוּהוּ בַּעֲלֵי הַדִּין בִּדְבָרִים.[12] כְּלָלוֹ שֶׁל דָּבָר, אָסוּר לַדַּיָּן לְקַבֵּל הֲנָאָה מִבַּעֲלֵי הַדִּין כְּלָל בִּשְׁבִיל

---

**to return [the bribe]** to the litigant.[9]

Chinuch discusses the scope of the prohibition:

וְשֶׁאָסוּר לַדַּיָּן לְהַגְדִּיל מַעֲלָתוֹ — **Also** included is the law that **it is forbidden for the judge to inflate his stature,** and the reputation of his court, לְכַוָּנָה כְּדֵי לְהַרְבּוֹת שָׂכָר לְסוֹפְרָיו — **with intent to increase the wages of his scribes.**[10]

וְשֶׁאֲפִלּוּ שֹׁחַד דְּבָרִים אָסוּר לִקַּח — Not only is accepting a monetary bribe prohibited, but **it is even forbidden to accept** a non-monetary bribe, such as **a bribe of words** (i.e., flattery).[11] אֶלָּא יַרְאֶה עַצְמוֹ כְּאִלּוּ אֵינוֹ מֵשִׂים לִבּוֹ כְּלָל אֶל הַדְּבָרִים — **Rather, [the judge] should demonstrate that he pays absolutely no attention to the** reverential **words** spoken to him, אִם אוּלַי יְכַבְּדוּהוּ בַּעֲלֵי הַדִּין בִּדְבָרִים — **if the litigants do indeed honor him with words.**[12]

Chinuch states the general rule:

כְּלָלוֹ שֶׁל דָּבָר — **The sum of the matter** is that אָסוּר לַדַּיָּן לְקַבֵּל הֲנָאָה מִבַּעֲלֵי הַדִּין כְּלָל בִּשְׁבִיל

---

## NOTES

9. *Rambam* ibid. This law has no explicit source in the Gemara, but it is based on the principle stated in *Temurah* (4b): *Anything which the Torah said not to do bears no legal significance if one does it.* Since the Torah commanded the judge not to accept bribery, the giving of the bribe (i.e., the transfer of money from a litigant to the judge) has no legal validity; thus, the judge is effectively holding another's money unlawfully and must return it (*Bach, Choshen Mishpat* §9 ד"ה ואם לקח; *Minchas Chinuch* §1).

[*Rambam* (ibid.) indicates that the judge is obligated to return the bribe only if the litigant demands its return (see *Sma* ibid. §3; *Minchas Chinuch* ibid.; see also *Pischei Teshuvah, Choshen Mishpat* 9:2). Chinuch, however, omits this detail, suggesting that the judge is legally required to return the bribe even if the litigant does not claim it (*Minchas Chinuch* ibid.).]

10. *Rambam* ibid. §3. Although a judge may not charge a fee for his judicial services (as Chinuch will indicate below; see also *Rambam* ibid. §5), his *court* may impose legal fees on the litigants in order to cover administrative costs, such as salaries for the bailiffs and scribes. However, the judge is enjoined not to purposefully embellish the credentials of his court so that his court can charge higher fees, gaining his attendants higher wages.

The source for this is the Gemara (*Shabbos* 56a) that relates that the sons of the prophet Samuel deviated from the way of their righteous father; whereas Samuel traveled to judge people in their cities, his sons would insist that the litigants come before them, intending to thereby increase the income of their bailiffs and scribes [who would charge the litigants for the extra effort and paperwork involved in summoning them to court]. Although Samuel's sons did not take the money for themselves, Scripture (*I Samuel* 8:3) refers to them as having been *"swayed by profit"* [and as akin to having accepted bribes (*Malbim* ad loc.)], because their actions indicated a propensity for profit, which is not in consonance with the Torah's directive (*Exodus* 18:21) that a judge be a שׂוֹנֵא בֶצַע, *one who despises money.* Although in our time it is the norm to summon litigants to court, *Rambam* (ibid.) maintains that the Gemara's teaching is still applicable, in the sense that a judge may not employ tactics to unduly increase the wages of his attendants (*Derishah, Choshen Mishpat* 9:8; cf. *Bach* there).

11. The Gemara (*Kesubos* 105b) derives this from the fact that Scripture uses the term שֹׁחַד, *bribery,* instead of בֶצַע, *[financial] gain,* indicating that any form of bribery — financial or otherwise — is forbidden. [For discussion as to whether this is a Scriptural basis for the law (and non-monetary bribes are thus Biblically forbidden) or rather only an allusion to a Rabbinic law, see *Maharsha* ad loc. ד"ה בד"ה and ד"ה אפילו שוחד דברים; לא למאן, and *Birkei Yosef, Choshen Mishpat* 9:10.]

[It is noteworthy that the Gemara (ibid.) goes on to record several examples of non-monetary bribes that involve services or non-monetary favors offered to the judge, but none of which involve *verbal* gestures. Nevertheless, Chinuch applies the ruling even to verbal bribery — i.e., flattery (see *Rambam* ibid. §3; *Sma, Choshen Mishpat* 9:4; cf. *Meiri* to *Kesubos* ibid.).]

12. I.e., the judge must be careful not to let himself be swayed even through expressions of honor used to address him, and as part of doing so, should demonstrate his indifference. [Indeed, the judge must beware of even a simple greeting bestowed by a litigant — if he does not normally greet him (*Sma, Choshen Mishpat* 9:4).]

Whereas regarding a monetary bribe or a bribe of services, "not accepting a bribe" simply means to decline the bribe, a bribe of words cannot be declined; how can the judge "not accept" it? Chinuch explains that by consciously dismissing the verbal "bribe," the judge is — in effect — not accepting it.

## 132 ❑ משפטים / מצוה פג: שלא לקח שחד

דִּינָיו, אֲבָל[13] אִם הַדַּיָּן הוּא בַּעַל מְלָאכָה, הִתִּירוּ לוֹ חֲכָמִים לִשְׁאוֹל מִבַּעֲלֵי הַדִּין שְׂכַר בַּטָּלָתוֹ מִמְּלַאכְתּוֹ בְּעוֹד שֶׁיַּעֲסֹק בְּדִינָם, וְהוּא שֶׁיְּהֵא הַדָּבָר נִכָּר שֶׁהוּא שְׂכַר הַבַּטָּלָה בִּלְבַד וְלֹא יוֹתֵר[14], וְיִטֹּל מִשְּׁנֵיהֶם בְּשָׁוֶה[15], וְיֶתֶר פְּרָטֶיהָ, בְּסַנְהֶדְרִין[16]. וְנוֹהֶגֶת בְּכָל מָקוֹם וּבְכָל זְמַן[17], בִּזְכָרִים, שֶׁהֵם דָּנִים[18].

---

**דִּינָיו** — it is forbidden for a judge to accept any benefit whatsoever from the litigants for the performance of **his adjudication.**

Not only may a judge not accept a bribe (to influence the judgment), he also may not accept basic payment from the litigants for handling the case.[13] Chinuch explains that there is a form of payment which the judge *may* accept, but it has strict guidelines: **אֲבָל אִם הַדַּיָּן הוּא בַּעַל מְלָאכָה** — Although a judge may not receive any form of payment from the litigants on account of his legal services, **if, however, the judge is a craftsman** and is interrupting his work to judge the case, **הִתִּירוּ לוֹ חֲכָמִים לִשְׁאוֹל מִבַּעֲלֵי הַדִּין** — the Sages (*Kesubos* 105a) **permitted him to request from the litigants** **שְׂכַר בַּטָּלָתוֹ מִמְּלַאכְתּוֹ בְּעוֹד שֶׁיַּעֲסֹק בְּדִינָם** — compensation **for being idle** and unable to engage **in his trade while he handles their case.** **וְהוּא שֶׁיְּהֵא הַדָּבָר נִכָּר שֶׁהוּא שְׂכַר הַבַּטָּלָה** — However, the judge may accept this payment **only when it is evident** **בִּלְבַד וְלֹא יוֹתֵר** — **that it is just the unemployment compensation, and not more.**[14] **וְיִטֹּל מִשְּׁנֵיהֶם בְּשָׁוֶה** — Moreover, **he must accept** this payment **from both [litigants] equally.**[15] **וְיֶתֶר פְּרָטֶיהָ בְּסַנְהֶדְרִין** — These laws, **and the additional details of [this mitzvah],** are elaborated in Tractate **Sanhedrin** (7b-8a).[16]

### ☞ Applicability of the Mitzvah ☜

**וְנוֹהֶגֶת בְּכָל מָקוֹם וּבְכָל זְמַן** — [This mitzvah] **applies in every location and in all times,**[17] **בִּזְכָרִים שֶׁהֵם דָּנִים** — and is applicable only **to males, for they** are the ones who **judge.**[18]

---

### NOTES

13. *Rambam* ibid. §5, based on *Bechoros* 29a. The law forbidding the acceptance of wages for judicial services is not due to the prohibition of bribery (our mitzvah). Rather, it is due to Moses' directive to the Jewish people that Torah shall, for all generations, be taught *as Hashem, my God, has commanded me* (*Deuteronomy* 4:5). The Gemara (*Bechoros* ibid., *Nedarim* 37a) understands this to mean that just as Moses was commanded by Hashem to teach the Torah to the Jewish people gratis (as he himself had received it from Hashem gratis), so too must the Jewish people teach it to their students gratis (see *Ran* and *Rosh* to *Nedarim* loc. cit.). Handing down a verdict based on Torah law is a form of teaching Torah, and therefore must be performed gratis.

[In earlier times, judges received a salary from a communal fund, which was permissible since they were not paid by the litigants, nor were they paid for the judicial services per se; rather, they were given a stipend for sustenance (*Kesubos* ibid. with *Tosafos* ד"ה גוזרי גזרות). Nowadays, it is customary for judges to receive remuneration for their services from the litigants, based on the following: Since the community has an obligation to provide its judges with a livelihood (*Shulchan Aruch, Choshen Mishpat* 9:3), a precondition can be made that this obligation will be discharged with money received from the litigants paying for each court case (*Nesivos HaMishpat* 9:6; see *Urim VeTumim* 9:9 for an alternative rationalization for judges to receive payment).]

14. I.e., it must be clear that the judge would have earned this sum of money had he not been occupied with this case. If it is unclear that the judge would have earned this much, or that he would have had the job at all, it is prohibited (*Kesubos* 105a).

15. *Rambam* ibid. (see *Kesef Mishneh* ad loc.). Receiving more money from one litigant than the other may influence the judge to rule in that person's favor (*Igros Moshe, Choshen Mishpat* II 26:3; see there for an additional explanation). [*Rambam* writes that the litigants must also pay in each other's presence.]

16. See also *Kesubos* 105a-b. The laws are codified in *Rambam, Hil. Sanhedrin* Ch. 23, and *Shulchan Aruch, Choshen Mishpat* §9.

17. I.e., it applies both in Eretz Yisrael and in the Diaspora, and whether the *Beis HaMikdash* is standing or not.

18. See Mitzvah 77. Chinuch pointed out in Mitzvah 77, however, that if litigants agree to accept a woman as their judge, she is authorized to judge their case. *Minchas Chinuch* (§4) notes that in such a case the woman would, presumably, be subject to the prohibition to accept a bribe. See also Mitzvah 75 note 32, and Mitzvah 81 note 5.

# 133 ◻ MISHPATIM / MITZVAH 83: THE PROHIBITION TO ACCEPT BRIBERY

וְהָעוֹבֵר עָלֶיהָ וְקִבֵּל שֹׁחַד, עָבַר עַל מִצְוַת מֶלֶךְ,[19] וְאֵינוֹ לוֹקֶה לְפִי שֶׁנִּתָּן לְהֶשְׁבּוֹן.[20]

---

וְהָעוֹבֵר עָלֶיהָ וְקִבֵּל שֹׁחַד — [A judge] who transgresses [the prohibition] and accepts a bribe עָבַר עַל מִצְוַת מֶלֶךְ — has transgressed a commandment of the King (i.e., God);[19] וְאֵינוֹ לוֹקֶה — but he does not incur *malkus* (lashes), לְפִי שֶׁנִּתָּן לְהֶשְׁבּוֹן — because [the bribe] is subject to restitution.[20]

---

## NOTES

19. I.e., the punishment for this sin is in the hands of Heaven, for no punishment is given by the courts (see end of Mitzvos 38, 39).

20. As stated earlier by Chinuch (at note 10), a judge who accepted a bribe must return it to the giver. Hence, this prohibition falls under the category of לָאו הַנִּיתָּן לְתַשְׁלוּמִין, *a prohibition that is subject to repayment*, which is excluded from the penalty of *malkus* (*Makkos* 16a; *Rambam, Hil. Sanhedrin* 18:2; see also Mitzvah 68). For discussion of Chinuch's opinion that the prohibition of bribery is a לָאו הַנִּיתָּן לְתַשְׁלוּמִין, see *R' Y. F. Perla, Sefer HaMitzvos of Rav Saadiah Gaon, Asei* 86-88, Vol. I, p. 311a. [Forms of bribery not applicable to restitution, such as flattery, would not carry the punishment of *malkus* either, as they involve no action (see end of Mitzvah 9).]

[As this prohibition forbids the very acceptance of a bribe, some maintain that the judge transgresses as soon as he accepts the bribe — even before the case has even begun (*Lechem Yehudah, Hil. Sanhedrin* 23:1; see, however, *Maharam Schik*). Needless to say, if the judge perverts justice as a result of the bribe, he transgresses other prohibitions as well, though none carry the penalty of *malkus* (see Mitzvos 233, 235).]

---

### ↝§ Insight: The Power of Bribery

*Tur* begins his discussion of the laws of bribery (*Choshen Mishpat* §9) with the enjoinder: מְאֹד מְאֹד צָרִיךְ הַדַּיָּין לִיזָּהֵר שֶׁלֹּא לִיקַּח שׁוֹחַד, *A judge must be extremely cautious not to accept a bribe* (see also *Shulchan Aruch* ibid.). *Bach* (ad loc.) explains that *Tur* employs this language because without extreme caution a judge is almost certain to stumble, since any favor afforded to the judge by a litigant — monetary or otherwise, significant or petty — constitutes bribery. As stated in the Gemara (*Kesubos* 105a), even one *perutah's* worth of benefit (i.e., a minute value) is forbidden. In fact, if a litigant so much as removed a feather from the judge's head or extended his hand to assist the judge when crossing a bridge, the judge is disqualified from judging his case (ibid. 105b). Chinuch writes that flattery, too, is a form of bribery. Indeed, the judge must beware of even a simple greeting bestowed by a litigant, if he does not normally greet him (*Sma, Choshen Mishpat* 9:4).

One might wonder: The Torah did not prohibit a sage from deciding on a halachic matter in which he has a personal interest. For example, one is allowed to examine his own animal for a *tereifah* defect (see Mitzvah 73) and decide whether it is kosher or not, and this is so even if he is poor and his livelihood depends on it. Evidently, the Torah is confident that the sage will decide the matter honestly and not be swayed by personal considerations. Why, then, is a judge disqualified if he accepts a small favor from a litigant? And why must he be careful not to accept even a greeting from a litigant? Will a minor favor or a simple greeting undermine the integrity of a wise and honest judge, who is trusted even regarding matters that might involve a significant financial loss to himself?

*Chazon Ish* (*Emunah U'Vitachon* 3:30) explains that over and above the natural effects of bias inherent in all people, a "bribe" is imbued with a force of *impurity* that, when accepted by a judge, dulls his heart and numbs his mind. When the Torah declares, *the bribe will blind the eyes of the wise*, it is not merely *indicating* this reality — it is *dictating* it. This accords with the Sages' dictum that "The Holy One, blessed is He, looked into the Torah and created the world"; i.e., the realities of the world are rooted in the Torah (see Mitzvah 77, at note 23). And while the Torah trusts the sage to transcend his *natural* biases (for example, in deciding his own halachic queries), no such confidence is extended once he has accepted a bribe and submitted to its pervasive power of swaying the mind. [See also *Kovetz Maamarim VeIgros* (R' Elchanan Wasserman), Vol. I, pp. 5-6.]

According to the *Satmar Rav*, R' Yoel Teitelbaum, a judge who accepts a bribe becomes such a devastating force of injustice that, in an effort to assist his beneficiary, he may even convince his *fellow judges* to see things in his twisted way. To bring out this idea, he presents a novel interpretation of the verse (*Deuteronomy* 16:19): וְלֹא תִקַּח שֹׁחַד כִּי הַשֹּׁחַד יְעַוֵּר עֵינֵי חֲכָמִים וִיסַלֵּף דִּבְרֵי צַדִּיקִם, *You shall not*

*accept a bribe, for the bribe will blind the eyes of the wise and corrupt the words of the righteous.* [According to this, literal, interpretation of the verse, צַדִּיקִם refers to *the righteous*. See above, note 3, for *Rashi's* exegetical interpretation.] Two difficulties come to mind regarding this verse: (1) How can a judge who accepts a bribe be called "righteous"? (2) The commandment not to accept a bribe is in the second-person singular ["לֹא תִקָּח; *you* (singular) *shall not accept*], whereas the outcome of the bribe's acceptance is expressed in the third-person plural ["יְעַוֵּר עֵינֵי "חֲכָמִים" וִיסַלֵּף דִּבְרֵי "צַדִּיקִם"; *will blind the eyes of the wise* (plural) *and corrupt the words of the righteous* (plural)]. The *Satmar Rav* explains that the verse reflects the fact that a *beis din* ordinarily consists of at least three judges. One judge might thus reason that no harm will result if he accepts a bribe, since even if he should unfairly favor one of the litigants, the other two judges who are unbiased will see the matter correctly and outvote him, so the court's ruling will turn out correct. To preclude this thought, the Torah enjoins the *single* judge not to accept a bribe, lest he be so influenced by the bribe that his passionate arguments on behalf of his beneficiary will sway the other judges to his corrupt view. Thus, the verse states: *You* (singular) *shall not accept a bribe, for the bribe will blind the eyes of the wise* (plural) *and corrupt the words of the righteous* (plural); i.e., *your* acceptance of the bribe will cause even the *other* judges — who actually are "wise" and "righteous," as they did not accept any bribe — to become blinded, and will cause their words to be corrupted (cited in *Teshuvos Be'er Moshe* Vol. IV §148:6).

## 135 ❑ MISHPATIM / MITZVAH 84: THE OBLIGATION REGARDING SHEMITTAH OF THE LAND

### מִצְוָה פד: מִצְוַת שְׁמִטַּת קַרְקָעוֹת [2,1]

לְהַפְקִיר כָּל מַה שֶּׁתּוֹצִיא הָאָרֶץ בַּשָּׁנָה הַשְּׁבִיעִית, שֶׁהִיא נִקְרֵאת מִפְּנֵי הַמַּעֲשֶׂה הַזֶּה שֶׁנִּתְחַיַּבְנוּ בָּהּ שְׁנַת הַשְּׁמִטָּה,[3] וְיִזְכֶּה בְּפֵרוֹתֶיהָ כָּל הָרוֹצֶה לִזְכּוֹת, שֶׁנֶּאֱמַר (שמות כ"ג, י"א) וְהַשְּׁבִיעִת תִּשְׁמְטֶנָּה[4] וּנְטַשְׁתָּהּ[5] וְאָכְלוּ אֶבְיֹנֵי עַמֶּךָ וְיִתְרָם תֹּאכַל חַיַּת הַשָּׂדֶה כֵּן תַּעֲשֶׂה

---

## ☙ Mitzvah 84 ❧
### The Obligation Regarding Shemittah of the Land

וְהַשְּׁבִיעִת תִּשְׁמְטֶנָּה וּנְטַשְׁתָּהּ וְאָכְלוּ אֶבְיֹנֵי עַמֶּךָ וְיִתְרָם תֹּאכַל חַיַּת הַשָּׂדֶה כֵּן תַּעֲשֶׂה לְכַרְמְךָ לְזֵיתֶךָ

*And in the seventh [year], you shall release it and leave it [unharvested], and the destitute of your people shall eat, and the wildlife of the field shall eat what is left; so shall you do to your vineyard and your olive grove (Exodus 23:11).*

The Torah dictates that every seventh year be observed as a Sabbatical year, known as the *Shemittah* ("relinquishing") year — also referred to as *Sheviis* (literally, *seventh*). The mitzvos of *Shemittah* demand that we relinquish our ownership of the land's produce (this mitzvah), desist from working the land (Mitzvos 112, 326-327), and refrain from harvesting and gathering (any produce that does grow) in the typical fashion (Mitzvos 328-329).[1]

There is another year that shares many of the laws of *Shemittah*, as well as a number of additional laws. That year, known as *Yovel*, the Jubilee Year (see Mitzvos 330-335, 340), would occur every fiftieth year — i.e., the year that immediately follows seven *Shemittah* cycles.[2]

לְהַפְקִיר כָּל מַה שֶּׁתּוֹצִיא הָאָרֶץ בַּשָּׁנָה הַשְּׁבִיעִית — **We are commanded to relinquish ownership of all that the land produces in the seventh year;** שֶׁהִיא נִקְרֵאת מִפְּנֵי הַמַּעֲשֶׂה הַזֶּה שֶׁנִּתְחַיַּבְנוּ בָּהּ — **which is called, by virtue of this act** of relinquishing **in which we are obligated** during [this year], שְׁנַת הַשְּׁמִטָּה — **the** *Shemittah* **("relinquishing") year.**[3] וְיִזְכֶּה בְּפֵרוֹתֶיהָ כָּל הָרוֹצֶה לִזְכּוֹת — **Anyone who so desires may take possession of [the land's] produce,** שֶׁנֶּאֱמַר — **as it is stated** (*Exodus* 23:11): "וְהַשְּׁבִיעִת תִּשְׁמְטֶנָּה וּנְטַשְׁתָּהּ וְאָכְלוּ אֶבְיֹנֵי עַמֶּךָ וְיִתְרָם תֹּאכַל חַיַּת הַשָּׂדֶה כֵּן תַּעֲשֶׂה לְכַרְמְךָ לְזֵיתֶךָ" — **And in the seventh [year], you shall release it**[4] **and leave it**

---

### NOTES

1. Another aspect of the *Shemittah* year pertains to loans. There is a mitzvah-obligation to nullify debts owed to us at that time (Mitzvah 477), and a mitzvah-prohibition that forbids pressing the debtor for collection after *Shemittah* passes (Mitzvah 475, see Mitzvah 476 as well). In a related mitzvah, we are forbidden to withhold credit before *Shemittah* out of concern that the loan will be abrogated by *Shemittah* (Mitzvah 480).

2. However, as Chinuch notes in Mitzvah 330, *Yovel*, unlike *Shemittah*, is observed only when all of the tribes of Israel are in their ancestral lands. Therefore, once the first tribes were exiled (Reuben, Gad, and part of Manasseh), *Yovel* was no longer observed (see below, note 48).

The *Yovel* year itself is not counted as part of the following seven-year cycle; the year following *Yovel* is thus the first year of the next seven-year cycle, not the second year (*Rambam, Hil. Shemittah VeYovel* 10:7). [Between Temples, as well as currently, not only is *Yovel* not observed, it is not even counted at all. Therefore the cycle of six years of work and a seventh of *Shemittah* continues without the interruption of *Yovel* years (ibid. 10:5).]

3. The word שְׁמִטָּה, *Shemittah*, literally means *releasing*, as in (*Deuteronomy* 15:2): שָׁמוֹט כָּל בַּעַל מַשֵּׁה יָדוֹ אֲשֶׁר יַשֶּׁה בְּרֵעֵהוּ, *every creditor shall "release" his authority over what he has lent his fellow.* See next note.

4. [According to a number of commentators to the verse (*Targum Yonasan, Ramban;* see also *Rashi;* cf. *Ibn Ezra* and *Sforno*), the word תִּשְׁמְטֶנָּה, *you shall release it*, is a reference to the requirement to desist from working the land (see Mitzvos 112 and 326). From the wording of Chinuch here and of *Rambam, Sefer HaMitzvos, Asei* 134, however, it would appear that, in their opinion, the term תִּשְׁמְטֶנָּה conveys a requirement to release the produce of the land, and refers directly to the obligation to relinquish ownership of the produce of one's field. In fact, Chinuch (Mitzvah 112) and *Rambam* (*Sefer*

## 136 □ משפטים / מצוה פד: מצות שמטת קרקעות

לְכַרְמְךָ לְזֵיתֶךָ. וּלְשׁוֹן מְכִילְתָּא (דרשב״י כאן), וַהֲלֹא הַכֶּרֶם וְהַזַּיִת בִּכְלָל הָיָה, כְּלוֹמַר שֶׁרֹאשׁ הַפָּסוּק שֶׁאָמַר תִּשְׁמְטֶנָּה וּנְטַשְׁתָּהּ יִכְלֹל כָּל מַה שֶּׁיִּצְמַח בָּאָרֶץ, בֵּין פֵּרוֹת אִילָן אוֹ פֵּרוֹת אֲדָמָה, וְלָמָּה פֵּרְטָן הַכָּתוּב שְׁנֵי אֵלֶּה, לְהַקִּישׁ לַכֶּרֶם שְׁאָר מִינֵי אִילָן, לְלַמֵּד שֶׁכְּמוֹ שֶׁיֵּשׁ בַּכֶּרֶם עֲשֵׂה וְלֹא תַעֲשֶׂה, שֶׁהֲרֵי בְּפֵרוּשׁ נִכְתַּב עָלָיו (ויקרא כ״ה, ה׳) וְאֶת עִנְּבֵי נְזִירֶךָ לֹא תִבְצֹר[6], כְּמוֹ כֵן כָּל שְׁאָר הָאִילָן יֵשׁ בָּהֶן עֲשֵׂה וְלֹא תַעֲשֶׂה, וּלְפִיכָךְ פֵּרֵט כֶּרֶם וְזַיִת לְלַמֵּד עַל עִנְיָן זֶה, כִּי כַוָּנַת הַכָּתוּב דְּלָאו דַּוְקָא זַיִת לְבַד

---

[unharvested],[5] *and the destitute of your people shall eat, and the wildlife of the field shall eat what is left; so shall you do to your vineyard and your olive grove.*

Chinuch cites an exposition of this verse, which sheds light on a related prohibition: וַהֲלֹא הַכֶּרֶם וְהַזַּיִת בִּכְלָל הָיָה — **In the words of** *Mechilta* **of R' Shimon ben Yochai:** וּלְשׁוֹן מְכִילְתָּא — **Why, the vineyard and olive grove are already included in the generalization** at the beginning of the verse!

Chinuch interrupts his citation of *Mechilta* to explain: כְּלוֹמַר שֶׁרֹאשׁ הַפָּסוּק שֶׁאָמַר "תִּשְׁמְטֶנָּה וּנְטַשְׁתָּהּ" — *Mechilta* **means to say that the beginning of the verse, which states,** *you shall release it and leave it [unharvested]*, יִכְלֹל כָּל מַה שֶּׁיִּצְמַח בָּאָרֶץ — **encompasses** an obligation to relinquish ownership of **all that sprouts in the land,** בֵּין פֵּרוֹת אִילָן אוֹ פֵּרוֹת אֲדָמָה — **whether** it is **produce of the tree or produce of the ground** (i.e., grains, vegetables, and the like).

Chinuch continues with the teaching of *Mechilta*: וְלָמָּה פֵּרְטָן הַכָּתוּב שְׁנֵי אֵלֶּה — **Why, then,** if the verse has included all types of produce, **did the verse** go on to **specify these two** examples, i.e., the produce of the vineyard and the produce of the olive grove? לְהַקִּישׁ לַכֶּרֶם שְׁאָר מִינֵי אִילָן — **The verse makes specific mention of these so as to liken other types of** fruit **trees** (such as the olive) **to a vineyard,** לְלַמֵּד שֶׁכְּמוֹ שֶׁיֵּשׁ בַּכֶּרֶם עֲשֵׂה וְלֹא תַעֲשֶׂה — **and to thereby teach us that just as with regard to** harvesting the produce of **a vineyard** during *Shemittah*, **there is both a mitzvah-obligation** to leave it unharvested (as stated in this verse) **and a mitzvah-prohibition** against harvesting it — שֶׁהֲרֵי בְּפֵרוּשׁ נִכְתַּב עָלָיו — **as it is explicitly written in reference to [the vineyard]** (*Leviticus* 25:5): "וְאֶת עִנְּבֵי נְזִירֶךָ לֹא תִבְצֹר" — *and the grapes you had set aside for yourself you shall not pick*, which is a *prohibition* against harvesting a vineyard in the usual fashion;[6] — כְּמוֹ כֵן כָּל שְׁאָר הָאִילָן יֵשׁ בָּהֶן עֲשֵׂה וְלֹא תַעֲשֶׂה — **so too, all other** fruit **trees are subject to a mitzvah-obligation and a mitzvah-prohibition with regard** to harvesting their produce.

Chinuch explains further:
וּלְפִיכָךְ פֵּרֵט כֶּרֶם וְזַיִת — It is **for this reason** that **[the Torah] specifies the vineyard and olive grove** in this verse (*Exodus* 23:11), לְלַמֵּד עַל עִנְיָן זֶה — i.e., **to teach this matter,** that all trees — like grapevines — are included in the *prohibition* of picking in the usual fashion. And although this verse seemingly links only olive groves to vineyards, the prohibition applies to all trees, כִּי כַוָּנַת הַכָּתוּב דְּלָאו דַּוְקָא זַיִת לְבַד — **because the intention of the verse is not** to extend the prohibition stated regarding

---

### NOTES

*HaMitzvos, Asei* 135) derive the mitzvah-obligation to rest from working the land from an entirely different verse (*Exodus* 34:21): בֶּחָרִישׁ וּבַקָּצִיר תִּשְׁבֹּת, *you shall desist from plowing and harvesting.* See *Tzava Rav* to Mitzvah 112.]

5. Our rendering of the term וּנְטַשְׁתָּהּ as *and leave it [unharvested]* is based on *Ramban* and *Rashbam* to the verse (cf. *Rashi* and *Ibn Ezra*). This would appear consistent with Chinuch's presentation of this mitzvah. The verse thus requires one to both relinquish ownership of the produce of the field [תִּשְׁמְטֶנָּה],

and to refrain from harvesting it as he usually does [וּנְטַשְׁתָּהּ]. See end of this mitzvah, where Chinuch (from *Rambam, Sefer HaMitzvos, Asei* 134) states that one transgresses this commandment by either locking (i.e., securing) his field (thus displaying that he is not relinquishing ownership), or by gathering the entire harvest and bringing it into his house (see also *Rambam, Hil. Shemittah VeYovel* 4:24).

6. Thus, one who harvests his vineyard as usual has transgressed both a mitzvah-obligation (this mitzvah) and a mitzvah-prohibition (see Mitzvah 329).

# 137 ☐ MISHPATIM / MITZVAH 84: THE OBLIGATION REGARDING SHEMITTAH OF THE LAND

אֶלָּא הוּא הַדִּין לְכָל שְׁאָר פֵּרוֹת הָאִילָן, אֶלָּא שֶׁהִזְכִּיר אֶחָד מֵהֶם וְהוּא מְלַמֵּד לְכֻלָּן, שֶׁזֶּה מִן הַמִּדּוֹת שֶׁהַתּוֹרָה נִדְרֶשֶׁת בָּהֶן[7]. וּמִצְוָה זוֹ שֶׁהִיא לְהַפְקִיר כָּל פֵּרוֹתֶיהָ, וְהַמִּצְוָה הָאַחֶרֶת שֶׁצִּוָּנוּ הָאֵל לִשְׁבֹּת בָּהּ, כְּמוֹ שֶׁכָּתוּב בְּכִי תִשָּׂא (שמות ל״ד, כ״א) בֶּחָרִישׁ וּבַקָּצִיר תִּשְׁבֹּת, קֶשֶׁר אֶחָד לָהֶן.

מִשָּׁרְשֵׁי הַמִּצְוָה, לִקְבֹּעַ בְּלִבֵּנוּ וּלְצַיֵּר צִיּוּר חָזָק בְּמַחֲשַׁבְתֵּנוּ עִנְיַן חִדּוּשׁ הָעוֹלָם

---

vineyards (*Leviticus* 25:5) **specifically** to **olives alone;** שְׁאָר פֵּרוֹת הָאִילָן — **rather, the same** prohibition **applies to all other tree fruits** as well. אֶלָּא שֶׁהִזְכִּיר אֶחָד מֵהֶם וְהוּא מְלַמֵּד לְכֻלָּן — **[The Torah]** simply **lists one** [type of tree], i.e., olive, as a prototype, **and this serves to teach** the lesson **regarding them all,** שֶׁזֶּה מִן הַמִּדּוֹת שֶׁהַתּוֹרָה נִדְרֶשֶׁת בָּהֶן — **as this is one of the rules through which the Torah is elucidated** — that when a law is taught regarding one item in a category, it applies to all the items in its category.[7]

Chinuch notes the relationship between the current mitzvah and Mitzvah 112, "The Obligation to Rest the Land During the Shemittah Year":

וּמִצְוָה זוֹ שֶׁהִיא לְהַפְקִיר כָּל פֵּרוֹתֶיהָ — **This mitzvah, which is** the obligation **to relinquish ownership over all of [the land's] produce,** וְהַמִּצְוָה הָאַחֶרֶת שֶׁצִּוָּנוּ הָאֵל לִשְׁבֹּת בָּהּ — **as well as the other mitzvah wherein the Almighty commands us to desist** from performing agricultural work **during [the *Shemittah*** year]** (Mitzvah 112), כְּמוֹ שֶׁכָּתוּב בְּכִי תִשָּׂא — **as is written** in *Parashas Ki Sisa* (*Exodus* 34:21), "בֶּחָרִישׁ וּבַקָּצִיר תִּשְׁבֹּת" — **you shall desist from plowing and harvesting,** קֶשֶׁר אֶחָד לָהֶן — **share a common bond.** That is, both the mitzvah to relinquish ownership over the produce of one's land and the mitzvah to desist from working the land ultimately stem from the same idea, for both reflect the Sabbatical nature of this year, as we shall see shortly.

### ☞ Underlying Purpose of the Mitzvah ☜

מִשָּׁרְשֵׁי הַמִּצְוָה — **Among the underlying purposes of the mitzvah is** לִקְבֹּעַ בְּלִבֵּנוּ — **to instill in our hearts** וּלְצַיֵּר צִיּוּר חָזָק בְּמַחֲשַׁבְתֵּנוּ — **and draw a powerful image in our minds** עִנְיַן חִדּוּשׁ הָעוֹלָם — of **the matter of Creation of the universe.**

Chinuch proceeds to explain how *Shemittah* demonstrates belief in Creation:

---

### NOTES

7. The rule to which Chinuch refers is the eighth rule in Rabbi Yishmael's list of thirteen hermeneutic rules through which the Torah is elucidated (Introduction to *Sifra*) which is: כָּל דָּבָר שֶׁהָיָה בִּכְלָל וְיָצָא מִן הַכְּלָל לְלַמֵּד, לֹא לְלַמֵּד עַל עַצְמוֹ יָצָא, אֶלָּא לְלַמֵּד עַל הַכְּלָל כֻּלּוֹ יָצָא, *Anything that was included in a general statement, but was then singled out from the general statement in order to teach something, was not singled out to teach [only] about itself, but to apply its teaching to the entire generality.* Now, in the beginning of our verse (וְהַשְּׁבִיעִת תִּשְׁמְטֶנָּה וּנְטַשְׁתָּהּ, *And in the seventh [year], you shall release it and leave it [unharvested]*), vineyards and olive groves were "included in the general statement," which is an *obligation* to leave *all kinds* of produce unharvested; but later in the verse (כֵּן תַּעֲשֶׂה לְכַרְמְךָ לְזֵיתֶךָ, *so shall you do to your vineyard and your olive grove*), these species were "singled out" so as to liken olives to grapes — and to thereby apply the *prohibition* of harvesting in the usual fashion, which was written regarding grapes (*Leviticus* 25:5), to olives. But, as per the above rule that something singled out to impart a teaching does not merely teach about itself but rather about its entire category, here too, the lesson we applied to olives (that they are subject to the harvesting prohibition) applies to all other fruits as well (see *Me'il HaEphod* §2).

[It should be noted that although Chinuch limits this discussion to fruit of the tree, in truth the prohibition to harvest in the normal fashion applies to all produce, including produce of the ground, such as grains and vegetables. Such produce is subject to its own prohibition (Mitzvah 328). There, however, the Torah prohibition is stated broadly (*Leviticus* 25:5): אֶת סְפִיחַ קְצִירְךָ לֹא תִקְצוֹר, *The aftergrowth of your harvest you shall not reap*, without limiting it to a particular species. By contrast, in the companion prohibition regarding the fruits of trees (Mitzvah 329), the Torah mentions only grapes. It is for this reason that, with regard to fruit trees, we need *Mechilta*'s derivation (as quoted by Chinuch) to apply the prohibition of harvesting fruit (in the normal fashion) to all fruit trees.]

כִּי שֵׁשֶׁת יָמִים עָשָׂה ה' אֶת הַשָּׁמַיִם וְאֶת הָאָרֶץ (שמות כ', י"א), וּבַיּוֹם הַשְּׁבִיעִי שֶׁלֹּא בָּרָא דָּבָר הִכְתִּיב מְנוּחָה עַל עַצְמוֹ[8]. וּלְמַעַן הָסִיר וְלַעֲקֹר וּלְשָׁרֵשׁ מֵרַעְיוֹנֵנוּ דְּבַר הַקַּדְמוּת אֲשֶׁר יַאֲמִינוּ הַכּוֹפְרִים בַּתּוֹרָה וּבוֹ יֶהֶרְסוּ כָּל פִּנּוֹתֶיהָ וְיִפְרְצוּ חוֹמוֹתֶיהָ[9], בָּאָה חוֹבָה עָלֵינוּ לְהוֹצִיא כָּל זְמַנֵּנוּ יוֹם יוֹם וְשָׁנָה שָׁנָה עַל דָּבָר זֶה לִמְנוֹת שֵׁשׁ שָׁנִים וְלִשְׁבֹּת בַּשְּׁבִיעִית, וּבְכֵן לֹא יִתְפָּרֵד הָעִנְיָן לְעוֹלָם מִבֵּין עֵינֵינוּ תָּמִיד[10], וְהוּא בְּעִנְיָן שֶׁאָנוּ מוֹצִיאִין יְמֵי הַשָּׁבוּעַ בְּשֵׁשֶׁת יְמֵי עֲבוֹדָה וְיוֹם מְנוּחָה[11]. וְלָכֵן צִוָּה בָּרוּךְ הוּא לְהַפְקִיר כָּל מַה שֶּׁתּוֹצִיא הָאָרֶץ בְּשָׁנָה זוֹ מִלְּבַד הַשְּׁבִיתָה בָּהּ,

---

"כִּי שֵׁשֶׁת יָמִים עָשָׂה ה' אֶת הַשָּׁמַיִם וְאֶת הָאָרֶץ" — The observance of this mitzvah serves as a testimony *that in six days HASHEM made the heavens and the earth* (Exodus 20:11), וּבַיּוֹם הַשְּׁבִיעִי שֶׁלֹּא בָּרָא דָּבָר — and regarding the seventh day, on which He did not create anything, הִכְתִּיב מְנוּחָה עַל עַצְמוֹ — He instructed Moses to write in the Torah a terminology of resting in reference to Himself, as the verse states (ibid.): *and He rested on the seventh day.*[8] וּלְמַעַן הָסִיר וְלַעֲקֹר וּלְשָׁרֵשׁ מֵרַעְיוֹנֵנוּ — Now, in order to remove, uproot, and expunge from our thoughts דְּבַר הַקַּדְמוּת — the notion of an ever-existing [universe], a notion that the deniers אֲשֶׁר יַאֲמִינוּ הַכּוֹפְרִים בַּתּוֹרָה of Torah believe, וּבוֹ יֶהֶרְסוּ כָּל פִּנּוֹתֶיהָ וְיִפְרְצוּ חוֹמוֹתֶיהָ — and through which they attempt to destroy all of [the Torah's] watchtowers and breach its ramparts,[9] בָּאָה חוֹבָה עָלֵינוּ לְהוֹצִיא כָּל זְמַנֵּנוּ — it becomes incumbent upon us to spend all of our cycles of time, יוֹם יוֹם וְשָׁנָה שָׁנָה — both daily and yearly, עַל דָּבָר זֶה — in a manner that causes us to reflect upon this matter of God's creation of the world. לִמְנוֹת שֵׁשׁ שָׁנִים וְלִשְׁבֹּת בַּשְּׁבִיעִית — Hence, with regard to our years, we are to count six years of work and rest in the seventh. וּבְכֵן לֹא יִתְפָּרֵד הָעִנְיָן לְעוֹלָם מִבֵּין עֵינֵינוּ תָּמִיד — The matter of Creation will thus never depart from before our eyes, and will remain a steadfast part of our consciousness.[10] וְהוּא בְּעִנְיָן שֶׁאָנוּ מוֹצִיאִין יְמֵי הַשָּׁבוּעַ בְּשֵׁשֶׁת יְמֵי עֲבוֹדָה וְיוֹם מְנוּחָה — This is in the same fashion in which we spend the days of the week as six days of work and one day of rest.[11] וְלָכֵן צִוָּה בָּרוּךְ הוּא לְהַפְקִיר כָּל מַה שֶּׁתּוֹצִיא הָאָרֶץ בְּשָׁנָה זוֹ — Therefore, God, blessed is He, commanded that we relinquish ownership of all the produce that the land brings forth in this *Shemittah* year, מִלְּבַד הַשְּׁבִיתָה בָּהּ — aside from the command to rest from working

---

### NOTES

8. Although rest is a human concept and certainly cannot be applied to the Almighty, about Whom it is written (*Isaiah* 40:28): *He does not weary, He does not tire*, nevertheless Hashem uses the terminology of "rest" with regard to Himself so as to relay to the human ear a concept that we are capable of relating to and understanding (*Rashi, Exodus* 31:17).

9. The fact that the world has a Creator, as stated in the very first verse of the Torah, is obviously a most fundamental Jewish belief (see Chinuch in Mitzvos 25 and 32). Indeed, it is the first of *Rambam's* thirteen basic Jewish principles (*Commentary to Mishnah, Sanhedrin* 10:1), which, as *Rambam* explains, obligates us to believe that God is the Creator and Sustainer of all of existence. The polar opposite of this principle is the notion of an ever-existing universe, which many have ascribed to in order to deny the validity of Torah and undermine its very basis. By ascribing to such a belief, these individuals deny the existence of a Creator, for a universe that lacks a beginning lacks a Creator.

10. By marking the continual passage of time in ways that highlight the seventh unit, we constantly display our belief that the world was created in six days and that God rested on the seventh. The seven-year *Shemittah* cycle is an example of this. *Sefer HaBatim* (Mitzvah 130) notes other such examples of our marking of time in sevens. In terms of weeks, for instance, we count seven weeks between Pesach and Shavuos, as per the verse (*Deuteronomy* 16:9): שִׁבְעָה שָׁבֻעֹת תִּסְפָּר לָךְ, *You shall count seven weeks for yourselves*. In terms of months, the seventh month (Tishrei) contains Rosh Hashanah, Yom Kippur, Succos, and Shemini Atzeres, and therefore is in a certain sense a Sabbath, for most of it is sanctified. Finally, we count seven of the seven-year *Shemittah* cycles to arrive at the fiftieth year, *Yovel*. All these reckonings instill within us the belief in the Creation, and the knowledge that the world has a Creator, who created it in six days and rested on the seventh.

11. *Shemittah* is to years what the Sabbath is to days. In fact, we find that the Torah writes regarding *Shemittah* (*Leviticus* 25:2): שַׁבָּת לַה׳, *A Sabbath to HASHEM*, just as it does with regard to the weekly Sabbath (*Exodus* 20:11). This emphasis on it being the Sabbath (or rest) "to Hashem," in particular, indicates that our rest on the weekly Sabbath and the "Sabbath" of *Shemittah* are both a reflection of Hashem's "rest" on the Sabbath of Creation (*Ramban, Leviticus* 25:2; cf. *Rashi*); i.e., as He rested, so do we. We thereby inculcate the lesson of Creation, as Chinuch has explained.

## 139 ☐ MISHPATIM / MITZVAH 84: THE OBLIGATION REGARDING SHEMITTAH OF THE LAND

כְּדֵי שֶׁיִּזְכֹּר הָאָדָם כִּי הָאָרֶץ שֶׁמּוֹצִיאָה אֵלָיו הַפֵּרוֹת בְּכָל שָׁנָה וְשָׁנָה לֹא בְּכֹחָהּ וּסְגֻלָּתָהּ תּוֹצִיא אוֹתָם, כִּי יֵשׁ אָדוֹן עָלֶיהָ וְעַל אֲדוֹנֶיהָ, וּכְשֶׁהוּא חָפֵץ הוּא מְצַוֶּה אֵלָיו לְהַפְקִירָם.[12] וְעוֹד יֵשׁ תּוֹעֶלֶת נִמְצָא בַּדָּבָר, לִקְנוֹת בָּזֶה מִדַּת הַוַּתְרָנוּת, כִּי אֵין נָדִיב כְּנוֹתֵן מִבְּלִי תִּקְוָה אֶל הַגְּמוּל.[13] וְעוֹד יֵשׁ תּוֹעֶלֶת אַחֵר נִמְצָא בָּזֶה הָאָדָם, שֶׁיּוֹסִיף הָאָדָם בִּטָּחוֹן בְּשֵׁם בָּרוּךְ הוּא, כִּי כָּל הַמּוֹצֵא עִם לְבָבוֹ לָתֵת וּלְהַפְקִיר לְעוֹלָם כָּל גִּדּוּלֵי קַרְקְעוֹתָיו וְנַחֲלַת אֲבוֹתָיו הַגְּדֵלִים בְּכָל שָׁנָה אַחַת, וּמְלֻמָּד בְּכָךְ הוּא וְכָל הַמִּשְׁפָּחָה כָּל יָמָיו, לֹא תֶחֱזַק בּוֹ לְעוֹלָם מִדַּת הַכִּילוּת הַרְבֵּה וְלֹא מִעוּט הַבִּטָּחוֹן.[14]

---

the land **during [Shemittah]** (Mitzvah 112). כְּדֵי שֶׁיִּזְכֹּר הָאָדָם — **The purpose of this is so that,** by fulfilling these mitzvos, **man will remember** כִּי הָאָרֶץ שֶׁמּוֹצִיאָה אֵלָיו הַפֵּרוֹת בְּכָל שָׁנָה וְשָׁנָה — **that the land that brings forth produce for him year after year** לֹא בְּכֹחָהּ וּסְגֻלָּתָהּ תּוֹצִיא אוֹתָם — **is not bringing it forth** by virtue **of its own strength and constitution;** כִּי יֵשׁ אָדוֹן עָלֶיהָ וְעַל אֲדוֹנֶיהָ — **for,** in truth, **there is a Master over it and over** the man who is **its owner,** וּכְשֶׁהוּא חָפֵץ הוּא מְצַוֶּה אֵלָיו לְהַפְקִירָם — **and when [that Master] so desires, He commands [the landowner] to relinquish ownership over [the produce].** Hence, by relinquishing control of the land during *Shemittah,* we demonstrate in two ways our belief in God as the Creator and Master of the universe: (1) by virtue of the count, which indicates that at the time of Creation Hashem rested on the seventh day, and (2) by virtue of conducting ourselves in a manner that shows that we are not the masters of the land.[12]

Chinuch offers another underlying purpose of the mitzvah:

וְעוֹד יֵשׁ תּוֹעֶלֶת נִמְצָא בַּדָּבָר — **There is another benefit to be found in the matter** of relinquishing ownership in the *Shemittah* year, לִקְנוֹת בָּזֶה מִדַּת הַוַּתְרָנוּת — which is **to thereby acquire the trait of yielding,** i.e., a generous willingness to forgo that which we see as our due. כִּי אֵין נָדִיב כְּנוֹתֵן מִבְּלִי תִּקְוָה אֶל הַגְּמוּל — **Performing this mitzvah is an exercise of this trait, for there is none so generous as one who gives without the anticipation of compensation,** and one who generously yields the produce in *Shemittah,* as per this mitzvah, does so without anticipation of any worldly compensation.[13]

Chinuch offers a third underlying purpose of this mitzvah:

וְעוֹד יֵשׁ תּוֹעֶלֶת אַחֵר נִמְצָא בָּזֶה הָאָדָם — **There is yet another benefit to be found in such a person** who observes this mitzvah. שֶׁיּוֹסִיף הָאָדָם בִּטָּחוֹן בְּשֵׁם בָּרוּךְ הוּא — This benefit is **that the person will increase trust in Hashem, blessed is He,** כִּי כָּל הַמּוֹצֵא עִם לְבָבוֹ לָתֵת וּלְהַפְקִיר לְעוֹלָם — **for** anyone who can find in his heart the capacity **to give and relinquish to the world** כָּל גִּדּוּלֵי קַרְקְעוֹתָיו וְנַחֲלַת אֲבוֹתָיו הַגְּדֵלִים בְּכָל שָׁנָה אַחַת — **all the produce of his land and his ancestral inheritance that grows throughout an entire year,** וּמְלֻמָּד בְּכָךְ הוּא וְכָל הַמִּשְׁפָּחָה כָּל יָמָיו — **and he and his family are accustomed to doing so, all of his days,** לֹא תֶחֱזַק בּוֹ לְעוֹלָם מִדַּת הַכִּילוּת הַרְבֵּה וְלֹא מִעוּט הַבִּטָּחוֹן — **the trait of miserliness will never take hold in [such a person], nor will he ever be seized by lack of trust.** Rather, he will willingly give of his possessions to others, and trust in Hashem to provide his needs.[14]

---

### NOTES

12. This sentiment of Chinuch is shared by *Rabbeinu Bachya* (*Leviticus* 25:2). *Chizkuni* (ad loc.) adds that this is why the verse stresses that *Shemittah* is a שַׁבָּת לַה׳, a Sabbath "to HASHEM," for by resting from working the land in this year, we demonstrate that He is the true owner of the land.

13. This reason is also offered by *Rambam* in *Moreh Nevuchim* 3:39, where he lists this as one of the mitzvos meant to bring out kindness and compassion to the less fortunate. *R' S. R. Hirsch* (*Exodus* 23:11) notes how this idea is in fact an outgrowth of the previous one; by acknowledging that God is the sole Owner and Master of one's land, the person recognizes that he is ultimately like an alien who dwells in the land only through the tolerance of the Owner. That humbling feeling does away with the arrogance that stems from the pride of standing on one's own soil, and in that humbled state one can engender a frame of mind that lovingly includes the stranger, the poor, and even the animals ("*and the destitute of your people shall eat, and the wildlife of the field shall eat what is left*") in sharing the bounty of the land.

14. The Midrash (*Vayikra Rabbah* 1:1) compares those who observe *Shemittah* to angels, and applies to them the verse that states (*Psalms* 103:20): *Bless HASHEM, O His angels; the strong warriors who do His bidding.* They are praised so highly because the level of

מִדִּינֵי[15] הַמִּצְוָה, מַה הֵן הַדְּבָרִים מֵעֲבוֹדוֹת הָאָרֶץ שֶׁהֵן לָנוּ בְּחִיּוּב שְׁבִיתָה זוֹ מִן הַתּוֹרָה, כְּגוֹן זְרִיעָה וּזְמִירָה קְצִירָה בְּצִירָה,[16] וַאֲשֶׁר הֵן אֲסוּרוֹת מִדְּרַבָּנָן, כְּגוֹן מְזַבֵּל וְחוֹפֵר,[17] וַעֲבוֹדוֹת שֶׁבָּאִילָן כְּגוֹן חוֹתֵךְ מִמֶּנּוּ יַבֶּלֶת,[18] וּפוֹרֵק מִמֶּנּוּ עָלִין אוֹ בַּדִּין יְבֵשִׁין,[19] מְאַבֵּק בְּאָבָק[20] אוֹ מְעַשֵּׁן

## ⁓ Laws of the Mitzvah ⁓

Chinuch begins the discussion of the laws of the mitzvah with a list of agricultural activities that are forbidden in *Shemittah*, either Biblically or Rabbinically:[15]

מַה הֵן הַדְּבָרִים מִדִּינֵי הַמִּצְוָה — The particulars **of the laws of the mitzvah** include, for example, שֶׁהֵן לָנוּ בְּחִיּוּב שְׁבִיתָה זוֹ מִן הַתּוֹרָה מֵעֲבוֹדוֹת הָאָרֶץ — defining **which means of working the land are subject to this "resting" obligation under Biblical law**, כְּגוֹן זְרִיעָה וּזְמִירָה קְצִירָה בְּצִירָה — **such as planting, pruning, harvesting, and picking**,[16] וַאֲשֶׁר הֵן אֲסוּרוֹת מִדְּרַבָּנָן — **and which** means of work **are forbidden by Rabbinic decree**, כְּגוֹן מְזַבֵּל וְחוֹפֵר — **such as fertilizing and digging**, which are performed on the soil.[17] וַעֲבוֹדוֹת שֶׁבָּאִילָן כְּגוֹן חוֹתֵךְ מִמֶּנּוּ יַבֶּלֶת — Other Rabbinically prohibited activities include **work done to trees, such as cutting off growths**,[18] וּפוֹרֵק מִמֶּנּוּ עָלִין אוֹ בַּדִּין יְבֵשִׁין — **removing dried-out leaves or branches from it**,[19]

---

NOTES

conviction necessary to fulfill this mitzvah for an entire year is extraordinary. *R' Chaim Shmulevitz* (*Sichos Mussar*, 2004 §69) asserts that of all the reasons offered in explanation of this mitzvah, the one that is the most central is this notion that *Shemittah* is to develop our *bitachon* (trust) in Hashem. This development of *bitachon* is of such fundamental importance for each and every member of the Jewish people that the Torah demands the seemingly impossible — to leave our fields fallow for an entire year — in order that we develop the trust that He will provide for us.

15. Actually, the requirement to desist from working the land is the subject of a separate mitzvah-obligation (Mitzvah 112) and two mitzvah-prohibitions (Mitzvos 326 and 327), while our mitzvah obligates one to relinquish ownership over the land. Thus, as Chinuch himself notes in Mitzvah 112, the laws that follow, which deal with working the land, technically belong in a discussion of that mitzvah. Nevertheless, Chinuch found it appropriate to discuss these laws here, since the mitzvah of relinquishing ownership and that of desisting from working the land are intimately linked and "share a common bond," as he stated earlier.

16. These four activities are specifically prohibited in the verses (*Leviticus* 25:4-5): וּבַשָּׁנָה הַשְּׁבִיעִת ... שָׂדְךָ לֹא תִזְרָע וְכַרְמְךָ לֹא תִזְמֹר. אֵת סְפִיחַ קְצִירְךָ לֹא תִקְצוֹר וְאֶת עִנְּבֵי נְזִירֶךָ לֹא תִבְצֹר שְׁנַת שַׁבָּתוֹן יִהְיֶה לָאָרֶץ, *But in the seventh year ... your field you shall not sow and your vineyard you shall not prune. The aftergrowth of your harvest you shall not reap and the grapes you had set aside for yourself you shall not pick: it shall be a year of rest for the land* (see Mitzvos 326-329). These verses clearly forbid:

(1) sowing [i.e., planting], (2) pruning, (3) reaping [i.e., harvesting], and (4) picking [fruit]. [Harvesting and picking in small quantities, though, are permitted, as Chinuch mentions at the end of this mitzvah and in Mitzvos 328-329.]

The Torah specifically mentions "pruning," even though, by virtue of it being a form of promoting plant growth, it should ostensibly be included in the similar activity of sowing. Similarly, the Torah makes specific mention of "picking [fruit]" even though it too is ostensibly included in the activity of harvesting. The Torah does so to indicate that inferences should not be made, and that *only* those activities specifically detailed in the Torah are included in the mitzvah-prohibitions; no other agricultural labor may be assumed to be included, even if those labors would seem to be logical extensions of those that were mentioned (*Moed Katan* 3a; *Rambam, Hil. Shemittah VeYovel* 1:2-3). Thus, for example, sowing — which is the planting of seeds — does not include the planting of a sapling (*Rambam* ibid. 1:4; cf. *Rash, Sheviis* 1:1; *Chazon Ish, Sheviis* 17:20 ד"ה שם).

It should be noted that although plowing is not included in the above mitzvah-prohibitions, it is included in the mitzvah-obligation to desist from working the land, as Chinuch alludes in Mitzvah 112 (see *Minchas Chinuch* 112:1; *Mahari Korkos* to *Rambam* ibid. 1:1; cf. *Pe'as HaShulchan, Beis Yisrael* 20:1).

17. Only digging that improves the quality and arability of the soil is forbidden (*Rambam, Hil. Shemittah VeYovel* 1:4); digging to create a pit or cistern, or the like, is permitted (ibid. 2:14).

[With respect to work not encompassed by the Biblical prohibitions, the Sages, as a rule, forbade those agricultural activities that serve to promote additional growth, while they permitted those activities that serve to avert deterioration and loss to the existing plant life (see *Avodah Zarah* 50b and *Moed Katan* 3a with *Rashi*; cf. *Chidushei HaRan* to *Moed Katan* 3a and *Nimukei Yosef* there fol. 1a ד"ה משקין).]

18. A יַבֶּלֶת is a wart-like growth (see *Leviticus* 22:22) that develops on the surface of a plant where it has a wound or infection (*Y. Feliks*, commentary to *Yerushalmi Sheviis*, p. 95).

19. So as to lighten the burden of the tree [and thus strengthen the tree] (*Rav* and *Rash* to *Mishnah, Sheviis* 2:2).

# 141 ☐ MISHPATIM / MITZVAH 84: THE OBLIGATION REGARDING SHEMITTAH OF THE LAND

תַּחְתָּיו לְהָמִית הַתּוֹלַעַת²¹, סָךְ הַנְּטִיעוֹת²², קוֹטֵם²³ אוֹ מְפַסֵּג הָאִילָנוֹת²⁴, וּמַה שֶּׁהִתִּירוּ לַעֲשׂוֹת בְּגוֹן סוֹקְרִין בְּסִיקְרָא²⁵, וְעוֹדֵר תַּחַת הַגְּפָנִים²⁶, וְדִין עֲבוֹדַת בֵּית הַשְּׁלָחִין²⁷, וְשֶׁלֹּא יַעֲשֶׂה אַשְׁפָּה בְּתוֹךְ שָׂדֵהוּ עַד שֶׁיַּעֲבֹר זְמַן הַזִּבּוּל, וְאַחַר כָּךְ שֶׁתְּהֵא גְּדוֹלָה וְלֹא יְהֵא נִרְאֶה כִּמְזַבֵּל,

סָךְ תַּחְתָּיו לְהָמִית הַתּוֹלַעַת — **applying dust,**[20] **or fumigating underneath it to kill worms,**[21] הַנְּטִיעוֹת — **smearing the saplings,**[22] קוֹטֵם אוֹ מְפַסֵּג הָאִילָנוֹת — **putting ash** on the roots,[23] **or supporting the trees.**[24] All these are prohibited Rabbinically during *Shemittah*.

Chinuch proceeds to mention a number of agricultural activities that are permitted during *Shemittah*:

וּמַה שֶּׁהִתִּירוּ לַעֲשׂוֹת — The laws of *Shemittah* include, **as well, that which [the Sages] permitted** one **to do** for his plants, בְּגוֹן סוֹקְרִין בְּסִיקְרָא — **such as painting** a tree **with red paint,**[25] וְעוֹדֵר תַּחַת הַגְּפָנִים — **and hoeing underneath grape vines.**[26] וְדִין עֲבוֹדַת בֵּית הַשְּׁלָחִין — **Included as well is the law** with regard to **the work of an irrigated field.**[27]

Chinuch discusses the laws of stockpiling manure:

וְשֶׁלֹּא יַעֲשֶׂה אַשְׁפָּה בְּתוֹךְ שָׂדֵהוּ עַד שֶׁיַּעֲבֹר זְמַן הַזִּבּוּל — The laws of *Shemittah* include, **as well, that one may not make a manure heap in his field until the time of fertilizing has passed,**[28] וְאַחַר כָּךְ שֶׁתְּהֵא גְּדוֹלָה וְלֹא יְהֵא נִרְאֶה כִּמְזַבֵּל — **and** even **after such** time, **[the pile] must be** made **large,**

---

### NOTES

20. This refers to covering with dust any roots that have become exposed (*Rav, Sheviis* 2:2). Alternatively, it refers to sprinkling dust on the branches of the tree itself, which is beneficial for some fruit trees (*Rambam Commenatary* ad loc.).

21. Smoke was directed at trees so as to kill insects that might damage them (*Rav* and *Rambam Commentary* ibid.). Although the Sages generally permitted performing activities whose purpose was simply to maintain the tree (see note 17), they nevertheless forbade fumigation, as it has too strong an appearance of labor (*Chazon Ish, Sheviis* 17:19 ד"ה שם מדרבנן).

22. This refers to the application of dung to a portion of the exposed trunk whose bark was peeled, which has the effect of generating new growth (*Rash, Sheviis* 2:4, based on *Avodah Zarah* 50b). Alternatively, the Sages forbade smearing the sapling with a foul-smelling substance even if one's intention was simply to protect its soft areas from the foraging of birds (*Rambam, Hil. Shemittah VeYovel* 1:5), perhaps as a decree lest one come to perform the other type of smearing that actually generates new growth (*Chazon Ish* ibid. ד"ה והר"מ; see *Lechem Mishneh, Hil. Yom Tov* 8:10).

23. Ash was placed on roots to thwart evaporation (*Ri ben Malki Tzedek* ad loc.) or as a fertilizer (*Tiferes Yisrael* ad loc.). The translation of קוֹטֵם as "putting ash [on the roots]" follows *Rav* (*Sheviis* 2:4, in his first explanation), who relates this word to the Aramaic word קטמא, *ash*. Alternatively, קוֹטֵם means breaking off the tips of branches, as in (*Succah* 29b) נקטם ראשו, *its top was clipped off* (*Rav*, in his second explanation), which was done to cause more of the sap to flow through to the fruit (*R' Tanchum HaYerushalmi*, quoted in notes at the end of *Ri ben Malki Tzedek*, Mechon HaTalmud HaYisraeli ed.).

24. Trees that were overly supple would be braced and supported, so that they would not break (*Rashi, Moed Katan* 3a, as explained by *Kesef Mishneh, Hil. Shemittah VeYovel* 1:5). Alternatively, this refers to tying the branches to train them to grow upward as opposed to being left to grow outward, which would place a heavy strain on the trunk (*Chidushei HaRan* ibid.). This too was forbidden due to its having too strong an appearance of working the land (*Chazon Ish, Sheviis* 17:19 ד"ה שם מדרבנן).

25. It was customary that when a tree would prematurely drop its fruit, it would be painted with red paint so that people would see it and pray for its owner's sake that it become healthier (*Shabbos* 67a). Often, stones were placed on it as well to lessen the flow of sap, with the hope that it would thereby retain its fruit longer (ibid.). Both of these actions are permitted during *Shemittah* (*Tosefta, Sheviis* 1:10; *Rambam* ibid. 1:7).

26. Hoeing is permitted only to seal otherwise damaging cracks in the roots, but not as a stimulant for new growth (*Chazon Ish, Sheviis* 17:19; see *Mayim Chaim* to *Rambam, Hil. Shemittah VeYovel* 1:8, quoted in *Sefer HaLikkutim* [Frankel ed.]).

27. בֵּית הַשְּׁלָחִין, which means *a tired* or *thirsty field* (based on the Aramaic root שלה, *thirsty*), refers to a field that, due to its elevation, requires constant watering. The Sages permitted one to water such a field during *Shemittah* (Mishnah, *Moed Katan* 2a), because watering is not one of the Biblically forbidden activities (see note 16 above), and in cases of loss, the Sages permitted it. Not watering such irrigated fields would cause irreversible harm to the soil and trees (*Rambam, Hil. Shemittah VeYovel* 1:8,10). Alternatively, one may even water such fields to sustain the crops in them for the purpose of picking them after *Shemittah* passes (*Rav, Sheviis* 2:10, based on *Moed Katan* 6b; cf. *Chazon Ish, Sheviis* 16:4 in explanation of *Rambam*).

28. Fertilizing a field during *Shemittah* is forbidden Rabbinically (*Rambam, Hil. Shemittah VeYovel* 1:4).

וְשִׁעוּרָהּ מִמֵּאָה וַחֲמִשִּׁים סְאָה זֶבֶל וּלְמַעְלָה[29], וּמַה שֶּׁאָמְרוּ (מועד קטן דף ג' ע"ב) שֶׁהַחִיּוּב לְהִמָּנַע מֵעֲבוֹדַת הָאָרֶץ שְׁלֹשִׁים יוֹם קֹדֶם שָׁנָה שְׁבִיעִית, וְהִיא הֲלָכָה לְמֹשֶׁה מִסִּינַי[30], וְדִין שְׂדֵה אִילָן כַּמָּה זְמַן אָסוּר בַּעֲבוֹדָה מִשָּׁנָה שִׁשִּׁית[31], וּמַהוּ נִקְרָא שְׂדֵה אִילָן[32],

**וְשִׁעוּרָהּ מִמֵּאָה וַחֲמִשִּׁים סְאָה זֶבֶל וּלְמַעְלָה** — A manure pile is considered sufficiently large when **its measurement is one hundred and fifty se'ah of manure or greater.** [29]

Chinuch notes that some activities are forbidden even prior to the commencement of the seventh year: **וּמַה שֶּׁאָמְרוּ שֶׁהַחִיּוּב לְהִמָּנַע מֵעֲבוֹדַת הָאָרֶץ** — The laws of *Shemittah* include, **as well, that which [the Sages] said** (*Moed Katan* 3b) **that the requirement to refrain from working the land is** in effect **שְׁלֹשִׁים יוֹם קֹדֶם שָׁנָה שְׁבִיעִית** — **thirty days before the** start of the **seventh year; וְהִיא הֲלָכָה לְמֹשֶׁה מִסִּינַי** — **this is** part of **the Oral Law given to Moses at** Mount **Sinai** (*Halachah LeMoshe MiSinai*).[30] **וְדִין שְׂדֵה אִילָן כַּמָּה זְמַן אָסוּר בַּעֲבוֹדָה מִשָּׁנָה שִׁשִּׁית** — They include **as well the law regarding how much time** (i.e., from which point) **during the sixth year is it forbidden to work a "field of trees,"**[31] **וּמַהוּ נִקְרָא שְׂדֵה אִילָן** — **and what is** in fact called **a "field of trees."**[32]

---

NOTES

The Sages went a step further and placed restrictions on the storing of fertilizer in the field, as was common in earlier times, such as in compost heaps made from animal manure. They did so out of fear that onlookers would suspect the owner of violating the law against fertilizing and working his land. They therefore required anyone wishing to make such heaps to wait until the season for fertilizing had come to an end — at which time such piles would not arouse suspicion (Mishnah, *Sheviis* 3:1; *Rambam* ibid. 2:1).

29. That is, even after the season for fertilizing ends, one may only store his fertilizer in the field in large enough piles that by virtue of their size are clearly for purposes of future usage — i.e., piles of 150 *se'ah* or more (approximately 44 to 76 cubic feet [1.24-2.16 cubic meters], depending on various opinions). The creation of smaller heaps resembles fertilizing, and is therefore forbidden. Furthermore, there is a limit as to how many such heaps one may place in his field; the maximum is three heaps per *beis se'ah* (2,500 square *amos*; approximately 700-1,000 square yards [roughly 600-850 square meters], depending on various opinions). However, there is no limit to the size of each heap (Mishnah, *Sheviis* 3:2; *Rambam*, *Hil. Shemittah VeYovel* 2:1).

30. This *Halachah LeMoshe MiSinai* teaches that at the end of the sixth year — thirty days prior to Rosh Hashanah of the seventh year — one must desist from working the fields. The Sages enacted an additional safeguard, and prohibited plowing the field even earlier — from the time when it is no longer beneficial to the crops of the sixth year – i.e., from Pesach of the sixth year for a grain field, and from Shavuos of the sixth year for an orchard (see below). However, Rabban Gamliel and his court taught that, with the Destruction of the Temple, this *Halachah LeMoshe MiSinai* requiring a thirty-day pre-Rosh Hashanah restriction is no longer in effect, and the Rabbinic extension is certainly no longer binding. Hence, nowadays, such work in the fields would be permitted until Rosh Hashanah of the seventh year (*Moed Katan* 3b-4a; *Rambam*, *Hil. Shemittah VeYovel* 3:1).

31. As discussed in the previous note, when the *Beis HaMikdash* stood, one was allowed to plow around his trees only until Shavuos of the sixth year. Plowing done until that time is beneficial for the tree, as it allows moisture to penetrate deeper into the soil. However, after Shavuos, when the land is already dry, plowing was prohibited, since it would actually weaken the tree and would therefore be done only by one who was preparing the soil with the intention to unlawfully plant in the coming *Shemittah* year (*Yerushalmi Sheviis* 1:1, as per *Mahari Korkos* to *Hil. Shemittah VeYovel* 3:1).

Even when plowing was permitted (i.e., before Shavuos), it was permitted only in the area immediately around the tree. The rest of the field would follow the rules of grain fields and could be plowed only until Pesach. However, once a field has a concentration of enough healthy trees in it to be considered a "field of trees" (see next note), it is considered beneficial for those trees to plow the entire orchard (until Shavuos), not just the area immediately around each tree (see Mishnah *Sheviis* 1:2 with *Rav*).

32. A field the size of a *beis se'ah* (2,500 square *amos*) with at least three trees large enough to produce a significant amount of fruit (see next paragraph) is considered a "field of trees" (Mishnah, *Sheviis* 1:2), and one may plow the entire orchard for the sake of those three trees up until Shavuos of the sixth year. And, if an orchard has ten trees in a *beis se'ah*, it can be plowed (until Shavuos) irrespective of the yield of fruit (*Rambam* ibid. 1:5; see there for additional leniencies for sapling trees).

Trees large enough to "produce a significant amount of fruit" are those that are of the size that, if they were fig trees, could be expected to produce a yield of figs weighing sixty Italian *maneh* (Mishnah, *Sheviis* 1:2), which is approximately 63 pounds [28.8 kg.] (*Y. Feliks*, commentary to *Yerushalmi Sheviis*, p. 29). The trees do not have to be fig trees, nor do they even have to

## 143 ☐ MISHPATIM / MITZVAH 84: THE OBLIGATION REGARDING SHEMITTAH OF THE LAND

וְאִסוּר הַבְרָכָה[33] וְהַרְכָּבָה[34,35], וְאִם עָבַר וְעָשָׂה מַה יְהֵא בִּנְטִיעוֹתָיו[36], וּפֵרוֹת שְׁבִיעִית מַה דִּינָן[37], דְּכָל שֶׁהוּא מְיֻחָד לְמַאֲכַל אָדָם כְּגוֹן חִטִּים וּשְׂעוֹרִים וּפֵרוֹת

וְאִסוּר הַבְרָכָה וְהַרְכָּבָה — **The laws of** *Shemittah* **also include the prohibition of layering**[33] **and grafting,**[34] toward the end of the sixth year,[35] וְאִם עָבַר וְעָשָׂה מַה יְהֵא בִּנְטִיעוֹתָיו — **and if one violated** that prohibition **and did** such activities, **what would be** the law **with regard to his plantings.**[36]

Even produce of *Shemittah* that has grown and was picked permissibly (see Mitzvos 328 and 329) contains *Shemittah* sanctity and its use remains restricted by special laws. The laws governing the use of *Shemittah* produce are based on the verse (*Leviticus* 25:6): וְהָיְתָה שַׁבַּת הָאָרֶץ לָכֶם לְאָכְלָה, *The Sabbath produce of the land shall be yours to eat.* Now, on the one hand, the word לָכֶם, *yours,* implies that we may treat it as our own and use the produce in any way we choose. On the other hand, the next word, לְאָכְלָה, *to eat,* would seem to limit usage of the produce to eating. The Sages therefore expound the verse to permit any usage that resembles eating. Usage is said to resemble eating when the use of the item coincides with its elimination; i.e., when the produce is totally consumed at the time benefit is derived from it (*Succah* 40a). Thus, as a rule, *Shemittah* produce may be used for eating, drinking, anointing, or as lamp fuel (Mishnah, *Sheviis* 8:2).[37]

Chinuch addresses another limitation on usage of produce of *Shemittah* derived from the word לְאָכְלָה, *to eat*:

וּפֵרוֹת שְׁבִיעִית מַה דִּינָן — **The laws of the mitzvah also include those pertaining to produce** that has grown **in the seventh year, and what its law would be** with regard to the following: דְּכָל שֶׁהוּא מְיֻחָד לְמַאֲכַל אָדָם כְּגוֹן חִטִּים וּשְׂעוֹרִים וּפֵרוֹת — **Anything that is reserved for human consumption,**

---

### NOTES

be fruit trees; the fig tree is simply the standard (as it produces a large amount of heavy fruit), and any tree that has the equivalent thickness and size of such a fig tree would count toward the minimum three (Mishnah ibid 1:3, with *Tiferes Yisrael; Rambam* ibid.).

33. This refers to a technique in which a branch is laid down in the ground and covered with earth so that it can sprout new trees (*Rambam Commentary, Sheviis* 2:6).

34. Grafting refers to taking a branch from one tree and attaching it to another [of the same species] (*Rav, Sheviis* 2:6). This was done so as to combine in one tree the virtues of the new addition and the virtues of the host tree (e.g., one produces abundant fruit while the other is a hardier tree). [It should be noted that to graft a tree of one species onto a host tree of another species would be forbidden as *kilayim* (see Mitzvah 245).]

35. Layering, grafting, and surely the actual planting of trees, are all Rabbinically forbidden during *Shemittah* (*Rambam, Hil. Shemittah VeYovel* 1:4; see note 16 above). Furthermore, since such planting activities require two weeks to take root (Mishnah, *Sheviis* 2:6, as per the opinion accepted by halachah, see *Yevamos* 83a), and since it is prohibited to cause that such taking root occur during *Shemittah*, these activities may not be performed during the two weeks prior to *Shemittah* (Mishnah ibid., as per *Rabbeinu Tam,* quoted in *Rash* there). Other authorities take this prohibition even further, and maintain that when the prohibition regarding the thirty-day pre-*Shemittah* period was in place (see note 31), it was prohibited to cause such taking root to occur within that period as well, and such planting was thus forbidden from 44 days before the advent of *Shemittah* (*Rav* ad loc., based on *Rosh Hashanah* 10b). *Rambam* (*Hil. Shemittah VeYovel* 3:11) goes yet further, and maintains that the 44-day restriction is in place even nowadays (for reasons why, see *Mahari Korkos* ad loc., *Minchas Chinuch* 326:5, and ArtScroll Yad Avraham commentary to Mishnah, *Sheviis* 2:6); see also *Aruch HaShulchan HeAsid, Hil. Shemittah VeYovel* 18:5.

36. Trees that were planted, grafted, or layered in contravention to the above-stated law must be uprooted (Mishnah ibid.; *Rambam* ibid.). This is a Rabbinically imposed penalty designed to discourage laxity in *Shemittah* observance (see *Gittin* 54a). If the tree was not uprooted, its fruit nevertheless remains permitted (*Rambam* ibid.).

37. Additionally, it may be used for dyeing, as the produce used as a dye is used up at the same time it colors the fabric (*Bava Kamma* 101b with *Rashi* ד"ה יצאו).

Not all produce has *Shemittah* sanctity. Plants whose typical usage is one where the benefit does not coincide with the item's elimination are not subject to the laws of *Shemittah*. Firewood is an example, for its typical usage occurs only after it is consumed — i.e., the wood is burned to produce charcoal, which is *then* used for baking. Thus, firewood is not imbued with any *Shemittah* sanctity and may be used freely (*Succah* 40a).

אֵין עוֹשִׂין מֵהֶן מְלוּגְמָא אוֹ רְטִיָּה[38], שֶׁנֶּאֱמַר בָּהֶן לְאָכְלָה[39] (ויקרא כ״ה, ו׳), וְשֶׁאֵינוֹ מְיֻחָד לְמַאֲכַל אָדָם כְּגוֹן קוֹצִים וְדַרְדָּרִים עוֹשִׂין מֵהֶן מְלוּגְמָא לְאָדָם וְלֹא לַבְּהֵמָה[40], וְשֶׁאֵינוֹ מְיֻחָד לְאָדָם וְלִבְהֵמָה[41] כְּגוֹן פּוּאָה[42] וְאֵזוֹב וְקוֹרָנִית הֲרֵי הוּא תָּלוּי בְּמַחְשֶׁבֶת הָאָדָם, חֲשָׁבָן לַאֲכִילָה[43] דִּינָן כְּמַאֲכָל, חֲשָׁבָן לְעֵצִים דִּינָן כְּעֵצִים[44], וְיֶתֶר רַבֵּי פְרָטֶיהָ כֻּלָּן, מְבֹאָרִים בְּמַסֶּכְתָּא הַבְּנוּיָה עַל זֶה, וְהִיא מַסֶּכֶת שְׁבִיעִית[45].

**may not be made into a** — אֵין עוֹשִׂין מֵהֶן מְלוּגְמָא אוֹ רְטִיָּה **such as wheat, barley, and fruit, medicinal plaster nor into a salve.**[38] שֶׁנֶּאֱמַר בָּהֶן "לְאָכְלָה" — *Shemittah* produce may not be used in this manner, **for it is stated regarding [such produce]** (*Leviticus* 25:6): *The Sabbath produce of the land shall be yours to eat*, implying, to eat, but not to be used as medicine.[39] וְשֶׁאֵינוֹ מְיֻחָד לְמַאֲכַל אָדָם כְּגוֹן קוֹצִים וְדַרְדָּרִים — **Produce that is not reserved for human consumption,** but rather is typically reserved for animal fodder, **such as thorns and thistles,** עוֹשִׂין מֵהֶן מְלוּגְמָא לְאָדָם וְלֹא לַבְּהֵמָה — **may be made into a** medicinal **plaster for humans, but not for animals.**[40] וְשֶׁאֵינוֹ מְיֻחָד לְאָדָם וְלִבְהֵמָה — The law for produce **that is not** specifically **reserved for either humans or animals** (i.e., it is fit for either usage, but is not specifically designated for either of them),[41] כְּגוֹן פּוּאָה וְאֵזוֹב וְקוֹרָנִית — **such as madder,**[42] **hyssop, and oregano,** הֲרֵי הוּא תָּלוּי בְּמַחְשֶׁבֶת הָאָדָם — **depends on the person's intent;** חֲשָׁבָן לַאֲכִילָה דִּינָן כְּמַאֲכָל — **if he had intention to eat them,**[43] **their law is that of food,** and they may not be used as medicine. חֲשָׁבָן לְעֵצִים דִּינָן כְּעֵצִים — However, **if he had intention** to use **them as firewood, their law is that of firewood,** and they may be used without restriction.[44] וְיֶתֶר רַבֵּי פְרָטֶיהָ כֻּלָּן מְבֹאָרִים בְּמַסֶּכְתָּא — These laws, **and all of the many details of [***Shemittah***]** הַבְּנוּיָה עַל זֶה — **are set forth in the tractate that is based on this** mitzvah, וְהִיא מַסֶּכֶת שְׁבִיעִית — **which is Tractate *Sheviis*.**[45]

---

NOTES

38. I.e., different types of medicinal ointments and applications. [The word מְלוּגְמָא is a conjunction of the words מְלוֹא לוּגְמָא, *a cheek-full*, for such plasters were made by chewing a cheek-full of wheat or figs or the like, and then applying the masticated mass to one's wound (*Rambam, Commentary to Mishnah, Sheviis* 8:1).]

39. As noted above, usage of *Shemittah* produce is governed by laws derived from the phrase "to eat." Here this phrase is expounded to exclude all usages that – unlike eating – are needed by only a small percentage of the general populace. Since only a small percentage of people need to use such salves and ointments, such use is in violation of this verse (*Succah* 40b).

Other restrictions are also derived from the exclusionary phrase "to eat." One is that the produce is meant for eating and may therefore not be wasted (*Pesachim* 52b). Additionally, it may not be treated as merchandise and sold in a commercial fashion (*Avodah Zarah* 62a).

40. Such produce may be made into a medicinal salve, since the verse that excludes medicinal uses reads: וְהָיְתָה שַׁבַּת הָאָרֶץ לָכֶם לְאָכְלָה, *The Sabbath produce of the land shall be yours to eat*. The emphasis of "yours" indicates that only food that is "yours" – i.e., for human consumption – has this restriction. Animal fodder, however, may be used by humans for medicinal purposes (*Rav, Sheviis* 8:1). Nevertheless, such produce may not be used as medicine for animals. This is based on a different verse, which states (*Leviticus* 25:7): וְלִבְהֶמְתְּךָ וְלַחַיָּה אֲשֶׁר בְּאַרְצֶךָ תִּהְיֶה כָל תְּבוּאָתָהּ לֶאֱכֹל, *And for your animal and for the beast that is in your land shall all of its produce be to eat*, indicating that produce that is meant for animals and beasts to consume must be used as food for those animals (*"to eat"*), and not as medicine for them (*Rav* ibid.).

41. The designation of an item for human or for animal usage is determined by the general widespread use of that species (see *Rashi, Bava Kama* 102a ד״ה יצאו). However, some items have multiple uses, and it is normal to use them as either animal fodder, human food, or simply as fuel. Chinuch now addresses the law of such items.

42. Madder is a plant used to produce a red dye (*Rav, Sheviis* 5:4). [Our versions of the Mishnah from which Chinuch quotes this law (*Sheviis* 8:1) lists סִיאָה, *savory*, in place of פּוּאָה, *madder*. If our texts of Chinuch are accurate, Chinuch apparently had a different reading in that Mishnah. In the Amsterdam (5481) edition of Chinuch, the word פּוּאָה, *madder*, does not appear at all.]

43. That is, at the time that he picked the madder, hyssop, oregano, or the like, he intended to use it as food (see *Rashi, Bava Kamma* 102a ד״ה סתם עצים).

44. That is, if he picks them with the intent to use them as fuel, they then have the status of firewood, and are therefore not subject to the laws of *Shemittah* (*Sheviis* 8:1). [Firewood is not subject to the laws of *Shemittah*, because, as mentioned earlier (note 37), its benefit occurs only after the wood is consumed by the fire, i.e., at the point when it becomes charcoal. This is unlike eating, where the benefit occurs at the time of the item's consumption (*Succah* 40a).]

45. The laws of relinquishing ownership of the produce of one's land are codified in *Rambam, Hil. Shemittah*

## 145 ◻ MISHPATIM / MITZVAH 84: THE OBLIGATION REGARDING SHEMITTAH OF THE LAND

וְנוֹהֶגֶת בִּזְכָרִים וּנְקֵבוֹת[46] בְּאֶרֶץ יִשְׂרָאֵל בִּלְבַד, וּבִזְמַן שֶׁיִּשְׂרָאֵל שָׁם, שֶׁנֶּאֱמַר עָלֶיהָ (שם, שם, ב׳) כִּי תָבֹאוּ אֶל הָאָרֶץ[47], וּמִדְּרַבָּנָן אֲפִלּוּ בַּזְּמַן הַזֶּה בְּאֶרֶץ דַּוְקָא.[48]

### ☞ Applicability of the Mitzvah ☜

וְנוֹהֶגֶת בִּזְכָרִים וּנְקֵבוֹת בְּאֶרֶץ יִשְׂרָאֵל בִּלְבַד — [This mitzvah] applies to men and women,[46] but only in Eretz Yisrael, וּבִזְמַן שֶׁיִּשְׂרָאֵל שָׁם — and under Biblical law it applies only at the time that the majority of the Jews are living there, שֶׁנֶּאֱמַר עָלֶיהָ "כִּי תָבֹאוּ אֶל הָאָרֶץ" — as it is stated regarding [this mitzvah] (Leviticus 25:2): **When you come into the land** that I give you, the land shall observe a Sabbath rest for HASHEM.[47] וּמִדְּרַבָּנָן אֲפִלּוּ בַּזְּמַן הַזֶּה בְּאֶרֶץ דַּוְקָא — **Rabbinically, however, [this mitzvah] is applicable even nowadays** when the majority of Jews do not live in Eretz Yisrael, **but** it is applicable **only in the Land** (i.e., Eretz Yisrael).[48]

The original conquest of Eretz Yisrael by Joshua and the Jewish people (whom Chinuch will refer to as "those ascending from Egypt"),[49] which marked the beginning of the first commonwealth, also determined the area that was sanctified and thus subject to *Shemittah* restrictions. At the end of the first-commonwealth period, upon the exile of the Jews to Babylonia, this sanctification lapsed. The returnees from the Babylonian exile — under the leadership of Ezra at the start of the second commonwealth — reinstated the sanctification for the region under their control (*Rambam, Hil. Terumos* 1:5). That region, however, was smaller than the region that was originally sanctified by those ascending from Egypt. Consequently, the land of Eretz Yisrael proper is said to be divided into two distinct regions: (1) The larger area that had been controlled by those ascending from Egypt, and (2) the smaller area within that larger area that was controlled by those ascending from Babylonia. These areas have distinct laws with regard to *Shemittah* observance, as Chinuch now explains:

---

NOTES

*VeYovel* 4:34. More broadly, the other laws of *Shemittah* vis-à-vis one's land and produce are codified in *Rambam* ibid. Chapters 1-8.

46. As a general rule, women are not obligated in מִצְוֹת עֲשֵׂה שֶׁהַזְּמַן גְּרָמָא, time-specific mitzvah obligations (see General Introduction). Why then would women be obligated in this mitzvah-obligation which, by virtue of it occurring specifically in the seventh year, is ostensibly time-specific? Some explain that due to the fact that the produce of *Shemittah* retains it sanctity and restrictions even after the *Shemittah* year ends, this mitzvah may in fact not be considered time-specific (see *Minchas Chinuch* §1). Others suggest a resolution based on Chinuch's opinion (see Mitzvah 321 and *Mishneh LaMelech* and *Minchas Chinuch* to Mitzvah 297; cf. *Tosafos, Kiddushin* 34a ד"ה מעקה) that any mitzvah-obligation that has an associated mitzvah-prohibition applies to women too; for, since they are bound by the prohibition, they are bound by the mitzvah obligation as well. The current mitzvah is subject to the associated prohibitions against harvest (Mitzvos 328 and 329), and therefore, based on Chinuch's rule, applies to women as well (*Me'il HaEphod* §5; see also *Minchas Chinuch* 326:1). [For another explanation of why this mitzvah applies to women, see *Minchas Chinuch* here §1 ד"ה ולכאורה; see also *Minchas Yitzchak* §11.]

47. Chinuch seems to mean to infer from the verse that the laws of *Shemittah* pertaining to the land are applicable only when the Jewish people "come into" (i.e., reside in) Eretz Yisrael. Thus, when they are exiled from the Land, this mitzvah ceases to apply on the Biblical level. In Mitzvah 330, however, Chinuch provides a different source for this law, as explained in the following note.

48. In Mitzvah 330, Chinuch (quoting *Rambam, Hil. Shemittah VeYovel* 10:8-9) explains that the laws of *Shemittah* are Biblically in effect only as long as the laws of *Yovel* (Jubilee) are in effect (see *Yerushalmi Gittin* 4:3 [21b], quoted in *Rashi, Gittin* 36a ד"ה בשביעית; cf. *Kesef Mishneh, Hil. Shemittah VeYovel* 4:25). *Yovel* was in effect only when each tribe was settled in its apportioned land, but once Sennacherib exiled the tribes of Reuben, Gad, and part of Manasseh toward the end of the First Temple period, *Yovel* ceased to be in effect. Thus, throughout the Second Temple period, when only a minority of Jews were living in Eretz Yisrael, *Yovel* was not in effect and therefore *Shemittah* too remained a Rabbinic obligation (*Minchas Chinuch* §2).

There is an opinion that *Shemittah* is not contingent on the observance of *Yovel* and that it remains a Biblical obligation even nowadays (see *Sifra, Parashas Behar* 2:2; *Ittur* ד"ה פרוזבול; *Rambam, Hil. Shemittah VeYovel* 4:25 according to *Kesef Mishneh*; cf. *Mahari Korkos* 9:2 and *Chazon Ish* 3:8). Most authorities, however, agree with Chinuch that the observance of *Shemittah* is presently only Rabbinically mandated (*Tur* and *Beis Yosef, Yoreh Deah* 331:19[a]; *Gra, Yoreh Deah* 331:6; *Pe'as HaShulchan, Beis Yisrael* 23:23; *Chazon Ish* loc. cit.).

49. Those who come into Eretz Yisrael are always referred to as "ascending," in that Eretz Yisrael is the pinnacle of the world (*Kiddushin* 69a) in a spiritual sense (*Maharal* there).

וְכָל מָקוֹם שֶׁהֶחֱזִיקוּ בּוֹ עוֹלֵי בָבֶל עַד כְּזִיב וְלֹא כְּזִיב בִּכְלָל,[50] אָסוּר בַּעֲבוֹדָה, וְכָל הַסְּפִיחִין הַצּוֹמְחִין שָׁם אֲסוּרִין בַּאֲכִילָה,[51] כִּי הֵם קִדְּשׁוּ הַמְּקוֹמוֹת שֶׁהֶחֱזִיקוּ בָּהֶן לְעוֹלָם.[52] וְהַמְּקוֹמוֹת שֶׁהֶחֱזִיקוּ בָּהֶן כְּבָר עוֹלֵי מִצְרַיִם וְלֹא עוֹלֵי בָבֶל שֶׁהֵן מִכְּזִיב וְעַד הַנָּהָר[53] וְעַד אֲמָנָה,[54]

---

וְכָל מָקוֹם שֶׁהֶחֱזִיקוּ בּוֹ עוֹלֵי בָבֶל עַד כְּזִיב וְלֹא כְּזִיב בִּכְלָל — **Any place that those ascending from Babylonia took possession of** upon their return from the Babylonian exile, extending **up to Keziv,**[50] **but not including Keziv,** אָסוּר בַּעֲבוֹדָה — **are** all included in the **prohibition to work** the land. וְכָל הַסְּפִיחִין הַצּוֹמְחִין שָׁם אֲסוּרִין בַּאֲכִילָה — **All aftergrowth that sprouts there is prohibited for consumption,**[51] כִּי הֵם קִדְּשׁוּ הַמְּקוֹמוֹת שֶׁהֶחֱזִיקוּ בָּהֶן לְעוֹלָם — **for [those who returned from Babylonia] sanctified those places of which they took possession, for all time** into the future.[52] וְהַמְּקוֹמוֹת שֶׁהֶחֱזִיקוּ בָּהֶן כְּבָר עוֹלֵי מִצְרַיִם וְלֹא עוֹלֵי בָבֶל — **Those places that were taken into possession by those ascending from Egypt, but not** by **those ascending from Babylonia,** שֶׁהֵן מִכְּזִיב וְעַד הַנָּהָר וְעַד אֲמָנָה — **which are from Keziv to the river**[53] **and until Amanah,**[54]

---

## NOTES

50. Many assume Keziv to be a city that marked the northwest corner of the second commonwealth (*Kaftor VaFerach*, quoted in *Tos. Yom Tov, Sheviis* 6:1; *Shenos Eliyahu* there; evident from *Rambam, Hil. Terumos* 1:8), and associate it with the modern day אַכְזִיב, *Achzib* (see *Joshua* 19:29; *Tiferes Yisrael, Sheviis* 6:1), which is some 7½ miles (13½ km.) north of Acco (Acre). Others, however, assume that Keziv marked the northeast boundary of the second commonwealth (*Rash* and *Rav* to *Sheviis* 6:1). As Chinuch notes, Keziv itself remained outside the boundaries of the land controlled and sanctified by Ezra and those who ascended from Babylonia (*Rambam, Hil. Terumos* 1:8).

51. "Aftergrowth" refers to produce, such as grains and vegetables, that were not cultivated in *Shemittah*, but nevertheless sprouted from fallen seeds or from old roots. On a Biblical level, such produce may be consumed during *Shemittah*. However, the Sages feared that unscrupulous individuals would plant their fields during *Shemittah* and claim that the produce was actually aftergrowth. As such, they forbade the consumption of such produce (see Mitzvah 328; *Rambam, Hil. Shemittah VeYovel* 4:1-2). This Rabbinic prohibition was extended only to those areas that were controlled by those ascending from Babylonia, but (as Chinuch will note) not to the areas beyond, even if they were part of the original conquest of Joshua (based on *Mishnah, Sheviis* 6:1, as per *Rambam* ibid. 4:26; cf. *Rav* and *Rash*).

52. As opposed to the original conquest in the time of Joshua, where the resulting sanctification lapsed with the exile of the Jewish people (*Chullin* 6b, et al.), the sanctification by Ezra at the beginning of the second commonwealth never lapsed. The latter sanctification was on a higher level insofar as the first one simply came about through conquest, without a specific declaration, while the second sanctification was done via an explicit verbal declaration (*Rambam, Hil. Terumos* 1:5 with *Radvaz*; cf. *Kesef Mishneh* to *Hil. Beis HaBechirah* 6:16).

53. The river referred to is נַחַל מִצְרַיִם, the *Brook of Egypt* (*Rambam, Hil. Terumos* 1:8), which is a river on the southwest border of Eretz Yisrael (see *Joshua* 15:4), which *Radvaz* (ibid. 1:7) identifies with Wadi-El-Arish. Others maintain that it refers to the Nile (see *Rashi, Joshua* 13:3, and *Targum Yonasan, Bamidbar* 34:5). See *Derech Emunah, Tziyun HaHalachah, Terumos* 1:160, for further discussion.

Alternatively, according to those who maintain that Keziv was a city in the northeast of Eretz Yisrael (see note 50), the river referred to is one in that direction, possibly the Pharpar or Phige rivers near Damascus (*Tevuas HaAretz; Admas Kodesh*) or Wadi-al-Kasumiah in Lebanon (*Maharit*, Vol. I, 84).

54. Amanah is another name for הֹר הָהָר, *Mount Hor* (see *Numbers* 34:7), which is at the northwest corner of Eretz Yisrael (*Rashi* ad loc.; *Rav, Sheviis* 6:1; see *Rash* there who notes that this is not the Mount Hor where Aaron died, which is in the south of Eretz Yisrael; see, however, *Targum Yonasan, Numbers* 20:22 and 34:7-8). The precise location of this mountain is uncertain, with some placing it near the ancient city of Antioch (see *Targum Yerushalmi, Numbers* 34:7-8) while others identify it as being near Beirut (see *HaAretz Lig'vuloseha*, p. 10, printed as an appendix to *Ir HaKodesh VeHaMikdash* Vol. 5).

Assuming Keziv is a city marking the northwest corner of the second commonwealth, "from Keziv to the river and until Amanah" would then be a line that delineates the western boundary of Eretz Yisrael based on the conquest of those ascending from Babylonia. That is, if we were to draw a line from the river (in the south) through Keziv (in the middle) all the way up until Amanah (in the north), the coastal land to the west of that line would fall outside the boundaries of the second commonwealth. However, assuming Keziv is a city marking the northeast corner of the second commonwealth, "from Keziv to the river and until Amanah" refers to a corridor from Keziv eastward to the river and from Keziv westward to Amanah (see *Rav, Challah* 4:8; cf. *Rav, Sheviis* 6:1 and *Tos. Yom Tov* there).

אַף עַל פִּי שֶׁהֵן אֲסוּרִין הַיּוֹם מִדְּרַבָּנָן בַּעֲבוֹדָה בַּשְּׁבִיעִית, שֶׁהֶחְמִירוּ בָּהֶן, הַסְּפִיחִין שֶׁצּוֹמְחִים שָׁם מֻתָּרִין בַּאֲכִילָה אַחַר שֶׁלֹּא נִתְקַדֵּשׁ בְּעוֹלֵי בָּבֶל.[55] וּמִן הַנָּהָר וַאֲמָנָה וְהָלְאָה מֻתָּר בַּעֲבוֹדָה.[56] סוּרְיָא, וְהוּא מִן הַמְּקוֹמוֹת שֶׁכָּבַשׁ דָּוִד קֹדֶם שֶׁנִּכְבְּשָׁה אֶרֶץ יִשְׂרָאֵל כֻּלָּהּ, וְזֶהוּ הַנִּקְרָא לְרַבּוֹתֵינוּ זִכְרוֹנָם לִבְרָכָה כִּבּוּשׁ יָחִיד,[57] וְהָאָרֶץ הַזֹּאת הִיא כְּנֶגֶד אֲרַם נַהֲרַיִם[58] וַאֲרַם צוֹבָא[59] כָּל יַד פְּרָת עַד בָּבֶל, כְּגוֹן דַּמֶּשֶׂק וְאַחְלָב[60] וְחָרָן וּמְקוֹמוֹת אֲחֵרִים סְמוּכִין לְאֵלּוּ, אַף עַל פִּי שֶׁאֵין שְׁבִיעִית נוֹהֶגֶת בָּהֶן מִן הַתּוֹרָה, גָּזְרוּ עֲלֵיהֶן שֶׁיִּהְיוּ אוֹתָן מְקוֹמוֹת אֲסוּרִין בַּעֲבוֹדָה כְּאֶרֶץ יִשְׂרָאֵל.[61] אֲבָל עַמּוֹן וּמוֹאָב וּמִצְרַיִם וְשִׁנְעָר,[62]

אַף עַל פִּי שֶׁהֵן אֲסוּרִין הַיּוֹם מִדְּרַבָּנָן בַּעֲבוֹדָה בַּשְּׁבִיעִית — **even though they are Rabbinically forbidden nowadays** to be **worked in the seventh** year, שֶׁהֶחְמִירוּ בָּהֶן — **for [the Sages] were stringent with regard to them** by forbidding such work, הַסְּפִיחִין שֶׁצּוֹמְחִים שָׁם מֻתָּרִין בַּאֲכִילָה — nevertheless, **the aftergrowth that sprouts there is permitted for consumption,** אַחַר שֶׁלֹּא נִתְקַדֵּשׁ בְּעוֹלֵי בָּבֶל — **insofar as [those areas] were not sanctified by those ascending from Babylonia.**[55] וּמִן הַנָּהָר וַאֲמָנָה וְהָלְאָה מֻתָּר בַּעֲבוֹדָה — **Those places that are from the river and Amanah and beyond** were never sanctified, and **are permitted to be worked.**[56]

Having noted that the areas beyond the borders of Eretz Yisrael proper are not subject to the laws of *Shemittah*, Chinuch points out that there is in fact one exception:

סוּרְיָא — **As for the region of Suria,** וְהוּא מִן הַמְּקוֹמוֹת שֶׁכָּבַשׁ דָּוִד קֹדֶם שֶׁנִּכְבְּשָׁה אֶרֶץ יִשְׂרָאֵל כֻּלָּהּ — **which is among the areas conquered by** King **David before all of Eretz Yisrael had been conquered,** וְזֶהוּ הַנִּקְרָא לְרַבּוֹתֵינוּ זִכְרוֹנָם לִבְרָכָה כִּבּוּשׁ יָחִיד — **which our Sages, of blessed memory, call an "individual conquest,"** such land is not considered part of the borders of Eretz Yisrael proper.[57] וְהָאָרֶץ הַזֹּאת הִיא כְּנֶגֶד אֲרַם נַהֲרַיִם וַאֲרַם צוֹבָא כָּל יַד פְּרָת עַד בָּבֶל — **This land is inclusive of Aram Naharayim**[58] **and Aram Tzova,**[59] **along the entire bank of the Euphrates until Babylonia,** כְּגוֹן דַּמֶּשֶׂק וְאַחְלָב וְחָרָן וּמְקוֹמוֹת אֲחֵרִים סְמוּכִין לְאֵלּוּ — including areas **such as Damascus, Halab,**[60] **Haran, and other areas near these;** אַף עַל פִּי שֶׁאֵין שְׁבִיעִית נוֹהֶגֶת בָּהֶן מִן הַתּוֹרָה — **even though** the laws of *Shemittah* **do not apply to them Biblically,** גָּזְרוּ עֲלֵיהֶן שֶׁיִּהְיוּ אוֹתָן מְקוֹמוֹת אֲסוּרִין בַּעֲבוֹדָה כְּאֶרֶץ יִשְׂרָאֵל — **[our Sages] nevertheless decreed regarding [the areas mentioned], that those places are forbidden to be worked, similar to** the lands in **Eretz Yisrael.**[61] אֲבָל עַמּוֹן וּמוֹאָב וּמִצְרַיִם וְשִׁנְעָר — **However, Ammon, Moab, Egypt, and Shinar,**[62]

## NOTES

55. As already noted, with the exile at the end of the first commonwealth, the sanctification of the land lapsed. Since that sanctification was never reinstated for the regions beyond the area controlled by those ascending from Babylonia, technically speaking there should be no *Shemittah* restrictions in those areas altogether. Nevertheless, the Sages were stringent and applied all the *Shemittah* restrictions to those regions, with the exception of the Rabbinic strictures on aftergrowth.

56. That is, areas south of the river and north of Amanah were never part of even the first commonwealth, and therefore are not subject to any agricultural *Shemittah* restrictions.

57. Only lands conquered and annexed to Eretz Yisrael after all the land of Eretz Yisrael proper (i.e., those areas previously belonging to the seven Canaanite nations) was fully conquered, were able to attain the full status of Eretz Yisrael. Suria, however, was conquered by King David before all of Eretz Yisrael proper had been conquered, and it was therefore not sanctified (*Rambam, Hil. Terumos* 1:3, based on *Sifrei, Parashas Eikev* §15; see *Derech Emunah* there, *Beur HaHalachah* ד"ה הארצות for other views). Thus, under Biblical law, *Shemittah* does not apply in Suria. Nevertheless, the Sages imposed *Shemittah* restrictions, as Chinuch will explain shortly.

58. Generally taken to be the northern part of Syria, east of the Euphrates. [This passage in Chinuch is based on *Rambam, Hil. Terumos* 1:9.]

59. This is a region in northern Syria, west of the Euphrates, in the area of Aleppo (see next note).

60. *Tziyun HaHalachah, Hil. Terumos* 1:53. Also known as Aleppo.

61. They did so out of concern that if work were permitted in Suria, people would abandon Eretz Yisrael proper to settle there so as to avoid the *Shemittah* restrictions (*Rambam, Hil. Shemittah VeYovel* 4:27).

62. Ammon and Moab are regions to the east of the Jordan River, in modern-day Jordan. Egypt is located to the south and west of Eretz Yisrael. Shinar is Babylonia, and is in the northeast of Eretz Yisrael in the area of modern-day Iraq.

[According to some, the specific area of Ammon and

## משפטים / מצוה פד: מצות שמטת קרקעות

אַף עַל פִּי שֶׁהֵן חַיָּבִין בְּמַעֲשֵׂר, אֵין שְׁבִיעִית נוֹהֶגֶת בָּהֶן[63], וְכָל שֶׁכֵּן שֶׁאֵין נוֹהֶגֶת בִּשְׁאָר חוּצָה לָאָרֶץ.

וְעוֹבֵר עָלֶיהָ וְנָעַל כַּרְמוֹ אוֹ שָׂדֵהוּ בַּשְּׁבִיעִית, אוֹ אָסַף כָּל פֵּרוֹתָיו לְבֵיתוֹ בִּזְמַן שֶׁיִּשְׂרָאֵל עַל אַדְמָתָן, בִּטֵּל עֲשֵׂה[64]. וּמִכָּל מָקוֹם מֻתָּר לֶאֱסֹף מֵהֶן מְעַט מְעַט אֶל הַבַּיִת וְלֶאֱכֹל, וּבִלְבַד שֶׁתְּהֵא יַד הַכֹּל שָׁוָה בָּהֶן כְּאִלּוּ אֵין לַקַּרְקַע בְּעָלִים יְדוּעִים[65].

---

אַף עַל פִּי שֶׁהֵן חַיָּבִין בְּמַעֲשֵׂר — **even though they are subject to tithing** (i.e., produce that grows there must be tithed), אֵין שְׁבִיעִית נוֹהֶגֶת בָּהֶן — nevertheless, the laws of **the seventh year do not apply to [those regions]**.[63] וְכָל שֶׁכֵּן שֶׁאֵין נוֹהֶגֶת בִּשְׁאָר חוּצָה לָאָרֶץ — **All the more so,** the laws of the seventh year **do not apply to other areas outside of the Land of Israel** that are not even subject to the laws of tithing.

Having described the areas where the laws of *Shemittah* apply, Chinuch addresses the consequences of a transgression:

וְעוֹבֵר עָלֶיהָ וְנָעַל כַּרְמוֹ אוֹ שָׂדֵהוּ בַּשְּׁבִיעִית — **One who transgresses [this mitzvah] and locks his vineyard or field in the seventh** year, אוֹ אָסַף כָּל פֵּרוֹתָיו לְבֵיתוֹ — **or gathers all of its produce into his home** בִּזְמַן שֶׁיִּשְׂרָאֵל עַל אַדְמָתָן — **during the times when the Jews are** dwelling in **their land** (i.e., when the majority of Jews are living in Eretz Yisrael, as above), בִּטֵּל עֲשֵׂה — **has violated a** mitzvah-**obligation**.[64] וּמִכָּל מָקוֹם מֻתָּר לֶאֱסֹף מֵהֶן מְעַט מְעַט אֶל הַבַּיִת וְלֶאֱכֹל — **Nevertheless,** although one may not harvest the produce of his field in the normal manner during *Shemittah*, **one may gather** produce **into his home in small quantities and eat it,** וּבִלְבַד שֶׁתְּהֵא יַד הַכֹּל שָׁוָה בָּהֶן — **as long as all** others **share equal access to [the field's produce],** כְּאִלּוּ אֵין לַקַּרְקַע בְּעָלִים יְדוּעִים — **as though the land has no known owners.**[65]

---

### NOTES

Moab discussed here is the area of the Trans-Jordan opposite the northern area of Eretz Yisrael that had been conquered by Sichon and Og, and that was later taken by the Jews under the leadership of Moses when they defeated Sichon and Og (*Rashi, Chagigah* 3b; *Rambam Commentary, Yadayim* 4:3 ד״ה נמנו). Others argue that the land of Sichon and Og is bound by the same *Shemittah* restrictions as the rest of the lands conquered by those ascending from Egypt, and therefore define Ammon and Moab as the lands that were retained by those nations, to the south of the lands taken by Sichon and Og (*Rash, Rosh,* and *Rav* to *Yadayim* 4:3; see also *Mishneh LaMelech, Hil. Shemittah VeYovel* 4:27).]

63. The tithing requirement for Shinar was an ancient Rabbinic obligation instituted by the prophets (*Mishnah, Yadayim* 4:3), due to its proximity to Eretz Yisrael and the large amount of traffic to and from Shinar (*Rambam, Hil. Terumos* 1:1). The tithing obligation for the other lands mentioned by Chinuch was instituted somewhat later, in the era of the *Anshei Knesses HaGedolah* [Men of the Great Assembly] (*Rashi, Chagigah* 3b ד״ה פשוט; cf. *Rav* to *Yadayim* ibid.), when Jews began settling there (*Rambam* ibid. with *Radvaz*). The proximity of these lands to Eretz Yisrael and the major flow of traffic between them caused the prophets (and later the Sages) to fear that if no tithing requirements were imposed, people would come to err and be lenient with tithing in Eretz Yisrael itself (*Mahari Korkos* ibid., end of 1:5). However, they never instituted the laws of *Shemittah* in these lands (*Rambam, Hil. Shemittah VeYovel* 4:27).

64. This holds true even if he were to bar entry and harvest the produce with the intention to give it all away to the poor (*Mechilta, Mishpatim* §20). In truth, one should technically be required to break down the wall around his field for the duration of *Shemittah* to allow for uninhibited access. Nevertheless [since this can result in undue damage to the trees (*Zayis Raanan*)], the Sages decreed that one need not go that far (*Mechilta* ibid. as per *Kesef Mishneh, Hil. Shemittah VeYovel* 4:24).

65. The verse states (*Leviticus* 25:6): וְהָיְתָה שַׁבַּת הָאָרֶץ לָכֶם לְאָכְלָה לְךָ וּלְעַבְדְּךָ וְלַאֲמָתֶךָ וְלִשְׂכִירְךָ וּלְתוֹשָׁבְךָ הַגָּרִים עִמָּךְ, *The Sabbath produce of the land shall be yours to eat, for you, for your slave, and for your maidservant; and for your laborer and for your resident who dwell with you,* which clearly allows for the consumption of *Shemittah* produce. At the same time, the Torah restricts one's right to harvest the field, stating (ibid. v. 5): אֵת סְפִיחַ קְצִירְךָ לֹא תִקְצוֹר וְאֶת עִנְּבֵי נְזִירֶךָ לֹא תִבְצֹר, *The aftergrowth of your harvest you shall not reap and the grapes you had set aside for yourself you shall not pick.* Our Sages (*Sifra*) explain that this teaches that while consumption of the produce is permitted, we may not harvest nor reap in the normal fashion — such as harvesting the entire field and creating large piles, or picking the grapes and putting them in the large winepresses. Such a full-scale harvest would in effect be a flagrant exhibition of one's personal ownership (see Mitzvos 328 and 329; *Mishnah, Sheviis* 8:6 with *Commentary of Rambam*; *Rambam, Hil. Shemittah VeYovel* 4:1,22; cf. *Rash, Sheviis* ibid.).

## MISHPATIM / MITZVAH 84: THE OBLIGATION REGARDING SHEMITTAH OF THE LAND

**⊷§ Insight: Relinquishment of Ownership: Owner's Obligation or Divine Edict?**

*Minchas Chinuch* (§1) poses a fundamental question regarding the requirement to relinquish ownership of the land, expressed in the verse (*Exodus* 23:11): *And in the seventh [year], you shall release it.* Does this mean that the owner is commanded to actively relinquish ownership of his field's produce during *Shemittah* by *declaring* it ownerless (*hefker*), and it is only due to the owner's declaration that the produce is rendered *hefker*? Or, does it mean that the produce is automatically deemed *hefker* on the basis of a Divine edict (אַפְקַעְתָּא דְמַלְכָּא, *made ownerless by the King*), even without the owner's declaration, and what the Torah requires of the owner is to refrain from any *display* of ownership (such as locking his field or harvesting the produce as usual)?

The practical difference emerges in the case of an owner who does not relinquish ownership. If the mitzvah requires the owner to declare his produce ownerless, then it is presumable that until he fulfills the mitzvah, he retains possession of the produce; thus, if another person takes produce from the field of one who did not relinquish ownership, he will be stealing. If, on the other hand, the produce automatically becomes ownerless by Divine edict, one who takes the produce of such a field is not stealing, for it is in fact *hefker* even though the owner of the field neglects to observe the mitzvah of *Shemittah*.

There is another practical difference with regard to the tithing obligation. The halachah is that *Shemittah* produce is exempt from all tithing obligations, and may therefore be eaten without the usual tithing of *terumos* and *maasaros* (*Rambam, Hil. Matnos Aniyim* 6:5). This exemption, explains *Minchas Chinuch*, is based on the fact that *hefker* produce is not subject to tithing (see *Rosh Hashanah* 15a; *Rambam* ibid.). Now, if the owner is required to declare his produce ownerless, then if he fails to do so the produce will require tithing, as it is not *hefker*! If, however, *Shemittah* produce becomes *hefker* by Divine edict, then such produce is exempt from tithing even though the owner did not explicitly relinquish ownership.

*Minchas Chinuch* writes that it subsequently came to his attention that this question is actually the subject of a dispute between *R' Yosef Caro* (*Beis Yosef*) and *R' Yosef Trani* (*Maharit*). To understand this dispute, some background information is necessary: *R' Yosef Caro* and *R' Moshe Trani* (*Mabit*), who was the father of *Maharit*, disputed the status of the land of a non-Jew in Eretz Yisrael with respect to *Shemittah* (cited in *Avkas Rocheil* §22-25; *Teshuvos Maharit* I, 42). *Mabit* held produce of such land to be subject to the laws of *Shemittah*, and exempt from the laws of tithing, while *R' Yosef Caro* held the opposite, exempting the produce from the laws of *Shemittah* and requiring them to be tithed (see *Beis Yosef, Yoreh Deah* 331:9[a] ד"ה ואין בה תרומות ומעשרות for an additional condition). In his correspondence regarding this matter (*Avkas Rocheil* §24 ד"ה ועתה ראיתי, *Teshuvos Maharit* §42 ד"ה ואני), *R' Yosef Caro* suggests that the reason that produce of a non-Jew is subject to tithing is because, unlike the produce of a Jew, a non-Jew's produce does not become ownerless during *Shemittah* (for *Shemittah* does not apply to non-Jews), and it therefore lacks the exemption that applies to produce of Jews. *R' Yosef Caro* then goes further to suggest that perhaps even the produce of a Jew who unlawfully locked his field would also be subject to tithing during *Shemittah*. *Maharit* (ibid. §43 ד"ה ראשונה), responding on behalf of his father (*Mabit*), specifically attacks the notion that the *Shemittah* produce of a Jew that was not properly relinquished would be subject to tithing, and brings various proofs from *Talmud Bavli, Yerushalmi, Mechilta,* and *Sifrei,* that the *hefker* status of produce during *Shemittah* is not contingent on any act of the owner but takes effect automatically. One such proof is from *Bava Metzia* (39a), where the term אַפְקַעְתָּא דְמַלְכָּא, *made ownerless by the King* (i.e., God), is used in description of *Shemittah* produce! We thus see that whether this mitzvah demands active relinquishment of ownership is the subject of debate between *Beis Yosef* and *Maharit*.

There are those, however, who argue that *R' Yosef Caro* certainly agrees that the relinquishment of ownership occurs on its own, as is evident from various Tannaic and Talmudic sources. Indeed, in his dialogue with *Mabit* (*Avkas Rocheil* §24 ד"ה ועתה ראיתי, *Teshuvos Maharit* §42 ד"ה ואני), *R' Yosef Caro* himself writes that God made the produce of *Shemittah* ownerless [רַחֲמָנָא אַפְקְרָא]! Thus, *Beis Yosef* apparently concedes that even if the owner were to lock the field, the produce would remain *hefker* and would be free to be taken by all. His suggestion that a Jew's locked field may be subject to tithing in *Shemittah*, however, is based on the premise that to be exempt from tithing, the produce must *in actuality* be available for all to take. Thus, as long as the owner does not allow the public access to

the produce, it may be subject to tithing, despite the fact that it is actually *hefker* (see *Toras HaAretz* 8:18-24; *Mitzvas HaMelech, Asei* 134, Ch. 1, 3:3).

The question of whether produce grown on land of non-Jews in Eretz Yisrael is subject to the laws of *Shemittah* has triggered much discussion among later authorities. This matter is discussed at length by *Pe'as HaShulchan* (end of §23), who rules such produce exempt from the *Shemittah* laws (in accordance with the view of *Beis Yosef*), and *Chazon Ish* (*Sheviis,* end of §20), who rules such produce subject to the *Shemittah* laws (in accordance with the view of *Mabit*). The prevailing custom in Jerusalem has been in accord with the lenient view, but those who follow the rulings of the *Chazon Ish* abide by the stringent view.

## MISHPATIM / MITZVAH 85: THE OBLIGATION TO REST ON THE SABBATH

### מִצְוָה פה: מִצְוַת שְׁבִיתָה בְּשַׁבָּת

לִשְׁבֹּת מִמְּלָאכָה בְּיוֹם הַשַּׁבָּת[1], שֶׁנֶּאֱמַר (שמות כ״ג, י״ב) וּבַיּוֹם הַשְּׁבִיעִי תִּשְׁבֹּת[2].
כָּל עִנְיָנָהּ כָּתוּב לְמַעְלָה בַּלָּאו הַבָּא עַל זֶה[3].
וְנִכְפְּלָה מִצְוַת שַׁבָּת עַד י״ב פְּעָמִים[4].

## Mitzvah 85
## The Obligation to Rest on the Sabbath

שֵׁשֶׁת יָמִים תַּעֲשֶׂה מַעֲשֶׂיךָ וּבַיּוֹם הַשְּׁבִיעִי תִּשְׁבֹּת לְמַעַן יָנוּחַ שׁוֹרְךָ וַחֲמֹרֶךָ וְיִנָּפֵשׁ בֶּן אֲמָתְךָ וְהַגֵּר

*Six days shall you perform your activities, and on the seventh day you shall rest, so that your ox and donkey may rest, and your maidservant's son and the resident may be refreshed (Exodus 23:12).*

לִשְׁבֹּת מִמְּלָאכָה בְּיוֹם הַשַּׁבָּת — **We are commanded to desist from** performing ***melachah***[1] **on the Sabbath day,** שֶׁנֶּאֱמַר — **as it is stated** (Exodus 23:12): "וּבַיּוֹם הַשְּׁבִיעִי תִּשְׁבֹּת" — **and on the seventh day you shall rest.**[2]

### Laws of the Mitzvah

כָּל עִנְיָנָהּ — **All the particulars of [this mitzvah]** כָּתוּב לְמַעְלָה בַּלָּאו הַבָּא עַל זֶה — **are written above, in the prohibition that pertains to this** topic (Mitzvah 32).[3]
וְנִכְפְּלָה מִצְוַת שַׁבָּת עַד י״ב פְּעָמִים — **The mitzvah of the Sabbath is repeated** in the Torah **no less than twelve times.**[4]

---

### NOTES

1. *Melachah* is often translated as "work" or "labor," but this term actually refers to any of 39 specific types of activity prohibited on the Sabbath. For a list of the 39 Biblically prohibited *avos melachah* [i.e., primary categories of *melachah*], see above, Mitzvah 32 (the prohibition to perform *melachah* on the Sabbath), in Vol. I, p. 276.

2. Furthermore, as indicated in the final words of the verse, לְמַעַן יָנוּחַ שׁוֹרְךָ וַחֲמֹרֶךָ וְיִנָּפֵשׁ בֶּן אֲמָתְךָ וְהַגֵּר, *so that your ox and donkey may rest, and your maidservant's son and the resident may be refreshed,* this mitzvah includes an obligation to have one's animals and Canaanite slaves desist from *melachah* on the Sabbath (*Rambam, Sefer HaMitzvos, Asei* 154). For a thorough discussion of this subject, see Mitzvah 32, with notes 1-21.

3. That is, the mitzvah-obligation to "rest" is violated by performing *melachah*. Thus, one who performs *melachah* on the Sabbath has transgressed both the mitzvah-prohibition not to perform *melachah* (Mitzvah 32) and the mitzvah-obligation to rest (this mitzvah). [As Chinuch explained in Mitzvah 32 (at note 37), violation of this mitzvah-prohibition is punishable by execution. Although the violation of a mitzvah-*obligation* is not punishable in *beis din*, the extra exhortation of a mitzvah-obligation lends additional severity to the transgression (see *Shabbos* 114b; *Chullin* 66b et al.; see further, *Minchas Chinuch* §1).]

There are certain additional activities that are not considered *"melachos,"* and do not carry the penalty of execution, but are Biblically prohibited nonetheless. Included in this category are the act of *mechameir* (driving an animal forward as it performs a *melachah*, e.g., plowing; see Mitzvah 32) and going beyond the *techum* (the Sabbath boundary; see Mitzvah 24). It is a matter of dispute among the Rishonim whether one who desecrates the Sabbath by performing one of these non-*melachah* actions has also transgressed the mitzvah-obligation to "rest," or the obligation to rest is transgressed only through the performance of *melachah*. See *Rashba, Yevamos* 6a ד״ה וניגמר and *Tosafos* there ד״ה ניגמר; see also *Minchas Chinuch* §2 and above, 24:1. For an entirely different understanding of this mitzvah-obligation, see the Insight.

4. Literally, *until twelve times*. In addition to our verse, the commandment regarding the Sabbath is found in the following eleven verses in the Torah: (1) *Exodus* 31:13, (2) 31:14, (3) 31:15, (4) 31:16, (5) 34:21, (6) 35:2; (7) *Leviticus* 19:3, (8) 19:30, (9) 23:3, (10) 26:2; (11) *Deuteronomy* 5:12. [Nevertheless, as *Rambam* (*Sefer HaMitzvos, Shoresh* 9, p. 157, Frankel ed.) points out, this certainly does not mean that the mitzvah is counted twelve times in the count of 613 mitzvos, for repetitions of a mitzvah are not counted separately unless they

### NOTES

broaden its application. Rather, the repeated mention of the Sabbath commandment indicates its significance.]

Sabbath is also mentioned in a number of other places aside from those listed above (see *Exodus* 16:23, 29). Apparently, those places are not included in this list, because those verses are *descriptive* of the Sabbath, rather than commandments regarding the Sabbath (see *Rambam* ibid.).

As Chinuch wrote above, Mitzvah 32, the prohibition to perform *melachah* on the Sabbath applies in all locations and times. The same holds true with regard to this mitzvah-obligation. As for women, they are included in the prohibition to perform *melachah* on the Sabbath, for women are generally subject to *all* mitzvah-prohibitions (see General Introduction, VI). Now, one might suppose that women are not subject to the mitzvah-obligation to "rest" on the Sabbath, since women are generally exempt from time-specific mitzvah-obligations (see General Introduction ibid.). However, with regard to the corresponding mitzvah-obligation of resting from *melachah* on Yom Tov (Mitzvah 321), Chinuch writes that women are included [because the mitzvah-obligation to rest is related to the mitzvah-prohibition of performing *melachah*, as it pertains to the same activities]. *Minchas Chinuch* (§2) asserts that the same applies here, and that women are indeed subject to the mitzvah-obligation of resting from *melachah* on the Sabbath (see also *Sefer HaMitzvos HaKatzar* [Chofetz Chaim] *Asei* 20, and *Minchah Chadashah*). [See further in *Minchas Chinuch* with regard to the opinion of *Tosafos* regarding this matter; see also *Minchas Soless* ד"ה והנה בחינוך; and *Minchas Chinuch* below, 297:3.]

---

**✑ Insight: On the Seventh Day You Shall Rest**

This mitzvah instructs us to *rest* on the Sabbath. The term *rest*, however, is obscure. From which activities must we rest? Chinuch interprets *rest*, in this context, as desisting from performing *melachah*. This refers to the group of activities encompassed by the prohibition to perform *melachah* on the Sabbath (Mitzvah 32; see above, note 1). It emerges that there are both a mitzvah-prohibition (Mitzvah 32) and a mitzvah-obligation (this mitzvah) requiring one to abstain from performing *melachah* on the Sabbath, and one fulfills the *obligation* to rest by refraining from any activity already forbidden by force of the earlier *prohibition* to perform *melachah*. The extra exhortation of a mitzvah-obligation, on top of the mitzvah-prohibition, lends additional severity to the transgression (see *Rambam, Sefer HaMitzvos, Asei* 154 and *Hil. Shabbos* 1:1; see also above, note 3).

*Ramban*, however, notes that *Mechilta* (*Bo* §9) has a different understanding of the verse, maintaining that it commands us to "rest" from certain activities that are *not* included in the prohibition of *melachah*. *Ramban* explains as follows: It would theoretically be possible for a person to abide by the prohibition of *melachah* and refrain from all the activities included in that category, yet treat the Sabbath entirely like a weekday. This is because the prohibition of *melachah* (commonly translated as *work* or *labor*) does not apply to tasks that necessarily require exertion, but rather, encompasses a specific group of actions that were performed during construction of the *Mishkan* (Tabernacle). These include many forms of creative activity, such as cooking, kindling, building, and writing, among other acts. [The major categories of *melachah* are listed above, in Mitzvah 32, Volume I, p. 276.] Acts such as hauling loads, though involving strenuous activity, are not in the category of *melachah*. Similarly, engaging in commerce is not itself a *melachah* (though commercial transactions often involve *melachos* such as writing). Thus, a storekeeper could theoretically open his store on the Sabbath and spend the entire day buying and selling, and a laborer could hire himself out and spend the day loading, unloading, and delivering goods (within an *eruv* enclosure), all without violating the prohibition of *melachah*. The result would be that the Sabbath would hardly be different from a weekday! The Torah therefore added a commandment to *rest* on the Sabbath, meaning that one should treat it as a day of sanctity on which one is noticeably at rest and not engaged in the hustle and bustle of weekday activities. According to this interpretation, the obligation to rest does not merely add severity to the prohibition of *melachah*, but actually adds a new dimension to the sacredness of the Sabbath day (*Ramban, Leviticus* 19:2, 23:24 and *Derashah L'Rosh Hashanah*, pp. 218-219 in *Kisvei Ramban* Vol. I, Chavel ed.).

Now, aside from the actions that are Biblically forbidden, the Sages prohibited numerous additional activities on the Sabbath. These are known as the decrees of שְׁבוּת, *restfulness*. Among these prohibited activities are engaging in commerce (lest one perform the *melachah* of writing; *Rambam, Hil. Shabbos* 23:12), and moving stones (under the prohibition of *muktzeh*; *Rambam* ibid. 25:6). In light of *Ramban's* assertion that such activities are Biblically proscribed under the

mitzvah-obligation to "rest," what purpose do these Rabbinic "restfulness prohibitions" serve?

The answer is that the Biblical obligation of resting requires only that one preserve the character of the Sabbath as a day of rest and not treat it as a weekday by engaging in commerce or the like on a grand scale. Biblical law does not proscribe selling *one* item or hauling *one* load, as this single act does not violate the restful aura of the day. As long as an act is not in the category of *melachah*, it may be performed on an isolated basis; only *melachah* activities are *completely* forbidden. The Sages, however, prohibited engaging in even a *single* transaction, due to the concern that this might lead the buyer or seller to write and thus commit a *melachah*. Similarly, the Sages prohibited moving *muktzeh* items such as stones — including not only heavy boulders, but also small pebbles — even *once*, due to the concern that this might lead someone to violate the *melachah* of carrying from a private domain to a public domain. Thus, the Biblical command to "rest" requires us to treat the Sabbath as a *general* day of repose, whereas the Rabbinic decrees of "restfulness" prohibit the performance of specific activities even on an isolated basis (*Ramban, Derashos* ibid.; *Ritva, Rosh Hashanah* 32b; *Teshuvos Chasam Sofer, Orach Chaim* §208 ד"ה והנה, *Choshen Mishpat* §195, and *Even HaEzer* II §173; see also Mitzvah 32, at note 29).

Even according to this approach, however, one who performs an actual *melachah*, even on an isolated basis (e.g., he kindles one lamp), aside from transgressing the mitzvah-prohibition of performing *melachah* on the Sabbath (Mitzvah 32), he has also transgressed the mitzvah-obligation to "rest." Although, as has been explained, the simple meaning of the verse refers to resting from weekday activities in a general sense, in the final analysis, the Torah has prohibited *melachah,* and any performance of that which the Torah specifically prohibits must also be considered a lack of "resting" (*Chasam Sofer* to *Shabbos* 150a).

In summary, whereas Chinuch understands the verse *on the seventh day you shall rest* as a mitzvah-obligation to desist specifically from *melachah* activity, *Ramban* understands it as a mitzvah-obligation to preserve the character of the Sabbath day by resting from commercial activity and general toil, as well as desisting from *melachah* activity.

For further discussion, see *Rambam, Hil. Shabbos* 21:1 with *Maggid Mishneh,* and *Commentary to the Mishnah, Beitzah* 5:2; *Maharatz Chayes* to *Shabbos* 114b; and *Minchas Chinuch* 297:2 and 298:5 ד"ה ולפי.

## מִצְוָה פו: שֶׁלֹּא לִשָּׁבַע בַּעֲבוֹדָה זָרָה

שֶׁלֹּא נִשָּׁבַע בְּשֵׁם עֲבוֹדָה זָרָה[1] אֲפִלּוּ לְעוֹבְדֶיהָ[2], וְלֹא נַשְׁבִּיעַ לְגוֹי בָּהּ[3], שֶׁנֶּאֱמַר (שמות כ״ג, י״ג) וְשֵׁם אֱלֹהִים אֲחֵרִים לֹא תַזְכִּירוּ. וּבִכְלָל הָאַזְכָּרָה שָׁמַעְנוּ בֵּין נִשְׁבָּע בֵּין מַשְׁבִּיעַ[4], וְיֵשׁ מְפָרְשִׁים שֶׁעִקַּר לָאו זֶה אֵינוֹ בָּא אֶלָּא בְּעוֹסֵק עִם הַגּוֹי בְּיוֹם אֵידוֹ וּמַרְוִיחוֹ

---

## Mitzvah 86

## The Prohibition to Swear in the Name of an Avodah Zarah

וּבְכֹל אֲשֶׁר אָמַרְתִּי אֲלֵיכֶם תִּשָּׁמֵרוּ וְשֵׁם אֱלֹהִים אֲחֵרִים לֹא תַזְכִּירוּ לֹא יִשָּׁמַע עַל פִּיךָ

*Be careful regarding everything I have said to you. The name of alien gods you shall not mention, nor shall your mouth cause it to be heard (Exodus 23:13).*

Chinuch previously explained (Mitzvah 30) that a proper oath (שְׁבוּעָה) is one wherein the speaker lends credence and resolve to his words by swearing in the Name of God, effectively comparing the steadfastness of those words to the steadfastness of the Existence of God. Making an oath in God's Name carries great gravity and severity, and is one of the means of worshiping and honoring Him [see Mitzvah 435] (*Rambam, Hil. Shevuos* 11:1). This mitzvah discusses the misuse of this formula by swearing (or having others swear) in the name of an *avodah zarah* — i.e., a false deity — wherein the speaker is utilizing the supposed steadfastness of the *avodah zarah* to give his words credence.

שֶׁלֹּא נִשָּׁבַע בְּשֵׁם עֲבוֹדָה זָרָה — We are commanded **not to swear in the name of an *avodah zarah*,**[1] אֲפִלּוּ לְעוֹבְדֶיהָ — **even** when swearing **to those who worship it.**[2] וְלֹא נַשְׁבִּיעַ לְגוֹי בָּהּ — **We are also** commanded **not to have an idolater swear by [the *avodah zarah*].**[3] שֶׁנֶּאֱמַר "וְשֵׁם אֱלֹהִים אֲחֵרִים לֹא תַזְכִּירוּ" — These are both prohibited, **as it is stated** (Exodus 23:13): ***The name of alien gods you shall not mention,*** וּבִכְלָל הָאַזְכָּרָה שָׁמַעְנוּ בֵּין נִשְׁבָּע בֵּין מַשְׁבִּיעַ — **and** the term **"mentioning" denotes to us both swearing and causing others to swear** in the name of the *avodah zarah*.[4]

Chinuch presents a different understanding of the mitzvah:

וְיֵשׁ מְפָרְשִׁים שֶׁעִקַּר לָאו זֶה אֵינוֹ בָּא אֶלָּא בְּעוֹסֵק עִם הַגּוֹי בְּיוֹם אֵידוֹ — **Some explain that the essence of this prohibition refers solely to one who does business with an idolater on the day of his festival,**[5] וּמַרְוִיחוֹ — **causing [the idolater] to profit,** and the verse means to prohibit doing so

---

### NOTES

1. At the beginning of Mitzvah 28, Chinuch defines *avodah zarah* as any entity that is an object of worship, other than Hashem, the One God. See also the end of this mitzvah.

2. That is, even though the person swearing by the *avodah zarah* is not doing so because he ascribes any power or greatness to that idol, but rather, because he recognizes that the person to whom he is swearing believes in it, nevertheless it is forbidden. Even such swearing is included in this prohibition, for by swearing in the name of the *avodah zarah*, one invariably lends it credence (*Minchas Yitzchak* §1).

3. The prohibition also includes making a *neder* (i.e., a vow prohibiting something upon oneself; see below, note 13) in the name of an *avodah zarah*, or causing others to do so (see *Sanhedrin* 63b).

4. Causing others to mention something is also considered a form of "mentioning" (*Yad Ramah, Sanhedrin* 63b פיסקא ד״ה; see further, Gemara there, with *Tosafos* ד״ה שלא). [Some explain that this is based on the *hif'il*, causative, form of the word תַזְכִּירוּ, *mention*, wherein the word is taken to mean "cause to mention" (*Maharam Schif* here §1).]

Others, however, disagree with Chinuch and understand that the Biblical prohibition is only for a Jew himself to swear (or vow), but causing others to do so is prohibited by Rabbinic injunction (*Teshuvos Radvaz* 1:166; *Sma, Choshen Mishpat* 176:92; see also *Igros Moshe, Yoreh Deah* I §71).

5. [Literally, *the day of his calamity* — a pejorative term used for idolatrous festivals, based on the verse (Deuteronomy 32:35): *for the day of their calamity is at*

## 155 ☐ MISHPATIM / MITZVAH 86: NOT TO SWEAR IN THE NAME OF AN AVODAH ZARAH

דְּאָזִיל וּמוֹדֶה, וְקָא עָבַר עַל לֹא תַזְכִּירוּ,[6] כְּלוֹמַר שֶׁלֹּא יַזְכִּירוּם אֲחֵרִים עַל דֶּרֶךְ הַזְכָּרָה הָאֲסוּרָה לָהֶם, דְּהַיְנוּ עַל דַּעַת לְעָבְדָם, שֶׁהוּא אָסוּר אַף לָהֶם גַּם כֵּן מִן הַתּוֹרָה, שֶׁבְּנֵי נֹחַ מֻזְהָרִים עַל עֲבוֹדָה זָרָה.[7] וְעוֹד הוֹסִיפוּ זִכְרוֹנָם לִבְרָכָה הַרְחָקָה, וְאָמְרוּ בְּסַנְהֶדְרִין (דף ס״ג ע״ב) שֶׁלֹּא יֹאמַר אָדָם לַחֲבֵרוֹ שְׁמוֹר לִי בְּצַד עֲבוֹדָה זָרָה פְּלוֹנִית.[8]

on that day, **דְּאָזִיל וּמוֹדֶה** — **for [the idolater]**, having profited, **will** then **go and pay homage** to his *avodah zarah*, **וְקָא עָבַר עַל "לֹא תַזְכִּירוּ"** — **and** by bringing about the pagan's homage to his god, **[the Jew] violates** the prohibition of *the name of alien gods you shall not mention*.[6] **כְּלוֹמַר שֶׁלֹּא יַזְכִּירוּם אֲחֵרִים עַל דֶּרֶךְ הַזְכָּרָה הָאֲסוּרָה לָהֶם** — This is because the verse is understood **to mean that "others should not** be caused to **mention [their gods] in the manner of mentioning that is prohibited to them," דְּהַיְנוּ עַל דַּעַת לְעָבְדָם** — **meaning,** they should not be caused to recognize their gods **with the intent of worshiping them. שֶׁהוּא אָסוּר אַף לָהֶם גַּם כֵּן מִן הַתּוֹרָה** — Such an act of paying homage **is Biblically forbidden for even [non-Jews], as well, שֶׁבְּנֵי נֹחַ מֻזְהָרִים עַל עֲבוֹדָה זָרָה** — **in that Noahides** (i.e., non-Jews) **too are cautioned with regard to *avodah zarah*** (see end of Mitzvah 26).[7]

**וְעוֹד הוֹסִיפוּ זִכְרוֹנָם לִבְרָכָה הַרְחָקָה** — **[Our Sages],** of blessed memory, **went further and added a distancing** restriction, as a hedge for the Biblical prohibition, **וְאָמְרוּ בְּסַנְהֶדְרִין** — **and they said in** Tractate ***Sanhedrin*** (63b) **שֶׁלֹּא יֹאמַר אָדָם לַחֲבֵרוֹ שְׁמוֹר לִי בְּצַד עֲבוֹדָה זָרָה פְּלוֹנִית** — **that a person should not say to his fellow, "Wait for me next to such-and-such an *avodah zarah*."** Although no oath is being made, the Sages prohibited the very mention of the name of the particular *avodah zarah*, even in a case such as this, where it is being done in an innocuous manner, for the simple purpose of identifying a landmark.[8]

---

### NOTES

hand (*Avodah Zarah* 2a).] In Eretz Yisrael, the prohibition of doing business with an idolater starts even earlier (at least, by Rabbinic decree). It extends back to three days before the festival (Mishnah ibid. and Gemara there, 11b; *Rambam, Hil. Avodah Zarah* 9:1).

6. All agree that doing business with an idolater on a day when he will pay homage to his god is prohibited, as this is an explicit Mishnah (see *Avodah Zarah* 2a with *Rashi*). At issue is from where this prohibition is derived. According to the opinion that Chinuch cites here (see *Re'ah* to *Avodah Zarah* 2a), it is derived from this verse, וְשֵׁם אֱלֹהִים אֲחֵרִים לֹא תַזְכִּירוּ, *The name of alien gods you shall not mention*. Others, however, derive this prohibition (of causing an idolater to pay homage to his pagan deity) from the end of our verse, לֹא יִשָּׁמַע עַל פִּיךָ, *nor shall your mouth cause it to be heard* (*Rashi, Avodah Zarah* 6a ד״ה משום הרווחה; *Ran* to *Rif* ibid. fol. 1a ד״ה לפני), leaving the first part of the verse for the prohibition of swearing (or causing others to swear) in the *avodah zarah*'s name, as Chinuch uses it above (see *Rashi, Sanhedrin* 60b [ב ד״ה העובר; see, however, *Tosafos* there 63b ד״ה שלא).

7. See also Mitzvah 213 and *Minchas Chinuch* there. The prohibition of idolatry is the first of the seven Noahide laws listed by *Rambam* (*Hil. Melachim* 9:1).

In summary: According to the first view mentioned by Chinuch, which is followed by *Rambam* (*Hil. Avodah Zarah* 5:10) and others, the phrase, וְשֵׁם אֱלֹהִים אֲחֵרִים לֹא תַזְכִּירוּ, *The name of alien gods you shall not mention*, refers to the prohibition of swearing or causing others to swear in the name of an *avodah zarah*. However, according to the second opinion (*Re'ah*), the phrase, וְשֵׁם אֱלֹהִים אֲחֵרִים לֹא תַזְכִּירוּ, *The name of alien gods you shall not mention*, teaches that we are not to be the cause of an idolater's giving thanks and paying homage to his god, which results from engaging in business with him on the day of his festival. See Insight for a discussion regarding the scope of these prohibitions.

[It should be noted that according to *Re'ah* as well, swearing in the name of an *avodah zarah* is prohibited Biblically (as explicitly stated in the Mishnah, *Sanhedrin* 60b). He derives that prohibition, however, from the latter half of the verse: לֹא יִשָּׁמַע עַל פִּיךָ, *nor shall your mouth cause it to be heard* (*Minchas Yitzchak* §2; see *Re'ah* to *Avodah Zarah* 21b-22a).]

8. Chinuch will discuss some of the details of this Rabbinic prohibition below, in his discussion of this mitzvah's laws. [It should be noted that some are of the opinion that the prohibition of mentioning the name of an *avodah zarah* is actually Biblical, as per the literal reading of our verse, *The name of alien gods you shall not mention* (*Smag, Lo Saaseh* 32).]

מִשָּׁרְשֵׁי הַמִּצְוָה, לְהַרְחִיק כָּל עִנְיַן עֲבוֹדָה זָרָה בֵּין בְּמַעֲשֶׂה בֵּין בְּדִבּוּר עַד שֶׁלֹּא יַעֲלֶה זִכְרָהּ בִּלְבָבֵנוּ לְעוֹלָם. וְהִשְׁגִּיחוּ רַבּוֹתֵינוּ זִכְרוֹנָם לִבְרָכָה וְאָמְרוּ שֶׁבְּמ"ד מְקוֹמוֹת הִזְהִירָתְנוּ הַתּוֹרָה עָלֶיהָ לְרֹב מְאוּסָהּ, צֵא וַחֲשֹׁב.[9]

מִדִּינֵי הַמִּצְוָה, מַה שֶּׁאָמְרוּ שֶׁאֲפִלּוּ לְהַזְכִּיר שֵׁם עֲבוֹדָה זָרָה בְּדֶרֶךְ שְׁבוּעָה אָסוּר[10], וְשֶׁכָּל עֲבוֹדָה זָרָה הַכְּתוּבָה בְּסִפְרֵי הַקֹּדֶשׁ מֻתָּר לְהַזְכִּיר שְׁמָהּ[11], כְּגוֹן פְּעוֹר וּבֵל וּנְבוֹ וְכַיּוֹצֵא בָהֶן[12],

## ∽ Underlying Purpose of the Mitzvah ∾

לְהַרְחִיק כָּל עִנְיַן עֲבוֹדָה — מִשָּׁרְשֵׁי הַמִּצְוָה — **Among the underlying purposes of this mitzvah** זָרָה — **is to distance all matters** relating to *avodah zarah,* בֵּין בְּמַעֲשֶׂה בֵּין בְּדִבּוּר — **whether in deed or in speech,** עַד שֶׁלֹּא יַעֲלֶה זִכְרָהּ בִּלְבָבֵנוּ לְעוֹלָם — **to the point where the very memory** of [*avodah zarah*] **never enters our minds.** וְהִשְׁגִּיחוּ רַבּוֹתֵינוּ זִכְרוֹנָם לִבְרָכָה וְאָמְרוּ — **Our Sages, of blessed memory, took heed and noted** שֶׁבְּמ"ד מְקוֹמוֹת הִזְהִירָתְנוּ הַתּוֹרָה עָלֶיהָ לְרֹב מְאוּסָהּ — **that the Torah cautioned us regarding** [*avodah zarah*] **in forty-four** different **places;** this emphasis being **due to the great repulsiveness** of [*avodah zarah*]. צֵא וַחֲשֹׁב — **Go and count,** and you will find that it is so.[9]

## ∽ Laws of the Mitzvah ∾

מִדִּינֵי הַמִּצְוָה — **Among the laws of the mitzvah** is מַה שֶּׁאָמְרוּ — **that which [our Sages] said** (*Sanhedrin* 63b), שֶׁאֲפִלּוּ לְהַזְכִּיר שֵׁם עֲבוֹדָה זָרָה בְּדֶרֶךְ שְׁלֹּא שְׁבוּעָה אָסוּר — **that even to mention the name of an *avodah zarah* when it is not in the context of an oath is forbidden.**[10] וְשֶׁכָּל עֲבוֹדָה זָרָה הַכְּתוּבָה בְּסִפְרֵי הַקֹּדֶשׁ מֻתָּר לְהַזְכִּיר שְׁמָהּ — They also include the law **that it is permitted to mention the name of any *avodah zarah* that is written in the Holy Scriptures,**[11] כְּגוֹן פְּעוֹר — **such as *Pe'or*** (see *Numbers* 25:3 et al.), **or *Bel*** (see *Isaiah* 46:1), **or *Nebo*** (ibid.), וּבֵל וּנְבוֹ וְכַיּוֹצֵא בָהֶן — **and others like these.**[12]

---

### NOTES

9. The source for this statement is unclear. A similar statement appears in *Midrash Tanchuma* (*Vayikra* §2). However, our version of the Midrash states that there are forty-eight such references, not forty-four. The Midrash reads: "You will find that the Torah cautions us forty-eight times regarding [the proper treatment of] converts, and similarly cautions us the same number of times regarding idolatry." The Midrash goes on to explain that Hashem thus conveys to us that the convert's rejection of idolatry should be deemed sufficient cause for us to treat him well. [There are, in fact, discrepancies pertaining to the number of times that the Torah cautioned with regard to the treatment of converts as well; see above Mitzvah 64, and note 11 there.]

Notwithstanding the exact number of references to the prohibitions related to *avodah zarah,* it is clear that such paganism is considered detestable by the Torah, which states explicitly (*Deuteronomy* 7:26): שַׁקֵּץ תְּשַׁקְּצֶנּוּ וְתַעֵב תְּתַעֲבֶנּוּ, *you shall surely loath it, and you shall surely abominate it.* Moreover, anyone who believes in *avodah zarah* is considered to have denied the truth of the entire Torah (see Mitzvah 26), and has thereby distanced himself from all blessing (see Mitzvah 87).

10. The example given by the Gemara there (also mentioned by Chinuch earlier) is that a person may not say to his fellow, "Wait for me next to such-and-such an *avodah zarah.*" The prohibition, though, applies whenever a person mentions the name of an *avodah zarah,* whether he does so with cause, such as when he uses it as a landmark, or without cause, by simply mentioning its name (*Rosh, Sanhedrin* 7:3; *Shulchan Aruch, Yoreh Deah* 147:1). However, some note that this applies only to names that bear some connotation of godliness or regality. Names that are simply identifiers, such that they are names used by people in general, or names of holidays that bear no special terms of reverence, are not forbidden to be uttered (*Yerei'im* §245, quoted in *Hagahos Maimoniyos, Hil. Avodah Zarah* 5:3; *Beur HaGra, Yoreh Deah* 147:3).

11. However, swearing, or vowing in the names of even such gods remains forbidden. The only leniency applied to *avodah zarah* mentioned in *Tanach* (Scripture) is that we are permitted to mention their names (*Tosafos, Sanhedrin* 63b ד"ה שלא; *Mekor Mayim Chaim, Yoreh Deah* 147:1).

12. [For an explanation of this law, see *Yerei'im* §245.] It is furthermore permitted to mention the Aramaic names of *avodah zarah* as they appear in the *Targum* to such verses (*Birkei Yosef* to *Yoreh Deah* 147:4).

# 157 ☐ MISHPATIM / MITZVAH 86: NOT TO SWEAR IN THE NAME OF AN AVODAH ZARAH

וְשֶׁאָסוּר לִגְרֹם לַאֲחֵרִים שֶׁיִּדְּרוּ וִיקַיְּמוּ בְּשֵׁם עֲבוֹדָה זָרָה[13,14], אֲבָל אֵינוֹ לוֹקֶה אֶלָּא הַנּוֹדֵר וְהַמְקַיֵּם בִּשְׁמָהּ, דְּהַיְנוּ הַנִּשְׁבָּע בְּעַצְמוֹ וְלֹא הַמַּשְׁבִּיעַ, וְאַף עַל פִּי שֶׁהַמַּשְׁבִּיעַ כְּמוֹ כֵן בִּכְלַל הַלָּאו הוּא, לְפִי דַעַת הָרַמְבַּ"ם זִכְרוֹנוֹ לִבְרָכָה[15], וְיֶתֶר פְּרָטֶיהָ מְבֹאָרִים בְּפֶרֶק ז' מִסַּנְהֶדְרִין (דף ס' ע"ב, וס"ג ע"ב)[16].

וְנוֹהֶגֶת בְּכָל מָקוֹם וּבְכָל זְמַן, בַּזְּכָרִים וּנְקֵבוֹת.[17]

וְהָעוֹבֵר עָלֶיהָ וְנִשְׁבַּע בְּדָבָר מִכָּל הַנִּבְרָאִים שֶׁיַּאֲמִינוּ בָם הַכּוֹפְרִים הַסְּכָלִים, עַל צַד הַגַּדְלָה, חַיָּב מַלְקוּת[18], כֵּן כָּתַב הָרַב זִכְרוֹנוֹ לִבְרָכָה, וְאַף עַל פִּי

---

וְשֶׁאָסוּר לִגְרֹם לַאֲחֵרִים שֶׁיִּדְּרוּ וִיקַיְּמוּ בְּשֵׁם עֲבוֹדָה זָרָה — The laws include **also that it is forbidden to cause others to vow**[13] **or swear**[14] **in the name of an** *avodah zarah*. אֲבָל אֵינוֹ לוֹקֶה אֶלָּא הַנּוֹדֵר וְהַמְקַיֵּם בִּשְׁמָהּ — **However, only the one who vows or swears in its name receives** the penalty of *malkus*, דְּהַיְנוּ הַנִּשְׁבָּע בְּעַצְמוֹ וְלֹא הַמַּשְׁבִּיעַ — **that is, the one who swears himself, but not one who** simply **causes others to swear,** וְאַף עַל פִּי שֶׁהַמַּשְׁבִּיעַ כְּמוֹ כֵן בִּכְלַל הַלָּאו הוּא — **even though one who causes others to swear is also included in this prohibition.** לְפִי דַעַת הָרַמְבַּ"ם זִכְרוֹנוֹ לִבְרָכָה — **This, that only one who swears himself receives** *malkus*, **accords with the opinion of the Rambam, of blessed memory.**[15]

וְיֶתֶר פְּרָטֶיהָ מְבֹאָרִים בְּפֶרֶק ז' מִסַּנְהֶדְרִין — **These laws and the additional details of [this mitzvah] are set forth in the seventh chapter of** Tractate *Sanhedrin* **(60b, 63b).**[16]

## ☙ Applicability of the Mitzvah ☙

וְנוֹהֶגֶת בְּכָל מָקוֹם וּבְכָל זְמַן, בַּזְּכָרִים וּנְקֵבוֹת — **[This mitzvah] applies in every location and in all times to both men and women.**[17]

וְהָעוֹבֵר עָלֶיהָ וְנִשְׁבַּע בְּדָבָר מִכָּל הַנִּבְרָאִים שֶׁיַּאֲמִינוּ בָם הַכּוֹפְרִים הַסְּכָלִים — **One who violates it and swears by** (i.e., in the name of) **any created being in which the foolish heretics believe,** עַל צַד הַגַּדְלָה — **ascribing** to them **an aspect of greatness,** חַיָּב מַלְקוּת — **is liable to** *malkus* **(lashes),**[18] כֵּן כָּתַב הָרַב זִכְרוֹנוֹ לִבְרָכָה — **as the Master** (i.e., Rambam), **of blessed memory, writes** (*Sefer HaMitzvos, Lo Saaseh* 14). וְאַף עַל פִּי — **The** *malkus* **penalty applies even though**

---

### NOTES

13. A vow (*neder*) is a declaration that prohibits an item upon the one taking the vow. An example of a vow in the name of an *avodah zarah* would be if, for instance, one wished to abstain from bathing, and made a vow that all the produce of the world be forbidden to him in the name of such-and-such an *avodah zarah*, if he bathes (see *Rashi, Sanhedrin* 60b ד"ה הנודר בשמו). Chinuch adds here that not only is it forbidden for one to utter such a vow, but even to cause another — i.e., an idolater — to take such a vow is forbidden (*Sanhedrin* 63b with *Rashi* ד"ה לא יגרום).

14. Although the term קיום literally means *affirm*, according to many it is used by the Gemara (*Sanhedrin* 60b, 63b) to denote actual swearing (*Rambam, Hil. Avodah Zarah* 5:11; see also *Targum* to *Genesis* 21:23 et al.), and our translation follows this opinion. Others, however, explain the term more literally, understanding it to refer to the acceptance or affirmation of a vow stated by another (see *Yad Ramah, Sanhedrin* 60b ד"ה מתני). Accordingly, the case here would be where a Jew articulates the vow that he wishes the idolater to accept, and the idolater simply responds with an affirmation.

15. Commentators seek to understand *Rambam*'s reasoning behind this distinction (*Lechem Mishneh*, *Hil. Sanhedrin* 19:4 [7-8] ד"ה הנודר; *Dina D'Chayei, Lo Saaseh* 32 p. 31a ד"ה ועוד יש לתמוה). Some explain that it is because the inclusion of causing others to swear in the prohibition is based on the *hif'il*, causative, form of the word תַזְכִּירוּ, *mention*, wherein the word is taken to mean "cause to mention." Since this aspect of the prohibition is not the explicit meaning of the verse, it is not subject to *malkus* (see *Maharam Schik* §1).

16. These laws are codified in *Rambam, Hilchos Avodah Zarah* 5:10-11, and in *Shulchan Aruch, Yoreh Deah* §147. For the laws related to doing commerce with idolaters on (or shortly before) their festivals, see *Rambam* ibid. 9:1-5 and *Shulchan Aruch* ibid. §148.

17. I.e., it applies in Eretz Yisrael and the Diaspora, and whether the *Beis HaMikdash* is standing or not. In addition, it applies to both men and women, in accordance with the general rule pertaining to mitzvah-prohibitions.

18. Aside from violating this mitzvah-prohibition, one who swears in the name of an *avodah zarah* may also be in violation of the mitzvah-obligation of וּבִשְׁמוֹ תִּשָּׁבֵעַ, *and in His Name shall you swear* (*Deuteronomy* 10:20); see end of Mitzvah 435.

שֶׁאֵין בּוֹ מַעֲשֶׂה[19], מֵרֹב חֹמֶר עֲבוֹדָה זָרָה הוּא[20].

שֶׁאֵין בּוֹ מַעֲשֶׂה — **[the prohibition] involves no action,** and prohibitions that lack action are ordinarily not punishable with *malkus*.[19] מֵרֹב חֹמֶר עֲבוֹדָה זָרָה הוּא — **This** exception **is due to the great severity of** *avodah zarah* in general, and this prohibition's close association with that prohibition.[20]

---

### NOTES

19. That is, taking a vow or oath is not considered an action, since it is performed through speech. Generally speaking, for a prohibition to be punishable with *malkus* it must be done via action; see, for example, Mitzvah 11. This prohibition, however, is an exception, as Chinuch states in the name of *Rambam* (see *Kesef Mishneh, Hil. Avodah Zarah* 5:11; cf. *Raavad* there). See further.

20. Although taking an oath or vow in the name of an *avodah zarah* is not in itself a violation of idol worship (*Minchas Chinuch* §2), it nevertheless encroaches on that most grave sin. Therefore, this prohibition is an exception to the general rule that there is no *malkus* penalty when no action was performed.

Others suggest a different reason for the *malkus* penalty here, on the basis of the rule (see *Temurah* 3a-b) that one who swears falsely (and thus violates Mitzvah 227) is liable to *malkus*, notwithstanding the lack of action (see *Kesef Mishneh, Hil. Avodah Zarah* 5:11). Although one who swears in the name of an *avodah zarah* has not transgressed the prohibition of swearing falsely, nevertheless, there is a direct relationship between the prohibition of swearing falsely and that of swearing in the name of *avodah zarah*, as swearing in the name of *avodah zarah* is inherently false. Thus, the *malkus* penalty applies here as well (*Radvaz, Responsa* on *Rambam* §256). See also *Lechem Mishneh, Hil. Sanhedrin* 19:4, and *Minchas Chinuch* §1 and §4.

---

> **∽§ Insight: Business Dealings with Pagans**
>
> As Chinuch notes here, it is prohibited for a Jew to do business with an idolater on the day of his festival, since the idolater will pay homage to his god for the benefit he has received. This prohibition, to cause an idolater to pay homage to an idol, is apparently Biblical in origin, as it is derived, according to Chinuch, from the verse (*Exodus* 23:13), וְשֵׁם אֱלֹהִים אֲחֵרִים לֹא תַזְכִּירוּ, *the name of alien gods you shall not mention.* Others derive it from the end of the verse: לֹא יִשָּׁמַע עַל פִּיךָ, *nor shall your mouth cause it to be heard* (see note 6). Similarly, the prohibition to cause an idolater to swear in the name of his god, discussed by Chinuch above at length, is also Biblical in nature, and is also derived from the same verse.
>
> Notwithstanding the Biblical nature of these prohibitions, Rishonim apply what would seem to be rather broad leniencies to both. For one thing, Rabbinic authorities of certain European countries permitted, in their time, doing business with idolaters on pagan holidays, at least in part due to concerns of enmity (אֵיבָה). That is, since Jews of those countries actively did business with their idolatrous neighbors throughout the year, if they were to suddenly stop on the day of the festival, it would arouse feelings of enmity from these idolaters (*Tosafos, Avodah Zarah* 2a ד"ה אסור; *Rosh* ad loc. 1:1). Similarly, leniency was applied by some Rishonim with regard to causing an idolater to swear by his god, in that they permitted a Jew to demand an oath from the idolater for monies that the idolater denied owing to the Jew. The basis of this permit was that otherwise the Jew would never be able to recover his money (see *Tosafos, Sanhedrin* 63b ד"ה אסור לאדם in the name of *Rabbeinu Tam*, and *Rosh* there 7:3).
>
> R' Yechiel Michel Feinstein, in a letter to his uncle, R' Moshe Feinstein, questioned how it could be that these non-life-threatening concerns of enmity or monetary loss can be applied to permit Biblical prohibitions (*Igros Moshe, Yoreh Deah* I §71). Fear of the idolaters' hard feelings (in the case of business on the pagan holiday) or concerns of monetary loss (in the case of the idolatrous debtor) would not seem adequate to warrant the abrogating of Biblical prohibitions! In fact, the question becomes magnified if we consider the type of prohibitions that we are apparently dealing with in both of these cases. Both of these activities — assuming they are Biblically forbidden — would be subsumed under the general category of prohibitions related to idolatry. Now, idolatry is one of the few prohibitions for which a Jew must be ready to give his life rather than violate (*Sanhedrin* 74a; *Rambam, Hil. Yesodei HaTorah* 5:2), and in fact the same holds true even for a subcategory of idolatry

(*Rama, Yoreh Deah* 157:1) — ostensibly including these activities as well (see *Igros Moshe* loc. cit. and *Minchas Chinuch* §1). If one is required to give up his life rather than violate these prohibitions, surely fear of enmity or monetary loss would not be grounds to permit them!

In addressing these questions, R' Moshe Feinstein challenges the assumption that the acts of doing business with an idolater on his festival and of demanding an oath of him regarding his denial of a debt are Biblically prohibited. He explains that, in fact, based on the principle that דָּבָר שֶׁאֵין מִתְכַּוֵּן מוּתָּר, *something unintended is permitted* (*Nazir* 42a; *Yoma* 34b, et al.), neither of these could possibly be Biblically prohibited. The principle that "something unintended is permitted" states that one is permitted to engage in a permitted activity even though that activity may lead to a forbidden consequence, if that consequence is neither intended nor inevitable (*p'sik reisha*). In the case of doing business with the idolater, it is surely not the intention of the Jew that the idolater go and give homage to his idol, nor is it inevitable that he will do so. Therefore, on a Biblical level, such business is permitted, and any prohibition regarding such activities is Rabbinic in nature. It is therefore understandable that the Rabbinic authorities could allow for leniency in cases of enmity.

A similar reasoning applies in the case of an idolater who is denying a Jew's claim. The Jew, who simply wants to recover his money, is actually hoping that the idolater will back down and *not* take the oath, for if he does do so, the Jew will lose the money that he is owed. Hence, if the idolater does take the oath, that consequence is once again unintended, and surely not inevitable. It is therefore permitted to demand an oath from the idolater under such circumstances.

However, R' Moshe explains, there are cases of oaths where, if a Jew were to demand them from an idolater, the Jew would indeed be violating a Biblical prohibition; namely, oaths relating to the future. That is, if a Jew were to ask an idolater to swear by his god that he will follow through with some future commitment, such adjuring would be a violation of this prohibition, for here the consequence of the idolater taking an oath *is* intended. The Jew wants the idolater to back up his commitment by way of such an oath, and therefore this oath cannot be said to be "something unintended." It is specifically such an oath that our verse prohibits.

## מִצְוָה פז: שֶׁלֹּא לְהַדִּיחַ בְּנֵי יִשְׂרָאֵל אַחַר עֲבוֹדָה זָרָה

שֶׁלֹּא יִקְרָא אָדָם בְּנֵי־אָדָם לַעֲבוֹדַת עֲבוֹדָה זָרָה וְיָזְרֵז אוֹתָם עַל כָּךְ, וְאַף עַל פִּי שֶׁזֶּה הַקּוֹרֵא לֹא יַעַבְדֶנָּה וְלֹא יַעֲשֶׂה לָהּ פְּעֻלָּה מִן הַפְּעֻלּוֹת, רַק הַקְּרִיאָה לְבַד, וְזֶהוּ נִקְרָא מַדִּיחַ, וְכֵן אָמְרוּ בְּסַנְהֶדְרִין (דף ס״ג ע״ב) לֹא יִשָּׁמַע עַל פִּיךָ (שמות כ״ג, י״ג), אַזְהָרָה לַמַּדִּיחַ, וְכֵן אָמְרוּ גַּם בַּמְּכִילְתָּא.[1]

שֹׁרֶשׁ הַמִּצְוָה יָדוּעַ.[2]

דִּינֶיהָ בְּפֶרֶק עֲשִׂירִי מִסַּנְהֶדְרִין (דף קי״א ע״ב).[3]

---

## ~ Mitzvah 87 ~
## The Prohibition to Subvert Jewish People to Idolatry

וּבְכֹל אֲשֶׁר אָמַרְתִּי אֲלֵיכֶם תִּשָּׁמֵרוּ וְשֵׁם אֱלֹהִים אֲחֵרִים לֹא תַזְכִּירוּ לֹא יִשָּׁמַע עַל פִּיךָ
*Be careful regarding everything I have said to you; the name of alien gods you shall not mention, nor shall your mouth cause it to be heard (Exodus 23:13).*

שֶׁלֹּא יִקְרָא אָדָם בְּנֵי־אָדָם לַעֲבוֹדַת עֲבוֹדָה זָרָה — We are commanded that one **person shall not call other people to the worship of** *avodah zarah* (idolatry) וִיזָרֵז אוֹתָם עַל כָּךְ — **and encourage them to** engage in it. וְאַף עַל פִּי שֶׁזֶּה הַקּוֹרֵא לֹא יַעַבְדֶנָּה — This prohibition applies **even where the caller** himself **does not worship [***avodah zarah***],** וְלֹא יַעֲשֶׂה לָהּ פְּעֻלָּה מִן הַפְּעֻלּוֹת — **or perform any action on its behalf;** רַק הַקְּרִיאָה לְבַד — **the mere calling alone** is prohibited. וְזֶהוּ נִקְרָא מַדִּיחַ — This [person], who calls others to worship *avodah zarah*, **is called a** *madiach* (subverter); וְכֵן אָמְרוּ בְּסַנְהֶדְרִין — **and so did [the Sages] say in** Tractate *Sanhedrin* (63b): "לֹא יִשָּׁמַע עַל פִּיךָ" — The Torah's statement (*Exodus* 23:13), *And the name of alien gods you shall not mention,* **nor shall your mouth cause it to be heard,** אַזְהָרָה לַמַּדִּיחַ — **is the Scriptural injunction for a** *madiach*. וְכֵן אָמְרוּ גַּם בַּמְּכִילְתָּא — **They also stated so in** *Mechilta DeRashbi* (*Exodus* 23:13).[1]

### ~ Underlying Purpose of the Mitzvah ~

שֹׁרֶשׁ הַמִּצְוָה יָדוּעַ — **The underlying purpose of the mitzvah is well-known.**[2]

### ~ Laws of the Mitzvah ~

דִּינֶיהָ בְּפֶרֶק עֲשִׂירִי מִסַּנְהֶדְרִין — **Its laws are** found **in the tenth chapter of** Tractate *Sanhedrin* (111b ff.).[3]

---

NOTES

1. The term *madiach* (subverter) originates from the Torah's terminology in the context of the "subverted city" (*Deuteronomy* 13:14): יָצְאוּ אֲנָשִׁים בְּנֵי בְלִיַּעַל מִקִּרְבֶּךָ וַיַּדִּיחוּ אֶת יֹשְׁבֵי עִירָם לֵאמֹר נֵלְכָה וְנַעַבְדָה אֱלֹהִים אֲחֵרִים אֲשֶׁר לֹא יְדַעְתֶּם, *Lawless men have emerged from your midst, and they have* **subverted** *the dwellers of their city, saying "Let us go and worship the gods of others, that you have not known."* Such a city is known as an *ir hanidachas* (subverted city), and the subverter as a *madiach*. [The special laws of an *ir hanidachas* are discussed in Mitzvos 464-466.]

It emerges that our verse serves as a prohibition against subverting the residents of a city to idolatry. As we shall see, however, Chinuch maintains that the prohibition is not limited to the subversion of an entire city, but applies to anyone who incites other "people" (i.e., more than one person) to idolatry. This will be discussed further below.

2. In Mitzvah 25, Chinuch writes that the obligation to believe in the existence of Hashem does not require explanation, as it is obvious to all that this belief is the foundation of our faith, and that one who does not believe in it denies the basic principle of Judaism. That comment is relevant here as well, in the context of inducing people to forsake God and follow foreign deities. [See also Mitzvah 26 (at note 5), where Chinuch states that the denial in the belief in other deities is "the most essential principle of the Torah upon which everything is dependent."]

3. I.e., the chapter entitled *Cheilek*. [In our editions of *Talmud Bavli*, *Cheilek* is the *eleventh* chapter of

# 161 ☐ MISHPATIM / MITZVAH 87: THE PROHIBITION TO SUBVERT TO IDOLATRY

וּמִי שֶׁלֹּא הֵדִיחַ בָּעִנְיָן זֶה אֶלָּא אָדָם אֶחָד, אֵינוֹ נִקְרָא מַדִּיחַ אֶלָּא מֵסִית, וּבְסֵדֶר רְאֵה אָנֹכִי נִכְתֹּב אַזְהָרַת מֵסִית בְּעֶזְרַת הַשֵּׁם בְּלָאו כ״א (מצוה תסב), אֲבָל כְּשֶׁמַּדִּיחַ שְׁנֵי אֲנָשִׁים אוֹ יוֹתֵר, נִקְרָא מַדִּיחַ.[4]

וְזֶה שֶׁאַתָּה מוֹצֵא כָּל הַרְחָקוֹת אֵלּוּ בַּעֲבוֹדָה זָרָה, וְגֹדֶל הָעֹנֶשׁ בָּהּ[5] עַד שֶׁנִּכְפְּלָה בְּמ״ד

---

Chinuch has previously explained that one who encourages others to worship *avodah zarah* is known as a מַדִּיחַ, *madiach*. Now, Chinuch qualifies that definition, distinguishing between a person who incites many others and a person who incites just a single person to worship *avodah zarah*:

וּמִי שֶׁלֹּא הֵדִיחַ בָּעִנְיָן זֶה אֶלָּא אָדָם אֶחָד — **One who incites only a single person in this matter** of idol worship   אֵינוֹ נִקְרָא מַדִּיחַ אֶלָּא מֵסִית — **is not called a *madiach* (subverter), but a *meisis*** (instigator),   וּבְסֵדֶר רְאֵה אָנֹכִי נִכְתֹּב אַזְהָרַת מֵסִית בְּעֶזְרַת הַשֵּׁם בְּלָאו כ״א — **and in *Parashas Re'eh*, in Prohibition 21** of that *parashah* (Mitzvah 462), **we shall write, with the help of Hashem, the Scriptural injunction of the *meisis*.**   אֲבָל כְּשֶׁמַּדִּיחַ שְׁנֵי אֲנָשִׁים אוֹ יוֹתֵר נִקְרָא מַדִּיחַ — **However, if one incites two or more people** to idolatry, **he is called a *madiach*,** which is the subject of the present mitzvah.[4]

Chinuch addresses why the Torah deals with sins relating to *avodah zarah* with particular severity:

וְזֶה שֶׁאַתָּה מוֹצֵא כָּל הַרְחָקוֹת אֵלּוּ בַּעֲבוֹדָה זָרָה — **Now, that which you find all these distancing measures** in the Torah **regarding *avodah zarah*,**   וְגֹדֶל הָעֹנֶשׁ בָּהּ — **as well as the severity of its punishment,**[5]   עַד שֶׁנִּכְפְּלָה בְּמ״ד מְקוֹמוֹת בַּתּוֹרָה — **to the extent that [the prohibition of**

---

## NOTES

*Sanhedrin*. See *Tos. Yom Tov, Sanhedrin* 10:1.] The Mishnah and Gemara there deal with *ir hanidachas* (see note 1). *Rambam* codifies the special laws of the *ir hanidachas* in *Hil. Avodah Zarah* Ch. 4, and Chinuch presents them in Mitzvos 464-466.

As mentioned in note 1, the *madiach* (subverter) who is the subject of this prohibition is one who incites an entire city to idolatry and makes it an *ir hanidachas*, but according to Chinuch, this also includes anyone who incites more than a single person to idolatry. See the following note.

4. The inciter who is discussed in the context of the *ir hanidachas* (see note 1 for the verse) is known as a *madiach*, subverter. The law of one who leads an *individual* astray is addressed in a different verse (*Deuteronomy* 13:7), כִּי יְסִיתְךָ אָחִיךָ ... בַּסֵּתֶר לֵאמֹר נֵלְכָה וְנַעַבְדָה אֱלֹהִים אֲחֵרִים אֲשֶׁר לֹא יָדַעְתָּ אַתָּה וַאֲבֹתֶיךָ, *If your brother ... will instigate you* (singular) *secretly, saying, "Let us go and worship the gods of others"* — *that you did not know, you or your forefathers*. One who incites an individual is thus known as a *meisis*, instigator. He is not the subject of this mitzvah, but of Mitzvah 462. [For a practical difference as to which mitzvah refers to whom, see *Minchas Chinuch* 462:3.]

A fundamental difference between the *meisis* and the *madiach* is that the *meisis* (who speaks to one person) is liable to death even if the listener does not perform *avodah zarah* as a result of the incitement (see Mitzvah 462 with *Minchas Chinuch* there, §1), while the *madiach* (who speaks to two or more people) is liable only if his listeners heed his words and actually worship idols. In explanation of the basis for this distinction, *Minchas Yitzchak* and *Minchah Chadashah* suggest that since two people are more difficult to subvert than one, if an instigator addresses two people, his words carry less potency and do not suffice to render him liable, unless they are effective. But when he addresses a single person, his incitement carries far more weight, so even if it does not ultimately have the desired effect, he is liable on account of his words alone (see also *Lechem Mishneh, Hil. Avodah Zarah* 5:1).

Many authorities dispute Chinuch's assertion that one who incites more than one person is not considered a *meisis* but a *madiach,* and maintain that such a person is included in the category of *meisis* as long as he has not incited "many." [As for the number of people that is considered "many" in this context, some maintain that ten people are "many," while others assert that even three people are considered "many" (see *Beur R' Izaak Stein* to *Smag, Lo Saaseh* 26; *Mishnas Chachamim, Tzafnas Pane'ach* 22:6; *Minchas Chinuch* 462:4).]

Others insist that one who incites even "many" people is considered a *meisis,* as long as he has not incited the majority of a city, as in the case of an *ir hanidachas,* which is the specific context in which the Torah indicates that he is called a *madiach* (see *Minchas Chinuch* here and below, 462:4). For discussion, and for further distinctions between the laws of a *meisis* and those of a *madiach,* see *Avodas HaMelech, Hil. Avodah Zarah* 4:6, and *Chazon Ish, Sanhedrin* 24:10 ואם ד״ה. See Insight for analysis of Chinuch's view.

5. Idol worship normally carries the penalty of death by *sekilah* (stoning), which is the most severe form of execution (*Sanhedrin* 53a; *Rambam, Hil. Avodah Zarah* 3:1).

מְקוֹמוֹת בַּתּוֹרָה⁶, וְשֶׁתְּכַנֶּה הַתּוֹרָה לַשֵּׁם בָּרוּךְ הוּא קַנָּא עַל עוֹבְדֶיהָ⁷, אַל יַעֲלֶה בִּלְבָבְךָ שֶׁקִּנְאַת הָאֵל וְהַרְחָקוֹת אֵלּוּ נִכְתְּבוּ זוּלָתִי מִצַּד הָעוֹבְדִים⁸, כִּי הַשֵּׁם בָּרוּךְ הוּא וּבָרוּךְ שְׁמוֹ, בֵּין שֶׁיַּעַבְדוּ אוֹתוֹ בְּנֵי אָדָם, אוֹ יַעַבְדוּ מַלְאָךְ אוֹ גַּלְגַּל אוֹ כּוֹכָב אוֹ אֶחָד מִכָּל בְּרוּאָיו, אֵין שׁוּם צַד תּוֹסֶפֶת וְגֵרוּעַ נוֹפֵל בָּזֶה בִּכְבוֹדוֹ בָּרוּךְ הוּא, כִּי תַּכְלִית הַכָּבוֹד וְהַהוֹד לֹא נוֹסָף וְלֹא נִגְרַע בִּשְׁבִיל דָּבָר, אַף כִּי בְּמַעֲשָׂיו אֲנַחְנוּ פְּעֻלּוֹתָיו אַנְשֵׁי הַגּוּפוֹת. אַךְ תֵּדַע בֶּאֱמֶת כִּי כָּל עִנְיָנִים אֵלֶּה נֶאֱמָרִים עַל צַד הַמְקַבְּלִים, יֵאָמֵר כִּי בְּעֵת שֶׁהָאָדָם מוֹצִיא עַצְמוֹ לְגַמְרֵי וּמִתְפַּשֵּׁט מֵאֱמוּנַת הַשֵּׁם בָּרוּךְ הוּא, וּמוֹלִיךְ גּוּפוֹ וּמַתְפִּיס מַחְשְׁבוֹתָיו אַחֲרֵי הַהֶבֶל, לֹא יִהְיֶה רָאוּי כְּלָל לְהַנִּיחַ בּוֹ שׁוּם בְּרָכָה וְשׁוּם טוֹבָה, אֲבָל יִהְיֶה רָאוּי לְהַנִּיחַ עָלָיו כָּל מַה שֶּׁהוּא הֵפֶךְ הַבְּרָכָה, וְהוּא הַקְּלָלָה וְהַמְּאֵרָה וְהֶחֳלָאִים וְכָל רָעוֹת, כִּי הוּא נִתְרַחֵק תַּכְלִית הָרִחוּק מִכָּל גְּבוּלֵי הַטּוֹב, וְעַל כֵּן לֹא תַשִּׂיגֵהוּ כִּי אִם רַע מִכָּל צְדָדָיו⁹, וְעַל דֶּרֶךְ הַמָּשָׁל יֵאָמֵר עָלָיו כְּאִלּוּ הַשֵּׁם יִתְבָּרַךְ,

**וְשֶׁתְּכַנֶּה הַתּוֹרָה**[6] — **idolatry] appears repeatedly — as many as forty-four times — in the Torah, לַשֵּׁם בָּרוּךְ הוּא קַנָּא עַל עוֹבְדֶיהָ — and that the Torah refers to Hashem, blessed is He, as being "jealous" toward those who worship [idols],**[7] **and therefore exacts severe punishment from them, must be explained.** אַל יַעֲלֶה בִּלְבָבְךָ שֶׁקִּנְאַת הָאֵל וְהַרְחָקוֹת אֵלּוּ נִכְתְּבוּ זוּלָתִי מִצַּד הָעוֹבְדִים — But **do not think that the "jealousy" of God and these distancing measures were written** from any perspective **other than from the perspective of the worshipers,**[8] כִּי הַשֵּׁם בָּרוּךְ הוּא וּבָרוּךְ שְׁמוֹ — **for** in regard to **Hashem, blessed is He and blessed is His Name,** בֵּין שֶׁיַּעַבְדוּ אוֹתוֹ בְּנֵי אָדָם אוֹ יַעַבְדוּ מַלְאָךְ אוֹ גַּלְגַּל אוֹ כּוֹכָב אוֹ אֶחָד מִכָּל בְּרוּאָיו — regardless of **whether people worship Him, or they worship an angel, a** celestial **sphere, a star, or one of any of His** other **creations,** אֵין שׁוּם צַד תּוֹסֶפֶת וְגֵרוּעַ נוֹפֵל בָּזֶה בִּכְבוֹדוֹ בָּרוּךְ הוּא — **there is no increase or decrease whatsoever in His honor, blessed is He,** כִּי תַּכְלִית הַכָּבוֹד וְהַהוֹד לֹא נוֹסָף וְלֹא נִגְרַע בִּשְׁבִיל דָּבָר — **because the ultimate honor and glory** — which is Hashem's alone — **is not increased or decreased by anything,** אַף כִּי בְּמַעֲשָׂיו אֲנַחְנוּ פְּעֻלּוֹתָיו אַנְשֵׁי הַגּוּפוֹת — and **certainly** not by **the actions of His** own **works,** that is, **us** (i.e., human beings), **who are His creations, men of** physical **bodies.** אַךְ תֵּדַע — **Rather, you should know, in truth,** כִּי כָּל עִנְיָנִים אֵלֶּה נֶאֱמָרִים עַל צַד הַמְקַבְּלִים — **that all these matters were stated from the perspective of those receiving** God's goodness. יֵאָמֵר כִּי בְּעֵת שֶׁהָאָדָם מוֹצִיא עַצְמוֹ לְגַמְרֵי — **That is to say, when a person removes himself completely** from God, וּמִתְפַּשֵּׁט מֵאֱמוּנַת הַשֵּׁם בָּרוּךְ הוּא — **and strips himself of belief in Hashem, blessed is He,** וּמוֹלִיךְ גּוּפוֹ וּמַתְפִּיס מַחְשְׁבוֹתָיו אַחֲרֵי הַהֶבֶל — **and leads himself** astray, **and attaches his thoughts to the nonsense** of false beliefs, לֹא יִהְיֶה רָאוּי כְּלָל לְהַנִּיחַ בּוֹ שׁוּם בְּרָכָה וְשׁוּם טוֹבָה — **he is completely unfit to receive any blessing or goodness.** אֲבָל יִהְיֶה רָאוּי לְהַנִּיחַ עָלָיו כָּל מַה שֶּׁהוּא הֵפֶךְ הַבְּרָכָה — **Rather, he is fit to receive all that is the opposite of blessing,** וְהוּא הַקְּלָלָה וְהַמְּאֵרָה וְהֶחֳלָאִים וְכָל רָעוֹת — **that being, curse, attrition, illness, and every manner of harm,** כִּי הוּא נִתְרַחֵק תַּכְלִית הָרִחוּק מִכָּל גְּבוּלֵי הַטּוֹב — **because he has become distanced to the greatest extent from all boundaries of goodness,** וְעַל כֵּן לֹא תַשִּׂיגֵהוּ כִּי אִם רַע מִכָּל צְדָדָיו — **and therefore only harm will befall him from all his sides.**[9] וְעַל דֶּרֶךְ הַמָּשָׁל יֵאָמֵר עָלָיו כְּאִלּוּ הַשֵּׁם יִתְבָּרַךְ — Since the

---

## NOTES

6. See Mitzvah 86 and note 9 there.

7. For example, see *Exodus* 20:5 and *Deuteronomy* 32:21. The term "jealous," as used here, refers to an intolerance of faithlessness.

8. That is, one should not think that God distances people from worshiping idols because He is somehow affected by such actions, as Chinuch goes on to explain.

9. [Alternatively: *in all its aspects.*] God is the source of all blessing. Therefore, a person who does not believe in God, has — as a natural outcome of his actions — removed himself from all blessing and will meet with nothing but harm.

Rishonim observe that in the entire Torah, including the books of the Prophets, God is described as "jealous" only in the context of idol worship (*Rambam, Moreh Nevuchim* 1:36; *Ramban* to *Exodus* 20:3). *Ramban* cites *Mechilta* (to *Exodus* 20:5): "I (God) exact punishment with 'jealousy' from those who commit idolatry, but am gracious and merciful regarding other matters."

163 ◻ **MISHPATIM / MITZVAH 87: THE PROHIBITION TO SUBVERT TO IDOLATRY**

שֶׁהוּא אֲדוֹן הַטּוֹבָה, נַעֲשָׂה לוֹ לְאוֹיֵב וְעָצַר מִמֶּנּוּ כָּל הַטּוֹבוֹת, וּכְאִלּוּ הוּא מְקַנֵּא בּוֹ בְּהַנִּיחוֹ עֲבוֹדָתוֹ וְעוֹבֵד אֶת אֲחֵרִים. וְאוּלָם הָאֵל בָּרוּךְ הוּא לֹא אוֹיֵב לִבְרִיָּה וְלֹא יְקַנֵּא לְבֶן אָדָם, כִּי בְיָדוֹ לְהַחֲזִירָם כֻּלָּם עִם כָּל שְׁאָר הָעוֹלָם לְתֹהוּ וָבֹהוּ בַּהֲנָחַת חֶפְצוֹ בְּבִטּוּל,[10] כַּאֲשֶׁר בְּרָאָם בַּהֲנָחַת חֶפְצוֹ בַּבְּרִיאָה, אֲבָל יְכֻנֶּה שְׁמוֹ בָּרוּךְ הוּא בְּקִנְאָה עַל דֶּרֶךְ מַעֲשֵׂה בְּנֵי הָאָדָם, לְפִי שֶׁאֵין בֵּינֵיהֶם שִׂנְאָה גְדוֹלָה כְּמִי שֶׁמְּקַנֵּא בְּאִישׁ עַל שׁוּם דָּבָר אוֹ מְקַנֵּא בְּאִשְׁתּוֹ בִּזְנוּתָהּ עִם אֲחֵרִים, וְעַל כֵּן נִכְתְּבוּ בַּתּוֹרָה הַדִּמְיוֹנוֹת אֵלּוּ אֶצְלוֹ בָּרוּךְ הוּא, כְּדֵי שֶׁיְּבִינֵם אֹזֶן הַשּׁוֹמֵעַ.

וְנוֹהֵג אִסּוּר זֶה בְּכָל מָקוֹם וּבְכָל זְמַן,[11] בִּזְכָרִים וּנְקֵבוֹת.[12] אֲבָל דִּין הָעוֹבֵר עָלֶיהָ בֵּין אִישׁ וְאִשָּׁה, שֶׁהֵן בִּסְקִילָה,[13] אֵינוֹ אֶלָּא בְּמָקוֹם הָרָאוּי לַמִּשְׁפָּט שֶׁהוּא הָאָרֶץ הַנִּבְחֶרֶת.[14]

---

person becomes a paradigm of suffering, **it is said about him, by way of analogy, that it is as though Hashem, blessed be He,** שֶׁהוּא אֲדוֹן הַטּוֹבָה — **Who is the Master of goodness,** נַעֲשָׂה לוֹ לְאוֹיֵב וְעָצַר מִמֶּנּוּ כָּל הַטּוֹבוֹת — **has become an enemy to him and withholds all goodness from him,** וּכְאִלּוּ הוּא מְקַנֵּא בּוֹ בְּהַנִּיחוֹ עֲבוֹדָתוֹ וְעוֹבֵד אֶת אֲחֵרִים — **and it is as if [God] is jealous on his account because he has abandoned His worship and worships others** instead. וְאוּלָם הָאֵל בָּרוּךְ הוּא לֹא אוֹיֵב לִבְרִיָּה — **However, the Almighty, blessed is He, is not** in fact **an enemy to any creature,** כִּי בְיָדוֹ לְהַחֲזִירָם כֻּלָּם עִם כָּל שְׁאָר הָעוֹלָם — **and He is not jealous of** any man, לְתֹהוּ וָבֹהוּ בַּהֲנָחַת חֶפְצוֹ בְּבִטּוּל — **since it lies within His power to return all of [mankind], along with the rest of the entire world, to** its original state of **"emptiness and void,"**[10] **by directing His Will toward the** nullification **of the universe,** כַּאֲשֶׁר בְּרָאָם בַּהֲנָחַת חֶפְצוֹ בַּבְּרִיאָה — **just as He created them by directing His Will toward the creation** of the universe. אֲבָל יְכֻנֶּה שְׁמוֹ בָּרוּךְ הוּא בְּקִנְאָה עַל דֶּרֶךְ מַעֲשֵׂה בְּנֵי הָאָדָם — **Rather,** God, **blessed is He, is referred to as being "jealous"** only **by way of** analogy **to human behavior,** לְפִי שֶׁאֵין בֵּינֵיהֶם שִׂנְאָה גְדוֹלָה כְּמִי שֶׁמְּקַנֵּא בְּאִישׁ עַל שׁוּם דָּבָר — **for there is no greater hatred between [humans] as when one person is jealous of another over some matter,** אוֹ מְקַנֵּא בְּאִשְׁתּוֹ בִּזְנוּתָהּ עִם אֲחֵרִים — **or is jealous of his wife for** committing **adultery with others.** וְעַל כֵּן נִכְתְּבוּ בַּתּוֹרָה הַדִּמְיוֹנוֹת אֵלּוּ אֶצְלוֹ בָּרוּךְ הוּא — **Therefore, these images are drawn in the Torah, of [God], blessed is He,** כְּדֵי שֶׁיְּבִינֵם אֹזֶן הַשּׁוֹמֵעַ — **so that the ear of the listener may understand them,** through analogy to human emotions.

### ⸺ Applicability of the Mitzvah ⸺

וְנוֹהֵג אִסּוּר זֶה בְּכָל מָקוֹם וּבְכָל זְמַן — **This prohibition applies in every location and in all times**[11] בִּזְכָרִים וּנְקֵבוֹת — **to** both **men and women.**[12] That is, it is prohibited in all places and in all times to encourage others to engage in the worship of *avodah zarah*. אֲבָל דִּין הָעוֹבֵר עָלֶיהָ בֵּין אִישׁ וְאִשָּׁה — **However, the justice imposed upon one who transgresses [this prohibition], whether a man or a woman,** שֶׁהֵן בִּסְקִילָה — either **of** whom **is subject to** death through *sekilah* (stoning),[13] אֵינוֹ אֶלָּא בְּמָקוֹם הָרָאוּי לַמִּשְׁפָּט — **is** applicable **only in the place that is fit for the judgment** of capital cases, שֶׁהוּא הָאָרֶץ הַנִּבְחֶרֶת — **which is the Chosen Land** (Eretz Yisrael).[14]

---

NOTES

10. These are the words used by the Torah (*Genesis* 1:2) to describe the state of the world before it was fashioned in Creation.

11. I.e., in Eretz Yisrael and the Diaspora, and whether the *Beis HaMikdash* is standing or not.

12. In accordance with the general rule pertaining to mitzvah-prohibitions. See Insight for discussion of the statement that women are subject to this prohibition.

13. See *Deuteronomy* 13:11.

14. The imposition of capital punishment required a *beis din* comprised of 23 judges who had received *semichah* (i.e., ordination according to the procedure set forth in Mitzvah 491), which was conferred only in Eretz Yisrael, and is no longer conferred in our times. Moreover, capital punishment was administered only during the time of the *Beis HaMikdash*, when the Great Sanhedrin would convene in its designated chamber on the Temple Mount (i.e., the לִשְׁכַּת הַגָּזִית, *Chamber of Hewn Stone*); see *Rambam, Hil. Sanhedrin* 14:11. Once the Sanhedrin was exiled (40 years before the destruction of the *Beis HaMikdash*), it was no longer possible to implement capital punishment (*Rambam* ibid. §13). [See General Introduction (section VI) for further

particulars of the circumstances in which capital punishment was carried out in earlier times.]

Chinuch's statement that capital cases are tried only in Eretz Yisrael must be taken to mean that capital cases are tried in all places when the Great Sanhedrin judges in Eretz Yisrael (see *Minchas Chinuch* 77:9, cited there in note 45; for further discussion, see above, Mitzvah 47 note 16).

⋄§ **Insight: Chinuch's Opinion Regarding a Madiach**

Chinuch establishes that this mitzvah refers to a *madiach*, which he defines as someone who incites more than one person to engage in idolatry, and that the prohibition to incite a single individual to idolatry (i.e., to act as a *meisis*) is stated in Mitzvah 462. At the end of the mitzvah, Chinuch asserts that the prohibition stated here, as well as the punishment imposed for a violation, applies to women as well as men.

*Minchas Chinuch* (here and in Mitzvah 462) strongly questions the assertion that the prohibition of *madiach* applies to women. As was mentioned above, in note 1, the term *madiach* originates in the context of *ir hanidachas*, a subverted city — i.e., a city in which the majority of the residents were subverted to *avodah zarah* (see Mitzvah 464). There are many unique laws associated with an *ir hanidachas*, such as the rule that aside from the fact that those residents who worshiped *avodah zarah* are executed, all the property of the city is destroyed. Also, the guilty parties are executed through *sayif* (the sword), rather than *sekilah* (stoning), which is the usual punishment for the sin of *avodah zarah*. There also are many stipulations regarding the type of city that can become an *ir hanidachas* (e.g., its size), and the manner of subversion through which such a city acquires the status of an *ir hanidachas* (see *Sanhedrin* 111b-113a). In a case where these stipulations are not fulfilled, the special judgment of an *ir hanidachas* is not imposed. Rather, regardless of what percentage of the city's residents succumbed to idolatry, each individual is judged as a private sinner, and if he is found guilty, he is punished with *sekilah* and his property is left intact.

Included among the stipulations is that, even if the majority of a city's residents engage in idolatry, the city does not have the status of an *ir hanidachas* unless its residents were subverted by *two male residents* of that city (ibid. 111b). Thus, we see that the title *madiach*, which refers to one who subverts an *ir hanidachas*, applies only to men. How can Chinuch state that the prohibition against being a *madiach*, and the punishment for violating that prohibition, apply to both men and women?

Moreover, Chinuch indicates, at both the beginning and the end of the mitzvah, that the prohibition and the punishment of a *madiach* apply even to a single person who incites others to *avodah zarah*. But since, as mentioned, the law of *ir hanidachas* applies only when the city is subverted by at least *two* men, how can a single inciter be included in this prohibition and its punishment? Furthermore, Chinuch omits the stipulation that, in order for the punishment to apply, the *madiach* must be a resident of the city that he incites. Finally, the law of *ir hanidachas* applies only if the majority of a city's residents are subverted, yet Chinuch states that the prohibition of *madiach* applies to anyone who incites more than one person to *avodah zarah*.

*Minchas Chinuch* argues that in the case of incitement by a woman, or by a single man, or by a non-resident of the city, or incitement of less than the majority of the city, or in any other case where the city does not meet the standards of an *ir hanidachas*, the inciter has the status of a *meisis*, whose prohibition is stated in Mitzvah 462, not that of a *madiach*, whose prohibition is stated here.

In resolution of Chinuch's view, *Minchas Yitzchak* suggests that the special conditions required in order for a city to qualify as an *ir hanidachas* pertain only to the unique punishment imposed upon the *residents* who commit the mass transgression. *They* are not judged as a "subverted city" — i.e., mass transgressors as opposed to individual transgressors — except in certain conditions. These conditions do not, however, have any bearing on the one doing the subversion, i.e., the *madiach*. Rather, in any case where one incites more than a single individual to *avodah zarah*, the inciter is considered a *madiach*, rather than a *meisis*, and is subject to this prohibition and its punishment. [As explained above, in note 4, a crucial difference between a *madiach* and a *meisis* is that a *madiach* (who targets more than one person) is not liable unless he succeeds in convincing the people that he targeted to commit idolatry, whereas a *meisis* (who targets a single individual) is liable for merely attempting to incite the individual to idolatry.]

Thus, while the unique punishment of an *ir hanidachas* would not apply to the city if a woman (or two women) were to successfully incite most of the residents to worship idols, *she* would still be

in the category of a *madiach*. As long as she successfully subverted at least two people to idolatry, she has violated this prohibition, regardless of whether those whom she subverted are subject to the special laws of *ir hanidachas*. The same applies to a non-resident, or to a man acting alone. That is why Chinuch does not distinguish in regard to the *prohibition* of *madiach* between a man and a woman, or between a resident of the city and a non-resident, or between a case where the *madiach* acts alone and a case where he acts together with a partner.

## מִצְוָה פח: מִצְוַת חֲגִיגָה בָּרְגָלִים

לָחֹג בָּרְגָלִים, וְהוּא שֶׁנִּצְטַוֵּינוּ לַעֲלוֹת לְרֶגֶל לַמִּקְדָּשׁ שָׁלֹשׁ פְּעָמִים בַּשָּׁנָה, וְהֵן סָמוּךְ לְפֶסַח וְשָׁבוּעוֹת וְסֻכּוֹת,[1] כְּדֵי שֶׁנָּחֹג שָׁם, שֶׁנֶּאֱמַר (שמות כ"ג, י"ד)

---

## Mitzvah 88
# The Obligation to Celebrate the Pilgrimage Festivals

שָׁלֹשׁ רְגָלִים תָּחֹג לִי בַּשָּׁנָה

*Three pilgrimage festivals shall you celebrate for Me in the year* (Exodus 23:14).

In subsequent verses in this passage (vs. 15-17), the Torah identifies the three occasions that are to be celebrated annually as national pilgrimages to the Temple (*Beis HaMikdash*) in Jerusalem: the Festival of Matzos (Pesach), the Festival of the Harvest (Shavuos), and the Festival of the Ingathering (Succos). The passage further specifies that on these occasions all Jewish men must *appear before the Lord, Hashem* [i.e., in the Temple], and it cautions us not to appear before Him empty-handed. Elsewhere (*Deuteronomy* 16:10-11,14-15), the Torah mentions an additional requirement — to rejoice on these festivals, together with our families and with the needy.

As understood by the Oral Tradition (*Chagigah* 6b), which Chinuch will cite, these verses delineate three distinct elements of the רֶגֶל, *pilgrimage festival*, each of which constitutes a separate mitzvah-obligation: (1) חֲגִיגָה, *celebrating* the festival by observing it as an occasion of pilgrimage to Jerusalem and service at the Temple (this mitzvah); (2) רְאִיָּה, *appearing* before the Divine Presence by presenting ourselves in the Temple Courtyard with an offering on the opening day of the festival (Mitzvah 489); and (3) שִׂמְחָה, *rejoicing* throughout the festival (Mitzvah 488).

"Celebrating a festival for Hashem" denotes making a pilgrimage to His Holy Temple and joyously offering sacrifices to Him. This requires that one bring a special offering in honor of the festival. The offering is known as שַׁלְמֵי חֲגִיגָה, *shelamim of chagigah* (i.e., celebration), or simply, the *chagigah* offering. This pilgrimage and the accompanying offering are the subject of this mitzvah.

Chinuch notes further in Mitzvah 489 that a particular sacrificial offering is associated with *each* of the three mitzvos of the pilgrimage festival. "Celebrating," as just explained, obligates us to bring a *shelamim* as a *chagigah* offering. "Appearing" requires its own offering, for the Torah (v. 15 here, and *Deuteronomy* 16:16; Mitzvah 490) specifically prohibits appearing in the Temple empty-handed. The offering brought for this purpose is an *olah* offering known as the עוֹלַת רְאִיָּה, *olas re'iyah* (*olah of appearance*). "Rejoicing" is observed at the Temple by feasting on sacrificial meats (see *Deuteronomy* 27:7), and therefore, special offerings are brought for the purpose of fulfilling the mitzvah of rejoicing on the festival. These are regular *shelamim* offerings, and are known as שַׁלְמֵי שִׂמְחָה, *shelamim of simchah* (*rejoicing*). The *chagigah* and *re'iyah* offerings must be brought upon coming to the Temple Courtyard on the first day of each festival, though if not brought on that day, the opportunity for compensation exists for the remainder of the festival. The *shelamim of simchah* may be brought at any time on the festival, as needed.

While the specific focus of our mitzvah is the *chagigah* celebration, Chinuch in this context discusses aspects of all three of these mitzvos.

לָחֹג בָּרְגָלִים — It is a mitzvah **to celebrate on the pilgrimage festivals.** וְהוּא שֶׁנִּצְטַוֵּינוּ לַעֲלוֹת לְרֶגֶל לַמִּקְדָּשׁ שָׁלֹשׁ פְּעָמִים בַּשָּׁנָה — That is, **we are commanded to ascend in pilgrimage to the Holy Temple on three occasions each year,** וְהֵן סָמוּךְ לְפֶסַח וְשָׁבוּעוֹת וְסֻכּוֹת — **which are: immediately preceding Pesach, Shavuos, and Succos,**[1] כְּדֵי שֶׁנָּחֹג שָׁם — **in order to celebrate there** on these festivals, שֶׁנֶּאֱמַר — **as it is stated** (*Exodus* 23:14):

---

NOTES

1. Chinuch explains that the mitzvah to celebrate the pilgrimage festivals requires one to ascend to Jerusalem *before* each of the festivals, in order to be able to actually celebrate in the Temple *on* the first

## 167 ◻ MISHPATIM / MITZVAH 88: THE OBLIGATION TO CELEBRATE THE PILGRIMAGE FESTIVALS

שָׁלֹשׁ רְגָלִים תָּחֹג לִי בַּשָּׁנָה.[2] וּמֵעִנְיַן הַחֲגִיגָה הוּא שֶׁנַּעֲלֶה שָׁם בְּקָרְבָּן וְנַקְרִיבֵהוּ שְׁלָמִים לִכְבוֹד הֶחָג.[3] וְנִכְפְּלָה מִצְוָה זוֹ פְּעָמִים בַּתּוֹרָה,[4] וְאָמְרוּ זִכְרוֹנָם לִבְרָכָה בְּמַסֶּכֶת חֲגִיגָה (דף ו' ע״א) שָׁלֹשׁ מִצְווֹת נִצְטַוּוּ יִשְׂרָאֵל בָּרֶגֶל, חֲגִיגָה רְאִיָּה שִׂמְחָה.[5]

"שָׁלֹשׁ רְגָלִים תָּחֹג לִי בַּשָּׁנָה" — **Three pilgrimage festivals shall you celebrate for Me in the year.**[2]
וּמֵעִנְיַן הַחֲגִיגָה הוּא שֶׁנַּעֲלֶה שָׁם בְּקָרְבָּן — **Included in the** requirement of **celebration is that we are to ascend there with** an animal to be used as **a sacrifice** וְנַקְרִיבֵהוּ שְׁלָמִים לִכְבוֹד הֶחָג — **and offer it as a** *shelamim* **in honor of the festival.**[3]
וְנִכְפְּלָה מִצְוָה זוֹ פְּעָמִים בַּתּוֹרָה — **This mitzvah is repeated twice** more **in the Torah.**[4]

Chinuch explains that this is part of a group of three mitzvos that pertain to the celebration of the festivals:

וְאָמְרוּ זִכְרוֹנָם לִבְרָכָה בְּמַסֶּכֶת חֲגִיגָה — **[Our Sages], of blessed memory, stated in Tractate** *Chagigah* (6b): שָׁלֹשׁ מִצְווֹת נִצְטַוּוּ יִשְׂרָאֵל בָּרֶגֶל — **The people of Israel were commanded three** distinct **mitzvos in** reference to each **pilgrimage festival:** חֲגִיגָה — (1) *celebrating* the pilgrimage festival, רְאִיָּה — (2) *appearing* in the Temple before the Divine Presence (Mitzvah 489), שִׂמְחָה — and (3) *rejoicing* throughout the festival (Mitzvah 488).[5]

---

### NOTES

day of each festival. See note 3 for further discussion.

2. The word רְגָלִים, translated as *pilgrimage festivals,* literally means *feet,* and indicates that one must ascend the Temple Mount on foot in order to celebrate the festival there (see below, note 18). This is the source of the common description of the mitzvah as עֲלִיָּה לְרֶגֶל, *ascending on pilgrimage,* or *ascending on foot.*

3. Oral Tradition teaches that bringing the *chagigah* offering is a dimension of the mitzvah to celebrate (see *Chagigah* 10b). Chinuch implies that ascending from Jerusalem to the *Beis HaMikdash* together *with* an animal that will be used as the *chagigah* offering is part of the concept of pilgrimage. See further below, note 14.

Chinuch depicts the *chagigah* offering as a *detail* of this mitzvah, but not the entirety of the mitzvah. The mitzvah, in his opinion, is comprised of two elements: making the pilgrimage to the *Beis HaMikdash, and* sacrificing a *chagigah* offering upon arriving there (see *Minchas Yitzchak*). It should be noted that in Mitzvah 489 Chinuch describes the mitzvah of רְאִיָּה (*re'iyah*), *appearing [in the Temple],* as an obligation to ascend to the *Beis HaMikdash* and appear there on the festival with an *olah* offering (i.e., the *olas re'iyah*). It emerges, then, that visiting the *Beis HaMikdash* is obligatory under *each* of these mitzvos; the current mitzvah requires ascending to the *Beis HaMikdash* and "celebrating" there with a *chagigah,* and Mitzvah 489 requires ascending to the *Beis HaMikdash* and "appearing" there with an *olah*. [The *chagigah,* being a *shelamim* offering, is appropriate for "celebration," because the owner enjoys its meat. The *olah,* on the other hand, is burnt on the Altar in its entirety; hence, it is not celebratory, but simply an offering to Hashem brought on the occasion of appearing before Him in the Temple.]

Chinuch's approach follows that of *Rambam* in *Sefer HaMitzvos, Asei* 52-53, who explains that the pilgrimage is required both under the mitzvah of *chagigah* and under the mitzvah of *re'iyah*. In *Hilchos Chagigah* (1:1), however, *Rambam* takes a different approach. He explains that the pilgrimage is required specifically under the mitzvah of *re'iyah* (appearing in the Temple; Mitzvah 489), and the current mitzvah is simply an obligation to sacrifice a *chagigah* offering *when one comes to the Temple "to appear before Hashem"* — i.e., in fulfillment of Mitzvah 489. Thus, the *chagigah* offering is not a *detail* of the mitzvah of "celebrating," but is the very *essence* of the mitzvah. For discussion, see *Minchas Yitzchak* §1.

4. The obligation to ascend to the *Beis HaMikdash* on pilgrimage three times a year is mentioned in two additional passages in the Torah: *Exodus* 34:23 and *Deuteronomy* 16:16-17. In addition to these repetitions of the pilgrimage obligation, the requirement to celebrate is mentioned individually regarding each of the festivals: in reference to Pesach in *Exodus* 12:14; in reference to Shavuos in *Deuteronomy* 16:10; and in reference to Succos in *Leviticus* 23:39-41, *Numbers* 29:12, and *Deuteronomy* 16:15. [The term חַג, *chag,* in all these verses refers to the *chagigah* celebration (see *Chagigah* 8a-b, 9a, 10b).]

These repeated articulations of the mitzvah serve to emphasize its importance, but are not counted separately in the enumeration of the 613 mitzvos (see *Rambam, Sefer HaMitzvos, Shoresh* 9). Likewise, although the observance of this mitzvah is prescribed for three different times of the year, it is treated as a single mitzvah-obligation (*Rambam, Sefer HaMitzvos, Shoresh* 13; see R' Y. F. Perla, *Sefer HaMitzvos of R' Saadiah Gaon, Asei* 45 [Vol. I, p. 204b]).

5. The three obligations could have been viewed as components of a single mitzvah of pilgrimage. The Sages, however, identified them as three distinct mitzvah-obligations. As mentioned in the introduction to this mitzvah, each of these obligations carries a requirement to bring an offering.

מִשָּׁרְשֵׁי מִצְוָה זוֹ, לְפִי שֶׁאֵינוֹ בַּדִּין לָבוֹא בְּיָדַיִם רֵיקָנִיּוֹת לִפְנֵי הַמָּקוֹם בָּרוּךְ הוּא, וְאַף עַל פִּי שֶׁהָאֱמֶת כִּי אֵינוֹ צָרִיךְ דְּבַר מִיָּדֵינוּ, כְּמוֹ שֶׁכָּתוּב (תהילים נ׳, י״ב) אִם אֶרְעַב לֹא אֹמַר לָךְ, אַף עַל פִּי כֵן בְּדִמְיוֹן מַחֲשַׁבְתֵּנוּ אֲנַחְנוּ רוֹאִין כְּאִלּוּ נַעֲמֹד לְפָנָיו, וְהָאֱמֶת שֶׁהַנְּפָשׁוֹת קְרוֹבוֹת אֶל הַטּוֹב בַּמָּקוֹם הַהוּא יוֹתֵר מִשְּׁאָר מְקוֹמוֹת וְאוֹר פְּנֵי מֶלֶךְ נֹגַהּ עֲלֵיהֶם שָׁם, וְעַל כֵּן רָאוּי לָנוּ לַעֲשׂוֹת מַעֲשֵׂה הַקָּרְבָּן בָּעֵת הַהִיא, כִּי בִּפְעֻלַּת הַקָּרְבָּן נִתָּכֵן לְקַבָּלַת הַטּוֹבָה וְתִתְעַלֶּה נַפְשׁוֹתֵינוּ מַעֲלָה מַעֲלָה, כְּמוֹ שֶׁנִּכְתֹּב בְּעֶזְרַת הַשֵּׁם.

## ⁓ Underlying Purpose of the Mitzvah ⁓

In Mitzvah 489, Chinuch explains why we are obligated to come to the Temple three times a year: By visiting the House of God together with all of Israel, we demonstrate — and awaken in ourselves the awareness — that we are, collectively, His People, who alone were chosen from among all the nations to uphold His Law, and who therefore are the exclusive "members of His household." We thus are inspired to fear and love Him, and we become worthy of acquiring His blessing.[6]

Here, Chinuch explains why we must bring an offering on the occasion of our pilgrimage: מִשָּׁרְשֵׁי מִצְוָה זוֹ — **Among the underlying purposes of this mitzvah is** לְפִי שֶׁאֵינוֹ בַּדִּין לָבוֹא בְּיָדַיִם רֵיקָנִיּוֹת לִפְנֵי הַמָּקוֹם בָּרוּךְ הוּא — **that we are required to celebrate with offerings because it is not fitting to arrive empty-handed before the Omnipresent, blessed is He.**[7] וְאַף עַל פִּי שֶׁהָאֱמֶת כִּי אֵינוֹ צָרִיךְ דְּבַר מִיָּדֵינוּ — **Although the reality is that He has no need for anything that we possess,** כְּמוֹ שֶׁכָּתוּב — **as is written** with regard to sacrificial offerings (Psalms 50:12): אִם אֶרְעַב לֹא אֹמַר לָךְ — **Even were I hungry I would not tell you,** for Mine is the earth and its fullness,[8] אַף עַל פִּי כֵן בְּדִמְיוֹן מַחֲשַׁבְתֵּנוּ אֲנַחְנוּ רוֹאִין כְּאִלּוּ נַעֲמֹד לְפָנָיו — **nevertheless, in our mind's eye we are to envision ourselves,** in coming to the Temple, **as standing before Him** in tribute, and this requires us to respectfully offer a sacrifice.

Chinuch proceeds with a deeper explanation of this concept: וְהָאֱמֶת שֶׁהַנְּפָשׁוֹת קְרוֹבוֹת אֶל הַטּוֹב בַּמָּקוֹם הַהוּא יוֹתֵר מִשְּׁאָר מְקוֹמוֹת — **The reality is that** people's **souls are closer to the** ultimate **goodness in that place** (i.e., the Temple) **than in other places,** וְאוֹר פְּנֵי מֶלֶךְ נֹגַהּ עֲלֵיהֶם שָׁם — **and the Light of the King's Countenance shines upon them there.**[9] וְעַל כֵּן — **Consequently,** when we come to the Temple on pilgrimage, רָאוּי לָנוּ לַעֲשׂוֹת מַעֲשֵׂה הַקָּרְבָּן בָּעֵת הַהִיא — **it is appropriate for us to perform the sacrificial procedure at that time,** כִּי בִּפְעֻלַּת הַקָּרְבָּן נִתָּכֵן לְקַבָּלַת הַטּוֹבָה — **for through the act of making an offering we become suitable for receiving** that **goodness** וְתִתְעַלֶּה נַפְשׁוֹתֵינוּ מַעֲלָה מַעֲלָה — **and our souls are elevated ever higher,** כְּמוֹ שֶׁנִּכְתֹּב בְּעֶזְרַת הַשֵּׁם — **as we shall write, with the help of Hashem** (in Mitzvah 95).[10]

---

NOTES

6. See there for elaboration.

7. Just as decorum demands the presentation of a gift when coming before a king of flesh and blood, so too must we bring offerings when appearing before Hashem.

8. The Scriptural passage (in Psalm 50) contains an emphatic warning against wrongly misconceiving the sacrificial service as a mechanism through which man provides sustenance or power to the Divine; clearly, the Creator of the Universe has no need for our meager gifts. He is, of course, never hungry, and even if it could be imagined that He might be, He would not need our offerings, as everything in the universe is His. Rather, sacrificial offerings are meaningful only as an expression of heartfelt submission to Hashem and obedience to His Word (see *Menachos* 110a and *Bamidbar Rabbah*

21:16). Thus, the concept of "not arriving empty-handed" might seem incongruous.

9. The *Beis HaMikdash* is a place where man is blessed with spiritual clarity and keen awareness of Hashem (see Mitzvah 95, and the following note).

10. Chinuch explains in Mitzvah 95 that Hashem directs His flow of goodness through the *Beis HaMikdash,* for that is the place where people are closest to spirituality, and hence, most worthy of being beneficiaries of His goodness. Accordingly, Chinuch states here that when one comes to the *Beis HaMikdash* on pilgrimage, and thus attains an elevated spiritual state through basking "in the Light of the King's Countenance," he is called upon to refine his character even further by means of presenting an offering. In doing so, he becomes even

### 169 ☐ MISHPATIM / MITZVAH 88: THE OBLIGATION TO CELEBRATE THE PILGRIMAGE FESTIVALS

מִדִּינֵי[11] הַמִּצְוָה, מַה שֶּׁאָמְרוּ זִכְרוֹנָם לִבְרָכָה שֶׁקָּרְבָּנוֹת אֵלּוּ אֵין לָהֶן שִׁעוּר[12], אֶלָּא אֲפִלּוּ אֶחָד יַסְפִּיק, בֵּין בְּהֵמָה בֵּין עוֹף תּוֹר אוֹ גוֹזָל[13], וְשֶׁחַיָּב לַעֲלוֹת לִירוּשָׁלַיִם עַל כָּל פָּנִים בְּקָרְבָּן בְּיָדוֹ אוֹ בַּכֶּסֶף שֶׁיִּקְנֶה בּוֹ קָרְבָּן בִּירוּשָׁלַיִם, אֲבָל בְּשָׁוֶה כֶסֶף אֵינוֹ פָּטוּר[14],

---

### ⇜ Laws of the Mitzvah ⇝

Chinuch discusses laws pertaining to both of the offerings that must be brought when appearing in the Temple on the first day of each festival — the *chagigah* offering and the *re'iyah* offering:[11]

מִדִּינֵי הַמִּצְוָה — **The laws** related **to this mitzvah include** מַה שֶּׁאָמְרוּ זִכְרוֹנָם לִבְרָכָה — **that which [our Sages], of blessed memory, have stated** (Mishnah, *Peah* 1:1), שֶׁקָּרְבָּנוֹת אֵלּוּ אֵין לָהֶן שִׁעוּר — **that these offerings have no set amount**;[12] אֶלָּא אֲפִלּוּ אֶחָד יַסְפִּיק — **rather, even a single one suffices,** בֵּין בְּהֵמָה בֵּין עוֹף תּוֹר אוֹ גוֹזָל — **whether a beast or a bird,** namely, a turtledove or a young dove.[13]

וְשֶׁחַיָּב לַעֲלוֹת לִירוּשָׁלַיִם — **Also** included is the law **that one is obligated to ascend to Jerusalem** on pilgrimage עַל כָּל פָּנִים בְּקָרְבָּן בְּיָדוֹ — **with, in any event, an** actual **offering** (i.e., an animal or a bird) **in his hand,** אוֹ בַּכֶּסֶף שֶׁיִּקְנֶה בּוֹ קָרְבָּן בִּירוּשָׁלַיִם — **or** at least **with money with which to purchase an offering** upon arrival **in Jerusalem;** אֲבָל בְּשָׁוֶה כֶסֶף אֵינוֹ פָּטוּר — **but one cannot exempt** himself **by** bringing objects that have **monetary value** and are not actual currency.[14]

---

NOTES

more receptive to the Divine influence that permeates the *Beis HaMikdash,* and by extension, more worthy of benefiting from Hashem's goodness.

11. As has been noted on numerous occasions, Chinuch does not restrict his discussion to laws specific to the mitzvah at hand, but includes laws of related mitzvos as well. In our case, Chinuch writes explicitly in Mitzvah 489 (the obligation to appear in the Temple with a *re'iyah* offering) that he already discussed the laws of that mitzvah here, in Mitzvah 88. See further, note 13.

12. The Mishnah (*Peah* 1:1) lists הָרְאָיוֹן, *appearing,* among those things that have no fixed measure, meaning that the Torah sets neither a minimum nor a maximum to the number of animals — or the value of the animals — that shall be brought for the *re'iyah* offering. Although one is bidden to bring offerings in accordance with his wealth (*Deuteronomy* 16:17; see *Chagigah* 8b and *Rambam, Hil. Chagigah* 1:2), as long as one does not appear in the *Beis HaMikdash* empty-handed he has discharged the basic obligation. *Rambam* (ibid.) applies this rule to the *chagigah* as well.

Rabbinic law requires a minimum value of one silver *maah* for the *re'iyah* offering and two for the *chagigah* offering (*Chagigah* 7a; *Rambam* ibid.). [A *maah* is a silver coin whose weight equals 16 barleycorns (see *Kiddushin* 12a and *Rambam, Hil. Shekalim* 1:3 and *Hil. To'ein VeNit'an* 3:1).]

13. Since the offerings have no minimum measure, even a bird suffices (see the anonymous *Peirush* to *Rambam, Hil. Kiddush HaChodesh* 4:7).

Birds can be brought as *olah* offerings (see *Leviticus* 1:14), but never as *shelamim* offerings (see Mitzvah 141; see also *Rambam, Hil. Chagigah* 1:1). The commentators therefore question Chinuch's statement in our context of the *chagigah* (which is a *shelamim*) that

one may bring even a bird as his offering (*Mishneh LaMelech* here, et al.). Some suggest that when Chinuch states that a bird suffices, he refers specifically to the *re'iyah* offering, which is an *olah,* and not to the *chagigah* offering (*Minchas Yitzchak* §2; see Mitzvah 489). Indeed, *Rambam* (ibid.) rules that one must bring either an animal or a bird as a *re'iyah* offering, *and* an animal as a *chagigah* offering. [According to our texts of the Gemara, *Chagigah* 7a, the *re'iyah* offering must consist of an animal and not a bird (see *Rashi* there ד״ה בזבחים). *Rambam's* view (which Chinuch follows) seems to be based on a variant text of the Gemara (see *Kesef Mishneh, Hil. Chagigah* 1:1; see *Mahari Korkos* there for further discussion).]

In a novel approach, *Minchas Yitzchak* (§1, §6) suggests further that, according to Chinuch, although the mitzvah of *chagigah* is optimally performed by making the pilgrimage *and* bringing an offering, it can be fulfilled minimally (*bedi'avad*) by making the pilgrimage even without bringing an offering. Hence, the only offering that one *must* bring is the *olah* of *re'iyah.* Chinuch therefore states here that it suffices — at a minimum — to offer even a bird on the festival. See further below, note 26.

14. One may not rely on selling the objects in Jerusalem and thereby obtaining currency with which to purchase his offering; he must bring either the actual animal or bird for the offering, or money with which to purchase it. The rule that one should bring an offering or its value with him is part of the Biblical mitzvah (see above, note 3). The rule that the only item of value acceptable is *money* is a Rabbinic decree, instituted out of concern that if people would bring other items of value they might not be able to convert them to useful currency and ultimately would not be able to bring any

וְאִם לֹא הִקְרִיב קָרְבָּנוֹ בְּיוֹם רִאשׁוֹן שֶׁיֵּשׁ לוֹ תַּשְׁלוּמִין כָּל שִׁבְעָה, וּבִלְבַד שֶׁיִּהְיֶה הוּא שָׁם בַּיוֹם רִאשׁוֹן,[15] וְיֶתֶר פְּרָטֶיהָ מְבוֹאָרִים בְּמַסֶּכֶת חֲגִיגָה.[16] וְנוֹהֶגֶת בִּזְמַן הַבַּיִת, בִּזְכָרִים אֲבָל לֹא בִנְקֵבוֹת,[17] וְלֹא כָּל הַזְּכָרִים, שֶׁחִגֵּר[18]

וְאִם לֹא הִקְרִיב קָרְבָּנוֹ בְּיוֹם רִאשׁוֹן — Also included is the law that **if one did not bring his offering on the first day** of the festival, שֶׁיֵּשׁ לוֹ תַּשְׁלוּמִין כָּל שִׁבְעָה — **there is** the possibility of **compensating for it throughout** the **seven** days of the festival, וּבִלְבַד שֶׁיִּהְיֶה הוּא שָׁם בַּיוֹם רִאשׁוֹן — **provided that he was present there,** in the Temple, **on the first day.**[15]

וְיֶתֶר פְּרָטֶיהָ — These laws **and the additional details of [this mitzvah]** מְבוֹאָרִים בְּמַסֶּכֶת חֲגִיגָה — **are explained in** the first and second chapters of **Tractate Chagigah.**[16]

### ⇐ Applicability of the Mitzvah ⇒

וְנוֹהֶגֶת בִּזְמַן הַבַּיִת — **[This mitzvah] applies in the times of the Temple,** בִּזְכָרִים אֲבָל לֹא בִנְקֵבוֹת — **to men, but not to women.**[17]

וְלֹא כָּל הַזְּכָרִים — **However,** it does **not** apply to **all men,** שֶׁחִגֵּר — **as one who is lame,**[18]

---

NOTES

offerings (*Rambam, Hil. Chagigah* 1:3, as explained by *Oneg Yom Tov* §94 ד"ה ומטעם זה נראה לי).

It should be noted that the Gemara (*Bechoros* 51a) mentions this requirement in regard to הָרְאָיוֹן, *appearing*, which Rashi explains as referring specifically to the *re'iyah* offering. When making pilgrimage, one must bring along that offering or its value in currency [thus ensuring that he will not appear in the *Beis HaMikdash* empty-handed]. *Rambam* (*Hil. Chagigah* 1:3), however, cites this law in regard to קָרְבְּנוֹת הָרְאִיָּה, *the offerings of appearance,* in the plural form, which can be understood to encompass *both* offerings brought when appearing in the *Beis HaMikdash* — the *re'iyah olah* and the *chagigah shelamim* (see *Rambam* ibid. §1; cf. *Minchas Chinuch* §9).

With respect to Chinuch's position, it is unclear to which of these offerings he refers here. *Minchas Chinuch* (ibid.) assumes that he refers to the *chagigah* offering, but *Minchas Yitzchak* (§2) argues that he refers specifically to the *re'iyah* offering. [See note 11.]

15. The mitzvah to be present in the *Beis HaMikdash* and bring the *re'iyah* and *chagigah* offerings applies primarily on the inaugural day of the festival (*Rambam* ibid. 1:1, 2:6). One who was obligated in these offerings at that time, but did not bring them, may compensate for his omission by bringing the offerings on one of the remaining days of Pesach and Succos, including Shemini Atzeres. In the case of Shavuos, which is only one day long, he may bring the offerings on the six days following the festival. One who was not obligated on the first day of the festival, however, does not bring these offerings on another day (*Chagigah* 9a; *Rambam* ibid. 1:4-7). [See Chinuch below for a list of people who are exempt from the mitzvah; in some of those cases, the exemption might exist on the first day alone, but on that basis the person remains exempt throughout the festival.]

Here, Chinuch states that, even for one who was *not* exempt, compensation is possible only if he actually appeared in the *Beis HaMikdash* on the first day of the festival. Apparently, Chinuch maintains that the mitzvah of appearing in the *Beis HaMikdash* can be fulfilled *only* on the first day and has no compensation; thus, the obligation to bring the offering, which is tied to appearing in the *Beis HaMikdash,* can be triggered only on the first day. If that obligation sets in, then one who failed to bring the offering on the first day can bring it on a subsequent day of the festival; but if the obligation did not take effect on the first day, then the offering cannot be brought at all. Thus, if one appeared in the *Beis HaMikdash* on the first day without an offering, he may compensate by bringing the offering on another day, but if he failed to appear there on the first day, he has forfeited the mitzvah of *re'iyah* and has no basis to bring the offering (see *Turei Even, Chagigah* 2a ד"ה לאתויי חיגר ביום ראשון; cf. *Minchas Chinuch* 489:4; *Ohr Same'ach, Hil. Chagigah* 1:1).

[*Turei Even* (ibid.) assumes that this applies only to the *re'iyah* offering, but the *chagigah* may be brought throughout the festival even by one who did not appear in the *Beis HaMikdash* on the first day. See there for discussion.]

16. The laws are codified in *Rambam, Hil. Chagigah*.

17. The Torah (*Exodus* 23:17) specifically exempts women from these obligations, stating that כָּל זְכוּרְךָ, *all your menfolk,* are required to appear in the *Beis HaMikdash* on the festivals (*Chagigah* 4a). And anyone who is exempt from appearing is also exempt from bringing the associated offerings (*Rambam* ibid. 2:4; see note 21). [The Gemara (ibid.) explains why women are not automatically excluded by virtue of this being a מִצְוַת עֲשֵׂה שֶׁהַזְּמַן גְּרָמָא, *a mitzvah-obligation that is time-specific.*]

18. The word רְגָלִים (*pilgrimage festival*) in our verse is related to רֶגֶל (*foot*) and connotes *walking on foot* from Jerusalem to the top of the Temple Mount. Anyone who cannot walk up unassisted is exempt from making the pilgrimage and appearing in the *Beis HaMikdash,* as well as from making the associated sacrificial offerings (*Chagigah* 4a; see further, note 20).

# 171 ☐ MISHPATIM / MITZVAH 88: THE OBLIGATION TO CELEBRATE THE PILGRIMAGE FESTIVALS

וְסוּמָא אֲפִלּוּ בְּאַחַת מֵעֵינָיו,[19] וְחוֹלֶה וְזָקֵן וְעָנֹג הַרְבֵּה שֶׁאֵינוֹ יָכוֹל לַעֲלוֹת בְּרַגְלָיו,[20] כֻּלָּן פְּטוּרִין,[21] וְכֵן טֻמְטוּם וְאַנְדְּרוֹגִינוֹס[22] וַעֲבָדִים,[23] אֲבָל כָּל שְׁאָר הַזְּכָרִים חַיָּבִין, וַאֲפִלּוּ יֵשׁ לָהֶן אֻמָּנוּת מְכֹעָר כְּגוֹן מְקַמֵּץ וּמְצָרֵף[24] וְעַבְדָּן, מְטַהֲרִין גּוּפָן וּמַלְבּוּשָׁן וְעוֹלִין לִפְנֵי הַשֵּׁם יִתְבָּרַךְ, וְהֵם מְקֻבָּלִין לְפָנָיו כִּשְׁאָר יִשְׂרָאֵל,[25] שֶׁטִּנּוּף הַנֶּפֶשׁ הוּא הַמַּמְאִיס

---

וְחוֹלֶה וְזָקֵן וְעָנֹג הַרְבֵּה שֶׁאֵינוֹ יָכוֹל לַעֲלוֹת וְסוּמָא אֲפִלּוּ בְּאַחַת מֵעֵינָיו — or blind, even in one eye,[19] בְּרַגְלָיו — or ill, or elderly, or extremely delicate, such that he is unable to ascend the Temple Mount on foot[20] — כֻּלָּן פְּטוּרִין — all of these are exempt from this mitzvah.[21] וְכֵן טֻמְטוּם וְאַנְדְּרוֹגִינוֹס — Likewise, a *tumtum*, an *androgynos*,[22] וַעֲבָדִים — and Canaanite slaves, are all exempt.[23]

אֲבָל כָּל שְׁאָר הַזְּכָרִים חַיָּבִין — All other men, however, are obligated to celebrate the pilgrimage festival; וַאֲפִלּוּ יֵשׁ לָהֶן אֻמָּנוּת מְכֹעָר — and even those who have an unsavory occupation, כְּגוֹן מְקַמֵּץ וּמְצָרֵף וְעַבְדָּן — such as a dung-gatherer, a copper-miner,[24] or a tanner, מְטַהֲרִין גּוּפָן וּמַלְבּוּשָׁן וְעוֹלִין לִפְנֵי הַשֵּׁם יִתְבָּרַךְ — must cleanse their bodies and garments and ascend to the Temple to appear before Hashem, blessed be He, וְהֵם מְקֻבָּלִין לְפָנָיו כִּשְׁאָר יִשְׂרָאֵל — and they are accepted before Him just like the rest of the people of Israel.[25] שֶׁטִּנּוּף הַנֶּפֶשׁ הוּא הַמַּמְאִיס

---

## NOTES

19. A man who is even partially blind is not included in the mitzvah of רְאִיָּה, *appearance*, since he is unable to perceive fully the manifestation of the Divine Presence. Our Sages derive from Scripture that the mitzvah of *appearing* does not require merely that one appear before Hashem to be seen by Him. Rather: *Just as they (the people of Israel) come to be seen by Hashem, so do they come to see the splendor of His Holiness and of the House of His dwelling* (*Chagigah* 2a, as interpreted by *Rambam* ibid. 2:1).

20. As explained in note 18, the word רְגָלִים, *feet,* teaches that one who is unable to walk up to the Temple Mount unassisted is exempt from the mitzvah. This includes an "extremely delicate" person, that is, one who never walks without a cane (*Rambam* ibid., as explained by *Mishneh LaMelech*; cf. *Mahari Korkos* there).

Others explain that the "extremely delicate" person is one who is too fastidious to walk on his *bare feet*. No person may tread the sacred soil of the Temple Mount with shoes (*Berachos* 62b), and doing so constitutes "trampling God's Courtyards" (see *Isaiah* 1:12) rather than pilgrimage (*Rashi, Chagigah* 4b ד"ה מפנקי; *Tosafos* there ד"ה כי תבאו).

21. The Mishnah (*Chagigah* 2a) teaches merely that all these people are exempt from רְאִיָּה, *appearing [in the Beis HaMikdash]*, but Chinuch — following *Rambam* (ibid. 2:4) — maintains that whoever is exempt from appearing in the *Beis HaMikdash* is likewise exempt from bringing the associated offerings, whether the *re'iyah* or the *chagigah* offering (see end of note 3). *Tosafos* (*Chagigah* 2b ד"ה שומע), however, maintain that there can be a case of one who is exempt from the mitzvah of *appearing*, yet still obligated to bring a *chagigah* offering. For discussion, see *Minchas Chinuch* §6 ד"ה וחרש ff. [See *Rambam* ibid. for some additional exemptions that Chinuch omits, and see *Minchas Chinuch* ibid. for discussion.]

R' S. R. Hirsch (*Commentary* to *Exodus* 23:17) explains that the Torah exempts the blind, the infirm, and others of that type from this mitzvah, to demonstrate that the purpose of the pilgrimage to the *Beis HaMikdash* is not to provide an opportunity for people to seek salvation from their maladies. Rather, its purpose is to ingrain in the national consciousness that we are the people of God and must dedicate all our faculties to His service. Hence, the Torah summons specifically the able-bodied men, who represent the vitality of the nation, to appear before Hashem.

22. A *tumtum* is a person of indeterminate gender, and an *androgynos* is a hermaphrodite.

23. *Exodus* 23:17 states: שָׁלֹשׁ פְּעָמִים בַּשָּׁנָה יֵרָאֶה כָּל זְכוּרְךָ אֶל פְּנֵי הָאָדֹן ה׳, *Three times during the year shall all your menfolk appear before the Lord, Hashem*. The phrase *all your menfolk* refers only to those who are unambiguously male, and excludes the *tumtum* and *androgynos*. Furthermore, the phrase *before the Lord, Hashem*, refers to those whose only Master is Hashem, and excludes slaves, who are beholden to a human master (*Chagigah* 4a).

24. People in this occupation suffer from an unpleasant odor (see *Chagigah* 4a with *Rashi* ד"ה והמצרף נחשת). Alternatively, this refers to a copper-smelter (see *Kesubos* 77a with *Rashi* ד"ה חשלי דודי).

25. Because other people shun their company due to their persistent offensive odor, those who practice these occupations form separate congregations throughout the year (*Otzar HaGeonim* to *Chagigah* 4a; see also *Tosafos, Chullin* 57b ד"ה מטלית). Nonetheless, they are enjoined to bathe and wash their clothing so that they may participate in the national pilgrimage; in the eyes of Hashem, they are no different from anyone else. For discussion of this ruling, see *Chagigah* 4a and commentaries to *Rambam, Hil. Chagigah* 2:2.

בְּנֵי אָדָם לִפְנֵי הַמָּקוֹם, וְלֹא הָאֻמָּנוּת כָּל זְמַן שֶׁעוֹשִׂין אוֹתוֹ בִּנְאֱמָנוּת. וְעוֹבֵר עָלֶיהָ וְנִרְאָה בָּעֲזָרָה בְּיוֹם רִאשׁוֹן שֶׁל חַג וְלֹא הֵבִיא קָרְבָּן, בִּטֵּל עֲשֵׂה וְגַם עָבַר עַל לָאו שֶׁנֶּאֱמַר עַל זֶה (שמות כ״ג, ט״ו) [וְ]"לֹא יֵרָאוּ פָנַי רֵיקָם".[26]

בְּנֵי אָדָם לִפְנֵי הַמָּקוֹם — **For it is pollution of the spirit that renders people repulsive before the Omnipresent,** וְלֹא הָאֻמָּנוּת כָּל זְמַן שֶׁעוֹשִׂין אוֹתוֹ בִּנְאֱמָנוּת — **not the** person's **occupation, as long as it is performed with integrity.** וְעוֹבֵר עָלֶיהָ וְנִרְאָה בָּעֲזָרָה בְּיוֹם רִאשׁוֹן שֶׁל חַג וְלֹא הֵבִיא — **One who transgresses [this mitzvah],** קָרְבָּן — **and appears in the** Temple **Courtyard on the first day of the festival but does not bring an offering,** בִּטֵּל עֲשֵׂה — **has violated a** mitzvah-**obligation** וְגַם עָבַר עַל לָאו — **and also has transgressed a prohibition,** שֶׁנֶּאֱמַר עַל זֶה — **for it is stated in this context** (*Exodus* 23:15): "[וְ]לֹא יֵרָאוּ פָנַי רֵיקָם" — "**You shall not be seen before Me empty-handed.**"[26]

---

### NOTES

26. The commentators wonder about this statement: Chinuch writes explicitly below, in Mitzvah 490, that the prohibition to appear empty-handed pertains specifically to the *re'iyah* offering, not to the *chagigah* offering. This is also explicit in *Rambam* (ibid. 1:1; see also *Mechilta* to the verse). How can he state here, in the context of the *chagigah*, that one who fails to bring the offering violates the prohibition? (*Mishneh LaMelech* et al.).

Some suggest that Chinuch actually refers here to the *re'iyah* offering. As mentioned in note 13, it has been suggested that, according to Chinuch, the mitzvah of *celebrating* can be fulfilled minimally by merely making the pilgrimage to the *Beis HaMikdash* even without bringing a *chagigah* offering. The only offering that one *must* bring is the *olah* of *re'iyah*. Accordingly, Chinuch states here that if one appeared in the *Beis HaMikdash* without that offering, he is in violation of the prohibition to appear empty-handed (*Minchas Yitzchak* §6).

Others explain Chinuch to mean that since the verse specifically speaks of appearing in the *Beis HaMikdash* "empty-handed," one does not transgress this prohibition unless he appears without any offering *at all*. If he brings a *chagigah* offering, even if he does not bring a *re'iyah* offering, he is not in violation, since he is not empty-handed. Thus, Chinuch means that this prohibition is violated by omitting the *chagigah* offering *along with* the *re'iyah* offering (*Tzava Rav*, cited in notes to Mechon Yerushalayim edition of *Minchas Chinuch*; see also *Rashi, Deuteronomy* 16:16 with *Mizrachi*, cited ibid.).

Although Chinuch mentions only that one violates the mitzvah-obligation if he appears in the Temple without an offering, one also violates it if he fails to appear in the Temple altogether. The *prohibition* against appearing empty-handed is violated specifically if one appears there without an offering, but the *obligation* to celebrate the pilgrimage festivals is violated in any event (*Minchas Chinuch* §10). Possibly, Chinuch mentions only appearing without an offering because it is obvious that one who entirely fails to appear has violated the mitzvah-obligation (*Minchas Yitzchak* ibid.).

---

> **⊷§ Insight: May One Utilize the Chagigah Offering to Fulfill the Mitzvah of Rejoicing?**
>
> As noted in the introduction to this mitzvah, aside from the obligation to bring a *chagigah* offering (a celebratory *shelamim* offering) at one point during the festival, there is an additional mitzvah (Mitzvah 488) to rejoice on each day of the festival, which, when the *Beis HaMikdash* is standing, is fulfilled by partaking of sacrificial meat. *Rambam* (*Hil. Chagigah* 1:1), in his definition of the latter obligation, states that the mitzvah of rejoicing requires one "to bring other *shelamim* offerings, aside from the *chagigah* offering; these are called *shelamim of simchah* (rejoicing)." Many commentators understand this to mean that one who merely eats the meat of the *chagigah* has not fulfilled the mitzvah to rejoice, and to fulfill that mitzvah, one must utilize a separate offering designated for *simchah*.
>
> This implication, though, is problematic, for the Mishnah (*Chagigah* 7b) notes that the mitzvah of rejoicing on the festival can be fulfilled through eating the meat of a variety of offerings. Kohanim can "rejoice" by simply eating the portions that they receive from the offerings of Israelites, whether these are *chatas* offerings, *asham* offerings, *bechor* (firstborn) offerings, or *shelamim* offerings. The Israelites themselves can "rejoice" with their portions of the meat from any voluntary *shelamim* offerings that they bring over the festival, even those not consecrated for the sake of the *simchah*

obligation. Apparently, as long as the meat is sacrificial, one can utilize it to fulfill the obligation of rejoicing. Why, then, should consumption of the *chagigah's* meat not qualify as a fulfillment of the mitzvah of *simchah*?

*Avnei Nezer* (*Orach Chaim* 423:12) offers a novel explanation. He suggests that the *chagigah* is different from all the other offerings mentioned above because the *chagigah* obligation itself requires the owner to consume its meat. With respect to the other offerings, there is no personal obligation on the owner or on any particular Kohen to consume the meat. Although it is commanded that the meat of offerings be consumed, no individual is *personally obligated* to consume such meat; the mitzvah merely obligates a Kohen who actually *receives* a portion to eat it (see Mitzvah 102, at note 21). [The only clear exception is the *pesach* offering, which the owners are specifically commanded to eat (Mitzvah 6; see Insight A there).] *Avnei Nezer* suggests that the *chagigah* is also an exception, and the owner's consumption of its meat is an integral part of his fulfillment of the mitzvah of bringing the *chagigah* offering (see there for numerous proofs). As such, this consumption cannot also be utilized to fulfill the separate obligation of *simchah* (rejoicing). Since the owner is *personally* obligated to eat the meat of the *chagigah* by virtue of its own mitzvah, such eating cannot also be a simultaneous fulfillment of his separate obligation of *simchah*.

Numerous commentators offer a different explanation of *Rambam's* words. In their view, consumption of the *chagigah* meat is not a more specific obligation than consumption of the meat of any other offering. They explain, however, that the mitzvah of *simchah*, i.e., rejoicing on the festival with offerings, has two distinct aspects. One aspect is that one must *eat* sacrificial meat every day of the festival; this obligation can be fulfilled with the meat of any offering, including even the *chagigah*. Another, separate, aspect of the mitzvah of *simchah* is that one is required to *bring* an offering at some point during the festival, on any of its days, specifically for the purpose of rejoicing. This is called a *shalmei simchah* (*shelamim of rejoicing*) offering. There is, however, no specific requirement for the owner to eat its meat under this mitzvah; the meat is subject to consumption in accordance with the usual laws of a *shelamim*, and the special requirement is merely to *sacrifice* this offering.

Thus, the mitzvah of *simchah* requires that one *eat* sacrificial meat from *any* offering on *each* day of the festival, and also that one *sacrifice* a special *simchah* offering *once*, on *any* day of the festival. It is this latter aspect that *Rambam* addresses when he says that the *chagigah* offering does not suffice for the *simchah* obligation. Since the *chagigah* is brought in fulfillment of its own obligation, one cannot rely on it to also discharge his obligation to *bring* an offering of *simchah*. As for the separate requirement to rejoice by *eating* sacrificial meat, which applies every day of the festival, one can fulfill it even by consuming the meat of his *chagigah* offering, at whatever point of the festival he brings it (*Tzlach, Chagigah* 6b; *Avi Ezri, Hil. Chagigah* 2:10; see *Rambam, Sefer HaMitzvos, Asei* 54, and *Chinuch*, Mitzvah 488).

For a completely different understanding of *Rambam's* words, see *Chazon Ish, Orach Chaim* 129:10 ד"ה ר"מ פ"א, and the letter of *Chazon Ish* printed at the end of *Avi Ezri, Kodashim*. For further discussion of this topic, see *Ohr Same'ach, Hil. Chagigah* 2:10 ד"ה ומה, and *Aruch HaShulchan HeAsid, Hil. Chagigah* 196:6 and 199:21.

## מִצְוָה פט

## שֶׁלֹּא נִשְׁחַט שֶׂה הַפֶּסַח בְּאַרְבָּעָה עָשָׂר בְּנִיסָן בְּעוֹד שֶׁהֶחָמֵץ בִּרְשׁוּתֵנוּ

שֶׁלֹּא נִשְׁחַט שֶׂה הַפֶּסַח בְּאַרְבָּעָה עָשָׂר בְּנִיסָן בְּעוֹד שֶׁיִּהְיֶה חָמֵץ בִּרְשׁוּתֵנוּ עַד שֶׁנּוֹצִיאֶנּוּ[1], וּזְמַן בִּעוּרוֹ עַד חֲצִי הַיּוֹם, כְּמוֹ שֶׁדָּרְשׁוּ זִכְרוֹנָם לִבְרָכָה (פסחים דף ה׳ ע״א) אַךְ חִלֵּק[2,3].

# Mitzvah 89

## The Prohibition to Slaughter the Pesach Offering on the Fourteenth of Nissan While Chametz Is Still in Our Possession

לֹא תִזְבַּח עַל חָמֵץ דַּם זִבְחִי וְלֹא יָלִין חֵלֶב חַגִּי עַד בֹּקֶר

*You shall not offer the blood of My feast offering upon chametz; nor may the fat of My festive offering remain overnight until morning (Exodus 23:18).*

Two time-specific mitzvos are performed on the fourteenth of Nissan (Erev Pesach): Groups of Jews gather in the Temple Courtyard to bring the *pesach* offering (Mitzvah 5), and *chametz* is eliminated from our possession (Mitzvah 9). This prohibition addresses the relationship between these requirements:

שֶׁלֹּא נִשְׁחַט שֶׂה הַפֶּסַח בְּאַרְבָּעָה עָשָׂר בְּנִיסָן — **We are commanded not to slaughter the *pesach* lamb, which is brought on the fourteenth of Nissan,** בְּעוֹד שֶׁיִּהְיֶה חָמֵץ בִּרְשׁוּתֵנוּ — **while *chametz* is still in our possession;** עַד שֶׁנּוֹצִיאֶנּוּ — that is, the *pesach* offering may not be brought **until** the time at which we are obligated to **remove** [*chametz*] from our possession.[1] וּזְמַן בִּעוּרוֹ עַד חֲצִי הַיּוֹם — **Now, the time for destruction of [*chametz*] is by midday** of the fourteenth of Nissan, כְּמוֹ שֶׁדָּרְשׁוּ זִכְרוֹנָם לִבְרָכָה — **as [the Sages], of blessed memory, expounded** (*Pesachim* 4b-5a), based on the verse (*Exodus* 12:15): *but on the previous day* (i.e., the fourteenth of Nissan) *you shall eliminate leaven from your home.* אַךְ חִלֵּק — Our Sages said that the Scriptural phrase ***but*** etc. **divides** the fourteenth of Nissan into two equal parts: before midday (when ownership of *chametz* is still permitted), and after midday (when it is forbidden).[2] Since *chametz* may be in one's possession until midday, the *pesach* offering may not be slaughtered until after midday.[3]

---

### NOTES

1. The Torah does not mean to set a separate time for each individual *pesach* offering, depending on when its owners eliminate their *chametz*. Rather, the Torah here sets a uniform time for the *pesach* offering — it is to be brought once *chametz* is no longer *allowed* in our possession, but before that time, it may not be brought (see *Pesachim* 5a, and *Rashi* to *Exodus* 23:18, with *Divrei David*; see also *Tosafos*, *Pesachim* 108a ד״ה נימא, and see *Minchas Yitzchak*).

2. In Mitzvah 485, Chinuch explains further: The Torah cannot mean that *chametz* shall be eliminated at the first moment of the 14th of Nissan, for it is impossible to precisely calculate the first moment of the day. Perforce, *chametz* may be in our possession part of the day, and since the Torah does not delineate the precise duration of the permitted time, it stands to reason that possession of *chametz* is permitted throughout the earlier half of the day but forbidden throughout the later half; any other division would have no basis (see *Rashi*, *Pesachim* 5a, for other explanations).

[To prevent the possibility of accidentally missing this Scriptural deadline, the Sages required that *chametz* be eliminated one hour before midday (*Pesachim* 11b).]

3. This verse is not needed to teach that the time for bringing the *pesach* offering is in the afternoon, for the Gemara (*Pesachim* 61a) derives this from an earlier verse (*Exodus* 12:6), which states clearly: וְשָׁחֲטוּ אֹתוֹ כֹּל קְהַל עֲדַת יִשְׂרָאֵל בֵּין הָעַרְבָּיִם, *the entire congregation of the assembly of Israel shall slaughter it in the afternoon*. Rather, the earlier verse identifies the proper time for offering the *pesach*, while our verse adds a mitzvah-prohibition against slaughtering it before that time (see *Keren Orah*, *Zevachim* 12a ד״ה ומי איכא; see also *Minchas Yitzchak*).

## 175 ❑ MISHPATIM / MITZVAH 89: OFFERING THE PESACH WHILE POSSESSING CHAMETZ

שֶׁנֶּאֱמַר (שמות כ״ג, י״ח) **לֹא תִזְבַּח עַל חָמֵץ דַּם זִבְחִי, וּבָא הַפֵּרוּשׁ בּוֹ** (במכילתא כאן) לֹא תִשָּׁחֵט שֶׂה הַפֶּסַח וְיִהְיֶה עֲדַיִן חָמֵץ קַיָּם בִּרְשׁוּתְךָ.[4] וְנִכְפְּלָה זֹאת הַמְּנִיעָה בִּלְשׁוֹן אַחֵר בַּתּוֹרָה.[5] וְגַם כֵּן שָׁמַעְנוּ בִּכְלַל הַפֵּרוּשׁ שֶׁלֹּא יִהְיֶה חָמֵץ אֵצֶל הַשּׁוֹחֵט אוֹתוֹ וְלֹא אֵצֶל הַזּוֹרֵק דָּמוֹ וְלֹא אֵצֶל הַמַּקְטִיר חֶלְבּוֹ וְלֹא אֵצֶל אֶחָד מִבְּנֵי הַחֲבוּרָה הַנִּמְנִין עָלָיו.[7,6]

מִשָּׁרְשֵׁי הַמִּצְוָה, לְפִי שֶׁקְּבִיעוּת זְמַן בְּכָל הָעִנְיָנִים הוּא קִיּוּם עֲשִׂיָּתָן,

---

שֶׁנֶּאֱמַר — We are so commanded, **as it is stated** (*Exodus* 23:18): "**לֹא תִזְבַּח עַל חָמֵץ דַּם זִבְחִי** — *You shall not offer the blood of My feast offering upon chametz,* **וּבָא הַפֵּרוּשׁ בּוֹ** — and the explanation of [this verse], as transmitted to us by the Sages (*Mechilta* ad loc.), is that **לֹא תִשָּׁחֵט שֶׂה הַפֶּסַח וְיִהְיֶה עֲדַיִן חָמֵץ קַיָּם בִּרְשׁוּתְךָ** — you shall not slaughter the *pesach* lamb (*My feast offering*) while *chametz* is allowed to be **in existence in your possession,** i.e., before midday.[4] **וְנִכְפְּלָה זֹאת הַמְּנִיעָה בִּלְשׁוֹן אַחֵר בַּתּוֹרָה** — **This restriction is repeated with a** slightly **different expression** elsewhere **in the Torah.**[5]

Chinuch presents an additional injunction included in this verse:

**וְגַם כֵּן שָׁמַעְנוּ בִּכְלַל הַפֵּרוּשׁ** — **We have also received a tradition** from our Sages that another prohibition is **included in the interpretation** of the verse, **שֶׁלֹּא יִהְיֶה חָמֵץ אֵצֶל הַשּׁוֹחֵט אוֹתוֹ** — namely, **that there may not be** *chametz* **in the possession of the one who slaughters [the *pesach* offering],** **וְלֹא אֵצֶל הַזּוֹרֵק דָּמוֹ** — **nor in the possession of the [Kohen] who throws its blood** upon the Altar, **וְלֹא אֵצֶל הַמַּקְטִיר חֶלְבּוֹ** — **nor in the possession of the [Kohen] who offers up its fats** upon the Altar, **וְלֹא אֵצֶל אֶחָד מִבְּנֵי הַחֲבוּרָה הַנִּמְנִין עָלָיו** — **nor in the possession of any of the members of the group who have joined up for that** particular [*pesach* offering].[6] The verse thus has a dual meaning: First, it prohibits offering the *pesach* during the *time* when *chametz* is still allowed to be in our possession — i.e., before midday. Second, it prohibits the one who performs the *avodah* of slaughtering, throwing the blood, or offering the fats of the *pesach* offering, as well as any member of the group, from owning *chametz* at the time of the *avodah* — whenever the *avodah* of that group's offering is performed, even in the afternoon.[7]

### ⁓ Underlying Purpose of the Mitzvah ⁓

**מִשָּׁרְשֵׁי הַמִּצְוָה** — **Among the underlying purposes of this mitzvah is** **לְפִי שֶׁקְּבִיעוּת זְמַן בְּכָל הָעִנְיָנִים הוּא קִיּוּם עֲשִׂיָּתָן** — **that the setting of** definite **times for all matters guarantees their**

---

NOTES

4. Although this verse does not specify which offering it is referring to, *Mechilta* identifies *My feast offering* as the *pesach* offering, which is described elsewhere (*Exodus* 12:27) as a "*pesach* feast-offering to Hashem" (*Mechilta DeRashbi* to *Exodus* 23:18). Furthermore, a similar verse, which repeats this injunction (see next note), explicitly references the *pesach* offering. [See *Tzlach, Pesachim* 5a and 63a.]

5. *Exodus* 34:25 states: לֹא תִשְׁחַט עַל חָמֵץ דַּם זִבְחִי, *You shall not slaughter the blood of My feast offering upon chametz [nor may the feast offering of the Pesach festival be left overnight until morning].* [Since the two Scriptural injunctions are repetitive, they are not enumerated separately among the 613 Mitzvos (see *Rambam, Sefer HaMitzvos, Shoresh* 9).] See Insight.

6. See *Mechilta* to *Exodus* 23:18; *Tosefta, Pesachim* 4:4; and *Pesachim* 63b. [As we learned in Mitzvah 5, each *pesach* lamb is offered on behalf of a specific group of people, who registered on it in advance. None of these people may have *chametz* in their possession when the *avodah* (service) of their offering is performed.]

Chinuch indicates that this prohibition applies to those performing the *avodah* of the *pesach* offering as well as to any member of the group for whom the *avodah* is being performed (see also *Rambam, Sefer HaMitzvos, Lo Saaseh* 115, and *Ralbag* to *Exodus* 23:18; see *Rashi, Pesachim,* end of 63a). Others argue that this mitzvah-prohibition addresses only those performing the *avodah*, but not members of the group who are passive. In their view, whoever slaughters, throws the blood, or offers the fats upon the Altar is liable if he owns *chametz,* or if any member of the group for whom the *avodah* was performed owns *chametz;* passive members of the group, however, even if they own *chametz,* are not liable for transgressing this mitzvah (*Tosafos, Pesachim* 63b ד״ה או; see *Rambam, Hil. Korban Pesach* 1:5; *Me'il HaEphod* §8; *Yeshuos Malko, Hil. Korban Pesach* 1:5). They would, however, transgress Mitzvah 9, the obligation to be rid of one's *chametz* by midday of Erev Pesach. See also above, Mitzvah 11 note 2, and Mitzvah 20 note 3. See also Insight here.

7. See *Minchas Yitzchak* here.

## משפטים / מצוה פט: שלא נשחט הפסח בי"ד בניסן בעוד שהחמץ ברשותנו

יָדוּעַ הַדָּבָר אֵצֶל כָּל אָדָם, וְעַל כֵּן בְּדִבְרֵי הַפֶּסַח שֶׁהוּא דָבָר גָּדוֹל אֶצְלֵנוּ בְּקִיּוּם הַדָּת, כְּמוֹ שֶׁכָּתַבְנוּ לְמַעְלָה (מצוה כ"א),[8] צִוָּה הָאֵל בָּרוּךְ הוּא שֶׁנַּעֲשֶׂה עִנְיָנוֹ בְּסֵדֶר וּבִקְבִיעוּת זְמַן לְכָל דָּבָר וְדָבָר מִדְּבָרָיו, וְלֹא תָבוֹא מִצְוָה מִמִּצְוֹת עִנְיַן הַמּוֹעֵד הַזֶּה בִּגְבוּל חֲבֶרְתָּהּ, וְעַל כֵּן נִזְהַרְנוּ לְהַשְׁבִּית הֶחָמֵץ הַנִּמְאָס בְּעֵינֵינוּ לְשַׁעְתּוֹ תְּחִלָּה, וְאַחַר כָּךְ לְהַתְחִיל בְּקָרְבַּן הַפֶּסַח שֶׁהוּא הַתְחָלַת שִׂמְחַת הַמּוֹעֵד הַטּוֹב[9]. וְעוֹד אִם שָׁמַעְנוּ טוֹב מִזֶּה, נַחֲזִיק בּוֹ.[10]

מִדִּינֵי הַמִּצְוָה, מַה שֶּׁאָמְרוּ (פסחים דף ס"א ע"א) שֶׁזְּמַן שְׁחִיטָתוֹ אַחַר חֲצוֹת, וְאִם שְׁחָטוֹ קֹדֶם חֲצוֹת שֶׁפָּסוּל[11], וְאַף עַל פִּי שֶׁאַחַר חֲצוֹת הוּא זְמַנּוֹ, אֵינוֹ נִשְׁחָט לְכַתְּחִלָּה אֶלָּא אַחַר

---

proper **performance**; יָדוּעַ הַדָּבָר אֵצֶל כָּל אָדָם — indeed, **this concept is well-known to all people.** וְעַל כֵּן בְּדִבְרֵי הַפֶּסַח **Consequently, with respect to the matter of the Pesach** festival, שֶׁהוּא דָבָר גָּדוֹל אֶצְלֵנוּ בְּקִיּוּם הַדָּת כְּמוֹ שֶׁכָּתַבְנוּ לְמַעְלָה — **which is of great importance in ensuring the endurance of our faith, as we have written earlier** (in Mitzvah 21),[8] צִוָּה הָאֵל בָּרוּךְ הוּא שֶׁנַּעֲשֶׂה עִנְיָנוֹ בְּסֵדֶר וּבִקְבִיעוּת זְמַן לְכָל דָּבָר וְדָבָר מִדְּבָרָיו — **the Almighty, blessed is He, has commanded us to carry out** all **that is associated with it in an orderly manner, within the distinct time frame set for each and every element relating to it,** וְלֹא תָבוֹא מִצְוָה מִמִּצְוֹת עִנְיַן הַמּוֹעֵד הַזֶּה בִּגְבוּל חֲבֶרְתָּהּ — so that **none of the many mitzvos associated with this festival infringe on the boundary of another [mitzvah].** וְעַל כֵּן נִזְהַרְנוּ לְהַשְׁבִּית הֶחָמֵץ הַנִּמְאָס בְּעֵינֵינוּ לְשַׁעְתּוֹ תְּחִלָּה — **Accordingly, we are enjoined to first eliminate chametz, which, during this period** of the Pesach festival, **we find repulsive,** וְאַחַר כָּךְ לְהַתְחִיל בְּקָרְבַּן הַפֶּסַח שֶׁהוּא הַתְחָלַת שִׂמְחַת הַמּוֹעֵד הַטּוֹב — and **only afterward to begin** the service of **the pesach offering, which initiates the rejoicing of this favored festival.**[9]

Chinuch concludes:

וְעוֹד אִם שָׁמַעְנוּ טוֹב מִזֶּה נַחֲזִיק בּוֹ — **Still, if we should hear** a **better** explanation **than this** one, **we shall embrace it.**[10]

### ⇽ Laws of the Mitzvah ⇾

מִדִּינֵי הַמִּצְוָה — **Among the laws of this mitzvah is** מַה שֶּׁאָמְרוּ — **that which [the Sages] have stated** (*Pesachim* 61a), שֶׁזְּמַן שְׁחִיטָתוֹ אַחַר חֲצוֹת — **that the correct time for slaughtering [the offering] is after midday** of the fourteenth of Nissan, וְאִם שְׁחָטוֹ קֹדֶם חֲצוֹת שֶׁפָּסוּל — **and if one slaughtered it earlier than midday, it is invalid.**[11]

Chinuch now sets forth the preferred time for offering the *pesach* offering:

וְאַף עַל פִּי שֶׁאַחַר חֲצוֹת הוּא זְמַנּוֹ — **Although** immediately **after midday** of the fourteenth of Nissan **is**, indeed, **the time of** bringing **[the pesach offering],** so that a *pesach* offering brought at that time is valid, אֵינוֹ נִשְׁחָט לְכַתְּחִלָּה — **it should, preferably, not be slaughtered** אֶלָּא אַחַר

---

### NOTES

8. In Mitzvah 21, Chinuch writes that we received many mitzvah-prohibitions and mitzvah-obligations whose purpose is to recall the miracles of the Exodus, because the Exodus displayed God's total Omnipotence over His Creation, and is thus a great foundation of our faith (see there at length).

9. The Torah designates a distinct time frame for each mitzvah, in order to ensure the correct and wholehearted performance of these pivotal mitzvos. [Likewise, the time when the offering may be slaughtered ends before the time when the meat of the offering and matzos are to be consumed and the Exodus narrative is to be retold.]

10. Chinuch humbly acknowledges that other scholars may possess more profound explanations of the significance of slaughtering the *pesach* offering after the elimination of *chametz*. For other suggestions, see *Malbim* to Exodus 34:25 and R' Samson Raphael Hirsch to Exodus 23:18.

11. Chinuch (at the beginning of the mitzvah) explained the verse as teaching that the *pesach* offering may not be brought before the ban on owning *chametz* has taken effect, at midday. Here, he states that if it is brought earlier, it is invalid, and the group must bring another offering. [If, however, the *pesach* was slaughtered after midday while a member of the group had *chametz* in his possession, it is valid despite the transgression (see Chinuch below with note 16).]

# 177 ☐ MISHPATIM / MITZVAH 89: OFFERING THE PESACH WHILE POSSESSING CHAMETZ

תָּמִיד שֶׁל בֵּין הָעַרְבַּיִם, אַחַר שֶׁמַּקְטִירִים קְטֹרֶת שֶׁל בֵּין הָעַרְבַּיִם, גַּם לְאַחַר שֶׁמֵּיטִיב אֶת הַנֵּרוֹת[12], וְיֶתֶר פְּרָטֶיהָ, בִּפְסָחִים (פרק חמישי)[13].

וְנוֹהֶגֶת בִּזְמַן הַבַּיִת, בִּזְכָרִים וּבִנְקֵבוֹת[14].

וְהָעוֹבֵר עָלֶיהָ וְהִנִּיחַ מִדַּעְתּוֹ כַּזַּיִת חָמֵץ בִּרְשׁוּתוֹ בִּשְׁעַת הַקְרָבָתוֹ[15], אֶחָד שׁוֹחֵט אוֹ זוֹרֵק אוֹ מַקְטִיר הָאֲמוּרִין אוֹ אֲפִלּוּ אֶחָד מִכָּל בְּנֵי הַחֲבוּרָה הַנִּמְנִין בַּאֲכִילָתוֹ

---

אַחַר תָּמִיד שֶׁל בֵּין הָעַרְבַּיִם — **until after the afternoon** *tamid* **offering** has been brought; שֶׁמַּקְטִירִים קְטֹרֶת שֶׁל בֵּין הָעַרְבַּיִם — and even then it should not be offered until **after [the Kohanim] have offered up the afternoon** *ketores* (incense), גַּם לְאַחַר שֶׁמֵּיטִיב אֶת הַנֵּרוֹת — **and also after [the Kohen] has tended the lamps** of the Menorah.[12]

Chinuch concludes:

וְיֶתֶר פְּרָטֶיהָ בִּפְסָחִים — **The laws detailing the appropriate time for bringing the** *pesach* **offering, along with the additional details [of this mitzvah] are elaborated in Tractate** *Pesachim***, Chapter 5** (58a-59a, 61a, 63a-b).[13]

## ⸺ Applicability of the Mitzvah ⸺

וְנוֹהֶגֶת בִּזְמַן הַבַּיִת — **[This mitzvah] applies in the time of the Temple**, when the *pesach* offering is brought, בִּזְכָרִים וּבִנְקֵבוֹת — **to** both **men and women**.[14]

וְהָעוֹבֵר עָלֶיהָ — **One who transgresses [this prohibition]** וְהִנִּיחַ מִדַּעְתּוֹ כַּזַּיִת חָמֵץ בִּרְשׁוּתוֹ בִּשְׁעַת הַקְרָבָתוֹ — **and knowingly allows a** *kezayis* (olive's volume) **of** *chametz*[15] **to remain in his possession at the time when [the** *pesach* **offering] is brought,** אֶחָד שׁוֹחֵט אוֹ זוֹרֵק אוֹ מַקְטִיר הָאֲמוּרִין — **whether he is the one who slaughters the offering, or** the Kohen who **throws** the blood of the offering upon the Altar, **or** the Kohen who **offers up the sacrificial parts,** אוֹ אֲפִלּוּ אֶחָד מִכָּל בְּנֵי הַחֲבוּרָה הַנִּמְנִין בַּאֲכִילָתוֹ — **or even** if he is **one of the members of the group who are registered**

---

NOTES

12. In the course of a normal day's Temple service, the afternoon *tamid* offering is intended to be the final sacrificial offering of the day; afterward, the Kohanim offer up the evening *ketores* (Mitzvah 103) and arrange and kindle the lamps of the Menorah (Mitzvah 98).

On the 14th of Nissan, however, the *pesach* offering is to be slaughtered subsequent to all of these. The multiple Scriptural expressions (*Exodus* 12:6; *Deuteronomy* 16:6) that indicate that the *pesach* is to be offered as daylight wanes connote that this offering is to follow the last of the day's Temple procedures (see *Pesachim* 58a-59a; *Zevachim* 12a; *Rambam, Hil. Korban Pesach* 1:4.). Nonetheless, a *pesach* offering that was slaughtered prior to the offering of the afternoon *tamid* is valid (Mishnah, *Pesachim* 61a; *Rambam* ibid.).

13. The laws detailing the appropriate time for bringing the *pesach* offering, and the prohibition against the possession of *chametz* at the time the offering is brought, are codified in *Rambam, Hil. Korban Pesach* 1:4-5.

14. In accordance with the general rule pertaining to mitzvah-prohibitions. [The mitzvah at hand — not to offer the *pesach* while in possession of *chametz* — applies only to those obligated in offering the *pesach*. Although that mitzvah is a time-specific mitzvah-obligation, and women are generally exempt from such obligations, they are subject to the *pesach*-offering requirement (see Mitzvah 5 note 15 for the reason). And since they are obligated to offer the *pesach*, the prohibition against offering it while in possession of *chametz* can apply to them as well.]

15. One is not liable for offering the *pesach* while possessing *chametz* unless he possesses the measure of *chametz* that is the minimum in regard to the other *chametz* obligations and prohibitions: destroying *chametz* (Mitzvah 9), eating *chametz* (Mitzvah 12), and owning *chametz* (Mitzvos 11 and 20). Since the minimum measure of *chametz* with respect to those mitzvos is a *kezayis*, one is in violation of this mitzvah only if he is in possession of a *kezayis* of *chametz* (see *Yerushalmi Pesachim* 5:4, 41a-b, with 41b note 10 in Schottenstein ed.; *Rambam, Hil. Korban Pesach* 1:5; see also *Sfas Emes* to *Pesachim* 63a and *Minchas Chinuch* §3).

The prohibition is transgressed only if a complete *kezayis* is in the possession of one person associated with the *pesach* offering. If two or more people associated with the offering each owns less than a *kezayis* of *chametz*, but together they have a complete *kezayis*, they, and the one performing the *avodah*, are not in violation of this prohibition (*Minchas Soless* סד״ה והנה הצל״ח; cf. *Sho'eil U'Meishiv, Tinyana* III §107 ד״ה והנה; במה דאמרן; see *Yerushalmi* ibid., with *Mareh HaPanim* ד״ה תמן). [See *Minchas Chinuch* §3, who discusses whether the principle of חֲצִי שִׁעוּר אָסוּר מִן הַתּוֹרָה, [even] *a half-measure is Biblically prohibited*, is applicable here (see also Insight to Mitzvah 19).]

## משפטים / מצוה פט: שלא נשחט הפסח בי״ד בניסן בעוד שהחמץ ברשותנו

לוֹקֶה,[16] וְהַפֶּסַח כָּשֵׁר מִכָּל מָקוֹם.[17]

**to consume [that particular *pesach* offering],** לוֹקֶה — **incurs *malkus* (lashes).**[16] Chinuch concludes: וְהַפֶּסַח כָּשֵׁר מִכָּל מָקוֹם — Although the prohibition has been transgressed, **the *pesach* offering is, nevertheless, valid.**[17]

### NOTES

16. Chinuch stated above (at note 6) that this prohibition is directed not only at those performing the *avodah* of the *pesach* offering, but also at the members of the group (see there for a dissenting view). Here, he adds that the same is true with respect to the penalty of *malkus*: Any participant who is in possession of a *kezayis* of *chametz* while the *pesach* is offered, even if he himself did not perform the *avodah*, incurs *malkus* (see *Rambam, Sefer HaMitzvos, Lo Saaseh* 115; *Likkutei Halachos* to *Pesachim* 63b [*Zevach Todah* ד״ה הנך דקיימי עליה משום בל ילין).

[As was explained above, according to Chinuch the verse prohibits two things: (1) offering the *pesach* before midday, when possession of *chametz* is still permitted; (2) retaining possession of *chametz* at the time that one's *pesach* offering is actually brought. Here, he indicates that liability to *malkus* is incurred only for retaining *chametz* when the *pesach* offering is brought (after midday), but not for bringing the offering before midday. *Minchas Yitzchak* suggests that this is because *malkus* is incurred only for the inappropriate slaughter of a *valid* offering, such as one slaughtered after midday while in possession of *chametz* (see Chinuch further), but not for the slaughter of an invalid *pesach* offering, such as one slaughtered before midday (see above, note 11). For further discussion of this concept, see there, and see *Mishneh LaMelech, Hil. Korban Pesach* 1:5. For another explanation, see *Keren Orah, Zevachim* 11b ד״ה ומש״כ התוס׳.]

17. *Tosefta, Pesachim* 4:4. *Yerushalmi* (*Pesachim* 5:4, 40b) derives this from Scripture's use of the term זִבְחִי, *My feast-offering,* which indicates that even after a *pesach* is illicitly offered upon *chametz*, it remains "*My*" feast-offering, i.e., a valid offering (see *Tosafos* to *Pesachim* 63a ד״ה רבא אמר and *Temurah* 4b ד״ה השוחט; see also *Shaar HaMelech, Hil. Korban Pesach* 1:1). [See *Chidushei R' Akiva Eiger* (*Pesachim* 63b ד״ה ובזה אני מסופק) for a situation in which a *pesach* offered upon *chametz* may, in fact, be invalid.]

---

### ✥§ Insight: The Pesach Offering and Chametz

As pointed out in the introduction to this mitzvah, there are two time-specific mitzvos that are performed on the 14th of Nissan — the offering of the *pesach* and the elimination of *chametz* — and this mitzvah addresses a relationship between those two mitzvos. Specifically, it consists of a special prohibition for one to slaughter the *pesach* offering when there is still *chametz* in his possession.

R' Leib Malin (*Chidushei R' Aryeh Leib*, Vol. I §12) raises an interesting question regarding this mitzvah: The Torah sets forth many laws concerning *chametz*, and many laws concerning the *pesach* offering. Is this mitzvah rooted in the laws of *chametz*, or is it rooted in the laws of the *pesach* offering?

On the one hand, we may understand that counted among the many *chametz* prohibitions is this additional prohibition — to retain possession of *chametz* at the time when the *pesach* is offered. If this is the case, then even if one would violate the prohibition, this surely would not detract from the proper performance of the *pesach* service, since the offering is not the focus of the prohibition at all. It also follows that in a situation where one person slaughters the offering while there is *chametz* in the possession of another one of the participants in the *pesach* offering, it is the one who *owns* the *chametz* that violates the prohibition, not the one who slaughtered it.

On the other hand, we may understand that counted among the many conditions required to offer the *pesach* sacrifice is this additional one — that when it is offered, there must not be *chametz* in the possession of any of its participants. According to this approach, if one transgresses this prohibition he has performed the *pesach* service improperly by violating one of its conditions. And, in the above scenario, where one person slaughters the *pesach* while there is *chametz* in the possession of another participant, it is the one who *slaughtered* the *pesach* that violates the prohibition, not the owner of the *chametz*.

R' Leib notes that this would seem to be a point of disagreement between Chinuch and *Tosafos*. As mentioned above, in note 6, Chinuch indicates that this mitzvah prohibits *all* members of the

# 179 ☐ MISHPATIM / MITZVAH 89: OFFERING THE PESACH WHILE POSSESSING CHAMETZ

group who join to offer a *pesach* from owning *chametz* at the time it is offered — not only those who actually participate in the *avodah*. Chinuch emphasizes this again at the end of the mitzvah, where he states that any member of the group who "knowingly allows a *kezayis* of *chametz* to remain in his possession" at the time the *pesach* is offered has violated this mitzvah and incurs *malkus*. Thus, Chinuch apparently understands the prohibition as *chametz*-based. The moment when the *pesach* is offered is a time when anyone for whom it is offered is not allowed to possess *chametz*.

*Tosafos* (*Pesachim* 63b ד"ה או), however, maintain that the prohibition applies only to those who actually engage in the *avodah*, for example, by slaughtering the *pesach* offering. If any member of the group that will partake of the offering has *chametz* in his possession when its *avodah* is performed, then the one doing the *avodah* has transgressed this mitzvah. The one who has the *chametz*, however, does not transgress this mitzvah, unless he too joins in performing the *avodah* (see note 6). Thus, *Tosafos* apparently understand this prohibition as *pesach*-based. This is further borne out by the fact that *Tosafos* (ibid. 63a ד"ה השוחט) consider the possibility that possessing *chametz* causes the *pesach* offering to be invalidated. That possibility cannot exist unless we assume that this prohibition is rooted in the laws of the *pesach* offering and is one of the conditions by which it is offered.

After analyzing the matter at some length, R' Leib concludes that, in fact, this mitzvah contains *both* of these characteristics; it has aspects of a *chametz* prohibition as well as aspects of a *pesach*-offering prohibition. As Chinuch points out (at note 5), the prohibition is stated twice in the Torah, once in *Exodus* 23:18 (the verse upon which Chinuch expounds the mitzvah), and once in *Exodus* 34:25. Accordingly, R' Leib suggests that in the first verse we learn of a *chametz* prohibition, i.e., that it is prohibited to own *chametz* at the time that one's *pesach* is offered, and in the second verse we learn that this prohibition affects the offering as well, and it is prohibited to offer a *pesach* when one is in possession of *chametz*. See there for further discussion of how these two aspects of the prohibition are interrelated.

In connection with the above discussion, R' Leib cites a question regarding this mitzvah posed by *Minchas Chinuch* (§12): What is the law regarding offering the *emurin* (sacrificial parts burned on the Altar) of the *pesach* upon the Altar while owning *chametz* — at a time when it is permitted to own *chametz*? In the normal course of events this issue can never arise, since the *pesach* offering is offered after midday on Erev Pesach, by which time all *chametz* must be destroyed. *Minchas Chinuch* proposes, though, that the question can come up in the following case: *Emurin* may remain on the Altar for an indefinite time and be burned there even after many days (see Insight to Mitzvah 90). What if the *emurin* of the *pesach* offering remained atop the Altar all through the Pesach festival, until after the festival when it is again permitted to own *chametz*? May one perform the service of burning the *emurin* at that time while in possession of *chametz*? Although the circumstances are improbable, the underlying question remains: When the Torah forbade owning *chametz* at the time of the *pesach* offering, did the Torah refer only to prohibited *chametz*, or did it refer to all *chametz*, regardless of whether it is otherwise prohibited to be owned at the time?

*Minchas Chinuch* concludes that even permitted *chametz* is included in this prohibition. See *Chidushei R' Aryeh Leib* (ibid.) for discussion, and for how this inquiry is affected by the previous question regarding the definition of this mitzvah as a *pesach*-related or *chametz*-related prohibition.

## מִצְוָה צ: שֶׁלֹּא נַנִּיחַ אֵמוּרֵי הַפֶּסַח לְפָסֵל בְּלִינָה[1]

שֶׁלֹּא לְהַנִּיחַ אֵמוּרִין שֶׁל פֶּסַח עַד הַבֹּקֶר, שֶׁלֹּא יַקְרִיבוּ אוֹתוֹ, וְהֵן נִפְסָלִין בִּשְׁהִיָּה זוֹ וְנִקְרָאִין נוֹתָר[2], שֶׁנֶּאֱמַר (שמות כ״ג, י״ח) וְלֹא יָלִין חֵלֶב חַגִּי עַד בֹּקֶר[3], וְהוּא הַדִּין לִשְׁאָר אֵמוּרִין[4]

# Mitzvah 90
## The Prohibition to Leave the Sacrificial Parts of the Pesach Offering Overnight

לֹא תִזְבַּח עַל חָמֵץ דַּם זִבְחִי וְלֹא יָלִין חֵלֶב חַגִּי עַד בֹּקֶר

*You shall not offer the blood of My feast offering upon chametz; nor may the fat of My festive offering remain overnight until morning* (Exodus 23:18).

As Chinuch explained in Mitzvah 5, groups of Jews gather in the Temple Courtyard on the afternoon of the fourteenth of Nissan (Erev Pesach) to slaughter the *pesach* offering. In the previous mitzvah, we learned that the first part of the above verse forbids slaughtering the *pesach* when there is *chametz* in one's possession. The latter part of the verse constitutes another prohibition, pertaining to the fats of the offering.

Scripture (*Leviticus* 3:9-11,14-16; see Mitzvah 138) designates particular fats and internal organs of each sacrificial offering for burning upon the Altar. The requirement to offer up these parts (which are known as *emurin*[1]) applies to the *pesach* offering as well (*Pesachim* 64b; *Sifra* to *Leviticus* 3:16). Thus, while the meat of the *pesach* offering will be roasted and consumed by the members of the group that has brought it (as stated in Mitzvah 6), the *emurin* must be removed after slaughter and entrusted to the Kohanim, who are to offer them upon the Altar. It is of these fats, which are designated for the Altar, that this verse speaks.

שֶׁלֹּא לְהַנִּיחַ אֵמוּרִין שֶׁל פֶּסַח עַד הַבֹּקֶר — The Kohanim are commanded **not to leave the sacrificial portions** (*emurin*) **of the** *pesach* **offering until morning**. שֶׁלֹּא יַקְרִיבוּ אוֹתוֹ — **without offering them** upon the Altar, וְהֵן נִפְסָלִין בִּשְׁהִיָּה זוֹ וְנִקְרָאִין נוֹתָר — **and** in fact **they are disqualified** from being offered **by this delay, and are designated as** *nossar* (literally, *leftover*).[2] שֶׁנֶּאֱמַר ״וְלֹא יָלִין חֵלֶב חַגִּי עַד בֹּקֶר״ — Leaving the *emurin* of the *pesach* offering until morning is prohibited, **as it is stated**: (*Exodus* 23:18): *nor may the fat of My festive offering remain overnight until morning*.[3] וְהוּא הַדִּין לִשְׁאָר אֵמוּרִין — Although the verse specifies that the *fat* of the *pesach* offering may not be left overnight, **the same law applies to the other** *emurin* of the *pesach* offering,[4]

---

NOTES

1. The word אמורין, *emurin*, comes from the root אמר, *said*; i.e., the stated or commanded parts of an offering (*Rambam*, in his introduction to Mishnah *Zevachim*; see *Aruch* ערך מר and *Mishneh LaMelech*, *Hil. Maaseh HaKorbanos* 1:18, for other explanations).

2. *Nossar* refers to any offering part that has been disqualified by having been allowed to remain beyond the time prescribed for it to be offered or consumed. Once the *emurin* have been allowed to remain until morning, they are rendered *nossar* and may not be offered upon the Altar; rather, they must be incinerated in the place designated for the burning of disqualified offering parts (see *Rambam*, *Hil. Maaseh HaKorbanos* 7:3; see also *Sefer HaMitzvos*, *Lo Saaseh* 116; for discussion, see *Minchas Chinuch* 143:2 ד״ה הכלל).

It should be noted, however, that the disqualification of the *emurin* does not invalidate the entire offering; the obligation to bring an offering is fulfilled even when its *emurin* have not been offered up, as long as its blood has been applied to the Altar (*Zevachim* 7b; see Mishnah *Pesachim* 78b).

3. The *festive offering* mentioned in this verse is the *pesach* offering [which is referred to in the first half of the verse, as well; see Mitzvah 89] (*Rambam*, *Sefer HaMitzvos* ibid.; cf. *Ralbag* to the verse; *Mishneh LaMelech*, *Hil. Korban Pesach* 1:7). *The fat of My festive offering* refers to those fats that are designated as *emurin* and must be offered up. As described in Mitzvah 138, these are the hard fats around the body cavity and the fats upon the stomachs, kidneys, and flanks.

4. Aside from the fats mentioned in the previous note, the *emurin* include the kidneys, diaphragm, and a portion of the liver, and when the offering is a sheep, the tail as well (see Mitzvah 138).

# MISHPATIM / MITZVAH 90: LEAVING SACRIFICIAL PARTS OF THE PESACH OFFERING

וְלִשְׁאָר קָרְבָּנוֹת[5]. וּלְשׁוֹן מְכִילְתָּא (כאן), וְלֹא יָלִין חֵלֶב, בָּא הַכָּתוּב לְלַמֵּד עַל הַחֲלָבִים שֶׁנִּפְסָלִין בְּלִינָה[6]. וּכְבָר נִכְפְּלָה זֹאת הַמְּנִיעָה בְּמָקוֹם אַחֵר, שֶׁנֶּאֱמַר (שם ל״ד, כ״ה) וְלֹא יָלִין לַבֹּקֶר זֶבַח חַג הַפָּסַח[7].

מִשָּׁרְשֵׁי הַמִּצְוָה, כִּי כְבוֹד הַקָּרְבָּן לְהַקְרִיבוֹ בִּזְמַנּוֹ הַקָּבוּעַ אֵלָיו, וְהַמַּעֲבִיר הַמּוֹעֵד נִרְאֶה כְּמִתְיָאֵשׁ וּמַשְׁלִיךְ הַדָּבָר אַחֲרֵי גֵוֹו[8], וְאֵינֶנּוּ מִתְעוֹרֵר וּמִתְפַּיֵּס כַּוָּנוֹתָיו אֶל הָעֲבוֹדָה יָפָה[9], וּמִפְּנֵי כֵן נִפְסָלִין בְּכָךְ[10].

---

**וְלִשְׁאָר קָרְבָּנוֹת** — **as well as to** the *emurin* of **all other offerings;** all are included in this prohibition.[5] **וּלְשׁוֹן מְכִילְתָּא [כאן]** — **And,** although the verse states only that it is *prohibited* to leave the *emurin* overnight, this encompasses a disqualification as well, **as expressed by *Mechilta*** (to the verse): **וְלֹא יָלִין חֵלֶב** — When it states, **nor may the fat** of My festive offering **remain overnight** until morning, **בָּא הַכָּתוּב לְלַמֵּד עַל הַחֲלָבִים שֶׁנִּפְסָלִין בְּלִינָה** — **Scripture comes to teach that the fats** (i.e., *emurin*) of all sacrificial offerings **are disqualified** as *nossar* **by having been left overnight.**[6] **וּכְבָר נִכְפְּלָה זֹאת הַמְּנִיעָה בְּמָקוֹם אַחֵר** — **This injunction** against leaving *emurin* overnight **has actually been repeated elsewhere** in the Torah, **שֶׁנֶּאֱמַר "וְלֹא יָלִין לַבֹּקֶר זֶבַח חַג הַפָּסַח"** — **as it is stated** (*Exodus* 34:25): **nor may the feast offering of the Pesach festival be left overnight until morning.**[7]

### ~ Underlying Purpose of the Mitzvah ~

**מִשָּׁרְשֵׁי הַמִּצְוָה** — **Among the underlying purposes of this mitzvah is** **כִּי כְבוֹד הַקָּרְבָּן לְהַקְרִיבוֹ** **בִּזְמַנּוֹ הַקָּבוּעַ אֵלָיו** — **that respect for an offering** demands **that it be offered** upon the Altar promptly, **in its designated time, וְהַמַּעֲבִיר הַמּוֹעֵד נִרְאֶה כְּמִתְיָאֵשׁ וּמַשְׁלִיךְ הַדָּבָר אַחֲרֵי גֵוֹו** — **and one who lets the appointed time pass presents the appearance of one who is neglectful** of the offering **and "casts the matter behind his back."**[8] **וְאֵינֶנּוּ מִתְעוֹרֵר וּמִתְפַּיֵּס כַּוָּנוֹתָיו אֶל הָעֲבוֹדָה יָפָה** — **Moreover,** by tarrying, **he fails to rouse himself to thoroughly focus his attention upon the** sacred *avodah* (service) of the offering.[9] **וּמִפְּנֵי כֵן נִפְסָלִין בְּכָךְ** — **It is because of this that [the *emurin*] are** actually **rendered invalid through such** delay (as mentioned above).[10]

---

### NOTES

5. With the exception of the *olah* offering (which is wholly consumed by the fires of the Altar), the *emurin* of *all* animal offerings must be removed and offered up on the day the offering is brought, or during the subsequent night. The *pesach* offering is merely an example of an offering to which the prohibition against leaving any of these portions overnight applies.

   This prohibition pertains specifically to the *emurin* and is distinct from Mitzvos 8 and 142, which prohibit leaving over *meat* of the *pesach* or any other offering. "Meat" refers to the portions remaining after the *emurin* have been removed, which are designated for human consumption.

6. That is, since Scripture *prohibits* them from being left overnight until morning, we may infer that they become disqualified as *nossar* once morning arrives (since any sacrificial item that is left over automatically becomes *nossar*). Hence, they may not be offered on the Altar the next day, but must be incinerated (see note 2).

7. Here, Scripture unambiguously mentions the *pesach* offering. Chinuch and *Rambam* (ibid.) understand this verse as a repetition of the earlier injunction (in our verse) against leaving over its *emurin* (cf. *Tosafos, Pesachim* 59b ד״ה ולא; see *Mishneh LaMelech, Hil. Korban Pesach* 1:7, at length). [Since both verses refer to the same prohibition, these injunctions are not enumerated separately among the 613 Mitzvos (see *Sefer HaMitzvos, Shoresh* 9, and above, Mitzvah 85 note 4; see also *Mishneh LaMelech* ibid. ד״ה ודע דלסברת רבינו.]

8. Stylistic paraphrase of *I Kings* 14:9.

9. Performing the *avodah* lethargically is not only *indicative* of a lack of appreciation for the task, and poor concentration on it, but actually is *conducive* to this. As Chinuch frequently reiterates, a person's actions inevitably shape his attitudes (see Mitzvah 16, 95). Thus, the Torah sets a short deadline for offering the *emurin* so that the Kohanim should perform this *avodah* with alacrity and zeal.

10. That is, since leaving the *emurin* over for the next day would lead to their being offered up without the desired level of concentration and devotion, the Torah does not merely *prohibit* leaving them overnight, but also *disqualifies* them from being offered later.

## משפטים / מצוה צ: שלא נניח אמורי הפסח לפסל בלינה

**מִדִּינֵי**[11] **הַמִּצְוָה, מַה שֶּׁאָמְרוּ** (פסחים דף ס״ד ע״ב) **שֶׁמִּצְוָה לְהַקְטִיר אֵמוּרֵי כָּל זֶבַח וָזֶבַח בִּפְנֵי עַצְמוֹ, וּמַה שֶּׁאָמְרוּ**[12] (שם דף ס״ח ע״ב) **שֶׁמִּצְוַת הַקְטָרָתָן אַחַר שְׁחִיטָה סָמוּךְ, וְאִם לֹא הִקְטִיר כֵּן מַקְטִירָן כָּל הַלַּיְלָה עַד שֶׁיַּעֲלֶה עַמּוּד הַשַּׁחַר**[13]**, וְדַוְקָא**[14] **בְּשֶׁחָל אַרְבָּעָה עָשָׂר בְּנִיסָן לִהְיוֹת בְּשַׁבָּת, שֶׁחֶלְבֵי שַׁבָּת קְרֵבִין בְּיוֹם טוֹב**[15]**, אֲבָל אִם**

---

### ~ Laws of the Mitzvah ~

In connection with the prohibition to leave over the *emurin* beyond the time allotted for offering them up, which in effect requires that they be offered up within the allotted time and in accordance with the proper procedure, Chinuch discusses some laws of that procedure:[11]

מִדִּינֵי הַמִּצְוָה — **The laws of this mitzvah include** מַה שֶּׁאָמְרוּ — **that which [the Sages] have stated** (*Pesachim* 64b), שֶׁמִּצְוָה לְהַקְטִיר אֵמוּרֵי כָּל זֶבַח וָזֶבַח בִּפְנֵי עַצְמוֹ — **that it is a mitzvah to** offer up and **burn the *emurin* of each and every** individual offering on the Altar **separately.**[12] וּמַה שֶּׁאָמְרוּ — **Also** included is **that which [the Sages] have stated** (*Pesachim* 59b, 68b), שֶׁמִּצְוַת הַקְטָרָתָן אַחַר שְׁחִיטָה סָמוּךְ — **that the obligation of burning [the *emurin*]** on the Altar applies **immediately after the slaughtering** and blood appliations of the offering, i.e., it is a mitzvah for the Kohen to offer them up and burn them on that very day; וְאִם לֹא הִקְטִיר כֵּן — **but if he did not burn** the *emurin* on the Altar that day **as prescribed,** מַקְטִירָן כָּל הַלַּיְלָה עַד שֶׁיַּעֲלֶה עַמּוּד הַשַּׁחַר — he **may** offer up and **burn them** there **throughout the night** that follows, **until dawn breaks.**[13]

Chinuch proceeds to qualify the previous statement. While it is generally true that the *emurin* of offerings made on any particular day may be burned upon the Altar on the night that follows, in the case of the *pesach* offering there is another consideration that generally precludes this. The *pesach* is slaughtered on Erev Pesach (14 Nissan), and the night that immediately follows (15 Nissan) is the Yom Tov of Pesach. Burning items, whether on the Altar or elsewhere, is a form of *melachah* (forbidden activity) that is usually prohibited on the Sabbath and Yom Tov (see Mitzvos 32 and 298). And, although the Temple service overrides the Sabbath and Yom Tov restrictions, that is only for an offering slaughtered on the Sabbath or Yom Tov *itself*, but not for an offering slaughtered the day before.[14] Thus, the *emurin* of an offering made on Erev Pesach cannot be burned on the Altar on the night of 15 Nissan (Pesach), and must be burned before sundown on Erev Pesach. It is only in one specific case that the *emurin* may be burned on the Altar during the night of 15 Nissan:

וְדַוְקָא בְּשֶׁחָל אַרְבָּעָה עָשָׂר בְּנִיסָן לִהְיוֹת בְּשַׁבָּת — **The permit to burn the *emurin* of the *pesach*** offering "until morning" applies **specifically when the fourteenth of Nissan falls on the Sabbath.** שֶׁחֶלְבֵי שַׁבָּת קְרֵבִין בְּיוֹם טוֹב — **In this case,** burning the *emurin* during the night of the fifteenth is not a violation of the Yom Tov laws, **for** it is derived from Scripture that **the fats** (i.e., *emurin*) **of** an offering sacrificed on **the Sabbath may be offered** upon the Altar **on a Yom Tov** that immediately follows.[15] אֲבָל אִם

---

### NOTES

11. The obligation upon the Kohanim to offer up the *emurin* of each offering according to the designated procedure is actually included in the particular mitzvah-obligation detailing the *avodah* of that offering (see Mitzvos 115, 138, 140, 141; but see *Minchas Chinuch* here §3). Nevertheless, as is his custom, Chinuch includes some of the laws in his discussion of a related mitzvah.

12. That is, initially, the Kohen should not combine *emurin* removed from different *pesach* offerings and offer them up together; rather, he should place each of them on the Altar individually. This is implied by the verse that states regarding *emurin* (Leviticus 3:11): וְהִקְטִירוֹ הַכֹּהֵן הַמִּזְבֵּחָה, *The Kohen shall burn it* (i.e., one offering only) *upon the Altar* (*Pesachim* 64b). [The Gemara there also derives, from another verse, that it is a mitzvah to offer up and burn *all* the *emurin* of each individual offering together, at one time.]

13. The law that the *emurin* can be offered up during the night may be inferred from our verse, which prohibits only leaving over the fats of the *pesach* "until morning." Moreover, there is another verse (*Leviticus* 6:2; see Rashi there) that clearly permits the Kohen to burn the *emurin* of any offering throughout the night after the offering was slaughtered. Nevertheless, it is preferable — and is indeed a mitzvah — for him to burn the *emurin* on the Altar before the day ends (see *Pesachim* 59b, where this is derived from Scripture; see *Minchas Chinuch* §4).

14. *Pesachim* 59b; *Rambam, Hil. Temidin U'Mussafin* 1:7.

15. Just as the obligatory offerings of Yom Tov itself may be burned on the Altar during Yom Tov, even

## 183 □ MISHPATIM / MITZVAH 90: LEAVING SACRIFICIAL PARTS OF THE PESACH OFFERING

חָל אַרְבָּעָה עָשָׂר בְּנִיסָן בְּחֹל, אֵין מַקְטִירִין בַּלַּיְלָה, שֶׁאֵין מַקְטִירִין חֶלְבֵי חֹל בְּיוֹם טוֹב, דְּיוֹם טוֹב עֲשֵׂה וְלֹא תַעֲשֶׂה,[16] וְדוֹחֶה לָאו דְּלֹא יָלִין,[17] וְיֶתֶר פְּרָטֶיהָ בִּפְסָחִים[18] (דף נ״ט ע״ב).

וְנוֹהֶגֶת בִּזְמַן הַבַּיִת בִּזְכָרִים כֹּהֲנִים.[19]

וְהָעוֹבֵר וְלֹא הִקְרִיבָן[20] אֵינוֹ לוֹקֶה לְפִי שֶׁאֵין בּוֹ מַעֲשֶׂה.[21]

---

אֵין מַקְטִירִין חָל אַרְבָּעָה עָשָׂר בְּנִיסָן בְּחֹל — **But if the fourteenth of Nissan falls on a weekday,** בַּלַּיְלָה — **one may not burn** the *emurin* **during the night** of the fifteenth of Nissan, which is Yom Tov, שֶׁאֵין מַקְטִירִין חֶלְבֵי חֹל בְּיוֹם טוֹב — **because the fats of weekday** offerings **may not be burned** upon the Altar **on Yom Tov.**

In the latter case, if it occurred that the *emurin* were not offered up before sundown, refraining from offering them up during the night will inevitably result in a violation of the prohibition to leave them over "until morning." Chinuch explains why they may nevertheless not be offered up:

דְּיוֹם טוֹב עֲשֵׂה וְלֹא תַעֲשֶׂה — The imperative to offer up the *emurin* before morning does not override the restriction against performing *melachah* on Yom Tov, **because** performing *melachah* on **Yom Tov is forbidden by an injunctive obligation as well as a prohibition,**[16] וְדוֹחֶה לָאו דְּלֹא יָלִין — **and** accordingly, the restriction of *melachah* on Yom Tov **overrides the prohibition of nor may** the fat of My festive offering **remain overnight.**[17]

Chinuch concludes:

וְיֶתֶר פְּרָטֶיהָ בִּפְסָחִים — These laws, as well as **the remaining details of [this mitzvah], are** found in Tractate **Pesachim** (59b).[18]

### ⸎ Applicability of the Mitzvah ⸎

וְנוֹהֶגֶת בִּזְמַן הַבַּיִת — **[This prohibition] applies in the times of the Temple,** בִּזְכָרִים כֹּהֲנִים — **and** it is applicable **to male Kohanim,** who are the ones eligible to offer the *emurin* upon the Altar.[19]

וְהָעוֹבֵר וְלֹא הִקְרִיבָן — **[A Kohen] who violates** this prohibition **by failing to offer [the *emurin*]** within the allotted time[20] אֵינוֹ לוֹקֶה — **does not incur *malkus*** (lashes), לְפִי שֶׁאֵין בּוֹ מַעֲשֶׂה — **because [this transgression] does not entail action.**[21]

---

### NOTES

though this entails *melachah*, so may the offerings of the Sabbath be completed on Yom Tov, for the sanctity of the Sabbath is even greater than that of Yom Tov (see *Shabbos* 114a-b with *Chidushei HaRan*; *Rambam, Hil. Temidin U'Mussafin* 1:7). Hence, when Erev Pesach falls on a Sabbath, the *emurin* of the *pesach* offering — which is slaughtered on that Sabbath — may be burned during the following night, even though it is Yom Tov (*Pesachim* 59b; *Rambam, Hil. Korban Pesach* 1:8, and *Hil. Temidin U'Mussafin* 1:8).

16. The prohibition of *melachah* on Yom Tov is stated by Scripture both in the form of an *obligation* to rest [Mitzvah 297] and a *prohibition* to perform *melachah* [see Mitzvah 298].

17. Since the performance of *melachah* on Yom Tov is restricted by both a mitzvah-obligation and a mitzvah-prohibition, this restriction is of greater severity than that of leaving *emurin* overnight, which is stated only as a prohibition. Hence, if Erev Pesach falls on a weekday and the *emurin* are left until nightfall, such that burning them would violate the Yom Tov restriction while not burning them would violate the "leaving over"

restriction, the Yom Tov restriction is given priority and the *emurin* are not offered up (see *Pesachim* 59b; see also there, 83b-84a, for a related discussion, and see *Minchas Yitzchak*). See the Insight for further discussion.

18. The laws pertaining to this mitzvah are codified in *Rambam, Hil. Korban Pesach* 1:6-8.

19. *Pesachim* 63b. Specifically, the prohibition applies to the Kohanim who actually are fit to perform the *avodah*, not to those disqualified by blemishes or other factors (*Minchas Chinuch* §4 ד״ה ומה).

20. This refers to a Kohen who has the opportunity to offer up the *emurin* and neglects to do so, such that they are left over until morning; by failing to act he has transgressed the mitzvah (see Chinuch below, end of Mitzvah 401; see also below, Mitzvah 98 note 31).

21. As Chinuch frequently mentions, the penalty of *malkus* is not given for transgressions that occur through inaction [לָאו שֶׁאֵין בּוֹ מַעֲשֶׂה]. See, for example, Mitzvah 74. See also General Introduction, note 14. [For further discussion of the exemption from *malkus*, see *Mishneh LaMelech, Hil. Pesulei HaMukdashin* 18:9. See also *Minchas Chinuch* §5.]

### ✺§ Insight: Is There a Way to Permit Leaving Emurin Overnight?

Chinuch states (at notes 16-17) that when Erev Pesach falls on a weekday, the *emurin* of the offering must be burned on the Altar during that day, and if they remain until nightfall then they can no longer be offered up, because that night is Yom Tov, when burning is a prohibited *melachah*. Although this means that the prohibition to leave the *emurin* until morning will inevitably be violated, there is no choice, because burning them at night would violate both the mitzvah-obligation and mitzvah-prohibition to refrain from *melachah* on Yom Tov.

This law does not apply to the *pesach* alone, but actually has a much broader application. The *tamid* offering was brought every morning and afternoon, including Friday. If for some reason the limbs of the Friday *tamid* were not burned on the Altar that day, they could not be offered up once night had fallen, since it was then Sabbath (*Yoma* 46a; *Rambam, Hil. Temidin U'Mussafin* 1:7). Thus, according to Chinuch's approach, these limbs, too, would inevitably be left over until morning and would become disqualified.

Other Rishonim, however, have a different approach to this matter. The law is that if *emurin* were left *on top of the Altar* overnight (or even for several nights), they may be burned on the Altar the next day, or on subsequent days. Although if they had not been on the Altar they would be considered *nossar* (left over), since they were on the Altar they remain fit to be offered (*Zevachim* 87a; *Rambam, Hil. Pesulei HaMukdashin* 3:11). Accordingly, *Ritva* (*Yoma* 21a) states that whenever there were weekday *emurin* that could not be burned before nightfall of the Sabbath or Yom Tov (such as the limbs of the pre-Sabbath or pre-Yom Tov *tamid*), the Kohanim would place those limbs on the Altar and leave them there until after the Sabbath or Yom Tov, and *then* burn them. Thus, although the *emurin* could not be burned on the Sabbath or Yom Tov, due to the prohibition of *melachah*, this did not necessarily cause them to become disqualified.

According to *Ritva*, this is the intention of the Mishnah, *Avos* 5:5, which states that one of the miracles that occurred in the *Beis HaMikdash* was that the sacred meat never became rancid. Even though, at times, the meat (i.e., *emurin*) had to be left atop the Altar for several days (e.g., when the Sabbath and Yom Tov fell on consecutive days), and there it was exposed to the sun as well as the heat of the Altar pyre, the meat never spoiled. This is also the view of *Rashi* to *Avos* ibid. (cf. *Rabbeinu Yonah* there).

Why does Chinuch assert that when the *emurin* are not burned before the Sabbath or Yom Tov a disqualification must inevitably occur? Why does he not accept the view of *Rashi* and *Ritva*?

The explanation would seem to be as follows: The Gemara (*Zevachim* 87a) cites a debate as to the scope of the rule that *emurin* left atop the Altar overnight may be burned the next day. Rabbah maintains that "being left overnight" has no impact on items that are on top of the Altar; they do not become *nossar* and remain perfectly fit to be offered. Thus, even if they are removed from the Altar in the morning, it is permitted to bring them back up and burn them. Rava, however, understands that "being left overnight" does impact items that are on top of the Altar, and they become *nossar*, but nevertheless, *as long as they are still atop the Altar* they may be burned. This is a special dispensation that is based on the power of the Altar to "sanctify" even an invalid substance. If, however, these *emurin* are subsequently removed from the Altar, they may not be brought back up and burned, for they are *nossar*, and the dispensation to burn them expired when they were brought down (see *Rashi, Zevachim* 87a ד"ה רבא אמר לא יעלו). The halachah accords with this latter view of Rava (*Rambam, Hil. Pesulei HaMukdashin* 3:11).

*Tosafos* (*Rosh Hashanah* 30b ד"ה ונתקלקלו) state that according to Rabbah, who rules that the *emurin* do not become *nossar* while atop the Altar, in a situation where *emurin* cannot be burned by day it is permitted to initially (*lechatchilah*) bring them up to the top of the Altar and leave them there overnight, so that they may be burned on the next day or a subsequent day. But according to Rava, who rules that they do become *nossar*, they may not initially be left on the Altar overnight with the intention to offer them on a subsequent day, since they will be *inherently unfit*. There is merely a dispensation to burn them after the fact (*bedi'avad*) when they were left on the Altar overnight, not to leave them there in the first place (see *Turei Even* to *Tosafos* ibid.). Chinuch apparently follows this view. Hence, Chinuch states that if *emurin* of the *pesach* were not burned on Erev Pesach, it is inevitable that they will become disqualified and a transgression of "leaving over" will have been

## MISHPATIM / MITZVAH 90: LEAVING SACRIFICIAL PARTS OF THE PESACH OFFERING

committed. He does not consider it permissible to initially bring the *emurin* onto the Altar and leave them there for post-Yom Tov burning.

*Rashi* (*Pesachim* 59a ד"ה מעלה ומלינה), however, maintains that it is permitted to bring the *emurin* up onto the Altar overnight even according to Rava. Although Rava rules that the *emurin* become *nossar* and if removed from the Altar may not be brought back up, since, in the final analysis, while atop the Altar they may be burned, letting them stay atop the Altar overnight is not considered a transgression of "leaving over" — and is in fact permitted in the first place, in order to prevent the *emurin* from becoming disqualified (*Maharam Schik* here; *Chazon Ish, Zevachim* 19:44-45; see also *Rashi* to *Exodus* 23:18 ד"ה ולא ילין and *Turei Even* ibid.; cf. *Minchas Chinuch* §1 ד"ה אך קשה). Accordingly, *Rashi* and *Ritva* maintain that this was the standard practice followed in the *Beis HaMikdash* when pre-Sabbath or pre-Yom Tov *emurin* were not offered up: They were brought up onto the Altar and left there until after the Sabbath or Yom Tov, and then burned. Miraculously, it never occurred that the *emurin* became rancid while resting atop the Altar.

For further discussion of this subject, see *Minchas Chinuch* at length.

## מִצְוָה צא: מִצְוַת הֲבָאַת בִּכּוּרִים[1]

לְהָבִיא בִּכּוּרִים לַמִּקְדָּשׁ, וְהוּא הַפְּרִי הָרִאשׁוֹן שֶׁמִּתְבַּשֵּׁל בָּאִילָן[2] שֶׁחַיָּבִין אָנוּ לַהֲבִיאוֹ שָׁם וְלִתְּנוֹ לַכֹּהֲנִים, וְלֹא כָּל הָאִילָנוֹת בְּמִצְוָה זוֹ מִן הַתּוֹרָה,[3] אֶלָּא שִׁבְעַת הַמִּינִין בִּלְבַד שֶׁנִּשְׁתַּבְּחָה הָאָרֶץ בָּהֶן, וְהֵם חִטָּה וּשְׂעוֹרָה[4] גֶּפֶן וּתְאֵנָה וְרִמּוֹן זֵיתִים וּתְמָרִים,[5]

## Mitzvah 91
## The Obligation to Bring Bikkurim [to the Temple]

רֵאשִׁית בִּכּוּרֵי אַדְמָתְךָ תָּבִיא בֵּית ה' אֱלֹהֶיךָ

*The choicest first fruit of your land shall you bring to the House of Hashem, your God (Exodus 23:19).*

When a landowner sees the first of his fruits ripening in the growing season, he is obligated to designate them as "*bikkurim*" (literally, *ripening ones*) and bring them in a container to the Courtyard of the *Beis HaMikdash* (Holy Temple). There he performs the *bikkurim* service, in which he recites a special declaration (*Deuteronomy* 26:3-10), and sets down the *bikkurim* near the Altar. The produce is then distributed to the Kohanim serving in the *Beis HaMikdash*.

This mitzvah is mentioned both in the verse cited above, and, at greater length, in *Deuteronomy* 26:1-11. While the above verse contains the actual mitzvah-obligation to bring the *bikkurim* to the *Beis HaMikdash*, the longer *Deuteronomy* passage adds many details relating to this obligation, and contains the separate mitzvah-obligation to recite the *bikkurim* declaration (Mitzvah 606).[1] **לְהָבִיא בִּכּוּרִים לַמִּקְדָּשׁ** — It is an obligation **to bring** *bikkurim* **to the Holy Temple. וְהוּא הַפְּרִי הָרִאשׁוֹן שֶׁמִּתְבַּשֵּׁל בָּאִילָן** — This term, *bikkurim*, **refers to the fruit that ripens first on the tree**,[2] **שֶׁחַיָּבִין אָנוּ לַהֲבִיאוֹ שָׁם וְלִתְּנוֹ לַכֹּהֲנִים** — which we are obligated to bring there (i.e., to the Temple), **and give to the Kohanim. וְלֹא כָּל הָאִילָנוֹת בְּמִצְוָה זוֹ מִן הַתּוֹרָה** — **Not all trees are subject to this mitzvah by Biblical law;**[3] **אֶלָּא שִׁבְעַת הַמִּינִין בִּלְבַד שֶׁנִּשְׁתַּבְּחָה הָאָרֶץ בָּהֶן** — it applies **only** to fruits of **the Seven Species with which Eretz Yisrael is praised. וְהֵם חִטָּה וּשְׂעוֹרָה גֶּפֶן וּתְאֵנָה וְרִמּוֹן זֵיתִים וּתְמָרִים** — **These** species **are: wheat, barley,**[4] **grape, fig, pomegranate, olives, and dates.**[5]

---

NOTES

1. The *bikkurim* declaration consists of a set of verses of thanksgiving (*Deuteronomy* 26:5-10) that are recited by the one bringing the first fruits to the *Beis HaMikdash*. These two obligations, to bring *bikkurim* and to recite the *bikkurim* declaration, while related, are actually two separate mitzvos. There are a number of situations in which one must fulfill the mitzvah of bringing *bikkurim* but is exempt from reciting the declaration (see Mitzvah 606).

2. Chinuch uses the terms "fruit" and "tree" throughout this mitzvah because the majority of *bikkurim* produce is fruit — although, as Chinuch continues, the mitzvah of *bikkurim* applies to wheat and barley as well.

3. See below, note 15, regarding the Rabbinic obligation.

4. According to some authorities, the grains of spelt, oats, and rye are also included in the *bikkurim* obligation; see the Insight for further discussion.

5. The Torah writes, among the praises of Eretz Yisrael, that it is *a good land ... a land of wheat, barley, grape, fig, and pomegranate; a land of oil-olives and date-honey* (*Deuteronomy* 8:7-8). The "oil-olives" of this verse refer to high-quality olives that retain more oil while growing than other olives (see *Yerushalmi Bikkurim* 1:3 [4a in the Schottenstein edition]).

[Although the verse speaks of date-honey, as a rule, only the fruits themselves, and not any liquids produced from the fruit, are brought as *bikkurim*. Thus, only dates are brought for the *bikkurim* obligation, not honey produced from the dates (*Yerushalmi* ibid.). There are exceptions to this rule in regard to grape-wine and olive-oil; see *Rambam*, *Hil. Bikkurim* 2:4, with commentaries.]

## MISHPATIM / MITZVAH 91: THE OBLIGATION TO BRING BIKKURIM

שֶׁנֶּאֱמַר (שמות כ״ג, י״ט) רֵאשִׁית בִּכּוּרֵי אַדְמָתְךָ תָּבִיא וְגוֹ׳, וּבָא הַפֵּרוּשׁ שֶׁלֹּא נֶאֱמַר אֶלָּא עַל ז׳ פֵּרוֹת אֵלוּ⁶. וּלְפִי הַדּוֹמֶה כִּי בְּדֶרֶךְ זוֹ לָמְדוּ זִכְרוֹנָם לִבְרָכָה לוֹמַר כֵּן, כִּי אַחַר שֶׁלֹּא הִזְכִּירוּ פֵּרוֹת אֲחֵרִים חוּץ מֵאֵלּוּ בַּתּוֹרָה בְּשׁוּם מָקוֹם, וְצִוָּנוּ בָּרוּךְ הוּא לְהָבִיא מֵאַרְצֵנוּ בִּכּוּרֵי פֵּרוֹת סְתָם, בֶּאֱמֶת יֵשׁ לָדוּן כִּי עַל הַפֵּרוֹת שֶׁהוֹדִיעָנוּ בַּתּוֹרָה שֶׁהֵן בָּאָרֶץ וְשִׁשִּׁבְּחָה בָּהֶן, עַל אוֹתָן צִוָּנוּ⁷. וְאֶפְשָׁר כִּי יֵשׁ לְרַבּוֹתֵינוּ זִכְרוֹנָם לִבְרָכָה עוֹד הֶכְרֵחַ הַכָּתוּב בָּעִנְיָן⁸, אוֹ שֶׁמָּא דִּבְרֵי קַבָּלָה הֵם⁹.

וְכֵן הָיָה דַּרְכָּם לְהָבִיא אוֹתָן: הַסְּמוּכִין לִירוּשָׁלַיִם מְבִיאִין אוֹתָן רַכִּים, וְהָרְחוֹקִים מְיַבְּשִׁים אוֹתָן.

---

**שֶׁנֶּאֱמַר ״רֵאשִׁית בִּכּוּרֵי אַדְמָתְךָ תָּבִיא וְגוֹ׳ ״** — We are so commanded, **as it is stated** (*Exodus* 23:19): *The choicest first fruit of your land shall you bring* to the House of Hashem, your God. **וּבָא הַפֵּרוּשׁ שֶׁלֹּא נֶאֱמַר אֶלָּא עַל ז׳ פֵּרוֹת אֵלוּ** — **The explanation** of this verse, **as transmitted** to us by the Sages (*Mishnah, Bikkurim* 1:3) **is that** the ripening produce mentioned in **[the verse] refers only to these Seven** Species of **produce.**[6]

Chinuch suggests a possible source from which the Sages may have derived the law that the *bikkurim* obligation applies only to the Seven Species:

**וּלְפִי הַדּוֹמֶה כִּי בְּדֶרֶךְ זוֹ לָמְדוּ זִכְרוֹנָם לִבְרָכָה לוֹמַר כֵּן** — **It appears that [the Sages], of blessed memory, learned to state this** law, i.e., that *bikkurim* applies only to the Seven Species, **in the following way: כִּי אַחַר שֶׁלֹּא הִזְכִּירוּ פֵּרוֹת אֲחֵרִים חוּץ מֵאֵלּוּ בַּתּוֹרָה בְּשׁוּם מָקוֹם** — **For since no other** specific species of **produce is mentioned anywhere in the Torah aside from these, וְצִוָּנוּ בָּרוּךְ הוּא לְהָבִיא מֵאַרְצֵנוּ בִּכּוּרֵי פֵּרוֹת סְתָם** — **and [God], blessed is He, commanded us to bring from our land "produce,"** without specifying a particular species, **בֶּאֱמֶת יֵשׁ לָדוּן** — **it is certainly appropriate to reason כִּי עַל הַפֵּרוֹת שֶׁהוֹדִיעָנוּ בַּתּוֹרָה שֶׁהֵן בָּאָרֶץ וְשִׁשִּׁבְּחָה בָּהֶן** — **that it is** regarding **those fruits about which He informed us in the Torah that they are in the Land** (*Eretz Yisrael*), and on account of which He praised the Land — **עַל אוֹתָן צִוָּנוּ** — **regarding those fruits** only **were we commanded** to bring *bikkurim*.[7]

**וְאֶפְשָׁר כִּי יֵשׁ לְרַבּוֹתֵינוּ זִכְרוֹנָם לִבְרָכָה עוֹד הֶכְרֵחַ הַכָּתוּב בָּעִנְיָן** — **And** aside from this suggestion, **it is** also **possible that our Teachers, of blessed memory,** the Sages of the Oral Law, **have some other proof from Scripture regarding this subject,**[8] **אוֹ שֶׁמָּא דִּבְרֵי קַבָּלָה הֵם** — **or perhaps [this law] is** not derived from a specific Scriptural source, but is simply an Oral Law **received through transmission** from the earlier Sages.[9]

Chinuch returns to the description of the mitzvah:

**וְכֵן הָיָה דַּרְכָּם לְהָבִיא אוֹתָן** — **This is the manner in which they would bring [the *bikkurim* fruit]: הַסְּמוּכִין לִירוּשָׁלַיִם מְבִיאִין אוֹתָן רַכִּים** — **Those** whose produce grew **close to Jerusalem,** the place of the Temple, **would bring them** when **fresh** (literally, *soft*), **וְהָרְחוֹקִים מְיַבְּשִׁים אוֹתָן** — **and those** whose produce grew **far** from Jerusalem **would dry [the produce]** before bringing it, so that it would not spoil on the way.

---

### NOTES

6. The mitzvah is further limited to superior types of those species. Thus, for example, dates that grow on mountains, which are an inferior type of date, are not brought as *bikkurim* (Mishnah, *Bikkurim* 1:3).

7. Although the Torah does in fact make mention of other species of fruit (*Genesis* 43:11; *Leviticus* 23:40), Chinuch apparently refers here to produce mentioned in the context of the praise of Eretz Yisrael. [See *Me'il HaEphod* §3 for another possible explanation.]

8. In fact, *Sifrei* (*Deuteronomy* 26:2; cited by *Rashi* ad loc.) does derive this law from a Scriptural source (see also *Yerushalmi Bikkurim* 1:3, and less explicitly in *Menachos* 84b). Nevertheless, according to many authorities, the Scriptural derivation does not clearly specify the Seven Species, but merely limits the obligation of *bikkurim* to some particular species of produce. The identification of the Seven Species as the specific ones to which the Torah refers relies on some logical basis, as Chinuch supplies here (*Minchas Yitzchak* §1; *Minchas Soless*; see also *Gur Aryeh* to *Rashi* ibid.; for another explanation of Chinuch's words, see *Maharam Schik* §1).

9. While many laws of the Oral Torah can be derived in some way from Scripture, there are some that have no Scriptural source at all. They are, rather, part of an Oral Tradition beginning with Moses, who received these laws directly from God at Sinai [הֲלָכָה לְמֹשֶׁה מִסִּינַי].

## משפטים / מצוה צא: מצות הבאת בכורים

מִשָּׁרְשֵׁי הַמִּצְוָה, כְּדֵי לְהַעֲלוֹת דְּבַר הַשֵּׁם יִתְבָּרַךְ עַל רֹאשׁ שִׂמְחָתֵנוּ,[10] וְנִזְכֹּר וְנֵדַע כִּי מֵאִתּוֹ בָּרוּךְ הוּא יַגִּיעוּ לָנוּ כָּל הַבְּרָכוֹת בָּעוֹלָם, עַל כֵּן נִצְטַוִּינוּ לְהָבִיא לִמְשָׁרְתֵי בֵּיתוֹ רֵאשִׁית הַפְּרִי הַמִּתְבַּשֵּׁל בְּאִילָנוֹתָיו, וּמִתּוֹךְ הַזְכִּירָה וְקַבָּלַת מַלְכוּתוֹ וְהוֹדָאָתֵנוּ לְפָנָיו כִּי הַפֵּרוֹת וְיֶתֶר כָּל הַטּוֹבָה מֵאִתּוֹ יָבוֹאוּ,[11] נִהְיֶה רְאוּיִין לַבְּרָכָה וְיִתְבָּרְכוּ פֵּרוֹתֵינוּ.[12]

מִדִּינֵי הַמִּצְוָה, מַה שֶּׁאָמְרוּ זִכְרוֹנָם לִבְרָכָה (ביכורים פ"ב מ"א) שֶׁהֵן אֲסוּרִין לְזָר כִּתְרוּמָה[13] מִשֶּׁנִּכְנְסוּ לִירוּשָׁלַיִם,[14] וּמֵאֵי זֶה פֵּרוֹת מְבִיאִין מֵהֶם בִּכּוּרִים מִדְּרַבָּנָן,[15]

---

### ⇐ Underlying Purpose of the Mitzvah ⇒

מִשָּׁרְשֵׁי הַמִּצְוָה — **Among the underlying purposes of the mitzvah is** כְּדֵי לְהַעֲלוֹת דְּבַר הַשֵּׁם יִתְבָּרַךְ עַל רֹאשׁ שִׂמְחָתֵנוּ — **in order to elevate the Word of Hashem, blessed be He, over the pinnacle of our joy,**[10] i.e., to let the fulfillment of His command supersede our personal joy upon the ripening of our crop, וְנִזְכֹּר וְנֵדַע — **so that we may remember and know** כִּי מֵאִתּוֹ בָּרוּךְ הוּא יַגִּיעוּ לָנוּ כָּל הַבְּרָכוֹת בָּעוֹלָם — **that all the blessings in the world come to us from Him, blessed is He.** עַל כֵּן נִצְטַוִּינוּ לְהָבִיא לִמְשָׁרְתֵי בֵּיתוֹ — **We are therefore commanded to bring to the servants of His House**, i.e., the Kohanim, רֵאשִׁית הַפְּרִי הַמִּתְבַּשֵּׁל בְּאִילָנוֹתָיו — **the first fruits that ripen on the tree.** By bringing these fruits to the Temple at this time of joy, we are reminded that God is the Source of our blessings. וּמִתּוֹךְ הַזְכִּירָה וְקַבָּלַת מַלְכוּתוֹ — **And, through** this **remembrance** of Hashem **and acceptance of His sovereignty**, by following His commandment at a time that might otherwise be used for personal celebration, וְהוֹדָאָתֵנוּ לְפָנָיו כִּי הַפֵּרוֹת וְיֶתֶר כָּל הַטּוֹבָה מֵאִתּוֹ יָבוֹאוּ — **and** through **our acknowledgment before Him that the produce and all the rest of the good** that we have **comes to us from Him,**[11] נִהְיֶה רְאוּיִין לַבְּרָכָה וְיִתְבָּרְכוּ פֵּרוֹתֵינוּ — **we will be worthy of** further **blessing, and our produce will be blessed.**[12]

### ⇐ Laws of the Mitzvah ⇒

מִדִּינֵי הַמִּצְוָה — **Among the laws of the mitzvah is** מַה שֶּׁאָמְרוּ זִכְרוֹנָם לִבְרָכָה שֶׁהֵן אֲסוּרִין לְזָר כִּתְרוּמָה — **that which [the Sages], of blessed memory, stated** (Mishnah, *Bikkurim* 2:1; *Makkos* 19a), **that [*bikkurim* produce] is forbidden to non-Kohanim just as *terumah* produce is,**[13] וּמֵאֵי זֶה פֵּרוֹת מִשֶּׁנִּכְנְסוּ לִירוּשָׁלַיִם — **but only once [the *bikkurim*] enter the city of Jerusalem.**[14] מְבִיאִין מֵהֶם בִּכּוּרִים מִדְּרַבָּנָן — **Also** included is the law that clarifies **from which produce *bikkurim* is brought by Rabbinic law.**[15]

---

### NOTES

10. Stylistic paraphrase of *Psalms* 137:6; see *Ibn Ezra* and *Malbim* there.

11. This acknowledgment is expressed by the action of bringing the fruit to the *Beis HaMikdash*, and articulated in the declaration recited there in the *bikkurim* service (see above, note 1).

12. Chinuch elaborates further on this theme in his description of the underlying purpose for Mitzvah 606, the mitzvah of reciting the *bikkurim* declaration.

13. *Terumah* is the portion of one's crop [usually ¹⁄₅₀] given to the Kohen (Mitzvah 507). It is forbidden to non-Kohanim for consumption (Mitzvah 280). Since the Torah refers to *bikkurim* with the word "*terumah*" (*Deuteronomy* 12:17), we derive that *bikkurim* has the same forbidden status to non-Kohanim as *terumah* (*Rambam, Hil. Bikkurim* 3:1).

14. Chinuch (following *Rambam* ibid.) maintains that *bikkurim* produce attains the status of *terumah*, making it forbidden to non-Kohanim, only once it enters the walls of Jerusalem. According to other Rishonim, *bikkurim* attains this status only upon entering the Courtyard of the *Beis HaMikdash* (*Rash, Bikkurim* 2:1; see also *Rashi, Makkos* 19a ד"ה מאימתי; and *Tosafos* 18b ד"ה בכורים). [Even before it attains this status, the *bikkurim* may not be consumed, but the special ramifications connected with the *terumah* status, including the severe punishment for a non-Kohen who intentionally eats it, do not yet apply (see *Chazon Ish, Zeraim, Likkutim* 9:1 שם ד"ה, *Derech Emunah, Hil. Bikkurim* 3:2, in *Beur HaHalachah* חולין הוא הרי ד"ה).]

A Kohen is also prohibited from eating *bikkurim* produce before it is brought to the *Beis HaMikdash*. However, that is not due to its classification as *terumah* (since a Kohen is permitted to eat *terumah*), but due to a separate Biblical prohibition (see Mitzvah 449).

15. As Chinuch noted above, only produce of the Seven Species is included in the *bikkurim* obligation by

## 189 ☐ MISHPATIM / MITZVAH 91: THE OBLIGATION TO BRING BIKKURIM

וְשֶׁנִּתְּנִין הַבִּכּוּרִים לְאַנְשֵׁי מִשְׁמָר[16], וְשֶׁטְּעוּנִין כְּלִי[17], וְהוּא לַכֹּהֵן אִם הוּא שֶׁל עֵץ[18], וְשֶׁלֹּא יְבִיאֵם אָדָם בְּעִרְבּוּב אֶלָּא בְּדֶרֶךְ נוֹי, כְּגוֹן שֶׁמֵּשִׂים הוּצִין אוֹ עָלִין בַּסַּל בֵּין כָּל מִין וּמִין[19], וּמַקִּיף אֶשְׁכּוֹלוֹת עֲנָבִים לְסַל שֶׁל תְּאֵנִים עַל שְׂפָתוֹ[20], וּמְבִיאִין תּוֹרִים וּבְנֵי יוֹנָה לִכְבוֹד הַבִּכּוּרִים וְנוֹתְנִין אוֹתָן לַכֹּהֲנִים.[21]

---

Having cited laws pertaining to the produce itself, Chinuch turns to a number of laws regarding the procedure of offering the *bikkurim*:

וְשֶׁנִּתְּנִין הַבִּכּוּרִים לְאַנְשֵׁי מִשְׁמָר — **Also** included in the laws of the mitzvah is the rule **that** after the *bikkurim* service (including the *bikkurim* declaration) is completed, **the** *bikkurim* fruits **are given to the members of the** *mishmar* **of Kohanim serving in the Temple at the time that they are offered.**[16] וְשֶׁטְּעוּנִין כְּלִי — **Also, the law that [the** *bikkurim***] require a vessel,** i.e., one may not bring the *bikkurim* produce in one's hands,[17] וְהוּא לַכֹּהֵן אִם הוּא שֶׁל עֵץ — **and that [the vessel] is given to the Kohen, if it is** made **of wood.** [18] וְשֶׁלֹּא יְבִיאֵם אָדָם בְּעִרְבּוּב אֶלָּא בְּדֶרֶךְ נוֹי — **Also,** when bringing the *bikkurim*, **a person should not bring them in disarray, but rather, in a pleasing manner,** כְּגוֹן שֶׁמֵּשִׂים הוּצִין אוֹ עָלִין בַּסַּל בֵּין כָּל מִין וּמִין — **such as by placing palm leaves or** other **leaves in the** *bikkurim* **basket between each species** of produce,[19] וּמַקִּיף אֶשְׁכּוֹלוֹת עֲנָבִים לְסַל שֶׁל תְּאֵנִים עַל שְׂפָתוֹ — **and by encircling a basket of figs with clusters of grapes on the rim** of the basket to beautify it.[20] וּמְבִיאִין תּוֹרִים וּבְנֵי יוֹנָה לִכְבוֹד הַבִּכּוּרִים — **They would** also **bring turtledoves and young pigeons in honor of the** *bikkurim***,** וְנוֹתְנִין אוֹתָן לַכֹּהֲנִים — **and would give them** as gifts **to the Kohanim.**[21]

---

### NOTES

Biblical law. Here, Chinuch notes that by Rabbinic law one is obligated to bring *bikkurim* from other species as well (see also end of Mitzvah 449). Although this view is indicated by *Rashi* (commentary to *Nechemiah* 10:36), most commentators find it difficult, as it seems to be directly contradicted by *Yerushalmi Bikkurim* 1:3 [4a in Schottenstein edition]. For discussion of this difficulty and possible resolutions, see *Malbim* to *Nechemiah* loc. cit., and *Teshuvos Chasam Sofer, Orach Chaim* §197; see also *Chidushei HaRan, Chullin* 120b.

Some commentators suggest that Chinuch does not refer here to the Rabbinic obligation regarding other *species*, but to certain *places* where the *bikkurim* obligation is not Biblical but Rabbinic (*Tzava Rav, Minchas Yitzchak*; see further in *Minchas Yitzchak* for another possible explanation of these words of Chinuch).

16. The Kohanim who served in the *Beis HaMikdash* were divided into twenty-four groups, called *mishmaros* (watches; sing. *mishmar*), with each *mishmar* performing the *avodah* one week at a time, on a rotating basis. [This arrangement is the subject of Mitzvah 509.] The Kohanim of each *mishmar* received the priestly sacrificial gifts during their week of service. After the *bikkurim* service, the fruit is divided among the Kohanim of the *mishmar* of that week.

According to *Minchas Chinuch* (§9), a Kohen who offers *bikkurim* from his own land may keep the fruit for himself after the service is completed.

17. This is as per the instructions of the verse (*Deuteronomy* 26:2): וְשַׂמְתָּ בַטֶּנֶא, *and you shall put [the bikkurim fruit] in a basket* (*Sifrei* to verse).

18. If the *bikkurim* were brought in a metal vessel, the Kohen would take the *bikkurim* and return the vessel to the owner; if the vessel was a basket made of reeds or the like, it was retained by the Kohanim (*Rambam, Hil. Bikkurim* 3:8). Since those who brought homemade baskets were usually of modest means, the amount of their *bikkurim* gifts would typically be meager. The basket itself was therefore also given as part of the *bikkurim* offering, so that together with the fruit, it would constitute a substantial gift (*Sifrei* to *Deuteronomy* 26:4, following *Tos. Yom Tov, Bikkurim* 3:8; see also *Malbim* and *Gra* ad loc.). [According to *Lechem Shamayim* (*Bikkurim* 3:8), this practice was instituted so that the poor would not be embarrassed by their meager gifts in relation to the abundant and choice fruits of the rich. To augment their mitzvah of *bikkurim,* the poor were given the *opportunity* to donate their baskets as well.]

For another reason for this differentiation between the baskets, see *Derech Emunah, Bikkurim* 3:8, *Beur HaHalachah* ד"ה הרי הביכורים.

19. It is actually preferable to bring each of the species in its own vessel; the arrangement mentioned here applies only when one cannot do that and must bring all the fruits in one vessel (*Tosefta Bikkurim* 2:8; *Yerushalmi Bikkurim* 3:5 [26a in Schottenstein edition]; *Rambam* ibid.). For a specific order in which each kind of produce should be positioned within the vessel, see *Rambam* ibid. 3:7; see also the following note.

20. That is, additional clusters of grapes were placed on the rim to adorn the basket (*Yerushalmi* ibid). Alternatively, when both figs and grapes of *bikkurim* were offered, the figs were placed inside the basket, and the grapes were placed on the rim above it (*Rambam* ibid.).

21. According to *Rambam* (ibid. 3:9), two sets of birds were brought. One set was brought separately and presented as a gift to the Kohanim, and the other was brought together with the basket of fruit, and then

וְכֵיצַד[22] הָיוּ מַעֲלִין אוֹתָם[23], וְהַשִּׂמְחָה שֶׁהָיוּ עוֹשִׂין עֲלֵיהֶן הַמְּבִיאִין אוֹתָן[24] וְהַיּוֹצְאִים לִקְרָאתָם[25], וְהַמִּזְמוֹרִים שֶׁהָיוּ קוֹרִין סָמוּךְ לָעִיר[26], וְיֶתֶר פְּרָטֶיהָ, מְבֹאָרִים בְּמַסֶּכֶת בִּכּוּרִים[27]. וְנוֹהֶגֶת בִּזְמַן הַבַּיִת בִּזְכָרִים[28].

The *bikkurim* were brought to Jerusalem with much pomp and ceremony. Multitudes of Jews would gather from the various cities and bring their *bikkurim* together amid great celebration.[22] Chinuch mentions some details of this celebration:

וְכֵיצַד הָיוּ מַעֲלִין אוֹתָם — The laws of the mitzvah **also** include **how they would bring [the *bikkurim*] up** to Jerusalem and the Temple,[23] וְהַשִּׂמְחָה שֶׁהָיוּ עוֹשִׂין עֲלֵיהֶן הַמְּבִיאִין אוֹתָן — **and the celebration that would be made for** the bringing of **[the *bikkurim*] by those who brought it,**[24] וְהַיּוֹצְאִים לִקְרָאתָם — **and by those who would come out to greet them;**[25] וְהַמִּזְמוֹרִים שֶׁהָיוּ קוֹרִין סָמוּךְ לָעִיר — **and the psalms that they would recite when they neared the city** of Jerusalem.[26] וְיֶתֶר פְּרָטֶיהָ מְבֹאָרִים בְּמַסֶּכֶת בִּכּוּרִים — These, **and the remaining details of [the mitzvah], are set forth in Tractate *Bikkurim*.**[27]

### ⸺ Applicability of the Mitzvah ⸺

בִּזְכָרִים — וְנוֹהֶגֶת בִּזְמַן הַבַּיִת — **[This mitzvah] applies** only **in the times of the** Holy **Temple, and applies** only **to men.**[28]

---

### NOTES

presented as *olah* offerings. Chinuch here is apparently referring to the birds that were brought as gifts to the Kohanim.

According to many Rishonim, however, only one set of birds was customarily brought with the *bikkurim*, and the birds were presented as *olah* offerings (*Raavad* to *Rambam* loc. cit.; *Rash* and *Rosh* to *Bikkurim* 3:5; *Rashi* to *Menachos* 58a ד"ה והסלים).

22. Instead of bringing the *bikkurim* as individuals, they would gather to bring it in large groups for the greater glory of God, in keeping with the general rule that בְּרָב עַם הַדְרַת מֶלֶךְ, *With multitudes of people is the glory of the King* [*Proverbs* 14:28] (*Rambam*, *Hil. Bikkurim* 4:16). *Maharsha* writes (*Chidushim* to *Bikkurim*, printed after his *Chidushim* to *Berachos*) that this celebration was in fulfillment of the Biblical directive (*Deuteronomy* 26:11): וְשָׂמַחְתָּ בְּכָל הַטּוֹב אֲשֶׁר נָתַן לְךָ ה' אֱלֹהֶיךָ, *You shall rejoice with all of the goodness that Hashem, your God, has given you.* This verse appears at the conclusion of the Torah's description of the *bikkurim* ceremony.

23. After gathering from various cities, the group would arise early in the morning, and the appointee would announce (using the wording of *Jeremiah* 31:5): קוּמוּ וְנַעֲלֶה צִיּוֹן אֶל ה' אֱלֹהֵינוּ, *Let us rise and ascend to Zion, to Hashem, our God!* They would then ascend to Jerusalem in a procession.

24. The procession would be preceded by an ox, adorned with gold-covered horns and a wreath of olives on its head, and a flute would be played before them as they traveled. The entire way they would sing the verse (*Psalms* 122:1): שָׂמַחְתִּי בְּאֹמְרִים לִי בֵּית ה' נֵלֵךְ, *I rejoiced at those who said to me, "Let us go to the House of Hashem"* (Mishnah, *Bikkurim* 3:2 with *Tiferes Yisrael*; *Yerushalmi Bikkurim* 3:5 [22b in Schottenstein edition]; *Rambam*, *Hil. Bikkurim* 4:16).

25. When the procession neared Jerusalem, they would send an appointee to inform the people of Jerusalem that a *bikkurim* procession was readying to enter. Nobles of Jerusalem, leaders of the Kohanim, and heads of the various Temple offices would then come out to greet the procession (Mishnah ibid. 3:3; *Rambam* ibid.).

26. As they arrived in Jerusalem they would say (*Psalms* 122:2): עֹמְדוֹת הָיוּ רַגְלֵינוּ בִּשְׁעָרַיִךְ יְרוּשָׁלָיִם, *Our feet stood in your gates, O Jerusalem*. Other psalms were recited upon reaching the Temple Mount and entering the Courtyard of the Temple (Mishnah ibid.; *Rambam* ibid. §16-17).

In addition to the psalms sung by those bearing the *bikkurim*, the Leviim serving in the *Beis HaMikdash* would sing a special psalm (*Psalms* 30) when the *bikkurim* entered the *Beis HaMikdash*. This was an obligatory component of the *bikkurim* service (*Rambam*, *Hil. Bikkurim* 3:13-14).

27. The laws are codified in *Rambam*, *Hil. Bikkurim*, Chapters 1-5.

28. *Mishneh LaMelech* (glosses to Chinuch) points out that the Mishnah (*Bikkurim* 1:5) explicitly lists women among those *obligated* to bring *bikkurim* [from produce that grew in their own land], and exempts them only from the specific obligation to recite the *bikkurim* declaration in the *Beis HaMikdash*. He therefore explains that Chinuch here refers only to the Biblical obligation, from which women are indeed exempt, while the Mishnah refers to a later Rabbinic enactment obligating women to bring *bikkurim*. [Nevertheless, other Rishonim do not differentiate between the Biblical and Rabbinic obligation; see *Mishneh LaMelech* there.]

*Minchas Chinuch* (§10) explains that according to Chinuch, the reason women are Biblically exempt is that *bikkurim* is considered a time-specific mitzvah (from which women are generally exempt), since

# MISHPATIM / MITZVAH 91: THE OBLIGATION TO BRING BIKKURIM

וּבְפֵרוֹת אֶרֶץ יִשְׂרָאֵל[29] וְסוּרְיָא[30] וְעֵבֶר הַיַּרְדֵּן[31], אֲבָל לֹא בְּפֵרוֹת חוּצָה לָאָרֶץ. וְעוֹבֵר עָלֶיהָ בִּטֵּל עֲשֵׂה.

While mitzvos related to the land generally pertain only in Eretz Yisrael, there are an additional two territories that have a partial status of Eretz Yisrael, such that some of the mitzvos of Eretz Yisrael apply there, and some do not. These two territories are Suria and Transjordan.

"Suria" is a term that refers to all of the territories captured by King David in his military campaigns, and annexed by him to Eretz Yisrael (Chinuch, Mitzvah 507). "Transjordan" refers to the territories east of the Jordan River conquered by Moses and the Jewish people from Sichon, king of the Amorites, and Og, king of Bashan (Numbers 21:21-35). These territories were granted by Moses to the tribes of Reuben, Gad, and part of the tribe of Manasseh (ibid. 32:33).

וּבְפֵרוֹת אֶרֶץ יִשְׂרָאֵל וְסוּרְיָא וְעֵבֶר הַיַּרְדֵּן — The mitzvah of *bikkurim* applies **to the produce of Eretz Yisrael,**[29] **Suria,**[30] **and Transjordan,**[31] אֲבָל לֹא בְּפֵרוֹת חוּצָה לָאָרֶץ — **but not to produce** grown **outside of Eretz** Yisrael.

וְעוֹבֵר עָלֶיהָ בִּטֵּל עֲשֵׂה — **One who transgresses [this mitzvah]** and fails to bring *bikkurim* to the Temple **has violated a mitzvah-obligation.**

## NOTES

*bikkurim* are brought only from Shavuos until Chanukah (Mishnah, *Bikkurim* 1:6). [As for why the other authorities do not consider it so, see *Turei Even, Megillah* 20b ד״ה ולוידוי מעשר.]

29. The verse (*Exodus* 23:19) specifies with regard to *bikkurim*: רֵאשִׁית בִּכּוּרֵי אַדְמָתְךָ, *The choicest first-fruit of "your land"* (Rambam, Hil. Bikkurim 2:1; see also *Minchas Chinuch* §9 and glosses of R' Chaim Heller to *Sefer HaMitzvos*, Mitzvah 125 §5).

Aside from being considered part of Eretz Yisrael, there is an additional criterion for produce to be Biblically included in the *bikkurim* obligation — that the land from which it grows be fertile enough to be considered "flowing with milk and honey." [This appellation refers to the plentiful milk from its goats and the abundant honey dripping from its succulent figs and dates (see *Kesubos* 111b).] This criterion is inferred from the words of the *bikkurim* declaration, in which the bearer of *bikkurim* thanks God for bringing the Jewish people to "this land, a land flowing with milk and honey" (*Deuteronomy* 26:9). Thus, the *bikkurim* obligation does not pertain even to land that is part of Eretz Yisrael, if that area is not fertile enough to be referred to as "flowing with milk and honey" (see Mishnah, *Bikkurim* 1:10).

According to *Rashi* (*Deuteronomy* 18:2), the whole of Eretz Yisrael proper fulfills this criterion (*Minchas Soless*). *Ramban*, however, writes (*Exodus* 13:5) that there is a small part of Eretz Yisrael proper that is not considered to be "flowing with milk and honey," and that is therefore exempt by Biblical law from *bikkurim*. Even according to this opinion, however, these territories are obligated in *bikkurim* by Rabbinic law (see *Minchas Chinuch* §9).

30. Chinuch explains in Mitzvah 507 that while Suria does not have the status of Eretz Yisrael by Biblical law, the Sages decreed that certain mitzvos of Eretz Yisrael apply there as well (see there for further discussion; see also Mitzvah 84 note 57). The *bikkurim* obligation in Suria is thus not of Biblical, but of Rabbinic origin (see Mitzvah 606; cf. *Chazon Ish, Orlah* 11:20 and *Keren Orah, Menachos* 84b).

31. The obligation to bring *bikkurim* from Transjordan is also of Rabbinic origin (*Rambam, Hil. Bikkurim* 2:1; Mitzvah 606), although for a different reason than that of Suria. In contrast to Suria, by Biblical law Transjordan *does* share the status of Eretz Yisrael with regard to many mitzvos. Nevertheless, it is Biblically exempted from the *bikkurim* requirement because it lacks the criterion of "flowing with milk and honey" [see note 29] (*Kesef Mishneh* to *Rambam* ibid.; *Minchas Chinuch* §9; see also *Minchas Chinuch* ibid. regarding the opinion of *Ramban* [*Exodus* 13:5]).

### ◆§ Insight: The Seven Species: Bikkurim and the Laws of Blessings

Chinuch begins this mitzvah by pointing out that only the Seven Species with which Eretz Yisrael is praised are included in the *bikkurim* obligation. These species are enumerated in *Deuteronomy* (8:8): *A land of wheat, barley, grape, fig, and pomegranate; a land of oil-olives and date-honey* (see above, note 5). Although today, in the absence of the *Beis HaMikdash*, we no longer have the opportunity to offer *bikkurim*, the status of the Seven Species as the produce *"with which Eretz Yisrael is praised"* remains relevant, and plays an important role in the laws of blessings over food.

After eating fruit or vegetables, as after eating other foods, one recites a *berachah acharonah*

(after-blessing). The proper *berachah acharonah* for most fruits and vegetables is the *borei nefashos* blessing. However, after eating fruit that is among the Seven Species, the *berachah Mei'ein Shalosh* (the three-faceted blessing) is recited. This blessing is a concise version of all the blessings recited in *Bircas HaMazon* (Grace After Meals, recited after eating a bread meal). The reason for this difference is the special status that these fruits have as produce with which Eretz Yisrael is praised (*Tur, Orach Chaim* §208). [See below, Mitzvah 430, where Chinuch discusses whether this blessing is a Biblical or Rabbinic obligation.]

Another practical ramification of the Seven Species arises in the laws of precedence of blessings. When faced with a variety of foods from which one intends to eat, if all the foods share the same *berachah rishonah* (first-blessing), the blessing for the more significant food is recited first. One of the primary criteria for determining which food is more significant is whether a food is counted among the Seven Species. Thus, if one has, for example, an apple and a grape before him, and he intends to eat both, he recites the *berachah rishonah* (in this case, *borei pri ha'eitz*) upon the grape, since the grape is one of the Seven Species while the apple is not.

A question arises, however, with regard to three kinds of grain. It is an oft-repeated rule with regard to many areas of halachah that the primary grains are wheat, barley, rye, oats, and spelt. For example, only bread made from these five species of grain has the halachic status of bread (e.g., regarding the laws of *chametz* and matzah). The Gemara (*Pesachim* 35a) identifies spelt halachically as a sub-species of wheat, and rye and oats halachically as subspecies of barley. Following these definitions, it would seem that although not enumerated explicitly in the verse that lists the Seven Species, the grains rye, oats, and spelt are also to be counted among the Seven Species. Just as wheat and barley are "Seven Species" produce, these grains, which are subspecies of wheat and barley, should also share that status.

Indeed, *Maharsha* (to *Pesachim* 36b, *Tosafos* ד"ה אוציא) takes the position that one who has a field of rye, oats, or spelt is obligated to bring *bikkurim* from these grains, since they are included among the Seven Species by way of their identification with wheat and barley (see also *Tos. Ha-Rashba MiShantz, Pesachim* 36b ד"ה אוציא). *Tur* (ibid.) likewise writes that one of the reasons that the *Mei'ein Shalosh* blessing is recited after eating certain foods made from rye, oats, or spelt is that, due to their relation to wheat and barley, *"they too are among the species for which Eretz Yisrael is praised."*

Many Acharonim, however, take issue with this position. *Pnei Yehoshua* (to *Tosafos, Pesachim* ibid., cited by *Minchas Chinuch* §1) notes that the classic sources that speak of the Seven Species never mention rye, oats, or spelt. *Pnei Yehoshua* therefore writes that these species are identified as being in the wheat or barley family only with regard to laws where the *differentiation between species* plays a role (such as *terumah* and *challah*; see *Rashi* and *Tosafos* there). While halachic "bread" can be made from all of the five grains, the classification of "Seven Species" for *bikkurim* and other laws includes only those specific kinds of produce for which Eretz Yisrael is *explicitly* praised in the verse. These other species, despite their subspecies identification, are simply not considered praiseworthy features of Eretz Yisrael. [Indeed, *Pnei Yehoshua* points out that even among those Seven Species themselves, the inferior versions of those fruits are not included in the *bikkurim* obligation (such as inferior dates or figs; see note 6 above). If even these fruit are not considered to be "Seven Species" fruit, certainly the offshoots of the wheat and barley families are not included.]

This view seems to be reflected in a halachah that we find with regard to precedence of blessings. *Tur* and *Shulchan Aruch* write (*Orach Chaim* 168:4) that if one has before him barley bread and spelt bread, he should recite the blessing upon the barley bread "because it is from the Seven Species." This is a clear indication that spelt, as well as rye and oats, do not share this special status (see also ibid. 211:6).

Nevertheless, as we have seen above, *Tur* himself (*Orach Chaim* §208) counts these three species as produce for which Eretz Yisrael is praised, in regard to the *Mei'ein Shalosh* blessing. To explain this contradiction, some Acharonim take a third approach to this matter. *Magen Avraham* (168:6) writes that although, by virtue of their being a subspecies of wheat or barley, these species do have a Seven Species status, they are not considered "primary" Seven Species, but have only partial status as Seven Species. The reason for their lesser standing is that they are not listed explicitly in the verse.

Therefore, when the question is whether they qualify for the longer *Mei'ein Shalosh* blessing, and they are not then being judged in relation to any other produce, we consider them part of the Seven Species. However, when the question is which of the two species is primary, barley, which is one of the enumerated Seven Species, takes precedence over spelt, which is not mentioned explicitly in the verse (see also *Taz* 168:4; *Maharam Schik* 91:1).

[See *Orach Chaim* §168 and §211 for the many and varied rules that apply to the law of precedence of blessings.]

## מִצְוָה צב: שֶׁלֹּא לְבַשֵּׁל בָּשָׂר בְּחָלָב[1]

שֶׁלֹּא נְבַשֵּׁל בָּשָׂר בְּהֵמָה בְּחָלָב, שֶׁנֶּאֱמַר (שמות כ״ג, י״ט) לֹא תְבַשֵּׁל גְּדִי בַּחֲלֵב אִמּוֹ,[2] וּבָא הַפֵּרוּשׁ דְּלָאו דַּוְקָא גְּדִי אֶלָּא אֲפִלּוּ כָּל בָּשָׂר בְּהֵמָה בְּמַשְׁמָע, שֶׁאֵין לְשׁוֹן גְּדִי

# Mitzvah 92
# The Prohibition to Cook Meat With Milk

לֹא תְבַשֵּׁל גְּדִי בַּחֲלֵב אִמּוֹ
*You shall not cook a kid in the milk of its mother* (Exodus 23:19).

Although in its literal sense, the above verse speaks of a young goat and its mother's milk, its prohibition actually includes cooking the meat of any kosher domestic animal in the milk (or dairy product) of any such animal. As Chinuch explains below, the term *gedi*, while having the literal meaning of *a young goat*, can also be used to refer to any meat, and the Sages (*Chullin* 113a) determined that it is in this sense that the word is employed in our verse.

Oral Tradition teaches further that the verse's specification of "the milk of its mother" is merely an example of the most common way that meat would be cooked in milk (the tender meat of a slaughtered animal was most likely to be cooked in the surplus milk of its mother).[1] In actuality, the prohibition is not limited to the milk of its mother, but includes cooking the meat with any milk or dairy product.

In addition to the prohibition to *cook* meat with milk, there is another prohibition associated with meat and milk. A meat-and-milk mixture that was cooked together is forbidden for consumption or any other benefit (such as selling or giving it to a non-Jew). In Mitzvah 113, Chinuch outlines the Biblical parameters of that prohibition, and the Rabbinic safeguards that were enacted to ensure that the Biblical injunction is not violated. It is important to note that both of these prohibitions are independent of each other. As Chinuch points out in this mitzvah, the prohibition against cooking meat with dairy applies even if it is not subsequently eaten, and the prohibition against eating or benefiting from the cooked mixture applies even to one who did not cook it.

שֶׁלֹּא נְבַשֵּׁל בָּשָׂר בְּהֵמָה בְּחָלָב — We are commanded **not to cook meat of an animal with milk,** שֶׁנֶּאֱמַר ״לֹא תְבַשֵּׁל גְּדִי בַּחֲלֵב אִמּוֹ״ — **as it is stated** (Exodus 23:19): *You shall not cook a kid in the milk of its mother.*[2]

The literal translation of the word *gedi* is "young goat." Chinuch explains that in this verse, the meaning of the word is more inclusive:

וּבָא הַפֵּרוּשׁ — **The explanation** of this verse, **as transmitted** to us by the Sages (*Chullin* 113a-b) is דְּלָאו דַּוְקָא גְּדִי — **that** the verse does **not** refer **only** to **a young goat;** אֶלָּא אֲפִלּוּ כָּל בָּשָׂר בְּהֵמָה — **rather, even any** other **animal meat is included in the meaning** of the word in this context, בְּמַשְׁמָע — שֶׁאֵין לְשׁוֹן גְּדִי — **because** the term **"***gedi***"** in this verse **is not** to be understood as a reference

---

NOTES

1. *Rambam, Hil. Maachalos Asuros* 9:3; see *Rashbam* and *Ibn Ezra* to this verse for further elaboration. See also *Kli Yakar* and *HaKesav VeHaKabbalah* for discussion of the technical meanings of the terms used in this verse.

2. As explained in the introduction to this mitzvah, the prohibition is not limited to "the milk of its mother," but includes any milk. [When the term "milk" is used throughout this mitzvah, it includes all dairy products, such as butter, cream, and cheese.]

The *literal* meaning of the words לֹא תְבַשֵּׁל is *you shall not boil,* referring to boiling the meat in milk. Nevertheless, most other food preparations through which the food is altered by way of heat are included in the prohibition. See *Shulchan Aruch, Yoreh Deah* 87:1 with commentaries for an explanation of which of these are Biblically forbidden and which are Rabbinically forbidden. See also *Minchas Chinuch* §3 regarding other methods of preparation such as salting, pickling, and smoking.

# MISHPATIM / MITZVAH 92: THE PROHIBITION TO COOK MEAT WITH MILK

אֶלָּא לְשׁוֹן בְּהֵמָה, וְהוֹצִיאוּ בִּלְשׁוֹן גְּדִי לְפִי שֶׁהַבָּשָׂר דָּבָר רַךְ כִּגְדִי.[3] וְאֵיךְ אַתָּה לָמֵד כֵּן, מִמַּה שֶׁאַתָּה מוֹצֵא בְּכַמָּה מְקוֹמוֹת בַּתּוֹרָה שֶׁכָּתוּב גְּדִי וְהִצְרַךְ לְפָרֵשׁ גְּדִי עִזִּים, הָא לָמַדְתָּ שֶׁבַּמָּקוֹם שֶׁנֶּאֱמַר גְּדִי סְתָם, לָאו דַּוְקָא גְּדִי עִזִּים, אֶלָּא אַף כָּל בָּשָׂר בְּהֵמָה כַּיּוֹצֵא בּוֹ בְּמַשְׁמָע.[4]

מִשָּׁרְשֵׁי מִצְוָה זוֹ, לְפִי הַדּוֹמֶה שֶׁהוּא בְּעִנְיָן מַה שֶׁכָּתַבְנוּ בְּמִצְוַת מְכַשֵּׁפָה, כִּי יֵשׁ בָּעוֹלָם דְּבָרִים שֶׁנֶּאֱסַר לָנוּ תַּעֲרָבְתָּן בְּסִבַּת הָעִנְיָן שֶׁאָמַרְנוּ שָׁם,[5] וְאֶפְשָׁר שֶׁתִּתְעָרֵב הַבָּשָׂר עִם הֶחָלָב בְּמַעֲשֵׂה הַבִּשּׁוּל יִהְיֶה סִבַּת אִסּוּרוֹ מִן הַיְסוֹד הַהוּא.[6]

וְהוֹצִיאוּ — **but** is rather **a term for** the meat of any **animal.** אֶלָּא לְשׁוֹן בְּהֵמָה to a young goat, בִּלְשׁוֹן גְּדִי לְפִי שֶׁהַבָּשָׂר דָּבָר רַךְ כִּגְדִי — [The verse] **expresses** [this meaning] of meat **with the term "gedi" because meat is a tender item, as is a young goat.**[3] Thus, the word *gedi* is used here in a borrowed sense to refer to the meat of any animal.

Chinuch explains (from *Chullin* ibid.) the Scriptural basis for understanding the word *gedi* in this verse in its more inclusive sense:

וְאֵיךְ אַתָּה לָמֵד כֵּן — **How do you learn** that **this is true?** מִמַּה שֶׁאַתָּה מוֹצֵא בְּכַמָּה מְקוֹמוֹת בַּתּוֹרָה — **From that which you find in numerous places in the Torah** שֶׁכָּתוּב גְּדִי וְהִצְרַךְ לְפָרֵשׁ גְּדִי עִזִּים — where the word **"gedi" is written, and** [the Torah] **found it necessary to** further **clarify** the term by writing **"gedi izzim"** — *a kid of goats*; הָא לָמַדְתָּ שֶׁבַּמָּקוֹם שֶׁנֶּאֱמַר גְּדִי סְתָם לָאו דַּוְקָא גְּדִי עִזִּים — **you thus learn that when it says** only the word **"gedi" without specifying** the species, **it does not refer only to young goats;** אֶלָּא אַף כָּל בָּשָׂר בְּהֵמָה כַּיּוֹצֵא בּוֹ בְּמַשְׁמָע — **rather, even the meat of any** other **animal is likewise included.**[4]

## ◦ Underlying Purpose of the Mitzvah ◦

מִשָּׁרְשֵׁי מִצְוָה זוֹ — **Among the underlying purposes of this mitzvah** is לְפִי הַדּוֹמֶה שֶׁהוּא בְּעִנְיָן מַה שֶׁכָּתַבְנוּ בְּמִצְוַת מְכַשֵּׁפָה — **apparently, that it is similar to** the idea **that we have written with regard to the mitzvah of** executing **the sorceress** (Mitzvah 62), כִּי יֵשׁ בָּעוֹלָם דְּבָרִים שֶׁנֶּאֱסַר לָנוּ תַּעֲרָבְתָּן בְּסִבַּת הָעִנְיָן שֶׁאָמַרְנוּ שָׁם — that is, **that the world contains certain things that we are prohibited to mix together due to the reason that we stated there,** in that mitzvah.[5] וְאֶפְשָׁר שֶׁתִּתְעָרֵב הַבָּשָׂר עִם הֶחָלָב בְּמַעֲשֵׂה הַבִּשּׁוּל — **It is thus possible that** with regard to **the mixing of meat with milk through the act of cooking,** יִהְיֶה סִבַּת אִסּוּרוֹ מִן הַיְסוֹד הַהוּא — **the reason of the prohibition is based on that same foundation.**[6]

---

### NOTES

3. For further discussion, see below, Mitzvah 113. [For a discussion of the usage of the word *gedi* as meaning "meat," see *HaKesav VeHaKabbalah* to this verse.]

According to some Rishonim, the word *gedi*, often used in Scripture to refer to the young goat, technically means the young of *any* animal (*Rambam, Hil. Maachalos Asuros* 9:3 and *Rashi* to verse). [*Gur Aryeh* ad loc. writes that the original, true meaning of the word *gedi* is the young of any domestic animal. Its specific use as a reference to young goats came about because goats are the smallest of the domestic animals and the word most clearly fit their description; see also *Malbim* and *HaKesav VeHaKabbalah* to verse.] Even according to these opinions, however, the prohibition applies to any meat, not only to the meat of young animals; see the introduction to this mitzvah.

4. However, only the meat of kosher domestic animals is included in the Biblical prohibition, to the exclusion of, for example, deer or fowl; see below, Mitzvah 113, where Chinuch elaborates on the details and sources of these laws.

5. There, Chinuch discusses the concept that the various forces and phenomena of nature must each be preserved in its own role, and are not to be unnaturally blended or mixed. He explains there that this is the basis of the prohibition of sorcery, which involves tampering with the natural order. See there for the full discussion.

6. The mixing of meat and milk through cooking is considered an unnatural blend of disparate forces of the natural world. Chinuch applies this concept to the prohibitions governing other forms of mixtures as well, such as *kilayim*, i.e., the mixing of different seeds, animals, and fibers (Mitzvos 244, 245, and 551). [See *Kli Yakar* to the verse, who explains why the mixing of meat and milk is considered an unnatural blend; see also Insight to this mitzvah.]

וְקְצָת רְאָיָה לָזֶה לְפִי שֶׁבָּא הָאִסּוּר לָנוּ בְּמַעֲשֵׂה הַתַּעֲרֹבֶת אַף עַל פִּי שֶׁלֹּא נֹאכְלֶנּוּ, שֶׁנִּרְאֶה בָּזֶה שֶׁאֵין אִסּוּרוֹ מֵחֲמַת נֶזֶק אֲכִילָתוֹ כְּלָל, רַק שֶׁלֹּא נַעֲשֶׂה פְּעֻלַּת אוֹתוֹ הַתַּעֲרֹבֶת לְהַרְחָקַת אוֹתוֹ עִנְיָן שֶׁאָמַרְנוּ.[7] וְהִזְהִירָנוּ גַּם כֵּן בְּמָקוֹם אַחֵר שֶׁאִם אוּלַי נַעֲשָׂה הַתַּעֲרֹבֶת לְבַל נֹאכְלֵהוּ וְלֹא נֵהָנֶה בּוֹ, לְהַרְחִיק הָעִנְיָן, וַאֲפִלּוּ אֲכָלוֹ מִבְּלִי שֶׁנֶּהֱנָה מִמֶּנּוּ כְּלָל לוֹקֶה, מַה שֶּׁאֵין כֵּן בִּשְׁאָר כָּל אִסּוּרֵי הַמַּאֲכָלוֹת,[8] וְכָל זֶה מוֹרֶה שֶׁיְּסוֹד טַעֲמוֹ הוּא מֵחֲמַת הַתַּעֲרֹבֶת, וּכְעִנְיָן שֶׁאָמַרְנוּ בְּכִשּׁוּף.[9]

---

Chinuch supports this idea based on various unique aspects of the meat-and-milk prohibition: וְקְצָת רְאָיָה לָזֶה לְפִי שֶׁבָּא הָאִסּוּר לָנוּ — **Somewhat of a proof for this** explanation is the fact בְּמַעֲשֵׂה הַתַּעֲרֹבֶת אַף עַל פִּי שֶׁלֹּא נֹאכְלֶנּוּ — **that** in this mitzvah **a prohibition has been transmitted to us against performing the** very *act* **of mixing** meat and milk through cooking, **even without eating [the mixture] afterward.** שֶׁנִּרְאֶה בָּזֶה שֶׁאֵין אִסּוּרוֹ מֵחֲמַת נֶזֶק אֲכִילָתוֹ כְּלָל — **It is apparent from this that the prohibition** to cook meat and milk together **is not due at all to the harm** that one would suffer **from eating [such a mixture];** רַק שֶׁלֹּא נַעֲשֶׂה פְּעֻלַּת אוֹתוֹ הַתַּעֲרֹבֶת לְהַרְחָקַת אוֹתוֹ עִנְיָן שֶׁאָמַרְנוּ — **rather,** the intent is simply **that we should not perform the action of this mixing** itself, **due to the** necessity of **distancing that matter which we have described,** i.e., the blending of elements that must remain separate in accordance with the order that the Creator prescribed for His world.[7]

Having explained that the underlying purpose of this prohibition is not the harmful effect of eating a mixture of meat and milk, but the action of mixing meat with milk, Chinuch explains the purpose of the separate prohibition against eating or benefiting from such a mixture: וְהִזְהִירָנוּ גַּם כֵּן בְּמָקוֹם אַחֵר — **[God] has additionally enjoined us elsewhere** in the Torah (*Exodus* 34:26; see Mitzvah 113) שֶׁאִם אוּלַי נַעֲשָׂה הַתַּעֲרֹבֶת — **that even if** it should **perhaps** occur that **this mixture was made,** לְבַל נֹאכְלֵהוּ וְלֹא נֵהָנֶה בּוֹ — **we are not to eat it or benefit from it,** לְהַרְחִיק הָעִנְיָן — and the purpose of that prohibition is in order **to distance us from the endeavor** of mixing it.

Chinuch provides a further demonstration of the difference between the meat-and-milk prohibition and the prohibitions regarding other forbidden foods: וַאֲפִלּוּ אֲכָלוֹ מִבְּלִי שֶׁנֶּהֱנָה מִמֶּנּוּ כְּלָל לוֹקֶה — **Furthermore, even if one eats [the meat-and-milk mixture] without benefiting at all** from the act of eating, **he still incurs** *malkus* (lashes), if the violation was intentional, מַה שֶּׁאֵין כֵּן בִּשְׁאָר כָּל אִסּוּרֵי הַמַּאֲכָלוֹת — a law **that does not apply to any other of the food prohibitions.**[8] וְכָל זֶה מוֹרֶה שֶׁיְּסוֹד טַעֲמוֹ הוּא מֵחֲמַת הַתַּעֲרֹבֶת — **All this indicates that the foundation of the reason for [the prohibition]** against eating the mixture **is due to the** objectionable nature of the **mixture** itself, וּכְעִנְיָן שֶׁאָמַרְנוּ בְּכִשּׁוּף — **as we have explained with regard to sorcery.**[9]

---

NOTES

7. Eating other forbidden foods detrimentally affects the eater (see Chinuch, Mitzvah 73 for discussion). Here, Chinuch argues, this is not the case. Rather, the very action of blending meat and milk is what is improper. As Chinuch continues, the prohibition against eating the resulting mixture is to distance us from that improper action.

8. Eating food that has completely spoiled, or to which bitter ingredients were added, is not considered to be a usual manner of eating. With regard to other forbidden foods (such as the meat of nonkosher animals), one who eats it in that state therefore does not incur *malkus*. [Nevertheless, in the view of many authorities, such foods may not be eaten by Rabbinic law; see *The Laws of Kashrus*, Ch. 3, §1 (Mesorah Publications, 1994).] However, one who eats meat cooked with milk, even if bitter ingredients were added to it, does still incur *malkus* (*Pesachim* 25a; *Rambam, Hil. Maachalos Asuros* 14:10-11).

9. That is, it is clear from the fact that the act of cooking the mixture is prohibited, and from the unique laws that apply to the prohibition against eating the mixture, that the root of this prohibition is not the same as that relating to other forbidden foods. The latter are forbidden due to some detrimental aspect of their consumption, while meat and milk are prohibited due to the objectionable nature of the very act of mixing these ingredients through cooking.

## 197 ❑ MISHPATIM / MITZVAH 92: THE PROHIBITION TO COOK MEAT WITH MILK

זֶה נֶאֱמַר מִתּוֹךְ הַדְּחָק, וַעֲדַיִן צְרִיכִים אָנוּ לְמוֹדָעֵי הַמְקַבָּל[10]. וְהָרַמְבַּ"ם זִכְרוֹנוֹ לִבְרָכָה כָּתַב בְּעִנְיָן טַעַם אַחֵר, אָמַר כִּי יֵשׁ עוֹבְדֵי עֲבוֹדָה זָרָה יַעַבְדוּהָ בְּמַעֲשֵׂה תַּעֲרֹבֶת בָּשָׂר עִם חָלָב, וְלָכֵן הִרְחִיקָה הַתּוֹרָה אוֹתוֹ הַתַּעֲרֹבֶת[11], וְכָל זֶה אֵינֶנּוּ שׁוֶֹה לִי[12].

דִּינֵי הַמִּצְוָה נִכְתָּב בְּעֶזְרַת הַשֵּׁם בְּקִצּוּר, כְּמִנְהָגֵנוּ, בְּמִצְוַת אִסּוּר הָאֲכִילָה וְהַהֲנָאָה בְּסֵדֶר כִּי תִשָּׂא.

וְנוֹהֶגֶת בְּכָל מָקוֹם וּבְכָל זְמַן, בִּזְכָרִים וּנְקֵבוֹת[13].

וְעוֹבֵר עָלֶיהָ וּבִשֵּׁל בָּשָׂר בְּחָלָב, וְאַף עַל פִּי שֶׁלֹּא אֲכָלָן, לוֹקֶה[14].

---

Chinuch acknowledges that this reason by itself does not fully explain the underlying purpose of this mitzvah:

וַעֲדַיִן צְרִיכִים אָנוּ לְמוֹדָעֵי — זֶה נֶאֱמַר מִתּוֹךְ הַדְּחָק — **We present this** reason **out of difficulty,** הַמְקַבָּל — **but** in order to understand the matter more fully **we still require the knowledge of Kabbalah** regarding it.[10]

In closing, Chinuch cites the reason that *Rambam* offers for this mitzvah:

וְהָרַמְבַּ"ם זִכְרוֹנוֹ לִבְרָכָה כָּתַב בְּעִנְיָן טַעַם אַחֵר — ***Rambam*, of blessed memory** (*Moreh Nevuchim* III, Ch. 48), **wrote another reason regarding this matter** of the prohibition of cooking meat with milk: אָמַר כִּי יֵשׁ עוֹבְדֵי עֲבוֹדָה זָרָה יַעַבְדוּהָ בְּמַעֲשֵׂה תַּעֲרֹבֶת בָּשָׂר עִם חָלָב — **He said that there are idolaters who worship [their deities] by performing the act of mixing meat with milk** through cooking, i.e., this was once a part of an idolatrous service, וְלָכֵן הִרְחִיקָה הַתּוֹרָה אוֹתוֹ הַתַּעֲרֹבֶת — **and the Torah therefore distances** us from creating **this mixture.**[11] וְכָל זֶה אֵינֶנּוּ שׁוֶֹה לִי — **However, all this has no value to me**[12] as an explanation of this mitzvah.

### ☙ Laws of the Mitzvah ☙

דִּינֵי הַמִּצְוָה נִכְתָּב בְּעֶזְרַת הַשֵּׁם בְּקִצּוּר, כְּמִנְהָגֵנוּ — **We will write, with the help of God, a brief collection of the laws of the mitzvah, as is our practice** in this work, בְּמִצְוַת אִסּוּר הָאֲכִילָה וְהַהֲנָאָה בְּסֵדֶר כִּי תִשָּׂא — **in the mitzvah regarding the prohibition against eating or benefiting** from the meat and milk mixture (Mitzvah 113), **in *Parashas Ki Sisa*.**

### ☙ Applicability of the Mitzvah ☙

וְנוֹהֶגֶת בְּכָל מָקוֹם וּבְכָל זְמַן — **[This mitzvah] applies in every location and in all times,** בִּזְכָרִים וּנְקֵבוֹת — **to men and women.**[13]

וְעוֹבֵר עָלֶיהָ וּבִשֵּׁל בָּשָׂר בְּחָלָב — **One who violates [this prohibition] and cooks meat with milk,** וְאַף עַל פִּי שֶׁלֹּא אֲכָלָן — **even if he did not** subsequently **eat [the mixture],** לוֹקֶה — **incurs** *malkus* (lashes).[14]

---

### NOTES

10. *Rabbeinu Bachya* (*Exodus* 23:19), in the course of his discussion of this mitzvah, provides a Kabbalistic approach.

See the Insight below for a discussion of some of the approaches that various commentators have offered as to the underlying purpose of this mitzvah.

11. See similar explanations in commentaries of *Sforno* and *Malbim* to our verse.

12. Stylistic citation of *Esther* 5:13.

13. It applies in Eretz Yisrael and the Diaspora and whether the *Beis HaMikdash* is standing or not. It also applies to women as well as men, in accordance with the general rule pertaining to mitzvah-prohibitions (see General Introduction).

14. One incurs *malkus* for cooking a combined *kezayis* (olive's volume) of meat and milk (see *Chullin* 108b; *Rambam, Hil. Maachalos Asuros* 9:1). See *Minchas Chinuch* §2 for further discussion.

### ◆§ Insight: Understanding the Meat-and-Milk Prohibition

Chinuch concludes his discussion of the underlying purpose of this mitzvah with the caveat that a more complete understanding of this mitzvah is not possible without the benefit of Kabbalistic wisdom (see note 10). Indeed, many commentators describe this mitzvah as a *chok*, a Divine decree, a mitzvah that we must follow even without an understanding of its purpose (see *Ibn Ezra*, *Rabbeinu Bachya*, and *Kli Yakar* to verse). Nevertheless, aside from the reasons mentioned by Chinuch, many commentators offer rational explanations of the purpose of this mitzvah. Here, we present a brief review of these approaches.

*Ramban* (*Deuteronomy* 14:21) suggests that there is an aspect of cruelty involved in cooking a kid in the milk of its mother. Although the prohibition includes meat other than goat's meat, and includes cooking in milk other than the milk of its mother, this reason is still applicable. Every animal that suckles its young can be considered a "mother," and every animal can be seen as the young of an animal. Thus, cooking any meat in milk has overtones of an act of cruelty and is not an action worthy of the members of a holy nation (see *Ramban* there; see also *Ibn Ezra* to the *Exodus* verse [23:19]).

*Rashbam* to our verse writes that devouring an animal in the fluid that gave it life has an element of gluttony to it, and is an inherently shameful act. *Rashbam* connects this to the concepts behind the prohibition to slaughter an animal and its mother on the same day (Mitzvah 294), and the mitzvah to send a mother bird away before taking the chicks (Mitzvah 545). The Torah seeks to refine our characters, and such actions run counter to that goal. [As explained above in *Ramban's* reason, this understanding of the mitzvah can apply even with milk of animals other than the mother.]

Another approach connects this prohibition to the prohibition against eating blood (Mitzvah 148). *Rabbeinu Bachya* (to our verse) writes that consuming the blood of an animal can impart a cruel nature to a person (see also Chinuch to that mitzvah). The Gemara (*Bechoros* 6b) relates that the milk produced for lactation in the body originates as blood, and then changes to its final form for the purpose of nourishing the animal's young. Despite its origin, milk is permitted for consumption because its basic nature was changed from its original form by the body. However, when it is cooked together with meat, in some sense, it reverts back to its original nature, and has the detrimental effects that blood does upon consumption. [*Rabbeinu Bachya* also provides a Kabbalistic explanation for this mitzvah.]

*R' Samson Raphael Hirsch* (in his commentary to our verse) explains that the strict division of meat and dairy represents a great moral concept that is at the heart of what it means to be a Jew. Indeed, no other dietary law imprints itself on the Jewish home and the Jewish kitchen more than the separation of meat and milk. The lessons of this separation are meant to permeate our daily lives and thoughts. This lesson is explained by R' Hirsch through his clarification of the symbolic nature of both milk and meat. [These ideas are explained in his commentary at length; here we present only an outline of this section of the commentary.]

The functions of nourishment and reproduction are basic processes of all living things. In a plant, they constitute its primary life activities. An animal, although also carrying out these functions, lives on a higher plane of existence as well: it is given the ability to move and think. Still, although these abilities of an animal surely indicate a more advanced level of functioning than that of the plant, it does not essentially live on a higher level of existence. All the ability of movement and thought of an animal are placed in the service of the same goals — those of nourishment and procreation. The animal in essence is nothing more than a moving and breathing plant, its "animal characteristics" of movement and thought completely subjugated to its "vegetative characteristic" of nourishment and reproduction.

Man also comprises these two systems, the vegetative system of nourishment and reproduction, and the animal system of thought and action. Yet, Man lives on a completely different sphere than the other forms of life on earth. He is endowed with intelligence and spirit, qualities given to him so that he may elevate himself in the service of God. He is to do this by using his uniquely human abilities to rally *all* of his faculties, from the most physical to the most spiritual, to that end.

Milk, which is used for nourishment and for the perpetuation of the species, represents the simple, vegetative aspect of life. Meat, the muscle tissue of the animal, represents the more complex animal aspect of movement and thought. As explained, in an animal these two realms are completely

"mixed," as the higher system is used solely for the purpose of the lower, moving and thinking only to fulfill its most basic physical needs.

Man, however, may never allow himself to fall to the level where the milk-vegetative system and the meat-animal system are indistinguishable, working for a common purpose. He may never allow his higher functions of thought and action to become a mere vehicle for the pursuit of the most basic of his physical needs. When consuming meat and milk, we are to remind ourselves always that these two levels of existence must be kept separate, each an independent system, each called upon in the service of the highest qualities of *human* life — the ability to serve and reach for the Divine.

One must bear in mind, when speaking of "reasons" for any mitzvah, that clearly a human being cannot presume to have plumbed the full depths of understanding of this or any of God's mitzvos. In relation to this mitzvah in particular, *Rabbeinu Bachya* cites the words of the Sages that the true reason for the meat-and-milk prohibition will be revealed only in the World to Come. [*Rabbeinu Bachya* offers a Kabbalistic explanation of why this reason cannot be fully revealed in this world.] As Chinuch writes in his introduction to this work, one can merely endeavor to gain "glimpses" of the underlying purposes of the mitzvos, to bring them somewhat closer to our understanding and to gain a bit of appreciation for their immeasurable and eternal benefit (see Author's Introduction to Sefer HaChinuch in Volume I of this work, with note 119 there).

## מִצְוָה צג

### שֶׁלֹּא לִכְרֹת בְּרִית לְשִׁבְעָה עֲמָמִים וְכֵן לְכָל עוֹבֵד עֲבוֹדָה זָרָה[1]

שֶׁלֹּא נִכְרֹת בְּרִית, כְּלוֹמַר שֶׁלֹּא נַבְטִיחַ בְּאַהֲבָתֵנוּ אֶל הָעָם הָרָע הַכּוֹפְרִים שֶׁהֵם שִׁבְעָה עֲמָמִים שֶׁבַּתּוֹרָה שֶׁהָיוּ מַחֲזִיקִים בְּאַרְצֵנוּ טֶרֶם בּוֹאֵנוּ שָׁם[2], וְהֵן הַחִתִּי וְהָאֱמֹרִי וְכוּ'[3], שֶׁנֶּאֱמַר (שמות כ"ג, ל"ב) לֹא תִכְרֹת לָהֶם וְלֵאלֹהֵיהֶם בְּרִית, כְּלוֹמַר שֶׁלֹּא נַעֲשֶׂה עִמָּהֶם שָׁלוֹם וְנַנִּיחַ אוֹתָם לַעֲבֹד הָעֲבוֹדָה זָרָה[4].

---

## Mitzvah 93

## The Prohibition to Seal a Covenant With Any of the Seven Canaanite Nations, or With Any Worshipers of Avodah Zarah

לֹא תִכְרֹת לָהֶם וְלֵאלֹהֵיהֶם בְּרִית
*You shall not seal a covenant with them and their gods (Exodus 23:32).*

This mitzvah restrains us from creating a bond with the unrepentant seven Canaanite nations, who dwelled in Eretz Yisrael when the Jewish people entered the Land. These nations no longer exist, but their very essence was the embodiment of paganism and all its perverted and wicked trappings, including *avodah zarah* (idolatry) and practices such as passing their children through fire as offerings to their gods (Deuteronomy 12:31). The Torah makes it clear why it is imperative to remain apart from these nations (ibid. 20:18): *so that they will not teach you to act according to their abominations that they performed for their gods, and you will sin to HASHEM, your God.*[1]

שֶׁלֹּא נִכְרֹת בְּרִית — We are commanded **not to seal a covenant,** כְּלוֹמַר שֶׁלֹּא נַבְטִיחַ בְּאַהֲבָתֵנוּ — **that is to say, we are not to make a pledge of our friendship,** אֶל הָעָם הָרָע הַכּוֹפְרִים שֶׁהֵם שִׁבְעָה עֲמָמִים שֶׁבַּתּוֹרָה — **with the wicked heathen people who compose the seven** Canaanite **nations that are** listed **in the Torah,** שֶׁהָיוּ מַחֲזִיקִים בְּאַרְצֵנוּ טֶרֶם בּוֹאֵנוּ שָׁם — **who were in possession of our** promised **Land before we arrived there.**[2] וְהֵן הַחִתִּי וְהָאֱמֹרִי וְכוּ' — **These** seven Canaanite **nations are (1) the Hittite, (2) the Amorite etc.** [(3) the Perizzite, (4) the Hivvite, (5) the Jebusite, (6) the Canaanite, and (7) the Girgashite].[3] שֶׁנֶּאֱמַר — Entering into a covenant with them is forbidden, **as it is stated** (Exodus 23:32): "לֹא תִכְרֹת לָהֶם וְלֵאלֹהֵיהֶם בְּרִית" — *You shall not seal a covenant with them and their gods.* כְּלוֹמַר שֶׁלֹּא נַעֲשֶׂה עִמָּהֶם שָׁלוֹם — **That is to say, we are not to make peace with them,** וְנַנִּיחַ אוֹתָם לַעֲבֹד הָעֲבוֹדָה זָרָה — **while leaving them to worship** *avodah zarah* (idols).[4]

---

### NOTES

1. Should you learn from their abominable practices and mimic those practices, you would thereby *sin to HASHEM, your God* (Ramban). Along similar lines, the Torah states (Exodus 23:33): לֹא יֵשְׁבוּ בְּאַרְצְךָ פֶּן יַחֲטִיאוּ אֹתְךָ לִי כִּי תַעֲבֹד אֶת אֱלֹהֵיהֶם וגו', *They shall not dwell in your Land lest they cause you to sin against Me, that you will worship their gods,* etc.

2. Eretz Yisrael was deemed our Land for centuries before the Jews, led by Joshua, conquered it. In the בְּרִית בֵּין הַבְּתָרִים, *Covenant Between the Parts* (see Genesis Ch. 15), the Torah records (ibid. v. 18): *On that day HASHEM made a covenant with Abram, saying, "To your descendants have I given this Land."* The verse does not say "I *will* give this Land," but rather speaks of the Land as having been given already, from which our Sages derive that the Land was the heritage of the Jewish people from that time (Yerushalmi Challah 2:1 [10b]). This is because God's promise is as good as done (Rashi, Genesis 15:18).

3. See *Deuteronomy* 7:1-2.

4. If, however, they choose to reject idolatry, they may live among us in peace, as Chinuch will discuss shortly (see below, note 10). This in fact is implicit in the verse, which stresses "with them *and* their gods." It is specifically a covenant "with them *and* their gods" [i.e., one that allows them to continue their idolatrous worship

## MISHPATIM / MITZVAH 93: WITH WHOM ONE IS FORBIDDEN TO MAKE A COVENANT

מִשָּׁרְשֵׁי מִצְוָה זוֹ, לְאַבֵּד עֲבוֹדָה זָרָה וְכָל מְשַׁמְּשֶׁיהָ מִן הָעוֹלָם, וְאֵלּוּ הַשִּׁבְעָה עֲמָמִים הָיוּ עִקַּר עֲבוֹדָה זָרָה וִיסוֹדָהּ הָרִאשׁוֹן,[5] וְעַל כֵּן נֶעֶקְרוּ מֵאַרְצָם,[6] וְנִצְטַוֵּינוּ לְשָׁרֵשׁ אַחֲרֵיהֶם וּלְאַבֵּד זִכְרָם לְעוֹלָם, וּכְמוֹ שֶׁכָּתְבוּ עֲלֵיהֶם בַּתּוֹרָה (דברים כ׳, י״ז) הַחֲרֵם תַּחֲרִימֵם, וְהִיא מִצְוַת עֲשֵׂה בְּסֵדֶר וָאֶתְחַנָּן, וְשָׁם אַאֲרִיךְ בַּמִּצְוָה בְּעֶזְרַת הַשֵּׁם, וְנַגִּיד סִבַּת הֱיוֹת בָּעוֹלָם הָאֻמּוֹת הָרָעוֹת לָמָּה,[7] וְכִי מִצְוָה זוֹ בִּכְלַל הַמִּצְוֹת הַנּוֹהֲגוֹת.

וּמִן הָאַזְהָרָה בָּהֶם נִשְׁמָע אַזְהָרָה שֶׁלֹּא נִכְרֹת בְּרִית לְכָל עוֹבְדֵי עֲבוֹדָה זָרָה,[8]

---

### ⸺ Underlying Purpose of the Mitzvah ⸺

לְאַבֵּד עֲבוֹדָה זָרָה וְכָל — מִשָּׁרְשֵׁי מִצְוָה זוֹ — **Among the underlying purposes of this mitzvah** מְשַׁמְּשֶׁיהָ מִן הָעוֹלָם — **is to eliminate** *avodah zarah* **and all that is in its service from the world.** וְאֵלּוּ הַשִּׁבְעָה עֲמָמִים הָיוּ עִקַּר עֲבוֹדָה זָרָה וִיסוֹדָהּ הָרִאשׁוֹן — **These seven nations were the very essence of** *avodah zarah,* **and its most primary foundation.**[5] וְעַל כֵּן נֶעֶקְרוּ מֵאַרְצָם — **They were therefore** punished by God by being **uprooted from their land,**[6] וְנִצְטַוֵּינוּ לְשָׁרֵשׁ אַחֲרֵיהֶם וּלְאַבֵּד זִכְרָם לְעוֹלָם — **and we were** further **commanded to root out and destroy their** very **memory forever** (unless they would agree to abandon their idolatrous practices), וּכְמוֹ שֶׁכָּתְבוּ עֲלֵיהֶם בַּתּוֹרָה — **as is written regarding them in the Torah** (*Deuteronomy* 20:17), "הַחֲרֵם תַּחֲרִימֵם" — **You shall utterly destroy them.** וְהִיא מִצְוַת עֲשֵׂה בְּסֵדֶר וָאֶתְחַנָּן — **[This requirement] is a mitzvah-obligation** in its own right, recorded **in** *Parashas Va'eschanan* (Mitzvah 425). וְשָׁם אַאֲרִיךְ בַּמִּצְוָה בְּעֶזְרַת הַשֵּׁם — **I will expound upon the mitzvah at length there, with Hashem's help.** וְנַגִּיד סִבַּת הֱיוֹת בָּעוֹלָם הָאֻמּוֹת הָרָעוֹת לָמָּה — **Furthermore, we will relate** there **the purpose** that these **evil nations serve in the world,**[7] וְכִי מִצְוָה זוֹ בִּכְלַל הַמִּצְוֹת הַנּוֹהֲגוֹת — **and how that mitzvah** (Mitzvah 425) **is included among the mitzvos that apply** for future generations, notwithstanding the fact that these seven nations no longer exist.

Chinuch explains that the current mitzvah has limited application to other nations besides the seven Canaanite nations:

וּמִן הָאַזְהָרָה בָּהֶם נִשְׁמָע אַזְהָרָה שֶׁלֹּא נִכְרֹת בְּרִית לְכָל עוֹבְדֵי עֲבוֹדָה זָרָה — **From the prohibition against** sealing a covenant with **[the Canaanite nations], we derive a prohibition to seal a covenant with all those who worship** *avodah zarah.*[8]

---

### NOTES

of their gods] that is forbidden (*Ramban* ad loc., second explanation). See Insight.

5. As Chinuch explains in a later mitzvah (Mitzvah 425), these ancient seven nations were the first to adopt idolatry and all its related abominable practices. Hence, they are given the ignoble distinction of being declared the "essence of *avodah zarah* and its most primary foundation" (see *Rambam, Sefer HaMitzvos, Asei* 187).

6. After warning us not to become contaminated by the perverted idolatrous and immoral practices of the Canaanite nations, the Torah states (*Leviticus* 18:27-28): כִּי אֶת כָּל הַתּוֹעֵבֹת הָאֵל עָשׂוּ אַנְשֵׁי הָאָרֶץ אֲשֶׁר לִפְנֵיכֶם וַתִּטְמָא הָאָרֶץ. וְלֹא תָקִיא הָאָרֶץ אֶתְכֶם בְּטַמַּאֲכֶם אֹתָהּ כַּאֲשֶׁר קָאָה אֶת הַגּוֹי אֲשֶׁר לִפְנֵיכֶם, *For the inhabitants of the Land who are before you committed all these abominations, and the Land became contaminated. Let not the Land disgorge you for having contaminated it, as it disgorged the people that were before you.* See also ibid. 20:23.

7. Chinuch explains there that one should not be troubled by the question of why these evil nations exist, for in truth they were not destined to be evil. Like all people, they were given free choice and had the option to choose a path of righteousness, but willingly chose their evil ways. Whatever punishment they receive is a result of their persisting unrepentingly in those evil ways. Furthermore, it is likely that in the course of their history, some good, or at least a single good individual, emerged from them, giving purpose for the existence of the entire people. For further discussion, see Mitzvah 425.

8. That is, although the focus of the prohibition is with regard to the seven Canaanite nations (as stated in *Deuteronomy* 7:1-2), nevertheless, in Chinuch's opinion, making a covenant with any idolatrous nation is also prohibited by the Torah — though there surely is no obligation to destroy those nations (as Chinuch will immediately explain). This view is shared by others as well (*Rambam, Hil. Avodah Zarah* 10:1; *Tosafos, Yevamos* 23a ד״ה ההוא, first answer; see *Mechilta D'Rashbi;* see *Minchas Yitzchak* §1 for further discusssion). A number of other authorities, however, rule that we are prohibited from making a covenant only with the seven

# משפטים / מצוה צג: שלא לכרת ברית לז׳ עממים וכן לכל עובד ע״ז

אֲבָל יֵשׁ חִלּוּק בֵּין שִׁבְעָה עֲמָמִים לִשְׁאָר הָאֻמּוֹת עוֹבְדֵי עֲבוֹדָה זָרָה, כִּי שְׁאָר הָאֻמּוֹת אִם אֵין נִלְחָמִים עִמָּנוּ אֵין מִצְוָה עָלֵינוּ לְהָרְגָם, אֶלָּא שֶׁלֹּא יֵשְׁבוּ בְּאַרְצֵנוּ עַד שֶׁיַּעַזְבוּ עֲבוֹדַת עֲבוֹדָה זָרָה[9], וְאֵלּוּ הַשִּׁבְעָה עֲמָמִים נִצְטַוֵּינוּ לְהָרְגָם בְּכָל מָקוֹם שֶׁנּוּכַל לָהֶם אֶלָּא אִם כֵּן יַנִּיחוּ עֲבוֹדָה זָרָה[10], וְהָעִנְיָן לְפִי שֶׁהֵם הָיוּ עִקַּר הָעֲבוֹדָה זָרָה וִיסוֹדָהּ הָרִאשׁוֹן, כְּמוֹ שֶׁכָּתַבְתִּי[11]. וְכָל מִי שֶׁבָּא לְיָדוֹ אֶחָד מֵהֶם וְיָכוֹל לְהָרְגוֹ בְּלֹא סַכָּנָה וְלֹא הֲרָגוֹ, עוֹבֵר בְּלָאו.

וְזֶה שֶׁאָמַרְנוּ שֶׁעוֹבְדֵי עֲבוֹדָה זָרָה בְּשֶׁאֵין נִלְחָמִים עִמָּנוּ שֶׁלֹּא נַהַרְגֵם, דַּוְקָא עוֹבְדֵי עֲבוֹדָה זָרָה מִן הָאֻמּוֹת, אֲבָל יִשְׂרָאֵל עוֹבֵד עֲבוֹדָה זָרָה, כְּגוֹן הַמִּינִין וְהַמְשֻׁמָּדִין וְהָאֶפִּיקוֹרְסִין, מִצְוָה עָלֵינוּ לְהָרְגָם, לְפִי שֶׁהֵם מְצֵרִים לְיִשְׂרָאֵל, וּמוּטָב יֹאבְדוּ אֶלֶף כַּיּוֹצֵא בָם וְלֹא יִשְׂרָאֵל אֶחָד כָּשֵׁר.

מִדִּינֵי הַמִּצְוָה, מַה שֶּׁאָמְרוּ (סוטה דף ל״ה ע״ב) שֶׁמְּקַבְּלִין אוֹתָן אִם רָצוּ לַחֲזֹר בִּתְשׁוּבָה[12],

---

אֲבָל יֵשׁ חִלּוּק בֵּין שִׁבְעָה עֲמָמִים לִשְׁאָר הָאֻמּוֹת עוֹבְדֵי עֲבוֹדָה זָרָה — **However, there is a distinction between the seven** Canaanite **nations and all other nations that worship** *avodah zarah*. כִּי שְׁאָר הָאֻמּוֹת — **For** with regard to **other nations,** אִם אֵין נִלְחָמִים עִמָּנוּ — **if they do not wage war against us,** אֵין מִצְוָה עָלֵינוּ לְהָרְגָם — **we have no command to kill them** (even if they do not abandon *avodah zarah*); אֶלָּא שֶׁלֹּא יֵשְׁבוּ בְּאַרְצֵנוּ עַד שֶׁיַּעַזְבוּ עֲבוֹדַת עֲבוֹדָה זָרָה — **rather,** the only limitation that pertains to them is that **they are not to dwell in our Land** (i.e., Eretz Yisrael) **until they forsake the worship of** *avodah zarah*.[9] וְאֵלּוּ הַשִּׁבְעָה עֲמָמִים — **However, with regard to the seven** Canaanite **nations,** נִצְטַוֵּינוּ לְהָרְגָם בְּכָל מָקוֹם שֶׁנּוּכַל לָהֶם אֶלָּא אִם כֵּן יַנִּיחוּ עֲבוֹדָה זָרָה — **we are commanded to kill them wherever we can, unless they abandon** their worship of *avodah zarah*.[10] וְהָעִנְיָן לְפִי שֶׁהֵם הָיוּ עִקַּר הָעֲבוֹדָה זָרָה וִיסוֹדָהּ הָרִאשׁוֹן — **The reason** for this distinction **is because [the seven Canaanite nations] were the very essence of** *avodah zarah* **and its** most **primary foundation,** כְּמוֹ שֶׁכָּתַבְתִּי — **as I wrote** above.[11]

### ~ Laws of the Mitzvah ~

מִדִּינֵי הַמִּצְוָה מַה שֶּׁאָמְרוּ — **The laws of this mitzvah include that which [our Sages] stated** (*Sotah* 35b), שֶׁמְּקַבְּלִין אוֹתָן אִם רָצוּ לַחֲזֹר בִּתְשׁוּבָה — **that we may accept them if they want to repent** from their idolatrous ways.[12]

---

NOTES

Canaanite nations, and that a pact with any other idolatrous people is permitted (*Smag, Lo Saaseh* 47; see *Rambam, Sefer HaMitzvos, Lo Saaseh* 48).

9. By forsaking the practice of idolatry, one is permitted to become a גֵּר תּוֹשָׁב, *resident alien*, a non-Jew dwelling in Eretz Yisrael.

10. Chinuch's strict view regarding the seven Canaanite nations of old is disputed by prominent authorities. *Rambam* (*Hil. Avodah Zarah* 10:1, as explained by *Minchas Chinuch* §1) rules that even the seven Canaanite nations could be killed only if they waged war, but not outside the context of war.

Once they rejected *avodah zarah*, all agree that even these nations could live in Eretz Yisrael. In that case, the Torah's principal concern — (*Deuteronomy* 20:18): לְמַעַן אֲשֶׁר לֹא יְלַמְּדוּ אֶתְכֶם לַעֲשׂוֹת כְּכֹל תּוֹעֲבֹתָם אֲשֶׁר עָשׂוּ לֵאלֹהֵיהֶם, *so that they will not teach you to act according to all their abominations that they performed for their gods* — was alleviated, for they would clearly no longer influence the Jewish people to engage in idolatrous worship (*Minchas Yitzchak* §4, based on *Sifrei* ad loc.).

11. The text here follows the Vienna, *Minchas Yitzchak*, and *Minchas Chinuch* versions of Chinuch.

12. That is, if they are willing to repent from their idolatrous ways, they may live peacefully among us (*Sotah* 35b; *Sifrei* to *Deuteronomy* 20:18), and we may indeed make a covenant with them (*Ramban, Deuteronomy* 20:11; cf. *Malbim, Joshua* 9:3; *Maharam Schik* 528:3). However, they must undertake to observe the seven Noahide laws, as well as pay tribute and accept subservience to the governing Jewish people (see *Rambam, Hil. Melachim* 6:1).

According to many, the opportunity for the Canaanite nations to make peace with us was afforded to them by explicit overtures made by Joshua upon our entry into the Land. Letters were sent affording them the choice to make peace (as per the above terms), leave, or else wage war (*Rambam* ibid. 6:5; *Ramban, Deuteronomy* 20:10). Others, however, state that these offers were

## MISHPATIM / MITZVAH 93: WITH WHOM ONE IS FORBIDDEN TO MAKE A COVENANT

וְיֶתֶר פְּרָטֶיהָ, מְבֹאָרִין בְּסַנְהֶדְרִין.

וְיֶתֶר פְּרָטֶיהָ מְבֹאָרִין בְּסַנְהֶדְרִין — This law and the additional details of [this mitzvah] are set forth in *Sanhedrin*.[13]

### NOTES

made only to other idolatrous nations, but not to the seven Canaanite nations. With regard to the seven nations, the assumption was that any rejection of idolatry would not be sincere, unless they came on their own to make peace and accept these terms (*Rashi, Sotah* 35b ד"ה וכתבו, as understood by *Lechem Mishneh, Hil. Melachim* 6:1; *Rashbam, Deuteronomy* 20:16). See Insight below, as well as Mitzvah 527, for further discussion of these issues.

13. The details of this mitzvah are not discussed in Tractate *Sanhedrin*. Apparently this is a copyist's error, and the text should read, "are set forth in *Sotah* [35b]" (*Me'il HaEphod* §3). The laws of this mitzvah are codified in *Rambam, Hilchos Avodah Zarah* 10:1 and *Hilchos Melachim* 6:1-5.

With regard to the consequences of violating this mitzvah, insofar as it is a לָאו שֶׁאֵין בּוֹ מַעֲשֶׂה, *a prohibition that does not involve action* (for the mitzvah can be violated simply by way of a verbal promise), it is not punishable by *malkus* (*Minchas Chinuch* §4).

---

### ⋅§ Insight: The Gibeonites and the Treaty Based on Deception

The Book of *Joshua* (Ch. 9) relates that after Joshua's successful campaign against Jericho and Ai, the Hivvite inhabitants of Gibeon became apprehensive of the invading Jewish force. They therefore devised a ruse wherein they disguised themselves as emissaries from a faraway land who had been sent by their rulers to seal a covenant with the Jewish people. Although originally hesitant to make such a covenant out of fear that these emissaries were in truth from the land of Canaan itself, Joshua ultimately did seal a covenant with them, and the leaders of the Jewish people swore to let them live. After the ruse was discovered, and it became clear that the Gibeonites were actually a local Canaanite clan, the Jewish people became indignant and railed against their leaders for having made such a pact. Notwithstanding the fact that the oath was made under false pretexts and was therefore not valid, the Jews stood by it [for failure to do so would have led to a desecration of God's Name (*Gittin* 46a)]. However, Joshua did force the Gibeonites into the role of being hewers of wood and drawers of water for the nation and for the needs of the Altar of Hashem, from that time forward.

The story of the Gibeonites, whose fear led them to resort to such a ruse, seems to indicate that had they been straightforward as to their true identity — i.e., Hivvites, one of the seven Canaanite nations — their request would have been rejected. Indeed, the apprehension of the Jews that these emissaries were really not from a faraway land, but rather (*Joshua* 9:7), *Perhaps you dwell in my midst*, points to the fact that the Gibeonites' fear was well-founded. Some therefore deduce from this episode that the seven Canaanite nations were not given the option of making peace with the invading Jewish forces. That is, although the Torah calls for overtures of peace upon going to war (see *Deuteronomy* 20:10), such invitations were extended only to other peoples, but not to the seven Canaanite nations (*R' Eliyahu Mizrachi, Numbers* 21:29, in explanation of *Rashi, Deuteronomy* 20:10).

As mentioned above, in note 12, however, others disagree and state that the requirement to first offer peace is a prerequisite before going to war against all peoples, including the seven Canaanite nations (*Rambam, Hil. Melachim* 6:1; *Ramban, Deuteronomy* 20:11). That being the case, what then were the Gibeonites afraid of? Why did they not simply accept the offer of peace? Furthermore, if such treaties are offered in any case, why were the Jews so indignant and troubled by the fact that such a treaty was made?

With regard to the first question of why the Gibeonites were afraid, some explain that the offer of peace had not yet reached them and they were simply unaware that such an option was available to them (*Ramban* ibid.). Others suggest that although the offer of peace had reached them, they thought that it was, in fact, a ruse on the part of the Jewish nation. They argued that Jericho and Ai surely were offered the treaty, and yet they were destroyed. They concluded (falsely) that this offer must, therefore, not have been sincere (*Radak, Joshua* 9:7). Finally, others suggest that while they did

receive the offer to make peace, they had originally turned it down, and now that they had a change of heart, they thought that it was too late and the offer had expired (*Rambam* ibid., as explained by *Kesef Mishneh*).

As for the second question — i.e., why the Jews were upset that they were tricked into making the covenant, when they were supposed to offer peace — some commentators explain that the overture of peace offered to a nation with whom we have begun the prospect of waging war must include three basic concessions on their part: They must agree to (1) pay tribute, (2) accept subservience to the Jewish nation, and (3) keep the seven Noahide laws. Although the Gibeonites had implicitly accepted the last condition (see *Joshua* 9:9), they had not accepted the first two. However, their supposed status of being representatives of a nation from a "faraway land," with whom the Jewish people had no prospect of waging war, ostensibly made all such conditions unnecessary. Once their identity was discovered, and it was revealed that they in truth were a nation with whom the Jewish people were at war, their lack of accepting all the conditions was retroactively deemed unlawful. That is why Joshua required them to accept the role of being hewers of wood and drawers of water for the public, for that effectively put them into the position they would have assumed, had they been forthright from the beginning (*Ramban* ibid., as explained by *Lechem Mishneh, Hil. Melachim* 6:1; see *Rambam* ibid. 6:5 for a similar explanation; see further, *Dina DeChayei, Asei* 118 ד"ה מפני שכרתו; *Maharam Schik* 528:3; *Malbim, Joshua* 9:3).

# MISHPATIM / MITZVAH 94: NOT TO SETTLE AN IDOLATER IN OUR LAND

## מִצְוָה צד: שֶׁלֹּא לְהוֹשִׁיב עוֹבֵד עֲבוֹדָה זָרָה בְּאַרְצֵנוּ

שֶׁלֹּא לְשַׁכֵּן עוֹבְדֵי עֲבוֹדָה זָרָה בְּאַרְצֵנוּ, שֶׁנֶּאֱמַר (שמות כ״ג, ל״ג) לֹא יֵשְׁבוּ בְּאַרְצְךָ פֶּן יַחֲטִיאוּ אֹתְךָ לִי[1].

מִשָּׁרְשֵׁי הַמִּצְוָה, מַה שֶּׁנִּגְלֶה בַּכָּתוּב, בִּשְׁבִיל שֶׁלֹּא נִלְמַד מִכְּפִירָתָם[2].

מִדִּינֵי הַמִּצְוָה, כְּגוֹן מַה שֶּׁאָמְרוּ זִכְרוֹנָם לִבְרָכָה שֶׁאִלּוּ רָצוּ לְהַנִּיחַ עֲבוֹדָה זָרָה,

## ~ Mitzvah 94 ~

## The Prohibition to Settle a Worshiper of Avodah Zarah in Our Land

> לֹא יֵשְׁבוּ בְּאַרְצְךָ פֶּן יַחֲטִיאוּ אֹתְךָ לִי כִּי תַעֲבֹד אֶת אֱלֹהֵיהֶם כִּי יִהְיֶה לְךָ לְמוֹקֵשׁ
> *They shall not dwell in your Land lest they cause you to sin against Me, that you will worship their gods, for it will be a trap for you* (Exodus 23:33).

שֶׁלֹּא לְשַׁכֵּן עוֹבְדֵי עֲבוֹדָה זָרָה בְּאַרְצֵנוּ — **We are commanded not to cause worshipers of** *avodah zarah* (idols) **to dwell in our Land,** שֶׁנֶּאֱמַר "לֹא יֵשְׁבוּ בְּאַרְצְךָ פֶּן יַחֲטִיאוּ אֹתְךָ לִי" — **as it is stated** (*Exodus* 23:33): **They shall not dwell in your Land lest they cause you to sin against Me.**[1]

### ~ Underlying Purpose of the Mitzvah ~

מִשָּׁרְשֵׁי הַמִּצְוָה — **Among the underlying purposes of** this mitzvah מַה שֶּׁנִּגְלֶה בַּכָּתוּב — **is that which is revealed in the verse** itself, בִּשְׁבִיל שֶׁלֹּא נִלְמַד מִכְּפִירָתָם — that is, **so that we not learn from their heathen beliefs.**[2]

### ~ Laws of the Mitzvah ~

מִדִּינֵי הַמִּצְוָה — **Among the laws of the mitzvah are,** כְּגוֹן מַה שֶּׁאָמְרוּ זִכְרוֹנָם לִבְרָכָה — **for example, that which [our Sages], of blessed memory, have stated** (*Avodah Zarah* 64b), שֶׁאִלּוּ רָצוּ לְהַנִּיחַ עֲבוֹדָה זָרָה — **that if [these people] want to abandon** their worship of *avodah zarah,*

---

### NOTES

1. From its context, the verse seems to be referring specifically to the Canaanites who inhabited the land when the Israelites entered it (see *Exodus* 23:27-33). Nevertheless, Chinuch (following *Rambam, Hil. Avodah Zarah* 10:6; *Sefer HaMitzvos, Lo Saaseh* 51; see also *Tosafos, Avodah Zarah* 20a ד״ה דאמר) understands that this mitzvah applies to *all* worshipers of *avodah zarah,* and not just the seven Canaanite nations. This is because the reason the Torah gives here for this mitzvah — *lest they cause you to sin against Me* — applies equally to all worshipers of *avodah zarah* (*Kesef Mishneh* ad loc.; *Yere'im* §315). Others, however, disagree and rule that this prohibition applies only to the seven Canaanite nations, as per the simple reading of the verse and its context (*Raavad* ad loc.; *Rashi, Gittin* 45a ד״ה לא ישבו). [For further discussion of the extent of this prohibition, see *Rambam* and *Raavad, Hil. Avodah Zarah* 10:6.]

2. As the verse concludes (*Exodus* 23:33): *lest they cause you to sin against Me, that you will worship their gods, for it will be a trap for you.* [The Torah thus warns that we are not to place our trust in our own spiritual attainments, and thereby be deluded into thinking that we are impervious to evil influence; nor should we fool ourselves into thinking that we will be able to elevate idolaters rather than being dragged down to their level. We must recognize that their dwelling among us *will be a trap* for us (*R' S. R. Hirsch*).]

Historically, as a nation, we have failed to fulfill this commandment, as noted in Scripture (see *Judges* 1:29,33). This failure prompted Hashem to send us an emissary, who prophesied in His Name, saying (ibid. 2:2-3): *you did not hearken to My voice ... so I also said, "I shall not chase them out before you, and they will be unto you [as thorns in your] sides, and their gods will be a trap for you."* Thus, as a consequence of the failure of the Jewish people to fulfill this mitzvah, the Canaanite inhabitants of the Land brought great suffering upon them, and their negative influence was the pernicious seed that led to the spiritual decline of the Jewish nation, culminating in the destruction of the First Temple and exile of the Jews more than 800 years later.

## משפטים / מצוה צד: שלא להושיב עובד עבודה זרה בארצנו

אַף עַל פִּי שֶׁעֲבָדוּהָ מִתְּחִלָּתָן, שֶׁמֻּתָּרִין לִשְׁכֹּן בְּאַרְצֵנוּ,[3] וְזֶהוּ הַנִּקְרָא גֵּר תּוֹשָׁב, כְּלוֹמַר שֶׁהוּא גֵּר לְעִנְיָן שֶׁהֻתַּר לֵישֵׁב בְּאַרְצֵנוּ, כְּמוֹ שֶׁאָמְרוּ זִכְרוֹנָם לִבְרָכָה (ע״ז דף ס״ד ע״ב) אֵי זֶהוּ גֵּר תּוֹשָׁב, זֶה שֶׁקִּבֵּל שֶׁלֹּא לַעֲבֹד עֲבוֹדָה זָרָה.[4] וְאִם לֹא הִנִּיחַ עֲבוֹדָה זָרָה אֵין צָרִיךְ לוֹמַר שֶׁאֵין מוֹכְרִין לוֹ קַרְקַע שֶׁיִּשְׁכֹּן בְּאַרְצֵנוּ[5] אֶלָּא אֲפִלּוּ (לשכור) [לְהַשְׂכִּיר] לוֹ אָסוּר כָּל זְמַן שֶׁיִּשְׂכֹּר לְדִירָה,

---

שֶׁמֻּתָּרִין — אַף עַל פִּי שֶׁעֲבָדוּהָ מִתְּחִלָּתָן — then, **even though they had originally worshiped it**, **they are permitted to dwell in our Land.** לִשְׁכֹּן בְּאַרְצֵנוּ — וְזֶהוּ הַנִּקְרָא גֵּר תּוֹשָׁב — Such an individual **is called a "ger toshav,"** resident alien. כְּלוֹמַר שֶׁהוּא גֵּר לְעִנְיָן שֶׁהֻתַּר לֵישֵׁב בְּאַרְצֵנוּ — **That is to say, he is a *ger*** (i.e., convert) **with regard to being allowed to dwell in our Land**, but not that he is a full-fledged convert.[3] כְּמוֹ שֶׁאָמְרוּ זִכְרוֹנָם לִבְרָכָה — **This is as [our Sages],** of blessed memory, **have stated** (*Avodah Zarah* 64b): אֵי זֶהוּ גֵּר תּוֹשָׁב — **Who is** considered **a *ger toshav*?** זֶה שֶׁקִּבֵּל שֶׁלֹּא לַעֲבֹד עֲבוֹדָה זָרָה — **It is one who has accepted** upon himself **not to worship *avodah zarah*.**[4]

Chinuch addresses the matter of selling or renting land to an idolater who does *not* wish to forsake idolatry:

וְאִם לֹא הִנִּיחַ עֲבוֹדָה זָרָה — **Now, if he does not abandon** his worship of ***avodah zarah***, the Torah's concern is in force: *lest they cause you to sin against Me, that you will worship their gods, for it will be a trap for you.* אֵין צָרִיךְ לוֹמַר שֶׁאֵין מוֹכְרִין לוֹ קַרְקַע שֶׁיִּשְׁכֹּן בְּאַרְצֵנוּ — **In this case, therefore, it is unnecessary to state that we may not sell him real estate for** the purpose of **dwelling in our Land,** as that would clearly violate this prohibition.[5] אֶלָּא אֲפִלּוּ (לשכור) [לְהַשְׂכִּיר] לוֹ אָסוּר כָּל זְמַן שֶׁיִּשְׂכֹּר

---

### NOTES

3. The word *ger*, which literally means *stranger* or *alien*, can also be used in reference to a convert to Judaism. The word *toshav* means resident. Hence, the phrase *ger toshav* refers to one who, by rejecting idolatry in front of a *beis din* of three Torah scholars (see *Avodah Zarah* 64b; *Rambam, Hil. Melachim* 8:10), has effected a "conversion," but only in the sense that it allows him to be a *toshav* (resident) of the Land. See Insight.

4. *Minchas Chinuch* (§2) points out that Chinuch's definition here of a *ger toshav* would seem to be at odds with the accepted halachah. That is, although one who has accepted upon himself not to worship *avodah zarah* is termed a *ger toshav* according to R' Meir, the Sages disagree, and rule that to be classified as a *ger toshav* one needs to accept upon himself *all* seven Noahide laws, not merely the prohibition of *avodah zarah* (*Avodah Zarah* 64b). [The other Noahide laws are: the prohibitions of "blessing" (i.e., cursing) the Name of God, murder, illicit relations, theft, eating a limb torn from a living animal, and the obligation to set up courts.] The halachah follows the Sages' opinion (*Rambam, Hil. Avodah Zarah* 10:6; *Hil. Melachim* 8:10; cf. *Rambam, Sefer HaMitzvos, Lo Saaseh* 51). Hence, Chinuch's definition seems to contradict the halachah.

Others, however, come to the defense of Chinuch, and suggest that the dispute between R' Meir and the Sages is limited to the definition of a *ger toshav* vis-à-vis one particular issue — the obligation to support him (as the Gemara there seems to imply). The Torah imposes on us a special obligation to provide financial support to a *ger toshav* in need, as it is stated (*Leviticus* 25:35): וְהֶחֱזַקְתָּ בּוֹ, *you shall strengthen him*. It is to be eligible for this type of support that the Sages state that one needs to accept all seven Noahide laws. With regard to allowing him to settle in our Land, however, his rejection of *avodah zarah* is sufficient (*Me'il HaEphod* §2; *Minchas Yitzchak* §1; see also *Gittin* 45a; *Tosafos, Avodah Zarah* 64b ד״ה איזהו).

[This assertion is borne out by Chinuch himself, for when he mentions the requirement to support a needy *ger toshav* (in Mitzvah 426), he, too, states that to be defined as such, one would need to have accepted all seven Noahide laws. This is in contrast to his definition of *ger toshav* elsewhere (see Mitzvos 14 and 347), where he defines it as one who has merely rejected idolatry, as he does here (*Minchas Yitzchak*).]

5. A number of commentators (*Mishneh LaMelech* here; *Minchas Chinuch* §5) note that one who sells a home in Eretz Yisrael to an idolater is actually in violation of another prohibition, namely (*Deuteronomy* 7:2), וְלֹא תְחָנֵּם, *nor shall you show them favor* (see Mitzvah 426), for, as the Gemara (*Avodah Zarah* 20a) states, the phrase לֹא תְחָנֵּם can be expounded as reading: לֹא תִּתֵּן לָהֶם חֲנָיָה, *do not give them settlement* in the Land (see *Smag, Lo Saaseh* 48). However, it would appear from the language of *Rambam* in *Sefer HaMitzvos* (*Lo Saaseh* 51), from which Chinuch's words here are drawn, that these two mitzvos are related, and the exposition of לֹא תִּתֵּן לָהֶם חֲנָיָה, *do not give them settlement*, is in actuality defining the parameters of this mitzvah (see also *Minchas Yitzchak*).

[See *Rambam* in *Hil. Avodah Zarah* 10:4 and 10:6, where he seems to take a different approach to our mitzvah; see also *Chazon Ish, Sheviis* 24:1.]

## MISHPATIM / MITZVAH 94: NOT TO SETTLE AN IDOLATER IN OUR LAND

לְפִי שֶׁמַּכְנִיס שָׁם עֲבוֹדָה זָרָה,[6] אֲבָל לִסְחוֹרָתוֹ מֻתָּר וּבִלְבַד שֶׁלֹּא יַשְׂכִּיר לִשְׁלֹשָׁה בְּנֵי אָדָם, לְפִי שֶׁשְּׁלֹשָׁה דְּבַר קְבִיעוּת הוּא וְאֵין רָאוּי לְקָבְעָם.[7] וְחִלּוּק הַדִּינִין שֶׁאָמְרוּ זִכְרוֹנָם לִבְרָכָה (עבודה זרה דף כ"א ע"א) שֶׁיֵּשׁ בְּעִנְיָן זֶה בֵּין בָּתִּים לְשָׂדוֹת וּכְרָמִים[8] וּבֵין סוּרְיָא לְאֶרֶץ יִשְׂרָאֵל,[9,10]

לְדִירָה — **However, even to rent** real estate **to him is forbidden, whenever he rents it for residential** purposes, לְפִי שֶׁמַּכְנִיס שָׁם עֲבוֹדָה זָרָה — **for** it is assumed that **he will bring in his** *avodah zarah* (i.e., his idol) **there.**[6] אֲבָל לִסְחוֹרָתוֹ מֻתָּר — **However, if it is** merely a place **for him to store his merchandise, it is permitted** to rent to him, since there is no assumption that he will bring his idol there. וּבִלְבַד שֶׁלֹּא יַשְׂכִּיר לִשְׁלֹשָׁה בְּנֵי אָדָם — This permit, however, is **provided that one does not rent** houses adjoining each other **to three** idolatrous **people,** לְפִי שֶׁשְּׁלֹשָׁה דְּבַר קְבִיעוּת הוּא וְאֵין רָאוּי לְקָבְעָם — **for three** creates **a permanence, and it is not proper to give them permanence** among us.[7]

Chinuch notes some distinctions with regard to this prohibition, depending on the type of real estate the transaction involves and where the real estate is located: וְחִלּוּק הַדִּינִין שֶׁאָמְרוּ זִכְרוֹנָם לִבְרָכָה שֶׁיֵּשׁ בְּעִנְיָן זֶה — Another detail is **that which [our Sages], of blessed memory, have stated** (*Avodah Zarah* 21a) with regard to **the distinction in law that exists in this matter** בֵּין בָּתִּים לְשָׂדוֹת וּכְרָמִים — **between houses,** on the one hand, **and fields and vineyards,** on the other hand,[8] וּבֵין סוּרְיָא לְאֶרֶץ יִשְׂרָאֵל — as well as the distinction in law

---

### NOTES

6. Renting to an idol worshiper does not constitute "settling" him in the land (see *Rashi, Avodah Zarah* 20b ד"ה אין משכירין בתים), but is prohibited due to another consideration. A Jew may not bring an idol into his home, as per the verse (*Deuteronomy* 7:26): וְלֹא תָבִיא תוֹעֵבָה אֶל בֵּיתֶךָ, *you shall not bring an abomination into your home*. The Mishnah (*Avodah Zarah* 21a) teaches that it is therefore prohibited to rent one's home to an idolater as a residence, for it can be assumed that the idolater will bring his idol into the residence, which would cause the Jew to transgress the above prohibition.

According to many Rishonim, since the Jew himself does not bring in the *avodah zarah* for his own use, the prohibition in this case is merely Rabbinic (*Ramban, Ritva, Ran,* and *Rosh* to *Avodah Zarah* ibid.; see also *Tosafos* there, end of ד"ה אף). Others indicate that the Biblical prohibition applies even when the Jew merely allows an idolater to bring the *avodah zarah* into his house (*Rambam, Hil. Avodah Zarah* 10:4, as understood by *Minchas Chinuch* below, 429:1; cf. *Beis HaLevi* I 47:4). [*Chinuch* in Mitzvah 429 concurs with the former opinion (see *Minchas Chinuch* ibid.). See, however, note 14 below.]

This prohibition presumably applies even outside of Eretz Yisrael, as there would not seem to be a difference between Eretz Yisrael and the Diaspora with regard to the prohibition of bringing an idol into one's home. Accordingly, the commentators question how, already in earlier times, people would freely rent homes as residences to idolaters, seemingly in open violation of this law. They offer a number of distinctions between their situation and that prohibited by the Mishnah. Some explain that the idolaters of later times no longer placed idols in their residences on a consistent basis (*Tosafos, Avodah Zarah* 21a ד"ה אף; *Tur, Yoreh Deah* §151). Others suggest that the prohibition of having an idol in one's home applies only in Eretz Yisrael, since the above verse stresses בֵּיתֶךָ, *your home*, and only in our Land can a home truly be called ours (*Tosafos* ibid., quoting *Rabbeinu Chaim Kohen*). For additional resolutions, see *Tosafos* ibid. in the name of *Rabbeinu Elchanan*; *Smag, Lo Saaseh* 48; *Bach, Yoreh Deah* 151:9.

7. It is forbidden to rent three different buildings in one area to three idol worshipers (*Avodah Zarah* 21a with *Ritva*), if no Jewish homes remain between (*Meiri* ad loc.). Allowing a cluster of idolaters to take root in a Jewish neighborhood creates a danger for the Jews that remain, since these pagans might conspire to harm their Jewish neighbors (*Tosafos* ad loc. ד"ה אלפני; cf. *Meiri*).

*Chinuch*'s wording here, which implies that this prohibition against renting to three idolaters in a Jewish neighborhood applies specifically in Eretz Yisrael, is consistent with the opinion of *Rambam* (*Hil. Avodah Zarah* 10:3, as understood by *Dagul MeiRevavah* to *Shach, Yoreh Deah* 151:15). Others, however, contend that this issue applies outside Eretz Yisrael as well (*Ritva* ibid.; *Tur, Yoreh Deah* 151:8-9; *Shach* there §15).

8. The law is more restrictive with regard to fields and vineyards than with regard to non-residential houses (see below, note 10). The reason for this distinction is that with regard to non-residential houses, there is only one issue to contend with — the prohibition to settle an idol worshiper in the Land. With regard to fields and vineyards, however, there is an additional concern — that the field will be removed from the mitzvah of tithing, since the idolater will not tithe his produce (*Avodah Zarah* 21a). [That is, even if an idolater's ownership of a field in Eretz Yisrael does not *exempt* the

## 208 □ משפטים / מצוה צד: שלא להושיב עובד עבודה זרה בארצנו

וְיֶתֶר פְּרָטֶיהָ, מְבֹאָרִין בְּסַנְהֶדְרִין וַעֲבוֹדָה זָרָה (שם).[11]
וְנוֹהֶגֶת בִּזְכָרִים וּנְקֵבוֹת, בָּאָרֶץ.[12, 13]
וְעוֹבֵר עָלֶיהָ וּמָכַר קַרְקַע אוֹ שְׂכָרוֹ לָהֶם בְּמָקוֹם שֶׁאֵינוֹ רַשַּׁאי,[14] עָבַר עַל מִצְוַת מֶלֶךְ, וְאֵינוֹ לוֹקֶה, לְפִי שֶׁאֶפְשָׁר לִמְכֹּר לָהֶם קַרְקַע אוֹ לְהַשְׂכִּיר בְּלֹא עֲשִׂיַּת מַעֲשֶׂה.[15]

between the region of **Suria**, which adjoins Eretz Yisrael,[9] **and Eretz Yisrael** proper.[10] מְבֹאָרִין בְּסַנְהֶדְרִין וְיֶתֶר פְּרָטֶיהָ — These laws, **and the additional details of [this mitzvah]**, וַעֲבוֹדָה זָרָה — **are set forth in** Tractates *Sanhedrin* **and** *Avodah Zarah* (19b-21b).[11]

### ☞ Applicability of the Mitzvah ☜

וְנוֹהֶגֶת בִּזְכָרִים וּנְקֵבוֹת בָּאָרֶץ — **[This mitzvah] applies to men and women,**[12] **only in Eretz Yisrael.**[13] וְעוֹבֵר עָלֶיהָ וּמָכַר לָהֶם קַרְקַע — **One who transgresses [this mitzvah] and sells land to [idol worshipers],** אוֹ שְׂכָרוֹ לָהֶם בְּמָקוֹם שֶׁאֵינוֹ רַשַּׁאי — **or rents it to them where he is not permitted to,**[14] עָבַר עַל מִצְוַת מֶלֶךְ — **has violated the command of the King** (God). וְאֵינוֹ לוֹקֶה — **However, he does not receive** *malkus* (lashes) **for this violation**, לְפִי שֶׁאֶפְשָׁר לִמְכֹּר לָהֶם קַרְקַע אוֹ לְהַשְׂכִּיר בְּלֹא עֲשִׂיַּת מַעֲשֶׂה — **for it is possible to sell them real estate or to rent it to them without** having **to perform an action,** and as a rule, any violation that can be done without having to resort to action is not subject to *malkus* even when performed with an action.[15]

---

### NOTES

field from tithing (disputed in *Gittin* 47a), the idolater certainly will not tithe the produce *in practice* (*Lechem Mishneh, Hil. Avodah Zarah* 10:3).]

9. Suria is the region to the north of Eretz Yisrael that was conquered by King David and annexed to Eretz Yisrael at that time. Due to the fact that David conquered Suria before all of Eretz Yisrael proper was conquered, the conquest was considered premature and was deemed כִּבּוּשׁ יָחִיד, *an individual conquest.* Therefore, Suria did not attain the sanctified status of Eretz Yisrael proper (see Mitzvah 84, with note 57). Nevertheless, the Sages did impose some level of the restrictions of Eretz Yisrael on Suria (see following note).

10. In Eretz Yisrael, one may not sell his field, vineyard, or house to an idolater. One also may not rent his field or vineyard to an idolater (for the reason given in note 8), but one may rent him a house for non-residential purposes. In Suria, it is permitted even to sell a house to an idolater; and it is permitted to rent him a field or vineyard, though not to sell it outright. In all areas beyond Eretz Yisrael and Suria, it is permitted to sell all properties outright — houses, fields, and vineyards (*Rambam, Hil. Avodah Zarah* 10:3; but see above, end of note 7).

11. [This mitzvah is not discussed in Tractate *Sanhedrin,* and this word is apparently a copyist error (*Me'il HaEphod* §5).] These laws are codified in *Rambam, Hilchos Avodah Zarah* Ch. 10 and in *Shulchan Aruch, Yoreh Deah* 151:7-10.

12. In accordance with the general rule pertaining to mitzvah-prohibitions.

13. Chinuch is obviously referring to the location of the *property,* not of the buyer and seller. Thus, it is prohibited to sell real estate that is located in Eretz Yisrael to an idol worshiper, even if the buyer and seller are outside of Eretz Yisrael, and it is permitted to sell real estate located outside of Eretz Yisrael, even if the buyer and seller are situated in Eretz Yisrael.

14. [I.e., he rents them a house in Eretz Yisrael for purposes of residence (see note 6).] As mentioned in note 6, according to many Rishonim (including Chinuch in Mitzvah 429) the prohibition to rent residential property to an idol worshiper is Rabbinic in origin, because letting an idolater bring his *avodah zarah* into one's home is itself prohibited only Rabbinically. Chinuch's wording here, however, implies that renting is included in the Biblical prohibition (see also *Rambam, Sefer HaMitzvos, Lo Saaseh* 51). This matter requires further study.

15. As a rule, one who transgresses a לָאו שֶׁאֵין בּוֹ מַעֲשֶׂה, *a prohibition that does not involve action,* is not subject to *malkus*. In Chinuch's opinion, any prohibition that *can* be violated without having to resort to performing an action is considered a לָאו שֶׁאֵין בּוֹ מַעֲשֶׂה, *a prohibition that does not involve action,* even if one actually violates the prohibition with an action (see Insight to Mitzvah 68). Here too, since this transaction can be performed without action (e.g., with a simple verbal agreement, allowing the idol worshiper to take possession), one would be exempt from *malkus* even if he effected the transaction by means of an action (e.g., writing a document of sale). [See, however, *Minchas Chinuch* 426:5, who points out that Chinuch himself elsewhere seems to view a transaction as invariably involving an action, and therefore questions Chinuch's assertion here to the contrary.]

### ◈§ Insight: Becoming a Ger Toshav

In his discussion of the necessary steps involved to become a *ger toshav* (resident alien; see notes 3-4), *Rambam* (*Hil. Melachim* 8:11) states that it is not enough for a non-Jew to accept the Noahide commandments simply because he sees them as logical. Rather, to become a *ger toshav*, the non-Jew must accept these commandments because they were stated by God in the Torah, which He transmitted to us through His prophet Moses. This distinction must be understood: Why, if one accepted to abide by all the requisite commandments, should it be insufficient for him to do so because God transmitted these commandments through prophecy to Adam and Noah — or simply because he deems them morally proper? (See *Meshech Chochmah*, Deuteronomy 33:4 ד"ה התורה; *Ohr Same'ach, Hil. Isurei Biah* 14:7 ד"ה ולפ"ז.)

To explain this matter, let us analyze the matter of the *ger toshav*, as there appear to be two fundamentally different ways to understand this person's status. One approach is that a *ger toshav* is simply a non-Jew who has made the commitment to abide by the Seven Noahide Laws to which humanity is bound. Now, as noted above (see note 3), the process of becoming a *ger toshav* was performed in front of a *beis din*, by the person declaring before the court his acceptance of the Noahide Laws. According to this first approach, the requirement for the *ger toshav* to make this declaration in *beis din* is not an intrinsic part of the process, but is simply the mechanism by which he lets his commitment be known, so that we may recognize him as a *ger toshav* and accord him all the associated rights and privileges (see *Ran* to *Rif*, *Avodah Zarah* fol. 1b ד"ה דינרא, and *Chazon Ish*, *Yoreh Deah* 65:3).

The other approach to the matter is that a *ger toshav* is a separate entity entirely. While he is not a convert who has accepted to fulfill all of the commandments of the Torah, he is, nevertheless, not simply a non-Jew who has committed to keeping the Noahide commandments. Rather, he is viewed as an individual who has undergone a quasi-conversion. For this reason, he is called a *"ger,"* i.e., convert (see *Rabbeinu Gershom* to *Kereisos* 9a [printed on 10b] ד"ה כישראל). According to this view, the *ger toshav's* declaration before *beis din* is not simply a way of publicizing his commitment, but is actually the key to his transformation — for conversion always requires a *beis din* (*Shulchan Aruch*, *Yoreh Deah* 268:3).

It would appear that *Rambam* concurs with this latter position, and maintains that one who becomes a *ger toshav* is not simply accepting a code of morality, but is converting to some level of Judaism. *Rambam* therefore rules that, to effect this quasi-conversion, the *ger toshav* must undertake to fulfill the mitzvos in which he is obligated specifically because they were commanded in the Torah through Moses. Only in this manner can he acquire the unique "Jewishness" of a *ger toshav*, and not remain simply a morally correct non-Jew.

This discussion may have relevance to another issue, as well. The Gemara (*Arachin* 29a) states that a *ger toshav* is accepted only when the law of *Yovel* (the Jubilee year) is in force, which is when all the tribes of Israel are settled in their ancestral lands (see Mitzvos 330 and 426). Now, if a *ger toshav* is merely a person who has formally decided to abide by the Noahide Laws (in accordance with the first approach above), how can he not be "accepted"? What prevents his commitment from being effective? Indeed, *Raavad* (*Hil. Isurei Biah* 14:8) seems to understand this rule as a practical matter: The Torah obligates us to support a *ger toshav* financially (see above, note 4), and *this* obligation pertains only when the *Yovel* is in force, i.e., when all the tribes of Israel reside in their ancestral homeland. The reason is because otherwise fulfilling the obligation would simply be too difficult. The poor of the world would seek to gain *ger toshav* status, and would quickly deplete the resources of the Jewish people. Only when the nation is settled in Eretz Yisrael in its full numbers can it feasibly carry that burden, so it is only then that we "accept" a *ger toshav* in the sense of becoming obligated to support him financially. [See *Raavad* there for practical considerations that similarly affect certain other laws pertaining to the *ger toshav*, when *Yovel* is not in force. A non-Jew is, however, theoretically able to become a *ger toshav* even nowadays, in regard to laws not affected by those considerations.]

*Rambam* (*Hil. Isurei Biah* ibid.; *Hil. Avodah Zarah* 10:6), however, apparently understands the exclusion of accepting a *ger toshav* nowadays to apply to all the rules of a *ger toshav*; one cannot attain *ger toshav* status in any respect except when *Yovel* is in force (see *Minchas Chinuch* §2 and *Chazon*

*Ish* ibid.; cf. *Kesef Mishneh, Hil. Avodah Zarah* loc. cit.). The question thus returns: What prevents the person's commitment to abide by the Noahide Laws, which is what generates *ger toshav* status, from being effective?

The matter can be understood according to the above explanation that, in *Rambam's* view, a *ger toshav* actually undergoes a quasi-conversion. Apparently, the Torah limits this unique form of conversion to the era in which *Yovel* is in force. Although humanity is bound by the Seven Noahide Laws in all times, the partial-conversion to the status of "*ger toshav*" is linked to *Yovel*, and when *Yovel* is not in force, only one form of conversion remains — the one that involves a complete and unequivocal acceptance of all of the Torah's mitzvos.

[Based on *Masas Moshe* (R' Moshe Chevroni), *Kiddushin* 48:2; *Mishnas Yaavetz* (R' Betzalel Zolty) *Yoreh Deah* 3:1-2; *Kuntresei HaShiurim, Bava Metzia* 12:10-11; cf. *Chidushei HaGriz* to *Rambam*, p. 164.]

# פרשת תרומה
# Parashas Terumah

וְיִקְחוּ לִי תְּרוּמָה יֵשׁ בָּהּ שְׁתֵּי מִצְוֹת עֲשֵׂה
וְאַחַת מִצְוֹת לֹא תַעֲשֶׂה

*Parashas Terumah* contains two Mitzvah-Obligations
and one Mitzvah-Prohibitions.

---

CONTAINS THREE MITZVOS:
MITZVOS 95-97

---

95. מִצְוַת בִּנְיַן בֵּית הַבְּחִירָה — The Obligation to Build the Holy Temple
96. שֶׁלֹּא לְהוֹצִיא בַּדֵּי הָאָרוֹן מִמֶּנּוּ — The Prohibition to Remove the Poles From the Ark of the Covenant
97. מִצְוַת סִדּוּר לֶחֶם הַפָּנִים וּלְבוֹנָה — The Obligation to Arrange the *Lechem HaPanim* and the *Levonah*

## מִצְוָה צה: מִצְוַת בִּנְיַן בֵּית הַבְּחִירָה

לִבְנוֹת בַּיִת לְשֵׁם ה', כְּלוֹמַר שֶׁנִּהְיֶה מַקְרִיבִים שָׁם קָרְבְּנוֹתֵינוּ אֵלָיו, וְשָׁם תִּהְיֶה הָעֲלִיָּה לָרֶגֶל וְקִבּוּץ כָּל יִשְׂרָאֵל בְּכָל שָׁנָה[1], שֶׁנֶּאֱמַר (שמות כ"ה, ח') "וְעָשׂוּ לִי מִקְדָּשׁ"[2]. וְזֹאת הַמִּצְוָה כּוֹלֶלֶת עִמָּהּ הַכֵּלִים הַצְּרִיכִים בַּבַּיִת אֶל הָעֲבוֹדָה, כְּגוֹן הַמְּנוֹרָה וְהַשֻּׁלְחָן וְהַמִּזְבֵּחַ[3] וְכָל שְׁאָר הַכֵּלִים כֻּלָּם[4].

מִשָּׁרְשֵׁי מִצְוָה זוֹ, מַה שֶּׁתִּרְאֶה בְּסוֹף דְּבָרַי.

---

## ~ Mitzvah 95 ~
## The Obligation to Build the Holy Temple

וְעָשׂוּ לִי מִקְדָּשׁ וְשָׁכַנְתִּי בְּתוֹכָם
*They shall make a Sanctuary for Me, so that I may dwell among them (Exodus 25:8).*

לִבְנוֹת בַּיִת לְשֵׁם ה׳ — We are commanded **to construct a Temple** that is dedicated **to the Name of Hashem,** כְּלוֹמַר שֶׁנִּהְיֶה מַקְרִיבִים שָׁם קָרְבְּנוֹתֵינוּ אֵלָיו — **that is to say,** dedicated as the place **where we shall bring our sacrificial offerings before Him,** וְשָׁם תִּהְיֶה הָעֲלִיָּה לָרֶגֶל וְקִבּוּץ כָּל יִשְׂרָאֵל בְּכָל שָׁנָה — **and where the ascent in pilgrimage and the gathering of all of Israel each year,** on the three festivals, **shall be done;**[1] שֶׁנֶּאֱמַר "וְעָשׂוּ לִי מִקְדָּשׁ" — **as it is stated** (*Exodus* 25:8): *They shall make a Sanctuary for Me, so that I may dwell among them.*[2] וְזֹאת הַמִּצְוָה כּוֹלֶלֶת עִמָּהּ הַכֵּלִים הַצְּרִיכִים בַּבַּיִת אֶל הָעֲבוֹדָה — **In addition, this mitzvah includes** an obligation to construct **the utensils that are needed in the Temple for the** *avodah* (service); כְּגוֹן הַמְּנוֹרָה וְהַשֻּׁלְחָן וְהַמִּזְבֵּחַ וְכָל שְׁאָר הַכֵּלִים כֻּלָּם — **for example, the Menorah, the Table, the Altar,**[3] **and all the other utensils.**[4]

### ~ The Underlying Purpose of the Mitzvah ~

מִשָּׁרְשֵׁי מִצְוָה זוֹ, מַה שֶּׁתִּרְאֶה בְּסוֹף דְּבָרַי — **The underlying purpose of this mitzvah is what you shall see at the end of my words.**

Before proceeding, Chinuch expresses — in the form of a poem — his hesitation to discuss the purpose of this mitzvah. Paraphrasing verses throughout Scripture, Chinuch employs the restrictions that apply

---

NOTES

1. All of Israel is commanded to ascend in pilgrimage and gather in the *Beis HaMikdash* (Temple) on each of the three festivals of the year — Pesach, Shavuos, and Succos (Mitzvos 88 and 489); see *Rambam, Sefer HaMitzvos, Shoresh* 12. [Chinuch's language here is taken from *Sefer HaMitzvos, Asei* 20.]

2. Chinuch follows *Rambam* in *Sefer HaMitzvos, Asei* 20 (see *Kinas Soferim* ad loc.), and *Hil. Beis HaBechirah* 1:1 (see *Kesef Mishneh* ad loc.) in citing this verse as the source of the mitzvah. It should be noted, however, that Chinuch's (and *Rambam's*) discussion in this mitzvah pertains primarily to the *Beis HaMikdash* built in Jerusalem, though this verse was stated in reference to the *Mishkan* (Tabernacle) originally built in the Wilderness. In *Hil. Melachim* 1:1, *Rambam* cites the verse (*Deuteronomy* 12:5): לְשִׁכְנוֹ תִדְרְשׁוּ, *you shall seek out His Presence,* as the source of the obligation to build the *Beis HaMikdash.* See *Lechem Mishneh* and other commentaries there for discussion.

3. There were two Altars in the *Beis HaMikdash*: (1) The Outer Altar, which stood in the Temple Courtyard and on which almost all the offerings were made. This was also known as the מִזְבַּח הָעוֹלָה, *Altar for the Olah* (and other offerings). [Throughout this mitzvah, this will be referred to simply as "the Altar."] (2) The Inner Altar, also known as the מִזְבַּח הַזָּהָב, *Golden Altar,* or מִזְבַּח הַקְּטֹרֶת, *Incense Altar.* This Altar stood inside the Holy and was used primarily for the burning of the daily incense (*ketores*) offering. Both Altars are included in this mitzvah; see *Rambam, Sefer HaMitzvos* ibid. and *Hil. Beis HaBechirah* 1:6.

4. Such as the *Kevesh* (Ramp, upon which to ascend to the Altar), and the *Kiyor* (Laver, from which the Kohanim would wash before engaging in the *avodah*), and its base (see *Rambam, Hil. Beis HaBechirah* 1:6). For further discussion, see Insight.

# 213 ❏ TERUMAH / MITZVAH 95: THE OBLIGATION TO BUILD THE HOLY TEMPLE

וְאָכֵן[5] מִיִּרְאָתִי לְהִתְקָרֵב אֶל מִשְׁכַּן הַשֵּׁם,
כִּי יָדַעְתִּי כָּל הַקָּרֵב הַקָּרֵב,
אִם לֹא הִתְקַדֵּשׁ לְמַדַּי
לֹא יִרְאֶה הַבַּיִת וָחָי[6],
גַּם הַכֹּהֲנִים הַנִּגָּשִׁים אֶל ה' לַעֲבוֹדָה
יִתְקַדְּשׁוּ בְּבוֹאָם אֶל הַקֹּדֶשׁ לִפְנַי, וְהַלְוִיִּם אַחַי הִטַּהָרוּ,
וַיָּנֶף אַהֲרֹן אֹתָם תְּנוּפָה
טֶרֶם יִתְּנוּ קוֹלָם בְּהֵיכַל הַשֵּׁם[7],
אָמַרְתִּי גַּם אֲנִי אַגִּיד עֲצָתִי,

---

to one who performs the *Beis HaMikdash* service as a metaphor for his reservations in approaching this subject:[5]

וְאָכֵן מִיִּרְאָתִי לְהִתְקָרֵב אֶל מִשְׁכַּן הַשֵּׁם — **However, due to my fear of approaching the** subject of **Hashem's Tabernacle,**

כִּי יָדַעְתִּי כָּל הַקָּרֵב הַקָּרֵב — **for I know that everyone who approaches closer,**

אִם לֹא הִתְקַדֵּשׁ לְמַדַּי — **if he has not sanctified himself sufficiently,**

לֹא יִרְאֶה הַבַּיִת וָחָי — **will not see the House and live;**[6]

גַּם הַכֹּהֲנִים הַנִּגָּשִׁים אֶל ה' לַעֲבוֹדָה — and **even the Kohanim, who approach Hashem to perform the Service** in the *Beis HaMikdash*,

יִתְקַדְּשׁוּ בְּבוֹאָם אֶל הַקֹּדֶשׁ לִפְנַי — **must sanctify themselves as they enter the Sanctuary** and proceed **within;**

וְהַלְוִיִּם אַחַי הִטַּהָרוּ — **and the Leviim, my brethren, purified themselves,**

וַיָּנֶף אַהֲרֹן אֹתָם תְּנוּפָה — **and Aaron waved them in a Waving Ceremony**

טֶרֶם יִתְּנוּ קוֹלָם בְּהֵיכַל הַשֵּׁם — **before they raised their voices** in song **in the Sanctuary of Hashem;**[7]

אָמַרְתִּי גַּם אֲנִי אַגִּיד עֲצָתִי — **I said: I, too, will relate my rationale**

---

## NOTES

5. In his Introduction to this work (Vol. I, pp. 31-33; see note 119 there), the author of Chinuch explains at length that it is impossible for man to fathom Hashem's reasons for the mitzvos, and that it is with great trepidation that he undertakes to suggest the underlying purposes of the mitzvos. Here, he expresses even greater trepidation upon approaching the mitzvos pertaining to the *Beis HaMikdash* and the sacrificial offerings. Certainly it cannot be said that Hashem needs a "dwelling" or that He is hungry for the flesh of the sacrificial offerings (see *Menachos* 110a; see also Mitzvah 88 note 8). Clearly then, these mitzvos cannot be understood from man's material perspective, but must instead be appreciated on a more profound level. In this mitzvah, which is the first of many relating to the *Beis HaMikdash* and the *avodah* performed there, Chinuch dedicates a lengthy essay toward outlining the concepts that are the basis for understanding these mitzvos. See also *Kuzari* II §25; *Ramban, Toras Hashem Temimah* (*Kisvei Ramban*, Chavel ed., p. 163).

[To avoid burdening the reader with excessive footnotes, in the following section we have referenced Chinuch's Scriptural paraphrases only where analysis of the Scriptural verse illuminates Chinuch's words.]

6. See *Numbers* 17:28.

7. Based on ibid. 8:21. Chinuch refers here to the consecration ritual that the Leviim were required to undergo before they were permitted to perform their service in the *Mishkan* [for example, the singing of hymns]. This ritual involved being lifted and waved in different directions by Aaron (see ibid. vs. 5-22). Since the author of Chinuch was himself a Levi, as he identifies himself in his Introduction as "a Levi from Barcelona" (see Vol. I, p. 30, with note 116 there), he refers to the Leviim as his "brethren."

[According to an editorial gloss found in the Venice (1600) edition of Sefer HaChinuch, these words convey how the author, whose name was Aaron, elevated and purified his own thoughts, which he refers to as his "brothers" who accompany him (the name "Levi" is derived from the term *yilaveh, he will accompany* — see *Genesis* 29:34), in order to gain insight into the purpose of this mitzvah. According to this interpretation, Chinuch is providing a clue to his identity here, by indicating his name. This early gloss is cited to support the position of those who maintain that Chinuch was authored by R' Aharon HaLevi, the *Re'ah*. See General Introduction, and Glosses of R' C. D. Chavel to this passage of Chinuch. See, however, above, Mitzvah 73 note 34.]

וְאֶעֱרֹךְ הִתְנַצְּלוּתִי נֶגֶד זְקֵנַי,
וְאֶרְחַץ בְּנִקָּיוֹן כַּפָּי[8]
טֶרֶם אֶעֱלֶה בֵּית ה'.
יָדוּעַ הַדָּבָר וּמְפֻרְסָם בֵּינֵינוּ הָעָם מְקַבֵּל הַמִּצְוֹת,
כִּי שִׁבְעִים פָּנִים לַתּוֹרָה,[9]
וּבְכָל אַחַת מֵהֶן שָׁרָשִׁים גְּדוֹלִים וְרַבִּים,
וּלְכָל שֹׁרֶשׁ וָשֹׁרֶשׁ עֲנָפִים,
כָּל אֶחָד יִשָּׂא אֶשְׁכּוֹל גָּדוֹל שֶׁל פֵּרוֹת נֶחְמָדִים
לְהַשְׂכִּיל לְבָבוֹת,
יוֹם יוֹם יוֹצִיאוּ פֶּרַח לַשּׁוֹקְדִים עֲלֵיהֶם,[10]
פִּרְחֵי חָכְמָה וְשֵׂכֶל טוֹב,
כָּל עֵינַיִם מְאִירוֹת,
וְרָחֲבָה וְנָסְבָה עֹמֶק חָכְמָתָהּ
עַד שֶׁאֵין כֹּחַ בָּאָדָם לְהַשִּׂיג תַּכְלִיתָהּ,
כְּמוֹ שֶׁהֵעִיד הַמֶּלֶךְ הֶחָכָם (קהלת ז', כ"ג)
אָמַרְתִּי אֶחְכָּמָה וְהִיא רְחוֹקָה מִמֶּנִּי,[11]

---

**וְאֶעֱרֹךְ הִתְנַצְּלוּתִי נֶגֶד זְקֵנַי** — and set forth my justification before my elders,

**וְאֶרְחַץ בְּנִקָּיוֹן כַּפָּי** — and thus I will wash my hands in cleanliness[8]

**טֶרֶם אֶעֱלֶה בֵּית ה'** — before I ascend to Hashem's Temple.

**יָדוּעַ הַדָּבָר וּמְפֻרְסָם בֵּינֵינוּ הָעָם מְקַבֵּל הַמִּצְוֹת** — It is a matter of widespread knowledge among us, the nation that has received the mitzvos,

**כִּי שִׁבְעִים פָּנִים לַתּוֹרָה** — that "there are seventy facets to the Torah."[9]

**וּבְכָל אַחַת מֵהֶן שָׁרָשִׁים גְּדוֹלִים וְרַבִּים** — Now, each of these facets has many major root concepts,

**וּלְכָל שֹׁרֶשׁ וָשֹׁרֶשׁ עֲנָפִים** — and each and every root concept has numerous branches,

**כָּל אֶחָד יִשָּׂא אֶשְׁכּוֹל גָּדוֹל שֶׁל פֵּרוֹת נֶחְמָדִים** — each of which bears a great cluster of precious fruit

**לְהַשְׂכִּיל לְבָבוֹת** — that has the capacity to impart understanding to the heart.

**יוֹם יוֹם יוֹצִיאוּ פֶּרַח לַשּׁוֹקְדִים עֲלֵיהֶם** — Each day, they bring forth blossoms to those who are diligent over them,[10]

**פִּרְחֵי חָכְמָה וְשֵׂכֶל טוֹב** — blossoms of wisdom and keen insight

**כָּל עֵינַיִם מְאִירוֹת** — that are enlightening to every eye.

**וְרָחֲבָה וְנָסְבָה עֹמֶק חָכְמָתָהּ** — The profundity of its wisdom is broad and extensive,

**עַד שֶׁאֵין כֹּחַ בָּאָדָם לְהַשִּׂיג תַּכְלִיתָהּ** — such that man lacks the ability to fathom its entire essence,

**כְּמוֹ שֶׁהֵעִיד הַמֶּלֶךְ הֶחָכָם** — as the wise king (Solomon) attested (Ecclesiastes 7:23):

**"אָמַרְתִּי אֶחְכָּמָה וְהִיא רְחוֹקָה מִמֶּנִּי"** — I thought I could become wise, but it is beyond me.[11]

---

NOTES

8. Paraphrase of *Psalms* 26:6. Just as the Kohanim washed their hands [and feet] from the *Kiyor* (Laver) before performing *avodah* in the *Beis HaMikdash*, so must one be cleansed of sin before approaching any aspect of the Divine Service, in order for it to be accepted (*Metzudas David* and *Malbim* ad loc.). Chinuch thus alludes that with his following "justification," he means to cleanse himself of any suspicion of impropriety in approaching the task of explaining the purpose of this mitzvah.

9. That is, the Torah can be explained in seventy unique ways. See *Osiyos DeRabbi Akiva* and *Bamidbar Rabbah* 13:15.

10. One who toils in the study of Torah will continuously arrive at a new understanding of its words (see *Eruvin* 54a-b).

11. The many facets of the Torah encompass numerous interpretations and lessons, which, due to their complexity and overwhelming greatness, cannot be fathomed by the minds of mortal beings. Even King Solomon, the wisest of all men, acknowledged that the depths of its wisdom were beyond him.

# 215 □ TERUMAH / MITZVAH 95: THE OBLIGATION TO BUILD THE HOLY TEMPLE

וְעִם כָּל זֶה אֵין לְהַרְפּוֹת יְדֵי הָעוֹסֵק בָּהּ,

כִּי אִם מְעַט וְאִם הַרְבֵּה מִמֶּנָּה יֹאכַל כֻּלָּהּ מְתוּקָה[12],

וְאִם יֵשׁ כַּמָּה אֲשֶׁר מִפְּרִי עֵץ הַגָּן לֹא תַשִּׂיג יָדָם לָקַחַת,

יִקְחוּ לָהֶם עָלֵהוּ לִתְרוּפָה[13].

וְאָנֹכִי עִם דַּעְתִּי גֹּדֶל עֶרְכָּהּ וְרֹב עָמְקָהּ,

וְכִי פְלִיאָה מִמֶּנִּי נִשְׂגָּבָה,

פָּעַרְתִּי פִי לְדַבֵּר בָּהּ[14],

וְאֶסְמֹךְ בַּמֶּה שֶׁלִּמְּדוּנִי רַבּוֹתַי (ע״ז דף י״ט ע״א)

**לְגָרֵס אִינִישׁ וְאַף עַל גַּב דְּלָא יָדַע מַאי קָאָמַר,**

**שֶׁנֶּאֱמַר** (תהילים קי״ט, כ׳) **גָּרְסָה נַפְשִׁי לְתַאֲבָה[15].**

**דַּע[16] בְּנִי,** כִּי כָּל אֲשֶׁר יַגִּיעַ אֵצֶל הַשֵּׁם יִתְבָּרַךְ בַּעֲשׂוֹת בְּנֵי אָדָם כָּל מִצְווֹתָיו,

---

וְעִם כָּל זֶה אֵין לְהַרְפּוֹת יְדֵי הָעוֹסֵק בָּהּ — **But despite all this, one should not weaken the resolve of one who is involved in** studying it,

כִּי אִם מְעַט וְאִם הַרְבֵּה מִמֶּנָּה יֹאכַל כֻּלָּהּ מְתוּקָה — **for, whether one "eats" little or much of it, it is all sweet;**[12]

וְאִם יֵשׁ כַּמָּה אֲשֶׁר מִפְּרִי עֵץ הַגָּן לֹא תַשִּׂיג יָדָם לָקַחַת — **and though there may be many whose capabilities will not suffice** for them **to take from the fruit of the garden,**

יִקְחוּ לָהֶם עָלֵהוּ לִתְרוּפָה — **they will take for themselves its leaves, for healing.**[13]

וְאָנֹכִי עִם דַּעְתִּי גֹּדֶל עֶרְכָּהּ וְרֹב עָמְקָהּ — **Therefore, although I know [the Torah's] tremendous value and great profundity,**

וְכִי פְלִיאָה מִמֶּנִּי נִשְׂגָּבָה — **and that it is wondrous and exalted, beyond my** capacity,

פָּעַרְתִּי פִי לְדַבֵּר בָּהּ — **I have** nevertheless **opened my mouth wide to speak about it.**[14]

וְאֶסְמֹךְ בַּמֶּה שֶׁלִּמְּדוּנִי רַבּוֹתַי — **And I will rely upon what my teachers have taught me** (*Avodah Zarah* 19a):

לְגָרֵס אִינִישׁ וְאַף עַל גַּב דְּלָא יָדַע מַאי קָאָמַר — **A person should always recite** words of Torah, **even if he does not understand what he is saying,**

שֶׁנֶּאֱמַר גָּרְסָה נַפְשִׁי לְתַאֲבָה — **as it is stated** (*Psalms* 119:20): ***My soul shatters with yearning*** for Your statutes, always!*[15]

Having concluded his "justification," Chinuch turns to the underlying purpose of the mitzvah. He begins by discussing the purpose of mitzvos in general and, in doing so, addresses an unspoken question: It is obvious that God is Perfect and has no need for our service, and it is equally obvious that man is utterly incapable of giving Him anything; why, then, did He command us to perform the mitzvos?[16]

דַּע בְּנִי — **Know, my son,** כִּי כָּל אֲשֶׁר יַגִּיעַ אֵצֶל הַשֵּׁם יִתְבָּרַךְ בַּעֲשׂוֹת בְּנֵי אָדָם כָּל מִצְווֹתָיו — **that the entire** "benefit" **that reaches Hashem, blessed be He, when people perform any of His mitzvos,**

---

## NOTES

12. Stylistic citation of *Ecclesiastes* 5:11, which speaks of the good fortune of one who labors in the service of Hashem (*Targum* and *Rashi* ad loc.). Even if he achieves only a very limited understanding of the lofty concepts of the Torah, the student attains great spiritual fulfillment and pleasure.

13. Stylistic citation of *Ezekiel* 47:12. Even one who will not attain an understanding of the essence of the mitzvah [the "fruit"] may attain a superficial understanding [the "leaves"], which also represents a degree of spiritual accomplishment. [For discussion of the analogy to fruit and leaves, see the beginning of *Maalos HaTorah*

by R' Avraham, the brother of the Vilna Gaon.]

14. Stylistic citation of *Psalms* 119:131 (see *Malbim, Peirush HaMilos* ad loc., and *Isaiah* 5:14).

15. The Sages (*Avodah Zarah* 19a) expound the verse to mean that the eager soul "shatters" the Torah in its effort to digest its studies. By employing the term "shatter," which implies a less thorough breakdown of material than "grind," the Psalmist indicates that there is merit to study even if it will not lead to thorough comprehension.

16. Chinuch also discusses this matter at length in his Introduction to this work (Vol. 1, pp. 12-17).

אֵינֶנּוּ רַק שֶׁחָפֵץ הַשֵּׁם יִתְבָּרַךְ לְהֵיטִיב לָנוּ, וּבִהְיוֹת הָאָדָם מֻכְשָׁר וּמוּכָן בַּעֲשִׂיַּת אוֹתָם הַמִּצְווֹת לְקַבֵּל הַטּוֹבָה אָז יֵיטִיב אֵלָיו הַשֵּׁם, וְעַל כֵּן הוֹדִיעָם דֶּרֶךְ טוֹב לִהְיוֹתָם טוֹבִים, וְהִיא דֶרֶךְ הַתּוֹרָה כִּי בָהּ יִהְיֶה הָאָדָם טוֹב[17], נִמְצָא שֶׁכָּל הַמְקַיֵּם מִצְווֹתָיו הַשְּׁלֵמִים חֶפְצוֹ בַּאֲשֶׁר הוּא רָאוּי אָז לְקַבֵּל טוֹבָתוֹ, וְכָל שֶׁאֵינוֹ מֵכִין עַצְמוֹ לְכָךְ רָעָתוֹ רַבָּה, שֶׁיּוֹדֵעַ חֵפֶץ הַשֵּׁם יִתְבָּרַךְ בַּמֶּה, וְהוּא יַעֲשֶׂה מַעֲשָׂיו כְּנֶגֶד חֶפְצוֹ. וּפָרָשָׁה אַחַת נִכְתְּבָה בַתּוֹרָה לְהוֹדִיעֵנוּ עִקָּר זֶה לְבַד, וְהִיא מַה שֶּׁכָּתוּב בְּסֵדֶר וְהָיָה עֵקֶב (דברים י, י״ב), וְעַתָּה יִשְׂרָאֵל מָה ה׳ אֱלֹהֶיךָ שֹׁאֵל מֵעִמָּךְ וְגוֹ׳ עַד לְטוֹב לָךְ[18], כְּלוֹמַר אֵינֶנּוּ שׁוֹאֵל מֵעִמְּךָ דָּבָר בַּעֲשׂוֹתְךָ מִצְוֹתָיו, רַק שֶׁרָצָה בְטוּבוֹ הַגָּדוֹל לְהֵיטִיב לָךְ, וּכְמוֹ שֶׁכָּתוּב אַחֲרָיו (שם, י״ד) הֵן לַה׳ אֱלֹהֶיךָ הַשָּׁמַיִם וּשְׁמֵי הַשָּׁמַיִם הָאָרֶץ וְכָל אֲשֶׁר בָּהּ, כְּלוֹמַר וְאֵינוֹ צָרִיךְ לְמִצְוֹתֶיךָ, רַק מֵאַהֲבָתוֹ אוֹתְךָ לְזַכּוֹתְךָ[19].

---

**אֵינֶנּוּ רַק שֶׁחָפֵץ הַשֵּׁם יִתְבָּרַךְ לְהֵיטִיב לָנוּ** — is only that Hashem, blessed be He, wishes to bestow goodness upon us, **וּבִהְיוֹת הָאָדָם מֻכְשָׁר וּמוּכָן בַּעֲשִׂיַּת אוֹתָם הַמִּצְווֹת לְקַבֵּל הַטּוֹבָה** — and when man is readied and prepared, through performing those mitzvos, to receive goodness, **אָז יֵיטִיב אֵלָיו הַשֵּׁם** — then Hashem will bestow goodness upon him. **וְעַל כֵּן הוֹדִיעָם דֶּרֶךְ טוֹב** — For this reason, [Hashem] informed [mankind] of the good path, **לִהְיוֹתָם טוֹבִים** — so that they could become good; **וְהִיא דֶרֶךְ הַתּוֹרָה** — and this is the path of the Torah, **כִּי בָהּ יִהְיֶה הָאָדָם טוֹב** — for through [the Torah] a person becomes good.[17] **נִמְצָא שֶׁכָּל הַמְקַיֵּם מִצְווֹתָיו הַשְּׁלֵמִים חֶפְצוֹ** — It emerges, then, that anyone who fulfills [Hashem's] mitzvos has fulfilled His Will, **בַּאֲשֶׁר הוּא רָאוּי אָז לְקַבֵּל טוֹבָתוֹ** — because he is then worthy of receiving His goodness — which is His ultimate Will. **וְכָל שֶׁאֵינוֹ מֵכִין עַצְמוֹ לְכָךְ רָעָתוֹ רַבָּה** — But one who does not prepare himself for this goodness, and neglects to perform Hashem's mitzvos, is guilty of great evil, **שֶׁיּוֹדֵעַ חֵפֶץ הַשֵּׁם יִתְבָּרַךְ בַּמֶּה** — for he knows what the Will of Hashem, blessed be He, is, **וְהוּא יַעֲשֶׂה מַעֲשָׂיו כְּנֶגֶד חֶפְצוֹ** — yet he conducts his matters in a manner that is contrary to His Will. **וּפָרָשָׁה אַחַת נִכְתְּבָה בַתּוֹרָה לְהוֹדִיעֵנוּ עִקָּר זֶה לְבַד** — Indeed, a passage is written in the Torah specifically to teach us this principle, i.e., that the purpose of the mitzvos is not for Hashem's interest but for the benefit of mankind. **וְהִיא מַה שֶּׁכָּתוּב בְּסֵדֶר וְהָיָה עֵקֶב** — This is [the passage] that is written in *Parashas Eikev* (Deuteronomy 10:12-13), **״וְעַתָּה יִשְׂרָאֵל מָה ה׳ אֱלֹהֶיךָ שֹׁאֵל מֵעִמָּךְ״ וְגוֹ׳ עַד ״לְטוֹב לָךְ״** — beginning with the words, *Now, O Israel, what does HASHEM, your God, ask of you*, etc., and continuing through the words *for your benefit*.[18] **כְּלוֹמַר אֵינֶנּוּ שׁוֹאֵל מֵעִמְּךָ דָּבָר בַּעֲשׂוֹתְךָ מִצְוֹתָיו** — That is to say, Hashem is not requesting anything *from* you when commanding that you observe His mitzvos; **רַק שֶׁרָצָה בְטוּבוֹ הַגָּדוֹל לְהֵיטִיב לָךְ** — rather, due to His great goodness, He desires to bestow goodness upon you, so all that He asks of you is *"for your benefit."* **וּכְמוֹ שֶׁכָּתוּב אַחֲרָיו** — And indeed, so it is written afterward, in the verse that follows (ibid. v. 14): **״הֵן לַה׳ אֱלֹהֶיךָ הַשָּׁמַיִם וּשְׁמֵי הַשָּׁמַיִם הָאָרֶץ וְכָל אֲשֶׁר בָּהּ״** — *Behold! To HASHEM your God are the Heavens and the Highest Heavens, the earth and everything that is in it.* **כְּלוֹמַר וְאֵינוֹ צָרִיךְ לְמִצְוֹתֶיךָ** — That is to say, He has no need for your performance of mitzvos, since everything is His; **רַק מֵאַהֲבָתוֹ אוֹתְךָ לְזַכּוֹתְךָ** — rather, it is due to His love for you that He commanded you to perform them, so as to provide you with merit.[19]

---

### NOTES

17. Chinuch explains frequently throughout this work that only one who is imbued with goodness is qualified to benefit from the goodness of Hashem (see, for example, Mitzvos 66-67,88). Since Hashem desires that we benefit from Him, He instructed us to observe the mitzvos, so as to become better human beings and be worthy of His beneficence.

18. The passage reads: וְעַתָּה יִשְׂרָאֵל מָה ה׳ אֱלֹהֶיךָ שֹׁאֵל מֵעִמָּךְ כִּי אִם לְיִרְאָה אֶת ה׳ אֱלֹהֶיךָ לָלֶכֶת בְּכָל דְּרָכָיו וּלְאַהֲבָה אֹתוֹ וְלַעֲבֹד אֶת ה׳ אֱלֹהֶיךָ בְּכָל לְבָבְךָ וּבְכָל נַפְשֶׁךָ. לִשְׁמֹר אֶת מִצְוֹת ה׳ וְאֶת חֻקֹּתָיו אֲשֶׁר אָנֹכִי מְצַוְּךָ הַיּוֹם לְטוֹב לָךְ, *Now, O Israel, what does HASHEM, your God, ask of you? Only to fear HASHEM, your God, to go in all His ways and to love Him, and to serve HASHEM, your God, with all your heart and with all your soul. To observe the commandments of HASHEM and His decrees, which I command you today, for your benefit.*

19. This passage clearly stipulates the fundamental principle that Chinuch set forth regarding the mitzvos:

## 217 □ TERUMAH / MITZVAH 95: THE OBLIGATION TO BUILD THE HOLY TEMPLE

וְיֵשׁ בְּעוֹשֵׂי הַמִּצְווֹת יָשִׂימוּ מְגַמַּת פְּנֵיהֶם אֶל הַטּוֹבָה הַמְעֻתֶּדֶת אֲלֵיהֶם בַּעֲשִׂיָּתָן לְבַד, כִּי יָדְעוּ שֶׁבְּסִבָּתָן תָּנוּחַ עֲלֵיהֶם הַבְּרָכָה וְהַטּוֹב, וְאֶל הַכַּוָּנָה הַהִיא יִתְעַסְּקוּ בָּהֶן לְעוֹלָם, וְאֵלֶּה חֶלְקָם בַּחַיִּים וְזוֹכִין לְעֵדֶן גַּן אֱלֹהִים, וְאוּלָם לֹא הִגִּיעוּ אֶל תַּכְלִית הַכַּוָּנָה הַטּוֹבָה. אֲבָל יֵשׁ אֲשֶׁר זָכוּ וְנָתַן לָהֶם הַשֵּׁם יִתְבָּרַךְ לֵב לָדַעַת וּלְהַכִּיר בְּמִדּוֹתָיו הַמְעֻלּוֹת[20], וּמִתּוֹךְ הַכָּרָתָם יִתְקַשְּׁרוּ מוֹרָשֵׁי[21] לְבָבָם בְּאַהֲבָתוֹ קֶשֶׁר חָזָק וְאַמִּיץ, עַד שֶׁיָּשִׂימוּ כָּל כַּוָּנַת הֶכְנַת גּוּפָם כְּדֵי לְהַשְׁלִים חֵפֶץ הַשֵּׁם יִתְבָּרַךְ לְרֹב חִשְׁקָם אוֹתוֹ, וְאֶל הַתּוֹעֶלֶת הַמְעֻתֶּדֶת לָהֶם בָּעֵסֶק הַהוּא לֹא יָשִׁיתוּ לֵב, וְהִיא הַמַּעֲלָה הַגְּדוֹלָה שֶׁעָלוּ אֵלֶיהָ הָאָבוֹת הַקְּדוֹשִׁים הַשְּׁלֹשָׁה, וְהַרְבֵּה מִבְּנֵיהֶם אַחֲרֵיהֶם, זֵכֶר כֻּלָּם לִבְרָכָה, וְזֹאת הִיא הַמַּדְרֵגָה הָעֶלְיוֹנָה שֶׁאֶפְשָׁר לְבֶן אָדָם לַעֲלוֹת[22].

---

Chinuch introduces two levels of devotion that one may have when observing the mitzvos, one purer than the other. Although a person merits reward through all mitzvah observance, the higher form of devotion will bring one closer to God:

וְיֵשׁ בְּעוֹשֵׂי הַמִּצְווֹת יָשִׂימוּ מְגַמַּת פְּנֵיהֶם אֶל הַטּוֹבָה הַמְעֻתֶּדֶת אֲלֵיהֶם בַּעֲשִׂיָּתָן לְבַד — Now, among those who perform the mitzvos, there are those who set as their objective only the good that is destined for them through performing [the mitzvos], כִּי יָדְעוּ שֶׁבְּסִבָּתָן תָּנוּחַ עֲלֵיהֶם הַבְּרָכָה וְהַטּוֹב — for they know that as the result of performing [the mitzvos], blessing and goodness will rest upon them, since Hashem rewards those who fulfill His command, וְאֶל הַכַּוָּנָה הַהִיא יִתְעַסְּקוּ בָּהֶן לְעוֹלָם — and it is always with this intention that they engage in observance of [the mitzvos]. וְאֵלֶּה חֶלְקָם בַּחַיִּים — These people have a share in the Eternal Life, וְזוֹכִין לְעֵדֶן גַּן אֱלֹהִים — and they merit a place in Eden, the Garden of God. וְאוּלָם לֹא הִגִּיעוּ אֶל תַּכְלִית הַכַּוָּנָה הַטּוֹבָה — However, they have not attained the ultimate proper intention in performing the mitzvos. אֲבָל יֵשׁ אֲשֶׁר זָכוּ וְנָתַן לָהֶם הַשֵּׁם יִתְבָּרַךְ לֵב — On the other hand, there are those who have merited that Hashem, blessed be He, gave them a heart לָדַעַת וּלְהַכִּיר בְּמִדּוֹתָיו הַמְעֻלּוֹת — to know and to recognize His exalted Attributes,[20] וּמִתּוֹךְ הַכָּרָתָם — and through their recognition of those Attributes יִתְקַשְּׁרוּ מוֹרָשֵׁי לְבָבָם בְּאַהֲבָתוֹ קֶשֶׁר חָזָק וְאַמִּיץ — the innermost feelings[21] of their hearts become bound in love of [Hashem] with such a strong and fast bond עַד שֶׁיָּשִׂימוּ כָּל כַּוָּנַת הֶכְנַת גּוּפָם כְּדֵי לְהַשְׁלִים חֵפֶץ הַשֵּׁם יִתְבָּרַךְ — that they set the entire focus of their corporeal existence upon the goal of fulfilling the Will of Hashem, blessed be He, לְרֹב חִשְׁקָם אוֹתוֹ — due to their great desire to be close to Him, וְאֶל הַתּוֹעֶלֶת הַמְעֻתֶּדֶת לָהֶם בָּעֵסֶק הַהוּא לֹא יָשִׁיתוּ לֵב — while paying no heed to the benefit to which they are destined for engaging in that pursuit. וְהִיא הַמַּעֲלָה הַגְּדוֹלָה — This is the greatest level of service before God, שֶׁעָלוּ אֵלֶיהָ הָאָבוֹת הַקְּדוֹשִׁים הַשְּׁלֹשָׁה, וְהַרְבֵּה מִבְּנֵיהֶם אַחֲרֵיהֶם — and is the level to which the three holy Patriarchs (Abraham, Isaac, and Jacob) and many of their descendants after them, ascended, זֵכֶר כֻּלָּם לִבְרָכָה — may all their memories be blessed; וְזֹאת הִיא הַמַּדְרֵגָה הָעֶלְיוֹנָה שֶׁאֶפְשָׁר לְבֶן אָדָם לַעֲלוֹת — indeed, this is the highest level to which a human being can ascend.[22] In short, the reason Hashem gave us mitzvos is to enable us to attain closeness to Him and benefit from His goodness.

---

### NOTES

Hashem Himself has no gain when any mitzvah is performed, as the entire universe is His. He desires fulfillment of the mitzvos solely for *our* benefit. [See also *Ramban, Deuteronomy* 22:6.]

20. I.e., as a result of their devotion to Him, Hashem opened their hearts to attain a deeper recognition of His Attributes.

21. Literally, *legacies* (see *Job* 17:11 with *Rashi* et al.).

22. See *Ramban, Leviticus* 18:4, who explains in some detail the far greater reward that awaits those who attain this great level of devotion to Hashem. Actually, as *Mesillas Yesharim* (Ch. 1) explains, the closeness to Hashem that one attains is itself the ultimate goodness.

[The attitudes that Chinuch has described here are two of *four* attitudes that *Ramban* describes there. *Ramban* explains that the level of "Life" that one attains through observance of the mitzvos depends upon his attitude and devotion. See further, *Rambam, Hil. Teshuvah* Ch. 10, and *Mesillas Yesharim* Ch. 4.]

## 218 ❑ תרומה / מצוה צה: מצות בנין בית הבחירה

וּמֵעַתָּה בִּהְיוֹת הַנָּחַת דַּעְתֵּנוּ עַל זֶה בְּעִנְיַן מִצְווֹתָיו בָּרוּךְ הוּא, תְּחַיֵּב אוֹתָנוּ לֵאמֹר כִּי בִּנְיַן בַּיִת לַשֵּׁם יִתְבָּרַךְ, וַעֲשׂוֹתֵנוּ בָּה תְּפִלּוֹת[23] וְקָרְבָּנוֹת אֵלָיו, הַכֹּל לְהָכִין הַלְּבָבוֹת לַעֲבוֹדָתוֹ יִתְעַלֶּה, לֹא מֵהְיוֹתוֹ צָרִיךְ לָשֶׁבֶת בֵּין אֲנָשִׁים וְלָבוֹא בְּצֵל קוֹרוֹתָם, וְאִם אַרְזֵי לְבָנוֹן יִבְנוּהוּ אוֹ בְרוֹתִים, כִּי הַשָּׁמַיִם וּשְׁמֵי הַשָּׁמַיִם לֹא יְכַלְכְּלוּהוּ, וּבְרוּחוֹ יַעֲמֹדוּ, אַף כִּי הַבַּיִת אֲשֶׁר בָּנוּ בְנֵי אָדָם כְּבוֹדוֹ חָלִילָה, הֲלֹא יְדוּעִים הַדְּבָרִים וּבְרוּרִים שֶׁהַכֹּל לְהַכְשֵׁר גּוּפוֹתֵינוּ, כִּי הַגּוּפוֹת יַכְשְׁרוּ עַל יְדֵי הַפְּעֻלּוֹת, וּבְרַבּוֹת הַפְּעֻלּוֹת הַטּוֹבוֹת וְרֹב הַתְמָדָתָן מַחְשְׁבוֹת הַלֵּב מִטַּהֲרוֹת מִתְלַבְּנוֹת מְזֻקָּקוֹת. וְהַשֵּׁם חָפֵץ בְּטוֹבָתָן שֶׁל בְּרִיּוֹת[24] כְּמוֹ שֶׁאָמַרְנוּ, וְעַל כֵּן צִוָּנוּ לִקְבֹּעַ מָקוֹם שֶׁיִּהְיֶה טָהוֹר וְנָקִי בְּתַכְלִית הַנְּקִיּוּת, לְטַהֵר שָׁם מַחְשְׁבוֹת בְּנֵי אִישׁ וּלְתַקֵּן לִבָּם אֵלָיו בּוֹ[25], וְהוּא בָּרוּךְ הוּא בָּחַר אוֹתוֹ הַמָּקוֹם וֶהֱכִינוֹ אֶל הַטּוֹבָה לִבְנֵי אָדָם,

Chinuch now proceeds to the specific mitzvah of building the *Beis HaMikdash*: וּמֵעַתָּה בִּהְיוֹת הַנָּחַת דַּעְתֵּנוּ עַל זֶה בְּעִנְיַן מִצְווֹתָיו בָּרוּךְ הוּא — **And now that we have reached this conclusion with regard to the mitzvos [of Hashem], blessed is He,** in general, תְּחַיֵּב אוֹתָנוּ לֵאמֹר — **it compels us to say** further כִּי בִּנְיַן בַּיִת לַשֵּׁם יִתְבָּרַךְ — that **our constructing a Temple dedicated to Hashem, blessed be He,** וַעֲשׂוֹתֵנוּ בָּה תְּפִלּוֹת וְקָרְבָּנוֹת אֵלָיו — **and our conducting of prayers**[23] **and offerings in it before Him,** הַכֹּל לְהָכִין הַלְּבָבוֹת לַעֲבוֹדָתוֹ יִתְעַלֶּה — **are all in order to prepare the hearts** of man to **be focused upon His service, may He be exalted.** לֹא מֵהְיוֹתוֹ צָרִיךְ לָשֶׁבֶת בֵּין אֲנָשִׁים וְלָבוֹא בְּצֵל קוֹרוֹתָם — **It is not because He needs to dwell among men or to come beneath the shelter of their roof,** וְאִם אַרְזֵי לְבָנוֹן יִבְנוּהוּ אוֹ בְרוֹתִים — **even if they should construct it** most fittingly, **with cedars of Lebanon or with cypress.** כִּי הַשָּׁמַיִם וּשְׁמֵי הַשָּׁמַיִם לֹא יְכַלְכְּלוּהוּ — **Indeed, the Heavens and Highest Heavens cannot contain Him,** וּבְרוּחוֹ יַעֲמֹדוּ — **and they,** in fact, **exist** only **by His Will!** אַף כִּי הַבַּיִת אֲשֶׁר בָּנוּ בְנֵי אָדָם צָרִיךְ כְּבוֹדוֹ — **Surely,** then, is it absurd to think that **a building constructed by man** would be able to contain Him, or that **His Honor should need** such a building; חָלִילָה — **Heaven forbid** the thought! הֲלֹא יְדוּעִים הַדְּבָרִים וּבְרוּרִים שֶׁהַכֹּל לְהַכְשֵׁר גּוּפוֹתֵינוּ — **Thus, the matter is most obvious and clear — that all** this is commanded **in order to improve our corporeal nature;** כִּי הַגּוּפוֹת יַכְשְׁרוּ עַל יְדֵי הַפְּעֻלּוֹת — **for physical entities become improved through the actions** that they perform, וּבְרַבּוֹת הַפְּעֻלּוֹת הַטּוֹבוֹת וְרֹב הַתְמָדָתָן — **and as** their **proper actions increase, and through consistently** performing **them,** מַחְשְׁבוֹת הַלֵּב מִטַּהֲרוֹת מִתְלַבְּנוֹת מְזֻקָּקוֹת — **the thoughts of the heart become purified, cleansed, and refined.**[24] וְהַשֵּׁם חָפֵץ בְּטוֹבָתָן שֶׁל בְּרִיּוֹת כְּמוֹ שֶׁאָמַרְנוּ — **It follows that since Hashem wishes for the betterment of His creations, as we have said,** וְעַל כֵּן צִוָּנוּ לִקְבֹּעַ מָקוֹם שֶׁיִּהְיֶה טָהוֹר וְנָקִי — **He therefore commanded us to establish a place that is pure and** spiritually **clean,** בְּתַכְלִית הַנְּקִיּוּת — **with the ultimate** degree of **cleanliness,** לְטַהֵר שָׁם מַחְשְׁבוֹת בְּנֵי אִישׁ — **so that the thoughts of men should be purified there** וּלְתַקֵּן לִבָּם אֵלָיו בּוֹ — and **so that their hearts should become attuned toward Him there.**[25] וְהוּא בָּרוּךְ הוּא בָּחַר אוֹתוֹ הַמָּקוֹם — **[Hashem], blessed is He, chose the specific location** of the *Beis HaMikdash* (Holy Temple), וֶהֱכִינוֹ אֶל הַטּוֹבָה לִבְנֵי אָדָם — **and prepared it for the betterment**

---

### NOTES

23. The *Beis HaMikdash* was not only the venue for bringing sacrificial offerings, but was also designated as a place for prayer (see *Isaiah* 56:7). In fact, even today, prayers recited all over the world are directed to the place where the *Beis HaMikdash* stood (see *I Kings* 8:28-53; *Berachos* 30a; see also *Rashi, Genesis* 28:17 ד"ה וזה).

24. Chinuch returns here to the oft-repeated theme he set forth in Mitzvah 16, that man is affected by the actions that he performs. This is true with regard to man's intent as well. By repeatedly performing mitzvos with a pure intent, one will attain pure motives for all his actions.

25. Within the confines of the purity and sanctity of the *Beis HaMikdash*, man elevates his perspective and nurtures an ability to recognize God's Attributes and to engage in mitzvos out of love for Him, as Chinuch described above. See similarly above, Mitzvah 88, at note 9.

## 219 □ TERUMAH / MITZVAH 95: THE OBLIGATION TO BUILD THE HOLY TEMPLE

אוּלַי מִהְיוֹתוֹ אֶמְצָעוּת הָעוֹלָם בְּכִוּוּן, וְהָאֶמְצָעוּת נִבְחָר מִן הַקְּצָווֹת,[26] אוֹ מִן הַטַּעַם שֶׁיִּהְיֶה[27] בָּרוּךְ הוּא הַיּוֹדֵעַ. וּמִתּוֹךְ הֶכְשֵׁר הַמַּעֲשֶׂה וְטָהֳרַת הַמַּחֲשָׁבָה שֶׁיִּהְיֶה לָנוּ שָׁם, יַעֲלֶה שִׂכְלֵנוּ אֶל הַדְּבֵקוּת עִם הַשֵּׂכֶל הָעֶלְיוֹנִי[28], וְעַל דֶּרֶךְ הַפְּשָׁט עַל הַצַּד הַזֶּה נִפְרָשׁ שְׁרִיַּת הַשְּׁכִינָה בַּמָּקוֹם הַהוּא.[29] וְאַף עַל פִּי שֶׁהָאֱמֶת כִּי אָמְרוּ זִכְרוֹנָם לִבְרָכָה (מגילה כ"ח ע"א) קְדֻשָּׁתָן עֲלֵיהֶם אֲפִלּוּ כְּשֶׁהֵן שׁוֹמְמִין, שֶׁמַּשְׁמָע בָּזֶה שֶׁאֵין כָּל סִבַּת שְׁרִיַּת הַשְּׁכִינָה שָׁם מִצַּד הָעוֹבְדִים,[30]

---

**אוּלַי מִהְיוֹתוֹ אֶמְצָעוּת הָעוֹלָם בְּכִוּוּן** — **Perhaps** He chose this location **because it is precisely the center of the world,** **וְהָאֶמְצָעוּת נִבְחָר מִן הַקְּצָווֹת** — **and the center is more select than the edges,**[26] **אוֹ מִן הַטַּעַם שֶׁיִּהְיֶה** — **or,** perhaps He chose it **for** some other **reason that may exist.**[27] **בָּרוּךְ הוּא הַיּוֹדֵעַ** — **Blessed is He, Who knows** the reason!

Based on the above, Chinuch explains why the verse that is the source of this mitzvah states that when we build a Sanctuary for Hashem, He will "dwell" among us:

**וּמִתּוֹךְ הֶכְשֵׁר הַמַּעֲשֶׂה וְטָהֳרַת הַמַּחֲשָׁבָה שֶׁיִּהְיֶה לָנוּ שָׁם** — **By virtue of the rectitude of action and purity of thought that we will attain there,** **יַעֲלֶה שִׂכְלֵנוּ אֶל הַדְּבֵקוּת עִם הַשֵּׂכֶל הָעֶלְיוֹנִי** — **our spiritual essence will rise to become joined with the Higher Spiritual Essence.**[28] **וְעַל דֶּרֶךְ הַפְּשָׁט עַל הַצַּד הַזֶּה נִפְרָשׁ שְׁרִיַּת הַשְּׁכִינָה בַּמָּקוֹם הַהוּא** — **On a basic level, this is the manner through which we are to explain the "resting" of the Divine Presence in that place,** i.e., the *Beis HaMikdash.*[29]

Chinuch addresses a difficulty with his explanation.

**וְאַף עַל פִּי שֶׁהָאֱמֶת כִּי אָמְרוּ זִכְרוֹנָם לִבְרָכָה קְדֻשָּׁתָן עֲלֵיהֶם אֲפִלּוּ כְּשֶׁהֵן שׁוֹמְמִין** — **Now, although it is true that the Sages, of blessed memory, said** (see *Megillah* 28a) that **"the sanctity [of the Temples] remains upon them even when they are desolate,"** i.e., the Temple area retains its sanctity even when the First *Beis HaMikdash* as well as the Second are destroyed, **שֶׁמַּשְׁמָע בָּזֶה שֶׁאֵין כָּל סִבַּת שְׁרִיַּת הַשְּׁכִינָה שָׁם מִצַּד הָעוֹבְדִים** — **which implies that the reason why the Divine Presence "rests" there is not entirely because of the ones who are performing its service,**[30] this is not a difficulty.

---

### NOTES

26. The location of the *Beis HaMikdash* is considered to be the "center" of the world (see *Yoma* 54b with *Maharsha, Chidushei Aggados* ד"ה מאמצעיתו נברא). Since the center of a thing is viewed as its choicest part, whereas the extremities are somewhat less desirable, Hashem chose the "center" of the world as the place where spiritual purity would prevail and Man would be elevated to recognize His Attributes. This is, after all, the ultimate purpose for which the world was created, so it is appropriate that the choicest part of the world be designated for it.

27. *Rambam* (*Hil. Beis HaBechirah* 2:1-2) writes that Mount Moriah, where the *Beis HaMikdash* was built [as stated in *II Chronicles* 3:1], is the place where Abraham bound his son Isaac as an offering at the *Akeidah* [as stated in *Genesis* 22:2]. Moreover, the Altar was built on the precise spot where Abraham built his altar for the *Akeidah*; that was the same spot where Noah built an altar and brought offerings when he exited the Ark after the Flood [see *Genesis* 8:20]; that was the spot where Cain and Abel brought their offerings [*Genesis* 4:3-4], and where Adam brought an offering on the day of his creation [see *Chullin* 60a]; and that is the very spot from which Adam was created. Thus, man originated from the precise location where he receives atonement for his transgressions.

28. [Literally: *our intellect will rise to become joined with the Higher intellect.* Chinuch, throughout this mitzvah and often in this work, uses the term שֵׂכֶל, "intellect," to refer to spirituality, or to what we would call the spirit or soul. See note 32 to the Author's Introduction (Vol. I, p. 13). See also below, at note 46.]

29. Nowhere in the world can man recognize and incorporate within himself the Attributes of Hashem as he can in the *Beis HaMikdash*. In this simple sense, the *Beis HaMikdash* is considered a place where the Presence of God "rests"; since it is the place where man is most able to recognize and become joined with Hashem, from a human perspective it may be considered His "dwelling" (cf. *Ramban, Exodus* 29:46; *Rabbeinu Bachya* ad loc. and *Numbers* 15:41).

30. If holiness remains in the place of the *Beis HaMikdash* even when the Jewish people are no longer able to perform any service there, it would seem that the place carries intrinsic holiness. This is inconsistent with Chinuch's assertion that the Divine Presence "rests" there in the sense that through our performance of the *avodah* in that place we are inspired to recognize Hashem.

אֶפְשָׁר לוֹמַר כִּי אוֹתוֹ הַמָּקוֹם בְּחָרוֹ הָאֵל לְבָרֵךְ בְּנֵי הָאָדָם אֲשֶׁר בָּרָא מִמֶּנּוּ[31], כְּמוֹ שֶׁאָמַרְנוּ[32], וּכְמוֹ שֶׁהָיָה חֶפְצוֹ לִשְׁלֹחַ לִבְנֵי אָדָם נָבִיא לְהוֹרוֹתָם דֶּרֶךְ יֵלְכוּ בָהּ וְיִזְכּוּ לְקִיּוּם נַפְשׁוֹתָם, כְּמוֹ כֵן חָפֵץ בַּחֲסָדָיו הַגְּדוֹלִים לִקְבֹּעַ לָהֶם מָקוֹם בָּאָרֶץ שֶׁיִּהְיֶה נָכוֹן אֶל טוֹבַת הַבְּרִיּוֹת וּזְכוּתָם[33], וְכָל זֶה מֵחֲסָדָיו עַל בְּרִיּוֹתָיו. וּמִכָּל מָקוֹם לְעוֹלָם תִּתְרַבֶּה שָׁם הַבְּרָכָה וְהַקְּדֻשָּׁה לְפִי הַפְּעֻלּוֹת הַטּוֹבוֹת שֶׁיַּעֲשׂוּ שָׁם בְּנֵי־אָדָם, וְאָז עִם הַפְּעֻלּוֹת הַטּוֹבוֹת יִפְתְּחוּ מַעְיְנוֹת הַטּוֹב כְּנֶגְדּוֹ, כִּי בֶּאֱמֶת אֵינוֹ דוֹמֶה קְדֻשַּׁת הַמָּקוֹם בְּחָרְבָּנוֹ לִקְדֻשָּׁתוֹ בְּיִשּׁוּבוֹ[34].

וְהֻנַּחַת הַטַּעַם הַזֶּה בְּעִנְיַן הַבַּיִת תְּחַיֵּב אוֹתָנוּ גַּם כֵּן לִסְמֹךְ אֶל הַטַּעַם הַזֶּה בְּעַצְמוֹ לְפִי הַפְּשָׁט עִנְיַן הַקָּרְבָּנוֹת, וְשֵׁבֶט עוֹבֵד, וְכֵלִים יְקָרִים יְדוּעִים[35].

---

**אֶפְשָׁר לוֹמַר** — **It is possible to say** the following in explanation of the matter: Indeed, the place of the *Beis HaMikdash* has a degree of sanctity even without our performing any service there, but the reason is **כִּי אוֹתוֹ הַמָּקוֹם בְּחָרוֹ הָאֵל לְבָרֵךְ בְּנֵי הָאָדָם אֲשֶׁר בָּרָא מִמֶּנּוּ** — **that the Almighty chose that location** to be a place of sanctity **in order to** thereby **bless mankind, whom He created from there,**[31] **כְּמוֹ שֶׁאָמַרְנוּ** — **as we have said.**[32] **וּכְמוֹ שֶׁהָיָה חֶפְצוֹ לִשְׁלֹחַ לִבְנֵי אָדָם נָבִיא** — **For just as it was His Will to send mankind prophets,** **לְהוֹרוֹתָם דֶּרֶךְ יֵלְכוּ בָהּ** — **to teach [mankind] the proper path on which to go,** **וְיִזְכּוּ לְקִיּוּם נַפְשׁוֹתָם** — **so that they would merit continuity for their souls** in the World to Come, **כְּמוֹ כֵן חָפֵץ בַּחֲסָדָיו הַגְּדוֹלִים** — **so too did He will, in His great benevolence,** **לִקְבֹּעַ לָהֶם מָקוֹם בָּאָרֶץ** **שֶׁיִּהְיֶה נָכוֹן אֶל טוֹבַת הַבְּרִיּוֹת** — **to establish for them a place on earth** **וּזְכוּתָם** — **that would be prepared** with sanctity **for the betterment of mankind and** where they could achieve **merit;**[33] **וְכָל זֶה מֵחֲסָדָיו עַל בְּרִיּוֹתָיו** — **all this is** a manifestation **of [Hashem's] benevolence toward His creations.** **וּמִכָּל מָקוֹם לְעוֹלָם תִּתְרַבֶּה שָׁם הַבְּרָכָה וְהַקְּדֻשָּׁה** — **But nevertheless,** although the place is sanctified and blessed by Hashem even without our performance of any service, **the blessing and holiness will always increase there** **לְפִי הַפְּעֻלּוֹת הַטּוֹבוֹת שֶׁיַּעֲשׂוּ שָׁם בְּנֵי־אָדָם** — **commensurate with the worthy activities that people perform there;** **וְאָז עִם הַפְּעֻלּוֹת הַטּוֹבוֹת** — **and then, with the** increase in **worthy activities,** **יִפְתְּחוּ מַעְיְנוֹת הַטּוֹב כְּנֶגְדּוֹ** — **the wellsprings** **of God's goodness will open correspondingly.** **כִּי בֶּאֱמֶת אֵינוֹ דוֹמֶה קְדֻשַּׁת הַמָּקוֹם בְּחָרְבָּנוֹ לִקְדֻשָּׁתוֹ בְּיִשּׁוּבוֹ** — **For in truth, the holiness of the place** of the *Beis HaMikdash* **when it is destroyed is not comparable to its holiness when it is settled,** i.e., when the *Beis HaMikdash* is standing.[34]

Chinuch continues with this line of reasoning, explaining various aspects of the *Beis HaMikdash* service: **וְהֻנַּחַת הַטַּעַם הַזֶּה בְּעִנְיַן הַבַּיִת** — **Having established this** as the **reason for the** essential **matter of** building **the Temple,** **תְּחַיֵּב אוֹתָנוּ גַּם כֵּן לִסְמֹךְ אֶל הַטַּעַם הַזֶּה בְּעַצְמוֹ** — **we are compelled to similarly relate to this very reason** **לְפִי הַפְּשָׁט** — **the explanation, on a basic level,** **עִנְיַן הַקָּרְבָּנוֹת** — of **the subject of the sacrificial offerings,** **וְשֵׁבֶט עוֹבֵד** — of **having a designated tribe that performs the service** in the Temple (i.e., the Kohanim of the tribe of Levi), **וְכֵלִים יְקָרִים יְדוּעִים** — **and** of **having precious utensils,** whose description is **well known,** in the Temple.[35]

---

### NOTES

31. See note 27.

32. I.e., the purpose of designating a place where His Presence would "dwell" and be manifest is not for His benefit, but for the benefit of mankind, as asserted above.

33. Just as Hashem takes the initiative to bestow prophecy onto a prophet so that people will heed his admonitions and improve their actions, so too, He took the initiative to impart holiness to the location of the *Beis HaMikdash*, so that people would draw close to Him through basking in the Divine Presence that rests there.

34. Although some holiness is present even when the *Beis HaMikdash* is not there, that holiness is increased considerably when the *Beis HaMikdash* is standing and the *avodah* is being performed. This is consistent with the essential concept that Chinuch expressed — that Hashem's "Presence" in the *Beis HaMikdash* is an expression of our becoming joined with Him as a result of the purity we attain by performing the *avodah* there.

35. Having concluded that the purpose of the mitzvah to *build* a *Beis HaMikdash* is for the benefit of mankind, Chinuch explains that many of the mitzvos that pertain to the *service* in the *Beis HaMikdash* should be understood in a similar vein. [Chinuch will proceed to explain the concept of sacrificial offerings on the basis of his earlier words. In the mitzvos that follow, he will expand these ideas with regard to the obligations

**221 □ TERUMAH / MITZVAH 95: THE OBLIGATION TO BUILD THE HOLY TEMPLE**

הֲלֹא אָמַרְנוּ כִּי עִקְרֵי הַלְּבָבוֹת תְּלוּיִין אַחַר הַפְּעֻלּוֹת, וְעַל־כֵּן כִּי יֶחֱטָא אִישׁ, לֹא יִטְהַר לִבּוֹ יָפֶה בְּדָבָר שְׂפָתַיִם לְבַד, שֶׁיֹּאמַר בֵּינוֹ וְלַכֹּתֶל חָטָאתִי לֹא אוֹסִיף עוֹד, אֲבָל בַּעֲשׂוֹתוֹ מַעֲשֶׂה גָּדוֹל עַל דְּבַר חֶטְאוֹ, לָקַחַת מִמִּכְלְאוֹתָיו עַתּוּדִים וְלִטְרֹחַ לַהֲבִיאָם אֶל הַבַּיִת הַנָּכוֹן אֶל הַכֹּהֵן, וְכָל הַמַּעֲשֶׂה הַכָּתוּב בְּקָרְבְּנֵי הַחוֹטְאִים,[36] מִתּוֹךְ כָּל הַמַּעֲשֶׂה הַגָּדוֹל הַהוּא יִקְבַּע בְּנַפְשׁוֹ רֹעַ הַחֵטְא, וְיִמָּנַע מִמֶּנּוּ פַּעַם אַחֶרֶת.[37] וּכְעֵין טַעַם זֶה מָצָאתִי לָרַמְבַּ״ן זִכְרוֹנוֹ לִבְרָכָה עַל צַד הַפְּשָׁט, שֶׁכָּתַב בְּשֵׁם אֲחֵרִים, וְזֶה לְשׁוֹנוֹ,[38] כִּי בַּעֲבוּר שֶׁמַּעֲשֵׂה בְּנֵי אָדָם נִגְמָרִים בְּמַחֲשָׁבָה וּבְדִבּוּר וּבְמַעֲשֶׂה, צִוָּה הַשֵּׁם יִתְבָּרַךְ כִּי כַאֲשֶׁר יֶחֱטָא יָבִיא קָרְבָּן וְיִסְמֹךְ עָלָיו יָדָיו כְּנֶגֶד הַמַּעֲשֶׂה, וְיִתְוַדֶּה בְּפִיו כְּנֶגֶד הַדִּבּוּר, וְיִשְׂרֹף[39] בָּאֵשׁ הַקֶּרֶב וְהַכְּלָיוֹת שֶׁהֵם כְּלֵי הַמַּחֲשָׁבָה וְהַתַּאֲוָה, וּכְרָעַיִם כְּנֶגֶד יָדָיו וְרַגְלָיו שֶׁל אָדָם הָעוֹשִׂים

---

הֲלֹא אָמַרְנוּ כִּי עִקְרֵי הַלְּבָבוֹת תְּלוּיִין אַחַר הַפְּעֻלּוֹת — **Now, we have said that the essential** emotions **of a person's heart are linked to the actions** he performs. וְעַל־כֵּן — **It therefore follows that** כִּי יֶחֱטָא אִישׁ לֹא יִטְהַר לִבּוֹ יָפֶה בְּדָבָר שְׂפָתַיִם לְבַד — **if a person sins, his heart will not become completely cleansed through mere utterances of** his lips, שֶׁיֹּאמַר בֵּינוֹ וְלַכֹּתֶל — **by saying in** private, "**between him and the wall,**" where no one but God hears: חָטָאתִי לֹא אוֹסִיף עוֹד — "**I have sinned, and will not continue** to sin **further.**" אֲבָל בַּעֲשׂוֹתוֹ מַעֲשֶׂה גָּדוֹל עַל דְּבַר חֶטְאוֹ — **However, by engaging in an extensive procedure with regard to his sin,** לָקַחַת מִמִּכְלְאוֹתָיו עַתּוּדִים — in which **he must take goats from his pens,** וְלִטְרֹחַ לַהֲבִיאָם אֶל הַבַּיִת הַנָּכוֹן אֶל הַכֹּהֵן — **and trouble himself to bring them to the established Temple, to the Kohen,** וְכָל הַמַּעֲשֶׂה הַכָּתוּב בְּקָרְבְּנֵי הַחוֹטְאִים — **and** to follow **the entire procedure that is written regarding the offerings of sinners**[36] — מִתּוֹךְ כָּל הַמַּעֲשֶׂה הַגָּדוֹל הַהוּא יִקְבַּע בְּנַפְשׁוֹ רֹעַ הַחֵטְא — **through** engaging in **that entire extensive procedure, he will establish in his soul the evil** nature **of the sin,** וְיִמָּנַע מִמֶּנּוּ פַּעַם אַחֶרֶת — **and he will** thus **refrain from it on a future occasion.**[37]

Chinuch cites a similar explanation: וּכְעֵין טַעַם זֶה מָצָאתִי לָרַמְבַּ״ן זִכְרוֹנוֹ לִבְרָכָה — **I have found a similar reason** offered **by** *Ramban,* **of blessed memory,** עַל צַד הַפְּשָׁט — to explain the concept of sacrificial offerings **on a basic level;** שֶׁכָּתַב בְּשֵׁם אֲחֵרִים — **he writes** this **in the name of others,** וְזֶה לְשׁוֹנוֹ — **and the following is** a quotation of **his language:**[38] כִּי בַּעֲבוּר שֶׁמַּעֲשֵׂה בְּנֵי אָדָם נִגְמָרִים בְּמַחֲשָׁבָה וּבְדִבּוּר וּבְמַעֲשֶׂה — **For, since the actions of mankind are consummated through** the combination of **thought, speech, and action,** צִוָּה הַשֵּׁם יִתְבָּרַךְ — **Hashem, blessed be He, commanded** כִּי כַאֲשֶׁר יֶחֱטָא יָבִיא קָרְבָּן — **that when** a person **sins, he must bring an offering** to atone for all these components of his sin. וְיִסְמֹךְ עָלָיו יָדָיו כְּנֶגֶד הַמַּעֲשֶׂה — **He must lean his hands upon it, which corresponds to the action** of his sin, וְיִתְוַדֶּה בְּפִיו כְּנֶגֶד הַדִּבּוּר — **and must verbally confess** his sin, **which corresponds to the** sin's **speech** component. וְיִשְׂרֹף בָּאֵשׁ הַקֶּרֶב וְהַכְּלָיוֹת שֶׁהֵם כְּלֵי הַמַּחֲשָׁבָה וְהַתַּאֲוָה — **Then,** after slaughtering the offering, he[39] **must burn** upon the Altar **the innards and the kidneys, as they are the organs of thought and desire** that led him to sin, וּכְרָעַיִם כְּנֶגֶד יָדָיו וְרַגְלָיו שֶׁל אָדָם הָעוֹשִׂים

---

**NOTES**

pertaining to the holy utensils of the *Beis HaMikdash* and the specific services performed there. See Mitzvos 96-110; see also Mitzvah 186.]

36. As set forth in Mitzvos 121, 123, 128, and 129, among others.

37. Obviously, an offering does not undo the sin that preceded it, nor is it a gift to placate Hashem after having violated His Will. How then does it achieve atonement for the sin? Chinuch explains that, like other mitzvos, an offering serves to elevate man. By going through the trouble of bringing an offering, the sinner will focus on the great upheaval his sin has caused, and will be reluctant to repeat it. Having elevated himself above his sin in this manner, he achieves atonement. This, then, is another application of the principle that a man's actions affect his attitudes.

38. What follows is a direct quote from *Ramban*'s Commentary to *Leviticus* (1:9). *Ramban* develops the concept further elsewhere (*Toras Hashem Temimah, Kisvei Ramban,* Chavel ed., p. 163), where he cites this concept in the name of *Ibn Ezra.* See also *Rabbeinu Bachya, Leviticus* loc. cit.

39. I.e., the Kohen, who performs the service on behalf of the sinner.

## 222 ☐ תרומה / מצוה צה: מצות בנין בית הבחירה

כָּל מְלַאכְתּוֹ, וְיִזְרֹק הַדָּם עַל הַמִּזְבֵּחַ כְּנֶגֶד דָּמוֹ בְּנַפְשׁוֹ,[40] כְּדֵי שֶׁיַּחֲשֹׁב אָדָם בַּעֲשׂוֹתוֹ כָּל אֵלֶּה כִּי חָטָא לֵאלֹהִים בְּגוּפוֹ וְנַפְשׁוֹ, וְרָאוּי לוֹ שֶׁיִּשָּׁפֵךְ דָּמוֹ וְיִשָּׂרֵף גּוּפוֹ, לוּלֵי חֶסֶד הַבּוֹרֵא שֶׁלָּקַח מִמֶּנּוּ תְּמוּרָה וְכֹפֶר הַקָּרְבָּן, שֶׁיִּהְיֶה דָּמוֹ תַּחַת דָּמוֹ, נֶפֶשׁ תַּחַת נֶפֶשׁ, וְרָאשֵׁי אֵבְרֵי הַקָּרְבָּן כְּנֶגֶד רָאשֵׁי אֵבָרָיו,[41] וְהַמָּנוֹת לְהַחֲיוֹת בָּהֶן מוֹרֵי הַתּוֹרָה[42] שֶׁיִּתְפַּלְּלוּ עָלָיו, וְקָרְבַּן הַתָּמִיד[43] בַּעֲבוּר שֶׁלֹּא יִנָּצְלוּ הָרַבִּים מֵחֲטֹא תָּמִיד, וְאֵלֶּה דְּבָרִים מִתְקַבְּלִין מוֹשְׁכִין הַלֵּב כְּדִבְרֵי הַגָּדָה,[44] עַד כָּאן. וְהֶאֱרִיךְ הוּא עוֹד בָּעִנְיָן, וְכָתַב, וְעַל דֶּרֶךְ הָאֱמֶת יֵשׁ בַּקָּרְבָּנוֹת סוֹד נֶעְלָם וְכוּ׳, כְּמוֹ שֶׁכָּתוּב בְּפֵרוּשָׁיו בְּפָרָשַׁת וַיִּקְרָא.

---

כָּל מְלַאכְתּוֹ — **and also the legs** of some offerings, **corresponding to the hands and legs of man, which carry out all his activities.** וְיִזְרֹק הַדָּם עַל הַמִּזְבֵּחַ — **Furthermore, he must sprinkle the blood** of the offering **upon the Altar,** כְּנֶגֶד דָּמוֹ בְּנַפְשׁוֹ — **as it corresponds to the "blood of his soul."**[40] כְּדֵי שֶׁיַּחֲשֹׁב אָדָם בַּעֲשׂוֹתוֹ כָּל אֵלֶּה — This is **in order that a person should contemplate, while performing all these** procedures, כִּי חָטָא לֵאלֹהִים בְּגוּפוֹ וְנַפְשׁוֹ — **that he sinned to God** with **both his body and his soul,** וְרָאוּי לוֹ שֶׁיִּשָּׁפֵךְ דָּמוֹ וְיִשָּׂרֵף גּוּפוֹ — **and** that **it would be appropriate for his** own **blood to be spilled and his** own **body to be burned,** לוּלֵי חֶסֶד הַבּוֹרֵא — **were it not for the benevolence of the Creator,** שֶׁלָּקַח מִמֶּנּוּ תְּמוּרָה וְכֹפֶר הַקָּרְבָּן — **Who accepted from him a substitute and ransom** — that being **the** sacrificial **offering,** שֶׁיִּהְיֶה דָּמוֹ תַּחַת דָּמוֹ, נֶפֶשׁ תַּחַת נֶפֶשׁ — **whose blood is to be** sprinkled upon the Altar **instead of his blood, "a life for a life,"** וְרָאשֵׁי אֵבְרֵי הַקָּרְבָּן כְּנֶגֶד רָאשֵׁי אֵבָרָיו — **and the primary limbs of the sacrificial offering** are burned, **corresponding to [the sinner's] own primary limbs.**[41] וְהַמָּנוֹת לְהַחֲיוֹת בָּהֶן מוֹרֵי הַתּוֹרָה שֶׁיִּתְפַּלְּלוּ עָלָיו — **And the** remaining meat **portions** of the offering are designated **to sustain** the Kohanim, who are **the ones who teach the Torah** to the people,[42] **so that they will pray for him.** The preceding applies to an offering brought by an individual to atone for his personal sin. וְקָרְבַּן הַתָּמִיד — **The** twice-daily communal *tamid* **offering,** too,[43] although it is not associated with a specific sin, can be understood on this basis, בַּעֲבוּר שֶׁלֹּא יִנָּצְלוּ הָרַבִּים מֵחֲטֹא תָּמִיד — **because the masses cannot avoid sinning regularly,** and thus are always in need of a degree of atonement. וְאֵלֶּה דְּבָרִים מִתְקַבְּלִין — **Now, these are plausible words** מוֹשְׁכִין הַלֵּב כְּדִבְרֵי הַגָּדָה — that **"attract the heart like words of Aggadah."**[44] עַד כָּאן — **Until here** is a quote from *Ramban*. וְהֶאֱרִיךְ הוּא עוֹד בָּעִנְיָן — **He discussed the matter further at length,** וְכָתַב, וְעַל דֶּרֶךְ הָאֱמֶת יֵשׁ בַּקָּרְבָּנוֹת סוֹד נֶעְלָם וְכוּ׳ — **and** also **wrote** there: **"According to the true** (i.e., Kabbalistic) **approach, the** concept of the sacrificial **offerings contains a hidden secret etc.,"** כְּמוֹ שֶׁכָּתוּב בְּפֵרוּשָׁיו בְּפָרָשַׁת וַיִּקְרָא — **as is written in his commentary to *Parashas Vayikra*** (1:9).

Chinuch expands his explanation of how sacrificial offerings help a person avoid further sin:

---

### NOTES

40. See *Leviticus* 17:14.

41. *Rabbeinu Bachya* (ibid.) adds that there is precedent for understanding the concept of an offering in this manner, in the well-known Midrash that states (*Tanchuma, Shelach* §14, cited by *Rashi, Genesis* 22:13) that when Abraham offered a ram as a sacrifice in the place of Isaac, he prayed repeatedly with regard to each aspect of the service that it should be considered as though the service were being performed upon Isaac.

42. The meat of a *chatas* (sin) offering or an *asham* (guilt) offering may be eaten only by male Kohanim (see Mitzvah 102). They were the primary disseminators of Torah among the Jewish people — see *Deuteronomy* 17:9 and 33:10. [In Mitzvah 102 (at note 5), Chinuch cites the teaching of our Sages that the Kohanim's consumption of the meat of these offerings contributed to the atonement for the owners' sin.]

43. See Mitzvah 401.

44. Paraphrase of *Shabbos* 87a. [Aggadah is the portion of Torah that includes inspirational narratives and expositions of Scripture, which appeal to man's thoughts and emotions.]

וְעוֹד נוֹסִיף דְּבָרִים עַל צַד הַפְּשָׁט, וְנֹאמַר כִּי מִזֶּה הַשֹּׁרֶשׁ צִוָּנוּ הָאֵל לְהַקְרִיב לְעוֹלָם מֵהַדְּבָרִים שֶׁלֵּב אָדָם הוֹמֶה בָּהֶן, כְּמוֹ הַבָּשָׂר וְהַיַּיִן וְהַפַּת, כְּדֵי שֶׁיִּתְעוֹרֵר הַלֵּב יוֹתֵר עִם הָעֵסֶק בָּהֶם, וּלְעָנִי חִיֵּב לְהָבִיא מִמְעַט קִמְחוֹ אֲשֶׁר עֵינָיו וְלִבּוֹ עָלָיו כָּל הַיּוֹם.[45] וְעוֹד יֵשׁ הִתְעוֹרְרוּת אַחֵר לַלֵּב בְּקָרְבַּן הַבְּהֵמוֹת מִצַּד הַדִּמְיוֹן, שֶׁגּוּף הָאָדָם וְהַבְּהֵמָה יִדְמוּ בְּכָל עִנְיָנִים, לֹא יִתְחַלְּקוּ, רַק שֶׁבָּזֶה נָתַן הַשֵּׂכֶל[46] וְלֹא בָּזֶה, וּבִהְיוֹת גּוּף הָאָדָם יוֹצֵא מִגֶּדֶר הַשֵּׂכֶל בְּעֵת הַחֵטְא, יֵשׁ לוֹ לָדַעַת שֶׁנִּכְנַס בָּעֵת הַהִיא בְּגֶדֶר הַבְּהֵמוֹת אַחַר שֶׁלֹּא יְחַלְּקֵם רַק הוּא לְבַדּוֹ,[47] וְעַל כֵּן נִצְטַוָּה לָקַחַת גּוּף בָּשָׂר כְּגוּפוֹ, וְלַהֲבִיאוֹ אֶל הַמָּקוֹם הַנִּבְחָר לְעִלּוּי הַשֵּׂכֶל וּלְשָׂרְפוֹ שָׁם וּלְהַשְׁכִּיחַ זִכְרוֹ, כָּלִיל יִהְיֶה,[48] לֹא יִזָּכֵר וְלֹא יִפָּקֵד, תַּחַת גּוּפוֹ, כְּדֵי לְצַיֵּר בִּלְבָבוֹ צִיּוּר חָזָק שֶׁכָּל עִנְיָנוֹ שֶׁל גּוּף בְּלִי שֵׂכֶל אָבֵד וּבָטֵל לְגַמְרֵי,

---

**וְעוֹד נוֹסִיף דְּבָרִים עַל צַד הַפְּשָׁט** — Let us add further comments to that which was previously stated, continuing on the basic level, **וְנֹאמַר** — and say, **כִּי מִזֶּה הַשֹּׁרֶשׁ** — that due to this underlying purpose **צִוָּנוּ הָאֵל לְהַקְרִיב לְעוֹלָם מֵהַדְּבָרִים שֶׁלֵּב אָדָם הוֹמֶה בָּהֶן** — the Almighty commanded us to always bring offerings only from things that excite a person's heart, **כְּמוֹ הַבָּשָׂר וְהַיַּיִן וְהַפַּת** — such as meat, wine, and bread, **כְּדֵי שֶׁיִּתְעוֹרֵר הַלֵּב יוֹתֵר עִם הָעֵסֶק בָּהֶם** — in order that the heart be more inspired when engaged in the service of [the offerings]. **וּלְעָנִי חִיֵּב לְהָבִיא מִמְעַט קִמְחוֹ** — Similarly, He obligated a poor person who cannot afford an animal to bring an offering from the little flour that he possesses (Mitzvah 123), **אֲשֶׁר עֵינָיו וְלִבּוֹ עָלָיו כָּל הַיּוֹם** — upon which his eyes and heart are focused all day.[45]

**וְעוֹד יֵשׁ הִתְעוֹרְרוּת אַחֵר לַלֵּב בְּקָרְבַּן הַבְּהֵמוֹת** — There is yet another element of inspiration to the heart through the service of an animal offering, **מִצַּד הַדִּמְיוֹן** — from the perspective of imagery. **שֶׁגּוּף הָאָדָם וְהַבְּהֵמָה יִדְמוּ בְּכָל עִנְיָנִים** — For the bodies of a person and an animal are similar in all their features; **לֹא יִתְחַלְּקוּ, רַק שֶׁבָּזֶה נָתַן הַשֵּׂכֶל וְלֹא בָּזֶה** — there is no difference between them, except that into this one (man) [God] imparted spirituality[46] and into that one (an animal) He did not. **וּבִהְיוֹת גּוּף הָאָדָם יוֹצֵא מִגֶּדֶר הַשֵּׂכֶל בְּעֵת הַחֵטְא** — And, since man's physicality abandons the jurisdiction of his spirituality at the time when he commits a sin, **יֵשׁ לוֹ לָדַעַת שֶׁנִּכְנַס בָּעֵת הַהִיא בְּגֶדֶר הַבְּהֵמוֹת** — he must know that at that time he entered into the category of animals, **אַחַר שֶׁלֹּא יְחַלְּקֵם רַק הוּא לְבַדּוֹ** — since there is nothing that distinguishes between them (i.e., man and animal) other than [his spirituality] alone.[47] **וְעַל כֵּן נִצְטַוָּה לָקַחַת גּוּף בָּשָׂר כְּגוּפוֹ** — He is therefore commanded to take a body formed of flesh like his own body, **וְלַהֲבִיאוֹ אֶל הַמָּקוֹם הַנִּבְחָר לְעִלּוּי הַשֵּׂכֶל** — and to bring it to the place that was chosen for the enhancement of spirituality, i.e., the Temple, **וּלְשָׂרְפוֹ שָׁם וּלְהַשְׁכִּיחַ זִכְרוֹ** — to burn it there, and to thus obliterate any memory of it — **כָּלִיל יִהְיֶה** — "it shall be entirely [burned],"[48] **לֹא יִזָּכֵר וְלֹא יִפָּקֵד** — neither mentioned nor remembered thereafter — **תַּחַת גּוּפוֹ** — in lieu of his own body. **כְּדֵי לְצַיֵּר בִּלְבָבוֹ צִיּוּר חָזָק** — This is done in order to create in his mind a powerful image — **שֶׁכָּל עִנְיָנוֹ שֶׁל גּוּף בְּלִי שֵׂכֶל אָבֵד וּבָטֵל לְגַמְרֵי** — that any aspect

---

## NOTES

45. This fits with the concept that the purpose of the offerings is to arouse a person's heart to genuine repentance.

46. Literally, *intellect*. See note 28.

47. As the author explained at length in his introduction to Sefer HaChinuch (Vol. I, pp. 12-17), and as he reiterates in numerous other places in this work (e.g., Mitzvos 313, 421), man is comprised of two aspects: the physical and the spiritual. His physical dimension gives him animal desires, and it is the function of his spiritual dimension to hold his physicality in check, so as to remain faithful to the laws of the Torah and to attain closeness to God. One who sins has obviously allowed his physicality to overpower his spiritual dimension, and he is thus analogous to a beast.

[Although the sacrificial offerings generally atone only for unintentional sins (see below), it is nevertheless due to man's animalistic dimension that even the unintentional sins occur. For, on account of his corporeal instincts, man has a tendency to act in a manner that is inconsistent with the Will of Hashem, and it is this tendency that brought about even his unintentional sin (*Beis Elokim, Shaar HaTeshuvah* Ch. 6).]

48. Paraphrase of *Leviticus* 6:16.

וְיִשְׂמַח בְּחֶלְקוֹ בַּנֶּפֶשׁ הַמַּשְׂכֶּלֶת שֶׁחֲנָנוּ הָאֵל שֶׁהִיא קַיֶּמֶת לְעוֹלָם, וְגַם לַגּוּף הַשֻּׁתָּף עִמָּהּ יֵשׁ קִיּוּם בַּתְּחִיָּה בְּסִבָּתָהּ בְּלֶכְתּוֹ בַּעֲצָתָהּ, כְּלוֹמַר שֶׁיִּשָּׁמֵר מִן הַחֵטְא, וּבְקָבְעוֹ צִיּוּר זֶה בְּנַפְשׁוֹ יִזָּהֵר מִן הַחֵטְא הַרְבֵּה, וְהִבְטִיחָה הַתּוֹרָה שֶׁבַּמַּעֲשֶׂה הַגָּדוֹל הַזֶּה וּבְהַסְכָּמַת עוֹשֵׂהוּ שֶׁיִּתְנַחֵם עַל חֶטְאוֹ מִלֵּב וּמִנֶּפֶשׁ, תְּכֻפַּר אֵלָיו שִׁגְגָתוֹ. אֲבָל הַזְּדוֹנוֹת לֹא יַסְפִּיק לְכַפְּרָם דִּמְיוֹן זֶה, כִּי הַזָּד לֹא יִוָּכַח בְּדִמְיוֹנוֹת וּדְבָרִים, שֵׁבֶט לְגֵו כְּסִילִים.[49]

וְאַל יִקְשֶׁה עָלֶיךָ בְּהַנָּחַת טַעַם זֶה אֵיךְ נָבִיא קָרְבָּן נְדָבָה לְעוֹלָם,[50] כִּי טַעֲמֵנוּ זֶה יִסְבֹּל גַּם הַנְּדָבוֹת, שֶׁאַחַר שֶׁאָמַרְנוּ שֶׁהַקָּרְבָּן דִּמְיוֹן לְהַשְׁפָּלַת הַגּוּפוֹת וּלְעִלּוּי הַנְּפָשׁוֹת, אַף בְּלֹא חֵטְא יָדוּעַ יִמָּצֵא בּוֹ הַמַּקְרִיב תּוֹעֶלֶת לָקַחַת מוּסָר.

---

**of a body without spirituality is futile and totally void.** וְיִשְׂמַח בְּחֶלְקוֹ — **He will thus rejoice with his lot,** בַּנֶּפֶשׁ הַמַּשְׂכֶּלֶת שֶׁחֲנָנוּ הָאֵל — that is, **with the spiritual soul that the Almighty graciously granted him —** שֶׁהִיא קַיֶּמֶת לְעוֹלָם — **for [the soul] is everlasting,** וְגַם לַגּוּף הַשֻּׁתָּף עִמָּהּ יֵשׁ קִיּוּם בַּתְּחִיָּה בְּסִבָּתָהּ — **and because of it, the body that is partnered with it also can have everlasting** life in the Revivification of the Dead, בְּלֶכְתּוֹ בַּעֲצָתָהּ — **when it proceeds according to [the soul's] counsel;** כְּלוֹמַר שֶׁיִּשָּׁמֵר מִן הַחֵטְא — **that is to say, when [the body] is careful to avoid sin.** וּבְקָבְעוֹ צִיּוּר זֶה בְּנַפְשׁוֹ — **And by affixing this image** (i.e., the view of the temporal nature of corporeality and the everlasting nature of the soul) **in his mind,** יִזָּהֵר מִן הַחֵטְא הַרְבֵּה — **he will be extremely cautious to avoid sin.** וְהִבְטִיחָה הַתּוֹרָה — **Thus, the Torah guaranteed** שֶׁבַּמַּעֲשֶׂה הַגָּדוֹל הַזֶּה — **that through this great act** of bringing an offering and following through all its procedures, וּבְהַסְכָּמַת עוֹשֵׂהוּ שֶׁיִּתְנַחֵם עַל חֶטְאוֹ מִלֵּב וּמִנֶּפֶשׁ — **along with the resolution of the one making [the offering] that he regrets his sin with his heart and soul,** תְּכֻפַּר אֵלָיו שִׁגְגָתוֹ — **he will attain atonement for his unintentional sin.** אֲבָל הַזְּדוֹנוֹת — **However,** with regard to **intentional sins,** לֹא יַסְפִּיק לְכַפְּרָם דִּמְיוֹן זֶה — an exercise that is based upon **this symbolism is not sufficient to atone for them,** כִּי הַזָּד לֹא יִוָּכַח בְּדִמְיוֹנוֹת וּדְבָרִים — **for an intentional sinner is not chastened with imagery or words;** שֵׁבֶט "לְגֵו כְּסִילִים" — rather, as the verse states (*Proverbs* 26:3): ***a rod for the back of fools.***[49]

Chinuch addresses a difficulty one may have with the reason he offered for the sacrificial offerings: וְאַל יִקְשֶׁה עָלֶיךָ בְּהַנָּחַת טַעַם זֶה — **Let it not trouble you, with regard to this suggested reason** for the sacrificial offerings (that it is to remind the sinner of his animalistic tendencies): אֵיךְ נָבִיא קָרְבָּן נְדָבָה לְעוֹלָם — If so, **how** is it that **we ever bring a donated offering,** i.e., an offering that one donates voluntarily, not on account of a sin?[50] כִּי טַעֲמֵנוּ זֶה יִסְבֹּל גַּם הַנְּדָבוֹת — **This is not a difficulty, for this reason of ours does** indeed **accommodate the donated [offerings] as well.** שֶׁאַחַר שֶׁאָמַרְנוּ שֶׁהַקָּרְבָּן דִּמְיוֹן לְהַשְׁפָּלַת הַגּוּפוֹת וּלְעִלּוּי הַנְּפָשׁוֹת — **Since we have said that** bringing **an offering is symbolic of the diminishing of the** physical **bodies and the enhancement of the** spiritual **souls,** אַף בְּלֹא חֵטְא יָדוּעַ יִמָּצֵא בּוֹ הַמַּקְרִיב תּוֹעֶלֶת לָקַחַת מוּסָר — **one who brings an offering can derive benefit from it even without** having committed **any known sin, by taking** from it the very same **ethical lesson,** namely, the importance of elevating one's spirituality over his physicality. Since internalizing this principle is vital to all people, whether they have sinned or not, the Torah provides the opportunity to bring a donated offering whenever one desires.

Chinuch proceeds to examine yet another type of offering. As part of the Yom Kippur service (Mitzvah 185), the Kohen Gadol would cast lots over two identical he-goats. One of the goats would be brought as an offering in the *Beis HaMikdash,* and the other, upon which he would confess the sins of the entire

---

NOTES

49. This verse refers to an intentional sinner who deliberately ignores his spiritual dimension in favor of the physical, for which reason he can certainly be described as a fool. He will change his ways only upon experiencing painful retribution for his misdeeds (see *Metzudas David* and *Malbim* ad loc.).

50. For example, the *olah* offering (Mitzvah 115) and the *shelamim* offering (Mitzvah 141) are most often brought voluntarily.

## 225 ❏ TERUMAH / MITZVAH 95: THE OBLIGATION TO BUILD THE HOLY TEMPLE

וּבְקָרְבַּן עֲזָאזֵל שֶׁנִּשְׁלַח חַי אֶל מְקוֹם הַחָרְבָּן וְהַכִּלָּיוֹן, נֹאמַר בִּפְשַׁט הָעִנְיָן, לְבַל יְדַמֶּה הַחוֹטֵא הַגָּמוּר שֶׁאַחַר שֶׁיְּקַבֵּל נַפְשׁוֹ עֹנֶשׁ עַל חֲטָאָיו, תָּשׁוּב לַעֲמֹד בִּמְקוֹם הַטּוֹבִים אוֹ תִּהְיֶה לָהּ הַשְׁאֵרוּת וְטוֹבָה קְצָת וַאֲפִלּוּ יִהְיֶה כְּיָרָבְעָם בֶּן נְבָט וַחֲבֵרָיו,[51] כְּמוֹ שֶׁהוּא רוֹאֶה כָּל הַשָּׁנָה כֻּלָּהּ, שֶׁיֵּשׁ לְגוּף הַבְּהֵמָה, שֶׁהוּא לְדִמְיוֹן גּוּף הַחוֹטֵא, הַשְׁאֵרוּת קְצָת בֵּית הַשֵּׁם יִתְבָּרַךְ בָּאֵפֶר שֶׁנִּשְׁאָר שָׁם בְּעֵת הַשְּׂרֵפָה, לֹא יוֹצִיאוּהוּ מִן הַבַּיִת עַד אַחַר זְמַן הַרְבֵּה,[52] עַל כֵּן בַּשָּׂעִיר הַחַי הַנּוֹשֵׂא כָּל הָעֲוֹנוֹת, יִרְאוּ רֶמֶז כִּי הַחוֹטֵא שֶׁעֲוֹנוֹתָיו מְרֻבִּין, כְּמוֹ הָאֶפִּיקוֹרוֹסִין וְשֶׁכָּפְרוּ בַּתּוֹרָה וּבִתְחִיַּת הַמֵּתִים וְכָל הַמְּצֵרִים לְיִשְׂרָאֵל בִּכְלָל, לֹא יִרְאוּ בְטוֹבָה לְעוֹלָם.[53]

---

Jewish nation, was designated for *"Azazel,"* i.e., it was brought to the wilderness and thrown from a cliff to its death (see *Rashi, Leviticus* 16:8). Chinuch explains this service on the basis of his earlier theme: וּבְקָרְבַּן עֲזָאזֵל — **As for the *Azazel* offering,** שֶׁנִּשְׁלַח חַי אֶל מְקוֹם הַחָרְבָּן וְהַכִּלָּיוֹן — **which was sent** while **alive to a place of desolation and utter destruction,** נֹאמַר בִּפְשַׁט הָעִנְיָן — **we will say, with regard to the simple meaning of the matter,** as follows: לְבַל יְדַמֶּה הַחוֹטֵא הַגָּמוּר — It is **in order that a complete sinner** (i.e., one who is completely wicked) **not suppose** שֶׁאַחַר שֶׁיְּקַבֵּל נַפְשׁוֹ עֹנֶשׁ עַל חֲטָאָיו — **that after his soul will receive punishment for its sins** תָּשׁוּב לַעֲמֹד בִּמְקוֹם הַטּוֹבִים — **it will revert to stand in the same place as** the souls of **the righteous ones,** אוֹ תִּהְיֶה לָהּ הַשְׁאֵרוּת וְטוֹבָה קְצָת — **or** that **it will have some continuity or benefit** in the World to Come, וַאֲפִלּוּ יִהְיֶה כְּיָרָבְעָם בֶּן נְבָט וַחֲבֵרָיו — **even if he were** as wicked **as Jeroboam ben Nebat and his comrades.**[51] כְּמוֹ שֶׁהוּא רוֹאֶה כָּל הַשָּׁנָה כֻּלָּהּ — **One might reach this erroneous conclusion by thinking that his situation is analogous to what he sees throughout the year,** שֶׁיֵּשׁ לְגוּף הַבְּהֵמָה, שֶׁהוּא לְדִמְיוֹן גּוּף הַחוֹטֵא הַשְׁאֵרוּת קְצָת בֵּית הַשֵּׁם יִתְבָּרַךְ — **that the body of the animal** brought as an offering, **which symbolizes the body of the sinner, has some** degree of **continuity in the Temple of Hashem, blessed be He,** בָּאֵפֶר שֶׁנִּשְׁאָר שָׁם בְּעֵת הַשְּׂרֵפָה — in the form of **ashes that remain there at the time of** its **burning** upon the Altar, לֹא יוֹצִיאוּהוּ מִן הַבַּיִת עַד אַחַר זְמַן הַרְבֵּה — **which they do not remove from the Temple until a long time has elapsed.**[52] עַל כֵּן — **Therefore,** the Torah provides a service to counter this error, בַּשָּׂעִיר הַחַי הַנּוֹשֵׂא כָּל הָעֲוֹנוֹת — for **through** the service of **"the he-goat that lives"** (i.e., the one that is not slaughtered in the *Beis HaMikdash* but is sent to *Azazel*), **which** by virtue of the Kohen Gadol's confession upon it **"carries all the sins** of the Jews" from the entire year (*Leviticus* 16:22), and is sent to die in the wilderness, יִרְאוּ רֶמֶז — **they will see an indication** כִּי הַחוֹטֵא שֶׁעֲוֹנוֹתָיו מְרֻבִּין — **that a sinner whose offenses are profuse,** כְּמוֹ הָאֶפִּיקוֹרוֹסִין וְשֶׁכָּפְרוּ בַּתּוֹרָה וּבִתְחִיַּת הַמֵּתִים — **such as heretics or those who have denied** the truth of **the Torah or the Revivification of the Dead,** וְכָל הַמְּצֵרִים לְיִשְׂרָאֵל בִּכְלָל — **and all the oppressors of the Jews are** also **included** in this category, לֹא יִרְאוּ בְטוֹבָה לְעוֹלָם — **will never see the benefits** of the World to Come,[53]

---

### NOTES

51. Jeroboam ben Nebat was the first king of the Kingdom of Israel. [This was the Northern Kingdom, primarily comprised of the Ten Tribes of Israel (aside from Judah and Benjamin) that broke away from the Kingdom of Judah during the reign of Rehoboam, son of Solomon (see *I Kings* 12:20).] Jeroboam feared that his subjects would return to the rule of Rehoboam if they were allowed to go up to serve Hashem in the *Beis HaMikdash* in Jerusalem. He therefore outlawed the tri-annual pilgrimage to Jerusalem, and substituted pilgrimages to idolatrous centers in his own kingdom. Since he not only sinned alone, but also caused the public to sin, he is commonly mentioned as a prototype of the worst category of sinner (see, for example, *Avos* 5:18).

52. According to Chinuch (see Mitzvah 131 and *Minchas Chinuch* there §7), the ashes of all the burnt offerings would be gathered into a single pile upon the Altar, which would remain there for long periods of time. This can be viewed as an indication that once a sinner has endured his punishment he will have a share in the World to Come, just as the offering, which is symbolic of a sinner, remains in an exalted position once it has been burnt. One might think this is true for *any* sinner, regardless of the extent of his wickedness!

53. See Mishnah, *Sanhedrin* 90a.

וְתוֹלַעְתָּם לֹא תָמוּת וְאִשָּׁם לֹא תִכְבֶּה[54], כְּמַעֲשֵׂה הַשָּׂעִיר בְּנָשְׂאוֹ רִבּוּי עֲוֹנוֹת כָּל יִשְׂרָאֵל יֻשְׁלַךְ לְגַמְרֵי אֶל אֶרֶץ גְּזֵרָה, לֹא יִמָּצֵא בֵּית הַשֵּׁם לֹא לִשְׁחִיטָה וְלֹא לִזְרִיקָה, זִכְרוֹ יֹאבַד מִנִּי אָרֶץ[55]. וְזֶהוּ שֶׁאָמְרוּ זִכְרוֹנָם לִבְרָכָה (ירושלמי יומא פ״א ה״ג) כִּי בְּשָׁעָה שֶׁיִּשְׂרָאֵל מְרַצִּין לֹא הִגִּיעַ לַחֲצִי הָהָר עַד שֶׁנַּעֲשָׂה אֵבָרִים אֵבָרִים, לְהוֹדִיעָן דִּמְיוֹן הַחוֹטֵא הַגָּמוּר כִּי כֵן יֹאבַד מְהֵרָה וְיִהְיֶה כָּלֶה כִּלָּיוֹן גָּמוּר, לְמַעַן יִלְמְדוּ וְיִקְחוּ מוּסָר וְיֵיטִיבוּ דַרְכֵיהֶם, וְזֶהוּ הַסִּימָן הַטּוֹב לָהֶם, שֶׁאֵין מְלַמֵּד מוּסָר אֶלָּא הָאוֹהֵב, כְּמוֹ שֶׁכָּתוּב (משלי י״ג, כ״ד) וְאֹהֲבוֹ שִׁחֲרוֹ מוּסָר.

וּבְעִנְיַן חִלּוּק הַקָּרְבָּנוֹת בִּשְׁחִיטָתָן וּבְמַתְּנוֹת הַדָּם וּבְחֵלֶק הַכֹּהֲנִים[56], וְיֶתֶר פְּרָטֵיהֶן רַבִּים, אִם נֹאמַר לְפִי הַפְּשָׁט שֶׁהָיָה כֵן לִהְיוֹת מַחֲשֶׁבֶת הָעוֹבֵד מְכֻוָּנוֹת אֶל הָעֲבוֹדָה הָרַבָּה,

---

"וְתוֹלַעְתָּם לֹא תָמוּת וְאִשָּׁם לֹא תִכְבֶּה" — as Scripture states (*Isaiah 66:24*): **their decay will not cease and their fire** (i.e., the fire that consumes them) **will not be extinguished.**[54] כְּמַעֲשֵׂה הַשָּׂעִיר — **Thus,** the fate of a "complete" sinner will be **similar to what is done with the** he-goat, בְּנָשְׂאוֹ רִבּוּי עֲוֹנוֹת כָּל יִשְׂרָאֵל — **which, because it carries the many sins of all of Israel,** יֻשְׁלַךְ לְגַמְרֵי אֶל אֶרֶץ גְּזֵרָה — **is entirely cast away into an uninhabited wasteland;** לֹא יִמָּצֵא בֵּית הַשֵּׁם לֹא לִשְׁחִיטָה וְלֹא לִזְרִיקָה — **it has no presence in the Temple of Hashem, neither to be slaughtered, nor to** have its blood **sprinkled** upon the Altar; זִכְרוֹ יֹאבַד מִנִּי אָרֶץ — **its memory shall be lost from the land.**[55] וְזֶהוּ שֶׁאָמְרוּ זִכְרוֹנָם לִבְרָכָה — **This is** the meaning of **what** [the Sages], of blessed memory, **said** (*Yerushalmi, Yoma 6:3*), כִּי בְּשָׁעָה שֶׁיִּשְׂרָאֵל מְרַצִּין — **that** in times **when the Jews were pleasing to God** לֹא הִגִּיעַ לַחֲצִי הָהָר עַד שֶׁנַּעֲשָׂה אֵבָרִים אֵבָרִים — [the Azazel goat] would not even reach **half of** its descent from **the mountain before it became entirely dismembered.** לְהוֹדִיעָן דִּמְיוֹן הַחוֹטֵא הַגָּמוּר — **This would convey to** [the people] **a symbol** of the fate of **a complete sinner,** כִּי כֵן יֹאבַד מְהֵרָה וְיִהְיֶה כָּלֶה כִּלָּיוֹן גָּמוּר — indicating **that he will similarly perish quickly and be subject to utter destruction,** לְמַעַן יִלְמְדוּ וְיִקְחוּ מוּסָר וְיֵיטִיבוּ דַרְכֵיהֶם — **and its purpose was in order that** [the Jews] **should learn and accept reproof** from it, **and thus improve their ways.** וְזֶהוּ הַסִּימָן הַטּוֹב לָהֶם — **This is** why it is **a good omen for** [the Jews] when the goat is subject to quick and utter destruction, שֶׁאֵין מְלַמֵּד מוּסָר אֶלָּא הָאוֹהֵב — **for only a devoted friend offers reproof,** כְּמוֹ שֶׁכָּתוּב — **as it is stated** (*Proverbs 13:24*): "וְאֹהֲבוֹ שִׁחֲרוֹ מוּסָר" — **One who spares his rod hates his child, but he who loves him disciplines him** in his youth.

Chinuch acknowledges that his explanation is inadequate to explain all the particulars of the various offering services:

וּבְעִנְיַן חִלּוּק הַקָּרְבָּנוֹת — **As for the matter of the differences among** the laws of **the offerings,** בִּשְׁחִיטָתָן וּבְמַתְּנוֹת הַדָּם וּבְחֵלֶק הַכֹּהֲנִים — **with regard to their slaughter, the application of their blood** to the Altar, **and the portions** awarded **to the Kohanim,**[56] וְיֶתֶר פְּרָטֵיהֶן רַבִּים — **as well as their many additional details,** אִם נֹאמַר לְפִי הַפְּשָׁט — **if we were to state, in accordance with the simple explanation** that we have followed (i.e., that man's actions in making the offerings are meant to positively impact his attitude), שֶׁהָיָה כֵן לִהְיוֹת מַחֲשֶׁבֶת הָעוֹבֵד מְכֻוָּנוֹת אֶל הָעֲבוֹדָה הָרַבָּה — **that it is subject** to these details **in order that the thoughts of the one performing the**

---

### NOTES

54. The Gemara (*Rosh Hashanah* 17a) applies this verse to the worst sinners.

55. Unlike other offerings, which atone for individual sins, the *Azazel*-goat atones for the multitude of sins of the entire nation. The utter destruction it suffers outside of the *Beis HaMikdash* is a symbolic warning to those who are heavily laden with sin, that they will be entirely destroyed and have no share in the World to Come.

56. Certain offerings must be slaughtered in the northern portion of the Temple Courtyard, while others may be slaughtered anywhere in the Courtyard. The offerings also differ from one another in the manner in which their blood is applied to the Altar; and they differ in regard to which portions are awarded to the Kohanim, as well as in regard to the length of time for which they may be eaten. The basic distinctions are spelled out in the Mishnayos of *Zevachim* Ch. 5. See also Chinuch, Mitzvos 102 and 138-141.

כִּי הַחֲלוּקִין יַכְרִיחוּ כֵּיוָן הַמַּחֲשָׁבָה בַּדָּבָר, לֹא נַעֲלֶה בְּיָדֵינוּ רַק דִּבְרֵי נַעֲרוּת.[57]
וּכְלָל הַדְּבָרִים
כִּי גַּם בִּפְשָׁטִים
לֹא נִמְצָא יָדֵינוּ וְרַגְלֵינוּ בִּלְתִּי סַעַד הַמְקֻבָּלִים,
וַאֲלֵיהֶם נִכְרַע אַפַּיִם וְיִפְתְּחוּ לָנוּ בְּכָל אֵלֶּה הָעִנְיָנִים.
וְאוּלָם אֵין לִקְרוֹתֵנוּ מִכַּת הַכְּסִילִים
בְּהוֹצִיאֵנוּ כָּל רוּחֵנוּ בִּדְבָרִים,
כִּי בִּפְסֹלֶת רַב, מְעַט אֹכֶל נִמְצָא לְעִתִּים,[58]
גַּם כִּי רָאִינוּ לְרַבּוֹתֵינוּ זִכְרוֹנָם לִבְרָכָה כַּיּוֹצֵא בִּדְבָרֵינוּ אוֹמְרִים,
שֶׁאָמְרוּ בְּקָרְבַּן סוֹטָה,
הִיא עָשְׂתָה מַעֲשֶׂה בְּהֵמָה, לְפִיכָךְ תַּקְרִיב שְׂעוֹרִים[59] (סוטה דף י״ד ע״א),

---

כִּי הַחֲלוּקִין יַכְרִיחוּ כֵּיוָן הַמַּחֲשָׁבָה — *avodah* (service) **should be very focused upon the** *avodah*, בַּדָּבָר — **for distinctions** in the applicable laws **force the mind to be focused on the matter** at hand, לֹא נַעֲלֶה בְּיָדֵינוּ רַק דִּבְרֵי נַעֲרוּת — **we will emerge only with a childish explanation** of the matter.[57]

Chinuch continues in poetic rhyme:

וּכְלָל הַדְּבָרִים — **Thus, the general rule of these matters is**

כִּי גַּם בִּפְשָׁטִים — **that even on a basic** level of **explanation**

לֹא נִמְצָא יָדֵינוּ וְרַגְלֵינוּ בִּלְתִּי סַעַד הַמְקֻבָּלִים — **we cannot "find our hands or our feet"** to adequately understand the matter of the offerings **without the assistance of those versed in** *Kabbalah*.

וַאֲלֵיהֶם נִכְרַע אַפַּיִם — **We therefore kneel** with our **faces** to the ground **before them,**

וְיִפְתְּחוּ לָנוּ בְּכָל אֵלֶּה הָעִנְיָנִים — **and they will open our eyes with regard to all these matters.**

וְאוּלָם אֵין לִקְרוֹתֵנוּ מִכַּת הַכְּסִילִים — **Nevertheless, we are not to be labeled as part of the class of fools**

בְּהוֹצִיאֵנוּ כָּל רוּחֵנוּ בִּדְבָרִים — **for expending all** the efforts of **our spirit on** this **matter,** even though we have not succeeded in fully explaining it,

כִּי בִּפְסֹלֶת רַב, מְעַט אֹכֶל נִמְצָא לְעִתִּים — **for** even **in a great** amount of **waste, a small** amount of **edible matter can occasionally be found.**[58]

גַּם כִּי רָאִינוּ לְרַבּוֹתֵינוּ זִכְרוֹנָם לִבְרָכָה כַּיּוֹצֵא בִּדְבָרֵינוּ אוֹמְרִים — **Furthermore,** we are justified in offering the above explanation, **because we have seen that our Sages, of blessed memory, say things similar to ours.**

שֶׁאָמְרוּ בְּקָרְבַּן סוֹטָה — For example, **they said, with regard to the offering brought by a** *sotah* (*Sotah* 14a):

הִיא עָשְׂתָה מַעֲשֶׂה בְּהֵמָה, לְפִיכָךְ תַּקְרִיב שְׂעוֹרִים — **She committed an animalistic act; therefore,** the Torah commanded that **she shall bring an offering of barley.**[59]

---

### NOTES

57. I.e., this is an obvious oversimplification of a matter that has a much deeper meaning. See *Moreh Nevuchim* III, Ch. 26, where *Rambam* also explains that certain differences of the particulars of the offerings cannot be understood on a rational level. See Chinuch's further discussion of this point in Mitzvah 104.

58. "Edible matter" refers to a worthy explanation. Thus, Chinuch states that even if a large portion of his explanation needs to be rejected, his efforts were nevertheless worthwhile, for the sake of the degree of truth that can be found in his words. See the final lines of the Author's Introduction to this work (Vol. I, p. 33), where Chinuch makes similar remarks about his discussing the reasons for all the mitzvos.

59. A *sotah* is a married woman who was discovered to have secluded herself with another man after her husband had warned her not to do so; see Mitzvah 366. She is required to bring an offering of barley, and to follow the procedure that the Torah sets forth in *Numbers* 5:11-31, to determine her innocence or guilt. The Mishnah explains that her offering is comprised of barley rather than wheat — which is the usual ingredient of a

## תרומה / מצוה צה: מצות בנין בית הבחירה

וּבְקָרְבַּן מְצֹרָע,
הוּא עָשָׂה מַעֲשֵׂה פַּטִּיט, יַקְרִיב צִפֳּרִים[60] (ערכין דף ט"ז ע"ב),
וּבְדוֹמֶה לָזֶה אָמְרוּ זִכְרוֹנָם לִבְרָכָה בְּעִנְיַן הַנִּדָּה,
מִפְּנֵי מָה אָמְרָה תּוֹרָה לֵישֵׁב שִׁבְעָה נְקִיִּים[61],
שֶׁתְּהֵא חֲבִיבָה עָלָיו בְּיוֹתֵר[62] (נדה דף ל"א ע"ב),
וּבֶאֱמֶת שֶׁאֵין כָּל זֶה לְדַעְתָּם תַּכְלִית הַכַּוָּנָה בַּדְּבָרִים,
רַק לְהוֹדִיעַ כִּי עִנְיַן הַמִּצְוָה יִסְבֹּל הַרְבֵּה רְמָזִים
מִלְּבַד עִקָּרֶיהָ גְּדוֹלִים וַחֲזָקִים[63].

---

וּבְקָרְבַּן מְצֹרָע — **And regarding the offering of a** *metzora,* they said (Arachin 16b): הוּא עָשָׂה מַעֲשֵׂה פַּטִּיט, יַקְרִיב צִפֳּרִים — **He committed an act** that entailed **chatter; therefore, the Torah commanded that for his purification he shall bring birds,** which chatter![60] וּבְדוֹמֶה לָזֶה אָמְרוּ זִכְרוֹנָם לִבְרָכָה בְּעִנְיַן הַנִּדָּה — **And in a similar vein [the Sages], of blessed memory, said regarding a** *niddah* (Niddah 31b): מִפְּנֵי מָה אָמְרָה תּוֹרָה לֵישֵׁב שִׁבְעָה נְקִיִּים — **Why did the Torah say** that a woman who is a *niddah* must **wait seven clean [days]?**[61] שֶׁתְּהֵא חֲבִיבָה עָלָיו בְּיוֹתֵר — **So that she should be more beloved to [her husband].**[62] וּבֶאֱמֶת שֶׁאֵין כָּל זֶה לְדַעְתָּם תַּכְלִית הַכַּוָּנָה בַּדְּבָרִים — **Now, in truth, it is** obviously **not the intent of [the Sages] that any of this is the** Torah's **ultimate objective in** commanding these **matters.** רַק לְהוֹדִיעַ כִּי עִנְיַן הַמִּצְוָה יִסְבֹּל הַרְבֵּה רְמָזִים — **Rather,** it was their intention **to teach that the concept of** each **mitzvah carries much symbolism,** מִלְּבַד עִקָּרֶיהָ גְּדוֹלִים וַחֲזָקִים — **aside from its great and compelling fundamental purposes.**[63]

---

### NOTES

*minchah* (meal) offering — because barley is primarily used as fodder for animals. This is symbolic of her behavior: just as an animal does not cling to a particular mate, so too did she improperly seclude herself with a man other than her husband.

60. A *metzora* is a person who was afflicted with *tzaraas*, a skin affliction described in *Leviticus* Ch. 13. One of the causes of this malady is speaking *lashon hara* [disparaging talk] (see *Arachin* 16b and *Rambam, Hil. Tumas Tzaraas* 16:13 ff.). Since the inappropriate chatter that begets this affliction is symbolized by the continuous chirping of birds, he is required to bring birds for his purification. [The birds are not actually brought as an offering, but are part of the *metzora's* purification ritual, as set forth in *Leviticus* 14:1-7.]

61. A woman who experiences a menstrual flow becomes prohibited to have relations with her husband until the flow ceases, and she then counts seven "clean days" (i.e., consecutive days on which it is verified that there has been no flow), and immerses in a *mikveh*. For further details of this law, see Mitzvah 207.

[The requirement of seven "clean days" applies to every *niddah* nowadays under Rabbinic law. Biblically, this requirement applies only in the unique case of a *zavah*, as detailed by Chinuch in Mitzvah 207. In fact, the word נְקִיִּים, *clean days,* does not appear in the Gemara cited by Chinuch here, for that Gemara refers to the Biblical law of *niddah* (which requires only seven days in total). Apparently, in order to maintain the rhyme, Chinuch adds this word, referring to the Rabbinic requirement of waiting seven clean days even in the case of an ordinary *niddah*. In his previous citations regarding the *sotah* and *metzora*, as well, Chinuch modified the words of the Gemara to fit his rhyme scheme.]

62. By prohibiting a husband and wife from engaging in intimate behavior on an uninterrupted basis, the Torah ensures that their relationship will be refreshed each time relations become permissible.

We see in these three instances that the Sages provided rational explanations for laws of the Torah. Moreover, in the first two instances, the reasons closely parallel the rationale that Chinuch provided above for bringing offerings.

63. Certainly, the Sages recognized that those mitzvos have far greater significance than these simple lessons indicate, but this did not deter them from deriving even such basic lessons from them. Chinuch explains that he is following this precedent. Although he is aware that his explanation does not capture the full essence of the purpose of the offerings, he does not refrain from presenting the insight he has. See also Mitzvah 166.

# 229 ☐ TERUMAH / MITZVAH 95: THE OBLIGATION TO BUILD THE HOLY TEMPLE

מִדִּינֵי הַמִּצְוָה, מַה שֶּׁאָמְרוּ זִכְרוֹנָם לִבְרָכָה (זבחים דף קי״ב ע״ב) שֶׁקֹּדֶם שֶׁנִּבְנָה הַבַּיִת בִּירוּשָׁלַיִם הָיוּ מַקְרִיבִין קָרְבָּנוֹת בִּשְׁאָר מְקוֹמוֹתָם,[64] אֲבָל מִשֶּׁנִּבְנָה הַבַּיִת נֶאֶסְרוּ כָּל הַמְּקוֹמוֹת לִבְנוֹת בָּם בַּיִת לַשֵּׁם וּלְהַקְרִיב שָׁם, שֶׁנֶּאֱמַר (תהלים קל״ב, י״ד) ״זֹאת מְנוּחָתִי עֲדֵי עַד״.[65] וְאֵלּוּ הֵם הַדְּבָרִים שֶׁהֵם עִקָּר בְּבִנְיַן הַבַּיִת,[66] עוֹשִׂין בּוֹ קֹדֶשׁ וְקֹדֶשׁ קָדָשִׁים, וְיִהְיֶה לִפְנֵי הַקֹּדֶשׁ מָקוֹם אֶחָד וְהוּא הַנִּקְרָא אוּלָם, וּשְׁלָשְׁתָּן נִקְרָאִין הֵיכָל.[67] וְעוֹשִׂין מְחִצָּה אַחַת סָבִיב לַהֵיכָל רָחוֹק מִמֶּנּוּ כְּעֵין קַלְעֵי הֶחָצֵר שֶׁהָיוּ בַּמִּדְבָּר,[68] וְכָל הַמֻּקָּף בִּמְחִצָּה זוֹ שֶׁהוּא כְּעֵין חֲצַר אֹהֶל מוֹעֵד הוּא הַנִּקְרָא עֲזָרָה, וְהַכֹּל נִקְרָא מִקְדָּשׁ.[69]

---

## ⸺ Laws of the Mitzvah ⸺

מִדִּינֵי הַמִּצְוָה — **Among the laws of the mitzvah are the following:**
Chinuch begins by discussing where the *Beis HaMikdash* is to be built:
מַה שֶּׁאָמְרוּ זִכְרוֹנָם לִבְרָכָה — **First, is what [the Sages], of blessed memory, said** (*Zevachim* 112b), שֶׁקֹּדֶם שֶׁנִּבְנָה הַבַּיִת בִּירוּשָׁלַיִם הָיוּ מַקְרִיבִין קָרְבָּנוֹת בִּשְׁאָר מְקוֹמוֹתָם — **that before the Temple was built in Jerusalem they would bring offerings in other locations,**[64] אֲבָל מִשֶּׁנִּבְנָה הַבַּיִת — **but once the Temple was built** נֶאֶסְרוּ כָּל הַמְּקוֹמוֹת לִבְנוֹת בָּם בַּיִת לַשֵּׁם וּלְהַקְרִיב שָׁם — **it became prohibited to build a Temple** dedicated **to Hashem in any** other **location, or to bring offerings there;** שֶׁנֶּאֱמַר ״זֹאת מְנוּחָתִי עֲדֵי עַד״ — **as it is stated** (*Psalms* 132:14): **This is My resting place for ever and ever.**[65]

Chinuch continues with laws regarding the structure of the *Beis HaMikdash*:
וְאֵלּוּ הֵם הַדְּבָרִים שֶׁהֵם עִקָּר בְּבִנְיַן הַבַּיִת — **These are the items that are essential to the building of the Temple:**[66] עוֹשִׂין בּוֹ קֹדֶשׁ וְקֹדֶשׁ קָדָשִׁים — **One must build in it the Holy and Holy of Holies,** וְיִהְיֶה לִפְנֵי הַקֹּדֶשׁ מָקוֹם אֶחָד וְהוּא הַנִּקְרָא אוּלָם — **and there is to be before the Holy a designated area that is called the** *Ulam* (Antechamber); וּשְׁלָשְׁתָּן נִקְרָאִין הֵיכָל — **all of these three** together **are called the** *Heichal* (Sanctuary).[67] וְעוֹשִׂין מְחִצָּה אַחַת סָבִיב לַהֵיכָל — **We also** must **build a partition around the** *Heichal*, רָחוֹק מִמֶּנּוּ — **at a distance from it,** כְּעֵין קַלְעֵי הֶחָצֵר שֶׁהָיוּ בַּמִּדְבָּר — **corresponding to the curtains of the Courtyard** of the *Mishkan* (Tabernacle) **in the Wilderness.**[68] וְכָל הַמֻּקָּף בִּמְחִצָּה זוֹ — **The entire area that is surrounded by this partition,** שֶׁהוּא כְּעֵין חֲצַר אֹהֶל מוֹעֵד — **which corresponds to the Courtyard of the** *Mishkan*, הוּא הַנִּקְרָא עֲזָרָה — **is called the** *Azarah*, וְהַכֹּל נִקְרָא מִקְדָּשׁ — **and everything** together (i.e., the *Heichal* with the *Azarah*) **is called the** *Mikdash* (Sacred).[69]

---

### NOTES

64. On an altar known as a *bamah* (high place).

65. In this verse, "My resting place" refers to Jerusalem (*Har HaMoriah* to *Rambam, Hil. Beis HaBechirah* 1:3 §8). Once the Divine Presence came to "rest" in the *Beis HaMikdash* in Jerusalem, that would remain its "resting place" forevermore (see *Zevachim* 119a).

66. Although the *Beis HaMikdash* contained various additional rooms and chambers (see further in Chinuch), the minimum requirements of the mitzvah are fulfilled through building these essential areas (*Radvaz, Hil. Beis HaBechirah* 1:5; *Mikdash David* 1:3). [The following section of Chinuch (until וְהַכֹּל נִקְרָא מִקְדָּשׁ) is a direct quote of *Rambam, Hil. Beis HaBechirah* 1:5.]

67. There is disagreement among the Sages whether the *Ulam* possesses the greater level of sanctity of the *Heichal*, or shares the lesser sanctity of the Courtyard [*Azarah*] (see, for example, *Yoma* 44b). The wording here apparently follows the view that the *Ulam* has the higher level of sanctity (*Har HaMoriah* to *Rambam*, ibid., §10; see, however, *Likkutei Halachos* to *Zevachim* 55b in *Zevach Todah* ד״ה וחר). See *Minchas Chinuch* 141:5.

68. See *Exodus* 27:9 ff. The basic structure of the *Beis HaMikdash* (i.e., the *Azarah*, the Holy, and the Holy of Holies) and the arrangement of the utensils within it parallel the structure and arrangement of the *Mishkan*.

69. The Torah (*Numbers* 19:20) states that if one who is *tamei* (spiritually impure) enters מִקְדַּשׁ ה׳, *Hashem's* "*Mikdash*," he is liable to *kares* (excision) [if he entered intentionally, and to a *chatas* (sin) offering if he entered unintentionally; see Mitzvah 363]. As explained here, this term refers to the area of the *Azarah* and *Heichal* (*Derech Chochmah, Hil. Beis HaBechirah* 1:30; see also *Har HaMoriah* to *Rambam, Hil. Beis HaBechirah* 1:5 §11).

## 230 ❑ תרומה / מצוה צה: מצוות בנין בית הבחירה

וְעוֹשִׂין בַּמִּקְדָּשׁ הַכֵּלִים הַכְּתוּבִים בַּתּוֹרָה שֶׁצְּרִיכִים שָׁם.[70] וּמַה שֶּׁאָמְרוּ שֶׁכָּל כְּלֵי הַקֹּדֶשׁ שֶׁנִּקְּבוּ אוֹ נִסְדְּקוּ שְׁמִיָּד מַתִּיכִין אוֹתָן וְעוֹשִׂין אוֹתָן חֲדָשִׁים, וְסַכִּין שֶׁנִּשְׁמַט מַקַּתּוֹ אוֹ נִפְגַּם אֵין מְתַקְּנִין אוֹתוֹ אֶלָּא גּוֹנְזִין אוֹתוֹ מִיָּד,[71] שֶׁאֵין עֲנִיּוּת בִּמְקוֹם עֲשִׁירוּת,[72] וְעוֹשִׂין בְּתוֹךְ הָעֲזָרָה גְּבוּלִין, עַד כָּאן לְיִשְׂרָאֵל, עַד כָּאן לַכֹּהֲנִים,[73] וּבוֹנִין סָמוּךְ לָהּ בָּתִּים לְהִשְׁתַּמֵּשׁ בָּהֶן לְכָל צָרְכֵי הַמִּקְדָּשׁ, וְכָל אַחַת נִקְרֵאת לִשְׁכָּה.[74] וְיֶתֶר פְּרָטֶיהָ, כְּגוֹן בִּנְיַן הַבַּיִת כֵּיצַד,[75] וְתַבְנִיתוֹ וְכָל מִדּוֹתָיו,[76] וּבִנְיַן הַמִּזְבֵּחַ וּמִשְׁפָּטָיו,[77] מְבֹאָרִים בְּמַסֶּכֶת מִדּוֹת,[78]

---

וְעוֹשִׂין בַּמִּקְדָּשׁ הַכֵּלִים הַכְּתוּבִים בַּתּוֹרָה שֶׁצְּרִיכִים שָׁם — **We** must **also make in the** *Mikdash* **the utensils that are recorded in the Torah as being needed there.**[70]

וּמַה שֶּׁאָמְרוּ — **Also,** the laws of the mitzvah include **that which [the Sages], of blessed memory, have said** (*Zevachim* 88a), שֶׁכָּל כְּלֵי הַקֹּדֶשׁ שֶׁנִּקְּבוּ אוֹ נִסְדְּקוּ — **that if any of the holy utensils incur a hole or crack,** שְׁמִיָּד מַתִּיכִין אוֹתָן וְעוֹשִׂין אוֹתָן חֲדָשִׁים — **we immediately melt them down and make them anew,** rather than repair them; וְסַכִּין שֶׁנִּשְׁמַט מַקַּתּוֹ אוֹ נִפְגַּם — **and,** similarly, **if a knife slips out of its handle or incurs a nick,** אֵין מְתַקְּנִין אוֹתוֹ — **we do not repair it,** אֶלָּא גּוֹנְזִין אוֹתוֹ מִיָּד — **rather, we store it away immediately.**[71] שֶׁאֵין עֲנִיּוּת בִּמְקוֹם עֲשִׁירוּת — **The reason for** these laws is **because there is** to be **no appearance of poverty in a place** that warrants **opulence.**[72]

עַד כָּאן לְיִשְׂרָאֵל, וְעוֹשִׂין בְּתוֹךְ הָעֲזָרָה גְּבוּלִין — **We** also **affix boundaries within the** *Azarah,* עַד כָּאן לַכֹּהֲנִים — indicating "**until here** it is permissible **for an Israelite** to go" **and "until here** it is permissible **for Kohanim** to go."[73] וּבוֹנִין סָמוּךְ לָהּ בָּתִּים לְהִשְׁתַּמֵּשׁ בָּהֶן לְכָל צָרְכֵי הַמִּקְדָּשׁ — **Also, we build rooms near [the** *Azarah***], to be used for all the needs of the** *Beis HaMikdash***;** וְכָל אַחַת נִקְרֵאת לִשְׁכָּה — **each one is called a** *lishkah.*[74]

וְיֶתֶר פְּרָטֶיהָ — **These, and the additional details [of this mitzvah],** כְּגוֹן בִּנְיַן הַבַּיִת כֵּיצַד — for **example, how the Temple must be built,**[75] וְתַבְנִיתוֹ וְכָל מִדּוֹתָיו — **its design and all its dimensions,**[76] וּבִנְיַן הַמִּזְבֵּחַ וּמִשְׁפָּטָיו — **and** how **the Altar is built, and its laws,**[77] מְבֹאָרִים בְּמַסֶּכֶת מִדּוֹת — **are set forth in Tractate** *Middos.*[78]

---

### NOTES

70. See above, at notes 3-4; see also the Insight.

71. Apparently, a knife cannot be melted down and made anew like other utensils (*Derech Chochmah, Hil. Klei HaMikdash* 1:86). Since it is unfit for use in the *Beis HaMikdash,* and may neither be repaired, nor redeemed and used for any other purpose (see *Minchas Chinuch* above, end of 40:4), it must be stowed away and never used again (see *Rambam, Hil. Klei HaMikdash* 1:15 with *Derech Chochmah, Beur HaHalachah* there, for details regarding where they are stowed).

72. The honor of the House of God demands that if an item becomes damaged it is not to be mended, but must be replaced with a new one. [For discussion of various aspects of this law, see *Mishneh LaMelech, Hil. Klei HaMikdash* 1:14 and *Minchas Chinuch* §16.]

73. See *Keilim* 1:8-9 for a description of the areas that were off-limits to Israelites, and those that were off-limits even to Kohanim, except for the specific purpose of performing the *avodah* there. See *Middos* 35b (2:6) for a description of how separate areas within the *Azarah* were demarcated. [For discussion of the particulars of this law, see *Har HaMoriah, Hil. Beis HaBechirah* 1:7 §16; see also *Derech Chochmah* 1:46-47.]

74. Each *lishkah* was designated for a specific function; see Mitzvos 105, 118, 276, 350, and 377, where Chinuch refers to some of these rooms and their functions.

75. Such as the proper time for building the *Beis HaMikdash* and which materials may be used for its construction. See *Rambam, Hil. Beis HaBechirah* 1:8-12.

76. The Torah (*Exodus* 26:15-30, 27:9-15) provides the specifications of the *Mishkan* built in the Wilderness, but the dimensions of the *Beis HaMikdash* did not conform to those of the *Mishkan.* Similarly, the dimensions of the Second *Beis HaMikdash* were not identical to those of the First *Beis HaMikdash*, and the dimensions of the Third *Beis HaMikdash* will differ from both of those that preceded it. Each *Beis HaMikdash* was built according to the specifications of the prophet of that time (*Rambam* ibid. 1:1,4; see *I Kings,* Chs. 6-7 and *Ezekiel,* Chs. 40-42 ff.).

77. This refers to laws regarding the precise location of the Altar, and to laws regarding the materials and tools that are used in its construction. See *Rambam* ibid. 1:13-17, 2:1-18. For additional laws of the Altar, see Mitzvos 40 and 41.

78. The laws regarding the dimensions and structure of the *Beis HaMikdash* are set forth by *Rambam* ibid. Chapters 4-6. The laws of the Altar can be found in Chapter 2 there.

## TERUMAH / MITZVAH 95: THE OBLIGATION TO BUILD THE HOLY TEMPLE

וְכֵן תַּבְנִית הַמְּנוֹרָה וְהַשֻּׁלְחָן וּמִזְבַּח הַזָּהָב, וּמְקוֹמָם בַּהֵיכָל, בַּגְּמָרָא מְנָחוֹת (דף כ״ח ע״א רצ״ז ע״א ואילך) וְיוֹמָא (דף ל״ג ע״ב)[79].

וְנוֹהֶגֶת מִצְוָה זוֹ בִּזְמַן שֶׁרֹב יִשְׂרָאֵל עַל אַדְמָתָן[80]. וְזוֹ מִן הַמִּצְוֹת שֶׁאֵינָן מֻטָּלוֹת עַל הַיָּחִיד כִּי אִם עַל הַצִּבּוּר כֻּלָּן[81], כְּשֶׁיִּבָּנֶה הַבַּיִת בִּמְהֵרָה בְיָמֵינוּ יִתְקַיֵּם מִצְוַת עֲשֵׂה[82].

וְכֵן תַּבְנִית הַמְּנוֹרָה וְהַשֻּׁלְחָן וּמִזְבַּח הַזָּהָב — **Similarly, the structures of the Menorah, the Table, and the Golden Altar,** וּמְקוֹמָם בַּהֵיכָל — **and where they are placed in the** *Heichal*, בַּגְּמָרָא מְנָחוֹת וְיוֹמָא — **are set forth in the Talmud,** in Tractates ***Menachos*** (28a, 97a ff.) **and** ***Yoma*** (33b).[79]

### ᐳ Applicability of the Mitzvah ᐸ

וְנוֹהֶגֶת מִצְוָה זוֹ בִּזְמַן שֶׁרֹב יִשְׂרָאֵל עַל אַדְמָתָן — **[This mitzvah] applies** only **when the majority of the Jewish people are** residing **in their Land** (i.e., Eretz Yisrael),[80] וְזוֹ מִן הַמִּצְוֹת שֶׁאֵינָן מֻטָּלוֹת עַל הַיָּחִיד כִּי — **and this is among the mitzvos that are not incumbent upon any individual** אִם עַל הַצִּבּוּר כֻּלָּן — **but only upon the community as a whole.**[81]
כְּשֶׁיִּבָּנֶה הַבַּיִת בִּמְהֵרָה בְיָמֵינוּ — **When the Temple will be rebuilt,** may this take place **speedily, in our days,** יִתְקַיֵּם מִצְוַת עֲשֵׂה — **this mitzvah obligation will be fulfilled.**[82]

---

### NOTES

79. The laws of these utensils are codified in *Rambam* ibid. Ch. 3.

80. This ruling, that the mitzvah to build a *Beis HaMikdash* applies only when most Jews are residing in Eretz Yisrael, is somewhat difficult to understand, in light of the fact that during the period of the Second *Beis HaMikdash* most Jews did not reside in Eretz Yisrael; see Mitzvah 507 (see also *Tzitz Eliezer* Vol. 10, 1:11 and 2:1).

81. The mitzvah to build a *Beis HaMikdash* does not apply during nighttime hours, nor may work proceed on the Sabbath or festivals. Therefore, in accordance with the general rule that time-specific obligations do not apply to women, there may be reason to assume that women are not included in this mitzvah. *Rambam* (ibid. 1:12), however, states that just as women participated in construction of the *Mishkan* in the Wilderness, so too are they required to participate in the building of the *Beis HaMikdash*. See *Kehillos Yaakov, Shevuos* 10:2, for a number of resolutions of this issue.

82. There is disagreement among the Rishonim regarding the building of the Third *Beis HaMikdash*. *Rambam* (*Hil. Melachim* 11:1) maintains that it will be built through human effort, by Mashiach. *Rashi* and *Tosafos*, however, indicate in a number of places (see, for example, *Succah* 41a ד״ה אי נמי) that the Third *Beis HaMikdash* will be built in the Heavens, from where it will descend and become revealed to the human eye. See *Shoshanim LeDavid,* preface to Tractate *Middos,* who discusses how the miraculous construction of the Third *Beis HaMikdash* would constitute fulfillment of a mitzvah; see also *Siach Yitzchak* in *Siddur HaGra,* to *Mussaf* of Yom Tov ד״ה והראנו בבנינו; and *Derech Chochmah, Hil. Beis HaBechirah* 1:1, *Beur HaHalachah* ד״ה לעשות.

---

> **⋖§ Insight: Constructing the Utensils of the Beis HaMikdash**
>
> Chinuch (at note 4) writes that our mitzvah includes not only the obligation to build the *Beis HaMikdash* itself, but also the obligation to construct the utensils necessary for the *avodah* (service) performed in the *Beis HaMikdash*. Chinuch's position in this matter is based on that of *Rambam* in *Sefer HaMitzvos* (*Asei* 20; see also beginning of *Shoresh* 12), and reflected in *Rambam's* codification of this mitzvah in the beginning of *Hil. Beis HaBechirah* (1:6): "We are to fashion utensils for the Temple: an Altar for the olah and other offerings; a ramp with which to ascend the Altar ... the Kiyor (Laver) and its base for the Kohanim to wash their hands and feet for the avodah; an Altar for incense; a Menorah; a Shulchan ... " Since these utensils are necessary for the *avodah* in the *Beis HaMikdash*, each for its own purpose, they are all included in the general mitzvah to build the *Beis HaMikdash*.
>
> *Ramban* (Glosses to *Sefer HaMitzvos, Asei* 33), however, takes issue with this position, asserting that the obligation to construct the utensils of the *Beis HaMikdash* cannot be viewed as part of the mitzvah to build the *Beis HaMikdash* itself. *Ramban* argues that the utensils are not structurally a part of the *Beis HaMikdash*, nor are they halachically indispensable to the *avodah* performed there, for the *avodah* is valid even if the utensils are not present. *Ramban* therefore concludes that

the construction of these utensils is not subsumed under the general mitzvah to build the *Beis HaMikdash*.

Nevertheless, *Ramban* does not count the construction of the utensils as a separate mitzvah. Rather, he maintains that the construction of each of the utensils is considered a detail of the mitzvah service of which it is a part. Thus, for example, part of the mitzvah of the *Lechem HaPanim* (Mitzvah 97) is that the bread be placed on a specific form of *Shulchan*, which must therefore be constructed for this purpose; part of the mitzvah of lighting the Menorah (Mitzvah 98) is the requirement of a specific kind of candelabrum. Similarly, the construction of the Altars and the *Kiyor* are parts of the requirements of their respective *avodos* (Mitzvos 103, 106, and 115).

Now, the forgoing discussion is applicable to all the utensils of the *Beis HaMikdash* except for one: the Holy Ark. The Ark had no purpose as part of any specific *avodah* in the *Beis HaMikdash*. Its construction can therefore not be subsumed under any other mitzvah. Even *Rambam*, who maintains that the construction of all the utensils is considered a part of the mitzvah to build the *Beis HaMikdash*, indicates that the construction of the Ark is not included with the rest of the utensils. In *Rambam's* list of the various utensils that are a part of the construction of the *Beis HaMikdash* (*Hil. Beis HaBechirah* ibid.), he omits any mention of the Ark. This is because the other utensils are included only by dint of their necessity in the *avodah* of the *Beis HaMikdash*; the Ark, having no specific *avodah*, does not belong in this list (see *Shoshanim LeDavid*, *Menachos*, end of 11:6, and *Kli Chemdah*, *Terumah* §3).

*Ramban* addresses this unique quality of the Ark by asserting that the requirement to construct the Ark must indeed be counted as an independent mitzvah. *Rambam*, however, counts no such specific mitzvah. But if constructing the Ark is not included in the mitzvah to build the *Beis HaMikdash*, why, according to *Rambam*, is it not counted as another mitzvah among the 613 Mitzvos?

A solution may be offered on the basis of *Rambam's* rule (*Sefer HaMitzvos, Shoresh* III) that only a mitzvah that pertains for all times is counted in the 613 Mitzvos, while a mitzvah whose commandment is applicable only for a specific time or generation is not included in the count (see *Chinuch's* discussion of this rule in the next mitzvah). The commandment to construct the other utensils of the *Beis HaMikdash* is not limited to one time, since throughout the years, when a utensil is worn, lost or even destroyed, we are to replace that utensil as part of this mitzvah-commandment (see *Rashi, Exodus* 25:9). Such ravages of time, however, may have effected all the utensils — except the Ark. The Ark constructed by Moses was the same Ark that was used throughout the years of the *Mishkan* (Tabernacle) and first *Beis HaMikdash*. When the destruction of the first *Beis HaMikdash* appeared inevitable, King Josiah concealed the Ark for safekeeping, and it has remained in that place through the ages, until such time as the *Beis HaMikdash* will be rebuilt and it may be returned to its proper place (*Rambam, Hil. Beis HaBechirah* 4:1).

It emerges, then, that the commandment to construct the Ark applied only once, at the time of its original construction by Moses, for that very same Ark was destined to survive through the ages with no replacement or repair. Therefore, as a mitzvah that does not pertain for all time, it is not counted as one of the 613 Mitzvos (see *Ramban* to *Sefer HaMitzvos, Asei* 33 with *Megillas Esther* there; *Derech Chochmah, Hil. Beis HaBechirah* 1:5, end of *Beur HaHalachah* ד"ה ואלו).

# 233 ☐ TERUMAH / MITZVAH 96: NOT TO REMOVE THE POLES FROM THE ARK

≈ מִצְוָה צו: שֶׁלֹּא לְהוֹצִיא בַּדֵּי הָאָרוֹן מִמֶּנּוּ ≈

שֶׁלֹּא לְהוֹצִיא בַּדֵּי הָאָרוֹן מִתּוֹךְ הַטַּבָּעוֹת, שֶׁנֶּאֱמַר[1] (שמות כ״ה, ט״ו) בְּטַבְּעֹת הָאָרֹן יִהְיוּ הַבַּדִּים לֹא יָסֻרוּ מִמֶּנּוּ[2].

וּמְבֹאָר[3] הוּא שֶׁמִּצְוָה זוֹ בִּכְלַל מִצְווֹת הַנּוֹהֲגוֹת לְדוֹרוֹת הִיא, שֶׁאֵין פֵּרוּשׁ נוֹהֲגוֹת לְדוֹרוֹת שֶׁלֹּא יִפָּסֵק מִיִּשְׂרָאֵל מַעֲשֵׂה אוֹתָהּ מִצְוָה לְעוֹלָם בְּשׁוּם זְמַן, אֶלָּא כֵּן הוּא הָעִנְיָן, כָּל מִצְוָה שֶׁלֹּא נִצְטַוֵּינוּ עָלֶיהָ לַעֲשׂוֹתָהּ רַק בִּזְמַן יָדוּעַ וְלֹא יוֹתֵר,

## ≈ Mitzvah 96 ≈
## The Prohibition to Remove the Poles From the Ark of the Covenant

בְּטַבְּעֹת הָאָרֹן יִהְיוּ הַבַּדִּים לֹא יָסֻרוּ מִמֶּנּוּ
*The poles shall be in the rings of the Ark; they may not be removed from it* (Exodus 25:15).

The Torah required that the vessels of the *Mishkan* (Tabernacle) be outfitted with poles, which the Leviim used to carry the vessels when traveling in the Wilderness. Although the poles of the other vessels were removed when the *Mishkan* was standing, the Torah prohibits removing the poles of the Holy Ark at any time. Even in the era of the *Beis HaMikdash*, when the vessels were carried only in exceptional circumstances, it was forbidden to remove the poles.

שֶׁלֹּא לְהוֹצִיא בַּדֵּי הָאָרוֹן מִתּוֹךְ הַטַּבָּעוֹת — We are commanded **not to remove the poles of the Ark from within the rings** that were affixed to the Ark,[1] שֶׁנֶּאֱמַר ״בְּטַבְּעֹת הָאָרֹן יִהְיוּ הַבַּדִּים לֹא יָסֻרוּ מִמֶּנּוּ״ — **as it is stated** (Exodus 25:15): ***The poles shall be in the rings of the Ark; they may not be removed from it.***[2]

Chinuch explains why this prohibition is counted among the 613 Mitzvos:[3]

וּמְבֹאָר הוּא שֶׁמִּצְוָה זוֹ בִּכְלַל מִצְווֹת הַנּוֹהֲגוֹת לְדוֹרוֹת הִיא — **It is clear that this mitzvah is included among the mitzvos that apply throughout the generations,** and therefore belong to the 613 Mitzvos, שֶׁאֵין פֵּרוּשׁ נוֹהֲגוֹת לְדוֹרוֹת — **for the meaning of** "a mitzvah **that applies throughout the generations" is not** שֶׁלֹּא יִפָּסֵק מִיִּשְׂרָאֵל מַעֲשֵׂה אוֹתָהּ מִצְוָה לְעוֹלָם בְּשׁוּם זְמַן — **that the performance of the mitzvah will never cease from the Jewish people at any time.** אֶלָּא כֵּן הוּא הָעִנְיָן — **Rather, the idea is this:** כָּל מִצְוָה שֶׁלֹּא נִצְטַוֵּינוּ עָלֶיהָ לַעֲשׂוֹתָהּ רַק בִּזְמַן יָדוּעַ וְלֹא יוֹתֵר — **Any mitzvah that we were commanded to do for only a specific time and not longer,**

---

### NOTES

1. Two rings protruded from one side of the Ark and two rings from the opposite side. A pole was inserted through each pair of rings (*Exodus* 25:12-15, as understood by *Rashi* and *Ramban* ad loc.; see, however, *Tosafos* cited below, in the Insight).

2. *Rambam* (Hil. Klei HaMikdash 2:13) states that even if one removes just one of the poles, he violates this prohibition. See *Maayan HaChochmah, Lo Saaseh* 59, and *Toafos Re'eim* to *Sefer Yere'im* §316.

3. When setting forth the principles that determine which of the Torah's laws is counted among the 613 Mitzvos, *Rambam* states that only mitzvos that apply throughout the generations are included (*Sefer HaMitzvos, Shoresh* 3). Thus, the question arises: Since the prohibition of removing the poles from the Ark was relevant only when the Ark was being used in the *Mishkan* or *Beis HaMikdash*, why is it included in the count of the mitzvos? Chinuch addresses this difficulty.

[Actually, as Chinuch states throughout this work, there are many mitzvos among the 613 that apply only in the time of the *Beis HaMikdash* (e.g., Mitzvos 5-8, 13-17, 88-91), or when the Jewish nation resides in Eretz Yisrael (e.g., Mitzvos 42-45, 49-52, 84, 95). It is unclear why Chinuch waited until this mitzvah to discuss this point.]

## 234 ❏ תרומה / מצוה צו: שלא להוציא בדי הארון ממנו

בְּגוֹן מַה שֶּׁבָּתוּב (שמות י״ט, ט״ו) הָיוּ נְכֹנִים לִשְׁלֹשֶׁת יָמִים, וּכְמוֹ כֵן אַזְהָרָה דְסִינַי (שם ל״ד, ג׳) גַּם הַצֹּאן וְהַבָּקָר אַל יִרְעוּ אֶל מוּל הָהָר הַהוּא[4] וְכָל כַּיּוֹצֵא בָּזֶה, שֶׁלֹּא הָיְתָה הַצַּוָּאָה אֶלָּא לְשָׁעָה בִּלְבַד, אֵלּוּ יִקָּרְאוּ מִצְוֹת שֶׁאֵינָן נוֹהֲגוֹת לְדוֹרוֹת, אֲבָל כָּל מִצְוָה שֶׁלֹּא נִצְטַוִּינוּ עָלֶיהָ לִזְמַן יָדוּעַ, אַף עַל פִּי שֶׁיֵּשׁ לָהּ הֶפְסֵק בִּזְמַן מִן הַזְּמַנִּים מִצַּד גָּלוּתֵנוּ אוֹ בְּסִבַּת דָּבָר אַחֵר, כְּגוֹן עַכְשָׁו בַּעֲוֹנוֹתֵינוּ שֶׁאֵין לָנוּ אָרוֹן, מִצְוָה הַנּוֹהֶגֶת לְדוֹרוֹת נִקְרֵאת, לְפִי שֶׁכָּל זְמַן שֶׁיִּהְיֶה לָנוּ אָרוֹן אָנוּ חַיָּבִין לְבַל נָסִיר בַּדָּיו מִמֶּנּוּ, כְּדֵי שֶׁיּוֹצִיאוּהוּ בָּהֶם הַלְוִיִּם, אִם נִצְטָרֵךְ לַהֲבִיאוֹ מִמָּקוֹם לְמָקוֹם בְּסִבַּת מִלְחָמָה[5] אוֹ מֵאֵי זֶה סִבָּה שֶׁתָּבוֹא.[6]

---

בְּגוֹן מַה שֶּׁבָּתוּב "הָיוּ נְכֹנִים לִשְׁלֹשֶׁת יָמִים" — **such as that which is written** regarding the Revelation at Sinai (*Exodus* 19:15): ***Be prepared after a three-day period;*** *do not draw near a woman,* וּכְמוֹ כֵן אַזְהָרָה דְסִינַי — **and similarly, the injunction pertaining to** Mount Sinai (ibid. 34:3): "גַּם הַצֹּאן וְהַבָּקָר אַל יִרְעוּ אֶל מוּל הָהָר הַהוּא" — *no man should ascend with you nor may anyone be seen on the entire mountain;* **even the flock and the cattle may not graze facing that mountain,**[4] וְכָל כַּיּוֹצֵא בָּזֶה — **and anything similar to these,** שֶׁלֹּא הָיְתָה הַצַּוָּאָה אֶלָּא לְשָׁעָה בִּלְבַד — **where the commandment pertained for only a short time,** אֵלּוּ יִקָּרְאוּ מִצְוֹת שֶׁאֵינָן נוֹהֲגוֹת לְדוֹרוֹת — **those are called "mitzvos that do not apply throughout the generations."** אֲבָל כָּל מִצְוָה שֶׁלֹּא נִצְטַוִּינוּ עָלֶיהָ לִזְמַן יָדוּעַ — **However, any mitzvah that we were** ***not*** **commanded to do for** only **a specific time,** but could (theoretically) apply forever, אַף עַל פִּי שֶׁיֵּשׁ לָהּ הֶפְסֵק בִּזְמַן מִן הַזְּמַנִּים — **even if it is subject to interruption at one time or another** מִצַּד גָּלוּתֵנוּ אוֹ בְּסִבַּת דָּבָר אַחֵר — **due to our exile or some other cause,** כְּגוֹן עַכְשָׁו בַּעֲוֹנוֹתֵינוּ שֶׁאֵין לָנוּ אָרוֹן — **such as nowadays,** when **on account of our sins we do not have an Ark** and the prohibition against removing its poles is irrelevant, מִצְוָה הַנּוֹהֶגֶת לְדוֹרוֹת נִקְרֵאת — it is nevertheless **called a "mitzvah that applies throughout the generations,"** לְפִי שֶׁכָּל זְמַן שֶׁיִּהְיֶה לָנוּ אָרוֹן חַיָּבִין אָנוּ לְבַל נָסִיר בַּדָּיו מִמֶּנּוּ — **for whenever we will have an Ark, we will be obligated not to remove its poles from it,** כְּדֵי שֶׁיּוֹצִיאוּהוּ בָּהֶם הַלְוִיִּם — **so that the Leviim can use them to carry out** [the Ark] אִם נִצְטָרֵךְ לַהֲבִיאוֹ מִמָּקוֹם לְמָקוֹם — **if it will be necessary to bring it from place to place** בְּסִבַּת מִלְחָמָה — **because of a war**[5] אוֹ מֵאֵי זֶה סִבָּה שֶׁתָּבוֹא — or some **other cause that might arise.**[6]

---

### NOTES

4. These instructions were given to the Jewish people at the time of the Giving of the Torah. They had to refrain from marital relations for three days and they were not allowed to ascend the mountain while the Divine Presence was upon it. Since these laws were intended only for that one short time, they are not "mitzvos that apply throughout the generations."

5. The Jews took the Ark with them in their battles against their enemies, as in *Joshua* Ch. 6 and *II Samuel* 11:11.

Some Rishonim state that there were two Arks: a wooden one made by Moses that contained the pieces of the broken *Luchos* (i.e., the Tablets of Stone on which the Ten Commandments had initially been written), and a golden one made by Betzalel that contained the unbroken *Luchos* (i.e., the second Tablets). It was the Ark of Moses that was taken to the battlefield, while Betzalel's Ark remained in the *Mishkan* or its pre-Temple equivalent (see *Rashi* to *Numbers* 10:33 and *Deuteronomy* 10:1; *Tosafos* to *Eruvin* 63b ד״ה כל זמן).

Other Rishonim, however, maintain that there was a single Ark, namely, the one built by Betzalel, and it held both sets of Tablets (see *Ramban* to *Deuteronomy* ibid.). This dispute relates to the pre-Temple era. Once King Solomon built the *Beis HaMikdash,* all agree that only Betzalel's Ark was used. From that point on, no Ark was allowed to be taken to the battlefield (*Tosafos* ibid.).

6. The mitzvos that cannot be observed in our time, yet are included in the count of the 613 Mitzvos, are included because they are relevant at least in theory; they are inapplicable in practice only because of external factors. For example, we cannot bring sacrificial offerings because the *Beis HaMikdash* is not currently standing, but since it can be built at any time, bringing each of the offerings is considered one of the 613 Mitzvos. These mitzvos are thus unlike the commandments that Chinuch mentioned earlier, which were never intended to apply beyond a specific time.

# TERUMAH / MITZVAH 96: NOT TO REMOVE THE POLES FROM THE ARK

מִשָּׁרְשֵׁי הַמִּצְוָה, לְפִי שֶׁהָאָרוֹן מִשְׁכַּן הַתּוֹרָה[7] וְהִיא כָּל עִקָּרֵנוּ וּכְבוֹדֵנוּ, וְנִתְחַיַּבְנוּ לִנְהֹג בּוֹ כָּל כָּבוֹד וְכָל הָדָר בְּכָל יְכָלְתֵּנוּ, עַל כֵּן נִצְטַוֵּינוּ לְבַל נָסִיר בַּדֵּי הָאָרוֹן מִמֶּנּוּ, פֶּן נִהְיֶה צְרִיכִים לָצֵאת עִם הָאָרוֹן לְשׁוּם מָקוֹם בִּמְהִירוּת, וְאוּלַי מִתּוֹךְ הַטְּרָדָה וְהַחִפָּזוֹן לֹא נִבְדֹּק יָפֶה לִהְיוֹת בַּדָּיו חֲזָקִים כָּל הַצֹּרֶךְ, וְשֶׁמָּא חַס וְשָׁלוֹם יִפֹּל וְאֵין זֶה כְּבוֹדוֹ. אֲבָל בִּהְיוֹתָם בּוֹ מוּכָנִים לְעוֹלָם וְלֹא יָסוּרוּ מִמֶּנּוּ, נַעֲשֶׂה אוֹתָן חֲזָקוֹת הַרְבֵּה וְלֹא יְאֹרַע תַּקָּלָה בָּהֶן. וְעוֹד טַעַם אַחֵר, שֶׁכָּל כְּלֵי הַמִּקְדָּשׁ צוּרָתָן מְחֻיֶּבֶת לִרְמֹז עִנְיָנִים גְּדוֹלִים עֶלְיוֹנִים, כְּדֵי שֶׁיְּהֵא הָאָדָם נִפְעָל לְטוֹבָה מִתּוֹךְ מַחֲשַׁבְתּוֹ בָּהֶן, וְרָצָה הָאֵל לְטוֹבָתֵנוּ שֶׁלֹּא תִפָּסֵד אוֹתָהּ הַצּוּרָה אֲפִלּוּ לְפִי שָׁעָה[8].

## ⟢ Underlying Purpose of the Mitzvah ⟣

מִשָּׁרְשֵׁי הַמִּצְוָה — **Among the underlying purposes of the mitzvah is** לְפִי שֶׁהָאָרוֹן מִשְׁכַּן הַתּוֹרָה — **that the Ark is the abode of the Torah,**[7] וְהִיא כָּל עִקָּרֵנוּ וּכְבוֹדֵנוּ — **which is our entire essence and glory,** וְנִתְחַיַּבְנוּ לִנְהֹג בּוֹ כָּל כָּבוֹד וְכָל הָדָר בְּכָל יְכָלְתֵּנוּ — **and we must therefore treat it with every** form of **glory and honor, to the best of our ability.** עַל כֵּן נִצְטַוֵּינוּ לְבַל נָסִיר בַּדֵּי הָאָרוֹן מִמֶּנּוּ — **We are consequently commanded not to remove the poles from the Ark,** פֶּן נִהְיֶה צְרִיכִים לָצֵאת עִם הָאָרוֹן לְשׁוּם מָקוֹם בִּמְהִירוּת — **lest we need to go out somewhere with the Ark in a hurry,** וְאוּלַי מִתּוֹךְ הַטְּרָדָה וְהַחִפָּזוֹן לֹא נִבְדֹּק יָפֶה לִהְיוֹת בַּדָּיו חֲזָקִים כָּל הַצֹּרֶךְ — **and maybe in** our **preoccupation and rush we will not check properly that its poles are as strong as necessary,** וְשֶׁמָּא חַס וְשָׁלוֹם יִפֹּל — **and then [the Ark] might, Heaven forbid, fall,** וְאֵין זֶה כְּבוֹדוֹ — **which does not befit its glory.** אֲבָל בִּהְיוֹתָם בּוֹ מוּכָנִים לְעוֹלָם וְלֹא יָסוּרוּ מִמֶּנּוּ — **However, if [the poles] are ready in it at all times and are not removed from it,** נַעֲשֶׂה אוֹתָן חֲזָקוֹת הַרְבֵּה וְלֹא יְאֹרַע תַּקָּלָה בָּהֶן — **we will make them very strong, and no mishap will befall them.** וְעוֹד טַעַם אַחֵר — **Another reason** for this mitzvah is שֶׁכָּל כְּלֵי הַמִּקְדָּשׁ — **that** regarding **all the vessels of the Holy Temple,** צוּרָתָן מְחֻיֶּבֶת לִרְמֹז עִנְיָנִים גְּדוֹלִים עֶלְיוֹנִים — **their design is specifically commanded, to hint at great sublime concepts,** כְּדֵי שֶׁיְּהֵא הָאָדָם נִפְעָל לְטוֹבָה מִתּוֹךְ מַחֲשַׁבְתּוֹ בָּהֶן — **so that a person will become positively affected by thinking about them.** וְרָצָה הָאֵל — **And so the Almighty desired,** לְטוֹבָתֵנוּ — **for our own benefit,** שֶׁלֹּא תִפָּסֵד אוֹתָהּ הַצּוּרָה אֲפִלּוּ לְפִי שָׁעָה — **that this design not be lost for even a moment.**[8]

---

### NOTES

7. The Torah Scroll written by Moses was placed either within the Ark or next to it (see *Bava Basra* 14a-b). Furthermore, as stated in note 5, it contained the *Luchos* on which the Ten Commandments were written.

The decorative gold rim of the Ark represented the crown of the Torah (*Rashi* to *Exodus* 25:11; see *Yoma* 72b).

8. The poles of the Ark were not merely functional; rather, they were part of the Ark itself. As such, they could never be removed because then the essential form of the Ark would be lost.

*Ralbag* (*Exodus* 25:15) explains that the poles were an integral part of the Ark because their constant presence meant that the Ark never required any adjustment or modification. Even if the Ark had to be moved, nothing had to be added to it. The symbolism here is that just as the Ark is perfect, never requiring any adjustment, so too the Torah — which is inscribed upon the *Luchos* contained within the Ark — is perfect.

One who removes a pole from the Ark, thus violating this prohibition, incurs the penalty of *malkus* (*Rambam, Sefer HaMitzvos, Lo Saaseh* 86).

According to the current editions of Chinuch, Mitzvah 96 concludes without a section regarding the applicability of the mitzvah, which represents a change from the format of the entire work. A brief reference to its applicability appears at the end of Mitzvah 97; see note 29 there.

---

⧂§ **Insight: Preparing the Ark for Being Carried in the Wilderness**

In the course of their forty years of wandering in the Wilderness, whenever the Jewish people broke camp, the Kohanim prepared the vessels of the *Mishkan* for travel. Regarding the Ark, it is

stated (Numbers 4:6): וְנָתְנוּ עָלָיו כְּסוּי עוֹר תַּחַשׁ וּפָרְשׂוּ בֶגֶד כְּלִיל תְּכֵלֶת מִלְמָעְלָה וְשָׂמוּ בַדָּיו, *They shall place upon it a tachash-skin covering and spread a cloth entirely of turquoise wool over it, and they shall place its poles.* This verse seems inconsistent with this mitzvah. In light of the mitzvah's mandate that the poles be permanently attached to the Ark, how can we understand this directive to insert them before the people traveled?

Among the various solutions that have been suggested, the following have bearing on the parameters of this mitzvah:

*Minchah Chadashah* cites the opinion of *Smag* (*Lavin* 296), who states that the prohibition of removing the poles applied only when the Ark was not in its regular position, such as when the Israelites were traveling. But when the Ark came to rest at the places of destination, it was permissible to remove them. Presumably, argues *Minchah Chadashah*, *Smag* derived this position from this very verse, which implies that the poles were reinserted each time a new journey began.

Most authorities, though, maintain that the poles were *never* allowed to be removed. In their view, the Torah required that the poles remain in place at all times, so that, as *Chinuch* explained, the Ark would always be ready to be carried.

*Tosafos* (*Yoma* 72a ד"ה כתיב בטבעות הארון) solve the problem by suggesting that the Ark had *two* pairs of poles: one pair that constantly remained in place, as required by this mitzvah, and another pair that was used to carry the Ark. The latter were inserted before traveling and removed when the destination was reached. It is with regard to these poles that the Torah states וְשָׂמוּ בַדָּיו, *and they shall place its poles*. *Tosafos* infer this from the verse (*Exodus* 25:12): וְיָצַקְתָּ לּוֹ אַרְבַּע טַבְּעֹת זָהָב וְנָתַתָּה עַל אַרְבַּע פַּעֲמֹתָיו וּשְׁתֵּי טַבָּעֹת עַל צַלְעוֹ הָאֶחָת וּשְׁתֵּי טַבָּעֹת עַל צַלְעוֹ הַשֵּׁנִית, *You shall cast for it four rings of gold and place them on its four corners; two rings on its one side and two rings on its second side.* Many commentators explain that the second half of the verse (*two rings on its one side,* etc.) clarifies *where* the four rings mentioned earlier were to be placed (*Rashi, Ramban,* et al.). *Tosafos,* however, understand the second half as referring to a *different* set of rings. The first clause speaks of four rings that were placed on the *corners* of the Ark, whereas the second clause describes another four rings that were placed on the *sides* of the Ark. Thus, there were eight rings altogether. Each pair of rings held a pole, making for a total of four poles, two of which remained permanently in place and two of which were inserted only for traveling.

Several other suggestions have been offered to resolve the contradiction between the instruction to "place the poles" prior to travel and the prohibition that is the subject of this mitzvah.

*Ramban* (*Numbers* ibid.) explains that the directive *"and they shall place its poles"* refers not to the insertion of the poles into the rings of the Ark, but to putting the poles on the shoulders of the Ark's bearers. [*Tosafos* (ibid.) also cite this answer, but find it unsatisfactory, because this phrase is immediately preceded by the commandment to cover the Ark. Thus, if the verse is understood in this manner, it would imply that as soon as the Ark was covered it should be loaded onto the shoulders of the Leviim, who carried the Ark. Yet, the Torah forbade the Leviim to approach any of the vessels until *all* of them were wrapped, as indicated by *Numbers* 4:20 (*They shall not come to look as the holy is being covered*).]

Alternatively, *Ramban* suggests (see also *Meiri, Yoma* 72a) that "placing the poles" meant adjusting the poles *within* the rings into a position that would best facilitate the carrying of the Ark.

*Chizkuni* (*Exodus* 25:15) offers yet another approach: When Moses inserted the poles in the course of erecting the *Mishkan*, the prohibition of removing the poles did not immediately apply. The poles were removed after Moses put them in, and then the Kohanim reinserted them before the next journey, at which point the prohibition took effect. The reason for this arrangement is that God wanted the Kohanim to be the ones who inserted the poles permanently. The verse *"and they shall place the poles"* refers to the first (and only) time that the Kohanim put the poles in place, after which it was forbidden to ever take them out.

## מִצְוָה צז: מִצְוַת סִדּוּר לֶחֶם הַפָּנִים וּלְבוֹנָה[1]

לְהָשִׂים בְּבֵית הַמִּקְדָּשׁ לִפְנֵי ה' לֶחֶם תָּמִיד, שֶׁנֶּאֱמַר (שמות כ"ה, ל') וְנָתַתָּ עַל הַשֻּׁלְחָן לֶחֶם פָּנִים לְפָנַי תָּמִיד.

מִשָּׁרְשֵׁי הַמִּצְוָה, שֶׁצִּוָּנוּ הָאֵל בָּרוּךְ הוּא מִצְוָה תְּמִידִית בַּלֶּחֶם לְפִי שֶׁבּוֹ יִחְיֶה הָאָדָם, וְעַל כֵּן צָרִיךְ אֵלָיו לִהְיוֹת הַבְּרָכָה מְצוּיָה בּוֹ תָּמִיד, וּמִתּוֹךְ עִסְקֵנוּ בּוֹ לְקַיֵּם עָלָיו מִצְוַת הַשֵּׁם יִתְבָּרַךְ יִהְיֶה הָרָצוֹן וְהַבְּרָכָה חָלִים עָלֵינוּ וְיִתְבָּרֵךְ בְּמֵעֵינוּ, כִּי בְּכָל שֶׁעוֹשֶׂה בּוֹ הָאָדָם

# Mitzvah 97

## The Obligation to Arrange the Lechem HaPanim and the Levonah

וְנָתַתָּ עַל הַשֻּׁלְחָן לֶחֶם פָּנִים לְפָנַי תָּמִיד
*On the Table you shall place Lechem HaPanim before Me, always* (Exodus 25:30).

Among the regular services that were performed in the Temple (*Beis HaMikdash*) was the weekly arrangement of the *Lechem HaPanim* — literally, *bread of faces* — on the Table (*Shulchan*). The bread was so called because of the special shape of the loaves, which were formed similar to a squared-off "U" — with a flat bottom and two vertical "faces" (*Rashi, Exodus 25:29*). Twelve of these loaves were baked each Friday, and then, on the Sabbath, arranged upon the *Shulchan* in two stacks of six loaves each. They remained there until the next Sabbath, when they were removed and replaced with a fresh set of loaves. Two spoons filled with *levonah* (frankincense) were also placed on the *Shulchan*, one near each stack of loaves.[1] Upon the removal of the *Lechem HaPanim* from the *Shulchan* on the Sabbath, the *levonah* was burned on the Altar and the twelve loaves were eaten by the Kohanim. Although the loaves had been baked more than a week earlier, they miraculously remained fresh, as though they had just been baked. לְהָשִׂים בְּבֵית הַמִּקְדָּשׁ לִפְנֵי ה' לֶחֶם תָּמִיד — We are commanded **to place bread in the *Beis HaMikdash*** (Holy Temple) **before Hashem constantly,**[2] שֶׁנֶּאֱמַר — **as it is stated** (*Exodus* 25:30): "וְנָתַתָּ עַל הַשֻּׁלְחָן לֶחֶם פָּנִים לְפָנַי תָּמִיד" — *On the Table you shall place Lechem HaPanim before Me, always.*

### Underlying Purpose of the Mitzvah

שֶׁצִּוָּנוּ הָאֵל בָּרוּךְ הוּא מִצְוָה — **Among the underlying purposes of the mitzvah is** מִשָּׁרְשֵׁי הַמִּצְוָה — **that the Almighty, blessed is He, imposed upon us a mitzvah that is** to be **continuously** performed **with bread** לְפִי שֶׁבּוֹ יִחְיֶה הָאָדָם — **because a man's life is sustained through [bread],** וְעַל כֵּן צָרִיךְ אֵלָיו לִהְיוֹת הַבְּרָכָה מְצוּיָה בּוֹ תָּמִיד — **and hence, he needs that a blessing always be found in it.** וּמִתּוֹךְ עִסְקֵנוּ בּוֹ לְקַיֵּם עָלָיו מִצְוַת הַשֵּׁם יִתְבָּרַךְ — **Through busying ourselves with [bread] for the sake of fulfilling a mitzvah of Hashem, blessed be He,** יִהְיֶה הָרָצוֹן וְהַבְּרָכָה חָלִים עָלֵינוּ — **His good will and blessing will be visited upon us,** וְיִתְבָּרֵךְ בְּמֵעֵינוּ — **and [our own bread] will become blessed within our innards,** כִּי בְּכָל שֶׁעוֹשֶׂה בּוֹ הָאָדָם

---

### NOTES

1. See below, note 16.

[The Scriptural term לְבוֹנָה, *levonah*, is generally translated as frankincense — a resinous substance deriving from the sap of certain trees, which hardens into granules that are burned as incense. Whether the trees identified as the sources of frankincense are indeed identical to the ones from which *levonah* was taken is difficult to determine. However, *Aruch HaShulchan HeAsid* 19:8 cites from the *Siddur* of the *Shelah* that *levonah* indeed comes from the sap of a tree. See also *Tiferes Yisrael* in his *Chomer BaKodesh* (Introduction to *Seder Kodashim*) 2:67. We will refer to this simply as *levonah*.]

2. Although each set of twelve loaves remained on the *Shulchan* for only one week, the incoming loaves were put on the *Shulchan* at the very time the outgoing ones were removed (as Chinuch explains below, at note 25). Thus, *Lechem HaPanim* was "constantly" on the *Shulchan* before Hashem.

רְצוֹן הַשֵׁם יִתְבָּרֵךְ, בּוֹ הוּא מִתְבָּרֵךְ, וּלְפִי כָּל עִנְיָן וְעִנְיָן שֶׁיָּשִׂים מְגַמַּת פָּנָיו וּמַחְשְׁבוֹתָיו וַעֲסָקָיו בִּדְבַר מִצְוָה, לְפִיהֶן מַעְיַן הַבְּרָכָה נוֹבֵעַ עָלָיו. וְכֵן מָצָאתִי לְהָרַמְבַּ"ן ז"ל,[3] וּכְעִין מַה שֶּׁאָמְרוּ זִכְרוֹנָם לִבְרָכָה (ראש השנה דף ט"ז ע"א) הָבִיאוּ לְפָנַי עֹמֶר בַּפֶּסַח כְּדֵי שֶׁיִּתְבָּרְכוּ לָכֶם תְּבוּאָה שֶׁבַּשָּׂדוֹת, נַסְּכוּ לְפָנַי מַיִם בֶּחָג כְּדֵי שֶׁיִּתְבָּרְכוּ לָכֶם גִּשְׁמֵי שָׁנָה, תִּקְעוּ לְפָנַי שׁוֹפָר שֶׁל אַיִל כְּדֵי לִזְכֹּר עֲקֵדַת יִצְחָק.[4] וְעַל הַלֶּחֶם הַזֶּה בְּעַצְמוֹ אָמְרוּ (יומא דף ל"ט ע"א) כִּי מִפְּנֵי שֶׁהוּא תַּשְׁמִישׁ הַמִּצְוָה וּבוֹ נַעֲשָׂה רְצוֹן הָאֵל, הָיְתָה הַבְּרָכָה דְּבֵקָה בּוֹ בְּיוֹתֵר, וְכָל אֶחָד מִן הַכֹּהֲנִים שֶׁהִגִּיעַ לוֹ מִמֶּנּוּ כְּפוֹל הָיָה שָׂבֵעַ.[5]

---

רְצוֹן הַשֵׁם יִתְבָּרֵךְ — **because whatever** object **man uses in performing the Will of Hashem, blessed be He,** בּוֹ הוּא מִתְבָּרֵךְ — **he himself becomes blessed through it;** וּלְפִי כָּל עִנְיָן וְעִנְיָן שֶׁיָּשִׂים מְגַמַּת פָּנָיו וּמַחְשְׁבוֹתָיו וַעֲסָקָיו בִּדְבַר מִצְוָה — **and according to each and every specific matter with which [man] sets his direction, his thoughts, and his deeds toward the purpose of fulfilling a mitzvah,** לְפִיהֶן מַעְיַן הַבְּרָכָה נוֹבֵעַ עָלָיו — **in regard to those [matters], the wellsprings of blessing flow over him.** וְכֵן מָצָאתִי לְהָרַמְבַּ"ן ז"ל — **I found** a similar explanation **in the commentary of** *Ramban***, of blessed memory** (*Exodus* 25:24).[3] וּכְעִין מַה שֶּׁאָמְרוּ זִכְרוֹנָם לִבְרָכָה — **This explanation reflects what [the Sages] of blessed memory said** (*Rosh Hashanah* 16a): הָבִיאוּ לְפָנַי עֹמֶר בַּפֶּסַח — **God commanded: "Bring before Me the** *Omer* **offering on Pesach,** כְּדֵי שֶׁיִּתְבָּרְכוּ לָכֶם תְּבוּאָה שֶׁבַּשָּׂדוֹת — **so that the grain in the fields will be blessed for you.** נַסְּכוּ לְפָנַי מַיִם בֶּחָג — **Pour before Me the water libation on the Festival** of Succos, כְּדֵי שֶׁיִּתְבָּרְכוּ לָכֶם גִּשְׁמֵי שָׁנָה — **so that the annual rains will be blessed for you.** תִּקְעוּ לְפָנַי שׁוֹפָר שֶׁל אַיִל — **Blow before Me the shofar of a ram** on Rosh Hashanah, כְּדֵי לִזְכֹּר עֲקֵדַת יִצְחָק — **to commemorate the Binding of Isaac."**[4] וְעַל הַלֶּחֶם הַזֶּה בְּעַצְמוֹ אָמְרוּ — **Furthermore, regarding this Bread** (the *Lechem HaPanim*) itself, [the Sages] said (*Yoma* 39a) כִּי מִפְּנֵי שֶׁהוּא תַּשְׁמִישׁ הַמִּצְוָה — **that since it is a mitzvah article** וּבוֹ נַעֲשָׂה רְצוֹן הָאֵל — **through which the Will of the Almighty was performed,** הָיְתָה הַבְּרָכָה דְּבֵקָה בּוֹ בְּיוֹתֵר — **blessing adhered to it in abundance,** וְכָל אֶחָד מִן הַכֹּהֲנִים שֶׁהִגִּיעַ לוֹ מִמֶּנּוּ כְּפוֹל הָיָה שָׂבֵעַ — **such that any Kohen who received** even **a bean-sized portion of it was satiated** by eating it.[5]

Having explained that the *Lechem HaPanim* serves to bring blessing, Chinuch extends this idea to the entire service in the *Beis HaMikdash*:

---

NOTES

3. *Ramban* writes that after the Six Days of Creation, God's blessings ceased to create something out of nothing. Rather, they act to affect an entity that already exists, making it increase and grow. This is the purpose served by the *Lechem HaPanim*. The Divine blessing of material wealth devolves upon the *Lechem HaPanim*, which already exists, and from there it flows to all Israel.

4. God decides on Pesach how much grain will grow that year, on Succos how much rain will fall, and on Rosh Hashanah He judges each human being for his deeds (Mishnah, *Rosh Hashanah* 16a). We therefore bring the *Omer* offering (which is from the new crop of barley) on Pesach to beseech God for a favorable judgment on grain, we perform the ritual of *nisuch hamayim* (water libation) on Succos for a favorable judgment on water, and we blow the shofar on Rosh Hashanah so that God will remember *Akeidas Yitzchak* (the binding of Isaac, in whose place a ram was offered; see *Genesis* 22:13) and judge us favorably in its merit (see Gemara ibid.). The function of each service is to bring about blessing with regard to that particular item, which is how Chinuch explained the purpose of the *Lechem HaPanim*.

5. According to our version of that Gemara, a Kohen would be satiated by eating a *kezayis* (olive-sized portion) of the *Lechem HaPanim*, which is larger than a bean-sized portion. However, it is clear from the Gemara that even a bean-sized piece of the *Lechem HaPanim* effected some degree of satisfaction (see *Ritva* there).

[*Ritva* also records an alternative text of the Gemara, in which a *bean*-sized piece of the *Lechem HaPanim* is said to cause satiety. Although *Ritva* rejects this version because it does not appear in earlier manuscripts, it seems to have been Chinuch's reading of the Gemara.]

# TERUMAH / MITZVAH 97: TO ARRANGE THE LECHEM HAPANIM AND THE LEVONAH

וְאֵלֶּה הַדְּבָרִים, כְּגוֹן שֻׁלְחָן וּמְנוֹרָה וְלֶחֶם הַפָּנִים וְהַקָּרְבָּנוֹת, בְּכֻלָּן נִצְטַוֵּינוּ מִצַּד הַמְקַבְּלִים, וּכְעִנְיָן שֶׁכָּתַבְתִּי[6], אֵין סָפֵק וּפִקְפּוּק לְכָל מֵבִין עִם תַּלְמִיד[7], שֶׁאֵין חֲסַר תְּבוּנוֹת[8] בָּעוֹלָם יַחְשֹׁב שֶׁבְּסִדּוּר לֶחֶם בַּבַּיִת עַל שֻׁלְחָן, שֶׁנַּנִּיחֶנּוּ שָׁלֵם וְנִקָּחֶנּוּ שָׁלֵם וּמְבֹרָךְ, תְּקַבֵּל שׁוּם הֲנָאָה לְמַעְלָה חָלִילָה, לֹא בְמַרְאֶה וְלֹא בְרֵיחַ וְלֹא בְּשׁוּם צַד, רַק שֶׁצִּוָּנוּ בְּכָךְ לְחֶפְצוֹ בָּרוּךְ הוּא שֶׁנִּתְבָּרֵךְ מִמֶּנּוּ מֵרֹב מִדַּת טוּבוֹ[9]. גַּם הַלְּבוֹנָה הַבָּאָה עִם הַלֶּחֶם שֶׁנִּכְתַּב בָּהּ (ויקרא כ״ד, ז׳) אִשֶּׁה לַה', וְאָמְרוּ הַמְפָרְשִׁים שֶׁאֵין מִן הַלֶּחֶם לְגָבוֹהַּ כְּלוּם אֶלָּא הַלְּבוֹנָה שֶׁנִּקְטֶרֶת בְּכָל שַׁבָּת כְּשֶׁמְּסַלְּקִין הַלֶּחֶם[10], אֵין כַּוָּנָתָם חָלִילָה לִהְיוֹת חִלּוּק כְּלָל בֵּין הַלְּבוֹנָה וְהַלֶּחֶם לְמַעְלָה,

---

וְאֵלֶּה הַדְּבָרִים בְּגוֹן שֻׁלְחָן וּמְנוֹרָה וְלֶחֶם הַפָּנִים — **These elements** of the *Beis HaMikdash* service, וְהַקָּרְבָּנוֹת — **such as** those pertaining to **the Table, the Menorah, the *Lechem HaPanim*, and the offerings,** בְּכֻלָּן נִצְטַוֵּינוּ מִצַּד הַמְקַבְּלִים — **we were commanded in all of them only for the sake of those who received** the commandments (i.e., for our own sake, and not for God's), וּכְעִנְיָן שֶׁכָּתַבְתִּי — **as I have written** previously.[6] אֵין סָפֵק וּפִקְפּוּק לְכָל מֵבִין עִם תַּלְמִיד — **There is no doubt or question** about this **to any expert or student,**[7] שֶׁאֵין חֲסַר תְּבוּנוֹת בָּעוֹלָם יַחְשֹׁב — **for there is no fool**[8] **in the world who would think** שֶׁבְּסִדּוּר לֶחֶם בַּבַּיִת עַל שֻׁלְחָן — **that by arranging bread upon a table in the Temple,** שֶׁנַּנִּיחֶנּוּ שָׁלֵם וְנִקָּחֶנּוּ שָׁלֵם וּמְבֹרָךְ — **which we put down** when **whole and remove** when **whole and blessed,** תְּקַבֵּל שׁוּם הֲנָאָה לְמַעְלָה חָלִילָה — **the One Above receives any benefit, Heaven forbid,** לֹא בְמַרְאֶה וְלֹא בְרֵיחַ וְלֹא בְּשׁוּם צַד — **either from** its **appearance, or** from its **aroma, or** from **any other aspect** of it. רַק שֶׁצִּוָּנוּ בְּכָךְ — **Rather, [God] commanded us in these** forms of service לְחֶפְצוֹ בָּרוּךְ הוּא שֶׁנִּתְבָּרֵךְ מִמֶּנּוּ מֵרֹב מִדַּת טוּבוֹ — **out of His desire, blessed be He** — which emanates **from His great Attribute of Goodness** — **that we become blessed from Him.**[9]

Chinuch explains that the above is true even though the Torah might be understood to indicate otherwise:

גַּם הַלְּבוֹנָה הַבָּאָה עִם הַלֶּחֶם — **The preceding applies even to the *levonah* that accompanies the *Lechem* HaPanim,** שֶׁנִּכְתַּב בָּהּ "אִשֶּׁה לַה׳" — **about which it is written: *a fire-offering for* HASHEM** (*Leviticus* 24:7), וְאָמְרוּ הַמְפָרְשִׁים — **and the commentators** (Rashi ad loc.) **said** that the *levonah* is described as such שֶׁאֵין מִן הַלֶּחֶם לְגָבוֹהַּ כְּלוּם — **because no part of the *Lechem* HaPanim is offered up before the Most High,** אֶלָּא הַלְּבוֹנָה שֶׁנִּקְטֶרֶת בְּכָל שַׁבָּת כְּשֶׁמְּסַלְּקִין הַלֶּחֶם — **except the *levonah* that is burned** on the Altar **each Sabbath when the *Lechem HaPanim* is removed** from the Table. By explaining that the *levonah* is "for Hashem" because it is burned on the Altar, the commentators seem to imply that offerings burned on the Altar are for God's benefit.[10] However, this is not so. אֵין כַּוָּנָתָם חָלִילָה לִהְיוֹת חִלּוּק כְּלָל בֵּין הַלְּבוֹנָה וְהַלֶּחֶם לְמַעְלָה — In fact, **their intent was not, Heaven forbid, that there is any distinction at all between the *levonah* and the *Lechem* HaPanim** with

---

## NOTES

6. Chinuch discusses this principle at length in Mitzvah 95; see also Mitzvah 88.

7. Stylistic citation of *I Chronicles* 25:8.

8. Stylistic citation of *Proverbs* 28:16.

9. Given that the *Lechem HaPanim* merely lies upon the *Shulchan* until it is eaten by man, it *obviously* benefits only people, and not God. Chinuch extrapolates from there to all the *Beis HaMikdash* services. Even an offering that is not eaten by anyone, but is burned entirely on the Altar, does not provide pleasure to God, but serves to benefit man. [See Mitzvah 95, where Chinuch explains that the purpose of *all* the mitzvos is to bring about benefit to the Jewish people, and where he discusses the unique role of the *Beis HaMikdash* service in this regard.]

10. Had the Torah not distinguished between the bread and the *levonah*, we would have understood its words "for Hashem" as meaning that one must perform these mitzvos for the sake of Heaven, and not for personal, ulterior motives. However, since these words are in fact limited to the *levonah*, which is burned on the Altar (as opposed to the bread, which is eaten by man), it cannot carry this meaning, which would apply to both mitzvos alike. Hence, we might have suggested instead that "for Hashem" conveys that something burned on the Altar is a source of benefit to God. Chinuch proceeds to reject this interpretation.

וְקִיּוּם מִצְוַת הָאֵל בַּלֶּחֶם וּבַלְּבוֹנָה אֶחָד הוּא, כִּי כְּמוֹ שֶׁצִּוָּה הָאֵל בָּרוּךְ הוּא לְהַסְדִּיר הַלֶּחֶם לְפָנָיו וְנַעֲשָׂה רְצוֹנוֹ וְסִדְּרוּהוּ, כֵּן נַעֲשָׂה רְצוֹנוֹ בַּלְּבוֹנָה שֶׁצִּוָּה לְהַקְטִיר וְהִקְטִירוּהָ, קֶצֶב אֶחָד לַכֹּל. אֲבָל כָּל אֵלֶּה הָעִנְיָנִים יִכָּתְבוּ עַל צַד הָעוֹסְקִים, כִּי הַלֶּחֶם שֶׁנֶּאֱכַל לַכֹּהֲנִים אֵין לִכְתֹּב עָלָיו שֶׁכֻּלּוֹ לַשֵּׁם כִּי הֵם יֹאכְלוּהוּ, נִמְצָא שֶׁאֵין כֻּלּוֹ לַשֵּׁם כִּי אֲחֵרִים יַחְלְקוּ בוֹ, אֲבָל בְּכָל מַה שֶּׁלֹּא יֵהָנֶה בּוֹ הָאָדָם כְּלָל אֶלָּא שֶׁעוֹשֶׂה מִמֶּנּוּ מִצְוַת בּוֹרְאוֹ וְכָלָה לְגַמְרֵי בְּמִצְוָה, בָּזֶה נוּכַל לוֹמַר עָלָיו כִּי כֻלּוֹ לַה׳, כְּלוֹמַר שֶׁנִּכְנַס כֻּלּוֹ בְּמִצְוָתוֹ, לֹא אָכַל מִמֶּנּוּ אָדָם וְלֹא נֶהֱנָה בּוֹ הֲנָאָה גוּפָנִית כְּלָל.[11] וְעַל שֶׁהָרֵיחַ אֵינֶנּוּ מִן הַהֲנָאוֹת שֶׁל גּוּף רַק מֵהֲנָאַת הַנֶּפֶשׁ,[12] כִּי הַגּוּף לֹא יְקַבֵּל רַק הֲנָאַת הַמִּשּׁוּשׁ, יְכֻנֶּה לְעוֹלָם עִנְיַן הָרֵיחַ אֶל הַשֵּׁם בָּרוּךְ הוּא, אַף עַל פִּי שֶׁהוּא בָּרוּךְ הוּא וּבָרוּךְ שְׁמוֹ אֵינֶנּוּ לְרֹב מַעֲלָתוֹ וְגָדְלוֹ בְּגֶדֶר עִנְיָנִים אֵלֶּה כְּלָל

וְקִיּוּם מִצְוַת הָאֵל בַּלֶּחֶם וּבַלְּבוֹנָה אֶחָד הוּא — **Rather, in the matter of obeying the commandment of the Almighty, the *Lechem HaPanim* and the *levonah* are the same, with respect to the One Above.** כִּי כְּמוֹ שֶׁצִּוָּה הָאֵל בָּרוּךְ הוּא לְהַסְדִּיר הַלֶּחֶם לְפָנָיו — **for just as the Almighty, blessed is He, commanded us to arrange the *Lechem HaPanim* before Him,** וְנַעֲשָׂה רְצוֹנוֹ וְסִדְּרוּהוּ — **and His Will was fulfilled and [the bread] was arranged,** כֵּן נַעֲשָׂה רְצוֹנוֹ בַּלְּבוֹנָה — **so was His Will fulfilled with the *levonah*,** שֶׁצִּוָּה לְהַקְטִיר וְהִקְטִירוּהָ — **for He commanded us to burn it and it was burned;** קֶצֶב אֶחָד לַכֹּל — **there is one dimension to all** the components of this mitzvah. אֲבָל כָּל אֵלֶּה הָעִנְיָנִים יִכָּתְבוּ עַל צַד הָעוֹסְקִים — **Rather, all these things** (such as the description of burned offerings as being "for Hashem") **are written from the perspective of those who engage** in bringing the offerings. כִּי הַלֶּחֶם שֶׁנֶּאֱכַל לַכֹּהֲנִים אֵין לִכְתֹּב עָלָיו שֶׁכֻּלּוֹ לַשֵּׁם — **Regarding the *Lechem HaPanim*, which is eaten by the Kohanim, it could not be written that it is entirely for Hashem,** כִּי הֵם יֹאכְלוּהוּ — **because [the Kohanim] eat it.** נִמְצָא שֶׁאֵין כֻּלּוֹ לַשֵּׁם כִּי אֲחֵרִים יַחְלְקוּ בוֹ — **Thus, [the bread] is not entirely "for Hashem," since others have a share in it** as well. אֲבָל בְּכָל מַה שֶּׁלֹּא יֵהָנֶה בּוֹ הָאָדָם כְּלָל — **However, any** offering **from which man does not benefit at all,** אֶלָּא שֶׁעוֹשֶׂה מִמֶּנּוּ מִצְוַת בּוֹרְאוֹ — **rather, he uses it** only to fulfill **the commandment of his Creator,** וְכָלָה לְגַמְרֵי בְּמִצְוָה — **and it is entirely consumed in** the performance of **the mitzvah,** בָּזֶה נוּכַל לוֹמַר עָלָיו כִּי כֻלּוֹ לַה׳ — **in that case, we can say that it is entirely "for Hashem."** כְּלוֹמַר — **That is to say,** שֶׁנִּכְנַס כֻּלּוֹ בְּמִצְוָתוֹ — **all of it was used for its mitzvah** וְלֹא נֶהֱנָה בּוֹ הֲנָאָה גוּפָנִית — in the sense that **man did not eat from it,** לֹא אָכַל מִמֶּנּוּ אָדָם — nor did he derive any physical benefit from it.[11]

Chinuch explains another Scriptural expression that could be understood to imply that God benefits from the sacrificial offerings. This is the expression found numerous times in regard to the offerings (e.g., *Leviticus* 1:9), רֵיחַ נִיחוֹחַ לַה׳, *a satisfying aroma to HASHEM*:

וְעַל שֶׁהָרֵיחַ אֵינֶנּוּ מִן הַהֲנָאוֹת שֶׁל גּוּף — **And because smell is not** one **of the pleasures of the body,** רַק מֵהֲנָאַת הַנֶּפֶשׁ — **but only a pleasure of the soul,**[12] כִּי הַגּוּף לֹא יְקַבֵּל רַק הֲנָאַת הַמִּשּׁוּשׁ — **for a body cannot receive anything other than tangible pleasure,** יְכֻנֶּה לְעוֹלָם עִנְיַן הָרֵיחַ אֶל הַשֵּׁם בָּרוּךְ הוּא — **therefore, the concept of smell is frequently attributed to Hashem, blessed is He,** אַף עַל פִּי שֶׁהוּא בָּרוּךְ הוּא וּבָרוּךְ שְׁמוֹ — **even though [Hashem], blessed is He and blessed is His Name,** אֵינֶנּוּ לְרֹב מַעֲלָתוֹ וְגָדְלוֹ בְּגֶדֶר עִנְיָנִים אֵלֶּה כְּלָל — **due to His exalted stature and greatness, is not subject to these matters at all,**

---

NOTES

11. Chinuch has thus explained that when the Torah describes the *levonah* as an offering "for Hashem," it refers to the fact that the *levonah* is completely expended in the service of God, without any part being eaten or otherwise enjoyed by man.

12. The Gemara (*Berachos* 43b) states: "What is something from which the soul derives pleasure but the body does not derive pleasure? It is smell."

Since smells do not enter the body in the same tangible form as do food and drink, smell is considered, by comparison to eating, a "pleasure of the soul." The Hebrew word רֵיחַ, *smell*, is related to רוּחַ, *spirit*, because it is a "spiritual" type of pleasure (*Aruch HaShulchan, Orach Chaim* 216:1).

# 241 □ TERUMAH / MITZVAH 97: TO ARRANGE THE LECHEM HAPANIM AND THE LEVONAH

לְפִי שֶׁאֵינוֹ גּוּף וְלֹא כֹחַ בַּגּוּף, יָדוּעַ הוּא אֵצֶל כָּל מֵבִין, וּכְבָר פֵּרְשׁוּ זִכְרוֹנָם לִבְרָכָה, בְּכָל מָקוֹם שֶׁנֶּאֱמַר רֵיחַ נִיחוֹחַ לַה'[13], שֶׁאָמַרְתִּי וְנַעֲשָׂה רְצוֹנִי, וְכֵן וַיָּרַח ה' אֶת רֵיחַ הַנִּיחֹחַ (בראשית ח', כ"א) בַּדֶּרֶךְ הַזֶּה. זֶהוּ שֶׁנִּרְאָה לָנוּ בְּעִנְיַן סִדּוּר הַלֶּחֶם בְּבֵית הַשֵּׁם. וְהָרַמְבַּ"ם זִכְרוֹנוֹ לִבְרָכָה כָּתַב (מורה נבוכים ח"ג מ"ה) וְזֶה לְשׁוֹנוֹ, אֲבָל הַשֻּׁלְחָן וֶהֱיוֹת הַלֶּחֶם עָלָיו תָּמִיד לֹא אֵדַע לוֹ סִבָּה, וְאֵינִי יוֹדֵעַ לְאֵי זֶה דָּבָר אֲיַחֵס אוֹתוֹ עַד הַיּוֹם.

מִדִּינֵי הַמִּצְוָה, מַה שֶּׁאָמְרוּ זִכְרוֹנָם לִבְרָכָה (תורת כהנים אמור כ"ד, ז') שֶׁבְּכָל אַחַת מִן הַמַּעֲרָכוֹת[14] הָיוּ נוֹתְנִים כְּלִי שֶׁיֵּשׁ בּוֹ קֹמֶץ[15] לְבוֹנָה, שֶׁנֶּאֱמַר (ויקרא כ"ד, ז') וְנָתַתָּ עַל הַמַּעֲרֶכֶת, כְּלוֹמַר עַל כָּל אַחַת מֵהֶן לְבוֹנָה זַכָּה[16], וּכְלִי זֶה נִקְרָא בָּזָךְ, וְאָמְרוּ זִכְרוֹנָם לִבְרָכָה

---

לְפִי שֶׁאֵינוֹ גּוּף — because He is neither a body וְלֹא כֹחַ בַּגּוּף — nor a force that manifests itself within a body, יָדוּעַ הוּא אֵצֶל כָּל מֵבִין — as is known to any intelligent person. וּכְבָר פֵּרְשׁוּ זִכְרוֹנָם לִבְרָכָה — And [the Sages], of blessed memory, have already said (Sifra, Leviticus 1:9; see Rashi there) בְּכָל מָקוֹם שֶׁנֶּאֱמַר "רֵיחַ נִיחוֹחַ לַה'" — that wherever it is stated *a satisfying aroma to HASHEM* (Leviticus ibid.), it should be understood as meaning: שֶׁאָמַרְתִּי וְנַעֲשָׂה רְצוֹנִי — "I have spoken, and My Will was fulfilled."[13] וְכֵן "וַיָּרַח ה' אֶת רֵיחַ הַנִּיחֹחַ" בַּדֶּרֶךְ הַזֶּה — Similarly, the phrase *HASHEM smelled the pleasing aroma* (Genesis 8:21) should be understood **in this manner**.

Having suggested an explanation for the *Lechem HaPanim* service, Chinuch notes that this is, nonetheless, a difficult mitzvah to understand:

זֶהוּ שֶׁנִּרְאָה לָנוּ בְּעִנְיַן סִדּוּר הַלֶּחֶם בְּבֵית הַשֵּׁם — This is what seems correct **to us regarding the matter of arranging the *Lechem HaPanim* in the Temple of Hashem.** וְהָרַמְבַּ"ם זִכְרוֹנוֹ לִבְרָכָה כָּתַב וְזֶה לְשׁוֹנוֹ — However, *Rambam*, of blessed memory, wrote these words (*Moreh Nevuchim* III Ch. 45): אֲבָל הַשֻּׁלְחָן וֶהֱיוֹת הַלֶּחֶם עָלָיו תָּמִיד לֹא אֵדַע לוֹ סִבָּה — "But I do not know the reason **for the Table and** for the requirement **that there constantly be *Lechem HaPanim* upon it,** וְאֵינִי יוֹדֵעַ לְאֵי זֶה דָּבָר אֲיַחֵס אוֹתוֹ עַד הַיּוֹם — and, **until this very day, I do not know what purpose I can ascribe to it.**"

## ⤞ Laws of the Mitzvah ⤝

מִדִּינֵי הַמִּצְוָה — The laws of the mitzvah include מַה שֶּׁאָמְרוּ זִכְרוֹנָם לִבְרָכָה — what [the Sages], of blessed memory, have stated (Sifra, Leviticus 24:7), שֶׁבְּכָל אַחַת מִן הַמַּעֲרָכוֹת הָיוּ נוֹתְנִים כְּלִי — that for each stack of six loaves[14] they would place a vessel that contains שֶׁיֵּשׁ בּוֹ קֹמֶץ לְבוֹנָה — a *kometz*[15] of *levonah*, שֶׁנֶּאֱמַר — as it is stated (Leviticus ibid.): "וְנָתַתָּ עַל הַמַּעֲרֶכֶת" כְּלוֹמַר — You shall put upon the stack — meaning **to say, upon each one of** עַל כָּל אַחַת מֵהֶן לְבוֹנָה זַכָּה — [the stacks] — *pure levonah*.[16] וּכְלִי זֶה נִקְרָא בָּזָךְ — This vessel is called a *bazach* (spoon). וְאָמְרוּ זִכְרוֹנָם לִבְרָכָה — [The Sages], of blessed memory, stated further (Mishnah *Menachos* 27a)

---

### NOTES

13. Since smell is the most spiritual of man's sensations, it is the most appropriate sensation to use as a metaphor for what we perceive as God's "satisfaction" in having His Will obeyed.

14. See note 16.

15. A *kometz* is the quantity of particles that can be contained within the area formed by closing the tips of one's fingers against the palm of one's hand. [The scooping of the *kometz* is part of the service of the *menachos* (meal offerings). For further discussion, see Mitzvah 137, and Mitzvah 116 note 33.]

16. The twelve loaves of the *Lechem HaPanim* were arranged in two stacks of six loaves, as the Torah states (Leviticus 24:6): וְשַׂמְתָּ אוֹתָם שְׁתַּיִם מַעֲרָכוֹת שֵׁשׁ הַמַּעֲרָכֶת עַל הַשֻּׁלְחָן הַטָּהֹר לִפְנֵי ה', *You shall place them in two stacks, six to the stack, upon the pure Table before HASHEM*. The next verse states: וְנָתַתָּ עַל הַמַּעֲרֶכֶת לְבֹנָה זַכָּה, *You shall put pure frankincense (levonah) upon the stack.*

The Sages disagree as to where the spoons of *levonah* were placed. Some, citing the words עַל הַמַּעֲרֶכֶת, *upon the stack,* maintain that they were put on the uppermost loaf of each stack. Others maintain that they were placed directly upon the *Shulchan*, for, in their view, עַל means *next to,* in this context, as it does in *Numbers* 2:20, *Exodus* 40:3 [and other places] (see Mishnah *Menachos* 96a, Gemara ibid. 98a). *Rambam* follows the latter opinion (*Hil. Beis HaBechirah* 3:14, *Hil. Temidin U'Mussafin* 5:2).

## תרומה / מצוה צז: מצוות סדור לחם הפנים ולבונה

(מנחות דף כ״ז ע״א) שְׁשְׁנֵי הַסְּדָרִין מְעַכְּבִים זֶה אֶת זֶה,[17] וּשְׁנֵי הַבְּזִיכִין מְעַכְּבִין זֶה אֶת זֶה, וּמִיּוֹם שַׁבָּת לְיוֹם שַׁבָּת מוֹצִיאִין אֶת הַלֶּחֶם וּמְסַדְּרִין לֶחֶם אַחֵר מִיָּד,[18] וְזֶה שֶׁמּוֹצִיאִין הוּא שֶׁחוֹלְקִין שְׁתֵּי הַמִּשְׁמָרוֹת, הַנִּכְנֶסֶת וְהַיּוֹצֵאת,[19] עִם כֹּהֵן גָּדוֹל[20] וְאוֹכְלִין אוֹתוֹ,[21] וְכֵיצַד מְסַדְּרִין אוֹתוֹ, שֶׁאַרְבָּעָה נִכְנָסִין בַּלֶּחֶם וּבַבְּזִיכִין[22] וְאַרְבָּעָה מַקְדִּימִין לִפְנֵיהֶם לִטּוֹל הַלֶּחֶם מֵעַל הַשֻּׁלְחָן,[23] וְאָמְרוּ זִכְרוֹנָם לִבְרָכָה שֶׁהָיוּ מְכֻוָּנִין בַּהַנָּחָתוֹ לִהְיוֹת טֻפְחוֹ שֶׁל זֶה[24] בְּצַד טֻפְחוֹ שֶׁל זֶה, לְקַיֵּם מַה שֶּׁנֶּאֱמַר לְפָנַי תָּמִיד.[25]

וּשְׁנֵי – שְׁשְׁנֵי הַסְּדָרִין מְעַכְּבִים זֶה אֶת זֶה – that the two stacks of loaves are essential to each other הַבְּזִיכִין מְעַכְּבִין זֶה אֶת זֶה – and that the two spoons of frankincense are essential to each other.[17]

Chinuch now presents the procedure for the placement and removal of the *Lechem HaPanim*: וּמִיּוֹם שַׁבָּת לְיוֹם שַׁבָּת מוֹצִיאִין אֶת הַלֶּחֶם – Each and every Sabbath, the previous week's bread was removed from the Table וּמְסַדְּרִין לֶחֶם אַחֵר מִיָּד – and other bread was arranged there immediately.[18] וְזֶה שֶׁמּוֹצִיאִין – This set of loaves that had just been removed הוּא שֶׁחוֹלְקִין שְׁתֵּי הַמִּשְׁמָרוֹת, הַנִּכְנֶסֶת וְהַיּוֹצֵאת עִם כֹּהֵן גָּדוֹל – is the one that the two shifts of Kohanim — i.e., the incoming one and the outgoing one[19] — share with the Kohen Gadol,[20] וְאוֹכְלִין אוֹתוֹ – and they eat it.[21]

וְכֵיצַד מְסַדְּרִין אוֹתוֹ – Also included in the laws of the mitzvah is how [the *Lechem HaPanim*] is arranged each Sabbath: שֶׁאַרְבָּעָה נִכְנָסִין בַּלֶּחֶם וּבַבְּזִיכִין – Four Kohanim enter the Sanctuary with the *Lechem HaPanim* loaves and the spoons of the *levonah*,[22] וְאַרְבָּעָה מַקְדִּימִין לִפְנֵיהֶם – לִטּוֹל הַלֶּחֶם מֵעַל הַשֻּׁלְחָן – and four others precede them to take the previous week's loaves and *levonah* from upon the Table.[23] וְאָמְרוּ זִכְרוֹנָם לִבְרָכָה – [The Sages], of blessed memory, said (Mishnah *Menachos* 99b) שֶׁהָיוּ מְכֻוָּנִין בַּהַנָּחָתוֹ – that they would aim when putting [the new bread] down לִהְיוֹת טֻפְחוֹ שֶׁל זֶה בְּצַד טֻפְחוֹ שֶׁל זֶה – to have a handbreadth of one set of bread next to a handbreadth of the other set of bread,[24] לְקַיֵּם מַה שֶּׁנֶּאֱמַר "לְפָנַי תָּמִיד" – which served to fulfill that which is stated (Exodus 25:30): *before Me, always.*[25]

### NOTES

17. If one of the stacks of loaves was missing from the *Shulchan*, the other stack is invalid for the mitzvah; and if either spoonful of *levonah* was absent, the other spoonful is invalid.

That Mishnah (*Menachos* 27a) proceeds to teach that if the *Lechem HaPanim* is not present, the *levonah* cannot be used for the mitzvah; and, conversely, if the *levonah* is not present, the loaves cannot be used (see *Rav MiBartenura* and *Tiferes Yisrael* ad loc.).

18. See the introduction to this mitzvah and note 2 above.

19. The Kohanim were divided into shifts (*mishmaros*), with each shift serving in the *Beis HaMikdash* and eating the offerings one week at a time (see Mitzvah 509). The change from one *mishmar* to the next took place on the Sabbath. The *Lechem HaPanim,* which was allocated on the Sabbath, was divided between the incoming shift and the outgoing one.

20. The Kohen Gadol had a right to take half of the loaves, as derived from the verse (*Leviticus* 24:9): וְהָיְתָה לְאַהֲרֹן וּלְבָנָיו, *and it* [the *Lechem HaPanim*] *shall be to Aharon* [the Kohen Gadol] *and his sons* [the Kohanim] (*Rambam, Hil. Temidin U'Mussafin* 4:14; see *Yoma* 17b).

21. The *Lechem HaPanim* must be eaten in the Courtyard of the *Beis HaMikdash*. According to Biblical law, the Kohanim may eat it until the end of the following night (i.e., until daybreak on Sunday), but the Sages required them to complete it before midnight, as a precaution against missing the Biblical deadline (see Mishnah *Berachos* 2a; *Rambam, Hil. Maaseh HaKorbanos* 10:8).

22. Two of these four Kohanim each carried a stack of six loaves, and each of the other two carried one of the spoons of *levonah* (Mishnah *Menachos* 99b). [As to why so many Kohanim were required, see *Mikdash David* 22:2.]

23. Two Kohanim to remove the two stacks of loaves and two to remove the two spoons of *levonah* (ibid.).

[The authorities discuss which tasks were assigned to the outgoing *mishmar* and which to the incoming one. See *Succah* 56b with *Rashi* ד״ה ובזיכין and *Aruch LaNer*; *Sfas Emes* to *Menachos* 99b ד״ה וד׳ כהנים; and *Radvaz, Hil. Temidin U'Mussafin* 4:11.]

24. As one pair of Kohanim pulled out the previous week's bread, the other pair inserted the new bread. When each *tefach* (handbreadth) of the *Shulchan's* length was cleared of the old bread, it was immediately filled with the new.

25. Because the removal of the old loaves and the insertion of the new loaves took place simultaneously, the *Shulchan* could be said to have *Lechem HaPanim* on it "always."

# 243 ☐ TERUMAH / MITZVAH 97: TO ARRANGE THE LECHEM HAPANIM AND THE LEVONAH

וְצוּרַת הַלֶּחֶם²⁶ וְעִנְיַן הַנָּחָתוֹ כֵּיצַד הָיָה כְּדֵי שֶׁיְּהֵא הָאֲוִיר שׁוֹלֵט בּוֹ²⁷, וְיֶתֶר פְּרָטֶיהָ, מְבֹאָרִים בְּפֶרֶק י״א מִמְּנָחוֹת (דף צ״ד ע״א)²⁸.

וְנוֹהֶגֶת בִּזְמַן הַבַּיִת בְּזִכְרֵי הַכֹּהֲנִים, כִּי לָהֶם הָעֲבוֹדָה לֹא לְנָשִׁים.

שְׁלֹשֶׁת מִצְווֹת סֵדֶר זֶה אֵינָן נוֹהֲגוֹת הַיּוֹם²⁹.

---

וְעִנְיַן הַנָּחָתוֹ כֵּיצַד הָיָה כְּדֵי שֶׁיְּהֵא   וְצוּרַת הַלֶּחֶם — Also among the laws is **the shape of the bread**,[26] הָאֲוִיר שׁוֹלֵט בּוֹ — **and how its placement** on the Table **was** done **so that air would reach it**.[27] וְיֶתֶר פְּרָטֶיהָ מְבֹאָרִים בְּפֶרֶק י״א מִמְּנָחוֹת — These, **and other details of** [the mitzvah] **are set forth in the eleventh chapter of** Tractate **Menachos**.[28]

### ⸙ Applicability of the Mitzvah ⸙

וְנוֹהֶגֶת בִּזְמַן הַבַּיִת — **[This mitzvah] applies in the times of the Temple** בְּזִכְרֵי הַכֹּהֲנִים — **and is** incumbent **upon male Kohanim,** כִּי לָהֶם הָעֲבוֹדָה — **because the** Temple **service is** assigned **to them,** לֹא לְנָשִׁים — and **not to women.** שְׁלֹשֶׁת מִצְווֹת סֵדֶר זֶה — **The three mitzvos of this** *parashah* (the obligation to build the *Beis HaMikdash* [Mitzvah 95], the prohibition to remove the Poles from the Ark [Mitzvah 96], and the obligation to arrange the *Lechem HaPanim* and the *levonah* [Mitzvah 97]) אֵינָן נוֹהֲגוֹת הַיּוֹם — **do not apply nowadays.**[29]

---

### NOTES

26. See *Menachos* 94b for a dispute about the shape of the bread.

27. Between each loaf and the one above it, there were three horizontal rods (which were supported by vertical columns that extended above the surface of the *Shulchan*). These rods created space between the loaves in which air could circulate and prevent the loaves from becoming moldy (see *Menachos* 96a and *Rashi* to *Exodus* 25:29).

28. The laws of the *Lechem HaPanim* are codified by Rambam in *Hil. Temidin U'Mussafin*, Chapters 4-5.

29. When Chinuch wrote his work, he arranged the obligations and prohibitions of each *parashah* separately, first presenting all the obligations and then all the prohibitions. This format was followed in the early printings of Chinuch, but in later editions the order of the mitzvos was rearranged so that they are listed according to their sequence in the Torah. In the early editions, Chinuch's statement here was the closing sentence of the previous mitzvah — the prohibition of removing the poles from the Ark — which, as the only prohibition in the *parashah*, appeared as its final mitzvah. This statement served as the "applicability" section of that mitzvah. It mentions all three mitzvos, because none of them apply nowadays, and each for the same reason (namely, that the *Beis HaMikdash* is not standing and we have not merited to rebuild it). When the mitzvos were rearranged in the later editions, this statement was left at the end of *Parashas Terumah*, although the mitzvah to which it belonged ("The Prohibition to Remove the Poles of the Ark") was shifted.

---

> ⸙§ **Insight: Displaying the Lechem HaPanim to the Festival Pilgrims**
>
> The *Lechem HaPanim* loaves, which were placed on the *Shulchan* each Sabbath, could not be baked on the Sabbath, and were baked the day before. After being placed upon the *Shulchan*, they remained there for an entire week, until the next Sabbath, when they were replaced with new loaves. Thus, when the loaves were removed to be eaten by the Kohanim, they were no less than eight days old. Nevertheless, the Gemara (*Chagigah* 26b) derives from Scripture that the loaves were miraculously fresh and warm when they were removed, as though they had just been baked. The Gemara relates further that on the festivals of Pesach, Shavuos, and Succos, when Israelites made the pilgrimage to the Temple in Jerusalem, Kohanim would raise the *Shulchan* to display the still fresh and warm *Lechem HaPanim*, and proclaim to the people: "See how beloved you are in the eyes of God!" Witnessing this manifestation of God's love for them cultivated a reciprocal love on their part for God, leading them to increase their devotion to His service.
>
> The following problem must be addressed, however: The loaves had to remain on the *Shulchan* at all times — in fulfillment of the directive: *On the Table you shall place Lechem HaPanim before*

*Me, always* (see above, note 1). Yet the people were forbidden to approach the Sanctuary where the *Shulchan* stood. How, then, was it possible for them to know that the bread was fresh and warm? For this, it would not be enough to *see* the bread from a distance; they would have to feel and touch the loaves.

*Rambam* (*Hil. Metam'ei Mishkav U'Moshav* 11:11) implies that the Kohanim would remove the *Shulchan* from the Sanctuary and bring it to the people assembled in the Israelite's section of the Temple Courtyard (see *Mishneh LaMelech* ad loc.). However, this solution is problematic, because some Rishonim argue that removing the *Shulchan* from the Sanctuary is itself forbidden on account of the very verse quoted above, *On the Table you shall place Lechem HaPanim before Me, always.* By stating *before Me*, the Torah implies that the *Shulchan*, which was always laden with the *Lechem HaPanim*, had to remain inside the Sanctuary (*Teshuvos Radvaz* §2178, in explanation of *Rashi* to *Chagigah* 26a ד"ה ואומרים להם and *Tosafos* ibid. 26b ד"ה שלא).

To explain *Rambam*, it can be said that the Courtyard is also considered *"before Me"* (*Chasdei David* to *Tosefta Menachos* 11:7 ד"ה אך מ"מ). This is implied by the Torah's requirement that certain offerings be slaughtered לִפְנֵי ה', *before God* (for example, see *Leviticus* 1:5 and 4:4), even though they are slaughtered in the Courtyard.

Alternatively, *Rambam* may be of the opinion that removing the *Shulchan* from the Sanctuary for only a short while with the *Lechem HaPanim* still on it — and with intent to return it immediately — does not violate the requirement of *"before Me"* (*Siach Yitzchak, Chagigah* 26b).

There are, however, those who maintain that the *Shulchan* may never be removed from the Sanctuary at all. Following the latter view, *Ritva* (*Yoma* 21a ד"ה שסלוקו כסדורו) suggests that the *Lechem HaPanim* remained so hot that steam rose from it. Hence, the *Shulchan* had only to be lifted from the floor of the Sanctuary, and the Jews could witness the miracle of the fresh bread by seeing the steam from afar. [Although steam generally does not rise from bread except when it is cut open, this may have been part of the miracle (*Radvaz*).]

*Radvaz* finds both of these approaches unsatisfactory. He therefore proposes a third solution: The *Lechem HaPanim* was not displayed on every day of each festival, but only on the Sabbath, when the previous week's loaves were removed from the *Shulchan* and replaced with new ones. Before removing the old loaves, the Kohanim would raise the *Shulchan* and carry it to the opening of the Sanctuary. The *Shulchan* would thus remain in the Sanctuary (*"before Me"*), but in a place where it could be seen by the people. They would then remove the old loaves under the gaze of the people, and carry them out into the Courtyard, where the people could touch them and feel their warmth and freshness. Having seen the loaves from the moment the *Shulchan* was raised, they knew that these were indeed the loaves of the previous week, and then, by touching the loaves, they could attest to their freshness.

This explains how the miracle was witnessed on Pesach and Succos, each of which includes a Sabbath during its seven- or eight-day span. As for Shavuos, which lasts only one day, *Radvaz* suggests that if the festival occurred on a weekday then the above procedure was performed on the following Sabbath, and those who wished to observe the miracle of the warm and fresh *Lechem HaPanim* would remain in Jerusalem to witness it.

# פרשת תצוה
# Parashas Tetzaveh

וְאַתָּה תְּצַוֶּה יֵשׁ בָּהּ אַרְבַּע מִצְווֹת עֲשֵׂה
וְשָׁלֹשׁ מִצְווֹת לֹא תַעֲשֶׂה

Parashas Tetzaveh contains four Mitzvah-Obligations
and three Mitzvah-Prohibitions.

### CONTAINS SEVEN MITZVOS:
### MITZVOS 98-104

98. מִצְוַת עֲרִיכַת נֵרוֹת בַּמִּקְדָּשׁ — The Obligation to Arrange the Lamps of [the Menorah in] the Temple

99. מִצְוַת לְבִישַׁת בִּגְדֵי כֹהֲנִים — The Obligation [for Kohanim] to Don the Priestly Garments

100. שֶׁלֹּא יִזַּח הַחֹשֶׁן מֵעַל הָאֵפוֹד — The Prohibition to Detach the *Choshen* From the *Ephod*

101. שֶׁלֹּא לִקְרֹעַ הַמְּעִיל שֶׁל כֹּהֲנִים — The Prohibition to Tear the *Me'il* of the Kohen Gadol

102. מִצְוַת אֲכִילַת בְּשַׂר חַטָּאת וְאָשָׁם — The Obligation [Upon the Kohanim] to Eat the Meat of the *Chatas* and *Asham* Offerings

103. מִצְוַת הַקְטָרַת קְטֹרֶת — The Obligation [Upon the Kohanim] to Offer the Incense

104. שֶׁלֹּא לְהַקְטִיר וּלְהַקְרִיב עַל מִזְבַּח הַזָּהָב — The Prohibition to Burn or Offer [Anything but the Incense] on the Golden Altar

## מִצְוָה צח: מִצְוַת עֲרִיכַת נֵרוֹת הַמִּקְדָּשׁ

לְהֵיטִיב נֵרוֹת תָּמִיד לִפְנֵי הַשֵּׁם יִתְבָּרַךְ, שֶׁנֶּאֱמַר (שמות כ״ז, כ״א) יַעֲרֹךְ אֹתוֹ אַהֲרֹן וּבָנָיו,

# Mitzvah 98
## The Obligation to Arrange the Lamps of [the Menorah in] the Temple

וְאַתָּה תְּצַוֶּה אֶת בְּנֵי יִשְׂרָאֵל וְיִקְחוּ אֵלֶיךָ שֶׁמֶן זַיִת זָךְ כָּתִית לַמָּאוֹר לְהַעֲלֹת נֵר תָּמִיד. בְּאֹהֶל מוֹעֵד מִחוּץ לַפָּרֹכֶת אֲשֶׁר עַל הָעֵדֻת יַעֲרֹךְ אֹתוֹ אַהֲרֹן וּבָנָיו מֵעֶרֶב עַד בֹּקֶר לִפְנֵי ה׳ חֻקַּת עוֹלָם לְדֹרֹתָם מֵאֵת בְּנֵי יִשְׂרָאֵל

*Now you shall command the Children of Israel that they shall take for you pure, pressed olive oil for illumination, to kindle a lamp continually. In the Tent of Meeting, outside the partition that is near the Testimonial-tablets (Luchos), Aaron and his sons shall arrange it from evening until morning, before* HASHEM, *an eternal decree for their generations, from the children of Israel* (Exodus 27:20-21).

In the above passage, the Torah sets forth the service of the Menorah in the Temple (*Beis HaMikdash*), and makes reference to both *arranging* the lamps and *kindling* them. Chinuch will explain that the service is actually comprised of three tasks: removing residue from the previous lighting, preparing the lamps with new oil and wicks, and kindling the lamps. Chinuch follows *Rambam* (*Hil. Temidin U'Mussafin* 3:10-12; *Sefer HaMitzvos, Asei* 25), who views all these tasks as components of a single mitzvah, to which the Torah refers in the preceding verses as both "arranging" and "kindling." He will, however, cite another opinion, which maintains that these tasks actually comprise two separate mitzvos: (1) arranging the lamps, i.e., preparing them for kindling by removing the residue and inserting fresh wicks and oil; and (2) kindling the lamps.[1]

In addition to the terms *arranging* and *kindling*, the Torah uses another word to describe the Menorah service. In *Exodus* 30:7-8, while discussing the daily burning of incense (*ketores*) on the Inner Altar (Mitzvah 103), the Torah states: בַּבֹּקֶר בַּבֹּקֶר בְּהֵיטִיבוֹ אֶת הַנֵּרוֹת יַקְטִירֶנָּה, *every morning, when he "tends" the lamps, he shall burn it.* There is disagreement as to the precise intention of the verse in using this word (as Chinuch points out below, at notes 26-28), but Chinuch frequently uses "tend" as an inclusive term to refer to *all* aspects of the mitzvah.

לְהֵיטִיב נֵרוֹת תָּמִיד לִפְנֵי הַשֵּׁם יִתְבָּרַךְ — We are commanded **to tend lamps**[2] **continually**[3] **before Hashem, blessed be He,** i.e., in His Holy Temple, שֶׁנֶּאֱמַר "יַעֲרֹךְ אֹתוֹ אַהֲרֹן וּבָנָיו" — **as it is stated** (*Exodus* 27:21): **Aaron and his sons shall arrange it** … **before** HASHEM;

---

NOTES

1. This debate is not academic. We will learn below that there are significant ramifications to the question of whether these tasks comprise one mitzvah or two. See note 28.

2. *Rambam* writes "to *kindle* lamps" (*Sefer HaMitzvos, Asei* 25; see also *Hil. Temidin U'Mussafin* 3:12). Chinuch apparently uses "to *tend* lamps" so as to include the preparation of the lamps in the mitzvah. This will be discussed more thoroughly in the notes below and in the Insight.

3. The word תָּמִיד (*tamid*), which appears in the verse regarding our mitzvah, has two connotations. It can mean *continually* (on a regular basis), or it can mean *constantly* (without cessation). In the context of tending to the Menorah, which was not a constant mitzvah, but rather, a mitzvah performed according to a regular daily schedule, it means *continually* (*Rashi, Exodus* 27:20). For another explanation, see *Ramban* to the verse and *Minchas Chinuch* §15.

## 247 ☐ TETZAVEH / MITZVAH 98: TO ARRANGE THE LAMPS OF THE MENORAH

כְּלוֹמַר יַעֲרֹךְ הַנֵּר לִפְנֵי הַשֵּׁם יִתְבָּרַךְ, וְזֶהוּ מִצְוַת הֲטָבַת נֵרוֹת הַנִּזְכֶּרֶת בַּגְּמָרָא.[5]

מִשָּׁרְשֵׁי הַמִּצְוָה, שֶׁצִּוָּנוּ הַשֵּׁם יִתְבָּרַךְ לִהְיוֹת נֵר דּוֹלֵק בַּבַּיִת הַקָּדוֹשׁ לְהַגְדָּלַת הַבַּיִת לְכָבוֹד וּלְתִפְאֶרֶת בְּעֵינֵי הָרוֹאִים, כִּי כֵן דֶּרֶךְ בְּנֵי אִישׁ לְהִתְכַּבֵּד בְּבָתֵּיהֶם בְּנֵרוֹת דּוֹלְקִין[6], וְכָל עִנְיַן הַהַגְדָּלָה בּוֹ כְּדֵי שֶׁיַּכְנִיס הָאָדָם בְּלִבּוֹ כְּשֶׁיִּרְאֵהוּ מוֹרָא וַעֲנָוָה, וּכְבָר אָמַרְנוּ כִּי בְּמַעֲשֵׂה הַטּוֹב הַכָּשֵׁר הַנֶּפֶשׁ[7]. וְכָל זֶה סוֹבֵב עַל הַיְסוֹד הַבָּנוּי לָנוּ

---

**כְּלוֹמַר** — **that is to say,** **יַעֲרֹךְ הַנֵּר לִפְנֵי הַשֵּׁם יִתְבָּרַךְ** — [Aaron] or one of his descendants **shall arrange the lamp**[4] **before Hashem, blessed be He.** **וְזֶהוּ מִצְוַת הֲטָבַת נֵרוֹת הַנִּזְכֶּרֶת בַּגְּמָרָא** — **This is the mitzvah of "Tending the Lamps"** that is **often mentioned in the Gemara.**[5]

### ⁓ Underlying Purpose of the Mitzvah ⁓

**שֶׁצִּוָּנוּ הַשֵּׁם יִתְבָּרַךְ** ... **מִשָּׁרְשֵׁי הַמִּצְוָה** — **Among the underlying purposes of this mitzvah is** **לִהְיוֹת נֵר דּוֹלֵק בַּבַּיִת הַקָּדוֹשׁ** — **that Hashem, blessed be He, commanded us to have a lamp burning in the Holy Temple** **לְהַגְדָּלַת הַבַּיִת** — in order **to increase the grandeur of the Temple,** **לְכָבוֹד וּלְתִפְאֶרֶת בְּעֵינֵי הָרוֹאִים** — **to** make it attain **glory and splendor in the eyes of** its **beholders;** **כִּי כֵן דֶּרֶךְ בְּנֵי אִישׁ** — **for such is the way of mankind,** **לְהִתְכַּבֵּד בְּבָתֵּיהֶם בְּנֵרוֹת דּוֹלְקִין** — **to be glorified in their homes with burning lamps.**[6]
**וְכָל עִנְיַן הַהַגְדָּלָה בּוֹ** — **The entire objective of enhancing the grandeur of [the Temple] is** **כְּדֵי שֶׁיַּכְנִיס הָאָדָם בְּלִבּוֹ כְּשֶׁיִּרְאֵהוּ מוֹרָא וַעֲנָוָה** — **so that a person will introduce into his heart, when he sees [the Temple],** a sense of **awe and humility** before Hashem; **וּכְבָר אָמַרְנוּ כִּי בְּמַעֲשֵׂה הַטּוֹב הַכָּשֵׁר הַנֶּפֶשׁ** — **and we have already stated** (in Mitzvah 95) **that through** the **good deeds** that we perform in the Temple, with the purity of intent that we are able to attain there, our **souls become refined.**[7]

Chinuch qualifies the preceding explanation:

**וְכָל זֶה סוֹבֵב עַל הַיְסוֹד הַבָּנוּי לָנוּ** — **This entire** approach, that the purpose of the kindling service is to inspire awe and humility, **revolves around the principle we have established**

---

### NOTES

4. The term "it" in the verse (*shall arrange* "it") is undefined; Chinuch explains that this refers to the lamp that is mentioned in the previous verse (*to kindle* "*a lamp*"). [See *Ibn Ezra* to *Exodus* 27:21 for a different interpretation.] Although *lamp* in the verse is in the singular, it refers to all the lamps of the Menorah (*Malbim, Leviticus* 24:2; *Aruch HaShulchan HeAsid* 106:20; cf. *Ramban* ibid.).

5. For example, *Yoma* 14b and 33a-b, and *Menachos* 50a and 88b.

Interestingly, Chinuch discusses only tending lamps "before Hashem," and does not make any reference to the Menorah. *Ramban* (*Numbers* 8:2) asserts that the mitzvah of kindling lamps in the *Beis HaMikdash* applies specifically to the lamps of the Menorah — as stated explicitly in *Leviticus* 24:4 — and applies only when the Menorah is available. If there is no Menorah, no lamps are lit (see also *Rabbeinu Bachya, Leviticus* 24:4). In fact, according to *Ramban* (glosses to *Sefer HaMitzvos, Asei* 33), since kindling cannot be done without a Menorah, the obligation to make the Menorah is included in the mitzvah of kindling the lamps. *Rambam* (*Asei* 20) and Chinuch (Mitzvah 95), however, maintain that the obligation to make the Menorah (as well as the other Temple vessels and accoutrements) is included in the mitzvah of building the *Beis HaMikdash*. See *Minchas Chinuch* 95:8. See also Insight to Mitzvah 95.

6. Hashem surely does not need illumination in His Temple, since He is the ultimate Source of Light (see *Shabbos* 22b and *Bamidbar Rabbah* 15:2). Rather, since people consider illumination a sign of grandeur in their own homes, He commanded that the *Beis HaMikdash* be illuminated, so that people will be awed when seeing it.

7. See Mitzvah 95 at notes 20-29; see also below, Mitzvah 99 at note 13.

Chinuch established in Mitzvah 16 that "man is affected in accordance with his actions," and he relies on this principle as the basis for many mitzvos (e.g., Mitzvah 40,99). In Mitzvah 95, Chinuch explained further that the purpose of building a *Beis HaMikdash* is not to bring glory to God, for He does not need our honor; rather it is so that we should prepare a place of utmost spiritual cleanliness in which we can serve God with purity of intent, and thereby gain closeness to Him. Here, Chinuch would seem to mean that enhancing the glory of the *Beis HaMikdash* advances this purpose, as it instills awe and leads to performance of the service with greater devotion, which in turn brings about refinement of character and a closer connection to God.

248 ❑ **תצוה** / **מצוה צח: מצות עריכת נרות המקדש**

כִּי הַכֹּל נִגְזַר מִצַּד הַמְקַבְּלִים[8], עִם הֱיוֹתִי מַאֲמִין בֶּאֱמֶת כִּי יֵשׁ לַמְקֻבָּלִים בָּעִנְיָנִים אֵלֶּה חָכְמוֹת נִכְבָּדוֹת וְסוֹדוֹת נִפְלָאִים[9]. וְאוּלָם גַּם אֲנַחְנוּ נִכְתֹּב הַנִּרְאֶה כִּפְשׁוּטָן שֶׁל דְּבָרִים, וְהַכֹּל לְשֵׁם שָׁמַיִם[10].

דִּינֵי הַמִּצְוָה, כְּגוֹן מַה שֶּׁאָמְרוּ הַדְלָקַת הַנֵּרוֹת דּוֹחָה שַׁבָּת[11] כְּקָרְבָּנוֹת שֶׁקָּבוּעַ לָהֶם זְמַן, שֶׁנֶּאֱמַר בּוֹ תָּמִיד[12], וְשֶׁנּוֹתֵן לְכָל נֵר וָנֵר חֲצִי לֹג[13] שֶׁמֶן, שֶׁנֶּאֱמַר מֵעֶרֶב עַד בֹּקֶר[14], וְשִׁעֲרוּ חֲכָמִים שֶׁזֶּה הַשִּׁעוּר יַסְפִּיק בְּלֵילֵי טֵבֵת, וְכֵן נוֹתְנִין בְּכָל הַלֵּילוֹת,

---

כִּי הַכֹּל נִגְזַר מִצַּד הַמְקַבְּלִים — **that everything** pertaining to the Temple **is mandated for the benefit of those who are affected** by it.[8] עִם הֱיוֹתִי מַאֲמִין בֶּאֱמֶת — I present the underlying purpose of the mitzvos pertaining to the Temple and its *avodah* (service) in this light, **notwithstanding my sincere belief** כִּי יֵשׁ לַמְקֻבָּלִים בָּעִנְיָנִים אֵלֶּה חָכְמוֹת נִכְבָּדוֹת וְסוֹדוֹת נִפְלָאִים — **that regarding these matters** of the Temple *avodah* and the design of its vessels **the Kabbalists possess lofty insights of wisdom and wondrous esoteric concepts.**[9] וְאוּלָם גַּם אֲנַחְנוּ נִכְתֹּב הַנִּרְאֶה כִּפְשׁוּטָן שֶׁל דְּבָרִים — **Nevertheless, we too shall write what appears to be the simple explanation of** these **matters,** וְהַכֹּל לְשֵׁם שָׁמַיִם — **and all** this is done **for the sake of Heaven.**[10]

### ~ Laws of the Mitzvah ~

דִּינֵי הַמִּצְוָה — **The laws of the mitzvah** include, כְּגוֹן מַה שֶּׁאָמְרוּ — **for example, that which [the Sages] said** (*Sifra* to *Leviticus* 24:2-4), הַדְלָקַת הַנֵּרוֹת דּוֹחָה שַׁבָּת — that **kindling the lamps** of the Temple Menorah **overrides** the **Sabbath** restrictions,[11] כְּקָרְבָּנוֹת שֶׁקָּבוּעַ לָהֶם זְמַן — **just like** the slaughter and the burning of Temple **offerings that have a designated time** at which they must be brought overrides the Sabbath restrictions, שֶׁנֶּאֱמַר בּוֹ תָּמִיד — **because** the expression *tamid* ("continually") **is stated in regard to [the kindling].**[12] וְשֶׁנּוֹתֵן לְכָל נֵר וָנֵר חֲצִי לֹג שֶׁמֶן — **Also** included is the law **that [the Kohen] shall place a half-*log*[13] of oil in each lamp** of the Menorah, שֶׁנֶּאֱמַר מֵעֶרֶב עַד בֹּקֶר — **as it is stated** (*Exodus* 27:21): *Aaron and his sons shall arrange it* **from evening until morning,** meaning that they must place enough oil in the lamps for them to burn through the night.[14] וְשִׁעֲרוּ חֲכָמִים שֶׁזֶּה הַשִּׁעוּר יַסְפִּיק בְּלֵילֵי טֵבֵת — **and the Sages reckoned that this measure** (a half-*log*) **is sufficient for the** longest winter **nights of the** month of **Teves.** וְכֵן נוֹתְנִין בְּכָל הַלֵּילוֹת — **They place the same** amount of oil in the Menorah **on**

---

NOTES

8. See Mitzvah 95 at length.

9. See, for example, *Rabbeinu Bachya* to *Exodus* 25:38, *Tzeror HaMor* to *Exodus* 27:1 and *Numbers* 8:2-4, and *Malbim* throughout *Parashas Terumah*. For a lengthy treatise on the meaning of the Menorah and its service, see *R' S. R. Hirsch* to *Exodus* 25:39.

10. I.e., although some might view the Kabbalists' esoteric approach as more profound than Chinuch's "simple" approach, Chinuch presents his explanation for the sake of Heaven, since recognizing the practical aspect of these mitzvos also serves to enhance our appreciation of the Temple service, and of mitzvah observance in general. As the Mishnah (*Menachos* 110a) states in another context, whatever offering one makes to God is equally pleasing to Him, *"whether one gives more or less, as long as he directs his heart toward [his Father] in Heaven."*

11. That is, the lamps of the Menorah are kindled even on the Sabbath, despite the fact that kindling is a *melachah* (labor activity) that is ordinarily prohibited on the Sabbath [see Mitzvah 32]. See also *Rambam, Hil. Temidin U'Mussafin* 3:10.

12. Any offering that must be brought at a designated time (e.g., the daily *tamid* offering, the *pesach* offering) overrides the Sabbath restrictions that are involved in acts of *avodah* such as slaughtering the offering and burning its meat upon the Altar (*Temurah* 14a; *Rambam, Hil. Bi'as HaMikdash* 4:9). Chinuch explains that the service of kindling the Menorah is in the same category, since the Torah employs the word תָּמִיד, *continually*, in regard to this service, indicating that it must be performed every single day, including the Sabbath (see above, note 3). For further discussion, see *Chidushei R' Chaim HaLevi, Hil. Bi'as HaMikdash* 9:7.

13. A *log* is a unit of liquid measurement that ranges, according to various authorities, between 11.7 and 20.3 fl. oz. [approx. 350-600 cc.]. Half of this amount of oil is placed in each lamp.

14. The verse obviously cannot mean that the *act* of arranging should take all night. Rather, it means that the Kohen should supply each lamp with sufficient oil to burn through the night (*Menachos* 89a; *Mizrachi* to *Exodus* 27:21; see *Ibn Ezra* there).

# TETZAVEH / MITZVAH 98: TO ARRANGE THE LAMPS OF THE MENORAH

וְאִם יוֹתֵר אֵין בְּכָךְ כְּלוּם.[15] וּמֵעִנְיַן מִצְוַת הַהֲטָבָה הוּא הַדִּשּׁוּן,[16] וְדִשּׁוּן הַמְּנוֹרָה וַהֲטָבָתָהּ מִצְוָה עֲשֵׂה בַּבֹּקֶר וּבֵין הָעַרְבָּיִם,[17] וְהַדִּשּׁוּן הוּא שֶׁכָּל נֵר שֶׁכָּבָה מֵסִיר הַפְּתִילָה וְכָל הַשֶּׁמֶן שֶׁבַּנֵּר[18] וּמְקַנְּחוֹ, וְנוֹתֵן בּוֹ פְּתִילָה אַחֶרֶת וְשֶׁמֶן אַחֵר, וְנֵר שֶׁלֹּא כָבָה מְתַקְּנוֹ,[19]

---

**וְאִם יוֹתֵר אֵין בְּכָךְ כְּלוּם — and if there is** oil **left over all nights,** even the short nights of summer, in the morning, **it is of no consequence.**[15]

Chinuch now discusses some details of the mitzvah and how often it is performed:

**וּמֵעִנְיַן מִצְוַת הַהֲטָבָה הוּא הַדִּשּׁוּן — One component of the mitzvah of tending** the lamps **is the removal of residue** from the previous lighting.[16]

**וְדִשּׁוּן הַמְּנוֹרָה וַהֲטָבָתָהּ — This task of removing the residue from the Menorah and tending [its lamps],** i.e., preparing them with wicks and oil, and actually kindling them, **מִצְוָה עֲשֵׂה בַּבֹּקֶר וּבֵין הָעַרְבָּיִם — is a mitzvah-obligation** that is to be performed each day **in** both **the morning and the afternoon.**[17]

Chinuch proceeds to describe the process of preparing the lamps for kindling:

**וְהַדִּשּׁוּן הוּא — The removal of the residue is** done as follows: **שֶׁכָּל נֵר שֶׁכָּבָה מֵסִיר הַפְּתִילָה וְכָל הַשֶּׁמֶן שֶׁבַּנֵּר — From every lamp that has become extinguished, [the Kohen] removes the wick, as well as the oil** remaining **in the lamp.**[18] **וּמְקַנְּחוֹ — He then wipes [the lamp] clean, וְנוֹתֵן בּוֹ פְּתִילָה אַחֶרֶת וְשֶׁמֶן אַחֵר — and places in it another wick and other oil.** He does this with each lamp that was extinguished. **וְנֵר שֶׁלֹּא כָבָה מְתַקְּנוֹ — But** as for any **lamp that was not extinguished, he** merely **adjusts it,** by trimming the wick and adding oil.[19]

---

## NOTES

15. Some explain that at daybreak the lamps were extinguished and the leftover oil was discarded (see *Rashi*, *Menachos* 89a ד"ה ושיערו חכמים), while others explain that the lamps were allowed to continue burning into the day until the oil was used up (*Rashi*, *Shabbos* 22b ד"ה כמדת חברותיה; *Ramban*, *Shabbos* 22b; *Teshuvos HaRashba* Vol. I §309). See further below.

[The preceding follows the understanding that the lamps were required to burn only by night. There is, however, an opinion that the lamps were required to burn by night *and* by day. Chinuch below cites this opinion, and accordingly, he maintains that if a lamp was still burning in the morning, the Kohen would be spared the task of rekindling it, and would simply add oil to last through the day (see below, notes 17 and 19). In any event, according to all opinions, it did not matter that on the short summer nights there was oil remaining in the lamps in the morning.]

Still others maintain that there never was oil left over, for as the nights grew shorter they would make progressively thicker wicks, so that all the oil would be consumed by morning (*Rashi*, *Menachos* ibid.; *Tosafos* there ד"ה ושיערו; *Tos. Yeshanim*, *Yoma* 15a ד"ה תן לה מדתה; *Daas Zekeinim* and *Chizkuni* to *Exodus* 27:21).

16. See *Tamid* 30b, 33a. [For discussion of this requirement, see *Chidushei HaGriz* to *Rambam*, *Hil. Temidin U'Mussafin* p. 80, and *Even HaAzel* to *Rambam*, *Hil. Temidin U'Mussafin* 3:12.]

17. Chinuch here follows *Rambam* (ibid. 3:10 and *Sefer HaMitzvos*, *Asei* 25), who counts the "arranging" and "kindling" of the Menorah as a single mitzvah. Now, the Torah states (*Exodus* 30:7-8), regarding the *ketores* (incense) offering, which is brought twice daily: בַּבֹּקֶר בַּבֹּקֶר בְּהֵיטִיבוֹ אֶת הַנֵּרוֹת יַקְטִירֶנָּה וּבְהַעֲלֹת אַהֲרֹן אֶת הַנֵּרֹת בֵּין הָעַרְבַּיִם יַקְטִירֶנָּה, *every morning when he tends the lamps he shall burn it* [the *ketores*], *and when Aaron kindles the lamps in the afternoon he shall burn it.* Scripture speaks of "tending" the lamps in the morning and "kindling" them in the afternoon. Since "tending" and "kindling" refer to the same process (see *Rambam*, *Hil. Temidin U'Mussafin* 3:12), the verse must mean that the entire Menorah service is performed twice daily — in the morning and in the afternoon (*Kesef Mishneh* to *Rambam* loc. cit.). [The afternoon kindling, however, was the primary one, and that is why the verse cited at the beginning of this Mitzvah (*Exodus* 27:21) states that the lamps shall be arranged מֵעֶרֶב עַד בֹּקֶר, *from evening until morning* (*Ralbag*, *Exodus* 27:21; *Chazon Ish*, *Menachos* 36:8 ד"ה ונראה; see *Rambam* ibid. 3:11).]

Chinuch will later cite another opinion regarding this matter. See note 28.

18. The Kohen places the old oil and wicks in "the place of the ashes," an area located three *tefachim* east of the ramp of the Outer Altar, ten *amos* from the foot of the ramp (*Tamid* 28b; *Rambam* ibid. 3:12; cf. *Radvaz* to *Rambam* there §17; see *Chidushei HaGriz* ibid.).

19. [See *Menachos* 107a with *Rashi* ד"ה מחטטן.] Here too, Chinuch follows the opinion of *Rambam* (ibid.), who states that kindling does not have to be performed when it is not necessary. That is, if a lamp remains lit from the previous kindling, it need not be extinguished and rekindled with a new wick and oil; it need merely be adjusted so that it will continue to burn well (see *Lechem Mishneh* to *Rambam* loc. cit.). Other Rishonim, however, maintain that the mitzvah requires that the act of kindling be performed each time; thus, any lamp

וְנֵר אֶמְצָעִי אִם כָּבָה[20] מַדְלִיקוֹ מֵאֵשׁ שֶׁעַל מִזְבַּח הַחִיצוֹן[21], וְהָאֲחֵרִים מַדְלִיקִין זֶה מִזֶּה, שֶׁמּוֹשֵׁךְ הַפְּתִילָה וּמַטָּה אוֹתָהּ עַד שֶׁהָאוֹר נִתְפֶּשֶׂת בָּהּ[22], לְפִי שֶׁאֵין כְּבוֹד הַמִּצְוָה לְהַדְלִיקָן מִנֵּר אַחֵר.[23]

---

Chinuch now describes the actual kindling:

מַדְלִיקוֹ מֵאֵשׁ שֶׁעַל מִזְבַּח הַחִיצוֹן — וְנֵר אֶמְצָעִי אִם כָּבָה — **If the middle lamp was extinguished,**[20] — **[the Kohen] rekindles it from the fire that is on the Outer Altar.**[21] וְהָאֲחֵרִים מַדְלִיקִין זֶה מִזֶּה — **The other [lamps] are kindled one** directly **from the other;** שֶׁמּוֹשֵׁךְ הַפְּתִילָה וּמַטָּה אוֹתָהּ עַד שֶׁהָאוֹר נִתְפֶּשֶׂת בָּהּ — that is, **[the Kohen] extends the** unlit **wick** from its receptacle, **tilts it toward the flame of a burning lamp beside it until the flame catches onto it,** and returns it to rest in its receptacle.[22] לְפִי שֶׁאֵין כְּבוֹד הַמִּצְוָה לְהַדְלִיקָן מִנֵּר אַחֵר — **The lighting is done in this manner, because it is not** in keeping with **the honor of the mitzvah to kindle [the lamps] from another lamp** that is not sacred.[23]

---

NOTES

still burning at the time of the next lighting must be extinguished and then rekindled along with the rest of the lamps (*Rashi, Menachos* 86b and *Shabbos* 22b; *Ramban, Shabbos* 22b; *Teshuvos HaRashba* Vol. I §309). See the Insight for further discussion.

20. The middle lamp is the one that is called the נֵר מַעֲרָבִי, "western lamp." It was the middle lamp on the Menorah, but its wick was drawn toward its western lip, which faced the Holy of Holies (hence, the name "western lamp"); the other wicks were all drawn toward this middle one (*Menachos* 98b, as explained by *Rashi* ד"ה מצדד להו אצדודי). [According to *Rambam* (*Hil. Beis HaBechirah* 3:8), the cup of the middle lamp was tilted west toward the Holy of Holies, and the cups of the other lamps were tilted toward the middle one (see *Chidushei HaGriz, Parashas Beha'aloscha*).] Although the "western lamp" contained the same amount of oil as the others (i.e., only enough to burn "from evening until morning"), it would miraculously burn from one evening to the next. The Gemara (*Shabbos* 22b) states that this miracle served as *testimony for all mankind that the Divine Presence dwells among Israel*. After the death of Shimon HaTzaddik (a Kohen Gadol of the Second Temple Era), the Jews became unworthy of this miracle on a constant basis, and it would occur only intermittently. Hence, the Kohen might find the "western lamp" extinguished (*Yoma* 39a).

[The Gemara (*Menachos* 98b) cites two opinions as to how the Menorah was positioned in the *Beis HaMikdash*, and which of its lamps was the "western lamp." Chinuch follows the opinion that the Menorah stood in a north-south position, so that none of its lamps was more westerly than the others. However, the middle lamp (or its wick) faced westward, while the other lamps (or their wicks) faced the middle one. See diagram.]

21. The Gemara (*Yoma* 45b) derives this requirement from Scripture. [Chinuch follows his opinion stated above (see note 19), that if any lamp — including the middle one — was still burning, it did not have to be extinguished and rekindled. Hence, he states that *if* it was extinguished, it must be relit from the fire of the Outer Altar.]

Chinuch follows the opinion of *Rambam* (*Hil. Temidin U'Mussafin* 3:13) that the "western lamp," due to its unique status, may never be kindled except with fire from the Outer Altar. *Raavad* (ad loc.), however, disagrees and maintains that fire from the Outer Altar was required only if *all* the lamps were extinguished and the Menorah had to be lit anew, but if any of the lamps was burning, that flame was used to rekindle the "western lamp." [All agree that once the "western lamp" was lit, its flame would be used to kindle the lamp next to it, and so forth, in the manner that Chinuch shall describe (see *Tamid* 33a).]

22. The lamp cups were fixed to the branches of the Menorah; thus, the only way one lamp could be kindled directly from another was by extending the wick (*Rambam* ibid. §14, based on *Shabbos* 22b). [There is an opinion, however, that the lamp cups were removable (see *Menachos* 88b; see also *Rashi, Yoma* 24b ד"ה שסידר את המנורה).]

23. Rather than extending the unlit wick toward the burning lamp of the Menorah, it would have been simpler to light a taper from the burning lamp and use it to kindle the unlit wick. Chinuch explains that this was not done because it would be disrespectful to the mitzvah.

Chinuch writes that it would be disrespectful לְהַדְלִיקָן מִנֵּר אַחֵר, *to kindle them **from** another lamp*, which implies that the disrespect lies in using a non-sacred taper to kindle the Menorah lamps. From the Gemara's related discussion regarding the Chanukah lamps, however, it seems that

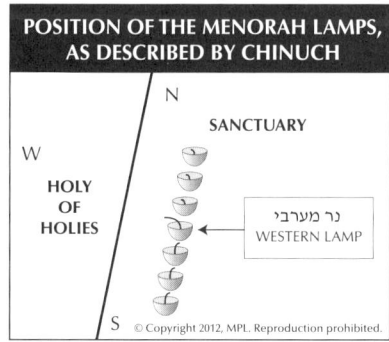

POSITION OF THE MENORAH LAMPS, AS DESCRIBED BY CHINUCH

# 251 □ TETZAVEH / MITZVAH 98: TO ARRANGE THE LAMPS OF THE MENORAH

וְיֶתֶר פְּרָטֶיהָ, מְבֹאָרִים בְּפֶרֶק שְׁמִינִי מִמְּנָחוֹת[24] (דף פ"ו ע"א) וּמְקוֹמוֹת מִתָּמִיד.[25]

זֶהוּ דַעַת הָרַמְבַּ"ם זִכְרוֹנוֹ לִבְרָכָה בְּמִצְוָה זוֹ שֶׁהֲטָבַת הַנֵּרוֹת הִיא הַדְלָקָתָן כְּמוֹ שֶׁפֵּרַשְׁנוּ,[26] אֲבָל דַּעַת מְפָרְשִׁים רַבִּים[27] שֶׁהֲטָבָה הִיא הַדִּשּׁוּן וְהַקִּנּוּחַ וְתִקּוּן הַפְּתִילוֹת, וְזוֹ הִיא מִצְוָה בִּפְנֵי עַצְמָהּ,[28] וְכֵן נִרְאֶה בְּפֶרֶק הַתְּכֵלֶת בְּמַסֶּכֶת מְנָחוֹת (דף נ' ע"א).[29]

---

Chinuch concludes: **מְבֹאָרִים בְּפֶרֶק** **וְיֶתֶר פְּרָטֶיהָ** — These laws, **as well as the additional details of [the mitzvah], שְׁמִינִי מִמְּנָחוֹת וּמְקוֹמוֹת מִתָּמִיד** — **are set forth in the eighth chapter of** Tractate *Menachos* (86a-b),[24] **and** in various **places in** Tractate *Tamid* (30b, 33a).[25]

## ⸺ Dispute Regarding the Mitzvah ⸺

**זֶהוּ דַעַת הָרַמְבַּ"ם זִכְרוֹנוֹ לִבְרָכָה בְּמִצְוָה זוֹ** — **This** preceding presentation, and indeed, our reckoning of the entire process of the Menorah service as only *one* of the 613 mitzvos, **is the opinion of the Rambam, of blessed memory, regarding this mitzvah, שֶׁהֲטָבַת הַנֵּרוֹת הִיא הַדְלָקָתָן כְּמוֹ שֶׁפֵּרַשְׁנוּ** — that is, **that** the mitzvah of "tending" the lamps is comprised not only of the *preparation* of the lamps for kindling, but also of **their** actual **kindling, as we have explained.**[26] **אֲבָל דַּעַת מְפָרְשִׁים רַבִּים** — **However, it is the opinion of many commentators**[27] **שֶׁהֲטָבָה הִיא הַדִּשּׁוּן וְהַקִּנּוּחַ וְתִקּוּן הַפְּתִילוֹת** — **that the** mitzvah of "tending" the lamps **is comprised only of the removal of residue, the** act of **wiping the lamps clean, and the preparation of the** new **wicks** and oil, **וְזוֹ הִיא מִצְוָה בִּפְנֵי עַצְמָהּ** — **and this is a mitzvah unto itself,** not part of the mitzvah of kindling the lamps.[28] **וְכֵן נִרְאֶה בְּפֶרֶק הַתְּכֵלֶת בְּמַסֶּכֶת מְנָחוֹת** — **Indeed, this seems** to be correct, as

---

### NOTES

the disrespect lies in lighting the *taper*, which is non-sacred, from a sacred Menorah lamp that is burning — even though the taper will then be used to kindle the other Menorah lamps (see *Shabbos* 22a-b with *Rashi* ד"ה טעמא דרב). *Minchas Chinuch* (§10) suggests emending the text of Chinuch to read לְהַדְלִיקָן בְּנֵר אַחֵר, *to kindle them with a different lamp*. I.e., it would be disrespectful to use a taper, since the taper would have to be lit from one of the sacred lamps.

Others explain that Chinuch's language is precise, because the law regarding the Temple Menorah is different from the law regarding the Chanukah lamps. We have seen that if the "western lamp" of the Menorah was extinguished, it must be rekindled from the flame of the Outer Altar. Thus, there is a specific requirement that this lamp of the Temple Menorah be kindled from a sacred source. It follows that the additional lamps, too, must be kindled directly from a sacred source — i.e., from the "western lamp" or another burning Menorah lamp. Lighting them from a non-sacred taper would diminish the honor of the mitzvah. Regarding the Chanukah lamps, however, there is no requirement to light them from a sacred source. In that case, therefore, the only concern is that it is disrespectful to light a taper *from* a mitzvah lamp (*Shevet HaLevi* Vol. V, *Kuntres HaMitzvos* §35).

24. Chinuch refers to Chapter *Kol Korbenos HaTzibbur*, which nowadays is the *ninth* chapter in Gemara *Menachos*, but is arranged as the *eighth* chapter in Mishnayos *Menachos*. Chinuch apparently had it as the eighth chapter in his edition of the Gemara as well, so he refers to it as the *eighth* chapter (see also *Sefer HaMitzvos, Asei* 25). In some editions of Chinuch, the text has been emended to read "the *ninth* chapter." [The laws are also discussed in the tenth chapter, 88b-89a.]

25. The laws are codified by *Rambam* primarily in *Hil. Temidin U'Mussafin* 3:10-17. See also *Hil. Bi'as HaMikdash* 9:7 and *Hil. Beis HaBechirah* 3:7-8.

26. See note 17.

27. See *Teshuvos HaRashba* Vol. I §309 at length, and ibid. §79; *Rashi* to *Exodus* 30:7-8 and to *Chagigah* 26b ד"ה מנורה לא כתיב בה תמיד; *Ramban* to *Exodus* 27:20 and *Shabbos* 22b; *Raavad*, *Hil. Avodas Yom HaKippurim* 2:2; see also *Meiri* to *Shabbos* 22b.

28. Thus, the Menorah service includes two distinct mitzvos: the obligation to clean and prepare the lamps, and the obligation to kindle them (see *Meiri* ibid.).

There is a significant practical difference as to whether "tending" and "kindling" are considered one mitzvah or two separate mitzvos. It was explained in note 17 that Scripture speaks of "tending" the lamps in the morning and "kindling" them in the afternoon. According to *Rambam's* understanding that these terms are synonymous and encompass the entire Menorah service, the verse means that this service in its entirety is performed twice daily — the lamps are cleaned out, prepared anew, and kindled each afternoon (toward evening), and the process is repeated each morning. According to the opinion that "tending" and "kindling" refer to different acts, however, the verse has another meaning entirely: The Kohanim must *tend* to the

## 252 ❑ תצוה / מצוה צח: מצות עריכת נרות המקדש

וְנוֹהֶגֶת בִּזְמַן הַבַּיִת, בַּכֹּהֲנִים[30].
וְכֹהֵן הָעוֹבֵר עָלֶיהָ וְלֹא עָרַךְ הַנֵּרוֹת כַּמִּצְוָה, בִּטֵּל עֲשֵׂה[31].

emerges from study of the relevant Talmudic passage **in Chapter** *HaTecheiles* **(Ch. 4) of Tractate** *Menachos* [50a].[29]

### ☙ Applicability of the Mitzvah ☙

וְנוֹהֶגֶת בִּזְמַן הַבַּיִת — **[This mitzvah] applies in the time of the Temple,** בַּכֹּהֲנִים — **to Kohanim.**[30] וְכֹהֵן הָעוֹבֵר עָלֶיהָ וְלֹא עָרַךְ הַנֵּרוֹת כַּמִּצְוָה — **A Kohen who transgressed [this mitzvah] and did not arrange the lamps according to** the guidelines of **the mitzvah** בִּטֵּל עֲשֵׂה — **has violated a** mitzvah-**obligation.**[31]

---

### NOTES

lamps — that is, remove the residue and prepare new wicks and oil — in the morning; and they must *kindle* the lamps in the afternoon. Thus, the Menorah is lit only *once* daily, as evening approaches, and it is cleaned out once daily, in the morning. [This applies to all the lamps except the "western" one, which is supposed to burn constantly] (see *Teshuvos HaRashba* ibid.; *Rashi* ibid.; *Ramban* ibid.; *Raavad* ibid.).

29. For a discussion of the proof and possible deflections of it, see *Teshuvos HaRashba* ibid.; *Lechem Mishneh*, *Hil. Temidin U'Mussafin* 3:12; and *Chazon Ish*, *Menachos* 36:8 ד"ה ונראה. [Although Chinuch states that he is inclined to agree with the latter view, he counts the Menorah service as only one mitzvah, in accordance with *Rambam's* view (and he presents the laws of the mitzvah accordingly). This is consistent with Chinuch's policy of following *Rambam's* count of the mitzvos in this work, as he stated in his Introduction (Vol. I, p. 34; see note 3 there).]

30. The Torah states explicitly (*Exodus* 27:21): יַעֲרֹךְ אֹתוֹ אַהֲרֹן וּבָנָיו, *Aaron and his sons* [i.e., the Kohanim] *shall arrange it.* See the Insight for further discussion.

31. Chinuch's intention here is somewhat obscure. Understood simply, he refers to a case where the mitzvah was neglected and the Menorah remained unlit. If so, it is unclear which Kohen has committed the transgression. Perhaps it is the Kohen who won the right to perform this mitzvah in the daily lottery (described in *Yoma* 25a). Or, perhaps, any Kohen who saw the Menorah unlit and had the opportunity to light it, but neglected to do so, is in violation (see Mitzvah 401 for a similar concept).

Alternatively, Chinuch may refer to a case where the Menorah was not left unlit, but was kindled in a manner inconsistent with the laws of the mitzvah (e.g., the residue was not removed), and he means that the Kohen who did the improper kindling has violated a mitzvah-obligation.

---

### ❧ Insight: May a Non-Kohen Kindle the Menorah?

Chinuch states (at note 30) that the mitzvah of tending the Menorah applies specifically to Kohanim. This point seems indisputable, even discounting the fact that the *avodos* of the *Beis HaMikdash* (with only minor exceptions) had to be performed by Kohanim. First, it was forbidden for a non-Kohen to enter the Sanctuary (*Heichal*), where the Menorah rested. Moreover, in regard to the Menorah service, the Torah states explicitly (*Exodus* 27:21): יַעֲרֹךְ אֹתוֹ אַהֲרֹן וּבָנָיו, *Aaron and his sons* [i.e., the Kohanim] *shall arrange it*; it further states (ibid. 30:8): וּבְהַעֲלֹת אַהֲרֹן אֶת הַנֵּרֹת בֵּין הָעַרְבַּיִם, *and when Aaron kindles the lamps in the evening*; and it also states (*Numbers* 8:2): דַּבֵּר אֶל אַהֲרֹן וְאָמַרְתָּ אֵלָיו בְּהַעֲלֹתְךָ אֶת הַנֵּרֹת, *Speak to Aaron and say to him: "When you kindle the lamps … "*

Nevertheless, *Rambam* (*Hil. Bi'as HaMikdash* 9:7) rules that while a non-Kohen may not *prepare* the Menorah lamps, nor enter the Sanctuary to kindle the Menorah, if a Kohen prepared the lamps and brought them out to the Temple Courtyard, a non-Kohen would be allowed to kindle them. This ruling is based on a statement in the Gemara (*Yoma* 24b) that "kindling is not an *avodah* (act of service)," which *Rambam* understands to mean that it need not be performed by a Kohen. Thus, as long as a Kohen performs the preparation of the lamps, which *is* considered an *avodah*, and the lamps are brought out to the Temple Courtyard, a non-Kohen may kindle them (see *Raavad* ad loc. for another explanation of the Gemara).

The obvious difficulty with *Rambam's* position is that the Torah repeatedly speaks of Kohanim performing the kindling. Moreover, *Minchas Chinuch* (§13) wonders how this fits with Chinuch's

statement that the mitzvah applies specifically to Kohanim. Since a non-Kohen may also perform it, this mitzvah is seemingly the responsibility of *all* the Jewish people!

*R' Chaim Soloveitchik* explains *Rambam's* position in a manner that resolves these difficulties: The Torah (*Exodus* 27:21) explicitly commands Aaron and his sons (the Kohanim) to "arrange" the lamps. It does not, however, command the Kohanim — or, for that matter, anyone — to actually *kindle* the lamps. [It merely speaks passively about the kindling — viz., *"when Aaron kindles the lamps"; "when you kindle the lamps"* (see *Ritva, Yoma* 24b).] We may infer that the essence of the mitzvah is not the *act* of kindling, but rather, *having* lamps burning. The Kohanim are commanded to perform the "arranging," which involves preparing the lamps for kindling, and seeing to it that they burn. The act of kindling, though, is not the essence of the mitzvah; *having* lamps burning is the essence of the mitzvah, and that is fulfilled passively. It is for this reason that the Gemara (ibid.) declares that "kindling is not an *avodah*." Only an act that is an *inherent* part of the service qualifies as an *avodah* that must be performed by a Kohen. The kindling is not an inherent part of the service, but merely a way of *causing* the mitzvah to be fulfilled, so it is not classified as an *avodah* (*Chidushei R' Chaim HaLevi, Hil. Bi'as HaMikdash* 9:7; see there for further discussion; see also *Chidushei HaGriz* to *Rambam, Hil. Temidin U'Mussafin* p. 82 ד"ה והנה ברמב"ם; *Chazon Ish, Menachos* 30:8 ד"ה והר"מ).

This explains why, as Chinuch pointed out (at note 5), the Gemara consistently refers to this mitzvah as the obligation of "tending" the lamps, not of "kindling" them. It also explains why Chinuch describes the mitzvah as pertaining specifically to Kohanim. The Kohanim are commanded to tend the lamps — i.e., to see to it that they burn, by performing the preparatory acts and by ensuring that they are lit. Regardless of who does the actual lighting, it is the Kohanim who bear responsibility for ensuring that the lamps burn — and that is the essence of the mitzvah.

The preceding understanding of the mitzvah finds expression in another law: Chinuch states (at note 19) that if a lamp was still burning when the time of the next kindling arrived, the Kohen would merely adjust the lamp (i.e., trim the wick and add oil); he was not required to extinguish and relight it. This ruling follows *Rambam* (*Hil. Temidin U'Mussafin* 3:12), and is consistent with the preceding explanation of *Rambam's* opinion — that the act of kindling is not a daily mitzvah at all, and the mitzvah is merely that the lamps *be burning*. Hence, if they already were burning from the previous day, there is no point in extinguishing and relighting them; the mitzvah is fulfilled by simply ensuring that they continue to burn. It was mentioned in note 19 that other Rishonim disagree with this ruling, and maintain that if any lamp was still burning at the time of the next kindling, the Kohen was required to extinguish and relight it, in order to fulfill the mitzvah of kindling the Menorah. These Rishonim apparently maintain that the *act* of kindling is essential to the mitzvah, and since the mitzvah must be performed *each day*, if the lamps were still burning from the previous day they had to be extinguished and relit (see *Chidushei HaGriz* ibid.).

The above explanation has another ramification: *Minchas Chinuch* (§14) asserts that, even according to *Rambam's* view that the kindling may be performed by a non-Kohen, it may not be performed by a deaf-mute, a deranged person, or a minor. He reasons that although the kindling does not qualify as *"avodah,"* it certainly is a "mitzvah," and since these individuals are deemed legally incompetent to perform mitzvos, they may not fulfill the mitzvah of kindling the Menorah lamps. According to the above explanation, however, it follows that the lamps may be kindled even by one of these individuals. Since the essential part of the mitzvah is not to perform the *act* of kindling, but to *have* kindled lamps, it makes no difference whether they are kindled by a competent person or an incompetent one. In the final analysis, all that matters is that the lamps of the Menorah are burning (*Chazon Ish* ibid.).

For further discussion of *Rambam's* ruling that the kindling may be done in the Temple Courtyard, see *Minchas Chinuch* §9, *Maharam Schik*, and *Chazon Ish* ibid. See also *Siach Yitzchak, Yoma* 24b to *Tos. Yeshanim* ד"ה הדלקת; and *Derashos Chasam Sofer, Chanukah* 5592.

## מִצְוָה צט: מִצְוַת לְבִישַׁת בִּגְדֵי הַכֹּהֲנִים

שֶׁנִּצְטַוּוּ הַכֹּהֲנִים לִלְבֹּשׁ בְּגָדִים מְיֻחָדִים[1] לִגְדֻלָּה וְכָבוֹד[2] וְאָז יַעַבְדוּ בַּמִּקְדָּשׁ, שֶׁנֶּאֱמַר (שמות כ"ח, ד'): וְעָשׂוּ בִגְדֵי קֹדֶשׁ לְאַהֲרֹן אָחִיךָ וּלְבָנָיו[3].

## Mitzvah 99
## The Obligation [for Kohanim] to Don the Priestly Garments

וְעָשִׂיתָ בִגְדֵי קֹדֶשׁ לְאַהֲרֹן אָחִיךָ לְכָבוֹד וּלְתִפְאָרֶת. וְאַתָּה תְּדַבֵּר אֶל כָּל חַכְמֵי לֵב אֲשֶׁר מִלֵּאתִיו רוּחַ חָכְמָה וְעָשׂוּ אֶת בִּגְדֵי אַהֲרֹן לְקַדְּשׁוֹ לְכַהֲנוֹ לִי. וְאֵלֶּה הַבְּגָדִים אֲשֶׁר יַעֲשׂוּ חֹשֶׁן וְאֵפוֹד וּמְעִיל וּכְתֹנֶת תַּשְׁבֵּץ מִצְנֶפֶת וְאַבְנֵט וְעָשׂוּ בִגְדֵי קֹדֶשׁ לְאַהֲרֹן אָחִיךָ וּלְבָנָיו לְכַהֲנוֹ לִי

*You shall make vestments of sanctity for Aaron your brother, for glory and splendor. And you shall speak to all the wise-hearted people whom I have invested with a spirit of wisdom, and they shall make the vestments of Aaron, to sanctify him to minister to Me. These are the vestments that they shall make: a Choshen (Breastplate), an Ephod (Apron), a Me'il (Robe), a Kesones (Tunic) of a box-like knit, a Mitznefes (Turban), and an Avneit (Sash); they shall make vestments of sanctity for Aaron your brother and his sons, to minister to Me (Exodus 28:2-4).*

These verses describe six of the eight Priestly Garments that are worn by the Kohen Gadol when serving in the Temple. Further in the passage (vs. 36-42), the Torah mentions two additional garments that must be made — a *Tzitz* (Headplate), and *Michnasayim* (Breeches).[1] Four of these garments are worn only by the Kohen Gadol, while the other four are worn by ordinary Kohanim as well, as Chinuch will explain. All these garments will be described below.

שֶׁנִּצְטַוּוּ הַכֹּהֲנִים לִלְבֹּשׁ בְּגָדִים מְיֻחָדִים לִגְדֻלָּה וְכָבוֹד — **The Kohanim are commanded to don garments designated for grandeur and glory,**[2] וְאָז יַעַבְדוּ בַּמִּקְדָּשׁ — **and** only then **to perform** *avodah* (service) **in the Temple,** שֶׁנֶּאֱמַר — **as it is stated** (*Exodus* 28:4): "וְעָשׂוּ בִגְדֵי קֹדֶשׁ לְאַהֲרֹן אָחִיךָ וּלְבָנָיו" — **They shall make vestments of sanctity for Aaron your brother and his sons,** *to minister to Me*.[3]

---

### NOTES

1. The *Tzitz* is not mentioned together with the other garments because it was not literally a "garment." The *Michnasayim* are not mentioned there because they were worn *to cover the flesh of nakedness* (ibid. v. 42), and not *for glory and splendor* (*Ibn Ezra* and *Baal HaTurim* to *Exodus* 28:4).

2. Chinuch apparently understands that when the verse (cited above) states that the purpose of the garments is לְכָבוֹד וּלְתִפְאָרֶת, *for glory and splendor,* it creates a halachic requirement: The garments must be *designated* for grandeur and glory — i.e., designed and worn in a manner that promotes grandeur and glory. Indeed, Rambam (*Hil. Klei HaMikdash* 8:4) rules that the stipulation *for glory and splendor* requires that the garments be in new condition, of nice appearance, and of proper size when worn by the Kohanim. [Chinuch will elaborate below on the reason for this requirement.]

3. This verse is also cited as the source of the mitzvah in early editions of *Sefer HaMitzvos, Asei* 33. In later editions, and in *Hil. Klei HaMikdash* 10:4, Rambam cites the earlier verse in the passage (28:2): *You shall make vestments of sanctity for Aaron your brother, for glory and splendor.*

Although these verses speak of *making* the garments, Chinuch defines this mitzvah as an obligation on the Kohanim to *wear* them when performing the *avodah* [for that is the ultimate objective] (see also *Sefer HaMitzvos* ibid.). In *Hil. Klei HaMikdash* 10:4, Rambam states that the mitzvah has two facets: (1) to *make* the garments, based on the above verse; (2) to *wear* the garments while performing the *avodah*, based on *Exodus* 29:8, which states: וְהִלְבַּשְׁתָּם וגו׳, *You shall dress them* (the Kohanim) etc. Nevertheless, making the garments is not reckoned as a separate mitzvah, in keeping with the rule that any obligation that is a preparatory step toward fulfilling a mitzvah is not reckoned as a separate mitzvah (*Sefer HaMitzvos, Shoresh* 10; see also Mitzvah 103 note 4).

# TETZAVEH / MITZVAH 99: TO DON THE PRIESTLY GARMENTS

מִשָּׁרְשֵׁי הַמִּצְוָה, הַיְסוֹד הַקָּבוּעַ לָנוּ כִּי הָאָדָם נִפְעָל לְפִי פְּעֻלּוֹתָיו וְאַחֲרֵיהֶם מַחְשְׁבוֹתָיו וְכַוָּנוֹתָיו[4], וְהַשָּׁלִיחַ הַמְכַפֵּר צָרִיךְ לְהַתְפִּיס כָּל מַחְשַׁבְתּוֹ וְכַוָּנָתוֹ אֶל הָעֲבוֹדָה[5], עַל כֵּן רָאוּי לְהִתְלַבֵּשׁ בִּגְדֵי מְיֻחָדִים אֵלֶיהָ, שֶׁבְּשֶׁיִּסְתַּכֵּל בְּכָל מָקוֹם שֶׁבְּגוּפוֹ מִיָּד יִהְיֶה נִזְכָּר וּמִתְעוֹרֵר בְּלִבּוֹ לִפְנֵי מִי הוּא עוֹבֵד, וְזֶה כְּעֵין תְּפִלִּין שֶׁנִּצְטַוּוּ הַכֹּל לְהַנִּיחַ בִּקְצָת הַגּוּף שֶׁיִּהְיֶה לְזִכְרוֹן מַחֲשֶׁבֶת הַכָּשֵׁר[6]. וְאַף עַל פִּי שֶׁגַּם הַכֹּהֵן הָיָה מֵנִיחַ תְּפִלִּין[7], לְגֹדֶל עִנְיָנוֹ הָיָה צָרִיךְ גַּם זֶה.

---

### ⸺ Underlying Purpose of the Mitzvah ⸺

מִשָּׁרְשֵׁי הַמִּצְוָה — **Among the underlying purposes of this mitzvah**, הַיְסוֹד הַקָּבוּעַ לָנוּ — **is the fundamental principle that we have established** (in Mitzvah 16), כִּי הָאָדָם נִפְעָל לְפִי פְּעֻלּוֹתָיו — **that a man is affected in accordance with his actions**, וְאַחֲרֵיהֶם מַחְשְׁבוֹתָיו וְכַוָּנוֹתָיו — **and his thoughts and his intentions follow** the direction of [those actions].[4]

וְהַשָּׁלִיחַ הַמְכַפֵּר — **Now, the agent who provides atonement** for a person who brings an offering, i.e., the Kohen who performs its *avodah*, צָרִיךְ לְהַתְפִּיס כָּל מַחְשַׁבְתּוֹ וְכַוָּנָתוֹ אֶל הָעֲבוֹדָה — **must focus all his thoughts and intentions on the** *avodah*.[5] עַל כֵּן רָאוּי לְהִתְלַבֵּשׁ בִּגְדֵי מְיֻחָדִים אֵלֶיהָ — **It is therefore appropriate that [the Kohen] dress himself in garments designated for [the** *avodah*], שֶׁבְּשֶׁיִּסְתַּכֵּל בְּכָל מָקוֹם שֶׁבְּגוּפוֹ — **so that when he gazes upon any part of his body**, מִיָּד יִהְיֶה נִזְכָּר וּמִתְעוֹרֵר בְּלִבּוֹ לִפְנֵי מִי הוּא עוֹבֵד — **he will immediately be reminded** of, and his heart will be awakened to, an awareness of the One **before Whom he is serving**.

וְזֶה כְּעֵין תְּפִלִּין — **This** idea is similar to one of the underlying purposes of the mitzvah of **tefillin**, שֶׁנִּצְטַוּוּ הַכֹּל לְהַנִּיחַ בִּקְצָת הַגּוּף — **which all** men **are commanded to place on** certain **parts of the body** (i.e., the head and the arm), שֶׁיִּהְיֶה לְזִכְרוֹן מַחֲשֶׁבֶת הַכָּשֵׁר — in order **that [the tefillin] should serve as a reminder to** engage in **proper thoughts**.[6] וְאַף עַל פִּי שֶׁגַּם הַכֹּהֵן הָיָה מֵנִיחַ תְּפִלִּין — **And although a Kohen, too, would wear tefillin**, so it might seem unnecessary for him to additionally wear special garments,[7] לְגֹדֶל עִנְיָנוֹ הָיָה צָרִיךְ גַּם זֶה — **nevertheless**, **because of the loftiness of the matter of his** sacred *avodah*, **he requires this** additional reminder (i.e., special garments) **as well**.

Chinuch expands this principle to explain certain laws regarding the priestly vestments:

---

NOTES

4. Throughout this work, Chinuch stresses the principle that a person's actions influence his attitude and inner tendencies. See Mitzvah 16 at length, as well as Mitzvos 40, 95, 98, et al.

5. Chinuch established in Mitzvah 95 that the intention with which an offering is brought is a critical element of its capacity to effect atonement. While his discussion there focused on the importance of the owner's attitude, it is surely essential for the Kohen who actually performs the *avodah* to do so with the purest of intentions. [See *Nedarim* 35b, *Yoma* 19a, and *Kiddushin* 23b, for discussion of whether the Kohanim act as agents of the Israelites who bring the offerings, or of the One Who commanded that they be offered.]

6. See below, Mitzvos 421-422, where Chinuch elaborates on this concept.

7. In earlier times people wore tefillin all day (see *Shulchan Aruch, Orach Chaim* 37:2). Since the tefillin serve as a constant reminder that one is in God's presence, the question arises as to why the special priestly garments were necessary.

[Actually, the Kohanim were not obligated to wear tefillin while performing the *avodah* (Chinuch below, Mitzvah 421; see *Zevachim* 19a with *Rashi* ד"ה ומן התפילין; *Rambam, Hil. Tefillin* 4:13; *Beis HaLevi* Vol. I §3:2). Nevertheless, it seems that they generally did wear the head-tefillin. They were *not allowed* to wear the arm-tefillin during the *avodah*, because those tefillin would constitute an interposition (*chatzitzah*) between their body and the *Kesones* (Tunic) of the priestly garments. They were, however, allowed to wear the head-tefillin, because there was space for tefillin between the forehead and the *Mitznefes* (Turban) that they wore (see *Arachin* 3b; see also *Minchas Chinuch* §16, and *Minchas Yitzchak* below, 421:3; for further discussion, see *Shitah Mekubetzes* to *Arachin* 3b §6, and *Shaagas Aryeh* §37). Had they not been commanded to wear the special vestments, then *chatzitzah* would not have been an issue, and they presumably would have worn the arm-tefillin as well.]

וּמִן הַטַּעַם הַזֶּה נֶאֱמַר שֶׁנִּתְחַיְּבוּ לִהְיוֹת אֹרֶךְ הַכֻּתֹּנֶת עַל כָּל גּוּפוֹ עַד לְמַעְלָה מִן הֶעָקֵב מְעַט, וְאֹרֶךְ בֵּית יָד שֶׁלָּהּ עַד פַּס יָדוֹ,[8] וְהַמִּצְנֶפֶת אָרְכָּהּ שֵׁשׁ עֶשְׂרֵה אַמָּה[9] וּמַקִּיפָהּ בְּרֹאשׁוֹ כְּדֵי שֶׁיִּרְאֶה אוֹתָהּ בְּכָל עֵת שֶׁיִּשָּׂא עֵינָיו, וְהָאַבְנֵט שֶׁחוֹגֵר בְּמָתְנָיו אָרְכּוֹ ל"ב אַמָּה,[10] וּמַקִּיפוֹ וּמַחֲזִירוֹ עַל גּוּפוֹ כֶּרֶךְ עַל כֶּרֶךְ[11] וְנִמְצָא שֶׁמַּרְגִּישׁ בּוֹ בְּכָל עֵת בִּזְרוֹעוֹתָיו, שֶׁמִּתּוֹךְ גָּבְהוֹ בְּרֹב הַהֶקֵּפִין, הַזְּרוֹעוֹת נוֹגְעוֹת בּוֹ עַל כָּל פָּנִים. וְכָל זֶה רְאָיָה לָמָּה שֶׁאָמַרְתִּי לְמוֹדֶה עַל הָאֱמֶת,[12] מִלְּבַד שֶׁיֵּשׁ בָּעִנְיָן כָּבוֹד לַבַּיִת וְלָעֲבוֹדָה בִּהְיוֹת הָעוֹבֵד מְלֻבָּשׁ בִּלְבוּשׁ מְיֻחָד לָעֲבוֹדָה, וּכְבָר כָּתַבְנוּ כִּי בְּהַגְדָּלַת הַבַּיִת וּבְמוֹרָאוֹ

שֶׁנִּתְחַיְּבוּ לִהְיוֹת אֹרֶךְ הַכֻּתֹּנֶת עַל כָּל וּמִן הַטַּעַם הַזֶּה נֶאֱמַר – **Based on this reasoning, we may say** גּוּפוֹ – **that** this is why **it is obligatory for the length of the** Kohen's ***Kesones*** (Tunic) **to extend over his entire body,** עַד לְמַעְלָה מִן הֶעָקֵב מְעַט – **until slightly above the heel,** וְאֹרֶךְ בֵּית יָד שֶׁלָּהּ עַד פַּס יָדוֹ – **and** for **the length of its sleeve** to reach **until the palm of his hand.**[8] His entire body must be covered with the *Kesones*, so that wherever he gazes he will have a reminder of his holy function. וְהַמִּצְנֶפֶת אָרְכָּהּ שֵׁשׁ עֶשְׂרֵה אַמָּה – Similarly, **the** proper **length of** the strip of fabric that is used to fashion **the *Mitznefes*** (Turban) **is sixteen *amos*,**[9] וּמַקִּיפָהּ בְּרֹאשׁוֹ – **and [the Kohen] wraps it around his head,** forming a very large turban, כְּדֵי שֶׁיִּרְאֶה אוֹתָהּ בְּכָל עֵת שֶׁיִּשָּׂא עֵינָיו – **so that whenever he lifts his eyes he will see it** and be reminded of his holy task. וְהָאַבְנֵט שֶׁחוֹגֵר בְּמָתְנָיו – Similarly, with respect to **the *Avneit*** (Sash) **that he girds around his hips,** אָרְכּוֹ ל"ב אַמָּה – **its** proper **length is thirty-two *amos*,**[10] וּמַקִּיפוֹ וּמַחֲזִירוֹ עַל גּוּפוֹ כֶּרֶךְ עַל כֶּרֶךְ – **and he wraps it around his body repeatedly, layer upon layer;**[11] וְנִמְצָא שֶׁמַּרְגִּישׁ בּוֹ בְּכָל עֵת בִּזְרוֹעוֹתָיו – **thus, it emerges that he feels [the *Avneit*] with his arms at all times,** שֶׁמִּתּוֹךְ גָּבְהוֹ בְּרֹב הַהֶקֵּפִין – **for on account of its thickness, resulting from the many windings** with which it was wrapped around his waist, הַזְּרוֹעוֹת נוֹגְעוֹת בּוֹ עַל כָּל פָּנִים – **his arms** (i.e., his elbows) **would inevitably touch it** constantly. In sum, each of these garments was designed in a manner that caused the Kohen to be constantly aware that he was wearing it, וְכָל זֶה רְאָיָה לָמָּה שֶׁאָמַרְתִּי – **all of which serves as a proof to what I have said** regarding the purpose of the garments in general, לְמוֹדֶה עַל הָאֱמֶת – to anyone **who admits to the truth.**[12]

Chinuch notes that there is another purpose for this mitzvah: מִלְּבַד שֶׁיֵּשׁ בָּעִנְיָן כָּבוֹד לַבַּיִת וְלָעֲבוֹדָה – **The preceding reason exists aside from the basic principle that it brings honor to the** Holy **Temple and to the *avodah*** בִּהְיוֹת הָעוֹבֵד מְלֻבָּשׁ בִּלְבוּשׁ מְיֻחָד לָעֲבוֹדָה – **when the one who serves is dressed in a garment** specifically **designated for the *avodah*;** וּכְבָר כָּתַבְנוּ – **and we have already written** (Mitzvah 95, 98) כִּי בְּהַגְדָּלַת הַבַּיִת וּבְמוֹרָאוֹ – **that through enhancement of the Temple's grandeur, and the** resulting **awe that people have for it,**

---

NOTES

8. *Rambam, Hil. Klei HaMikdash* 8:17; see *Zevachim* 18a-b and *Yoma* 72b.

9. *Rambam* ibid. §19. *Mitznefes* is the term for the headwear of the Kohen Gadol. The headwear of the ordinary Kohen is called a *Migbaas*. Both of these are described more fully below, in note 26. [Sixteen *amos* equals between 25 and 31 feet (approx. 7.6-9.5 meters), depending on various opinions.]

10. *Rambam* ibid., from *Yerushalmi Yoma* 7:3. [Thirty-two *amos* equals between 50 and 62 feet (approx. 15.2-19 meters), depending on various opinions. *Rambam* adds that the width of the *Avneit* was equal to three finger-breadths.]

11. Scripture states (*Ezekiel* 44:18): לֹא יַחְגְּרוּ בַּיָּזַע, *They shall not gird themselves where one perspires,* which the Gemara (*Zevachim* 18b-19a) understands to mean that the Kohanim should not wrap the *Avneit* below the loins or above the elbows, because those areas are prone to sweat. Hence, the *Avneit* had to be wrapped around the portion of the torso that is opposite the elbows, i.e., the waist. Since its 32-*amah* length was sufficient to encircle the torso many times, it would form many layers around the waist (*Rambam* ibid. 10:2).

12. Interestingly, it is derived from Scripture that the Kohen Gadol was *required* to constantly keep his attention on the *Tzitz* (Headplate) that he wore, because the Name of Hashem was inscribed upon it (*Yoma* 7b; see Insight). No such requirement is mentioned regarding the other vestments, but nevertheless, Chinuch posits that they were designed in a manner that ensured that the Kohanim would always remain aware of them.

# TETZAVEH / MITZVAH 99: TO DON THE PRIESTLY GARMENTS

יִתְרַכְּכוּ שָׁם לִבּוֹת הַחוֹטְאִים וְיָשׁוּבוּ אֶל ה'.[13]

דִּינֵי הַמִּצְוָה, כְּגוֹן בְּאוּר הַמַּלְבּוּשִׁים שֶׁהֵן שְׁלֹשֶׁת מִינִין, בִּגְדֵי כֹּהֵן הֶדְיוֹט מִין אֶחָד, וּבִגְדֵי כֹּהֵן גָּדוֹל שְׁנֵי מִינִין, בִּגְדֵי זָהָב וּבִגְדֵי לָבָן, וְשֶׁל כֹּהֵן הֶדְיוֹט הֵם אַרְבָּעָה כֵּלִים וּשְׁמָם כֵּן: כְּתֹנֶת וּמִכְנָסַיִם וּמִגְבַּעַת וְאַבְנֵט. הַכְּתֹנֶת הִיא כְּעֵין חָלוּק רָחָב שֶׁל יִשְׁמְעֵאלִים,[14] וְהַמִּכְנָסַיִם צוּרָתָן יְדוּעָה בְּכָל מָקוֹם, וְהָיוּ שֶׁלָּהֶם גְּדוֹלִים מִמָּתְנַיִם וְעַד יְרֵכַיִם, כְּלוֹמַר עַד הַיְּרֵכַיִם שֶׁהוּא הַנִּקְרָא גִּינוּ"י. אָמְנָם הַמִּגְבַּעַת הוּא כְּלִי שֶׁמַּנִּיחִין עַל הָרֹאשׁ עָשׂוּי כְּכוֹבַע,[15] הָאַבְנֵט הוּא כְּמִין אֵזוֹר שֶׁחוֹגְרִין בּוֹ אֶלָּא שֶׁהֵם הָיוּ מַקִּיפִין בּוֹ הַרְבֵּה הֶקֵּפִין מַה שֶׁאֵין אָנוּ עוֹשִׂין כֵּן בָּאֵזוֹר. וְאַרְבַּעַת כֵּלִים אֵלֶּה שֶׁל פִּשְׁתָּן[16] הָיוּ לְבָנִים[17] וְחוּטָן כָּפוּל שִׁשָּׁה,[18]

יִתְרַכְּכוּ שָׁם לִבּוֹת הַחוֹטְאִים וְיָשׁוּבוּ אֶל ה' — **the hearts of sinners** who visit the Temple **will become softened and they will return to Hashem** in repentance.[13]

### ⸺ Laws of the Mitzvah ⸺

דִּינֵי הַמִּצְוָה — **The laws of the mitzvah** include, כְּגוֹן בְּאוּר הַמַּלְבּוּשִׁים — **for example, a description of the** priestly **vestments,** שֶׁהֵן שְׁלֹשֶׁת מִינִין — **which are of three categories:** בִּגְדֵי כֹּהֵן וּבִגְדֵי כֹּהֵן גָּדוֹל שְׁנֵי הֶדְיוֹט מִין אֶחָד — **The vestments of an ordinary Kohen are one category,** מִינִין — **and the vestments of the Kohen Gadol** are divided into **two categories,** בִּגְדֵי זָהָב וּבִגְדֵי לָבָן — one known as **the Golden Vestments and** the other known as **the White Vestments.**

Chinuch describes the vestments of the ordinary Kohen:

וְשֶׁל כֹּהֵן הֶדְיוֹט הֵם אַרְבָּעָה כֵּלִים — **[The vestments] of the ordinary Kohen consist of four garments,** וּשְׁמָם כֵּן — **whose names are as follows:** כְּתֹנֶת וּמִכְנָסַיִם וּמִגְבַּעַת וְאַבְנֵט — (1) *Kesones* (Tunic); (2) *Michnasayim* (Breeches); (3) *Migbaas* (Headwear); and (4) *Avneit* (Sash). הַכְּתֹנֶת הִיא כְּעֵין חָלוּק רָחָב שֶׁל יִשְׁמְעֵאלִים — **The** *Kesones* (Tunic) **is similar to the wide robe of the Ishmaelites.**[14] וְהַמִּכְנָסַיִם צוּרָתָן יְדוּעָה בְּכָל מָקוֹם — With respect to **the** *Michnasayim* (Breeches), **their form is known everywhere,** וְהָיוּ שֶׁלָּהֶם גְּדוֹלִים מִמָּתְנַיִם וְעַד יְרֵכַיִם — except that, as the Torah states (*Exodus* 28:42), **those of [the Kohanim]** were **large enough to extend *from the hips to the thighs*,** כְּלוֹמַר עַד הַיְּרֵכַיִם שֶׁהוּא הַנִּקְרָא גִּינוּ"י — **that is, to** the bottom of **the thigh, which is the knee.** אָמְנָם הַמִּגְבַּעַת הוּא כְּלִי שֶׁמַּנִּיחִין עַל הָרֹאשׁ — **As for the** *Migbaas*, **it is a garment that is placed upon the head,** עָשׂוּי כְּכוֹבַע — **and is formed like a hat.**[15] הָאַבְנֵט הוּא כְּמִין אֵזוֹר שֶׁחוֹגְרִין בּוֹ — **The** *Avneit* **is a kind of belt used for girding oneself,** אֶלָּא שֶׁהֵם הָיוּ מַקִּיפִין בּוֹ הַרְבֵּה הֶקֵּפִין — except that, as has been explained, **[the Kohanim] wrapped it about themselves with many windings,** מַה שֶׁאֵין אָנוּ עוֹשִׂין כֵּן בָּאֵזוֹר — **which we do not** usually **do with a belt.** וְאַרְבַּעַת כֵּלִים אֵלֶּה שֶׁל פִּשְׁתָּן — **These four garments were made of linen,**[16] הָיוּ לְבָנִים — **they were white,**[17] וְחוּטָן כָּפוּל שִׁשָּׁה — **and their threads were plied** with **six strands.**[18]

---

## NOTES

13. See above, Mitzvah 98 note 7.

14. As Chinuch described above, it covers the entire length of the Kohen's body and has long sleeves. [The Gemara (*Zevachim* 19a) and *Rambam* (ibid. 10:6-7) indicate that the Kohen's garments were tight-fitting, and there was not supposed to be any gap between his flesh and the garments. Chinuch's reference to the "wide" Ishmaelite robes is thus unclear.]

15. This will be described more fully below. See note 26.

16. The Torah consistently (e.g., *Exodus* 28:39, 42) refers to these articles as made of שֵׁשׁ or בַּד, both of which refer to *flax* (*Zevachim* 18b; *Rambam* ibid. 8:1,13).

17. *Rambam* ibid. 8:1. [*Minchas Chinuch* (101:3) suggests that these vestments were allowed to be dyed, but are nevertheless called "white" vestments because they were *permitted* to be undyed (as opposed to certain vestments of the Kohen Gadol, which were required to be dyed, as we shall learn). *Kiryas Sefer* (*Hil. Klei HaMikdash* 8:3), however, asserts that the term בַּד refers specifically to linen fiber that is in its natural, undyed, state. See also *Toras Kohanim, Tazria* 13:3-4, cited by *Rash, Negaim* 11:3.]

18. The term שֵׁשׁ (*linen*), with which the Torah describes the vestments, also means *six*. This alludes to the fact that each thread was plied with six strands twisted together (see *Yoma* 71b; *Rambam* ibid.). [According to *Rambam* (ibid. §14), using six strands is essential only in the specific instances where the Torah employs the term שֵׁשׁ. Where it employs the term בַּד, using six

# תצוה / מצוה צט: מצוות לבישת בגדי הכהנים

וְהָאַבְנֵט לְבַדּוֹ רָקוּם בְּצֶמֶר[19], וּבְאֵלּוּ הָיָה עוֹבֵד לְעוֹלָם כֹּהֵן הֶדְיוֹט[20], וּמֻתָּר לְלָבְשָׁן בַּיּוֹם[21] בֵּין בִּשְׁעַת עֲבוֹדָה בֵּין שֶׁלֹּא בִּשְׁעָתָהּ, דְּמֻתָּר לֵהָנוֹת בָּהֶן[22], חוּץ מִן הָאַבְנֵט לְפִי שֶׁהוּא שַׁעַטְנֵז[23] וּלְפִיכָךְ אָסוּר שֶׁלֹּא בִּשְׁעַת עֲבוֹדָתָהּ[24].

---

וְהָאַבְנֵט לְבַדּוֹ רָקוּם בְּצֶמֶר — The *Kesones, Michnasayim,* and *Migbaas* were made purely of linen, **but the *Avneit*, alone, was** made of linen **embroidered with wool.**[19]

Chinuch discusses when these vestments were worn:

וּבְאֵלּוּ הָיָה עוֹבֵד לְעוֹלָם כֹּהֵן הֶדְיוֹט — It is while clothed **in these** vestments that **an ordinary Kohen would always perform** *avodah* in the Temple.[20]

וּמֻתָּר לְלָבְשָׁן בַּיּוֹם — Moreover, **[a Kohen] was permitted to wear them** throughout **the day** (on any day when it was his turn to perform the *avodah*),[21] בֵּין בִּשְׁעַת עֲבוֹדָה בֵּין שֶׁלֹּא בִּשְׁעָתָהּ — **whether** it was **during the time of** his actually performing ***the avodah*, or outside the time of** his performing **[the *avodah*],** דְּמֻתָּר לֵהָנוֹת בָּהֶן — **as it was permissible** for a Kohen **to derive** personal **benefit from [the vestments].**[22] חוּץ מִן הָאַבְנֵט לְפִי שֶׁהוּא שַׁעַטְנֵז — **This applies to all the vestments except the *Avneit*, because it was *shaatnez*,**[23] וּלְפִיכָךְ אָסוּר שֶׁלֹּא בִּשְׁעַת עֲבוֹדָה — **and** a Kohen **was therefore prohibited** to wear it **outside the time when** he was performing **the *avodah*.**[24]

---

## NOTES

strands is *preferred,* but a garment made from threads of one strand is valid. *Rashi* (*Zevachim* 18b), however, maintains that six-ply thread is essential in all instances (*Kesef Mishneh* to *Rambam* ibid.). See *Mishneh LaMelech, Hil. Klei HaMikdash* 8:3, for a lengthy discussion of this subject.]

19. The Torah (*Exodus* 28:39) describes the *Avneit* as מַעֲשֵׂה רֹקֵם, *embroiderer's work,* and elsewhere (ibid. 39:29) states that it contained linen as well as תְּכֵלֶת, *turquoise wool,* אַרְגָּמָן, *purple wool,* and תּוֹלַעַת שָׁנִי, *scarlet wool.* This surely applied to the Kohen Gadol's *Avneit.* The Gemara (*Yoma* 12b) cites a dispute whether it also applied to the *Avneit* worn by ordinary Kohanim, or theirs was made of pure linen. Chinuch follows *Rambam* (ibid. 8:1), who rules that the *Avneit* of an ordinary Kohen also contained a mixture of linen and wool. Although such a mixture is ordinarily forbidden as *shaatnez* (*Leviticus* 19:19), Scripture explicitly *requires* this in the case of the Kohanim's vestments (see *Yoma* 69a; see further, note 24).

[Chinuch understands the verse *embroiderer's work* to mean "embroidered with wool." The intention is somewhat unclear, since the *Avneit* was not merely embroidered with wool, but was actually woven from equal amounts of each type of thread — linen, turquoise wool, purple wool, and scarlet wool (see *Mishneh LaMelech* ibid. 8:1-2). Chinuch below (at note 30) implies that, aside from the woolen thread inside it, the *Avneit* additionally had embroidery on top. For further discussion, see *Mishneh LaMelech* ibid., *Minchas Chinuch* §2 ד״ה ומבואר and end of §8, and *Haamek Davar* to *Exodus* 28:39.]

20. The Kohen was commanded to do so by this mitzvah. Moreover, as Chinuch will explain below (at notes 35-37), if a Kohen performed the *avodah* without wearing all these vestments, the *avodah* is invalid.

21. *Rambam* ibid. 8:11.

22. Although, ordinarily, one who derives personal benefit from Temple property is guilty of *me'ilah* (misappropriation; see *Leviticus* 5:14-16), a Kohen who wears the vestments outside the time of the *avodah* has not committed any sin (*Yoma* 69a; *Rambam* ibid. 8:11). This is based on the principle (*Kiddushin* 54a): לֹא נִיתְּנָה תּוֹרָה לְמַלְאֲכֵי הַשָּׁרֵת, *the Torah was not given to the ministering angels.* I.e., since the Kohanim are human and it is impossible for them to remove their vestments at the precise moment that they finish the *avodah,* they are granted a dispensation from the prohibition of *me'ilah.*

There is disagreement among Rishonim as to the extent of this dispensation. Chinuch seems to follow *Rambam* (ibid.; see also *Rashi* to *Kiddushin* 66a ד״ה הקם), who permits a Kohen to wear the vestments for the entire day that he is designated to serve in the *Beis HaMikdash,* even when he is not actually performing any *avodah.* Since he is in any event unable to limit his wearing of the vestments to the precise times of actual *avodah,* the Torah permitted him to wear them throughout the day. *Tosafos* (*Kiddushin* ibid. ד״ה הקם, *Yoma* ibid. ד״ה בגדי), however, maintain that the Kohen may don the vestments only for the purpose of the *avodah,* and the dispensation allows him merely to continue wearing them after he completes his *avodah* until such time as he is comfortably able to remove them. He may not, however, wear them during the remainder of the day. For discussion, see *Beis HaLevi* Vol. I §2:14.

It should be noted that, in any event, the Kohanim were permitted to wear the vestments only within the Temple precincts (*Yoma* ibid.), meaning the entire Temple Mount (*Tos. Yeshanim* ad loc. ד״ה ובמקדש).

23. See note 19.

24. When the Kohen performed the *avodah,* his obligation to wear the vestments — including the *Avneit* — overrode the *shaatnez* prohibition (see *Yevamos* 3b).] The moment he finished the *avodah,* however, he was required to remove the *Avneit.* The dispensation

## TETZAVEH / MITZVAH 99: TO DON THE PRIESTLY GARMENTS

וְשֶׁל כֹּהֵן גָּדוֹל הֵם שְׁמוֹנָה, וּשְׁמָם כֵּן: כֻּתֹּנֶת וּמִכְנָסַיִם וְאַבְנֵט, כְּשֵׁם הַשְּׁלֹשָׁה שֶׁל כֹּהֵן הֶדְיוֹט[25], וּמִצְנֶפֶת לְכֹהֵן גָּדוֹל בִּמְקוֹם מִגְבַּעַת שֶׁל כֹּהֵן הֶדְיוֹט, שֶׁזֶּה וָזֶה עַל הָרֹאשׁ נָתוּן, אֶלָּא שֶׁהַמִּצְנֶפֶת הוּא עָשׂוּי כְּמוֹ בֶּגֶד אָרֹךְ שֶׁצּוֹנְפִין בּוֹ הַנָּשִׁים רֹאשָׁן, וְכֹהֵן גָּדוֹל צוֹנֵף בָּהּ, וְהַמִּגְבַּעַת עָשׂוּי כְּמִין כּוֹבַע[26], הֲרֵי אַרְבָּעָה שֶׁל כֹּהֵן גָּדוֹל, שֶׁהָיוּ אַרְבַּעְתָּן שֶׁל פִּשְׁתָּן לְבַדּוֹ[27] לְבָנִים וְחוּטָן כָּפוּל שִׁשָּׁה[28], וּמַעֲשֵׂה רוֹקֵם הָיוּ עֲשׂוּיִין[29] אֲבָל לֹא הָיָה דוּמֶה רְקִימָתָן לִרְקִימַת

---

*Chinuch now enumerates the vestments of the Kohen Gadol:*

וְשֶׁל כֹּהֵן גָּדוֹל הֵם שְׁמוֹנָה — [The vestments] of the Kohen Gadol consisted of **eight** garments, וּשְׁמָם כֵּן — whose **names are as follows:** כֻּתֹּנֶת וּמִכְנָסַיִם וְאַבְנֵט כְּשֵׁם הַשְּׁלֹשָׁה שֶׁל כֹּהֵן הֶדְיוֹט — (1) *Kesones*, (2) *Michnasayim*, and (3) *Avneit*, which are **named the same as the three** corresponding garments **of the ordinary Kohen,** and are similar to them.[25] וּמִצְנֶפֶת לְכֹהֵן גָּדוֹל — (4) **The Kohen Gadol's** headwear, known as a *Mitznefes*, בִּמְקוֹם מִגְבַּעַת שֶׁל כֹּהֵן הֶדְיוֹט — **was in place of the** *Migbaas* worn by **the ordinary Kohen,** שֶׁזֶּה וָזֶה עַל הָרֹאשׁ נָתוּן — **for** both **this one** (the *Mitznefes*) **and that one** (the *Migbaas*) **were placed upon the head,** אֶלָּא שֶׁהַמִּצְנֶפֶת הוּא עָשׂוּי כְּמוֹ בֶּגֶד אָרֹךְ שֶׁצּוֹנְפִין בּוֹ הַנָּשִׁים רֹאשָׁן — **except that the** *Mitznefes* **was fashioned like a long,** narrow, strip of **cloth that women wrap around their heads,** as a turban, וְכֹהֵן גָּדוֹל צוֹנֵף בָּהּ — **and the Kohen Gadol would wrap** his head **with it** in a similar fashion, וְהַמִּגְבַּעַת עָשׂוּי כְּמִין כּוֹבַע — **whereas the** *Migbaas* worn by the ordinary Kohen **was formed like a hat.**[26]

הֲרֵי אַרְבָּעָה שֶׁל כֹּהֵן גָּדוֹל — **Thus,** we have enumerated **four** of the eight **vestments of the Kohen Gadol,** שֶׁהָיוּ אַרְבַּעְתָּן שֶׁל פִּשְׁתָּן לְבַדּוֹ — **all four of which were** made **solely of linen.**[27] לְבָנִים וְחוּטָן כָּפוּל שִׁשָּׁה — These vestments, like the parallel ones of the ordinary Kohanim, **were white, their threads were plied** with **six** strands,[28] וּמַעֲשֵׂה רוֹקֵם הָיוּ עֲשׂוּיִין — **and they were made with embroiderer's work;**[29] אֲבָל לֹא הָיָה דוּמֶה רְקִימָתָן לִרְקִימַת הָאַבְנֵט שֶׁל כֹּהֵן

---

### NOTES

for wearing the vestments outside the time of *avodah* pertained only to the *me'ilah* restriction, but not to the *shaatnez* prohibition (*Kesef Mishneh, Hil. Klei HaMikdash* 8:11-12).

Chinuch's view here follows *Rambam* (ibid.). *Raavad* (ad loc.), however, maintains that a Kohen was allowed to wear even his *Avneit* all day. See also *Rambam* and *Raavad* in *Hil. Kilayim* 10:32.

[Some suggest that, even according to *Rambam,* only an ordinary Kohen was forbidden to wear his *Avneit* outside the time of the *avodah,* but the Kohen Gadol was allowed to wear it at all times, because, aside from the necessity of vestments for the *avodah,* it was a mitzvah for the Kohen Gadol to be clothed in his eight vestments all day. For discussion, and various explanations of this matter, see *Radvaz* to *Hil. Kilayim* ibid.; *Beis HaLevi* ibid. §3:2; *Aruch HaShulchan HeAsid* 29:11; *Even HaAzel, Hil. Klei HaMikdash* 8:11. See also *Shaagas Aryeh* §29, who discusses this matter at length.]

25. These garments were basically made the same way for the Kohen Gadol as for the ordinary Kohanim, though some commentators maintain that there were minor differences between them. For discussion, see *Minchas Chinuch* §3 ד"ה וכהן and §7 ד"ה ועיין.

26. *Rambam* (ibid. 8:2,19) states that both the *Mitznefes* of the Kohen Gadol and the *Migbaas* of the ordinary Kohen were identical 16-*amah*-long strips of cloth (see note 9), and the only difference between them was in the way they were worn. The Kohen Gadol would wrap the cloth around his head like a bandage, so for him it was called a מִצְנֶפֶת, which is cognitive to צָנִיף, turban. The ordinary Kohen would shape it like a hat, so for him it was called מִגְבַּעַת, which is cognitive to מִקְבַּעַת or כּוֹבַע, hat/helmet (see also *Ramban, Exodus* 28:31, and *Kesef Mishneh* to *Rambam* loc. cit.). *Raavad* (ad loc.), however, argues that only the *Mitznefes* of the Kohen Gadol was a head-wrapping; the *Migbaas* of the ordinary Kohen was a peaked cap. Chinuch seems to follow *Raavad's* opinion (*Minchas Chinuch* §8).

For other opinions as to the forms of these head-coverings, see *Rashi, Exodus* 28:4, and *Tosafos, Yoma* 12b ד"ה אלא. See also *Minchas Chinuch* §2 ד"ה מגבעת.

27. This statement is problematic, since the Kohen Gadol's *Avneit* definitely was not pure linen (see note 19). *Minchas Chinuch* (§8) suggests that this clause was inserted here by an errant copyist and actually belongs below (at note 33), where Chinuch discusses the special linen vestments that the Kohen Gadol wore on Yom Kippur.

28. See above, notes 17-18.

29. Actually, Scripture (*Exodus* 28:39) mentions "embroiderer's work" only in connection with the *Avneit*, and *Rambam* (ibid. 8:2) cites this stipulation only regarding that garment. *Minchas Chinuch* (ibid.) therefore asserts that this clause, too, is a copyist's error, and it actually should say that *the Avneit* was made with embroiderer's work.

הָאַבְנֵט שֶׁל כֹּהֵן הֶדְיוֹט[30]. וְעוֹד הָיוּ לוֹ אַרְבָּעָה אֲחֵרִים שֶׁל זָהָב[31], וּשְׁמָם חֹשֶׁן אֵפוֹד מְעִיל צִיץ[32]. וּבְכָל הַשְּׁמוֹנָה הָיָה עוֹבֵד עֲבוֹדַת חוּץ, אֲבָל בִּפְנִים שֶׁהוּא לִפְנִים מִן הַפָּרֹכֶת לֹא הָיָה עוֹבֵד לְעוֹלָם כִּי אִם בְּבִגְדֵי הַבַּד[33]. וְאַחַר שֶׁעָבַד בָּהֶן בְּיוֹם הַכִּפּוּרִים אֶחָד אֵינוֹ חוֹזֵר וְעוֹבֵד בָּהֶן לְעוֹלָם, שֶׁנֶּאֱמַר וְהִנִּיחָם שָׁם[34]. וְכָל זְמַן שֶׁיַּעֲבֹד הַכֹּהֵן, בֵּין הֶדְיוֹט בֵּין גָּדוֹל,

---

הֶדְיוֹט — **but their embroidery was not the same as the embroidery on the *Avneit* of an ordinary Kohen.**[30]

וְעוֹד הָיוּ לוֹ אַרְבָּעָה אֲחֵרִים שֶׁל זָהָב — **In addition** to the above vestments of the ordinary Kohen, **[the Kohen Gadol] had four other [vestments], of gold.**[31] וּשְׁמָם חֹשֶׁן אֵפוֹד מְעִיל צִיץ — **Their names are: (1) *Choshen*** (Breastplate), **(2) *Ephod*** (Apron), **(3) *Me'il*** (Robe), **and (4) *Tzitz*** (Headplate).[32]

וּבְכָל הַשְּׁמוֹנָה הָיָה עוֹבֵד עֲבוֹדַת חוּץ — **It was while clothed in all eight** of these vestments that **[the Kohen Gadol] would perform the "outer *avodah*,"** i.e., the standard year-round *avodah* that was performed on the Altar that stood in the Temple Courtyard, or on the Altar, Menorah, or Table (*Shulchan*) that stood in the Holy. אֲבָל בִּפְנִים — **But** on Yom Kippur, **when** he performed the **"inner *avodah*,"** שֶׁהוּא לִפְנִים מִן הַפָּרֹכֶת — **which is** the *avodah* done in the Holy of Holies, **within the curtain** that separated it from the rest of the *Heichal*, לֹא הָיָה עוֹבֵד לְעוֹלָם כִּי אִם בְּבִגְדֵי הַבַּד — he **would never serve except** while clothed **in the** four **linen vestments.**[33]

Chinuch adds a point:

וְאַחַר שֶׁעָבַד בָּהֶן בְּיוֹם הַכִּפּוּרִים אֶחָד — **After [the Kohen Gadol] served** while clothed in **[the linen vestments] on one Yom Kippur,** אֵינוֹ חוֹזֵר וְעוֹבֵד בָּהֶן לְעוֹלָם — he would never serve in them **again,** שֶׁנֶּאֱמַר — **as it is stated** regarding the conclusion of the Yom Kippur service (*Leviticus* 16:23): "וְהִנִּיחָם שָׁם" — *He shall remove the linen vestments that he wore when he entered the Sanctuary,* **and he shall leave them there.**[34]

Chinuch discusses the consequences of performing the *avodah* without donning the special vestments:

וְכָל זְמַן שֶׁיַּעֲבֹד הַכֹּהֵן — **Any time that a Kohen performs *avodah*** in the *Beis HaMikdash,* בֵּין הֶדְיוֹט בֵּין גָּדוֹל — **whether** he is an **ordinary** Kohen **or** the Kohen **Gadol,**

---

NOTES

30. I.e., the Kohen Gadol's *Avneit,* though made of the same materials as the ordinary Kohen's *Avneit,* had a different style of embroidery on it. [This ruling of Chinuch accords with manuscript editions of *Rambam* (ibid.). Some printed editions of *Rambam* read that the Kohen Gadol's *Avneit* was *identical* to that of the ordinary Kohen. See *Mishneh LaMelech* ad loc.]

31. These were not made entirely of gold, but each of them contained some gold. Hence, they were called בִּגְדֵי זָהָב, *the Golden Vestments.* [In fact, the entire set of (eight) vestments that the Kohen Gadol wore all year round was called his set of "Golden Vestments" (*Rambam* ibid. 8:2, but see *Kesef Mishneh* there).]

32. These items are described in the Insight below.

33. For the special Yom Kippur *avodah* performed in the Holy of Holies, the Kohen Gadol did not wear his Golden Vestments, but wore four linen vestments that paralleled the four always worn by an ordinary Kohen (i.e., *Kesones, Michnasayim, Avneit,* and *Mitznefes*). On that occasion, though, even his *Avneit* was made of pure linen (*Leviticus* 16:4). On Yom Kippur, therefore, the Kohen Gadol had to change his clothing numerous times, for whenever he performed an "outer *avodah*" he wore the Golden Vestments, and whenever he entered the Holy of Holies to perform an "inner *avodah*" he could wear only the linen ones. [See above, note 27.]

34. This teaches that the linen vestments had to be put away permanently, never to be used again for any purpose (*Yoma* 12b, 24a; *Rambam* ibid. 8:5). The Golden Vestments, however, could be used repeatedly until they wore out, at which point they, too, were stored away permanently (*Rambam* ibid.; see *Kiryas Sefer* there). By contrast, when the vestments of ordinary Kohanim wore out, they would be unraveled, and their thread would be used to make wicks for the Menorah or for the torches lit at the *Beis HaSho'evah* celebration on Succos (*Rambam* ibid 8:5-6, based on *Succah* 51a; see *Kesef Mishneh* and *Mishneh LaMelech* there, and *Minchas Chinuch* §9).

[Actually, the Kohen Gadol had two separate sets of linen vestments made for each Yom Kippur, one for each entry into the Holy of Holies, and he would put away each set after wearing it only *once* (Mishnah, *Yoma* 34b).]

## TETZAVEH / MITZVAH 99: TO DON THE PRIESTLY GARMENTS

בִּפְחוֹת מִבְּגָדָיו הַמְיֻחָדִין לָעֲבוֹדָה הַהִיא אוֹ בְּיוֹתֵר מֵהֶן,[35] עֲבוֹדָתוֹ פְּסוּלָה, וְגַם יִתְחַיֵּב מִיתָה בִּידֵי שָׁמַיִם,[36] כְּמוֹ שֶׁלָּמְדוּ הַדָּבָר רַבּוֹתֵינוּ זִכְרוֹנָם לִבְרָכָה (סנהדרין דף פ"ג ע"ב) מֵ"וְחָגַרְתָּ אוֹתָם אַבְנֵט וְגוֹ' וְהָיְתָה לָהֶם כְּהֻנָּה, בִּזְמַן שֶׁבִּגְדֵיהֶם עֲלֵיהֶם כְּהֻנָּתָם עֲלֵיהֶם, אֵין בִּגְדֵיהֶם עֲלֵיהֶם אֵין כְּהֻנָּתָם עֲלֵיהֶם, וְיֵחָשְׁבוּ כְּזָר הָעוֹבֵד שֶׁהוּא בְּמִיתָה,[37]

---

בִּפְחוֹת מִבְּגָדָיו הַמְיֻחָדִין לָעֲבוֹדָה הַהִיא — if he performs it while clothed **in less than the** prescribed **number of vestments designated for that** particular performance of **avodah,** אוֹ בְּיוֹתֵר מֵהֶן — **or in more than** [the prescribed number of vestments] **for that** performance of *avodah,*[35] עֲבוֹדָתוֹ פְּסוּלָה — **his** *avodah* **is invalid.** וְגַם יִתְחַיֵּב מִיתָה בִּידֵי שָׁמַיִם — **Furthermore, he incurs the penalty of death at the hands of Heaven,**[36] כְּמוֹ שֶׁלָּמְדוּ הַדָּבָר רַבּוֹתֵינוּ זִכְרוֹנָם לִבְרָכָה — **as our Sages, of blessed memory, have derived this matter** (*Sanhedrin* 83b) מֵ"וְחָגַרְתָּ אֹתָם אַבְנֵט וְגוֹ' וְהָיְתָה לָהֶם כְּהֻנָּה" — **from** the verse (*Exodus* 29:9): **You shall girdle them** — Aaron and his sons — **with an Avneit, etc., and this shall be for them a [state of] priesthood.** The verse implies that their state of priesthood, insofar as serving in the *Beis HaMikdash*, is dependent upon their being clothed in the *Avneit* and other priestly vestments. Thus, we learn that בִּזְמַן שֶׁבִּגְדֵיהֶם עֲלֵיהֶם כְּהֻנָּתָם עֲלֵיהֶם — **at the time when their vestments are upon them, their status as Kohanim is upon them,** אֵין בִּגְדֵיהֶם עֲלֵיהֶם אֵין כְּהֻנָּתָם עֲלֵיהֶם — **but when their vestments are not upon them, their status as Kohanim is not upon them,** וְיֵחָשְׁבוּ כְּזָר הָעוֹבֵד — **and instead, they are considered** to have the status of **a non-Kohen who performs the** *avodah,* שֶׁהוּא בְּמִיתָה — regarding **whom** the law is that he **is liable to death** at the hands of Heaven (as stated in *Numbers* 18:7).[37]

---

### NOTES

35. For example, the Kohen Gadol performs *avodah* while wearing the vestments of an ordinary Kohen (less than the number prescribed for him), or an ordinary Kohen performs *avodah* while wearing the vestments of a Kohen Gadol (more than the number prescribed for him), or any of them wears two of any vestment (e.g., two *Avneits*), or fails to wear one of the prescribed vestments (*Rambam* ibid. 10:4-5). [Regarding a Kohen who wears an extra, non-sacred, garment, see *Zevachim* 19a and *Rambam* ibid. 10:8.]

36. *Sanhedrin* 83a, *Zevachim* 17b; *Rambam* ibid. [This refers to premature death; see General Introduction, note 17.]

37. [See Mishnah, *Sanhedrin* 81b.] Thus, a Kohen who fails to don the priestly vestments before performing his *avodah,* as prescribed, has not merely committed a transgression; he actually has desecrated the *avodah,* rendering it unfit and incurring the same punishment as a non-Kohen who performs *avodah.* For further discussion, see *Tosafos* to *Zevachim* 17b ד"ה אין. See also the following note.

It should be noted, though, that even a non-Kohen is not liable to death at the hands of Heaven for every element of the *avodah.* The Gemara (*Yoma* 24a) derives from Scripture that, although a non-Kohen is prohibited in the first place to perform almost all *avodos,* and renders them invalid, he does not incur the stated penalty unless he performs an *avodah* that *completes a sacrificial process.* This includes only four specific *avodos,* each of which constitutes the final step in its particular service: (1) זְרִיקָה — applying blood to the Altar, which is the final step in the blood service of an animal or bird offering; (2) הַקְטָרָה — burning sacrificial items upon the Altar, which is the concluding step in the offering service; (3) נִסּוּךְ הַיַּיִן — pouring the libation of wine (which accompanied certain offerings) upon the Altar; (4) נִסּוּךְ הַמַּיִם — pouring the water libation (that was brought with the morning *tamid* each day of Succos) upon the Altar (*Yoma* 24a; *Rambam, Hil. Bi'as HaMikdash* 9:2; see *Chinuch* below, Mitzvah 390). Similarly, a Kohen who performs any of these four *avodos* without donning his vestments as prescribed incurs the penalty of death at the hands of Heaven (*Maasai LaMelech, Hil. Klei HaMikdash* 10:4; see also *Shaar HaMelech* there).

[It is noteworthy that the Torah explicitly mentions the penalty of death (at the hands of Heaven) regarding a Kohen Gadol who fails to don the *Me'il* (*Exodus* 28:35), and regarding any Kohen who fails to don *Michnasayim* (ibid. v. 43). Some suggest that this automatically applies to all the other vestments as well (*Rashi* to both verses, based on *Tanchuma, Acharei Mos* §6). The Gemara (*Sanhedrin* 83b, which *Chinuch* cites), however, assumes otherwise. It is therefore forced to explain that a Kohen lacking *any one* of the vestments (not only the *Me'il* or *Michnasayim*) is liable to death because he has the status of a non-Kohen. For discussion of this matter, including reasons to distinguish between the *Me'il* and *Michnasayim* and the other garments, see *Tosafos* to *Sanhedrin* 83b ד"ה אין, and *Ramban, Exodus* 28:35.]

וְיֶתֶר פְּרָטֶיהָ, מְבֹאָרִים בְּפֶרֶק שְׁנֵי מִזְבְּחִים (דף י״ח ע״א) וּבִמְקוֹמוֹת מְכֻפָּרִים (דף ע״א ע״ב) וְסֻכָּה (דף ה׳ ע״א).

וְנוֹהֶגֶת מִצְוָה זוֹ בִּזְמַן הַבַּיִת בְּזִכְרֵי כְהֻנָּה.
וְעוֹבֵר עָלֶיהָ וְעָבַד מְחֻסַּר בְּגָדִים אוֹ יוֹתֵר, חַיָּב מִיתָה בִּידֵי שָׁמַיִם כְּמוֹ שֶׁכָּתַבְנוּ.[38]

מְבֹאָרִים בְּפֶרֶק שְׁנֵי מִזְבְּחִים וְיֶתֶר פְּרָטֶיהָ — These, **and the additional details of [this mitzvah],** וּבִמְקוֹמוֹת מְכֻפָּרִים — **are elaborated in the second chapter of** Tractate *Zevachim* (17b-19b), **and in** various **places in** Tractate *Yoma* (e.g., 12b, 24a-b, 71b-73a) וְסֻכָּה — **and** Tractate *Succah* (5a, 51a).

### ☙ Applicability of the Mitzvah ❧

וְנוֹהֶגֶת מִצְוָה זוֹ בִּזְמַן הַבַּיִת — **This mitzvah applies in the time of the** *Beis HaMikdash*, בְּזִכְרֵי כְהֻנָּה — **to male Kohanim,** who are the only ones eligible to perform the *avodah*. וְעוֹבֵר עָלֶיהָ וְעָבַד מְחֻסַּר בְּגָדִים אוֹ יוֹתֵר — **[A Kohen] who transgresses [this commandment]** — **and performs** *avodah* in the *Beis HaMikdash* while clothed **in less than or more than** the prescribed number of **vestments** חַיָּב מִיתָה בִּידֵי שָׁמַיִם — **is liable to death at the hands of Heaven,** כְּמוֹ שֶׁכָּתַבְנוּ — **as we have** just **written.**[38]

---

### NOTES

38. Obviously, the Kohen has violated the mitzvah-obligation to don the priestly vestments before performing *avodah*. But he also has violated a prohibition. Since he has the status of a non-Kohen, he transgresses the mitzvah-prohibition that forbids a non-Kohen to perform *avodah* (Mitzvah 390). Hence, it is possible for a Kohen to incur another penalty for this transgression. If he is forewarned not to perform the *avodah* without his vestments, he incurs *malkus* (lashes) at the hands of *beis din* for violating the prohibition (Rambam, *Hil. Sanhedrin* 19:2). The Heavenly death penalty applies in a case where *malkus* are not meted out (see Mishnah, *Makkos* 23a). *Minchas Chinuch* (§16 ד״ה ואם) wonders why Chinuch does not mention the possibility of incurring *malkus*.

---

### ❧ Insight: The Kohen Gadol's Golden Vestments

Chinuch has explained that, in addition to the four vestments worn by an ordinary Kohen when he performed the *avodah* (the *Kesones, Michnasayim, Migbaas,* and *Avneit*), the Kohen Gadol wore four vestments that contained gold — the *Choshen, Ephod, Me'il* and *Tzitz*. The four vestments worn by all Kohanim were described by Chinuch above: The *Kesones*, a Tunic; the *Michnasayim*, Breeches; the *Migbaas*, a Headcovering; and the *Avneit*, a Sash. The following is a description of the four special "golden" vestments worn by the Kohen Gadol:

(a) **Choshen** — The *Choshen* was a breastplate woven from threads containing three types of wool (תְּכֵלֶת, turquoise wool; אַרְגָּמָן, purple wool; and תּוֹלַעַת שָׁנִי, scarlet wool), linen, and gold. Each thread used to weave the *Choshen* contained 28 strands. First, six strands of turquoise wool were twisted together with one strand of gold to form a seven-ply thread. Similar seven-ply threads were made of purple wool, scarlet wool, and linen, all combined with gold, so that there were four types of seven-ply threads. These four threads were then combined to form a single thread of 28 strands that was used to weave the *Choshen*.

The *Choshen* was one *amah* long by a half-*amah* wide, and it was folded over to form a square of a half-*amah* by a half-*amah*. [A half-*amah* equals between 9 and 11.4 inches (24-29 cm.), approximately.] Twelve precious stones were set in boxes attached to the front of the *Choshen*, with the name of one of the twelve Tribes of Israel inscribed on each stone (*Yoma*

71b-72a; *Rambam, Hil. Klei HaMikdash* 9:5-7; see *Minchas Chinuch* §3 ד"ה החושן for details). Inside the fold, the *Urim VeTumim* was inserted. This was a slip of parchment upon which the Name of Hashem was written. When consulted by the Kohen Gadol regarding certain issues, the *Urim VeTumim* would cause the letters etched on the stones to light up and spell out a message (see *Rashi* and *Ramban* to *Exodus* 28:30, and *Rambam* ibid. 10:10-12). Other aspects of the *Choshen* are discussed in Mitzvah 100.

**(b) Ephod** — The *Ephod* was made of the same material as the *Choshen*, but the form of this garment is a matter of dispute. According to some Rishonim, the *Ephod* was an apron-like garment that covered the Kohen Gadol's back from his waist to his heels. It had a belt woven into it at its upper edge, so that it could be tied in front of him. It also had straps that extended up to the Kohen Gadol's shoulders, and golden chains attached to these straps hung down on the Kohen Gadol's chest. The lower end of each chain was attached to a ring at the upper end of the *Choshen*, and held the *Choshen*. On each shoulder strap there was a golden setting, and these settings contained precious stones inscribed with the names of the twelve tribes (*Rashi, Exodus* 28:6; *Rambam* ibid. 9:9; for , see *Minchas Chinuch* §3 ד"ה והיה).

Other Rishonim describe the *Ephod* as being a short vest-like garment that did not extend below the waist. It covered the Kohen Gadol's back, had a belt at his waist and straps upon his shoulders, with golden chains as described above, and was open in front to leave place for the *Choshen* (*Siddur* of *R' Saadiah Gaon*, Yom Kippur Avodah [p. 271 in Me'kitzei Nirdamim ed., Jerusalem 5739]; see *Chizkuni, Exodus* 28:27). Chinuch, in his description in the beginning of Mitzvah 100 (see note 3 there), seems to follow this latter view.

Further details regarding the *Ephod* and its attachment to the *Choshen* are discussed in Mitzvah 100.

**(c) Me'il** — The *Me'il* was a long garment that the Kohen Gadol wore over his *Kesones* (Tunic) and under his *Choshen* and *Ephod*. It reached almost to the ground. The *Me'il* was woven of threads each consisting of twelve strands of תְּכֵלֶת, turquoise wool. According to *Rashi* (*Exodus* 28:4), the construction of the *Me'il* was similar to that of the *Kesones* (closed at the sides, with sleeves), except that it was worn as an outer garment, rather than directly on the body. *Rambam* (ibid. 9:3) and *Ramban* (*Exodus* 28:31), however, maintain that it was similar to a cape, with no sleeves, and was joined only at the neckline.

There were seventy-two ornamental pomegranates, fashioned from turquoise, purple, and scarlet wool, hung at the hem of the *Me'il*, along with seventy-two ornamental golden bells. According to *Rashi* (ibid. 28:33-34) and *Rambam* (ibid. 8:4), the bells hung between the pomegranates, with bells and pomegranates alternating along the entire hem. According to *Ramban* (*Exodus* 28:33-34.), however, the bells hung *inside* the pomegranates. Further details regarding the *Me'il* are discussed in Mitzvah 101.

**(d) Tzitz** — The *Tzitz* was a headplate made of gold, two fingerbreadths wide, that encircled the Kohen Gadol's forehead from ear to ear. Inscribed on it were the words קֹדֶשׁ לה׳, *Holy to Hashem*. It was held in place by threads of turquoise wool, which were inserted in holes bored into it and were tied behind the Kohen Gadol's head (*Exodus* 28:36-37 with *Rashi*; *Rambam* ibid. 9:1-2). [For discussion of how the words *Holy to Hashem* were inscribed, see *Rambam* ibid., *Rashba* to *Shabbos* 63b, and *Minchas Chinuch* §6.]

**THE EIGHT GARMENTS OF THE KOHEN GADOL**

## מִצְוָה ק: שֶׁלֹּא יִזַּח הַחֹשֶׁן מֵעַל הָאֵפוֹד[1]

שֶׁלֹּא נָסִיר הַחֹשֶׁן מֵעַל הָאֵפוֹד, וְעִנְיַן חֹשֶׁן וְאֵפוֹד כְּבָר זְכַרְנוּם לְמַעְלָה שֶׁהֵם שְׁנַיִם מִשְּׁמוֹנָה בִּגְדֵי כֹהֵן גָּדוֹל,[2] וְהַחֹשֶׁן הָיָה נָתוּן כְּנֶגֶד לִבּוֹ שֶׁל כֹּהֵן לְפָנָיו, וְהָאֵפוֹד מֵאֲחוֹרָיו מְכֻוָּן כְּנֶגֶד הַחֹשֶׁן שֶׁלְּפָנָיו.[3]

# Mitzvah 100
## The Prohibition to Detach the Choshen From the Ephod

וְרָכְסוּ אֶת הַחֹשֶׁן מִטַּבְּעֹתָיו אֶל טַבְּעֹת הָאֵפוֹד בִּפְתִיל תְּכֵלֶת לִהְיוֹת עַל חֵשֶׁב הָאֵפוֹד וְלֹא יִזַּח הַחֹשֶׁן מֵעַל הָאֵפוֹד

*They shall attach the Choshen from its rings to the rings of the Ephod with a turquoise woolen cord so that it will remain above the belt of the Ephod, and the Choshen shall not be detached from upon the Ephod (Exodus 28:28).*

In the previous mitzvah, Chinuch discussed the general obligation upon Kohanim to wear the priestly garments, and he described some of those garments. In this mitzvah, Chinuch focuses on two of the garments of the Kohen Gadol, the *Choshen* and the *Ephod*.

Among all of the eight priestly garments, only the *Choshen* and the *Ephod* were fastened to each other. In this mitzvah, Chinuch explains the position of the *Choshen* and the *Ephod* as they were worn by the Kohen Gadol and how they were fastened together, in the context of the specific prohibition of this mitzvah — that we are not to detach the *Choshen* from its connection to the *Ephod*.[1]

שֶׁלֹּא נָסִיר הַחֹשֶׁן מֵעַל הָאֵפוֹד — We are commanded **not to remove the *Choshen* from upon the *Ephod*.**

Chinuch describes the positions of these two garments relative to each other as they were worn by the Kohen Gadol:

וְעִנְיַן חֹשֶׁן וְאֵפוֹד — **The description of** the arrangement of **the *Choshen* and the *Ephod*** is as follows: כְּבָר זְכַרְנוּם לְמַעְלָה שֶׁהֵם שְׁנַיִם מִשְּׁמוֹנָה בִּגְדֵי כֹהֵן גָּדוֹל — **We have already mentioned above** (Mitzvah 99) **that [these garments] are two of the eight priestly vestments worn by the Kohen Gadol.**[2] וְהַחֹשֶׁן הָיָה נָתוּן כְּנֶגֶד לִבּוֹ שֶׁל כֹּהֵן לְפָנָיו — **The *Choshen* was placed opposite the heart of the Kohen** Gadol, **in front of him,** i.e., on his chest, וְהָאֵפוֹד מֵאֲחוֹרָיו מְכֻוָּן כְּנֶגֶד הַחֹשֶׁן שֶׁלְּפָנָיו — **and the *Ephod*** was positioned **on his back, directly corresponding to the *Choshen* that was in front of him.**[3]

As described in the Torah (*Exodus* 28:7-12, 22-27), the *Ephod* had two shoulder straps attached to the top of the back and ending on the front of the shoulders of the Kohen Gadol. These straps held two golden boxes containing the two *shoham* stones upon which the names of the tribes of Israel were written. The *Choshen*, which rested on the Kohen Gadol's chest, was suspended from the shoulder straps of the

---

NOTES

1. Had the words of the verse been שֶׁלֹּא יִזַּח, [They shall] tie the *Choshen* to the *Ephod*] *so that* it shall not be detached, we might have understood that this phrase is merely an explanation of the need for the additional lower attachment. Since the verse actually says, וְלֹא יִזַּח, **and it shall not be detached,** it is understood as an independent clause, conveying a prohibition against detaching the two garments (*Yoma* 72a).

2. For general descriptions of all eight garments of the Kohen Gadol, see Insight to previous mitzvah.

3. Chinuch seems to describe the *Ephod* as a garment worn on the back from the shoulders to the waist, similar to a vest without a front. See Insight to the previous mitzvah for another opinion (of *Rashi* and *Rambam*) concerning the description of the *Ephod*.

## 266 ❑ תצוה / מצוה ק: שלא יזח החשן מעל האפוד

וְהָיָה[4] בָּאֵפוֹד מִמַּעֲשֵׂה הָאֵפוֹד בְּעַצְמוֹ כְּמִין שְׁתֵּי יָדוֹת יוֹצְאוֹת מִמֶּנּוּ,[5] שֶׁחוֹגֵר עַצְמוֹ הַכֹּהֵן בָּהֶן, וְהוּא נִקְרָא חֵשֶׁב הָאֵפוֹד,[6] וְאוֹתוֹ חֵשֶׁב הָאֵפוֹד, אַחַר שֶׁחָגַר עַצְמוֹ בּוֹ וְנָתַן הַחֹשֶׁן עַל לִבּוֹ, הָיָה עוֹמֵד תַּחַת הַחֹשֶׁן. וְצִוָּה הַכָּתוּב לִקְשֹׁר טַבָּעוֹת שֶׁהָיוּ קְבוּעִים בַּחֹשֶׁן עִם טַבָּעוֹת שֶׁהָיוּ קְבוּעִין בָּאֵפוֹד בִּפְתִיל תְּכֵלֶת,[7] כְּדֵי שֶׁיִּהְיֶה נָתוּן הַחֹשֶׁן עַל הַחֵשֶׁב דֶּרֶךְ קְבִיעוּת וְהָדָר, שֶׁאִם לֹא יִקְשֹׁר אוֹתָם בְּאוֹתָם טַבָּעוֹת, יִהְיֶה הַחֹשֶׁן נָד וְנִבְדָּל מֵחֵשֶׁב הָאֵפוֹד וְנוֹקֵשׁ עַל לוּחַ לִבּוֹ שֶׁל כֹּהֵן, וְעַל זֶה נֶאֱמַר[8] (שמות כ״ח, כ״ח), "וְלֹא יִזַּח הַחֹשֶׁן מֵעַל הָאֵפוֹד,

---

*Ephod* by two golden chains. These chains were attached at one end to the golden boxes on the shoulder straps of the *Ephod*, and at the other end they were threaded through two rings that were attached to the two upper corners of the *Choshen*. Additionally, there were two rings attached to the lower corners of the *Choshen*, and another two rings attached to the *Ephod* at the lower back, so that the *Choshen* could be fastened to the *Ephod* at the bottom as well.[4] Chinuch proceeds to provide further details about the construction of the *Ephod* and how the *Choshen* was attached to it at the bottom:

וְהָיָה בָּאֵפוֹד מִמַּעֲשֵׂה הָאֵפוֹד בְּעַצְמוֹ — **There was** an additional piece **on the *Ephod*, fashioned of** the same weave as **the *Ephod* itself,** i.e., not woven separately and then attached, but woven together with it of the same material, כְּמִין שְׁתֵּי יָדוֹת יוֹצְאוֹת מִמֶּנּוּ — fashioned **like two straps extending from it** at the waist,[5] שֶׁחוֹגֵר עַצְמוֹ הַכֹּהֵן בָּהֶן — **with which the Kohen** Gadol **girded himself.** וְהוּא נִקְרָא חֵשֶׁב הָאֵפוֹד — **This** protrusion of material from the *Ephod* **was called "the belt of the *Ephod*"** (see *Exodus* 28:8, 27-28).[6] וְאוֹתוֹ חֵשֶׁב הָאֵפוֹד — **Now, that belt of the *Ephod*,** אַחַר שֶׁחָגַר עַצְמוֹ בּוֹ וְנָתַן הַחֹשֶׁן עַל לִבּוֹ — **after [the Kohen Gadol] girded himself with it and placed the *Choshen* on his heart,** הָיָה עוֹמֵד תַּחַת הַחֹשֶׁן — **would be positioned** directly **under the *Choshen*.** וְצִוָּה הַכָּתוּב — **Scripture commanded** us (ibid. vs. 26-28) לִקְשֹׁר טַבָּעוֹת שֶׁהָיוּ קְבוּעִים בַּחֹשֶׁן עִם טַבָּעוֹת שֶׁהָיוּ קְבוּעִין בָּאֵפוֹד — **to tie the rings that were set in** the lower part of **the *Choshen* to the rings that were set in the *Ephod*** at the lower back בִּפְתִיל תְּכֵלֶת — **by** means of **a cord of *techeiles*** that passed through both sets of rings.[7] כְּדֵי שֶׁיִּהְיֶה נָתוּן הַחֹשֶׁן עַל הַחֵשֶׁב דֶּרֶךְ קְבִיעוּת וְהָדָר — This connection was made **in order that the *Choshen* would remain** securely on the Kohen Gadol's chest **above the belt** of the *Ephod* **in a fixed and beautiful manner;** שֶׁאִם לֹא יִקְשֹׁר אוֹתָם בְּאוֹתָם טַבָּעוֹת — **for if he would not tie [the *Choshen* and *Ephod*] together by** way of **those** lower **rings,** יִהְיֶה הַחֹשֶׁן נָד וְנִבְדָּל מֵחֵשֶׁב הָאֵפוֹד — **the *Choshen* would shift and be removed from** its position above **the belt of the *Ephod*** וְנוֹקֵשׁ עַל לוּחַ לִבּוֹ שֶׁל כֹּהֵן — **and,** with the Kohen Gadol's movements, **it would** sway and **strike against the chest of the Kohen** Gadol.[8]

Chinuch cites and explains the source verse for this prohibition:

וְעַל זֶה נֶאֱמַר — **It is regarding this** fastening of the *Choshen* in its position that **Scripture states** (*Exodus* 28:28): "וְלֹא יִזַּח הַחֹשֶׁן מֵעַל הָאֵפוֹד" — **... and the *Choshen* shall not be detached from

---

## NOTES

4. See diagrams.

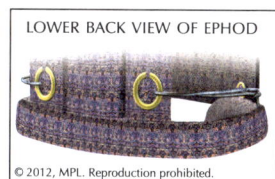

LOWER BACK VIEW OF EPHOD

5. These straps extended from the bottom of the "vest" section of the *Ephod*, as two strips of material forming a belt in front of the wearer.

6. The word *cheshev* (חֵשֶׁב) is related to the similar root חבש, *to bind*. Hence, חֵשֶׁב הָאֵפוֹד means *the belt of the Ephod* (see *Chizkuni*, *Exodus* 28:8).

7. That is, one cord looped through the lower right ring of the *Choshen* and attached to the corresponding ring on that side of the *Ephod* in back of the Kohen Gadol, and another cord looped through the lower left ring of the *Choshen* and attached to the corresponding ring on that side of the *Ephod* in back of the Kohen Gadol.

8. If the *Choshen* had been connected to the *Ephod* only by way of the upper rings, the *Choshen* would swing free with every movement of the Kohen, which is disrespectful to the *Choshen*. The tying of the *Choshen* by its lower rings to the lower rings of the *Ephod* firmly secured the *Choshen* in its place despite any movement of the Kohen Gadol (see following note).

# 267 ☐ TETZAVEH / MITZVAH 100: NOT TO DETACH THE CHOSHEN FROM THE EPHOD

בְּלוֹמַר מֵעַל חֵשֶׁב הָאֵפוֹד[9], וְתַרְגּוּמוֹ לָא יִתְפָּרֵק[10]. וְהַמְפָרֵק חִבּוּרָן בִּשְׁעַת עֲבוֹדָה לוֹקֶה מִלָּאו זֶה[11].

מִשָּׁרְשֵׁי הַמִּצְוָה, שֶׁרָצָה הַשֵּׁם לְטוֹבָתֵנוּ לְזַכּוֹתֵנוּ בְּהַגְדָּלַת אוֹתוֹ הַבַּיִת הַקָּדוֹשׁ, וְלִהְיוֹת כָּל אֲשֶׁר בּוֹ מְכֻוָּן וְקָבוּעַ עַל מְכוֹנוֹ[12], בֵּין עִנְיַן כֵּלָיו שֶׁיִּהְיוּ בְּתַכְלִית הַשְּׁלֵמוּת, בֵּין עִנְיַן כְּלֵי הַמְשָׁרְתִים כְּגוֹן מַלְבּוּשִׁים אֵלֶּה שֶׁהֵם מִלְבָּשִׁים בָּהֶן בִּשְׁעַת הָעֲבוֹדָה, שֶׁהַכֹּל יִהְיֶה נָכוֹן וְשָׁלֵם בְּתַכְלִית הַשְּׁלֵמוּת, לֹא יֶחְסַר שׁוּם נוֹי בְּכָל הַדְּבָרִים, וּבֶאֱמֶת כִּי מִנּוּי הָעִנְיָן הוּא שֶׁלֹּא יִהְיֶה הַחֹשֶׁן נָע וָנָד עַל לוּחַ לִבּוֹ אֶלָּא יַעֲמֹד שָׁם קָבוּעַ כְּמִין חֹמֶר[13], וְעַד שָׁמְעֵנוּ טוֹב מִזֶּה נַחֲזִיק בָּזֶה[14].

---

*upon the Ephod;* בְּלוֹמַר מֵעַל חֵשֶׁב הָאֵפוֹד — that is, it shall not be detached **from** its position **above the belt of the Ephod.**[9] וְתַרְגּוּמוֹ לָא יִתְפָּרֵק — **The** *Onkelos* **translation of [this verse] is,** *and it shall not be taken apart* **from the Ephod.**[10] וְהַמְפָרֵק חִבּוּרָן בִּשְׁעַת עֲבוֹדָה — **One who takes apart the connection [of the** *Choshen* **and the** *Ephod***] during the time of** *avodah* (service) **in the Temple** לוֹקֶה מִלָּאו זֶה — **incurs** the penalty of *malkus* (lashes), **based on this prohibition.**[11]

## ⤳ Underlying Purpose of the Mitzvah ⤳

מִשָּׁרְשֵׁי הַמִּצְוָה — **Among the underlying purposes of the mitzvah** שֶׁרָצָה הַשֵּׁם לְטוֹבָתֵנוּ לְזַכּוֹתֵנוּ — is the principle **that Hashem desires, for our benefit and to bring us merit,** בְּהַגְדָּלַת אוֹתוֹ הַבַּיִת הַקָּדוֹשׁ — **the enhancement** of the grandeur **of that Holy Temple,** וְלִהְיוֹת כָּל אֲשֶׁר בּוֹ מְכֻוָּן וְקָבוּעַ עַל מְכוֹנוֹ — **and that everything in it should be exact and fixed in its proper place.**[12] בֵּין עִנְיַן כֵּלָיו שֶׁיִּהְיוּ בְּתַכְלִית הַשְּׁלֵמוּת — **This applies** **both to the matter of its vessels,** regarding which it is desired **that they should be in a state of complete perfection,** בֵּין עִנְיַן כְּלֵי הַמְשָׁרְתִים — and also **to the matter of the articles of those who serve** in the Temple, כְּגוֹן מַלְבּוּשִׁים אֵלֶּה — שֶׁהֵם מִלְבָּשִׁים בָּהֶן בִּשְׁעַת הָעֲבוֹדָה — **such as these garments in which [the Kohanim] are clothed during the** Temple *avodah,* שֶׁהַכֹּל יִהְיֶה נָכוֹן וְשָׁלֵם — **regarding which it is desired that everything should be steady and perfect,** בְּתַכְלִית הַשְּׁלֵמוּת — **in a state of complete perfection,** לֹא יֶחְסַר שׁוּם נוֹי בְּכָל הַדְּבָרִים — **and** that **no** dimension of **beauty should be lacking in any** of these things. וּבֶאֱמֶת כִּי מִנּוּי הָעִנְיָן הוּא — **Now, certainly it is in keeping with the beauty of the matter** שֶׁלֹּא יִהְיֶה הַחֹשֶׁן נָע וָנָד עַל לוּחַ לִבּוֹ — **that the** *Choshen* **not move and shift on the chest of [the Kohen Gadol];** אֶלָּא יַעֲמֹד שָׁם קָבוּעַ כְּמִין חֹמֶר — **rather,** the *Choshen* **should remain fixed in place, like a beautiful ornament.**[13] וְעַד שָׁמְעֵנוּ טוֹב מִזֶּה נַחֲזִיק בָּזֶה — **Until we hear an** underlying reason for this prohibition **better than this** one, **we will hold fast to this** reason.[14]

---

### NOTES

9. Chinuch indicates that the prohibition applies specifically to detaching the lower rings (see also *Sefer Yere'im, Lo Saaseh* 317). *Rambam* (*Hil. Klei HaMikdash* 9:10), however, seems to include both parts of the attachment of the *Ephod* to the *Choshen*, the lower *and* the upper rings, in the prohibition of this verse (see *Radvaz* ad loc. and *Maharam Shick* to this mitzvah).

10. Chinuch cites the *Onkelos* translation in this case due to the unfamiliarity of the word יִזַּח, which does not appear in that form in any other context in Scripture. For a discussion of the exact meaning of this word, see *Rashi* and *Ramban* to verse.

11. *Minchas Chinuch* (§2) finds no source for Chinuch's statement that the prohibition applies only during the time of *avodah*. In fact, *Minchas Chinuch* writes that all indications are that one is liable for disconnecting these two vestments at any time. For some explanations of Chinuch's position, see *Maharam Shick, Minchas Yitzchak,* and *Toafos Re'eim* to *Sefer Yere'im, Lo Saaseh* 317.

See also *Radvaz, Hil. Klei HaMikdash* 9:10, regarding whether the prohibition includes only completely detaching the two vestments, or if merely loosening the connection is also included.

12. In Mitzvah 95, Chinuch elaborates on why it is important for the *Beis HaMikdash* to be beautiful and perfect, and how this condition of the *Beis HaMikdash* is in fact for our benefit and merit.

13. See *Rashi, Kiddushin* 22b ד"ה חומר.

14. See *Metzudas David* (by *Radvaz*), Mitzvah 318, for a discussion of Chinuch's reason for the mitzvah, and a Kabbalistic approach to the underlying purpose of the mitzvah. For further discussion see *Shelah, Parashas Tetzaveh, Torah Ohr* §2; *Malbim* to Exodus 28:28.

## 268 ❑ תצוה / מצוה ק: שלא יזח החשן מעל האפוד

דִּינֵי הַמִּצְוָה, כְּגוֹן מַעֲשֵׂה הַחֹשֶׁן וְהָאֵפוֹד[15] וְסֵדֶר לְבִישָׁתָן, וְיֶתֶר פְּרָטֶיהָ, מְבֹאָרִים בְּמִדּוֹת.[16]

וְנוֹהֶגֶת מִצְוָה זוֹ, שֶׁלֹּא נָסִיר הַחֹשֶׁן מֵעַל הָאֵפוֹד, בִּזְמַן הַבַּיִת, בִּזְכָרִים וּנְקֵבוֹת, כְּלוֹמַר שֶׁאֶחָד אִישׁ אוֹ אִשָּׁה שֶׁפֵּרֵק חִבּוּרָם, לוֹקֶה.

### ～ Laws of the Mitzvah ～

דִּינֵי הַמִּצְוָה – **The laws of the mitzvah** include, כְּגוֹן מַעֲשֵׂה הַחֹשֶׁן וְהָאֵפוֹד – for example, the **workmanship of the** *Choshen* **and** *Ephod*,[15] וְסֵדֶר לְבִישָׁתָן – **and the** correct **order of donning [these vestments].** וְיֶתֶר פְּרָטֶיהָ – These laws, **and the additional details of [this mitzvah]**, מְבֹאָרִים בְּמִדּוֹת – are delineated in *Middos*.[16]

### ～ Applicability of the Mitzvah ～

וְנוֹהֶגֶת מִצְוָה זוֹ שֶׁלֹּא נָסִיר הַחֹשֶׁן מֵעַל הָאֵפוֹד – **This mitzvah,** namely, that we are **not to remove the** *Choshen* **from upon the** *Ephod*, applies בִּזְמַן הַבַּיִת – **in the time of the Temple** (i.e., when it is standing). בִּזְכָרִים וּנְקֵבוֹת – It further applies to **both men and women,** כְּלוֹמַר – **meaning to say,** שֶׁאֶחָד אִישׁ אוֹ אִשָּׁה שֶׁפֵּרֵק חִבּוּרָם לוֹקֶה – **that either a man or a woman who detaches the connection of [the** *Choshen* **to the** *Ephod***] incurs** the penalty of *malkus*.

### NOTES

15. For discussion of this matter, see Insight to the previous mitzvah.

16. Laws pertaining to the priestly vestments do not appear in our version of Tractate *Middos*. Some suggest that the word מִדּוֹת is a result of a copyist's error and should read מַכּוֹת, referring to Tractate *Makkos*, where the prohibition to remove the *Ephod* from the *Choshen* is discussed, on 22a (glosses to Mechon Yerushalayim edition). It has also been suggested that Chinuch (as well as other Rishonim) was in possession of a collection of Mishnaic texts (*Baraisos*), which described the priestly vestments, and that this collection was called "*Middos*" (see *Bigdei Kehunah*, by R' Moshe Shachor, p.13).

The laws pertaining to the *Ephod* and the *Choshen* are codified in *Rambam, Hil. Klei HaMikdash,* Chapters 9-10.

---

> **◆§ Insight: A Deeper Look at the Vestments**
>
> The current mitzvah, as well as the previous and following mitzvos, relates to the priestly garments worn by the Kohanim as part of their service. The Gemara (*Arachin* 16a) explains that not only do the particular services in the *Beis HaMikdash* effect atonement for various sins, but the wearing of the eight garments by the Kohen Gadol (described at length in the previous mitzvah) also serves to atone for particular sins or shortcomings of the Jewish people. Each of the garments has its spiritual effect on one area of spiritual failing, as the Gemara there explains.
>
> The wearing of the *Kesones* (Tunic) atones for the sin of murder. The tunic, worn next to the flesh of one's torso, is the garment most readily soaked with the blood of its owner upon his murder. For this reason, when Joseph's brothers wished to show their father that Joseph had met a violent end, they took his tunic (*kesones*) and dipped it into blood (*Genesis* 37:31). The Kohen's wearing of a sacred *Kesones* on his flesh atones for the soaking of the murder victim's tunic (*Maharal* and *Maharsha* to *Zevachim* 88b; see *Rashi* there).
>
> The *Michnasayim* (Breeches) atoned for the sin of illicit relations, as they are described as (*Exodus* 28:42): מִכְנְסֵי בָד לְכַסּוֹת בְּשַׂר עֶרְוָה, *linen breeches to cover the flesh of nakedness*. This is homiletically interpreted to mean that the breeches "conceal" (i.e., atone for) sins related to the uncovering of nakedness (*Rashi, Zevachim* ibid.).
>
> The *Mitznefes* (Turban), worn high on the person of the Kohen, atoned for the sin of haughtiness — a sin associated with self-ascribed loftiness. Head coverings are used as a means of fostering reverence for God (see *Shabbos* 156b), mitigating such feelings of self-adulation (*Maharsha* ibid.;

*Malbim, Parashas Tetzaveh* רמזי בגדי הקדש).

The *Avneit* (Sash) atoned for sinful thoughts of the heart, as it was wrapped around the Kohen's torso, near his heart (*Rashi* ibid.). Moreover the *Avneit* was 32 cubits long, which is the numerical value (*gematria*) of the word לֵב, *heart* [ל = 30, ב = 2] (*Vayikra Rabbah* 10:6; *Malbim* ibid.).

The *Choshen* (Breastplate), described as the (*Exodus* 28:15) חֹשֶׁן מִשְׁפָּט, *Breastplate of Judgment*, effected atonement for sins related to perversion of justice. [The Choshen lies on the heart, the symbolic seat of a person's capacity of judgment.]

The *Ephod* (Apron or Vest) was a garment often associated with idolatrous practice [see *Judges* 17:5]; in its use now in the service of the One, true God, it effects atonement for the sin of idolatry.

The *Me'il* (Robe), whose hem was ringed by small golden bells, effected atonement for the sin of *lashon hara* (disparaging speech). God says, "Let that which makes noise (the bells) atone for the sin of noise (prohibited speech)."

Finally, the *Tzitz* (Headplate), which was worn on the מֵצַח, *forehead*, atoned for sins of brazenness, as the word מֵצַח is associated with shameless sin (see *Jeremiah* 3:3).

Now, it must be understood that this does not mean that as long as the Kohen Gadol served with the priestly garments all individuals were completely forgiven for any of the above sins. Some commentators explain that the atonement discussed here was effective only for sins committed inadvertently (*Maharsha* ibid.). Others state that these garments brought about atonement even for willful transgressions, but only in conjunction with the sinner's penitence (*Tosafos, Sanhedrin* 37b סוף ד"ה מיום; *Rosh*, cited in *Shitah Mekubetzes, Arachin* 16a §9). Finally, some add that, at least with regard to the more heinous sins listed above (e.g., murder and illicit relations), these garments served to mitigate the peripheral effects of these sins on the nation as a whole, rather than atoning for the individual who committed them (*Rashi* ibid.).

The way in which offerings bring about atonement is explained at length by various Rishonim, among them Chinuch, above, in Mitzvah 95. What connection is there, however, between the wearing of specific garments by the Kohen Gadol and atonement for sins? To appreciate this connection, we must first understand that clothing, in Scripture, is generally used as an analogy for character traits; just as the body is clothed in garments, so is the soul clothed in its personality and character (see *Ecclesiastes* 9:8). Clothing is referred to as מַד, *measure* (see *Leviticus* 6:3), as it is made to the person's dimensions. Similarly, the "garments of the soul" are referred to as מִדּוֹת, *traits*, as they too are given in appropriate measure to help the individual bring out his inherent luster and strengths (*Malbim* ibid.; see also *Maharsha, Berachos* 16b ד"ה ותציץ).

The garments of the Kohen are primarily a representation of their inner counterparts — the traits and character. When the Kohen Gadol dons these eight vestments, he looks to their spiritual inner counterparts and allows their true holiness and splendor to envelop him, transform him, and rectify that parallel world — the world of traits, from which all our actions flow. And, in doing so, he reveals that he, as well as the nation that he represents, identify their essence with these noble qualities. The sins that may have been committed are shown to be merely outward failures, not inherent spiritual deficiencies.

This understanding gives new meaning to the verse (*Psalms* 132:9): כֹּהֲנֶיךָ יִלְבְּשׁוּ צֶדֶק, *Let your Kohanim be clothed in righteousness* — for in truth, when the Kohanim donned their vestments, they were cloaked in more than mere fabric. They were to turn their attention to the inner world of the מִדּוֹת (traits), and thereby clothe their souls, and those of the people, with righteousness (*Malbim* ibid.).

## מִצְוָה קא: שֶׁלֹּא לִקְרֹעַ הַמְּעִיל שֶׁל כֹּהֲנִים

שֶׁלֹּא לְהַכְרִית פִּי הַמְּעִיל שֶׁל כֹּהֵן גָּדוֹל, שֶׁנֶּאֱמַר (שמות כ"ח, ל"ב) **לֹא יִקָּרֵעַ**[1].

מִשָּׁרְשֵׁי הַמִּצְוָה, לְפִי שֶׁהַקְּרִיעָה דָּבָר שֶׁל גְּנַאי אֶצְלֵנוּ וְעִנְיַן הַשְׁחָתָה[2], וְאַף כִּי בְּפִי הַבֶּגֶד, נִתְרַחַקְנוּ מִן הַדָּבָר וְהֻזְהַרְנוּ עָלָיו בְּלָאו כְּדֵי שֶׁיִּלְבָּשֵׁהוּ הַלּוֹבְשׁוֹ בְּאֵימָה בְּיִרְאָה וּבְנַחַת וְדֶרֶךְ כָּבוֹד, שֶׁיִּירָא מִלְּקָרְעוֹ וּמִלְּהַשְׁחִית בּוֹ דָּבָר[3].

---

## ⸺ Mitzvah 101 ⸺
# The Prohibition to Tear the Me'il of the Kohen Gadol

> וְהָיָה פִי־רֹאשׁוֹ בְּתוֹכוֹ שָׂפָה יִהְיֶה לְפִיו סָבִיב מַעֲשֵׂה אֹרֵג כְּפִי תַחְרָא יִהְיֶה־לּוֹ לֹא יִקָּרֵעַ
> *Its head-opening shall be folded over within it, its opening shall have a border all around of weaver's work — it shall be for it like the opening of a coat of mail — it shall not be torn* (Exodus 28:32).

The subject of this mitzvah is the *Me'il* (Robe), one of the four special garments of the Kohen Gadol. [A description and diagram of this garment can be found in the Insight to Mitzvah 99.] The above verse describes how the neck-opening of the *Me'il* was to be fashioned: it was to be woven as part of the garment, with the fabric doubled at the opening and folded toward the inside. This reinforced the opening and would prevent it from tearing.

The last words of the verse, לֹא יִקָּרֵעַ, *it shall not be torn*, aside from representing the reason for the reinforced weave at the neck-opening, also constitutes a separate prohibition to tear the area of the neck-opening of the *Me'il*.

שֶׁלֹּא לְהַכְרִית פִּי הַמְּעִיל שֶׁל כֹּהֵן גָּדוֹל — We are commanded **not to cut the neck-opening of the *Me'il* of the Kohen Gadol,** שֶׁנֶּאֱמַר "לֹא יִקָּרֵעַ" — **as it is stated** with regard to this opening (Exodus 28:32): ***it shall not be torn*.**[1]

### ⸺ Underlying Purpose of the Mitzvah ⸺

מִשָּׁרְשֵׁי הַמִּצְוָה — **Among the underlying purposes of this mitzvah** is that לְפִי שֶׁהַקְּרִיעָה דָּבָר שֶׁל גְּנַאי אֶצְלֵנוּ וְעִנְיַן הַשְׁחָתָה — **since tearing** a garment **is for us a disgraceful matter and an act of destruction,**[2] וְאַף כִּי בְּפִי הַבֶּגֶד — **and certainly this is the case with regard to the opening of the garment,** i.e., the neckline, which is clearly noticeable, נִתְרַחַקְנוּ מִן הַדָּבָר וְהֻזְהַרְנוּ עָלָיו בְּלָאו — **we were distanced from this matter and were forbidden from [tearing it] with this prohibition.** כְּדֵי שֶׁיִּלְבָּשֵׁהוּ הַלּוֹבְשׁוֹ בְּאֵימָה בְּיִרְאָה — This is **in order that the** Kohen Gadol **who wears [the *Me'il*], should wear it with** a feeling of **awe and trepidation,** וּבְנַחַת וְדֶרֶךְ כָּבוֹד — **and will** treat it **gently and with reverence,** שֶׁיִּירָא מִלְּקָרְעוֹ וּמִלְּהַשְׁחִית בּוֹ דָּבָר — **for he will fear to tear it or destroy any part of it.**[3]

---

### NOTES

1. Had the words of the verse have been שֶׁלֹּא יִקָּרֵעַ, *so that it shall not be torn*, we might have understood that this phrase is merely an explanation of the need for a reinforced neck opening. Since the verse actually says, לֹא יִקָּרֵעַ, *it shall not be torn*, it is understood as an independent clause, conveying a prohibition against tearing the neck opening (*Yoma* 72a; see similarly above, Mitzvah 100 note 1). [See also *Rashi*, Exodus 28:32 with *Ba'er Heiteiv*, and *Lev Same'ach* to *Sefer HaMitzvos*, *Shoresh* 5.]

See Insight regarding the applicability of this prohibition to other priestly garments.

2. Torn clothing represents either general slovenliness or a state of mourning (see, for example, mitzvos 150, 171, 264), neither of which are in keeping with the Torah's description of the priestly garments as being לְכָבוֹד וּלְתִפְאָרֶת, *for glory and splendor* (Exodus 28:2); see *Rambam, Hil. Klei HaMikdash* 8:4 and 5:6.

3. *Minchas Chinuch* (§1) notes that from *Chinuch*'s comments here it would seem that this prohibition applies only to tearing it in a destructive manner, and

## 271 ☐ TETZAVEH / MITZVAH 101: THE PROHIBITION TO TEAR THE ME'IL

וְנוֹהֶגֶת בִּזְמַן הַבַּיִת[4] בִּזְכָרִים וּבִנְקֵבוֹת, כְּלוֹמַר שֶׁכָּל מִי שֶׁקְּרָעוֹ, בֵּין אִישׁ בֵּין אִשָּׁה, אוֹ אֲפִלּוּ הִכְרִיתוֹ בְּמִסְפָּרַיִם[5] בְּמֵזִיד, לוֹקֶה.

### ☞ Applicability of the Mitzvah ☜

וְנוֹהֶגֶת בִּזְמַן הַבַּיִת — This mitzvah **applies in the time of the Temple** (i.e., when the Temple is standing);[4] בִּזְכָרִים וּבִנְקֵבוֹת — and it applies **to both men and women,** כְּלוֹמַר שֶׁכָּל מִי שֶׁקְּרָעוֹ — meaning to say, that anyone who tears [the opening of the *Me'il*], בֵּין אִישׁ בֵּין אִשָּׁה — **whether a man or a woman,** אוֹ אֲפִלּוּ הִכְרִיתוֹ בְּמִסְפָּרַיִם — **or even if he cuts it with scissors,**[5] בְּמֵזִיד לוֹקֶה — if he has done so **deliberately, incurs** the penalty of *malkus* (lashes).

### NOTES

not, for example, to tearing for the purpose of repairing it. See Insight for further discussion.

4. *Minchas Chinuch* (§2) suggests that Chinuch means this only in a practical sense (since after the destruction of the *Beis HaMikdash*, the priestly garments were not accessible). Technically, however, if after the Temple's destruction, one would be in possession of the *Me'il* of the Kohen Gadol, it would still be forbidden to tear its opening.

5. This phrasing would seem to indicate that one violates the prohibition even when tearing it in a non-destructive manner, such as to repair it (*Ner Mitzvah* 10:25; cf. *Yitzchak Yeranein, Hil. Klei HaMikdash* 9:3). See Insight.

---

**◆§ Insight: The Prohibition to Tear Other Priestly Garments**

As Chinuch explains, the source of the prohibition to tear the opening of the *Me'il* is the verse that discusses specifically the neck-opening of this garment (cited at the beginning of the mitzvah), which concludes: לֹא יִקָּרֵעַ, *it shall not be torn* (Exodus 28:32). Chinuch mentions no other application of this prohibition other than the specific law that one may not tear the neck-opening of the *Me'il*. *Minchas Chinuch* (§1) points out, however, that the Gemara (*Yoma* 72a) presents this very prohibition as applying to the tearing of *any* of the priestly garments: *Rachava said in the name of R' Yehudah, "One who tears one of the priestly vestments incurs malkus* (lashes), *for [the verse] states, 'it shall not be torn.'"* Apparently, R' Yehudah maintains that although the subject of that verse happens to be the *Me'il*, the prohibition against tearing applies equally to all of the priestly garments. If that is the case, why does Chinuch mention only the *Me'il* as the subject of the prohibition?

A careful reading of *Rambam's* presentation of this prohibition can shed light on the matter. *Rambam* writes (*Hil. Klei HaMikdash* 9:3): One who rips the opening of the *Me'il* incurs *malkus*, as the verse states: "it shall not be torn." So too with regard to all priestly garments — one who rips them **in a destructive manner** incurs *malkus*.

In setting down this law, *Rambam* includes all priestly garments in the prohibition, but he distinguishes between the *Me'il* and the other garments. With regard to the *Me'il*, he states simply that one incurs *malkus* for tearing it, but with regard to other priestly garments, he specifies that one incurs *malkus* for tearing them *in a destructive manner*. This implies that if one would tear one of the other priestly garments constructively, for example, in the process of repairing the garment, he would not violate the prohibition. From where does *Rambam* derive this essential difference between the *Me'il* and the other garments?

*Minchas Chinuch* (§1) suggests that the above ruling of R' Yehudah (in *Yoma* 72a), that the prohibition applies to all priestly garments, is the subject of dispute. The Gemara in *Zevachim* (95a) discusses a procedure in which it becomes necessary to tear a priestly garment that had become soiled. The Gemara cites Reish Lakish, who wonders how this procedure can be carried out with the *Me'il*, which one is forbidden to tear. Reish Lakish does not, however, ask this question regarding the other priestly garments. Clearly, writes *Minchas Chinuch*, Reish Lakish disagrees with R' Yehudah and maintains that this prohibition applies to the *Me'il* only. Reish Lakish understands that the verse לֹא יִקָּרֵעַ, *it shall not be torn*, applies only to the *Me'il*, which is the subject of that verse.

*Minchas Chinuch* suggests further that *Rambam* rules in accordance with Reish Lakish, and not R' Yehudah, that the prohibition of לֹא יִקָּרֵעַ, *it shall not be torn*, applies only to the *Me'il* and not to

any of the other priestly garments. If so, why does *Rambam* write that it is prohibited to tear any of the other priestly garments? *Minchas Chinuch* suggests that this prohibition is in fact arrived at from another source altogether.

The Torah (*Deuteronomy* 12:1-4) establishes an obligation to destroy all places of idolatrous worship, and then concludes with the following prohibition (v. 4): לֹא תַעֲשׂוּן כֵּן לַה' אֱלֹהֵיכֶם, *You shall not do so to HASHEM, your God*. This constitutes a prohibition to destroy any object belonging to the *Beis HaMikdash* (*Makkos* 22a). [Another aspect of this prohibition is that one may not erase the Name of God; both of these aspects of the prohibition are discussed by Chinuch in Mitzvah 437.] Surely, the priestly garments, which belong to the *Beis HaMikdash* and are used in the Divine service, are also included in this prohibition. Thus, one who ruins any of the priestly garments has violated the prohibition, *You shall not do so to HASHEM*.

It emerges that when *Rambam* speaks of the prohibition to tear the opening of the *Me'il* and the prohibition to tear any other priestly garment, he is in fact speaking of two separate prohibitions, one from the verse לֹא יִקָּרֵעַ, *it* (the *Me'il*) *shall not be torn*, and the other from the verse לֹא תַעֲשׂוּן כֵּן לַה' אֱלֹהֵיכֶם, *you shall not do so to HASHEM, your God*, which forbids destroying any of the belongings of the *Beis HaMikdash*. Now, the verse לֹא יִקָּרֵעַ, *it shall not be torn*, makes no mention of the kind of tearing that is forbidden; it simply forbids the action of tearing the opening of the *Me'il*. Thus it is forbidden to tear it for any reason whatsoever, even to repair it. In contrast, the verse לֹא תַעֲשׂוּן כֵּן לַה' אֱלֹהֵיכֶם, *you shall not do so to HASHEM, your God*, speaks specifically about destructive actions: we are commanded to destroy idolatrous places, but not to do so to the belongings of God. Thus, one incurs *malkus* for tearing other priestly garments only if he does so in a destructive manner.

Chinuch, following *Rambam*, also rules that the specific prohibition of the verse לֹא יִקָּרֵעַ, *it shall not be torn*, applies to the *Me'il* only. Therefore, in this mitzvah, where he discusses what is forbidden by *this* verse, Chinuch makes no mention of the prohibition relating to the tearing of any of the other priestly garments.

[See *Minchas Chinuch* there at length, where the opinions of other Acharonim on these issues are discussed.]

## TETZAVEH / MITZVAH 102: TO EAT THE MEAT OF THE CHATAS AND ASHAM OFFERINGS

### מִצְוָה קב: מִצְוַת אֲכִילַת בְּשַׂר חַטָּאת וְאָשָׁם [4,3,2,1]

## Mitzvah 102
## The Obligation [Upon the Kohanim] to Eat the Meat of the Chatas and Asham Offerings

וְאָכְלוּ אֹתָם אֲשֶׁר כֻּפַּר בָּהֶם לְמַלֵּא אֶת יָדָם לְקַדֵּשׁ אֹתָם וְזָר לֹא יֹאכַל כִּי קֹדֶשׁ הֵם

*They shall eat them so that atonement may be attained through them, to inaugurate them, to sanctify them; a non-Kohen shall not eat, for they are holy* (Exodus 29:33).

This verse refers to the *miluim* (inauguration) offerings, which were offered by Aaron and his sons as part of the process through which they were inaugurated into their service as Kohanim (see *Exodus* 29:1-37). With regard to these offerings, Aaron and his sons had a dual role: They were the *owners* for whom the offerings atoned, and they themselves also were the Kohanim who performed the atonement service. The verse commands them, in their role as Kohanim, to eat the meat of these offerings, so that in their role as owners they shall attain atonement; they were thereby inaugurated into the Divine service and acquired the sanctity reserved for Kohanim.[1]

As Chinuch will explain, the verse conveys the concept that "The Kohanim eat [the meat of an offering] and the owner thereby attains atonement." Although the primary aspect of atonement via an offering is achieved through the application of its blood to the Altar, the consumption of its meat by God's appointed ministers, the Kohanim, is the culmination of its offering-service, and this adds an element to the atonement and completes it.[2] While the Torah mentions this in the context of the *miluim* offerings, the concept of atonement through consumption of the offering — and the command for Kohanim to actually consume the offerings — is not limited to the particular case of *miluim*, but applies to other offerings as well. The verse is understood as a general mitzvah-obligation upon Kohanim to eat offerings and thereby effect atonement for the owners who brought those offerings.

There are two categories of offerings brought in the Temple: *kodshei kodashim* ("most holy" offerings — which include the *olah, chatas, asham,* and communal *shelamim* offerings), and *kodashim kalim* (offerings of lesser holiness — which include all other animal offerings). *Kodshei kodashim* are generally brought for atonement, and are subject to greater restrictions than *kodashim kalim*, which generally are not brought for atonement. Among these restrictions is the rule that the meat of *kodshei kodashim* (other than the *olah,* whose meat is burned on the Altar) is given to the Kohanim, and may be eaten only by male Kohanim, within the confines of the Temple Courtyard. The meat of *kodashim kalim* is treated more leniently: A portion is given to the Kohanim and may be eaten by them and members of their households, while the remainder is given to the owner of the offering, and may be eaten by all Israelites; all the meat may be eaten anywhere in Jerusalem.

The offerings to which our verse refers were *kodshei kodashim*.[3] Hence, the verse directs the Kohanim

---

NOTES

1. *Malbim, Exodus* 29:33. This understanding of the verse follows Chinuch in this mitzvah; *Rambam* in *Sefer HaMitzvos, Asei* 89 and *Hil. Maaseh HaKorbanos* 10:1; and *Rashi, Yevamos* 40a ד"ה ק; see also *Pesachim* 59b. [See *Rashi* to the verse for a different understanding.] The "atonement" referred to here is not forgiveness for a specific sin, but a purging of their non-Kohen status (*Rashi* to the verse). [The word כִּפֶּר, *atone*, literally means "wipe away" (see *Rashi, Genesis* 32:21).]

2. *Tosafos, Zevachim* 6a ד"ה והלא; *Rashi, Yevamos* 40a ד"ה ק. See further, note 13.

3. The verse actually refers to a *shelamim* offered by Aaron and his sons during the *miluim* procedure. Although personal *shelamim* offerings are generally in the category of *kodashim kalim*, those offered as part of the *miluim* procedure were *kodshei kodashim* [and, as the verse states clearly, they "atoned" for Aaron and his sons] (*Rashi, Exodus* 29:31, 33).

## תצוה / מצוה קב: מצות אכילת בשר חטאת ואשם

שֶׁנִּצְטַוּוּ הַכֹּהֲנִים לֶאֱכֹל בָּשָׂר קְצָת מִן הַקָּרְבָּנוֹת כְּגוֹן הַחַטָּאת וְהָאָשָׁם, שֶׁנֶּאֱמַר עֲלֵיהֶם (שמות כ״ט, ל״ג) וְאָכְלוּ אֹתָם אֲשֶׁר כֻּפַּר בָּהֶם, וְאָמְרוּ זִכְרוֹנָם לִבְרָכָה (פסחים דף נ״ט ע״ב) כֹּהֲנִים אוֹכְלִים וּבְעָלִים מִתְכַּפְּרִים.[5] וְעִנְיַן מַעֲשֵׂה הַחַטָּאת וְהָאָשָׁם אֵיךְ הָיוּ עוֹשִׂין אוֹתָן וּמְקוֹם וּזְמַן אֲכִילָתָם, בַּסֵּדֶר שֶׁלּוֹ נִכְתְּבֶנּוּ בְּעֶזְרַת הַשֵּׁם. וּכְלַל הַדָּבָר שֶׁכָּל בְּשַׂר קָרְבַּן הַחַטָּאת וְהָאָשָׁם הָיָה נֶאֱכָל לְזִכְרֵי כְּהֻנָּה בָּעֲזָרָה[6] חוּץ מִן הָאֵמוּרִין שֶׁבָּהֶן[7] וְאֵין לַבְּעָלִים בָּהֶן כְּלוּם, וְשָׁם יִתְפָּרֵשׁ גַּם כֵּן מַה הֵן הָאֵמוּרִין[8].

---

to eat the meat of *kodshei kodashim*, through which the owner receives atonement. Chinuch will discuss whether it is also a mitzvah for Kohanim to eat the portions of the *kodashim kalim* offerings that they receive.[4]

לֶאֱכֹל בָּשָׂר קְצָת מִן הַקָּרְבָּנוֹת שֶׁנִּצְטַוּוּ הַכֹּהֲנִים — **The Kohanim are commanded to eat the meat of some of the offerings,** כְּגוֹן הַחַטָּאת וְהָאָשָׁם — specifically, *kodshei kodashim* offerings **such as the** *chatas* **and the** *asham*, which effect atonement, שֶׁנֶּאֱמַר עֲלֵיהֶם — **for it is stated in regard to [such offerings]** (*Exodus* 29:33): וְאָכְלוּ אֹתָם אֲשֶׁר כֻּפַּר בָּהֶם — **They shall eat them so that atonement may be attained through them.** וְאָמְרוּ זִכְרוֹנָם לִבְרָכָה — **[Our Sages], of blessed memory, have stated** (*Pesachim* 59b) in explanation of this verse that כֹּהֲנִים אוֹכְלִים וּבְעָלִים מִתְכַּפְּרִים — **the Kohanim eat** the meat of the offering **and,** by virtue of their eating, **the owners** who brought the offering **attain atonement** for the sin for which it was brought.[5]

Chinuch notes that this mitzvah is focused on consumption of the meat, but other aspects of the *chatas* and *asham* offerings are discussed elsewhere:

וְעִנְיַן מַעֲשֵׂה הַחַטָּאת וְהָאָשָׁם — **As regards the procedures of the** *chatas* **and** *asham* **offerings,** אֵיךְ הָיוּ עוֹשִׂין אוֹתָן — namely, **how [the Kohanim] would perform** the *avodah* (service) of **[these offerings],** וּמְקוֹם וּזְמַן אֲכִילָתָם — **and** what was **the** proper **place and time for their consumption,** בַּסֵּדֶר שֶׁלּוֹ נִכְתְּבֶנּוּ בְּעֶזְרַת הַשֵּׁם — **we will write** all of **it in the** *parashah* that discusses it (*Parashas Tzav*; Mitzvos 138,140), **with the help of Hashem.** וּכְלַל הַדָּבָר שֶׁכָּל בְּשַׂר קָרְבַּן הַחַטָּאת — **With respect to consumption, the sum of the matter is** וְהָאָשָׁם הָיָה נֶאֱכָל לְזִכְרֵי כְּהֻנָּה בָּעֲזָרָה — **that all the meat of the** *chatas* **and** *asham* **offerings was eaten by male Kohanim, in the Temple Courtyard,**[6] חוּץ מִן הָאֵמוּרִין שֶׁבָּהֶן — **except for the** *emurin* (i.e., sacrificial parts) **of [the offerings],** which were burned on the Altar;[7] וְאֵין לַבְּעָלִים בָּהֶן כְּלוּם — **and the owners received none** of the meat **of [these offerings].** וְשָׁם יִתְפָּרֵשׁ גַּם כֵּן מַה הֵן הָאֵמוּרִין — **There,** in *Parashas Tzav* (Mitzvah 138), **it will also be explained which** parts of the offering **are the** *emurin*.[8]

---

### NOTES

4. Aside from our mitzvah, which pertains to sacrificial *meat*, there is a mitzvah for the Kohanim to eat their portion of the *minchah* (meal) offering, which is also *kodshei kodashim*. That is the subject of Mitzvah 134.

5. I.e., the atonement is *completed* through the Kohanim's consumption of the meat (see sources cited in note 2).

Aside from the *chatas* and *asham* offerings, which Chinuch mentions, there was only one other case of a *kodshei kodashim* offering whose meat was eaten: the communal *shelamim* brought on Shavuos (see *Leviticus* 23:19-20, and Mitzvah 307). [Whereas personal *shelamim* offerings were *kodashim kalim*, the communal *shelamim* was *kodshei kodashim* (*Zevachim* 54b-55a).] That offering did not atone in the conventional sense, but it served to effect permission for the new harvest of grain to be offered in the *Beis HaMikdash*. Chinuch does not discuss that offering, implying that it was not in the same category as the *chatas* and *asham* with respect to the mitzvah-obligation mentioned here. See also *Rambam*, *Sefer HaMitzvos*, Asei 89; see further, *Hil. Maaseh HaKorbanos* 10:1,3.

6. The time limit for this consumption is discussed below, in note 18.

7. For the etymology of the word אמורין, *emurin*, see Mitzvah 90 note 1.

8. Specific parts of the animal must be burned on the Altar: the (hard) fats around the body cavity and the fats upon the stomachs, kidneys, and flanks. The Kohanim were not allowed to eat their portions of meat before the *emurin* were burned on the Altar (*Pesachim* 59b; *Rambam* ibid. 9:11).

## TETZAVEH / MITZVAH 102: TO EAT THE MEAT OF THE CHATAS AND ASHAM OFFERINGS

וּבִכְלָל⁹ מִצְוָה עֲשֵׂה זֶה גַּם כֵּן שֶׁיֹּאכְלוּ חֶלְקָם הַמַּגִּיעַ אֲלֵיהֶם מִכָּל הַקָּרְבָּנוֹת שֶׁנִּקְרָאִין קָדָשִׁים קַלִּים,¹⁰ וְכֵן אֲכִילַת הַתְּרוּמָה בִּכְלָל הַמִּצְוָה.¹¹ וְאוּלָם אֵין אֲכִילַת קָדָשִׁים קַלִּים וּתְרוּמָה כְּמוֹ אֲכִילַת בְּשַׂר חַטָּאת וְאָשָׁם, שֶׁבַּאֲכִילַת חַטָּאת וְאָשָׁם תִּשְׁלַם כַּפָּרַת הַמִּתְכַּפֵּר,¹² כְּמוֹ שֶׁאָמְרוּ זִכְרוֹנָם לִבְרָכָה, כֹּהֲנִים אוֹכְלִין וּבְעָלִים מִתְכַּפְּרִין, וַאֲכִילַת קָדָשִׁים קַלִּים וּתְרוּמָה לֹא יוֹסִיף וְלֹא יִגְרַע בְּמִצְוַת הַמַּקְרִיב וְהַנּוֹתֵן.¹³

---

Since the verse commanding the Kohanim to eat sacrificial meat states that this consumption brings about atonement, it is clear that the command was given with reference to offerings that effect atonement, namely, the *chatas* and *asham*, which are *kodshei kodashim*.[9] However, the Kohanim also receive specific portions of *kodashim kalim* offerings. Chinuch now discusses the consumption of those portions, as well as other sacred food that the Kohanim receive:

שֶׁיֹּאכְלוּ חֶלְקָם — וּבִכְלָל מִצְוַת עֲשֵׂה זֶה גַּם כֵּן — **Also included in this mitzvah-obligation is** the rule הַמַּגִּיעַ אֲלֵיהֶם מִכָּל הַקָּרְבָּנוֹת שֶׁנִּקְרָאִין קָדָשִׁים קַלִּים — **that [the Kohanim] should eat the portions that are their due from all the offerings that are classified as *kodashim kalim*.**[10] וְכֵן אֲכִילַת הַתְּרוּמָה בִּכְלָל הַמִּצְוָה — **Similarly, the consumption of *terumah* is included in this mitzvah.**[11] וְאוּלָם אֵין אֲכִילַת קָדָשִׁים קַלִּים וּתְרוּמָה כְּמוֹ אֲכִילַת בְּשַׂר חַטָּאת וְאָשָׁם — **However, the consumption of *kodashim kalim* and *terumah* is not** of the same significance **as the consumption of the meat of the *chatas* and *asham*;** שֶׁבַּאֲכִילַת חַטָּאת וְאָשָׁם תִּשְׁלַם כַּפָּרַת הַמִּתְכַּפֵּר — **for it is through the** Kohanim's **consumption of the *chatas* and *asham* meat that the atonement of the one who is being forgiven** for his sin through this offering (i.e., the owner) **is completed,**[12] כְּמוֹ שֶׁאָמְרוּ זִכְרוֹנָם לִבְרָכָה — **as [our Sages], of blessed memory, have stated** (*Pesachim* ibid.): כֹּהֲנִים אוֹכְלִין וּבְעָלִים מִתְכַּפְּרִין — **the Kohanim eat** the meat of an offering, **and the owners** of the offering thereby **attain atonement** of the sin for which it was brought. וַאֲכִילַת קָדָשִׁים קַלִּים וּתְרוּמָה — **The consumption of *kodashim kalim* and *terumah*** by the Kohanim, **however,** לֹא יוֹסִיף וְלֹא יִגְרַע בְּמִצְוַת הַמַּקְרִיב וְהַנּוֹתֵן — **neither adds to, nor detracts from, the mitzvah of the one bringing** the offering **or the one giving** the *terumah*.[13]

---

### NOTES

9. *Rambam, Sefer HaMitzvos*, Asei 89; *Radvaz, Hil. Maaseh HaKorbanos* 10:1.

10. The Kohanim received the חָזֶה וְשׁוֹק, *breast and [right] thigh* (*Leviticus* 7:31-34) from all *kodashim kalim* offerings [except the *maaser* and *pesach*]. Additionally, they received four of the forty loaves brought with the *todah* offering (ibid. 7:14), the cooked foreleg and two loaves from the *shelamim* offering of a *nazir* (*Numbers* 6:19-20), and the entire *bechor* [firstborn] offering (ibid. 18:18). These portions were prohibited to Israelites, but could be eaten by Kohanim *and* members of their households, anywhere in Jerusalem (Mishnah, *Zevachim* 55a). The remainder of the meat was given to the owners, and could be eaten by all Israelites, anywhere in Jerusalem (Mishnah ibid.). Chinuch states that the consumption of the Kohanim's portions is a subcategory of our mitzvah. See below, note 13.

11. *Terumah* was a portion of the crop (generally 2 percent) that was awarded to Kohanim, and was allowed to be consumed by Kohanim and members of their households, as well as their animals (see Mitzvah 280 and Mitzvah 507). Chinuch states that the consumption of *terumah* is a subcategory of our mitzvah. See note 13.

12. As mentioned in the introduction to this mitzvah, the primary aspect of the atonement is achieved through the application of the offering's blood to the Altar. The consumption of the meat by God's emissaries adds an element to the atonement and completes it. See the following note.

13. With regard to *kodashim kalim* and *terumah,* the owner's role is completed when the Kohanim receive their portions. Even if the Kohanim should fail to eat those portions, the owner has fulfilled the mitzvah completely. The Kohanim's consumption — albeit a mitzvah — is unrelated to the owner's obligation. With regard to *kodshei kodashim,* however, the Kohanim's consumption — which effects atonement — is considered an element of the *avodah* (see *Yoma* 68b with *Rabbeinu Chananel*). If the Kohanim fail to eat the meat, the service of the offering was not completed in the ideal fashion and, as a result, the owner's atonement — which was his purpose in bringing the offering — is somewhat incomplete. Nevertheless, the owner is not required to bring another offering to atone for his sin, as the essential part of the atonement is accomplished through the application of the offering's blood to the Altar (*Divrei Malkiel* 5:28; *Avi Ezri II, Hil. Maaseh HaKorbanos* 10:1; see *Tosafos, Zevachim* 6a ד"ה והלא, and *Rashi, Yevamos* 40a ד"ה ה"ק; see, however, *Rashi,*

## 276 ❑ תצוה / מצוה קב: מצות אכילת בשר חטאת ואשם

מִשָּׁרְשֵׁי הַמִּצְוָה, הַיְסוֹד הַקָּבוּעַ אֶצְלֵנוּ כִּי כָּל פְּעֻלּוֹת הַקָּרְבָּנוֹת לְהַכְשִׁיר מַחְשְׁבוֹתֵינוּ וְכַוָּנוֹתֵינוּ לְטוֹב, וּלְהַשְׁפִּיל נֶפֶשׁ הַמִּתְאַוָּה אֲשֶׁר בָּנוּ, וּלְהַגְדִּיל וּלְחַזֵּק נֶפֶשׁ הַשֵּׂכֶל אֶל הַמִּצְוֹת[14], וְעַל כֵּן נִצְטַוֵּינוּ לְהִתְנַהֵג בְּכָל עִנְיְנֵי הַבַּיִת וְהַקָּרְבָּנוֹת דֶּרֶךְ מַעֲלָה וּגְדֻלָּה וְכָבוֹד, לְמַעַן תָּנוּחַ בִּלְבָבֵנוּ יִרְאָה וַעֲנָוָה וְשִׁפְלוּת הָרוּחַ בִּהְיוֹתֵנוּ שָׁם, גַּם בְּזָכְרֵנוּ אוֹתוֹ מִמְּקוֹמֵנוּ[15]. וּבֶאֱמֶת כִּי מִן הַנְהָגַת הַכָּבוֹד אֶל הַקָּרְבָּן שֶׁהַכַּפָּרָה תְּלוּיָה בּוֹ,

### ⇜ Underlying Purpose of the Mitzvah ⇝

Although the fulfillment of this mitzvah is limited to Kohanim, as are most mitzvos connected with the *Beis HaMikdash* (Temple), the underlying purpose is relevant to all Jews. Chinuch begins with a statement about the *avodah* in general:

מִשָּׁרְשֵׁי הַמִּצְוָה — **Among the underlying purposes of the mitzvah is** הַיְסוֹד הַקָּבוּעַ אֶצְלֵנוּ **the fundamental principle that we have established** (in Mitzvah 95) כִּי כָּל פְּעֻלּוֹת הַקָּרְבָּנוֹת לְהַכְשִׁיר מַחְשְׁבוֹתֵינוּ וְכַוָּנוֹתֵינוּ — **that all of the actions** related **to the offerings** in the Temple לְטוֹב — **are** commanded in order **to train our thoughts and intentions to virtuousness,** וּלְהַשְׁפִּיל נֶפֶשׁ הַמִּתְאַוָּה אֲשֶׁר בָּנוּ — **to subjugate the desirous spirit that is within us,** וּלְהַגְדִּיל וּלְחַזֵּק נֶפֶשׁ הַשֵּׂכֶל אֶל הַמִּצְוֹת — **and to enhance and encourage the intelligent spirit** that is within us **toward** the fulfillment of **the mitzvos.**[14] וְעַל כֵּן נִצְטַוֵּינוּ — **Therefore,** in keeping with this objective, **we were commanded** לְהִתְנַהֵג בְּכָל עִנְיְנֵי הַבַּיִת וְהַקָּרְבָּנוֹת דֶּרֶךְ מַעֲלָה וּגְדֻלָּה וְכָבוֹד — **to treat all matters pertaining to the Temple and the offerings in a manner of nobility, grandeur, and respect,** לְמַעַן תָּנוּחַ בִּלְבָבֵנוּ יִרְאָה וַעֲנָוָה וְשִׁפְלוּת הָרוּחַ בִּהְיוֹתֵנוּ שָׁם — **so that reverence, humility, and submissiveness of spirit** before Hashem **will settle in our hearts when we are there,** גַּם בְּזָכְרֵנוּ אוֹתוֹ מִמְּקוֹמֵנוּ — **and even when we reflect on [the Temple] from our own locations.**[15]

Chinuch proceeds to explain how this principle applies to our mitzvah:

וּבֶאֱמֶת כִּי מִן הַנְהָגַת הַכָּבוֹד אֶל הַקָּרְבָּן שֶׁהַכַּפָּרָה תְּלוּיָה בּוֹ — **Now, truly,** as **part of the respectful conduct** with which we must act **toward an offering upon which** our **atonement depends,**

---

### NOTES

*Pesachim* 59b ד״ה מכדי and *Tosafos* there ד״ה יכול נטמאו; *Rashba, Yevamos* 90a; see also *Mikdash David* 14:7).

*Rambam* (*Sefer HaMitzvos*, Asei 89) notes that while the Torah (in our verse) commands that the Kohanim eat their portions of *kodshei kodashim*, it never commands that they eat their portions of *kodashim kalim* or *terumah*. [It merely mentions the consumption of those items in the course of setting restrictions as to when, and where, and by whom they may be eaten (see *Leviticus* 22:1-16 et al.).] *Rambam* therefore concludes that the consumption of those sacred foods is not a full-fledged mitzvah-*obligation*. Nevertheless, a Kohen who eats his portion of *kodashim kalim* or *terumah* performs a meritorious deed, for consuming those sacred foods is "an adjunct" to our mitzvah of eating *kodshei kodashim*. For further discussion, see note 21.

It is noteworthy that Chinuch and *Rambam* (ibid.) do not mention the *owner's* consumption of his portion of *kodashim kalim* as being a mitzvah. *Rashi* (*Pesachim* 59a ד״ה בשאר ימות השנה), however, maintains that our mitzvah applies to *all* portions of offerings: Just as it obligates the Kohanim to eat their portions, so too, it obligates the owners to eat the portions of *kodashim kalim* that they receive. *Ramban* (glosses to *Sefer HaMitzvos*, additional mitzvos, Added Asei 1) has yet another view. He concedes that our verse refers specifically to the Kohanim, but argues that there is *another* mitzvah (*Deuteronomy* 14:23) that obligates the owners to eat their portions of *kodashim kalim*. For further discussion of this matter, see Insight A.

14. The struggle between man's "intelligent spirit" (i.e., his spirituality and good inclination — *yetzer tov*) and his "desirous spirit" (i.e., his earthiness and evil inclination — *yetzer hara*) defines his sojourn in this world. The intelligent spirit draws him toward the Truth, which encompasses service of God and adherence to His ways, while the desirous spirit drags him toward animalistic desires (Chinuch, Mitzvah 313; see *Bereishis Rabbah* 14:3 and *Rambam, Hil. Teshuvah* 5:1-4). The majority of the Torah's laws are devices designed by the Great Counselor to correct man's attitudes and perfect his ways (*Rambam, Hil. Temurah* 4:13), and as Chinuch often notes, this is particularly so with regard to the mitzvos involving the *avodah* in the *Beis HaMikdash*. See his lengthy discussion of this subject in Mitzvah 95.

15. Thus, the grandeur of the *Beis HaMikdash* affects us in a positive manner long after we have visited there.

## 277 □ TETZAVEH / MITZVAH 102: TO EAT THE MEAT OF THE CHATAS AND ASHAM OFFERINGS

לִהְיוֹתוֹ נֶאֱכָל אֶל הַמְשָׁרְתִים בְּעַצְמָם וְלֹא שֶׁיִּתְּנוּהוּ לְעַבְדֵיהֶם וּלְכַלְבָּם אוֹ יִמְכְּרוּהוּ לְכָל קוֹנֶה[16], וְכֵן מִן הַכָּבוֹד הוּא שֶׁיֵּאָכֵל בְּמָקוֹם קָדוֹשׁ[17], וְכֵן שֶׁלֹּא יַשְׁהוּ אֲכִילָתוֹ הַרְבֵּה כְּדֵי שֶׁלֹּא יַסְרִיחַ וְיִהְיֶה הַנֶּפֶשׁ קָצָה בּוֹ[18], הֲלֹא כָּל זֶה מַרְאֶה בָּעִנְיָן גְּדֻלָּה וַחֲשִׁיבוּת.

דִּינֵי הַמִּצְוָה, בִּמְקוֹמָן נַאֲרִיךְ בָּהֶן קְצָת כְּמִנְהָגֵנוּ.[19]

---

לִהְיוֹתוֹ נֶאֱכָל אֶל הַמְשָׁרְתִים בְּעַצְמָם — **it is appropriate that** the meat of **[the offering] be eaten by** the Kohanim, who are **the attendants** of the Temple, **themselves,** וְלֹא שֶׁיִּתְּנוּהוּ לְעַבְדֵיהֶם וּלְכַלְבָּם — **and not that they give it to their servants or their dogs,** אוֹ יִמְכְּרוּהוּ לְכָל קוֹנֶה — **or that they sell it to any buyer.** This is a basis of the law that the *chatas* and *asham* offerings may be eaten only by male Kohanim.[16]

Having explained the central law of our mitzvah, Chinuch applies the above concept to other laws regarding the consumption of the offerings that atone:

וְכֵן מִן הַכָּבוֹד הוּא — **Likewise, it is part of the** appropriate **respect** due an offering that effects atonement שֶׁיֵּאָכֵל בְּמָקוֹם קָדוֹשׁ — **that it be eaten in a holy place;** this is a basis of the law that the meat of the *chatas* and *asham* may be eaten only within the confines of the Temple Courtyard.[17]

וְכֵן שֶׁלֹּא יַשְׁהוּ אֲכִילָתוֹ הַרְבֵּה — **Similarly,** part of the respect due the offering is **that they should not delay its consumption very long,** כְּדֵי שֶׁלֹּא יַסְרִיחַ וְיִהְיֶה הַנֶּפֶשׁ קָצָה בּוֹ — **so that it should not become rancid and the soul will be repulsed by it.** This is a basis of the law that the meat of the *chatas* and *asham* may be eaten only on the day they are offered and the night that follows.[18]

הֲלֹא כָּל זֶה מַרְאֶה בָּעִנְיָן גְּדֻלָּה וַחֲשִׁיבוּת — **Surely, all this demonstrates grandeur and importance regarding the matter** of offerings that effect atonement.

### ⸺ Laws of the Mitzvah ⸺

דִּינֵי הַמִּצְוָה — **As regards the laws of the mitzvah,** בִּמְקוֹמָן נַאֲרִיךְ בָּהֶן קְצָת כְּמִנְהָגֵנוּ — **we will elaborate on them somewhat in their proper places** (i.e., in the mitzvos pertaining to the service of each of these offerings), **in accordance with our custom.**[19]

---

### NOTES

16. Since, as Chinuch stated above, an element of atonement depends upon consumption of the offering, it is surely fitting that only the male Kohanim who actually serve in the *Beis HaMikdash* should eat the meat.

This reason pertains specifically to *kodshei kodashim*, which are the primary subject of our mitzvah. *Kodshei kodashim* are brought for atonement, and may in fact be eaten only by male Kohanim. The portions of *kodshei kalim* awarded to Kohanim (as described in note 10) may be eaten by all members of the Kohanim's households. *Terumah* may be fed even to the Kohanim's animals (see note 11). Moreover, the Kohen who receives *terumah* may sell it to another Kohen (or even to a non-Kohen, provided it will be eaten only by a Kohen or members of his household). Thus, while even *terumah* and *kodashim kalim* are prohibited to non-Kohanim, and are accorded measures of respect reflecting their particular levels of sanctity, *kodshei kodashim* are treated with an added measure of respect, bringing home to us the reverence with which we must view the atonement service.

17. The Torah (*Leviticus* 6:19; 7:6) specifies that the *chatas* and *asham* must be eaten בְּמָקוֹם קָדוֹשׁ, *in a holy place,* referring to the Courtyard of the *Beis HaMikdash* (see Mishnah, *Zevachim* 52b). Chinuch explains that this is because their consumption effects atonement [and fittingly should be done in the place designated for atonement]. *Kodashim kalim,* however, may be eaten anywhere in the city of Jerusalem (*Zevachim* 55a; *Rambam, Hil. Maaseh HaKorbanos* 10:5). *Terumah* may be eaten even outside Jerusalem. [See Mitzvah 446, where Chinuch adds that *kodshei kodashim* must be eaten within the Courtyard so that when the Kohanim eat the meat they will concentrate on the fact that this effects atonement for the owner.]

18. Meat of *kodashim kalim* offerings, by contrast, may in most cases be eaten until nightfall of the next day (see *Leviticus* 7:16). Although the meat does not spoil after one day — for *kodashim kalim* surely may not be left to spoil — the Torah imposed an added degree of stringency for *kodshei kodashim,* reflecting the reverence due to offerings that effect atonement. [Even in the case of *kodashim kalim,* the Torah indicates that it is preferable that they be consumed on the day they are offered; it is merely that if not finished that day they may be consumed for one additional day (*Ramban, Leviticus* 7:16, citing *Sifra* there).]

Under Biblical law, *kodshei kodashim* may be eaten until daybreak the next morning, but the Sages forbade consumption after midnight. This is a protective measure, enacted to ensure that no one would come to eat the meat after daybreak (Mishnah, *Berachos* 2a).

19. Details regarding the service of the *chatas* and

## 278 ❏ תצוה / מצוה קב: מצות אכילת בשר חטאת ואשם

וְנוֹהֶגֶת מִצְוָה זוֹ בִּזְמַן הַבַּיִת, בְּזִכְרֵי כְהֻנָּה.[20]
וְעוֹבֵר עָלֶיהָ וְלֹא אָכַל חֶלְקוֹ הַמַּגִּיעוֹ מֵהֶן בִּזְמַן הַמֻּגְבָּל לוֹ, בִּטֵּל עֲשֵׂה[21] וְנֶעֱנָשׁ עוֹד מִצַּד כַּפָּרַת הַבְּעָלִים שֶׁתְּלוּיָה בּוֹ, כְּמוֹ שֶׁאָמַרְנוּ.[22]
וְהָרַמְבַּ״ן זִכְרוֹנוֹ לִבְרָכָה לֹא יִמְנֶה מִצְוָה זוֹ, כִּי אָמַר שֶׁזֶּה חֵלֶק מֵחֶלְקֵי מִצְוַת הַקָּרְבָּנוֹת

---

### ~ Applicability of the Mitzvah ~

בְּזִכְרֵי כְהֻנָּה – to **male Kohanim.**[20] וְנוֹהֶגֶת מִצְוָה זוֹ בִּזְמַן הַבַּיִת – **This mitzvah applies in the times of the Temple,** וְעוֹבֵר עָלֶיהָ וְלֹא אָכַל חֶלְקוֹ הַמַּגִּיעוֹ מֵהֶן – **[A Kohen] who transgresses [this commandment] and does not eat the portion [of a** *chatas* **or** *asham***] that he has received,** בִּזְמַן הַמֻּגְבָּל לוֹ – **in the time prescribed for it** to be eaten, בִּטֵּל עֲשֵׂה – **has violated a mitzvah-obligation.**[21] וְנֶעֱנָשׁ עוֹד מִצַּד כַּפָּרַת הַבְּעָלִים שֶׁתְּלוּיָה בּוֹ – **And,** aside from the Heavenly punishment that he incurs for violating Hashem's commandment, **he will additionally be punished on account of** failing to complete **the owners' atonement, which was contingent upon [his consumption]** of the meat, כְּמוֹ שֶׁאָמַרְנוּ – **as we have said.**[22]

### ~ Dispute Regarding the Mitzvah ~

Chinuch has followed *Rambam* (*Sefer HaMitzvos, Asei* 89) in counting the consumption of *kodshei kodashim* as a distinct mitzvah, independent of the mitzvah to perform the actual *avodah*. He now cites a dissenting opinion:

וְהָרַמְבַּ״ן זִכְרוֹנוֹ לִבְרָכָה לֹא יִמְנֶה מִצְוָה זוֹ – ***Ramban,* of blessed memory, does not count this mitzvah** as one of the 613 Mitzvos, כִּי אָמַר שֶׁזֶּה חֵלֶק מֵחֶלְקֵי מִצְוַת הַקָּרְבָּנוֹת הוּא – **because [*Ramban*] has said** (glosses to *Sefer HaMitzvos,* end of *Shoresh* 12) **that this** (the consumption of sacrificial meat by the Kohanim) **is but one detail among the** many **details of the** overall **mitzvah of** performing all the procedures of **the** various **offerings.**[23]

---

### NOTES

*asham*, including some details about their consumption, are set forth in Mitzvos 138, 140, and 446. Details regarding the consumption of the Kohanim's portions of *kodashim kalim* are provided in Mitzvah 141. The laws regarding the consumption of all types of *kodashim* are codified by *Rambam* in *Hil. Maaseh HaKorbanos* Ch. 10.

20. Only male Kohanim are *permitted* to eat the meat of *kodshei kodashim* offerings (*Leviticus* 6:19,7:6). Hence, only male Kohanim are subject to our mitzvah, which *commands* that these offerings be eaten (*Sefer HaMitzvos, Asei* 89; *Radvaz, Hil. Maaseh HaKorbanos* 10:1). [As mentioned in note 13, the *commandment* contained here pertains specifically to *kodshei kodashim* (see *Minchas Yitzchak;* cf. *Minchas Chinuch* §1).]

21. As has been mentioned (note 13), *Rambam* observes that the Torah commands the Kohanim to eat their portions of *kodshei kodashim* (i.e., the *chatas* and *asham*), but never *commands* them to eat their portions of *kodashim kalim* or *terumah*, so while the consumption of those sacred foods is meritorious, as an adjunct to our mitzvah, it is not a mitzvah-*obligation*. It follows that if a Kohen neglects to eat a portion of *kodashim kalim* or *terumah* that he receives, he has not *transgressed* anything, but has merely forfeited the opportunity to merit a mitzvah (*Minchas Yitzchak;* see also *Minchas Soless;* see, however, *Minchas Chinuch* §1).

22. Chinuch implies that even if another Kohen ate a portion, by this Kohen neglecting to eat *his* portion he withholds complete atonement from the owner. Thus, full atonement is contingent upon consumption of *all* the meat.

23. *Ramban* asserts that the mitzvah upon Kohanim to perform the *avodah* of the various offerings encompasses all the associated details, including — as Chinuch explains — the consumption of *kodshei kodashim* meat. See the following note.

[*Ramban* actually disputes *Rambam* on two points: (1) *Rambam* reckons the sacrificial procedure of each offering (e.g., *chatas, olah*) as a separate mitzvah (see *Sefer HaMitzvos, Asei* 63-67), whereas *Ramban* argues (beginning of *Shoresh* 12) that there is but a single broad mitzvah-obligation to make *all* the offerings in the proper manner — a *chatas* according to the laws of *chatas,* an *olah* according to the laws of *olah,* and so forth. (2) *Rambam* counts the consumption of *kodshei kodashim* as a distinct mitzvah (*Asei* 89), independent of the mitzvah to perform the actual *avodah* of each offering, whereas *Ramban* argues (end of *Shoresh* 12) that it is subsumed in the general mitzvah to perform the *avodah*. Thus, *Ramban* maintains that there is but one mitzvah that encompasses the *avodah* and consumption of the various offerings.]

# TETZAVEH / MITZVAH 102: TO EAT THE MEAT OF THE CHATAS AND ASHAM OFFERINGS

הוּא²³, שֶׁצִוָּה הַשֵּׁם יִתְבָּרַךְ בָּהֶם מִי יֹאכְלֵם וּלְמִי יִהְיוּ, וְהָאֱמֶת שֶׁהַכַּפָּרָה תְּלוּיָה בָּזֶה²⁴.

שֶׁצִוָּה הַשֵּׁם יִתְבָּרַךְ בָּהֶם — **For,** as *Ramban* explains, among the laws of the offerings, **Hashem, blessed be He, has commanded** us **regarding them** מִי יֹאכְלֵם וּלְמִי יִהְיוּ — **who shall eat them and to whom they shall belong;** וְהָאֱמֶת שֶׁהַכַּפָּרָה תְּלוּיָה בָּזֶה — **and,** *Ramban* concludes, **the truth is that the** complete **atonement** of the owners **is contingent upon this** (the Kohanim's consumption of the meat).[24]

---

NOTES

24. Chinuch understands *Ramban* to mean that since the owner's complete atonement is contingent upon the Kohanim's consumption, their consumption must not be an independent obligation, but rather, must be part of the general mitzvah-obligation to carry out all aspects of the atonement service. It should be noted, however, that *Ramban* does not state this explicitly, and other authorities dispute Chinuch's understanding of *Ramban's* opinion. For discussion of this matter, see Insight A.

---

◆§ **Insight A: Ramban's Opinion Regarding Our Mitzvah**

Chinuch concludes with the assertion that *Ramban* does not count the obligation to eat *kodshei kodashim* as a distinct mitzvah-obligation, for he considers it part of the larger mitzvah of performing *all* aspects of the *avodah* in accordance with the stated laws. While Chinuch bases this assertion on *Ramban's* words in his glosses to *Sefer HaMitzvos* (end of *Shoresh* 12), *Ramban* does not state this explicitly. *Ramban* there actually discusses the owner's obligation to give the Kohanim the meat of the offerings. He explains that although there are mitzvah-obligations to give certain gifts to Kohanim (see Mitzvos 506, 508), there is no distinct mitzvah-obligation to *give* them their portions of the offerings. Rather, since the owner's atonement is contingent upon the Kohanim's consumption of the meat, giving them the meat is one of the procedures of the offering, and is part of the general mitzvah to perform all those procedures properly. Chinuch understands *Ramban* to mean that the Kohanim's consumption, too, is therefore subsumed in the larger mitzvah that encompasses all aspects of the *avodah*.

While Chinuch's inference seems logical, there is a serious difficulty with this understanding of *Ramban's* position. At the end of *Sefer HaMitzvos*, *Ramban* lists the mitzvos that he deleted from *Rambam's* count, and there he makes no mention of deleting the mitzvah upon the Kohanim to eat *kodshei kodashim*. How, then, can Chinuch state that *Ramban* deletes this mitzvah from the count? (*Maayan HaChochmah*; *Malbim*, Exodus 29:33).

Chinuch's view may be resolved as follows: In *Ramban's* list of mitzvah-obligations that he *added* to *Rambam's* count (*Sefer HaMitzvos*, end of *Mitzvos Asei*), *Ramban* includes (*Added Asei* 1) the obligation to eat *maaser sheni* and *kodashim kalim* offerings in Jerusalem (*Deuteronomy* 14:32; see above, end of note 13). *Ramban* explains that just as *Rambam* counts the obligation upon Kohanim to eat their portions of *kodshei kodashim* as a mitzvah, he (*Ramban*) counts the obligation upon the *owners* to eat their portions of *maaser sheni* and *kodashim kalim* as a mitzvah. *Ramban* concludes "and it seems that these are counted as *two* mitzvos" — meaning that the consumption of *maaser sheni* and the consumption of *kodashim kalim* constitute separate mitzvah-obligations. It emerges that in his "*Added Asei* 1," *Ramban* actually adds *two* mitzvah-obligations. Why does he count them as *one* added mitzvah? Apparently, the reason is because *Ramban* omits the mitzvah upon Kohanim to eat *kodshei kodashim*, which *Rambam* counted! This is replaced with the mitzvah upon the owners to eat *kodashim kalim*, with the result that *Ramban* has, in counting this verse, added only a single mitzvah — eating *maaser sheni* — to the total (*Minchas Yitzchak*, *Minchah Chadashah*).

This, however, begs the question: Why would *Ramban* count the owner's consumption of *kodashim kalim* as a mitzvah yet decline to count the Kohanim's consumption of *kodshei kodashim*? The answer lies in the reason Chinuch (quoting *Ramban*) gives for omitting the Kohanim's consumption of *kodshei kodashim*: Since the owners' complete atonement is dependent upon the Kohanim's consumption of the meat, their consumption *cannot* be counted as a separate mitzvah, for it is included in the general requirement to perform *all* details of the *avodah* that bring about

atonement (see *Yoma* 68b [beginning of Ch. 7] with *Rabbeinu Chananel*). The owner's consumption of *kodashim kalim*, however, does not bring about atonement, and is unrelated to the *avodah* of the offering (see note 13). Rather, it constitutes a rite in and of itself, which the Torah has commanded the owner to fulfill, *independent* of the Kohen's performance of the offering service. Hence, it can be — and is — counted as a separate mitzvah.

For further discussion of this subject, see *Minchas Chinuch* to Added *Mitzvos of Ramban*, Mitzvah 1 §2; *Tzlach, Beitzah* 19b ד"ה ומדי עסקי; *Likkutei Halachos, Pesachim* 59a; *Aruch HaShulchan HeAsid* 81:1-5.

### ◆§ Insight B: The Mitzvah That Chinuch Omitted

The verse that is the source of our mitzvah (*Exodus* 29:33) contains two statements: (1) וְאָכְלוּ אֹתָם אֲשֶׁר כֻּפַּר בָּהֶם לְמַלֵּא אֶת יָדָם לְקַדֵּשׁ אֹתָם, *They shall eat them so that atonement may be attained through them, to inaugurate them, to sanctify them;* (2) וְזָר לֹא יֹאכַל כִּי קֹדֶשׁ הֵם, *a non-Kohen shall not eat for they are holy.* Rambam, in *Sefer HaMitzvos*, counts these statements as two separate mitzvos. In *Asei* 89, he derives from the first part of the verse an *obligation* upon Kohanim to eat their portions of *kodshei kodashim* offerings; and in *Lo Saaseh* 148, he derives from the latter part of the verse a *prohibition* on a non-Kohen to eat of *kodshei kodashim* offerings (see also *Makkos* 18b). Chinuch, surprisingly, includes in his reckoning of the mitzvos only the obligation upon Kohanim to eat *kodshei kodashim*, but omits the prohibition on non-Kohanim to eat them (see *Mishneh LaMelech*, glosses to Mitzvah 487 [489 in early editions]).

Several commentators suggest that Chinuch understands the latter part of the verse as referring specifically to the *miluim* (inauguration) offerings, which are mentioned earlier in the passage (see the introduction to this mitzvah). The verse forbids a non-Kohen to eat *those* offerings, but it does not refer to any other offerings, even of *kodshei kodashim*. [Although a non-Kohen surely may not eat of *kodshei kodashim*, that is not the subject of this verse.] Since the prohibition of this verse applied only at the time that Aaron and his sons were inaugurated into the Temple service, but does not apply to later generations, it cannot be counted among the 613 Mitzvos [see *Sefer HaMitzvos, Shoresh* 3] (*Maayan HaChochmah, Maharam Schik*).

This explanation is unclear, however, for the first part of the verse also refers to the *miluim* offerings, yet since it states *"so that atonement may be attained through them,"* its directive is understood as applying to all offerings that atone — i.e., all *kodshei kodashim*. It follows that since the latter part of the verse similarly states *"for they are holy"* — meaning that they are *kodshei kodashim* (see *Rashi* ad loc.) — its directive should be understood as applying to all offerings of *kodshei kodashim*. This matter requires further study. [For a possible resolution, see *Maharam Schik*, Mitzvah 103.]

To compensate for his omission of this prohibition, Chinuch includes in his count of the 613 Mitzvos a prohibition that *Rambam* does not reckon. This is Mitzvah 487, which emerges from the verse (*Deuteronomy* 16:5) לֹא תוּכַל לִזְבֹּחַ אֶת הַפָּסַח בְּאַחַד שְׁעָרֶיךָ, *You may not slaughter the pesach offering in one of your cities*. Chinuch explains there that this constitutes a prohibition to make the *pesach* offering on a private *bamah* (altar), even during the pre-Temple period when other offerings were allowed to be brought on a *bamah*. For discussion of why *Rambam* does not count this as a mitzvah, see the Responsum of R' *Avraham ben HaRambam* printed in Frankel ed. of *Sefer HaMitzvos*, p. 544; *Mishneh LaMelech* ibid.; and *Maayan HaChochmah* to Mitzvah 487.

Regardless of *why* Chinuch disagrees with *Rambam* in these matters, his omission of the prohibition in our verse, and his addition of a prohibition that *Rambam* omitted, is perplexing. Chinuch states repeatedly in this work that he has exclusively followed *Rambam's* reckoning of the 613 mitzvos, as set forth in *Sefer HaMitzvos*, even in instances where he disagrees with *Rambam* (see Chinuch's introductory Order and Count of the Mitzvos, and Mitzvos 138, 153). Why would he veer from *Rambam's* view in this instance? Moreover, whatever his reasoning, how could he have failed to even mention this deviation from his policy? Why, at the end of Mitzvah 111, Chinuch takes pains to explain why he bases that mitzvah on a different verse than *Rambam* did. Surely, he ought to explain here why he completely disregards *Rambam's* reckoning of a mitzvah! The only plausible explanation seems to be that Chinuch's version of *Sefer HaMitzvos* had a variant text that provided the basis for his reckoning. See Introduction to Heller ed. of *Sefer HaMitzvos* regarding Chinuch's text of that work; see also *R' Daniel HaBavli's* Inquiry to *R' Avraham ben HaRambam*, cited in Frankel ed. of *Sefer HaMitzvos*, pp. 542-543.

# TETZAVEH / MITZVAH 103: THE OBLIGATION TO OFFER THE INCENSE

## ❦ מִצְוָה קג: מִצְוַת הַקְטָרַת קְטֹרֶת ❦

שֶׁנִּצְטַוּוּ הַכֹּהֲנִים[1] לְהַקְטִיר קְטֹרֶת סַמִּים פַּעֲמַיִם בְּכָל יוֹם עַל מִזְבַּח הַזָּהָב,[2] שֶׁנֶּאֱמַר (שמות ל׳, ז׳) וְהִקְטִיר עָלָיו אַהֲרֹן קְטֹרֶת סַמִּים בַּבֹּקֶר בַּבֹּקֶר בְּהֵיטִיבוֹ אֶת הַנֵּרֹת וְגוֹ׳. וּבְכָל שָׁנָה וְשָׁנָה מִצְוָה עֲלֵיהֶם לַעֲשׂוֹת מִמֶּנָּה כְּדֵי לְהַקְטִיר בָּהּ כְּמוֹ שֶׁאָמַרְנוּ.[3]

---

## ❦ Mitzvah 103 ❦
## The Obligation [Upon the Kohanim] to Offer the Incense

וְהִקְטִיר עָלָיו אַהֲרֹן קְטֹרֶת סַמִּים בַּבֹּקֶר בַּבֹּקֶר בְּהֵיטִיבוֹ אֶת הַנֵּרֹת יַקְטִירֶנָּה. וּבְהַעֲלֹת אַהֲרֹן אֶת הַנֵּרֹת בֵּין הָעַרְבַּיִם יַקְטִירֶנָּה קְטֹרֶת תָּמִיד לִפְנֵי ה׳ לְדֹרֹתֵיכֶם

*Aaron shall burn the spice incense upon it (the Golden Altar); every morning, when he tends the lamps he shall burn it. And when Aaron kindles the lamps in the afternoon he shall burn it, continual incense before HASHEM, for your generations (Exodus 30:7-8).*

**לְהַקְטִיר קְטֹרֶת סַמִּים פַּעֲמַיִם בְּכָל יוֹם עַל מִזְבַּח** שֶׁנִּצְטַוּוּ הַכֹּהֲנִים — **The Kohanim**[1] **are commanded הַזָּהָב — to burn** a portion of **spice incense** (*ketores*) **twice each day on the Golden Altar**,[2] **שֶׁנֶּאֱמַר — as it is stated** (*Exodus* 30:7): ״וְהִקְטִיר עָלָיו אַהֲרֹן קְטֹרֶת סַמִּים בַּבֹּקֶר בַּבֹּקֶר בְּהֵיטִיבוֹ אֶת הַנֵּרֹת וְגוֹ׳״ — *Aaron shall burn the spice incense upon it* (the Golden Altar); *every morning, when he tends the lamps he shall burn it. And when Aaron kindles the lamps in the afternoon he shall burn it,* **etc.**

Chinuch points out that there is another requirement associated with this mitzvah: **וּבְכָל שָׁנָה וְשָׁנָה מִצְוָה עֲלֵיהֶם — Also, each and every year it is a mitzvah upon [the Kohanim] לַעֲשׂוֹת מִמֶּנָּה כְּדֵי לְהַקְטִיר בָּהּ — to produce** a quantity **of [***ketores***] sufficient** for them **to burn** the daily portions on the Altar throughout that year, **כְּמוֹ שֶׁאָמַרְנוּ — in accordance with** the obligation **that we have** just **mentioned.**[3]

---

### NOTES

1. Chinuch implies that this mitzvah is solely the obligation of the Kohanim, not an obligation of the general community that is *carried out* by the Kohanim who serve in the *Beis HaMikdash* as emissaries of the nation. See Insight A for discussion of this point.

2. The "Golden Altar" was a wooden altar plated with gold, located inside the *Heichal* (Temple Sanctuary), and was also known as the Inner Altar. It was used mainly for the daily *ketores* service, though the blood of certain offerings (including those of the Yom Kippur service) was sprinkled on it. The blood of the vast majority of offerings was applied to the Outer Altar (made of stone), which was located in the Temple Courtyard, and the sacrificial parts of animal, bird, and meal offerings were burned exclusively on the Outer Altar.

3. Chinuch will state below that the amount of *ketores* offered each day equaled the weight of 100 *dinars*, also known as a "*maneh*" (see below, note 17). Half of this amount was burned on the Golden Altar in the morning and half in the afternoon. The recipe for *ketores* called for mixing various spices in specific amounts, and the total amount of spice in the mixture was 368 *maneh*. Thus, the annual production provided a *maneh* for each of the 365 days of the solar year, and three additional *maneh* from which the Kohen Gadol would scoop up a double handful on Yom Kippur to use in that day's special *ketores* service in the Holy of Holies (*Kereisos* 6a; *Rambam, Hil. Klei Hamikdash* 2:3). [See *Kereisos* 6a-b for discussion of what was done with the remainder of those three *maneh*.]

Although it was preferable that the entire annual amount be produced at once (see Mitzvah 110, at note 7), if a smaller amount of *ketores* was mixed it was valid, as long as it contained the spices in the correct proportions (*Kereisos* 6b). *Rashi* (ad loc. ד״ה במתכונתה) maintains that, at a minimum, the amount produced had to measure a *maneh*, sufficient for one entire day's *ketores* offerings. *Rambam* (ibid. 2:8), however, rules that it sufficed to produce a half-*maneh* recipe, sufficient for either the morning or the afternoon burning. In fact, it seems from *Rambam* (ibid. 2:9 and *Commentary to Kereisos* 1:1) that the *ketores* was valid even if produced in small batches of less than a half-*maneh*

## 282 ❏ תצוה / מצוה קג: מצות הקטרת קטרת

וַעֲשִׂיָּתָהּ וְהַמִּצְוָה שֶׁנַּעֲשֵׂית בָּהּ בְּכָל יוֹם נֶחְשָׁב לְמִצְוָה אַחַת, לְפִי שֶׁסּוֹף מִצְוַת עֲשִׂיָּתָהּ אֵינָהּ אֶלָּא לְהַקְטִיר בָּהּ, וְאַף עַל פִּי שֶׁשְּׁנֵי כְתוּבִים שֶׁל מִצְוָה מָצָאנוּ בֵּין הָעֲשִׂיָּה וְהַהַקְטָרָה, שֶׁנֶּאֱמַר בְּסֵדֶר כִּי תִשָּׂא (שם ל׳, ל״ד) קַח לְךָ סַמִּים וְגוֹ׳ עַל עֲשִׂיָּתָהּ, וְכָאן כָּתוּב וְהִקְטִיר עָלָיו אַהֲרֹן וְגוֹ׳, אַף עַל פִּי כֵן רָאִיתִי לְמְחַשְּׁבֵי הַמִּצְוֹת שֶׁחוֹשְׁבִין הַכֹּל מִצְוָה אַחַת, אֵין בָּזֶה מַחֲלֹקֶת בֵּינֵיהֶם כְּלָל.[4]

אֲבָל יַחְלְקוּ בָּהּ בְּעִנְיָן אַחֵר, כִּי הָרַמְבַּ״ם זִכְרוֹנוֹ לִבְרָכָה קְטֹרֶת יְמַנֶּה שֶׁל שַׁחֲרִית וְשֶׁל עַרְבִית מִצְוָה אַחַת,[5] וְהָרַמְבַּ״ן זִכְרוֹנוֹ לִבְרָכָה כָּתַב שֶׁהֵן נִמְנוֹת שְׁתַּיִם, וּרְאָיוֹתָיו בְּסִפְרוֹ.[6]

---

Chinuch addresses whether the production of *ketores* should be enumerated as a separate mitzvah: וַעֲשִׂיָּתָהּ וְהַמִּצְוָה שֶׁנַּעֲשֵׂית בָּהּ בְּכָל יוֹם נֶחְשָׁב לְמִצְוָה אַחַת — **However, the production of [the *ketores*] and the mitzvah** of burning **that was performed with it daily are considered one mitzvah**-obligation in the count of the 613 Mitzvos, לְפִי שֶׁסּוֹף מִצְוַת עֲשִׂיָּתָהּ אֵינָהּ אֶלָּא לְהַקְטִיר בָּהּ — **because the ultimate** purpose **of the mitzvah to produce [the *ketores*] is simply to burn it** upon the Golden Altar. וְאַף עַל פִּי שֶׁשְּׁנֵי כְתוּבִים שֶׁל מִצְוָה מָצָאנוּ בֵּין הָעֲשִׂיָּה וְהַהַקְטָרָה — **Thus, although we find two** separate **verses containing commands regarding the production and the burning** of the *ketores*, שֶׁנֶּאֱמַר בְּסֵדֶר כִּי תִשָּׂא ״קַח לְךָ סַמִּים וְגוֹ׳ ״ עַל עֲשִׂיָּתָהּ — **as it is stated in *Parashas Ki Sisa*** (ibid 30:34) ***Take for yourself spices***, **etc., referring to** the mitzvah of **producing [the *ketores*]**, וְכָאן כָּתוּב ״וְהִקְטִיר עָלָיו אַהֲרֹן וְגוֹ׳ ״ — **and it is written here,** in *Parashas Tetzaveh*, ***Aaron shall burn the spice incense upon it*** **etc.**, referring to the mitzvah of burning the *ketores*, אַף עַל פִּי כֵן רָאִיתִי לְמְחַשְּׁבֵי הַמִּצְוֹת שֶׁחוֹשְׁבִין הַכֹּל מִצְוָה אַחַת — **nevertheless, I have seen that the [authorities] who reckon the 613 mitzvos are unanimous in that they count the entire matter** of the *ketores* as only **one mitzvah;** אֵין בָּזֶה מַחֲלֹקֶת בֵּינֵיהֶם כְּלָל — **there is no disagreement between them whatsoever** regarding this point.[4]

### ☞ Dispute Regarding the Mitzvah ☜

אֲבָל יַחְלְקוּ בָּהּ בְּעִנְיָן אַחֵר — **There is, however, disagreement among [the authorities] in regard to a different matter;** כִּי הָרַמְבַּ״ם זִכְרוֹנוֹ לִבְרָכָה קְטֹרֶת יְמַנֶּה שֶׁל שַׁחֲרִית וְשֶׁל עַרְבִית מִצְוָה אַחַת — **for *Rambam*, of blessed memory** (*Sefer HaMitzvos*, Asei 28; *Hil. Temidin U'Mussafin* 3:1), **counts the *ketores*** offering **of the morning and** the *ketores* offering **of the afternoon as a single mitzvah**,[5] וְהָרַמְבַּ״ן זִכְרוֹנוֹ לִבְרָכָה כָּתַב שֶׁהֵן נִמְנוֹת שְׁתַּיִם — **but *Ramban*, of blessed memory, writes that [the two offerings] are counted as two** separate mitzvos, וּרְאָיוֹתָיו בְּסִפְרוֹ — **and his proofs are** set forth **in his book** (i.e., his glosses to *Sefer HaMitzvos*).[6]

---

### NOTES

each (*Chidushei HaGriz, Hil. Klei HaMikdash* 2:8). This is also implied by Chinuch below, in Mitzvah 110. For further discussion, see Mitzvah 110 note 6 and the sources cited there.

It is noteworthy that while only Kohanim could perform the burning of the *ketores*, as this was considered an *avodah* (Temple service; pl. *avodos*), even non-Kohanim could mix the spices to produce the *ketores* (*Minchas Chinuch* §11). Nevertheless, the compounding had to take place within the precincts of the Temple Courtyard (*Kereisos* 6a; *Rambam* ibid. 2:6). In practice, the *ketores* was prepared in a special chamber of the Temple called *Beis Avtinas*, named for the family in charge of its preparation (see *Yoma* 18b-19a with *Rashi*). See further below, Mitzvah 110 note 7.

4. In *Sefer HaMitzvos*, *Shoresh* 10, *Rambam* cites this mitzvah as illustrative of the general rule that whenever a commandment involves a preparatory step toward fulfilling a mitzvah, that preparatory step is not reckoned as a separate mitzvah. *Ramban* ad loc. agrees with *Rambam* regarding this point (see also *Smag*, *Asei* 167; see *Kinas Soferim* to *Shoresh* 10 for further discussion).

Interestingly, *Rambam* remarks that *Halachos Gedolos* does count preparatory requirements as separate mitzvos, and that he (*Rambam*) rejects this view. *Ramban*, however, responds that *Rambam* misunderstood the intent of *Halachos Gedolos*, for he too does not mean to count preparatory requirements as separate mitzvos. This, apparently, is why Chinuch emphasizes that there is no dispute at all regarding this matter.

5. This is also the opinion of *Smag*, *Aseh* 167 and others (see *Bris Moshe* to *Smag*).

6. See *Ramban's* list of *Mitzvos Omitted by Rambam* ד״ה ואתה אם תבין (at the end of *Sefer HaMitzvos*, p. 412 in

# TETZAVEH / MITZVAH 103: THE OBLIGATION TO OFFER THE INCENSE

מִשָּׁרְשֵׁי מִצְוָה זוֹ, גַּם כֵּן[7] לְהַגְדִּיל כְּבוֹד הַבַּיִת וְלִהְיוֹת מַעֲלָתוֹ וּמוֹרָאוֹ עַל פְּנֵי[8] כָּל אָדָם, וְאִי אֶפְשָׁר לְהַגְדִּיל דָּבָר בְּלֵב בֶּן אָדָם וּמַחֲשַׁבְתּוֹ רַק בִּדְבָרִים שֶׁהוּא חוֹשֵׁב אוֹתָם לִגְדֻלָּה וְיִמָּצֵא בָּהֶם תַּעֲנוּג וְשִׂמְחָה, וְיָדוּעַ כִּי עִנְיַן הָרֵיחַ הַטּוֹב הוּא דָּבָר שֶׁנֶּפֶשׁ אָדָם נֶהֱנֵית בּוֹ וּמִתְאַוָּה אֵלָיו וּמוֹשֵׁךְ הַלֵּב הַרְבֵּה, וְרֵיחַ קְטֹרֶת הָיָה הַטּוֹב שֶׁאֶפְשָׁר לַעֲשׂוֹת עַל יְדֵי אָדָם,[9] עַד שֶׁאָמְרוּ זִכְרוֹנָם לִבְרָכָה בְּפֶרֶק אָמַר לָהֶם הַמְמֻנֶּה (תמיד פ״ג דף ל׳ ע״ב, יומא דף ל״ט ע״ב)[10], כִּי מְרִיחוֹ הָיוּ מְרִיחִין בּוֹ בִּשְׁעַת הַקְטָרָה מֵרֵיחוֹ עַד יְרוּשָׁלַיִם.[11]

---

### ☞ Underlying Purpose of the Mitzvah ☜

לְהַגְדִּיל — מִשָּׁרְשֵׁי מִצְוָה זוֹ גַּם כֵּן — **Among the underlying purposes of this mitzvah, too,**[7] כְּבוֹד הַבַּיִת וְלִהְיוֹת מַעֲלָתוֹ וּמוֹרָאוֹ עַל פְּנֵי כָּל אָדָם — **is to increase the grandeur of the Temple, so that** a sense of **its loftiness and awesomeness will be** established in the consciousness[8] **of every person.** וְאִי אֶפְשָׁר לְהַגְדִּיל דָּבָר בְּלֵב בֶּן אָדָם וּמַחֲשַׁבְתּוֹ — **Now, it is impossible to increase** the appreciation of **an object in man's heart and his thoughts** רַק בִּדְבָרִים שֶׁהוּא חוֹשֵׁב אוֹתָם לִגְדֻלָּה — **except by** enhancing it with **things that he considers glorious,** בָּהֶם תַּעֲנוּג וְשִׂמְחָה — **and in which he finds pleasure and joy;** וְיָדוּעַ כִּי עִנְיַן הָרֵיחַ הַטּוֹב הוּא — **and it is** well **known that a pleasant aroma is something** דָּבָר שֶׁנֶּפֶשׁ אָדָם נֶהֱנֵית בּוֹ וּמִתְאַוָּה אֵלָיו — **that the soul of man enjoys and desires** וּמוֹשֵׁךְ הַלֵּב הַרְבֵּה — **and** that **it attracts his heart very much.** The Kohanim are therefore commanded to burn the *ketores* twice daily, וְרֵיחַ קְטֹרֶת הָיָה הַטּוֹב שֶׁאֶפְשָׁר לַעֲשׂוֹת עַל יְדֵי אָדָם — for **the aroma of the *ketores* was the most pleasant** aroma **that can be produced by man.** The presence of this wonderful fragrance throughout the Temple grounds caused people to be attracted to the Temple and to respect it.[9] עַד שֶׁאָמְרוּ זִכְרוֹנָם לִבְרָכָה בְּפֶרֶק אָמַר לָהֶם הַמְמֻנֶּה — The aroma of the *ketores* was so intense and fragrant that [the Sages], of blessed memory, said in Tractate *Tamid*, **Chapter *Amar Lahem HaMemuneh*** (*Tamid* 30b),[10] כִּי מְרִיחוֹ הָיוּ מְרִיחִין בּוֹ בִּשְׁעַת הַקְטָרָה — **that they would smell the aroma of [the *ketores*], at the time of its burning,** מֵרֵיחוֹ עַד יְרוּשָׁלַיִם — **all the way from Jericho to Jerusalem.**[11]

---

### NOTES

Frankel ed.). *Ramban* argues that the morning and afternoon *ketores* offerings should be counted as separate mitzvos because they are performed at different times, and they are not dependent on each other, i.e., if one is omitted the other must still be performed (see *Chinuch* below, at note 14). [Based on this reasoning, *Ramban* also counts the morning and afternoon *tamid* offerings, and the morning and evening *Shema* recitations, as separate mitzvos. See further, *Ramban* to *Shoresh* 11, and *Kinas Soferim* to *Asei* 39.]

7. *Chinuch* apparently means that this mitzvah has the same underlying purpose as the one he set forth for Mitzvah 98 (the first mitzvah in this *Parashah*).

8. Literally, *upon the face*.

9. *Rambam* makes this point in *Moreh Nevuchim* 3:45, where he elaborates on how the utensils of the *Beis HaMikdash* and the laws relating to it promote feelings of awe and exaltedness. With respect to the *ketores*, he adds another dimension: Since many animal and bird offerings were slaughtered and eviscerated in the *Beis HaMikdash* each day, and their fats and flesh were burned on the Outer Altar, without any intervention the *Beis HaMikdash* might have the unpleasant smell of a meat market. The Torah commanded that the *ketores* be offered twice daily, in the morning and afternoon, to provide a pleasant aroma to the *Beis HaMikdash* and the clothing of all who work there, ensuring that people would be attracted to the *Beis HaMikdash*, and not repulsed by the odor of animal innards. For further discussion of the purpose of the pleasant smell, see Insight B.

10. The reference is to Chapter 3 of Tractate *Tamid*, and not the chapter by the same name in Tractate *Yoma* (Ch. 3). There is, however, a similar statement in Chapter 4 of *Yoma* (39b); see the following note.

11. While this alone does not prove that the scent was pleasant, the fact that the Gemara dwells on this indicates that it was desirable for the aroma to travel that great distance. In *Yoma* (ibid.), the Gemara states explicitly that the women in Jericho did not have to perfume themselves, because the fragrance of the *ketores* offered in the Temple wafted over their city and served to perfume them.

## 284 ❑ תצוה / מצוה קג: מצות הקטרת קטרת

מִדִּינֵי הַמִּצְוָה מַה שֶּׁאָמְרוּ (עיין כריתות דף ו' ע"א) שֶׁפִּטּוּם הַקְּטֹרֶת הָיָה (חמשה) [אַחַד] עָשָׂר סַמָּנִין אַרְבָּעָה מֵהֶן מְפֹרָשִׁין בַּתּוֹרָה (ואחד עשר) [וְשִׁבְעָה] קַבָּלָה,[12] וּמַה שֶּׁאָמְרוּ שֶׁהַקְּטֹרֶת נַעֲשֵׂית בֵּין עַל יְדֵי כֹהֵן גָּדוֹל אוֹ הֶדְיוֹט,[13] וְאָמְרוּ שֶׁאִם לֹא הִקְטִיר בַּבֹּקֶר מַקְטִיר בֵּין הָעַרְבַּיִם[14] כָּל הַשִּׁעוּר שֶׁל יוֹם אֶחָד[15] שֶׁהוּא מִשְׁקַל

---

### ⌘ Laws of the Mitzvah ⌘

**מִדִּינֵי הַמִּצְוָה** — Among the laws of the mitzvah is **מַה שֶּׁאָמְרוּ** — that which [the Sages] said (see *Kereisos* 6a), **שֶׁפִּטּוּם הַקְּטֹרֶת הָיָה (חמשה) [אַחַד] עָשָׂר סַמָּנִין** — that the *ketores* mixture consisted of eleven spices, **אַרְבָּעָה מֵהֶן מְפֹרָשִׁין בַּתּוֹרָה** — four of which are explicitly enumerated in the Torah, **(ואחד עשר) [וְשִׁבְעָה] קַבָּלָה** — and the other seven of which are known through Oral Tradition.[12] **וּמַה שֶּׁאָמְרוּ** — Also included is that which [the Sages] said (see Mishnah, *Yoma* 26a), **שֶׁהַקְּטֹרֶת נַעֲשֵׂית** — **בֵּין עַל יְדֵי כֹהֵן גָּדוֹל אוֹ הֶדְיוֹט** — that the daily burning of the *ketores* may be performed by either the Kohen Gadol or an ordinary [Kohen].[13] **וְאָמְרוּ** — [The Sages] further stated (Mishnah, *Menachos* 49a), **שֶׁאִם לֹא הִקְטִיר בַּבֹּקֶר** — that if [a Kohen] did not perform the burning of *ketores* in the morning, **מַקְטִיר בֵּין הָעַרְבַּיִם** — he may perform the burning in the afternoon,[14] **כָּל הַשִּׁעוּר שֶׁל יוֹם אֶחָד** — and, in that case, in the afternoon he burns the total amount required for one day,[15]

---

### NOTES

12. [The emendations of the text follow the first printed edition of Chinuch (Venice 1523) and *Minchas Chinuch* §2, who notes that the standard printed version is obviously erroneous; see *Kereisos* 6b and *Rambam, Hil. Klei HaMikdash* 2:1-3.]

The four spices mentioned in the Torah (*Exodus* 30:34) are: [צֳרִי] נָטָף, *stacte*; [צִפֹּרֶן] שְׁחֵלֶת, *onycha*; חֶלְבְּנָה, *galbanum*; and לְבֹנָה, *frankincense*. The seven known through Oral Tradition are: מוֹר, *myrrh* (but see Mitzvah 107 note 12); קְצִיעָה, *cassia*; שִׁבֹּלֶת נֵרְדְּ, *spike-lavender*; כַּרְכֹּם, *saffron*; קוֹשְׁטְ, *costus*; קִלּוּפָה, *aromatic bark*; and קִנָּמוֹן, *cinnamon* (*Kereisos* 6a, recited in the *Pittum HaKetores* in the Siddur; see there for the measure of each spice in the mixture). [It is noteworthy that *galbanaum* had a foul aroma, and from its inclusion in the *ketores* the Sages (ibid. 6b) derive that even sinners should be included in our communal prayers. Thus, the *ketores* expresses the concept of Jewish unity.]

*Rambam* (ibid.) and *Chinuch* indicate that the *ketores* must contain specifically these eleven spices. *Rashi* (*Kereisos* 6b ד"ה י"א סמנים), however, while agreeing that the Oral Tradition dictates that the *ketores* contain eleven spices, maintains that only the four spices mentioned explicitly in the Torah are mandatory ingredients, but the other seven may consist of any aromatic substances, as long as the resultant mixture produces smoke that rises in a straight column (see also *Ramban, Exodus* 30:34).

13. Although the verse cited at the beginning of this mitzvah states that Aaron (who was Kohen Gadol) shall burn the *ketores* daily, it does not mean to exclude an ordinary Kohen from performing this service. [See *Ramban, Exodus* 30:7, who discusses why the Torah mentions Aaron.] In practice, each day lots were cast to determine which Kohen would merit the right to burn the *ketores*. Only Kohanim who had never done this *avodah* were permitted to participate in the lot, because anyone who merited performing the *ketores* service would become wealthy, and it was desired that this benefit be spread among as many people as possible (see *Yoma* 26a). See Insight B for further discussion.

14. Chinuch encapsulates two points in this phrase: (1) If the morning *ketores* burning was omitted, they still perform the afternoon burning, for the two burnings are not interdependent (see Mishnah, *Menachos* 49a). (2) If the specific Kohen who won the right to perform the morning *ketores* service was negligent and failed to perform it, he is not penalized from entering the lottery for the afternoon service (see *Rambam, Hil. Temidin U'Mussafin* 4:8), and if he wins that lottery he may perform the afternoon burning. There was no need to impose a penalty, for since this service brought wealth in its wake, the Kohanim were eager to perform it, so there was no concern that others would also be negligent (see *Radvaz* to *Hil. Temidin U'Mussafin* 3:1).

15. This is a matter of dispute in the Mishnah, *Menachos* 49a, and Chinuch rules in accordance with the Tanna R' Shimon, who maintains that the full amount is offered.

[*Rambam's* opinion regarding this matter is not entirely clear. Some commentators understand *Rambam* (*Hil. Temidin U'Mussafin* 3:1) as ruling that if the morning *ketores* was not offered, they offer only the usual amount in the afternoon, not the full amount for the day (see *Radvaz* and *Lechem Mishneh* ad loc.). Others understand *Rambam* to mean that they offer the full daily complement in the afternoon (*Batei Keneisiyos, Beis Avtinas* §39 [Vol. I, p. 56b ד"ה וחדשות]). Since Chinuch generally follows *Rambam's* opinion, it would seem that he understands *Rambam* in accordance with the latter view (cf. *Minchas Chinuch* §10).]

מֵאָה דִינָרִין[16], וּמִשְׁקַל הַדִּינָר יָדוּעַ[17], וּבְכָל יוֹם הָיָה מַקְטִיר חֶצְיָן בַּבֹּקֶר וְחֶצְיָן בָּעֶרֶב אַחַר תָּמִיד שֶׁל בֵּין הָעַרְבַּיִם[18], קֹדֶם הֲטָבַת הַנֵּרוֹת כֻּלָּן, אַחַר הֲטָבַת חָמֵשׁ פְּתִילוֹת מֵהֶן, כִּי לֹא הָיָה מַדְלִיקָן רְצוּפִין[19]. וְכָךְ הָיוּ עוֹשִׂין עִנְיָן זֶה, כֹּהֵן שֶׁזָּכָה לְהַקְטִיר הַקְּטֹרֶת[20] נוֹטֵל כְּלִי מָלֵא קְטֹרֶת גָּדוּשׁ וּטְנִי שְׁמוֹ[21], וּפוֹרְשִׁין כָּל הָעָם מִן הַהֵיכָל[22] וּמִבֵּין הָאוּלָם וְלַמִּזְבֵּחַ[23],

---

וּמִשְׁקַל – שֶׁהוּא מִשְׁקַל מֵאָה דִינָרִין – **which is the weight of one hundred *dinarim*, or one *maneh*;**[16] הַדִּינָר יָדוּעַ – **and the weight of a *dinar* is well known.**[17]

Chinuch now addresses the specific requirements and time frame of the mitzvah:

וּבְכָל יוֹם הָיָה מַקְטִיר חֶצְיָן בַּבֹּקֶר – **Each day [the Kohen] would offer half of [the daily portion of *ketores*]** (i.e., a half-*maneh*) **in the morning,** וְחֶצְיָן בָּעֶרֶב אַחַר תָּמִיד שֶׁל בֵּין הָעַרְבַּיִם – **and half of it in the afternoon, after** the service of **the afternoon *tamid* offering.**[18] קֹדֶם הֲטָבַת הַנֵּרוֹת כֻּלָּן – Both in the morning and in the afternoon, the *ketores* would be offered **before the tending of all the lamps** of the Menorah; אַחַר הֲטָבַת חָמֵשׁ פְּתִילוֹת מֵהֶן – that is, it was offered **after the tending of five wicks of [the seven Menorah lamps],** but before the tending of the last two, כִּי לֹא הָיָה מַדְלִיקָן רְצוּפִין – **for [the lamps] were not kindled consecutively.**[19]

Chinuch describes the *ketores* service:

וְכָךְ הָיוּ עוֹשִׂין עִנְיָן זֶה – **This is how this procedure was performed:** כֹּהֵן שֶׁזָּכָה לְהַקְטִיר הַקְּטֹרֶת – **The Kohen who won the right to** perform the mitzvah of **burning the *ketores*** [20] נוֹטֵל כְּלִי מָלֵא קְטֹרֶת גָּדוּשׁ וּטְנִי שְׁמוֹ – **takes a vessel that is full and overflowing with *ketores*, and [the vessel] is called a *teni*,**[21] וּפוֹרְשִׁין כָּל הָעָם מִן הַהֵיכָל וּמִבֵּין הָאוּלָם וְלַמִּזְבֵּחַ – **and all the people** other than that Kohen **remove themselves from the *Heichal* (Sanctuary and its Antechamber**[22]**), as well as** the area of the Courtyard **between the *Ulam* (Antechamber) and the** Outer **Altar,**[23]

---

NOTES

16. Ordinarily, they would burn half a *maneh* of *ketores* in the morning and half a *maneh* in the afternoon (see above, note 3, and Chinuch further). In the event that the morning *ketores* was not offered, they would burn the entire *maneh* in the afternoon.

17. A *dinar* was a silver coin that had the weight of 96 barleycorns (see *Rambam, Hil. Eruvin* 1:12). [In modern terms, this equals slightly less than five grams (see *Shiurin Shel Torah, Shiurei HaMitzvos* ד"ה פרוטה). Thus, a *maneh* (the total amount of *ketores* offered daily) equals nearly 500 grams, or slightly more than one pound.]

The *maneh* measure is not specified in the Torah. *Rashi* (*Zevachim* 109b ד"ה אמר רבה) states that under Biblical law it sufficed to burn a *kezayis* (olive's volume) of *ketores* in the morning and a *kezayis* in the afternoon, and it was the Sages who mandated that half a *maneh* be offered each time. *Tosafos* (*Kereisos* 6b ד"ה המפטם), however, state that the *maneh* measure is mandated Biblically, by *Halachah LeMoshe MiSinai*. For discussion, see *Mishneh LaMelech, Hil. Temidin U'Mussafin* 3:2, and *Minchas Chinuch* §5,8. See also the sources cited below, Mitzvah 110 note 6.

18. In the morning, as well, the *ketores* service came after the *tamid* service, but Chinuch does not need to mention this, since the morning *tamid* preceded all the other daily *avodos*. He does specify that in the afternoon the *ketores* followed the *tamid*, as this is a somewhat novel point, since other offerings generally could not be brought after the *tamid* (see Mitzvah 401).

19. We learned in Mitzvah 98 (see note 17 there) that, according to Chinuch, the Menorah lamps were cleaned out, prepared anew, and kindled twice daily, in the morning and in the afternoon. The Gemara (*Yoma* 33a-b) establishes that the Menorah service was performed in two stages, with another *avodah* intervening between the two stages: First, five lamps were cleaned and rekindled, then another *avodah* was performed, and only then were the remaining two lamps cleaned and rekindled (see there for the reason). It is a matter of dispute (*Yoma* 14b, 33b) which *avodah* intervened, but *Rambam* (*Hil. Temidin U'Mussafin* 6:3-4,11) rules in accordance with the opinion that the *ketores* service was performed in the midst of the Menorah service, both in the morning and in the afternoon. Chinuch follows *Rambam's* view.

20. As mentioned above (note 13), this right was awarded by lottery.

21. *Minchas Chinuch* (§11) emends the text to read בָּזָךְ, *bazach*. The *teni* was the vessel used to clean the ashes of the previously burnt *ketores* from the Golden Altar (see *Tamid* 30b, 32b; *Rambam* ibid. 3:4).

22. The term *Heichal* refers to the entire structure of the Sanctuary, including the Holy of Holies, the Holy, and the Antechamber [*Ulam*] (Chinuch in Mitzvah 95, at note 67).

23. See *Keilim* 1:9, *Yoma* 44a, *Rambam* ibid. §3.

שֶׁנֶּאֱמַר (ויקרא ט״ז, י״ז) וְכָל אָדָם לֹא יִהְיֶה בְּאֹהֶל מוֹעֵד וְגוֹ׳,[24] וּמַקְטִיר כַּדֶּרֶךְ שֶׁמְפֹרָשׁ שָׁם בַּגְּמָרָא, שֶׁמַּשְׁלִיךְ הַקְּטֹרֶת בְּנַחַת עַל הַגֶּחָלִים אֲשֶׁר (במחתת) [בְּמִזְבֵּחַ] הַזָּהָב[25] וּמִשְׁתַּחֲוֶה וְיוֹצֵא.[26] וְיֶתֶר פְּרָטֶיהָ וְכֵיצַד הִיא נַעֲשֵׂית, וּמַה שֶּׁהָיוּ אוֹמְרִין בִּשְׁחִיקַת הַסַּמָּנִין הֵיטֵב הָדֵק הָדֵק הֵיטֵב, לְפִי שֶׁאָמְרוּ רַבּוֹתֵינוּ זִכְרוֹנָם לִבְרָכָה (כריתות שם) כִּי הַקּוֹל יָפֶה לַסַּמָּנִין בְּעוֹד שֶׁשּׁוֹחֲקִין אוֹתָם,[27] הַכֹּל בִּכְרִיתוֹת (שם) וּבְתָמִיד (דף ל״ב ע״ב ול״ג ע״א).[28]

וְנוֹהֶגֶת בִּזְמַן הַבַּיִת בְּזִכְרֵי כְהֻנָּה,[29] וְהַמַּקְטִיר כְּדִינוֹ קִיֵּם עֲשֵׂה זֶה.[30]

שֶׁנֶּאֱמַר "וְכָל אָדָם לֹא יִהְיֶה בְּאֹהֶל מוֹעֵד וְגוֹ׳" — **as it is stated** (*Leviticus* 16:17): *There shall not be any person in the Tent of Meeting* when he comes to provide atonement in the Holy, etc.[24] וּמַקְטִיר כַּדֶּרֶךְ שֶׁמְפֹרָשׁ שָׁם בַּגְּמָרָא — **He** enters the Holy and **burns** the *ketores* on the Golden Altar **in the manner prescribed by the Gemara there** (*Tamid* 33a); שֶׁמַּשְׁלִיךְ הַקְּטֹרֶת בְּנַחַת עַל הַגֶּחָלִים אֲשֶׁר (במחתת) [בְּמִזְבֵּחַ] הַזָּהָב — that is, **he gently tosses the** *ketores* **onto the coals that are on the Golden Altar**,[25] וּמִשְׁתַּחֲוֶה וְיוֹצֵא — **and he** then **bows down and exits**.[26]

Chinuch concludes:

וְכֵיצַד הִיא נַעֲשֵׂית — These laws, **and the additional details of [this mitzvah]**, וְיֶתֶר פְּרָטֶיהָ **including how [the** *ketores***] is made**, וּמַה שֶּׁהָיוּ אוֹמְרִין בִּשְׁחִיקַת הַסַּמָּנִין — **and what they would chant while the spices** for the *ketores* **were being ground**, הֵיטֵב הָדֵק הָדֵק הֵיטֵב — namely, *"hadeik heiteiv, heiteiv hadeik"* (grind thoroughly, thoroughly grind), לְפִי שֶׁאָמְרוּ רַבּוֹתֵינוּ זִכְרוֹנָם לִבְרָכָה — **in keeping with the statement of our Sages, of blessed memory** (*Kereisos* 6b), כִּי הַקּוֹל יָפֶה לַסַּמָּנִין בְּעוֹד שֶׁשּׁוֹחֲקִין אוֹתָם — **that sound is beneficial for spices while they are being ground**;[27] הַכֹּל בִּכְרִיתוֹת וּבְתָמִיד — **all** these laws **are set forth in** Tractate *Kereisos* (6a-b) **and in** Tractate *Tamid* (32b-33a).[28]

## ☞ Applicability of the Mitzvah ☜

וְנוֹהֶגֶת בִּזְמַן הַבַּיִת — **[This mitzvah] applies in the time of the Temple** (i.e., when the *Beis HaMikdash* is standing), בְּזִכְרֵי כְהֻנָּה — **to male Kohanim**.[29] וְהַמַּקְטִיר כְּדִינוֹ קִיֵּם עֲשֵׂה זֶה — **[A Kohen] who burns** the *ketores* on the Golden Altar **in accordance with its prescribed procedure has fulfilled a mitzvah-obligation**.[30]

---

### NOTES

24. The verse requires only that all exit the Holy when an *avodah* is performed there, but the Sages decreed that they also exit the adjacent areas [i.e., the Antechamber and the area between it and the Outer Altar], lest someone inadvertently enter the Holy during the service (*Yoma* 44b).

25. The coals were brought there for this purpose by another Kohen, who won the right by lottery to take a shovelful of coals from the Outer Altar and place them upon the Golden Altar (*Tamid* 33a; Rambam ibid. §4-7). Yet another Kohen won the right to clean the ashes of the previous *ketores* from the Golden Altar (ibid.).

26. *Tamid* ibid. The Kohen was allowed to bow and exit as soon as he had thrown the *ketores* upon the coals; he did not have to wait until it actually went up in smoke (see *Chidushei HaGriz* to Rambam, p. 77a ד״ה והנה חזיתי).

27. Some explain that sound waves somehow have a salutary effect on ground spices (see *Tosafos* and *Rabbeinu Gershom*, *Kereisos* 6b; *Rashi*, *Arachin* 10b; *Siddur R' Yaakov Emden*, *Pittum HaKetores*). Among the other reasons given for this phenomenon is that the rhythmic chant helps the grinder to grind the spices evenly, avoiding the problem of having some spices ground more finely than others (*Abarbanel* to *Exodus* 30:36).

28. The laws of producing the *ketores* are codified by Rambam in *Hil. Klei HaMikdash* 2:1-8, and the laws of burning it are codified in *Hil. Temidin U'Mussafin* 3:1-9. Chinuch mentions some additional laws pertaining to the production of *ketores* in Mitzvah 110, The Prohibition to Replicate the Incense.

29. Only male Kohanim were fit to perform the *avodah*. [Here, too, Chinuch stresses the specific responsibility of the Kohanim, rather than the community (see note 1). See Insight A for further discussion.]

30. Interestingly, here Chinuch states the positive aspect, that a Kohen who *does* perform the mitzvah of burning *ketores* has *fulfilled* a mitzvah-obligation, whereas at the end of Mitzvah 98 (Arranging the Menorah Lamps) he states the negative aspect — that a Kohen who *does not* perform the mitzvah of arranging the lamps has *violated* a mitzvah-obligation. Perhaps the reason is because, as mentioned in note 14, Kohanim would never be negligent in regard to the *ketores*, since whoever merited to perform this *avodah* was blessed with wealth. See further, Insight B.

## TETZAVEH / MITZVAH 103: THE OBLIGATION TO OFFER THE INCENSE

**◈§ Insight A: Does the Mitzvah Pertain to the Kohanim or the Community?**

Chinuch states at the beginning of this mitzvah that the Kohanim are the ones who are commanded to burn the *ketores* on the Golden Altar twice daily. At the end of the mitzvah, he states similarly that the obligation applies to male Kohanim. These comments stand in contrast to Chinuch's remarks in Mitzvah 401, where he discusses the requirement of the daily *tamid* offerings. There, Chinuch begins by stating that the *Jewish people* are commanded to bring these offerings *through the Kohanim*, who are the servants of Hashem. And, at the end of that mitzvah, he emphasizes that the *tamid* obligation rests upon the entire community, and if the offering is not brought, then every member of the nation who can rectify the matter bears responsibility. *Rambam* makes the same distinction in *Sefer HaMitzvos*. In *Asei* 28, he states that the Torah commanded the *Kohanim* to offer the *ketores*, yet in *Asei* 39 he states that the Torah commanded *us* (i.e., the community) to bring the *tamid* offerings.

To be sure, regarding the *ketores* the Torah states (*Exodus* 30:7-8) that Aaron (i.e., a Kohen) shall burn it, whereas in regard to the *tamid* the Torah (*Numbers* 28:2) addresses the command to the "Children of Israel." However, the Gemara (*Zevachim* 109b) states clearly that the Kohanim offer the *ketores* on behalf of the entire community. Seemingly, then, this obligation is no different from the *tamid* obligation, which is performed by the Kohanim on behalf of the community with whom that responsibility ultimately lies. What is the basis to distinguish between these two mitzvos?

*Chidushei HaGriz (Hil. Klei HaMikdash* 2:8) suggests the following explanation: Although both the *tamid* and the *ketores* are communal offerings, they are fundamentally different in the nature of their obligations. The *tamid* obligation is, at its essence, a requirement upon the community to *gain atonement* twice each day through this offering. This is because the community's *tamid* obligation is no different from the obligation of an individual to bring an offering in which he is obligated. Just as a private individual is, in certain instances, commanded to make offerings for the purpose of atonement, so too, is the community commanded to make the *tamid* offerings in order to gain a degree of atonement. And just as the owner of a private offering fulfills *his* obligation when the Kohanim offer it in the manner necessary for it to effect atonement, so too, the communal owners of the *tamid* offering fulfill *their* obligation when the Kohanim offer it properly and it effects the communal atonement. The *acts* involved in offering it must be performed by the Kohanim, since they are the ones authorized to perform the *avodah* in the *Beis HaMikdash*. But the *mitzvah* of bringing the offering is credited to the owner — whether the individual or the community — for whom it atones. [Certainly, the Kohanim also discharge a mitzvah by sacrificing the offerings, but that is a separate mitzvah of performing the *avodah* as mandated. The offering itself is credited to the owner, since the purpose of the offering is the atonement it affords.]

The *ketores* obligation is inherently different. Whereas in the case of animal and bird offerings (and *minchah* offerings), the essence of the mitzvah is for the owner to achieve atonement, and the sacrificial service is the *means* of gaining atonement, in the case of *ketores* the essence of the mitzvah is the performance of the service; i.e., the *avodah* of burning the *ketores* on the Golden Altar is the end unto itself. That is why the Torah (*Exodus* ibid.) commands simply: Aaron shall burn the *ketores* every morning [without adding any of the qualifiers that it commonly states regarding other offerings; e.g., *a fire-offering to Hashem*]. It means to convey that the mitzvah is fulfilled by the *act* of burning the *ketores*, not by any *achievement* of atonement.

It follows that, although both the *tamid* and the *ketores* are offered on behalf of the community, on the practical level they are very different. The mitzvah of offering the *tamid* is discharged by the community, since the essence of this mitzvah is the achievement of atonement, and it is they who gain atonement through it. The mitzvah of burning the *ketores*, however, is discharged by the Kohanim, for the essence of this mitzvah is the *avodah* of bringing it up in smoke upon the Altar, and the *avodah* is performed by the Kohanim. This is why the Torah addresses the mitzvah to "Aaron," and is also why *Rambam* and Chinuch state that the mitzvah applies specifically to the Kohanim. See *Chidushei HaGriz* ibid. for further elaboration.

**◈§ Insight B: Ketores and Bris Milah**

The Gemara (*Yoma* 26a) teaches that each Kohen was given the opportunity to perform the *ketores* service only once in his lifetime; no Kohen was allowed to repeat this *avodah* (except the Kohen Gadol, who was entitled to perform any *avodah* whenever he wanted — *Yoma* 14a; see *Rambam, Hil.*

*Klei HaMikdash* 5:12). The reason is because anyone who merited performing the *ketores* service would be blessed with wealth, as the Torah states (*Deuteronomy* 33:10-11): יָשִׂימוּ קְטוֹרָה בְּאַפֶּךָ ... בָּרֵךְ ה' חֵילוֹ, *They place incense before Your Presence ... Bless, O Hashem, his resources*. The desire to spread the blessing of wealth among as many Kohanim as possible led them to institute a rule that each performance of the *ketores* service would be done by a different Kohen.

We find a similar practice in regard to *bris milah*. The verse preceding the ones just cited (ibid. v. 9) mentions *milah*, stating וּבְרִיתְךָ יִנְצֹרוּ, *and Your covenant they preserved*. *Rama* (*Yoreh Deah* 265:11) cites *Maharil*, who infers that the covenant of *milah* is comparable to the *ketores* service, and thus, the *sandak* who holds the child on his lap during the *milah* is considered like one who offers *ketores*. *Maharil* states that it is therefore customary for a father to avoid honoring the same person with the role of *sandak* for two of his sons, just as no Kohen was given the opportunity to repeat the *ketores* service. [While it is acceptable for one person to serve as *sandak* twice for different fathers, each father generally does not give the same person two opportunities (see *Beis Hillel* to *Yoreh Deah* loc. cit.; cf. *Beur HaGra* there §46).] Many commentators wonder why the *sandak* is singled out here. If anything, the rule should seemingly apply to the *mohel* who actually performs the *milah*!

*Maharam Schik* (Mitzvah 104) offers a novel explanation, based on Chinuch's interpretation of the purpose of the *ketores* service. Chinuch states that the Kohanim were commanded to burn *ketores* twice daily in order to enhance the glory of the *Beis HaMikdash* by permeating it with a wonderful aroma, and to thus ensure that people will want to visit the *Beis HaMikdash*. Surely, Chinuch does not mean that this is the only purpose of the mitzvah, for the Torah (*Numbers* 17:11-13) teaches that the *ketores* has the power to halt a plague (see also *Shabbos* 89a). [Moreover, the Gemara (*Arachin* 16a) states that the *ketores* brought about atonement for the sin of *lashon hara*.] Clearly, there is an esoteric element to the mitzvah. Rather, Chinuch provides us with a *practical* purpose for the *ketores* burning. As he states explicitly in Mitzvah 98, although the Kabbalists possess lofty insights into the various aspects of the Temple service, he focuses on the simple explanations.

Now, the Mishnah (*Peah* 1:1) teaches that there are certain mitzvos whose fruits a person enjoys in this world though their principal remains intact for him in the World to Come. *Rambam*, in his Commentary there, explains that these are mitzvos that bring benefit to people, such as acts of גְּמִילוּת חֲסָדִים, *lovingkindness*. When a person performs this type of mitzvah, he causes others to emulate him, thus bringing about the common benefit. *Maharam Schik* elaborates that when one's performance of a mitzvah influences others to follow in his ways, he is rewarded in the World to Come for the mitzvah itself, which is primary, but is also rewarded in this world for influencing others to do good and bringing benefit to all. The Kohanim who offered the *ketores* performed this type of mitzvah. They fulfilled the Will of Hashem and accomplished great things in the hidden, Heavenly spheres; for that, their reward was reserved in the World to Come. But, by enhancing the glory of the *Beis HaMikdash*, they also influenced other people to flock to that holy place. For this accomplishment, they deserved to be rewarded in this world. The blessing of wealth was a fitting reward, as it caused their own stature to be enhanced, enabling them to further spread their positive influence on others.

A *sandak* fulfills a similar role. His participation is not essential to the mitzvah, for *milah* can be performed without a *sandak*. It is the *mohel* who is the primary protagonist. What the *sandak* accomplishes is that he adds honor and glory to the mitzvah, for by taking the child on his lap he demonstrates love and admiration for the performance of *milah*. Since, with his secondary role, he enhances others' appreciation for Hashem's command, he fulfills a task similar to the secondary achievement of the Kohanim who offered the *ketores* in the *Beis HaMikdash*. It is thus fitting that he be rewarded in a manner similar to the reward the Kohanim received for their secondary accomplishment.

## 289 ❑ TETZAVEH / MITZVAH 104: NOT TO BURN ANYTHING BUT INCENSE ON THE ALTAR

### מִצְוָה קד: שֶׁלֹּא לְהַקְטִיר וּלְהַקְרִיב עַל מִזְבַּח הַזָּהָב

שֶׁלֹּא לְהַקְרִיב בְּמִזְבַּח הַזָּהָב שֶׁבַּהֵיכָל[1] כִּי אִם קְטֹרֶת שֶׁבְּכָל יוֹם, זוּלָתִי הַזָּאַת הַדָּמִים מִיּוֹם הַכִּפּוּרִים לְיוֹם הַכִּפּוּרִים[2], שֶׁנֶּאֱמַר (שמות ל׳, ט׳) לֹא תַעֲלוּ עָלָיו קְטֹרֶת זָרָה וְעֹלָה וּמִנְחָה וְנֵסֶךְ לֹא תִסְּכוּ עָלָיו[3].

## ☙ Mitzvah 104 ☙
### The Prohibition to Burn or Offer [Anything but the Incense] on the Golden Altar

לֹא תַעֲלוּ עָלָיו קְטֹרֶת זָרָה וְעֹלָה וּמִנְחָה וְנֵסֶךְ לֹא תִסְּכוּ עָלָיו
*You shall not bring upon it foreign incense, or an olah offering or a minchah offering; nor may you pour a libation upon it (Exodus 30:9).*

In the previous mitzvah, Chinuch set forth the mitzvah-obligation to offer incense (*ketores*) twice daily on the Golden Altar in the *Beis HaMikdash*. In this mitzvah, Chinuch discusses the prohibition related to bringing any other offerings upon this Altar.

שֶׁלֹּא לְהַקְרִיב בְּמִזְבַּח הַזָּהָב שֶׁבַּהֵיכָל — We are commanded **not to offer** any offering **on the Golden Altar in the** *Heichal* (Sanctuary),[1] כִּי אִם קְטֹרֶת שֶׁבְּכָל יוֹם — **other than the daily** *ketores* **offerings.** זוּלָתִי הַזָּאַת הַדָּמִים מִיּוֹם הַכִּפּוּרִים לְיוֹם הַכִּפּוּרִים — This applies to all animal, bread, or incense offerings, **with the exception of the** annual **sprinkling of the** sacrificial **blood** of the special "inner" offerings **every Yom Kippur.**[2] שֶׁנֶּאֱמַר "לֹא תַעֲלוּ עָלָיו קְטֹרֶת זָרָה וְעֹלָה וּמִנְחָה וְנֵסֶךְ לֹא תִסְּכוּ עָלָיו" — We are so commanded, **as it is stated** with regard to the Golden Altar (*Exodus* 30:9): **You shall not bring upon it foreign incense, or an olah offering or a minchah offering; nor may you pour a libation upon it.**[3]

### ☙ Underlying Purpose of the Mitzvah ☙

Chinuch considers this particular mitzvah-obligation one component of the general mitzvos relating to the Temple (*Beis HaMikdash*), and, as such, does not offer a specific reason for this mitzvah. In this section, Chinuch discusses the limitations of trying to discern reasons for those mitzvos or components of mitzvos that can be classified as "details" of more general commandments:[4]

---

### NOTES

1. See previous mitzvah, note 2, for a description of the Golden Altar, its location, and function.

2. Literally, *from Yom Kippur to Yom Kippur*. Among the services performed with the blood of the special offerings of Yom Kippur was its sprinkling upon the Golden Altar (*Leviticus* 16:18-19). See the following note.

3. The following verse continues, *Aaron will atone [upon the Altar] once a year, from the blood of the chatas offering of the atonements* .... This once-a-year application of blood refers to the Yom Kippur offerings, whose blood was sprinkled upon the Golden Altar.

The Yom Kippur offerings were the only *regularly scheduled* offerings whose blood was sprinkled on the Golden Altar. There were, however, other exceptional cases in which blood was sprinkled on that Altar. This applied in the case of an offering brought for a communal transgression resulting from an erroneous ruling by the Sanhedrin (Mitzvah 120), as well as the case of a *chatas* offering brought by a Kohen Gadol who committed a transgression (*Leviticus* 4:7, 18; Mishnah, *Zevachim* 47a). The verse mentions only the Yom Kippur offerings because the others were not offered unless certain conditions were fulfilled, and were extremely rare (*Ibn Ezra*; see *Meshech Chochmah* for further discussion).

4. To understand the following section of Chinuch, it is important to note that Chinuch's discussion of the reasons of mitzvos is limited to the reasons that can be ascertained עַל דֶּרֶךְ הַפְּשָׁט, *following the plain understanding* of the Torah, i.e., the level of Torah understanding that is most readily accessible to most people. Chinuch points this out many times in his work (see, for example, Author's Introduction, Mitzvah 95, and Mitzvah 397), and underscores this point repeatedly in the following section. Reasons for the mitzvos that are derived from the deeper levels of Torah understanding, which are the province of the more erudite scholars, are not the focus of this work. See also the following note.

## תצוה / מצוה קד: שלא להקטיר ולהקריב על מזבח הזהב

כְּבָר כָּתַבְנוּ לְמַעְלָה (בשרשי מצוה צ"ה) תְּשׁוּבָה לְשׁוֹאֵל עַל צַד הַפְּשָׁט, עַל עִנְיַן מִצְוֹת בִּנְיַן הַבַּיִת הַקָּדוֹשׁ לָאֵל בָּרוּךְ הוּא, וְעִנְיַן הֱיוֹת שָׁם כֵּלִים יְקָרִים לַעֲבוֹדָה וְשֻׁלְחָן וּמְנוֹרָה, וְאַחֲרֵי זֹאת אֵין לִיגַע מַחְשַׁבְתֵּנוּ בַּמֶּה שֶׁאֵינוּ צָרִיךְ וּלְחַפֵּשׂ טַעַם לָמָּה יְצַוֶּה הָאֵל לְבַל נַקְטִיר בְּמִזְבַּח הַזָּהָב קְטֹרֶת זָרָה, שֶׁאִם כֵּן יְחַיְּבוּנוּ לְחַפֵּשׂ לָמָּה צִוָּה אוֹתָנוּ לִהְיוֹת נֵרוֹת הַמְּנוֹרָה שִׁבְעָה וְלֹא שְׁמוֹנָה, וְאֶל הַפְּרָטִים אֵין חֵקֶר וְלֹא תַּשִּׂיג בָּהֶן הַמַּחֲשָׁבָה לְעוֹלָם. וְאִם תִּלְחָצֵנִי לְהָשִׁיב בִּפְרָטִים עַל כָּל פָּנִים, אֹמַר עַל צַד הַפְּשָׁט, אִם לֹא שֶׁהַקַּבָּלָה תַּכְרִיחַ לְפִי דִּבְרֵי רַבּוֹתֵינוּ לִבְרָכָה זִכְרוֹנָם הַקְּדוֹשִׁים הַמְקֻבָּלִים, שֶׁלֹּא יִהְיֶה בַּפְּרָטִים טַעַם אַחֵר, אֶלָּא נֹאמַר שֶׁאַחַר שֶׁנִּתְחַיַּבְנוּ לִבְנוֹת בַּיִת וְלַעֲשׂוֹת כֵּלִים, נִצְטַוִּינוּ בָּהֶם עַל צַד אֶחָד מִן הַצְּדָדִין, וּבָא בָּהֶן אֶחָד מִן הַחֶשְׁבּוֹנוֹת שֶׁאִי אֶפְשָׁר לְמַעֲשֶׂה לְבִלְתִּי אֶחָד מֵהֶן,[5]

---

כְּבָר כָּתַבְנוּ לְמַעְלָה תְּשׁוּבָה לְשׁוֹאֵל — **We have already written above** (Mitzvos 95, 97, 98) **a response to one who** might **inquire,** עַל צַד הַפְּשָׁט — **according to the plain understanding** of the reasons of the mitzvos of the Torah, עַל עִנְיַן מִצְוֹת בִּנְיַן הַבַּיִת הַקָּדוֹשׁ לָאֵל בָּרוּךְ הוּא — **about the subject of** the underlying reasons **for the mitzvos of building a Temple for the Almighty, blessed is He,** וְעִנְיַן הֱיוֹת שָׁם כֵּלִים יְקָרִים לַעֲבוֹדָה וְשֻׁלְחָן וּמְנוֹרָה — **and the matter of** our having been commanded that **there should exist there** (in the Temple) specific **precious utensils** to be used **for the** Divine **service, and the Table** (*Shulchan*) **and the Menorah.** וְאַחֲרֵי זֹאת אֵין לִיגַע מַחְשַׁבְתֵּנוּ בַּמֶּה שֶׁאֵינוּ צָרִיךְ — **After** having provided these reasons, **we should not weary our minds needlessly,** וּלְחַפֵּשׂ טַעַם לָמָּה יְצַוֶּה הָאֵל לְבַל נַקְטִיר בְּמִזְבַּח הַזָּהָב קְטֹרֶת זָרָה — **to search for a reason why the Almighty would command us not to offer foreign incense upon the Golden Altar.** שֶׁאִם כֵּן — **For if** we would do **so,** i.e., if we would try to explain this detail of the incense mitzvah, יְחַיְּבוּנוּ לְחַפֵּשׂ לָמָּה צִוָּה אוֹתָנוּ לִהְיוֹת נֵרוֹת הַמְּנוֹרָה שִׁבְעָה וְלֹא שְׁמוֹנָה — [such line of inquiry] **would also obligate us to search** for reasons for all the details of the mitzvos, such as **why** [God] **commanded us that the Menorah have seven lamps, and not eight;** וְאֶל הַפְּרָטִים אֵין חֵקֶר וְלֹא תַּשִּׂיג בָּהֶן הַמַּחֲשָׁבָה לְעוֹלָם — certainly we cannot attempt to explain the details, because **there would be no end to the investigation** into details of the mitzvos, **and the mind will never grasp** the definitive reasons **for them.** Investigation into the particulars of the mitzvos would not yield fruitful results, as we could never fully understand the reasons for all of the fine details of the mitzvos. We therefore need not weary ourselves in searching for reasons for these details.

Chinuch continues by pointing out another limitation to the endeavor of ascertaining reasons for particular details of mitzvos:

וְאִם תִּלְחָצֵנִי לְהָשִׁיב בִּפְרָטִים עַל כָּל פָּנִים — **And if you should press me to respond** with an explanation **regarding the details** of mitzvos **in any case,** אֹמַר עַל צַד הַפְּשָׁט — **I would state, according to the plain understanding** of the reasons of the Torah, as follows: אִם לֹא שֶׁהַקַּבָּלָה תַּכְרִיחַ לְפִי דִּבְרֵי רַבּוֹתֵינוּ לִבְרָכָה זִכְרוֹנָם הַקְּדוֹשִׁים הַמְקֻבָּלִים — **If Kabbalistic wisdom, according to the teachings of our holy Sages of Kabbalah, of blessed memory, does not compel** us to say otherwise, שֶׁלֹּא יִהְיֶה בַּפְּרָטִים טַעַם אַחֵר — **we may say** according to the plain understanding **that there is no** specific **reason for the details** of the mitzvos other than the primary reason for the mitzvah itself. אֶלָּא נֹאמַר שֶׁאַחַר שֶׁנִּתְחַיַּבְנוּ לִבְנוֹת בַּיִת וְלַעֲשׂוֹת כֵּלִים — **Rather, we would say, that since we were obligated** in the primary mitzvah **to build the Temple and fashion utensils,** נִצְטַוִּינוּ בָּהֶם עַל צַד אֶחָד מִן הַצְּדָדִין — **we were commanded** to build and fashion **them in one** specific **way out of the many** possible **ways** that they could be built; וּבָא בָּהֶן אֶחָד מִן הַחֶשְׁבּוֹנוֹת — **and** of the many possible numbers of details that each one could have had, [the mitzvos] took the form of **one of these numbers,** שֶׁאִי אֶפְשָׁר לְמַעֲשֶׂה לְבִלְתִּי אֶחָד מֵהֶן — **for it is not possible to execute** any of these **without** doing so in **one of [the possible ways].**[5]

---

NOTES

5. To explain with the example that Chinuch mentioned above: The Torah wished for us to fashion a Menorah, one detail of which is that the Menorah contain seven lamps. According to this "simple" approach, there may

# 291 ☐ TETZAVEH / MITZVAH 104: NOT TO BURN ANYTHING BUT INCENSE ON THE ALTAR

וְאוּלָם אַחַר שֶׁנִּצְטַוֵּינוּ בָּהֶם בָּאָה הַצַּוָּאָה עֲלֵיהֶם לַעֲשׂוֹתָם כְּמִצְוָה דֶּרֶךְ קֶבַע לְעוֹלָם, וְלֹא נוֹסִיף וְלֹא נִגְרַע, כִּי הַתּוֹסֶפֶת וְהַגֵּרוּעַ בִּמְכֻוָּן בִּשְׁלֵמוּת קִלְקוּל, וְכָל מִצְוֹתָיו בָּרוּךְ הוּא שְׁלֵמוֹת וּתְמִימוֹת. וְאוּלָם שָׁמַעְתִּי כִּי יֵשׁ לַמְקֻבָּלִים בְּכָל אֶחָד מִן הַפְּרָטִים טְעָמִים נִפְלָאִים וְסוֹדוֹת עֲמֻקִּים.[6]

וְנוֹהֶגֶת מִצְוָה זוֹ שֶׁלֹּא לְהַקְרִיב בְּמִזְבַּח הַזָּהָב כִּי אִם קְטֹרֶת, בִּזְמַן הַבַּיִת בַּכֹּהֲנִים.[7]

---

Chinuch adds that although, on this basic level of understanding, there may be no inherent explanation for the particular details of a mitzvah, there is still an underlying imperative to follow these details exactly as prescribed:

וְאוּלָם אַחַר שֶׁנִּצְטַוֵּינוּ בָּהֶם — However, **after we have been commanded** to build and fashion [the **Temple and its utensils**] with their specific details, בָּאָה הַצַּוָּאָה עֲלֵיהֶם לַעֲשׂוֹתָם כְּמִצְוָה דֶּרֶךְ קֶבַע לְעוֹלָם — **we received the commandment regarding them to execute them as commanded, in that fixed way, always.** וְלֹא נוֹסִיף וְלֹא נִגְרַע — **We are not** permitted **to add or subtract** anything from these precise instructions, כִּי הַתּוֹסֶפֶת וְהַגֵּרוּעַ בִּמְכֻוָּן בִּשְׁלֵמוּת קִלְקוּל — **for any additions or subtractions in that which is exactly perfect is the ruination** of that thing; וְכָל מִצְוֹתָיו בָּרוּךְ הוּא שְׁלֵמוֹת וּתְמִימוֹת — **and all the commandments [of God], blessed is He, are complete and perfect.** וְאוּלָם שָׁמַעְתִּי — **Nevertheless,** although the above can be said on the level of the plain understanding of the mitzvos, **I have heard** כִּי יֵשׁ לַמְקֻבָּלִים בְּכָל אֶחָד מִן הַפְּרָטִים — **that the Masters of Kabbalah possess, regarding all the details** of the mitzvos, טְעָמִים נִפְלָאִים וְסוֹדוֹת עֲמֻקִּים — **wondrous reasons and profound secrets.**[6]

## ⮞ Applicability of the Mitzvah ⮜

וְנוֹהֶגֶת מִצְוָה זוֹ שֶׁלֹּא לְהַקְרִיב בְּמִזְבַּח הַזָּהָב כִּי אִם קְטֹרֶת — **This mitzvah,** in which we are commanded **not to offer upon the Golden Altar** any offerings **except for the** daily **ketores, applies** בִּזְמַן הַבַּיִת — **in the time of the Temple** (i.e., when the *Beis HaMikdash* is standing); בַּכֹּהֲנִים — and the mitzvah applies **to Kohanim,** who are the ones who perform the *avodah* (service) in the Temple.[7]

---

NOTES

be no specific reason for there to be exactly seven lamps on the Menorah. Rather, God wished us to execute the Menorah specifically in accordance with His command, and He chose one of the possibilities with regard to the number of lamps, and commanded us to do it in that way. The fact that we are commanded to make it with seven lamps is in itself not evidence that there is a specific reason for that number, since there had to be a certain number in any case. Thus, the question "Why seven?" is not necessarily a valid one, since it could as well be asked of any other number that the Torah would have prescribed. Rather, the Torah simply chose one and commanded us to execute it in that way (as Chinuch continues to explain below). This same idea can be applied to other details of mitzvos as well.

It is important to understand these words of Chinuch in context of his other remarks regarding the reasons for mitzvos. In Mitzvah 95, Chinuch describes at length the reasons for many details of various offerings made in the *Beis HaMikdash*, and then states that the full explanation of all the details requires an understanding of Kabbalistic wisdom (see also below in this very mitzvah, at note 6). And, at the end of Mitzvah 96, Chinuch states that the specific, detailed form of each utensil in the *Beis HaMikdash* alluded to great and sublime matters in the Heavenly spheres. Chinuch makes similar remarks at the end of his Author's Introduction to this work, and in numerous other places. Thus, there is no doubt that Chinuch acknowledges that there is endless Divine wisdom inherent in *every detail* of the Torah's mitzvos. Chinuch's statement here is intended only to discourage attempting to explain the details of the mitzvos with the simplistic, straightforward (non-Kabbalistic) approach that he uses throughout this work to explain the more general reasons for mitzvos. See Insight for further discussion.

6. One deeper approach to this Mitzvah can be found in *Akeidas Yitzchak, Shaar* 48.

7. *Minchas Chinuch* (§3) understands Chinuch to mean that if a non-Kohen offers something on the Golden Altar he does not violate this prohibition, since he is completely unfit to perform the *avodah* of any offering. Similarly, the specific prohibitions to perform *avodah* while inebriated (Mitzvah 152) or while *tamei* (Mitzvah 278) apply to Kohanim who are fit to perform *avodah* while sober and *tahor*, not to those who are in any event unfit to perform *avodah*. [For a related discussion, see Insight to Mitzvah 125.]

## תצוה / מצוה קד: שלא להקטיר ולהקריב על מזבח הזהב

וְהָעוֹבֵר עַל זֶה וְהִקְרִיב אוֹ זָרַק בּוֹ, כִּי אִם דָּבָר הָרָאוּי לְהַקְרִיב בּוֹ כְּמוֹ שֶׁאָמַרְנוּ, חַיָּב מַלְקוֹת.

---

וְהָעוֹבֵר עַל זֶה וְהִקְרִיב אוֹ זָרַק בּוֹ — [A Kohen] who transgresses this prohibition and brings an offering or sprinkles blood on [the Golden Altar], כִּי אִם דָּבָר הָרָאוּי לְהַקְרִיב בּוֹ כְּמוֹ שֶׁאָמַרְנוּ — other than something that is meant to be offered upon it (e.g., the daily *ketores* and the blood of the Yom Kippur offerings), **as we have stated** above, חַיָּב מַלְקוֹת — **incurs** the penalty of *malkus* (lashes).

---

### ◆§ Insight: Understanding the Details

*Chinuch's* statement in this mitzvah that we should be satisfied with understanding a mitzvah's general scheme, and not weary our minds to try and propose reasons for the details of a mitzvah, is a paraphrase of the opinion of *Rambam* in *Moreh Nevuchim* (3:26). While *Rambam* praises the study of the reasons behind mitzvos in general (see *Hilchos Me'ilah* 8:8), he states such study is fruitless and often counterproductive regarding the details of the mitzvos.

*Rambam* bases this idea on a statement of the Midrash (*Bereishis Rabbah* 44:1) regarding the mitzvah of *shechitah* (ritual slaughter). The Midrash asks: What difference does it make to God whether we slaughter an animal by its throat (as dictated by halachah) or we simply sever its head from the nape of the neck? The Midrash answers that the mitzvos are given to refine us, as the verse states (*Psalms* 18:31), אִמְרַת ה' צְרוּפָה, *the words of God are refining*.

According to *Rambam*, the question and answer of this Midrash refer to the many details of the mitzvos. The Midrash wonders what possible difference these details can make to God; is there a reason to slaughter specifically from the throat in contrast to the back of the neck? To this, the Midrash responds that in fact the details of the mitzvos need not have any other reason except simply to purify us by virtue of our compliance with God's command. Of all the possible ways a mitzvah could be designed, God chose one of the possibilities; our duty thereafter is to obey the mitzvah specifically as He commanded us, and this very obedience refines us. [After taking this position in this mitzvah, however, *Chinuch* does point out that even the details may have explanations based on the wisdom of Kabbalah. Furthermore, in other mitzvos *Chinuch* himself does suggest reasons for the details of mitzvos using his usual straightforward approach (see, for example, Mitzvos 96 and 124). See also notes 4-5 above.]

*Ramban*, in his commentary to *Deuteronomy* (22:6), has a completely different understanding of this very same Midrash. According to *Ramban*, when the Midrash asks what difference there is whether we slaughter from the throat or the nape of the neck, it does not mean to ask "What is the difference *at all* (i.e., why such detail)," but rather, "What difference does it make *to God*?" I.e., what does our fulfillment of mitzvos do for an Omnipotent, Eternal God? Does Scripture not state (*Job* 35:6,7): אִם חָטָאתָ מַה תִּפְעָל בּוֹ ... אִם צָדַקְתָּ מַה תִּתֶּן לוֹ אוֹ מַה מִיָּדְךָ יִקָּח, *If you have sinned how have you affected Him? ... If you were righteous what have you given Him, or what has He taken from your hand?* To *this* question, the Midrash answers that, indeed, the purpose of all mitzvos is ultimately for our benefit, not for God's. The mitzvos are meant to refine us in various ways, whether by protecting us from physical harm or false philosophies, or by imparting positive traits and improving our character, or by having us recall the miracles of the past so that we can develop a more meaningful understanding of God's ways. The verse cited by the Midrash, אִמְרַת ה' צְרוּפָה, *the words of God are refining*, means that much like a silversmith removes the dross from silver so as to refine it, so do the mitzvos of the Torah purify and benefit those who practice them.

This concept, that the mitzvos were given to us for our benefit and not for God's, is mentioned many times by *Chinuch* as well (particularly in Mitzvah 95). *Rambam*, too, agrees with this concept (see, for example, *Hilchos Temurah* 4:13). The disagreement between *Rambam* and *Ramban* centers only on the understanding of the above Midrash: *Ramban* understands the Midrash as reflecting the idea that mitzvos are solely for our benefit, and *Rambam* explains the Midrash as the source for his idea that a study of the reasoning of mitzvah details is unwarranted. *Chinuch* himself, in Mitzvah 545,

writes at length concerning both of these approaches; see there for elaboration.

Other Rishonim, however, have a completely different approach to the details of the mitzvos. According to their understanding, a mitzvah is a reflection of a certain spiritual reality, which through its existence and our performance of it, elevates us and gives us spiritual life. This spiritual reality relies on its details no less than on its generalities, much as physical things do. A plant, for example, needs all of its components in order to exist and carry on as a life-giving entity, not only its "general" ones. The myriad details of its many life-systems and the minute structure of its cells are just as essential as its basic height and color and shape. So too, are mitzvos independent realities, albeit spiritual ones, which form a cohesive whole through all of their components, general and particular. To observe a mitzvah without performance of all its details is to impair the spiritual influence of that mitzvah, and sometimes to counter it entirely (see *Kuzari* 1:99; see also *Teshuvos HaRashba* I §94). [This latter view of the Rishonim is firmly embraced by *R' Samson Raphael Hirsch*, in his *Horeb, Chumash Commentary*, and other works, where he endeavors to show the remarkable significance and symbolism of even the smallest details of the mitzvos.]

# פרשת כי תשא
# Parashas Ki Sisa

כִּי תִשָּׂא יֵשׁ בָּהּ אַרְבַּע מִצְווֹת עֲשֵׂה
וְחָמֵשׁ מִצְווֹת לֹא תַעֲשֶׂה

*Parashas Ki Sisa* contains four Mitzvah-Obligations
and five Mitzvah-Prohibitions.

---

CONTAINS NINE MITZVOS:
MITZVOS 105-113

---

105. מִצְוַת נְתִינַת מַחֲצִית הַשֶּׁקֶל בַּשָּׁנָה — The Obligation to Give the Half-*Shekel* Annually
106. מִצְוַת קִדּוּשׁ יָדַיִם וְרַגְלַיִם בִּשְׁעַת עֲבוֹדָה — The Obligation [Upon Kohanim] to Sanctify Their Hands and Feet When Serving [in the Temple]
107. מִצְוַת מְשִׁיחַת כֹּהֲנִים גְּדוֹלִים וּמְלָכִים בְּשֶׁמֶן הַמִּשְׁחָה — The Obligation of Anointing Kohanim Gedolim and Kings With the Anointment Oil
108. שֶׁלֹּא יָסוּךְ זָר בְּשֶׁמֶן הַמִּשְׁחָה — The Prohibition to Anoint an Outsider With the Anointment Oil
109. שֶׁלֹּא לַעֲשׂוֹת כְּמַתְכֹּנֶת שֶׁמֶן הַמִּשְׁחָה — The Prohibition to Replicate the Anointment Oil
110. שֶׁלֹּא לַעֲשׂוֹת כְּמַתְכֹּנֶת הַקְּטֹרֶת — The Prohibition to Replicate the Incense
111. שֶׁלֹּא לֶאֱכֹל וְלִשְׁתּוֹת תִּקְרֹבֶת עֲבוֹדָה זָרָה — The Prohibition to Consume Idolatrous Offerings
112. מִצְוַת שְׁבִיתַת הָאָרֶץ בִּשְׁנַת הַשְּׁמִטָּה — The Obligation to Rest the Land During the *Shemittah* Year
113. שֶׁלֹּא לֶאֱכֹל בָּשָׂר בְּחָלָב — The Prohibition to Eat a Mixture of Meat and Milk

## מִצְוָה קה: מִצְוַת נְתִינַת מַחֲצִית הַשֶּׁקֶל בְּשָׁנָה[1,2]

שֶׁיִּתֵּן כָּל אֶחָד מִיִּשְׂרָאֵל מִבֶּן עֶשְׂרִים שָׁנָה וָמַעְלָה[3] בֵּין עָנִי בֵּין עָשִׁיר מַחֲצִית הַשֶּׁקֶל, שֶׁהוּא מִשְׁקַל עֲשָׂרָה גֵּרָה[4] כֶּסֶף, בְּכָל שָׁנָה לְיַד הַכֹּהֲנִים[5], שֶׁנֶּאֱמַר (שמות ל׳, י״ג)

# Mitzvah 105
## The Obligation to Give the Half-Shekel Annually

זֶה יִתְּנוּ כָּל הָעֹבֵר עַל הַפְּקֻדִים מַחֲצִית הַשֶּׁקֶל בְּשֶׁקֶל הַקֹּדֶשׁ עֶשְׂרִים גֵּרָה הַשֶּׁקֶל מַחֲצִית הַשֶּׁקֶל תְּרוּמָה לַה׳

*This shall they give — everyone who passes through the census — a half-shekel of the sacred shekel, the shekel is twenty gerahs, half a shekel as a portion to* HASHEM *(Exodus 30:13).*

When the Jewish people were counted in the Wilderness, God commanded Moses not to count them directly, but rather to collect a silver half-*shekel* from each of those included in the census, and thereby reckon their number. The silver thus collected was to be used in the construction of the *Mishkan* (Tabernacle). The above verse is taken from the passage in which this commandment is set forth.

Although the direct meaning of the passage refers to the census taken at that time, the Sages (*Megillah* 29b) found reference in these verses to an independent annual tax of a half-*shekel*.[1] The funds raised in this tax were designated for the communal offerings in the Temple (*Beis HaMikdash*) and related expenses. Since the source of this mitzvah is found in the passage that speaks of the census, many of the laws relating to the mitzvah can also be traced to the verses in this passage, as Chinuch sets forth below.[2]

שֶׁיִּתֵּן כָּל אֶחָד מִיִּשְׂרָאֵל מִבֶּן עֶשְׂרִים שָׁנָה וָמַעְלָה — We are commanded **that every Jew who is twenty years of age or older**[3] **must give,** בֵּין עָנִי בֵּין עָשִׁיר — **whether he is poor or rich,** מַחֲצִית הַשֶּׁקֶל שֶׁהוּא מִשְׁקַל עֲשָׂרָה גֵּרָה כֶּסֶף בְּכָל שָׁנָה — the value of **a half-*shekel*, which equals the weight of ten silver *gerah*,**[4] **each year,** לְיַד הַכֹּהֲנִים — **to the hands of the Kohanim.**[5] שֶׁנֶּאֱמַר

---

### NOTES

1. This obligation is explicitly mentioned elsewhere in Scripture: *II Chronicles* 24:6 and *Nehemiah* 10:33-34; see *Ramban* to the *Exodus* verse.

2. See *Rashi* and *Ramban* to the cited verses. See also the lengthy discussion of this matter by *Rash Sirilio* in the introduction to his commentary to Tractate *Shekalim*.

It should be noted that not all Rishonim are in agreement about which specific verses in the passage refer to the mitzvah of the half-*shekel*. This disagreement has several ramifications with regard to various laws pertaining to the half-*shekel* obligation; see, for example, note 6, below.

[According to the Vilna Gaon (*Aderes Eliyahu* to *Exodus* ibid.), the source of the mitzvah of giving the annual half-*shekel* is not found in this passage at all, but is known to us through *Halachah LeMoshe MiSinai*, Oral Tradition from Sinai. Accordingly, any references in the Gemara to these verses in the context of the annual half-*shekel* obligation are merely Scriptural *allusions* to this mitzvah, not Scriptural *sources*.]

3. See below, note 6.

4. See below, at note 28, where Chinuch explains how much silver this is.

5. That is, the treasurers of the Temple. [Although even Israelites may hold this office (*Minchas Chinuch* §9), Chinuch presumably refers to Kohanim since they would most often be the treasurers of the *Beis HaMikdash*.]

Chinuch below (at note 35) follows the view of *Rambam* (*Hil. Shekalim* 1:5) that the obligation of the half-*shekel* consists of giving half of a coin that is current at the time. *Rambam* (ibid.) writes that one gives this coin even if it weighs more than the *shekel* used in the times of Moses — though not if the weight of the current coin is *less* than the *shekel* of Moses. [As for which of the current coins should be used as the standard, *Chazon Ish* (*Choshen Mishpat* 16:16) suggests that the largest silver coin of the time should be used. Alternatively, the standard should be the coin that is the closest in value to the *shekel* used in the times of Moses. For another suggestion, and a discussion of this topic, see *Shekel HaKodesh* (R' Chaim Kanievsky), *Beur HaHalachah* 1:5 ד״ה מחצית.]

*Ramban* (to *Exodus* 30:13) and *Raavad* (Glosses to

## KI SISA / MITZVAH 105: THE OBLIGATION TO GIVE THE HALF-SHEKEL

זֶה יִתְּנוּ כָּל הָעֹבֵר עַל הַפְּקֻדִים.⁶ וְהָיוּ מַנִּיחִין הַכֹּל בְּלִשְׁכָּה אַחַת שֶׁבַּמִּקְדָּשׁ וּמִשָּׁם הָיוּ מוֹצִיאִין לִקְנוֹת תְּמִידִין⁸,⁷ וּמוּסָפִין⁹ וְכָל קָרְבָּן הַקָּרֵב עַל הַצִּבּוּר,¹⁰ וְנִסְכֵּיהֶם,¹¹ וְהַמֶּלַח שֶׁמּוֹלְחִין בּוֹ אֶת הַקָּרְבָּנוֹת,¹² וַעֲצֵי הַמַּעֲרָכָה,¹³ וְלֶחֶם הַפָּנִים,¹⁴ וְשָׂכָר

---

**"זֶה יִתְּנוּ כָּל הָעֹבֵר עַל הַפְּקֻדִים"** — We are so commanded, **as it is stated** (*Exodus* 30:13): ***This shall they give — everyone who passes through the census*** — *a half-shekel of the sacred shekel, the shekel is twenty gerahs,* etc.[6]

Chinuch details the designations of the funds that were collected through the annual half-*shekel* collection.

**וְהָיוּ מַנִּיחִין הַכֹּל בְּלִשְׁכָּה אַחַת שֶׁבַּמִּקְדָּשׁ** — [The treasurers] would place all the collected monies in a chamber in the Temple, **וּמִשָּׁם הָיוּ מוֹצִיאִין לִקְנוֹת** — and they would withdraw money from there for the purpose of buying the following items for Temple use:

Chinuch begins with the regular communal offerings in the *Beis HaMikdash*:[7]

**תְּמִידִין** — The animals for **the** daily ***tamid*** **offerings**;[8] **וּמוּסָפִין** — **the** ***mussaf*** (literally, *additional*) **offerings**;[9] **וְכָל קָרְבָּן הַקָּרֵב עַל הַצִּבּוּר** — and any other **offering that is offered for the community** of Israel;[10] **וְנִסְכֵּיהֶם** — as well as the accompanying *nesachim* offerings.[11]

Chinuch continues with other necessities related to the offerings, as well as additional communal offerings that were brought on various occasions:

**וְהַמֶּלַח שֶׁמּוֹלְחִין בּוֹ אֶת הַקָּרְבָּנוֹת** — Also purchased with funds from this account was **the salt with which they would salt the offerings**;[12] **וַעֲצֵי הַמַּעֲרָכָה** — **and the wood** that was needed **for the pyres** on the Altar, upon which the offerings were burnt;[13] **וְלֶחֶם הַפָּנִים** — **the** *Panim* **Breads**;[14] **וְשָׂכָר**

---

### NOTES

*Rambam* ibid.), however, maintain that the annual obligation is fixed at half the value of the *shekel* that was used in the times of Moses. This amount is defined further below.

6. Chinuch understands that this verse, as well as the following two verses, refer to the annual half-*shekel* obligation (see introduction to this mitzvah). Thus, rich and poor are obligated in this amount and those under 20 are exempt, as the verses state (vs. 14-15): *Everyone who passes through the census, from twenty years of age and up, shall give the portion of Hashem. The wealthy shall not increase and the destitute shall not decrease from half a shekel — to give the portion of Hashem, to atone for your souls.* [*Rama, Orach Chaim* 694:1 follows this opinion; cf. *Magen Avraham* ad loc.]

According to *Rambam* (*Hil. Shekalim* 1:7, as understood by *Minchas Chinuch* §1 and *Shaar HaMelech* ad loc.) and *Ramban* to v. 12, however, the verse that limits the obligation to those 20 and older is not speaking of the annual half-*shekel* obligation, but of the specific census that occurred in the days of Moses. Accordingly, the annual mitzvah to give the half-*shekel* applies to all adults, even to those younger than 20 (see also *Tos. Yom Tov, Shekalim* 1:4).

7. "Communal offerings" refer to those obligatory offerings in the *Beis HaMikdash* that the entire community of Israel are responsible to bring, and are offered by the Kohanim on behalf of the community.

8. The *tamid* (literally, *constant*) offerings were the two yearling sheep that were offered in the *Beis HaMikdash* every day of the year, one in the morning and one in the afternoon (*Numbers* 28:1-8; Mitzvah 401).

9. On the Sabbath, Rosh Chodesh, and each day of every Yom Tov, additional communal offerings are brought, aside from the daily *tamid* offerings. The type and number of animals offered on each occasion is set out in *Numbers* 28:9-29:38. [Each of these offerings individually constitutes its own mitzvah: these are set out below in Mitzvos 299, 312, 314, 320, 322, 402, 403, and 404.]

10. This phrase includes other communal offerings not included in this list, such as the two lambs that were brought as part of the Shavuos offerings, the daily incense (*ketores*) offering, and the special incense offering of Yom Kippur [Mitzvos 103 and 185] (see commentaries of *R' Meshullam* and *Talmid Rashbash* to *Shekalim* 9b; *Rav* to Mishnah *Shekalim* 4:1).

11. Every *olah* and *shelamim* offering must be accompanied by a *minchah* (meal) offering and a wine libation; these accompanying offerings are referred to collectively as *nesachim* (literally, *libations*). Any communal offering that was offered as an *olah* or *shelamim* thus also required accompanying *nesachim* offerings.

12. All offerings were salted before being offered upon the Altar (Mitzvos 118-119). The salt for private offerings was purchased by this fund as well (see below, Mitzvah 118, for the reason).

13. This wood was provided by the Temple, even for the offerings of private individuals; see previous note. [This wood would ordinarily be donated by certain families (see *Taanis* 28a); the half-*shekel* fund would be used only in the case where the donated wood did not suffice (see *Rambam, Hil. Shekalim* 4:1).]

14. Every Sabbath, twelve loaves of specially baked

הָעוֹשֶׂה לֶחֶם הַפָּנִים[15], וְהָעֹמֶר[16], וּשְׁתֵּי הַלֶּחֶם[17], וּפָרָה אֲדֻמָּה[18], וְשָׂעִיר הַמִּשְׁתַּלֵּחַ[19], וְלָשׁוֹן שֶׁל זְהוֹרִית[20].

מִשָּׁרְשֵׁי הַמִּצְוָה, שֶׁרָצָה הַקָּדוֹשׁ בָּרוּךְ הוּא לְטוֹבַת כָּל יִשְׂרָאֵל וְלִזְכוּתָם שֶׁיִּהְיֶה יַד כֻּלָּם שָׁוָה בִּדְבַר הַקָּרְבָּנוֹת הַקְּרֵבִים לְפָנָיו כָּל הַשָּׁנָה בְּהַתְמָדָה, וּבָעִנְיָנִים אֵלּוּ הַנִּזְכָּרִים,

הָעוֹשֶׂה לֶחֶם הַפָּנִים — the wages of those who make the *Panim* Bread;[15] וְהָעֹמֶר — the *Omer* offering;[16] וּשְׁתֵּי הַלֶּחֶם — the Two Loaves of bread that were offered on Shavuos;[17] וּפָרָה אֲדֻמָּה — the Red Cow;[18] וְשָׂעִיר הַמִּשְׁתַּלֵּחַ — the he-goat that is sent to *Azazel* on Yom Kippur;[19] וְלָשׁוֹן שֶׁל זְהוֹרִית — and the strip of red wool.[20]

### ◆ Underlying Purpose of the Mitzvah ◆

מִשָּׁרְשֵׁי הַמִּצְוָה — Among the underlying purposes of the mitzvah שֶׁרָצָה הַקָּדוֹשׁ בָּרוּךְ הוּא לְטוֹבַת כָּל יִשְׂרָאֵל וְלִזְכוּתָם — is that the Holy One, Blessed is He, wished, for the good of all of Israel and to increase their merit, שֶׁיִּהְיֶה יַד כֻּלָּם שָׁוָה בִּדְבַר הַקָּרְבָּנוֹת הַקְּרֵבִים לְפָנָיו כָּל הַשָּׁנָה בְּהַתְמָדָה — that they should all have an equal share in the offerings that were regularly offered before Him the entire year, וּבָעִנְיָנִים אֵלּוּ הַנִּזְכָּרִים — and in these other items

---

### NOTES

*lechem hapanim* [*Panim* Bread] were arranged on the golden *Shulchan* (Table) in the Temple, in two tiers of six loaves each. They remained on the *Shulchan* until the next Sabbath, when they would be replaced with twelve fresh loaves; see above, Mitzvah 97, for a full description of this mitzvah.

15. The shape of these loaves was unusual, and it took great skill to bake them in a manner that would allow them to be removed from the oven whole and fully baked (see *Yoma* 38a; see also above, Mitzvah 97 note 26). The craftsmen who baked them were compensated monetarily for their efforts.

16. On the second day of Pesach, a special offering, consisting of an *omer* (a measure equal to the volume of 43.2 eggs) of crushed barley grains was brought as a meal offering in the *Beis HaMikdash* (see *Leviticus* 2:14-16 and 23:9-13). See below, Mitzvah 302, for a description of this mitzvah.

17. This Shavuos offering consisted of two leavened (*chametz*) loaves, made of flour from the newly ripened crop of wheat (see *Leviticus* 23:16-17); see Mitzvah 307.

18. The ashes of a *Parah Adumah,* or Red Cow, were used in the purification of one who was contaminated with *tumah* (ritual impurity) stemming from a corpse. After the cow was slaughtered and burnt, its ashes were mixed with spring water, which was then sprinkled upon the affected person. Upon then immersing in a *mikveh*, he would become purified of the *tumah* (*Numbers* 19:1-22). See further, Mitzvah 397.

The *Parah Adumah* had to be completely red, without even two black hairs. Such cows were extremely rare, and thus commanded a very high price (see *Kiddushin* 31a).

19. In addition to the many offerings sacrificed in the *Beis HaMikdash* on Yom Kippur, part of the Yom Kippur service involved a he-goat (specially designated by lot for this purpose) that was sent to Azazel (i.e., a precipice in the desert; see *Yoma* 67a), where it was thrown from a cliff (*Leviticus* 16:22; see Mitzvah 95, at notes 51-55, for a discussion of this atonement ceremony).

20. Strips of red wool were used in the *Beis HaMikdash* on three different occasions: (1) Upon the burning of the *Parah Adumah* (see above, note 19), a bundle consisting of a piece of cedar wood and stalks of hyssop, bound together with a strip of red wool, was thrown into the blaze. (2) On Yom Kippur, a strip of red wool was used to distinguish between the two he-goats, which were identical in appearance, as one of the he-goats was designated for *Azazel* and one was offered in the *Beis HaMikdash*. (3) In addition, part of a strip of red wool would be tied between the horns of the *Azazel* goat, and part to a rock. As the *Azazel* goat fell down the cliff, the red strip, which symbolized the sins of the Jewish nation, would miraculously turn white to symbolize that they were forgiven.

The Mishnah (*Shekalim* 4:2) lists a strip of red wool among the items purchased with the half-*shekel* fund, and Rishonim differ as to which of these three uses is referred to. See commentaries to Mishnah ad loc. and to *Yerushalmi Shekalim* 10b; *Rambam, Hil. Shekalim* 4:1 with *Mishneh LaMelech*; *Shekel HaKodesh, Beur HaHalachah* to *Rambam* ibid.

The half-*shekel* funds were used to pay for numerous other things. For a full list, see *Rambam, Hil. Shekalim,* Ch. 4. [Another Temple account, separate and distinct from the half-*shekel* fund, was the one used for the upkeep of the Temple (*bedek habayis*). That account was not funded by any tax. Rather, people donated to it voluntarily, giving either money, or material fit for use in upkeep of the Temple, or articles that would be sold for profit by the Temple treasurer.]

## KI SISA / MITZVAH 105: THE OBLIGATION TO GIVE THE HALF-SHEKEL

וְשֶׁיִּהְיוּ הַכֹּל, אֶחָד עָנִי וְאֶחָד עָשִׁיר, שָׁוִים בְּמִצְוָה אַחַת לְפָנָיו לְהַעֲלוֹת זִכְרוֹן כֻּלָּן עַל יְדֵי הַמִּצְוָה שֶׁהֵם כְּלוּלִים בָּהּ יַחַד לְטוֹבָה לְפָנָיו. וַעֲלִיַּת הַזִּכָּרוֹן, הַכֹּל נֶאֱמַר מִצַּד הַמְקַבֵּל, עַל הַדֶּרֶךְ שֶׁכְּתַבְנוּ לְמַעְלָה (מצוה צ״ז)[21].

מִדִּינֵי הַמִּצְוָה, כְּגוֹן מַה שֶּׁאָמְרוּ זִכְרוֹנָם לִבְרָכָה (שקלים פ״א מ״א) שֶׁבְּאֶחָד בַּאֲדָר[22] מַשְׁמִיעִים עַל הַשְּׁקָלִים[23], וְשֶׁאֲפִלּוּ דַל שֶׁבַּדַּלִּים חַיָּב בּוֹ, וְאִם אֵין לוֹ, שׁוֹאֵל[24] מֵאֲחֵרִים אוֹ מוֹכֵר כְּסוּתוֹ שֶׁעָלָיו וְנוֹתְנוֹ, שֶׁנֶּאֱמַר (שמות ל׳, ט״ו) וְהַדַּל לֹא יַמְעִיט[25],

---

וְשֶׁיִּהְיוּ הַכֹּל אֶחָד עָנִי וְאֶחָד עָשִׁיר — mentioned above that were purchased with the half-*shekel* funds. שָׁוִים בְּמִצְוָה אַחַת לְפָנָיו — **In addition,** He wished **that all of Israel, both poor and rich, should have an equal part in one mitzvah** that they perform **before Him,** לְהַעֲלוֹת זִכְרוֹן כֻּלָּן עַל יְדֵי הַמִּצְוָה שֶׁהֵם כְּלוּלִים בָּהּ יַחַד לְטוֹבָה לְפָנָיו — **so that, through the mitzvah in which they are all included, the remembrance of all of them would be elevated favorably before Him.**

Chinuch qualifies the above statement, which speaks of a "remembrance" before God:

וַעֲלִיַּת הַזִּכָּרוֹן — **The idea that one's remembrance rises** before God, i.e., that He focuses on certain people or concepts at certain times, הַכֹּל נֶאֱמַר מִצַּד הַמְקַבֵּל עַל הַדֶּרֶךְ שֶׁכְּתַבְנוּ לְמַעְלָה — does not mean that God remembers certain things at one time and not at others; rather, **all such expressions are meant from the perspective of the receivers** of the action, in our case, the Jewish people, **as we have written above** (Mitzvah 30, 74, 97).[21]

### ~ Laws of the Mitzvah ~

מַה שֶּׁאָמְרוּ זִכְרוֹנָם — **Among the laws of the mitzvah** are, כְּגוֹן — **for example,** מִדִּינֵי הַמִּצְוָה — **that which** [the Sages], of blessed memory, have stated (*Shekalim* 1:1), **that on the first day** of Adar [**the *Beis Din*]**[22] **announces** the collection of **the *shekalim*;**[23] וְשֶׁאֲפִלּוּ דַל שֶׁבַּדַּלִּים חַיָּב בּוֹ — **and that even the poorest of the poor is obligated** to give the half-*shekel*, וְאִם אֵין לוֹ שׁוֹאֵל מֵאֲחֵרִים — **and if he does not have** enough money, **he should borrow**[24] **from others** אוֹ מוֹכֵר כְּסוּתוֹ שֶׁעָלָיו וְנוֹתְנוֹ — **or** he must **sell** even **the garment that he is wearing and give** [the half-*shekel*], שֶׁנֶּאֱמַר "וְהַדַּל לֹא יַמְעִיט" — **as it is stated** (*Exodus* 30:15): **the destitute shall not decrease** from half a shekel.[25]

Chinuch mentions some laws relating to the payment itself:

---

#### NOTES

21. Chinuch explains in a number of places that God never experiences changes of state in any way. When the Torah or the Sages speak of His anger or His mercy it does not mean that He is at times "angry" or at others "merciful." These are merely expressions of the different ways that *we experience* God's actions. Thus, when it is stated that God "remembers" the Jewish people favorably, this does not mean that there is only a specific time when they have His attention. Rather, it is merely a description of the situation wherein at a certain time the Jewish people experience God's favor. This situation is described in human terms as God's favorable "remembrance" of the Jewish people.

22. See *R' Meshullam, Shekalim* 2a; cf. *Talmid Rashbash, Shekalim* ibid.; see following note.

23. The *beis din* of Jerusalem would send out agents to wherever Jews lived, to remind them of their obligation to give a half-*shekel* before the month of Nissan commences.

The first of Nissan marked the start of a new year for contributions to the Temple treasury, and from that date onward the various communal offerings were purchased with these new funds. [The money remaining in the previous year's *shekel* fund was used to fund certain specific Temple projects; see *Shekalim* 10b-11a.] The *beis din* announced the collection on the first of the previous month, Adar, to provide people with a thirty-day advance reminder to bring their *shekalim* (see *Yerushalmi Shekalim* 1a).

24. Translation follows *Shekel HaKodesh, Beur HaHalachah* to 1:1 ד״ה אפילו עני.

25. With regard to most other mitzvah-obligations, there is no requirement to borrow or to sell one's garment in order to fulfill them; see *Rama, Orach Chaim* 656:1. The absolute obligation in this case, which requires even the most destitute to sell their clothing if necessary, stems from the specific Scriptural instruction that *the destitute shall not decrease*. For full discussion, see *Shekel HaKodesh, Beur HaHalachah* ibid.

וְאֵינוֹ נִתָּן בְּפִרְעוֹנוֹת הַרְבֵּה אֶלָּא הַכֹּל בְּפַעַם אַחַת[26], וְהוּא מִשְׁקַל שְׁמוֹנִים גַּרְעִינֵי שְׂעוֹרָה[27], שֶׁהַשֶּׁקֶל הַשָּׁלֵם הָיָה בִּימֵי מֹשֶׁה מִשְׁקַל מֵאָה וְשִׁשִּׁים שְׂעוֹרָה[28]. וְהַכֹּל חַיָּבִין לִתְּנָם, כֹּהֲנִים לְוִיִּם וְיִשְׂרְאֵלִים, גֵּרִים וַעֲבָדִים מְשֻׁחְרָרִין[29], אֲבָל לֹא נָשִׁים[30] וַעֲבָדִים וּקְטַנִּים[31]. וְאִם נָתְנוּ מְקַבְּלִין מֵהֶן[32], אֲבָל לֹא מִן הַגּוֹיִם, חֵלֶק וְנַחֲלָה לֹא יִהְיֶה לָהֶם בְּתוֹכֵנוּ[33].

---

וְאֵינוֹ נִתָּן בְּפִרְעוֹנוֹת הַרְבֵּה אֶלָּא הַכֹּל בְּפַעַם אַחַת — [The half-*shekel* payment] **may not be given in many** smaller **payments, rather, the entire amount** must be given **at one time**.[26] וְהוּא מִשְׁקַל שְׁמוֹנִים גַּרְעִינֵי שְׂעוֹרָה — [The half-*shekel*] **equals the weight of eighty barleycorns** of pure silver;[27] שֶׁהַשֶּׁקֶל הַשָּׁלֵם הָיָה בִּימֵי מֹשֶׁה מִשְׁקַל מֵאָה וְשִׁשִּׁים שְׂעוֹרָה — **for the whole-*shekel* in the times of Moses equaled the weight of 160 barleycorns** of pure silver; thus the half-*shekel* coin equaled half that amount.[28]

Chinuch sets forth who is obligated and who is exempt from this mitzvah:

כֹּהֲנִים לְוִיִּם וְיִשְׂרְאֵלִים גֵּרִים וְהַכֹּל חַיָּבִין לִתְּנָם — **Every** Jew **is obligated to give the** [half-*shekel*]: וַעֲבָדִים מְשֻׁחְרָרִין — **Kohanim, Levites, Israelites, proselytes, and freed** Canaanite **slaves**;[29] אֲבָל לֹא נָשִׁים וַעֲבָדִים וּקְטַנִּים — **but not women**,[30] Cannanite **slaves, or minors**.[31] וְאִם נָתְנוּ מְקַבְּלִין מֵהֶן — **However, if** [those who are exempt] **give** the half-*shekel* of their own volition, **it is accepted**.[32] אֲבָל לֹא מִן הַגּוֹיִם חֵלֶק וְנַחֲלָה לֹא יִהְיֶה לָהֶם בְּתוֹכֵנוּ — **However, we do not** accept donations to the half-*shekel* fund **from idolaters**, even if they offer such donations, for **they shall have no lot or portion among us** with regard to the communal offerings of the Jewish people in the *Beis HaMikdash*.[33]

---

NOTES

26. This halachah is first mentioned by *Rambam, Hil. Shekalim* 1:1. *Kiryas Sefer* writes that the source of the law is the wording of the above verse, לֹא יַמְעִיט מִמַּחֲצִית הַשֶּׁקֶל, *he shall not decrease from half a shekel*. If the intention of the verse was only that the poor may not give less, it would have said יִתֵּן מַחֲצִית הַשֶּׁקֶל, *he should give half a shekel*; the words *he shall not decrease* indicate not only that he may he not decrease from the amount, but also that he may not pay less than the full amount in any one payment. [According to R' Y. F. Perla (*Sefer HaMitzvos* of Rav Saadiah Gaon, *Asei* 20; Vol. I, p. 296), the *Aruch* (v. טבע ב׳) maintains that it is permitted to give the half-*shekel* in multiple payments.]

27. The barleycorn was a standard unit of weight for precious metals and gems in earlier times. [See following note.]

28. *Minchas Chinuch* §4 points out that this is an error in the printed edition; the actual amount of the whole *shekel* is 320 barleycorns, as *Rambam* writes (*Hil. Shekalim* 1:2) [and as Chinuch himself writes in Mitzvah 350]. Thus, the half-*shekel* is equal to 160 barleycorns of pure silver.

As Chinuch mentions below, the half-*shekel* obligation refers to half of the coin that is current in that time (see above, note 5). The weight given here for the amount of the half-*shekel* in the times of Moses is important because it serves as the minimum half-*shekel* donation. That is, in a case where the common coin of that time is worth less than the *shekel* of Moses' time, the mitzvah would require one to give the higher amount (*Minchas Chinuch* §4).

In today's terms, the half-*shekel* has been identified as being either 7.1 or 8 grams of silver (depending on the various opinions on the matter), which is the equivalent of approximately a quarter of a troy ounce (used for precious metals). For further discussion, see *Middos V'Shiurei Torah* 22:9-12 (R' Chaim Benisch, Bnei Brak, 2000).

29. When the Canaanite slave is emancipated, he attains the status of a full Jew, like any convert.

30. According to some authorities, the giving of the half-*shekel* is considered a time-specific mitzvah (since it must be performed before Nissan), from which women are generally exempt (*Meiri, Shekalim*, 1:2; see *Shekel HaKodesh* 1:46 with *Beur HaHalachah* 1:7 ד״ה אבל לא נשים). *Minchas Chinuch* §1 writes that it is not time-specific (presumably since it *can* be given at any time during the year), but that women are excluded from the obligation by a specific Scriptural exemption (see *Rambam, Sefer HaMitzvos, Asei* 171; and *Rav* to Mishnah *Shekalim* 1:3).

31. According to Chinuch above, the exemption of minors (found in the Mishnah, *Shekalim* 1:3) refers to anyone under 20; see above, note 6.

32. Some commentators raise the following question: The communal offerings must be bought with communal funds and may not be bought with private donations. Since the individuals listed here are actually exempt, when they give their half-*shekels* to the *Beis HaMikdash*, they would have the status of private donations. How can they be accepted in this fund? Some suggest that upon giving their half-*shekel*, these individuals must first donate it to the community at large, whereupon the money can be used for communal purposes (see *Minchas Chinuch* §1; see there also with regard to the legality of accepting such donations from minors).

33. Although idolaters may donate certain private offerings to the *Beis HaMikdash* (see *Rambam, Hil.*

# KI SISA / MITZVAH 105: THE OBLIGATION TO GIVE THE HALF-SHEKEL

וְעוֹד[34] אָמְרוּ זִכְרוֹנָם לִבְרָכָה שֶׁכָּל מִי שֶׁאֵינוֹ נוֹתֵן חֲצִי שֶׁקֶל מִמַּה שֶׁהָיָה מַטְבֵּעַ בְּאוֹתוֹ זְמַן[35] וְנוֹתֵן בַּעֲבוּרוֹ כֶּסֶף בְּמִשְׁקָלוֹ אוֹ פְּרוּטוֹת, שֶׁמּוֹסִיף עַל מִשְׁקַל שִׁקְלוֹ זֶה מְעַט[36], וְאוֹתוֹ הַמְעַט נִקְרָא קַלְבּוֹן[37], וְאוֹתוֹ הַמְעַט הוּא שְׂכַר הַשֻּׁלְחָנִי שֶׁמִּשְׁתַּכֵּר כְּשֶׁהוּא מַחֲלִיף חֲצִי שֶׁקֶל שֶׁהָיָה טָבוּעַ בִּשְׁבִיל פְּרוּטוֹת[38]. וּלְפִיכָךְ שְׁנַיִם שֶׁהֵבִיאוּ שֶׁקֶל שָׁלֵם בֵּין שְׁנֵיהֶם, חַיָּבִים בְּקַלְבּוֹן, שֶׁאִלּוּ רָצוּ לְהַחֲלִיפוֹ צְרִיכִין הָיוּ לִתֵּן הַקַּלְבּוֹן לַשֻּׁלְחָנִי, וּכְמוֹ כֵן יִתְּנוּהוּ לַגִּזְבָּר, לְפִי שֶׁבַּחֲצִי שֶׁקֶל חִיְּבָם הַכָּתוּב, וְלָכֵן חַיָּבִים בּוֹ אוֹ בְּעֶרְכּוֹ בְּכִוּוּן[39]. וְכֵן מַה שֶּׁאָמְרוּ זִכְרוֹנָם לִבְרָכָה

---

One need not give the exact denomination of the half-*shekel*; any amount of coins that equal the required amount may be given.[34] However, when one does not give the exact denomination, there is a separate "surcharge" that must be given along with the half-*shekel*, as Chinuch explains:

**שֶׁכָּל מִי שֶׁאֵינוֹ נוֹתֵן חֲצִי שֶׁקֶל** — [The Sages], of blessed memory, also stated **וְעוֹד אָמְרוּ זִכְרוֹנָם לִבְרָכָה** — that anyone who does not give for his half-*shekel* obligation the actual **coin that is current at that time**,[35] **וְנוֹתֵן בַּעֲבוּרוֹ כֶּסֶף בְּמִשְׁקָלוֹ אוֹ פְּרוּטוֹת** — and **instead gives** other silver **coins equal in weight to it, or** he gives *perutos* (smaller copper coins) that equal the required amount, **שֶׁמּוֹסִיף עַל מִשְׁקַל שִׁקְלוֹ זֶה מְעַט** — **must add, beyond this** amount of his "*shekel*" that he is giving, **a small amount.**[36] **וְאוֹתוֹ הַמְעַט נִקְרָא קַלְבּוֹן** — **This small** added **amount is called a** *kalbon*.[37]

Chinuch explains why the *kalbon* must be added:

**וְאוֹתוֹ הַמְעַט הוּא שְׂכַר הַשֻּׁלְחָנִי** — **This small amount** of the *kalbon* is in place of **the moneychanger's fee,** **שֶׁמִּשְׁתַּכֵּר כְּשֶׁהוּא מַחֲלִיף חֲצִי שֶׁקֶל שֶׁהָיָה טָבוּעַ בִּשְׁבִיל פְּרוּטוֹת** — which [the moneychanger] would earn by changing a half-*shekel* coin for *perutos*.[38]

**וּלְפִיכָךְ שְׁנַיִם שֶׁהֵבִיאוּ שֶׁקֶל שָׁלֵם בֵּין שְׁנֵיהֶם** — **Therefore, if two people bring a complete *shekel* to** the Temple officers as payment **for both** of their half-*shekel* obligations, **חַיָּבִים בְּקַלְבּוֹן** — **they are obligated,** between the two of them, to provide **an** additional **kalbon;** **שֶׁאִלּוּ רָצוּ לְהַחֲלִיפוֹ צְרִיכִין הָיוּ** **לִתֵּן הַקַּלְבּוֹן לַשֻּׁלְחָנִי** — **for if they wanted to change it** into two half-*shekel* coins for each of their individual obligations, **they would have had to give** the amount of **the *kalbon* to the moneychanger,** **וּכְמוֹ כֵן יִתְּנוּהוּ לַגִּזְבָּר** — **so they must likewise give [that amount]** to the Temple **treasurer.** **לְפִי שֶׁבַּחֲצִי שֶׁקֶל חִיְּבָם הַכָּתוּב** — **In both cases,** whether one is giving a higher or lower denomination than the half-*shekel* coin, the reason for the *kalbon* is the same: It is **because Scripture obligated people to give a half-*shekel*,** **וְלָכֵן חַיָּבִים בּוֹ אוֹ בְּעֶרְכּוֹ בְּכִוּוּן** — **and they are therefore obligated to give either [that coin], or its exact value.** Since other denominations are worth less (because half-*shekel* coins are in higher demand),[39] the *kalbon* offsets this difference in value.

Chinuch concludes with a law relating to half-*shekel* donations that were lost:

**וְכֵן מַה שֶּׁאָמְרוּ זִכְרוֹנָם לִבְרָכָה** — **Also** included in these laws is **that which [the Sages], of blessed**

---

## NOTES

*Maaseh HaKorbanos* 3:2), they have no share in the standard communal offerings, which are the obligation and privilege of the Jewish people alone.

34. See *Shekel HaKodesh, Beur HaHalachah* 1:1 ד״ה מחצית השקל כסף.

35. The mitzvah of the half-*shekel*, according to Chinuch, obligates one to give the value of half of the current coin to the Temple (see note 5 above).

36. According to *Shekel HaKodesh* (3:27), the amount to be added equals a twenty-fourth of the amount he is giving for the half-*shekel* obligation.

37. The term קַלְבּוֹן (*kalbon*) is an acronym formed of the words קַל, *light*, and בֵּין, *between*; thus the word denotes a small ("light") sum representing the difference "between" the value of the half-*shekel* coins and that of the other denominations totaling that sum (as Chinuch explains below); see *Rav, Shekalim* 1:6.

In certain situations one may be exempt from the *kalbon* obligation even when not giving the exact denomination; see *Rambam, Hil. Shekalim* 3:1-7.

38. At the time of the collection of the half-*shekels*, half-*shekel* coins were in high demand. One who wanted to change other denominations, whether higher or lower, for a half-*shekel* coin would have to pay a small charge to the moneychanger for the service. If one chooses to give other denominations to the *Beis HaMikdash* instead of an actual half-*shekel* coin, he must add the amount of the moneychanger's fee to his donation.

39. See *Rambam, Hil. Shekalim* 3:1.

## 302 ❑ כי תשא / מצוה קה: מצוות נתינת מחצית השקל

(שם פ״ב מ״א) בְּמִי שֶׁאָבַד שִׁקְלוֹ בַּדֶּרֶךְ מַה דִּינוֹ⁴⁰, וְיֶתֶר רַבֵּי פְּרָטֶיהָ, מְבֹאָרִים בְּמַסֶּכְתָּא הַבְּנוּיָה עַל זֶה וְהִיא מַסֶּכֶת שְׁקָלִים.⁴¹

וְנוֹהֶגֶת בִּזְמַן הַבַּיִת, שֶׁחַיָּבִין לָתֵת אוֹתָם כָּל יִשְׂרָאֵל בֵּין הָעוֹמְדִין בָּאָרֶץ אוֹ חוּצָה לָאָרֶץ, וְשֶׁלֹּא בִּזְמַן הַבַּיִת אֵין חַיָּב בָּהּ אָדָם וַאֲפִלּוּ הָעוֹמְדִין בָּאָרֶץ.⁴² וְהָעוֹבֵר עָלֶיהָ וְלֹא נְתָנוֹ, בִּטֵּל עֲשֵׂה, וְעָנְשׁוֹ גָּדוֹל, שֶׁפֵּרֵשׁ עַצְמוֹ מִן הַצִּבּוּר, וְאֵינוֹ בִּכְלַל כַּפָּרָתָן.⁴³

וְעַכְשָׁו בַּעֲווֹנוֹתֵינוּ שֶׁאֵין לָנוּ מִקְדָּשׁ וְלֹא שְׁקָלִים, נָהֲגוּ כָּל יִשְׂרָאֵל לְזֵכֶר הַדָּבָר לִקְרוֹת בְּבֵית הַכְּנֶסֶת בְּכָל שָׁנָה וְשָׁנָה פָּרָשָׁה זוֹ שֶׁל כִּי תִשָּׂא עַד וְלָקַחְתָּ אֶת כֶּסֶף הַכִּפֻּרִים,

---

**בְּמִי שֶׁאָבַד שִׁקְלוֹ בַּדֶּרֶךְ מַה דִּינוֹ** — regarding what the law is for one whose half-*shekel* was lost while en route to the Temple.[40] **וְיֶתֶר רַבֵּי פְּרָטֶיהָ מְבֹאָרִים בְּמַסֶּכְתָּא הַבְּנוּיָה עַל זֶה וְהִיא מַסֶּכֶת שְׁקָלִים** — These, and the many other details of [the mitzvah] are set forth in the tractate based upon this mitzvah, which is Tractate *Shekalim*.[41]

### ⌒ Applicability of the Mitzvah ⌒

**וְנוֹהֶגֶת בִּזְמַן הַבַּיִת** — This mitzvah applies in the times of the Temple, i.e., when the *Beis HaMikdash* stands, **שֶׁחַיָּבִין לָתֵת אוֹתָם כָּל יִשְׂרָאֵל בֵּין הָעוֹמְדִין בָּאָרֶץ אוֹ חוּצָה לָאָרֶץ** — at which time all of Israel is obligated to give [the half-*shekels*], both those Jews residing in Eretz Yisrael, and those residing outside of Eretz Yisrael. **וְשֶׁלֹּא בִּזְמַן הַבַּיִת אֵין חַיָּב בָּהּ אָדָם וַאֲפִלּוּ הָעוֹמְדִין בָּאָרֶץ** — When it is not in the times of the Temple, no one is obligated in [this mitzvah], even those who reside in Eretz Yisrael.[42] **וְהָעוֹבֵר עָלֶיהָ וְלֹא נְתָנוֹ בִּטֵּל עֲשֵׂה וְעָנְשׁוֹ גָּדוֹל** — One who transgresses this mitzvah and does not give the half-*shekel* (when the *Beis HaMikdash* is standing) has violated this mitzvah-obligation, and his punishment is great, **שֶׁפֵּרֵשׁ עַצְמוֹ מִן הַצִּבּוּר וְאֵינוֹ בִּכְלַל כַּפָּרָתָן** — for he has separated himself from the general community, who are participants in the communal offerings, and he is therefore not included in their atonement.[43] **וְעַכְשָׁו בַּעֲווֹנוֹתֵינוּ שֶׁאֵין לָנוּ מִקְדָּשׁ וְלֹא שְׁקָלִים** — Nowadays, when, due to our sins, we no longer have a Temple in which to bring offerings, nor the mitzvah to give the *shekalim* for these offerings, **נָהֲגוּ כָּל יִשְׂרָאֵל לְזֵכֶר הַדָּבָר** — it is the practice of all of Israel, in remembrance of [this mitzvah], **לִקְרוֹת בְּבֵית הַכְּנֶסֶת בְּכָל שָׁנָה וְשָׁנָה פָּרָשָׁה זוֹ** — to read aloud in the synagogue, each and every year, this Torah passage in which the mitzvah of *shekalim* is written, **שֶׁל כִּי תִשָּׂא עַד וְלָקַחְתָּ אֶת כֶּסֶף הַכִּפֻּרִים** — that is, from the beginning of *Parashas Ki Sisa*, which reads, *Hashem spoke, to Moses saying: When you take a census* etc. (30:11-12), until the end of the verse, *You shall take the silver of*

---

### NOTES

40. One whose half-*shekel* already reached the Temple treasurer has fulfilled his obligation, and is no longer responsible for it, even if it was subsequently lost. However, if one sent his half-*shekel* with an agent (or, as in the case of the Mishnah [*Shekalim* 2:1], if a city sent an agent with all of their half-*shekels*) to the Temple, and it was lost en route, there are various factors that determine responsibility. These factors include what level of responsibility the agent accepted, what the circumstances of the loss were (avoidable or unavoidable), and when the loss occurred (before the *shekel* fund was drawn upon in the Temple or afterward). See *Rambam, Hil. Shekalim* 3:8-9 for the various details of this law.

41. The laws are codified in *Rambam, Hil. Shekalim*.

42. As explained, the purpose of this mitzvah is to provide funds for the communal offerings, which obviously are not brought when there is no *Beis HaMikdash*.

43. The offerings are a source of atonement for the community of Israel; one who intentionally excludes himself from participation in the offerings is therefore not a recipient of that atonement (see *Meiri, Shekalim* 2:2). [See Insight regarding the share in the communal offerings of those who are exempt from the half-*shekel* obligation.]

## KI SISA / MITZVAH 105: THE OBLIGATION TO GIVE THE HALF-SHEKEL

בְּשַׁבָּת שֶׁהוּא לִפְנֵי רֹאשׁ חֹדֶשׁ אֲדָר לְעוֹלָם.[44]

*the atonements* etc. (v. 16). בְּשַׁבָּת שֶׁהוּא לִפְנֵי רֹאשׁ חֹדֶשׁ אֲדָר לְעוֹלָם — This passage is read annually, **always on the Sabbath before Rosh Chodesh Adar** (the first day of Adar).[44]

### NOTES

44. This is in remembrance of the *shekalim* announcement, which, as Chinuch noted above, was made on the first day of Adar. If Rosh Chodesh Adar itself falls on the Sabbath, the *shekalim* passage is read that Sabbath (*Rambam, Hil. Tefillah* 13:20; *Shulchan Aruch, Orach Chaim* 685:1). [According to *Rashi* (*Megillah* 29a ד"ה קורין בפרשת שקלים), this custom did not originate as a mere remembrance. Rather, the Torah passage of *shekalim* was read on the Sabbath before Rosh Chodesh Adar even when the *Beis HaMikdash* stood, for this was a way of announcing that the time for bringing the *shekalim* was upon them. See also Gemara there, 29b, 30a.]

There is an additional custom, recorded by *Rama* (*Orach Chaim* 694:1), that was instituted as a remembrance for the mitzvah of the half-*shekel*: Before Purim, each person gives three halves of the standard coin of that time and place to charity. See there, with *Mishnah Berurah*, for the details of this custom.

---

**ఆξ Insight: The Half-Shekel Obligation and the Mussaf Prayer**

Women are exempt from the obligation to give the annual half-*shekel* (Chinuch, above; see note 30). Some authorities have inferred that since the primary purpose of the half-*shekel* collection is to fund the communal offerings in the *Beis HaMikdash*, the fact that women are exempt from the half-*shekel* obligation indicates that they are not included in the obligation upon the community to bring these communal offerings. Other authorities differ, maintaining that the exemption from one is not sufficient proof of an exemption from the other. Although today the communal offerings can no longer be brought, this dispute does have practical ramifications in the context of the laws of prayer. Following is a discussion of these two views as they relate to women's obligation in the *Mussaf* prayer.

Like men, women are obligated to pray daily. This includes, according to most authorities, the obligation to recite the morning and afternoon prayers (see *Shulchan Aruch, Orach Chaim* 106:1 with *Mishnah Berurah* §4). Although this is a time-specific obligation, from which women are generally exempt, the *necessity* to beseech God for His mercy is one that applies to men and women equally, and this necessity provides a basis to *obligate* women to pray (*Mishnah Berurah* ibid.). However, this reasoning applies only to the standard daily prayers, whose primary purpose is entreaty. The *Mussaf* prayer was instituted not primarily to beg God's mercy, but as an expression of praise to Him, in representation of the *Mussaf* offering in the *Beis HaMikdash* (see *Rabbeinu Yonah, Berachos* fol. 13a in *Rif* ד"ה ויש; see above, note 9, regarding this offering). Thus, the standard reason to include women in the prayer obligation does not seem to apply to the *Mussaf* prayer.

If women are obligated as men are in all the communal offerings, there is a reason to obligate women in the *Mussaf* prayer, since it is representative of the *Mussaf* offering in which women are obligated. Thus, the question of whether women must recite the *Mussaf* prayer today is contingent upon the question of whether they are included in the obligation of all the communal offerings in the times of the *Beis HaMikdash*. It has been proposed that the exemption of women from the half-*shekel* obligation indicates that women have no obligation in the communal offerings, and that they are therefore exempt from reciting the *Mussaf* prayer (see *Teshuvos R' Akiva Eiger* §9, and *R' Akiva Eiger* on *Shulchan Aruch, Orach Chaim* 106:2).

Many Acharonim take exception to this line of reasoning (see, for example, *Amudei Ohr* §7; *Be'er Yitzchak, Orach Chaim* 20:3 and *Zecher Yitzchak* §2). One of the primary challenges put forth relates to the view of the Tanna Ben Buchri (cited in the Mishnah, *Shekalim* 1:3), who maintains that Kohanim and Leviim are exempt from contributing to the half-*shekel* fund. [The halachah does not follow this view, and Chinuch (at note 29) lists Kohanim and Leviim among those obligated to give the half-*shekel*.] Following the above logic — that those who are exempt from the half-*shekel* must be exempt from the communal offerings — the entire tribe of Levi would seem to have no part in the communal offerings according to Ben Buchri! Taking this one step further, all Kohanim and Leviim would also be exempted from the *Mussaf* prayers. Yet (as *Amudei Ohr* demonstrates) it is

clear from the Gemara (*Succah* 53a) that the Leviim did recite an obligatory *Mussaf* prayer in the *Beis HaMikdash*. This seems to indicate that no direct line can be drawn from the half-*shekel* exemption to an exemption from the *Mussaf* prayer. Even those whom the Torah exempted from donating the half-*shekel* were included in the atonement afforded by the communal offerings, and were exempt only from the *tax* imposed to pay for those offerings. And since they received atonement through the *Mussaf* offering, they are obligated in the *Mussaf* prayer as well. It follows that even though women are exempt from the half-*shekel*, they may still be included in the obligation to recite the *Mussaf* prayer.

*Kehillos Yaakov* (*Zevachim* §4), however, notes that there is a difference between the men of the tribe of Levi and women. Even according to Ben Buchri, who exempts Kohanim and Leviim from the specific mitzvah of the half-*shekel*, they are certainly obligated in the mitzvah of the communal offerings, just as they are obligated in all mitzvos. Thus, theoretically, were the half-*shekel* fund to be depleted in the middle of the year, and a collection imposed on the community to fund the remaining communal offerings, Kohanim and Leviim — as part of the community obligated to bring these offerings — would be equally responsible to contribute. Ben Buchri exempts them only from the specific mitzvah-obligation of giving the annual half-*shekel*, which is required of all others even if there already are sufficient funds for the communal offerings. But surely they are just as responsible as all other Jews to ensure that the communal offerings, including *Mussafin*, are brought. This, in turn, causes them to be obligated in the *Mussaf* prayer.

The obligation of women in the communal offerings, however, cannot be assumed, because the communal offerings are time-specific mitzvos, from which women are generally exempt. [The *Mussafin* are brought on specific days, and even the daily *tamid* offerings cannot be brought at night.] Now, if women were obligated to contribute to the half-*shekel* fund, this would have led us to conclude that they are obligated in the communal offerings as well, in exception to the general rule regarding time-specific mitzvos. But since women are exempt from the half-*shekel* obligation, we revert to the general rule that women are exempt from the obligations of the communal offerings, just as they are exempt from all time-specific mitzvos. Thus, support can be found for the exemption of women from the *Mussaf* prayer, not due to their exemption from the mitzvah of the half-*shekel*, but rather, because they are actually exempt from all communal offerings, and among them the *Mussaf* offering.

The question of the obligation of women in the *Mussaf* prayer involves other points of debate as well. For further discussion, see *Tzlach, Berachos* 26a; *Sdei Chemed, Maareches Yom Tov,* 2:6; *Mishnah Berurah* 106:4.

## KI SISA / MITZVAH 106: TO SANCTIFY HANDS AND FEET WHEN SERVING

### מִצְוָה קו: מִצְוַת קִדּוּשׁ יָדַיִם וְרַגְלַיִם בִּשְׁעַת עֲבוֹדָה

לִרְחֹץ הַיָּדַיִם וְהָרַגְלַיִם בְּכָל עֵת הִכָּנֵס לַהֵיכָל,[1] וְהַבָּא לַעֲבֹד עֲבוֹדָה, וְזֹאת הִיא מִצְוַת קִדּוּשׁ יָדַיִם וְרַגְלַיִם,[2] שֶׁנֶּאֱמַר (שמות ל׳, י״ט) וְרָחֲצוּ אַהֲרֹן וּבָנָיו מִמֶּנּוּ אֶת יְדֵיהֶם וְאֶת רַגְלֵיהֶם בְּבֹאָם אֶל אֹהֶל מוֹעֵד וְגוֹ׳ אוֹ בְגִשְׁתָּם אֶל הַמִּזְבֵּחַ וְגוֹ׳.[3]

---

## Mitzvah 106

### The Obligation [Upon Kohanim] to Sanctify Their Hands and Feet When Serving [in the Temple]

וְרָחֲצוּ אַהֲרֹן וּבָנָיו מִמֶּנּוּ אֶת יְדֵיהֶם וְאֶת רַגְלֵיהֶם. בְּבֹאָם אֶל אֹהֶל מוֹעֵד יִרְחֲצוּ מַיִם וְלֹא יָמֻתוּ אוֹ בְגִשְׁתָּם אֶל הַמִּזְבֵּחַ לְשָׁרֵת לְהַקְטִיר אִשֶּׁה לַה׳

*From it (the Kiyor, i.e., Laver), Aaron and his sons shall wash their hands together with their feet. Whenever they come to the Tent of Meeting, they shall wash with water and not die, or when they approach the Altar to serve, to raise up in smoke a fire-offering to Hashem (Exodus 30:19-20).*

**לִרְחֹץ הַיָּדַיִם וְהָרַגְלַיִם בְּכָל עֵת הִכָּנֵס לַהֵיכָל** — The Kohanim are commanded **to wash** their **hands and** their **feet any time they enter the** *Heichal* (Sanctuary),[1] **וְהַבָּא לַעֲבֹד עֲבוֹדָה** — **and upon coming to perform the** Divine *avodah* (service, pl. *avodos*) in the Temple, even if they perform that *avodah* in the Courtyard; **וְזֹאת הִיא מִצְוַת קִדּוּשׁ יָדַיִם וְרַגְלַיִם** — **this is** referred to as **the mitzvah of "sanctification of the hands and feet."**[2] **שֶׁנֶּאֱמַר "וְרָחֲצוּ אַהֲרֹן וּבָנָיו מִמֶּנּוּ אֶת יְדֵיהֶם וְאֶת רַגְלֵיהֶם** — Kohanim are so commanded, **as the verse states** (*Exodus* 30:19-20): *From it, Aaron and his sons shall wash their hands together with their feet.* **בְּבֹאָם אֶל אֹהֶל מוֹעֵד וְגוֹ׳ אוֹ בְגִשְׁתָּם אֶל הַמִּזְבֵּחַ וְגוֹ׳** — *Whenever they come to the Tent of Meeting ... or when they approach the Altar to serve, etc.*[3]

---

### NOTES

1. See Mitzvah 95 (at note 67), where Chinuch describes the components of the Temple complex. The *Heichal* refers to the Temple building (in contrast to the Courtyard).

2. It is so called because by washing the hands and feet in the procedure outlined below, the Kohanim sanctify their hands and feet for the Divine service.

Note that Chinuch mentions two actions that require a prior washing of the hands and feet: (1) Entering the *Heichal*; this applies even if one enters the *Heichal* without the intention to perform an *avodah* there (although it is forbidden to enter without performing some service — see Mitzvah 184); and (2) performing the *avodah* anywhere in the *Beis HaMikdash*. This includes *avodah* that is performed outside the *Heichal*, such as those *avodos* that were performed on the Outer Altar, situated in the Temple Courtyard (*Minchas Chinuch* §1). See further, following note.

3. The mitzvah addresses "Aaron and his sons," i.e., the Kohanim of that generation, as well as the Kohanim of all further generations (as v. 21 states: לְדֹרֹתָם, *for their generations* — *Noda BiYehudah* II, *Orach Chaim* §87).

Chinuch cites the two parts of the verse that indicate the two requirements of washing the hands and feet discussed in the previous note: (1) "*When they come to the Tent of Meeting*," referring to the interior of the *Mishkan* (Tabernacle), which corresponds, in the Temple complex, to the *Heichal* building; and (2) "*When they approach the Altar to serve*" refers to serving at the Altar in the Courtyard of the *Mishkan*, which corresponds to service at the Altar situated in the Courtyard of the *Beis HaMikdash* (see *Tosafos, Yoma* 5b ד״ה להביא; *Minchas Chinuch* §1).

[Chinuch's view is disputed by other Rishonim, who maintain that these verses do not mean to require sanctification for merely *entering* the *Heichal*; rather, only performing an *avodah* requires prior sanctification by Biblical law (though there is a Rabbinic requirement of sanctification before entering the *Heichal*; see *Keilim* 1:9 with commentaries). According to this view, the word לְשָׁרֵת, *to serve*, in the above verse (אוֹ בְגִשְׁתָּם אֶל הַמִּזְבֵּחַ לְשָׁרֵת, *or when they approach the Altar to serve*), qualifies both the phrase "*when they approach the Altar*," and "*when they come to the Tent of Meeting*." That is, whether the Kohanim are going to serve at the Altar or in the *Heichal*, they are obligated to wash their hands and feet (*Rashi* to verse; see *Zevachim* 19b and *Minchas Chinuch* ibid.). According to *Minchas Chinuch*, this is also the opinion of *Rambam, Hil. Bi'as HaMikdash* 5:1.]

מִשָּׁרְשֵׁי הַמִּצְוָה, הַיְסוֹד הַקָּבוּעַ שֶׁאָמַרְנוּ לְהַגְדִּיל כְּבוֹד הַבַּיִת וְכָל הַמְּלָאכוֹת הַנַּעֲשׂוֹת שָׁם, עַל כֵּן רָאוּי לְנַקּוֹת הַיָּדַיִם, שֶׁהֵן הָעוֹשׂוֹת בַּמְּלָאכָה, בְּכָל עֵת יִגְּעוּ הַכֹּהֲנִים בְּעִנְיְנֵי הַבַּיִת[4]. וּמִזֶּה הַשֹּׁרֶשׁ אָמְרוּ זִכְרוֹנָם לִבְרָכָה (זבחים דף י״ט ע״ב) שֶׁאֵין הַכֹּהֵן צָרִיךְ לְקַדֵּשׁ יָדָיו בֵּין עֲבוֹדָה לַעֲבוֹדָה אֶלָּא פַּעַם אַחַת בַּבֹּקֶר, וְעוֹבֵד כָּל הַיּוֹם וְכָל הַלַּיְלָה, וְהוּא שֶׁלֹּא יִישַׁן וְלֹא יַטִּיל מַיִם וְלֹא יַסִּיחַ דַּעְתּוֹ[5]. נִרְאֶה מִכָּל זֶה שֶׁאֵין הַכַּוָּנָה בִּרְחִיצָה מִתְּחִלָּה אֶלָּא לְהַגְדִּיל כְּבוֹד הַבַּיִת, שֶׁאֲפִלּוּ הָיָה טָהוֹר וְנָקִי בִּתְחִלַּת בּוֹאוֹ שָׁם צָרִיךְ לִרְחֹץ, וּמִשֶּׁהִתְחִיל בַּעֲבוֹדָה אֵין צָרִיךְ עוֹד לִרְחִיצָה בֵּין עֲבוֹדָה לַעֲבוֹדָה, זוּלָתִי בְּיוֹם הַכִּפּוּרִים לְרֹב חֻמְרוֹ שֶׁל יוֹם[6],

## ⸺ Underlying Purpose of the Mitzvah ⸺

מִשָּׁרְשֵׁי הַמִּצְוָה הַיְסוֹד הַקָּבוּעַ שֶׁאָמַרְנוּ — **Among the underlying purposes of the mitzvah is the firm foundation that we have mentioned** regarding many of the mitzvos relating to the Holy Temple (Mitzvos 95, 98, 103), לְהַגְדִּיל כְּבוֹד הַבַּיִת וְכָל הַמְּלָאכוֹת הַנַּעֲשׂוֹת שָׁם — namely, that their goal is **to raise** in our eyes **the prestige of the Temple and** the prestige of **all the activities that were done there.** עַל כֵּן רָאוּי לְנַקּוֹת הַיָּדַיִם שֶׁהֵן הָעוֹשׂוֹת בַּמְּלָאכָה — **It is therefore fitting to clean the hands, for it is** [the hands] **that execute all the** required **actions,** בְּכָל עֵת יִגְּעוּ הַכֹּהֲנִים בְּעִנְיְנֵי הַבַּיִת — **anytime** that **the Kohanim touch anything related to the** Holy **Temple.**[4] The purpose of this washing is not simple cleanliness, but to promote an awareness of the honor of the *Beis HaMikdash* (Holy Temple) and the various activities performed therein.

Chinuch cites certain laws regarding this washing to illustrate how the purpose of honoring the *Beis HaMikdash* and its service is reflected in the laws of the mitzvah:

וּמִזֶּה הַשֹּׁרֶשׁ אָמְרוּ זִכְרוֹנָם לִבְרָכָה — **As a reflection of this underlying purpose** of the mitzvah [**the Sages**], **of blessed memory, have stated** (*Zevachim* 19b) שֶׁאֵין הַכֹּהֵן צָרִיךְ לְקַדֵּשׁ יָדָיו בֵּין עֲבוֹדָה לַעֲבוֹדָה — **that a Kohen need not sanctify his hands between** one *avodah* **and** another *avodah* that he performs in the Temple, even if they became soiled with blood or fat as a result of the first *avodah*; אֶלָּא פַּעַם אַחַת בַּבֹּקֶר וְעוֹבֵד כָּל הַיּוֹם וְכָל הַלַּיְלָה — **rather, he washes once in the morning and he can** then **serve the entire day and the night** immediately following, without requiring any additional washing, וְהוּא שֶׁלֹּא יִישַׁן וְלֹא יַטִּיל מַיִם וְלֹא יַסִּיחַ דַּעְתּוֹ — **as long as he does not sleep, pass water** (urinate), **or divert his attention** from the cleanliness of his hands the entire time.[5] נִרְאֶה מִכָּל זֶה — **It seems from all of this,** i.e., from the obligation to wash in the morning, and the lack of any additional requirement to wash throughout the day, שֶׁאֵין הַכַּוָּנָה בִּרְחִיצָה מִתְּחִלָּה אֶלָּא לְהַגְדִּיל כְּבוֹד הַבַּיִת — **that the only intention of the initial washing is to raise the prestige of the** Holy **Temple,** שֶׁאֲפִלּוּ הָיָה טָהוֹר וְנָקִי בִּתְחִלַּת בּוֹאוֹ שָׁם צָרִיךְ לִרְחֹץ — **for even if** [a Kohen] **was pure** (of any ritual impurity) **and clean when he first comes** [to the Temple], **he is still required to wash** before engaging in any *avodah*, וּמִשֶּׁהִתְחִיל בַּעֲבוֹדָה אֵין צָרִיךְ עוֹד לִרְחִיצָה בֵּין עֲבוֹדָה לַעֲבוֹדָה — **yet once he has begun the** *avodah*, **he does not require any new washing between** his performance of one *avodah* **and** his performance of another *avodah*, even if his hands became soiled through the first *avodah*. זוּלָתִי בְּיוֹם הַכִּפּוּרִים לְרֹב חֻמְרוֹ שֶׁל יוֹם — **The only exception is on Yom Kippur,** when the Kohen Gadol performs the sanctification of the hands and feet ten times throughout the day, **due to the great stringency of the Yom Kippur day.**[6]

---

### NOTES

4. Since Kohanim serve barefoot, it is a sign of respect to wash the feet as well, as the feet are often soiled (*Ramban* to verse 19). [Throughout this mitzvah, Chinuch uses the phrase "sanctification of the hands," referring to sanctification of both hands and feet.]

5. After washing the hands, one must take heed to keep them from becoming soiled in a mundane manner. If he diverted his attention from this, he must wash again.

Urinating often results in one's hands being soiled (see *Yoma* 29b-30a), and therefore requires one to wash again afterward. Likewise, while sleeping one cannot keep his hands from touching parts of his body that are usually covered, so another washing is required upon awakening (see *Minchas Chinuch* §4).

6. The greater severity of the day demands greater care to wash at each interval, out of concern that the

לְפִי שֶׁבָּל עֵסֶק עֲבוֹדַת הַבַּיִת אָנוּ מַחֲזִיקִין וְרוֹאִין בְּלִבֵּנוּ, טָהוֹר וְנָקִי וְקָדוֹשׁ.[7]

מִדִּינֵי הַמִּצְוָה, מַה שֶּׁאָמְרוּ זִכְרוֹנָם לִבְרָכָה (שם דף כ' ע"ב) שֶׁהַיּוֹצֵא חוּץ לְחוֹמַת הָעֲזָרָה טָעוּן קִדּוּשׁ יָדַיִם, וְאִם קִדֵּשׁ יָדָיו הַיּוֹם, צָרִיךְ לַחֲזֹר וּלְקַדֵּשׁ לְמָחָר, אַף עַל פִּי שֶׁלֹּא יָשַׁן כָּל הַלַּיְלָה, שֶׁהַיָּדַיִם נִפְסָלוֹת בְּלִינָה.[8] וְשֶׁמִּצְוָה לְכַתְּחִלָּה לִרְחֹץ בְּשַׁחֲרִית פָּנָיו יָדָיו וְרַגְלָיו,[9] וְשֶׁמִּצְוָה לְקַדֵּשׁ בְּמֵי הַכִּיּוֹר, וְאִם קִדֵּשׁ מֵאֶחָד מִכְּלֵי שָׁרֵת כָּשֵׁר

**לְפִי שֶׁבָּל עֵסֶק עֲבוֹדַת הַבַּיִת אָנוּ מַחֲזִיקִין וְרוֹאִין בְּלִבֵּנוּ טָהוֹר וְנָקִי וְקָדוֹשׁ** — The reason a new washing is ordinarily not required, even though the Kohen's hands may have become soiled when performing a previous *avodah*, is **because we hold and view all involvement in the Temple *avodah* as pure and clean and holy.**[7]

## ⇐ Laws of the Mitzvah ⇒

**מִדִּינֵי הַמִּצְוָה מַה שֶּׁאָמְרוּ זִכְרוֹנָם לִבְרָכָה** — **Among the laws of the mitzvah is that which the Sages, of blessed memory, have stated** (see *Zevachim* 19b, 20b), **שֶׁהַיּוֹצֵא חוּץ לְחוֹמַת הָעֲזָרָה טָעוּן קִדּוּשׁ יָדַיִם** — **that one who** performs the sanctification and then **goes out beyond the walls of the** Temple **Courtyard requires a** new **sanctification of the hands** upon returning; **וְאִם קִדֵּשׁ יָדָיו הַיּוֹם צָרִיךְ** — **and that if one sanctified his hands one day, he is required to sanctify them again the following day,** לַחֲזֹר וּלְקַדֵּשׁ לְמָחָר — **אַף עַל פִּי שֶׁלֹּא יָשַׁן כָּל הַלַּיְלָה** — **even if he did not sleep the entire** intervening **night,** שֶׁהַיָּדַיִם נִפְסָלוֹת בְּלִינָה — **because** the sanctification of **the hands becomes invalidated with the passing of the night.**[8] **וְשֶׁמִּצְוָה לְכַתְּחִלָּה לִרְחֹץ בְּשַׁחֲרִית פָּנָיו יָדָיו וְרַגְלָיו** — It is also **a mitzvah, preferably, to wash one's face, hands, and feet in the morning.**[9]

A special vessel, the *Kiyor* (Laver), was designated to facilitate the sanctification of the hands and feet, as the verse states (*Exodus* 30:18-19): *You shall make a copper Laver and its base of copper, for washing … From it, Aaron and his sons shall wash …* This vessel was a large cauldron-like copper utensil, set upon a base and filled with water, with spouts at the bottom through which the water flowed (*Rashi* ad loc.). It was situated in the courtyard of the *Beis HaMikdash*. Chinuch discusses the laws associated with the *Kiyor*:

**וְשֶׁמִּצְוָה לְקַדֵּשׁ בְּמֵי הַכִּיּוֹר** — The appropriate way to fulfill **the mitzvah is to sanctify** the hands and feet **with the water of the *Kiyor*,** וְאִם קִדֵּשׁ מֵאֶחָד מִכְּלֵי שָׁרֵת כָּשֵׁר דִּיעֲבַד — **but if [a**

---

### NOTES

Kohen Gadol may have touched something unclean (see *Chizkuni, Leviticus* 16:4).

7. Even if something were to adhere to the hands or feet of the Kohen from the *avodah* that he has performed, we do not regard it as something that needs to be washed off, due to the great reverence with which we view all the activities of the *Beis HaMikdash*.

8. The verse states that the Kohanim must wash their hands and feet "*when they approach the Altar.*" Since a new arrangement of wood is placed on the Altar each morning, when the Kohen comes to perform a service in the morning he is considered to be making a new "approach" to the Altar. A Kohen must therefore wash his hands and feet each morning in the *Beis HaMikdash*, and may not rely on his washing of the previous day (*Zevachim* 19b with *Rashi* ד"ה דכתיב בגשתם; see also *Minchas Chinuch* §3).

9. *Minchas Chinuch* §12 points out that the Gemara in *Shabbos* (50b), which is the source of this practice, refers to an obligation upon every person to wash his face, hands, and feet daily for the honor of God (see

*Magen Avaraham, Orach Chaim* 4:1 with *Pri Megadim*). It is not speaking specifically about the mitzvah of sanctifying the hands and feet of the Kohanim in the *Beis HaMikdash*. *Minchas Chinuch* therefore concludes that this phrase was mistakenly inserted into the Chinuch, and actually does not apply to the laws of the sanctification of the hands in this mitzvah.

*Minchas Soless* suggests that, in fact, Chinuch does intend this phrase to refer to Kohanim. Chinuch reasons that since there is a mitzvah for everyone to wash his hands, feet, and face daily in honor of God, certainly a Kohen who actually comes into God's House to serve Him must do likewise. See also *Minchas Yitzchak*.

[Perhaps Chinuch indeed refers to the general obligation for a person to wash his hands and face daily, but considers this obligation an outgrowth of the mitzvah of sanctifying the hands before the *avodah*. This would be in keeping with the teaching of *Rashba* (*Teshuvos* I:191) that the general obligation to wash one's hands in the morning is based on the obligation of a Kohen to wash before he begins his service (see Insight).]

דִּיעֲבַד[10], אֲבָל לֹא מִכְּלִי חֹל אֲפִלּוּ דִּיעֲבַד. וְשֶׁאֵין מַכְנִיסִין יְדֵיהֶן לְתוֹכוֹ אֶלָּא שׁוֹפְכִין מִמֶּנּוּ עַל יְדֵיהֶם, וְגַם זֶה דֶּרֶךְ כָּבוֹד[11], וְאֵין[12] אָנוּ מַצְרִיכִין כֵּן בְּעִנְיַן נְטִילַת יָדַיִם לְחֻלִּין[13] לִטֹּל מִן הַכְּלִי וְלֹא בְּתוֹכוֹ, שֶׁאַף עַל פִּי שֶׁאָנוּ מַצְרִיכִין כְּלִי לִנְטִילַת חֻלִּין, וִיסוֹד הַדָּבָר הוּא מִפְּנֵי שֶׁמְּצָאנוּ כְּלִי לִנְטִילָה בַּקֹּדֶשׁ[14], מִכָּל מָקוֹם בַּקְּדֻשָּׁה הוּא דְּמַעֵט רַחֲמָנָא מִמֶּנּוּ וְלֹא בְּתוֹכוֹ,

---

**Kohen] performed the sanctification** by pouring water **from any** other **of the** consecrated **service vessels** of the *Beis HaMikdash*, the sanctification **is valid after the fact**.[10] אֲבָל לֹא מִכְּלִי חֹל אֲפִלּוּ דִּיעֲבַד — **However,** it is **not** valid if poured **from an ordinary vessel** (i.e., one not consecrated for Temple use), **even after the fact.**

Chinuch cites a law pertaining to the washing procedure: וְשֶׁאֵין מַכְנִיסִין יְדֵיהֶן לְתוֹכוֹ — **[The Kohanim] are not to** wash by **inserting their hands into** the water that is in **[the *Kiyor*]**, אֶלָּא שׁוֹפְכִין מִמֶּנּוּ עַל יְדֵיהֶן — **rather, they must pour the water from [the *Kiyor*] onto their hands.** וְגַם זֶה דֶּרֶךְ כָּבוֹד — The reason for **this** law, **too, is** because this **a respectful manner** of washing for the Divine Service.[11]

There is a Rabbinic requirement to wash the hands before eating bread, referred to as *netilas yadayim*, *washing the hands*. As Chinuch will explain below, this Rabbinic requirement, which applies to every person, is related to the Biblical obligation on Kohanim to sanctify their hands before engaging in the Divine service. Nevertheless, the specific laws regarding the procedure for *netilas yadayim* (i.e., washing the hands for bread) are not precisely the same as the laws regarding the procedure of *kiddush yadayim* (i.e., sanctifying the hands for the *avodah*). Chinuch points out a distinction:[12]

וְאֵין אָנוּ מַצְרִיכִין כֵּן בְּעִנְיַן נְטִילַת יָדַיִם לְחֻלִּין — Although with regard to sanctification of the hands, the water must specifically be *poured* upon the hands, **we do not require this with regard to the *netilas yadayim*** (washing of the hands) **for ordinary [bread]**;[13] לִטֹּל מִן הַכְּלִי וְלֹא בְּתוֹכוֹ — that is, there is no requirement **to wash** the hands specifically by pouring **from a vessel and not** by inserting the hands **into it.** שֶׁאַף עַל פִּי שֶׁאָנוּ מַצְרִיכִין כְּלִי לִנְטִילַת חֻלִּין — **Now, although we require that the washing for ordinary** bread **be** done **with a vessel** (e.g., one may not pour water from one hand to another), וִיסוֹד הַדָּבָר הוּא מִפְּנֵי שֶׁמְּצָאנוּ כְּלִי לִנְטִילָה בַּקֹּדֶשׁ — **and the basis for that** requirement **is because we find** that **the washing for holy** purposes, i.e., the washing for the sanctification of the hands in the *Beis HaMikdash*, does require **a vessel** (either the *Kiyor* or another of the sanctified vessels of the Temple, as above),[14] מִכָּל מָקוֹם בַּקְּדֻשָּׁה הוּא דְּמַעֵט רַחֲמָנָא — **nevertheless, it is** only **with regard to** washing for a **holy** purpose that **the Merciful One,** i.e., God, **excluded** washing by inserting the hands into a vessel, "מִמֶּנּוּ" וְלֹא בְּתוֹכוֹ — as He commanded in regard to this mitzvah (verse 19): **"From it,** Aaron and his sons shall wash," from which we learn that they must wash by

---

### NOTES

10. However, the washing must have been done within the boundaries of the Temple Courtyard (*Rambam, Hil. Bi'as Mikdash* 5:10). [According to *Ramban, Exodus* 30:19, one may even *initially* use other consecrated vessels for the sanctification. Indeed, the Mishnah (*Yoma* 43b) teaches that on Yom Kippur the Kohen Gadol would sanctify his hands and feet with water from a special golden pitcher.]

11. That it is a respectful manner of washing is the underlying *purpose* for the law (in keeping with the general underlying purpose for this mitzvah); the Scriptural *source* of this law is discussed below.

12. *Netilas yadayim* (the washing of hands, for bread) involves very specific procedures, which are outlined in *Shulchan Aruch, Orach Chaim* §157-165. It should be noted that in the coming segment Chinuch follows the opinion of *Rashba* (*Toras HaBayis* 6:3) with regard to the law of *netilas yadayim,* but common practice does not concur with his view. See below, note 15.

13. Chinuch refers to the washing for bread as "washing for *chullin*," or *ordinary* food, to distinguish it from the required washing of the hands upon sanctified food, i.e., *terumah,* which he will mention below. [*Terumah* is the portion of one's crop given to the Kohen (Mitzvah 507). It is forbidden for a Kohen to eat *terumah* when he is in a state of impurity (Mitzvah 279).]

14. I.e., since the washing for the sanctification of the hands (and feet) in the *Beis HaMikdash* requires a vessel, the Sages deemed it appropriate to require a vessel for the washing over bread as well (see *Rashba* to *Chullin* 107a ד"ה מגופת). The connection between the washing in the *Beis HaMikdash* and the washing over bread will be clarified below.

## 309 ❑ KI SISA / MITZVAH 106: TO SANCTIFY HANDS AND FEET WHEN SERVING

אֲבָל בְּחֻלִּין אֵין לָנוּ מִעוּט[15], וְאַף[16] עַל פִּי שֶׁנְּטִילַת הַחֻלִּין מִשּׁוּם סֶרֶךְ הַקֳּדָשִׁים הִיא, וּכְמוֹ שֶׁאָמְרוּ זִכְרוֹנָם לִבְרָכָה (חולין דף ק״ו ע״א) מִשּׁוּם סֶרֶךְ תְּרוּמָה, מִכָּל מָקוֹם אֵין לָנוּ לְהַשְׁווֹתָם לְגַמְרֵי בְּכָל דִּינֵיהֶם, וְדַי לָנוּ לְחַיֵּב בִּנְטִילָה וּבִכְלִי בְּחֻלִּין מִשּׁוּם סֶרֶךְ זֶה, וּלְהַנִּיחַ מִעוּט דְּמִמֶּנּוּ שֶׁנֶּאֱמַר בּוֹ בִּמְקוֹמוֹ, וַאֲפִלּוּ בִּתְרוּמָה עַצְמָהּ נְטִילַת יָדַיִם בָּהּ מִדְּרַבָּנָן הוּא, כִּי מִן הַתּוֹרָה לֹא נִמְצָא טָהֳרָה רַק בְּכָל הַגּוּף בְּבַת אַחַת[17],

---

אֲבָל בְּחֻלִּין אֵין לָנוּ מִעוּט — **But with regard to** the washing for **ordinary [bread], we have no** such **exclusion,** and therefore this particular law does not apply.[15]

Aside from the requirement upon every person to wash the hands before eating bread, the Sages required Kohanim to wash their hands before eating any food of *terumah*. Indeed, as Chinuch will state, the requirement for all Jews to wash their hands before eating a bread meal was enacted in order to ensure that Kohanim would be accustomed to washing their hands before eating *terumah*.[16] Since *terumah* is a sanctified food, the washing for *terumah*, and by extension the washing for all bread, is associated with the washing for the sacred *avodah* in the *Beis HaMikdash*. Accordingly, Chinuch analyzes the distinction he just made between these washing requirements:

וְאַף עַל פִּי שֶׁנְּטִילַת הַחֻלִּין מִשּׁוּם סֶרֶךְ הַקֳּדָשִׁים הִיא — **Now, although** the reason for **the washing for eating ordinary [food] is due to an association with** eating **sanctified [food]**, וּכְמוֹ שֶׁאָמְרוּ זִכְרוֹנָם לִבְרָכָה מִשּׁוּם סֶרֶךְ תְּרוּמָה — **as [the Sages], of blessed memory, said** (*Chullin* 106a) that the enactment of *netilas yadayim* for all bread was made **due to its association with** the required washing upon eating the sanctified food of ***terumah***, מִכָּל מָקוֹם אֵין לָנוּ לְהַשְׁווֹתָם לְגַמְרֵי בְּכָל דִּינֵיהֶם — **still, we need not make them** (i.e., the washing for a holy purpose and the washing of hands for ordinary bread) **completely identical in all their laws.** וְדַי לָנוּ לְחַיֵּב בִּנְטִילָה וּבִכְלִי בְּחֻלִּין מִשּׁוּם סֶרֶךְ זֶה — **Rather, it is sufficient for us to require washing for ordinary [bread], and** also to require that that washing be performed **with a vessel, based on this association** with the consumption of sanctified foods, וּלְהַנִּיחַ מִעוּט דְּמִמֶּנּוּ שֶׁנֶּאֱמַר בּוֹ בִּמְקוֹמוֹ — **and to leave the exclusion of "*from it*" stated with regard to [sanctifying the hands in the Temple],** from which we learn that one may not simply insert his hands in the vessel to wash, **in its place**; that restriction need not apply to ordinary washing as well. וַאֲפִלּוּ בִּתְרוּמָה עַצְמָהּ נְטִילַת יָדַיִם בָּהּ מִדְּרַבָּנָן הוּא — **In fact, even with regard to *terumah* itself,** where the hand-washing requirement for food originates, **the *netilas yadayim* obligation** before eating **it is of Rabbinic origin** and is not a Biblically mandated procedure, כִּי מִן הַתּוֹרָה לֹא נִמְצָא טָהֳרָה רַק בְּכָל הַגּוּף בְּבַת אַחַת — **for in Biblical law there is no** law of impurity or **purification** that applies to the hands themselves, but **only to the entire body at once.** Since the entire concept of removing impurity from the hands is wholly Rabbinic in origin, and not an actual derivation of the sanctification procedure in the *Beis HaMikdash*, there is no reason to apply all details of the sanctification to this Rabbinic procedure.[17]

---

### NOTES

15. The view that one may wash for bread by inserting his hands into the vessel is disputed by other Rishonim. *Shulchan Aruch* (*Orach Chaim* 159:8) cites both views; see *Mishnah Berurah* there (§56) regarding the practical halachah in this case.

16. See *Aruch HaShulchan*, *Orach Chaim* 158:3, for the reason that the general enactment was applied only to a bread meal. [Another reason for the enactment of *netilas yadayim* before a meal is to preserve the cleanliness of the food that one eats, as cleanliness is associated with purity and holiness (see *Mishnah Berurah* 158:1).]

17. In Biblical law, contact with impurity (*tumah*) by one part of the body renders the entire body ritually impure (*tamei*), even if the point of contact was the hands. Purification too, such as immersion in a *mikveh* (ritual bath), effects purity for the entire body at once, not only for the hands. Nevertheless, the Sages decreed that, in certain circumstances, the hands of a person who is otherwise in a ritually pure state may be considered impure, and that such impurity could be removed by washing the hands according to a specific procedure. [For an overview of the reasons for this decree and the various circumstances in which it applies, see Schottenstein edition of *Talmud Bavli*, *Chagigah* 18b, note 4. A detailed overview of this subject can also be

# 310 □ כי תשא / מצוה קו: מצוות קדוש ידים ורגלים

וּמַה שֶּׁאָמְרוּ זִכְרוֹנָם לִבְרָכָה (שם) שֶׁהַנְּטִילָה מִדִּכְתִיב (ויקרא ט"ו, י"א) וְיָדָיו לֹא שָׁטַף בַּמַּיִם וְגוֹ׳, אַסְמַכְתָּא בְּעָלְמָא הוּא[18], כֵּן כָּתוּב בְּסֵפֶר הַמִּצְוֹת שֶׁל הָרַמְבַּ״ן זִכְרוֹנוֹ לִבְרָכָה (בהשגתו לשורש ראשון בתשובה השנית)[19].

וְכֵן מַה שֶּׁאָמְרוּ זִכְרוֹנָם לִבְרָכָה (זבחים דף כ"א ע"ב) כַּמָּה מַיִם צָרִיךְ לִהְיוֹת בַּכִּיּוֹר, אֵין פָּחוֹת מִשִּׁעוּר מַיִם הָרְאוּיִין לִנְטִילַת אַרְבָּעָה אֲנָשִׁים, שֶׁנֶּאֱמַר (שמות ל, י"ט) וְרָחֲצוּ אַהֲרֹן וּבָנָיו מִמֶּנּוּ אֶת יְדֵיהֶם, וְהָיוּ אַהֲרֹן אֶלְעָזָר וְאִיתָמָר וּפִינְחָס עִמָּהֶם[20].

---

Chinuch cites a source that apparently contradicts the above statement that the law of *netilas yadayim* is purely of Rabbinic origin:

וּמַה שֶּׁאָמְרוּ זִכְרוֹנָם לִבְרָכָה שֶׁהַנְּטִילָה מִדִּכְתִיב "וְיָדָיו לֹא שָׁטַף בַּמַּיִם וְגוֹ׳" — **And** as for **that which the Sages, of blessed memory, stated** (ibid.), **that the washing of the hands** for ordinary bread **is derived from the verse** (*Leviticus* 15:11): *And he did not wash his hands in water … shall be impure*, which seems to indicate that there is a situation in which the hands themselves can be purified through washing by Biblical law, אַסְמַכְתָּא בְּעָלְמָא הוּא — this is not a technical derivation of a law from Scripture as with other Scriptural derivations; rather, **it is simply a** Scriptural **allusion** to a law that is actually Rabbinic in origin.[18] כֵּן כָּתוּב בְּסֵפֶר הַמִּצְוֹת שֶׁל הָרַמְבַּ״ן זִכְרוֹנוֹ לִבְרָכָה — **So it is written in the Book of Mitzvos of Ramban, of blessed memory** (glosses to *Sefer HaMitzvos* of *Rambam*, *Shoresh* 1).[19]

Chinuch returns to laws relating to the sanctification procedure in the Temple:

וְכֵן מַה שֶּׁאָמְרוּ זִכְרוֹנָם לִבְרָכָה — **Also** included in the laws of the mitzvah is **that which [the Sages], of blessed memory, have stated** (*Rambam, Hil. Bi'as HaMikdash* 5:13, from *Zevachim* 19b): כַּמָּה מַיִם צָרִיךְ לִהְיוֹת בַּכִּיּוֹר — **How much water must be in the Kiyor** in order to perform the sanctification from it? אֵין פָּחוֹת מִשִּׁעוּר מַיִם הָרְאוּיִין לִנְטִילַת אַרְבָּעָה אֲנָשִׁים — **Not less than the amount of water that is adequate for the washing of** the hands and feet of **four people**, i.e., for four Kohanim to perform the sanctification from it, שֶׁנֶּאֱמַר "וְרָחֲצוּ אַהֲרֹן וּבָנָיו מִמֶּנּוּ אֶת יְדֵיהֶם" — **as the verse states** (*Exodus* 30:19), *From it, Aaron and his sons shall wash their hands*. This teaches that when washing "*from it*," i.e., from the *Kiyor*, it must have enough for Aaron and his sons. וְהָיוּ אַהֲרֹן אֶלְעָזָר וְאִיתָמָר וּפִינְחָס עִמָּהֶם — **This** yields a total of four, because at the time that the Torah's command to wash from the *Kiyor* was first performed **there were** four Kohanim performing the service: **Aaron, and** his sons **Elazar and Ithamar, and with them Phinehas**, son of Elazar.[20]

---

### NOTES

found in the introduction to Tractate *Yadayim* in the Artscroll Mishnah Series, Yad Avraham.]

Chinuch does not state clearly whether the pouring stipulation applies to the washing for *terumah* or not. On the one hand, the verse *from it*, which requires pouring, is stated in the context of the Biblically required sanctification for the *avodah*. On the other hand, the washing for *terumah*, though Rabbinic in origin, is a "washing for a holy purpose." Chinuch's view in this regard requires further study.

18. The Gemara that Chinuch cited (*Chullin* 106a) itself implies that the verse is merely an *asmachta*, i.e., allusion, to the law. See *Niddah* 43a, where the actual Scriptural teaching of that verse is explained.

[The Sages at times attached a verse to a Rabbinic teaching as a way of preserving and remembering the law (see *Rambam*, Introduction to Mishnah Commentary). *Maharal* writes (*Be'er HaGolah*, beginning of *Be'er* §1) that the Sages actually found support for the concept of the impurity of the hands in this verse (see there at length for how it is derived), but although the *concept* is indeed a Biblical one, its *formal enactment* as a law was left to the Sages, giving it the final status of a Rabbinic enactment and not a Biblical law.]

19. Chinuch often refers to *Ramban*'s extensive glosses to *Sefer HaMitzvos* as "*Ramban*'s Book of Mitzvos." The passage he cites here is in *Shoresh* 1 ד"ה ובתשובה השנית, pp. 38-40 in Frankel ed.

20. This is a quote from *Rambam, Hil. Bi'as HaMikdash* 5:13. It is, however, difficult, for on the first day on which Aaron and his sons performed the *avodah*, Aaron's elder sons, Nadav and Abihu, were still alive. Moreover, according to many, Phinehas was at that time not yet qualified to perform *avodah* (see *Zevachim* 101b). For another explanation of how the number of four Kohanim is derived from the verse, see *Rashi* to *Zevachim* 19b ד"ה משה ואהרן, and *Kesef Mishneh* to *Rambam* ibid. For resolution of *Rambam*'s view, see *Teshuvos Chasam Sofer, Orach Chaim* §173, and *Aruch HaShulchan HeAsid* 42:6. See also *Minchas Soless*.

# KI SISA / MITZVAH 106: TO SANCTIFY HANDS AND FEET WHEN SERVING

וְכָל מַיִם כְּשֵׁרִין לְקִדּוּשׁ, בֵּין מֵי מַעְיָן אוֹ מֵי מִקְוֶה[21], וְנִפְסָלִין בְּלִינָה[22]. וְכֵיצַד מִצְוַת קִדּוּשׁ, מַנִּיחַ יָדוֹ הַיְמָנִית עַל רַגְלוֹ הַיְמָנִית וְיָדוֹ הַשְּׂמָאלִית עַל רַגְלוֹ הַשְּׂמָאלִית, וְרוֹחֵץ עוֹמֵד וְלֹא יוֹשֵׁב[23], לְפִי שֶׁמִּכְּלַל הָעֲבוֹדָה הוּא קִדּוּשׁ יָדַיִם וְרַגְלַיִם, וְכָל עֲבוֹדוֹת הַמִּקְדָּשׁ מְעֻמָּד הֵן, שֶׁנֶּאֱמַר (דברים י״ח, ה׳) לַעֲמֹד לְשָׁרֵת, וְכָל זֶה לְמַעֲלַת הַבַּיִת, וְיֶתֶר פְּרָטֶיהָ מְבֹאָרִים בְּפֶרֶק שֵׁנִי מִזְּבָחִים (דף י״ט ע״ב ואילך)[24].

וְנוֹהֶגֶת בִּזְמַן הַבַּיִת, בְּזִכְרֵי כְהֻנָּה בִּלְבַד[25]. וְעוֹבֵר עָלֶיהָ וְלֹא קִדֵּשׁ יָדָיו וְרַגְלָיו שַׁחֲרִית, אוֹ שֶׁיָּצָא מִן הַמִּקְדָּשׁ וְהִסִּיחַ דַּעְתּוֹ וְחָזַר וְעָבַד בְּלֹא קִדּוּשׁ, חַיָּב מִיתָה בִּידֵי שָׁמַיִם[26],

Chinuch cites laws relating to the water used for sanctification:

וְכָל מַיִם כְּשֵׁרִין לְקִדּוּשׁ בֵּין מֵי מַעְיָן אוֹ מֵי מִקְוֶה — **All water is valid for** use in **the sanctification, both spring water and gathered water,**[21] וְנִפְסָלִין בְּלִינָה — **and** the water, once it has been gathered in the *Kiyor* (or other holy vessel) **becomes invalidated** for future washing **upon remaining overnight.**[22]

Chinuch describes the sanctification procedure:

וְכֵיצַד מִצְוַת קִדּוּשׁ — **How is the mitzvah of sanctification** of the hands and feet performed? מַנִּיחַ יָדוֹ הַיְמָנִית עַל רַגְלוֹ הַיְמָנִית — **[The Kohen] places his right hand upon his right foot** וְיָדוֹ הַשְּׂמָאלִית עַל רַגְלוֹ הַשְּׂמָאלִית — **and his left hand upon his left foot,** וְרוֹחֵץ עוֹמֵד וְלֹא יוֹשֵׁב — **and he washes standing, not sitting.**[23] לְפִי שֶׁמִּכְּלַל הָעֲבוֹדָה הוּא קִדּוּשׁ יָדַיִם וְרַגְלַיִם — **The reason the washing must be performed while standing is because the sanctification of the hands and feet is included in the service** of the Holy Temple, וְכָל עֲבוֹדוֹת הַמִּקְדָּשׁ מְעֻמָּד הֵן — **and all services** performed **in the Holy Temple must be** done **while standing,** שֶׁנֶּאֱמַר "לַעֲמֹד לְשָׁרֵת" — **as it is stated** (*Deuteronomy* 18:5): *For him* (i.e., the Kohen) *has HASHEM chosen from among all your tribes* ***to stand to serve.*** וְכָל זֶה לְמַעֲלַת הַבַּיִת — **All of this is due to the greatness of the Holy Temple.** וְיֶתֶר פְּרָטֶיהָ — **These and the remaining details [of the mitzvah]** מְבֹאָרִים בְּפֶרֶק שֵׁנִי מִזְּבָחִים — **are set forth in the second chapter of** *Zevachim* (19b-22b).[24]

## ⌐ Applicability of the Mitzvah ¬

וְנוֹהֶגֶת בִּזְמַן הַבַּיִת — **[This mitzvah] applies in the times of the** Holy **Temple,** בְּזִכְרֵי כְהֻנָּה בִּלְבַד — **to male Kohanim only.**[25]

וְעוֹבֵר עָלֶיהָ וְלֹא קִדֵּשׁ יָדָיו וְרַגְלָיו שַׁחֲרִית — **One who transgresses [this mitzvah], and does not sanctify his hands and feet in the morning** before performing *avodah* or entering the *Heichal*, אוֹ שֶׁיָּצָא מִן הַמִּקְדָּשׁ וְהִסִּיחַ דַּעְתּוֹ — **or, even if he** had sanctified his hands and feet, but subsequently **left the Holy Temple and diverted his attention** from keeping his hands clean, וְחָזַר וְעָבַד בְּלֹא קִדּוּשׁ — **and he then returned and did** *avodah* in the Temple **without** first performing the **sanctification** again, חַיָּב מִיתָה בִּידֵי שָׁמַיִם — **is liable to death at the hands of Heaven.**[26]

---

### NOTES

21. I.e., the water put into the *Kiyor* for sanctification need not be spring water, which emerges from the ground by its own force; water that has gathered and pooled from the rain or other source may also be used. The actual washing itself, however, must use water that comes directly from the *Kiyor* (or another holy vessel), as Chinuch writes above.

22. Anything that is contained in a holy vessel becomes sanctified. One of the effects of this sanctification is that it becomes halachically invalidated upon remaining overnight. Thus the water in the *Kiyor* becomes invalidated with daybreak and can no longer be used for sanctification (*Rambam, Hil. Beis HaBechirah* 3:18). [Accordingly, the *Kiyor* would have to be refilled daily.

For various methods that were used to circumvent this issue in the *Beis HaMikdash*, see *Rambam,* ibid. and *Hil. Bi'as HaMikdash* 5:14-15.]

23. The *Kiyor* had faucets, which could be opened to allow a flow of water. With the faucets open, the Kohen would bend over with his hands upon his feet and wash them (see *Rambam, Hil. Bi'as HaMikdash* 5:16 and *Commentary to the Mishnah, Zevachim* 2:1).

24. The laws of the sanctification of the hands and feet are codified in *Rambam, Hil. Bi'as HaMikdash,* Ch. 5.

25. This is because it is they who are charged with performing the *avodah* in the *Beis HaMikdash*.

26. I.e., the violator dies prematurely by Heavenly punishment.

וַעֲבוֹדָתוֹ פְּסוּלָה[27], בֵּין כֹּהֵן גָּדוֹל אוֹ הֶדְיוֹט[28].

וַעֲבוֹדָתוֹ פְּסוּלָה — Furthermore, if he served in the Temple in that state, **his *avodah* is invalid**;[27] בֵּין כֹּהֵן גָּדוֹל אוֹ הֶדְיוֹט — this applies to **both the Kohen Gadol and** an **ordinary Kohen**.[28]

## NOTES

27. I.e., the *avodah* is not accepted, and must be performed again.

28. That is, it applies both to the *avodos* that require a Kohen Gadol, such as the service of Yom Kippur, and to the *avodos* that can be done even by an ordinary Kohen (see *Rashi, Zevachim* 19b ד"ה שחרית).

### ◆§ Insight: The Morning Netilas Yadayim

Chinuch explains that the laws that govern the *netilas yadayim* (washing of the hands) for bread share some similarities with the laws governing the sanctification of the hands in the *Beis HaMikdash*. This is because the original obligation of *netilas yadayim* pertained to the eating of *terumah*, which, as sanctified food, is associated with the sacred service of the *Beis HaMikdash*. As Chinuch points out, since the washing in the *Beis HaMikdash* required a vessel (the *Kiyor* or another holy vessel), a vessel is also required when washing for bread. Another similarity pertains to the water itself: Discolored water is invalid for use in the *Kiyor*, and is therefore also invalid for the *netilas yadayim* for bread (*Re'ah* to *Berachos* 53b, cited by *Beis Yosef, Orach Chaim* 160:1; see *Birkei Yosef* there at length).

Aside from the *netilas yadayim* for bread, there is an additional, apparently unrelated *netilas yadayim* obligation. When one arises in the morning one must wash his hands and recite the blessing *al netilas yadayim* (*Berachos* 60b). What is the source of this obligation?

The Gemara (*Shabbos* 108b, as explained by *Rashi*) teaches that before washing the hands in the morning, one should be extremely careful not to touch the eyes, ears, nose, mouth, or any other opening of the body, because an impure spirit rests upon the hands. The *Zohar* (*Vayeishev* 184b, cited by *Beis Yosef, Orach Chaim* 4:8) explains that when a person sleeps he experiences, on some level, the impurity of death. Upon arising, the impure spirit departs, but leaves a trace on the hands. By washing the hands three times in an alternate pattern, the hands become sanctified and all traces of impurity depart. *Mishnah Berurah* (4:8) writes, however, that although it is imperative to perform this ritual, the Sages would not have enacted a special Rabbinic *obligation* that requires the recitation of a blessing were it only for this reason. *Mishnah Berurah* (ibid. §1) therefore cites two views from the Rishonim to explain the reason for the Rabbinic enactment of the morning *netilas yadayim*.

*Rosh* (*Berachos* 9:23 and *Teshuvos* §4) maintains that the morning *netilas yadayim* is a part of the general obligation to clean one's hands before prayers (see *Berachos* 15a). When a person sleeps, his hands move inadvertently and are assumed to have touched parts of the body that are usually covered. Since touching these areas causes the hands to be considered "unclean," the Sages instituted a special obligation for one to wash his hands in the morning to ensure that his hands are clean for the morning prayers.

Since, according to *Rosh*, the reason for this washing is merely to ensure cleanliness, the requirements to use a vessel and to pour the water onto the hands, which apply to *netilas yadayim* for bread, would not apply to the morning *netilas yadayim*. As long as one cleans his hands, it is sufficient (*Pri Megadim, Mishbetzos Zahav* 4:1). Indeed, *Rosh* himself points out that if water is unavailable one may clean his hands in another way, such as with a dry cloth.

*Rashba* (*Teshuvos* §191), however, points to a Gemara (*Chullin* 106b), which indicates that the morning *netilas yadayim* does indeed require a vessel, like the *netilas yadayim* for bread. This demonstrates that there is more to this washing than just cleanliness. *Rashba* therefore introduces another reason for this *netilas yadayim*.

The purpose of our creation is for us to bring honor to God and serve Him. Each morning, upon awakening, a person is considered to have been created anew by God (see *Midrash Rabbah, Eichah* 3:8), thus renewing our purpose in our creation as well. Throughout our morning blessings, we thank God for this renewal in all of its details, including sight, mobility, intellect, and energy. The Jew

who awakens and begins his service of God anew each day is in this way like the Kohen approaching the *Beis HaMikdash* to begin his Divine service. The Sages obligated every person to wash upon awakening in emulation of the Kohen who washes his hands from the *Kiyor* each morning before the *avodah*. [The Kohanim, who serve barefoot, also wash their feet (see note 5 above; *Sifrei, Korach* §116, with commentary *Sifrei DeVei Rav*).]

Since the morning *netilas yadayim* is analogous to the washing in the *Beis HaMikdash*, some of the procedures of that washing pertain here as well. It is for this reason that one must use a vessel for the morning *netilas yadayim*, just as the Kohen washed his hands from the *Kiyor* or another holy vessel (as Chinuch explained regarding the *netilas yadayim* for bread). And while one is required to wash his hands before other prayers as well (as cited earlier from *Berachos* 15a), that requirement is only to ensure cleanliness, and a vessel would not be required.

A number of practical differences arise based on these different reasons for the morning *netilas yadayim* obligation. For example, one who sleeps all night while wearing gloves will not touch any part of his body with his hands during the night. According to *Rosh*, who maintains that the reason for the morning hand-washing is for cleanliness, the gloved sleeper would not be obligated to wash his hands in the morning. According to *Rashba*, however, the obligation applies in any case, since anyone who sleeps at night is considered a new creation in the morning, readying himself to serve his Creator (*Pri Megadim, Eishel Avraham* 4:1).

Another difference applies to one who remained awake the entire night. According to *Rosh*, who maintains that the morning washing is not an independent obligation, but only a part of the general obligation to ensure cleanliness of the hands for prayers, one who was awake need not wash, for he knows that his hands remained clean throughout the night. According to *Rashba*, however, there is a special Rabbinic enactment of *netilas yadayim* in the morning. This enactment would therefore apply to all, including even one to whom the reason for this enactment does not apply (*Shulchan Aruch, Orach Chaim* 4:13 with *Mishnah Berurah*; cf. *Taz* 4:9 and *Beur HaGra* 4:14).

Since these two cases are matters of dispute, one must wash his hands, but not recite the blessing upon washing, following the general rule that one does not recite blessings in cases of doubt (see *Rama, Orach Chaim* ibid. with *Mishnah Berurah* §1 and §30).

## מִצְוָה קז: מִצְוַת מְשִׁיחַת כֹּהֲנִים גְּדוֹלִים וּמְלָכִים בְּשֶׁמֶן הַמִּשְׁחָה

לַעֲשׂוֹת שֶׁמֶן הַמִּשְׁחָה עַל הָעִנְיָן שֶׁצִּוְּתָה הַתּוֹרָה לַעֲשׂוֹתוֹ, שֶׁנֶּאֱמַר (שמות ל', כ"ה) וְעָשִׂיתָ אֹתוֹ שֶׁמֶן מִשְׁחַת קֹדֶשׁ¹, שֶׁיִּהְיֶה מוּכָן לִמְשֹׁחַ בּוֹ כָּל כֹּהֵן גָּדוֹל שֶׁיִּתְמַנֶּה², כְּמוֹ שֶׁכָּתוּב (ויקרא כ"א, י') וְהַכֹּהֵן הַגָּדוֹל וְגוֹ' אֲשֶׁר יוּצַק עַל רֹאשׁוֹ שֶׁמֶן הַמִּשְׁחָה³.

---

## ☞ Mitzvah 107 ☜
# The Obligation of Anointing Kohanim Gedolim and Kings With the Anointment Oil

וְאַתָּה קַח לְךָ בְּשָׂמִים רֹאשׁ מָר דְּרוֹר חֲמֵשׁ מֵאוֹת וְקִנְּמָן בֶּשֶׂם מַחֲצִיתוֹ חֲמִשִּׁים וּמָאתָיִם וּקְנֵה בֹשֶׂם חֲמִשִּׁים וּמָאתָיִם. וְקִדָּה חֲמֵשׁ מֵאוֹת בְּשֶׁקֶל הַקֹּדֶשׁ וְשֶׁמֶן זַיִת הִין. וְעָשִׂיתָ אֹתוֹ שֶׁמֶן מִשְׁחַת קֹדֶשׁ רֹקַח מִרְקַחַת מַעֲשֵׂה רֹקֵחַ שֶׁמֶן מִשְׁחַת קֹדֶשׁ יִהְיֶה

*You shall take for yourself choice spices: five hundred [portions] of mar-deror; fragrant kinnamon — half of it, two hundred and fifty; two hundred and fifty of fragrant kaneh; five hundred of kiddah, in the sacred shekel weight; and a hin of olive oil. You shall make of it oil of sacred anointment, a blended compound, the handiwork of a perfumer; it shall remain oil of sacred anointment (Exodus 30:23-25).*

In these verses, Moses was commanded to collect these ingredients and to use them in formulating the anointment oil. In the subsequent verses (26-30), he was instructed to use this oil to anoint the *Mishkan* (Tabernacle) and its vessels, and Aaron and his sons, thereby consecrating them for the *avodah* (Temple service). Finally, he was to impress upon the Jewish people the holy and eternal nature of the oil and say to them as follows (v. 31): שֶׁמֶן מִשְׁחַת קֹדֶשׁ יִהְיֶה זֶה לִי לְדֹרֹתֵיכֶם, *This shall remain for Me oil of sacred anointment for your generations.*

לַעֲשׂוֹת שֶׁמֶן הַמִּשְׁחָה עַל הָעִנְיָן שֶׁצִּוְּתָה הַתּוֹרָה לַעֲשׂוֹתוֹ — We are commanded **to make the anointment oil** (*shemen hamishchah*) **according to the formula with which the Torah instructed that it be made,** שֶׁנֶּאֱמַר — **as it is stated** (*Exodus* 30:25): "וְעָשִׂיתָ אֹתוֹ שֶׁמֶן מִשְׁחַת קֹדֶשׁ" — *You shall make of it oil of sacred anointment,* etc.,[1] שֶׁיִּהְיֶה מוּכָן לִמְשֹׁחַ בּוֹ כָּל כֹּהֵן גָּדוֹל שֶׁיִּתְמַנֶּה — **so that it should be available for anointing every Kohen Gadol who is appointed,**[2] כְּמוֹ שֶׁכָּתוּב — **as it is written** (*Leviticus* 21:10): "וְהַכֹּהֵן הַגָּדוֹל וְגוֹ' אֲשֶׁר יוּצַק עַל רֹאשׁוֹ שֶׁמֶן הַמִּשְׁחָה" — ***The Kohen who is exalted above his brethren*** (i.e., the Kohen Gadol), **upon whose head the anointment oil has been poured**;[3]

---

### NOTES

1. The ingredients of the *shemen hamishchah*, and the process by which it is prepared, are described by Chinuch below.

2. Chinuch states that the mitzvah is *to make* the anointment oil so that it will be *available* for anointing each new Kohen Gadol; he does not explicitly state that there is a mitzvah to actually anoint the Kohen Gadol. For discussion of this matter, see the Insight.

3. In this verse, the Torah indicates that a Kohen Gadol is installed into his high office by being anointed with the *shemen hamishchah*. The verse continues: וּמִלֵּא אֶת יָדוֹ לִלְבֹּשׁ אֶת הַבְּגָדִים, *and who has been inaugurated to don the vestments.* In addition to being anointed with the *shemen hamishchah*, for his investiture the Kohen Gadol dons the eight priestly vestments (as opposed to the four of an ordinary Kohen; see Mitzvah 99). If there is no *shemen hamishchah* (as was the case throughout the Second Temple Era; see note 21), the Kohen Gadol can assume his office through donning the eight vestments alone (*Rambam, Hil. Klei HaMikdash* 1:8, 4:12-13). [Such a Kohen Gadol is called מְרוּבֵּה בְגָדִים, *one of additional vestments*, whereas a Kohen Gadol who was also anointed with the *shemen hamishchah* is called כֹּהֵן מָשִׁיחַ, *an anointed Kohen*. These two types of Kohanim Gedolim are subject to the same laws and duties, except that the unique *chatas* offering that the Torah prescribes for a transgression by הַכֹּהֵן הַמָּשִׁיחַ, *the anointed Kohen* (*Leviticus* 4:3), is brought only by one who was anointed with the *shemen hamishchah*

# KI SISA / MITZVAH 107: ANOINTING KOHANIM GEDOLIM AND KINGS

וְכֵן מוֹשְׁחִין בּוֹ קְצָת הַמְּלָכִים,[4] וְכֵן גַּם כֵּן מָשְׁחוּ בּוֹ הַכֵּלִים שֶׁל בֵּית־הַמִּקְדָּשׁ,[5] וְלֹא יִצְטָרְכוּ לִמְשֹׁחַ לֶעָתִיד אֶלָּא בָּעֲבוֹדָה יִתְקַדְּשׁוּ,[6] וְזֶהוּ שֶׁכָּתוּב (שמות ל׳, ל״א) יִהְיֶה זֶה לִי לְדֹרֹתֵיכֶם,[7] כֵּן אָמְרוּ זִכְרוֹנָם לִבְרָכָה בַּסִּפְרִי.[8]

מִשָּׁרְשֵׁי הַמִּצְוָה, שֶׁרָצָה הָאֵל בָּרוּךְ הוּא שֶׁנַּעֲשֶׂה פְּעֻלָּה בְּנַפְשׁוֹתֵינוּ בַּיּוֹם שֶׁנַּעֲלֶה לְהִתְחַנֵּךְ

---

וְכֵן מוֹשְׁחִין בּוֹ קְצָת הַמְּלָכִים – **and similarly, with [this oil] we anoint some kings** at the time of their inauguration.[4]
וְכֵן גַּם כֵּן מָשְׁחוּ בּוֹ הַכֵּלִים שֶׁל בֵּית־הַמִּקְדָּשׁ – **Additionally, with [this oil] they anointed the original vessels of the Holy Temple;**[5] וְלֹא יִצְטָרְכוּ לִמְשֹׁחַ לֶעָתִיד – **but they will not need to anoint the vessels of the Temple in the future,** when it is rebuilt; אֶלָּא בָּעֲבוֹדָה יִתְקַדְּשׁוּ – **rather, [those vessels] will become consecrated through** their usage in the Temple **service.**[6] וְזֶהוּ שֶׁכָּתוּב – "יִהְיֶה זֶה לִי לְדֹרֹתֵיכֶם" – **This is** alluded to in **the verse** (Exodus 30:31): ***This shall remain for Me oil of sacred anointment for your generations.***[7] כֵּן אָמְרוּ זִכְרוֹנָם לִבְרָכָה בַּסִּפְרִי – **Thus said [the Sages], of blessed memory, in** *Sifrei* (to Numbers 7:1).[8]

## ☞ Underlying Purpose of the Mitzvah ☜

Chinuch begins by explaining the purpose of anointing the Kohen Gadol upon his inauguration:

מִשָּׁרְשֵׁי הַמִּצְוָה – **Among the underlying purposes of the mitzvah** is שֶׁרָצָה הָאֵל בָּרוּךְ הוּא – **that the Almighty, Blessed is He, desired** שֶׁנַּעֲשֶׂה פְּעֻלָּה בְּנַפְשׁוֹתֵינוּ – **that we should perform a procedure with ourselves,** בַּיּוֹם שֶׁנַּעֲלֶה לְהִתְחַנֵּךְ בִּכְבוֹד עֲבוֹדָתוֹ הַקְּדוֹשָׁה – **on the day that**

---

### NOTES

(see *Mishnah, Horayos* 11b; for further discussion, see *Minchas Chinuch* §6).]

An ordinary Kohen is not anointed. As we will see in Mitzvah 108, however, the Kohen who is designated to address the nation before battle (see *Deuteronomy* 20:2-9) is also anointed with the *shemen hamishchah*. He is thus called מְשׁוּחַ מִלְחָמָה, *the anointed for battle* (see Mitzvah 108 note 17).

4. As Chinuch explains in Mitzvah 108 (at notes 18-23), only kings of the House of David were anointed with the *shemen hamishchah,* and even among them, generally, only those who did not inherit the throne from their father were anointed. By contrast, *every* Kohen Gadol is anointed, even if he is a son of the previous Kohen Gadol (*Kereisos* 5b, *Horayos* 11b).

[To be sure, if the son of a deceased Kohen Gadol is qualified for the position, he has precedence over other Kohanim (see *Leviticus* 16:32 with *Rashi*). Unlike a king, however, he does not simply inherit the position, but requires a new investiture through the process of anointment (*Meiri* to *Horayos* 11b ד״ה אע״פ; for discussion, see *Mishnas Yaavetz, Yoreh Deah* §36; cf. *Chidushei HaGriz* to *Kereisos* 5b ד״ה בגמ׳ ואפי׳ כ״ג). See also Mitzvah 108 notes 16, 20, 21.]

5. Actually, the vessels made for the *Beis HaMikdash* were not anointed (see the following note). Chinuch must be referring to the vessels of the *Mishkan* (Tabernacle), which Moses was instructed to anoint at the inauguration of the *Mishkan* (*Exodus* 30:26-29). Most of these eventually became vessels of the *Beis HaMikdash* (*Minchas Yitzchak*).

6. The original sacred vessels that were made for the *Mishkan* required anointment, but this requirement did not apply to any vessels subsequently made for either the *Mishkan* or the *Beis HaMikdash*. Those became consecrated automatically the first time they were used in the Temple service. The same holds true regarding the vessels that will be made for the future *Beis HaMikdash*. It is derived from Scripture that by virtue of Moses' initial anointment of each type of vessel, any vessel subsequently made to replace one of the original vessels automatically attains sanctity simply by being used in the Temple service (see *Sifrei*, cited by Chinuch below; *Shevuos* 15a; *Rambam, Sefer HaMitzvos, Asei* 35, and *Hil. Klei HaMikdash* 1:12; see also *Teshuvos Chasam Sofer, Orach Chaim* §37).

7. The expression *for your generations* indicates that the anointment of the original sacred vessels with the *shemen hamishchah* had an impact for all future generations. As explained in the previous note, by virtue of that anointment, all replacement vessels attained the same sanctity as the original ones, as soon as they were used in the *avodah* (*Shevet HaLevi* Vol. 5, *Kuntres HaMitzvos* §40).

8. *Sifrei* states that future vessels would not require anointment, but actually derives this from a different verse than the one Chinuch quotes. In any event, *Sifrei* clearly teaches that when Moses anointed the original vessels of the *Mishkan*, he generated the sanctity that would imbue all future Temple vessels. Chinuch explains that this is alluded to in the verse, *oil of sacred anointment for your generations* (*Shevet HaLevi* ibid.). [See *Minchas Yitzchak* for another explanation of Chinuch's words that requires emendation of the text.]

בִּכְבוֹד עֲבוֹדָתוֹ הַקְּדוֹשָׁה, תּוֹרָה בָּנוּ גְדֻלָּה וְשֶׁבַח, וְזֶהוּ מְשִׁיחַת הַשֶּׁמֶן, לְפִי שֶׁעִנְיַן הַמְּשִׁיחָה בְּשֶׁמֶן הַטּוֹב לֹא יַעֲשׂוּהָ רַק הַמְּלָכִים וְהַשָּׂרִים הַגְּדוֹלִים.[9] וְגַם מִיסוֹד הַמִּצְוָה, לִהְיוֹתוֹ מוּכָן בַּבַּיִת לְעֵת הַצֹּרֶךְ,[10] לְמַעֲלַת הַמָּקוֹם, כִּי יָדוּעַ עַל דֶּרֶךְ מָשָׁל כִּי מִמַּעֲלַת בַּעַל הַבַּיִת הַנִּכְבָּד לִהְיוֹת מוּכָן בַּבַּיִת בָּהּ כָּל הַצָּרִיךְ וְלֹא תִתְעַכֵּב שָׁם מְלָאכָה עַד הָכֵן הַצָּרִיךְ אֵלֶיהָ.[11]

דִּינֵי הַמִּצְוָה, כְּגוֹן מַעֲשֵׂה הַשֶּׁמֶן כֵּיצַד נַעֲשָׂה, מוֹר,[12] וְקִנָּמוֹן[13] קִדָּה[14] חֲמֵשׁ מֵאוֹת

---

**תּוֹרָה בָּנוּ גְדֻלָּה** — we rise up to be initiated into the high **honor of** performing **His holy service,** **וְשֶׁבַח** — that **will exhibit in us greatness and excellence,** so that we will be inspired to perform that service devotedly. **וְזֶהוּ מְשִׁיחַת הַשֶּׁמֶן** — **This** act to which we refer **is anointment with the anointing oil,** which demonstrates greatness, **לְפִי שֶׁעִנְיַן הַמְּשִׁיחָה בַּשֶּׁמֶן הַטּוֹב לֹא יַעֲשׂוּהָ רַק הַמְּלָכִים וְהַשָּׂרִים הַגְּדוֹלִים** — since the practice of being anointed with fine oil is generally **afforded only to kings and great noblemen.**[9]

Chinuch proceeds to explain the significance of having the oil readily available:

**לִהְיוֹתוֹ מוּכָן בַּבַּיִת** — **Additionally,** it is **a fundamental feature of the mitzvah** **וְגַם מִיסוֹד הַמִּצְוָה** — **לְעֵת הַצֹּרֶךְ** — **that [the oil] should** always **be available in the** Holy **Temple for the time when it will be needed,**[10] **לְמַעֲלַת הַמָּקוֹם** — **as** this brings **distinction to that** holy **place. כִּי יָדוּעַ עַל דֶּרֶךְ מָשָׁל** — **For, by way of analogy, it is known** **כִּי מִמַּעֲלַת בַּעַל הַבַּיִת הַנִּכְבָּד לִהְיוֹת מוּכָן בַּבַּיִת** **כָּל הַצָּרִיךְ בָּהּ** — that it is a mark of **distinction for an esteemed householder to have available** in his **house anything that may** at some time **be needed there, וְלֹא תִתְעַכֵּב שָׁם מְלָאכָה עַד** **הָכֵן הַצָּרִיךְ אֵלֶיהָ** — **so that no chore should be delayed there until** such time as they are able to **prepare that which [the chore] requires.** Similarly, having the anointment oil available in the Temple for the occasions when it is needed is a mark of distinction to the Temple.[11]

## ~ Laws of the Mitzvah ~

**דִּינֵי הַמִּצְוָה** — **The laws of the mitzvah include,** **כְּגוֹן מַעֲשֵׂה הַשֶּׁמֶן כֵּיצַד נַעֲשָׂה** — **for example,** the guidelines for the formulation of the oil, as follows: **מוֹר וְקִנָּמוֹן קִדָּה** — **The** ingredients include aromatic spices, namely, **mor,**[12] **kinnamon,**[13] and **kiddah,**[14] **חֲמֵשׁ מֵאוֹת**

---

NOTES

9. The indulgence of fine oil distinguishes nobility from the common folk. Chinuch explains that the symbolic act of being anointed with the *shemen hamishchah* is intended to instill in that individual the sense that, in taking up the high office of the Kohen Gadol (or King), he is assuming an elevated status in the service of Hashem. This will inspire him to carry out his duties with a higher sense of purpose and devotion (see *Moreh Nevuchim* III:45, cited in footnote to Mechon Yerushalayim edition of *Minchas Chinuch*).

See Mitzvah 99, where Chinuch expresses a similar idea regarding the obligation to don the priestly garments. It is all rooted in Chinuch's principle that "man is affected in accordance with his actions" (Mitzvos 16, 95, et al.). See also Mitzvah 366, where Chinuch discusses the prominence of oil relative to all other liquids.

10. The *shemen hamishchah* was stored in the *Beis HaMikdash*, at the side of the Ark in the Holy of Holies (see *Rashi* to I Kings 1:39, and to *Yoma* 52b ד"ה תשימו בארגז).

11. Thus, having the oil available in the *Beis HaMikdash* serves (together with other mitzvos of the *Beis HaMikdash*; e.g., Mitzvos 95, 98, 103, 388) to create an atmosphere of prestige and grandeur in that holy place, which will bring those who come there to greater devotion and humility in the service of Hashem.

12. This is called *mar-deror* in the Torah (see the verse at the beginning of the mitzvah). *Rambam* (Hil. Klei HaMikdash 1:3) identifies this as musk — a fragrant extract of the musk deer, a species of deer native to India; it has an extraordinarily complex aroma and is a key constituent in many perfumes (see *Radvaz* ad loc. and *Ramban* to Exodus 30:23). Others, however, identify *mar-deror* as myrrh, a fragrant gum resin that exudes from the *Commiphora myrrh*, a small, prickly tree species native to the Mideast (*Ramban* ibid.; see also *Raavad,* Hil. Klei HaMikdash loc. cit., with *Radvaz*). For discussion of this dispute and its ramifications, see Insight to Mitzvah 109.

13. *Rambam* (ibid.) describes *kinnamon* as a woody substance with a pleasant scent that is imported from the Indian Islands. In his Commentary to the Mishnah, *Kereisos* 1:1 [end], he refers to it as *kishr saliha*, the Arabic equivalent of cinnamon (see R' Y. Kafich's annotation there). This identification is also the opinion of *Rashi* (Exodus 30:23). *Ramban* (ibid.), however, identifies *kinnamon* as a type of fragrant straw; see also *Malbim* there.

14. *Rambam* (ibid.) identifies *kiddah* as *kosht,* or costus,

## KI SISA / MITZVAH 107: ANOINTING KOHANIM GEDOLIM AND KINGS

שֶׁקֶל[15] מִכָּל אֶחָד, אֶלָּא שֶׁהַקִּנְּמוֹן נִשְׁקַל בֵּין שְׁתֵּי פְעָמִים לְהַרְבּוֹת בּוֹ שְׁתֵּי הַכְרָעוֹת[16], וְקָנֶה בְשֵׂם[17] חֲמִשִּׁים וּמָאתַיִם שֶׁקֶל, וְכֻלָּן נִמְצָאִים בְּאִיֵּי הֹדּוּ[18], וְשֶׁמֶן זַיִת שִׁעוּר הִין שֶׁהוּא שְׁנֵים עָשָׂר לֹג[19], וְאַחַר שֶׁיִּתְבַּשֵּׁל הַכֹּל כְּדֵי צָרְכּוֹ חוֹזֵר הַכֹּל לְמִדַּת הַשֶּׁמֶן שֶׁהוּא שְׁנֵים עָשָׂר לֹג[21],

---

אֶלָּא שֶׁהַקִּנְּמוֹן נִשְׁקַל בֵּין שְׁתֵּי — שֶׁקֶל מִכָּל אֶחָד — **five hundred** *shekel*-**weights**[15] **of each;** פְעָמִים — **except that the** *kinnamon* **was weighed in two batches** that measured two hundred and fifty *shekel*-weights each, לְהַרְבּוֹת בּוֹ שְׁתֵּי הַכְרָעוֹת — in order **to increase its amount by two scale-tilting bits.**[16] וְקָנֶה בְשֵׂם חֲמִשִּׁים וּמָאתַיִם שֶׁקֶל — **The fourth spice is the fragrant** *kaneh*,[17] and its amount is **two hundred and fifty** *shekel*-**weights,** in total. וְכֻלָּן נִמְצָאִים בְּאִיֵּי הֹדּוּ — **All these [spices] are native to the Indian islands** (i.e., the Indian subcontinent).[18] וְשֶׁמֶן זַיִת שִׁעוּר הִין שֶׁהוּא שְׁנֵים עָשָׂר לֹג — The base for the anointment oil consisted of **olive oil in the measure of a** *hin,* **which is** the same as **twelve** *log*.[19] The spices were ground up individually, and then combined and soaked in pure, sweet water until it absorbed all of their fragrance; then the oil was added and the entire mixture was boiled.[20] וְאַחַר שֶׁיִּתְבַּשֵּׁל הַכֹּל כְּדֵי צָרְכּוֹ — **After everything was** fully **cooked as required,** and the water had boiled off, חוֹזֵר הַכֹּל לְמִדַּת הַשֶּׁמֶן שֶׁהוּא שְׁנֵים עָשָׂר לֹג — **all** the oil **that remained would** miraculously **retain the** original **volume of the oil, which is twelve** *log*.[21]

---

### NOTES

an aromatic root of a tall herb (*Saussurea costus*) that even today grows only in the Kashmir highlands ("costus" in Greek means "from the East," referring to the Indian lower Himalaya from where the spice was imported). Others identify it as *ketziah,* or cassia, a cinnamon-like bark (*Ramban* ibid. and *Rashi* ibid.; see also *Kesef Mishneh* to *Rambam* loc. cit.).

15. The *shekel* was a silver coin used in ancient times. Since its value was determined by its weight, Scripture uses it as a unit of weight. A *shekel*-weight is approximately 16 grams, or .56 oz. (see Appendix I to ArtScroll Yad Avraham edition of Mishnayos *Shekalim*).

16. The spices for the *shemen hamishchah* were weighed on a balance scale, and with each weighing, there was a requirement to add a bit of extra spice so that the scale would not be perfectly balanced, but would tilt in the direction of the spice. Thus, the amount of spice actually used was slightly more than the amount set forth in Scripture. Weighing the *kinnamon* in two batches caused its total amount to be increased by *two* "tilting bits."

The requirement to do this is derived from the manner in which Scripture expresses the total weight mandated for the *kinnamon* spice. Whereas for the other spices the Torah gives the total weight (e.g., *five hundred*), in regard to *kinnamon,* it does not state "five hundred," but rather: *half of it, two hundred and fifty* (the verse is cited at the beginning of the mitzvah). This indicates that the *kinnamon* must be brought in two batches of 250 *shekel*-weights each. Since there would seem to be no difference whether it is brought in one batch of 500 or two batches of 250, the Gemara (*Kereisos* 5a) infers that the spices are to be weighed each time with a "tilting of the scale," i.e., with some extra spice to weigh down the pan of the balance scale that contains the spice. Thus, weighing the *kinnamon* in two batches becomes meaningful (see, however, *Shekalim* 16a).

[Similarly, when one weighs out merchandise for a customer, there is a mitzvah to make the scale tilt in the buyer's favor (see *Bava Basra* 88b and *Rambam, Hil. Geneivah* 8:12-15).]

17. *Rambam* (*Hil. Klei HaMikdash* ibid.) identifies *kaneh* — literally "cane" — as a reddish straw with a pleasant scent and therapeutic properties; this appears to be the palmarosa plant, also known as the Indian rosha grass (*HaChai VeHaTzome'ach BaTorah,* Jerusalem 1984; see also *The Living Torah* by R' Aryeh Kaplan, to Exodus 30:23-24, for discussion of all these spices). *Ramban* (ibid. v. 34), however, identifies *kaneh* as cinnamon.

18. Chinuch appears to follow *Rambam* (ibid.), who similarly describes these spices as indigenous to the Indian region. [However, several of the other opinions mentioned in the preceding notes also include spices not native to India.]

19. A *log* is a unit of liquid that ranges, according to various authorities, between 11.6 and 20.4 fl. oz. (345-600 cc.). Chinuch explains that the measure that Scripture calls a *hin* is equivalent to the more commonly known measure of twelve *log*.

20. *Kereisos* 5a-b; *Rambam* ibid. §2. These details of the actual production of the oil are not explicit in Scripture. However, by commanding that the oil be made *a blended compound, the handiwork of a perfumer* (Exodus 30:25), the Torah indicates that the oil should be made using the method of perfumers known at the time (*Ramban* ibid.; see also *Aruch HaShulchan HeAsid* 15:8-10).

21. Considering the fact that some oil is absorbed by the pot, some by the spices, and some of it boils off (albeit not as much as the water), it was a miracle that the remaining oil would still measure exactly twelve *log,* the same amount as was originally placed in the pot (*Kereisos* 5b). Moreover, even after the oil was used for anointing the *Mishkan* and all its vessels, and Aaron

## 318 □ כי תשא / מצוה קז: מצות משיחת כהנים גדולים ומלכים

וְסִימָן יִהְיֶה זֶה (שמות ל׳, ל״א), זֶ״ה בְּגִימַטְרִיָּא שְׁנֵים עָשָׂר הֱוֵי[22], וְיֶתֶר פְּרָטֶיהָ, מְבֹאָרִים בְּפֶרֶק רִאשׁוֹן מִכְּרִיתוֹת (דף ה׳ ע״ב)[23].

וְנוֹהֶגֶת בִּזְמַן הַבַּיִת, וְהִיא מִמִּצְווֹת הַמֻּטָּלוֹת עַל הַצִּבּוּר כְּמוֹ בִּנְיַן הַבַּיִת וְכֵלָיו[24].

---

וְסִימָן "יִהְיֶה זֶה" — This is **indicated by** the Torah's words (*Exodus* 30:31): *This* (זֶה) **shall remain** for Me oil of sacred anointment for your generations, זֶ״ה בְּגִימַטְרִיָּא שְׁנֵים עָשָׂר הֱוֵי — for the word זֶה (*this*) has the **gematria** (numeric value) **of twelve.**[22]

וְיֶתֶר פְּרָטֶיהָ — These laws, as well as **the additional details of [the mitzvah],** מְבֹאָרִים בְּפֶרֶק רִאשׁוֹן מִכְּרִיתוֹת — **are elaborated in the first chapter of** Tractate *Kereisos* (5a-b).[23]

### ⇜ Applicability of the Mitzvah ⇝

וְנוֹהֶגֶת בִּזְמַן הַבַּיִת — **[This mitzvah] applies in the time of the Temple,** וְהִיא מִמִּצְווֹת הַמֻּטָּלוֹת עַל הַצִּבּוּר — **and is among the mitzvah-obligations that are incumbent upon the community** as a whole, כְּמוֹ בִּנְיַן הַבַּיִת וְכֵלָיו — **similar to** the mitzvah-obligation of **construction of the Temple and its vessels** (Mitzvah 95).[24]

---

### NOTES

and his sons, on seven consecutive days during the initial inaugural services (*miluim*), as well as numerous Kohanim Gedolim and kings for many centuries, it still miraculously retained its original measure of twelve *log* (*Kereisos* ibid.; see Mitzvah 109). [The oil was concealed along with the Holy Ark, by King Yoshiyahu (Josiah), toward the end of the First Temple Era, and will again be available in its entirety when Mashiach comes (*Horayos* 11b-12a; see Mitzvah 109).]

22. The word זֶה, *This,* in the verse refers to the anointing oil, and it is composed of the letters ז, whose numeric value is 7, and ה, whose numeric value is 5. Hence, the total value of the word, 12, indicates that the twelve-*log* volume of the *shemen hamishchah* shall remain intact after it is produced and throughout all generations.

23. See also *Horayos* 11b-12a, and *Shekalim* 16a. The laws are codified in *Rambam, Hil. Klei HaMikdash* 1:1-12.

*Minchas Chinuch* (§3) wonders why *Rambam* [and Chinuch] describe the details of how the *shemen hamishchah* was produced. As Chinuch notes in Mitzvah 109, since the original twelve *log* that Moses made will remain intact throughout all generations, there never will be a need to produce any more of it. Why, then, is it relevant for us to know how it is produced? *Minchas Chinuch* answers that it is on account of the prohibition (Mitzvah 109) for anyone to make his own mixture of aromatic oil in the same formula as the *shemen hamishchah. Rambam* explains how the *shemen hamishchah* was made so that we will know what we are *forbidden* to do. [See also *Aruch LaNer, Kereisos* 5a. For another approach, see *R' Y. F. Perla, Sefer HaMitzvos of Rav Saadiah Gaon, Onesh* 11, Vol. III, p. 51a.]

24. The command to produce and preserve the *shemen hamishchah* was given to Moses as part of the general mandate to construct the *Mishkan* and its vessels. We repeatedly find the *shemen hamishchah* mentioned among the contributions for the *Mishkan* (e.g., *Exodus* 25:6) and in the account of its construction (e.g., ibid. 37:29). It is thus evident that this mitzvah is related to the obligation to build the *Beis HaMikdash,* and applies only in the time when it is standing. For this reason, *Rambam* includes the laws of the *shemen hamishchah* among the laws of the Temple accessories, in *Hil. Klei HaMikdash.*

As is true regarding the building of the *Beis HaMikdash,* the entire community of Israel bears the responsibility to see to it that the mitzvah is carried out by those who have the ability to do so (see end of Mitzvah 401). For further discussion of this obligation, see the Insight.

---

### ◆§ Insight: What Is Included in the Mitzvah?

There is considerable discussion among the commentators as to what requirements, precisely, are encompassed by our mitzvah. Chinuch begins his presentation by stating that we are commanded to *make* the anointment oil so that it will be available for anointing each new Kohen Gadol. This formulation of the mitzvah follows *Rambam, Hil. Klei HaMikdash* 1:1. The question that arises is: Since the original *shemen hamishchah* that Moses prepared was destined to miraculously remain intact for all generations (see notes 21-22), the commandment to produce *shemen hamishchah* was relevant only in Moses' time. Accordingly, this commandment should seemingly not be included in

the count of the 613 Mitzvos, since one of the principles of reckoning mitzvos is that only something commanded for all generations counts as a "Mitzvah" (see *Sefer HaMitzvos, Shoresh* 3)!

In *Sefer HaMitzvos, Asei* 35, Rambam presents the mitzvah differently. There, he states that we are commanded *to have anointment oil available* for the anointment of Kohanim Gedolim. *Rambam* states that this is derived from the verse (*Exodus* 30:31): שֶׁמֶן מִשְׁחַת קֹדֶשׁ יִהְיֶה זֶה לִי לְדֹרֹתֵיכֶם, *This shall remain for Me oil of sacred anointment for your generations*, which is understood as a command to *preserve* the *shemen hamishchah* for all generations. The implication is that the essence of this mitzvah is not the *making* of the *shemen hamishchah*, but rather, its preservation, i.e., keeping it in readiness and guarding it from being lost. This requirement surely applies in all generations (*Aruch LaNer, Kereisos* 5a).

Chinuch, while mentioning that we are commanded to *make* the *shemen hamishchah*, apparently agrees that preserving it is part of the mitzvah. This is evident from his description of the Mitzvah's underlying purpose, where he explains why it is important for anointment oil to always be available in the *Beis HaMikdash* (see above, notes 10-11). Accordingly, the mitzvah can be classified as one of the 613 Mitzvos, since at least one of its components is applicable in all generations, not only in Moses' time. Apparently, when Chinuch states, at the beginning of the mitzvah, that we are commanded "to make the anointment oil ... so that it should be available for anointing every Kohen Gadol," he means that the mitzvah encompasses both making the *shemen hamishchah* and ensuring its availability. Perhaps this is also the intention of Rambam in *Hil. Klei HaMikdash*, such that his words there are compatible with those in *Asei* 35.

Rambam presents yet another formulation of the mitzvah in *Shoresh* 10 of *Sefer HaMitzvos*. In that *Shoresh* (Introductory Rule), he establishes the principle that an act done as preparation for fulfilling another obligation cannot be counted as one of the 613 Mitzvos. As an example, he notes that preparing the *shemen hamishchah* does not count as a separate mitzvah, because this is done merely to prepare the material needed to fulfill the obligation of anointing Kohanim Gedolim, kings, and sacred vessels. Thus, the primary aspect of the mitzvah is *using* the *shemen hamishchah* for anointment, and this surely applies through the generations, when conditions are met, and not only in Moses' time. Making the *shemen hamishchah*, as well as guarding it, are merely preparatory obligations that are subsumed in the mitzvah to perform anointment whenever required (see *Kinas Soferim* to *Shoresh* 10).

Interestingly, Chinuch titles this mitzvah "The Obligation of Anointing Kohanim Gedolim and Kings With the Anointment Oil." This implies that he, too, considers the act of anointing an essential aspect of this mitzvah — if not the essence of the mitzvah. [Presumably, he omits the anointment of the sacred vessels because that applied only in Moses' time.] Although the Torah does not explicitly command that Kohanim Gedolim and kings be anointed, the very fact that it states *This shall remain for Me "oil of sacred anointment"* implies that the mitzvah encompasses using it for the purpose of anointment. Indeed, numerous commentators understand that the reason *Rambam* and Chinuch view this as a mitzvah that applies for all generations (when the Temple is standing) is because it includes the act of anointing, which we are commanded to do when we invest a Kohen Gadol, or a king of the Davidic dynasty (see *Minchas Chinuch* §1; *Aruch HaShulchan HeAsid* 16:1-3; *Chidushei HaGriz* to *Kereisos* 5b ד"ה מה דלא מנה; for a dissenting view, see *Radvaz*, introduction to *Hil. Klei HaMikdash*).

In summary, the procedures associated with the *shemen hamishchah* encompass three subjects: *making* it, *preserving* it, and *using* it for anointment. In the course of this mitzvah, Chinuch mentions all three subjects, and Rambam also mentions all three — though Rambam mentions them in three different places in his works. Assuming that Rambam's words are complementary, it emerges that our mitzvah encompasses all three aspects of the *shemen hamishchah* laws (see further, *Chidushei HaGriz* ibid.).

[It is noteworthy that although the *shemen hamishchah* prepared by Moses never diminished, there was a period when no oil was available for anointment. Toward the end of the First Temple Era, when King Yoshiyahu (Josiah) realized that the destruction of the *Beis HaMikdash* was imminent, he concealed the Holy Ark along with the *shemen hamishchah* and various other sacred items (see end of note 21). The location of these items will be revealed when Mashiach comes. Thus, in the last years of the First Temple Era, and throughout the entire Second Temple Era, they did not have *shemen hamishchah*. Why did they not produce new *shemen hamishchah*, using the

original formula? *Tosafos* (*Nazir* 47a ד"ה וכן) explain that since the Torah states (ibid.), regarding the *shemen hamishchah* prepared by Moses, **This** *shall remain for Me oil of sacred anointment for your generations,* we learn that *only* that oil was valid for anointment. Any new mixture would not be valid, even if prepared according to the original formula (see also *Minchas Chinuch* §1; cf. *R' Y. F. Perla, Sefer HaMitzvos of Rav Saadia Gaon, Onesh* 11, Vol. III, p. 50b-51a). Thus, it would seem that the reason King Yoshiyahu concealed the *shemen hamishchah,* before it could fall into enemy hands, was to ensure that it would be available in the future era for anointment of the Messianic King and the Kohen Gadol who will be installed at that time (see *Yerushalmi Shekalim* 6:1, which states similarly regarding the Holy Ark). Although by concealing the *shemen hamishchah* he made it temporarily unavailable, in the larger scheme he actually fulfilled the requirement of preserving it for future generations.]

# KI SISA / MITZVAH 108: NOT TO ANOINT AN OUTSIDER WITH THE ANOINTMENT OIL

## ≈ מִצְוָה קח: שֶׁלֹּא יָסוּךְ זָר בְּשֶׁמֶן הַמִּשְׁחָה ≈

שֶׁלֹּא לִמְשֹׁחַ[1] בְּשֶׁמֶן הַמִּשְׁחָה שֶׁעָשָׂה מֹשֶׁה[2] אֶלָּא כֹּהֲנִים לְבַד[3], שֶׁנֶּאֱמַר (שמות ל׳, ל״ב) עַל בְּשַׂר אָדָם לֹא יִיסָךְ[4], וְנִתְבָּאֵר בַּכָּתוּב שֶׁמִּי שֶׁמָּשַׁח בּוֹ בְּמֵזִיד[5] חַיָּב כָּרֵת,

---

## ≈ Mitzvah 108 ≈
## The Prohibition to Anoint an Outsider With the Anointment Oil

שֶׁמֶן מִשְׁחַת קֹדֶשׁ יִהְיֶה זֶה לִי לְדֹרֹתֵיכֶם. עַל בְּשַׂר אָדָם לֹא יִיסָךְ ... קֹדֶשׁ הוּא קֹדֶשׁ יִהְיֶה לָכֶם ... וַאֲשֶׁר יִתֵּן מִמֶּנּוּ עַל זָר וְנִכְרַת מֵעַמָּיו

*This shall remain for Me oil of sacred anointment, for your generations. It shall not be smeared on a person's flesh ... it is holy, it shall remain holy for you ... [anyone] who shall put it upon an outsider shall be cut off from his people (Exodus 30:31-33).*

---

As explained in the previous mitzvah, the anointment oil (*shemen hamishchah*) was made for the purpose of consecrating the vessels of the *Mishkan* and inaugurating the Kohanim into the Temple service, and for anointing future Kohanim Gedolim and kings. This mitzvah prohibits applying this sacred oil to a person's flesh for any other purpose. Anyone whose anointment is not authorized by the Torah is considered an "outsider," and is included in the prohibition set forth in these verses.

שֶׁלֹּא לִמְשֹׁחַ בְּשֶׁמֶן הַמִּשְׁחָה שֶׁעָשָׂה מֹשֶׁה — We are commanded **not to anoint**[1] anyone **with the anointment oil that Moses made,**[2] אֶלָּא כֹּהֲנִים לְבַד — **except** those **Kohanim** who require anointment,[3] שֶׁנֶּאֱמַר "עַל בְּשַׂר אָדָם לֹא יִיסָךְ" — **as it is stated** (*Exodus* 30:32): ***It shall not be smeared on a person's flesh.***[4]

Chinuch sets forth the penalty for transgressing this prohibition:

וְנִתְבָּאֵר בַּכָּתוּב שֶׁמִּי שֶׁמָּשַׁח בּוֹ בְּמֵזִיד חַיָּב כָּרֵת — **It is explicated in Scripture that one who**

---

### NOTES

1. The term לִמְשֹׁחַ, *to anoint,* can refer either to a ceremonial anointment, such as that performed on a Kohen Gadol or king, or to a simple act of smearing for pleasure (see *Rashi* to *Exodus* 30:29). In the context of our prohibition, it refers to any form of applying the oil, including merely pouring it on the body (see further, note 6).

Although Chinuch here writes that we are commanded "not *to anoint*," which suggests that only the act of *applying* the oil (whether to oneself or to another) is prohibited, it is clear from his words below that one who *is* anointed with the *shemen hamishchah* also transgresses this prohibition. See note 8.

2. The prohibition applies exclusively to the original *shemen hamishchah* that Moses formulated, as Chinuch will explain below (at note 14).

3. That is, the Kohanim for whom anointment with the *shemen hamishchah* was prescribed by the Torah, as set forth in the previous mitzvah — the original Kohanim (Aaron and his sons) and subsequent Kohanim Gedolim. In this mitzvah, Chinuch will mention an additional Kohen who requires anointment.

It is unclear why Chinuch omitted "kings," since they, too, are anointed with the *shemen hamishchah* under certain conditions, as Chinuch indicates in the previous mitzvah and later in this mitzvah. *Rambam* (*Sefer HaMitzvos, Lo Saaseh* 84) writes "except Kohanim Gedolim and kings."

4. Since the verse specifies "a *person's* flesh," one who smears the anointment oil on an animal or other object is not liable (*Kereisos* 6b; *Rambam, Hil. Klei HaMikdash* 1:6; see there for additional limitations). Nevertheless, it is prohibited, by Rabbinic decree, to apply the sacred oil to any object.

[The preceding pertains to this mitzvah, which is the specific prohibition against smearing with the *shemen hamishchah*. Authorities debate whether one who uses the *shemen hamishchah* improperly is, additionally, liable for transgressing the general prohibition of *me'ilah*, i.e., the prohibition against using sacred property for mundane purposes (Mitzvah 127). If there is liability for *me'ilah*, then it will apply even if the oil is smeared on an inanimate object. For discussion of this issue, see *Minchas Chinuch* §5; *Teshuvos Avnei Nezer, Yoreh Deah* 313:8; *Yeshuos Malko, Hil. Klei HaMikdash* 1:5; *Teshuvos Imrei Yosher* 2:7.]

שֶׁנֶּאֱמַר (שם, ל"ג) וַאֲשֶׁר יִתֵּן מִמֶּנּוּ עַל זָר וְנִכְרְתָה[6], וְאִם נִמְשַׁח בּוֹ בְּשׁוֹגֵג[7] חַיָּב חַטָּאת קְבוּעָה[8], פֵּרוּשׁ קְבוּעָה, כְּלוֹמַר שֶׁאֵין חִלּוּק בּוֹ בֵּין הַדַּל וְהֶעָשִׁיר אֶלָּא דָּבָר קָבוּעַ הוּא לַכֹּל[9].

מִשָּׁרְשֵׁי מִצְוָה זוֹ, גַּם כֵּן[10] לְהַגְדָּלַת הַבַּיִת וְכָל אֲשֶׁר בּוֹ[11], וְלָכֵן אֵין רָאוּי

**deliberately anointed** himself or another[5] **with [the oil],** when not authorized to do so, **is liable to kares** (excision), שֶׁנֶּאֱמַר "וַאֲשֶׁר יִתֵּן מִמֶּנּוּ עַל זָר וְנִכְרְתָה" — **as it is stated** (ibid., v. 33): *... and [anyone] who shall put it upon an outsider shall be cut off from his people.*[6] וְאִם נִמְשַׁח בּוֹ בְּשׁוֹגֵג — **And, if one was anointed with it unknowingly,**[7] חַיָּב חַטָּאת קְבוּעָה — **he is liable to a fixed chatas offering.**[8]

Chinuch explains:

פֵּרוּשׁ קְבוּעָה — **The meaning of** a *"fixed" chatas* **is,** כְּלוֹמַר שֶׁאֵין חִלּוּק בּוֹ בֵּין הַדַּל וְהֶעָשִׁיר — so **to say, that regarding [this offering] there is no difference between** the obligation of **a poor person and** that of **a wealthy person;** אֶלָּא דָּבָר קָבוּעַ הוּא לַכֹּל — **rather, [the obligation] is a fixed matter for all** transgressors.[9]

### ⸺ Underlying Purpose of the Mitzvah ⸺

מִשָּׁרְשֵׁי מִצְוָה זוֹ גַּם כֵּן — **Among the underlying purposes of the mitzvah, too,** like the previous mitzvah and others pertaining to the Holy Temple (*Beis HaMikdash*),[10] לְהַגְדָּלַת הַבַּיִת וְכָל אֲשֶׁר בּוֹ — **is to increase the grandeur of the Temple and all that is in it** in people's eyes.[11] וְלָכֵן אֵין רָאוּי

---

### NOTES

5. *Rambam, Hil. Klei HaMikdash* 1:6.

6. The verse containing the prohibition (which mentions *smearing* the oil on a person's flesh) and the one containing the penalty (which mentions *putting* the oil on an outsider) complement one another. It is prohibited to either *smear* or *put* the oil on any person other than those designated for sacred anointment, and one who does either of these acts incurs the penalty of *kares* (see *Kereisos* 6b with *Aruch LaNer* ד"ה מה סיכה and *Sfas Emes* ד"ה וכמה יסוך; for an exception, see *Minchas Chinuch* §2 ד"ה והנותן).

7. E.g., he was unaware that the oil with which he is being anointed is the *shemen hamishchah* (see *Rashi* to *Keresios* 2a ד"ה ועל לא הודע).

8. *Mishnah, Kereisos* 2a. Although the verse expresses only the *kares* penalty, it is a rule that any prohibition that is punishable by *kares* if violated deliberately carries *chatas* liability when transgressed inadvertently (see Mitzvah 121).

By stating "And if one *was anointed* with it," Chinuch indicates that *being anointed* with the *shemen hamishchah* is a transgression of the prohibition, just like *doing the anointing*. Accordingly, if one person anointed another, each of them incurs a penalty, commensurate with his personal awareness of the transgression. If both were deliberate, they both incur *kares*; if both were unknowing, they are each liable to a *chatas* offering; and if one of them was deliberate and the other unknowing, then the former incurs *kares* and the latter brings a *chatas* (*Tosefta, Makkos* 3:1). However, the one who is anointed incurs this liability only if he actively assists in the application, for example, by extending his arm (*Chasdei David* to *Tosefta* loc. cit., *Radvaz* to *Rambam* ibid., and *Minchas Chinuch* §3, based on *Makkos* 20a; see also *Asvan D'Oraisa* §20 ד"ה וע"ע בתוספתא; see, however, *Aruch HaShulchan HeAsid* 17:6-7).

It is unclear why Chinuch chose to illustrate the מֵזִיד (deliberate) scenario with the anointer and the שׁוֹגֵג (unknowing) scenario with the anointed. For a possible explanation, see the related discussion of *R' Y. F. Perla, Sefer HaMitzvos of Rav Saadiah Gaon, Onesh* 11, Vol. III, p. 52a-b.

9. That is, anyone who commits this transgression (or one of the other *kares*-bearing transgressions) inadvertently is obligated to bring an animal offering consisting of a female sheep or goat (see Mitzvah 121). This is the standard *chatas* offering, and contrasts with the "variable" *chatas* offering, brought for transgressing certain prohibitions, which carries different levels of liability depending on a person's financial status (see Mitzvah 123).

10. Chinuch apparently means that this mitzvah has the same underlying purpose as the one he set forth for the previous mitzvah (Mitzvah 107), as well as Mitzvos 98 and 103 (see following note).

11. Chinuch expresses numerous times (e.g., Mitzvos 98, 103) that many mitzvos relating to the *Beis HaMikdash* are intended to create an atmosphere of grandeur, which will inspire awe and humility in the hearts of those who come there to serve Hashem. In the previous mitzvah (at notes 10-11), Chinuch explained that the availability of the *shemen hamishchah* in the *Beis HaMikdash* contributes to the overall distinguished aura of the place. The current mitzvah, too, serves that function, as Chinuch proceeds to explain.

# 323 ☐ KI SISA / MITZVAH 108: NOT TO ANOINT AN OUTSIDER WITH THE ANOINTMENT OIL

לְהֶדְיוֹטוֹת לְהִשְׁתַּמֵּשׁ בְּאוֹתוֹ הַשֶּׁמֶן הַנִּכְבָּד שֶׁבַּבַּיִת רַק הַנִּבְחָרִים בָּעָם לְבַד שֶׁהֵם כֹּהֲנִים וּמְלָכִים, וּבְכֵן בְּהִמָּנַע הֶהָמוֹן מִמֶּנּוּ יִיקַר בְּעֵינֵיהֶם עַד מְאֹד וְיִתְאַוּוּ אֵלָיו, כִּי גֹּדֶל עֵרֶךְ הַדְּבָרִים בְּלֵב רֹב בְּנֵי אָדָם לְפִי מְעוּט הִמָּצְאָם אֶצְלָם.[12]

מִדִּינֵי הַמִּצְוָה, כְּגוֹן מַה שֶּׁאָמְרוּ זִכְרוֹנָם לִבְרָכָה שֶׁחִיּוּב הַכָּרֵת וְהַקָּרְבָּן אֵינוֹ עַד שֶׁיָּסוּךְ מִמֶּנּוּ שִׁעוּר כַּזַּיִת[13], וְשֶׁלֹּא חִיְּבוּנוּ הַכָּתוּב אֶלָּא עַל אוֹתוֹ שֶׁעָשָׂה מֹשֶׁה וְלֹא עַל אַחֵר שֶׁיַּעֲשֶׂה שׁוּם אָדָם[14], וְקַבָּלָה בְּיָדֵינוּ שֶׁנֵּס נַעֲשָׂה בּוֹ שֶׁיַּסְפִּיק לְעוֹלָם.[15]

---

לְהֶדְיוֹטוֹת לְהִשְׁתַּמֵּשׁ בְּאוֹתוֹ הַשֶּׁמֶן הַנִּכְבָּד שֶׁבַּבַּיִת — **For this reason, it is improper for common folk to use this exalted oil that is** housed **in the Temple;** רַק הַנִּבְחָרִים בָּעָם לְבַד שֶׁהֵם כֹּהֲנִים וּמְלָכִים — **rather,** it should be used **only** for anointing **the choicest of the nation, which are** specific **Kohanim and kings.** וּבְכֵן בְּהִמָּנַע הֶהָמוֹן מִמֶּנּוּ — **And so, with the masses having been denied** use of [the anointment oil] through this prohibition, יִיקַר בְּעֵינֵיהֶם עַד מְאֹד וְיִתְאַוּוּ אֵלָיו — **it will become most precious in their eyes, and they will** wistfully **long for it,** כִּי גֹּדֶל עֵרֶךְ הַדְּבָרִים בְּלֵב רֹב בְּנֵי אָדָם — **because the degree of value** that **things have in most people's hearts** לְפִי מְעוּט הִמָּצְאָם אֶצְלָם — **corresponds to the scarcity of the availability of [those things] to them.**[12]

### ⇒ Laws of the Mitzvah ⇐

מִדִּינֵי הַמִּצְוָה — **Included among the laws of the mitzvah is,** כְּגוֹן מַה שֶּׁאָמְרוּ זִכְרוֹנָם לִבְרָכָה — **for example, that which [the Sages], of blessed memory, stated** (Kereisos 6b), שֶׁחִיּוּב הַכָּרֵת וְהַקָּרְבָּן — אֵינוֹ עַד שֶׁיָּסוּךְ מִמֶּנּוּ שִׁעוּר כַּזַּיִת — **that liability to** either *kares* or a *chatas* **offering is not** incurred **until one smears** at least **a** *kezayis* (olive's volume) of [the anointment oil] on a person.[13] וְשֶׁלֹּא חִיְּבוּנוּ הַכָּתוּב אֶלָּא עַל אוֹתוֹ שֶׁעָשָׂה מֹשֶׁה — **Also included is the law** (ibid. 5a) **that Scripture does not hold us liable** to *kares* or to a *chatas* offering **except for** the unauthorized application of **that** particular anointment oil **which Moses made,** וְלֹא עַל אַחֵר שֶׁיַּעֲשֶׂה שׁוּם אָדָם — **but not for the** application of **another** anointment oil **that any** other **person makes.**[14] Nevertheless, the prohibition against unauthorized use of the anointment oil applies in all generations, וְקַבָּלָה בְּיָדֵינוּ שֶׁנֵּס נַעֲשָׂה בּוֹ שֶׁיַּסְפִּיק לְעוֹלָם — **for we have received a Tradition that a miracle occurred with [this oil]** in **that it** never became depleted and **would last forever.**[15]

---

### NOTES

12. [Obviously, it is not the purpose of the mitzvah that people should desire to *use* the *shemen hamishchah*, for the Torah does not wish to tempt people with sin. Rather, the purpose is to create a feeling of awe for the *shemen hamishchah*, by making the masses recognize that it is a unique item reserved for select individuals who may use it only on very special occasions. This reverence for the *shemen hamishchah* will, in turn, increase respect for the *Beis HaMikdash*, where it is stored and used. See Mitzvah 107 notes 10-11.]

13. This is inferred from Scripture's use of the word *put* (anyone who shall "*put*" it upon an outsider) — a term that in Scripture generally refers to "putting" a *kezayis* (see *Kereisos* 6b with *Rashi* ד"ה נתינה בעלמא כזית). Although the term *smear*, in Scripture, does not necessarily refer to a *kezayis*, in this case we apply the minimum measure of *kezayis* to smearing as well, since here these two terms are complementary (*Rambam, Hil. Klei HaMikdash* 1:5,10 with *Kesef Mishneh* to §10; see above, note 6). [Chinuch follows *Rambam's* opinion. However, *Raavad* there (§10) disagrees and maintains that the measure of *kezayis* pertains only to *putting*, but *smearing* carries liability in any amount.]

By stating that no *penalty* is imposed if less than a *kezayis* was applied, Chinuch implies that it is nonetheless prohibited. For discussion, see *Minchas Chinuch* §2; *Aruch LaNer* to *Kereisos* 7a ד"ה לא איתחל; *Minchas Yitzchak* to Mitzvah 8 §1.

14. That is, if someone formulates an oil compound identical to the *shemen hamishchah* that Moses prepared, it does not fall under this prohibition. We will learn in the following mitzvah that the one who makes that compound is liable to *kares*, but the oil thus made is not subject to the prohibition against personal anointment (*Kereisos* 5a; see *Chidushei HaGriz* there ד"ה והנה; see also *Ohr HaChaim, Exodus* 30:32).

Although Chinuch here states only that there is no *liability* for smearing a person with duplicate oil, from his description of the prohibition at the beginning of the mitzvah ("not to anoint anyone with the anointment oil that Moses made"), it is evident that there also is no *prohibition* to do so (see *Minchas Yitzchak* ibid.).

15. As Chinuch elaborates in Mitzvah 109 (at note 3), although Moses' *shemen hamishchah* was used to anoint the *Mishkan* and all its vessels, and Aaron and his sons, and many subsequent Kohanim Gedolim and

## כי תשא / מצוה קח: שלא יסוך זר בשמן המשחה

וּמַה שֶּׁאָמְרוּ זִכְרוֹנָם לִבְרָכָה (כריתות דף ה׳ ע״ב) שֶׁאֵין מוֹשְׁחִין בּוֹ לְדוֹרוֹת כָּל הַכֹּהֲנִים הַמִּתְחַנְּכִים לָעֲבוֹדָה[16] אֶלָּא כֹּהֵן גָּדוֹל וּמְשׁוּחַ מִלְחָמָה[17] וּמַלְכֵי בֵּית דָּוִד[18], וְכָל שְׁאָר מְלָכִים אֵינָם נִמְשָׁחִין בְּזֶה הַשֶּׁמֶן אֶלָּא בְּשֶׁמֶן אֲפַרְסְמוֹן[19], וְהַחִלּוּק שֶׁיֵּשׁ בְּמַעֲשֵׂה מְשִׁיחַת הַמֶּלֶךְ לְמַעֲשֵׂה מְשִׁיחַת הַכֹּהֵן.[20]

Chinuch now discusses the instances in which anointment with the *shemen hamishchah* is permitted, and indeed mandated, for inaugural purposes:

וּמַה שֶּׁאָמְרוּ זִכְרוֹנָם לִבְרָכָה — **Included also is that which [the Sages], of blessed memory, stated** (ibid. 5b), שֶׁאֵין מוֹשְׁחִין בּוֹ לְדוֹרוֹת כָּל הַכֹּהֲנִים הַמִּתְחַנְּכִים לָעֲבוֹדָה — **that in the generations** subsequent to the initial installation of Aaron and his sons as Kohanim, **we do not anoint all Kohanim that are initiated into the** Temple **service;**[16] אֶלָּא כֹּהֵן גָּדוֹל וּמְשׁוּחַ מִלְחָמָה — **rather, we anoint only a Kohen Gadol,** when he is inaugurated into that position, **and a** Kohen **anointed for battle.**[17]

In addition, certain kings are anointed with the anointment oil:

וּמַלְכֵי בֵּית דָּוִד — **And,** in regard to anointing kings, only **kings of the House of David** are anointed with the sacred oil,[18] וְכָל שְׁאָר מְלָכִים אֵינָם נִמְשָׁחִין בְּזֶה הַשֶּׁמֶן — **but all other kings,** such as those of the House of Israel, **are not anointed with this oil,** אֶלָּא בְּשֶׁמֶן אֲפַרְסְמוֹן — **but** rather, **with** pure **balsam oil.**[19]

וְהַחִלּוּק שֶׁיֵּשׁ בְּמַעֲשֵׂה מְשִׁיחַת הַמֶּלֶךְ לְמַעֲשֵׂה מְשִׁיחַת הַכֹּהֵן — **Also** included in the laws is **the difference that exists between the procedure of anointing a king and the procedure of anointing a Kohen** (i.e., the Kohen Gadol or the Kohen anointed for battle).[20]

### NOTES

kings, miraculously it always retained its full original measure of 12 *log* (see also above, Mitzvah 107, with note 21). [Hence, the prohibition to smear an outsider with *this* oil applies in all times (see below, note 25). It can thus be counted among the 613 Mitzvos, which contain only commandments that apply in all generations (see *Sefer HaMitzvos, Shoresh* 3).]

16. The original Kohanim — Aaron and his sons — were anointed, as stated in *Exodus* 30:30 and *Leviticus* 8:12,30. Subsequent Kohanim, however, did not require anointment, for since the *avodah* (service) of ordinary Kohanim is an inherited duty, they draw from the sanctity imbued in their fathers [see similarly above, Mitzvah 107 note 5, regarding the sacred vessels]. The position of Kohen Gadol, however, is not inherited; thus a new Kohen Gadol requires anointment (*Abarbanel, Exodus* 30:22 ד״ה העיקר הז׳; *Sforno* to *Numbers* 3:3; *Teshuvos Chikrei Lev, Orach Chaim* II §118; see also below, note 21).

17. This refers to the Kohen who was designated to address the nation before battle (see *Deuteronomy* 20:2-9). His title, מְשׁוּחַ מִלְחָמָה, *the anointed for battle,* indicates that he was anointed with the *shemen hamishchah* (*Kesef Mishneh, Hil. Klei HaMikdash* 1:7; but see *Yad Eisan* there). He does not wear the eight vestments of a Kohen Gadol, but is similar to a Kohen Gadol in many respects, as he is subject to a number of restrictions that otherwise pertain only to a Kohen Gadol (see *Horayos* 12b and *Yoma* 73a). [Some state that if this Kohen was subsequently appointed a Kohen Gadol, he would not require a new anointment (*Chidushei HaGrach al HaShas* בענין משוח מלחמה; cf. *Teshuvos Chikrei Lev* ibid.; see *Chidushei HaGriz, Zevachim* 101b).]

18. Numerous verses in Scripture indicate that King David and his son Solomon were anointed with the *shemen hamishchah* (see *I Samuel* 16:13, *I Kings* 1:39, *Psalms* 89:21). [Although the Torah states with regard to this mitzvah (v. 33): וַאֲשֶׁר יִתֵּן מִמֶּנּוּ עַל זָר וְנִכְרַת, *and [anyone] who shall put it upon an outsider* [זָר] *shall be cut off,* and the term זָר, *outsider,* generally denotes a non-Kohen, in this case it refers to one who is an "outsider" to the mitzvah of anointment — i.e., one who is neither a Kohen Gadol nor a king of the House of David (*Rashi, Exodus* 30:33; see further *Ramban* there, and *Tos. HaRosh* to *Horayos* 11b ד״ה ובו נמשחו).]

When the Torah permits the anointment of a Kohen Gadol or king with the *shemen hamishchah*, it is only for inaugural purposes. Smearing the oil on these individuals for any other purpose is prohibited (see *Kereisos* 6b; for further details, see *Rambam, Hil. Klei HaMikdash* 1:10, and *Ramban* ibid.; see also *Minchas Chinuch* §4).

19. It is derived from Scripture that only kings of the House of David were qualified for anointment with the *shemen hamishchah* (see *Kereisos* 5b). Other kings were ceremoniously anointed with pure balsam oil, which was not sacred like the *shemen hamishchah*, but was highly valued as a unique oil of Eretz Yisrael (see *Berachos* 43a with *Rashi* ד״ה שמן ארצנו).

For discussion on the difference between the monarchy of the House of David and that of the House of Israel with regard to the *shemen hamishchah*, see *Chidushei HaGriz* to *Kereisos* 5b ד״ה בגמ׳ מלכי ישראל and to *Parashas Shoftim*; *Meshech Chochmah* to *Exodus* 30:31. [Many authorities maintain that King Saul was anointed with the *shemen hamishchah*. See Insight for discussion.]

20. For a king, the *shemen hamishchah* was smeared around his head like a crown (*Kereisos* 5b, as understood

# KI SISA / MITZVAH 108: NOT TO ANOINT AN OUTSIDER WITH THE ANOINTMENT OIL

וּמַה שֶּׁאָמְרוּ זִכְרוֹנָם לִבְרָכָה (שם) שֶׁאֵין מוֹשְׁחִין מֶלֶךְ בֶּן מֶלֶךְ[21] אֶלָּא אִם כֵּן יֵשׁ עָלָיו מַחֲלֹקֶת[22], וְעַל כֵּן נִמְשַׁח שְׁלֹמֹה[23], וְיֶתֶר פְּרָטֶיהָ, מְבֹאָרִים בְּפֶרֶק [רִאשׁוֹן] [שְׁלִישִׁי] מִכְּרִיתוֹת (שם)[24].

וְנוֹהֶגֶת מִצְוָה זוֹ שֶׁל אִסּוּר מְשִׁיחַת הַשֶּׁמֶן בְּכָל מָקוֹם שֶׁיִּמָּצֵא וּבְכָל זְמַן[25], בִּזְכָרִים וּנְקֵבוֹת[26].

וּמַה שֶּׁאָמְרוּ זִכְרוֹנָם לִבְרָכָה — **Also, that which [the Sages], of blessed memory, said** (*Kereisos* ibid.), שֶׁאֵין מוֹשְׁחִין מֶלֶךְ בֶּן מֶלֶךְ — **that,** even among the House of David, **we do not anoint a king** who is **the son of a king** and succeeds his father,[21] אֶלָּא אִם כֵּן יֵשׁ עָלָיו מַחֲלֹקֶת — **unless there is contention over him,** i.e., his ascent to the throne is disputed,[22] וְעַל כֵּן נִמְשַׁח שְׁלֹמֹה — **and it is for this** reason that King **Solomon was anointed** even though he succeeded his father, David.[23] וְיֶתֶר פְּרָטֶיהָ מְבֹאָרִים בְּפֶרֶק — These laws, **as well as the additional details of [the mitzvah],** [שְׁלִישִׁי] [רִאשׁוֹן] מִכְּרִיתוֹת — **are elaborated in the first chapter of** Tractate *Kereisos* (5a-7a).[24]

## ☞ Applicability of the Mitzvah ☜

וְנוֹהֶגֶת מִצְוָה זוֹ שֶׁל אִסּוּר מְשִׁיחַת הַשֶּׁמֶן — **This mitzvah, namely, the prohibition of anointing** an unauthorized individual **with the** anointment **oil, applies** בְּכָל מָקוֹם שֶׁיִּמָּצֵא וּבְכָל זְמַן — **in every location in which [the oil] is present and in all times** in which it is present,[25] בִּזְכָרִים וּנְקֵבוֹת — and is applicable **to** both **men and women.**[26]

---

### NOTES

by *Rashi*; cf. *Rambam Commentary* to *Kereisos* 1:1). For a Kohen Gadol [or a Kohen anointed for battle], the oil was first poured on his head and then applied between his eyes in the form of the Greek letter *chi* (*Kereisos* ibid.; *Rambam, Hil. Klei HaMikdash* 1:9).

The exact shape of the letter *chi* is the subject of controversy. Many maintain that it was an X shape. Others identify it with the lower-case Greek upsilon (ō) or capital Upsilon (Ō). Yet others describe it as the capital Pi (Đ), Lambda (Ë) or Omega (Ù). For a lengthy discussion of this dispute, see *Tosafos* to *Menachos* 75a ד"ה כמין כי; *Tiferes Yisrael* to *Zevachim* 10:8; *Yalkut Shinuyei Nuschaos* in Frankel ed. of *Rambam, Hil. Klei HaMikdash* 1:9.

An additional difference is that the anointment of a king takes place adjacent to a spring, as a portent that his reign should endure for generations like the endless flow of a spring (*Keresios* 5b), whereas the anointment of a Kohen Gadol does not; it presumably takes place in the *Beis HaMikdash*. [This distinction is based on the fact that the monarchy is an inheritance that passes from father to son (see following note), but the position of Kohen Gadol is not an inheritance, as explained above in note 16, and in Mitzvah 107 note 4 (*Maharsha* to *Horayos* 12a; *Abarbanel* to *Exodus* 30:22 ד"ה העיקר הי"א).]

Finally, a Kohen Gadol is anointed only by day, as indicated by the verse (*Leviticus* 6:13): בְּיוֹם הִמָּשַׁח אֹתוֹ, on the "day" of his anointment. A king, however, can be anointed at any time (*Minchas Chinuch* §7; but see *Abarbanel* ibid. ד"ה העיקר הי"ב).

21. A king who succeeds his father to the throne takes it as an inheritance, as implied by the verse (*Deuteronomy* 17:20): לְמַעַן יַאֲרִיךְ יָמִים עַל מַמְלַכְתּוֹ הוּא וּבָנָיו בְּקֶרֶב יִשְׂרָאֵל ... so that he will prolong the days of his kingship, "he and his sons," in the midst of Israel. Since he inherits the throne, he does not require anointment. [A Kohen Gadol, however, requires anointment even when he succeeds his father, as mentioned in note 16. For further discussion, see Mitzvah 107 with note 4.]

22. When the monarchy is contested, it ceases to be an inheritance, and a new royal line needs to be established with the successor; hence, anointment is required (*Kereisos* 5b as understood by *Rashi* ד"ה בזמן ששלום בישראל; see, however, *Rambam* ibid. §11; *Teshuvos Avnei Nezer, Yoreh Deah* 312:3; *Chidushei HaGriz* to *Kereisos* 5b ד"ה בגמ' מפני מה).

23. Although King Solomon was David's chosen successor, his half-brother Adoniyah attempted to block his ascent to the throne and claim it for himself. When David intervened and ordered Solomon's immediate inauguration, a new anointment was required because of the dispute (see *I Kings* Ch. 1 and *Kereisos* ibid.).

[*Chinuch*'s account of all these laws seemingly belongs in the previous mitzvah (Mitzvah 107), which refers to the *obligation* to anoint Kohanim Gedolim and kings. It is unclear why he chose to write them here, in the context of the *prohibition* to anoint others. Perhaps, it is to indicate that those individuals who do not *require* anointment with the *shemen hamishchah* are *forbidden* to receive it, under pain of *kares* (see above, end of note 18).]

24. The laws are codified in *Rambam, Hil. Klei HaMikdash* 1:5-12.

25. Given that the prohibition applies only to the *shemen hamishchah* that Moses made (as Chinuch stated above), it is limited to the availability of that particular oil. Thus, after the oil was concealed by King Yoshiyahu (see Mitzvah 107 note 21), the prohibition was not applicable in the practical sense. When the location of the oil becomes known again in the times of Mashiach, the prohibition will resume practical applicability.

26. In accordance with the general rule pertaining to mitzvah-prohibitions.

וְעוֹבֵר עָלֶיהָ וְסָךְ מִמֶּנּוּ כַּזַּיִת, בְּמֵזִיד חַיָּב כָּרֵת, בְּשׁוֹגֵג חַיָּב חַטָּאת קְבוּעָה.[27]

וְעוֹבֵר עָלֶיהָ וְסָךְ מִמֶּנּוּ כַּזַּיִת — Regarding **one who transgresses [the prohibition] and smears a *kezayis* of it** on himself or another person, בְּמֵזִיד חַיָּב כָּרֵת — **if he did so deliberately, he is liable to *kares*,** בְּשׁוֹגֵג חַיָּב חַטָּאת קְבוּעָה — and **if he did so unknowingly, he is liable to a fixed *chatas* offering.**[27]

---

NOTES

27. See above, notes 8-9.

---

### ☙ Insight: The Anointment of King Saul

Chinuch (at note 18) cites the halachah that only kings of the Davidic line may be anointed with the sacred anointment oil. The Gemara (*Kereisos* 5b) derives this from God's statement to the prophet Samuel when he encountered David for the first time: קוּם מְשָׁחֵהוּ כִּי זֶה הוּא, *Arise and anoint him, for this is he!* (*I Samuel* 16:12) The Gemara explains that this alludes to the fact that only the kings of "*this*" monarchy may be crowned with the anointment oil. All other kings, such as those who later ruled over the ten tribes of Israel after the kingdom was split, may be anointed only with balsam oil (see note 18).

Nevertheless, many Rishonim maintain that King Saul, who reigned prior to David and who was not even from the royal tribe of Judah, was indeed anointed with the anointing oil (see *Rambam, Hil. Melachim* 1:7; *Meiri, Horayos* 11b ד"ה משיחה; cf. *Radak* to *I Samuel* 10:1). How are we to understand the use of the anointing oil in that case, seemingly in violation of the clear ruling restricting its use to kings of the Davidic line?

Various answers have been suggested to resolve this difficulty.

*Meiri* (ibid.) writes that, in fact, the Jewish monarchy is meant to be the exclusive function of the tribe of Judah (see *Genesis* 49:10). When the Jewish people requested their first king, however, there was no one in that tribe with all the spiritual qualities necessary to fill this crucial position. Only Saul of the tribe of Benjamin — spiritually unmatched in all of Israel and physically imposing — fit the requirements. Saul was therefore chosen as a substitute leader to "stand in" for a Judean monarch. Since King Saul served to fill the position until a king would rise from the House of David, his reign was viewed as a figurative extension of the Davidic line, and as such, he was fit to be crowned with the special anointing oil reserved for the house of David. [See *Tiferes Yisrael* to *Shekalim* (6:1 *Boaz* §1), who suggests that the name "Saul" (שָׁאוּל), whose literal meaning in Hebrew is *borrowed*, alludes to Saul's status as a monarch, since he was "borrowed," as it were, from the tribe of Benjamin until David's reign.]

*Chidushei HaGriz* to *Kereisos* (5b ד"ה בגמ' מלכי בית דוד) suggests that the Gemara's reference to kings of the House of David as the only legal recipients of the anointing oil actually applies more generally to all primary monarchs of Israel. This excludes, for example, the kings of the Ten Tribes who reigned simultaneously with the Davidic monarchs, as they were considered ancillary monarchs, and could therefore not be anointed with this oil. But at the time of Saul's inauguration as the first king of Israel, there was no monarchy other than his. Therefore, as the primary monarch it was appropriate for him to be anointed with the oil.

Alternatively, it stands to reason that even if we take this law literally to refer to the progeny of David, the limitation upon the oil applied only once David had been chosen as the king of Israel. With the selection of David as king, the Davidic line was chosen, and all other lines of dynastic succession were precluded (see *Mechilta, Parshas Bo* הקדמה ד"ה בארץ מצרים). The law prohibiting other kings to use the anointing oil therefore applied only from the time of David's coronation and on. Indeed, the verse cited above, from which the Gemara derives this law, refers specifically to the anointing of David himself. Saul, who was crowned before David, was therefore not subject to this prohibition (*Chidushei HaGriz* ibid.; see *Rashi* and *Tosafos* to *Kereisos* 5b).

*Meshech Chochmah* (*Exodus* 30:31) finds a Scriptural allusion to the restriction of the anointing oil to the Davidic monarchs as well as to the exception of King Saul's coronation. The Torah writes

### KI SISA / MITZVAH 108: NOT TO ANOINT AN OUTSIDER WITH THE ANOINTMENT OIL

regarding the sacred oil (*Exodus* 30:31): שֶׁמֶן מִשְׁחַת קֹדֶשׁ יִהְיֶה זֶה לִי לְדֹרֹתֵיכֶם, *This shall remain for Me oil of sacred anointment for your generations.* The word לְדֹרֹתֵיכֶם, *for your generations,* indicates that the anointing oil may be used only for monarchies that can last for perpetuity, like the Davidic line. Israelite monarchs are barred from utilizing this oil, since their dynasties, by definition, will not last for perpetuity (see *Rambam* ibid. 1:9; cf. *Raavad* ad loc.). With respect to Saul, however, Scripture indicates (*I Samuel* 13:13) that had he not sinned, his monarchy would have continued in dynastic succession. [Although David's line was always to be the primary monarchy in Israel, *Ramban* explains (*Genesis* 49:10) that Saul's descendants would have either ruled over a portion of the tribes, or served as viceroys under the Davidic monarchs.] Since Saul's rule, too, had the possibility to continue "*for your generations,*" much as the Davidic line did, it was indeed appropriate for Saul's reign to begin with anointment with this sacred oil.

## מִצְוָה קט: שֶׁלֹּא לַעֲשׂוֹת בְּמַתְכֹּנֶת שֶׁמֶן הַמִּשְׁחָה

שֶׁלֹּא לַעֲשׂוֹת שֶׁמֶן הַמִּשְׁחָה, שֶׁנֶּאֱמַר (שמות ל׳, ל״ב) וּבְמַתְכֻּנְתּוֹ לֹא תַעֲשׂוּ[1].

מִשָּׁרְשֵׁי הַמִּצְוָה, מַה שֶּׁכָּתַבְנוּ בְּאִסּוּר מְשִׁיחָתוֹ[2].

עִנְיַן הַמִּצְוָה, שֶׁאָמְרוּ זִכְרוֹנָם לִבְרָכָה (כריתות ה׳ ע״ב) כִּי מֵעוֹלָם לֹא נַעֲשָׂה מִמֶּנּוּ אֶלָּא אוֹתוֹ שֶׁעָשָׂה מֹשֶׁה בַּמִּדְבָּר, וְאָמְרוּ שֶׁנֵּס נַעֲשָׂה בּוֹ שֶׁכֻּלּוֹ קַיָּם לֶעָתִיד לָבוֹא, וּמַה שֶּׁהוֹצִיאוּ

---

## Mitzvah 109

## The Prohibition to Replicate the Anointment Oil

וּבְמַתְכֻּנְתּוֹ לֹא תַעֲשׂוּ כָּמֹהוּ קֹדֶשׁ הוּא קֹדֶשׁ יִהְיֶה לָכֶם

*... and in its measure you shall not make [another] like it; it is holy, it shall remain holy for you* (Exodus 30:32).

שֶׁלֹּא לַעֲשׂוֹת שֶׁמֶן הַמִּשְׁחָה — We are commanded **not to make** a mixture of **the anointment oil** other than that which Moses made, שֶׁנֶּאֱמַר — **as it is stated** regarding the anointment oil (*Exodus* 30:32): וּבְמַתְכֻּנְתּוֹ לֹא תַעֲשׂוּ — *... and in its measure you shall not make [another] like it.*[1]

### Underlying Purpose of the Mitzvah

מִשָּׁרְשֵׁי הַמִּצְוָה — **Among the underlying purposes of the mitzvah** is מַה שֶּׁכָּתַבְנוּ בְּאִסּוּר מְשִׁיחָתוֹ — **that which we wrote** above (Mitzvah 108) **regarding the prohibition** against **anointing** with [the anointment oil that Moses made].[2]

### Laws of the Mitzvah

Chinuch, in this instance, prefaces the actual laws of the mitzvah with a description of its concept: עִנְיַן הַמִּצְוָה — **The concept of this mitzvah** שֶׁאָמְרוּ זִכְרוֹנָם לִבְרָכָה — **is that which [the Sages], of blessed memory, stated** (*Menachos* 98a), כִּי מֵעוֹלָם לֹא נַעֲשָׂה מִמֶּנּוּ אֶלָּא אוֹתוֹ שֶׁעָשָׂה מֹשֶׁה בַּמִּדְבָּר — **that no [anointment oil] was ever made** for sacred use **aside from [the mixture] that Moses made in the Wilderness;** וְאָמְרוּ שֶׁנֵּס נַעֲשָׂה בּוֹ שֶׁכֻּלּוֹ קַיָּם לֶעָתִיד לָבוֹא — **and they stated further** (*Kereisos* 5b) **that a miracle occurred with [this oil],** such **that** it was never depleted and **all of it** shall **remain intact for the Future Era,** when the Third Temple will be built, וּמַה שֶּׁהוֹצִיאוּ

---

NOTES

1. The prohibition pertains only to the exact replication of the *shemen hamishchah* (anointment oil) formula (see below).

There is disagreement as to the scope of this mitzvah. According to *Rambam* (*Hil. Klei HaMikdash* 1:4), it is Biblically prohibited only to replicate the *shemen hamishchah* for *personal* use; replicating it for nonpersonal use (e.g., with intention to learn how to produce it for the *Beis HaMikdash*) is prohibited by Rabbinic decree. Others maintain that after Moses prepared the original *shemen hamishchah,* it became prohibited for anyone to replicate it for *any* purpose. See note 4 for elaboration and discussion of Chinuch's view.

2. In Mitzvah 108, Chinuch explained that the Torah prohibited personal use of the *shemen hamishchah* so that people would hold it in high regard, and as a result would have more reverence for the *Beis HaMikdash,* where it is stored. If the *shemen hamishchah* could be replicated, this purpose would be defeated, because one could enjoy a similar experience elsewhere. The prohibition against making an identical oil compound precludes such a possibility, making the *shemen hamishchah* an exclusive feature of the *Beis HaMikdash.* [See also *Moreh Nevuchim* III:45, cited in footnote 5 to Mitzvah 108 in the Mechon Yerushalayim edition of *Minchas Chinuch.*]

## KI SISA / MITZVAH 109: THE PROHIBITION TO REPLICATE THE ANOINTMENT OIL

מִמֶּנּוּ לִמְשִׁיחַת הַמִּשְׁכָּן וְכֵלָיו, הַבְּרָכָה הִשְׁלִימוֹ⁴. וְשֶׁאֵין חַיָּבִין עַל עֲשִׂיָּתוֹ אֶלָּא בְּשֶׁעֲשָׂאָהוּ בְּסְכוּם סַמְמָנָיו⁵, וְזֶהוּ לָשׁוֹן בְּמַתְכֻּנְתּוֹ, מִלְּשׁוֹן חֶשְׁבּוֹן⁶, כְּלוֹמַר בְּחֶשְׁבּוֹן סַמְמָנָיו⁷,

מִמֶּנּוּ לִמְשִׁיחַת הַמִּשְׁכָּן וְכֵלָיו — **and whatever** amount **was dispensed of it for the anointment of the** *Mishkan* (Tabernacle) **and its vessels,** as well as the anointment of Kohanim Gedolim and kings throughout the generations, הַבְּרָכָה הִשְׁלִימוֹ — **the** Divine **blessing has replenished.**[3] Hence, there is no need to ever produce more of this oil.[4]

Having explained the concept of the mitzvah, Chinuch presents its basic law:

וְשֶׁאֵין חַיָּבִין עַל עֲשִׂיָּתוֹ אֶלָּא בְּשֶׁעֲשָׂאָהוּ בְּסְכוּם סַמְמָנָיו — **One is liable** (to the penalty described below) **for replicating [the anointment oil] only if he made it with the** exact **amount of spices** and oil as the one that Moses made.[5] וְזֶהוּ לָשׁוֹן בְּמַתְכֻּנְתּוֹ מִלְּשׁוֹן חֶשְׁבּוֹן — **This is** indicated by the Torah's usage of **the expression** *bemaskunto* (in the verse, *and "bemaskunto" [in its measure] you shall not make [another] like it*), **which is synonymous with** "its **total quantity,"**[6] כְּלוֹמַר בְּחֶשְׁבּוֹן סַמְמָנָיו — meaning **to say** that what is prohibited is to replicate the anointment oil **according to the** precise **quantity of its** component **spices** and oil.[7]

---

NOTES

3. The *shemen hamishchah* made by Moses was used initially to anoint the *Mishkan* and all its vessels, as well as Aaron and his sons upon their inauguration into the priesthood, as stated in *Exodus* 30:26-30. This was done on each of the שִׁבְעַת יְמֵי הַמִּלּוּאִים, *seven days of inauguration* [*miluim*] (*Kereisos* 5b). It was further used to anoint every Kohen Gadol, every Kohen "anointed for battle," and numerous kings of the House of David during the First Temple Era, as described in Mitzvah 108. [The *shemen hamishchah* was concealed by King Yoshiyahu (Josiah) before the destruction of the Temple, and was not available during the Second Temple Era (see Mitzvah 107 note 21).] Despite its extensive use, the entire 12-*log* mixture that Moses formulated (as described in Mitzvah 107) was miraculously extant until the times of King Yoshiyahu (Josiah), and all of it will remain intact in the Messianic Era, when the oil will once again be found and returned to use (*Kereisos* ibid.). The Torah itself predicts this miracle, as explained above, Mitzvah 107 note 22.

[Chinuch's description of the miracle indicates that the *shemen hamishchah* did, in fact, diminish with each anointing, but the miracle caused it to subsequently be replenished. Others maintain that the oil never diminished in the first place (see *Iyun Yaakov* to *Horayos* 11b ד"ה ומשום, and *Ben Yehoyada* there, 12a ד"ה שמא ח"ו (מעלתי.]

4. By relating these facts here, Chinuch seems to imply that our verse means to prohibit replicating this formula of oil for *any* purpose, including use in the *Beis HaMikdash*. The Torah, knowing that the oil would miraculously remain intact, categorically forbids its reformulation. This is how the prohibition is understood by *Ralbag, Exodus* 30:32, and *Abarbanel, Exodus* 30:22. [See also *Tosafos, Nazir* 47a ד"ה בשלמא, who state further that only the original *shemen hamishchah* made by Moses was valid for anointment, and no replication of it would be valid. See further, end of Insight to Mitzvah 107.]

*Rambam* (*Hil. Klei HaMikdash* 1:4), however, maintains that although producing such oil for the *Beis HaMikdash* was unnecessary, if a person made it with the intention of donating it to the *Beis HaMikdash* (or to learn the production process) he would not be liable for a violation. Only replication for personal use is Biblically prohibited (see also *Tosafos*, cited in *Shitah Mekubetzes* to *Kereisos* 5a §14; see further, *Minchas Chinuch* §2). [For discussion of whether, according to *Rambam's* opinion, a replication made for Temple use would actually be valid for anointment, see *R' Y. F. Perla* to *Sefer HaMitzvos of Rav Saadiah Gaon, Onesh* 11 (Vol. 3, p. 51a); and *Chidushei HaGriz* to *Kereisos* 5a.]

5. For a detailed description of the various ingredients of the *shemen hamishchah* and their prescribed quantities, see Mitzvah 107 (see also note 23 there).

6. The Torah uses the same term in regard to the quota of bricks that Jews in Egypt were required to produce by Pharaoh's decree. *Exodus* 5:8 states: ...וְאֶת מַתְכֹּנֶת הַלְּבֵנִים תָּשִׂימוּ עֲלֵיהֶם, *but the quota of bricks ... you shall impose upon them* (see *Rashi* there and to *Exodus* 30:32).

7. Chinuch seems to understand that the entire law is derived from the term בְּמַתְכֻּנְתּוֹ, which he renders *according to the total quantity of its contents*. From the Gemara (*Kereisos* 5a) and *Rambam* (ibid.), however, it appears that this law is derived as follows: The verse states: וּבְמַתְכֻּנְתּוֹ לֹא תַעֲשׂוּ כָּמֹהוּ, *and in its measure you shall not make [another] like it*. The term וּבְמַתְכֻּנְתּוֹ, *and in its measure*, teaches that in order for the prohibition to apply the ingredients must be mixed in the same proportion as those of Moses' anointment oil — i.e., the stipulated amount of each spice per 12 *log* of olive oil. This could still mean that it is prohibited to make a double recipe, or a half-recipe, using that proportion of spices and oil. [Indeed, the similar prohibition to replicate the *ketores* (Mitzvah 110) encompasses even making a part-recipe of it (see Chinuch there, at note 6).] The additional word כָּמֹהוּ, *like it*, in our verse, teaches that the prohibition to replicate the *shemen*

וְיֶתֶר פְּרָטֶיהָ, מְבֹאָרִים בְּפֶרֶק רִאשׁוֹן מִכְּרִיתוֹת (שם).
וְנוֹהֶגֶת מִצְוָה זוֹ שֶׁל אִסּוּר עֲשִׂיַת הַשֶּׁמֶן בְּכָל מָקוֹם וּבְכָל זְמַן, בַּזְּכָרִים וּנְקֵבוֹת.
וְעוֹבֵר עָלֶיהָ וְעָשָׂה מִמֶּנּוּ, בְּמֵזִיד חַיָּב כָּרֵת, בְּשׁוֹגֵג חַיָּב חַטָּאת קְבוּעָה.

מְבֹאָרִים בְּפֶרֶק רִאשׁוֹן מִכְּרִיתוֹת וְיֶתֶר פְּרָטֶיהָ — These, **and additional details of [the mitzvah], are elaborated in the first chapter of** Tractate *Kereisos* (5a-b).[8]

## ⁓ Applicability of the Mitzvah ⁓

וְנוֹהֶגֶת מִצְוָה זוֹ שֶׁל אִסּוּר עֲשִׂיַת הַשֶּׁמֶן — **This mitzvah, namely, the prohibition of producing** a replication of **the** anointment **oil, applies** בְּכָל מָקוֹם וּבְכָל זְמַן — **in every location and in all times,** בַּזְּכָרִים וּנְקֵבוֹת — **to** both **men and women.**[9] וְעוֹבֵר עָלֶיהָ וְעָשָׂה מִמֶּנּוּ — **Regarding one who transgresses [this mitzvah] and produces** a replication of **[the anointment oil],** בְּמֵזִיד חַיָּב כָּרֵת — **if he does so deliberately, he is liable to** *kares* (excision),[10] בְּשׁוֹגֵג חַיָּב חַטָּאת קְבוּעָה — **and if he does so inadvertently,**[11] **he is liable to** bring **a fixed** *chatas* **offering.**[12]

---

### NOTES

*hamishchah* pertains only to making a batch of oil *precisely* like the original *shemen hamishchah* mixture, using specifically 12 *log* of oil and the actual amount of each spice listed in the Torah (see *Minchas Chinuch* here §3 and below, 110:6; see also *Rashi, Exodus* 30:32 with *Mizrachi* and *Gur Aryeh*).

Although Chinuch sets forth this stipulation with regard to the penalty, it is apparent that this also pertains to the prohibition itself, since the verse states וּבְמַתְכֻּנְתּוֹ לֹא תַעֲשׂוּ כָּמֹהוּ, *and in its measure you shall not make [another] like it*.

8. The laws are codified in *Rambam, Hil. Klei HaMikdash* 1:4.

9. I.e., it applies both in Eretz Yisrael and in the Diaspora, whether the *Beis HaMikdash* is standing or not.

And, like all mitzvah-prohibitions, it is incumbent upon women as well as men (see General Introduction).

10. The liability to *kares* is expressed by Scripture in the verse (*Exodus* 30:33): אִישׁ אֲשֶׁר יִרְקַח כָּמֹהוּ ... וְנִכְרַת מֵעַמָּיו, *Anyone who shall compound its like … shall be cut off from his people.*

11. E.g., he intended to take other ingredients but inadvertently used the ingredients of the *shemen hamishchah* instead (*Rashi* to *Kereisos* 2a ד"ה ועל לא הודע).

12. This follows the rule that any prohibition that is punishable by *kares* if violated deliberately carries *chatas* liability when transgressed inadvertently (see Mitzvah 121).

For the definition of "fixed *chatas* offering," see Mitzvah 108 at note 9, and Mitzvah 121.

---

> **⥽ Insight: The Kosher Status of Musk**
>
> As Chinuch states, one violates the prohibition against replicating the *shemen hamishchah* only if he uses the exact same ingredients (and proportions) as those used by Moses in his production of the actual *shemen hamishchah*. Chinuch listed those ingredients in Mitzvah 107, and one of them was *mor*, or as the Torah refers to it, *mar-deror* (*Exodus* 30:23). There is some question as to the identity of this ingredient.
>
> *Rambam* (*Hil. Klei HaMikdash* 1:3) identifies *mor* as "the blood gathered in [an internal cavity of] an animal native to India, whose identity is well known, which people everywhere use as a perfume." As the commentators explain (*Radvaz* ad loc.; *Ramban, Exodus* 30:23), *Rambam* refers to musk, a secretion of the male musk deer. *Raavad* (ad loc.), however, disagrees with *Rambam's* identification of *mor* as musk, for he argues that blood — which by definition is not kosher — would not be used as an ingredient in the sacred anointment oil. He therefore suggests that the *mor* of this verse is the same as that referenced in *Song of Songs* (5:1), which he explains to be a plant derivative. This plant is identified as *myrrh* (*Ramban* ibid.) — a fragrant gum resin that exudes from a small, prickly tree species native to the Middle East.
>
> Others, though, defend *Rambam* and explain that musk, although ultimately derived from the blood of the animal, is in its final form no longer considered blood, for it has been transformed into a distinct product (*Ramban* ibid.). In fact, upon drying, the reddish-brown paste within the

musk pod becomes a black granular material (called "musk grain"), which some describe as more characteristic of earth than of blood (*Radvaz* loc. cit.).

The above discussion has ramifications beyond the identification of the ingredient *mor*, as it relates directly to the question of whether musk is considered kosher, and hence, whether it may be used as an additive to food. Some Rishonim argue that since musk is a derivative of blood, it must be viewed as nonkosher, and may not be used as a food additive (*R' Meir HaLevi* [*Ramah*], cited by *Rabbeinu Yonah*, *Berachos* fol. 31b; *Rosh*, *Berachos* 6:35). Others disagree and maintain that musk is considered kosher, since in its current state it is not blood, but rather a bodily excretion formed of blood that decomposed, and the fact that it originated as blood is no longer relevant (*Rabbeinu Yonah* ibid.; *Radvaz* ibid.).

This question is debated by later authorities as well. See *Taz, Orach Chaim* 216:2; *Magen Avraham* 216:3; *Elyah Rabbah* 216:4; *Mishnah Berurah* 216:7; *Chazon Ish, Bechoros* 16:15.

The question of whether we must look at the root source of musk — or, for that matter, any ingredient — or we may simply view the ingredient as per its current state, is one that has broader consequence in the laws of *kashrus*. One classic example relates to the consumption on Pesach of foods with ingredients that are derived from *chametz*, but have taken on an entirely different form. An example of such an ingredient is citric acid (often used as a flavoring additive or an acidifier). Citric acid is commonly produced by feeding a glucose solution sometimes derived from grain (which can be *chametz*) to a mold (*Aspergillus niger*), which, after a number of days, generates a liquid byproduct. This byproduct is treated with other chemicals (lime and sulfuric acid) to produce the finished citric acid product. Whether or not citric acid and other such ingredients may be used on Pesach would depend, at least in part, on the above question regarding musk — namely, whether we relate to musk based on its current form or the forbidden form from which it was derived.

Another example relates to the Ashkenazic custom to refrain from eating *kitniyos* (legumes) on Pesach (see *Rama, Orach Chaim* 453:1). What is the status of products that are derived from *kitniyos* (legumes), but have taken on an entirely different form? Examples of these include ascorbic acid and aspartame, which are produced from corn after a multi-stage conversion process. The permissibility of such ingredients depends, at least in part, on the above question of how we relate to a product that is derived from a forbidden item but has taken on an entirely new form.

For further discussion of this issue, see *Ginas Veradim, Kelalim, Klal* 51; *Teshuvos Chesed LeAvraham* (*R' Avraham Teumim*) *II, Orach Chaim* §48; *Teshuvos Minchas Yitzchak* Vol. 5 §5; *Tzitz Eliezer* Vol. 6 §16. See also *Teshuvos Minchas Yitzchak* Vol. 7 §27, *Shevet HaLevi* Vol. 4 §47 and Vol. 5 §56 ד"ה וגם יש, and *Yechaveh Daas* Vol. 2 §62.

## מִצְוָה קי: שֶׁלֹּא לַעֲשׂוֹת בְּמַתְכֹּנֶת הַקְּטֹרֶת

שֶׁלֹּא לַעֲשׂוֹת קְטֹרֶת כִּדְמוּת קְטֹרֶת, כְּלוֹמַר שֶׁתִּהְיֶה הַרְכָּבָתוֹ עַל עִנְיַן הַמִּשְׁקָלִים[1] וְיִתְכַּוֵּן לְהַקְטִיר עַצְמוֹ בָּהּ, שֶׁנֶּאֱמַר (שמות ל, לז), (ו)בְּמַתְכֻּנְתָּהּ לֹא תַעֲשׂוּ לָכֶם, וְנֶאֱמַר עָלֶיהָ (שם, שם, לח), אִישׁ אֲשֶׁר יַעֲשֶׂה כָמוֹהָ לְהָרִיחַ בָּהּ, כְּלוֹמַר שֶׁיִּתְכַּוֵּן בַּעֲשִׂיָּתָהּ לְהַקְטִיר עַצְמוֹ[2].

מִשָּׁרְשֵׁי הַמִּצְוָה, מַה שֶּׁכָּתַבְנוּ בְּאִסּוּר מְשִׁיחַת הַשֶּׁמֶן[3].

## Mitzvah 110
## The Prohibition to Replicate the Incense

וְהַקְּטֹרֶת אֲשֶׁר תַּעֲשֶׂה בְּמַתְכֻּנְתָּהּ לֹא תַעֲשׂוּ לָכֶם קֹדֶשׁ תִּהְיֶה לְךָ לַה'
*The incense that you shall make — in its measure you shall not make for yourselves; it shall remain holy to you, for Hashem* (Exodus 30:37)

In Mitzvah 103, Chinuch described the obligation of the Kohanim to produce the Temple incense (*ketores*) and offer it on the Golden Altar. The *ketores* is compounded of eleven spices, in a recipe containing precise measures for the various spices in the mixture (see there with note 12). In this mitzvah, Chinuch discusses the prohibition to replicate this particular formula for personal use.

שֶׁלֹּא לַעֲשׂוֹת קְטֹרֶת כִּדְמוּת קְטֹרֶת — We are commanded **not to make incense** that is **identical to the** *ketores* used in the Temple (*Beis HaMikdash*); כְּלוֹמַר שֶׁתִּהְיֶה הַרְכָּבָתוֹ עַל עִנְיַן הַמִּשְׁקָלִים — that **is to say,** incense **whose composition is** of the same spices **in the same proportions as those** of the *ketores*,[1] וְיִתְכַּוֵּן לְהַקְטִיר עַצְמוֹ בָּהּ — and this prohibition applies specifically where **one intends to** subsequently **use [the incense] to create** a pleasant **aroma for himself.** שֶׁנֶּאֱמַר — Replicating the *ketores* is prohibited, **as it is stated** (*Exodus* 30:37): "(ו)בְּמַתְכֻּנְתָּהּ לֹא תַעֲשׂוּ לָכֶם" — *The incense that you shall make — in its measure you shall not make for yourselves;* וְנֶאֱמַר עָלֶיהָ — **and** we know that this prohibition applies only when there is intent to enjoy its aroma, since **it is** further **stated regarding [this matter],** in the subsequent verse (ibid. v. 38): "אִישׁ אֲשֶׁר יַעֲשֶׂה כָמוֹהָ לְהָרִיחַ בָּהּ" — *Whoever makes [another] like it "to smell it"* shall be cut off from his people (i.e., shall incur *kares*, excision); כְּלוֹמַר שֶׁיִּתְכַּוֵּן בַּעֲשִׂיָּתָהּ לְהַקְטִיר עַצְמוֹ — **that is to say,** the penalty applies to one **who produces it with the intention to** burn it in order to **create** a pleasant **aroma for himself.**[2]

### Underlying Purpose of the Mitzvah

מִשָּׁרְשֵׁי הַמִּצְוָה — **Among the underlying purposes of the mitzvah** is מַה שֶּׁכָּתַבְנוּ בְּאִסּוּר מְשִׁיחַת הַשֶּׁמֶן — **that which we wrote with** regard to **the prohibition** against **anointing** with the anointment oil (Mitzvah 108).[3]

---

NOTES

1. As Chinuch will state below, it is prohibited to compound even a small amount of incense if the proportion of its spices is the same as that of the *ketores*. See below, note 6.

2. Although this verse discusses the penalty, Chinuch maintains that its stipulation of intent "to smell it" pertains to the prohibition stated in the previous verse as well. Thus, only replicating the *ketores* with intent to enjoy its aroma is prohibited; doing so for other purposes that Chinuch will discuss below is permitted (see *Rashi* to *Exodus* 30:38; *Be'er Sheva* to *Kereisos* 5a ד"ה הוא לכם; *Aruch LaNer* to *Kereisos* 5a ד"ה או למוסרו; *Chazon Nachum* to *Mishnayos Kereisos* 1:1).

[Others maintain that the prohibition to replicate the *ketores* applies in all cases, and the stipulation of "to smell it" pertains only to the *kares* penalty; one who replicates it for one of the other purposes discussed below is exempt from *kares*, but has committed a transgression (*Ohr HaChaim* to *Exodus* 30:37; *Tzafnas Pane'ach, Tinyana* p. 29a; see also the language of *Rambam, Hil. Klei HaMikdash* 2:10, and *Har HaMoriah* to *Hil. Klei HaMikdash* 1:4 §10).]

It is prohibited to replicate the *ketores* with *intent* to smell it, even if one does not actually smell it (*Rambam* ibid. 2:9).

3. In Mitzvah 108, Chinuch stated that it is human

# 333 ☐ KI SISA / MITZVAH 110: THE PROHIBITION TO REPLICATE THE INCENSE

מִדִּינֵי הַמִּצְוָה, מַה שֶּׁאָמְרוּ זִכְרוֹנָם לִבְרָכָה (כריתות דף ה׳ ע״א) שֶׁהָעוֹשֶׂה אוֹתָהּ לְהִתְלַמֵּד אוֹ לְמָכְרָהּ לַצִּבּוּר[4] פָּטוּר[5], וְהָעוֹשֶׂה אֲפִלּוּ קְצָת מִמֶּנָּה, כָּל זְמַן שֶׁנַּעֲשֶׂה אוֹתוֹ קְצָת לְפִי מִשְׁקֶלֶת הַקְּטֹרֶת שֶׁחַיָּב[6], וּמַה שֶּׁאָמְרוּ שֶׁהַקְּטֹרֶת הָיְתָה נַעֲשֵׂית בִּזְמַן הַבַּיִת בְּכָל שָׁנָה וְשָׁנָה[7],

## ⸙ Laws of the Mitzvah ⸙

**מִדִּינֵי הַמִּצְוָה — Among the laws of the mitzvah is מַה שֶּׁאָמְרוּ זִכְרוֹנָם לִבְרָכָה — that which [the Sages], of blessed memory, stated** (Kereisos 5a), **שֶׁהָעוֹשֶׂה אוֹתָהּ לְהִתְלַמֵּד — that one who makes [the incense] in order to become practiced** in the proper manner of preparation of ketores, **אוֹ לְמָכְרָהּ לַצִּבּוּר — or** in order **to sell it to the community**[4] for use in the Temple as ketores, **פָּטוּר — is exempt** from liability.[5]

**וְהָעוֹשֶׂה אֲפִלּוּ קְצָת מִמֶּנָּה — Also** among the laws is that **if one makes even a small portion of** [incense] with the ingredients of the ketores, **כָּל זְמַן שֶׁנַּעֲשֶׂה אוֹתוֹ קְצָת לְפִי מִשְׁקֶלֶת הַקְּטֹרֶת — as long as that small portion was made** with its ingredients **matching the proportions of** the ingredients of **the ketores, שֶׁחַיָּב — he is liable.**[6]

Chinuch now mentions two laws that pertain to the ketores of the Beis HaMikdash:

**וּמַה שֶּׁאָמְרוּ — Also** included in the laws is **that which [the Sages] said** (ibid. 6a), **שֶׁהַקְּטֹרֶת הָיְתָה נַעֲשֵׂית בִּזְמַן הַבַּיִת בְּכָל שָׁנָה וְשָׁנָה — that in the time of the Holy Temple, the ketores was made on an annual basis,** i.e., once a year, in an amount sufficient for that entire year,[7]

---

### NOTES

nature to appreciate that which is not readily available and which is not regularly experienced (see there for how this pertains to the anointment oil [shemen hamishchah]). Now, as Chinuch explained in Mitzvah 103, the underlying purpose of the ketores was to permeate the Beis HaMikdash with its extraordinary aroma, creating an atmosphere both dignified and pleasant that would move people to greater devotion in the service of Hashem. The prohibition to replicate the ketores for personal use precludes the possibility of experiencing its aroma elsewhere, thereby enhancing its effect in the Beis HaMikdash. [See also Moreh Nevuchim 3, Ch. 45, cited in footnote 5 to Mitzvah 108 in the Mechon Yerushalayim edition of Minchas Chinuch.]

4. Some texts read: לְמָסְרָהּ לַצִּבּוּר, to "give" it to the community, as a donation (see footnote §4 in the Mechon Yerushalayim edition of Minchas Chinuch; see also the text of the Gemara, Kereisos 5a and 6a).

5. Actually, according to Chinuch, replicating the ketores for these purposes — or any similar purpose — is not merely excluded from liability, but is actually permissible, as explained in note 2 (see Minchas Chinuch §4).

[For discussion of whether incense that one donates to the Beis HaMikdash is actually valid as ketores, see Mishneh LaMelech, Hil. Klei HaMikdash 2:6; Har HaMoriah there 1:4 §10; Aruch HaShulchan HeAsid 19:25; see also above, Mitzvah 103, end of note 3.]

6. Chinuch follows Rambam's opinion (Hil. Klei HaMikdash 2:9; Commentary to Kereisos 1:1) that compounding incense in any quantity for personal use is prohibited if the proportion of the spices is similar to that of the ketores. This would be considered replicating the ketores, since the ketores itself can be compounded in any quantity [as explained above, Mitzvah 103 note 3] (see Chidushei HaGriz to Rambam, Hil. Klei HaMikdash 2:8, and to Menachos 49a ד״ה והנה בגמרא).

[Rashi (Kereisos 6b ד״ה במסכונתה), however, maintains that the ketores for the Beis HaMikdash must be compounded in at least the amount needed for one day's offering, which is a maneh (see Mitzvah 103 note 3); hence, one is not liable for replicating the ketores unless he compounds at least that measure of incense. For further discussion, see Tosafos, Kereisos 6b ד״ה המפטם, Shitah Mekubetzes there §4; Sfas Emes there; Likkutei Halachos there in Ein Mishpat §90; Mishneh LaMelech, Hil. Klei HaMikdash 2:8 and Hil. Temidin U'Mussafin 3:2; Minchas Chinuch §3; R' Y. F. Perla, Sefer HaMitzvos of Rav Saadiah Gaon, Asei 3-4, Vol. I, p. 78b-79a.]

The prohibition to replicate the ketores differs from the prohibition to replicate the shemen hamishchah (Mitzvah 109) in this regard. With respect to the shemen hamishchah, there is a set quantity required for its manufacture (see Mitzvah 107), and thus, replicating it is prohibited only when done in that same quantity (see Mitzvah 109, at notes 5-7). The ketores, however, does not have a set quantity for its manufacture (as was just explained, according to Chinuch), so replicating it in any amount for personal use is prohibited and carries the kares liability (see Kereisos 5a).

7. The preferred way of performing the mitzvah of compounding the ketores was to make an entire year's quantity in one batch (Tosafos, Shevuos 11a ד״ה הואיל; cf. Ri Migash and Rashash there; see Minchas Chinuch 103:5). See above, beginning of Mitzvah 103 with note 3.

## 334 □ כי תשא / מצוה קי: שלא לעשות במתכנת הקטרת

וְאִם חִסַּר הָעוֹשֶׂה אוֹתָהּ אַחַת מִסַּמְמָנֶיהָ חַיָּב מִיתָה,[8] וְיֶתֶר פְּרָטֶיהָ, מְבֹאָרִים בְּפֶרֶק רִאשׁוֹן מִכְּרִיתוֹת (שם).[9]

וְנוֹהֶגֶת מִצְוָה זוֹ שֶׁל אִסּוּר עֲשִׂיָּתָהּ בְּכָל מָקוֹם וּבְכָל זְמַן, בִּזְכָרִים וּנְקֵבוֹת.[10] וְעוֹבֵר עָלֶיהָ וְעָשָׂה מִמֶּנָּה לְפִי מִשְׁקָלָהּ לְהָרִיחַ בָּהּ, בְּמֵזִיד חַיָּב כָּרֵת,[11] בְּשׁוֹגֵג[12] חַיָּב חַטָּאת קְבוּעָה.[13] אֲבָל הַמֵּרִיחַ בָּהּ לְבַד וְלֹא עֲשָׂאָהּ אֵינוֹ חַיָּב כָּרֵת,[14] אֶלָּא דִּינוֹ כְּדִין כָּל הַנֶּהֱנֶה מִן הַהֶקְדֵּשׁ.[15]

---

וְאִם חִסֵּר הָעוֹשֶׂה אוֹתָהּ אַחַת מִסַּמְמָנֶיהָ — and that **if the one making [the *ketores*] for the Temple omitted any of its spices,** חַיָּב מִיתָה — **he is liable to death** at the hands of Heaven.[8] וְיֶתֶר פְּרָטֶיהָ — These, **and the remaining details of [the mitzvah],** מְבֹאָרִים בְּפֶרֶק רִאשׁוֹן מִכְּרִיתוֹת — **are elaborated in the first chapter of** Tractate *Kereisos* (5a, 6a-b).[9]

### ☙ Applicability of the Mitzvah ☙

וְנוֹהֶגֶת מִצְוָה זוֹ שֶׁל אִסּוּר עֲשִׂיָּתָהּ — **This mitzvah, namely, the prohibition of replicating [the *ketores*]** for personal use, **applies** בְּכָל מָקוֹם וּבְכָל זְמַן — **in every location and in all times,** בִּזְכָרִים וּנְקֵבוֹת — **and is applicable** **to** both **men and women.**[10] וְעוֹבֵר עָלֶיהָ — **Regarding one who transgressed [the prohibition]** וְעָשָׂה מִמֶּנָּה לְפִי מִשְׁקָלָהּ לְהָרִיחַ בָּהּ — **and made** a replica **of [the *ketores*] in accordance with its proportions,** in order **to smell it,** בְּמֵזִיד חַיָּב כָּרֵת — **if he did so deliberately, he is liable to** *kares* (excision),[11] בְּשׁוֹגֵג חַיָּב חַטָּאת קְבוּעָה — **and if he did so inadvertently,**[12] **he is liable to a fixed** *chatas* offering.[13] אֲבָל הַמֵּרִיחַ בָּהּ לְבַד וְלֹא עֲשָׂאָהּ — **However, one who merely smelled [the *ketores*]** burning in the *Beis HaMikdash* with intent to benefit from it, **but did not make** a replica of it for that purpose, אֵינוֹ חַיָּב כָּרֵת — **is not liable to** *kares*;[14] אֶלָּא דִּינוֹ כְּדִין כָּל הַנֶּהֱנֶה מִן הַהֶקְדֵּשׁ — **rather, he is subject to the law that applies to anyone who derives benefit from sacred property.**[15]

---

### NOTES

8. Chinuch seems to be saying that the one who *prepares* the deficient *ketores* is liable. However, this presents a difficulty, since the Gemara in *Yoma* (53a) clearly indicates that it is the Kohen who knowingly *offers* the deficient *ketores* who is liable, not the one who makes it (see also *Rashi, Kereisos* 6a ד"ה חייב מיתה). Chinuch's intention requires further study. For discussion, see *Abir Yaakov* to *Kereisos* 6a ד"ה חיסר. See also the Insight below.

[It is additionally unclear why Chinuch mentions this point here, in the mitzvah that discusses the prohibition to *replicate* the *ketores*, and not in Mitzvah 103, which discusses the obligation to *make* the *ketores*. Perhaps he means to allude that if one replicates the *ketores* but omits even one of these spices, he is exempt.]

9. These laws are codified in *Rambam, Hil. Klei HaMikdash* 2:8-10.

10. It applies in both Eretz Yisrael and the Diaspora, whether the *Beis HaMikdash* is standing or not. And, in accordance with the general rule pertaining to mitzvah-prohibitions, it applies to women as well as men.

11. The liability to *kares* is explicit in the verse (*Exodus* 30:38): *Whoever makes [another] like it to smell it shall be cut off from his people.*

12. E.g., he intended to take other ingredients but inadvertently used the ingredients of the *ketores* instead (*Rashi* to *Kereisos* 2a ד"ה ועל לא הודע).

13. This is in accordance with the rule that that any prohibition that is punishable by *kares* if violated deliberately carries *chatas* liability when transgressed inadvertently (see Mitzvah 121).

14. This stands in contrast to the law regarding the *shemen hamishchah,* which is that one incurs *kares* not only for replicating it, but also for smearing it on oneself or another person (see Mitzvos 108-109). [Smearing (the *shemen hamishchah*) is a transgression that involves action, so the Torah imposes *kares* for it; smelling (the *ketores*) does not involve action, so the Torah does not impose *kares* for it (*Rashi* to *Kereisos* 2a, end of first ד"ה ופסח ומילה מצות עשה, at *Shitah Mekubetzes* §28).]

15. *Kereisos* 6a. He has committed the sin of *me'ilah* (misuse of Temple property; Mitzvah 127), and is required to bring an offering known as אֲשַׁם מְעִילוֹת, the *asham* of *me'ilah* (*Pesachim* 26a with *Rashi* ד"ה אלא שמעל). This applies only if he smelled the *ketores* while it was still extant and burning. Once the *ketores* has been consumed by the fire and only its ascending column of fragrant smoke remains, one who smells it does not commit *me'ilah*. Nonetheless, this is prohibited (*Pesachim* ibid.; *Rambam, Hil. Me'ilah* 5:16; see *Tosafos* to *Kereisos* 6a ד"ה קול).

It must be noted that one is liable for having derived benefit from the *ketores* only if he purposefully came closer in order to smell the fragrance. It is permitted for people in the vicinity of the *Beis HaMikdash* to enjoy the fragrant aroma of the *ketores* while going about their business (see *Yoma* 39b with *Tosafos* ד"ה כלה שבירושלים; see also above, Mitzvah 103 note 11).

### ✥§ Insight: Reciting Pittum HaKetores

Chinuch (at note 8) cites the law that if one omits one or more of the *ketores* spices, he incurs the penalty of death at the hands of Heaven. This law has bearing on our daily prayers. It is customary in many communities to recite the paragraph פִּטּוּם הַקְּטֹרֶת (*Pittum HaKetores*), *The Ketores Mixture*, which describes the ingredients of the *ketores*, at the end of the daily *Shacharis* prayer. As a general rule, when we recite Scriptural or Talmudic passages that describe the processes of bringing the various offerings, it is reckoned on a certain level as if we had actually brought those offerings (see *Menachos* 110a; see further, *Maharal, Nesiv HaTorah* Ch. 9 ד"ה ועל החבור). It follows that the recitation of the *Pittum HaKetores* paragraph comes in place of the *ketores* offering in the *Beis HaMikdash*. Indeed, *Noda BiYehudah* (*Orach Chaim* I §10) assumes that just as a Kohen who offered the *ketores* would merit wealth (see Insight B to Mitzvah 103), so too, is one who recites the *Pittum HaKetores* ordained to be blessed with wealth. Moreover, *Elyah Rabbah* (132:5) cites *Piskei Tosafos,* who assert that just as the *ketores* halted a plague in Moses' time (see *Numbers* 17:6-15), so too does reciting the *Pittum HaKetores* have the power to halt a plague.

Since reciting the *Pittum HaKetores* is in a sense tantamount to actually offering the *ketores* in the *Beis HaMikdash*, *Mahari Abuhav* (cited by *Beis Yosef, Orach Chaim* §133) states that this paragraph should not be recited orally but only from a written text, lest one omit one of its spices and be "liable to death" on account of having "offered" a deficient *ketores*. *Mahari Abuhav* notes further that some communities refrain from reciting this paragraph altogether, and he suggests that this stems from the apprehension that it will be recited hurriedly and some omission may occur. *Beis Yosef* (ibid.), however, dismisses *Mahari Abuhav's* concern, for several reasons:

The source of the law that omission of a spice from the *ketores* mixture carries the punishment of death is a Baraisa cited in *Kereisos* 6a which states simply, "if he left out any of its spices, he is liable to death," without indicating to whom this refers. *Rashi* (ad loc.) explains that the severe penalty applies specifically in a case where the Kohen Gadol offers this deficient *ketores* in the Holy of Holies on Yom Kippur (see *Leviticus* 16:12-13). He is liable to death because, since the *ketores* is not valid, he is considered to have entered the Holy of Holies for no purpose, and anyone who enters there without sanction incurs the penalty of death at the hands of Heaven (ibid. v. 2; see *Yoma* 53a). Thus, according to *Rashi*, death is not incurred for offering a deficient *ketores*, but for what turned out to be an unnecessary entry into the Holy of Holies. *Beis Yosef* therefore contends that, even if omitting one of the spices while reciting *Pittum HaKetores* is tantamount to offering a deficient *ketores*, it surely cannot be considered as having unnecessarily entered the Holy of Holies.

*Rambam* (*Hil. Klei HaMikdash* 2:8), however, seems to understand that the Baraisa's ruling is not limited to the case of the Yom Kippur *ketores* offered in the Holy of Holies, but applies even to the daily offering of *ketores* on the Golden Altar (Mitzvah 103). According to *Rambam*, the death penalty is incurred because a deficient *ketores* is considered a קְטֹרֶת זָרָה, *unauthorized incense*, which one is prohibited to offer under Mitzvah 104 (see *Exodus* 30:9). Although Scripture does not explicitly impose a penalty of death for this violation, *Beis Yosef* explains that it is inferred from the fate that Nadab and Abihu, the sons of Aaron, suffered when they offered an unauthorized *ketores* (see *Leviticus* 10:1-2 with *Sforno*). [For analysis of the dispute between *Rashi* and *Rambam*, see *Mishneh LaMelech, Hil. Klei HaMikdash* 2:3, and *Even HaAzel* there 2:8.]

Presumably, *Mahari Abuhav* follows *Rambam's* opinion that the penalty of death for a deficient *ketores* applies to the daily offering, and he therefore cautions against a deficient recitation of this offering. Nevertheless, *Beis Yosef* argues that although the recitation stands in place of the *ketores* offering in the *Beis HaMikdash*, there is no basis to assume that omitting the name of a spice from the recitation has the same gravity as omitting an actual spice from the *ketores* offering. *Magen Avraham* (132:5) adds that, in any case, the penalty of death is imposed only for *deliberately* omitting a spice, while here the concern is that one might *inadvertently* omit a spice. [For additional rebuttals of *Mahari Abuhav's* concern, see *Beis Yosef* ibid. and *Chochmas Shlomo* [*Kluger*] to end of *Orach Chaim* 132.]

*Rama* (*Orach Chaim* 132:2), however, accepts *Mahari Abuhav's* ruling and writes that it is therefore customary [in many communities] not to recite *Pittum HaKetores* at the end of the *Shacharis* prayer on weekdays, when people might omit some words due to their hurrying to work. [It is, however,

recited almost universally on the Sabbath and Yom Tov.] As for the above arguments against *Mahari Abuhav*, *Teshuvos Maharshal* (§64) indicates that we are not concerned that a reciter who omits a spice will actually incur death at the hands of Heaven; rather, the intention is that since offering a deficient *ketores* carries this severe penalty [at least in some instances], and the recitation stands in place of the actual offering, it behooves us to take pains to avoid even reciting it deficiently, as such a recitation would be highly inappropriate. *Rama's* language seems consistent with this approach. [The expression "liable to death" is often used figuratively to connote the seriousness of a matter (see *Sdei Chemed, Kelalim, Maareches Ches* §92).]

In practice, Sephardim and those who pray *Nusach Sefard* — as well as all Askenazim in Eretz Yisrael — follow the opinion of *Beis Yosef* and recite the *Pittum HaKetores* daily, while those in the Diaspora who pray *Nusach Ashkenaz* follow *Rama* and recite it only on the Sabbath and Yom Tov. Nevertheless, *Aruch HaShulchan* (133:4) advises that those of *Nusach Ashkenaz* who make an effort to recite the *Pittum HaKetores* daily are praiseworthy, and with respect to *Mahari Abuhav's* concern, one can adopt the practice of counting the eleven spices on the fingers while reciting them, to ensure that all eleven are accounted for. This custom is mentioned in numerous sources (see, for example, *Kaf HaChaim, Orach Chaim* 48:4, and *Chasan Sofer, Shaar HaKorbanos VeHaKapparah* §6).

*Ben Ish Chai* has a novel approach to this matter (see *Od Yosef Chai, Halachos, Parashas Mikeitz* §7). He suggests that it is because of *Mahari Abuhav's* concern that we preface the *Pittum Haketores* recitation with the phrase: אַתָּה הוּא שֶׁהִקְטִירוּ אֲבוֹתֵינוּ לְפָנֶיךָ אֶת קְטֹרֶת הַסַּמִּים, *It is You* [Hashem] *before Whom our forefathers burned the ketores of spices*. Fearing the prospect of omitting one of the spices, we declare that our recitation is not in place of the *ketores* offering, but is, rather, an account of our forefathers' devotion to the mitzvah of *ketores* in the time when the *Beis HaMikdash* stood. In this way, a faulty recitation cannot have negative consequences, since the recitation is merely commemorative. However, Hashem knows that in our hearts we desire to please Him, and that it is our fear of omitting a spice that prompts us to state this disclaimer, so He lovingly accepts our recitation as if we had offered the *ketores* in His *Beis HaMikdash*.

For further discussion of the great significance attached to the recitation of the *Pittum HaKetores*, see *Machazik Berachah, Orach Chaim* 48:2, and *Kaf HaChaim* 132:18-23.

## KI SISA / MITZVAH 111: THE PROHIBITION TO CONSUME IDOLATROUS OFFERINGS

### מִצְוָה קיא: שֶׁלֹּא לֶאֱכֹל וְלִשְׁתּוֹת תִּקְרֹבֶת עֲבוֹדָה זָרָה

שֶׁלֹּא לֶאֱכֹל וְלִשְׁתּוֹת תִּקְרֹבֶת עֲבוֹדָה זָרָה, שֶׁנֶּאֱמַר (שמות ל״ד, י״ב-ט״ו) הִשָּׁמֶר לְךָ פֶּן תִּכְרֹת בְּרִית לְיוֹשֵׁב הָאָרֶץ וְגוֹ׳, וְזָבְחוּ לֵאלֹהֵיהֶם וְקָרָא לְךָ וְאָכַלְתָּ מִזִּבְחוֹ[1].

מִשָּׁרְשֵׁי הַמִּצְוָה, לְהַרְחִיק וּלְסַלֵּק כָּל עִנְיַן עֲבוֹדָה זָרָה וְכָל דָּבָר הַמְיֻחָס אֵלֶיהָ מִבֵּין עֵינֵינוּ וּמִמַּחֲשַׁבְתֵּנוּ, וּבִיסוֹד רִחוּק הָעֲבוֹדָה זָרָה כָּתַבְנוּ לְמַעְלָה מַה שֶּׁיָּדַעְנוּ בּוֹ.

## Mitzvah 111

# The Prohibition to Consume Idolatrous Offerings

הִשָּׁמֶר לְךָ פֶּן תִּכְרֹת בְּרִית לְיוֹשֵׁב הָאָרֶץ אֲשֶׁר אַתָּה בָּא עָלֶיהָ פֶּן יִהְיֶה לְמוֹקֵשׁ בְּקִרְבֶּךָ ... פֶּן תִּכְרֹת בְּרִית לְיוֹשֵׁב הָאָרֶץ וְזָנוּ אַחֲרֵי אֱלֹהֵיהֶם וְזָבְחוּ לֵאלֹהֵיהֶם וְקָרָא לְךָ וְאָכַלְתָּ מִזִּבְחוֹ

*Be vigilant lest you seal a covenant with the inhabitant of the land to which you come, lest it be a snare among you ... Lest you seal a covenant with the inhabitants of the land and they stray after their gods, and slaughter to their gods, and he invite you and you eat from his slaughter (Exodus 34:12-15).*

In *Parashas Yisro*, in the Ten Commandments (*Exodus* 20:3-5), we were given the basic prohibitions of idolatry (Mitzvos 26-29): not to believe in any deity other than Hashem, not to make an idol, and not to bow down or perform any other act of worship to an *avodah zarah* — which Chinuch defines (beginning of Mitzvah 28) as any entity that is an object of worship, other than Hashem, the One God. In *Parashas Mishpatim* (*Exodus* 23:13, 24, 32-33), the Torah adds several mitzvos pertaining to idolatry, including the prohibition to make a treaty with any worshipers of *avodah zarah* (Mitzvah 93; see also Mitzvos 86, 87, 94). This mitzvah is repeated in our *parashah*, in the passage cited above, and with it we are given an additional commandment pertaining to *avodah zarah*:

שֶׁלֹּא לֶאֱכֹל וְלִשְׁתּוֹת תִּקְרֹבֶת עֲבוֹדָה זָרָה — We are commanded **not to eat or drink** from anything that was presented as **an offering to an** *avodah zarah,* שֶׁנֶּאֱמַר — as it is stated (*Exodus* 34:12-15): "הִשָּׁמֶר לְךָ פֶּן תִּכְרֹת בְּרִית לְיוֹשֵׁב הָאָרֶץ וְגוֹ׳, וְזָבְחוּ לֵאלֹהֵיהֶם וְקָרָא לְךָ וְאָכַלְתָּ מִזִּבְחוֹ" — *Be vigilant lest you seal a covenant with the inhabitants of the land, etc., and they slaughter to their gods, and he invite you and you eat from his slaughter.*[1]

### Underlying Purpose of the Mitzvah

מִשָּׁרְשֵׁי הַמִּצְוָה — **Among the underlying purposes of the mitzvah is** לְהַרְחִיק וּלְסַלֵּק כָּל עִנְיַן עֲבוֹדָה זָרָה — **to distance and remove any matter of idolatry** וְכָל דָּבָר הַמְיֻחָס אֵלֶיהָ — **and anything attributed to it** מִבֵּין עֵינֵינוּ וּמִמַּחֲשַׁבְתֵּנוּ — **from the focus of our eyes and from our thoughts.** וּבִיסוֹד רִחוּק הָעֲבוֹדָה זָרָה — As for the importance of **the fundamental principle of distancing idolatry** from ourselves, כָּתַבְנוּ לְמַעְלָה מַה שֶּׁיָּדַעְנוּ בּוֹ — **we have written above** (Mitzvah 87) **what we know about it.**

---

NOTES

1. Chinuch explains at the end of the mitzvah that the phrases הִשָּׁמֶר, *Be vigilant,* and פֶּן, *lest,* convey a prohibition. [Since sealing a covenant with the idolatrous inhabitants of the land was previously prohibited (Mitzvah 93), the prohibition here pertains to eating from that which the idolater slaughtered to his god.] Chinuch also states at the end of the mitzvah that in citing this verse as the source of the prohibition, he follows the opinion of *Ramban,* but *Rambam* derives this prohibition from a different verse.

## כי תשא / מצוה קיא: שלא לאכל ולשתות תקרבת עבודה זרה

מִדִּינֵי הַמִּצְוָה, מַה שֶּׁאָמְרוּ זִכְרוֹנָם לִבְרָכָה (עבודה זרה דף נ״א ע״ב) שֶׁכָּל דָּבָר שֶׁעָשׂוּ מִמֶּנּוּ תִּקְרֹבֶת לַעֲבוֹדָה זָרָה אָסוּר, וַאֲפִלּוּ מַיִם וּמֶלַח, כְּלוֹמַר שֶׁאַף עַל פִּי שֶׁמַּיִם וּמֶלַח הֵם דְּבָרִים קַלִּים[2] וְאֶפְשָׁר לוֹמַר בָּהֶם שֶׁאֵינָן לְתִקְרֹבֶת וְלֹא הֻנִּיחוּם לִפְנֵי הָעֲבוֹדָה זָרָה לְכַוָּנַת כָּבוֹד כְּלָל, אַף עַל פִּי כֵן אָסוּר. וְכֵן אָסְרוּ זִכְרוֹנָם לִבְרָכָה (שם דף כ״ט ע״ב) לְרֹב רִחוּק זֶה כָּל יַיִן שֶׁל גּוֹיִם אַף עַל פִּי שֶׁלֹּא יָדַעְנוּ בּוֹ שֶׁנִּסְּכוּהוּ לַעֲבוֹדָה זָרָה, וְהוּא נִקְרָא לָהֶם סְתָם יֵינָם[3], אֶלָּא שֶׁחִלְּקוּ זִכְרוֹנָם לִבְרָכָה (שם דף ע״ד ע״א) בֵּין הַנֶּסֶךְ בְּיָדוּעַ לִסְתָם יֵינָם, שֶׁהַיָּדוּעַ אִסּוּרוֹ בְּמַשֶּׁהוּ מִן הַתּוֹרָה וְלוֹקִין עָלָיו,

### ⁓ Laws of the Mitzvah ⁓

מִדִּינֵי הַמִּצְוָה — **Among the laws of the mitzvah of blessed memory, have said** (*Avodah Zarah* 51b), מַה שֶּׁאָמְרוּ זִכְרוֹנָם לִבְרָכָה — **is what [the Sages],** שֶׁכָּל דָּבָר שֶׁעָשׂוּ מִמֶּנּוּ תִּקְרֹבֶת לַעֲבוֹדָה זָרָה אָסוּר — **that anything that was used as an offering to an** *avodah zarah* **is forbidden** for consumption, וַאֲפִלּוּ מַיִם וּמֶלַח — including **even water or salt.** כְּלוֹמַר — **That is to say,** שֶׁאַף עַל פִּי שֶׁמַּיִם וּמֶלַח — that even though water and salt הֵם דְּבָרִים קַלִּים — **are insubstantial items,**[2] וְאֶפְשָׁר לוֹמַר בָּהֶם — and one could say about them שֶׁאֵינָן לְתִקְרֹבֶת — **that they are not genuinely used as offerings,** וְלֹא הֻנִּיחוּם לִפְנֵי הָעֲבוֹדָה זָרָה לְכַוָּנַת כָּבוֹד כְּלָל — **and they were not placed before the idol with any intention of honoring it,** אַף עַל פִּי כֵן אָסוּר — **nevertheless, they are forbidden.**

Based on the preceding principle, it is prohibited to drink wine that was poured as a libation for an idol (יֵין נֶסֶךְ, *yein nesech* wine). Chinuch mentions a Rabbinic extension of this prohibition: וְכֵן אָסְרוּ זִכְרוֹנָם לִבְרָכָה לְרֹב רִחוּק זֶה כָּל יַיִן שֶׁל גּוֹיִם — **Likewise, due to this great degree of distance** that we must keep from idolatry, **[the Sages], of blessed memory** (ibid. 29b), **prohibited** *all* **wine of idolaters,** אַף עַל פִּי שֶׁלֹּא יָדַעְנוּ בּוֹ שֶׁנִּסְּכוּהוּ לַעֲבוֹדָה זָרָה — **even though we do not know about it that it was** actually **poured as a libation for an idol.** וְהוּא נִקְרָא לָהֶם סְתָם יֵינָם — **This is what [the Sages] call "their ordinary wine,"** i.e., ordinary wine of idolaters.[3] אֶלָּא שֶׁחִלְּקוּ זִכְרוֹנָם לִבְרָכָה בֵּין הַנֶּסֶךְ בְּיָדוּעַ לִסְתָם יֵינָם — **However, [the Sages], of blessed memory** (ibid. 74a), **differentiated,** in regard to the severity of the prohibition, **between wine that is known to have been poured as a libation** for an idol (i.e., *nesech* wine), which is prohibited Biblically, and **[idolaters'] ordinary wine,** which is prohibited by decree of the Sages. שֶׁהַיָּדוּעַ אִסּוּרוֹ בְּמַשֶּׁהוּ מִן הַתּוֹרָה — **The difference is that** with respect to **[wine] that is known** to have been poured for an idol (*nesech* wine), **its prohibition applies to** even **a minute amount, under Biblical law,** וְלוֹקִין עָלָיו — **and one incurs** *malkus* **(lashes) for**

---

NOTES

2. Water and salt are considered "insubstantial" in relation to other food items because they do not provide nourishment as other foods do (see Mishnah, *Eruvin* 26b, and Gemara there 30a). In the context of *avodah zarah*, they are not viewed as an offering that "beautifies" the idol in the same manner as other foods (see Rashi, *Avodah Zarah* 51b ד״ה אפילו מים ומלח, and *Tosafos* ad loc.).

3. Chinuch indicates here (and again below, after note 8) that the Rabbinic prohibition of סְתָם יֵינָם, *[idolaters'] ordinary wine*, was instituted out of concern that the wine had been used as a libation for their idols. This explanation is based on the Gemara, *Avodah Zarah* 29b. The Gemara elsewhere (ibid. 36b), however, states that wine owned by an idolater was prohibited by the Sages for a different reason: to prevent intermarriage with idolaters. *Rashba* (*Toras HaBayis* 5:1) explains that initially, as a hedge against intermarriage, the Sages prohibited the ordinary wine of idolaters only for consumption, just as they likewise prohibited the bread and oil of idolaters for consumption, for the same reason (see *Avodah Zarah* 36b). However, after the Sages saw that the practice of wine libations was very prevalent among idolaters, they decreed that the ordinary wine of idolaters be prohibited even for benefit, out of concern that it actually was used for a libation. Wine that is *known* to have been poured as a libation is Biblically prohibited for benefit as *nesech* wine.

[*Tosafos* (ibid. 29b ד״ה יין) and *Ramban* (ibid. 36b) have another approach. They explain that the possibility of libations is not a major concern, since only a small percentage of idolaters actually make libations to their idols. Rather, the reason for the prohibition is purely so that there should be a hedge against intermarriage. Thus, it would have been sufficient to prohibit the wine for consumption only. Nevertheless, since ordinary wine of an idolater is similar to actual *nesech* wine, which is prohibited for benefit, the Sages prohibited all wine of idolaters for benefit.]

מִדִּכְתִיב (דברים י״ג, י״ח) וְלֹא יִדְבַּק בְּיָדְךָ מְאוּמָה מִן הַחֵרֶם,[4] וּבְסִתְמָם יֵינָם שֶׁאֵין אִסּוּרוֹ אֶלָּא מִדִּבְרֵיהֶם אֵין בְּחִיּוּב שְׁתִיָּתוֹ אֶלָּא מַכַּת מַרְדּוּת,[5] וּבְשׁוֹתֵהוּ מִמֶּנּוּ רְבִיעִית,[6] אֲבָל בְּפָחוֹת מֵרְבִיעִית אֵין בּוֹ מַכַּת מַרְדּוּת,[7] וּמִכָּל מָקוֹם הוּא מִדִּבְרֵיהֶם אֲפִלּוּ בְּמַשֶּׁהוּ בַּהֲנָאָה.[8] וּבִשְׁאָר דְּבָרִים שֶׁבָּעוֹלָם חוּץ מִיַּיִן לֹא הֶחֱמִירוּ זִכְרוֹנָם לִבְרָכָה לֶאֱסֹר כָּל הַנִּמְצָא בְּיָדָם בְּסִתְמָם מִפְּנֵי חֲשָׁשׁ תִּקְרֹבֶת עֲבוֹדָה זָרָה אוֹ חֲשָׁשׁ עֲבוֹדָה זָרָה עַצְמָהּ, זוּלָתִי בִּדְבָרִים שֶׁבָּהֶם נִכָּר שֶׁהֵם עֲשָׂאוּם לְכָךְ, כְּגוֹן מַה שֶּׁאָמְרוּ זִכְרוֹנָם לִבְרָכָה (שם דף מ׳ ע״ב)

---

**וְלֹא** — as derived **from the verse** (*Deuteronomy* 13:18): **מִדִּכְתִיב** — drinking a minute amount of it, **יִדְבַּק בְּיָדְךָ מְאוּמָה מִן הַחֵרֶם** — *Nothing of the banned property may adhere to your hand.*[4] **וּבְסִתְמָם יֵינָם שֶׁאֵין אִסּוּרוֹ אֶלָּא מִדִּבְרֵיהֶם** — But concerning [idolaters'] ordinary wine, which is prohibited only by decree of [the Sages], **אֵין בְּחִיּוּב שְׁתִיָּתוֹ אֶלָּא מַכַּת מַרְדּוּת** — the liability for drinking of it is only the punishment of *makkas mardus* (lashes of discipline),[5] **וּבְשׁוֹתֵהוּ מִמֶּנּוּ רְבִיעִית** — and this punishment is incurred only in a case where one drinks the measure of a *revi'is*[6] of it; **אֲבָל בְּפָחוֹת מֵרְבִיעִית אֵין בּוֹ מַכַּת מַרְדּוּת** — but a case where one drinks less than a *revi'is* [of idolater's ordinary wine] does not carry the punishment of *makkas mardus*.[7] **וּמִכָּל מָקוֹם הוּא מִדִּבְרֵיהֶם אֲפִלּוּ בְּמַשֶּׁהוּ בַּהֲנָאָה** — Nevertheless, although one is not punished for drinking less than a *revi'is* [idolaters' ordinary wine] is forbidden initially by decree of [the Sages] even in a minute amount, for any form of benefit.[8]

Chinuch notes that although the Biblical prohibitions to benefit from idols and from idolatrous offerings pertain to any item that was worshiped as an *avodah zarah* or that was offered before an *avodah zarah*, when the Sages issued their decree regarding something that *may* have been used in idolatrous service they limited it to wine:

**וּבִשְׁאָר דְּבָרִים שֶׁבָּעוֹלָם חוּץ מִיַּיִן** — Regarding all other things that exist in the world, other than wine, **לֹא הֶחֱמִירוּ זִכְרוֹנָם לִבְרָכָה לֶאֱסֹר כָּל הַנִּמְצָא בְּיָדָם בְּסִתְמָם** — [the Sages], of blessed memory, were not so stringent as to prohibit every "ordinary" item that is found in the possession of [idolaters], i.e., every item not known to have been used for idolatrous service; **מִפְּנֵי חֲשָׁשׁ תִּקְרֹבֶת עֲבוֹדָה זָרָה** — neither did they prohibit an ordinary item because of the suspicion that it may have been used as an offering to an *avodah zarah,* **אוֹ חֲשָׁשׁ עֲבוֹדָה זָרָה עַצְמָהּ** — nor did they prohibit an ordinary item because of the suspicion that it itself was worshiped as an actual *avodah zarah.* **זוּלָתִי בִּדְבָרִים שֶׁבָּהֶם נִכָּר** **שֶׁהֵם עֲשָׂאוּם לְכָךְ** — Thus, any ordinary item found in the possession of an idolater, other than wine, is permitted for benefit, **except for items that are recognizable as having been made by them for this purpose** (i.e., to be used for worship). **כְּגוֹן** — An example of the latter is **מַה שֶּׁאָמְרוּ זִכְרוֹנָם לִבְרָכָה**

---

### NOTES

4. This verse refers to idols [and their accessories], which are "banned property," i.e., prohibited for benefit. The phrase *"Nothing" of the banned property* teaches that any item prohibited on account of idolatry is forbidden in the minutest amount (*Rambam, Hil. Maachalos Asuros* 11:1-2; see also *Ramban's* Glosses to *Sefer HaMitzvos, Lo Saaseh* 194).

5. *Makkas mardus* is the term used to describe Rabbinically authorized lashes — as opposed to the term *malkus*, which describes lashes prescribed by Biblical law (see General Introduction, note 16). *Makkas mardus* was a less severe punishment than *malkus*, either because fewer lashes were meted out (*R' Saadiah Gaon,* cited in *Otzar HaGeonim, Nazir* 23a), or because the strap used caused less pain (*Ran to Kesubos,* fol. 16b in *Rif*).

6. A liquid measure of between 2.9 and 5.1 fluid ounces (between 86 and 150 cc).

7. *Rambam, Hil. Maachalos Asuros* 11:3. [For discussion of *Rambam's* source for this ruling, see *Lechem Mishneh, Mirkeves HaMishneh* and *Avi Ezri* ad loc.]

8. Ordinary wine of idolaters is treated more leniently than *nesech* wine only in regard to punishment after the fact. Initially, however, the law of idolater's ordinary wine parallels that of the Biblically prohibited *nesech* wine. Just as it is forbidden to drink a minute amount of *nesech* wine, or to derive benefit from it, so, too, is it forbidden to drink a minute amount of idolaters' ordinary wine, or to derive any type of benefit from it (see *Lechem Mishneh* ibid.; see also *Minchas Chinuch* §5).

[It should be noted that although both *nesech* wine and idolaters' ordinary wine are prohibited for benefit, one incurs punishment (either *malkus* or *makkas mardus*) only for drinking the wine, but not for deriving other benefit from it (see *Rambam* ibid. 11:1-3).]

## 340 □ כי תשא / מצוה קיא: שלא לאכל ולשתות תקרבת עבודה זרה

בְּעִנְיַן הַצְּלָמִים, שֶׁסְּתָם הַצְּלָמִים לַעֲבוֹדָה זָרָה יַעֲשׂוּם, וּלְפִיכָךְ אָסְרוּ אוֹתָם[9], וַאֲפִלּוּ הַמּוֹצֵא אוֹתָם מֻשְׁלָכִים אֵינוֹ רַשַּׁאי לְטַלְּטֵם כִּי אִם בִּתְנָאִים יְדוּעִים, כְּמוֹ שֶׁפֵּרְשׁוּ הֵם זִכְרוֹנָם לִבְרָכָה (שם דף מ״א ע״א)[10], וְכֵן נִרְאֶה בְּוַדַּאי בְּכָל דָּבָר שֶׁהַיִּשְׂרָאֵל חוֹשֵׁב שֶׁנַּעֲשָׂה בּוֹ תִּקְרֹבֶת שֶׁאָסוּר לוֹ לִקָּחוֹ מֵהֶם.[11]

וְעוֹד עָשׂוּ הַרְחָקוֹת רַבּוֹת בְּעִנְיַן הַיַּיִן לְפִי שֶׁהוּא עִקַּר שִׂמְחַת הַזֶּבַח לָהֶם, וְעוֹד שֶׁהַתּוֹרָה הִזְכִּירָה אִסּוּרוֹ בְּפֵרוּשׁ, כְּמוֹ שֶׁכָּתוּב בְּפָרָשַׁת הַאֲזִינוּ (דברים ל״ב, ל״ח) יִשְׁתּוּ יֵין נְסִיכָם[12], וְעַל כֵּן הֶחְמִירוּ זִכְרוֹנָם לִבְרָכָה בּוֹ וְאָמְרוּ לְהַרְחָקַת הָעִנְיָן, שֶׁאֲפִלּוּ יֵין שֶׁל יִשְׂרָאֵל מִיָּד שֶׁיִּגַּע בּוֹ גּוֹי יְהֵא אָסוּר אֲפִלּוּ בַּהֲנָאָה.[13] וְאַל יִקְשֶׁה עָלֶיךָ אֵיךְ יוּכַל הַגּוֹי לֶאֱסֹר יַיִן שֶׁל יִשְׂרָאֵל,

---

בְּעִנְיַן הַצְּלָמִים — **what [the Sages], of blessed memory, have stated** (*Avodah Zarah* 40b) **regarding statues,** שֶׁסְּתָם הַצְּלָמִים לַעֲבוֹדָה זָרָה יַעֲשׂוּם — **that "ordinary" statues** (i.e., statues whose purpose is unknown) **are** presumed to have been **made for idolatry;** וּלְפִיכָךְ אָסְרוּ אוֹתָם — **[the Sages] therefore prohibited [statues]** for benefit, even if it is not known that they have been worshiped, whenever such a possibility exists.[9] וַאֲפִלּוּ הַמּוֹצֵא אוֹתָם מֻשְׁלָכִים — **And even if one finds [the statues] discarded,** אֵינוֹ רַשַּׁאי לְטַלְּטֵם כִּי אִם בִּתְנָאִים יְדוּעִים — **he is not permitted to take them, except under certain known conditions,** כְּמוֹ שֶׁפֵּרְשׁוּ הֵם זִכְרוֹנָם לִבְרָכָה — **as explained by [the Sages], of blessed memory** (ibid. 41a).[10] וְכֵן נִרְאֶה בְּוַדַּאי — **Similarly, it would definitely seem** בְּכָל דָּבָר שֶׁהַיִּשְׂרָאֵל חוֹשֵׁב שֶׁנַּעֲשָׂה בּוֹ תִּקְרֹבֶת — **regarding anything** in the possession of idolaters **that a Jew believes was used as an offering** to an *avodah zarah*, שֶׁאָסוּר לוֹ לִקָּחוֹ מֵהֶם — **that it is forbidden for him to buy it from [the idolaters],** even though the idolatrous usage has not been confirmed. Just as the Sages were stringent with regard to "ordinary" statues because of the likelihood that they were made for idolatry, so too must each individual act stringently with regard to any item that he feels was likely used for idolatry.[11]

Chinuch returns to the matter of wine of idolaters:
וְעוֹד עָשׂוּ הַרְחָקוֹת רַבּוֹת בְּעִנְיַן הַיַּיִן — **In addition** to the prohibition to drink or benefit from idolaters' ordinary wine, **[the Sages] instituted many more "distancing" restrictions concerning wine,** on account of the following factors: לְפִי שֶׁהוּא עִקַּר שִׂמְחַת הַזֶּבַח לָהֶם — **(1) because [wine] is the mainstay of their rejoicing over an offering** to their idols, וְעוֹד שֶׁהַתּוֹרָה הִזְכִּירָה אִסּוּרוֹ בְּפֵרוּשׁ — **and additionally, (2) because the Torah explicitly mentioned the prohibition of [wine used as a libation],** כְּמוֹ שֶׁכָּתוּב בְּפָרָשַׁת הַאֲזִינוּ — **as it is written in *Parashas Haazinu*** (Deuteronomy 32:38): יִשְׁתּוּ יֵין נְסִיכָם — **they would drink the wine of their libations.**[12] וְעַל כֵּן הֶחְמִירוּ זִכְרוֹנָם לִבְרָכָה בּוֹ — Therefore, [the Sages], of blessed memory, were very **stringent concerning [wine of idolaters].** וְאָמְרוּ לְהַרְחָקַת הָעִנְיָן — One law that **[the Sages] stated** (*Avodah Zarah* 57b-58a, 60b), in order **to distance** us exceedingly from **the matter** of wine used for an idolatrous libation, is שֶׁאֲפִלּוּ יֵין שֶׁל יִשְׂרָאֵל מִיָּד שֶׁיִּגַּע בּוֹ גּוֹי יְהֵא אָסוּר — **that even wine of a Jew, if an idolater** merely **touches it, immediately becomes forbidden,** אֲפִלּוּ בַּהֲנָאָה — **not** only for drinking, **but even for** any other **benefit.**[13]

Chinuch addresses a question regarding this law:
וְאַל יִקְשֶׁה עָלֶיךָ — **Do not let** the following question **disturb you:** אֵיךְ יוּכַל הַגּוֹי לֶאֱסֹר יַיִן שֶׁל יִשְׂרָאֵל

---

### NOTES

9. See *Shulchan Aruch, Yoreh Deah* 141:1, with commentaries, for numerous qualifications of this law.

10. When a statue has been discarded, there is a possibility that even if it was worshiped, the idolater nullified it (i.e., canceled its status as an object of worship). Hence, one might think that it is permitted. Actually, though, it is permitted only in certain conditions, as described by *Rambam* ibid. 7:7 and *Shulchan Aruch* ibid. §2 with *Shach* §7.

11. For related laws, see *Shulchan Aruch* ibid. §3.

12. I.e., in addition to the prohibition in our verse, *Lest you ... eat from his slaughter*, which refers to consumption of any food or beverage that was offered before an *avodah zarah*, the Torah specifically speaks of drinking the wine of their libations. As Chinuch states at the end of the mitzvah, *Rambam* sees in this verse a source of the prohibition to partake of *nesech* wine.

13. To ensure that Jews not drink or derive benefit from actual *nesech* wine, the Sages decreed that even wine that an idolater merely touched is prohibited (*Rama, Yoreh Deah* 123:1). For details of this law, see *Yoreh Deah* 124:10-27.

## KI SISA / MITZVAH 111: THE PROHIBITION TO CONSUME IDOLATROUS OFFERINGS

וְהָא קַיְמָא לָן אֵין אָדָם אוֹסֵר דָּבָר שֶׁאֵינוֹ שֶׁלּוֹ (חולין דף מ' ע״ב)‏[14], שֶׁלֹּא נֶאֱמַר זֶה אֶלָּא כְּגוֹן מִשְׁתַּחֲוֶה לִבְהֶמַת חֲבֵרוֹ שֶׁלֹּא עָשָׂה מַעֲשֶׂה בְּגוּף הַדָּבָר, אֲבָל כָּל זְמַן שֶׁיַּעֲשֶׂה מַעֲשֶׂה בְּגוּף הַדָּבָר וַאֲפִלּוּ מַעֲשֶׂה מוּעָט כִּי הַאי דִּנְגִיעָה, יֵשׁ לוֹ כֹּחַ לֶאֱסֹר דָּבָר שֶׁאֵינוֹ שֶׁלּוֹ מִדְּרַבָּנָן, שֶׁהֶחְמִירוּ בַּדָּבָר, אֲבָל לֹא מִדְּאוֹרַיְתָא עַד שֶׁיַּעֲשֶׂה מַעֲשֶׂה גָּדוֹל כְּגוֹן שְׁחִיטַת בְּהֵמָה שֶׁהוּא מַעֲשֶׂה גָּדוֹל‏[15], וְכֵן אִם נִסֵּךְ הַיַּיִן לִפְנֵי הָעֲבוֹדָה זָרָה מַמָּשׁ,

---

**How can the idolater render the Jew's wine prohibited** by touching it? וְהָא קַיְמָא לָן אֵין אָדָם אוֹסֵר דָּבָר שֶׁאֵינוֹ שֶׁלּוֹ — **Why, we have an established principle** (ibid. 44a, et al.) that **a person cannot make a prohibition take hold on something that is not his own!** Since the wine does not belong to the idolater, how can he cause it to become prohibited through touching it?[14] שֶׁלֹּא נֶאֱמַר זֶה אֶלָּא כְּגוֹן מִשְׁתַּחֲוֶה לִבְהֶמַת חֲבֵרוֹ — This is not a difficulty, for **this** principle **was stated only regarding a case of** someone **bowing to his fellow's animal,** or the like, שֶׁלֹּא עָשָׂה מַעֲשֶׂה בְּגוּף הַדָּבָר — **where he did not perform an action on the body of the object** that is becoming prohibited. אֲבָל כָּל זְמַן שֶׁיַּעֲשֶׂה מַעֲשֶׂה בְּגוּף הַדָּבָר — **But whenever one performs an action on the body of the object,** וַאֲפִלּוּ מַעֲשֶׂה מוּעָט כִּי הַאי דִּנְגִיעָה — **even** if it is **a minor action like that of touching,** יֵשׁ לוֹ כֹּחַ לֶאֱסֹר דָּבָר שֶׁאֵינוֹ שֶׁלּוֹ מִדְּרַבָּנָן — [a non-owner] **does have the capacity to prohibit a thing that is not his,** at least **by Rabbinic decree,** שֶׁהֶחְמִירוּ בַּדָּבָר — **for** [the Sages] **were stringent regarding this matter.** אֲבָל לֹא מִדְּאוֹרַיְתָא — **Now,** the non-owner does **not** render the object prohibited **by Biblical law** עַד שֶׁיַּעֲשֶׂה מַעֲשֶׂה גָּדוֹל — **until he performs a major action** on the body of the object, כְּגוֹן שְׁחִיטַת בְּהֵמָה — **such as slaughtering an animal** as an offering to an *avodah zarah,* שֶׁהוּא מַעֲשֶׂה גָּדוֹל — **which is** considered **a major action;**[15] וְכֵן אִם נִסֵּךְ הַיַּיִן לִפְנֵי הָעֲבוֹדָה זָרָה מַמָּשׁ — **and likewise,**

---

### NOTES

14. To clarify the question: The principle that "a person cannot make a prohibition take hold on something that is not his own" applies in specific situations. When an item becomes prohibited purely on account of a physical circumstance, it makes no difference who brought about that circumstance, as the item becomes prohibited in any event. For example, if someone cooks his fellow's meat in milk (see Mitzvah 92), the meat becomes prohibited for consumption and benefit even though it does not belong to the one who cooked it, because the prohibition stems from the fact that the meat was physically cooked in milk. When, however, an item becomes prohibited on account of an action performed with a specific *intention*, the prohibition takes effect only if the action was performed by the owner. A stranger's intent cannot have any impact on his fellow's item (*Tosafos, Yevamos* 83b ד״ה אין אדם אוסר; see *Rash, Kilayim* 7:4).

In our case, the Rabbinic decree prohibiting wine touched by an idolater is an extension of the Biblical prohibition of *nesech* wine (see previous note). *Nesech* wine itself is prohibited only because when the idolater poured it before his idol, he intended to make it an offering to the idol; merely pouring wine without such intent does not render it "an idolatrous offering." It follows that the basis to prohibit a Jew's wine that was touched by an idolater is that the wine is treated as if the idolater intended to make it a libation to an idol. But since the basis of this prohibition is the idolater's intent, how can it take effect on wine that is not his?

15. That is, under Biblical law, if one performs a major action with his fellow's object (e.g., slaughtering the fellow's animal), he can render it prohibited, even though in order for the prohibition to take effect that action must be accompanied by a specific intention (e.g., to thereby serve an idol). By Rabbinic decree, this applies even if one performs a minor action (e.g., touching), as long as the action is done with the body of the object that is being rendered forbidden. It is only where one does not perform any action at all with that body (e.g., one bows down to his fellow's animal and declares it an idol) that we say "one cannot make a prohibition take hold on something that is not his own." Hence, if an idolater touches a Jew's wine, he can render it prohibited Rabbinically, since he has performed an action — albeit a minor one — with the wine itself.

[Chinuch follows the opinion of *Raavad, Hil. Avodah Zarah* 8:1, and *Rashba* in *Toras HaBayis* 1:1 (10a in Josefov edition), based on *Avodah Zarah* 54a and *Chullin* 40b-41a; see also *Shulchan Aruch, Yoreh Deah* 145:8. Others, however, maintain that a person cannot make a prohibition take hold on his fellow's object even through a major action, at least under Biblical law (see *Rambam, Hil. Avodah Zarah* loc. cit.; and *Re'ah* in *Bedek HaBayis* to *Toras HaBayis* ibid., and in *Chidushei Re'ah* to *Avodah Zarah* 59b; for further discussion, see the sources cited in *Minchas Chinuch* §6). This is one of numerous instances in which Chinuch contradicts the writings of *Re'ah*, which undermines the assumption of many Acharonim that the Sefer HaChinuch was authored by *Re'ah* (see further above, Mitzvah 73 note 34).]

## 342 □ כי תשא / מצוה קיא: שלא לאכל ולשתות תקרבת עבודה זרה

גַּם זֶה הוּא מַעֲשֶׂה גָדוֹל,[16] אֲבָל נְגִיעָה בְּיַיִן שֶׁלֹּא בִּפְנֵי עֲבוֹדָה זָרָה, מַעֲשֶׂה מוּעָט הוּא, וּמִכֵּיוָן שֶׁהוּא מוּעָט וְאֵין הָאָסוּר אֶלָּא מִדְּרַבָּנָן, הִתִּירוּ זִכְרוֹנָם לִבְרָכָה (עבודה זרה דף נ״ט ע״ב) לִטֹּל תַּשְׁלוּם מַה שֶּׁאָסַר מִיַּד הָאוֹסֵר,[17] וְאַף עַל פִּי שֶׁבַּגּוּף הַדָּבָר שֶׁאָסַר הֶחְמִירוּ לְאָסְרוֹ בַּהֲנָאָה, בְּתַשְׁלוּמִין לֹא הֶחְמִירוּ, לְפִי שֶׁאֵין הַתַּשְׁלוּמִין אֶלָּא כְּעֵין תַּשְׁלוּמֵי נֶזֶק וְאֵינוֹ נֶהֱנֶה מִן הַדָּבָר הָאָסוּר אֶלָּא שֶׁלּוֹקֵחַ תַּשְׁלוּמֵי נִזְקוֹ מִיַּד הָאוֹסֵר.[18]

וְכֵן הֶחְמִירוּ זִכְרוֹנָם לִבְרָכָה הַרְבֵּה בְּרִחוּק יַיִן שֶׁנִּתְנַסֵּךְ מַמָּשׁ לַעֲבוֹדָה זָרָה

---

**if [an idolater] poured the wine** of a Jew as a libation **before an actual *avodah zarah*,** גַּם זֶה הוּא מַעֲשֶׂה גָדוֹל — **that, too, is** considered **a major action,** and he renders the wine prohibited Biblically as *nesech* wine.[16] אֲבָל נְגִיעָה בְּיַיִן שֶׁלֹּא בִּפְנֵי עֲבוֹדָה זָרָה — **However, merely touching the wine, not in front of an *avodah zarah*,** מַעֲשֶׂה מוּעָט הוּא — **is** considered **a minor action** and prohibits the wine only by Rabbinic decree.

Having explained that the prohibition of wine touched by an idolater is only Rabbinic, Chinuch points out a certain leniency pertaining to it:

וּמִכֵּיוָן שֶׁהוּא מוּעָט וְאֵין הָאָסוּר אֶלָּא מִדְּרַבָּנָן — **Since [touching] is** considered **a minor** action, **and the** resulting **prohibition is only Rabbinic,** הִתִּירוּ זִכְרוֹנָם לִבְרָכָה לִטֹּל תַּשְׁלוּם מַה שֶּׁאָסַר מִיַּד הָאוֹסֵר — **[the Sages], of blessed memory** (ibid. 59b), **permitted** the owner of the wine **to accept payment for [the wine] that became prohibited from the one who rendered it prohibited.**[17] וְאַף עַל פִּי שֶׁבַּגּוּף — **Although,** with respect to the object itself that [the idolater] rendered prohibited הַדָּבָר שֶׁאָסַר (i.e., the wine), הֶחְמִירוּ לְאָסְרוֹ בַּהֲנָאָה — **[the Sages] were** so **stringent** as **to prohibit** deriving any form of **benefit from it,** including monetary benefit, such as by selling it to another person, בְּתַשְׁלוּמִין לֹא הֶחְמִירוּ — **with respect to** accepting **payment** for it from the one who rendered it forbidden **they were not stringent.** לְפִי שֶׁאֵין הַתַּשְׁלוּמִין אֶלָּא כְּעֵין תַּשְׁלוּמֵי נֶזֶק — This is **because the payment is merely a form of compensation for the damage** inflicted, וְאֵינוֹ נֶהֱנֶה מִן הַדָּבָר הָאָסוּר — **and** by accepting this payment, [the owner] **is not** considered to be **deriving benefit from the prohibited object;** אֶלָּא שֶׁלּוֹקֵחַ תַּשְׁלוּמֵי נִזְקוֹ מִיַּד הָאוֹסֵר — **rather, he is collecting compensation for his damages from the one who rendered** the wine **prohibited.**[18]

Chinuch discusses additional stringencies that the Sages imposed on wine and other objects used for idolatrous worship:

וְכֵן הֶחְמִירוּ זִכְרוֹנָם לִבְרָכָה הַרְבֵּה — **Likewise, [the Sages], of blessed memory, were** very **stringent** בְּרִחוּק יַיִן שֶׁנִּתְנַסֵּךְ מַמָּשׁ לַעֲבוֹדָה זָרָה — in **distancing wine that was actually poured as a libation for**

---

### NOTES

16. This point, too, is not unanimous. Chinuch follows *Rashi* to *Chullin* 40b ד״ה אין אדם אוסר, who considers the pouring of wine to be a "major" action. *Rabbeinu Chananel* (cited by *Rosh, Chullin* 2:14 and *Ran* there fol. 8b ד״ה גרסינן בגמרא) considers it to be a "minor" action.

17. This is a novel leniency. Since the wine is prohibited for benefit, and thus may not be sold, one might have assumed that the owner may not accept payment for it, since he is in effect "selling" it to the one making the payment. The Sages nevertheless permitted the victim to exact payment from the idolater who rendered it prohibited by touching it, for the reason that Chinuch proceeds to explain.

18. In the words of the Gemara, the idolater who rendered the wine prohibited to its Jewish owner in effect "burned" (i.e., destroyed) it. Thus, the Jew is not *selling* him *nesech* wine, but taking restitution for the permissible wine that he destroyed (*Rashi* ad loc.). This is permitted even if the idolater refuses to pay unless he receives the wine, since the payment is ultimately deemed restitution for the damage rather than settlement of a sale (*Tosafos* ad loc.).

[Chinuch indicates that the permit to accept compensation applies only because the wine is prohibited Rabbinically, but would not apply where it became prohibited Biblically — e.g., if it was actually poured as a libation. This accords with the position of *Re'ah* in *Bedek HaBayis* (5:2; in Josefov ed. 48a ד״ה עוד כתב כל מקום שאמרו; see also *Chidushei Re'ah* to *Avodah Zarah* 59b). *Rashba* (*Mishmeres HaBayis* ad loc.), however, maintains that the permit applies in all cases. For discussion of Chinuch's view, see *Minchas Chinuch* §8 and *Minchas Yitzchak* §9.]

# KI SISA / MITZVAH 111: THE PROHIBITION TO CONSUME IDOLATROUS OFFERINGS

אוֹ בְּכָל דָּבָר שֶׁהוּא מֵעֲבוֹדָה זָרָה יוֹתֵר מִכָּל אִסּוּרִין שֶׁבַּתּוֹרָה,[19] שֶׁאֵין לְךָ דָּבָר שֶׁאָסוּר בַּהֲנָאָה בְּכָל הַתּוֹרָה שֶׁנִּתְעָרֵב בְּהֶתֵּר וְאֵינֶנּוּ נִכָּר, שֶׁלֹּא יְהֵא לוֹ תַקָּנָה לַהֲנָאָתוֹ,[20] וַאֲפִלּוּ לַח בְּלַח, עִם מַה שֶּׁאָמַר רַבָּן שִׁמְעוֹן בֶּן גַּמְלִיאֵל בַּגְּמָרָא (שם דף ע״ד ע״א) שֶׁיִּמָּכֵר כֻּלּוֹ לַגּוֹיִם חוּץ מִדְּמֵי הָאִסּוּר שֶׁבּוֹ,[21] וְהוּא שֶׁיְּהֵא מִן הַדְּבָרִים שֶׁאֵינָן נִקָּחִין מִן הַגּוֹיִם[22] כְּדֵי שֶׁלֹּא יְבַשֵּׁל בָּהֶן שׁוּם אָדָם מִיִּשְׂרָאֵל שֶׁיִּקָּחֵנוּ מִן הַגּוֹי,[23] אֲבָל בְּיֵין נֶסֶךְ גָּמוּר וּבְכָל דִּבְרֵי עֲבוֹדָה זָרָה

---

**an *avodah zarah*** (i.e., *nesech* wine), אוֹ בְּכָל דָּבָר שֶׁהוּא מֵעֲבוֹדָה זָרָה — **or any substance that was part of an *avodah zarah* or an accessory to an *avodah zarah*,** יוֹתֵר מִכָּל אִסּוּרִין שֶׁבַּתּוֹרָה — **more than** we are distanced from **all other substances that the Torah prohibits.**[19] One stringency that the Sages imposed pertains to cases in which the wine or other idolatrous substance became intermingled with another, permitted, substance. שֶׁאֵין לְךָ דָּבָר שֶׁאָסוּר בַּהֲנָאָה בְּכָל הַתּוֹרָה — **For you do not have in the entire Torah** any other case of **a substance that is prohibited for benefit** שֶׁנִּתְעָרֵב בְּהֶתֵּר **וְאֵינֶנּוּ נִכָּר — that,** when **intermingled with** a similar **permitted** substance to the extent **that it is not recognizable** in the mixture, שֶׁלֹּא יְהֵא לוֹ תַקָּנָה לַהֲנָאָתוֹ — **does not have a remedy** that will enable one **to** derive **benefit from [the mixture].**[20] וַאֲפִלּוּ לַח בְּלַח — **Even** if was a prohibited **fluid that became mixed with** a permitted **fluid,** so that they are completely intermingled and the prohibited substance cannot possibly be separated from the permitted substance, it is possible to derive benefit from the permitted portion of the mixture, עִם מַה שֶּׁאָמַר רַבָּן שִׁמְעוֹן בֶּן גַּמְלִיאֵל בַּגְּמָרָא — **by means of what Rabban Shimon ben Gamliel stated in the Gemara** (ibid. 74a), שֶׁיִּמָּכֵר כֻּלּוֹ לַגּוֹיִם חוּץ מִדְּמֵי הָאִסּוּר שֶׁבּוֹ — **that the entire [mixture] can be sold to idolaters without** charging them for **the value of the prohibited substance in it.**[21] וְהוּא שֶׁיְּהֵא מִן הַדְּבָרִים שֶׁאֵינָן נִקָּחִין מִן הַגּוֹיִם — Parenthetically, there is a limitation to this permit, inasmuch as the mixture may be sold to an idolater only **provided that it consists of one of the substances that [Jews] would not buy from idolaters.**[22] If the mixture is of a substance that a Jew would buy from an idolater, one may not sell it to an idolater when it contains a prohibited portion, כְּדֵי שֶׁלֹּא יְבַשֵּׁל בָּהֶן שׁוּם אָדָם מִיִּשְׂרָאֵל שֶׁיִּקָּחֵנוּ מִן הַגּוֹי — **so that no Jewish person should stumble** and commit a transgression **through it, by buying it from the idolater** and subsequently consuming it.[23] In any event, subject to the preceding qualification, the device of "selling the entire mixture to idolaters without charging them for the value of the prohibited substance in it" may be relied upon for mixtures containing any substance that the Torah prohibits for benefit, other than *nesech* wine and other *avodah zarah* substances. אֲבָל בְּיֵין נֶסֶךְ גָּמוּר — **However, concerning actual *nesech* wine** that was mixed into kosher wine, וּבְכָל דִּבְרֵי עֲבוֹדָה זָרָה — **and** likewise, **concerning all substances of *avodah zarah*** that became intermingled with permitted substances,

---

## NOTES

19. An idol and its accessories are Biblically prohibited for benefit, as is *nesech* wine. Chinuch proceeds to explain that, by Rabbinic decree, these items are treated more stringently than any other substance that the Torah prohibits for benefit.

20. In every instance in which an item prohibited for benefit became intermingled with permitted items, there is a mechanism that enables one to derive benefit from at least the percentage of the mixture that consists of the permitted items.

21. For example, if a liter of a beverage that is prohibited for benefit became mixed with two liters of a permitted beverage, and the three-liter mixture is worth three dollars, it may be sold to an idolater for two dollars — which is the value of the permitted portion of the mixture. Thus, the owner is able to derive the full benefit of the permitted portion of the mixture, without benefiting from the prohibited portion.

22. For example, a Jew would not buy meat from an idolater (without proper kosher certification). Thus, if a piece of prohibited meat became mixed with two pieces of permitted meat, the entire mixture may be sold to an idolater for the price of the permitted portion, since there is no fear that the idolater will then sell the mixture to another Jew.

23. For example, if prohibited wheat (such as wheat of *kilayim*; see note 31) became mixed with a greater amount of permitted wheat, one may not sell the mixture to an idolater for the price of the permitted portion. Since wheat is generally kosher, a Jew might buy the mixture from the idolater not realizing that it contains a prohibited portion. If he then consumes the entire mixture, it will emerge that the Jew who sold it to the idolater brought about his fellow's transgression (see *Avodah Zarah* 65b).

## 344 □ כי תשא / מצוה קיא: שלא לאכל ולשתות תקרבת עבודה זרה

אֵין לָהֶם תַּקָּנָה בִּמְכָר כֻּלּוֹ לַגּוֹיִם וְכוּ׳, וְכָל שֶׁכֵּן שֶׁאֵין לָהֶן תַּקָּנָה בְּיוֹלִיךְ הֲנָאָה לְיָם הַמֶּלַח[24]. וּמִיהוּ דַּוְקָא כְּשֶׁנִּתְעָרֵב יֵין נֶסֶךְ מַמָּשׁ, וַאֲפִלּוּ טִפָּה מִמֶּנּוּ, בְּקַנְקַן מַחֲזִיק כַּמָּה סְאִין[25], הוּא דִּין זֶה שֶׁאֵין תַּקָּנָה לַהֲנָאָתוֹ לְעוֹלָם, אֲבָל אִם נִתְעָרֵב מִמֶּנּוּ חָבִית אַחַת בְּחָבִיּוֹת אֲחֵרוֹת שֶׁל יַיִן כָּשֵׁר, כֵּיוָן שֶׁלֹּא נִתְעָרֵב גּוּף הָאִסּוּר מַמָּשׁ אֶלָּא כָּל אֶחָד בִּפְנֵי עַצְמוֹ הוּא עוֹמֵד, יֵשׁ לוֹ תַּקָּנָה בְּתַקָּנַת רַבָּן שִׁמְעוֹן בֶּן גַּמְלִיאֵל שֶׁיִּמָּכֵר כֻּלּוֹ לַגּוֹיִם וְכוּ׳, וְכֵן בִּסְתָם יֵינָם יֵשׁ לוֹ תַּקָּנָה בְּתַקָּנַת רַבָּן שִׁמְעוֹן בֶּן גַּמְלִיאֵל, וַאֲפִלּוּ נִתְעָרֵב מַמָּשׁ, כְּדִין שְׁאָר אִסּוּרִין, כֵּיוָן שֶׁאֵינוֹ יֵין נֶסֶךְ גָּמוּר[26].

---

אֵין לָהֶם תַּקָּנָה בִּמְכָר כֻּלּוֹ לַגּוֹיִם וְכוּ׳ — the law is that **they cannot be remedied by** means of the device of **"selling the entire [mixture] to idolaters,** etc. [without charging them for the value of the prohibited substance in it]." וְכָל שֶׁכֵּן שֶׁאֵין לָהֶן תַּקָּנָה בְּיוֹלִיךְ הֲנָאָה לְיָם הַמֶּלַח — **And certainly, they cannot be remedied by** means of the alternative device of **taking the** monetary value of the forbidden **benefit to the Dead Sea** and casting it in.[24]

Chinuch qualifies this stringency: וּמִיהוּ דַּוְקָא כְּשֶׁנִּתְעָרֵב יֵין נֶסֶךְ מַמָּשׁ — **However,** this applies **only when the** *nesech* **wine was actually mixed** into kosher wine, וַאֲפִלּוּ טִפָּה מִמֶּנּוּ בְּקַנְקַן מַחֲזִיק כַּמָּה סְאִין — **even** if it was only **a droplet of** [*nesech* wine] that became mixed **into a vessel containing many** *se'ah*[25] measures of kosher wine; הוּא דִּין זֶה שֶׁאֵין תַּקָּנָה לַהֲנָאָתוֹ לְעוֹלָם — **only** then is this law applicable — namely, **that there is no remedy for** deriving **benefit from [the mixture] whatsoever.** אֲבָל אִם נִתְעָרֵב מִמֶּנּוּ חָבִית אַחַת בְּחָבִיּוֹת אֲחֵרוֹת שֶׁל יַיִן כָּשֵׁר — **If, however,** the mixture constituted **one barrel of** [*nesech* wine] that **became intermingled with other barrels of kosher wine,** כֵּיוָן שֶׁלֹּא נִתְעָרֵב גּוּף הָאִסּוּר מַמָּשׁ — **since the actual body of the forbidden substance was not intermingled** with the body of the kosher substance, אֶלָּא כָּל אֶחָד בִּפְנֵי עַצְמוֹ הוּא עוֹמֵד — **rather, each one** of the substances **is standing by itself,** within its respective barrel, יֵשׁ לוֹ תַּקָּנָה — **the permitted portion of [the mixture] can be remedied for benefit** בְּתַקָּנַת רַבָּן שִׁמְעוֹן בֶּן גַּמְלִיאֵל שֶׁיִּמָּכֵר כֻּלּוֹ לַגּוֹיִם וְכוּ׳ — **by** means of **the remedy of Rabban Shimon ben Gamliel,** who stated **that the entire [mixture] can be sold to idolaters, etc.** [without charging them for the value of the prohibited substance in it]. וְכֵן בִּסְתָם יֵינָם — **Likewise, in** the case of **ordinary wine of [idolaters]** that was mixed into kosher wine, although the idolaters' wine is prohibited, יֵשׁ לוֹ תַּקָּנָה בְּתַקָּנַת רַבָּן שִׁמְעוֹן בֶּן גַּמְלִיאֵל — **the permitted portion of [the mixture] can be remedied** for benefit **by means of the** aforementioned remedy **of Rabban Shimon ben Gamliel,** וַאֲפִלּוּ נִתְעָרֵב מַמָּשׁ — and this applies **even if [the idolaters' ordinary wine] was actually mixed** into the kosher wine, in the same vessel. כְּדִין שְׁאָר אִסּוּרִין — **In this respect, the law regarding idolaters' ordinary wine is the same as the law regarding other prohibited substances** that are not of the *avodah zarah* category. The Sages did not impose the above stringency on idolaters' ordinary wine, כֵּיוָן שֶׁאֵינוֹ יֵין נֶסֶךְ גָּמוּר — **since it is not actual** *nesech* **wine.**[26]

---

### NOTES

24. In certain limited instances, the Sages permit a person to keep a mixture containing a prohibited item and to benefit from the entire mixture, on the basis of "taking the benefit to the Dead Sea" — i.e., tossing coins equaling the value of the prohibited item into the Dead Sea, or destroying them in some other fashion. By forfeiting the value of the prohibited benefit, one becomes permitted to use the mixture (see *Avodah Zarah* 49b with *Milchamos Hashem* and *Ritva*; and *Rambam, Hil. Avodah Zarah* 7:13). This represents a greater leniency than the previous device of "selling it to an idolater without charging him the value of the prohibited substance in it," since the owner actually keeps the prohibited substance and benefits from it. Chinuch states that this is certainly not permitted for *nesech* wine and other *avodah zarah* substances.

It emerges that if even a small amount of actual *nesech* wine became mixed into a large amount of permitted wine, the entire mixture is prohibited for benefit, and the owner has no means of salvaging the value of his permitted wine. This is a stringency that the Sages imposed in the specific cases of *nesech* wine and other *avodah zarah* substances, due to the necessity of maintaining a great distance from these items.

25. A *se'ah* is a measure containing between approximately 9 and 15 liters.

26. Both of these exceptions to the above rule are mentioned in the Gemara, *Avodah Zarah* 74a.

## 345 ❑ KI SISA / MITZVAH 111: THE PROHIBITION TO CONSUME IDOLATROUS OFFERINGS

וְעוֹד יֵשׁ לְךָ לָדַעַת, שֶׁכָּל אִסּוּרִין שֶׁבַּתּוֹרָה שֶׁאוֹסְרִין תַּעֲרֻבְתָּן בַּהֲנָאָה אֵין אוֹסְרִין אוֹתָן אֶלָּא אִם כֵּן יֵשׁ מִן הָאִסּוּר שֶׁנִּתְעָרֵב בַּהֶתֵּר בִּכְדֵי נְתִינַת טַעַם בַּהֶתֵּר,[27] זוּלָתִי אִם יִהְיֶה אוֹתוֹ אִסּוּר דָּבָר חָשׁוּב, כִּי כָּל דָּבָר חָשׁוּב כְּגוֹן חֲתִיכָה הָרְאוּיָה לְהִתְכַּבֵּד וְכַיּוֹצֵא בָהּ, אוֹסְרִין בְּכָל שֶׁהֵן, אֲבָל כָּל שֶׁאֵינוֹ דָּבָר חָשׁוּב[28] אֵינוֹ אוֹסֵר תַּעֲרֻבְתּוֹ בַּהֲנָאָה אֶלָּא אִם כֵּן יִהְיֶה בּוֹ בִּכְדֵי נְתִינַת טַעַם, כְּמוֹ שֶׁאָמַרְנוּ,

---

Chinuch identifies another stringency pertaining to *nesech* wine:

וְעוֹד יֵשׁ לְךָ לָדַעַת – **You must know further** שֶׁכָּל אִסּוּרִין שֶׁבַּתּוֹרָה שֶׁאוֹסְרִין תַּעֲרֻבְתָּן בַּהֲנָאָה – **that all substances prohibited** for benefit **by the Torah, which cause mixtures in which they are contained to** also **be prohibited for benefit,** אֵין אוֹסְרִין אוֹתָן – **do not render [the mixtures] prohibited** אֶלָּא אִם כֵּן יֵשׁ מִן הָאִסּוּר שֶׁנִּתְעָרֵב בַּהֶתֵּר בִּכְדֵי נְתִינַת טַעַם בַּהֶתֵּר – **unless there is enough of the forbidden substance intermingled with the permitted substance to impart flavor to the permitted substance.**[27] זוּלָתִי אִם יִהְיֶה אוֹתוֹ אִסּוּר דָּבָר חָשׁוּב – **This holds true in all cases, except where that prohibited substance is considered to be an "item of significance."** כִּי כָּל דָּבָר חָשׁוּב – **For** the rule is that any **"item of significance,"** כְּגוֹן חֲתִיכָה הָרְאוּיָה לְהִתְכַּבֵּד וְכַיּוֹצֵא בָהּ – **such as a piece** of meat **that is fit** to be used as a serving **to honor** a guest, **and the like,** אוֹסְרִין בְּכָל שֶׁהֵן – **renders** a mixture **prohibited in any amount,** even if no flavor of the prohibited substance is detected in the mixture.[28] אֲבָל כָּל שֶׁאֵינוֹ דָּבָר חָשׁוּב – **But** as for **anything that is not an "item of significance,"** אֵינוֹ אוֹסֵר תַּעֲרֻבְתּוֹ – בַּהֲנָאָה אֶלָּא אִם כֵּן יִהְיֶה בּוֹ בִּכְדֵי נְתִינַת טַעַם – **it does not render the mixture in which it is contained prohibited for benefit unless there is enough of it** within the mixture **to impart flavor** to the permitted portion of the mixture, כְּמוֹ שֶׁאָמַרְנוּ – **as we have stated.** And when the prohibited substance became intermingled with a permitted substance of its own kind, such that flavor of the prohibited substance is indiscernible from that of the permitted substance, the rule is as follows: If the mixture contains sixty units of the permitted substance for the one unit of prohibited substance, then the prohibited substance is nullified and the mixture is permitted; but if it contains less than sixty units of the permitted substance

---

### NOTES

27. This refers to a case where a forbidden substance of one kind is mixed into a permitted substance of a different kind, meaning that the substances have flavors that are distinguishable from each other. The mixture is rendered forbidden if the flavor of the forbidden substance can be detected in the permitted substance. For instance, nonkosher meat that was cooked in a vegetable soup renders the entire soup forbidden (even after the nonkosher meat is removed) if meat flavor can be detected in the soup. Now, a Jew may not taste the mixture, for if there is flavor it is prohibited, but the determination is possible through tasting by an idolater. Alternatively, if the mixture contains 60 units of permitted substance for one unit of forbidden substance, it is assumed that the forbidden substance did not impart flavor to the permitted substance. In that case, the forbidden substance is nullified and the mixture is permitted (*Shulchan Aruch, Yoreh Deah* 98:1; see *Chullin* 97b).

If the two substances are of the same kind, the determination cannot be made through tasting, since the flavor of the forbidden substance is indistinguishable from that of the permitted substance. In such cases, everything depends on the proportion of the items in the mixture. When the ratio of permitted substance to forbidden substance is 60:1, the mixture is permitted, and when the ratio is less than 60:1, the mixture is prohibited (*Yoreh Deah* ibid.).

[*Rama* (*Yoreh Deah* ibid.) rules that nowadays we do not rely on tasting by an idolater, and even in the case of unlike substances everything depends on whether the mixture contains 60 units of permitted substance to one unit of forbidden substance. Chinuch, however, apparently relies on tasting, so he states that no forbidden substance renders a mixture prohibited unless it imparts flavor to the mixture.]

28. Thus, if a "significant" portion of prohibited meat became mixed into a stew containing a hundred such portions of permitted meat, the entire stew is forbidden. The details of this law appear in *Yoreh Deah* §101. [The same law applies if an entire creature (e.g., a prohibited insect) became mixed into a stew of kosher food. An entire creature has the same status as an "item of significance" (see *Yoreh Deah* §100).]

It should be noted that if the forbidden piece of meat is recognizable and is removed from the mixture, then the remaining flavor that was emitted into the mixture by the nonkosher meat can be nullified, as described in the previous note. The leftover flavor does not have the status of "a significant item," and thus is subject to nullification; i.e., if the flavor is not discernible in the mixture, or the amount of kosher food is 60 times more than the nonkosher food, then the mixture is permitted. Only when the piece that is fit to honor a guest is unidentifiable within the mixture is the entire mixture automatically prohibited.

## 346 ❑ כי תשא / מצוה קיא: שלא לאכל ולשתות תקרבת עבודה זרה

חוּץ[29] מִיֵּין נֶסֶךְ וְכָל עִנְיְנֵי עֲבוֹדָה זָרָה שֶׁאוֹסְרִין בְּמַשֶּׁהוּ בַּהֲנָאָה כָּל שֶׁנִּתְעָרֵב עִמָּהֶם[30], וְאֵין שׁוּם דָּבָר אַחֵר בָּעוֹלָם יוֹצֵא מִכְּלָל זֶה חוּץ מִכִּלְאֵי הַכֶּרֶם [וְעָרְלָה][31] וְחָמֵץ בְּפֶסַח לְדַעַת קְצָת מְפָרְשִׁים[32], שֶׁהֵן אוֹסְרִין בַּהֲנָאָה תַּעֲרָבְתָּן בְּאֶחָד וּמָאתַיִם בֵּין בְּמִינָן בֵּין שֶׁלֹּא בְּמִינָן[33], [וּתְרוּמָה] (ו)עוֹלָה בְּאֶחָד וּמֵאָה[34]. וּלְעִנְיַן הַתַּקָּנָה שֶׁיֵּשׁ לָהֶם

---

חוּץ מִיֵּין נֶסֶךְ וְכָל עִנְיְנֵי [29] for the one unit of prohibited substance, then the entire mixture is prohibited. עֲבוֹדָה זָרָה — This rule applies to all substances prohibited by the Torah **except for *nesech* wine and all forbidden substances of *avodah zarah*;** שֶׁאוֹסְרִין בְּמַשֶּׁהוּ בַּהֲנָאָה כָּל שֶׁנִּתְעָרֵב עִמָּהֶם — for with regard to these items, the rule is that **they render anything that became intermingled with them prohibited for benefit in any amount,** even when they are not "items of significance."[30]

Chinuch mentions several other items that are exceptions to the general rule, in that they render a mixture prohibited even if they are insufficient to impart flavor, or they are outnumbered in the mixture by 60:1. None of these items, though, has the same degree of stringency as that assigned to *nesech* wine: וְאֵין שׁוּם דָּבָר אַחֵר בָּעוֹלָם יוֹצֵא מִכְּלָל זֶה — **There is no other prohibited item whatsoever** that is **excluded from this rule** of nullification in sixty permitted units, חוּץ מִכִּלְאֵי הַכֶּרֶם [וְעָרְלָה] — **except for *kilayim* of the vineyard and *orlah*,**[31] וְחָמֵץ בְּפֶסַח לְדַעַת קְצָת מְפָרְשִׁים — **and according to some commentators, *chametz* on Pesach, too.**[32] שֶׁהֵן אוֹסְרִין בַּהֲנָאָה תַּעֲרָבְתָּן בְּאֶחָד וּמָאתַיִם — **For these** prohibited substances **render** an entire **mixture in which they are contained prohibited for benefit unless** the mixture contains **two hundred and one** portions, i.e., two hundred units of the permitted substance against one unit of the prohibited substance, בֵּין בְּמִינָן בֵּין שֶׁלֹּא בְּמִינָן — **whether** they mix **with** a permitted substance of **their own kind, or** they mix **with** a permitted substance **not of their own kind.**[33] [וּתְרוּמָה] (ו)עוֹלָה בְּאֶחָד וּמֵאָה — **The same law applies to *terumah*,** but with one difference: ***Terumah* becomes nullified in** a mixture of **one hundred and one** (i.e., one hundred units of the permitted substance against one unit of the prohibited substance), instead of two hundred and one. None of these substances, though, has the same degree of stringency as *nesech* wine and other *avodah zarah* substances, which render a mixture prohibited in *any* amount.[34] וּלְעִנְיַן הַתַּקָּנָה שֶׁיֵּשׁ לָהֶם — **And** furthermore,

---

### NOTES

29. See note 27.

30. See Mishnah, *Avodah Zarah* 73a. This applies when the mixture is one of like substances, e.g., *nesech* wine became mixed with kosher wine. The law is that *nesech* wine is not nullified in 60 portions of kosher wine. Rather, even one drop of *nesech* wine prohibits an entire barrel of kosher wine. Regarding mixtures of unlike substances, e.g., *nesech* wine in water, the Mishnah rules that if the flavor of the wine is not discernible in the mixture then it is nullified (*Minchas Yitzchak* §13). [Chinuch's unequivocal statement that the mixture is prohibited would seem to mean that, even in cases of unlike substances, if there is no idolater available to taste the mixture, it is prohibited in any amount (based on the commentators cited below, note 33).]

There is disagreement whether this stringency (of non-nullification) applies only to actual *nesech* wine (*Rabbeinu Tam*, cited by *Tosafos*, *Avodah Zarah* 73a ד"ה יין), or even to ordinary wine of idolaters (*Ritva* and *Ran* there). Chinuch apparently follows the former opinion, for he mentions only "*nesech* wine." See *Yoreh Deah* 134:2 for the practical halachah.

31. *Kilayim* of the vineyard are grains or greens planted in a vineyard. Such plantings are forbidden, and the produce of such plantings (i.e., the grains or greens, as well as the grapes) — known as כִּלְאֵי הַכֶּרֶם, *mixtures of the vineyard* — are prohibited for benefit (see *Mitzvos* 548-549). *Orlah* fruits are those that grow in the first three years after a tree is placed into the ground. They are prohibited for benefit (*Mitzvah* 246).

32. See *Ritva*, *Avodah Zarah* 74a ד"ה ולייתני, and *Pesachim* 30a ד"ה אמר רבא; see further, note 34.

33. Actually, the law of 200:1 applies only in mixtures of their own kind. In mixtures not of their own kind, the law is that they render the mixture prohibited only if they impart flavor (see *Avodah Zarah* 73b). What Chinuch means is that if they are mixed not in their own kind and there is no idolater available to taste the mixture and determine whether flavor was imparted (see note 27), then we require 200 parts of the permitted substance in order to permit the mixture (*Minchas Yitzchak* §14 ד"ה ומ"ש רבינו דכלאי הכרם, based on *Rambam*, *Commentary* to *Avodah Zarah* 5:8 and *Hil. Maachalos Asuros* 15:30; see also *Ohr Same'ach* there, *Teshuvos Maharibach* §88, and *Ohr Gadol* to *Orlah* 2:1; cf. *Minchas Chinuch* §9 and *Chazon Ish, Orlah* 8:12).

34. This is Chinuch's opinion, but according to the actual halachah, *chametz* on Pesach also renders a mixture prohibited in any amount (see *Tur* and *Shulchan Aruch, Orach Chaim* 447:1).

# 347 ❑ KI SISA / MITZVAH 111: THE PROHIBITION TO CONSUME IDOLATROUS OFFERINGS

כְּבָר אָמַרְנוּ כִּי לְכָל הָאֲסוּרִין יֵשׁ תַּקָּנָה בְּתַקָּנַת רַבָּן שִׁמְעוֹן בֶּן גַּמְלִיאֵל חוּץ מִכָּל אִסּוּרֵי עֲבוֹדָה זָרָה שֶׁנִּתְעָרֵב גּוּף הָאִסּוּר מַמָּשׁ שֶׁאֵין לוֹ שׁוּם תַּקָּנָה לְעוֹלָם, וְזֶהוּ מֵחֹמֶר עֲבוֹדָה זָרָה.[35] וַהֲפֹךְ וַהֲפֹךְ בַּגְּמָרָא, כִּי כָל זֶה תִּמְצָא בָּהּ מְבֹאָר עִם הַפֵּרוּשִׁים הַטּוֹבִים, וּשְׁמֹר הַדְּבָרִים כִּי בְהַרְבֵּה מְקוֹמוֹת בַּתַּלְמוּד תִּצְטָרֵךְ אֲלֵיהֶם, וְעַל כֵּן הֶאֱרַכְתִּי בָּהֶן שֶׁלֹּא כְּמִנְהָגַי בְּקוּנְטְרֵיסִין אֵלּוּ.[36]

וְעוֹד הִרְחִיקוּנוּ זִכְרוֹנָם לִבְרָכָה (עבודה זרה דף ס"ב ע"א) מֵאִסּוּר יֵין נֶסֶךְ לוֹמַר שֶׁאֲפִלּוּ שְׂכַר שֶׁל יֵין נֶסֶךְ יְהֵא אָסוּר בַּהֲנָאָה.[37]

---

these substances (*kilayim* of the vineyard, *orlah*, and *terumah*) are also less severe than *nesech* wine **regarding the remedy that is available for** deriving benefit from **them,** when they are intermingled with a permitted substance and there is insufficient permitted substance in the mixture to nullify them. כְּבָר אָמַרְנוּ כִּי לְכָל הָאֲסוּרִין יֵשׁ תַּקָּנָה בְּתַקָּנַת רַבָּן שִׁמְעוֹן בֶּן גַּמְלִיאֵל — For **we have already stated that for all prohibited substances** that became intermingled with permitted substances, the permitted portion of the mixture **can be remedied** for benefit **by** means of **the** aforementioned **remedy of Rabban Shimon ben Gamliel** (selling the mixture to idolaters without charging them for the value of the prohibited substance within it), חוּץ מִכָּל אִסּוּרֵי עֲבוֹדָה זָרָה — **except for any prohibited substances** of *avodah zarah,* שֶׁנִּתְעָרֵב גּוּף הָאִסּוּר מַמָּשׁ — in a case **where the body of the prohibited substance actually became intermingled** with a permitted substance, שֶׁאֵין לוֹ שׁוּם תַּקָּנָה לְעוֹלָם — **for** in that case alone **[the mixture] has no remedy whatsoever.** וְזֶהוּ מֵחֹמֶר עֲבוֹדָה זָרָה — **This is due to the severity of** *avodah zarah* over and above all other prohibited substances.[35]

Chinuch concludes his discussion of mixtures:

וַהֲפֹךְ וַהֲפֹךְ בַּגְּמָרָא — **Delve, and delve** deeper, **into the** relevant sections of **Gemara** that deal with these issues, כִּי כָל זֶה תִּמְצָא בָּהּ מְבֹאָר עִם הַפֵּרוּשִׁים הַטּוֹבִים — **for you will find all this clearly taught in** it when you study it **with the fine commentaries.** וּשְׁמֹר הַדְּבָרִים כִּי בְהַרְבֵּה מְקוֹמוֹת בַּתַּלְמוּד תִּצְטָרֵךְ אֲלֵיהֶם — **And preserve these matters** that I taught here in your memory, **for you will need them** in order to understand the discussions **in many places in the Talmud.** וְעַל כֵּן הֶאֱרַכְתִּי בָּהֶן שֶׁלֹּא כְּמִנְהָגַי בְּקוּנְטְרֵיסִין אֵלּוּ — **I have therefore elaborated them at length, in a departure from my usual practice in these pamphlets.**[36]

Chinuch now discusses yet another unique stringency pertaining to *nesech* wine:

וְעוֹד הִרְחִיקוּנוּ זִכְרוֹנָם לִבְרָכָה מֵאִסּוּר יֵין נֶסֶךְ — **[The Sages], of blessed memory, further distanced us from the prohibition of** *nesech* **wine** לוֹמַר שֶׁאֲפִלּוּ שְׂכַר שֶׁל יֵין נֶסֶךְ יְהֵא אָסוּר בַּהֲנָאָה — **by saying** (Mishnah, *Avodah Zarah* 62a) **that even wages earned from** the handling of *nesech* **wine shall be prohibited for benefit.**[37]

---

## NOTES

35. To summarize the laws of mixtures discussed by Chinuch:

(1) Generally, when a prohibited substance becomes mixed with a permitted substance, it renders the mixture prohibited only if (a) it imparts flavor to the entire mixture, or (b) it is not outnumbered in the mixture by 60:1. In the cases of *kilayim* of the vineyard and *orlah*, when mixed with their own kind (or no idolater is available to taste them) they must be outnumbered by 200:1, and in the case of *terumah* by 100:1. With respect to *nesech* wine and other *avodah zarah* substances, however, the mixture is prohibited in any amount.

(2) Generally, when a substance that is prohibited for benefit is contained in a mixture and has not been nullified, one may sell the mixture to an idolater without charging for the value of the prohibited portion, and thus recoup the value of the permitted portion without deriving benefit from the prohibited substance. This is allowed for all prohibited substances except *nesech* wine and other *avodah zarah* substances.

36. Apparently, Chinuch originally published this work in individual pamphlets each containing one or more mitzvos.

37. For example, if an idolater hires a Jew to pour his *nesech* wine into barrels or to transport the wine, the worker's wage is prohibited for benefit. This is a penalty imposed by the Sages specifically in the case of *nesech* wine [and other *avodah zarah* substances], due to the stringency associated with *avodah zarah*. There is no parallel prohibition to benefit from wages earned through working with other prohibited substances [though it is forbidden to profit by selling substances that are prohibited for benefit] (see Gemara

## 348 □ כי תשא / מצוה קיא: שלא לאכל ולשתות תקרבת עבודה זרה

גַּם הִפְלִיגוּ בְּרִחוּקוֹ לוֹמַר שֶׁאֲפִלּוּ הַנִּשְׂכָּר לִשְׁבֹּר חָבִיּוֹת שֶׁשְּׁכָרוֹ אָסוּר מִפְּנֵי שֶׁהוּא רוֹצֶה בְּקִיּוּמוֹ זְמַן מוּעָט, כְּלוֹמַר שֶׁרוֹצֶה שֶׁיִּהְיֶה קַיָּם בֶּחָבִיּוֹת עַד שֶׁיִּשְׁבְּרֵם הוּא כְּדֵי שֶׁיַּרְוִיחַ שְׂכָרוֹ עַל הַשְּׁבִירָה,[38] כִּי הֵם זִכְרוֹנָם לִבְרָכָה רָצוּ לַעֲקֹר מִמַּחֲשַׁבְתֵּנוּ שֶׁלֹּא נִהְיֶה חֲפֵצִים בְּקִיּוּמוֹ אֲפִלּוּ רֶגַע אֶחָד לְרֹב מְאוּסֵנוּ בְּכָל מִינֵי עֲבוֹדָה זָרָה,[39] [וְהָיְתָה הַתְּשׁוּבָה, יִשָּׁבֵר וְתָבֹא עָלָיו בְּרָכָה, שֶׁמְּמַעֵט אֶת הַתִּפְלָה.[40]]

---

Chinuch discusses an interesting application of this law that was contemplated (though ultimately rejected) by the Sages:

גַּם הִפְלִיגוּ בְּרִחוּקוֹ לוֹמַר — **Moreover, [the Sages] went so far in distancing [*nesech* wine] as to suggest** (ibid. 63b) — שֶׁאֲפִלּוּ הַנִּשְׂכָּר לִשְׁבֹּר חָבִיּוֹת יֵין נֶסֶךְ — **that even if one was hired to break barrels** filled with ***nesech* wine**, so that the wine will drain away and be destroyed, שֶׁשְּׁכָרוֹ אָסוּר מִפְּנֵי שֶׁהוּא רוֹצֶה בְּקִיּוּמוֹ זְמַן מוּעָט — **his wages** should be **prohibited** — **because he is interested in the existence of [the wine]**, albeit **for a short while;** כְּלוֹמַר שֶׁרוֹצֶה שֶׁיִּהְיֶה קַיָּם בֶּחָבִיּוֹת עַד שֶׁיִּשְׁבְּרֵם הוּא — **that is, he wants the wine to remain in existence in the barrels until he breaks them,** כְּדֵי שֶׁיַּרְוִיחַ שְׂכָרוֹ עַל הַשְּׁבִירָה — **so that he will** be able to **earn his wage from the breakage.**[38] כִּי הֵם זִכְרוֹנָם לִבְרָכָה רָצוּ לַעֲקֹר מִמַּחֲשַׁבְתֵּנוּ — This was suggested **because [the Sages],** of blessed memory, **wanted to completely uproot** idolatry **from our thoughts,** שֶׁלֹּא נִהְיֶה חֲפֵצִים בְּקִיּוּמוֹ אֲפִלּוּ רֶגַע אֶחָד — **such that we should not be interested in its existence even for a single moment,** לְרֹב מְאוּסֵנוּ בְּכָל מִינֵי עֲבוֹדָה זָרָה — **due to our being utterly repulsed by all kinds of *avodah zarah*.**[39] [וְהָיְתָה הַתְּשׁוּבָה — **The reply** to this suggestion, however, as recorded in the Gemara (ibid.), **was:** יִשָּׁבֵר וְתָבֹא עָלָיו בְּרָכָה — **Let him break** the barrels, **and may a blessing come upon him,** שֶׁמְּמַעֵט אֶת הַתִּפְלָה — **for he is decreasing** the existence of **"the futility,"** i.e., *avodah zarah*.[40] Despite this

---

### NOTES

there 62a-b; for further discussion, see *Tosafos* there ד"ה מ"ט, *Ran* and *Ritva* there).

The preceding pertains to actual *nesech* wine. For the law pertaining to wages earned through working with ordinary wine of idolaters, see *Yoreh Deah* 137:1 with *Rama*.

38. If the barrels of wine would break without his intervention, the Jew would receive no payment. He therefore wishes the barrels to remain intact until he breaks them and earns his wage. The Gemara suggests that since this person's work incorporates a tacit desire that the *nesech* wine continue to exist, his wage should be prohibited for benefit (*Rashi* ad loc.).

To clarify: The Torah commands the destruction of idols and their accessories (*Deuteronomy* 12:2-3), which includes *nesech* wine, and inherent in that command is a prohibition against contributing to their continued existence. The Sages went so far as to prohibit any benefit that is dependent upon the continued existence of an *avodah zarah* substance (for examples, see *Avodah Zarah* 64a and *Yoreh Deah* 132:7). This is known as רוֹצֶה בְּקִיּוּמוֹ, *desiring its continued existence* (see *Ramban* and *Rashba*, *Avodah Zarah* 63b, and *Ritva* 62a ד"ה אמר רבי אבהו). In our case, since the Jewish worker's wage is dependent upon the *nesech* wine remaining in existence until he breaks the barrels, and he desires that continued existence, the Gemara suggests that perhaps his wage should be prohibited — even though he is actually being paid to destroy the wine! Although the Gemara concludes that the wage is permitted, as Chinuch shall explain, the fact that the Gemara even considers the possibility that it is prohibited illustrates the extent of the prohibition to benefit from *nesech* wine.

39. *Avodah zarah* is considered loathsome and abominable, and the Torah commands us to view it as such, stating (*Deuteronomy* 7:26): שַׁקֵּץ תְּשַׁקְּצֶנּוּ וְתַעֵב תְּתַעֲבֶנּוּ, *you shall surely loath it, and you shall surely abominate it*. Accordingly, the Sages prohibited us to "desire its continued existence," as explained in the preceding note, and the suggestion at hand was made in consideration of that law.

40. That is, "desiring the existence" of idols or their accessories is prohibited only when one desires it for some positive purpose, such as to return them to their owners or to sell them. If, however, one wishes them to remain intact only so that he can destroy them, his desire does not fall under this prohibition (*Beis Yosef*, *Yoreh Deah* 133:7).

[In describing the law of "desiring its continued existence," Chinuch clearly indicates that this is a Rabbinic prohibition that was enacted only regarding *avodah zarah* substances (see also *Ramban* et al. cited in note 37). For an opinion that it applies to other prohibited substances as well, see *Tosafos, Avodah Zarah* 32a, end of ד"ה והא הכא, and *Tur* and *Shulchan Aruch, Orach Chaim* 450:7. For a thorough discussion of these views, see *Pri Chadash, Orach Chaim* 450:7.]

## 349 ☐ KI SISA / MITZVAH 111: THE PROHIBITION TO CONSUME IDOLATROUS OFFERINGS

וְיֶתֶר פְּרָטֶיהָ הָרַבִּים, כְּגוֹן מִי עוֹשֶׂה יֵין נֶסֶךְ לְאָסְרוֹ אֲפִלּוּ בַּהֲנָאָה, וּמִי אוֹסְרוֹ בִּשְׁתִיָּה דַּוְקָא,[41] וּמֵאֵימָתַי נַעֲשֶׂה יֵין נֶסֶךְ,[42] וְדִינֵי מַגָּעוֹ שֶׁל גּוֹי בְּכַוָּנָה וְשֶׁלֹּא בְּכַוָּנָה,[43] וְכֹחוֹ וְכֹחַ כֹּחוֹ[44] וְסִיּוּעַ יִשְׂרָאֵל עִמּוֹ,[45] וְאֵי זוֹ שְׁמִירָה תַּסְפִּיק לָנוּ בְּיֵינֵנוּ בְּבֵיתוֹ שֶׁל גּוֹי[46] אוֹ בְּבֵיתֵנוּ אִם יֵשׁ שָׁם גּוֹי, אוֹ בְּקָרוֹן וְהִנִּיחַ שָׁם גּוֹי, כְּגוֹן הַנִּכְנָס וְהַיּוֹצֵא, שֶׁמֻּתָּר הַיַּיִן,[47]

---

conclusion, the Gemara's discussion regarding this case illustrates the extent of the prohibition to benefit from *nesech* wine and other *avodah zarah* substances.]

Chinuch continues his discussion of the laws of the mitzvah by briefly listing numerous additional points:

וְיֶתֶר פְּרָטֶיהָ הָרַבִּים — **There are many additional details of [this mitzvah],** כְּגוֹן מִי עוֹשֶׂה יֵין נֶסֶךְ לְאָסְרוֹ אֲפִלּוּ בַּהֲנָאָה — including, **for example,** the law of **who renders** *nesech* **wine prohibited even for benefit** by touching it, וּמִי אוֹסְרוֹ בִּשְׁתִיָּה דַּוְקָא — **and who renders it prohibited only for drinking.**[41] וּמֵאֵימָתַי נַעֲשֶׂה יֵין נֶסֶךְ — **Also,** the law defining **at what point** juice pressed from grapes is considered to be "wine" so that **it can be rendered** prohibited as *nesech* **wine.**[42] וְדִינֵי מַגָּעוֹ שֶׁל גּוֹי בְּכַוָּנָה וְשֶׁלֹּא בְּכַוָּנָה — **Also, the laws regarding** cases of direct **contact** with wine **by an idolater,** and the difference whether it was done **intentionally or unintentionally;**[43] וְכֹחוֹ וְכֹחַ כֹּחוֹ — the laws regarding cases where there was no direct contact but the wine was propelled by **[the idolater's] force, or** by **the force of his force** (i.e., his secondary force);[44] וְסִיּוּעַ יִשְׂרָאֵל עִמּוֹ — **and the law regarding** cases where **a Jew assisted [the idolater]** in propelling the wine.[45]

וְאֵי זוֹ שְׁמִירָה תַּסְפִּיק לָנוּ בְּיֵינֵנוּ — **Also** included are the laws regarding **what type of supervision is sufficient for us regarding our wine,** בְּבֵיתוֹ שֶׁל גּוֹי — when it is **in the house of an idolater,**[46] אוֹ בְּבֵיתֵנוּ אִם יֵשׁ שָׁם גּוֹי — **or** when the wine is **in our house, but an idolater is present there,** אוֹ בְּקָרוֹן וְהִנִּיחַ שָׁם גּוֹי — **or** when the wine is **in a wagon and [the Jew] left an idolater there with the wine.** כְּגוֹן הַנִּכְנָס וְהַיּוֹצֵא — **For instance,** in the latter cases, if **[a Jew] is going in and out** of the place where the wine is kept, שֶׁמֻּתָּר הַיַּיִן — **then the wine is permitted,** for this degree of supervision suffices.[47]

---

### NOTES

41. For details, see *Yoreh Deah* §124.

42. The juice is considered "wine" for this purpose as soon as it begins to flow away from the pile of pressed grapes in the winepress (see *Avodah Zarah* 55b and *Yoreh Deah* 123:17).

43. Direct contact by an idolater renders wine prohibited for benefit, provided three conditions are present: (1) The contact is intentional; (2) the idolater is aware that it is wine; and (3) the contact does not occur in the course of some other activity, such as measuring the amount of wine in a vat. In other cases, the wine is prohibited only for drinking but is permitted for benefit, so it may be sold to idolaters (*Yoreh Deah* 124:10 ff.; see *Avodah Zarah* 57a-58b).

44. An idolater's "force" refers to a case where, for example, he poured wine out of a vessel — thus propelling it from the vessel without touching it (see *Avodah Zarah* 72b). The "force of his force" (i.e., a secondary force) refers to a case where he turns a press screw that in turn, lowers a beam onto the grapes (ibid. 57a). In both cases, the wine is prohibited for drinking but permitted for benefit (see *Yoreh Deah* 125:1-2; see *Tur* there for other views).

[Although idolatrous libations were performed by pouring wine from a vessel, this form of libation was done only in the actual presence of the idol. When a libation was performed not in the idol's presence, it generally took the form of agitating the wine with one's hand (שִׁכְשׁוּךְ; see Gemara ibid. 59b). Hence, where the idolater poured the wine not in the idol's presence, there is no concern of actual *nesech* wine, which is Biblically prohibited for benefit. The Sages, however, decreed that it be prohibited for consumption, lest the idolater touch it (see *Rosh, Avodah Zarah* 4:13, and *Ritva* there 72b).]

45. When a Jew helps to pour the wine, it is permitted, for the decree against wine propelled by an idolater's force was instituted only for cases where his force alone propels the wine. Nevertheless, a Jew should not initially pour wine together with an idolater, lest he tire and momentarily let the idolater pour the wine by himself (see *Tosafos* ibid. 60a ד"ה עובד כוכבים and *Yoreh Deah* 125:3; see Gemara ibid. 72b).

46. The basic rule is that the wine must have a double seal, such as being placed in a sealed container that is within another sealed container, or it must be placed in a sealed container that is under lock and key. For details, see *Yoreh Deah* 130:1-2.

47. Even if the idolater is left alone with the wine for a period of time, as long as he does not know the Jew's schedule, such that he fears that the Jew may return at any moment and is therefore afraid to touch the Jew's wine, it remains permitted (see Mishnah, *Avodah Zarah* 69a). For details, see *Yoreh Deah* 129:1 ff.

וְדִינֵי הָאִסּוּר שֶׁיֵּשׁ לָנוּ בִּכְלֵי יֵינָן[48], וְדִינֵי הֶכְשֵׁירָן[49], וְרֻבֵּי הַפְּרָטִים שֶׁבָּאוּ לָנוּ גַּם כֵּן בִּכְלֵי בִּשּׁוּלֵיהֶן וְהוּא הָעִנְיָן הַנִּקְרָא גְּעוּלֵי גוֹיִם[50], וְדִינֵי רִחוּקֵנוּ שֶׁלֹּא לְשַׁקֵּץ נַפְשֵׁנוּ גַּם כֵּן בְּעִנְיָנִים הַנִּגְרָרִין אַחַר דְּבָרִים אֵלּוּ הַמְּאוּסוֹת, כְּגוֹן מַה שֶׁאָמְרוּ זִכְרוֹנָם לִבְרָכָה (מכות דף ט״ז ע״ב) שֶׁלֹּא לֶאֱכוֹל וְלִשְׁתּוֹת בְּכֵלִים מְאוּסִים כְּגוֹן כְּלֵי הַשֶּׁתֶן וְהַצּוֹאָה וְקַרְנָא דְאוּמָּנָא לְפִי שֶׁיֵּשׁ בַּדָּבָר שִׁקּוּץ הַנֶּפֶשׁ[51], וְיֶתֶר פְּרָטֶיהָ אֵלּוּ מְבֹאָרִים בַּפְּרָקִים הָאַחֲרוֹנִים שֶׁל עֲבוֹדָה זָרָה וּקְצָת מֵהֶן בְּחוּלִּין[52]. וְנוֹהֶגֶת אַזְהָרָה זוֹ בְּכָל מָקוֹם וּבְכָל זְמַן, בְּזָכָרִים וּנְקֵבוֹת[53].

---

וְדִינֵי הָאִסּוּר שֶׁיֵּשׁ לָנוּ בִּכְלֵי יֵינָן — **Also** included are **the laws pertaining to the prohibition imposed on us concerning** the use of [idolaters'] **wine vessels** for storing kosher wine, due to those vessels having absorbed nonkosher wine,[48] וְדִינֵי הֶכְשֵׁירָן — **and the laws of how to purify [these vessels]** for kosher use via the various methods of removing nonkosher absorption.[49] וְרֻבֵּי הַפְּרָטִים שֶׁבָּאוּ לָנוּ גַּם כֵּן בִּכְלֵי בִּשּׁוּלֵיהֶן — **Also, the many details transmitted to us** by the Sages **concerning the related** prohibition of using **their cooking utensils** that absorbed the flavor of the nonkosher food cooked in them, וְהוּא הָעִנְיָן הַנִּקְרָא גְּעוּלֵי גוֹיִם — **which is the topic called "the emissions** of utensils **of idolaters."**[50]

Chinuch mentions another subject that is not technically included in this mitzvah, but is conceptually related to it:

וְדִינֵי רִחוּקֵנוּ שֶׁלֹּא לְשַׁקֵּץ נַפְשֵׁנוּ גַּם כֵּן בְּעִנְיָנִים הַנִּגְרָרִין אַחַר דְּבָרִים אֵלּוּ הַמְּאוּסוֹת — **And,** related to this topic are **the laws that distance us** from all forms of repulsive behavior and teach us **not to abominate ourselves with matters that are** conceptually **associated with these repulsive things** (i.e., *avodah zarah* substances); כְּגוֹן מַה שֶׁאָמְרוּ זִכְרוֹנָם לִבְרָכָה — **for instance, that which [the Sages], of blessed memory, have stated** (see *Makkos* 16b) שֶׁלֹּא לֶאֱכוֹל וְלִשְׁתּוֹת בְּכֵלִים מְאוּסִים — that we are **not to eat or drink from repulsive vessels,** כְּגוֹן כְּלֵי הַשֶּׁתֶן וְהַצּוֹאָה — **such as receptacles for urine or feces,** וְקַרְנָא דְאוּמָּנָא — **or a bloodletter's tube,** לְפִי שֶׁיֵּשׁ בַּדָּבָר שִׁקּוּץ הַנֶּפֶשׁ — **because this matter is** a means of **abominating oneself.**[51] וְיֶתֶר פְּרָטֶיהָ אֵלּוּ מְבֹאָרִים בַּפְּרָקִים הָאַחֲרוֹנִים שֶׁל עֲבוֹדָה זָרָה — **These** and **many additional details of** [this mitzvah] **are explained in the last** two **chapters of** Tractate *Avodah Zarah* (55a-76b); וּקְצָת מֵהֶן בְּחוּלִּין — **and some of [the above details],** namely, the laws concerning mixtures of forbidden and permitted substances, are found **in** Tractate *Chullin* (97b-100a).[52]

## ~ Applicability of the Mitzvah ~

וְנוֹהֶגֶת אַזְהָרָה זוֹ בְּכָל מָקוֹם וּבְכָל זְמַן — **This prohibition applies in every location and in all times,** בְּזָכָרִים וּנְקֵבוֹת — **to** both **men and women.**[53]

---

### NOTES

48. See *Yoreh Deah* §137.

49. See ibid. §135, 138; *Avodah Zarah* 33a-34a and 74b-75b.

50. Utensils used by idolaters for cooking nonkosher food have absorbed some of the flavor of that food and must be purged of it before they may be used for cooking kosher food, lest they impart the nonkosher flavor to the kosher food (see *Avodah Zarah* 75b-76b, and *Yoreh Deah* §120-121, for discussion of the purging processes). [The purging is called הַגְעָלָה, from the same root as the word תִגְעַל in the verse (*Leviticus* 26:11): וְלֹא תִגְעַל נַפְשִׁי אֶתְכֶם, *My Spirit will not repel you* (Rashi and Ramban to that verse; cf. Rambam, *Commentary to Mishnah*, *Zevachim* 7:1). Hence, the term גְּעוּלֵי גוֹיִם, *emissions* of utensils *of idolaters*.]

51. *Minchas Chinuch* (§10) points out that these last laws are not included in this mitzvah, but are actually an adjunct of Mitzvah 164, the prohibition to eat certain abominable creatures, which emerges from the verse (*Leviticus* 11:43): אַל תְּשַׁקְּצוּ אֶת נַפְשֹׁתֵיכֶם וגו׳, *Do not abominate yourselves* etc. Apparently, Chinuch mentions them here because, as he stated above, idolatrous substances are also "abominable" (see note 39).

52. The laws of deriving benefit from *avodah zarah* substances are codified in *Rambam, Hil. Avodah Zarah*, Chapters 7-8, and *Shulchan Aruch, Yoreh Deah* §139-146. The laws regarding *nesech* wine and idolaters' ordinary wine are codified in *Rambam, Hil. Maachalos Asuros*, Chapters 11-13, and *Shulchan Aruch, Yoreh Deah* §123-138. The laws regarding mixtures of prohibited and permitted substances are codified in *Rambam* ibid., Chapters 15-16, and *Shulchan Aruch* ibid. §98-111.

53. It applies in Eretz Yisrael and the Diaspora, and whether the *Beis HaMikdash* is standing or not. It also

# 351 ⬜ KI SISA / MITZVAH 111: THE PROHIBITION TO CONSUME IDOLATROUS OFFERINGS

וְעוֹבֵר עָלֶיהָ וְאָכַל כָּל שֶׁהוּא אוֹ שָׁתָה אֲפִלּוּ טִפַּת יֵין נֶסֶךְ גָּמוּר לוֹקֶה, שֶׁאֵין דִּין דְּבָרִים אֵלּוּ כְּדִין שְׁאָר אִסּוּרֵי מַאֲכָלוֹת, שֶׁהֵן בִּכְזַיִת וְדִין שְׁתִיָּה בִּרְבִיעִית[54], לְפִי שֶׁעַל עֲבוֹדָה זָרָה הִזְהִירָה תּוֹרָה וְאָמְרָה (דברים י״ג, י״ח) וְלֹא יִדְבַּק בְּיָדְךָ מְאוּמָה מִן הַחֵרֶם, כְּלוֹמַר וַאֲפִלּוּ כָּל שֶׁהוּא[55].

בְּזֹאת הַמְנִיעָה שֶׁל יֵין נֶסֶךְ הָרַמְבַּ״ם זִכְרוֹנוֹ לִבְרָכָה (בספר המצוות) וְהָרַמְבַּ״ן זִכְרוֹנוֹ לִבְרָכָה (בהשגותיו) שְׁנֵיהֶם יוֹדוּ שֶׁיֵּשׁ בָּזֶה לָאו, וְשֶׁהוּא נִמְנֶה בְּחֶשְׁבּוֹן הַלָּאוִין, אָמְנָם נֶחְלְקוּ בּוֹ בְּעִנְיָן זֶה, כִּי הָרַמְבַּ״ם זִכְרוֹנוֹ לִבְרָכָה יוֹצִיא אִסּוּר יֵין נֶסֶךְ מִן הַמִּקְרָא שֶׁכָּתוּב בְּפָרָשַׁת הַאֲזִינוּ שֶׁנֶּאֱמַר (דברים ל״ב, ל״ח) יִשְׁתּוּ יֵין נְסִיכָם, וְאִסּוּר שְׁאָר תִּקְרֹבֶת עֲבוֹדָה זָרָה מִלֹּא יִדְבַּק בְּיָדְךָ מְאוּמָה מִן הַחֵרֶם (שם י״ג, י״ח), וּמִלֹּא תָבִיא תוֹעֵבָה (שם ז׳, כ״ו), וְהָרַמְבַּ״ן זִכְרוֹנוֹ לִבְרָכָה כָּתַב, כִּי מִפָּסוּק זֶה דְּהִשָּׁמֶר לְךָ וְגוֹ׳ (שמות ל״ד, י״ב) נִלְמַד אִסּוּר כָּל תִּקְרֹבֶת עֲבוֹדָה זָרָה וְיֵין נֶסֶךְ בִּכְלָל[56]. וַאֲנִי כָּתַבְתִּי זֶה הַמִּקְרָא כְּדַעְתּוֹ

---

וְעוֹבֵר עָלֶיהָ — **One who transgresses [this prohibition]** וְאָכַל כָּל שֶׁהוּא — **and eats a minute amount** of a substance that was offered to an *avodah zarah*, אוֹ שָׁתָה אֲפִלּוּ טִפַּת יֵין נֶסֶךְ גָּמוּר — **or drinks even a drop of actual *nesech* wine,** i.e., wine that was offered in libation for an idol, לוֹקֶה — **incurs** the punishment of ***malkus*** (lashes). שֶׁאֵין דִּין דְּבָרִים אֵלּוּ כְּדִין שְׁאָר אִסּוּרֵי מַאֲכָלוֹת — **For the law regarding these substances** of *avodah zarah* **is not like the law regarding other forbidden foods,** שֶׁהֵן בִּכְזַיִת וְדִין שְׁתִיָּה בִּרְבִיעִית — **which are subject to** a minimum measure for liability, insofar as the law for eating is that one incurs *malkus* only when he consumes **a *kezayis*** (olive's volume), **and the law for drinking is** that one incurs *malkus* only when he imbibes **a *revi'is*.**[54] לְפִי שֶׁעַל עֲבוֹדָה זָרָה הִזְהִירָה תּוֹרָה וְאָמְרָה — **With respect to *avodah zarah* substances, however, there is no minimum measure, because concerning *avodah zarah*, the Torah warned and stated** (*Deuteronomy* 13:18): "וְלֹא יִדְבַּק בְּיָדְךָ מְאוּמָה מִן הַחֵרֶם" — "***Nothing of the banned property shall adhere to your hand,*** כְּלוֹמַר וַאֲפִלּוּ כָּל שֶׁהוּא — meaning, **not even a minute amount.**[55]

### ~ Dispute Regarding the Mitzvah ~

בְּזֹאת הַמְנִיעָה שֶׁל יֵין נֶסֶךְ — **Regarding this prohibition of *nesech* wine,** הָרַמְבַּ״ם זִכְרוֹנוֹ לִבְרָכָה וְהָרַמְבַּ״ן זִכְרוֹנוֹ לִבְרָכָה שְׁנֵיהֶם יוֹדוּ שֶׁיֵּשׁ בָּזֶה לָאו — ***Rambam,* of blessed memory, and *Ramban,* of blessed memory, both agree** (*Sefer HaMitzvos, Lo Saaseh* 194, and Glosses there) **that it is the subject of a** mitzvah-prohibition, וְשֶׁהוּא נִמְנֶה בְּחֶשְׁבּוֹן הַלָּאוִין — **and that it is counted within the number of the** 365 mitzvah-prohibitions. אָמְנָם נֶחְלְקוּ בּוֹ בְּעִנְיָן זֶה — **However, they disagree concerning it in the following matter:** כִּי הָרַמְבַּ״ם זִכְרוֹנוֹ לִבְרָכָה יוֹצִיא אִסּוּר יֵין נֶסֶךְ מִן הַמִּקְרָא שֶׁכָּתוּב בְּפָרָשַׁת הַאֲזִינוּ — **For *Rambam,* of blessed memory, derives the prohibition of *nesech* wine from a verse that is written in *Parashas Haazinu,*** שֶׁנֶּאֱמַר — **where it is stated** (*Deuteronomy* 32:38): "יִשְׁתּוּ יֵין נְסִיכָם" — **"they would drink the wine of their libations,"** וְאִסּוּר שְׁאָר תִּקְרֹבֶת עֲבוֹדָה זָרָה מִלֹּא יִדְבַּק "בְּיָדְךָ מְאוּמָה מִן הַחֵרֶם" — **and he derives the prohibition of other idolatrous offerings from the verse** (*Deuteronomy* 13:18): ***Nothing of the banned property*** *shall cleave to your hand,"* וּמִלֹּא תָבִיא תוֹעֵבָה — **and from the verse** (ibid. 7:26): *You shall not bring an abomination into your home.* וְהָרַמְבַּ״ן זִכְרוֹנוֹ לִבְרָכָה כָּתַב — ***Ramban,* of blessed memory, however, disagrees and writes** כִּי מִפָּסוּק זֶה דְּהִשָּׁמֶר לְךָ וְגוֹ׳ — **that from this verse** that we cited above (*Exodus* 34:12-15), *Be vigilant,* etc. [lest ... he invite you and you eat from his slaughter] **is derived the prohibition of all idolatrous offerings, including *nesech* wine.**[56] וַאֲנִי כָּתַבְתִּי זֶה הַמִּקְרָא כְּדַעְתּוֹ — **I** 

---

#### NOTES

applies to women as well as to men, in accordance with the general rule pertaining to mitzvah-prohibitions.

54. See above, note 6, for the definition of this measure.

55. See above, note 4.

56. *Ramban* understands the two verses, *Nothing of the banned property shall cleave to your hand,* and

## 352 ❑ כי תשא / מצוה קיא: שלא לאכל ולשתות תקרבת עבודה זרה

שֶׁלֹּא כְּמִנְהָגִי בְּכָל הַסֵּפֶר, כִּי כֻלָּם כְּתַבְתִּים כְּדַעַת הָרַמְבַּ״ם זִכְרוֹנוֹ לִבְרָכָה,[57] אֲבָל בְּכָאן רָאִיתִי שֶׁהַפָּסוּק הַזֶּה נָאֶה מְאֹד לִדְרשׁ מִמֶּנּוּ הָעִנְיָן, וְעוֹד שֶׁיֵּשׁ בּוֹ אַזְהָרָה, וּכְמוֹ שֶׁאָמְרוּ זִכְרוֹנָם לִבְרָכָה (עירובין דף צ״ו ע״א) כָּל מָקוֹם שֶׁנֶּאֱמַר בּוֹ הִשָּׁמֶר פֶּן וְאַל, אֵינוֹ אֶלָּא לֹא תַעֲשֶׂה, וּבַפָּסוּק יִשְׁתּוּ יֵין נְסִיכָם אֵין שָׁם אַזְהָרָה.[58] גַּם רָאִיתִי גְּדוֹלִים מִמּוֹנֵי הַמִּצְוֹת שֶׁכָּתְבוּ כֵן.[59]

---

**wrote** above that **this verse** in *Exodus* is the Scriptural source of the prohibition, and I therefore placed this prohibition here, in *Parashas Ki Sisa,* **in accordance with [***Ramban's***] opinion,** שֶׁלֹּא כְּמִנְהָגִי **בְּכָל הַסֵּפֶר** — **unlike my** usual **practice throughout this book,** כִּי כֻלָּם כְּתַבְתִּים כְּדַעַת הָרַמְבַּ״ם זִכְרוֹנוֹ לִבְרָכָה — **for I recorded all [the mitzvos]** and their Scriptural sources **in accordance with the opinion of** *Rambam,* **of blessed memory.**[57] אֲבָל בְּכָאן רָאִיתִי שֶׁהַפָּסוּק הַזֶּה נָאֶה מְאֹד לִדְרשׁ מִמֶּנּוּ הָעִנְיָן — **Here, however, I saw this verse** in *Exodus* (*Be vigilant lest ... you eat from his slaughter*) **as very fitting** to be the source **for expounding the matter of** the prohibition to derive benefit from idolatrous offerings. וְעוֹד שֶׁיֵּשׁ בּוֹ אַזְהָרָה — **Furthermore,** I see this verse as the source of the mitzvah-prohibition, **for it contains an injunction,** וּכְמוֹ שֶׁאָמְרוּ זִכְרוֹנָם לִבְרָכָה — **as [the Sages],** of blessed memory, **said** (*Eruvin* 96a et al): כָּל מָקוֹם שֶׁנֶּאֱמַר בּוֹ ״הִשָּׁמֶר״, ״פֶּן״ וְ״אַל״ — **in any context where** the expressions "**be vigilant,**" "**lest,**" **or** "**do not,**" **are stated** in the Torah, אֵינוֹ אֶלָּא לֹא תַעֲשֶׂה — **[the expression] constitutes nothing other than a prohibition.** Thus, the verse *Be vigilant lest ... you eat from his slaughter* constitutes a genuine mitzvah-prohibition, וּבַפָּסוּק ״יִשְׁתּוּ יֵין נְסִיכָם״ אֵין שָׁם אַזְהָרָה — **whereas** in the verse *they would drink the wine of their libations,* which *Rambam* cited as the source of this prohibition, **there is no injunction,** but merely a description of idol worship.[58] גַּם רָאִיתִי גְּדוֹלִים מִמּוֹנֵי הַמִּצְוֹת שֶׁכָּתְבוּ כֵן — **Moreover, I saw that** some of the **great ones among those who counted the mitzvos** also **wrote this,** i.e., they cited the verse *Be vigilant,* etc. as the source of this mitzvah.[59] For these reasons I have recorded this verse as the source of the prohibition to consume all idolatrous offerings, including *nesech* wine.

---

### NOTES

*You shall not bring an abomination into your home,* to be referring to the idols themselves, not to offerings brought before them (Glosses to *Sefer HaMitzvos, Lo Saaseh* 194).

57. Chinuch writes in his Introduction (Vol. I, p. 34) that this book is based on *Rambam's* count of the 613 mitzvos in his *Sefer HaMitzvos.* See also below, Mitzvos 138 and 153. In this instance, too, he does not deviate from *Rambam's* count, for as he stated, *Rambam* agrees that *nesech* wine and other idolatrous offerings are prohibited by a mitzvah-prohibition that is counted as one of the 613 Mitzvos. He differs with *Rambam* here with respect to identifying the verse that is the source of this prohibition.

58. For possible explanations of why *Rambam* understands this verse as the source of the prohibition on idolatrous offerings, see Glosses of *Chazon Ish* to *Avi Ezri, Hil. Maachalos Asuros* 11:1-3, and *Haamek She'eilah* §162. For *Rambam's* understanding of the injunction *Be vigilant lest ... you eat from his slaughter,* see his comments in *Hil. Shechitah* 4:11.

59. See *Smag, Lo Saaseh* 148.

---

### ⤳§ Insight: Yayin Mevushal (Cooked Wine)

In the course of this mitzvah, we learned that a Jew's wine that was so much as merely touched by an idolater becomes prohibited. There is, however, an exception that is regularly relied upon nowadays: יַיִן מְבֻשָּׁל, *cooked wine.* The Gemara (*Avodah Zarah* 30a) states: "Cooked wine is not subject to the *nesech* prohibition." I.e., if an idolater touches cooked wine of a Jew, he does not render it prohibited. Similarly, if an idolater owns cooked wine that he obtained from a Jew, it is not prohibited.

Why is cooked wine not included in the prohibition? Numerous explanations are found in the Rishonim. *Rambam* (*Hil. Maachalos Asuros* 11:9) states that it is because cooked wine was unfit for use as a libation in the *Beis HaMikdash,* and similarly, idol worshipers do not use cooked wine in their

religious rites. Numerous Rishonim understand this to mean that we are therefore not concerned that the idolater may have intended to make it a libation when he touched it. They wonder, though, on what basis we can assume that just because cooked wine was not used in the *Beis HaMikdash*, idolaters also never use cooked wine in their rites (see *Ramban* et al. to *Avodah Zarah* 30a). Some Acharonim explain *Rambam* to mean that the Biblical prohibition of *nesech* wine (i.e., wine actually used for an idolatrous libation) applies only to wine that would be suitable for a libation in the *Beis HaMikdash*, and therefore (by Scriptural decree) wine that is unfit for the *Beis HaMikdash* does not become prohibited as *nesech* even if an idolater actually used it as a libation for his idol. It follows that the Rabbinic decree against wine of idolaters also does not apply to cooked wine (*Chazon Ish, Yoreh Deah* 56:4; see also *Avnei Nezer, Yoreh Deah* 116:5).

*Rosh* (*Avodah Zarah* 2:13), however, raises another objection to *Rambam's* view: The Gemara (ibid. 36b) states that, aside from the concern for an idolatrous libation, there was an additional rationale for the Rabbis' prohibiting idolaters' wine, namely, to prevent intermarriage with their daughters (see above, note 3). This concern certainly exists as much with regard to cooked wine as with regard to uncooked wine! *Rosh* therefore suggests that the reason cooked wine was not included in the decree against idolaters' wine is that it was uncommon for wine to be cooked. Since, as a rule, Rabbinic decrees do not apply to uncommon cases [מִלְתָא דְּלָא שְׁכִיחָא לָא גָּזְרוּ בֵּיהּ רַבָּנָן], the decree against idolaters' wine (and wine touched by an idolater) was not instituted with respect to cooked wine. [Even if in later generations it became more common to cook wine, since the initial Rabbinic decree did not apply to such wine and no new decree was ever issued, it remains permitted in all times (*Minchas Shlomo* I §25:3; *Teshuvos Minchas Yitzchak* Vol. VII §61; see, similarly, *Ritva, Avodah Zarah* 29b ד"ה אמר רב אשי).]

[For a resolution of *Rosh's* challenge to *Rambam*, see *Chidushei R' Akiva Eiger* to *Yoreh Deah* 123 on *Taz* §3, and *Shaar HaMelech* to *Hil. Maachalos Asuros* 11:3.]

A third rationale is mentioned by *Rashba* (*Toras HaBayis* 5:3 [50d in Josefov edition]; *Teshuvos HaRashba* Vol. IV §149; see also Vol. 1 §813). *Rashba* states that cooking wine changes its flavor to the point that it is no longer called simply "wine," but rather "cooked wine." Accordingly, the Rabbinic prohibition, which was enacted regarding idolaters' *wine*, does not apply to *cooked wine*. [Some take this a step further and rule that one does not recite the blessing *borei pri hagafen* over cooked wine (but rather, *shehakol*) and that is unfit for *Kiddush*, because it is not considered "wine" at all (*Tur, Orach Chaim* 272:8, in the name of *Rashi* and others; *Rabbeinu Manoach* to *Rambam, Hil. Chametz U'Matzah* 7:10; cf. *Teshuvos HaRashba* ibid.).]

There is some question as to the extent to which wine must be heated in order for it to be considered "cooked" and excluded from the decree against idolaters' wine. *Ramban* (*Avodah Zarah* 30a) mentions two standards: (1) מִשֶּׁהִרְתִּיחַ, from when it begins to bubble, and (2) מִשֶּׁיִּתְמַעֵט מִמִּדָּתוֹ עַל יְדֵי הָאוּר, from when it begins to diminish in quantity due to [vaporization from the heat of] the fire. Other Rishonim, however, suggest that these two standards may actually be describing the same point (see *Toras HaBayis* ibid. [50c in Josefov edition], and *Ran* to *Rif, Avodah Zarah* fol. 10a ד"ה יין מבושל; see also *Shach, Yoreh Deah* 123:7). *Shulchan Aruch* (*Yoreh Deah* 123:3) rules that wine is considered cooked when it begins to bubble. See, however, *Meiri, Avodah Zarah* 30a ד"ה לא הוזכר, who cites several additional definitions of "cooked" in this context.

Latter-day authorities deal at length with the question of whether the leniency regarding cooked wine applies to wines (and grape juices; see above, note 42) that have been pasteurized. [Pasteurization is a process by which a beverage is heated to a specific temperature for a certain period of time in order to kill microorganisms that could cause disease, spoilage, or unwanted fermentation. Commercially sold grape juices nowadays are generally pasteurized, and so are some wines.] At issue is whether the degree of heat generated during pasteurization suffices for the wine to be halachically considered "cooked," and whether the manner in which pasteurization is done qualifies as "cooking." R' Moshe Feinstein (*Igros Moshe, Yoreh Deah* III §31) ruled that wines and grape juices that have been pasteurized are considered "cooked" (see also *Teshuvos Minchas Yitzchak* ibid.). Other authorities, however, disagree with this view; see *Minchas Shlomo* I §25, and *Ohr LeZion* (*R' Ben Tzion Abba Shaul*) Vol. II §20:18 ד"ה ויש לדעת. For an extensive treatment of the issue, see *Yabia Omer* Vol. XVIII §15; see also *Shevet HaLevi* Vol. II §51.

## מִצְוָה קיב: מִצְוַת שְׁבִיתַת הָאָרֶץ בִּשְׁנַת הַשְּׁמִטָּה

לְבַטֵּל עֲבוֹדַת הָאָרֶץ בַּשָּׁנָה הַשְּׁבִיעִית, שֶׁנֶּאֱמַר (שמות ל״ד, כ״א) בֶּחָרִישׁ וּבַקָּצִיר תִּשְׁבֹּת, וּבָא הַפֵּרוּשׁ שֶׁעַל שָׁנָה הַשְּׁבִיעִית נֶאֱמַר, שֶׁנִּצְטַוֵּינוּ שֶׁלֹּא לַעֲסֹק בָּהּ כְּלָל בַּעֲבוֹדַת הָאָרֶץ.[1]

---

## Mitzvah 112

### The Obligation to Rest the Land During the Shemittah Year

שֵׁשֶׁת יָמִים תַּעֲבֹד וּבַיּוֹם הַשְּׁבִיעִי תִּשְׁבֹּת בֶּחָרִישׁ וּבַקָּצִיר תִּשְׁבֹּת

*Six days shall you work and on the seventh day you shall desist; you shall desist from plowing and harvesting (Exodus 34:21).*

---

This mitzvah is the one of numerous mitzvos that deals with the agricultural laws of the *Shemittah* (Sabbatical) year. [See introduction to Mitzvah 84 for an enumeration of the various mitzvos pertaining to *Shemittah*.]

לְבַטֵּל עֲבוֹדַת הָאָרֶץ בַּשָּׁנָה הַשְּׁבִיעִית — **We are commanded to suspend work of the land during the seventh year** (i.e., *Shemittah*), שֶׁנֶּאֱמַר "בֶּחָרִישׁ וּבַקָּצִיר תִּשְׁבֹּת" — **as it is stated** (*Exodus* 34:21): ***you shall desist from plowing and harvesting.*** וּבָא הַפֵּרוּשׁ — **The explanation** of this expression, **as transmitted** to us by the Sages (*Rosh Hashanah* 9a), **is** שֶׁעַל שָׁנָה הַשְּׁבִיעִית נֶאֱמַר — **that it is stated in reference to the seventh year,** שֶׁנִּצְטַוֵּינוּ שֶׁלֹּא לַעֲסֹק בָּהּ כְּלָל בַּעֲבוֹדַת הָאָרֶץ — meaning **that we are** thereby **commanded not to engage in working the land at all in** [the *Shemittah* year].[1]

---

### NOTES

1. The verse, which in full reads, *Six days shall you work and on the seventh day you shall desist; you shall desist from plowing and harvesting*, seems to refer to the obligation to desist from these activities on the weekly Sabbath, not on *Shemittah*. Nevertheless, as Chinuch notes, our Sages explained the verse to be discussing the obligation to rest the land during *Shemittah*. [According to some, this is due to the fact that the obligation to desist from these activities on the weekly Sabbath is already included in the directive (*Exodus* 20:10): וְיוֹם הַשְּׁבִיעִי שַׁבָּת לַה׳ אֱלֹהֶיךָ לֹא תַעֲשֶׂה כָל מְלָאכָה, *But the seventh day is Sabbath to HASHEM, your God, you shall not do any work* (*Yerushalmi Sheviis* 1:1; see also *Rashi, Moed Katan* 2b ד״ה חרישה בשביעית). Others assert that it is problematic to say that our verse, which states "*you shall desist from plowing and harvesting*" is referring to the weekly Sabbath, for if it were, why then were only these two of the thirty-nine *melachos* (i.e., activities prohibited on the Sabbath; see Mitzvah 32) singled out? (*Rashi, Rosh Hashanah* 9a ד״ה אין צריך לומר; cf. *Ramban* and *Rashbam* to *Exodus* 34:21). Accordingly, the verse is interpreted as referring to *Shemittah*.]

Although Chinuch and *Rambam* (*Sefer HaMitzvos*, *Asei* 135) state unequivocally that this verse (*you shall desist from plowing and harvesting*) is referring to *Shemittah*, in truth, this explanation follows the opinion of R' Akiva (*Rosh Hashanah* 9a). R' Yishmael, however, disagrees (ibid.), and sees the verse as referring to the laws of the weekly Sabbath. Moreover, even R' Akiva, who understands the subject of the verse to be *Shemittah*, seemingly does not apply it to *Shemittah* itself, but to the period leading up to and following *Shemittah*. That is, he sees our verse as prohibiting plowing in the period immediately prior to *Shemittah*, and prohibiting harvesting *Shemittah* produce in the year following *Shemittah*. How then can Chinuch and *Rambam* use this verse as the source for the mitzvah to rest the land during the *Shemittah* year?

R' Avraham ben HaRambam (*Maaseh Nissim* §9 — printed in *Sefer HaMitzvos*, Frankel ed., p. 256), in defense of his father's position, addresses this issue and notes that, in truth, it is not only R' Akiva who sees the verse as referring to *Shemittah*, but it is clear from *Mechilta* (*Mechilta D'Rashbi*, *Exodus* 34:21) that others as well take this position, including R' Yehudah and R' Shimon. Furthermore, although R' Akiva sees the verse as referring to the prohibitory periods before and after *Shemittah*, that is not to be understood as being to the exclusion of *Shemittah* itself — wherein such activities must all the more so be forbidden (see also *Ran, Chidushim, Rosh Hashanah* 9a; *Mahari Korkos, Hil. Shemittah VeYovel* 1:1).

## 355 ☐ KI SISA / MITZVAH 112: TO REST THE LAND DURING THE SHEMITTAH YEAR

וְנִכְפְּלָה הַמִּצְוָה בָּזֶה בְּאָמְרוֹ בְּמָקוֹם אַחֵר (ויקרא כ״ה, ה׳) שְׁנַת שַׁבָּתוֹן יִהְיֶה לָאָרֶץ, וְכֵן וְשָׁבְתָה הָאָרֶץ שַׁבָּת לַה׳ (שם, ב׳). וּכְבָר כָּתַבְתִּי כָּל עִנְיָנָהּ מְשֻׁלָּם לְמַעְלָה בְּסֵדֶר אִם כֶּסֶף תַּלְוֶה[2] בְּמִצְוַת וְהַשְּׁבִיעִת תִּשְׁמְטֶנָּה וּנְטַשְׁתָּהּ (שמות כ״ג, י״א), שֶׁבָּאָה לְצַוּוֹת עַל הֶפְקֵר פֵּרוֹת שָׁנָה זוֹ לַכֹּל,[3] וְאַף עַל פִּי שֶׁכָּאן הָיָה מְקוֹמוֹ.

וְנִכְפְּלָה הַמִּצְוָה בָּזֶה בְּאָמְרוֹ בְּמָקוֹם אַחֵר — **The command with regard to this** suspension of agricultural labor in *Shemittah* **is repeated when [the Torah] states elsewhere** (*Leviticus* 25:5): שְׁנַת שַׁבָּתוֹן יִהְיֶה לָאָרֶץ — ***it shall be a year of rest for the land.*** " וְכֵן – "וְשָׁבְתָה הָאָרֶץ שַׁבָּת לַה׳ — It is similarly stated (ibid. v. 2), ***the land shall observe a Sabbath rest for HASHEM,*** which conveys the same idea, prohibiting working the land during the *Shemittah* year.

In Mitzvah 84 (*The Obligation Regarding Shemittah of the Land*), Chinuch writes that Mitzvah 84 and this mitzvah "share a common bond," and, when addressing the laws of that mitzvah, he goes on to discuss the laws of this mitzvah. Chinuch references that discussion:

וּכְבָר כָּתַבְתִּי כָּל עִנְיָנָהּ מְשֻׁלָּם — **I have already fully written all of [this mitzvah's] aspects,** including its laws, לְמַעְלָה בְּסֵדֶר אִם כֶּסֶף תַּלְוֶה בְּמִצְוַת וְהַשְּׁבִיעִת תִּשְׁמְטֶנָּה וּנְטַשְׁתָּהּ — **above,** in ***Parashas Im Kesef Talveh,***[2] **in the** related **mitzvah** (Mitzvah 84) that emerges from the verse (*Exodus* 23:11): ***And in the seventh [year], you shall release it and leave it [unharvested],*** שֶׁבָּאָה לְצַוּוֹת עַל הֶפְקֵר פֵּרוֹת שָׁנָה זוֹ לַכֹּל — **which comes to command** us **regarding relinquishing the produce of this year to all,** so that anyone may come and freely take of it.[3] וְאַף עַל פִּי שֶׁכָּאן הָיָה מְקוֹמוֹ — The particulars of the mitzvah have been discussed there, **even though the** proper **place for that** discussion **would have been here.**

---

### NOTES

2. According to Chinuch's custom, *Parashas Mishpatim* was divided into two *Parashiyos*: *Mishpatim* [*Exodus* 21:1-22:23] and *Im Kesef* [*Exodus* 22:24-24:18] (see above, Introduction to *Parashas Im Kesef*).

3. As mentioned above, Chinuch, in Mitzvah 84, includes in his discussion the laws relating to working the land. There he notes that both men and women are bound by the *Shemittah* mitzvos. Furthermore, he notes that on a Biblical level, these mitzvos apply only when the majority of Jews and all the tribes are living in Eretz Yisrael on their ancestral lands, and how in the absence of those conditions, the observance of the agricultural restrictions of *Shemittah* is a Rabbinic obligation.

With regard to the transgression of this mitzvah, one who works the field in a forbidden manner during *Shemittah* has transgressed this mitzvah-obligation. Aside from this mitzvah-obligation, working the field during *Shemittah* is also the subject of a mitzvah-prohibition (Mitzvah 326), while working trees during *Shemittah* is prohibited by force of a separate prohibition (Mitzvah 327).

[*Minchas Chinuch* notes one exception, which, in the opinion of Chinuch, is covered only by this mitzvah-obligation but is not subject to the prohibitory verses — namely, plowing (see Mitzvah 84, note 15). The exact source of the prohibition to plow during the *Shemittah* year is the subject of controversy. Many, like Chinuch, see it as being a violation of the mitzvah-obligation that emerges from the verse of our mitzvah, *you shall desist from plowing* (*Rashi, Moed Katan* 2b חרישה בשביעית; see also *Rash, Sheviis* 2:2; *Tosafos, Gittin* 44b ד״ה נטייבה), or from the verse (*Leviticus* 25:2): *the land shall observe a Sabbath rest,* that Chinuch cites above (*Mahari Korkos, Hil. Shemittah VeYovel* 1:1 in explanation of *Rambam*; *Aruch HaShulchan HeAsid* 19:3). Others, however, argue that plowing during *Shemittah* is only Rabbinically prohibited (*Rambam,* according to *Tos. Yom Tov, Sheviis* 2:2 and *Aruch HaShulchan HaAsid* 19:11; cf. *Mahari Korkos* loc. cit.; see also *Chazon Ish, Sheviis* 19:1).]

---

### ⌘ Insight: Shemittah — Relating to the Person or the Land?

A question that must be addressed with regard to this mitzvah — the mitzvah that the land rest on *Shemittah* — is how the mitzvah is defined. Is the mitzvah focused on the individual, meaning that the Torah commanded that *the person* refrain from working the land during *Shemittah,* or is it focused on the land, meaning that one must ensure that *the land* rests during *Shemittah*? This question has several practical ramifications. One possible halachic implication of this question pertains to allowing a non-Jew to perform work in one's field on *Shemittah*: If the mitzvah is that the individual

rest, there would presumably be no prohibition in allowing a non-Jew to work the land (without specifically instructing him to do so), since a non-Jew is not commanded to observe *Shemittah*. If, on the other hand, the mitzvah demands that the land should rest (as the title of this mitzvah, *The Obligation to Rest the Land* . . . , would seem to suggest), allowing a non-Jew to work one's land during *Shemittah* would also be a violation of this mitzvah. This latter approach is taken by *Minchas Chinuch* (§2), who understands that this mitzvah obligates us to ensure that our land is not worked, irrespective of who is working it.

*Minchas Chinuch* notes that this approach is in fact borne out by the terminology of the verses in *Leviticus* (25:2,5) that Chinuch cited above. The verses state: שְׁנַת שַׁבָּתוֹן יִהְיֶה לָאָרֶץ, *it shall be a year of rest for the land*, and: וְשָׁבְתָה הָאָרֶץ שַׁבָּת לַה', *the land shall observe a Sabbath rest for* HASHEM. These verses clearly focus on the land and the obligation to allow it to lie fallow (see also *Maharshal, Bava Metzia* 90a ד"ה אבל, and *Tos. Rid, Avodah Zarah* 15b ד"ה אמר ליה). [This is in contrast to the *prohibition* of working the land (Mitzvah 326), which is violated only when the person himself does the work, as there the wording of the prohibition focuses on the individual (*Leviticus* 25:4): שָׂדְךָ לֹא תִזְרָע, *you shall not sow your field,* as opposed to being focused on the land, "you shall not allow your field to be sown."]

A similar concept is found with regard to the requirement that one's animal rest on the Sabbath. The verse states (*Exodus* 23:12): *so that your ox and donkey may rest,* which teaches the obligation to make sure that our animal does not work, even if we are not the ones working the animal. Even allowing a non-Jew to work one's animal is a violation of this mitzvah-obligation (*Rambam, Hil. Shabbos* 20:1,3).

*Minchas Chinuch* notes that the idea that this mitzvah is that the land should rest is indeed stated rather clearly in the Gemara (*Avodah Zarah* 15b), which teaches that the obligation to allow one's field to rest is similar to the obligation to allow one's animal to rest on the Sabbath (see *Rashi* there ד"ה אדם מצווה). This would indicate that just as on the Sabbath, the mitzvah obligates us to make sure that our animal does not work, so too, we are obligated to make sure that our fields are not worked on *Shemittah,* even if we are not the ones working them (cf. *Teshuvos Maharit* 2:52; see also *Avi Ezri II, Hil. Shemittah VeYovel* 3:8 §2).

This notion that the mitzvah requires that the land should rest enables us to understand an otherwise seemingly peculiar law with regard to *Shemittah*. As Chinuch referenced in Mitzvah 84 (see note 34 there and Mishnah, *Sheviis* 2:6), not only is one prohibited from planting during *Shemittah*, but one may not even plant a tree immediately prior to *Shemittah*, for it takes up to two weeks for a tree to take root, and we may not allow the taking root to occur during *Shemittah*. On the Sabbath we find no such equivalent prohibition. That is, one may plant something during the week without concern that it will take root on the Sabbath. *Minchas Chinuch* (298:15) explains the distinction as above: With regard to the *melachah* (forbidden activity) of planting on the Sabbath, the prohibition is on the person, and as long as he performed his act of planting before the Sabbath, the fact that the land continues to interact with the seed and bring about the rooting on the Sabbath is irrelevant. However, with regard to *Shemittah,* the fact that the taking root occurs during *Shemittah* in effect means that the land is "working," putting one in direct conflict with the mitzvah.

## 🙠 מִצְוָה קיג: שֶׁלֹּא לֶאֱכֹל בָּשָׂר בְּחָלָב 🙠

שֶׁלֹּא לֶאֱכֹל בָּשָׂר בְּחָלָב שֶׁנִּתְבַּשְּׁלוּ¹ בְּיַחַד², שֶׁנֶּאֱמַר (שמות ל״ד, כ״ו) לֹא תְבַשֵּׁל גְּדִי בַּחֲלֵב אִמּוֹ³, וְזֶה הַכָּתוּב בָּא לֶאֱסֹר הָאֲכִילָה וְהַהֲנָאָה בְּבָשָׂר בְּחָלָב⁴. וְאַל יִקְשֶׁה עָלֶיךָ אִם כֵּן לָמָּה לֹא נֶאֱמַר בְּפֵרוּשׁ אִסּוּרוֹ בְּלֹא תֹאכַל וְהוֹצִיאוֹ בִּלְשׁוֹן בִּשּׁוּל, שֶׁהַתְּשׁוּבָה בָּזֶה מִפְּנֵי שֶׁנִּתְחַדְּשָׁה אֲכִילָתוֹ מֵאִסּוּר שְׁאָר אֲכִילַת אִסּוּרִין, שֶׁשְּׁאָר אִסּוּרִין אֵין חִיּוּבָן אֶלָּא אִם כֵּן

---

## 🙠 Mitzvah 113 🙠
# The Prohibition to Eat a Mixture of Meat and Milk

לֹא תְבַשֵּׁל גְּדִי בַּחֲלֵב אִמּוֹ
*You shall not cook a kid in the milk of its mother (Exodus 34:26).*

The above verse, from which the prohibition of the meat-and-milk mixture (*basar bechalav*) is derived, appears in the Torah three times (*Exodus* 23:19 and 34:26; *Deuteronomy* 14:21). The Gemara (*Chullin* 115b) explains that this teaches that there are three aspects to the meat-and-milk prohibition: One may not *create* such a mixture by cooking meat and milk together, one may not *eat* a mixture of meat and milk that were cooked together, and one may not derive *benefit* from such a mixture. The prohibition of cooking meat and milk together is contained in the first appearance of the verse, and was set forth in Mitzvah 92. This mitzvah refers to the other two aspects of this prohibition — eating and deriving benefit from a mixture of meat and milk. As Chinuch will explain, although these aspects of the prohibition are expressed by two separate verses, they are nevertheless counted as a single mitzvah.

שֶׁלֹּא לֶאֱכֹל בָּשָׂר בְּחָלָב שֶׁנִּתְבַּשְּׁלוּ בְּיַחַד — We are commanded **not to eat meat and milk**[1] **that have been cooked**[2] **together,** "שֶׁנֶּאֱמַר ״לֹא תְבַשֵּׁל גְּדִי בַּחֲלֵב אִמּוֹ — as it is stated (*Exodus* 34:26): *You shall not cook a kid in the milk of it mother.*[3] וְזֶה הַכָּתוּב בָּא לֶאֱסֹר הָאֲכִילָה וְהַהֲנָאָה בְּבָשָׂר בְּחָלָב — **And** although the verse states a prohibition to cook, **this verse** actually **comes to prohibit eating or deriving** any form of **benefit from the meat-and-milk mixture.**[4]

Chinuch explains why the Torah uses the phrase "*do not cook*" in expressing this prohibition.

וְאַל יִקְשֶׁה עָלֶיךָ אִם כֵּן לָמָּה — **Now, do not find it difficult** — **that if it is so,** that this verse actually prohibits *eating,* **why** then **is [this meat-and-milk] prohibition not explicitly stated with** the phrase **"you shall not eat,"** וְהוֹצִיאוֹ בִּלְשׁוֹן בִּשּׁוּל — **and it is** instead **expressed in terms of cooking?** שֶׁהַתְּשׁוּבָה בָּזֶה — **For the answer to this is,** מִפְּנֵי שֶׁנִּתְחַדְּשָׁה אֲכִילָתוֹ מֵאִסּוּר שְׁאָר אֲכִילַת אִסּוּרִין — **because the** prohibition of **eating [this mixture] is uniquely** different **from other eating prohibitions.** שֶׁשְּׁאָר אִסּוּרִין אֵין חִיּוּבָן אֶלָּא אִם כֵּן

---

### NOTES

1. In this context, the term חָלָב, *milk,* includes not only milk, but other dairy products, such as cheese, cream, or butter.

2. See Mitzvah 92 note 2, regarding the definition of "cooked" in this context.

3. As Chinuch explained in Mitzvah 92, although the Torah states the prohibition of cooking meat and milk specifically with regard to the meat of a kid, in truth it applies to the meat of any kosher domestic animal. Similarly, it applies to dairy products of any animal from this category. This is true of the prohibition of eating and deriving benefit from the meat-and-milk mixture as well. See Chinuch below in his discussion of the laws of the mitzvah.

4. [This includes both physical enjoyment, such as warming oneself with a fire that is fueled by the mixture, and monetary gain, such as selling it to an idolater.] Although the verse refers to *cooking* the kid in milk, the Sages explain that since the Torah has previously stated that cooking meat and milk together is prohibited (*Exodus* 23:19), the repetition of the verse must be coming to teach a prohibition of eating and deriving benefit from the meat-and-milk mixture, as Chinuch will proceed to explain.

### כי תשא / מצוה קיג: שלא לאכל בשר בחלב

נֶהֱנֶה בַּאֲכִילָתָן, וְכָאן אֲפִלּוּ לֹא נֶהֱנֶה בַּאֲכִילָה מִכֵּיוָן שֶׁבְּלָעוֹ וַאֲפִלּוּ יִבְלָעֶנּוּ חַם וְשׂוֹרֵף גְּרוֹנוֹ בּוֹ וְכַיּוֹצֵא בָזֶה שֶׁאֵין לוֹ הֲנָאָה בּוֹ, מִכָּל מָקוֹם לוֹקֶה, כְּמוֹ שֶׁאָמְרוּ זִכְרוֹנָם לִבְרָכָה בְּפֶרֶק שֵׁנִי מִפְּסָחִים (דף כ״ה ע״א) לְהָכִי לֹא כָתַב רַחֲמָנָא אֲכִילָה בְּגוּפֵיהּ לְמֵימְרָא שֶׁלּוֹקִין עָלָיו שֶׁלֹּא כְּדֶרֶךְ הֲנָאָתוֹ[5]. וּמִכָּל מָקוֹם אֵין לוֹקִין עָלָיו אֶלָּא דֶּרֶךְ בִּשּׁוּל כַּלָּשׁוֹן שֶׁהוֹצִיא הַכָּתוּב אִסּוּרוֹ[6].

וְאַף עַל פִּי שֶׁאָמְרוּ זִכְרוֹנָם לִבְרָכָה (חולין דף קט״ו ע״ב) שֶׁזֶּה שֶׁנִּכְתַּב בַּתּוֹרָה אִסּוּר הַבִּשּׁוּל שָׁלֹשׁ פְּעָמִים שֶׁהוּא לְלַמֵּד אִסּוּר אֲכִילָה וְאִסּוּר בִּשּׁוּל וְאִסּוּר הֲנָאָה, אֵין רָאוּי לָנוּ לִמְנוֹת

---

נֶהֱנֶה בַּאֲכִילָתָן — **For** with regard to **other prohibitions there is no liability unless one has pleasure from eating [the prohibited foods],** וְכָאן אֲפִלּוּ לֹא נֶהֱנֶה בַּאֲכִילָה — **while here,** one is liable **even if he derives no pleasure from eating** it; מִכֵּיוָן שֶׁבְּלָעוֹ — for **by** merely **swallowing it,** וַאֲפִלּוּ יִבְלָעֶנּוּ חַם וְשׂוֹרֵף גְּרוֹנוֹ בּוֹ — **even if he swallows it when it is very hot and he scalds his throat with it,** וְכַיּוֹצֵא בָזֶה שֶׁאֵין לוֹ הֲנָאָה בּוֹ — **or in a similar manner, in which he derives no pleasure from it,** מִכָּל מָקוֹם לוֹקֶה — **he nevertheless incurs** *malkus* (lashes), כְּמוֹ שֶׁאָמְרוּ זִכְרוֹנָם לִבְרָכָה בְּפֶרֶק שֵׁנִי מִפְּסָחִים — **as** [the Sages], of blessed memory, **said in the second chapter of** Tractate *Pesachim* (25a). לְהָכִי לֹא כָתַב רַחֲמָנָא אֲכִילָה בְּגוּפֵיהּ — **It is for this reason that the Torah did not write "eating" with regard to [this prohibition];** לְמֵימְרָא שֶׁלּוֹקִין עָלָיו שֶׁלֹּא כְּדֶרֶךְ הֲנָאָתוֹ — that is, it omitted this term **in order to indicate that one incurs** *malkus* for consuming **[this mixture]** even if its consumption was **not in the manner that it provides benefit.**[5] וּמִכָּל מָקוֹם אֵין לוֹקִין עָלָיו אֶלָּא דֶּרֶךְ בִּשּׁוּל — **Nevertheless, one does not incur** *malkus* for eating it **unless** the meat-and-milk mixture came about **through cooking,** כַּלָּשׁוֹן שֶׁהוֹצִיא הַכָּתוּב אִסּוּרוֹ — **as is** indicated from **the terminology through which Scripture expressed the prohibition —** *you shall not "cook."*[6]

Chinuch goes on to discuss the prohibition of deriving benefit from the meat-and-milk mixture, and whether that should be counted as an additional prohibition:

וְאַף עַל פִּי שֶׁאָמְרוּ זִכְרוֹנָם לִבְרָכָה — **Now, although [the Sages], of blessed memory, have stated** (*Chullin* 115b) שֶׁזֶּה שֶׁנִּכְתַּב בַּתּוֹרָה אִסּוּר הַבִּשּׁוּל שָׁלֹשׁ פְּעָמִים — **that [the reason] the prohibition of cooking** meat and milk together **was written in the Torah three times** שֶׁהוּא לְלַמֵּד אִסּוּר אֲכִילָה וְאִסּוּר בִּשּׁוּל וְאִסּוּר הֲנָאָה — **is to teach** that there is **a prohibition of eating, a prohibition of cooking, and a prohibition of deriving benefit** from this mixture, אֵין רָאוּי לָנוּ לִמְנוֹת

---

#### NOTES

5. Had the Torah expressed the commandment by referring to a prohibition of "eating," that would have implied that this prohibition is subject to the standard laws that pertain to prohibitions of eating. Thus, if one ate the meat-and-milk mixture in a manner that does not give pleasure, such as when it was scalding hot or the like, he would not bear any liability. By expressing this prohibition in an atypical manner, the Torah teaches that it is not subject to the standard laws. [See Mitzvah 92, at notes 8-9, where Chinuch discusses the underlying reason for this uniqueness.]

6. The use of the term "cook" teaches us that the prohibition applies only if the mixture was cooked. It does not apply (on a Biblical level) if the meat-and-milk mixture was created in any manner other than being cooked together (such as if the meat and milk were soaked or salted together for an extended period). [Nevertheless, the Sages prohibited eating all mixtures of meat and dairy no matter how they came about.]

[Chinuch wrote earlier that by not expressing the prohibition with the term "eat" (addressing instead *cooking* meat and milk), the Torah indicates that if one ate the meat-and-milk mixture in a manner that does not give pleasure, he nevertheless would be subject to the prohibition (see previous note). Here, Chinuch explains that the verse refers to *cooking* in order to indicate that the Biblical prohibition applies only where the meat and dairy were cooked together. Apparently, although, as a rule, we can derive only one exegesis from the Torah's use of one term over another, nevertheless, here, the Torah could have expressed the prohibition without referring specifically to cooking. Thus, by not expressing the prohibition with the term "eating," the Torah indicates that the prohibition applies even if one ate the meat-and-milk mixture in a manner that does not give pleasure, while by using the term "cook" (rather than some other term), the Torah indicates that the Biblical prohibition applies only if the mixture was cooked (see *Sfas Emes, Pesachim* 25a; cf. *Aruch HaShulchan, Yoreh Deah* 87:5-6).]

## KI SISA / MITZVAH 113: NOT TO EAT A MIXTURE OF MEAT AND MILK

בְּחֶשְׁבּוֹן הַלָּאוִין אֶלָּא הַשְּׁנַיִם, לְפִי שֶׁאִסוּר אֲכִילָה וַהֲנָאָה דָּבָר אֶחָד הוּא, וּכְמוֹ שֶׁאָמְרוּ זִכְרוֹנָם לִבְרָכָה (פסחים דף כ״א ע״ב), כָּל מָקוֹם שֶׁנֶּאֱמַר לֹא תֹאכַל, לֹא תֹאכְלוּ, אֶחָד אִסּוּר אֲכִילָה וְאֶחָד אִסּוּר הֲנָאָה בְּמַשְׁמָע, כִּי הַתּוֹרָה תּוֹצִיא כָּל הַהֲנָאוֹת דֶּרֶךְ כְּלָל בִּלְשׁוֹן אֲכִילָה לְפִי שֶׁהִיא הֲנָאָה תְּמִידִית לָאָדָם וְצָרִיךְ אֵלֶיהָ, וּכְעִנְיָן שֶׁכָּתוּב (שמות כ״ד, י״א) וַיֶּחֱזוּ אֶת הָאֱלֹהִים וַיֹּאכְלוּ וַיִּשְׁתּוּ, שֶׁכִּנָּה הַהֲנָאָה לַאֲכִילָה.⁸

וְאִם תִּתְפַּשׁ עָלַי, אִם כֵּן לָמָּה נִכְתְּבוּ שְׁלֹשָׁה לָאוִין, דִּשְׁנַיִם יַסְפִּיקוּ לְפִי זֶה שֶׁאָמַרְתִּי, יֵשׁ לַהֲשִׁיבְךָ דְוַדַּאי אִם נִכְתַּב בְּמָקוֹם אֶחָד לֹא תְבַשֵּׁל שֶׁיְּלַמֵּד עַל אִסוּר בִּשּׁוּל, וּבְמָקוֹם אַחֵר לֹא תֹאכַל, שֶׁיִּכְלֹל אִסּוּר הֲנָאָה וַאֲכִילָה כְּמוֹ שֶׁאָמַרְנוּ, הָיָה בַּדִּין שֶׁלֹּא יִכְתֹּב הַשְּׁלִישִׁי, שֶׁאֵין צֹרֶךְ עוֹד בּוֹ, שֶׁכְּבָר הָיִינוּ לְמֵדִים אֲכִילָה וַהֲנָאָה בְּלֹא תֹאכַל,

---

בְּחֶשְׁבּוֹן הַלָּאוִין אֶלָּא הַשְּׁנַיִם — nevertheless, **it is appropriate for us to count only two** of them (i.e., cooking and eating) **in the tally of the mitzvah-prohibitions.** לְפִי שֶׁאִסוּר אֲכִילָה וַהֲנָאָה דָּבָר אֶחָד הוּא — **This is because the prohibitions of eating and deriving benefit are one and the same thing,** וּכְמוֹ שֶׁאָמְרוּ זִכְרוֹנָם לִבְרָכָה — **as [the Sages], of blessed memory, have stated** (*Pesachim* 21b): כָּל מָקוֹם שֶׁנֶּאֱמַר "לֹא תֹאכַל" "לֹא תֹאכְלוּ" — **Wherever it is stated** in the Torah, *you* (singular) *shall not eat* or *you* (plural) *shall not eat*, אֶחָד אִסּוּר אֲכִילָה וְאֶחָד אִסּוּר הֲנָאָה בְּמַשְׁמָע — it **denotes both a prohibition of eating and a prohibition of deriving benefit.** כִּי הַתּוֹרָה תּוֹצִיא כָּל הַהֲנָאוֹת דֶּרֶךְ כְּלָל בִּלְשׁוֹן אֲכִילָה — **For the Torah generally expresses all forms of benefit with the term "eating,"** לְפִי שֶׁהִיא הֲנָאָה תְּמִידִית לָאָדָם וְצָרִיךְ אֵלֶיהָ — **because [eating] is a source of constant benefit to man and** is something **that he always needs.**[7] וּכְעִנְיָן שֶׁכָּתוּב — This is **along the lines of that which is written** (*Exodus* 24:11): "וַיֶּחֱזוּ אֶת הָאֱלֹהִים וַיֹּאכְלוּ וַיִּשְׁתּוּ" — **and they gazed at God, and they ate and they drank,** שֶׁכִּנָּה הַהֲנָאָה לַאֲכִילָה — **where [the verse] employs** the term **"eat"** as an expression **for** other forms of **benefit.**[8] Thus, when the Torah expresses the prohibition of eating, the prohibition is not limited to eating, but includes other forms of benefit as well. Accordingly, the prohibitions of eating and deriving benefit cannot be counted as distinct mitzvos.

Chinuch addresses an obvious difficulty:

וְאִם תִּתְפַּשׂ עָלַי — **If you will challenge me,** by asking, אִם כֵּן לָמָּה נִכְתְּבוּ שְׁלֹשָׁה לָאוִין — "**If so, why were three prohibitory** verses **written,** דִּשְׁנַיִם יַסְפִּיקוּ לְפִי זֶה שֶׁאָמַרְתִּי — **when two verses would suffice,"** according to what I have said, that the prohibition of eating includes a prohibition on other forms of benefit as well, יֵשׁ לַהֲשִׁיבְךָ — **the following response may be offered to you:** דְוַדַּאי אִם נִכְתַּב בְּמָקוֹם אֶחָד לֹא תְבַשֵּׁל שֶׁיְּלַמֵּד עַל אִסוּר בִּשּׁוּל — **Certainly, if in one place it would have been written "you shall not cook,"** which would teach the prohibition of cooking meat and milk together, וּבְמָקוֹם אַחֵר לֹא תֹאכַל שֶׁיִּכְלֹל אִסוּר הֲנָאָה וַאֲכִילָה כְּמוֹ שֶׁאָמַרְנוּ — **and in another place** the Torah would have stated **"you shall not eat,"** which would encompass both **a prohibition of deriving benefit** from the meat-and-milk mixture **and** a prohibition of **eating it, as we have said,** הָיָה בַּדִּין שֶׁלֹּא יִכְתֹּב הַשְּׁלִישִׁי — **it would have been correct that [the Torah] not write the third** prohibition. שֶׁאֵין צֹרֶךְ עוֹד בּוֹ — **For** in that case **there would be no further need for it,** שֶׁכְּבָר הָיִינוּ לְמֵדִים אֲכִילָה וַהֲנָאָה בְּלֹא תֹאכַל — **as we would have already learned** that both **eating and deriving** other forms of **benefit** are prohibited **from** the verse **"you shall not eat,"**

---

### NOTES

7. The Gemara thus derives that when the Torah expresses a prohibition of eating, it is intended not only as a prohibition of eating but of any other form of benefit as well. [This rule, however, has numerous exceptions, with few, if any, applications in other cases (see Gemara there).] Chinuch will proceed to explain why a separate verse is needed to teach that it is prohibited to derive benefit from meat-and-milk, once the verse teaches that *eating* (which by extension includes having benefit) of meat-and-milk is prohibited.

8. This verse, which speaks of the Divine Revelation at Mount Sinai, describes the experience of the Elders as they took in the vision, as "eating and drinking" (see *Onkelos* and *Targum Yonasan*). This is an example of how the Torah describes even the most sublime form of pleasure in terms of "eating and drinking."

מִן הַכְּלָל שֶׁבְּיָדֵינוּ דְּבִכְלַל אֲכִילָה הֲנָאָה בְּמַשְׁמָע, אֲבָל עַכְשָׁו שֶׁלֹּא הִזְכִּירָהּ בּוֹ אֲכִילָה בְּשׁוּם מָקוֹם, לֹא הָיִינוּ לְמֵדִים הַהֲנָאָה אֶלָּא עִם הַלָּאו הַשְּׁלִישִׁי[9]. וְאֵין לְךָ לִשְׁאֹל עוֹד, וְלָמָּה לֹא כָּתַב רַחֲמָנָא לֹא תֹאכַל מֵהֶם בְּאֶחָד וְיַסְפִּיק בִּשְׁנַיִם, שֶׁכְּבָר הוֹדַעְתִּיךָ כִּי לְעִנְיָן נִצְטָרֵךְ שֶׁלֹּא יַזְכִּיר בּוֹ הַכָּתוּב לְשׁוֹן אֲכִילָה, מִפְּנֵי שֶׁהַחִיּוּב בּוֹ אֲפִלּוּ שֶׁלֹּא כְּדֶרֶךְ הֲנָאָתוֹ[10]. לָמַדְנוּ מֵעַתָּה כִּי מַה שֶּׁאָמְרוּ זִכְרוֹנָם לִבְרָכָה חַד לְאִסּוּר אֲכִילָה וְחַד לְאִסּוּר הֲנָאָה וְחַד לְאִסּוּר בִּשּׁוּל, אֵין הַכַּוָּנָה בָּהֶם שֶׁיִּהְיֶה נֶחְשָׁב הַכָּתוּב הַשְּׁלִישִׁי לְלָאו אַחֵר, אֶלָּא שֶׁנִּצְטָרֵךְ לִלְמֹד מִמֶּנּוּ הֲנָאָה.

מִן הַכְּלָל שֶׁבְּיָדֵינוּ דְּבִכְלַל אֲכִילָה הֲנָאָה בְּמַשְׁמָע — on the basis of the accepted principle that included in "eating" is all forms of benefit. אֲבָל עַכְשָׁו שֶׁלֹּא הִזְכִּירָהּ בּוֹ אֲכִילָה בְּשׁוּם מָקוֹם — But now that the term "eating" is not mentioned anywhere with regard to this prohibition, לֹא הָיִינוּ לְמֵדִים הַהֲנָאָה אֶלָּא עִם הַלָּאו הַשְּׁלִישִׁי — we would not derive the prohibition of deriving benefit if not for the third prohibition.[9] וְאֵין לְךָ לִשְׁאֹל עוֹד — And you cannot ask further: וְלָמָּה לֹא כָּתַב רַחֲמָנָא לֹא תֹאכַל מֵהֶם בְּאֶחָד — Why did the Torah not write "do not eat" in one of [the verses] instead of *you shall not cook...*, which would teach that deriving benefit is also prohibited, וְיַסְפִּיק בִּשְׁנַיִם — and thus suffice with two verses to express the prohibitions of the meat-and-milk mixture? שֶׁכְּבָר הוֹדַעְתִּיךָ — For I have already informed you כִּי לְעִנְיָן נִצְטָרֵךְ שֶׁלֹּא יַזְכִּיר בּוֹ הַכָּתוּב לְשׁוֹן אֲכִילָה — that there is a reason why it was necessary for Scripture not to mention the term "eating" with regard to [this prohibition]; מִפְּנֵי שֶׁהַחִיּוּב בּוֹ אֲפִלּוּ שֶׁלֹּא כְּדֶרֶךְ הֲנָאָתוֹ — that is, because the Torah wishes to convey that [this prohibition's] liability applies even if its consumption was not in its manner of providing benefit.[10] In summary: All three verses are necessary to teach the three prohibited acts: cooking, eating, and deriving benefit. Had the Torah stated only twice that one may not cook meat with milk, we would not have known that the mixture is prohibited for benefit, for the prohibition of eating derived from the term "You shall not cook" does not include deriving benefit. Had the Torah written two verses, and specifically stated in one of them "You shall not cook," the prohibition of deriving benefit would be included, but we would not know that eating in a manner that does not give pleasure is prohibited. Therefore, the Torah stated *You shall not cook ...* three times.

Chinuch returns to his original discussion — why the three verses regarding the meat-and-milk mixture are counted as only two mitzvos:

כִּי מַה שֶּׁאָמְרוּ זִכְרוֹנָם לִבְרָכָה חַד לְאִסּוּר אֲכִילָה וְחַד לְאִסּוּר — **Thus we have learned** לָמַדְנוּ מֵעַתָּה הֲנָאָה וְחַד לְאִסּוּר בִּשּׁוּל — that when [the Sages], of blessed memory, said that **one** of the verses serves as a source **for a prohibition of eating, one for a prohibition of deriving benefit, and one for a prohibition of cooking,** אֵין הַכַּוָּנָה בָּהֶם שֶׁיִּהְיֶה נֶחְשָׁב הַכָּתוּב הַשְּׁלִישִׁי לְלָאו אַחֵר — the **intent** with the repetition of [these verses] **was not** in order **that the third verse be considered a separate prohibition.** אֶלָּא שֶׁנִּצְטָרֵךְ לִלְמֹד מִמֶּנּוּ הֲנָאָה — **Rather,** the intent was **that** [the third verse] is needed so that we can **learn from it** a prohibition with regard to **deriving benefit.** That is, although the fact that both eating and deriving benefit are prohibited is derived from separate verses, nevertheless, due to the unique relationship between the two (i.e., eating and deriving benefit), once the

---

NOTES

9. That is, although the term "eating" is used by the Torah as a reference to all forms of benefit, that is only when the Torah specifies eating. Here, however, although the second appearance of the verse "*Do not cook ...*" can only be understood as a prohibition of eating the meat-and-milk mixture, nevertheless, since the actual term "eating" is never used, we would not know that other forms of benefit are also prohibited, and we would have assumed that, as with many other prohibitions, the prohibition here is limited to eating. It is therefore necessary for the Torah to write a third verse, to teach the prohibition of deriving benefit from the meat-and-milk mixture.

10. The Torah refrained from explicitly expressing a prohibition of "eating" the meat-and-milk mixture, in order to convey the law that one is liable for consuming it in any manner, even if it does not provide any pleasure. Therefore, since the Torah refrained from stating "do not eat," there is a need for a third appearance of this prohibition, to teach that it extends to other forms of benefit as well.

# KI SISA / MITZVAH 113: NOT TO EAT A MIXTURE OF MEAT AND MILK

וּבָרוּךְ שֶׁבָּחַר בְּדִבְרֵיהֶם.[11]

מִשָּׁרְשֵׁי הַמִּצְוָה, כָּתַבְנוּ בְּאִסּוּר הַבִּשּׁוּל בְּפָרָשַׁת וְאֵלֶּה הַמִּשְׁפָּטִים, עַל צַד הַפְּשָׁט מַה שֶּׁיָּכֹלְנוּ.[12]

מִדִּינֵי הַמִּצְוָה, מַה שֶּׁאָמְרוּ זִכְרוֹנָם לִבְרָכָה (חולין דף קי"ג ע"א) שֶׁאֵין אָסוּר בָּשָׂר בְּחָלָב מִן הַתּוֹרָה אֶלָּא בִּבְשַׂר בְּהֵמָה טְהוֹרָה אֲבָל לֹא בִּבְהֵמָה טְמֵאָה[13] וְלֹא בְּחַיָּה אֲפִלּוּ טְהוֹרָה,[14]

---

Torah teaches, by writing an additional verse, that deriving benefit from the meat-and-milk mixture is prohibited, we understand that the prohibition to derive benefit is an extension of the prohibition to eat the mixture.

Having explained the Sages' understanding of the puzzling repetition of the verses of our mitzvah, Chinuch concludes with praise to God for endowing the Sages with the wisdom to interpret the words of the Torah:

וּבָרוּךְ שֶׁבָּחַר בְּדִבְרֵיהֶם — **Blessed is** God, **Who chose the words of [the Sages]!**[11]

### ☙ Underlying Purpose of the Mitzvah ☙

מִשָּׁרְשֵׁי הַמִּצְוָה כָּתַבְנוּ בְּאִסּוּר הַבִּשּׁוּל — **We have written** some **of the underlying purposes of this mitzvah** above, **in** the mitzvah pertaining to **the prohibition of cooking** meat and milk together, בְּפָרָשַׁת וְאֵלֶּה הַמִּשְׁפָּטִים — **set forth in** *Parashas Mishpatim* [Mitzvah 92]; עַל צַד הַפְּשָׁט מַה שֶּׁיָּכֹלְנוּ — that is, **what we were able to** attain **on a simple level.**[12]

### ☙ Laws of the Mitzvah ☙

מִדִּינֵי הַמִּצְוָה — **Among the laws of this mitzvah** are laws pertaining to the type of meat included in the prohibition.

Chinuch explained in Mitzvah 92 that the prohibition of cooking meat and milk together, although expressed in the verse with regard to the meat of a kid, is not limited to such meat. The same applies with regard to the prohibition of this mitzvah. Chinuch discusses the types of meat included:

מַה שֶּׁאָמְרוּ זִכְרוֹנָם לִבְרָכָה — **The laws include that which [the Sages], of blessed memory, said** (*Chullin* 113a-b), שֶׁאֵין אָסוּר בָּשָׂר בְּחָלָב מִן הַתּוֹרָה אֶלָּא בִּבְשַׂר בְּהֵמָה טְהוֹרָה — **that the Biblical prohibition with regard to the meat-and-milk mixture applies only to the meat of a kosher domestic animal.** אֲבָל לֹא בִּבְהֵמָה טְמֵאָה — **It does not, however,** apply **to** the meat of **a nonkosher animal,**[13] וְלֹא בְּחַיָּה אֲפִלּוּ טְהוֹרָה — **nor to** the meat of **even a kosher non-domestic animal,**[14]

---

### NOTES

11. Chinuch here paraphrases *Avos* 6:1.

12. There, Chinuch indicates that meat and dairy represent disparate forces of nature, and that the unnatural blending of nature's distinct forces is detrimental to the world and its inhabitants. The Torah therefore prohibited producing this blend, and, to further safeguard against its production, even prohibited eating or deriving benefit from it. Nevertheless, Chinuch there adds that proper understanding of the purpose of this mitzvah can be attained only by those versed in the study of *Kabbalah*.

13. Obviously, this has no practical ramification with regard to the permissibility of eating the mixture in its normal manner, as the mixture may in any case not be eaten since it contains meat of a nonkosher animal. It would, however, have pertinence with regard to cooking or having benefit from such a mixture, and there is thus no Biblical prohibition of cooking or having benefit from a mixture of meat of a nonkosher animal and milk. [Cooking such a mixture may nevertheless be Rabbinically prohibited; see *Rama, Yoreh Deah* 87:4.]

[For this reason, one may purchase and use pet food that contains milk that was cooked together with meat of a nonkosher animal (e.g., horse or pig). Nevertheless, many authorities maintain that while meat of a nonkosher animal is not subject to the meat-and-milk prohibition, meat of a kosher animal that was not slaughtered with *shechitah* (ritual slaughter), and is thus prohibited to be eaten, is nevertheless subject to the meat-and-milk prohibition, and one may thus not have benefit from a mixture of such meat cooked with milk; see *Pischei Teshuvah, Yoreh Deah* 87:6.]

14. Similarly, the Biblical prohibition applies only to cooking meat in the milk of a kosher domestic animal, not to cooking meat (even of a kosher domestic animal) in milk of a nonkosher or non-domestic animal (*Rambam*,

וְלֹא בְּעוֹף בֵּין טָהוֹר בֵּין טָמֵא, וְנִסְמְכוּ בָזֶה בְּמַה שֶּׁכָּתוּב שָׁלֹשׁ פְּעָמִים בַּתּוֹרָה גְּדִי שֶׁהוּא לָשׁוֹן מְחֻדָּשׁ, שֶׁהָיָה לוֹ לִכְתֹּב בָּשָׂר. וּבָא הַפֵּרוּשׁ עַל זֶה[15], גְּדִי וְלֹא בְהֵמָה טְמֵאָה, גְּדִי וְלֹא חַיָּה[16], גְּדִי וְלֹא עוֹף, וּלְפִיכָךְ[17] אָמְרוּ זִכְרוֹנָם לִבְרָכָה כִּי שְׁלֹשָׁה אֵלֶּה מֻתָּר לְבַשְּׁלָם בְּחָלָב[18] וּמֻתָּרִים בַּהֲנָאָה, אֲבָל בַּאֲכִילָה[19] אָסְרוּם זִכְרוֹנָם לִבְרָכָה לִגְדֹּר בְּשַׂר בְּהֵמָה שֶׁאִסּוּרוֹ דְּבַר תּוֹרָה, כְּדֵי שֶׁלֹּא יִתְחַלֵּף לִבְנֵי אָדָם בָּשָׂר בְּבָשָׂר[20],

---

וְלֹא בְּעוֹף בֵּין טָהוֹר בֵּין טָמֵא — **nor to** the meat of **fowl, regardless of whether kosher or nonkosher.** וְנִסְמְכוּ בָזֶה בְּמַה שֶּׁכָּתוּב שָׁלֹשׁ פְּעָמִים בַּתּוֹרָה גְּדִי — **[The Sages] drew support** for this position **from the fact that** the specific term **"a kid"** (gedi) **is written in the Torah three times** with respect to the prohibitions pertaining to meat-and-milk, once in each of the three appearances of the verse *"You shall not cook a kid in the milk of its mother,"* שֶׁהָיָה לוֹ לִכְתֹּב, **for this term is unique,** שֶׁהוּא לָשׁוֹן מְחֻדָּשׁ — וּבָא הַפֵּרוּשׁ עַל זֶה — **as** [the Torah] **should have written** the more general term, **"meat." And the explanation of this, as transmitted** to us by the Sages, is that each appearance of the term "kid" indicates an exception to the meat-and-milk prohibitions:[15] גְּדִי וְלֹא בְהֵמָה טְמֵאָה — **One mention** of the term "kid" teaches that the prohibitions apply to meat of a kosher animal such as **a kid, but not to a nonkosher animal;** גְּדִי וְלֹא חַיָּה — another mention of the term "kid" teaches that the prohibitions apply to a domestic animal such as **a kid, but not to a non-domestic animal;**[16] גְּדִי וְלֹא עוֹף — and the third mention of the term teaches that the prohibitions apply to an animal such as **a kid, but not to fowl.**

Although the Torah entirely excludes the meat of the aforementioned animals from the meat-and-milk prohibitions, the Sages did include it with respect to certain restrictions.[17] Chinuch explains: וּלְפִיכָךְ אָמְרוּ זִכְרוֹנָם לִבְרָכָה — **In accordance with this** exegesis, **[the Sages], of blessed memory, said** כִּי שְׁלֹשָׁה אֵלֶּה מֻתָּר לְבַשְּׁלָם בְּחָלָב — **that it is permitted to cook these three** types of meat (i.e., that of nonkosher animals, of non-domestic animals, and of fowl) **with milk,**[18] וּמֻתָּרִים בַּהֲנָאָה — **and** that **it is permitted to derive benefit from [the mixture].** אֲבָל בַּאֲכִילָה — **However, with regard to eating** a mixture of meat of non-domestic animals or of fowl with milk,[19] אָסְרוּם זִכְרוֹנָם לִבְרָכָה — **[the Sages] prohibited [those mixtures],** לִגְדֹּר בְּשַׂר בְּהֵמָה שֶׁאִסּוּרוֹ דְּבַר תּוֹרָה — **as a safeguard** (i.e., a distancing measure) so that one not come to eat a mixture that contains **the meat of a domestic animal, whose** meat-and-milk **prohibition is of Biblical origin.** כְּדֵי שֶׁלֹּא יִתְחַלֵּף לִבְנֵי אָדָם בָּשָׂר בְּבָשָׂר — That is, **so that people should not confuse** one type of **meat** (i.e., that of a domestic animal), which may *not* be cooked with milk, **with** another type of **meat** (i.e., that of a non-domestic animal or fowl), which may be cooked with milk. In order to avoid such confusion, the Sages prohibited eating even a mixture of meat of non-domestic animals or of fowl cooked with milk.[20]

---

### NOTES

*Hil. Maachalos Asuros* 9:3). [See *Rama* ibid. with regard to whether this is permitted on the Rabbinic level.]

15. As noted by Chinuch in Mitzvah 92, the Gemara explains that while the term גְּדִי, *gedi*, is commonly used when referring to a young goat, in truth, the term can be used in reference to other animals as well. Thus, the meat-and-milk prohibitions apply not just to the meat of a kid, but also to the meat of other animals. The question, however, arises: If all meat is included in these prohibitions, why does the Torah specify the meat of a kid? The Gemara answers that this is to limit the prohibitions; that is, to teach that they apply only to meat that is similar to the meat of a kid, as Chinuch proceeds to explain.

16. The class of חַיָּה, *chayah*, which we have rendered as "non-domestic animal," includes animals such as deer (as opposed to בְּהֵמָה, *beheimah*, "domestic animal," which refers to animals such as cattle and sheep).

17. The prohibition of eating the meat-and-milk mixture is unique, for, when taken alone, each component of the mixture is permitted. Thus, since people always partake separately of meat and dairy, the Sages were concerned that they would inadvertently allow them to become mixed together and would even come to eat the mixture. They therefore imposed numerous safeguards for this prohibition, some of which Chinuch mentions below (see *Shach, Yoreh Deah* 88:2).

18. See *Rama, Yoreh Deah* 87:4 with *Taz* and other commentaries.

19. Chinuch is obviously not discussing the first type of meat discussed above (that of a nonkosher animal), for eating a mixture of meat of a nonkosher animal cooked with milk is prohibited in any case due to the prohibition of eating nonkosher meat (see *Shach, Yoreh Deah* 87:2; cf. *Bach* there).

20. The Sages were concerned that if the meat of

## 363 ❑ KI SISA / MITZVAH 113: NOT TO EAT A MIXTURE OF MEAT AND MILK

וּלְפִיכָךְ, מִפְּנֵי שֶׁהַדָּבָר קָרוֹב שֶׁבָּשָׂר בְּבָשָׂר מִתְחַלֵּף, הֶחֱמִירוּ גַּם בִּגְדֵר זֶה כְּמוֹ שֶׁהֶחֱמִירוּ בִּבְשַׂר הַבְּהֵמָה מַמָּשׁ בִּקְצָת עִנְיָנִים, שֶׁאָסְרוּ בָּהֶם שֶׁלֹּא לְהַעֲלוֹתָם עַל הַשֻּׁלְחָן כְּלָל.[21] וּלְפִי דַעַת קְצָת מִן הַמְפָרְשִׁים חִיְּבוּ בָּהֶם גַּם כֵּן שְׁהִיָּה בֵּין אֲכִילָתָם לַאֲכִילַת הַגְּבִינָה, כְּמוֹ בְּעִקַּר הָאִסּוּר, דְּהַיְנוּ בְּשַׂר בְּהֵמָה,[22] אֲבָל בִּבְשַׂר דָּגִים וַחֲגָבִים[23] לֹא גָדְרוּ בָּהֶם כְּלָל,

---

This stringency is taken yet further:

וּלְפִיכָךְ — **And due to this** concern, מִפְּנֵי שֶׁהַדָּבָר קָרוֹב שֶׁבָּשָׂר בְּבָשָׂר מִתְחַלֵּף — that is, **since it is a likely matter for** one type of **meat to be confused with** another type of meat, הֶחֱמִירוּ גַּם בִּגְדֵר זֶה — **they were additionally stringent with regard to this safeguard,** prohibiting eating meat of non-domestic animals or fowl with milk, כְּמוֹ שֶׁהֶחֱמִירוּ בִּבְשַׂר הַבְּהֵמָה מַמָּשׁ בִּקְצָת עִנְיָנִים — **in the very same manner as they were stringent with regard to the meat of a domestic animal** that is included in the Biblical prohibition, **with regard to certain matters.** That is, although the actual mixture is only Rabbinically prohibited, nevertheless, certain safeguards that the Sages applied to a meat of domestic animals (which is Biblically subject to the prohibition), were also applied to meat of non-domestic animals or fowl (which is Rabbinically prohibited to be mixed with milk), as follows: שֶׁאָסְרוּ בָּהֶם שֶׁלֹּא לְהַעֲלוֹתָם עַל הַשֻּׁלְחָן כְּלָל — **That is, they prohibited even placing [the meat]** of animals that are not subject to the Biblical prohibition **upon a table** together with dairy, just as they prohibited this with regard to the meat of a kosher domestic animal.[21] וּלְפִי דַעַת קְצָת מִן הַמְפָרְשִׁים חִיְּבוּ בָּהֶם גַּם כֵּן שְׁהִיָּה בֵּין אֲכִילָתָם לַאֲכִילַת הַגְּבִינָה — **Furthermore, in the opinion of some commentators, [the Sages] also mandated a waiting period between eating [the meat]** of animals that are not subject to the Biblical prohibition **and eating cheese** or other dairy, כְּמוֹ בְּעִקַּר הָאִסּוּר — **just as** they required a waiting period **in the** case of the **actual** (i.e., Biblical) **prohibition,** דְּהַיְנוּ בְּשַׂר בְּהֵמָה — **that is,** after eating **the meat of a** kosher domestic **animal.**[22] לֹא גָדְרוּ בָּהֶם כְּלָל — **But as for the meat of fish and grasshoppers,**[23] אֲבָל בִּבְשַׂר דָּגִים וַחֲגָבִים —

---

### NOTES

non-domestic animals or of fowl would be eaten with dairy, this could result in someone mistakenly eating even meat of a domestic animal that had been cooked with dairy. Therefore, the Sages imposed a prohibition on it (see also *Rambam, Hil. Maachalos Asuros* 9:4).

21. The Sages did not allow meat of a kosher domestic animal to be present on the table upon which one is eating dairy, and vice-versa. They extended this stringency even to fowl or meat of a non-domestic animal, despite the fact that these are not governed by the Biblical prohibition. [The Sages generally did not create safeguards for Rabbinic prohibitions, as this would be deemed a גְּזֵירָה לִגְזֵירָה, "safeguard to a safeguard." In this case, however, due to the very great possibility of confusion between the various types of meat, they extended their decree even to meat of non-domestic animals and fowl. For further discussion of why this (and the following) multi-layered safeguard is not considered a גְּזֵירָה לִגְזֵירָה, see *Chullin* 104a-b with *Toras Chaim* and *Rosh Yosef; Lechem Mishneh, Hil. Maachalos Asuros* 9:20.]

22. As Chinuch explained above, the Biblical meat-and-milk prohibition applies only where the meat and dairy were cooked together. However, the Sages prohibited eating any meat and dairy together, and required a cleansing procedure, and at times, a waiting period, between eating one and the other. According to the authorities cited by Chinuch here, these prohibitions and requirements apply even after partaking of the meat of non-domestic animals and fowl, despite the fact that they are not governed by the Biblical meat-and-milk prohibition.

Nowadays, most communities refrain from eating dairy for six hours after eating meat, whether of domestic or non-domestic animals or of fowl, and refrain from eating meat after a dairy meal without thoroughly cleaning and rinsing the mouth and ensuring that no dairy residue remains upon the hands (see *Rambam, Hil. Maachalos Asuros* 9:26-28; *Yoreh Deah* 89:1-2 with commentaries). Additionally, it is customary among Ashkenazic Jews to wait six hours before eating meat after eating certain types of hard cheese (see *Rama, Yoreh Deah* 89:2).

23. The Torah permits the consumption of grasshoppers that display certain features; see Mitzvah 158. [As will be noted there, due to a lack of tradition with regard to which species are permissible, most communities do not permit the consumption of grasshoppers, even when they exhibit the permissible features.]

# 364 ❏ כי תשא / מצוה קיג: שלא לאכל בשר בחלב

שֶׁאֵין בְּשָׂרָם דּוֹמֶה כְּלָל לַבָּשָׂר בַּבְּהֵמָה וְלֹא יָבוֹאוּ בְּנֵי אָדָם לִטְעוֹת בָּזֶה.
וְעוֹד[25,24] הֶחְמִירוּ בְּעִנְיָן זֶה שֶׁאָמְרוּ גַּם כֵּן שֶׁיֵּשׁ אִסּוּר מְחֻדָּשׁ בָּהּ יוֹתֵר מִשְּׁאָר אִסּוּרֵי מַאֲכָלוֹת לְפִי קְצָת מִן הַפֵּרוּשִׁים, שֶׁבְּעִנְיָנֵנוּ בָּשָׂר בְּחָלָב אִם נִתְעָרֵב חָלָב עִם הַבָּשָׂר וְאֵין בַּחֲתִיכַת הַבָּשָׂר שֶׁנִּתְעָרֵב בּוֹ שִׁשִּׁים כְּנֶגֶד הֶחָלָב, אָנוּ רוֹאִים שְׁנֵיהֶם כַּחֲתִיכַת אִסּוּר, וְאִם נָפְלָה אוֹתָהּ חֲתִיכָה בִּקְדֵרַת בָּשָׂר אוֹ בִּקְדֵרַת חָלָב, מְשַׁעֲרִין בְּכֻלָּהּ, וְזֶהוּ אָמְרָם זִכְרוֹנָם לִבְרָכָה

---

שֶׁאֵין בְּשָׂרָם דּוֹמֶה כְּלָל לַבָּשָׂר — [the Sages] did not create any safeguard at all prohibiting them, בַּבְּהֵמָה — for their flesh is not at all similar to the flesh of an animal, וְלֹא יָבוֹאוּ בְּנֵי אָדָם לִטְעוֹת בָּזֶה — and people would not come to err because of it. Therefore, one may eat kosher fish or grasshoppers cooked in milk.

The presence of any prohibited food in a mixture may cause the entire mixture to become prohibited.[24] However, in many instances, the halachah is that if there are sixty units of permitted food per unit of prohibited matter, the prohibited item does not impart flavor to the mixture, and does not effect a prohibition upon the permitted food. Similarly, if dairy falls into a meat soup and there are sixty units of soup that correspond to the dairy (or if meat falls into a dairy soup that contains sixty units of the size of the meat), the flavor of the dairy (or meat) is nullified and the mixture is permitted.[25] Chinuch sets forth an additional stringency that applies to the meat-and-milk prohibition, which relates to the law of nullification (*bitul*):

וְעוֹד הֶחְמִירוּ בְּעִנְיָן זֶה — [The Sages] imposed a further stringency with regard to this matter of meat-and-milk mixtures, שֶׁאָמְרוּ גַּם כֵּן שֶׁיֵּשׁ אִסּוּר מְחֻדָּשׁ בָּהּ — as they also said that [the meat-and-milk mixture] contains a unique prohibition, יוֹתֵר מִשְּׁאָר אִסּוּרֵי מַאֲכָלוֹת לְפִי קְצָת מִן הַפֵּרוּשִׁים — which, according to some commentaries, prohibits more than with regard to other prohibited foods. שֶׁבְּעִנְיָנֵנוּ בָּשָׂר בְּחָלָב — For, in the matter of the meat-and-milk prohibition, אִם נִתְעָרֵב חָלָב עִם הַבָּשָׂר וְאֵין בַּחֲתִיכַת הַבָּשָׂר שֶׁנִּתְעָרֵב בּוֹ — if milk became mixed into meat, שִׁשִּׁים כְּנֶגֶד הֶחָלָב — and the piece of meat into which [the milk] was mixed does not contain sixty times the volume of the milk that has fallen into it, אָנוּ רוֹאִים שְׁנֵיהֶם כַּחֲתִיכַת אִסּוּר — we view the entire mixture comprised of both [the milk and meat] as being a piece of forbidden food. וְאִם נָפְלָה אוֹתָהּ חֲתִיכָה בִּקְדֵרַת בָּשָׂר אוֹ בִּקְדֵרַת חָלָב — Thus, if that piece falls further into a pot of meat or into a pot of milk, and we wish to determine whether it is nullified, מְשַׁעֲרִין בְּכֻלָּהּ — we must measure it on the basis of its entirety. That is, if the piece of meat into which the milk was mixed subsequently fell into a pot of meat, it does not suffice if the meat in the second pot contains sixty times the volume of the milk that originally fell into the first piece of meat. Similarly, if the piece of meat into which the milk was mixed subsequently fell into a pot of milk, it does not suffice if the milk in the second pot contains sixty times the volume of the original piece of meat. Rather, the entire meat-and-milk mixture is considered a prohibited entity, and the second pot must contain sixty times the entire piece of meat together with the milk that it absorbed in order for it to be nullified. וְזֶהוּ אָמְרָם זִכְרוֹנָם לִבְרָכָה — And this is referred to by [our Sages], of blessed memory (*Chullin* 108a), as

---

### NOTES

24. In such a case, even if the prohibited food was removed and only its flavor remains, the food remains prohibited (see Mitzvah 111 note 27). In fact, even a pot in which a prohibited item or in which meat or milk has been cooked can absorb flavor and later impart flavor into food subsequently cooked in that pot. Other utensils used in the kitchen can also be similarly affected. For this reason, every Jewish home must maintain separate sets of utensils, one for use with meat and another for use with dairy, lest a utensil that had absorbed meat flavor later impart it to a dairy food, or vice versa.

25. Nevertheless, the prohibited substance (or milk or meat that fell into the dish) must be removed unless it has totally dissolved and is unrecognizable in the mixture. See similarly, Mitzvah 111 note 27. [The reader is reminded that no practical halachic conclusions may be drawn from the laws of the mitzvos presented by Chinuch or from our discussion of these laws. This certainly applies here, as the halachos pertaining to nullification are subject to many variables that can be ruled on only by competent halachic authorities.]

# KI SISA / MITZVAH 113: NOT TO EAT A MIXTURE OF MEAT AND MILK

(חולין דף ק״ח ע״א) חֲתִיכָה עַצְמָהּ נַעֲשֵׂית נְבֵלָה[26], וְהַטַּעַם מִפְּנֵי שֶׁתַּעֲרָבְתָּם אוֹסַרְתָּם, וּלְפִיכָךְ אַחַר שֶׁנִּתְעָרְבוּ הֲרֵי הֵן כַּחֲתִיכַת נְבֵלָה. וּבִשְׁאָר אִסּוּרִין אֵינוֹ כֵן, שֶׁאִסּוּר שֶׁנִּתְעָרֵב בַּחֲתִיכַת הֶתֵּר וְאֵין בַּחֲתִיכָה שִׁשִּׁים לְבַטֵּל הָאִסּוּר וְאַחַר כָּךְ נָפְלָה לִקְדֵרָה, אֵין מְשַׁעֲרִין אֶלָּא בְּשִׁעוּר הָאִסּוּר שֶׁנָּפַל בָּהּ וְהִיא בְּעַצְמָהּ תְּסַיֵּעַ לְעַלּוֹת הָאִסּוּר, לְפִי שֶׁאוֹתָהּ חֲתִיכָה לֹא נַעֲשֵׂית נְבֵלָה וְנִמְצָא הַהֶתֵּר שֶׁבָּהּ כְּמוֹ שְׁאָר הַהֶתֵּר שֶׁבַּקְּדֵרָה וּמְסַיֵּעַ לְהַעֲלוֹת הָאִסּוּר[27].

---

חֲתִיכָה עַצְמָהּ נַעֲשֵׂית נְבֵלָה — "**the piece itself becomes** intrinsically **prohibited** in the same manner **as** *neveilah*."[26] וְהַטַּעַם — **The reason** for this uniqueness is מִפְּנֵי שֶׁתַּעֲרָבְתָּם אוֹסַרְתָּם — **because** in the case of the meat-and-milk prohibition, **it is the blend** that is formed when the meat and milk are combined **that causes them to be prohibited,** וּלְפִיכָךְ אַחַר שֶׁנִּתְעָרְבוּ הֲרֵי הֵן כַּחֲתִיכַת נְבֵלָה — **and therefore, after they have become mixed together, they become** intrinsically prohibited in the same manner **as a piece of** *neveilah*. The principle of *chatichah naaseis neveilah* (the piece becomes prohibited as *neveilah*) was therefore said with regard to the meat-and-milk mixture, where both the meat and the dairy are entirely permitted on their own, and it is *the mixture* that is the subject of the prohibition. Thus, once the mixture has been formed, neither of its components can be viewed independently, and they cannot become nullified separately.

וּבִשְׁאָר שֶׁנִּתְעָרֵב אִסּוּרִין אֵינוֹ כֵן — **In** the case of **other prohibitions,** though, **this is not so,** שֶׁאִסּוּר שֶׁנִּתְעָרֵב בַּחֲתִיכַת הֶתֵּר — **for if a prohibited entity becomes mixed into a permitted piece** of food, וְאֵין בַּחֲתִיכָה שִׁשִּׁים לְבַטֵּל הָאִסּוּר — **and the piece does not contain sixty** corresponding units with which **to nullify the prohibited entity,** וְאַחַר כָּךְ נָפְלָה לִקְדֵרָה — **and afterward [that piece],** i.e., the one that had absorbed the prohibited entity, **falls into** another **pot,** אֵין מְשַׁעֲרִין אֶלָּא בְּשִׁעוּר הָאִסּוּר שֶׁנָּפַל בָּהּ — **we measure only the** actual **amount of the prohibited entity that fell into it.** וְהִיא בְּעַצְמָהּ תְּסַיֵּעַ לְעַלּוֹת הָאִסּוּר — **In fact, [the permitted food] itself will** actually **contribute to nullifying the prohibited entity.** That is, not only is the volume of the permitted piece (which the prohibited entity originally fell into) not included when calculating the total amount of prohibited matter, but, in fact, the volume of the original piece is included, along with the other permitted matter in the pot, in the calculations used to determine whether the permissible food contains sixty times the prohibited food. לְפִי שֶׁאוֹתָהּ חֲתִיכָה לֹא נַעֲשֵׂית נְבֵלָה — This is **because that piece did not become prohibited** intrinsically, **as** *neveilah* is; וְנִמְצָא הַהֶתֵּר שֶׁבָּהּ כְּמוֹ שְׁאָר הַהֶתֵּר שֶׁבַּקְּדֵרָה — **and thus, the permitted portion of [the piece] is the same as the rest of the permitted contents of the pot,** וּמְסַיֵּעַ לְהַעֲלוֹת הָאִסּוּר — **and it can contribute** (by being included in the calculations used to determine whether the permissible food contains sixty times the prohibited food) **to nullify the prohibited entity.**[27]

---

## NOTES

26. That is, one might have thought that the prohibition is dependent upon the presence of the meat and milk *independently,* and thus, if either the meat or milk is nullified, the mixture is permitted. The Sages teach that this is not the case, and that the prohibition is not viewed as being limited to a single part of the mixture. Rather, the *entire* piece is considered prohibited, for the reason that Chinuch shall explain. Since the entire piece of meat that has absorbed the milk became prohibited, if it later falls into a pot of meat, the pot must contain sixty times the entire piece of meat in order for the piece to be nullified. Otherwise the entire mixture into which it now fell will become prohibited, even though the mixture contains enough meat to nullify the initial dairy presence.

   As Chinuch writes, this principle, that a permitted entity that has absorbed flavor from a prohibited entity is considered to be intrinsically prohibited, is known as *chatichah naaseis neveilah,* "the piece becomes prohibited as *neveilah.*" [The Gemara uses the prohibition of eating *neveilah* (i.e., an animal that died without being slaughtered in the proper manner; Mitzvah 472) as an example of something that is intrinsically prohibited.]

   The implication of Chinuch's words above ("The Sages imposed ...") is that this prohibition is Rabbinic in origin. Other authorities, however, maintain that the principle of *chatichah naaseis neveilah* with regard to the meat-and-milk prohibition is Biblical in origin (see *Yoreh Deah* 92:2 with commentaries).

27. Thus, in the case of prohibitions other than meat-and-milk, even if so much of the prohibited matter was absorbed into permitted matter that it could not be nullified, the permitted matter does not become intrinsically prohibited, but is prohibited only due to the foreign presence that it contains. Therefore, in the subsequent mixture that contains additional permitted

וְאָמְנָם הַחֲתִיכָה עַצְמָהּ אִם הִיא נִכֶּרֶת, אֲסוּרָה לְעוֹלָם בְּדַעַת קְצָת הַמְפָרְשִׁים[28].
וְאָמְרוּ[29] זִכְרוֹנָם לִבְרָכָה (תמורה דף ל״ג ע״ב) שֶׁאֶפְרוֹ שֶׁל בָּשָׂר בְּחָלָב אָסוּר כְּאֵפֶר כָּל אִסּוּרֵי
הֲנָאָה, שֶׁטְּעוּנִין קְבוּרָה[30], וְאָמְרוּ גַּם כֵּן (חולין דף קי״ג ע״ב) שֶׁלֹּא אָסְרָה תּוֹרָה בָּשָׂר בְּחָלָב

---

וְאָמְנָם הַחֲתִיכָה עַצְמָהּ — **But** although the permitted portion of the piece that fell into the pot is included in the calculations used to determine whether the permissible food contains sixty times the prohibited food insofar as the contents of the pot are concerned, **nevertheless, the piece itself** that originally absorbed the prohibited matter and became prohibited, אִם הִיא נִכֶּרֶת אֲסוּרָה לְעוֹלָם — **if it is identifiable, remains prohibited forever** בְּדַעַת קְצָת הַמְפָרְשִׁים — **in the opinion of some commentators.**[28]

The Mishnah (*Temurah* 33b) divides items that are prohibited for benefit into two groups: those that must be buried and those that must be burned.[29] The prohibited meat-and-milk mixture is listed among those items that must be buried. Chinuch addresses a case of a prohibited meat-and-milk mixture that had been burned:

שֶׁאֶפְרוֹ שֶׁל וְאָמְרוּ זִכְרוֹנָם לִבְרָכָה — **[The Sages], of blessed memory, stated** (see *Temurah* 34a), בָּשָׂר בְּחָלָב אָסוּר — **that the ashes of a meat-and-milk mixture** that was burned **are prohibited** for all use, כְּאֵפֶר כָּל אִסּוּרֵי הֲנָאָה שֶׁטְּעוּנִין קְבוּרָה — **as** is the law regarding **the ashes of all** those items **that are prohibited for benefit that require burial.**[30]

Chinuch sets forth a number of situations where the meat-and-milk prohibition does not apply:

וְאָמְרוּ גַּם כֵּן — **[The Sages] also stated** (*Chullin* 113b) שֶׁלֹּא אָסְרָה תּוֹרָה בָּשָׂר בְּחָלָב אֶלָּא

---

NOTES

matter, the prohibited matter can become nullified based on a calculation of its *original* volume, and if the *total* volume of permitted matter contains sixty times the original prohibited matter, the flavor of the prohibited matter is nullified.

[Chinuch indicated earlier that this leniency represents the opinion of some commentators. Others, however, maintain that the principle of *chatichah naaseis neveilah* applies not only to the meat-and-milk prohibition, but — on a Rabbinic level — to other prohibitions as well. In their opinion, whenever a mixture becomes prohibited due to a prohibited entity that became mixed into it, the entire mixture is viewed as being intrinsically prohibited, regardless of the type of prohibition. Thus, if it subsequently became mixed into another food, the determination of whether *bitul* applies must be made based on whether there is enough permissible material in the second mixture to nullify the *entire* original mixture. See *Tosafos, Chullin* 100a ד״ה בשקדם וסלקו; *Tur* and *Beis Yosef, Yoreh Deah* 92:4; *Shulchan Aruch* with *Rama* ad loc.]

28. In the opinion of these authorities, once a food absorbs a prohibited entity, to the extent that the permitted food does not contain sixty times its volume, and it becomes prohibited, it remains prohibited even after the prohibited entity had become extracted from it [this is known as אֶפְשָׁר לְסוֹחֲטוֹ אָסוּר]. Thus, although, when the first piece fell into the second pot, the prohibited flavor was extracted from the piece that had initially absorbed it and became dispersed throughout the entire contents of the second mixture (which contains sixty times the prohibited matter), the piece itself that originally absorbed the prohibited entity remains prohibited (see *Tur, Yoreh Deah* 106). Other authorities, however, dispute this position and maintain that even the piece that absorbed the prohibited flavor becomes permitted once the prohibited entity is extracted from it (אֶפְשָׁר לְסוֹחֲטוֹ מוּתָּר). However, this dispute applies only with regard to prohibitions other than meat-and-milk. With regard to the meat-and-milk prohibition, if, for example a piece of meat was cooked together with milk, all authorities agree that the piece of meat remains prohibited even if it later fell into a pot of meat containing sixty times its volume.

29. Items that are prohibited for benefit must be either burned or buried, so that people will not come to transgress by deriving benefit from them. As explained by the Gemara (*Temurah* 34a), and by the commentators to the Mishnah (ibid. 33b), in certain instances the Torah mandates specifically that an item shall be burned, while in others it does not. In the latter cases, the Sages ordered that the item shall be buried.

30. When an item is Biblically mandated for burning (see previous note), the law is that once it has been burned in accordance with its mitzvah, the remaining ashes are permitted for benefit. When an item is not mandated for burning, the law is that even if it is burned the ashes remain prohibited for benefit (Gemara ibid.). Since the Torah does not command that a milk-and-meat mixture be burned, if one does burn it the ashes are prohibited. In fact, the Mishnah (ibid.) rules that it should specifically be buried and not burned, lest one think that the ashes are permitted for benefit (Gemara ibid.; but see *Rosh, Pesachim* 2:3).

# KI SISA / MITZVAH 113: NOT TO EAT A MIXTURE OF MEAT AND MILK

אֶלָּא בְּחָלָב שֶׁל בְּהֵמָה חַיָּה אֲבָל בַּחֲלֵב הַמֵּתָה אֵינוֹ נֶאֱסָר[31], וּלְפִיכָךְ הַכָּחָל מֻתָּר מִן הַתּוֹרָה בַּחֲלָבוֹ, אֶלָּא שֶׁחֲכָמִים אֲסָרוּהוּ לִגְדֵּר עַד שֶׁיְּמָרֵק חֲלָבוֹ מִמֶּנּוּ, כְּמוֹ שֶׁנִּתְבָּאֵר בִּמְקוֹמוֹ (שם דף ק"ט ע"א)[32]. וְחָלָב הַנִּמְצָא בְּקֵבַת הַבְּהֵמָה, יֵשׁ בּוֹ שְׁנֵי הֶתֵּרִין, אֶחָד שֶׁהוּא בִּכְלָל חָלָב שֶׁל מֵתָה, וְעוֹד שֶׁאֵינוֹ אֶלָּא כְּפֶרֶשׁ בְּעָלְמָא שֶׁכְּבָר נִתְעַכֵּל שָׁם, וּלְפִיכָךְ מֻתָּר לְכַתְּחִלָּה, וְאֵין צָרִיךְ לוֹמַר שֶׁהַנִּמְצָא שָׁם קָרוּשׁ מֻתָּר, שֶׁהוּא וַדַּאי כְּפֶרֶשׁ, אֶלָּא אֲפִלּוּ הַצָּלוּל הִתִּירוּ הַגְּאוֹנִים[33]. הַמְבַשֵּׁל שָׁלִיל בְּחָלָב חַיָּב, וְכֵן הָאוֹכְלוֹ[34], אֲבָל הַמְבַשֵּׁל שִׁלְיָא אוֹ עוֹר וְגִידִין וַעֲצָמוֹת וְעִקְרֵי

---

בְּחָלָב שֶׁל בְּהֵמָה חַיָּה — that the Torah prohibited the meat-and-milk mixture only when the meat is cooked in milk that came from a live animal. אֲבָל בַּחֲלֵב הַמֵּתָה אֵינוֹ נֶאֱסָר — However, meat cooked in the milk of a dead [animal] does not become prohibited.[31] וּלְפִיכָךְ הַכָּחָל מֻתָּר מִן הַתּוֹרָה בַּחֲלָבוֹ — Therefore, the udder of a slaughtered animal is Biblically permitted to be eaten with its milk, i.e., the milk that it contained when it was slaughtered, because that milk is not subject to the prohibition. אֶלָּא שֶׁחֲכָמִים אֲסָרוּהוּ לִגְדֵּר — But the Sages prohibited it, as a safeguard for the meat-and-milk prohibition, עַד שֶׁיְּמָרֵק חֲלָבוֹ מִמֶּנּוּ — unless it is cleansed of its milk, כְּמוֹ שֶׁנִּתְבָּאֵר בִּמְקוֹמוֹ — as is set forth by the Gemara in its place (Chullin 109a). וְחָלָב הַנִּמְצָא בְּקֵבַת הַבְּהֵמָה — As for the milk that is found in the stomach of an animal (e.g., a calf) after it was slaughtered, יֵשׁ בּוֹ שְׁנֵי הֶתֵּרִין — there are two reasons to permit it: אֶחָד שֶׁהוּא בִּכְלָל חָלָב שֶׁל מֵתָה — First, because it is included in the category of the milk of a dead [animal],[32] וְעוֹד שֶׁאֵינוֹ אֶלָּא כְּפֶרֶשׁ בְּעָלְמָא — and furthermore, because it is considered merely like fecal matter, שֶׁכְּבָר נִתְעַכֵּל שָׁם — as it had already been digested there, in the animal's stomach. וּלְפִיכָךְ מֻתָּר לְכַתְּחִלָּה — Therefore, such milk is permitted even initially. וְאֵין צָרִיךְ לוֹמַר שֶׁהַנִּמְצָא שָׁם קָרוּשׁ מֻתָּר — Now, not only is milk that is found there in congealed form permitted, שֶׁהוּא וַדַּאי כְּפֶרֶשׁ — for that is certainly like fecal matter, אֶלָּא אֲפִלּוּ הַצָּלוּל — but, in fact, הִתִּירוּ הַגְּאוֹנִים — the Geonim permitted even [milk] that is still fluid.[33] הַמְבַשֵּׁל שָׁלִיל בְּחָלָב חַיָּב — One who cooks a fetus in milk is liable for having violated the meat-and-milk prohibition, וְכֵן הָאוֹכְלוֹ — and the same applies for one who eats [a fetus cooked in milk].[34] אֲבָל הַמְבַשֵּׁל שִׁלְיָא — But one who cooks the afterbirth, אוֹ עוֹר וְגִידִין וַעֲצָמוֹת וְעִקְרֵי

---

### NOTES

31. When expressing our mitzvah, the Torah states: לֹא תְבַשֵּׁל גְּדִי בַּחֲלֵב אִמּוֹ, *You shall not cook a kid in the milk of its mother.* The Gemara explains that the final phrase, בַּחֲלֵב אִמּוֹ, *the milk of its mother,* indicates that the prohibition applies only to milk that emerged when the animal was alive, when it could still be described as a "mother."

32. This reason is not found in other Rishonim, and is in fact problematic. The milk in the animal's stomach had already emerged from the *mother* and acquired an identity as "milk of a live animal" at the time when it was ingested. It is therefore not considered as the "milk of a dead animal," and should be prohibited. Moreover, as pointed out by *Minchas Chinuch* and *R' Akiva Eiger* (glosses to *Rambam, Hil. Maachalos Asuros* 9:15), this is in direct contradiction to the Gemara (*Chullin* 109b; see *Rashi* ad loc. ד"ה זה כנוס במעיו), which differentiates between milk of the udder and milk that is found in the stomach of a slaughtered animal, based on the argument we mentioned here.

33. Chinuch's position, that even milk that is found in a fluid state in the stomach of a slaughtered animal loses its status as milk, accords with the position of a number of Rishonim, including *Rambam* (*Hil. Maachalos Asuros* 9:15). Other Rishonim, however, maintain that only if the milk is congealed when it was found in the stomach is it no longer subject to the meat-and-milk prohibition; yet others maintain that the milk found in the stomach remains governed by the meat-and-milk prohibition even after it became congealed (see *Yoreh Deah* 87:9 and *Shach* ad loc. §25).

[In the opinion of *Re'ah* (*Bedek HaBayis,* beginning of 3:4), milk that is discovered in the stomach may not be mixed with meat even if it had already congealed. *Tzava Rav* cites this law as a proof that the Chinuch was not authored by *Re'ah*. See General Introduction, Section VII, for further discussion regarding the authorship of Chinuch. See also Mitzvah 73 note 34, and Mitzvah 111 note 15.]

34. Chinuch is referring to an unborn fetus, which was discovered in the womb of a slaughtered animal. The Gemara (*Chullin* 113b) explains that the term "a kid" that is repeated in connection with the meat-and-milk prohibitions comes to extend these prohibitions to even an unborn fetus.

קַרְנַיִם וּטְלָפַיִם פָּטוּר.[35] וְיֶתֶר פְּרָטֵי הַמִּצְוָה, מְבֹאָרִים בְּפֶרֶק שְׁמִינִי מֵחֻלִּין (דף ק״ג ע״ב ואילך).[36]
וְנוֹהֶגֶת בְּכָל מָקוֹם וּבְכָל זְמַן, בִּזְכָרִים וּנְקֵבוֹת.[37]
וְהָעוֹבֵר עָלֶיהָ וְאָכַל כַּזַיִת מִן הַבָּשָׂר וְהֶחָלָב שֶׁנִּתְבַּשְּׁלוּ יַחַד, בְּמֵזִיד,[38] לוֹקֶה. אֲבָל נֶהֱנָה בּוֹ כְּגוֹן שֶׁנְּתָנוֹ[39] אוֹ מְכָרוֹ, אֵינוֹ לוֹקֶה, לְפִי שֶׁאֶפְשָׁר לַהֲנָאָה בְּלִי מַעֲשֶׂה, וְכָל שֶׁאֵין בּוֹ מַעֲשֶׂה אֵין לוֹקִין עָלָיו.[40] וַאֲפִלּוּ סָךְ מִמֶּנּוּ אֶפְשָׁר דְּלָא לָקֵי לְפִי שֶׁהוּא שֶׁלֹּא כְּדֶרֶךְ הֲנָאָתוֹ,

קַרְנַיִם וּטְלָפַיִם — **or the hide, sinews, bones, or the base of the horns and hooves,** with dairy, פָּטוּר — **is exempt** of any liability.[35] וְיֶתֶר פְּרָטֵי הַמִּצְוָה מְבֹאָרִים בְּפֶרֶק שְׁמִינִי מֵחֻלִּין — These, **and the additional details of this mitzvah, are set forth in the eighth chapter of** Tractate *Chullin.*[36]

## ~ Applicability of the Mitzvah ~

וְנוֹהֶגֶת בְּכָל מָקוֹם וּבְכָל זְמַן — **[This mitzvah] applies in every location and in all times,** בִּזְכָרִים וּנְקֵבוֹת — **and is incumbent upon** both **men and women.**[37] וְהָעוֹבֵר עָלֶיהָ וְאָכַל כַּזַיִת מִן הַבָּשָׂר וְהֶחָלָב שֶׁנִּתְבַּשְּׁלוּ יַחַד — **One who violates [this prohibition]** בְּמֵזִיד — **and intentionally eats a** *kezayis* **(olive's volume) of meat and milk that were cooked together**[38] לוֹקֶה — **incurs** the penalty of *malkus* (lashes). אֲבָל נֶהֱנָה בּוֹ — **But one who derived benefit from [the meat-and-milk mixture],** כְּגוֹן שֶׁנְּתָנוֹ אוֹ מְכָרוֹ — **for example, if he gave it as a gift**[39] **or he sold it,** אֵינוֹ לוֹקֶה — **does not incur** *malkus.* לְפִי שֶׁאֶפְשָׁר לַהֲנָאָה בְּלִי מַעֲשֶׂה — This is **because** — although he performed an action to derive the benefit — **it is possible to** derive benefit from the mixture **without** performing **an action,** וְכָל שֶׁאֵין בּוֹ מַעֲשֶׂה אֵין לוֹקִין עָלָיו — **and,** as a rule, **any** prohibition **that does not** necessarily **involve action, one does not incur** *malkus* **for** violating **it.**[40] וַאֲפִלּוּ סָךְ מִמֶּנּוּ — **In fact, even if one smeared** his skin **with [the mixture],** אֶפְשָׁר דְּלָא לָקֵי — **perhaps he does not incur** *malkus,* לְפִי שֶׁהוּא שֶׁלֹּא כְּדֶרֶךְ הֲנָאָתוֹ — **for that is**

---

NOTES

35. The term "a kid" that appears in the verse of our mitzvah refers to the meat, the portion of the animal that is commonly cooked and eaten. It does not, however, refer to these portions listed above, which are not commonly eaten; even the base of the horns and the hooves, which are soft enough to be eaten, are excluded. [See, however, *Shach, Yoreh Deah* 87:22, who rules that there is a Rabbinic prohibition of partaking of meat-and-milk mixtures that are comprised of these portions of an animal.]

36. The laws of the mitzvah are codified in *Rambam, Hil. Maachalos Asuros* Ch. 9, and *Shulchan Aruch, Yoreh Deah* §87-97.

37. The mitzvah applies in Eretz Yisrael and in the Diaspora regardless of whether the *Beis HaMikdash* is standing or not, and, in accordance with the general rule pertaining to mitzvah-prohibitions, applies to women as well as men.

38. That is, whether he ate a *kezayis* of the meat of the mixture or a *kezayis* of the milk, or a *kezayis* of both combined (see *Minchas Chinuch* §1).

39. Although one who gives a gift does not receive anything tangible in return, he nevertheless benefits from the goodwill of the recipient (see *Pesachim* 22a).

40. As we have seen numerous times throughout this work, one who transgresses a לָאו שֶׁאֵין בּוֹ מַעֲשֶׂה, a prohibition that does not involve action, does not incur *malkus*. Chinuch's position is that this exemption from *malkus* applies not only to one who actually violates a prohibition without performing an action, but even to one who violates a prohibition that *can* be violated without performing an action. Thus, if the prohibition can be violated without an action, even one whose violation *did* entail an action does not incur *malkus* (see, for example, Mitzvah 94). Accordingly, even if one violated the prohibition with an action, by selling it or giving it away, he is nevertheless not liable, for since there are instances where one can derive benefit from meat-and-milk without an action (e.g., warming oneself with a fire that is fueled by the mixture), the prohibition of deriving benefit from meat-and-milk never bears *malkus*. For further discussion of this concept, see Insight to Mitzvah 68.

[*Eating* meat-and-milk, however, is considered a distinct prohibition with regard to this issue, since it is derived from a separate verse. This is despite the fact that the prohibition of eating and the prohibition of deriving benefit from meat-and-milk are included in a single mitzvah. Thus, one who eats a mixture of meat-and-milk (which must be performed with an action) is liable to *malkus*, despite the fact that there are instances where *deriving benefit* from meat-and-milk can be transgressed without performing an action (*Sdei Chemed, Maareches HaLamed* §12 ד״ה מכל המקומות; see, however, *Derech HaMelech — R' Dov Rapaport*, Lemberg 1892).]

# 369 ❏ KI SISA / MITZVAH 113: NOT TO EAT A MIXTURE OF MEAT AND MILK

שֶׁאֵינוֹ עָשׂוּי לָסוּךְ[41], וְיֵשׁ לָדוּן בּוֹ גַּם כֵּן שֶׁיִּלְקֶה[42].

**שֶׁאֵינוֹ עָשׂוּי לָסוּךְ — as [such a mixture] is not the usual manner of deriving benefit from it,** not normally **used for smearing** on one's skin.[41] **וְיֵשׁ לָדוּן בּוֹ גַּם כֵּן שֶׁיִּלְקֶה —** On the other hand, **it can also be reasoned that one should incur** *malkus* **for this** act of smearing the mixture.[42]

---

### NOTES

41. Chinuch's statement here that even if one smeared the mixture he may nevertheless be exempt from *malkus*, since it is not the usual manner of deriving benefit, is difficult to understand. For although smearing does entail an action, nevertheless, Chinuch has just explained that since there are instances where the prohibition of deriving benefit from meat-and-milk does not entail an action, the prohibition is considered a לָאו שֶׁאֵין בּוֹ מַעֲשֶׂה, *a prohibition that does not involve action,* and does not bear the *malkus* penalty (see previous note). How, then, can Chinuch entertain the possibility that there should be *malkus* for smearing?

A number of Acharonim explain that, while, as a general rule, Chinuch maintains that if a prohibition can be violated without an action, even one who violated the prohibition with an action does not incur *malkus*, nevertheless, this applies only when the prohibition is being transgressed in a manner that can be done without action as well [for in such a case his action is insignificant as it is not required for the transgression of the prohibition]. If, however, he transgresses the prohibition in a manner that cannot be performed without an action, as is the case with regard to smearing, he would be liable to *malkus*; see also above, Insight B to Mitzvah 11, and Insight to Mitzvah 68 (see *Minchas Chinuch* §5, *Minchas Yitzchak* §11, *Heichal Melech*, bottom of fol. 76a; see also *Sdei Chemed, Maareches HaLamed* §12 ד"ה וראיתי). See also next note.

42. Chinuch does not state the basis for the reasoning that there should be liability to *malkus* here. *Minchas Yitzchak* suggests that just as the prohibition of meat-and-milk includes eating in an atypical manner (see note 5 above), it similarly includes deriving benefit in an atypical manner, as well (see *Dina D'Chayei* fol. 130a).

Others understand Chinuch's discussion regarding smearing a meat-and-milk mixture to be based on a principle set forth by the Mishnah, *Shabbos* 86a. The Mishnah, based on a Biblical source, establishes that smearing on one's skin is considered a form of drinking, which, as the Gemara explains (*Yoma* 76b), is the reason why such smearing is prohibited on Yom Kippur. Thus, one who smeared the prohibited meat-and-milk mixture on his skin would receive *malkus* because of the prohibition of *consuming* (i.e., eating or drinking) meat-and-milk. Thus, even though there is normally no *malkus* at all for deriving benefit, and even if the prohibition of deriving benefit applies only when one has benefitted in a typical manner, nevertheless, one would be liable for smearing the prohibited meat-and-milk mixture on his skin. For, as Chinuch explained above, one is liable for eating or drinking meat-and-milk even in an unusual manner, such as when it is scalding hot. Since smearing is a form of drinking, one would be liable for smearing the mixture, even though that is not the common way it is ingested (*Me'il HaEphod;* see there further for an explanation of Chinuch's original reasoning that one is not liable; see also *Sdei Chemed, Maareches HaLamed* §12 ד"ה מכל המקומות). It should be noted, however, that not all agree that smearing is considered as drinking on the *Biblical* level; see *Beur Halachah* 326:10 ד"ה בשאר. See also Mitzvos 313 and 610.

---

> ### ❧ Insight: A Chanukah Candle of Meat-and-Milk
>
> Halachic authorities address an interesting question, relating to the mitzvah of kindling lights on Chanukah, that pertains to the prohibition of deriving benefit from a meat-and-milk mixture. We shall address a number of issues of this case, which can shed light on the basic understanding of the meat-and-milk prohibition.
>
> At issue is whether one may fulfill the mitzvah of kindling Chanukah lights with a candle made of milk and meat that were cooked together (e.g., butter that was cooked in a meat pot from which it absorbed meat flavor, such that the butter becomes prohibited due to the meat-and-milk prohibition).
>
> *Shaar Ephraim* (*Orach Chaim* §38, cited in *Shaarei Teshuvah, Orach Chaim* 673:1) rules that although a meat-and-milk mixture is Biblically prohibited for benefit, it is permissible to light a candle containing a meat-and-milk mixture in order to fulfill the mitzvah of kindling the Chanukah lights. This is due to the rule that מִצְווֹת לָאו לֵיהָנוֹת נִיתְּנוּ, *mitzvos were not given for [the purpose of] deriving benefit [from them]* (*Rosh Hashanah* 28a, et al.). That is, discharging a mitzvah does not fall under the category of personal "benefit"; it is, rather, a fulfillment of God's decree (*Rashi* ad loc.). Therefore,

an item that is prohibited for benefit may be used for a mitzvah, as the resulting fulfillment of the mitzvah does not constitute "benefit."

Numerous Acharonim (*Elyah Zuta, Orach Chaim* 673:2, cited by *Pri Megadim, Sifsei Daas, Yoreh Deah* 87:2; see also *Shaarei Teshuvah* ibid.), however, point out that while *Shaar Ephraim* has explained why the prohibition of *deriving benefit* from a meat-and-milk mixture does not apply here, lighting such a candle should still be prohibited, because by lighting the candle one inevitably heats up the meat-and-milk mixture and melts it. This constitutes *cooking* meat and milk together, which, as we have seen in Mitzvah 92, is Biblically prohibited!

This difficulty may be resolved based on a rule stated in regard to cooking on the Sabbath: Although cooking is a *melachah* (work-activity) prohibited on the Sabbath (see Mitzvah 32), this prohibition does not apply to an item that has been cooked once before, for as a rule, אֵין בִּישׁוּל אַחַר בִּישׁוּל, *there is no cooking after cooking*. Assuming that this rule can also be applied to the laws of the meat-and-milk mixture (see *Pri Megadim, Yoreh Deah, Mishbetzos Zahav* 105:2 ד"ה עוד למדתי; *Rabbeinu Gershom* to *Chullin* 108b), it would emerge that the candle *may* be lit, since the meat-and-milk mixture contained within it has already been cooked together, and thus, no further prohibition is transgressed by rekindling the mixture.

However, upon further study, this does not suffice to fully alleviate the difficulty. *Shulchan Aruch* (*Orach Chaim* 318:4) writes, with respect to the laws of the Sabbath, that, while reheating a solid food that was previously cooked does not qualify as the *melachah* of "cooking," reheating a liquid that had been cooked and then cooled down is considered an act of "cooking." *Rama* (318:15) is more lenient, but nevertheless rules that if the liquid has *completely* cooled then reheating it is prohibited. Hence, it should be prohibited to light the meat-and-milk candle, as the candle is made of a liquid (melted butter), that, after being cooked, has cooled off completely, so reheating it would be considered "cooking" (see *Elyah Zuta* ibid.).

One can argue that since the candle is currently in solid form, it has the status of a solid food, which is not subject to re-cooking (see *Magen Avraham* 318:31, 40, and *Mishnah Berurah* 318:100). However, numerous authorities maintain that something that will dissolve when heated has the status of a liquid, which is subject to re-cooking (*Levush, Orach Chaim* 318:16; *Taz* 318:20; see *Chayei Adam, Hilchos Shabbos* 20:7). Must we assume that according to the latter opinion, it is in fact prohibited to light a candle made of a meat-and-milk mixture, in conflict with the lenient ruling of *Shaar Ephraim*?

A novel resolution to this issue is offered by *Badei HaShulchan* (*Beurim* 87:1 ד"ה בישול), who explains that the Biblical prohibition of cooking meat and milk together can be understood as being inherently different from the prohibition of cooking on the Sabbath. The *melachah* of cooking on the Sabbath is defined as the process of transforming an "uncooked" food into a "cooked" food. In this regard, a liquid that has been cooked and has cooled down no longer retains its status as a "cooked" food, so reheating it can be viewed as cooking on the Sabbath (see *Hagahos R' Akiva Eiger* to *Shulchan Aruch, Orach Chaim*, end of §253; cf. *Igros Moshe, Orach Chaim* IV §74, *Bishul* 2). By contrast, with regard to the meat-and-milk prohibition, the prohibition is not the "cooking" per se; rather, what the Torah forbids is *creating* a meat-and-milk mixture through cooking. If the forbidden mixture already exists, even if it is a liquid that has cooled down, there is no longer a prohibition to reheat it, since even when cooled it remains a forbidden mixture of meat and milk, and cooking it again does not create a new forbidden entity. Therefore, in the opinion of *Shaar Ephraim*, one is permitted to cook it further. Accordingly, in the case under discussion, since the candle already has the status of a forbidden meat-and-milk mixture, its kindling is permitted.

For further discussion of the law regarding kindling the Chanukah lights with such a mixture, see *Mishnah Berurah* 673:2, *Aruch HaShulchan* 673:5, and *Igros Moshe, Orach Chaim* I §191.

# פרשת ויקהל
## Parashas Vayakhel

---
**CONTAINS ONE MITZVOS:**
**MITZVOS 114**
---

114. שֶׁלֹּא יַעֲשׂוּ בֵּית דִּין מִשְׁפַּט מָוֶת בְּשַׁבָּת — The Prohibition Upon *Beis Din* to Carry Out Capital Punishment on the Sabbath

## מִצְוָה קיד: שֶׁלֹּא יַעֲשׂוּ בֵּית דִּין מִשְׁפַּט מָוֶת בְּשַׁבָּת

וַיַּקְהֵל מֹשֶׁה יֵשׁ בָּהּ מִצְוַת לֹא תַעֲשֶׂה אַחַת, וְהִיא שֶׁלֹּא יַעֲשׂוּ הַדַּיָּנִין דִּינִים בְּשַׁבָּת, כְּלוֹמַר שֶׁמִּי שֶׁנִּתְחַיֵּב מִיתָה בְּבֵית דִּין לֹא יְמִיתוּהוּ בְּשַׁבָּת, שֶׁנֶּאֱמַר (שמות ל"ה, ג') לֹא תְבַעֲרוּ אֵשׁ בְּכֹל מֹשְׁבֹתֵיכֶם בְּיוֹם הַשַּׁבָּת, וּבָא הַפֵּרוּשׁ עָלָיו בָּזֶה שֶׁלֹּא יִשְׂרְפוּ בֵּית דִּין בְּשַׁבָּת מִי שֶׁנִּתְחַיֵּב שְׂרֵפָה[1], וְהוּא הַדִּין לִשְׁאָר מִיתוֹת[2]. וְיֵשׁ[3] לָנוּ לִדְרֹשׁ מִמֶּנּוּ דָּבָר זֶה,

# Mitzvah 114

## The Prohibition Upon Beis Din to Carry Out Capital Punishment on the Sabbath

לֹא תְבַעֲרוּ אֵשׁ בְּכֹל מֹשְׁבֹתֵיכֶם בְּיוֹם הַשַּׁבָּת

*You shall not kindle a fire in any of your dwelling places on the Sabbath day* (*Exodus* 35:3).

As was explained in the General Introduction (end of section VI), the Torah has established various penalties for those who intentionally violate its laws, with certain serious transgressions being subject to the death penalty. In this mitzvah, the Torah prohibits *beis din*, which was charged with the responsibility of implementing the penalties for those who violate the law, from administering the death penalty on the Sabbath.

וַיַּקְהֵל מֹשֶׁה יֵשׁ בָּהּ מִצְוַת לֹא תַעֲשֶׂה אַחַת — *Parashas Vayakhel* contains one mitzvah-prohibition, וְהִיא שֶׁלֹּא יַעֲשׂוּ הַדַּיָּנִין דִּינִים בְּשַׁבָּת — which is that the judges may not implement justice on the Sabbath. כְּלוֹמַר שֶׁמִּי שֶׁנִּתְחַיֵּב מִיתָה בְּבֵית דִּין — That is to say, if one has been found liable to the death penalty by *beis din*, לֹא יְמִיתוּהוּ בְּשַׁבָּת — they may not execute him on the Sabbath, שֶׁנֶּאֱמַר — as it is stated (*Exodus* 35:3): "לֹא תְבַעֲרוּ אֵשׁ בְּכֹל מֹשְׁבֹתֵיכֶם בְּיוֹם הַשַּׁבָּת" — *You shall not kindle a fire in any of your dwelling places on the Sabbath day.* וּבָא הַפֵּרוּשׁ עָלָיו בָּזֶה — The explanation of this, as transmitted to us by the Sages, is שֶׁלֹּא יִשְׂרְפוּ בֵּית דִּין בְּשַׁבָּת מִי שֶׁנִּתְחַיֵּב שְׂרֵפָה — that *beis din* may not administer *sereifah* (burning) to one who is liable to execution by *sereifah*.[1] וְהוּא הַדִּין לִשְׁאָר מִיתוֹת — And, although the verse of our mitzvah refers only to *sereifah*, **the same applies to the other forms of execution.**[2]

According to its simple meaning, the verse, *You shall not kindle a fire in any of your dwelling places on the Sabbath day,* prohibits lighting *any* fire on the Sabbath, which is one of the 39 primary *melachos* (forbidden activities) prohibited on the Sabbath (see above, Mitzvah 32).[3] Chinuch explains why the Sages interpreted this verse as referring to *sereifah*:

וְיֵשׁ לָנוּ לִדְרֹשׁ מִמֶּנּוּ דָּבָר זֶה — **Now,** although this is not the simple understanding of the verse,

---

NOTES

1. The procedure for the *sereifah* penalty calls for melting a piece of lead, and pouring the molten lead down the condemned person's throat (see Mitzvah 261). Melting the lead requires that a fire be lit, which comprises the *melachah* (forbidden activity) of kindling. Additionally, melting the lead on the Sabbath is included in the *melachah* of "cooking" (see *Yevamos* 6b, with *Rashi* ד"ה פתילה), and taking any life on the Sabbath, whether of a human or of an animal, is also a *melachah*. Our verse prohibits *beis din* from kindling a fire or engaging in any other step in the *sereifah* process. See also below, note 9.

2. The Torah sets forth four forms of execution, which are dependent on the specific prohibition that was transgressed. These are *sekilah* (Mitzvah 555), *sereifah* (Mitzvah 261), *hereg* (Mitzvah 50), and *chenek* (Mitzvah 47).

3. A list of the primary *melachos* appears in Vol. 1, p. 276. *Kindling* [מַבְעִיר] is the 37th *melachah* on that list.

## 373 ☐ VAYAKHEL / MITZVAH 114: NOT TO CARRY OUT CAPITAL PUNISHMENT ON THE SABBATH

שֶׁהֲרֵי לְגוּפֵיהּ אֵינוֹ צָרִיךְ, שֶׁהֲרֵי כְּבָר כָּתוּב בְּמָקוֹם אַחֵר (שמות כ, י) לֹא תַעֲשֶׂה כָל מְלָאכָה, וְהַבְעָרָה לְצֹרֶךְ מְלָאכָה הִיא[4], אֶלָּא לְלַמֵּד עִנְיָן בִּפְנֵי עַצְמוֹ נִכְתַּב, וּפֵרְשׁוּ בוֹ שֶׁבָּא לְלַמֵּד אֶת זֶה שֶׁאָמַרְנוּ[5]. וְכֵן לְשׁוֹן הַמְּכִילְתָּא (כאן), לֹא תְבַעֲרוּ אֵשׁ, שְׂרֵפָה בִּכְלָל הָיְתָה וְיָצְאָת לְלַמֵּד[6], מַה שְּׂרֵפָה מְיֻחֶדֶת שֶׁהִיא אַחַת מִמִּיתוֹת בֵּית דִּין וְאֵינָהּ דּוֹחָה אֶת הַשַּׁבָּת, אַף כָּל שְׁאָר מִיתוֹת בֵּית דִּין לֹא יִדְחוּ אֶת הַשַּׁבָּת.

---

**because – שֶׁהֲרֵי לְגוּפֵיהּ אֵינוֹ צָרִיךְ** nevertheless, **we have** reason **to deduce this matter from it,** [the verse] is not needed for itself, i.e., for its simple meaning — that it is prohibited to light any fire on the Sabbath — **as it has already been written elsewhere – שֶׁהֲרֵי כְּבָר כָּתוּב בְּמָקוֹם אַחֵר** (*Exodus* 20:10), **"לֹא תַעֲשֶׂה כָל מְלָאכָה" – you shall not perform any melachah** on the *Sabbath day* (see *Mitzvah* 32), **and kindling a flame for a useful purpose is a melachah – וְהַבְעָרָה לְצֹרֶךְ מְלָאכָה הִיא,** and thus included in *that* verse.[4] **Rather, since – אֶלָּא לְלַמֵּד עִנְיָן בִּפְנֵי עַצְמוֹ נִכְתַּב,** the prohibition of this verse has already been taught in another verse, it must be that [this verse] was **written to teach us a matter of its own, – וּפֵרְשׁוּ בוֹ שֶׁבָּא לְלַמֵּד אֶת זֶה שֶׁאָמַרְנוּ and [the Sages] explain with regard to [this verse] that it is coming to teach that which we have stated,** that *beis din* may not administer *sereifah* on the Sabbath.[5]

Chinuch goes on to explain how it is derived that other forms of execution are also included in this prohibition:

**וְכֵן לְשׁוֹן הַמְּכִילְתָּא – These are the words of the *Mechilta*** to this verse: **"לֹא תְבַעֲרוּ אֵשׁ" – It is** stated, **You shall not kindle a fire. – שְׂרֵפָה בִּכְלָל הָיְתָה – Now, *sereifah* was included** among the forms of execution imposed by *beis din* **וְיָצְאָת לְלַמֵּד – and was singled out** in order **to teach** a law in its regard (i.e., that *sereifah* is prohibited on the Sabbath). In such cases, when the Torah singles out a rule with regard to one item in a category, the Torah does so in order to teach that law regarding its entire category.[6] **מַה שְּׂרֵפָה מְיֻחֶדֶת – That is, just as *sereifah* is unique שֶׁהִיא אַחַת מִמִּיתוֹת בֵּית דִּין** in **that it is one of the types of execution by *beis din*, וְאֵינָהּ דּוֹחָה אֶת הַשַּׁבָּת – and it does not override** the laws of **the Sabbath,** as taught in this verse, **אַף כָּל שְׁאָר מִיתוֹת בֵּית דִּין לֹא יִדְחוּ אֶת הַשַּׁבָּת – so too, all other forms of execution by *beis din* do not override** the laws of **the Sabbath.**

---

### NOTES

4. Chinuch specifies "kindling of a flame *for a purpose,*" because on the Biblical level, the prohibition of performing *melachah* on the Sabbath applies only to acts that are *productive* in nature, rather than *destructive* in nature; see *Mitzvah* 32, Insight B (§2). See end of next note for further discussion.

5. Since lighting a fire is among the *melachos* that are prohibited on the Sabbath, there is no need for a specific prohibition to prohibit lighting a fire. The Sages therefore explain that this verse must be specifically addressing lighting a fire for the sake of administering the *sereifah* penalty.

[The basis to say that this verse is referring to *beis din* is from the reference here to "dwelling places" (בְּכֹל מֹשְׁבֹתֵיכֶם, *in any of your dwelling places*), which also appears as a reference to *beis din* in the verse (*Numbers* 35:29): וְהָיוּ אֵלֶּה לָכֶם לְחֻקַּת מִשְׁפָּט לְדֹרֹתֵיכֶם בְּכֹל מוֹשְׁבֹתֵיכֶם, *These shall be for you a decree of justice for your generations, in all your dwelling places* (see *Makkos* 7a). The Gemara (*Yevamos* 6b) explains that by including this phrase here, the Torah indicates that our mitzvah is also referring to *beis din*.]

As stated in the previous note, the prohibition of performing *melachah* on the Sabbath applies only to actions that are *productive,* rather than *destructive,* in nature. The question then arises: How can taking the life of a human being (which is a destructive act) be considered a *melachah*? Now, with regard to *sereifah,* we may say that melting the lead is considered a productive act (see *Rashi, Shabbos* 106a ד״ה בישול; cf. *Tosafos* there ד״ה מה לי), but the question remains with regard to the other methods of execution, which, as Chinuch stated above, are also included in this prohibition (see further in Chinuch). This question is addressed by *Tosafos* (*Sanhedrin* 35a ד״ה אין), who explain that since the sinner achieves atonement for his sin once he is punished by *beis din*, administering the death penalty can actually be considered a productive act, and is therefore included in the prohibition.

6. One of the principles of Scriptural exposition is that where the Torah taught a law with regard to a general category, and then singles out one of the items in the set and teaches a specific law in its regard, it is for the purpose of teaching that specific law with regard to all the items in the category [כָּל דָּבָר שֶׁהָיָה בִּכְלָל וְיָצָא מִן הַכְּלָל ... לְלַמֵּד עַל הַכְּלָל כֻּלּוֹ יָצָא] (see introduction to *Toras Kohanim*).

## 374 □ ויקהל / מצוה קיד: שלא יעשו בית דין משפט מות בשבת

וְעִם[7] כָּל זֶה שֶׁלָּמַדְנוּ בְּפָסוּק זֶה, יֵשׁ לִדְרֹשׁ בּוֹ מַה שֶּׁדְּרָשׁוּ בּוֹ עוֹד גַּם כֵּן, הַבְעָרָה לְחַלֵּק יָצָאת (יבמות דף ו' ע״ב), כְּלוֹמַר שֶׁהָעוֹשֶׂה בְּשַׁבָּת הַרְבֵּה אֲבוֹת מְלָאכָה בְּבַת אַחַת בְּהֶעְלֵם אֶחָד שֶׁיִּהְיֶה חַיָּב חַטָּאת עַל כָּל מְלָאכָה וּמְלָאכָה בִּפְנֵי עַצְמָהּ[8]. וּבַגְּמָרָא דִּבְנֵי מַעֲרָבָא (ירושלמי סנהדרין פ״ד ה״ו) אָמְרוּ, בְּכֹל מוֹשְׁבוֹתֵיכֶם, רַבִּי אִילָא בְּשֵׁם רַבִּי יַנַּאי מִכָּאן לְבָתֵּי דִינִין שֶׁלֹּא יְהוּ דָנִין בְּשַׁבָּת[9].

A *chatas* (sin offering; see Mitzvah 132) is brought by one who desecrates the Sabbath inadvertently. Chinuch discusses an additional law that is derived from this verse with regard to the number of *chatas* obligations required for one who has inadvertently sinned repeatedly:[7] וְעִם כָּל זֶה שֶׁלָּמַדְנוּ בְּפָסוּק זֶה — **In addition to all that we have derived from this verse,** לִדְרֹשׁ בּוֹ מַה שֶּׁדְּרָשׁוּ בּוֹ עוֹד גַּם כֵּן — **we can still expound [the verse] as [the Sages] further expounded it** (*Yevamos* 6b), הַבְעָרָה לְחַלֵּק יָצָאת — **that the prohibition against kindling was singled out to separate [the liability]** of each *melachah* from the liability of the others. כְּלוֹמַר שֶׁהָעוֹשֶׂה — **That is to say, that if one** inadvertently **performs many** different **primary** *melachos* **on the Sabbath at once,** בְּהֶעְלֵם אֶחָד — that is, **in a single period of unawareness** of their prohibition, שֶׁיִּהְיֶה חַיָּב חַטָּאת עַל כָּל מְלָאכָה וּמְלָאכָה בִּפְנֵי עַצְמָהּ — **he is liable to** bring **a** *chatas* **for each and every** *melachah* **individually.**[8]

Chinuch cites a Talmudic exposition of the verse:

וּבַגְּמָרָא דִּבְנֵי מַעֲרָבָא אָמְרוּ — **[The Sages] said in** *Talmud Yerushalmi* (*Sanhedrin* 4:6): בְּכֹל מוֹשְׁבוֹתֵיכֶם — It is stated, *You shall not kindle a fire* **in any of your dwelling places** on the Sabbath day. רַבִּי אִילָא בְּשֵׁם רַבִּי יַנַּאי — **R' I'la stated in the name of R' Yannai:** מִכָּאן לְבָתֵּי דִינִין שֶׁלֹּא יְהוּ דָנִין בְּשַׁבָּת — **From here** we derive **a** prohibition **upon the** *beis din* **courts that they may not implement justice on the Sabbath.**[9]

---

NOTES

7. Generally, if one transgresses a *chatas*-bearing prohibition in error (for example, if one mistakenly ate *cheilev* [forbidden fat; Mitzvah 147]) and then repeats *the same* transgression before becoming aware of his earlier error ("in a single period of unawareness"), he is liable to bring only a single *chatas* (see Mitzvah 121 with note 15). If, however, the two transgressions were of two separate prohibitions — for example, he mistakenly ate *cheilev* and then consumed blood of an animal (Mitzvah 148) — he is liable to a separate *chatas* offering for each prohibition transgressed. As Chinuch will proceed to write, one who transgresses multiple prohibitions on the Sabbath is subject to a somewhat different set of rules.

8. As stated in the previous note, with regard to other *chatas*-bearing prohibitions, if one transgresses inadvertently and then repeats his transgression in a "single period of unawareness," he is liable to only a single *chatas*. Now, with regard to the Sabbath, the Torah specified a prohibition of a single *melachah* (i.e., kindling), even though it was already included in the general prohibition of performing *all* the *melachos*. This specification is understood as teaching a rule not only in regard to kindling, but also in regard to the entire category of prohibited *melachos* (*Mechilta*; see above, note 6). The verse thus indicates that although all 39 primary *melachos* are prohibited by a single mitzvah-prohibition (see Mitzvah 32 — *The Prohibition to Perform Melachah on the Sabbath*), the Torah views them individually, and imposes a separate *chatas* liability for each of them, as if it were the subject of an individual prohibition. Thus, if one performed a *melachah* without awareness that it was prohibited and then performed a different *melachah*, he is required to bring a separate *chatas* for each *melachah* violated, even if he performed the second before he became aware of his error in performing the first *melachah*.

[However, if he performed the *melachos* because he was unaware of the fact that it was the Sabbath day, rather than because he was unaware that his act was a *melachah*, or if in his second transgression he repeated the first *melachah*, he is liable to only a single *chatas* offering, provided that both transgressions were performed in a "single period of unawareness."]

Now, as noted by Chinuch, we are deriving both the law imposing a separate *chatas* liability for each *melachah* performed and the law that *beis din* may not perform an execution on the Sabbath from the same verse. Although, ordinarily, two distinct laws cannot be derived from a single phrase, in this case, the Torah could have taught the prohibition to carry out capital punishment on the Sabbath by stating simply "You shall not perform *melachah* in any of your dwelling places." By singling out the prohibition of *kindling*, the Torah teaches an additional law — the separate liability for each *melachah* (*Tosafos*, *Yevamos* 6b ד״ה טעמא; see also *Tosafos*, *Shabbos* 70a ד״ה הבערה ללאו יצאה).

9. The wording of *Mechilta* cited above by Chinuch would indicate that our mitzvah prohibits only

# 375 ☐ VAYAKHEL / MITZVAH 114: NOT TO CARRY OUT CAPITAL PUNISHMENT ON THE SABBATH

מִשָּׁרְשֵׁי הַמִּצְוָה, שֶׁרָצָה שֵׁם יִתְבָּרַךְ לְכַבֵּד הַיּוֹם הַזֶּה שֶׁיִּמְצְאוּ בוֹ מְנוּחָה הַכֹּל גַּם הַחוֹטְאִים וְהַחַיָּבִים. מָשָׁל לְמֶלֶךְ גָּדוֹל שֶׁקָּרָא בְּנֵי הַמְּדִינָה יוֹם אֶחָד לִסְעָדָה שֶׁאֵינוֹ מוֹנֵעַ הַפֶּתַח מִכָּל אָדָם, וְאַחַר יוֹם הַסְּעָדָה יַעֲשֶׂה מִשְׁפָּט, כֵּן הַדָּבָר הַזֶּה שֶׁהַשֵּׁם בָּרוּךְ הוּא צִוָּנוּ לְקַדֵּשׁ וּלְכַבֵּד יוֹם הַשַּׁבָּת לְטוֹבָתֵנוּ וְלִזְכוּתֵנוּ, כְּמוֹ שֶׁכָּתַבְתִּי לְמַעְלָה[10], וְזֶה גַּם כֵּן מִכְּבוֹדוֹ שֶׁל יוֹם הוּא.

וְנוֹהֶגֶת מִצְוָה זוֹ בִּזְמַן הַבַּיִת[11] בִּזְכָרִים, שֶׁהֵם בַּעֲלֵי הַמִּשְׁפָּט[12] וְחַיָּבִים לְהִזָּהֵר לְבַל יַעֲשׂוּ

---

## ~ Underlying Purpose of the Mitzvah ~

שֶׁרָצָה הַשֵּׁם יִתְבָּרַךְ לְכַבֵּד מִשָּׁרְשֵׁי הַמִּצְוָה — **Among the underlying purposes of the mitzvah is** שֶׁיִּמְצְאוּ הַיּוֹם הַזֶּה — **that Hashem, blessed be He, desired to glorify this day,** i.e., the Sabbath, בּוֹ מְנוּחָה הַכֹּל — **so that all should find rest in it,** גַּם הַחוֹטְאִים וְהַחַיָּבִים — **even the sinners and those liable** to punishment. מָשָׁל לְמֶלֶךְ גָּדוֹל — **This is analogous to a great king,** שֶׁקָּרָא בְּנֵי הַמְּדִינָה יוֹם אֶחָד לִסְעָדָה — **who invited the citizens of his nation to a feast on a single day.** שֶׁאֵינוֹ מוֹנֵעַ הַפֶּתַח מִכָּל אָדָם — **On that day, [the king] will not deny entry to any person,** even to the guilty, וְאַחַר יוֹם הַסְּעָדָה יַעֲשֶׂה מִשְׁפָּט — **and** only **after the day of the feast will he implement justice** upon them. כֵּן הַדָּבָר הַזֶּה — **So too,** with regard to **this matter,** שֶׁהַשֵּׁם בָּרוּךְ הוּא צִוָּנוּ לְקַדֵּשׁ וּלְכַבֵּד יוֹם הַשַּׁבָּת — **Hashem, blessed is He, commanded us to sanctify and honor the Sabbath day,** לְטוֹבָתֵנוּ וְלִזְכוּתֵנוּ כְּמוֹ שֶׁכָּתַבְתִּי לְמַעְלָה — **for our benefit and merit, as I have written above;**[10] וְזֶה גַּם כֵּן מִכְּבוֹדוֹ שֶׁל יוֹם הוּא — **and this** restriction **is also an aspect of the honor of the** Sabbath **day.**

## ~ Applicability of the Mitzvah ~

וְנוֹהֶגֶת מִצְוָה זוֹ בִּזְמַן הַבַּיִת — **This mitzvah applies during the times of the Temple,**[11] בִּזְכָרִים — **and is incumbent only upon males,** שֶׁהֵם בַּעֲלֵי הַמִּשְׁפָּט — **for they have the responsibility to impose justice,**[12] וְחַיָּבִים לְהִזָּהֵר לְבַל יַעֲשׂוּ דִין בְּשַׁבָּת — **and they are obligated to be careful to refrain from implementing justice on the Sabbath.**

---

### NOTES

administering the death penalty. Some understand that *Yerushalmi* expands the scope of the prohibition to include administering any form of punishment (see *Elyah Rabbah* 339:2; *Avnei Nezer* I §46). Others, however, understand that *Yerushalmi,* too, refers only to implementing the death penalty [and possibly *malkus,* as well; see *Rambam, Hil. Shabbos* 24:7] (see *Teshuvos HaGeonim* §10; *Birkei Yosef, Orach Chaim* 339:3 and *Machazik Berachah* there; see also *Minchas Chinuch* §1). Indeed throughout his discussion of the laws of this mitzvah, Chinuch appears to be addressing only implementing the death penalty on the Sabbath (see, however, *Elyah Rabbah* ibid. and *Pri Megadim,* beginning of preface to *Hilchos Shabbos*).

10. For discussion of the underlying purposes of the mitzvos that pertain to the Sabbath, see Mitzvos 31 and 32.

11. The imposition of capital punishment was possible only during the time of the *Beis HaMikdash,* when the Great Sanhedrin would convene in its designated chamber on the Temple Mount (i.e., the לִשְׁכַּת הַגָּזִית, *Chamber of Hewn Stone*); see *Rambam, Hil. Sanhedrin*

14:11. Once the Sanhedrin was exiled (40 years before the destruction of the *Beis HaMikdash*), it was no longer possible to implement capital punishment (*Rambam* ibid. §13). [According to those who maintain that administering *malkus* on the Sabbath is included in this prohibition (see above, note 9), the prohibition would apply even after the destruction of the *Beis HaMikdash.* Nevertheless, since a *beis din* can administer *malkus* only if it is comprised of judges who received the *semichah* that was granted in earlier times (i.e., ordination according to the procedure set forth in Mitzvah 491), this has no practical relevance today. Nevertheless, this mitzvah may have relevance even today according to the opinion (cited above, note 9) that *all* forms of punishment are included in this prohibition; see *Avnei Nezer* I §46 and *Mishnah Berurah* 339:13.]

It should be noted, however, that on a Rabbinic level, it is prohibited to judge any judicial cases as well as to perform various court-related activities on the Sabbath; see *Orach Chaim* 339:4 with commentaries for further details.

12. See Mitzvah 77 at note 40. See Insight.

## ויקהל / מצוה קיד: שלא יעשו בית דין משפט מות בשבת

דִּין בְּשַׁבָּת. וְאִם עָבְרוּ וְצִוּוּ לִשְׂרֹף בְּרִיָּה בְּשַׁבָּת, עָבְרוּ עַל לָאו זֶה. וְאֵין לוֹקִין עָלָיו אִם לֹא עָשׂוּ בּוֹ מַעֲשֶׂה.[13] וְאִם עָשׂוּ בּוֹ מַעֲשֶׂה, כְּגוֹן שֶׁשְּׂרָפוּהוּ הֵם בִּידֵיהֶם, אִם יֵשׁ עֵדִים וְהַתְרָאָה נִסְקָלִין[14], בְּשׁוֹגֵג מְבִיאִים חַטָּאת לְכַפָּרָה.[15]

וְאִם עָבְרוּ וְצִוּוּ לִשְׂרֹף בְּרִיָּה בְּשַׁבָּת — **If [the judges of a court] transgressed, and they instructed their agents to perform *sereifah* or another form of capital punishment upon a human being on the Sabbath,** עָבְרוּ עַל לָאו זֶה — **they have violated this prohibition.** וְאֵין לוֹקִין עָלָיו אִם לֹא עָשׂוּ בּוֹ מַעֲשֶׂה — **However, they do not incur *malkus* (lashes) for this [transgression] if they** themselves **did not perform an action** in committing **it, but merely issued the instruction to their** agents.[13] וְאִם עָשׂוּ בּוֹ מַעֲשֶׂה — **If they did perform an action** in violating **it,** כְּגוֹן שֶׁשְּׂרָפוּהוּ הֵם בִּידֵיהֶם — **for example, if they themselves carried out the *sereifah*,** אִם יֵשׁ עֵדִים וְהַתְרָאָה נִסְקָלִין — **if there are witnesses** to their act **and** they received **a warning** before transgressing, **they incur *sekilah* (stoning) for their act of Sabbath desecration.**[14] בְּשׁוֹגֵג מְבִיאִים חַטָּאת לְכַפָּרָה — **If** they transgressed **unintentionally, they must bring a *chatas* offering to atone** for their sin.[15]

### NOTES

13. Chinuch indicates here that this mitzvah applies not only to judges who administer the penalty themselves, but also to judges who instruct their agents to do so (for discussion, see Insight). It is only that judges who instruct their agents to administer a penalty do not themselves incur *malkus*, as their prohibition did not entail an action. This is consistent with the general rule that a לָאו שֶׁאֵין בּוֹ מַעֲשֶׂה, *a prohibition that does not involve action*, does not bear a corporal penalty.

14. One who deliberately performs *melachah* on the Sabbath is liable to *sekilah* (see General Introduction for the circumstances in which capital punishment was carried out in earlier times). Accordingly, if the judges themselves administer *sereifah* they are liable to this penalty. [As noted above (note 9), according to some, this prohibition includes implementing other punishments of *beis din*, as well. Presumably then, if *beis din* were to transgress the prohibition by carrying out some other punishment with their own hands, for example, they administered *malkus* in a manner that does not transgress any of the 39 *melachos* of the Sabbath for which one incurs *sekilah*, they themselves would be liable to *malkus*, for having transgressed *this* prohibition in a manner that entails an action. See, however, *Minchas Chinuch*, end of §1; cf. *Minchas Soless*.]

15. One who unintentionally performs *melachah* on the Sabbath must bring a *chatas* offering; see above, end of Mitzvah 32, with notes 39 and 40.

---

**⊷§ Insight: Capital Punishment on the Sabbath — The Focus of the Prohibition**

It is prohibited to take any life on the Sabbath, whether of a human or of an animal. Nevertheless, the Gemara (*Yevamos* 6b; see also *Mechilta* cited by Chinuch) states that since the Torah specifically obligates *beis din* to administer capital punishment to those who are liable to the death penalty, one might have thought that this obligation applies even on the Sabbath. The verse of this mitzvah teaches that the obligation to administer the death penalty applies only on weekdays, but on the Sabbath it is prohibited.

Now, the verse states with regard to building the *Beis HaMikdash* (*Leviticus* 19:30): אֶת שַׁבְּתֹתַי תִּשְׁמֹרוּ וּמִקְדָּשִׁי תִּירָאוּ, *My Sabbaths you shall observe and My Sanctuary you shall revere*. From this verse, the Sages derive (*Yevamos* 6b) that the mitzvah to build the *Beis HaMikdash* does not override the laws of the Sabbath. That verse is not counted as one of the 613 Mitzvos, which is understandable, since the verse is not teaching a prohibition per se. It is simply teaching that building the *Beis HaMikdash* is not an exception to the general rule, and is included in the *general prohibition* of performing *melachah* on the Sabbath. The question therefore arises: Why is the verse that teaches that *beis din* may not implement the death penalty on the Sabbath counted as a mitzvah? Here, too, it would seem that the verse is not teaching a new prohibition, but is simply teaching that implementing the death penalty on the Sabbath is not an exception to the general rule, and is included in the *general prohibition* of performing *melachah* on the Sabbath (see *Minchas Chinuch* §1; *Maayan HaChochmah*, Redelheim, 1904 ed., top of fol. 25a; see *Minchah Chadashah* for further discussion; see note 9 above for a different view on this matter).

*R' Y. F. Perla* (*Sefer HaMitzvos* of *R' Saadiah Gaon*, *Lo Saaseh* 178, Vol. 2, p. 392 ד"ה וראיתי) addresses

## VAYAKHEL / MITZVAH 114: NOT TO CARRY OUT CAPITAL PUNISHMENT ON THE SABBATH

פָּרָשַׁת אֵלֶּה פְקוּדֵי אֵין בָּהּ מִצְוָה.
נִשְׁלַם סֵפֶר וְאֵלֶּה שְׁמוֹת
בְּעֶזְרַת נוֹתֵן כֹּחַ וְתַעֲצוּמוֹת
תְּהִלָּה לְיוֹצֵר נְשָׁמוֹת
אָחֵל סֵפֶר וַיִּקְרָא
בְּסִיּוּעַ רָם וְנִשָּׂא.

פָּרָשַׁת אֵלֶּה פְקוּדֵי אֵין בָּהּ מִצְוָה — *Parashas Pekudei* does not contain mitzvos.
נִשְׁלַם סֵפֶר וְאֵלֶּה שְׁמוֹת — The elucidation of mitzvos in **the Book of** *Exodus* **has been completed**
בְּעֶזְרַת נוֹתֵן כֹּחַ וְתַעֲצוּמוֹת — **with the help of He Who grants strength and vigor;**
תְּהִלָּה לְיוֹצֵר נְשָׁמוֹת — for this, I give **praise to the Creator of souls.**
אָחֵל סֵפֶר וַיִּקְרָא — Now, **I shall commence the Book of** *Leviticus*
בְּסִיּוּעַ רָם וְנִשָּׂא — **with the assistance of the Exalted and Lofty.**

---

this question, and explains that our verse, in fact, teaches a unique prohibition. The focus of the prohibition of implementing justice on the Sabbath is not the *act* of execution (which certainly entails performing *melachah* that is prohibited on the Sabbath). Rather, the verse prohibits the judges of *beis din* from having a death sentence carried out *on their behalf* on the Sabbath. Thus, even if they do not actively participate in carrying out the execution, and do not themselves violate the prohibition of performing *melachah* on the Sabbath in any way, implementing the judgment by having it done on their behalf is a violation of this mitzvah. This, in fact, is evident from Chinuch's words at the close of the mitzvah, where he states that if the judges instruct their agent to administer *sereifah* they violate this prohibition. Clearly, by stating *You shall not kindle a fire in any of your dwelling places on the Sabbath day*, the Torah not only indicates that the execution itself is prohibited (and is not an exception to the general prohibition of *melachah*), but also specifically prohibits the judges of the court from issuing the directive to carry it out. Therefore, unlike the prohibition of building the *Beis HaMikdash* on the Sabbath, the activity prohibited by this verse is not included in the prohibition of performing *melachah* on the Sabbath, and is reckoned as a separate mitzvah.

This explanation of the focus of the prohibition resolves an additional difficulty: Chinuch states that since our mitzvah pertains to imposing penalties, it applies only to the judges of a *beis din*, and since women are not responsible for imposing justice, they are not included in this prohibition. *Minchah Chadashah* (§3), however, points out that in the case of one who was sentenced to death by *beis din* because he intentionally killed a person, it is a mitzvah for his execution to be administered by the victim's next of kin (see *Rambam, Hil. Rotze'ach* 1:2), who can presumably be a woman. A similar law applies in certain other cases as well (see *Rambam, Hil. Avodas Kochavim* 5:4). Thus, *Minchah Chadashah* asks, our mitzvah has an application even in regard to lay people, including women, as it prohibits them from administering the death penalty on the Sabbath. Why does Chinuch write that the mitzvah applies only to judges, and why does he limit its applicability to men?

According to the above explanation, however, this difficulty is resolved. Regardless of who carries out the execution, this mitzvah applies only to the judges on whose behalf it is administered. The focus of the mitzvah is not the actual performance of execution on the Sabbath, as that is included in the standard prohibition of performing *melachah* on the Sabbath; rather, its focus is a prohibition on the judges to have the death penalty administered. Since only men can serve as judges, only they are subject to this mitzvah. Obviously, though, anyone who actually carries out an execution on the Sabbath will have violated the general prohibition of performing *melachah* on the Sabbath.

# ספר ויקרא
## Book of Vayikra/Leviticus

## פרשת ויקרא
## Parashas Vayikra

וַיִּקְרָא יֵשׁ בָּהּ אַחַת עֶשְׂרֵה מִצְווֹת עֲשֵׂה
וְחָמֵשׁ מִצְווֹת לֹא תַעֲשֶׂה

*Parashas Vayikra* contains eleven Mitzvah-Obligations
and five Mitzvah-Prohibitions.

### CONTAINS SIXTEEN MITZVOS:
### MITZVOS 115-130

115. מִצְוַת מַעֲשֵׂה הָעוֹלָה — The Obligation Regarding the Process of the *Olah* Offering
116. מִצְוַת קָרְבַּן מִנְחָה — The Obligation Regarding the *Minchah* Offering
117. שֶׁלֹּא לְהַקְרִיב שְׂאוֹר אוֹ דְּבַשׁ — The Prohibition to Bring Leaven or Honey as an Offering
118. שֶׁלֹּא לְהַקְרִיב קָרְבָּן בְּלֹא מֶלַח — The Prohibition to Bring Up an Offering Without Salt
119. מִצְוַת מְלִיחַת הַקָּרְבָּן — The Obligation to Salt the Offering
120. מִצְוַת קָרְבַּן בֵּית דִּין אִם טָעוּ בְּהוֹרָאָה — The Obligation Upon *Beis Din* to Bring an Offering for an Erroneous Ruling
121. מִצְוַת קָרְבַּן חַטָּאת לְיָחִיד שֶׁשָּׁגַג בְּמִצְוַת לֹא תַעֲשֶׂה שֶׁחַיָּבִין עָלֶיהָ כָּרֵת — The Obligation Upon an Individual Who Inadvertently Committed a *Kares*-Bearing Prohibition to Bring a *Chatas* Offering
122. מִצְוַת עֵדוּת — The Obligation Regarding Testimony
123. מִצְוַת קָרְבַּן עוֹלֶה וְיוֹרֵד — The Obligation of the *Olah V'Yoreid* Offering
124. שֶׁלֹּא לְהַבְדִּיל הָרֹאשׁ בְּחַטַּאת הָעוֹף — The Prohibition to Sever the Head of a Bird *Chatas* Offering
125. שֶׁלֹּא לִתֵּן שֶׁמֶן זַיִת בְּמִנְחַת חוֹטֵא — The Prohibition to Place Olive Oil Upon a Sinner's *Minchah* Offering
126. שֶׁלֹּא לִתֵּן לְבוֹנָה בְּמִנְחַת חוֹטֵא — The Prohibition to Place *Levonah* Upon a Sinner's *Minchah* Offering

127. מִצְוַת תּוֹסֶפֶת חֹמֶשׁ לָאוֹכֵל מִן הַהֶקְדֵּשׁ אוֹ מוֹעֵל בָּהּ – The Obligation to Add a Fifth [to the Payment] for [Improper] Consumption of Temple Property or Its Misappropriation
128. מִצְוַת קָרְבַּן אָשָׁם תָּלוּי – The Obligation of the Pending-*Asham* Offering
129. מִצְוַת קָרְבַּן אָשָׁם וַדַּאי – The Obligation of the Definite-*Asham* Offering
130. מִצְוַת הֲשָׁבַת גֵּזֶל – The Obligation to Return a Stolen Item

## VAYIKRA / MITZVAH 115: THE PROCESS OF THE OLAH OFFERING

### מִצְוָה קטו: מִצְוַת מַעֲשֵׂה הָעוֹלָה [2,1]

## Mitzvah 115
## The Obligation Regarding the Process of the Olah Offering

אִם עֹלָה קָרְבָּנוֹ מִן הַבָּקָר זָכָר תָּמִים יַקְרִיבֶנּוּ אֶל פֶּתַח אֹהֶל מוֹעֵד יַקְרִיב אֹתוֹ לִרְצֹנוֹ לִפְנֵי ה׳

*If one's offering is an olah from the cattle, he shall offer an unblemished male; he shall bring it to the entrance of the Tent of Meeting, voluntarily, before* HASHEM *(Leviticus 1:3).*

In Mitzvah 95, "The Obligation to Build the Holy Temple" (*Beis HaMikdash*), Chinuch discussed at length the significance of the *Beis HaMikdash* service (*avodah*) and the offerings brought there, the purpose of the offerings in general, and the impact of their service on our relationship with Hashem. The Book of *Leviticus* contains many mitzvos pertaining to the offerings, including some that deal with the procedures for making the various offerings, others that deal with the circumstances in which one can incur an obligation to bring a specific offering, and others yet that deal with various requirements and prohibitions associated with the *avodah* of those offerings and other aspects of the *Beis HaMikdash* service. For this reason, *Leviticus* is often referred to in Talmudic and Midrashic literature as תּוֹרַת כֹּהֲנִים (*Toras Kohanim*), The Law of Kohanim, for it is the Kohanim who largely bear the responsibility of carrying out the mitzvos pertaining to the Temple service.

For each category of offering, the Torah outlines a distinct procedure, including specific rules as to how its blood is applied to the Altar and which parts of it are burned on the Altar. There also are rules governing when, by whom, and for how long the meat of each offering may be eaten.

The first mitzvah in *Leviticus* deals with the procedure of bringing the *olah* offering.[1] The *olah* is a category of offering wherein the animal is entirely consumed by the fire of the Altar, with no portion of its flesh going to the Kohanim or to its owner (the Kohanim, though, receive its hide). *Olah* offerings could be brought voluntarily, as discussed in the first chapter of *Leviticus* (see *Rashi, Leviticus* 1:2 ד״ה אדם), but in certain situations were obligatory.[2] In the case of voluntary *olah* offerings, although one did not need a specific reason for bringing it, people would often bring the offering in response to having violated a mitzvah that bears no other stated penalty (such as a mitzvah-obligation), or as an atonement for sinful thoughts. [For further discussion of the motivations for bringing an *olah*, see Insight.]

*Olah* offerings were also brought by the community at large in fulfillment of various communal obligations; for example, the *tamid* (daily communal offering) that was offered in the morning and evening of each day (Mitzvah 401) was an *olah* offering, as were practically all the *mussaf* offerings brought on festivals (Mitzvah 299, et al.), Rosh Chodesh (Mitzvah 403), and the Sabbath (Mitzvah 402). This mitzvah addresses the specific procedure of the *olah* service (for whichever of the above reasons it is

---

### NOTES

1. The word עֹלָה (*olah*) denotes *going up* or *elevation*. According to some, this refers to the fact that the offering is completely burned on the Altar, and thus *goes up* in flames (*Rashi, Exodus* 18:12). Alternatively, owing to the fact that the *olah* offering is entirely consumed on the Altar, it is viewed as being an offering of superior quality; hence its name stems from this qualitative superiority [עֶלְיוֹנָה] (*Tanchuma, Tzav* §1; see *Chizkuni, Leviticus* 1:3). Others explain that the name does not relate to the offering's procedure, but rather to the sin for which the offering comes to atone, i.e., sinful thoughts that *arise* in a person's mind (*Ramban* and *Ibn Ezra, Leviticus* 1:4). See Insight for further discussion.

2. For example, an *olah* was required of a woman who had given birth (Mitzvah 168), of every person after being healed from *tzaraas* (Mitzvah 176), and of every man upon appearing in the *Beis HaMikdash* at each festival (Mitzvah 489).

## 384 □ ויקרא / מצוה קטו: מצות מעשה העולה

לַעֲשׂוֹת הָעוֹלָה כְּמִשְׁפָּטָהּ, שֶׁנֶּאֱמַר (ויקרא א׳, ג׳) אִם עֹלָה קָרְבָּנוֹ וְגוֹ׳, כְּמוֹ שֶׁכָּתוּב בַּפָּרָשָׁה.[3]

מִשָּׁרְשֵׁי הַמִּצְוָה, מַה שֶּׁכָּתַבְתִּי[4] בְּמִצְוַת הַבַּיִת עַל עִנְיַן הַקָּרְבָּנוֹת, סֵדֶר וְיִקְחוּ לִי.[5]

מִדִּינֵי הַמִּצְוָה, מַה שֶּׁאָמְרוּ זִכְרוֹנָם לִבְרָכָה בְּמַעֲשֵׂה הָעוֹלָה שֶׁהָיְתָה נַעֲשֵׂית כֵּן, שׁוֹחֲטִין אֶת הַבְּהֵמָה בָּעֲזָרָה,[6] וְהַשְּׁחִיטָה כְּשֵׁרָה אֲפִלּוּ בְּזָרִים, וּמְקַבָּלַת הַדָּם וָאֵילָךְ מִצְוַת כְּהֻנָּה,[7]

---

being brought), and the obligation to perform that service in accordance with the procedure delineated in the Torah.

לַעֲשׂוֹת הָעוֹלָה כְּמִשְׁפָּטָהּ — We are commanded **to perform** the procedure of **the** *olah* **offering in accordance with its laws,** שֶׁנֶּאֱמַר "אִם עֹלָה קָרְבָּנוֹ וְגוֹ׳" — **as it is stated** (*Leviticus* 1:3): *If one's offering is an olah, etc.* — כְּמוֹ שֶׁכָּתוּב בַּפָּרָשָׁה — That is, we are to perform the sacrificial service **as per what is written in the passage** there.[3]

### ☞ Underlying Purpose of the Mitzvah ☜

מִשָּׁרְשֵׁי הַמִּצְוָה — **Among the underlying purposes of** this **mitzvah** מַה שֶּׁכָּתַבְתִּי בְּמִצְוַת הַבַּיִת — **is that which I wrote** above, in *Parashas Terumah*,[4] עַל עִנְיַן הַקָּרְבָּנוֹת סֵדֶר וְיִקְחוּ לִי — in Mitzvah 95 — **the obligation** to build **the Holy Temple** — **with regard to the subject of the offerings** in general.[5]

### ☞ Laws of the Mitzvah ☜

מַה שֶּׁאָמְרוּ זִכְרוֹנָם לִבְרָכָה בְּמַעֲשֵׂה הָעוֹלָה — מִדִּינֵי הַמִּצְוָה **Among the laws of the mitzvah** שֶׁהָיְתָה נַעֲשֵׂית כֵּן — **is that which [our Sages], of blessed memory, stated** (*Zevachim* 31b-32a) **with regard to the procedure of the** *olah* **offering, that it was performed as follows:** שׁוֹחֲטִין אֶת הַבְּהֵמָה בָּעֲזָרָה — **First, they would slaughter the animal in the** Temple **Courtyard.**[6] וְהַשְּׁחִיטָה כְּשֵׁרָה אֲפִלּוּ בְּזָרִים — **Now, the slaughter is valid even** if done by **a non-Kohen;** וּמְקַבָּלַת הַדָּם וָאֵילָךְ מִצְוַת כְּהֻנָּה — **however, the** *avodos* **(sacrificial services) from** that of the **receiving of the blood and onward are the exclusive charge of the Kohanim.**[7]

---

NOTES

3. The Torah passage that discusses the *olah* offering, *Leviticus* 1:3-17, lists in detail its laws and procedures, many of which Chinuch will reference shortly.

4. What is commonly known as *Parashas Terumah* is referred to by Chinuch as סֵדֶר וְיִקְחוּ לִי, based on the words at the beginning of the *Parashah*: וְיִקְחוּ לִי תְּרוּמָה, *let them take for Me a portion*.

5. In Mitzvah 95, "The Obligation to Build the *Beis HaMikdash*," Chinuch digresses to discuss some of the underlying purposes of offerings in general. In his discussion there, he focuses mostly on the *chatas* (sin) offering, and notes that it is human nature to be moved more by actions than by mere words. The act of taking one's own animal, a portion of his very sustenance, and bringing it with great effort to the *Beis HaMikdash*, will help him internalize the gravity of his error, much more than a simple confession could ever do. Chinuch notes further that in the slaughtering and burning of an animal, one recognizes that his own animalistic side, when it is not coupled with the guiding strength of the intellect, has no true value. This latter idea, Chinuch notes, helps explain offerings that are not sin offerings as well, for the message of the weakening of the influence of the body and the elevation of the spirit is one that is always poignant and relevant.

Some note an additional point regarding the *olah* offering in particular. As discussed in the introduction to this mitzvah, an *olah* is often brought to atone for sinful thoughts. Hence, the *olah* offering has a unique quality in that it is to be wholly burned to Hashem and shared with no one else, for other than the person himself, only Hashem is privy to this particular shortcoming (*Ramban, Leviticus* 1:4). See Insight for further discussion.

6. More specifically, the slaughtering of an *olah* offering is performed in the area of the Courtyard to the north of the Altar, as per (*Leviticus* 1:11): וְשָׁחַט אֹתוֹ עַל יֶרֶךְ הַמִּזְבֵּחַ צָפֹנָה לִפְנֵי ה׳, *He shall slaughter it at the northern side of the Altar before HASHEM*. This was where all sacrifices known as *kodshei kodashim* (most-holy offerings), which includes the *olah,* are slaughtered, while offerings known as *kodashim kalim* (*offerings of lesser holiness*) could be slaughtered anywhere in the Temple Courtyard (*Mishnah, Zevachim*, Ch. 5; *Rambam, Hil. Maaseh HaKorbanos* 5:2-4). [For further description of these categories, see introduction to Mitzvah 102.]

7. From the flow of the verse that states (*Leviticus* 1:5): וְשָׁחַט אֶת בֶּן הַבָּקָר לִפְנֵי ה׳ וְהִקְרִיבוּ בְּנֵי אַהֲרֹן הַכֹּהֲנִים אֶת הַדָּם וְזָרְקוּ אֶת הַדָּם עַל הַמִּזְבֵּחַ סָבִיב אֲשֶׁר פֶּתַח אֹהֶל מוֹעֵד, *He shall slaughter the bull before HASHEM; and the sons of*

## 385 ☐ VAYIKRA / MITZVAH 115: THE PROCESS OF THE OLAH OFFERING

וְזוֹרֵק הַכֹּהֵן הַדָּם[8] וּמַפְשִׁיט אוֹתָהּ[9] וּמְנַתְּחָהּ אֵיבָרִים שְׁלֵמִים, דִּכְתִיב (שם, שם ו) לִנְתָחֶיהָ, וּפֵרְשׁוּ זִכְרוֹנָם לִבְרָכָה וְלֹא נְתָחֶיהָ לִנְתָחִים. וּכְשֶׁמְּנַתֵּחַ מֵסִיר גִּיד הַנָּשֶׁה מִן הַיָּרֵךְ[10] וּמַקְטִיר[11] כָּל הַנְּתָחִים עַל גַּבֵּי הַמִּזְבֵּחַ.[12]

---

וְזוֹרֵק הַכֹּהֵן הַדָּם — **The Kohen throws the blood,**[8] וּמַפְשִׁיט אוֹתָהּ — **skins [the offering],**[9] וּמְנַתְּחָהּ אֵיבָרִים שְׁלֵמִים — **and then cuts it into whole limbs.** דִּכְתִיב "לִנְתָחֶיהָ" — **That the limbs are to be left whole is learned from a verse; as it is written** (ibid. 1:6): *he shall cut it **into its pieces**,* וּפֵרְשׁוּ זִכְרוֹנָם לִבְרָכָה — **and [our Sages], of blessed memory, explained** (*Chullin* 11a) that the emphasis of *"its" pieces* teaches us: וְלֹא נְתָחֶיהָ לִנְתָחִים — **but not its pieces into pieces.** That is, the limbs are not to be broken down even further into smaller portions, but rather, are to be offered whole. וּכְשֶׁמְּנַתֵּחַ מֵסִיר גִּיד הַנָּשֶׁה מִן הַיָּרֵךְ — **The laws include also that when he cuts up** the animal into its limbs, **he is to remove the *gid hanasheh*** (the "displaced sinew") **from the thigh.**[10] וּמַקְטִיר כָּל הַנְּתָחִים עַל גַּבֵּי הַמִּזְבֵּחַ — **He** then **burns**[11] **all the limbs on top of the Altar.**[12]

---

### NOTES

*Aaron, the Kohanim, shall bring the blood and throw the blood on the Altar, all around*, we derive that a Kohen is needed for the *avodos* starting from the "bringing of the blood" (i.e., receiving in a vessel the blood that flows out from the incision; *Zevachim* 4a) and onward. However, the slaughter, referenced in the first half of the verse, before the requirement for Kohanim is mentioned, does not require a Kohen (*Zevachim* 32a). In addition, any procedure that is not deemed an *avodah* may be performed by a non-Kohen, including skinning, dissection, and rinsing of the offering's innards (*Ramban, Leviticus* 1:6; *Minchas Chinuch* §19).

8. The Kohen takes the vessel in which he had received the blood from the slaughter, walks over to the Altar and, standing on the floor of the Courtyard, throws the blood from the basin against the northeast corner of the Altar, so that some blood falls on the northern wall and some on the eastern wall of the Altar. He repeats that procedure at the southwest corner, so that some blood falls on the southern wall and some on the western wall of the Altar. With these two applications, he fulfills the verse (*Leviticus* 1:5) which requires him to *throw the blood on the Altar, all around*. That is, by way of throwing the blood on those two corners, it is applied "all around," in that every side (east, north, west, south) of the Altar has had the blood applied to it (*Rashi* ad loc., quoting *Sifra*; *Rambam* ibid. 5:6). The blood of animal *olah* offerings is applied (using a different procedure) to the lower half of the Altar's walls, while that of fowl (discussed in detail below) is applied to the upper half (see Mishnah, *Kinnim* 1:1).

9. Smaller animals (e.g., sheep and goats) would be hung by their left hind leg on specially designed hooks located on pillars in the Courtyard. Oxen would be flayed in a similar fashion; however, they were not hung on the hooks, but were skinned while lying on the Courtyard floor (*Rambam* ibid. 6:5).

[Although Chinuch here speaks of the Kohen as being the one to skin and dissect the animal, in truth neither of these procedures *required* a Kohen (see above, note 7). Chinuch speaks of a Kohen as performing these tasks simply because that was the norm (see *Me'il HaEphod* §3).]

10. The *gid hanasheh* refers to the sciatic nerve. Since it is forbidden to be eaten (see Mitzvah 3), the *gid hanasheh* also may not be burned on the Altar. This is derived from the verse (*Ezekiel* 45:15): מִמַּשְׁקֵה יִשְׂרָאֵל לְמִנְחָה וּלְעוֹלָה וְלִשְׁלָמִים, *from the feast of Israel, for a minchah* (meal-offering), *an olah, and a shelamim* (peace offering), which teaches that what is offered on the Altar should (in general) be that which is fit for "the feast of Israel," i.e., permitted for consumption by a Jew. Therefore, after bringing the thigh up to the Altar, the *gid hanasheh* is removed and thrown onto the ash mound in the center of the Altar, but is not burned (*Chullin* 90b; *Rambam* ibid. 6:4).

[The removal of the *gid hanasheh* could not be done before bringing the thigh up to the Altar, for the act of removing the *gid hanasheh* requires one to cut deeply into the thigh. Such dissection would mar the appearance of the limb, and it would be disrespectful for it to be brought up the ramp in such a fashion (*Chullin* ibid.). *Minchas Chinuch* (§23) notes that Chinuch's wording here is difficult, as it implies that the removal of the *gid hanasheh* occurs below, in the Courtyard, at the time of the dissection of the animal into its limbs, which is not the case.]

11. Literally, *causes to go up in smoke*.

12. Kohanim were chosen by lot for all the *avodos* (of the communal offerings), including the privilege of bringing the limbs to the Altar ramp. This privilege was assigned to a number of Kohanim, which varied depending on the type of animal that had been offered (see below, notes 17-19). The limbs were then brought up from the ramp to the top of the Altar by a single Kohen, also chosen by lot (*Yoma* 26a; *Rashi* ad loc. 26b ד"ה עצמו; *Tosafos* there ד"ה דתנן; cf. *Tosafos Yeshanim* ibid. 26b ד"ה דלא, who maintain that several Kohanim were chosen for the latter task as well). The Kohen who brought up the limbs would stand at the edge of the ramp and throw them onto the Altar fire (*Zevachim* 62b; *Rambam* ibid. 6:4).

## 386 □ ויקרא / מצוה קטו: מצות מעשה העולה

וְצֶמֶר שֶׁבְּרָאשֵׁי הַכְּבָשִׂים וְשֵׂעָר שֶׁבִּזְקַן הַתְּיָשִׁים[13], וְהָעֲצָמוֹת וְהַגִּידִים וְהַקַּרְנַיִם וְהַטְּלָפַיִם, בִּזְמַן שֶׁהֵם מְחֻבָּרִים מַקְטִירִים הַכֹּל, שֶׁנֶּאֱמַר (שם, שם ט) "וְהִקְטִיר הַכֹּהֵן אֶת הַכֹּל", פֵּרְשׁוּ לֹא יַעֲלוּ, שֶׁנֶּאֱמַר (דברים י"ב, כ"ז) "וְעָשִׂיתָ עֹלֹתֶיךָ הַבָּשָׂר וְהַדָּם"[14]. וְסֵדֶר הַנִּתּוּחַ כֵּיצַד הָיָה[15], וַהֲדָחַת בְּנֵי הַמֵּעַיִם כֵּיצַד[16], וּבְכַמָּה בְּנֵי אָדָם מוֹלִיכִין אֶת הָאֵיבָרִים לַמִּזְבֵּחַ[17], שֶׁאָמְרוּ זִכְרוֹנָם לִבְרָכָה כִּי הַכֶּבֶשׂ בְּשִׁשָּׁה[18], וְהַשּׁוֹר בְּאַרְבָּעָה

---

Chinuch discusses the laws regarding the peripheral parts of the animal's body: וְצֶמֶר שֶׁבְּרָאשֵׁי הַכְּבָשִׂים וְשֵׂעָר שֶׁבִּזְקַן הַתְּיָשִׁים — **As for the wool on the heads of the sheep, and the hair of the beards of the he-goats,**[13] וְהָעֲצָמוֹת וְהַגִּידִים וְהַקַּרְנַיִם וְהַטְּלָפַיִם — **as well as the bones, sinews, horns, and hooves** of the animals, the rule is as follows: בִּזְמַן שֶׁהֵם מְחֻבָּרִים מַקְטִירִים הַכֹּל — **as long as they are still attached** to the limb that is to be offered, they are **all offered** together with the limbs, שֶׁנֶּאֱמַר "וְהִקְטִיר הַכֹּהֵן אֶת הַכֹּל" — **as it is stated** (*Leviticus* 1:9): *the Kohen shall burn it all* on the Altar; the term *all* indicates that even these peripheral parts of the animal are burned. פֵּרְשׁוּ לֹא יַעֲלוּ — **However, if they became detached** from the limb to be offered, **they are not brought up** to the Altar, שֶׁנֶּאֱמַר "וְעָשִׂיתָ עֹלֹתֶיךָ הַבָּשָׂר וְהַדָּם" — **as it is stated** (*Deuteronomy* 12:27): *You shall perform your olah offerings, the flesh and the blood,* upon the Altar of HASHEM; the phrase "the flesh and blood" indicates that no offering is to be made of *just* the peripheral hair or bone.[14]

וְסֵדֶר הַנִּתּוּחַ כֵּיצַד הָיָה — The laws also include **the procedure for how the dissection** of the offering **was** performed,[15] וַהֲדָחַת בְּנֵי הַמֵּעַיִם כֵּיצַד — **and how the rinsing of the intestines** was performed.[16]

Chinuch addresses the procedure for bringing the offering's pieces up onto the Altar: וּבְכַמָּה בְּנֵי אָדָם מוֹלִיכִין אֶת הָאֵיבָרִים לַמִּזְבֵּחַ — The laws include, as well, **how many people were to bring the limbs** of the offering **to the Altar** ramp,[17] שֶׁאָמְרוּ זִכְרוֹנָם לִבְרָכָה כִּי הַכֶּבֶשׂ בְּשִׁשָּׁה — as **[our Sages], of blessed memory, said** (*Yoma* 25a, 26b) **that** the limbs of **a sheep are** brought to the Altar ramp **by six** Kohanim,[18] וְהַשּׁוֹר בְּאַרְבָּעָה וְעֶשְׂרִים — **while** those of **an ox are** brought

---

### NOTES

13. Unlike the rest of the animal, the head of the *olah* was not skinned, because it was cut off before the skinning of the animal was performed, and thus was not included in the skinning requirement. Therefore, it generally still had the wool or hair connected to it (*Rashi, Zevachim* 85b ד"ה הצמר).

14. These two verses seemingly contradict one another, for one verse implies that the entire animal is offered (*the Kohen shall burn it all*), while the other implies that only the flesh and blood are offered (*You shall perform your olah offerings, the flesh and the blood*). The Sages teach, however, that in truth they are in consonance. As Chinuch explains, when these peripheral parts (i.e., the wool, hair, bones, etc.) are still attached to their associated limbs, they are offered together with that limb. If, however, they become detached, they are not to be brought up separately; rather, the limb is burned without its peripheral parts (*Mishnah, Zevachim* 85b).

15. The animal was flayed and dissected into its various limbs in keeping with the verse (*Leviticus* 1:6): *He shall skin the olah offering and cut it into its pieces.* See *Mishnah, Tamid* 4:2-3, and *Rambam, Hil. Maaseh HaKorbanos* 6:5, 7-9, for the sequence of dissecting. As each piece was cut away from the animal, it was given to the appropriate Kohen who had been awarded the right to bring it up to the Altar ramp.

16. The intestines were rinsed out at least three times on marble tables situated in the Courtyard adjacent to where the animal was slaughtered. The stomachs, too, were washed thoroughly, but since they contained more refuse, they were taken into an enclosed chamber (the "Rinsing Chamber") and washed there, so that their waste would not sully the other innards (*Mishnah, Tamid* 4:2, with *Rav*). Alternatively, they were washed there so as not to empty that refuse into the Temple Courtyard (*Rosh, Tamid* 31a).

17. As noted previously (see note 12), two lots were drawn for the offering of the limbs: One to determine which Kohanim would bring them to the ramp, and a second to determine which Kohen (or Kohanim) would throw them from the ramp to the fire (*Mishnah, Yoma* 25a, 26a). Chinuch here is discussing the Kohanim chosen to bring them to the ramp.

18. Each of the six Kohanim would carry a different portion of the sheep up to the Altar ramp in order of the portion's meatiness, with the more meaty limbs being brought first. The head, though, was the exception, for despite its lack of meat, it was nevertheless the first to be brought, as derived from Scriptural sources by the Gemara (*Yoma* 25b: *Radvaz* ibid. 6:12). [To compensate

וְעֶשְׂרִים[19] בְּעוֹלוֹת צִבּוּר, וְעוֹלוֹת יָחִיד בִּפְחוֹתוֹת[20]. וְעִנְיַן עוֹלַת הָעוֹף כֵּיצַד נַעֲשֵׂית[21] וְיֶתֶר פְּרָטֶיהָ, מְבֹאָרִים בִּזְבָחִים (ס"ד ע"ב)[22].

---

**by twenty-four.**[19] **בְּעוֹלוֹת צִבּוּר** — The above numbers refer to an animal that is brought **as a communal** *olah* offering, **וְעוֹלוֹת יָחִיד בִּפְחוֹתוֹת** — but the *olah* offering **of an individual requires less** Kohanim to bring it up to the Altar.[20]

Chinuch has discussed the animal variety of *olah* offerings. At times, an *olah* would be brought from fowl as well, as follows:

**וְעִנְיַן עוֹלַת הָעוֹף כֵּיצַד נַעֲשֵׂית** — The laws include **also the matter of how a bird *olah* offering was performed.**[21]

**וְיֶתֶר פְּרָטֶיהָ, מְבֹאָרִים בִּזְבָחִים** — These, **as well as the additional details of [this mitzvah], are set forth in** Tractate ***Zevachim*** (64b, 85b).[22]

---

### NOTES

for the lack of meat, the head of the sheep was brought together with the right hind leg (ibid.).]

The order and breakdown of the limbs among the six Kohanim are detailed in the Mishnah, *Yoma* 25a and *Rambam* ibid. 6:10-16. [Two more Kohanim were involved as well, albeit not with the limbs, with one Kohen bringing up the meal offering and another bringing up the wine libation that accompanied every *olah* (ibid.). Curiously, Chinuch neglects to account for these two here, even though he does include the carriers of the meal and wine offerings in the count of the ox below (see *Minchas Yitzchak* §7).]

Goats and rams may also be brought as an *olah*. The breakdown and assignment of Kohanim for a goat is the same as that of a sheep (*Rambam*, ibid 6:17). A ram, being an adult sheep, has larger innards (*Meiri, Yoma* 26a ד"ה ולענין פסק; cf. *Ritva*, ibid. 26b), and additionally required larger accompanying meal and wine offerings. It therefore requires three additional Kohanim: one additional Kohen to help carry the innards [for a total of two Kohanim for that function], and two additional Kohanim to carry the ram's accompanying flour and wine offering [for a total of four Kohanim for that function] (Mishnah ibid. 26b; *Rambam* ibid 6:16).

19. The ox, which is a larger animal than a sheep, requires more Kohanim to bring its limbs up onto the Altar ramp. In fact, some limbs required several Kohanim, and a total of eighteen Kohanim were involved in bringing its limbs up onto the Altar ramp. [The order and breakdown of the various limbs and the number of Kohanim required are detailed in the Mishnah, *Yoma* 26b and *Rambam* ibid. 6:18.] In addition, the accompanying flour offering is brought up by three Kohanim, and the wine by another three Kohanim, bringing the total to 24 Kohanim.

20. That is, when it comes to the offering of an individual, there is no fixed number of Kohanim necessary to bring the limbs up to the Altar. On the one hand, it can be performed by even a single Kohen (Mishnah, *Yoma* 26b with *Rashi* ד"ה אם רצה); on the other hand, it can be performed by more than the six or twenty-four needed for a communal sheep or ox offering (*Rambam* ibid. 6:19). No lots were drawn for the privilege of bringing up the limbs of an individual's *olah* (*Rashi* loc. cit.).

According to some, the owner himself would choose the Kohen (or Kohanim) he wanted to honor with that task (*Kol HaRamaz* ad loc.; glosses of R' Yechezkel Landau ad loc.; see *Rashi, Temurah* 32a ד"ה הקדש), while others maintain that it was the prerogative of the first available Kohen or Kohanim (*Minchas Chinuch* §22; see also *Mishneh LaMelech, Hil. Temidin U'Mussafin* 4:9).

21. One may bring a bird *olah* offering by bringing either a turtledove or young dove (*Leviticus* 1:14). The laws and procedures for a bird *olah* are different in many respects from those of an animal *olah* offering. In terms of the laws, for example, a bird *olah* can be either female or male and need not be unblemished (although it may not be missing a limb), while the animal *olah* must be specifically male and unblemished (*Temurah* 14a). Furthermore, unlike its animal counterpart, no flour or wine libations accompanied the bird *olah* (*Menachos* 90b).

The procedure for offering a bird *olah*, as recorded in *Leviticus* 1:14-17, has little in common with that of the animal *olah* discussed until this point. The procedure for a bird *olah* is as follows: The Kohen ascends to the top of the Altar with the live bird, and, standing at the southeast corner, he pierces the back of its neck with his pointed thumbnail, cutting all the way through, separating the head from the rest of the body, in a type of slaughter known as מְלִיקָה, *melikah*. The head and body are then pressed against the upper portion of the Altar's wall so as to apply the blood to the Altar. The head is then salted and thrown onto the Altar's fire. The Kohen then cuts a hole beneath the bird's neck and removes the crop together with the skin and feathers that cover it, as well as the entrails that emerge with them, and throws them onto the "place of the ashes" (a spot near the southern wall of the Altar to which a token quantity of ashes was removed from the Altar each day). Then, using just his hands, the Kohen tears the bird open along its spine, salts it, and throws it onto the Altar's fire (Mishnah, *Zevachim* 64b; *Rambam, Hil. Maaseh HaKorbanos* 6:20-22).

22. The dissection of the animal is described in Chapter 4 of *Tamid*, and the procedure for offering the limbs is discussed in *Yoma* 25a-27a. These laws are codified in *Rambam, Hil. Maaseh HaKorbanos*, Ch. 6.

## ויקרא / מצוה קטו: מצות מעשה העולה

וְנוֹהֶגֶת בִּזְמַן הַבַּיִת בְּזִכְרֵי כְהֻנָּה.[23] וְכֹהֵן שֶׁעָבַר וְלֹא עֲשָׂאָהּ כַּסֵּדֶר הַזֶּה בִּטֵּל עֲשֵׂה.

### ◆ Applicability of the Mitzvah ◆

וְנוֹהֶגֶת בִּזְמַן הַבַּיִת בְּזִכְרֵי כְהֻנָּה — **[This mitzvah] applies in Temple times,** and applies only **to male Kohanim,** for only they may perform this sacrificial service.[23] וְכֹהֵן שֶׁעָבַר וְלֹא עֲשָׂאָהּ כַּסֵּדֶר הַזֶּה בִּטֵּל עֲשֵׂה — **A Kohen who transgresses** this mitzvah **and does not perform** the service of the *olah* offering **as per this procedure has violated** this mitzvah-**obligation.**

#### NOTES

23. Anyone, including a non-Jew, may vow and bring an *olah* offering (*Rambam* ibid. 3:2). However, only male Kohanim could perform the actual *avodah* (service) of offering the animal. This is derived from the oft-repeated phrase, *sons of Aaron*, stated in the context of the various sacrificial services (*Leviticus* 1:5, et al.), from which we derive that only the "sons" of Aaron (males) may perform the service, but not the daughters of Aaron (*Kiddushin* 36a). See *Chinuch* above, with note 7, for which parts of the service require specifically a male Kohen.

---

**◆§ Insight: Olah — The Offering and Its Message**

As noted in the introduction to this mitzvah, an *olah* is often brought simply as a voluntary offering. Nevertheless, based on the verse (*Leviticus* 1:4), וְנִרְצָה לוֹ לְכַפֵּר עָלָיו, *and [the olah] shall be acceptable for him, to atone for him,* our Sages note that even the voluntary *olah* offering contains an aspect of atonement. They explain that the typical motivation behind bringing such an offering is the person's desire to rectify a failure for which there is no prescribed consequence or means of atonement. This includes a case where one failed to fulfill a mitzvah-obligation, or one violated a prohibition that bears no other stated penalty — such as a לָאו הַנִּיתָּק לַעֲשֵׂה, *a prohibition that can be remedied by the fulfillment of an obligation* (*Sifra* to *Leviticus* 1:4; see note 14 to General Introduction for other such prohibitions). In addition, one may be motivated to bring an *olah* to atone for sinful thoughts, though they were never carried out into action (*Vayikra Rabbah* 7:3).

Some explain that the above two shortcomings — i.e., failure to fulfill a mitzvah-obligation and sinful thoughts — are strongly related. Sinful thoughts are not so much an active giving over of oneself to sin as they are the product of a mind left unoccupied with more constructive thoughts. When a person desists from using his time and mental energy positively, when he desists from directing his thoughts to the fulfillment of mitzvos and Torah study, thoughts of sin and vain imaginations are the natural consequence; see *Rambam*, end of *Hil. Isurei Biah* (R' S. R. Hirsch, *Numbers* 15:39). The rectification of that is the *olah* offering, for the very name *olah* (which means "elevation") expresses a desire to elevate oneself and rise above one's current state (ibid. *Leviticus* 1:3).

◆§◆

The Torah allows for the voluntary *olah* to be brought from one's cattle, flock (sheep, goats, or rams), or birds. Now, there are certain obligatory offerings regarding which the Torah gives a range of different types of offerings that may be brought, such as the variable *chatas* offering (see Mitzvah 123) and the offerings brought by a woman who recently gave birth (Mitzvah 168), and generally the determining factor as to which offering is brought is the financial status of its owner. Wealthier owners were required to bring the animal offerings, while the less affluent would bring what they could afford — bird, or (in the case of the variable *chatas* offering) even flour. With regard to the voluntary *olah*, though, no such distinction of wealth is stated; the Torah merely provides the choice of bringing a large animal (cattle), a small animal (sheep or goats), or a bird. How does one determine which species to choose for one's *olah*?

*Rabbeinu Bachya* (*Leviticus* 1:3, based on *Zohar, Leviticus* 8:2) suggests that, in line with the obligatory offerings mentioned above, the choice of species for the voluntary *olah* should also ideally reflect the owner's financial status. The connection of each level of offering (cattle, flock, and bird) to a corresponding financial status, though, runs deeper than simply the matter of what one can afford. *Rabbeinu Bachya,* who stresses the above-stated idea that an *olah* is brought to correct for sinful thoughts, explains that sinful thoughts are often correlated to one's financial class. The

wealthy, whose ego can easily be swayed by their riches, should bring the largest option — i.e., cattle — for they are the most likely to have had sinful thoughts arising from arrogance. An average fellow, whose sins of ego are less common and egregious, brings a more modest animal from his flock, while the humble poor man, for whom such sins are few and far between, brings the smallest of the categories, a bird.

R' S. R. Hirsch (*Leviticus* 1:3 and 1:17), though, suggests a different set of criteria for the choice of species. In keeping with his focus on the *olah* offering's expression of a desire for spiritual elevation, R' Hirsch explains that each animal represents a different striving of the spirit. Cattle (working animals) represent man in his function of dynamic activity in the service of his Master. Animals of the flock (passive creatures) represent man in his receptive role, wherein his vital needs are provided by his Shepherd. Together, they represent the essence of a person's life: his work and his fortune. If one's motivation in bringing an *olah* stems from his recognition of a personal shortcoming in his fulfillment of Divinely ordained tasks, then it is appropriate that he bring cattle. If the motivation stems from a feeling that he has fallen short in his indebtedness to and recognition of the Shepherd Whose Hand has sustained him, then it is appropriate that his *olah* come from the flock.

The *olah* offering of birds expresses a different idea. Throughout Scripture, a bird is used as a metaphor for a defenseless individual (see *Proverbs* 26:2, 27:8, *Isaiah* 16:2), in the shadow of death (*Lamentations* 3:52, *Ecclesiastes* 9:12), moaning in his suffering (*Isaiah* 38:14; 59:11, *Nahum* 2:8). Thus, a bird represents a person going through intense torment. This downtrodden individual wants to reach his *olah*-ascent by way of his very suffering! Indeed the procedures of the *olah* offering of birds (see above, note 21) exemplify the violent lot of its owner's life; the piercing of the bird's neck, the rending of its body, and the pressing out of its vitality (blood) against the Altar's wall all signify the owner's struggle. Yet, unlike its counterparts pertaining to the animal *olah*, these procedures for the bird *olah* are performed at the height of the Altar, suggesting the idea that in his holding onto the Torah paradigm (represented by the top of the Altar) in spite of his suffering, the owner of this offering creates a unique spiritual reality. His lot of suffering — taken in stride and experienced in loving devotion to God and His Torah — brings him to a unique height, imbuing his offering with a most precious status in the eyes of his Creator.

## מִצְוָה קטז: מִצְוַת קָרְבַּן מִנְחָה

לַעֲשׂוֹת מְלֶאכֶת הַמִּנְחָה עַל הָעִנְיָן הַנִּזְכָּר בַּתּוֹרָה בְּפָרָשִׁיּוֹתֶיהָ, שֶׁנֶּאֱמַר (ויקרא ב׳, א׳) וְנֶפֶשׁ כִּי תַקְרִיב קָרְבַּן מִנְחָה, וּכְתִיב (שם, שם ה׳) וְאִם מִנְחָה עַל הַמַּחֲבַת, וּכְתִיב עוֹד (שם, שם ז׳) וְאִם מִנְחַת מַרְחֶשֶׁת.[1]

וְעִנְיַן הַמְּנָחוֹת הוּא קָרְבָּן הַבָּא מִמִּינֵי הַקְּמָחִים וְלֹא מִבַּעֲלֵי חַיִּים.

וּכְבָר כָּתַבְתִּי לְמַעְלָה, כִּי הַקָּרְבָּן בְּבַעֲלֵי חַיִּים הוּא בֶּאֱמֶת דִּמְיוֹן חָזָק אֵצֶל הָאָדָם

## Mitzvah 116
# The Obligation Regarding the Minchah Offering

וְנֶפֶשׁ כִּי תַקְרִיב קָרְבַּן מִנְחָה לַה׳ סֹלֶת יִהְיֶה קָרְבָּנוֹ וְיָצַק עָלֶיהָ שֶׁמֶן וְנָתַן עָלֶיהָ לְבֹנָה ... וְכִי תַקְרִב קָרְבַּן מִנְחָה מַאֲפֵה תַנּוּר סֹלֶת חַלּוֹת מַצֹּת בְּלוּלֹת בַּשֶּׁמֶן וּרְקִיקֵי מַצּוֹת מְשֻׁחִים בַּשָּׁמֶן. וְאִם מִנְחָה עַל הַמַּחֲבַת קָרְבָּנֶךָ סֹלֶת בְּלוּלָה בַשֶּׁמֶן מַצָּה תִהְיֶה ... וְאִם מִנְחַת מַרְחֶשֶׁת קָרְבָּנֶךָ סֹלֶת בַּשֶּׁמֶן תֵּעָשֶׂה

*When a person offers a minchah (meal) offering to HASHEM, his offering shall be of fine flour; he shall pour oil upon it and place levonah upon it ... When you offer a minchah offering that is baked in an oven, it shall be of fine flour: unleavened loaves mixed with oil, or unleavened wafers smeared with oil. If your offering is a minchah on the griddle-pan, it shall be of fine flour mixed with oil, it shall be unleavened ... If your offering is a minchah in a deep pan, it shall be made of fine flour with oil (Leviticus 2:1,4-5,7).*

As in the previous mitzvah, which sets forth the procedure for bringing a certain category of offering (the *olah*), in this mitzvah the Torah sets forth the procedure for another category — the *minchah* (meal) offering [pl. *menachos*]. A *minchah* offering may be brought voluntarily, and there are various types of voluntary *menachos*, enumerated in the verses cited above, each of which Chinuch will describe. There also are numerous instances of obligatory *menachos*, all of which Chinuch will discuss in the course of this mitzvah.

לַעֲשׂוֹת מְלֶאכֶת הַמִּנְחָה — **We are commanded to carry out the procedure of the *minchah* offering** עַל הָעִנְיָן הַנִּזְכָּר בַּתּוֹרָה בְּפָרָשִׁיּוֹתֶיהָ — **in the manner described in the Torah in the passages addressing [the *minchah* offering],** שֶׁנֶּאֱמַר ״וְנֶפֶשׁ כִּי תַקְרִיב קָרְבַּן מִנְחָה״ — **as it is stated** (*Leviticus* 2:1): **When a person offers a *minchah* to HASHEM, his offering shall be of fine flour,** etc.; וּכְתִיב ״וְאִם מִנְחָה עַל הַמַּחֲבַת״ — **and it is written** (ibid. v. 5): **If your offering is a *minchah* on the griddle-pan,** etc.; וּכְתִיב עוֹד ״וְאִם מִנְחַת מַרְחֶשֶׁת״ — **and it is further written** (ibid. v. 7): **If your offering is a *minchah* in a deep pan,** etc. All these passages discuss various forms of *minchah* offerings.[1]
וְעִנְיַן הַמְּנָחוֹת — **The** general **description of the *minchah* offerings is that** הוּא קָרְבָּן הַבָּא מִמִּינֵי הַקְּמָחִים — **it is an offering that is brought from** various **types of flour,** וְלֹא מִבַּעֲלֵי חַיִּים — **rather than from living creatures.** All the different types of *menachos* will be described below.

## ✽ Underlying Purpose of the Mitzvah ✽

כִּי הַקָּרְבָּן בְּבַעֲלֵי חַיִּים הוּא וּכְבָר כָּתַבְתִּי לְמַעְלָה — **I have already written above** (Mitzvah 95), בֶּאֱמֶת דִּמְיוֹן חָזָק אֵצֶל הָאָדָם — **that an offering of living creatures truly evokes a powerful**

---

NOTES

1. It is unclear why Chinuch omits verse 4 of the passage, which describes the "oven-baked *minchah* offering." See the verse at the introduction to the mitzvah.

# 391 ◻ VAYIKRA / MITZVAH 116: THE OBLIGATION REGARDING THE MINCHAH OFFERING

לְהַכְנִיעַ וּלְהַשְׁפִּיל הַנֶּפֶשׁ הַמִּתְאַוָּה וְהַחוֹטֵאת², כְּמוֹ שֶׁהוּא רוֹאֶה שֶׁבַּעַל חַיּוּת כְּמוֹתוֹ אֶלָּא שֶׁאֵין בּוֹ שֵׂכֶל נִשְׂרָף וְכָלֶה, וּכְמוֹ כֵן הַנֶּפֶשׁ הַחוֹטֵאת מִצַּד חֶלְשַׁת הַשֵּׂכֶל תִּכְלֶה וְתֹאבַד גַּם כֵּן אִם תַּתְמִיד בִּפְעֻלּוֹת בַּהֲמִיּוֹת שֶׁהֵן הַחֲטָאִים, כִּי הַחֵטְא לֹא יָבוֹא רַק מִשֹּׁרֶשׁ הַבַּהֲמִי³.

וְהַקָּרְבָּן בַּמֶּה שֶׁהוּא שֶׁאֵינוֹ בַּעַל חַיִּים, אַף עַל פִּי שֶׁהוּא בָּא גַּם כֵּן לְהַכְנָעַת הַיֵּצֶר, שֶׁיִּרְאֶה הָאָדָם כִּי בִּשְׁבִיל חֶטְאוֹ נִצְטָרֵךְ לִשְׂרֹף מָמוֹנוֹ וּלְכַלּוֹתוֹ, בֶּאֱמֶת אֵין דִּמְיוֹנוֹ חָזָק כְּמוֹ בְּבַעֲלֵי הַחַיִּים. וּמִן הַדּוֹמֶה לְפִי הַפְּשָׁט, כִּי עַל כֵּן יִקָּרֵא מִנְחָה⁴, מִפְּנֵי שֶׁעִנְיָנָהּ מְעַט מִקָּרְבַּן בַּעַל חַיִּים כְּמוֹ שֶׁמִּנְחוֹת בְּנֵי אָדָם יִהְיוּ בְּמוּעָט בְּרֹב הַפְּעָמִים,

---

**image in** the mind of **the person** who brings it, לְהַכְנִיעַ וּלְהַשְׁפִּיל הַנֶּפֶשׁ הַמִּתְאַוָּה וְהַחוֹטֵאת — the purpose of which is **to humble and lower the desirous and sinful spirit** that resides within man.[2]

כְּמוֹ שֶׁהוּא רוֹאֶה שֶׁבַּעַל חַיּוּת כְּמוֹתוֹ אֶלָּא שֶׁאֵין בּוֹ שֵׂכֶל נִשְׂרָף וְכָלֶה — **This is accomplished through** animal offerings, for, as explained there, by bringing it **one sees that just as a living being,** which is physically **like him but lacks** human **intellect, is burned and destroyed,** וּכְמוֹ כֵן הַנֶּפֶשׁ הַחוֹטֵאת מִצַּד חֶלְשַׁת הַשֵּׂכֶל תִּכְלֶה וְתֹאבַד גַּם כֵּן — **so, too, will the person who sins due to the weakness of** his **intellect** in controlling his baser self **also be destroyed and lost,** אִם תַּתְמִיד בִּפְעֻלּוֹת בַּהֲמִיּוֹת שֶׁהֵן הַחֲטָאִים — **if he persists in his beastly activities; namely, the sins** that he commits. כִּי הַחֵטְא לֹא יָבוֹא רַק מִשֹּׁרֶשׁ הַבַּהֲמִי — **The reason why sins are analogous to animalistic activities is because sin comes about only by way of the beast-like root** within man.[3]

Chinuch addresses the purpose of an offering of flour, which seemingly lacks the power to convey the above message of humbling the animalistic side of man:

וְהַקָּרְבָּן בַּמֶּה שֶׁהוּא שֶׁאֵינוֹ בַּעַל חַיִּים — **Now, an offering** — of whatever type it may be — **which is not a living creature,** אַף עַל פִּי שֶׁהוּא בָּא גַּם כֵּן לְהַכְנָעַת הַיֵּצֶר — **although it, too,** surely **comes** as an offering **in order to humble the** evil **inclination,** שֶׁיִּרְאֶה הָאָדָם כִּי בִּשְׁבִיל חֶטְאוֹ נִצְטָרֵךְ לִשְׂרֹף מָמוֹנוֹ וּלְכַלּוֹתוֹ — **in that the person will see that due to his sin it was necessary to burn** a portion of **his property and destroy it,** בֶּאֱמֶת אֵין דִּמְיוֹנוֹ חָזָק כְּמוֹ בְּבַעֲלֵי הַחַיִּים — **in truth, its image is not as powerful as that** evoked by means of offerings **of living creatures.** Nevertheless, it fulfills the purpose of imparting the message of the negative effect of sin — albeit to a lesser degree than animal offerings do.

Chinuch explains the reason for the name *"minchah,"* based on his above explanation of the relatively weaker message imparted by the *minchah* offering.

וּמִן הַדּוֹמֶה לְפִי הַפְּשָׁט — **It would appear, based on the simple understanding** of the matter, כִּי עַל כֵּן יִקָּרֵא מִנְחָה — **that this is why [a meal offering] is called a *"minchah,"*** which means *tribute,*[4] מִפְּנֵי שֶׁעִנְיָנָהּ מְעַט מִקָּרְבַּן בַּעַל חַיִּים — **for its feature** in being able to impart the message of the gravity of sin **is less** effective **than** that of **an offering of a living being,** כְּמוֹ שֶׁמִּנְחוֹת בְּנֵי אָדָם יִהְיוּ בְּמוּעָט בְּרֹב הַפְּעָמִים — **similar to the tributes of people** — i.e., the token gifts presented by one person to another — **which are usually small.**[5]

---

### NOTES

2. Man is comprised of two aspects: the physical and the spiritual. His physical ("desirous") dimension is motivated entirely by animalistic desires. It is the function of his spiritual dimension (which Chinuch will refer to as "intellect") to hold his physical desires in check, so as to remain faithful to the laws of the Torah.

3. The "desirous spirit" is also referred to by Chinuch as the "beastly spirit" (see below, Mitzvah 120), for a beast is not capable of any spiritual yearnings, and is motivated only by its physical needs and desires. This, explains Chinuch, is one reason why a sinner is required to bring an offering. Sin occurs when one succumbs to desire. By offering the meat of an animal in the *Beis HaMikdash*, a sinner is reminded of the transient nature of his beastly spirit, and that it is only through his spirituality that man is distinguished from beast (see Mitzvah 95, note 47).

4. As in *Genesis* 43:11, וְהוֹרִידוּ לָאִישׁ מִנְחָה, *bring [it] down to the man as a tribute,* where Jacob refers to the gift to be brought down to the Egyptian ruler (Joseph) with the word מִנְחָה, *minchah* (see also *Rashbam* and *Chizkuni, Leviticus* 2:1).

5. According to this explanation, the word *minchah* (tribute) conveys the fact that this offering is simply

וְעוֹד מִפְּנֵי שֶׁהַרְבֵּה מֵהֶן בָּאוֹת נְדָבָה, וּמַה שֶּׁאֵינוֹ בְּחִיּוּב אֵצֶל בְּנֵי אָדָם יִקְרָאוּ מִנְחָה.[6]
וְאֵלּוּ הֵן כָּל מִינֵי הַמְּנָחוֹת שֶׁהָיוּ מַקְרִיבִין בִּזְמַן הַבַּיִת הַבָּאוֹת בִּפְנֵי עַצְמָן, כְּלוֹמַר שֶׁאֵינָן בָּאוֹת לְמִנְחַת נְסָכִים, רוֹצֶה לוֹמַר בִּגְרִירַת קָרְבָּן אַחֵר,[7] שָׁלֹשׁ מְנָחוֹת הֵן שֶׁהֵן בָּאוֹת בִּשְׁבִיל כָּל הַצִּבּוּר, וְהֵן עֹמֶר בְּפֶסַח,[8]

Chinuch offers another explanation for the term "*minchah*":
וְעוֹד מִפְּנֵי שֶׁהַרְבֵּה מֵהֶן בָּאוֹת נְדָבָה — **Furthermore,** it may be called *"minchah"* **due to the fact that many [*minchah* offerings] are brought as a donation** (rather than in fulfillment of a required obligation), וּמַה שֶּׁאֵינוֹ בְּחִיּוּב אֵצֶל בְּנֵי אָדָם יִקְרָאוּ מִנְחָה — **and that which people are not bound by obligation** to do, **they will call a "tribute."**[6]

### ⸺ Laws of the Mitzvah ⸺

Chinuch lists the various types of *minchah* offerings:
וְאֵלּוּ הֵן כָּל מִינֵי הַמְּנָחוֹת שֶׁהָיוּ מַקְרִיבִין בִּזְמַן הַבַּיִת הַבָּאוֹת בִּפְנֵי עַצְמָן — **The following are all the various types of *minchah* offerings that would be offered in the time of the** Holy Temple (*Beis HaMikdash*) **as independent** offerings. כְּלוֹמַר שֶׁאֵינָן בָּאוֹת לְמִנְחַת נְסָכִים — **That is to say,** they are "independent" in the sense **that they are not brought as a *minchah* of libations,** רוֹצֶה לוֹמַר בִּגְרִירַת קָרְבָּן אַחֵר — **meaning** that they are not brought **by way of another offering** as a mere accompaniment to that offering, but are, rather, independently brought *minchah* offerings.[7]

Chinuch begins with the communal *minchah* offerings:
שָׁלֹשׁ מְנָחוֹת הֵן שֶׁהֵן בָּאוֹת בִּשְׁבִיל כָּל הַצִּבּוּר — **There are three *minchah* offerings that are brought for the sake of the entire community.** וְהֵן עֹמֶר בְּפֶסַח — **They are:** (1) **the *Omer* offering on Pesach,**[8]

---

### NOTES

a token offering with respect to its ability to impart the message of the gravity and effect of sin. Just as a tribute is generally a token or small amount, so too is this a diminutive offering in its ability to convey its message.

Others connect the *minchah* offering to the notion of a tribute as follows: A tribute is generally sent to a ruler as a sign of homage and as a means of conveying a sense of dependence and subjugation. So too, one who brings a *minchah* offering, along with its oil and *levonah* [defined above, Mitzvah 97, note 1], demonstrates that all of his sustenance (represented by flour), comfort (represented by oil), and satisfaction (represented by *levonah*) are gifts bestowed upon him by Hashem (R' S. R. Hirsch, *Leviticus* 2:1).

6. According to this explanation, the word "*minchah*" denotes a voluntary gift, since, generally speaking, *minchah* offerings are donative in nature. Although a *minchah* offering will at times be obligatory, e.g., the sinner's *minchah* or the *sotah's minchah* (see below), nevertheless, many, if not most, *menachos* that are brought on any given day are not brought in fulfillment of such obligations.

[Nevertheless, Chinuch's first explanation (that the name *minchah* reflects the limited message regarding the gravity of sin) is appropriate, since every offering effects a measure of atonement or acceptance for a person (see similarly above, introduction to Mitzvah 115).]

For further discussion of the significance of the *minchah* offering, see Insight A.

7. Many animal offerings (e.g., the *tamid* [communal daily offerings] and festival *mussaf* offerings, as well as personal voluntary *olah* and *shelamim* offerings) require an accompanying *minchah* of flour and a wine libation (i.e., an offering of wine poured on the Altar). The amount of flour, oil, and wine offered depends on whether the animal brought as an offering is a bull, ram, or sheep, as enumerated in *Numbers* Ch. 15. The flour and oil are mixed and offered in their entirety upon the Altar (*Rambam, Hil. Maaseh Ha-Korbanos* 2:1). Chinuch notes that he is not discussing *minchah* offerings that are normally brought as an adjunct to an animal offering; rather, he is referring to *minchah* offerings that are brought independently. [It should be noted, however, that a person may also voluntarily donate a *minchah* of libations in any of the appropriate measures, without attaching it to an animal offering (*Menachos* 104b; *Rambam* ibid. 14:1).]

8. On the second day of Pesach, an *omer*'s volume (also known as an *issaron* or tenth-*ephah,* which is the equivalent of the volume of 43.2 eggs) of fine barley flour was brought to the *Beis HaMikdash* in fulfillment of the verses in *Leviticus* 23:10-11. The offering was waved (back and forth, up and down) by the Kohen. The rest of the *avodah* (service) is similar to that of other *menachos;* see Chinuch below, at notes 31-34 (see Mitzvah 302 for further details).

This offering is also called the מִנְחַת בִּכּוּרִים (*minchas bikkurim*), *a meal offering of the first grain* (*Leviticus*

# VAYIKRA / MITZVAH 116: THE OBLIGATION REGARDING THE MINCHAH OFFERING

שְׁתֵּי הַלֶּחֶם בַּעֲצֶרֶת⁹, לֶחֶם הַפָּנִים בְּכָל שַׁבָּת¹⁰, וּשְׁלָשְׁתָּן נִקְרָאוֹת מִנְחָה¹¹. וְתֵשַׁע שֶׁל יָחִיד, וְאֵלּוּ הֵן: א. מִנְחַת חוֹטֵא, וְהִיא הַמִּנְחָה שֶׁיַּקְרִיב הֶעָנִי כְּשֶׁיִּתְחַיֵּב חַטָּאת וְלֹא תַגִּיעַ יָדוֹ¹². ב. מִנְחַת סוֹטָה, וְהִיא מִנְחַת הַקְּנָאוֹת הַכְּתוּבָה בְּפָרָשַׁת נָשֹׂא (במדבר ה׳, ט״ו)¹³. ג. הַמִּנְחָה שֶׁיַּקְרִיב כָּל כֹּהֵן כְּשֶׁיִּכָּנֵס לַעֲבוֹדָה שֶׁמַּקְרִיב אוֹתָהּ בְּיָדוֹ,

לֶחֶם הַפָּנִים בְּכָל שַׁבָּת — and (2) the offering of **the Two Loaves on Shavuos**,[9] שְׁתֵּי הַלֶּחֶם בַּעֲצֶרֶת — (3) the *Lechem HaPanim*, **each Sabbath.**[10] וּשְׁלָשְׁתָּן נִקְרָאוֹת מִנְחָה — These three communal flour offerings **are all called "***minchah*" **offerings.**"[11]

Chinuch enumerates the personal *minchah* offerings:

וְתֵשַׁע שֶׁל יָחִיד — **There are nine** *minchah* offerings **that** may be brought by **a private individual.** וְאֵלּוּ הֵן — **They are:** א. מִנְחַת חוֹטֵא — **(1) The "sinner's** *minchah*," וְהִיא הַמִּנְחָה שֶׁיַּקְרִיב הֶעָנִי כְּשֶׁיִּתְחַיֵּב חַטָּאת וְלֹא תַגִּיעַ יָדוֹ — **which is the** *minchah* **that a poor man offers when he is liable to a** *chatas* (sin) offering, **but cannot afford** to bring an animal.[12] ב. מִנְחַת סוֹטָה — **(2) The "***sotah's minchah*," וְהִיא מִנְחַת הַקְּנָאוֹת הַכְּתוּבָה בְּפָרָשַׁת נָשֹׂא — **which is the "***Minchah* **of Jealousies"** written in *Parashas Naso* (Numbers 5:15).[13] ג. הַמִּנְחָה שֶׁיַּקְרִיב כָּל כֹּהֵן כְּשֶׁיִּכָּנֵס לַעֲבוֹדָה — **(3) The** *minchah* **that every Kohen offers when he** initially **enters** into Temple service, שֶׁמַּקְרִיב אוֹתָהּ בְּיָדוֹ — **which he offers with his own hands** (i.e., he does not have it offered by another Kohen on

---

## NOTES

2:14; see *Toras Kohanim, Dibura DiNedavah, Parshasa* 13:4); only after it was offered was the new crop of grain (*chadash*) permitted for general consumption (see Mitzvos 303-305).

9. Two leavened loaves of bread from fine wheat flour were brought to the *Beis HaMikdash* on Shavuos, as directed in *Leviticus* 23:16-17. The loaves were waved in the Courtyard as per the verse (ibid. v. 17) לֶחֶם תְּנוּפָה, *bread that shall be waved*. After the waving [and the offering of the accompanying animal offerings (see *Rambam, Hil. Temidin U'Mussafin* 8:11)], the breads were eaten by the Kohanim (see Mitzvah 307 for more details).

This offering of the Two Loaves is referred to by the Torah (ibid. v. 16) as a מִנְחָה חֲדָשָׁה, *a new meal offering*, as it was the first *minchah* to be brought from the new wheat crop (*Rashi* ad loc.).

10. Twelve loaves of bread were placed on the *Shulchan* (Table) in the *Beis HaMikdash* each Sabbath, and they remained there until the next Sabbath, when they were replaced with new loaves. Two vessels containing *levonah* were also on the *Shulchan*. After the loaves were removed, the *levonah* was offered on the Altar, and the loaves were then distributed among the Kohanim to be eaten (see Mitzvah 97 for further details).

11. The *Omer* offering and the Two Loaves are each referred to as a "*minchah*" in the verses cited, respectively, in notes 8 and 9. The *Lechem HaPanim* is not called a "*minchah*" in Scripture, but since it is made of flour, it is in the category of *minchah*, and hence, is subject to the prohibition of making a *minchah* [other than the Two Loaves] of leavened dough; see Mitzvah 117 with note 1, and Mitzvah 135 (*Toras Kohanim, Dibura DiNedavah, Parshasa* 12:2; *Rambam, Hil. Maaseh HaKorbanos* 12:19).

12. One who violates a sin for which he is liable to bring a *chatas* is generally obligated to bring an animal offering, irrespective of his financial status (see Mitzvah 121). However, there are a number of sins that are exceptions to this rule and their violation subjects one to liability to bring an *oleh v'yoreid* (variable *chatas*) offering. The type of *oleh v'yoreid* offering brought depends on the penitent's financial status; the wealthy bring an animal, the poor bring birds, and the poorest bring a *minchah* offering (Mitzvah 123; see *Leviticus* 5:11). It is this last category that Chinuch refers to here when he speaks of the sinner's *minchah* offering.

The sinner's *minchah* consisted of a tenth-*ephah* volume of fine flour, but was unique in that it did not have oil or *levonah* added to it (see Mitzvos 125 and 126). After the *kometz* (fistful; see note 33 below), was offered on the Altar, the rest of the *minchah* was eaten by the Kohanim (*Leviticus* 5:12-13 with *Rashi* ad loc.).

13. A *sotah* is a married woman who is suspected of having had an adulterous relationship with a particular man, having secluded herself with that man after her husband had warned her not to do so. In order to determine her innocence or guilt, the *sotah* would undergo a ritual (described in *Numbers* 5:11-31), which included drinking of a specially prepared mixture and bringing a *minchah* offering, called the *Minchah* of Jealousies (ibid. v. 15; see Mitzvah 365 for more details of the *sotah* procedure). This offering was composed of a tenth-*ephah* of coarse barley flour, and was to contain neither oil nor *levonah* (see Mitzvos 366 and 367). The offering was waved, brought near to the Altar and then had a *kometz* of flour removed and offered upon the Altar. The remainder of the *minchah* was eaten by the Kohanim (*Rambam, Hil. Sotah* 3:15).

וְהִיא הַנִּקְרֵאת מִנְחַת חִנּוּךְ.[14] ד. הַמִּנְחָה שֶׁמַּקְרִיב כֹּהֵן גָּדוֹל בְּכָל יוֹם, וְהִיא נִקְרֵאת מִנְחַת חֲבִתִּין.[15] ה. מִנְחַת[16] הַסֹּלֶת,[17] וְהִיא בָּאָה בְּנֶדֶר וּנְדָבָה.[18] ו. מִנְחַת הַמַּחֲבַת,

---

his behalf). וְהִיא הַנִּקְרֵאת מִנְחַת חִנּוּךְ – [This *minchah*] is called the *"minchah* of initiation."[14] ד. הַמִּנְחָה שֶׁמַּקְרִיב כֹּהֵן גָּדוֹל בְּכָל יוֹם – (4) The *minchah* that the Kohen Gadol offers every day, וְהִיא נִקְרֵאת מִנְחַת חֲבִתִּין – which is called the *"minchas chavitin."*[15]

The next five *minchah* offerings are those that an individual may voluntarily offer, and, as Chinuch wrote above, these made up a large part of the independent *minchah* offerings brought in the *Beis HaMikdash*.[16]

ה. מִנְחַת הַסֹּלֶת – (5) The "fine-flour *minchah*,"[17] וְהִיא בָּאָה בְּנֶדֶר וּנְדָבָה – which is brought in fulfillment of a vow or donation.[18] ו. מִנְחַת הַמַּחֲבַת – (6) The "griddle-pan *minchah*,"

---

## NOTES

14. This *minchah*, as well as the following one (i.e., the *minchas chavitin*) is described in *Leviticus* 6:13-15. Both *minchah* offerings were made from a tenth-*ephah* of fine flour with 3 *log* (each *log* equals six egg-volumes) of oil, and both went through a multi-step process, including scalding in hot water, frying, and baking, after which they were offered in their entirety upon the Altar together with their *kometz* of *levonah*. However, unlike the *minchas chavitin* of the Kohen Gadol which was brought daily, the *minchah* of initiation was brought only once, at the very beginning of a Kohen's Temple service. The *minchah* of initiation consisted of ten loaves that were offered whole and all at once (*Rambam, Hil. Maaseh HaKorbanos* 13:4 with *Radvaz*), as opposed to the *chavitin,* which was divided (see next note).

Another situation in which the *minchah* of initiation was brought was when a Kohen was appointed to be Kohen Gadol. Although he had brought a *minchah* of initiation on the first day he served as a regular Kohen, he would bring another one on the day of his installation into his new position as Kohen Gadol. That *minchah* was in addition to the daily *chavitin* offering that he would bring from that day forward (*Rambam, Hil. Klei HaMikdash* 5:16).

15. *Minchas chavitin* is the Kohen Gadol's daily *minchah* offering that consisted of twelve loaves that were split in half, with twelve half-loaves offered in the morning and twelve in the afternoon. It is called "*chavitin*" by virtue of the griddle (*machavas*) upon which it is fried [see previous note] (*Rashi, Menachos* 50b ד"ה חביתי). This *minchah* is the subject of Mitzvah 136, where Chinuch discusses its details at greater length.

16. The minimum size for all the *minchah* offerings that follow is a tenth-*ephah* of flour (an *issaron*), but one may donate as much as he likes beyond that, as long as he retains the ratio of one *log* of oil per tenth-*ephah* of flour. However, the *levonah* remains steady at one *kometz* per vessel-full of flour, even if the vessel holds as much as sixty *issaron* [which is the maximum that may be put in a single vessel] (see below, Mitzvah 126).

17. Like most *minchah* offerings, the fine-flour *minchah* (discussed in *Leviticus* 2:1-3) has three applications of oil. First, some of the *log* of oil is placed in the empty vessel, then the flour is added and some more of the oil poured in and the flour is mixed with it. Finally, the mixture is placed in a sacred service vessel (כְּלִי שָׁרֵת), and the remainder of the oil is poured over it, after which the *levonah* is added (*Rambam* ibid. 13:5). The fine-flour *minchah* is distinct from the other voluntary *minchah* offerings, though, in that the fine-flour *minchah* is not baked or fried before the performance of *kemitzah* (i.e., the removal of the fistful to be burned; see note 33 below). Rather, *kemitzah* is performed on the raw flour-and-oil mixture, as per the verse (*Leviticus* 2:2): וְקָמַץ מִשָּׁם מְלֹא קֻמְצוֹ מִסָּלְתָּהּ וּמִשַּׁמְנָהּ, *he shall scoop the kometz from it, from its fine flour and from its oil.* It is for this reason that it is called the fine-flour *minchah* [even though most *menachos* were made from fine flour; see note 23], for it is offered simply as raw flour (*Rashi, Leviticus* 2:1). The remainder of the flour is distributed among the Kohanim to eat after they bake it as matzah (*Leviticus* 6:9; see *Rashi* ibid. 2:4 and *Mishneh LaMelech, Hil. Maaseh HaKorbanos* 13:10 ד"ה ודע שראיתי להרב).

18. The person who wishes to bring this type of *minchah* may declare, "I take upon myself to bring a fine-flour *minchah*." An obligation taken upon oneself in such a manner is known as a *neder* (vow). Later, he sets aside flour to fulfill his pledge by stating, "This is for my vow." Alternatively, he may do this all in one stage by declaring, "This *issaron* of flour is for a fine-flour *minchah*," designating from the very start the flour that is to be brought as a *minchah*. This is known as a *nedavah* (donation).

There is an important distinction between the *neder* (vow) and the *nedavah* (donation). In the case of the *neder,* if the designated flour is lost, he must bring other flour in its place in order to fulfill his original obligation to bring a *minchah*. However, with regard to the *nedavah,* if the flour is lost it need not be replaced, as he obligated himself only to bring "this flour." See *Rambam, Hil. Maaseh HaKorbanos* 14:4-5.

## VAYIKRA / MITZVAH 116: THE OBLIGATION REGARDING THE MINCHAH OFFERING

וְהִיא בָּאָה בְּנֶדֶר וּנְדָבָה. ז. מִנְחַת מַרְחֶשֶׁת, וְהִיא בָּאָה בְּנֶדֶר וּנְדָבָה.[20] ח. מִנְחַת מַאֲפֵה תַנּוּר וְהִיא חַלּוֹת,[21] וְהִיא בָּאָה בְּנֶדֶר וּנְדָבָה. ט. מִנְחַת מַאֲפֵה תַנּוּר וְהִיא רְקִיקִין,[22] וּבָאָה בְּנֶדֶר וּנְדָבָה.

מְנָחוֹת אֵלּוּ, מֵהֶן סֹלֶת חִטִּים וּמֵהֶן שְׂעוֹרִים,[23] מֵהֶן נֶאֱכָלוֹת לַכֹּהֲנִים חוּץ מִן הַקְּמִיצָה,[24] וּמֵהֶן שֶׁהֵן נִשְׂרָפוֹת כֻּלָּן.[25] וְאַחַת מֵהֶן חָמֵץ, וְהִיא שְׁתֵּי הַלֶּחֶם שֶׁמְּבִיאִין בְּיוֹם עֲצֶרֶת,

---

ז. מִנְחַת מַרְחֶשֶׁת — וְהִיא בָּאָה בְּנֶדֶר וּנְדָבָה — which is also brought in fulfillment of a vow or donation.[19] וְהִיא בָּאָה בְּנֶדֶר וּנְדָבָה — (7) The "deep-pan minchah," which is also brought in fulfillment of a vow or donation.[20] ח. מִנְחַת מַאֲפֵה תַנּוּר וְהִיא חַלּוֹת — (8) The "oven-baked minchah" that is made as unleavened loaves,[21] וְהִיא בָּאָה בְּנֶדֶר וּנְדָבָה — which is also brought in fulfillment of a vow or donation. ט. מִנְחַת מַאֲפֵה תַנּוּר וְהִיא רְקִיקִין — (9) The oven-baked minchah that is made as unleavened wafers,[22] וּבָאָה בְּנֶדֶר וּנְדָבָה — which is also brought in fulfillment of a vow or donation.

Chinuch discusses some of the differences between the various menachos:

מְנָחוֹת אֵלּוּ, מֵהֶן סֹלֶת חִטִּים וּמֵהֶן שְׂעוֹרִים — Particulars of these minchah offerings vary, with some of them consisting of fine wheat flour, and some of them consisting of barley.[23] מֵהֶן נֶאֱכָלוֹת לַכֹּהֲנִים חוּץ מִן הַקְּמִיצָה — Some of them are eaten by the Kohanim, other than the kometz (i.e., fistful) that is taken and offered on the Altar,[24] וּמֵהֶן שֶׁהֵן נִשְׂרָפוֹת כֻּלָּן — while some of them are burned in their entirety.[25]

Chinuch addresses whether these minchah offerings are leavened or unleavened:

וְאַחַת מֵהֶן חָמֵץ — Only one of [these minchah offerings] is chametz (i.e., made of leavened dough), וְהִיא שְׁתֵּי הַלֶּחֶם שֶׁמְּבִיאִין בְּיוֹם עֲצֶרֶת — namely, the Two Loaves that are brought on Shavuos,

---

### NOTES

19. The procedure for this minchah (discussed in Leviticus 2:5-6) also begins with some of the oil being placed in a vessel, the addition of the fine flour and additional oil, and the mixture of the two (see above, note 17). The mixture is then kneaded with lukewarm water (Rambam ibid. 12:21; cf. Rashi ms., Menachos 74b ד״ה קודם, who says the water is added earlier), and then fried as ten unleavened loaves upon a machavas (griddle) — a rimless pan for which this minchah is named. After being fried, the minchah is broken into pieces, placed in a sacred service vessel and the remainder of the oil is poured over it, after which the levonah is placed upon it (Rambam ibid. 13:6,10). This is followed by kemitzah. The kometz and levonah are offered upon the Altar (ibid. 12), and the remainder is eaten by the Kohanim.

20. The deep-pan minchah (discussed in Leviticus 2:7-9) follows the same procedure as the previous minchah, the griddle-pan minchah, aside from the utensil in which the ten loaves are cooked. The loaves of the deep-pan minchah are cooked in a rimmed utensil known as a marcheshes. Unlike the griddle-pan minchah, where the rimless utensil allows for the oil to burn off and the loaves to become hard and brittle, the depth of the marcheshes utensil retains the oil and therefore produces a softer, more spongy product (Rambam ibid. 13:7).

21. As its name suggests, the oven-baked minchah of loaves (discussed in Leviticus 2:4) is made in an oven. The procedure for the preparation of its dough is somewhat different from the previous ones in that the oil is not added in stages, but is mixed into the flour all at once (Rambam ibid. 13:8; Rashi, Menachos 74b ד״ה וחכמים; cf. Rashi ms. there ד״ה יציקה). In a procedure that is similar to that of the previous minchah offerings, the mixed flour is then kneaded with lukewarm water, baked as ten loaves, broken up into a sacred vessel, and levonah is placed upon them. This is followed by kemitzah. The kometz and levonah are offered upon the Altar and the remainder eaten by the Kohanim.

22. The oven-baked minchah of wafers is similar to the oven-baked minchah of loaves but differs in how it is prepared. In the case of the wafers, the flour is first kneaded with lukewarm water and baked, and only afterward is the oil added to the finished wafers (as opposed to the loaves, where the procedure is reversed). Furthermore, the log of oil is not mixed in, but rather smeared upon the wafers a little at a time until it is all absorbed (Rambam, Hil. Maaseh HaKorbanos 13:9; cf. Kesef Mishnah). The loaves and wafers, according to some, differ as well in terms of their thickness, with the loaves being thicker than the wafers, as their names indicate (Ibn Ezra, Exodus 29:2).

23. All minchah offering were made of fine wheat flour other than the Omer and the sotah's minchah, which were made of barley flour. The Omer and sotah's minchah differ from each other, with the Omer being made of finely sifted barley flour and the sotah's minchah of coarser, unsifted barley flour (Mishnah, Sotah 14a).

24. See note 33 below for a description of this procedure.

25. Any personal minchah offering of a Kohen is to be burned in entirety, as the verse states (Leviticus 6:16):

שֶׁגַּם הֵן נִקְרָאִין מִנְחָה[26,27], וְאֵינָן קְרֵבִין לְגַבֵּי מִזְבֵּחַ. וְעַל שְׁתֵּי הַלֶּחֶם אֵינוֹ נֶאֱמָר בַּתּוֹרָה בְּשֶׁאָסְרָהּ דֶּרֶךְ כְּלָל, כָּל הַמִּנְחָה אֲשֶׁר תַּקְרִיבוּ לַה' לֹא תֵעָשֶׂה חָמֵץ (ויקרא ב', י"א), פְּרָט בְּאֵלּוּ וְהוֹצִיאָם מִן הַכְּלָל, וַעֲלֵיהֶם נֶאֱמַר שָׁם (שם י"ב) קָרְבַּן רֵאשִׁית תַּקְרִיבוּ אֹתָם לַה', כְּלוֹמַר בְּאֵלּוּ לֹא אָסַרְתִּי לָכֶם הֶחָמֵץ.[28] וּמִכָּל מָקוֹם אֶל הַמִּזְבֵּחַ לֹא הָיוּ עוֹלִין מִכֵּיוָן שֶׁהָיָה בָּהֶן חָמֵץ, וּכְמוֹ שֶׁנֶּאֱמַר בָּהֶן (שם, שם) וְאֶל הַמִּזְבֵּחַ לֹא יַעֲלוּ לְרֵיחַ נִיחֹחַ.[29] כָּל הַשְּׁאָר הָיוּ מַצָּה.[30] וְסֵדֶר הֲבָאָתָן כָּךְ הִיא, אָדָם מֵבִיא סֹלֶת מִתּוֹךְ בֵּיתוֹ בִּכְלִי כֶסֶף

---

שֶׁגַּם הֵן נִקְרָאִין מִנְחָה — **which,** like the other offerings listed above, **are also referred to with** the term **"***minchah* **offering,"**[26] but nevertheless, are prepared as *chametz* — unlike any other offering that is called a *"minchah."*[27] וְאֵינָן קְרֵבִין לְגַבֵּי מִזְבֵּחַ — **[These loaves], however, are not offered on the Altar,** but rather, are entirely eaten by the Kohanim. וְעַל שְׁתֵּי הַלֶּחֶם אֵינוֹ נֶאֱמַר בַּתּוֹרָה בְּשֶׁאָסְרָהּ דֶּרֶךְ כְּלָל — **Now, it was not** in reference to **the Two Loaves** of Shavuos **that the Torah spoke, when it broadly forbade** the usage of leavened dough in *menachos*, in the verse (*Leviticus* 2:11; *Mitzvah* 117), "כָּל הַמִּנְחָה אֲשֶׁר תַּקְרִיבוּ לַה' לֹא תֵעָשֶׂה חָמֵץ" — **Any** *minchah* **that you offer to HASHEM shall not be prepared leavened,** *for you shall not offer any leavening or honey as a fire-offering to HASHEM.* פְּרָט בְּאֵלּוּ וְהוֹצִיאָם מִן הַכְּלָל — **[The Torah] specified these** loaves **and excluded them from** that **general rule,** וַעֲלֵיהֶם נֶאֱמַר שָׁם — **for with regard to [these loaves] it is stated there** in the very next verse (ibid. v. 12): "קָרְבַּן רֵאשִׁית תַּקְרִיבוּ אֹתָם לַה'" — **You shall offer them** (i.e., leavening and honey) **as a first-fruit offering to HASHEM.** כְּלוֹמַר בְּאֵלּוּ לֹא אָסַרְתִּי לָכֶם הֶחָמֵץ — **The verse means to say: With regard to these** loaves, which are the "first-fruit offering," **I** (Hashem) **did not prohibit you from** bringing *chametz.*"[28] וּמִכָּל מָקוֹם אֶל הַמִּזְבֵּחַ לֹא הָיוּ עוֹלִין — **Although these loaves are an exception to the rule and were prepared as** *chametz*, **they nevertheless were not brought up to the Altar,** מִכֵּיוָן שֶׁהָיָה בָּהֶן חָמֵץ — **since they contained** *chametz*. וּכְמוֹ שֶׁנֶּאֱמַר בָּהֶן — **This caveat is** noted by the end of the above verse, **as it is stated** there (ibid.) **with regard to [these loaves]:** "וְאֶל הַמִּזְבֵּחַ לֹא יַעֲלוּ לְרֵיחַ נִיחֹחַ" — **but they may not go up on the Altar for a satisfying aroma.**[29] כָּל הַשְּׁאָר הָיוּ מַצָּה — **All the other** *minchah* offerings, though, **were unleavened.**[30]

Chinuch now discusses how a typical *minchah* is brought:

וְסֵדֶר הֲבָאָתָן כָּךְ הִיא — **The following is the procedure of bringing [the** *minchah* **offerings]:** אָדָם מֵבִיא סֹלֶת מִתּוֹךְ בֵּיתוֹ — **A person brings fine flour from his home,** בִּכְלִי כֶסֶף

---

### NOTES

וְכָל מִנְחַת כֹּהֵן כָּלִיל תִּהְיֶה לֹא תֵאָכֵל, *Every* minchah *of a Kohen is to be entirely [burned]; it shall not be eaten* (see Mitzvah 137). Therefore, *kemitzah* is not performed on a Kohen's *minchah* offering; rather, the entire *minchah* is brought up to the Altar's fire. This applies to the "*minchah* of initiation" and "*minchas chavitin*" mentioned above, as well as a sinner's *minchah* brought by a poor Kohen, and any voluntary *minchah* that he may bring. The *minchah* of a female Kohen (i.e., the daughter of a Kohen), though, is treated like that of a non-Kohen, and is eaten after the *kometz* is offered upon the Altar (see Mitzvah 134; Rambam, Hil. Maaseh HaKorbanos 12:9-10).

26. See note 11.

27. [There was actually one other leavened offering, as the *todah* was accompanied by forty loaves, ten of which were prepared as *chametz* (*Leviticus* 7:12-13). However, those accompanying loaves are not considered a "*minchah*" (*Menachos* 46b).]

28. That is, although the Two Loaves of Shavuos are termed a "*minchah*," and the Torah states that "any *minchah* that you offer to Hashem shall not be prepared leavened," they are the exception, for the Torah goes on to write that leaven may be offered as "a first-fruit offering." This "first-fruit offering" is a reference to the Two Loaves of Shavuos (*Menachos* 58a), for they were the first *minchah* offering of the new wheat crop, and are thus known as (*Leviticus* 23:16) מִנְחָה חֲדָשָׁה, a *"new" meal offering* (Rashi, *Menachos* 57b ד"ה אותם).

29. The verse in full reads: *You shall offer them as a first-fruit offering to Hashem, but they may not go up on the Altar for a satisfying aroma.* Therefore, although the Two Loaves are the exception to the rule prohibiting *minchah* offerings of *chametz*, and we are indeed to "offer them as a first-fruit offering," nevertheless no part of them "goes up on the Altar for a satisfying aroma"; rather they are entirely eaten by the Kohanim.

30. Even the portion eaten by the Kohanim is to be unleavened (*Menachos* 55a; see Mitzvah 135; see also Mitzvah 117 at note 24).

# VAYIKRA / MITZVAH 116: THE OBLIGATION REGARDING THE MINCHAH OFFERING

אוֹ זָהָב אוֹ שֶׁל מַתֶּכֶת³¹ וּמוֹלִיכָהּ אֵצֶל הַכֹּהֵן, וְהַכֹּהֵן מוֹלִיכָהּ אֵצֶל הַמִּזְבֵּחַ³², וְקוֹמֵץ מִמֶּנָּה הַכֹּהֵן בְּרָאשֵׁי אֶצְבְּעוֹתָיו, וּמַקְטִיר הַקֹּמֶץ כֻּלּוֹ בַּמִּזְבֵּחַ³³, וְהַשְּׁאָר נֶאֱכָל לַכֹּהֲנִים.³⁴

---

**וּמוֹלִיכָהּ אֵצֶל הַכֹּהֵן** – **אוֹ זָהָב אוֹ שֶׁל מַתֶּכֶת – in a vessel of silver, gold, or** some other **metal,**[31] **and brings it to the Kohen** in the Holy Temple. **וְהַכֹּהֵן מוֹלִיכָהּ אֵצֶל הַמִּזְבֵּחַ** – **After the flour is** prepared in accordance with the procedures appropriate for the particular *minchah* being brought, **the Kohen brings [the *minchah*] near to the Altar.**[32] **וְקוֹמֵץ מִמֶּנָּה הַכֹּהֵן בְּרָאשֵׁי אֶצְבְּעוֹתָיו** – **The Kohen** then **scoops a *kometz* from it with the tips of his fingers, וּמַקְטִיר הַקֹּמֶץ כֻּלּוֹ בַּמִּזְבֵּחַ** – **and burns the entire *kometz* upon the Altar.**[33] **וְהַשְּׁאָר נֶאֱכָל לַכֹּהֲנִים** – **The remainder** of the *minchah* **is eaten by the Kohanim.**[34]

---

NOTES

31. The vessel should be one that is fit to be dedicated as a sacred service vessel (even if it would not end up being dedicated as such). Therefore, it is to be metal and not some lesser material, for metal vessels are significant (*Sotah* 14b; *Rambam, Hil. Maaseh HaKorbanos* 13:12). [The exception to this rule is the *sotah's minchah,* which was brought in an inferior palm-tree fiber basket (Mishnah, *Sotah* 14a), as an indication of the lowliness of her act (see *Dvar Shaul, Sotah* 16:1).] When the flour was brought to the *Beis HaMikdash,* it was prepared according to the mode of preparation appropriate for that particular *minchah* (e.g., mixed with oil, cooked, etc.) and then transferred to an actual service vessel to be sanctified (*Rambam* ibid. 13:5,12; cf. *Mishneh LaMelech* to 13:5 ד״ה ואח״כ, who quotes some authorities who require a service vessel for the preparation as well). The *levonah* was then placed upon it, at which point it was ready for the Kohen to bring it close to the Altar (see next note).

32. As part of the procedure of offering a *minchah,* it is to be brought near the southwest corner of the Altar. This is based on the verse (*Leviticus* 6:7): וְזֹאת תּוֹרַת הַמִּנְחָה הַקְרֵב אֹתָהּ בְּנֵי אַהֲרֹן לִפְנֵי ה׳ אֶל פְּנֵי הַמִּזְבֵּחַ, *This is the law of the meal offering: The sons of Aaron shall bring it before HASHEM, to the front of the Altar.* The phrase "before Hashem" implies the western side of the Altar, which was the side that faced the Sanctuary. However, the phrase "the front of the Altar" implies the southern side, for that is the side with the ramp that served as the entrance onto the Altar. To fulfill the verse in its entirety, the *minchah* is brought to the southwest corner. The vessel is to touch the corner, although the flour itself did not need to make contact with the Altar (*Sotah* 14b; *Rambam, Hil. Maaseh HaKorbanos* 13:12). This requirement of bringing the *minchah* close to the Altar is specifically for those that were offered (or had a portion offered) upon the fire (*Rambam,* ibid. 12:6), but not for the *Lechem HaPanim* or the Two Loaves of Shavuos, neither of which had any part offered upon the Altar (see *Radvaz* ad loc.).

33. The *kometz* [*fistful;* also referred to in the Torah as the אַזְכָּרָה, *memorial portion*] is the portion of the *minchah* offering that is removed from the rest of the *minchah,* and then offered up upon the Altar's fire. This is in fulfillment of the verse (*Leviticus* 2:2): וְקָמַץ מִשָּׁם מְלֹא קֻמְצוֹ מִסָּלְתָּהּ וּמִשַּׁמְנָהּ עַל כָּל לְבֹנָתָהּ וְהִקְטִיר הַכֹּהֵן אֶת אַזְכָּרָתָהּ הַמִּזְבֵּחָה, *He shall scoop up his fistful from it, from its fine flour and from its oil, as well as all its levonah; and the Kohen shall burn its memorial portion upon the Altar.* In a later mitzvah (Mitzvah 137), Chinuch describes the procedure of *kemitzah* (i.e., the removal of the *kometz*) as being the way one normally scoops up something with his fist, closing all his fingers (other than his thumb) over his palm. In this, he apparently follows *Rambam's* understanding of this procedure (*Commentary to Mishnah, Menachos* 1:2, and *Hil. Maaseh HaKorbanos* 13:13). Others contend that *kemitzah* involves scooping with only the three middle fingers of the hand, but not the little finger (*Rashi, Leviticus* 2:2; *Rav, Menachos* 1:2; *Smag, Asin* 186 – based on *Menachos* 11a; see however *Kesef Mishneh* to *Rambam* ibid.).

Regardless of how many fingers were involved, the procedure for *kemitzah* is as follows: The *levonah* is moved to one side, so that none of it is taken in the *kometz,* and the Kohen then scoops the four (or three) fingers-full of flour (neither more nor less) from a place where the oil is abundant, in keeping with the verse (ibid.), *from its fine flour and from its oil.* [In the case of *minchah* offerings that are baked before the *kemitzah,* the loaves are first folded into four quarters and then separated into those quarter-pieces so as to facilitate the *kemitzah* (*Rambam, Hil. Maaseh HaKorbanos* 13:10).] The *kometz* is then placed into a service vessel, into which all of the *levonah* is transferred as well, the combination of which is then brought up to the Altar to be salted (see Mitzvah 118) and then poured onto the Altar's fire (*Sotah* 14b). [See *Minchas Chinuch* 137:2, regarding Chinuch's statement that the "tips" of the fingers were used.]

34. Eating the remainder of the *minchah* is a separate mitzvah (Mitzvah 134). The Kohanim are permitted to eat the remainder only after most of the *kometz* has been ignited upon the Altar (*Rambam* ibid. 12:13), and they are to eat it only within the Temple Courtyard (ibid. 10:3).

## 398 ויקרא / מצוה קטז: מצות קרבן מנחה

זֶהוּ סֵדֶר הַנֶּאֱכָלוֹת. וְסֵדֶר הַנִּשְׂרָפוֹת[35], וְהַמְּלָאכוֹת שֶׁנַּעֲשׂוֹת בַּמְּנָחוֹת עַל יְדֵי זָרִים וְהַנַּעֲשׂוֹת בָּהֶן עַל יְדֵי כֹּהֲנִים[36], וְיֶתֶר פְּרָטֶיהָ, מְבֹאָרִין בְּמַסֶּכְתָּא הַבְּנוּיָה עַל זֶה, וְהִיא מַסֶּכֶת מְנָחוֹת.[37]

וְנוֹהֶגֶת עֲשִׂיַּת הַמְּנָחוֹת בִּזְמַן הַבַּיִת בְּזִכְרֵי כְהֻנָּה[38]. וְכֹהֵן שֶׁעָבַר וְשִׁנָּה מַעֲשֵׂה הַמִּנְחָה הַמְפֹרָשׁ בָּהּ, בִּטֵּל עֲשֵׂה.[39]

---

זֶהוּ סֵדֶר הַנֶּאֱכָלוֹת — **This is the procedure of the [*minchah* offerings] whose remainders are eaten** by the Kohanim. וְסֵדֶר הַנִּשְׂרָפוֹת — **As for the procedure for those that are** entirely **burned** and not eaten by Kohanim,[35] וְהַמְּלָאכוֹת שֶׁנַּעֲשׂוֹת בַּמְּנָחוֹת עַל יְדֵי זָרִים — **as well as which of the tasks performed with the *menachos* may be done by non-Kohanim,** וְהַנַּעֲשׂוֹת בָּהֶן עַל יְדֵי כֹּהֲנִים — **and which of them may be done by Kohanim** alone,[36] וְיֶתֶר פְּרָטֶיהָ — **as well as the additional details of [this mitzvah],** מְבֹאָרִין בְּמַסֶּכְתָּא הַבְּנוּיָה עַל זֶה — they **are set forth in the tractate that is dedicated to this** subject, וְהִיא מַסֶּכֶת מְנָחוֹת — **which is Tractate *Menachos*.**[37]

### ~ Applicability of the Mitzvah ~

וְנוֹהֶגֶת עֲשִׂיַּת הַמְּנָחוֹת בִּזְמַן הַבַּיִת — **The mitzvah involving the performance of** the service of **the *minchah* offerings applies in the times of the** Holy **Temple,** בְּזִכְרֵי כְהֻנָּה — **and applies exclusively to male Kohanim.**[38] וְכֹהֵן שֶׁעָבַר וְשִׁנָּה מַעֲשֵׂה הַמִּנְחָה הַמְפֹרָשׁ בָּהּ — **A Kohen who transgresses by deviating from the procedure of the *minchah* offering that is specified in its regard** בִּטֵּל עֲשֵׂה — **has violated** this mitzvah-**obligation.**[39]

---

### NOTES

35. This refers to *minchah* offerings of male Kohanim (see note 25).

36. Only male Kohanim may perform the actual *avodah* of the *minchah*. This is derived from the oft-repeated phrase, בְּנֵי אַהֲרֹן, *sons of Aaron*, stated in the context of the various sacrificial services (*Leviticus* 2:2, et al.), from which we derive that only the *sons* of Aaron (i.e., males) may perform the *avodah*, but not the daughters of Aaron (*Kiddushin* 36a). Nevertheless, from the flow of the verses, which state (*Leviticus* 2:1,2): וְיָצַק עָלֶיהָ שֶׁמֶן, וְנָתַן עָלֶיהָ לְבֹנָה וֶהֱבִיאָהּ אֶל בְּנֵי אַהֲרֹן הַכֹּהֲנִים וְקָמַץ מִשָּׁם מְלֹא קֻמְצוֹ *he shall pour upon it* (i.e., the flour) *oil, and place upon it levonah, and he shall bring it to the sons of Aaron, the Kohanim, and [the Kohen] shall take the kometz*, the implication is that a Kohen is not needed for the mixing and preparation of the *minchah*, and is only needed for the *kemitzah* and beyond (*Menachos* 18b; *Rambam, Hil. Maaseh HaKorbanos* 12:23). [In addition, the bringing of the *minchah* near to the southwest corner of the Altar (although prior to the *kemitzah*) requires a Kohen (*Ramban, Leviticus* 2:1; see also *Radvaz, Hil Maaseh HaKorbanos* 13:12 ד"ה ונותן הפתיתים).]

37. These laws are codified in *Rambam, Hilchos Maaseh HaKorbanos* Chs. 12, 13, and 17.

38. Any Jew could vow and bring a *minchah* offering (*Rambam, Hil. Maaseh HaKorbanos* 3:2). However, only male Kohanim could perform the actual *avodah*; see above, note 36.

39. However, his failure to perform those procedures does not necessarily invalidate the offering. Certain procedures are essential for the validation of the offering, while others are simply the correct way to perform the mitzvah, but their absence does not invalidate the offering after the fact (see *Rambam, Hil. Maaseh HaKorbanos* 13:11 with with commentaries).

---

> **∞§ Insight A: The Preciousness of the Minchah Offering**
>
> The voluntary *minchah* offering, being the least expensive of all offerings, was generally brought by the poor and indigent (*Menachos* 104b). The poor man, unable to scrape together the funds to bring even a bird offering, and surely not an offering of sheep or cattle, would simply offer what he had — a meager amount of flour and oil. Notwithstanding the paltry nature of his offering, the Torah specifically mentions Aaron, the Kohen Gadol, with regard to its procedure (see *Leviticus* 2:3), expressing the idea that even the Kohen Gadol should be happy to bring this offering, and should not scorn it as being beneath his dignity (*Baal HaTurim, Leviticus* 2:1). Indeed, our Sages note that the term רֵיחַ נִיחוֹחַ לַה', *a satisfying aroma to Hashem*, which appears in conjunction with the animal and

bird offerings (*Leviticus* 1:9,17), appears regarding the *minchah* offering as well (ibid. 2:2). The use of this expression with regard to the *minchah* indicates that it, too, is pleasing to Hashem. In the words of the Mishnah (*Menachos* 110a): אֶחָד הַמַּרְבֶּה וְאֶחָד הַמַּמְעִיט וּבִלְבַד שֶׁיְּכַוֵּן לִבּוֹ לַשָּׁמַיִם, *whether one gives a lot or one gives a little, [his offering is equally pleasing to God,] provided that he directs his heart toward his Father in Heaven*. Large and small offerings are equal in God's eyes, for He looks to the stirring of the heart of the supplicant who brings the offering, rather than to the size of the offering itself (*Sfas Emes, Leviticus* 5636).

In truth, though, the *minchah* offering was not only on par with its animal offering counterparts, but in a certain respect was even greater. The poor man's taking his daily allotment of sustenance and offering it to Hashem is an act of self-sacrifice simply not present in the animal offerings coming from those of greater financial means. [The minimum measurement of flour for the *minchah* — a tenth-*ephah* — was the same measurement as the daily allotment of manna in the Wilderness (*R' S. R. Hirsch, Leviticus* 2:1).] This, in fact, is the meaning of a phrase unique to the *minchah* offering (*Leviticus* 2:1): וְנֶפֶשׁ כִּי תַקְרִיב קָרְבַּן מִנְחָה לַה׳, *when a "soul" offers a minchah offering to Hashem*, regarding which our Sages state (*Menachos* 104b): אָמַר הַקָּדוֹשׁ בָּרוּךְ הוּא מַעֲלֶה אֲנִי עָלָיו כְּאִילוּ הִקְרִיב נַפְשׁוֹ, *The Holy One, blessed is He, says, "I will consider it as though he offered his own soul."* No animal offering shares this expression of offering a "soul," for it is specifically the donation of the poor man (i.e., the *minchah*), and its attendant self-sacrifice, that is regarded with such great esteem.

Regarding animal offerings, the blood that is offered on the Altar is equated with the soul of the animal (see *Leviticus* 17:11), and by extension, the soul of the one bringing the offering (see *R' S.R. Hirsch* ad loc.). *Minchah* offerings, though, by definition lack any such blood-service. Where, then, is this symbolic aspect of the offering of the soul of its owner? The answer, according to the above, is clear. The soul of the owner is offered in *every* aspect of the minchah offering. His selfless act, giving of what little he has in order to connect to his Creator, is the ultimate offering of his soul.

In a similar vein, *Kli Yakar* (*Leviticus* 2:1) cautions us not to construe the Torah's placement of the laws of the *minchah* after the animal and bird offerings as implying that the *minchah* is somehow of lesser significance. Rather, the opposite is the case. The *minchah* offering, being brought by the poor, downtrodden, and humble of spirit is by definition brought by those who are the least likely to sin and rebel against God, for their egos are not inflated by their wealth. It is for this reason that the *minchah* offering is listed last, for the poor man is the least likely to require spiritual rectification. Indeed, all the offerings are listed in descending order of monetary value, with the offering of cattle listed first, followed by the offering of the flock, then by the offering of fowl, and finally by the *minchah*, because those who must resort to the less expensive offerings are, successively, less likely to be in need of rectification. However, if and when the poorest person does bring his *minchah* offering, he has succeeded in bringing the offering that is most precious in God's eyes. He has brought the offering described as being (ibid. v. 3): קֹדֶשׁ קָדָשִׁים מֵאִשֵּׁי ה׳, *most holy from the fire-offerings of* HASHEM, for the one who brings it, brings his very soul!

### ⚜ Insight B: Why the Afternoon Service Is Called Minchah

The second of the three daily prayers, the afternoon prayer service, is known as *Minchah*. Why is it that we refer to the afternoon prayer as *"Minchah"*? What connection, if any, does this prayer have with the *minchah* offering?

Now, some actually see the term *"Minchah"* as being unrelated to the offering that shares the same name, but rather as a term that describes the afternoon, which is the time of day in which the *Minchah* prayer is recited. The afternoon is called מִנְחָה (*"minchah"*), which is cognate of מְנוּחָה (*menuchah*; i.e., rest), because that is when the sun is heading toward its "resting" position, and its powerful light is beginning to abate (*Ramban, Exodus* 12:6; see *Targum Onkelos* to *Genesis* 3:8).

Others, however, do indeed see a connection between the *minchah* offering and the afternoon prayer of the same name. Chinuch mentions two possible reasons for the term *minchah* in reference to the meal offering: It refers either (1) to the diminutive aspect of this offering, or (2) to its voluntary nature. The commentators connect the *Minchah* afternoon prayers to both of these aspects, as follows:

Some commentators note that the afternoon prayers are the shortest of the three daily prayers, and are thus appropriately referred to as *"Minchah,"* as per the term's meaning of "diminutive" (*Sifsei*

*Chachamim, Berachos* 26a ד"ה תפילת המנחה). Others connect the afternoon prayers to the "voluntary" aspect conveyed by the word *minchah*, for unlike the morning prayers, which bring atonement for the previous evening's sins, and the evening prayers, which bring atonement for the previous day's sins, the afternoon prayers are less compelling in comparison. As such, the recital of these prayers, while certainly obligatory, can be more aptly described as a tribute than as an integral service (*Emunas Shmuel* [R' Shmuel Keidinover] §20, quoted in *Eliyahu Rabbah* §232; see *Kedushas Levi, Chayei Sarah* ד"ה או יאמר for a similar approach).

Other explanations that connect the *Minchah* prayer to the *minchah* offering include one offered by *Tosafos* (*Pesachim* 107a ד"ה סמוך למנחה), who explain that *"Minchah"* is a reference to the *minchah* offering that *accompanied* the afternoon *tamid* (see above, note 7). Although the *tamid* of the morning had an accompanying *minchah* offering as well, the afternoon's accompanying *minchah* was particularly unique, as it was specifically at the time of the offering of that "*minchah* of libations" that Elijah the prophet was answered in his prayers in the confrontation with the false prophets of Baal on Mount Carmel (see *I Kings* Ch. 18). The verses state (ibid. vs. 36-37): וַיְהִי בַּעֲלוֹת הַמִּנְחָה וַיִּגַּשׁ אֵלִיָּהוּ הַנָּבִיא וַיֹּאמַר ... עֲנֵנִי ה', *And it was at the time of the [afternoon] minchah-offering, Elijah the prophet approached and said ... "Answer me, Hashem."* Elijah approached Hashem in prayer specifically at that time, for he recognized the propitious nature of that moment — and indeed, his prayer was answered. The Gemara thus states that one should always be diligent regarding the *Minchah* prayer, since it was at that time that Elijah the prophet was answered (*Berachos* 6b).

The unique character of that time was, in fact, imbued into it centuries earlier by Abraham and Isaac, for it was during that time of day that *Akeidas Yitzchak* (the "Binding of Isaac") took place, after which Abraham prayed that its merit should always stand his children in good stead (*HaRif* in *Ein Yaakov, Berachos* ad loc.). In fact, if we look more deeply at the *Akeidah*, we will see a further connection — not just to the timing of *Minchah*, but to the *minchah* offering as well. Isaac, who willingly accepted being the *olah* offering at the *Akeidah*, epitomized self-sacrifice. Now, while the *minchah* offering that was brought together with the *tamid* in the morning and afternoon was a communal obligation, *minchah* offerings were generally brought by individuals as donations. As noted in Insight A, self-sacrifice is the very hallmark of such a *minchah* offering — whose indigent owner must selflessly struggle to scrape together the means through which to bring his offering. His offering is therefore given the unique equivalence in God's eyes as his having offered up his very soul — a theme that connects the devotee who offers the *minchah* with his illustrious ancestor, Isaac, to whom the formulation of the *Minchah* prayer service is actually attributed (*Berachos* 26b). Isaac, who embodies the ideal of the *minchah* offering, instilled that characteristic into the prayer that shares the same name.

## מִצְוָה קיז: שֶׁלֹּא לְהַקְרִיב שְׂאוֹר אוֹ דְּבַשׁ

שֶׁלֹּא לְהַקְרִיב שְׂאוֹר וּדְבַשׁ עַל גַּבֵּי הַמִּזְבֵּחַ, שֶׁנֶּאֱמַר (ויקרא ב׳, י״א) כִּי כָל שְׂאוֹר וְכָל דְּבַשׁ לֹא תַקְטִירוּ מִמֶּנּוּ אִשֶּׁה לַיי׳. וְנִכְפְּלָה הַמְּנִיעָה בְּרֹאשׁ הַפָּסוּק, שֶׁנֶּאֱמַר כָּל הַמִּנְחָה אֲשֶׁר תַּקְרִיבוּ לַיי׳ לֹא תֵעָשֶׂה חָמֵץ.

---

## Mitzvah 117
## The Prohibition to Bring Leaven or Honey as an Offering

כָּל הַמִּנְחָה אֲשֶׁר תַּקְרִיבוּ לַה׳ לֹא תֵעָשֶׂה חָמֵץ כִּי כָל שְׂאֹר וְכָל דְּבַשׁ לֹא תַקְטִירוּ מִמֶּנּוּ אִשֶּׁה לַה׳

*Any meal-offering (minchah) that you offer to HASHEM shall not be prepared leavened, for you shall not burn any leaven or any honey as a fire offering to HASHEM (Leviticus 2:11).*

In this verse, the Torah declares that we may not leaven the *minchah* offering (pl. *menachos*), as it is forbidden to offer leaven or honey upon the Altar.[1] This prohibition against offering leaven or honey upon the Altar is not limited to *menachos*; it is prohibited to burn leaven or honey on the Altar as part of *any* offering (i.e., to add it to an offering), or as an offering in its own right, as we shall see.

שֶׁלֹּא לְהַקְרִיב שְׂאוֹר וּדְבַשׁ עַל גַּבֵּי הַמִּזְבֵּחַ — We are commanded **not to offer leaven**[2] **or honey upon the Altar,** שֶׁנֶּאֱמַר — **as it is stated** (*Leviticus* 2:11): "כִּי כָל שְׂאוֹר וְכָל דְּבַשׁ לֹא תַקְטִירוּ מִמֶּנּוּ אִשֶּׁה לַה׳" — **for you shall not burn any leaven or any honey as a fire offering to HASHEM.**[3]

וְנִכְפְּלָה הַמְּנִיעָה בְּרֹאשׁ הַפָּסוּק — **The restriction,** with respect to offering a leavened *minchah* on the Altar, **is twofold,** extending to its very preparation, as indicated **in the beginning of the verse,** שֶׁנֶּאֱמַר — **where it is stated:** *Any minchah that you offer to HASHEM shall not be prepared as chametz* (leavened).[4]

---

### NOTES

1. The preparation of the *minchah* offering, during which there is concern for leavening, is described in Mitzvah 116, notes 17-22.

The simple reading of the verse implies that the restriction on preparing a leavened *minchah* is only on account of its subsequent burning on the Altar. However, the Torah's command not to leaven a *minchah* actually constitutes an independent prohibition [reckoned by Chinuch as Mitzvah 135], which forbids the very *preparation* of a leavened *minchah*, and which applies also to *menachos* not offered on the Altar (such as the *Lechem HaPanim*; see Mitzvah 116 with notes 9-10). That said, the verse does teach that a *minchah* offered on the Altar is subject also to the prohibition against burning anything leavened on the Altar, and is thus prohibited twofold from becoming leavened, as Chinuch writes below.

2. שְׂאוֹר, *leaven,* refers to the agent that causes leavening, sometimes called "sourdough." *Chametz* (a leavened product) is also included in the prohibition, as indicated in the beginning of the verse cited above, that a *minchah* that was *prepared* leavened would be forbidden to be offered on the Altar (*Minchas Chinuch* §1).

3. Although leaven and honey may not be offered on the Altar, they are essential in certain offerings not burned on the Altar (but eaten by the Kohanim), as stated in the next verse (v. 12): *You shall offer them* (leaven or honey) *as a first-produce offering to HASHEM, but they may not go up upon the Altar for a satisfying aroma.* The "first-produce offering" refers to the Two Loaves of Shavuos, the first offering to be brought from the new wheat crop (which is brought as *chametz*, as stated in *Leviticus* 23:17; see Mitzvah 116, at notes 26-28); and *bikkurim*, the first fruits of the Seven Species that are brought to the *Beis HaMikdash* each year (Mitzvah 91), of which some species constitute "honey" [see notes 5-6 below] (*Rashi* ad loc., from *Sifra*).

4. While it is prohibited to offer leaven on the Altar even by itself, and for any purpose, the Torah adds a restriction with regard to leaven in a *minchah* offering, i.e., that its very preparation is forbidden (see note 1). Thus, with respect to a *minchah* offering, one is further distanced from burning leaven (i.e., *chametz*) on the Altar,

וְהַדְּבַשׁ הוּא שֵׁם כּוֹלֵל לַדְּבַשׁ הַיָּדוּעַ,[5] וְכֵן דְּבַשׁ תְּמָרִים שֶׁהוּא סְתַם הַדְּבַשׁ שֶׁל תּוֹרָה, וְכֵן מֵהַל הַיּוֹצֵא מִן הַפֵּרוֹת הַמְּתוּקִין.[6] וּבִכְלָל לֹא תַקְטִירוּ, הוּא גַם כֵּן שֶׁלֹּא לָתֵת מִמֶּנּוּ בְּפִטּוּם הַקְּטֹרֶת,[7] וּכְמוֹ שֶׁהַפַּטָּמִים אוֹמְרִים יָפֶה הָיָה הַדְּבַשׁ לַקְּטֹרֶת אֶלָּא שֶׁאֲסָרַתּוּ הַתּוֹרָה.[8]

---

Chinuch defines the word "honey" in the verse:

וְהַדְּבַשׁ הוּא שֵׁם כּוֹלֵל לַדְּבַשׁ הַיָּדוּעַ — **The "honey"** mentioned here **is a general term** that includes **the known honey** (bee's honey), וְכֵן דְּבַשׁ תְּמָרִים שֶׁהוּא סְתַם הַדְּבַשׁ שֶׁל תּוֹרָה — **as well as the honey of dates, which is the standard honey of the Torah,**[5] וְכֵן מֵהַל הַיּוֹצֵא מִן הַפֵּרוֹת הַמְּתוּקִין — **as well as the juice that issues from** other **sweet fruits.**[6]

The prohibition is not limited to offerings brought on the Outer Altar:

וּבִכְלָל "לֹא תַקְטִירוּ" — **Included in** this commandment, *You shall not burn ... any honey as a fire offering to* HASHEM, הוּא גַם כֵּן שֶׁלֹּא לָתֵת מִמֶּנּוּ בְּפִטּוּם הַקְּטֹרֶת — **is also that it is forbidden to add [honey] to the compound of the *ketores*** (incense; Mitzvah 103), which is burned on the Inner Altar,[7] וּכְמוֹ שֶׁהַפַּטָּמִים אוֹמְרִים — **as the compounders** of the *ketores* would say: יָפֶה הָיָה הַדְּבַשׁ לַקְּטֹרֶת אֶלָּא שֶׁאֲסָרַתּוּ הַתּוֹרָה — **"Honey would have been beneficial for the *ketores*, but the Torah forbade it."**[8]

---

## NOTES

since he is prohibited from leavening the *minchah* in the first place. In contrast, honey is restricted only from burning on the Altar.

[A simple reading of Chinuch's words indicates that there are two prohibitions in the verse against *offering* a leavened *minchah*. This, however, is untenable (see *Even HaAzel, Hil. Isurei HaMizbe'ach* 5:1 §7 ד"ה אכן; see also Chinuch below, at note 28). We have therefore interpreted his words to mean that there is a twofold prohibition in the verse with respect to leaven.]

5. In the verse (*Deuteronomy* 8:8), אֶרֶץ זֵית שֶׁמֶן וּדְבָשׁ, *a land of oil-olives and honey,* the term *honey* refers to date honey (*Rashi* to *Deuteronomy* 26:2 and *Berachos* 41b). See following note.

6. In the verse (*Leviticus* 2:11), כִּי כָל שְׂאֹר וְכָל דְּבַשׁ לֹא תַקְטִירוּ מִמֶּנּוּ אִשֶּׁה לַה׳, *for you shall not burn any leaven or any honey as a fire offering to* HASHEM, the term דְּבַשׁ refers not only to the honey of dates, but also to the sweet nectar of any fruit [such as the syrup that exudes from figs] (*Rashi* to the verse). In fact, the prohibition to burn honey on the Altar includes the fruits themselves, as is evident from *Shevuos* 12a-b (see *Mishneh LaMelech, Hil. Isurei HaMizbe'ach* 5:1).

With respect to the distinction between these verses, some explain that the unqualified term דְּבַשׁ refers specifically to date honey (as in *Deuteronomy* 8:8), but in the current prohibition (*Leviticus* 2:11) it is understood as a reference to all sweet things because the verse states *any* honey (*Sifsei Chachamim, Otzar HaPeirushim* ed.; cf. *Teshuvos Chasam Sofer, Orach Chaim* §197). Others explain that the unqualified term דְּבַשׁ refers to all sweets (as in the current prohibition), but in the verse *a land of oil-olives and honey* it is understood as a specific reference to dates because that very same verse lists a number of other sweet fruits (such as grapes, figs, and pomegranates), and that listing would be superfluous if דְּבַשׁ referred to all sweet fruits, so it is obvious that in that case דְּבַשׁ refers specifically to dates, from which honey is commonly produced (*Chasam Sofer* to *Nedarim* 55a).

In any event, it is clear from the Gemara (*Shevuos* 12a-b) that the prohibition to offer *"honey"* on the Altar encompasses all sweet fruits and their nectars. Chinuch's ruling that it also encompasses bee's honey, however, is a matter of dispute. *Radvaz* (*Teshuvos* 3:962) rules in accordance with Chinuch, but others disagree, because, in their view, this is not the standard meaning of דְּבַשׁ in the Torah (*Sdei Chemed, Pe'as HaSadeh, Maareches HaDalet* §41 in the name of *Batei Kenesiyos*; see there for a comprehensive discussion of this subject).

7. *Sifra* to the verse.

*Minchas Chinuch* (§5) writes that it would also be forbidden to mix honey into the Yom Kippur *ketores* that is burned on a shovel (*machtah*) in the Holy of Holies (see *Leviticus* 16:12-13), even though it is not offered on any Altar. However, see *Chidushei HaGriz* to *Yoma*, p. 34 ד"ה מש"כ במנחת חנוך.

8. Honey would have increased the pungency of the aroma of the *ketores*; as stated in *Yerushalmi Yoma* 4:5 [30a in Schottenstein edition]: *The compounders [of the ketores] in Jerusalem used to say: "Had one put a bit of honey into it, the entire world would be unable to resist its scent"* (a similar statement appears in the *ketores* passages recited in the daily prayers). [*Radvaz, Hil. Klei HaMikdash* 2:8, suggests that the compounders of the *ketores* in Jerusalem would say this to any so-called expert in perfumery who would advise them to add honey to the *ketores* to enhance its fragrance. They would retort that this "secret" was, in fact, well known to the Sages, except that the Torah forbade it.]

Chinuch refers to honey (with regard to adding it to the *ketores*) because it is beneficial to the *ketores*, but leaven would be equally forbidden (see *Rambam, Hil. Isurei HaMizbe'ach* 5:2 with *Kesef Mishneh*).

shָרְשֵׁי מִצְוָה זוֹ נֶעְלָמִים מְאֹד לִמְצֹא אֲפִלּוּ רֶמֶז קָטָן מֵהֶן, וְאוּלָם מִפְּנֵי שֶׁכְּבָר הוֹדַעְתִּי בְּפֶתַח דְּבָרַי[9] שֶׁכַּוָּנָתִי בְּאֵלּוּ הַטְּעָמִים שֶׁאֲנִי כּוֹתֵב לְהַרְגִּיל הַנְּעָרִים וּלְהַטְעִים לָהֶם בִּתְחִלַּת בּוֹאָם לִשְׁמֹעַ דִּבְרֵי סֵפֶר, כִּי יֵשׁ לְדִבְרֵי הַתּוֹרָה טְעָמִים וְתוֹעָלוֹת, וִיקַבְּלוּם עַל דֶּרֶךְ הֶרְגֵּל שֶׁלָּהֶם וּכְפִי חֻלְשַׁת שִׂכְלָם, וְאַל יִהְיוּ לָהֶם הַמִּצְוֹת בִּתְחִלָּה כְּדִבְרֵי הַסֵּפֶר הֶחָתוּם[10], פֶּן יִבְעֲטוּ בָהֶם מִתּוֹךְ כָּךְ בְּנַעֲרוּתָם וְיָנִיחוּם לְעוֹלָם וְיֵלְכוּ בַּהֶבֶל, עַל כֵּן אֶכְתֹּב בָּהֶם כָּל אֲשֶׁר יַעֲלֶה בִּתְחִלַּת הַמַּחֲשָׁבָה, וְאַל יִתְפֹּשׂ עָלַי תּוֹפֵשׂ בְּשׁוּם דָּבָר אַחֲרֵי יֵדַע הַכַּוָּנָה.

וְאֹמַר כִּי עִנְיְנֵי הַקָּרְבָּן כֻּלָּם לְעוֹרֵר מַחֲשֶׁבֶת הַמַּקְרִיב, וּלְפִי הַמַּעֲשֶׂה הַהוּא יִקַּח דִּמְיוֹנוֹתָיו בְּנַפְשׁוֹ, הַכֹּל כַּאֲשֶׁר כְּתַבְנוּ כְּבָר[11], וְעַל כֵּן בְּהַרְחִיק הֶחָמֵץ, שֶׁהוּא נַעֲשָׂה בִּשְׁהִיָּה גְּדוֹלָה[12], מִקָּרְבָּנוֹ, יִקַּח דִּמְיוֹן לִקְנוֹת מִדַּת הַזְּרִיזוּת וְהַקַּלּוּת וְהַמְּהִירוּת בְּמַעֲשֵׂי הַשֵּׁם בָּרוּךְ הוּא,

---

### ☞ Underlying Purpose of the Mitzvah ☜

שָׁרְשֵׁי מִצְוָה זוֹ נֶעְלָמִים מְאֹד לִמְצֹא אֲפִלּוּ רֶמֶז קָטָן מֵהֶן — **The underlying purposes of this mitzvah are too concealed to catch even a slight glimpse of them.** וְאוּלָם מִפְּנֵי שֶׁכְּבָר הוֹדַעְתִּי בְּפֶתַח דְּבָרַי — **However,** I will propose a reason, **because I have already made known at the opening of my words,** i.e., in the Introduction to this work,[9] שֶׁכַּוָּנָתִי בְּאֵלּוּ הַטְּעָמִים שֶׁאֲנִי כּוֹתֵב — **that my intention in writing these reasons** לְהַרְגִּיל הַנְּעָרִים וּלְהַטְעִים לָהֶם בִּתְחִלַּת בּוֹאָם לִשְׁמֹעַ דִּבְרֵי סֵפֶר — **is to ingrain in the youth, and to have them taste at the** very **beginning of their coming to hear the words of** holy **books,** כִּי יֵשׁ לְדִבְרֵי הַתּוֹרָה טְעָמִים וְתוֹעָלוֹת — **that the matters of the Torah have reasons and purposes.** וִיקַבְּלוּם עַל דֶּרֶךְ הֶרְגֵּל שֶׁלָּהֶם — **Let [the youth] absorb [the reasons] on the level to which they are accustomed** וּכְפִי חֻלְשַׁת שִׂכְלָם — **and in accordance with their** as yet **undeveloped minds,** וְאַל יִהְיוּ לָהֶם הַמִּצְוֹת בִּתְחִלָּה כְּדִבְרֵי הַסֵּפֶר הֶחָתוּם — **and let the mitzvos not be** perceived **by them at the start** of their studies **like words of a sealed book,**[10] פֶּן יִבְעֲטוּ בָהֶם מִתּוֹךְ כָּךְ בְּנַעֲרוּתָם — **lest they reject them because of this in their youth,** וְיָנִיחוּם לְעוֹלָם — **and** subsequently **abandon them forever** וְיֵלְכוּ בַּהֶבֶל — **and** follow the ways of **futility.** עַל כֵּן אֶכְתֹּב בָּהֶם כָּל אֲשֶׁר יַעֲלֶה בִּתְחִלַּת הַמַּחֲשָׁבָה — **Therefore, I shall write about [the mitzvos] whatever comes** to mind **at first thought,** וְאַל יִתְפֹּשׂ עָלַי תּוֹפֵשׂ בְּשׁוּם דָּבָר — **and let no critic criticize me for any** reason I suggest for a mitzvah אַחֲרֵי יֵדַע הַכַּוָּנָה — **now that he knows** my **intent.**

Having made this disclaimer, Chinuch presents a reason for the restriction of offering leaven: וְאֹמַר כִּי עִנְיְנֵי הַקָּרְבָּן כֻּלָּם לְעוֹרֵר מַחֲשֶׁבֶת הַמַּקְרִיב — **I suggest that all the aspects of an offering are intended to inspire the thoughts of the one bringing** it. וּלְפִי הַמַּעֲשֶׂה הַהוּא יִקַּח דִּמְיוֹנוֹתָיו בְּנַפְשׁוֹ — **Based on the particular action** involved in the offering, **he will internalize the perceptions** that it arouses **within him,** הַכֹּל כַּאֲשֶׁר כְּתַבְנוּ כְּבָר — **all as we have already written.**[11] וְעַל כֵּן בְּהַרְחִיק הֶחָמֵץ שֶׁהוּא נַעֲשָׂה בִּשְׁהִיָּה גְּדוֹלָה מִקָּרְבָּנוֹ — **Regarding the prohibition of** *chametz* in a *minchah* offering, it can **thus** be said that **through keeping** *chametz*, **which is made with much delay,**[12] **away from his offering,** יִקַּח דִּמְיוֹן לִקְנוֹת מִדַּת הַזְּרִיזוּת וְהַקַּלּוּת וְהַמְּהִירוּת בְּמַעֲשֵׂי הַשֵּׁם בָּרוּךְ הוּא — **one will take an example** that will inspire him **to acquire the traits of alacrity, nimbleness, and swiftness in the** performance of **acts** in the service **of Hashem, blessed is He.**

---

### NOTES

9. See the Author's Introduction, Vol. 1, pp. 30-31. [Chinuch states there that he wrote the book for his son and his son's friends.]

10. Stylistic citation of *Isaiah* 29:11.

11. See Mitzvah 95, at notes 35-63. [This concept, developed at length in Mitzvah 95, is reiterated in many of the subsequent mitzvos pertaining to the various services performed in the *Beis HaMikdash*.]

12. Leavened bread (*chametz*) represents sluggishness because it requires the slow and lengthy process of leavening, whereas unleavened bread (*matzah*), which is baked without delay, represents alacrity.

וּכְמוֹ שֶׁאָמְרוּ זִכְרוֹנָם לִבְרָכָה הֱוֵי קַל כַּנֶּשֶׁר וְרָץ כַּצְּבִי וְגִבּוֹר כָּאֲרִי לַעֲשׂוֹת וְכוּ'. וְנִתְחַיֵּב[13] הָעִנְיָן בְּמִנְחַת הַיְחִידִים יוֹתֵר מִמִּנְחַת הַצִּבּוּר לְפִי שֶׁהַיֵּאוּשׁ וְהָעַצְלָה נִמְצָא בְּיָחִיד יוֹתֵר, כִּי הָרַבִּים יַזְהִירוּ זֶה אֶת זֶה, וְלָכֵן לֹא תַּקְפִּיד הַתּוֹרָה עַל זֶה בְּמִנְחַת הַצִּבּוּר הַבָּאָה מִזְּמַן לִזְמַן, כְּגוֹן שְׁתֵּי הַלֶּחֶם שֶׁל עֲצֶרֶת[14], אֲבָל בְּלֶחֶם הַפָּנִים אַף עַל פִּי שֶׁהוּא נִקְרָא גַם כֵּן מִנְחַת צִבּוּר[15], מֵחֲמַת שֶׁהִיא מִנְחָה תְּמִידִית בְּכָל שַׁבָּת וְשַׁבָּת, תַּקְפִּיד הַתּוֹרָה בָּהּ, וְנִצְטַוִּינוּ גַם כֵּן בָּהּ שֶׁתִּהְיֶה מַצָּה.

וּבְעִנְיַן הַרְחָקַת הַדְּבַשׁ נֹאמַר אֶל הַיְלָדִים רַבִּים כְּדֵי לְיַסְּרָם, שֶׁהוּא סִבָּה לְדִמְיוֹן שֶׁיְּמַעֵט הָאָדָם מִלִּרְדֹּף אַחַר הַמַּאֲכָלִים הַמְּתוּקִים לְחִכּוֹ כְּמִנְהַג הַזּוֹלְלִים

**הֱוֵי קַל** — **וּכְמוֹ שֶׁאָמְרוּ זִכְרוֹנָם לִבְרָכָה** — It is **as [our Sages], of blessed memory, said** (*Avos* 5:20): **כַּנֶּשֶׁר וְרָץ כַּצְּבִי וְגִבּוֹר כָּאֲרִי לַעֲשׂוֹת וְכוּ'** — **"Be light as an eagle, swift as a deer, and strong as a lion to do** the will of your Father in Heaven."

Chinuch explains why, based on the above reasoning, the Two Loaves of Shavuos *are* brought as *chametz* (as stated in *Leviticus* 23:17):[13]

**וְנִתְחַיֵּב הָעִנְיָן בְּמִנְחַת הַיְחִידִים יוֹתֵר מִמִּנְחַת הַצִּבּוּר** — **This aspect** of the offering, i.e., that it must not be allowed to become *chametz*, in order to inspire one to alacrity in the service of Hashem, **is more essential with respect to the** *minchah* **offerings of individuals than the** *minchah* **offering of the community,** **לְפִי שֶׁהַיֵּאוּשׁ וְהָעַצְלָה נִמְצָא בְּיָחִיד יוֹתֵר** — **because apathy and laziness are more common in an individual** than in a community, **כִּי הָרַבִּים יַזְהִירוּ זֶה אֶת זֶה** — **since the many** members of the community **alert** and inspire **one another**. **וְלָכֵן לֹא תַּקְפִּיד הַתּוֹרָה עַל זֶה בְּמִנְחַת הַצִּבּוּר הַבָּאָה מִזְּמַן לִזְמַן** — **Therefore, the Torah is not particular about [the presence of** *chametz***]** and the lesson that it imparts **in the case of a communal** *minchah* **that is brought from time to time,** **כְּגוֹן שְׁתֵּי הַלֶּחֶם שֶׁל עֲצֶרֶת** — **such as the Two Loaves of** *Atzeres* (Shavuos).

Nevertheless, the prohibition *does* apply to the *Lechem HaPanim*,[14] despite it being a communal offering. Chinuch explains why:

**אֲבָל בְּלֶחֶם הַפָּנִים אַף עַל פִּי שֶׁהוּא נִקְרָא גַם כֵּן** — **However, in the case of the** *Lechem HaPanim*, **מֵחֲמַת שֶׁהִיא מִנְחָה תְּמִידִית** **מִנְחַת צִבּוּר** — **even though it, too, is called a communal** *minchah*,[15] **בְּכָל שַׁבָּת וְשַׁבָּת** — still, **since it is a constant** *minchah* **that is brought on each and every Sabbath,** **תַּקְפִּיד הַתּוֹרָה בָּהּ** — **the Torah is particular regarding it** that it should not be *chametz*; **וְנִצְטַוִּינוּ גַם כֵּן בָּהּ שֶׁתִּהְיֶה מַצָּה** — **and so, regarding it, too, we are commanded that it consist of matzah** (i.e., unleavened loaves).

Having posited a reason for the Torah's banning of *chametz* in an offering, Chinuch continues with a suggested rationale for the restriction on honey:

**וּבְעִנְיַן הַרְחָקַת הַדְּבַשׁ** **נֹאמַר אֶל הַיְלָדִים** — **As for the matter of distancing honey** from the Altar, **רַבִּים** — **we may tell our** young and **tender children,** **כְּדֵי לְיַסְּרָם** — **in order to discipline them,** **שֶׁהוּא סִבָּה לְדִמְיוֹן שֶׁיְּמַעֵט הָאָדָם מִלִּרְדֹּף אַחַר הַמַּאֲכָלִים הַמְּתוּקִים לְחִכּוֹ** — **that it promotes the idea that a person should limit his pursuit of foods that are sweet to his palate,** **כְּמִנְהַג הַזּוֹלְלִים**

---

### NOTES

13. [This offering is described in Mitzvah 116, at notes 26-28.] Presumably, Chinuch does not seek an explanation as to why the prohibition to offer leaven on the Altar does not apply to the Two Loaves, for they are *not offered* on the Altar (see above, note 3). Rather, having posited that the prohibition of offering leaven on the Altar stems from the idea that one can draw inspiration from his offering to acquire the trait of alacrity, an idea that applies as well to the prohibition of *preparing* a leavened *minchah* (Mitzvah 135; see above, note 1), Chinuch explains why this idea does not extend to the Two Loaves (cf. *Tzava Rav* cited in note 8 to Mechon Yerushalayim ed. of *Minchas Chinuch*).]

14. The *Lechem HaPanim* (*Panim* breads) were twelve loaves of bread that were placed on the *Shulchan* (Table) in the *Beis HaMikdash* on the Sabbath and remained there until the following Sabbath, when they were eaten by the Kohanim (see Mitzvah 97). They must not be *chametz*, as derived from Scripture in *Menachos* 57a.

15. Chinuch had indicated in Mitzvah 116 that the *Lechem HaPanim* is a *minchah* offering (see note 11 there).

וְהַסּוֹבְאִים יִמָּשְׁכוּ לְעוֹלָם אַחַר כָּל מָתוֹק, וְלֹא יִתֵּן לִבּוֹ כִּי אִם אֶל הַמַּאֲכָלִים הַמּוֹעִילִים לְגוּפוֹ וּצְרִיכִים לְמִחְיָתוֹ וְשׁוֹמְרִים בְּרִיאוּת אֵיבָרָיו. וְלָזֶה רָאוּי לְכָל בַּעַל שֵׂכֶל לְכַוֵּן בִּמְזוֹנוֹ וּשְׁתִיָּתוֹ, לֹא לִכְוָנַת הֲנָאַת מִשּׁוּשׁ הַגָּרוֹן[16]. וְלוּ חָכְמוּ בְּנֵי אָדָם יַשְׂכִּילוּ זֹאת[17], כִּי כָּל עִנְיַן חוּשׁ הַמִּשּׁוּשׁ[18] חֶרְפָּה הִיא לָהֶם, כָּל שֶׁכֵּן שֶׁאֵין רָאוּי לָהֶם לְכַוֵּן אֵלָיו וְלֵהָנוֹת בּוֹ, רַק הַצָּרִיךְ אֶל הַטֶּבַע בְּהֶכְרֵחַ. וּמֵאַנְשֵׁי הַחָכְמָה כָּתְבוּ חוּשׁ הַמִּשּׁוּשׁ אֲשֶׁר הוּא חֶרְפָּה לָנוּ[19].

וְעוֹד שָׁמַעְתִּי טַעַם בְּאִסּוּר שְׂאוֹר וּדְבַשׁ, לְפִי שֶׁהַשְּׂאוֹר מַגְבִּיהַּ עַצְמוֹ, וְכֵן הַדְּבַשׁ מַעֲלֶה רְתִיחָתוֹ הַרְבֵּה, וְלָכֵן נִתְרַחֲקוּ, לִרְמֹז כִּי תוֹעֲבַת יְיָ כָּל גְּבַהּ לֵב[20]. וְעוֹד רָאִיתִי בְּפֵרוּשׁ הָרַמְבַּ"ן זִכְרוֹנוֹ לִבְרָכָה שֶׁכָּתַב כֵּן, וְזֶה לְשׁוֹנוֹ, וּבַעֲבוּר שֶׁהַקָּרְבָּנוֹת לִרְצוֹן הַשֵּׁם הַנִּכְבָּד,

וְהַסּוֹבְאִים יִמָּשְׁכוּ לְעוֹלָם אַחַר כָּל מָתוֹק — as is the practice of the gluttons and the inebriated, who are always drawn after all that is sweet. וְלֹא יִתֵּן לִבּוֹ כִּי אִם אֶל הַמַּאֲכָלִים הַמּוֹעִילִים לְגוּפוֹ — One should rather set his heart only on foods that are beneficial to his body וּצְרִיכִים לְמִחְיָתוֹ — and necessary for his sustenance, וְשׁוֹמְרִים בְּרִיאוּת אֵיבָרָיו — and that maintain the health of his limbs. וְלָזֶה רָאוּי לְכָל בַּעַל שֵׂכֶל לְכַוֵּן בִּמְזוֹנוֹ וּשְׁתִיָּתוֹ — It is to this purpose that every intelligent person should aim while consuming his food and drink, לֹא לִכְוָנַת הֲנָאַת מִשּׁוּשׁ הַגָּרוֹן — and not to the purpose of enjoying the tactile sensations of his gullet.[16] וְלוּ חָכְמוּ בְּנֵי אָדָם יַשְׂכִּילוּ זֹאת — If people were wise, they would understand the following[17] point, כִּי כָּל עִנְיַן חוּשׁ הַמִּשּׁוּשׁ חֶרְפָּה הִיא לָהֶם — that the entire matter of the sense of touch[18] is a disgrace to them, כָּל שֶׁכֵּן שֶׁאֵין רָאוּי לָהֶם לְכַוֵּן אֵלָיו וְלֵהָנוֹת בּוֹ — all the more is it improper for them to aim for it and derive enjoyment through it, רַק הַצָּרִיךְ אֶל הַטֶּבַע בְּהֶכְרֵחַ — except that which is absolutely required for the nature of one's body. וּמֵאַנְשֵׁי הַחָכְמָה כָּתְבוּ — Indeed, some men of wisdom have written: חוּשׁ הַמִּשּׁוּשׁ אֲשֶׁר הוּא חֶרְפָּה לָנוּ — "The sense of touch, which is a disgrace to us ..."[19]

Chinuch now adds a reason that covers both leaven and honey:

וְעוֹד שָׁמַעְתִּי טַעַם בְּאִסּוּר שְׂאוֹר וּדְבַשׁ — In addition, I have heard the following reason for the prohibition of leaven and honey: לְפִי שֶׁהַשְּׂאוֹר מַגְבִּיהַּ עַצְמוֹ — It is because leaven causes itself (i.e., the dough) to rise, וְכֵן הַדְּבַשׁ מַעֲלֶה רְתִיחָתוֹ הַרְבֵּה — and honey is similar insofar as it rises greatly when it is boiling. וְלָכֵן נִתְרַחֲקוּ — For this reason, that they mimic puffed-up haughtiness, they were distanced from the Altar, לִרְמֹז כִּי תוֹעֲבַת ה' כָּל גְּבַהּ לֵב — to hint that every haughty heart is the abomination of HASHEM (Proverbs 16:5).[20]

Chinuch concludes with Ramban's insight to our mitzvah:

וְעוֹד רָאִיתִי בְּפֵרוּשׁ הָרַמְבַּ"ן זִכְרוֹנוֹ לִבְרָכָה שֶׁכָּתַב כֵּן — I have also seen in the commentary of Ramban, of blessed memory (to Leviticus 23:17), that he wrote the following, וְזֶה לְשׁוֹנוֹ — and these are his words: וּבַעֲבוּר שֶׁהַקָּרְבָּנוֹת לִרְצוֹן הַשֵּׁם הַנִּכְבָּד — Since the offerings are brought

---

## NOTES

16. See Rambam, Hil. Dei'os 3:2.

17. Stylistic citation of Deuteronomy 32:29.

18. In earlier times, the sense of taste was identified with the sense of touch (as opposed to the current classification of the five senses).

19. Rambam [citing Aristotle] in Moreh Nevuchim 2:36 (also, 2:40, 3:8,49; cf. Ramban, Iggeres HaKodesh Ch. 2). Rambam explains that the sense of touch in humans is much the same as it is in animals, whereas humans and animals differ considerably in regard to the other senses, such as scent and vision (Chinuch expresses a similar idea with respect to the sense of smell in Mitzvah 97, at note 12). Thus, the sense of touch is a disgrace to us, as it diminishes man's uniquely spiritual nature. Chinuch adds that indulging in the sense of touch further connects one to that aspect of his being and distances him from his true essence.

20. The distancing of leaven and honey from the Altar reflects the idea that what they represent is unacceptable to Hashem. [This idea appears in Pesikta Zutresa to Leviticus 2:11; see also Insights to Mitzvah 12 and Mitzvah 118.]

לֹא יָבוֹאוּ מִן הַדְּבָרִים אֲשֶׁר לָהֶם הַיָּד הַחֲזָקָה לְשַׁנּוֹת הַטִּבְעִיִּים, וְכֵן לֹא יָבוֹאוּ מִן הַדְּבָרִים הַמְּתוּקִים לְגַמְרֵי כְּמוֹ הַדְּבַשׁ, רַק מִן הַמְזוּגִים, כַּאֲשֶׁר אָמְרוּ זִכְרוֹנָם לִבְרָכָה בִּבְרִיאַת עוֹלָם שֶׁתֵּף מִדַּת רַחֲמִים בְּמִדַּת הַדִּין וּבְרָאוֹ, עַד כָּאן.[21]

דִּינֵי הַמִּצְוָה, כְּגוֹן מַה שֶּׁאָמְרוּ זִכְרוֹנָם לִבְרָכָה שֶׁכָּל הַמְּנָחוֹת הַקְּרֵבוֹת לְגַבֵּי הַמִּזְבֵּחַ בָּאוֹת מַצָּה,[22] כְּמוֹ שֶׁאָמַרְנוּ, וְכֵן שְׁיָרֵי הַמְּנָחוֹת שֶׁאוֹכְלִין הַכֹּהֲנִים, אַף עַל פִּי שֶׁהֵן מֻתָּרִין לֶאֱכֹל אוֹתָן בְּכָל מַאֲכָל וּבִדְבַשׁ,[23] אֵין אוֹכְלִין אוֹתָן חָמֵץ, שֶׁנֶּאֱמַר (שם ו', י') לֹא תֵאָפֶה חָמֵץ חֶלְקָם, וְיֵשׁ בְּמַשְׁמַע אֲפִלּוּ חֶלְקָם לֹא יַחֲמִיצוּ.[24] וְאִם הֶחֱמִיץ שְׁיָרֶיהָ לוֹקֶה,

---

**לֹא יָבוֹאוּ מִן הַדְּבָרִים אֲשֶׁר לָהֶם הַיָּד הַחֲזָקָה** to gain **the goodwill of Hashem, the Honored One,** **לְשַׁנּוֹת הַטִּבְעִיִּים** — **they may not come from things that have a strong hand in altering the natural conditions** (i.e., leaven), **וְכֵן לֹא יָבוֹאוּ מִן הַדְּבָרִים הַמְּתוּקִים לְגַמְרֵי כְּמוֹ הַדְּבַשׁ** — **nor may they come from things that are utterly sweet, like honey;** **רַק מִן הַמְזוּגִים** — rather, they must contain **only things that are balanced** (literally, mixed). **כַּאֲשֶׁר אָמְרוּ זִכְרוֹנָם לִבְרָכָה בִּבְרִיאַת עוֹלָם** — **This is as [the Sages], of blessed memory, said regarding the Creation of the World** (*Bereishis Rabbah* 12:15), **שֶׁתֵּף מִדַּת רַחֲמִים בְּמִדַּת הַדִּין וּבְרָאוֹ** — **[Hashem] combined His Attribute of Mercy with His Attribute of Justice and created it.** **עַד כָּאן** — **Until here are the words of** *Ramban*.[21]

### ⁓ Laws of the Mitzvah ⁓

**דִּינֵי הַמִּצְוָה** — **The laws of the mitzvah** **כְּגוֹן מַה שֶּׁאָמְרוּ זִכְרוֹנָם לִבְרָכָה** — **include, for example, that which [the Sages], of blessed memory, said** (*Menachos* 52b; *Rambam, Hil. Maaseh HaKorbanos* 12:14), **שֶׁכָּל הַמְּנָחוֹת הַקְּרֵבוֹת לְגַבֵּי הַמִּזְבֵּחַ בָּאוֹת מַצָּה** — **that all *menachos* offered on the Altar are brought as *matzah*, and must not be *chametz*,**[22] **כְּמוֹ שֶׁאָמַרְנוּ** — **as we have said** (in Mitzvah 116).

Of the *menachos* offered on the Altar, generally, only a *kometz* (fistful) is burned on the Altar, while the remainder is eaten by the Kohanim (Mitzvah 134; see also Mitzvah 116). Chinuch teaches that this remainder must also not become leavened:

**וְכֵן שְׁיָרֵי הַמְּנָחוֹת שֶׁאוֹכְלִין הַכֹּהֲנִים** — **And the same** applies to **the remnants of the *menachos*,** which are not burned on the Altar, but are **eaten by the Kohanim;** **אַף עַל פִּי שֶׁהֵן מֻתָּרִין לֶאֱכֹל אוֹתָן בְּכָל מַאֲכָל וּבִדְבַשׁ** — **although [the Kohanim] are allowed to eat [the remnants] with any food, and even with honey,**[23] **אֵין אוֹכְלִין אוֹתָן חָמֵץ** — **they may not eat them** in the form of ***chametz,*** **שֶׁנֶּאֱמַר** — **as it is stated** (*Leviticus* 6:10): **It shall not be baked leavened; their portion,** *I have given it from My fire-offerings,* **וְיֵשׁ בְּמַשְׁמַע אֲפִלּוּ חֶלְקָם לֹא יַחֲמִיצוּ** — **which,** in addition to the literal meaning of the verse, **can be understood** as teaching that **even their portion,** i.e., the remnants of the *minchah,* **[the Kohanim] shall not render *chametz.***[24] **וְאִם הֶחֱמִיץ שְׁיָרֶיהָ** **לוֹקֶה** — **If one did make [the *minchah's*] remnants *chametz,* he incurs *malkus*** (lashes).

---

### NOTES

21. As these words of *Ramban* are of an esoteric nature (see *Rabbeinu Bachya* to *Leviticus* 2:11), Chinuch quotes him verbatim without commentary. See Insight for a related discussion.

22. While there are *menachos*, such as the Two Loaves, that may (and indeed, must) be prepared as *chametz*, all *menachos* offered on the Altar must be prepared as *matzah*, on account of the prohibition to offer leaven on the Altar.

23. *Sotah* 15a; see there for the Scriptural source.

24. *Sotah* ibid., *Menachos* 55a. The verse reads (in part): לֹא תֵאָפֶה חָמֵץ חֶלְקָם נָתַתִּי אֹתָהּ מֵאִשָּׁי, which literally means: *It* (the *minchah* itself) *shall not be baked as chametz;*

*their portion* (the remnants), *I have given it from My fire-offerings.* Thus, in its literal sense, the verse does not indicate a prohibition on rendering the Kohanim's portion into *chametz*. However, the words *their portion* are interpreted here as a continuation of the immediately preceding phrase, thereby rendering the verse: *It shall not be baked leaven — their portion.* That is, even the Kohanim's portion of the *minchah,* i.e., what remains after the *kometz* is burned on the Altar, must not be allowed to become *chametz* (*Rashi* to *Yevamos* 40a and *Sotah* ibid. ד"ה לא תאפה חמץ חלקם; see also Mitzvah 135).

[Clearly, as the remnants are eaten by the Kohanim, the remnants are not subject to the prohibition to offer

# VAYIKRA / MITZVAH 117: NOT TO BRING LEAVEN OR HONEY AS AN OFFERING

וְלוֹקִין[25] עַל כָּל עֲשִׂיָּה וַעֲשִׂיָּה שֶׁבָּהּ. כֵּיצַד, לָשָׁה חָמֵץ אוֹ עֲרָכָהּ חָמֵץ אוֹ קִטְּפָהּ[26] חָמֵץ אוֹ אֲפָאָהּ חָמֵץ לוֹקֶה, שֶׁנֶּאֱמַר (שם ב׳, י״א) לֹא תֵעָשֶׂה חָמֵץ, וְנֶאֱמַר (שם ו׳, י׳) לֹא תֵאָפֶה חָמֵץ, לְחַיֵּב עַל מַעֲשֶׂה יְחִידִי שֶׁבַּעֲשִׂיָּתָהּ חָמֵץ (חִיֵּב)[27] מַלְקוּת.[28]

וְאֵין לוֹתְתִין חִטִּים שֶׁל מְנָחוֹת, שֶׁמָּא יַחֲמִיצוּ[29], וְאַף עַל פִּי כֵן אָמְרוּ זִכְרוֹנָם לִבְרָכָה

---

Chinuch explains that one need not perform the entire preparation of the leavened *minchah* to incur *malkus*:[25]

וְלוֹקִין עַל כָּל עֲשִׂיָּה וַעֲשִׂיָּה שֶׁבָּהּ — **One incurs *malkus* for any** one **of the** numerous **acts involved in** preparing **[the leavened *minchah*].** כֵּיצַד — **How so?** לָשָׁה חָמֵץ — **Whether one kneaded [the dough] as *chametz*,** אוֹ עֲרָכָהּ חָמֵץ — **or shaped it** into a loaf **as *chametz*,** אוֹ קִטְּפָהּ חָמֵץ — **or smoothed it out**[26] **as *chametz*,** אוֹ אֲפָאָהּ חָמֵץ — **or baked it as *chametz*,** לוֹקֶה — he **incurs *malkus*;** שֶׁנֶּאֱמַר "לֹא תֵעָשֶׂה חָמֵץ" — **for it is stated** (ibid. 2:11): ***it shall not be prepared as chametz,*** וְנֶאֱמַר "לֹא תֵאָפֶה חָמֵץ" — **and it is** also **stated** (ibid. 6:10): ***it shall not be baked chametz.*** Although the Torah had already mentioned "preparation" in general, it singles out "baking" לְחַיֵּב עַל מַעֲשֶׂה יְחִידִי שֶׁבַּעֲשִׂיָּתָהּ חָמֵץ (חִיֵּב)[27] מַלְקוּת — **in order to render one liable to *malkus* for even one action in the preparation of a leavened [*minchah*].**[28]

Chinuch notes that, on account of this prohibition, one must take precautions to ensure that the *minchah* offering does not become leavened:

וְאֵין לוֹתְתִין חִטִּים שֶׁל מְנָחוֹת — **Another law is that one may not soak the wheat** kernels intended **for *minchah* offerings** before they are ground, שֶׁמָּא יַחֲמִיצוּ — **lest they become *chametz*.**[29] וְאַף עַל פִּי כֵן אָמְרוּ זִכְרוֹנָם לִבְרָכָה — **Nevertheless, [the Sages], of blessed memory, said** (*Menachos* 55a)

---

## NOTES

leaven on the Altar. However, Chinuch's language, "The same [law that *menachos* brought on the Altar must not be *chametz*] applies to the remnants ...," suggests that, at least in concept, the restriction on leavening the remnants *is* rooted in the prohibition of burning leaven on the Altar. Indeed, *Chizkuni* (to *Leviticus* 6:10) understands the continuation of the verse: *their portion* (the remnants), *"I have given it from My fire-offerings,"* as an explanation as to why the remnants of a *minchah* may not be leavened. Since they are the Kohanim's portion "*from My offering,*" they carry the same restriction as "*My offering,*" for which Scripture states, *you shall not burn any leaven,* etc. (see also *Abarbanel* and *Meshech Chochmah* to the verse, and *Oznayim LaTorah* there).]

25. [This (as well as the next) segment in Chinuch pertains to the leavening of *minchah* offerings in general, and not only to the remnants (see *Rambam, Hil. Maaseh HaKorbanos* 12:14).]

As noted by *Mishneh LaMelech* (in his Glosses to Chinuch), these laws belong in Mitzvah 135. Nonetheless, they are presented here by Chinuch because, as indicated at note 4, an aspect of the prohibition against leavening a *minchah* is to prevent its subsequent burning as *chametz* on the Altar; as such, it relates to the subject of our mitzvah. This practice by Chinuch — to include laws and details of one mitzvah among the laws of another mitzvah so long as they are related — is common throughout this work (see General Introduction, note 9).

26. This refers to smoothing the surface of the dough with water (*Rashi, Menachos* 55b ד״ה לאתויי קיטוף). *Rabbeinu Gershom* (ibid.) defines קטוף as *tearing off* pieces from the large dough for the individual loaves.

27. Emendation follows manuscripts cited in Mechon Yerushalayim ed.

28. *Menachos* 55b; *Rambam, Hil. Maaseh HaKorbanos* 12:14-15. On the basis of the first verse, *it shall not be prepared leavened,* which speaks of "preparation" in general, it could have been thought that only one who performed the entire preparation (kneading, shaping, smoothing, and baking) of a leavened *minchah* would be liable to *malkus*. However, the second verse, *It shall not be baked leavened,* imposes *malkus* for the act of baking alone. Following the example of "baking," each individual step in a *minchah's* preparation also bears the penalty of *malkus*. This is a manifestation of one of the rules of Biblical exegesis (see Introduction to *Sifra*): "When part of a generality is singled out from that generality for separate treatment, then all the other parts of that generality are also subject to that treatment" כָּל דָּבָר שֶׁהָיָה בִּכְלָל וְיָצָא מִן הַכְּלָל לְלַמֵּד ... לְלַמֵּד] עַל הַכְּלָל כֻּלּוֹ יָצָא] (see also Mitzvah 114 note 6). Hence, not only does baking carry the penalty of *malkus*, but so does each of the other stages of preparation. Even if a person performs just one of these actions, he is liable to *malkus* (cf. *Tosafos, Menachos* ibid. ד״ה אף אני; *Sfas Emes* to *Menachos* ibid. ד״ה אפייה בכלל היתה; *Chidushei HaGriz* to *Menachos* ibid.) If he did all four actions, he incurs four sets of *malkus* (*Rambam* ibid.).

29. *Pesachim* 36a, 40a. A cleaner flour is produced when the wheat kernels are soaked in a little water before they are ground to remove their husks (*Rashi, Pesachim* 36a ד״ה לותתין). Although the *minchah* offering

## ויקרא / מצוה קיז: שלא להקריב שאור או דבש

שֶׁהַמְּנָחוֹת הַנֶּאֱפוֹת הָיוּ נִלּוֹשׁוֹת בְּפוֹשְׁרִין, וּמְשַׁמְּרִין אוֹתָן שֶׁלֹּא יַחְמִיצוּ[30], שֶׁהַכֹּהֲנִים זְרִיזִין הֵן[31]. וְשְׂאוֹר וּדְבַשׁ אֲסוּרִין בְּכָל שֶׁהוּא[32], שֶׁנֶּאֱמַר (שם ב, יא) "לֹא תַקְטִירוּ מִמֶּנּוּ", כְּלוֹמַר אֲפִלּוּ כָּל שֶׁהוּא[33]. וְאֵינוֹ חַיָּב אֶלָּא אִם כֵּן הִקְטִירָן עִם הַקָּרְבָּן אוֹ לְשֵׁם הַקָּרְבָּן[34], וְאֶחָד הַמַּקְטִיר עַצְמָן אוֹ תַּעֲרָבְתָּן לוֹקֶה[35], אֲבָל הִקְטִירָן בִּפְנֵי עַצְמָן לְשֵׁם עֵצִים פָּטוּר, שֶׁנֶּאֱמַר (שם, שם י"ב) "וְאֶל הַמִּזְבֵּחַ לֹא יַעֲלוּ לְרֵיחַ נִיחֹחַ", לְרֵיחַ נִיחוֹחַ אִי אַתָּה מַעֲלֶה אֲבָל אַתָּה מַעֲלֶה לְשֵׁם עֵצִים[36]. וְיֶתֶר פְּרָטֶיהָ, מְבֹאָרִין בְּמַסֶּכֶת מְנָחוֹת (נ"ב ע"ב – נ"ח ע"ב)[37].

---

שֶׁהַמְּנָחוֹת הַנֶּאֱפוֹת הָיוּ נִלּוֹשׁוֹת בְּפוֹשְׁרִין — that the baked *minchah* offerings were kneaded in lukewarm water, וּמְשַׁמְּרִין אוֹתָן שֶׁלֹּא יַחְמִיצוּ — and [Kohanim] would guard them to ensure that they did not become *chametz*,[30] שֶׁהַכֹּהֲנִים זְרִיזִין הֵן — for the Kohanim are diligent in their work and are careful that the dough should not become *chametz*. The soaking of the kernels prior to their grinding, however, is not necessarily performed by diligent people, since it is not done in the Temple.[31]

Chinuch now resumes the discussion of the prohibition against offering leaven or honey on the Altar: וְשְׂאוֹר וּדְבַשׁ אֲסוּרִין בְּכָל שֶׁהוּא — Leaven and honey are forbidden in the slightest amount to be brought on the Altar,[32] שֶׁנֶּאֱמַר "לֹא תַקְטִירוּ מִמֶּנּוּ" — as it is stated: *you shall not burn "from" it*; כְּלוֹמַר אֲפִלּוּ כָּל שֶׁהוּא — that is to say, even the slightest amount.[33] וְאֵינוֹ חַיָּב אֶלָּא אִם כֵּן הִקְטִירָן עִם הַקָּרְבָּן — One is not liable unless he burned them together with the offering, אוֹ לְשֵׁם הַקָּרְבָּן — or as an offering in their own right.[34] וְאֶחָד הַמַּקְטִיר עַצְמָן אוֹ תַּעֲרָבְתָּן לוֹקֶה — Whether one burns them by themselves, or burns mixtures in which they are contained, he incurs *malkus*.[35] אֲבָל הִקְטִירָן בִּפְנֵי עַצְמָן לְשֵׁם עֵצִים פָּטוּר — However, if one burned them by themselves as "wood," i.e., he used them as fuel on the Altar's pyre, he is exempt from punishment, שֶׁנֶּאֱמַר "וְאֶל הַמִּזְבֵּחַ לֹא יַעֲלוּ לְרֵיחַ נִיחֹחַ" — for it is stated (*Leviticus* 2:12): *... and to the Altar they shall not go up as a pleasant aroma*, לְרֵיחַ נִיחוֹחַ אִי אַתָּה מַעֲלֶה — which implies: You may not bring them up as a pleasant aroma, i.e., an offering, אֲבָל אַתָּה מַעֲלֶה לְשֵׁם עֵצִים — but you may bring them up as "wood."[36] וְיֶתֶר פְּרָטֶיהָ מְבֹאָרִין בְּמַסֶּכֶת מְנָחוֹת — These laws, as well as the additional details of [the mitzvah], are set forth in Tractate *Menachos* (52b-53a, 55a-58b).[37]

---

### NOTES

would be enhanced by this process, it is forbidden, since it can cause the kernels to leaven.

30. Mishnah, *Menachos* 55a. Lukewarm water produces a smooth-textured dough, and the mitzvah is thus fulfilled in the finest manner (*Chazon Ish, Menachos* 35:1). However, since warm water greatly accelerates the leavening process (see Rashi to *Pesachim* 36a ד"ה פושרין), the Kohen preparing the *minchah* must continually work the dough to forestall its leavening [this is the meaning of "to guard the dough"] (Rashi, *Menachos* 53a ד"ה מנין לכל המנחות).

31. See Mitzvah 116, where Chinuch writes that the *minchah* was to be brought to the *Beis HaMikdash* in the form of flour.

[*Minchas Yitzchak* (§10) points out that the Gemara (*Pesachim* 36a) retracts its statement that the kneading was performed by Kohanim, since a non-Kohen may also knead the *minchah*. Rather, kneading is different from soaking the kernels in that it must be performed in the Temple Courtyard, and would thus be performed in the presence of Kohanim, who would guide the kneader in preventing the dough from becoming leavened (see also Rambam ibid §21).]

32. *Rambam, Hil. Isurei HaMizbe'ach* 5:1 (see, however, *Kesef Mishneh* ad loc.; *Minchas Chinuch* §3).

33. Chinuch's derivation from מִמֶּנּוּ, *from it*, appears in Ramban (to *Leviticus* 2:11). However, *Minchas Chinuch* §6 finds this difficult because the Gemara (*Menachos* 58a) clearly infers this ruling from the word כָּל, *any*, which is stated in regard to both leaven and honey ("any" leaven or "any" honey).

34. See below, note 37. ["As an offering" means that the person burned it on the Altar for that purpose, not that it would be a valid offering.]

35. *Menachos* 58a.

36. *Zevachim* 77b-77a. The phrase cited here וְאֶל הַמִּזְבֵּחַ לֹא יַעֲלוּ לְרֵיחַ נִיחֹחַ, *and to the Altar they shall not go up as a pleasant aroma* (*Leviticus* 2:12), is contained in a verse that immediately follows the prohibition of burning leaven or honey on the Altar. The implication is that leaven and honey may not be burned "as a pleasant aroma" (an expression that denotes an offering; see Mitzvah 97, at note 13), but they may be burned as fuel.

37. The laws are codified in *Rambam, Hil. Isurei HaMizbe'ach* 5:1-5 and *Hil. Maaseh HaKorbanos* 12:14-21.

# 409 ☐ VAYIKRA / MITZVAH 117: NOT TO BRING LEAVEN OR HONEY AS AN OFFERING

וְהָרַמְבַּ"ם זִכְרוֹנוֹ לִבְרָכָה חָשַׁב שְׂאוֹר וּדְבַשׁ אִסּוּר לְלָאו אֶחָד, כְּלוֹמַר שֶׁאִם הִקְרִיב שְׂאוֹר וּדְבַשׁ שְׁנֵיהֶם יַחַד אֵינוֹ לוֹקֶה אֶלָּא אַחַת, וְכֵן אִם הִקְרִיב כָּל אֶחָד בִּפְנֵי עַצְמוֹ לוֹקֶה עַל כָּל אֶחָד מַלְקוּת אַחַת. וְנָתַן טַעַם לִדְבָרָיו שֶׁזֶּהוּ לָאו שֶׁבִּכְלָלוֹת,[38] וּבְלָאו שֶׁבִּכְלָלוֹת כָּזֶה לוֹקִין מַלְקוּת אַחַת עַל שְׁנֵי דְבָרִים.[39]

וְהָרַב רַבֵּנוּ מֹשֶׁה בַּר נַחְמָן זִכְרוֹנוֹ לִבְרָכָה חָלַק עָלָיו לַחֲשֹׁב שְׂאוֹר וּדְבַשׁ שְׁנֵי לָאוִין, וְאָמַר שֶׁאֵינוֹ רוֹאֶה כָּאן לָאו שֶׁבִּכְלָלוֹת, שֶׁהֲרֵי בְּחָמֵץ מְיֻחָד לָאוֶיהָ בְּפֵרוּשׁ, שֶׁנֶּאֱמַר (שם ו, י) לֹא תֵאָפֶה חָמֵץ, וְאִם כֵּן לָאו דִּדְבַשׁ אַף עַל גַּב דְּאָבָא שְׂאוֹר בַּהֲדֵהּ, יֵשׁ לָנוּ לוֹמַר הַדְּבַשׁ

---

## ⸔ Dispute Regarding the Mitzvah ⸕

וְהָרַמְבַּ"ם זִכְרוֹנוֹ לִבְרָכָה חָשַׁב שְׂאוֹר וּדְבַשׁ אִסּוּר לְלָאו אֶחָד — **Rambam**, of blessed memory (*Sefer HaMitzvos, Lo Saaseh* 98), **reckoned the prohibition of** offering **leaven and honey as one prohibition;** כְּלוֹמַר שֶׁאִם הִקְרִיב שְׂאוֹר וּדְבַשׁ שְׁנֵיהֶם יַחַד — **that is to say, that if one offered both leaven and honey together,** אֵינוֹ לוֹקֶה אֶלָּא אַחַת — **he would incur only one set of** *malkus*; וְכֵן אִם הִקְרִיב כָּל אֶחָד בִּפְנֵי עַצְמוֹ — **and so, too, if he offered each one on its own,** לוֹקֶה עַל כָּל אֶחָד מַלְקוּת אַחַת — **he would incur a separate** *malkus* **for each one.** וְנָתַן טַעַם לִדְבָרָיו שֶׁזֶּהוּ לָאו שֶׁבִּכְלָלוֹת — [Rambam] **gave a reason for his opinion;** namely, that **this is a generalized prohibition,**[38] וּבְלָאו שֶׁבִּכְלָלוֹת כָּזֶה — **and in the case of a generalized prohibition, such as this one,** לוֹקִין מַלְקוּת אַחַת עַל שְׁנֵי דְבָרִים — **one incurs a single set of** *malkus* **for two things.**[39] וְהָרַב רַבֵּנוּ מֹשֶׁה בַּר נַחְמָן זִכְרוֹנוֹ לִבְרָכָה חָלַק עָלָיו — **However,** *Ramban*, **of blessed memory** (Glosses to *Sefer HaMitzvos* ibid.), **disagreed with [Rambam],** לַחֲשֹׁב שְׂאוֹר וּדְבַשׁ שְׁנֵי לָאוִין — **and in his view, we are to reckon leaven and honey as two prohibitions;** thus, if one were to burn both leaven and honey together, he would be liable to two sets of *malkus*. וְאָמַר שֶׁאֵינוֹ רוֹאֶה כָּאן לָאו שֶׁבִּכְלָלוֹת — **With respect to** *Rambam's* **opinion, [Ramban] said that he does not see a generalized prohibition here,** שֶׁהֲרֵי בְּחָמֵץ מְיֻחָד לָאוֶיהָ בְּפֵרוּשׁ — **because with regard to** *chametz*, **it has an explicit prohibition specific to it** שֶׁנֶּאֱמַר "לֹא תֵאָפֶה חָמֵץ" — **as it is stated** (ibid. 6:10): *it shall not be baked leavened.* וְאִם כֵּן לָאו דִּדְבַשׁ אַף עַל גַּב דְּאָבָא שְׂאוֹר בַּהֲדֵהּ — **Therefore,** regarding **the prohibition of honey, even though leaven is** mentioned **together with it,** יֵשׁ לָנוּ לוֹמַר הַדְּבַשׁ נִדְרָשׁ אוֹתוֹ לְחוּדֵהּ — **we should say that the honey prohibition is interpreted** as a separate commandment **on its own.**[40]

---

### NOTES

38. לָאו שֶׁבִּכְלָלוֹת, *generalized prohibition,* is a general injunction that includes several specific prohibitions. For example, the Torah states (Leviticus 7:23): כָּל חֵלֶב שׁוֹר וְכֶשֶׂב וָעֵז לֹא תֹאכֵלוּ, *Any cheilev* (hard fat) *of ox, sheep, and goats you shall not eat,* addressing all the prohibitions with a single injunction ("*you shall not eat*"), rather than addressing each one individually.

[It should be noted that the term לָאו שֶׁבִּכְלָלוֹת takes on somewhat different meanings in different contexts. See *Rambam, Sefer HaMitzvos, Shoresh* 9 and *Ramban ad loc.; Tos. Rid* to *Pesachim* 41a; *Sfas Emes* to *Kereisos* 4a; see also *Teshuvos HaRashba* I §141.]

39. In our case, the verse, *you shall not burn any leaven or any honey as a fire offering,* uses one commandment ("*you shall not burn*") to cover both leaven and honey. Since there is only a single commandment, one who burns both leaven and honey on the Altar incurs only one set of *malkus*.

40. [Although the prohibition that is specific to leaven refers to its preparation, an aspect of this prohibition is to prevent its subsequent burning as *chametz* on the Altar, as indicated by Chinuch at note 4.] *Ramban* reasons that since *chametz* is subject to its own prohibition, it is unlikely that our verse, *you shall not burn any leaven or any honey,* means to put *chametz* and honey under a single, general classification. Rather, it is issuing one independent prohibition for *chametz* and another independent prohibition for honey. This means, in practice, that one who burned *chametz* and honey together on the Altar would be guilty of violating two prohibitions, for which he would be liable to two sets of *malkus*.

[*Ramban* notes that even if this verse *does* express a general prohibition, a person who burns both items would incur two sets of *malkus* anyway: one set for transgressing the specific prohibition of *chametz* alone (*it shall not be baked chametz*), and one set for transgressing the general prohibition of *chametz*/honey (*you shall not burn any leaven or any honey*). For a defense of *Rambam's* position, see *Megillas Esther ad loc.*]

410 □ ויקרא / מצוה קיז: שלא להקריב שאור או דבש

נִדְרָשׁ אוֹתוֹ לְחוּדֵהּ[40], וְנִמְצָא לָאו בְּכָל אֶחָד, וְיֶתֶר רְאָיוֹתֵיהֶם בְּסִפְרָם[41]. וְנוֹהֶגֶת בִּזְמַן הַבַּיִת בִּזְכָרִים בַּכֹּהֲנִים, כִּי לָהֶם הָעֲבוֹדָה[42].

**וְנִמְצָא לָאו בְּכָל אֶחָד** — It emerges then, according to *Ramban,* **that there is a prohibition for each one,** honey and leaven.

**וְיֶתֶר רְאָיוֹתֵיהֶם בְּסִפְרָם** — **The rest of [***Rambam's* and *Ramban's***] proofs,** in support of their respective positions, appear **in their book** (*Sefer HaMitzvos, Shoresh* 9 and *Lo Saaseh* 98 with *Ramban's Glosses*).[41]

### ☙ Applicability of the Mitzvah ☙

**וְנוֹהֶגֶת בִּזְמַן הַבַּיִת** — **[This mitzvah] applies** only **in the time of the Temple** (*Beis HaMikdash*), **בִּזְכָרִים בַּכֹּהֲנִים** — and only **to male Kohanim,** **כִּי לָהֶם הָעֲבוֹדָה** — **as the** *avodah* (service) **is** entrusted **to them.**[42]

---

NOTES

41. See above, Mitzvah 7, at note 19 and on, for a lengthy parallel discussion of *Rambam's* and *Ramban's* opinions regarding such cases.

42. That is, since only male Kohanim perform the *avodah* in the *Beis HaMikdash*, which includes burning offerings on the Altar, the injunction of burning leaven or honey pertains to them alone.

[This implies that if a non-Kohen — who is completely unfit to perform *avodah* — burns leaven or honey on the Altar, he is not in violation of this prohibition. *Minchas Chinuch* (§10) remarks that this law is not found in the works of *Rambam,* and there is no clear Talmudic source for it. He notes, however, that numerous mitzvos pertaining to the *manner* of performing the *avodah* (Mitzvos 106, 152, and 275-278) apply only to Kohanim, who are the ones qualified to perform *avodah* in the first place. It should further be noted that the same holds true with regard to other mitzvos (aside from this one) that prohibit the offering of *specific items* on the Altar, viz., Mitzvos 104, 118-119, and 125. In all these cases, Chinuch writes that the mitzvos apply only to Kohanim, and not to non-Kohanim, who are unfit to offer *anything* on the Altar. See Mitzvah 104 note 7 and Mitzvah 118 note 17. For a related discussion, see Insight to Mitzvah 125.]

---

**ఞ Insight: Honey and Sugar in Kiddush Wine**

The Gemara states (*Bava Basra* 97a) that one may recite the Sabbath *Kiddush* only over wine that is fit to be poured on the Altar as *nesachim* (a libation-offering). As indicated in the Gemara there (97b), wine that has a foul odor or was left uncovered is unacceptable for *Kiddush* as a result of this rule, since such wine is invalid for use as *nesachim*.

Based on this Gemara, *Rambam* (*Hil. Shabbos,* 29:14) rules that if wine was mixed with honey or leaven — even it was a minute amount that has no effect on the flavor of the wine — it is disqualified for *Kiddush*. As we learn in this mitzvah, honey may not be offered upon the Altar. Since wine with honey mixed in it would be invalid for use as *nesachim*, it follows that such wine is equally invalid for use in *Kiddush*.

Many Rishonim, however, disagree with this view and rule that wine mixed with honey, though invalid for *nesachim*, is acceptable for *Kiddush* (see *Rambam* ibid., *Raavad* ad loc.; *Ramban* and *Ritva* to *Bava Basra* ibid.; *Teshuvos HaRashba* Vol. 1 §24). Their primary proof is from a statement in *Yerushalmi Pesachim* 10:1 that *konditon* wine (a wine that is spiced with honey and pepper) is valid for *Kiddush*. Moreover, as evident from *Yerushalmi* there, such wine is acceptable even if the honey affects its taste and smell (*Beis Yosef, Orach Chaim* §272, citing *Rabbeinu Yerucham*).

How are we to understand the latter opinion in light of the above Gemara, which states that wine that is not valid for *nesachim* may not be used for *Kiddush*? *Maggid Mishneh* (to *Rambam* ibid.) explains that in the case of wine mixed with honey, there is no specific disqualification on the wine per se. It is only that one cannot, practically, offer the wine upon the Altar once honey is mixed in, because by doing so one would be offering the *honey* upon the Altar — but it is the honey that is prohibited, not the wine itself. This is different than, for example, wine that has a foul odor, where the wine itself is invalid for *nesachim* due to its own condition. Since this is the case, these Rishonim

maintain that wine mixed with honey may be used for *Kiddush*, since the wine itself is still valid for *nesachim*, and the added presence of honey is not a factor in regard to *Kiddush*.

*Rambam*, on the other hand, apparently maintains that when honey is mixed with wine it renders the wine *itself* invalid for *nesachim*. That is why *Rambam* considers the wine unfit for *Kiddush* as well (*Chidushei HaGriz* to *Menachos* 57b ד"ה הרמב"ם). [For further analysis of this idea, as well as of the dissenting view as explained by *Maggid Mishneh*, see *Masas HaMelech* by *R' S. M. Diskin* on *Haggadah Shel Pesach*, p. 82; see also *Shiurei R' Pesach MiKobrin*, Vol. II, *Inyanim* §10.]

The very fact that the Rishonim debate the validity of *Kiddush* wine mixed with honey is cited by *Radvaz* as proof in an entirely different discussion relating to this mitzvah. As indicated in note 6, it is clear from the Gemara (*Shevuos* 12 a-b) that the prohibition to offer דְּבַשׁ ("*honey*") on the Altar encompasses all sweet fruits and their nectars. There is a dispute, however, between *Radvaz* (*Teshuvos* 3:962) and *Batei Kenesiyos* (cited by *Sdei Chemed, Pe'as HaSadeh, Maareches HaDalet* §41) as to whether bee's honey is subject to the prohibition. While *Batei Kenesiyos* limits the Biblical prohibition to date honey or other fruit nectar, *Radvaz* maintains that it applies to bee's honey as well (this is Chinuch's opinion; see there at note 5). Among the numerous proofs he brings to support his opinion, *Radvaz* remarks that the debate among the Rishonim regarding honey in *Kiddush* wine is itself proof that bee's honey is forbidden on the Altar. This is because in the regions where these Rishonim lived, date or fig honey was unheard of, whereas bee's honey was readily available. Furthermore, *Radvaz* argues, *konditon* wine, which is the centerpiece of the Rishonim's refutation of *Rambam's* view (see above), is spiced with bee's honey. Clearly, the Rishonim spoke of nothing other than bee's honey, and they consider it unfit for being offered on the Altar.

There are authorities who maintain that sugar, too, is subject to the prohibition of offering דְּבַשׁ on the Altar, since it is extracted from plants (either sugar cane or sugar beets) and is thus in the category of fruit nectar (*Halachos Ketanos*, Vol. I §218; *Ner Mitzvah*, cited by *Sdei Chemed* ibid.; see, however, *Tziyunim LaTorah* ibid. p. 121). It follows that, according to *Rambam's* opinion that wine mixed with honey is invalid for *Kiddush*, wine mixed with sugar would likewise be invalid (*Pri Megadim, Mishbetzos Zahav* 272:3; *Mishnah Berurah* 272:21). For the halachah, see *Shulchan Aruch, Orach Chaim* 272:8 with *Rama*. For further discussion, see *Teshuvos VeHanhagos*, Vol. I §253; *Teshuvos Ohr LeTzion*, Vol. II 20:18; *Teshuvos Minchas Yitzchak*, Vol. IX 26:3.

## מִצְוָה קיח: שֶׁלֹּא לְהַקְרִיב קָרְבָּן בְּלֹא מֶלַח[1]

שֶׁלֹּא לְהַשְׁבִּית מֶלַח מֵעַל הַקָּרְבָּן אוֹ הַמִּנְחָה[2], כְּלוֹמַר שֶׁלֹּא יַקְרִיבוּ הַכֹּהֲנִים שׁוּם קָרְבָּן אוֹ שׁוּם מִנְחָה אֶלָּא אִם כֵּן יָשִׂימוּ בָּהֶן מֶלַח, שֶׁנֶּאֱמַר (ויקרא ב׳, י״ג) "וְלֹא תַשְׁבִּית מֶלַח בְּרִית אֱלֹהֶיךָ מֵעַל מִנְחָתֶךָ, וְכָתוּב גַּם כֵּן (שם) "עַל כָּל קָרְבָּנְךָ תַּקְרִיב מֶלַח[3].

---

# Mitzvah 118

## The Prohibition to Bring Up an Offering Without Salt

וְכָל קָרְבַּן מִנְחָתְךָ בַּמֶּלַח תִּמְלָח וְלֹא תַשְׁבִּית מֶלַח בְּרִית אֱלֹהֶיךָ מֵעַל מִנְחָתֶךָ עַל כָּל קָרְבָּנְךָ תַּקְרִיב מֶלַח

*You shall salt your every offering of meal with salt; you may not withhold the salt of your God's covenant from upon your meal offering — on your every offering shall you offer salt (Leviticus 2:13).*

This verse contains both a mitzvah-*prohibition* to withhold salt from any offering (i.e., to bring up an offering on the Altar unless it has been salted), and a mitzvah-*obligation* to salt every offering. The prohibition of withholding the application of salt from offerings is the subject of this mitzvah, while the obligation to add salt to the offerings is the subject of Mitzvah 119.[1]

שֶׁלֹּא לְהַשְׁבִּית מֶלַח מֵעַל הַקָּרְבָּן אוֹ הַמִּנְחָה — We are commanded **not to withhold** the application of **salt from upon** any animal **offering or** *minchah* (meal) offering;[2] כְּלוֹמַר — **that is to say,** שֶׁלֹּא יַקְרִיבוּ הַכֹּהֲנִים שׁוּם קָרְבָּן אוֹ שׁוּם מִנְחָה — we are commanded **that the Kohanim shall not offer up any** animal **offering or** *minchah* offering on the Altar, אֶלָּא אִם כֵּן יָשִׂימוּ בָּהֶן מֶלַח — **unless they** first **apply salt to [these offerings],** שֶׁנֶּאֱמַר — **as it is stated** (Leviticus 2:13): "וְלֹא תַשְׁבִּית מֶלַח בְּרִית אֱלֹהֶיךָ מֵעַל מִנְחָתֶךָ" — *you may not withhold the salt of your God's covenant from upon your meal offering.* Although this phrase specifies the *minchah* (meal offering) alone, וְכָתוּב גַּם כֵּן — **it is also stated,** in that very same verse, "עַל כָּל קָרְבָּנְךָ תַּקְרִיב מֶלַח" — *on your every offering shall you offer salt.*[3]

---

### NOTES

1. See Insight for explanation of the verse's reference to "the salt of God's covenant."

2. Chinuch uses the expression, שֶׁלֹּא לְהַשְׁבִּית מֶלַח, "not to withhold [the application of] salt," following the verse cited above. However, this is essentially a prohibition against *bringing* an offering without first salting it, as Chinuch immediately explains (see also below, note 20).

3. The phrase *on your every offering* expands the application of this verse to offerings other than the *minchah*. Although the *prohibition* against bringing up an offering without salt specifies the *minchah*, and it is the *obligation* to add salt that includes other offerings, since the obligation applies to all offerings, it is reasonable to interpret the prohibition as similarly applying to all offerings (*Mahari Korkos, Hil. Isurei HaMizbe'ach* 5:11-12).

[The Gemara (*Menachos* 20a) explains further that since the verse begins with the phrase *every* offering, then specifies the *minchah*, and finally concludes with a repetition of *every* offering, it contains a כְּלָל וּפְרָט וּכְלָל, *a generalization followed by a specification followed by another generalization.* In such instances, the rule is that we include every offering that is *similar* to the *minchah*, namely, every offering that is burned upon the Altar with firewood, whether an animal, a bird, or *levonah* (frankincense; see Mitzvah 97 note 1). Anything offered on the Altar but not burned with firewood, such as the blood of offerings and the libations of wine, are excluded from the salting requirement (see further, Mitzvah 119 with note 8). For further discussion, see *Sifra* to our verse with *Malbim*; *Lechem Mishneh, Hil. Isurei HaMizbe'ach* 5:11; *Mikdash David* §13, beginning.)

# 413 ❑ VAYIKRA / MITZVAH 118: NOT TO BRING UP AN OFFERING WITHOUT SALT

מִשָּׁרְשֵׁי הַמִּצְוָה, כָּתַבְתִּי לְמַעְלָה בְּרֹאשׁ הַסֵּדֶר.[4]

מִדִּינֵי הַמִּצְוָה, אָמְרוּ זִכְרוֹנָם לִבְרָכָה (מנחות כ״א ע״א) שֶׁמִּצְוָה לִמְלֹחַ הַבָּשָׂר יָפֶה כְּעֵין מוֹלֵחַ בָּשָׂר לִצְלִי[5] שֶׁמּוֹלְחוֹ מִשְּׁנֵי צְדָדָיו[6], וּבְדִיעֲבַד אֲפִלּוּ מָלַח כָּל שֶׁהוּא כָּשֵׁר.[7]

## ⌁ Underlying Purpose of the Mitzvah ⌁

כָּתַבְתִּי לְמַעְלָה בְּרֹאשׁ — **מִשָּׁרְשֵׁי הַמִּצְוָה — Regarding the underlying purposes of the mitzvah,** הַסֵּדֶר — **I have written** some of them **above, at the beginning of the** *parashah,* i.e., in Mitzvah 119.[4]

## ⌁ Laws of the Mitzvah ⌁

Chinuch discusses select laws regarding the salting of the offerings. [Additional laws are discussed in Mitzvah 119.]

**מִדִּינֵי הַמִּצְוָה — Among the laws of the mitzvah** is אָמְרוּ זִכְרוֹנָם לִבְרָכָה — **that which [the Sages], of blessed memory, have stated** *(Menachos 21a),* שֶׁמִּצְוָה לִמְלֹחַ הַבָּשָׂר יָפֶה — **that it is a mitzvah to salt the meat well,** כְּעֵין מוֹלֵחַ בָּשָׂר לִצְלִי — **in the manner in which one salts** non-sacrificial meat to prepare it **for roasting,**[5] שֶׁמּוֹלְחוֹ מִשְּׁנֵי צְדָדָיו — **in** which case **he salts it from both sides.**[6] וּבְדִיעֲבַד — **After the fact,** however, אֲפִלּוּ מָלַח כָּל שֶׁהוּא כָּשֵׁר — **even if he salted it the slightest amount, it is acceptable.**[7]

---

NOTES

4. As mentioned in the General Introduction, originally, *Sefer HaChinuch* was arranged with all the mitzvah-obligations in each *parashah* first, followed by all the mitzvah-prohibitions in that *parashah*. In contemporary editions, the obligations and prohibitions are intermingled, with all the mitzvos arranged according to the order of the verses in which they appear in the Torah. Thus, Mitzvah 119 (The *Obligation* to Salt the Offering), which is based on the end of the above verse, originally appeared before this mitzvah (The *Prohibition* to Bring an Offering Without Salt), which is based on the beginning of the verse. Chinuch therefore states that he discussed the underlying purposes of this mitzvah above, but in contemporary editions it appears below, in what is now known as Mitzvah 119.

5. Before meat may be consumed, its blood must be removed. This is accomplished through salting, for salt draws out the blood (see Mitzvah 148). According to many authorities, meat that is to be *cooked* requires salting, but meat that is to be roasted over a flame does not require salting, for the heat of the fire causes the blood to ooze out automatically during the roasting (see *Tur* and *Beis Yosef, Yoreh Deah* 76:1). Chinuch here, however, is quoting *Rambam* (*Hil. Isurei HaMizbe'ach* 5:11), and *Rambam* himself maintains (*Hil. Maachalos Asuros* 6:12) that meat must be salted even for roasting. Even according to *Rambam,* roasting is more lenient, for whereas meat may not be cooked until it is left to stand in salt for a period of time, meat may be roasted immediately upon being salted. Thus, Chinuch is saying that one must salt the offerings well, as one does before roasting to remove the blood — but, as when salting meat that is to be roasted, he need not wait, but may offer it up immediately (see also *Mordechai,*

*Chullin* §720). [Some suggest that sacrificial meat *must* be burned on the Altar immediately after its salting, before the salt dissolves, because the mitzvah is to bring up the offerings with *salt* in solid form, not liquified salt residue (*Chasdei David* to *Tosefta Menachos* 6:2 ד״ה ואמנם; see *Sifra* to the verse).]

[Chinuch's view requires further study, for in Mitzvah 148 he seems to follow the opinion that only meat that is to be cooked needs salting, while meat that is to be roasted does not require salting at all.]

6. The salting of the meat of offerings is clearly not done to draw out the blood, as even *minchah* offerings, which contain no blood, must be salted (*Mordechai* ibid.). Nevertheless, Chinuch (and *Rambam* ibid.) seems to require a greater degree of salting for meat offerings than for *minchah* offerings. He states that the *meat* of offerings should be salted "well," as it would be salted for human consumption, which implies that for *minchah* offerings a minimal salting suffices. It would seem that since grains do not require much salting for human consumption, less salting suffices for the Altar as well (*Even HaAzel, Hil. Isurei HaMizbe'ach* 5:11 §2 ד״ה והנה מה; see also *Chidushei HaGriz, Menachos* 21a). This corresponds with Chinuch's explanation of the underlying purpose of the mitzvah (in Mitzvah 119) — that we must treat the offerings with no less attention than we do our own food.

7. *Rambam* ibid. This statement presents a difficulty, since Chinuch states in Mitzvah 119 (as does *Rambam* ibid. §12) that all offerings except the *minchah* are acceptable after the fact even if they were not salted *at all.* Why, then, need he mention here that the meat is acceptable if salted the slightest amount? Presumably, what he means to say is that once the meat has been

### 414 ❑ ויקרא / מצוה קיח: שלא להקריב קרבן בלא מלח

וּמֶלַח שֶׁמּוֹלְחִין בּוֹ הַקָּרְבָּנוֹת הוּא מִשֶּׁל צִבּוּר[8], כְּמוֹ הָעֵצִים, וְאֵין הַיָּחִיד מֵבִיא מֶלַח אוֹ עֵצִים לַקָּרְבָּנוֹת[9], וְכָל זֶה מֵהַגְדָּלַת הַבַּיִת, דִּבְמָקוֹם עֲשִׁירוּת לֵיכָּא עֲנִיּוּת[10].

וּבִשְׁלֹשָׁה מְקוֹמוֹת הָיוּ נוֹתְנִין הַמֶּלַח, בְּלִשְׁכַּת הַמֶּלַח[11], וְעַל גַּבֵּי הַכֶּבֶשׁ וּבְרֹאשׁוֹ שֶׁל מִזְבֵּחַ. בְּלִשְׁכַּת הַמֶּלַח הָיוּ מוֹלְחִין [עוֹרוֹת הַקֳּדָשִׁים][12], וְעַל גַּבֵּי הַכֶּבֶשׁ הָיוּ מוֹלְחִין[13] הָאֵיבָרִים,

---

Chinuch discusses the salt that is used:

הוּא מִשֶּׁל צִבּוּר — **is** provided **from the communal** funds,[8] וּמֶלַח שֶׁמּוֹלְחִין בּוֹ הַקָּרְבָּנוֹת — **The salt with which the offerings are salted** כְּמוֹ הָעֵצִים — **as is the wood** used for fire to burn the offerings on the Altar; וְאֵין הַיָּחִיד מֵבִיא מֶלַח אוֹ עֵצִים לַקָּרְבָּנוֹת — **an individual is not to bring salt or wood for the offerings.**[9] וְכָל זֶה מֵהַגְדָּלַת הַבַּיִת — **This is all** a means **of elevating the stature of the Temple** (Beis HaMikdash), דִּבְמָקוֹם עֲשִׁירוּת לֵיכָּא עֲנִיּוּת — **for in a place of wealth, there should be no** conduct that typifies **poverty.**[10]

Chinuch discusses where the salting was done:

וּבִשְׁלֹשָׁה מְקוֹמוֹת הָיוּ נוֹתְנִין הַמֶּלַח — **Salt was placed in three locations** in the Temple: בְּלִשְׁכַּת הַמֶּלַח — **in the Chamber of Salt,**[11] וְעַל גַּבֵּי הַכֶּבֶשׁ — **and on the ramp** leading up to the Altar, וּבְרֹאשׁוֹ שֶׁל מִזְבֵּחַ — **and on the top of the Altar** itself. בְּלִשְׁכַּת הַמֶּלַח הָיוּ מוֹלְחִין [עוֹרוֹת הַקֳּדָשִׁים וְעַל גַּבֵּי הַכֶּבֶשׁ הָיוּ מוֹלְחִין] הָאֵיבָרִים — **In the Chamber of Salt, they would salt the hides of the offerings;**[12] **on the ramp, they would salt the limbs** of the offerings;[13]

---

#### NOTES

salted even a bit, the one who offers it up has not transgressed this prohibition. If not salted at all, however, the offering itself is acceptable, but the one who offered it up has committed a transgression [as Chinuch states at the end of this mitzvah] (Zecher Yitzchak §45).

8. I.e., from the half-*shekels* that were donated annually for the purpose of communal offerings (see Mitzvah 105, at note 12).

9. Private salt and wood were not acceptable for use with offerings brought on the Altar; only communal salt and wood were acceptable (see *Menachos* 21b-22a, where this is derived from Scripture). To be sure, an individual was allowed the privilege of *donating* salt and wood to the Temple, but in that case it became Temple property and could then be provided to anyone bringing an offering. In no instance would *private* salt or wood be used with an offering (see *Rambam, Hil. Klei HaMikdash* 8:7; see further, *Mishneh LaMelech, Hil. Klei HaMikdash* 6:10; *Even HaAzel, Hil. Temidin U'Mussafin* 9:11; see, however, *Minchas Chinuch* §7). [An individual was also allowed to donate wood as an offering on its own [קָרְבָּן הָעֵצִים] (*Menachos* 106b; see Mitzvah 119 note 7).]

10. The honor of the *Beis HaMikdash* demands that we make it a place of glorious affluence (see *Rambam, Hil. Beis HaBechirah* 1:11), and any indication of frugality would detract from that atmosphere. If an individual had to provide his own salt and wood, it would appear as though the *Beis HaMikdash* could not afford to supply these complements.

[The principle that "in a place of wealth, there should be no poverty" is mentioned several times in the Gemara (e.g., *Shabbos* 102b; *Kesubos* 106b), but it is Chinuch's innovation to use this principle to explain why the salt and wood had to come from communal funds.

As mentioned in the previous note, the Gemara derives this law from Scripture.]

11. This was one of three chambers located on the southern side of the Temple Courtyard (*Yoma* 19a).

12. The hides of the offerings were not burned on the Altar. Those of *kodshei kodashim* (most-holy offerings) were given to the Kohanim, and those of *kodashim kalim* (offerings of lesser holiness) were given to the owner of the offering (Mishnah, *Zevachim* 103a). The hides given to the Kohanim were softened with the salt that was in the Chamber of Salt. Although this salting was done for personal and not sacrificial purposes, the Kohanim were granted permission to use the Temple's salt for the portions of offerings that they received — whether the meat of offerings that they ate, or the hides of offerings that they were given (*Menachos* 21b).

[The text of Chinuch here follows the emendation of *Mishneh LaMelech* in his Glosses, based on *Menachos* 21b and *Rambam, Hil. Isurei HaMizbe'ach* 5:13. It should be noted, however, that the Mishnah in Tractate *Middos* 5:3 (as well as *Rambam, Hil. Beis HaBechirah* 5:17) states that the salt was merely *stored* in the Chamber of Salt, but the actual salting of the hides took place in the adjacent Parvah Chamber. *Tosafos* (*Menachos* 21b ד"ה בלשכת המלח) explain that this is the intent of the Gemara in *Menachos* as well; see also *Lechem Mishneh* to *Hil. Isurei HaMizbe'ach* ibid. For another view, see *Tos. Yeshanim, Yoma* 19a.]

13. This refers to the limbs of the *olah*, which were burned on the Altar. The *emurin* (specific parts of every animal offering that were burned on the Altar; see Mitzvah 138) were also salted on the ramp (*Radvaz, Hil. Maaseh HaKorbanos* 7:1; see *Tosafos, Menachos* 21b ד"ה והקטרת; see, however, *Tosefta Menachos* 6:2).

# 415 ❑ VAYIKRA / MITZVAH 118: NOT TO BRING UP AN OFFERING WITHOUT SALT

וּבְרֹאשׁוֹ שֶׁל מִזְבֵּחַ מוֹלְחִין הַקֹּמֶץ וְהַלְּבוֹנָה[14] וְהַמְּנָחוֹת הַנִּשְׂרָפוֹת וְעוֹלַת הָעוֹף,[15] וְיֶתֶר פְּרָטֶיהָ מְבֹאָרִין בְּפֶרֶק שְׁבִיעִי שֶׁבִּזְבָחִים.[16]

וְנוֹהֶגֶת בִּזְמַן הַבַּיִת בְּזִכְרֵי כְהֻנָּה, כִּי לָהֶם לְהַשְׁלִים צָרְכֵי הַקָּרְבָּן.[17] וְכֹהֵן הָעוֹבֵר עָלֶיהָ וְהִקְרִיב קָרְבָּן אוֹ מִנְחָה בְּלֹא מֶלַח כְּלָל[18] בָּטֵל עֲשֵׂה, וְגַם עוֹבֵר עַל לָאו זֶה[19] וְלוֹקֶה,

---

**הַקֹּמֶץ וְהַלְּבוֹנָה** — the *kometz* and the *levonah,* which are the portions of standard *minchah* offerings that are burned on the Altar, **וּבְרֹאשׁוֹ שֶׁל מִזְבֵּחַ מוֹלְחִין** — and on the top of the Altar, they would salt **וְהַמְּנָחוֹת הַנִּשְׂרָפוֹת** — and the entirety of those *minchah* offerings that were completely burned on the Altar,[14] **וְעוֹלַת הָעוֹף** — and the *olah* of fowl.[15] **וְיֶתֶר פְּרָטֶיהָ מְבֹאָרִין בְּפֶרֶק שְׁבִיעִי שֶׁבִּזְבָחִים** — These laws, and the additional details of [the mitzvah], are elaborated in the seventh chapter of Tractate *Zevachim*.[16]

## ☞ Applicability of the Mitzvah ☜

**וְנוֹהֶגֶת בִּזְמַן הַבַּיִת** — [This mitzvah] applies in the times of the Temple, **בְּזִכְרֵי כְהֻנָּה** — to male Kohanim, **כִּי לָהֶם לְהַשְׁלִים צָרְכֵי הַקָּרְבָּן** — for the responsibility of fulfilling the requirements of the offerings is theirs.[17] **וְכֹהֵן הָעוֹבֵר עָלֶיהָ וְהִקְרִיב קָרְבָּן אוֹ מִנְחָה בְּלֹא מֶלַח** — A Kohen who transgresses [this mitzvah] and offers up an animal offering or a *minchah* offering without any[18] salt **בָּטֵל עֲשֵׂה** — has violated a mitzvah-obligation (Mitzvah 119), **וְגַם עוֹבֵר עַל לָאו זֶה** — and also transgresses this mitzvah-prohibition,[19] **וְלוֹקֶה** — for which he incurs *malkus* (lashes). Although *malkus* are imposed only for a transgression that involves action, this transgression carries the penalty of *malkus*,

---

### NOTES

14. In the case of a standard *minchah* offering, the Kohen would scoop out a *kometz* (fistful) of the meal and oil, and burn that on the Altar together with the *levonah* that was a required component of the *minchah*. The remainder of the meal was eaten by the Kohanim (*Leviticus* 6:9; see Mitzvah 134). *Minchah* offerings brought by Kohanim, and the *minchas nesachim* (a *minchah* brought as an accessory to an animal offering; see *Numbers* 15:1-16), were entirely burned on the Altar (see Mitzvah 116; *Rambam Hil. Maaseh HaKorbanos* 13:12). Those portions burned on the Altar required prior salting. [The salt was kept at the southwestern corner of the Altar (*Tosefta Menachos* 6:2).]

15. An *olah* of fowl was burned on the Altar, so it required salting; a *chatas* of fowl, however, was not burned on the Altar, but was eaten in its entirety by the Kohanim (Mishnah, *Zevachim* 64b), so it did not require salting as part of this mitzvah. [There is an opinion that the portions of the offerings eaten by Kohanim required salting as part of this mitzvah (*Re'ah* in *Bedek HaBayis* to *Toras HaBayis* 3:3 p. 71b), but many others disagree (see *Rashba* in *Mishmeres HaBayis* to *Toras Habayis* ibid.; *Rosh, Pesachim* 2:23; and *Minchas Chinuch* §11).]

The specific place designated for the salting of each item accorded with the treatment of the item: The hides were not offered on the Altar, so they were not salted on the Altar, but in a designated chamber in the Temple. The limbs (and *emurin*) that were offered upon the Altar were salted on the Altar's ramp, immediately before they were brought up on the Altar and burned (see *Chasdei David* cited in note 5). The other items were salted on the Altar itself, away from the limbs that were salted on the ramp, so as to keep them clean from the blood of the limbs (see *Tosafos, Menachos* 21b ד"ה והקטרה).

16. The reference to the seventh chapter of *Zevachim* follows some editions of *Rambam, Sefer HaMitzvos, Lo Saaseh* 99 (see Frankel ed.). Other editions state that the laws of the mitzvah are elaborated "in Tractate *Pesachim*" — which discusses some laws regarding the salting of (non-sacrificial) meat for ordinary consumption (74b, 76a). However, the laws of this mitzvah do not appear in either of these places, but in Tractate *Menachos* (18a-21b,106b), as Chinuch states in Mitzvah 119. See note 11 there.

17. Since this prohibition pertains to the Temple *avodah* (service), and is transgressed through bringing up an offering without salt, it applies only to those authorized to bring offerings up on the Altar, not to non-Kohanim, whose bringing up of an offering is inherently unacceptable. Moreover, the salting is done in areas of the Temple that are not accessible to non-Kohanim [e.g., the Altar] (*Minchas Chinuch* §9; see *Menachos* 20a). [See similarly, end of Mitzvos 104, 117, and 125. For a related discussion, see Insight to Mitzvah 125.]

18. See Chinuch above, at note 7; and see note 7.

19. A Kohen need not bring up the entire offering without salt to transgress these mitzvos; he transgresses by bringing up a *kezayis* (olive's volume) without salt, for that is an amount significant enough to make his deed qualify as an act of "offering up" (*Minchas Chinuch* §8).

## ויקרא / מצוה קיח: שלא להקריב קרבן בלא מלח

שֶׁהֲרֵי מַעֲשֶׂה יֵשׁ כָּאן כְּשֶׁהוּא מַקְרִיב הַבָּשָׂר הַתָּפֵל שֶׁהֻזְהַר עָלָיו שֶׁלֹּא לְהַקְרִיבוֹ בְּלֹא מֶלַח.[20]

---

שֶׁהֲרֵי מַעֲשֶׂה יֵשׁ כָּאן כְּשֶׁהוּא מַקְרִיב הַבָּשָׂר הַתָּפֵל — **because there is a** forbidden **action** committed **here, when one offers up bland,** unsalted **meat,** שֶׁהֻזְהַר עָלָיו שֶׁלֹּא לְהַקְרִיבוֹ בְּלֹא מֶלַח — **which he was cautioned not to offer** upon the Altar **without salt.**[20]

---

### NOTES

20. Although the Torah phrases this prohibition as *you may not "withhold" the salt of your God's covenant* (and "withholding" does not involve action), since all offerings must ultimately be brought up on the Altar, the verse in effect prohibits the Kohanim from *bringing up* offerings that are unsalted. Thus, the prohibition is violated through action (*Rambam, Sefer HaMitzvos, Lo Saaseh* 99; see *Chazon Ish, Menachos* 25:18).

---

#### ⸙ Insight: Covenant of Salt

Scripture calls the salt offered with the sacrificial offerings מֶלַח בְּרִית אֱלֹהֶיךָ, *the salt of your God's covenant* (*Leviticus* 2:13, cited at the beginning of this mitzvah). Understood according to the plain meaning, *God's covenant* is a reference to the eternal covenant of the sacrificial offerings, which must be accompanied by salt as a symbol of preservation and endurance, as Chinuch states in Mitzvah 119 (see *Daas Zekeinim* and *Ramban* to the verse; cf. *Ibn Ezra* there).

*Rashi* (to the verse), however, cites another explanation from the Midrash: On the Second Day of Creation, when God created the firmament to separate the lower (i.e., earthly) waters from the upper (i.e., heavenly) waters, the lower waters cried because they would be "distant" from Him. He therefore promised the lower waters that salt — which is a product of seawater — would be offered upon the Altar with every offering, and that a libation of water would be poured upon the Altar during the festival of Succos. Thus, the people of Israel are commanded to uphold (as it were) the covenant that God made with the lower waters, by including salt in their offerings (see also *Rabbeinu Bachya* and *Gur Aryeh* to the verse; *Midrash Aseres HaDibros* §1; *Bereishis Rabbah* 5:4 with *Eitz Yosef* and *Nechmad LeMareh*; *Tikkunei Zohar* §5).

Based on this Midrash, *Chasam Sofer* (to the verse) gives a homiletic interpretation of the Torah's *requirement* to incorporate salt in the Altar offerings (Mitzvah 119), and the contrasting *prohibition* against offering up any leaven or honey (Mitzvah 117). The Sages (Mishnah, *Avos* 4:21) identify three drives that "remove a person from this world": קִנְאָה, *envy*; תַּאֲוָה, *desire*; and כָּבוֹד, *honor*. *Chasam Sofer* explains that the Torah alludes to an important distinction between these three destructive tendencies. Leaven, which can be understood to represent egotism and the pursuit of honor (as Chinuch states in Mitzvah 117), may not be offered upon the Altar of God, indicating that preoccupation with earning the respect of others is a corrupting trait that cannot be directed to the service of Hashem. Likewise, the cloying sweetness of honey — which symbolizes unbridled desire for pleasures (see Chinuch ibid.) — has no place on the Altar; hedonism cannot be sublimated to Godliness.

Salt represents envy, as it recalls the wish of the lower waters to share the status of the upper waters. Although envy is typically a destructive tendency, nevertheless, there is a "good" form of this trait that can and should be channeled to serve Hashem. "Envy between scholars increases wisdom," say the Sages (*Bava Basra* 21a); healthy competition can motivate great achievement in Torah. Likewise, envy of the יִרְאַת ה', *fear of Hashem*, exhibited by others, can prod a person to emulate their ways. As Scripture states (*Proverbs* 23:17): אַל יְקַנֵּא לִבְּךָ בַּחַטָּאִים כִּי אִם בְּיִרְאַת ה' כָּל הַיּוֹם, *Let not your heart envy sinners, rather those who revere HASHEM all the day* (see *Megillah* 6b). Thus, *Chasam Sofer* explains, salt may — and indeed, *must* — be offered upon the Altar, to indicate that envy of this sort, which parallels the lower waters' aspiration to attain closeness to God in no less a measure than the upper waters, stimulates and enhances one's Divine service.

# VAYIKRA / MITZVAH 119: THE OBLIGATION TO SALT THE OFFERING

## מִצְוָה קיט: מִצְוַת מְלִיחַת הַקָּרְבָּן

לְהַקְרִיב מֶלַח עַל כָּל הַקָּרְבָּנוֹת, כְּלוֹמַר שֶׁיִּתֵּן מֶלַח בִּבְשַׂר הַקָּרְבָּן וְכֵן בְּקֶמַח הַמְּנָחוֹת, שֶׁנֶּאֱמַר (ויקרא ב', י"ג) עַל כָּל קָרְבָּנְךָ תַּקְרִיב מֶלַח.[1]

כְּבָר אָמַרְנוּ בְּמִצְוַת בִּנְיָן הַבַּיִת, כִּי מִשָּׁרְשֵׁי מִצְוַת הַקָּרְבָּן לְהַכְשִׁיר וּלְהַיְשִׁיר נֶפֶשׁ הַמַּקְרִיב אוֹתוֹ, וְעַל כֵּן לְעוֹרֵר נַפְשׁוֹ שֶׁל מַקְרִיב נִצְטַוָּה בְּהַקְרָבַת דְּבָרִים הַטּוֹבִים וְהָעֲרֵבִים וְהַחֲבִיבִים עָלָיו, וּכְמוֹ שֶׁכָּתַבְנוּ לְמַעְלָה. וְהַמֶּלַח בּוֹ גַּם כֵּן מֵהַשֹּׁרֶשׁ הַזֶּה,[2]

## Mitzvah 119

# The Obligation to Salt the Offering

וְכָל קָרְבַּן מִנְחָתְךָ בַּמֶּלַח תִּמְלָח וְלֹא תַשְׁבִּית מֶלַח בְּרִית אֱלֹהֶיךָ מֵעַל מִנְחָתֶךָ עַל כָּל קָרְבָּנְךָ תַּקְרִיב מֶלַח

*You shall salt your every offering of meal with salt; you may not withhold the salt of your God's covenant from upon your meal offering — on your every offering shall you offer salt (Leviticus 2:13).*

This verse contains both a mitzvah-obligation to salt the offering before it is offered up on the Altar, and a mitzvah-prohibition not to withhold salt from the offerings. The preceding mitzvah discussed the *prohibition* of withholding the application of salt from the offerings. The subject of this mitzvah is the *obligation* to salt every offering.

לְהַקְרִיב מֶלַח עַל כָּל הַקָּרְבָּנוֹת — We are commanded **to offer salt on all the offerings.** כְּלוֹמַר **This means to say** שֶׁיִּתֵּן מֶלַח בִּבְשַׂר הַקָּרְבָּן — **that one shall place salt on the meat of an animal offering,** וְכֵן בְּקֶמַח הַמְּנָחוֹת — **as well as on the flour of the** *menachos* (meal offerings; sing. *minchah*) before they are offered up on the Altar; שֶׁנֶּאֱמַר — **as it is stated** (*Leviticus* 2:13): עַל כָּל קָרְבָּנְךָ תַּקְרִיב מֶלַח — **on your every offering shall you offer salt.**[1]

## Underlying Purpose of the Mitzvah

Chinuch notes how this mitzvah corresponds with the general underlying purpose of the offerings:

כְּבָר אָמַרְנוּ בְּמִצְוַת בִּנְיָן הַבַּיִת — **We have already stated in the mitzvah to build the Temple** (*Beis HaMikdash*) [Mitzvah 95], כִּי מִשָּׁרְשֵׁי מִצְוַת הַקָּרְבָּן — **that among the underlying purposes of the mitzvah** pertaining to **offerings** is the idea that an offering is brought לְהַכְשִׁיר וּלְהַיְשִׁיר נֶפֶשׁ הַמַּקְרִיב אוֹתוֹ — **to make the soul of the one bringing it worthy and upstanding.** וְעַל כֵּן לְעוֹרֵר נַפְשׁוֹ שֶׁל מַקְרִיב — **Therefore, in order to arouse the spirit of the one bringing** the offering, so that he may acquire these good traits, נִצְטַוָּה בְּהַקְרָבַת דְּבָרִים הַטּוֹבִים וְהָעֲרֵבִים וְהַחֲבִיבִים עָלָיו — he **was commanded to offer** in the Temple **items that are fine, pleasing, and dear to him,** וּכְמוֹ שֶׁכָּתַבְנוּ לְמַעְלָה — **as we have written earlier,** in Mitzvah 95.[2] וְהַמֶּלַח בּוֹ גַּם כֵּן מֵהַשֹּׁרֶשׁ הַזֶּה — **The** requirement to have **salt in [the offering] is also based on**

---

### NOTES

1. Chinuch will clarify below that the requirement of salting applies not only to animal and *minchah* offerings, but also to most other items offered on the Altar (see also *Rambam, Hil. Maaseh HaKorbanos* 16:14).

2. See there, at note 45. Although the quality of the items we offer does not matter to Hashem, we are commanded to offer items that have value to *us*, so that the offering will have a greater effect on us: through offering our most precious items to Hashem, we will be inspired (see *Rambam, Hil. Isurei HaMizbe'ach* 7:11).

כְּדֵי שֶׁתִּהְיֶה אוֹתָהּ פְּעֻלָּה שְׁלֵמָה, לֹא תֶחְסַר לְפִי הַנְהָגַת הָאָדָם דָּבָר, כִּי אָז יִתְעוֹרֵר לִבּוֹ אֵלָיו יוֹתֵר, כִּי כָל דָּבָר מִבְּלִי מֶלַח לֹא יֶעֱרַב לְאִישׁ לֹא טַעֲמוֹ וְלֹא אַף רֵיחוֹ. וּמִלְּבַד זֶה יֵשׁ בַּמֶּלַח עִנְיָן אַחֵר רוֹמֵז, כִּי הַמֶּלַח מְקַיֵּם כָּל דָּבָר וּמַצִּיל עַל הַהֶפְסֵד וְהָרִקָּבוֹן, וְכֵן בְּמַעֲשֵׂה הַקָּרְבָּן יִנָּצֵל הָאָדָם מִן הַהֶפְסֵד, וְתִשָּׁמֵר נַפְשׁוֹ וְתִשָּׁאֵר קַיֶּמֶת לָעַד.[3]

מִדִּינֵי הַמִּצְוָה, מַה שֶּׁאָמְרוּ זִכְרוֹנָם לִבְרָכָה (מנחות כ׳ ע״א) כִּי כָּל הַקָּרְבָּנוֹת נִמְלָחִין קֹדֶם שֶׁיַּעֲלוּ לַמִּזְבֵּחַ[4], וְאֵין לְךָ דָּבָר שֶׁקָּרֵב לַמִּזְבֵּחַ בְּלֹא מֶלַח חוּץ מִן הַנְּסָכִים[5]

---

**this same underlying purpose.** כְּדֵי שֶׁתִּהְיֶה אוֹתָהּ פְּעֻלָּה שְׁלֵמָה — It is **in order that this act** of bringing the offering **should be complete,** לֹא תֶחְסַר לְפִי הַנְהָגַת הָאָדָם דָּבָר — and **not lacking anything** that would be expected **by** the standards of normal **human conduct;** כִּי אָז יִתְעוֹרֵר לִבּוֹ אֵלָיו יוֹתֵר — **for then,** by bringing an offering in a manner that is deemed complete by human standards, [**the person's**] **heart will be more aroused to** appreciate the opportunity to bring the [the **offering**] than it would be if the offering were somehow lacking by human standards. כִּי כָל דָּבָר מִבְּלִי מֶלַח לֹא יֶעֱרַב לְאִישׁ — Therefore, we are commanded to apply salt to the offerings, **because any item** of food **without salt is not pleasing to a person** — לֹא טַעֲמוֹ וְלֹא אַף רֵיחוֹ — **neither its taste, nor even its scent** — and to attain the true purpose of bringing the offering, it must consist of something that is pleasing.

Chinuch offers another underlying purpose for this mitzvah:

וּמִלְּבַד זֶה — **Aside from this** reason, יֵשׁ בַּמֶּלַח עִנְיָן אַחֵר רוֹמֵז — **there is another concept** that is **alluded to through** the use of **salt,** כִּי הַמֶּלַח מְקַיֵּם כָּל דָּבָר — the fact **that salt preserves all things** וּמַצִּיל עַל הַהֶפְסֵד וְהָרִקָּבוֹן — **and saves** them **from loss and spoilage.** וְכֵן בְּמַעֲשֵׂה הַקָּרְבָּן — Similarly, through the performance of the offering, יִנָּצֵל הָאָדָם מִן הַהֶפְסֵד — **the person is saved from ruin,** וְתִשָּׁמֵר נַפְשׁוֹ וְתִשָּׁאֵר קַיֶּמֶת לָעַד — **and his soul will be protected and will endure eternally.**[3]

### ~ Laws of the Mitzvah ~

Chinuch mentions select laws related to the salting of the offerings. [Some laws were mentioned earlier, in Mitzvah 118.]

מִדִּינֵי הַמִּצְוָה — **Among the laws of the mitzvah** is מַה שֶּׁאָמְרוּ זִכְרוֹנָם לִבְרָכָה — **that which** [the Sages], of blessed memory, have said (*Menachos* 20a), כִּי כָּל הַקָּרְבָּנוֹת נִמְלָחִין קֹדֶם שֶׁיַּעֲלוּ לַמִּזְבֵּחַ — **that all offerings are salted before they are brought up to the Altar,**[4] וְאֵין לְךָ — and **there is nothing** דָּבָר שֶׁקָּרֵב לַמִּזְבֵּחַ בְּלֹא מֶלַח — **that is offered on the Altar without salt,** חוּץ מִן הַנְּסָכִים — **except for the** wine **libations** brought as an accessory to the offerings,[5]

---

NOTES

3. By bringing an offering, a person is saved from the "ruination" of his soul, which was tainted by sin, and is now purified through the atonement effected by his bringing of the necessary offering. Although this reason seemingly applies to sin offerings alone, feelings of repentance and humility before God are engendered by voluntary offerings as well, as Chinuch explains in Mitzvah 95.

4. The Gemara merely teaches that all offerings are salted, as Chinuch proceeds to explain. The statement that they are salted "before they are brought up on the Altar" is a quotation of *Rambam, Hil. Isurei HaMizbe'ach* 5:11. Now, in Mitzvah 118, Chinuch stated that there were three places in the *Beis HaMikdash* where the salt was applied, and certain parts of the offerings were actually salted after they were brought up to the Altar, on top of the Altar itself (see note 15 there). Chinuch's statement here presumably means that all offerings were salted before they were *burned* on the Altar. [See however, *Aruch HaShulchan HeAsid* 59:1.]

5. This refers to the wine libations that are brought with certain animal offerings (*Numbers* 15:1-13). These were brought to the Altar and poured onto the Altar itself (*Rambam, Hil. Maaseh HaKorbanos* 2:1). No salt was added to this wine before it was poured onto the Altar.

[One may also donate wine as an offering of its own, in which case it is poured on the Altar as well. In such a case, the requirement of salting does apply to it, and salt is added to the wine before it is poured on the Altar (*Rambam* ibid. 16:14 with *Kesef Mishneh*; see also *Minchas Chinuch* §5 and *Mikdash David, Kodashim* §13 ד״ה וזה דהנסכים for further details).]

# 419 □ VAYIKRA / MITZVAH 119: THE OBLIGATION TO SALT THE OFFERING

וְהַדָּם[6] וְהָעֵצִים[7], וְדָבָר זֶה קַבָּלָה וְאֵין לוֹ מִקְרָא[8]. וְאִם עָבַר וְהִקְרִיב בְּלֹא מֶלַח, הַקָּרְבָּן כָּשֵׁר וְנִרְצָה[9], חוּץ מִן הַמִּנְחָה שֶׁהַמֶּלַח מְעַכְּבָהּ, שֶׁנֶּאֱמַר בָּהּ בְּפֵרוּשׁ (שם) "וְלֹא תַשְׁבִּית מֶלַח בְּרִית אֱלֹהֶיךָ מֵעַל מִנְחָתֶךָ". וְיֶתֶר פְּרָטֶיהָ, מְבֹאָרִים בְּסִפְרָא וּבִמְקוֹמוֹת מִמְּנָחוֹת (י"ח ע"א — כ"א ע"ב)[11].

---

וְהַדָּם [6] — **the blood** of the offerings, וְהָעֵצִים — **and the wood.**[7] וְדָבָר זֶה קַבָּלָה וְאֵין לוֹ מִקְרָא — **This matter is a Tradition** transmitted orally at Sinai, **and has no** source in a **verse.**[8] וְאִם עָבַר וְהִקְרִיב בְּלֹא מֶלַח — **If one transgressed** this mitzvah-obligation **and offered** something on the Altar **without salt,** הַקָּרְבָּן כָּשֵׁר וְנִרְצָה — **the offering is nevertheless valid and** will be **accepted favorably** before Hashem.[9] חוּץ מִן הַמִּנְחָה שֶׁהַמֶּלַח מְעַכְּבָהּ — This applies to all offerings **except for the** *minchah*, **for which the salt is essential** to its validity, שֶׁנֶּאֱמַר בָּהּ בְּפֵרוּשׁ — **as it is explicitly stated with regard to [the** *minchah***]** (*Leviticus* 2:13): "וְלֹא תַשְׁבִּית מֶלַח בְּרִית אֱלֹהֶיךָ מֵעַל מִנְחָתֶךָ" — **you may not withhold the salt of your God's covenant from upon your meal offering** (i.e., *minchah*).[10]

וְיֶתֶר פְּרָטֶיהָ — **These laws, and the additional details [of the mitzvah]** מְבֹאָרִים בְּסִפְרָא — **are set forth in the** *Sifra* (to this verse), וּבִמְקוֹמוֹת מִמְּנָחוֹת — **and in** several **places in** Tractate *Menachos* (18a-21b, 106b).[11]

---

## NOTES

6. Although the blood of every offering is applied to the Altar, and the blood itself, being the primary element of the offering, is called an "offering" (see *Rashi, Menachos* 20a ד"ה עצים), no salt is added to it.

7. Wood used to fuel the Altar flame is certainly not salted, as it is not an offering. Chinuch here is teaching that even wood donated as an offering on its own [קָרְבַּן הָעֵצִים] (*Menachos* 106b), and not merely a provision for the performance of the offerings, is not salted (*Minchas Chinuch* §3).

[An explanation as to why these three items (wine, blood, and wood) are excluded from the requirement of salting can be offered in light of the underlying purpose presented above: since these are generally not salted for human use, there is no need that they be salted for the Altar (see *Ramban, Leviticus* 2:11).]

8. In saying that "this matter" (i.e., the exclusion of these three offerings from salting) is an Oral Tradition without a Scriptural source, Chinuch echoes the expression of *Rambam* (*Hil. Isurei HaMizbe'ach* 5:11). However, the Gemara (*Menachos* 20a) states clearly that these three items are excluded from the requirement of salting based on the choice of words in the verse cited above (*Leviticus* 2:13), which includes only those items that are similar to the *minchah* (for elaboration, see Mitzvah 118 note 2). Why, then, do *Rambam* and Chinuch state that there is no Scriptural source for this law?

Some explain that the reference in *Rambam* [and presumably, in Chinuch, as well] to this law as an Oral Tradition without a Scriptural source is directed specifically at the exclusion of *wood* from the requirement of salting. Since wood is considered an offering (see previous note) and shares certain characteristics with the *minchah* (e.g., it is burned on the Altar), it is not excluded by the words of the verse cited above, and should rightfully be included in the requirement. Thus, the only basis to exclude wood from the requirement of salting is the Oral Tradition (see *Kesef Mishneh, Lechem Mishneh, Mahari Korkos* to Rambam ibid.; see also *Rambam, Commentary to Mishnah, Menachos* 3:2).

9. I.e., not only is the offering valid despite its lacking salt, it even effects atonement for the one bringing it (see *Even HaAzel, Hil. Isurei HaMizbe'ach* 5:11-12, §6).

10. With regard to every offering, the verse states the obligation of salting only once: עַל כָּל קָרְבָּנְךָ תַּקְרִיב מֶלַח, *on your every offering shall you offer salt*. With regard to the *minchah*, however, the verse repeats the salting obligation: וְכָל קָרְבַּן מִנְחָתְךָ בַּמֶּלַח תִּמְלָח וְלֹא תַשְׁבִּית מֶלַח ... מֵעַל מִנְחָתֶךָ, *You shall salt your every offering of meal; you may not withhold the salt ... from upon your meal offering*. As a rule, when the Torah repeats a requirement with regard to offerings, it is for the purpose of indicating that the requirement is essential to its validity. Thus, the extra mention of the obligation of salting teaches us that not only is the salt required for the *minchah,* but it is essential to its validity (see *Radvaz* and *Kesef Mishneh, Hil. Isurei HaMizbe'ach* 5:12; see also *Even HaAzel, Hil. Isurei HaMizbe'ach* 5:11-12, §5). See Insight for further discussion of the unique status of *minchah* offerings in this regard.

11. The laws are codified in *Rambam, Hil. Isurei HaMizbe'ach* 11-13.

וְנוֹהֶגֶת בִּזְמַן הַבַּיִת בְּזִכְרֵי כְהֻנָּה.[12] וְעוֹבֵר עַל זֶה וְהִקְרִיב מִנְחָה אוֹ קָרְבָּן בְּלֹא מֶלַח כְּלָל[13] בִּטֵּל עֲשֵׂה[14], וְעוֹד שֶׁהוּא עוֹבֵר עַל לָאו, דִּכְתִיב (שם) וְלֹא תַשְׁבִּית מֶלַח וְגו'.

## ⇐ Applicability of the Mitzvah ⇒

בְּזִכְרֵי כְהֻנָּה — to male Kohanim.[12] וְנוֹהֶגֶת בִּזְמַן הַבַּיִת — [This mitzvah] applies in the times of the Temple, וְעוֹבֵר עַל זֶה — [A Kohen] who transgresses this [law], וְהִקְרִיב מִנְחָה אוֹ קָרְבָּן — and brings a *minchah* or animal **offering without any salt**,[13] בִּטֵּל עֲשֵׂה — has violated a mitzvah-obligation.[14] וְעוֹד שֶׁהוּא עוֹבֵר עַל לָאו — Moreover, he has transgressed a mitzvah-**prohibition** (Mitzvah 118), דִּכְתִיב "וְלֹא תַשְׁבִּית מֶלַח וְגו'" — for it is stated (*Leviticus* 2:13), ***you may not withhold the salt***, etc.

### NOTES

12. See above, Mitzvah 118 note 17.
13. See above, Mitzvah 118 with note 7.
14. As explained in Mitzvah 118 (note 19), one transgresses this mitzvah with the bringing up of a *kezayis* (olive's volume) of an offering without salt.

---

⇜§ **Insight: Why Is Salting the Offerings Counted as a Distinct Mitzvah?**

The passages in *Leviticus* that delineate the procedures for the various sacrificial offerings contain many detailed requirements. While these requirements are stated as imperatives (*the Kohen shall slaughter . . . the Kohen shall flay*, etc.), Chinuch, following *Rambam's* methodology, does not count each of them as a separate mitzvah, for he considers these requirements to be *details* of each mitzvah, rather than separate mitzvah-obligations. Thus, the *entire* procedure pertaining to each offering is enumerated as a single mitzvah-obligation. Examples of this include Mitzvah 115 (*The Obligation to Make the Olah Offering*) and Mitzvah 116 (*The Obligation of the Minchah Offering*). [See *Sefer HaMitzvos, Shoresh* 12, where *Rambam* articulates this principle and critiques *Halachos Gedolos*, whose count of mitzvos does include the individual components of the sacrificial procedures; cf. *Ramban*, Glosses ad loc. See also above, Mitzvah 102 with notes 23-24.]

Now, in keeping with *Rambam's* principle, it would seem appropriate that *this* mitzvah, *The Obligation to Salt the Offering*, also be omitted from the count of the 613 Mitzvos, as salting is one of the particular requirements of the offerings. Nonetheless, as we see here, Chinuch, following *Rambam* (*Sefer HaMitzvos, Asei* 62), *does* enumerate this as a distinct mitzvah-obligation. *Rambam* (*Sefer HaMitzvos, Shoresh* 12) explains this matter and writes that the requirement of עַל כָּל קָרְבָּנְךָ תַּקְרִיב מֶלַח, *on your every offering shall you offer salt*, applies to *all* offerings; it is not part of the procedure of any particular one. Thus, rather than being one of the details of any particular offering, it is a separate, general Scriptural obligation: to salt all offerings that are brought upon the Altar.

However, *Rambam's* position requires study, for further in the same passage in *Sefer HaMitzvos* (*Shoresh* 12), when listing the particulars of the mitzvah of offering a *minchah* that are *not* to be counted as independent mitzvos, *Rambam* actually includes salting the *minchah* as one of it particulars — along with pouring in the oil, mixing the meal and oil, removing the *kometz*, etc. This stands in apparent contradiction to *Rambam's* earlier assertion that salting the offerings is a separate mitzvah and not a detail of the specific mitzvah pertaining to each of the offerings.

*Chidushei HaGriz* (*Menachos* 67b ד"ה והנה הרמב"ם בספר המצות) explains that this apparent contradiction in *Rambam's* words actually highlights an important difference between the obligation expressed in the verse with regard to the *minchah* and the obligation pertaining to other offerings, as follows:

The verse contains a duplicate exhortation to salt the offerings: וְכָל קָרְבַּן מִנְחָתְךָ בַּמֶּלַח תִּמְלָח... עַל כָּל קָרְבָּנְךָ תַּקְרִיב מֶלַח, *you shall salt your every offering of meal with salt . . . on your every offering shall you offer salt*. The first phrase, *you shall salt your every offering* **of meal** *with salt*, which refers specifically to the *minchah* offering, teaches that salt is an integral component of that offering. Since this phrase is specific, it not understood as a separate mitzvah-obligation, but rather, as describing one of the

requirements of the *minchah* offering. Accordingly, *Rambam* indicates that *this* imperative is *not* counted among the 613 Mitzvos. In contrast, the final phrase of the verse, *on your every offering shall you offer salt,* is a general statement referring to *all* offerings. Hence, it is not understood as describing a detail of all the mitzvos pertaining to those offerings. Rather, it constitutes a distinct mitzvah-obligation to include salt in every offering (as stated above).

Based on the above, *Chidushei HaGriz* offers a rationale for one of the laws that Chinuch stated in this mitzvah — that any offering that was brought without salt is valid after the fact, except the *minchah*. *Chidushei HaGriz* explains: Since salting is generally not an integral part of the offerings, but is required under a separate mitzvah, it follows that even where the mitzvah of salting has been neglected, the offering is still valid. It is only in the case of the *minchah* — where Scripture indicates that the inclusion of salt is an intrinsic component of the offering — that the offering is rendered invalid if one failed to include salt.

# מִצְוָה קכ: מִצְוַת קָרְבַּן בֵּית דִּין אִם טָעוּ בְּהוֹרָאָה[1]

שֶׁיַּקְרִיבוּ סַנְהֶדְרֵי גְּדוֹלָה קָרְבָּן[2] אִם טָעוּ וְהוֹרוּ שֶׁלֹּא כַּהֲלָכָה בַּעֲבֵרוֹת חֲמוּרוֹת שֶׁחַיָּבִין עֲלֵיהֶן כָּרֵת[3], וְעָשׂוּ הַקָּהָל אוֹ רֻבָּן עַל פִּיהֶן, שֶׁנֶּאֱמַר (ויקרא ד׳, י״ג) וְאִם כָּל עֲדַת יִשְׂרָאֵל יִשְׁגּוּ וְנֶעְלַם דָּבָר מֵעֵינֵי הַקָּהָל וְגוֹ׳.

## Mitzvah 120

## The Obligation Upon Beis Din to Bring an Offering for an Erroneous Ruling

וְאִם כָּל עֲדַת יִשְׂרָאֵל יִשְׁגּוּ וְנֶעְלַם דָּבָר מֵעֵינֵי הַקָּהָל וְעָשׂוּ אַחַת מִכָּל מִצְוֹת ה׳ אֲשֶׁר לֹא תֵעָשֶׂינָה וְאָשֵׁמוּ. וְנוֹדְעָה הַחַטָּאת אֲשֶׁר חָטְאוּ עָלֶיהָ וְהִקְרִיבוּ הַקָּהָל פַּר בֶּן בָּקָר לְחַטָּאת וְהֵבִיאוּ אֹתוֹ לִפְנֵי אֹהֶל מוֹעֵד

*If the entire assembly of Israel shall err, and a matter became obscured from the eyes of the congregation, and they commit one from among all the commandments of HASHEM that may not be done, and they become guilty. When the sin regarding which they committed becomes known, the congregation shall offer a young bull as a sin-offering, and they shall bring it before the Tent of Meeting* (*Leviticus* 4:13-14).

The Great Sanhedrin, which had its official seat in the Chamber of Hewn Stone (לִשְׁכַּת הַגָּזִית) in the *Beis HaMikdash* (Holy Temple), was the highest judicial court in Eretz Yisrael. It was comprised of seventy-one judges, of whom the greatest one was chosen to be the head (see Mitzvah 491). This mitzvah addresses the requirement of bringing an atonement offering in the event that the Great Sanhedrin erred in a ruling that caused the nation to sin.[1] This offering is known as פַּר הֶעְלֵם דָּבָר שֶׁל צִבּוּר, *the bull for a communal error.*

**שֶׁיַּקְרִיבוּ סַנְהֶדְרֵי גְּדוֹלָה קָרְבָּן** – It is a mitzvah-obligation **that the Great Sanhedrin bring an offering**[2] **אִם טָעוּ וְהוֹרוּ שֶׁלֹּא כַּהֲלָכָה** – **if they** (i.e., the members of Sanhedrin) **erred and ruled** in a manner that is **not in accordance with halachah,** permitting an act that is actually prohibited. **בַּעֲבֵרוֹת חֲמוּרוֹת שֶׁחַיָּבִין עֲלֵיהֶן כָּרֵת** – This offering is required if the erroneous permissive ruling was issued **with regard to** one of **the grave sins that bear the penalty of *kares*** (excision),[3] **וְעָשׂוּ הַקָּהָל אוֹ רֻבָּן עַל פִּיהֶן** – **and the** entire **community** of the Jewish people, **or its majority, acted on** the basis of **their word** and thus transgressed, **שֶׁנֶּאֱמַר** – **as it is stated** (*Leviticus* 4:13): **"וְאִם כָּל עֲדַת יִשְׂרָאֵל יִשְׁגּוּ וְנֶעְלַם דָּבָר מֵעֵינֵי הַקָּהָל וְגוֹ׳ "** – ***If the entire assembly of Israel shall err, and a matter became obscured from the eyes of the congregation* etc.,** *the congregation shall offer a young bull as a sin offering.* The "eyes of the congregation" are the sages of the Great Sanhedrin, whose function it is to "see" (i.e., ascertain) what the Torah permits and what is prohibited. If a matter of law became obscured from them, and as a result "the entire assembly of Israel" (or its majority, which is tantamount to its entirety) transgresses, the *bull for a communal error* must be brought.

NOTES

1. This mitzvah applies only to a ruling of the Great Sanhedrin. Other courts, including those comprised of twenty-three members (known as סַנְהֶדְרֵי קְטַנָּה, *small Sanhedrin;* see Mitzvah 491), were not obligated in this mitzvah.

2. Although the obligation lies upon *beis din,* it is not actually *beis din* that brings this offering. Rather, the offering is brought on their behalf, as Chinuch states below, at note 20. See the Insight for discussion.

3. That is, mitzvah-prohibitions that would carry the penalty of *kares* if transgressed intentionally. Examples of such prohibitions include the consumption of *cheilev* (forbidden fat; Mitzvah 147) or blood (Mitzvah 148), as well as numerous instances of prohibited relations, such as when the woman is a *niddah* (Mitzvah 207).

# 423 ☐ VAYIKRA / MITZVAH 120: BEIS DIN TO BRING AN OFFERING FOR AN ERRONEOUS RULING

כְּבָר כָּתַבְתִּי לְמַעְלָה כִּי מִכַּוָּנוֹת הַקָּרְבָּן לְהַכְנָעַת נֶפֶשׁ הַמִּתְאַוָּה וּלְהַגְדִּיל נֶפֶשׁ הַשִּׂכְלִית, וְעַל כֵּן בְּהַגִּיעַ אֶל הַגְּדוֹלִים טָעוּת בְּדָבָר, יָדוּעַ כִּי בְּחֶלְשַׁת הַשֵּׂכֶל אֵרַע לָהֶם וּרְאוּיִים לְחַזְּקוֹ עַל כָּל פָּנִים, וְעַל כֵּן יָבוֹאוּ אֶל הַבַּיִת אֲשֶׁר שֶׁפַע הַשֵּׂכֶל עָלָיו וְיַעֲשׂוּ מַעֲשֵׂה הַקָּרְבָּן וְיָשׁוּבוּ אֶל לִבָּם בְּכֹחַ הַפְּעֻלָּה גְרִיעוּת הַנֶּפֶשׁ הַבַּהֲמִית הַטּוֹעָה וַחֲשִׁיבוּת הַשִּׂכְלִית הַמְיֻשֶּׁרֶת וְהַזַּכָּה, וּמִתּוֹךְ מַחֲשֶׁבֶת טָהֳרָה זוֹ יַשְׁגִּיחוּ וְיַשְׂכִּילוּ בְּכָל הוֹרָאוֹתָם לְעוֹלָם.

מִדִּינֵי הַמִּצְוָה, כְּגוֹן מַה שֶּׁאָמְרוּ זִכְרוֹנָם לִבְרָכָה (הוריות ד׳ ע״ב) שֶׁיֵּשׁ טָעוּת בְּהוֹרָאוֹת בֵּית דִּין, שֶׁהַבֵּית דִּין חַיָּבִין לְהָבִיא הַקָּרְבָּן וְלֹא עַל הָעוֹשֶׂה עַל פִּיהֶם,[5] וְיֵשׁ שֶׁהָעוֹשֶׂה חַיָּב וְלֹא הֵם.

---

## ☙ Underlying Purpose of the Mitzvah ❧

כְּבָר כָּתַבְתִּי לְמַעְלָה — **I have already written above** (Mitzvos 95, 102) כִּי מִכַּוָּנוֹת הַקָּרְבָּן — **that among the objectives of** bringing **an offering** לְהַכְנָעַת נֶפֶשׁ הַמִּתְאַוָּה — **is for the desirous spirit** of man **to be subdued,** וּלְהַגְדִּיל נֶפֶשׁ הַשִּׂכְלִית — **and for the intelligent spirit** of man **to be enhanced.**[4] וְעַל כֵּן בְּהַגִּיעַ אֶל הַגְּדוֹלִים טָעוּת בְּדָבָר — **Thus, when the great ones** of the generation **come to err in a matter** of halachah, יָדוּעַ כִּי בְּחֶלְשַׁת הַשֵּׂכֶל אֵרַע לָהֶם — **it is obvious that** this **occurred to them due to a weakness of the intelligent** spirit, וּרְאוּיִים לְחַזְּקוֹ עַל כָּל פָּנִים — **and it is appropriate for them to strengthen** [this spirit] **however** possible. וְעַל כֵּן יָבוֹאוּ אֶל הַבַּיִת — **They therefore are to come to the Temple,** אֲשֶׁר שֶׁפַע הַשֵּׂכֶל עָלָיו — **upon which there is the** Divine **influence of the intelligent** spirit, וְיַעֲשׂוּ מַעֲשֵׂה הַקָּרְבָּן — **and perform the procedure of the offering.** וְיָשׁוּבוּ אֶל לִבָּם בְּכֹחַ הַפְּעֻלָּה — **They will take to heart through the performance** of this act, גְרִיעוּת הַנֶּפֶשׁ הַבַּהֲמִית הַטּוֹעָה — **the lowliness of the errant beastly spirit,** וַחֲשִׁיבוּת הַשִּׂכְלִית הַמְיֻשֶּׁרֶת וְהַזַּכָּה — **and the worthiness of the intelligent** spirit, **which is straight and pure.** וּמִתּוֹךְ מַחֲשֶׁבֶת טָהֳרָה זוֹ — **Thus, as a result of this purifying thought,** יַשְׁגִּיחוּ וְיַשְׂכִּילוּ בְּכָל הוֹרָאוֹתָם לְעוֹלָם — **they will forever be vigilant and successful in all their rulings.**

## ☙ Laws of the Mitzvah ❧

מִדִּינֵי הַמִּצְוָה — **The laws of the mitzvah** include, כְּגוֹן מַה שֶּׁאָמְרוּ זִכְרוֹנָם לִבְרָכָה — **for example, that which** [the Sages], **of blessed memory, stated** (Horayos 4b), שֶׁיֵּשׁ טָעוּת בְּהוֹרָאוֹת בֵּית דִּין — **that there are** situations where there was **an error in the rulings of** beis din (which is the subject of this mitzvah), שֶׁהַבֵּית דִּין חַיָּבִין לְהָבִיא הַקָּרְבָּן — **for which** beis din **is liable to bring the** communal-error **offering,** וְלֹא עַל הָעוֹשֶׂה עַל פִּיהֶם — **while** there is **no** obligation **upon the one who acted on** the basis of **their word** and committed the transgression to bring a personal offering.[5] וְיֵשׁ שֶׁהָעוֹשֶׂה חַיָּב וְלֹא הֵם — **However, there are** other situations **where the one who acted** upon the

---

### NOTES

4. Chinuch refers to man's spiritual dimension and his physical dimension as his "intelligent spirit" and "desirous spirit," respectively. See Mitzvah 102 note 14.

The "desirous spirit" is also referred to by Chinuch (below) as the "beastly spirit," for a beast is not capable of any spiritual yearnings, and is motivated only by its physical needs and desires. This, as explained by Chinuch in Mitzvah 95, is one reason that a sinner is required to bring an offering. Sin occurs when one succumbs to desire. By offering the meat of an animal in the Beis HaMikdash, a sinner is reminded of the transient nature of his beastly spirit, and that it is only through his spirituality that man is distinguished from beast. See note 47 there.

5. Ordinarily, when an individual errs and unintentionally violates a kares-bearing prohibition, he must bring a chatas offering (sin offering — Mitzvah 121). However, when the transgression was the result of an error of beis din (and the situation warrants that an offering be brought by beis din, as per the particulars that Chinuch will proceed to detail), only beis din is obligated to bring a communal-error offering, while the individuals who sinned as a result of the erroneous ruling are not liable. [See Chinuch above, Mitzvah 78 (at notes 13-14), for an explanation of why the individual is totally absolved in a case where the sin was transgressed due to the ruling of beis din.]

## 424 ❑ ויקרא / מצוה קכ: מצות קרבן בית דין אם טעו בהוראה

וְאֵלּוּ מִן הַתְּנָאִים הַצְּרִיכִים בַּדָּבָר שֶׁיִּהְיוּ בֵּית דִּין חַיָּבִין וְלֹא הָעוֹשִׂים עַל פִּיהֶם,[6] שֶׁיִּהְיוּ הַמּוֹרִים שֶׁל שִׁבְעִים וְאֶחָד,[7] וְיִהְיֶה רֹאשׁ הַיְשִׁיבָה עִמָּהֶם בְּשָׁעָה שֶׁהוֹרוּ[8], וְיִהְיוּ כֻלָּם רְאוּיִין לְהוֹרָאָה[9], שֶׁנֶּאֱמַר (במדבר ט״ו, כ״ד) אִם מֵעֵינֵי הָעֵדָה, עַד שֶׁיִּהְיוּ לָהֶם לְעֵינַיִם, כְּלוֹמַר רְאוּיִין לְהוֹרָאָה, וְיִטְעוּ רֻבָּם בְּדָבָר זֶה שֶׁהוֹרוּ בּוֹ,[10] וְיוֹרוּ בְּפֵרוּשׁ, שֶׁיֹּאמְרוּ לָעָם מֻתָּרִין אַתֶּם לַעֲשׂוֹת,[11]

word of *beis din* **is liable** to bring a personal *chatas* offering (Mitzvah 121) **and they** (i.e., the members of *beis din*) are **not** liable to bring a communal-error offering.

וְאֵלּוּ מִן הַתְּנָאִים הַצְּרִיכִים בַּדָּבָר — **These are** some **of the conditions that must be** present **in the situation** שֶׁיִּהְיוּ בֵּית דִּין חַיָּבִין וְלֹא הָעוֹשִׂים עַל פִּיהֶם — for *beis din* **to be liable** to a communal-error bull, **and for those who committed** the transgression **on** the basis of **their word to not** be liable to personal *chatas* offerings.[6]

Chinuch begins the list of conditions by outlining a number of stipulations that apply to the composition of the *beis din*:

שֶׁיִּהְיוּ הַמּוֹרִים שֶׁל שִׁבְעִים וְאֶחָד — **It must be that those who ruled** erroneously **were** ruling as members **of** the *beis din* that contains **seventy-one** judges, i.e., the Great Sanhedrin,[7] וְיִהְיֶה רֹאשׁ הַיְשִׁיבָה עִמָּהֶם בְּשָׁעָה שֶׁהוֹרוּ — **and the Head of the Academy must have been** present **with them when they ruled** erroneously.[8] וְיִהְיוּ כֻלָּם רְאוּיִין לְהוֹרָאָה — **They must all be eligible for judgeship,**[9] שֶׁנֶּאֱמַר — **for it is stated** (Numbers 15:24): ״אִם מֵעֵינֵי הָעֵדָה״ — *If from the eyes of the assembly* it was done unintentionally, עַד שֶׁיִּהְיוּ לָהֶם לְעֵינַיִם — which implies that the obligation to bring a communal-error offering does not apply **until [the judges] are [the assembly's] "eyes,"** כְּלוֹמַר רְאוּיִין לְהוֹרָאָה — meaning **to say** that they are all **eligible for judgeship,** for the Sanhedrin can be considered the "eyes of the assembly" only if it is comprised entirely of eligible members.

Chinuch outlines various conditions pertaining to the actual ruling:

וְיִטְעוּ רֻבָּם בְּדָבָר זֶה שֶׁהוֹרוּ בּוֹ — **It must be that a majority among them** (i.e., among the members of *beis din*) **erred in the matter upon which they ruled.**[10] וְיוֹרוּ בְּפֵרוּשׁ — **It** also must be **that they ruled explicitly,** שֶׁיֹּאמְרוּ לָעָם מֻתָּרִין אַתֶּם לַעֲשׂוֹת — **by telling the people "you are permitted to perform"** the act that had been in question.[11]

---

### NOTES

6. As we shall see further in Chinuch, *all* of the conditions that follow must be present in order for *beis din* to become liable. If even one condition is not present, *beis din* is exempt, and each individual who followed their ruling is obligated to bring his own *chatas* offering.

7. This mitzvah applies only to the Great Sanhedrin, not to any other *beis din*; see Chinuch above. Additionally, the full count of 71 judges must have been present when their erroneous ruling was issued (*Horayos* 3b; *Lechem Mishneh, Hil. Shegagos* 13:1).

8. If the Head of the Academy (i.e., the most prominent sage) was not present at the time of their ruling, even if another had been installed in his place temporarily, they do not become obligated to bring this offering (*Rashi, Horayos* 4b ד״ה או שלא היה; *Lechem Mishneh* ibid.).

9. See Mitzvah 491, where Chinuch cites various factors that can disqualify one from serving on a *beis din*. If one who was ineligible had mistakenly been appointed to the *beis din*, and *beis din* then issued an erroneous ruling, they would not bring an offering for that ruling. As mentioned, in any such case, each individual who transgressed must bring a personal *chatas* offering.

10. That is, *beis din* is obligated to bring a communal-error bull even if their erroneous ruling was not the result of a unanimous decision, but was based on the view of a majority of its members. [Notwithstanding the fact that the ruling need not have been unanimous, there nevertheless may not have been any dissent *voiced* to the ruling. Accordingly, the obligation to bring a communal-error bull applies only if the minority remained silent and did not challenge the majority's decision (*Rambam, Hil. Shegagos* 13:1; see *Horayos* 3b).]

11. However, if after *beis din* arrived at its conclusion, but before they issued an explicit ruling, the conclusion became known to the public, and as a result the people transgressed the prohibition, *beis din* is not obligated to bring a communal-error offering (*Rambam* ibid.).

A logical consequence of this rule pertains to a case in which *beis din* rules that an act is not subject to *kares*, but it is nevertheless prohibited Biblically or Rabbinically, and it ultimately turned out that *beis din* was mistaken and the act is actually subject to *kares*. Even if a majority of the nation transgressed because they thought that this sin does not carry the penalty of *kares*, there is no obligation upon *beis din* to bring a communal-error offering, for the ruling that the act is not subject to *kares* certainly does not constitute "permission to perform" (see *Minchas Chinuch* §5).

# VAYIKRA / MITZVAH 120: BEIS DIN TO BRING AN OFFERING FOR AN ERRONEOUS RULING

וְיַעֲשׂוּ כָּל הַקָּהָל אוֹ רֻבָּם עַל פִּיהֶם עַל פִּיהֶם,[12] וְיִהְיוּ הָעוֹשִׂין שׁוֹגְגִין עַל פִּיהֶם וּמְדַמִּין שֶׁהַדָּבָר שֶׁהוֹרוּ בֵּית דִּין כְּדָת הוֹרוּ, וְלֹא שֶׁיָּדְעוּ אוֹתָן עוֹשִׂין שֶׁטָּעוּ וְעָשׂוּ אַף עַל פִּי כֵן.[14,15]

---

וְיַעֲשׂוּ כָּל הַקָּהָל אוֹ רֻבָּם עַל פִּיהֶם — **It must also** be that **the entire community** of the Jewish people, **or its majority, acted** and transgressed **on** the basis of **their word.**[12] וְיִהְיוּ הָעוֹשִׂין שׁוֹגְגִין עַל פִּיהֶם — It **also** must be that **those who committed** the transgression **erred due to the word of [beis din]**, and not due to their own error.[13] וּמְדַמִּין שֶׁהַדָּבָר שֶׁהוֹרוּ בֵּית דִּין כְּדָת הוֹרוּ — **Also,** it must be that **they supposed that the ruling of** *beis din* **was a correct ruling,** וְלֹא שֶׁיָּדְעוּ אוֹתָן עוֹשִׂין שֶׁטָּעוּ וְעָשׂוּ אַף עַל פִּי כֵן — **and not that those who committed** the act **knew that [the** *beis din*] **had erred but nevertheless acted** in accordance with their ruling.[14] Since, in such a case, the sin of these individuals cannot be directly attributed to the error of *beis din*, they cannot be counted among those who form a majority to impose an obligation upon *beis din*.[15]

Chinuch cites an additional condition that must be present in order for only *beis din* to be liable to bring an offering:

---

### NOTES

12. This refers to all or most of the Jews who reside in Eretz Yisrael (*Horayos* 3a). Jews who reside outside of Eretz Yisrael are not included in determining whether a majority of the Jewish people have sinned.

With regard to the requirement of bringing this offering, a majority of the nation can be formed in two ways. Certainly, if most residents of Eretz Yisrael acted in accordance with the ruling of *beis din*, then *beis din* is obligated to bring a communal-error bull. In addition, if the members of a majority of the *tribes* of Israel followed its ruling, *beis din* is obligated to bring the bull offering. This is true even if those tribes do not amount to a majority of the residents in Eretz Yisrael, such as if the members of the seven smallest tribes sinned, and their population accounted for less than half of the total population (*Rambam* ibid. 13:2). [Although for some purposes the tribe of Joseph is divided into two tribes, Ephraim and Menasseh, when determining whether a majority of tribes have sinned they are counted as a single tribe (*Rambam* ibid.).]

13. For example, *beis din* erroneously ruled that *cheilev* (forbidden fat) of the maw (stomach) is permitted. Subsequently, one mistook a portion of *cheilev* of the maw for a type of permissible fat, and ate it without realizing that it is *cheilev* of the maw. This person must bring his own *chatas* offering, since his transgression cannot be attributed to *beis din*, for he would have sinned even without the error of *beis din* (see *Mahari Korkos, Hil. Shegagos* 12:2).

14. If, among those who form the majority that have sinned, there are people who knew that *beis din* erred, but thought that they were obligated to follow even an erroneous ruling of the Sanhedrin (see next note), *beis din* does not bring the communal-error bull. In fact, even if there is a majority without these people and *beis din* is bringing the communal-error bull anyway, it does not atone for the sin of these individuals who knew that *beis din* had erred. Rather, each of them must bring his own *chatas* offering.

*Minchas Yitzchak* explains that Chinuch is referring specifically to learned people, who were aware of *beis din's* error. Since their sin was not a direct result of *beis din's* error, they cannot form the majority that imposes an obligation on *beis din* to bring an offering. One who is unlearned, however, is not excluded from the count of those who form the majority, for he may certainly follow the ruling of *beis din,* and, in fact, is required to follow *beis din's* ruling, even if in his eyes it is a mistake, as he can never be confident regarding his own opinion. Accordingly, if he committed a transgression based on the ruling of *beis din*, it must be viewed as the result of *beis din's* error, and he is counted among those who form the majority that will obligate *beis din* to bring a communal-error bull (see *Rambam* ibid. 13:5, *Minchas Chinuch* §2).

15. A basic issue must be addressed here. Normally, the halachah *requires* one to follow the ruling of the Sanhedrin even if one is certain that their ruling is erroneous (see Mitzvos 495-496; see also above Mitzvah 78). Why, then, in this case, is it considered an error to follow *beis din's* ruling when one is convinced that it is incorrect?

*Ramban* (*Sefer HaMitzvos, Shoresh* 1, p. 26 in Frankel ed.) explains that if the Sanhedrin issues a ruling, and one who is learned is of the opinion that it is incorrect, he is obligated to present his arguments to the Sanhedrin so that they may retract their ruling if they agree with him. Until he has done so, he may not act leniently on the matter. The obligation to follow the ruling of the Sanhedrin applies only once he has presented his arguments to the Sanhedrin and they were rejected. At that point, he may no longer follow his view. In the case addressed here, however, he has followed the ruling of the Sanhedrin without first presenting his arguments to them. Since he has not followed the required protocol, his error cannot be attributed to *beis din,* and he is not exempted through their offering. [For other resolutions to this difficulty, see *Chikrei Lev* (*Yoreh Deah* I §84) and *Rambam, Commentary to Mishnah, Sanhedrin* 11:2.]

וְעוֹד שֶׁיּוֹרוּ לְבַטֵּל מִקְצָת מִצְוָה וּלְקַיֵּם קְצָתָהּ, אֲבָל לֹא לַעֲקֹר כָּל מִצְוָה אַחַת[16], שֶׁנֶּאֱמַר (ויקרא ד', י"ג), וְנֶעְלַם דָּבָר, וְלֹא כָּל הַגּוּף[17], וְזֶהוּ גְּזֵרַת הַכָּתוּב. וְאֶפְשָׁר כִּי טַעַם הָעִנְיָן שֶׁשִּׁגְגַת עֲקִירַת כָּל גּוּף הַמִּצְוָה אֵין לָחוּשׁ שֶׁלֹּא תִתְגַּלֶּה בִּמְהֵרָה[18].

וּכְשֶׁיִּוָּדַע לָהֶם הַחַטָּאת, שֶׁיֵּדְעוּ גּוּפוֹ שֶׁל דָּבָר שֶׁהוֹרוּ בּוֹ בִּשְׁגָגָה וְלֹא שֶׁיִּסְתַּפְּקוּ עַל אֵי זֶה דָּבָר אֵרְעָה לָהֶם הַשְּׁגָגָה, וְאַף עַל פִּי שֶׁיֵּדְעוּ כִּי בְּוַדַּאי שָׁגְגוּ בְּאַחַת[19], וְאַף שֶׁהוֹדִיעוּם הַחוֹטְאִים וְאָמְרוּ לָהֶם בָּזוֹ שְׁגַגְתֶּם, כֵּיוָן שֶׁהֵם אֵינָם זוֹכְרִים אוֹתוֹ דָבָר בְּכֵיוָן פְּטוּרִין, שֶׁנֶּאֱמַר (שם, שם י"ד) וְנוֹדְעָה הַחַטָּאת, כְּלוֹמַר לָהֶם וְלֹא שֶׁיּוֹדִיעוּם אֲחֵרִים.

---

**וְעוֹד** — It must **also** be **שֶׁיּוֹרוּ לְבַטֵּל מִקְצָת מִצְוָה וּלְקַיֵּם קְצָתָהּ** — **that they ruled** in a manner **that would negate some of** the laws of **a mitzvah and would uphold some of its** laws, **אֲבָל לֹא לַעֲקֹר כָּל מִצְוָה אַחַת** — **but not** in a manner that would **uproot any single mitzvah entirely;**[16] **שֶׁנֶּאֱמַר** — **for it is stated** (Leviticus 4:13): "וְנֶעְלַם דָּבָר" — **and a matter shall become obscured, וְלֹא כָּל הַגּוּף** — which implies that only some aspect of a mitzvah was the subject of error, **not the entire body** of a mitzvah.[17] **וְזֶהוּ גְּזֵרַת הַכָּתוּב** — **This** condition **is a Scriptural decree,** with no reason offered. **וְאֶפְשָׁר כִּי טַעַם הָעִנְיָן** — **But perhaps the reason behind the matter is שֶׁשִּׁגְגַת עֲקִירַת כָּל גּוּף הַמִּצְוָה** — **that** with regard to **an error** by the Sanhedrin **that uproots the entire body of a mitzvah, אֵין לָחוּשׁ שֶׁלֹּא תִתְגַּלֶּה בִּמְהֵרָה** — **there is no** basis for a **concern that it would not be discovered quickly** and that it actually would lead the community to transgress.[18]

Chinuch presents a final condition that must be present in order for *beis din* to be liable to this offering:

**וּכְשֶׁיִּוָּדַע לָהֶם הַחַטָּאת** — **When the transgression becomes known to [*beis din*], שֶׁיֵּדְעוּ גּוּפוֹ שֶׁל דָּבָר שֶׁהוֹרוּ בּוֹ בִּשְׁגָגָה** — it is necessary **that they become aware of the specific matter** (i.e., prohibition) **about which they had ruled in error, וְלֹא שֶׁיִּסְתַּפְּקוּ עַל אֵי זֶה דָּבָר אֵרְעָה לָהֶם הַשְּׁגָגָה** — **and not that they be in doubt regarding in which matter the error occurred to them, וְאַף עַל פִּי שֶׁיֵּדְעוּ כִּי בְּוַדַּאי שָׁגְגוּ בְּאַחַת** — **even though they know that they certainly erred regarding one** of the prohibitions.[19] **וְאַף שֶׁהוֹדִיעוּם הַחוֹטְאִים** — **And even if those who transgressed notified them, וְאָמְרוּ לָהֶם בָּזוֹ שְׁגַגְתֶּם** — **and told them, "You erred regarding this** prohibition," **כֵּיוָן שֶׁהֵם אֵינָם זוֹכְרִים אוֹתוֹ דָבָר בְּכֵיוָן** — **since [the members of *beis din*]** themselves **do not recall the exact issue, פְּטוּרִין** — **they are absolved** from bringing an offering for an erroneous ruling, **שֶׁנֶּאֱמַר** — **as it is stated** (Leviticus 4:14): "וְנוֹדְעָה הַחַטָּאת" — **when the sin becomes known** etc., *the congregation shall offer a young bull.* **כְּלוֹמַר** — **That is to say,** the indication of the term *becomes known* is **לָהֶם** — that *beis din* incurs liability to bring an offering only when it becomes known **to them** on their own, **וְלֹא שֶׁיּוֹדִיעוּם אֲחֵרִים** — **but not when it is made known to them by others.**

---

NOTES

16. For example, if *beis din* had erroneously ruled that it is *entirely* permitted to bow down to idols, they would not become obligated to bring an offering for an erroneous ruling. If, however, they ruled only that it is permitted to kneel before an idol, while conceding that totally prostrating oneself before the idol is prohibited (see Mitzvah 28, with note 7 and Insight there), they would be obligated in this offering (*Rambam, Hil. Shegagos* 14:2).

17. This exegesis is explained in *Horayos* 4a.

18. If the ruling of *beis din* would uproot the entire corpus of a mitzvah, the error would likely be discovered before a majority of the nation had sinned. [The Torah therefore did not impose a liability upon *beis din* to bring an offering in the event of this type of error, even if it indeed occurred that a majority of the nation transgressed.]

19. For example, *beis din* issued an erroneous ruling regarding *cheilev* (forbidden fat), and subsequently, the majority of the nation transgressed *both* the prohibition of *cheilev* and the prohibition of consuming blood. When the national transgressions became known, *beis din* could not recall whether their error was in the matter of *cheilev* or in the matter of blood. In this case, although they certainly did err in a manner that led to a public transgression, since they do not recall the exact nature of their error, they do not bring a communal-error bull (see *Horayos* 5a with *Rashi* ד"ה ידעו שהורו, and *Rambam* ibid. 14:4 with *Mahari Korkos*).

## 427 ◻ VAYIKRA / MITZVAH 120: BEIS DIN TO BRING AN OFFERING FOR AN ERRONEOUS RULING

כָּל אֵלֶּה הַתְּנָאִים צְרִיכִין לִהְיוֹת בַּדָּבָר שֶׁיִּתְחַיְּבוּ הַבֵּית דִּין בְּקָרְבָּן וְלֹא הָעוֹשִׂים עַל פִּיהֶם. וְאָמְרִי שֶׁיִּתְחַיְּבוּ הַבֵּית דִּין קָרְבָּן, רוֹצֶה לוֹמַר שֶׁיָּבִיאוּ קָרְבָּן שִׁבְטֵי יִשְׂרָאֵל כְּנֶגְדָּם, כְּמוֹ שֶׁמְּבֹאָר בְּהוֹרָיוֹת (ה׳ ע״ב)[20], וְאִם בְּהוֹרָאַת עֲבוֹדָה זָרָה שָׁגְגוּ, מְבִיאִים שְׁנֵים עָשָׂר שְׁבָטִים שְׁנֵים עָשָׂר פָּרִים לְעוֹלָה וּשְׁנֵים עָשָׂר שְׂעִירִים לְחַטָּאת, וְאִם בְּהוֹרָאַת שְׁאָר כְּרֵתוֹת שֶׁחַיָּבִים עַל שִׁגְגָתָם חַטָּאת, מְבִיאִים שְׁנֵים עָשָׂר פָּרִים.[21]

וְאִם חָסֵר אַחַת, הָעוֹשֶׂה עַל פִּיהֶם חַיָּב חַטָּאת קְבוּעָה,[22] וְהֵן פְּטוּרִין, שֶׁלֹּא חִיְּבָה הַתּוֹרָה בֵּית דִּין בְּקָרְבָּן זֶה אֶלָּא כְּשֶׁהֵם בִּשְׁלֵמוּתָם,[23] לְפִי שֶׁיֵּשׁ בָּזֶה הוֹרָאָה לְחַטֵּאת כָּל הָעָם

---

כָּל אֵלֶּה הַתְּנָאִים צְרִיכִין לִהְיוֹת בַּדָּבָר — **All these conditions must be** present **in the situation,** שֶׁיִּתְחַיְּבוּ הַבֵּית דִּין בְּקָרְבָּן — **in order for beis din to become liable to** bring **an offering** for the communal transgression וְלֹא הָעוֹשִׂים עַל פִּיהֶם — **and** for **those who acted on** the basis of **their word** and transgressed to **not be liable.** If any of the conditions are missing, beis din is not liable, but rather, each person who transgressed is liable to bring a personal chatas offering.

Chinuch details who is required to bring the communal-error offering:

וְאָמְרִי שֶׁיִּתְחַיְּבוּ הַבֵּית דִּין קָרְבָּן — **My statement that "beis din becomes liable to** bring **an offering"** רוֹצֶה לוֹמַר — **means to say** שֶׁיָּבִיאוּ קָרְבָּן שִׁבְטֵי יִשְׂרָאֵל כְּנֶגְדָּם — **that** each of **the tribes of Israel must bring an offering on their behalf,** not that the members of beis din themselves bring this offering, כְּמוֹ שֶׁמְּבֹאָר בְּהוֹרָיוֹת — **as is set forth in** Tractate *Horayos* (5b).[20]

Chinuch now addresses the actual offering, and the difference in this regard between the sin of idolatry and other sins:

וְאִם בְּהוֹרָאַת עֲבוֹדָה זָרָה שָׁגְגוּ — **If they erred in a ruling regarding idolatry,** מְבִיאִים שְׁנֵים עָשָׂר שְׁבָטִים — **the twelve tribes** of Israel must bring שְׁנֵים עָשָׂר פָּרִים לְעוֹלָה — a total of **twelve bulls as olah offerings** וּשְׁנֵים עָשָׂר שְׂעִירִים לְחַטָּאת — **and twelve goats as chatas offerings.** וְאִם בְּהוֹרָאַת שְׁאָר כְּרֵתוֹת שֶׁחַיָּבִים עַל שִׁגְגָתָם חַטָּאת — **And if** they erred **in a ruling regarding other** prohibitions that bear liability of **kares, for which there is** ordinarily **an obligation upon** an individual **who erred in** any of **them to bring a chatas offering,** מְבִיאִים שְׁנֵים עָשָׂר פָּרִים — **they must bring** a total of **twelve bulls** as chatas offerings, but no goats.[21]

וְאִם חָסֵר אַחַת — **But if** even **one** of the aforementioned conditions was missing, הָעוֹשֶׂה עַל פִּיהֶם — חַיָּב חַטָּאת קְבוּעָה — **then each person who committed** the transgression **on the basis of [the beis din's] word is liable to** bring **a fixed chatas offering,**[22] וְהֵן פְּטוּרִין — **and they** (the beis din) **are absolved** from bringing a communal-error bull, שֶׁלֹּא חִיְּבָה הַתּוֹרָה בֵּית דִּין בְּקָרְבָּן זֶה אֶלָּא — כְּשֶׁהֵם בִּשְׁלֵמוּתָם — **for the Torah obligated beis din** to bring **this offering only when [beis din] is "whole."**[23] לְפִי שֶׁיֵּשׁ בָּזֶה הוֹרָאָה לְחַטֵּאת כָּל הָעָם — **And the reason for this qualification is because**

---

### NOTES

20. Each of the twelve tribes must bring a bull to atone for the communal transgression. See Insight for further discussion.

21. There are two passages in the Torah regarding the obligation to bring an offering when the error of beis din led to widespread transgression. In one (*Numbers* 15:24), the Torah requires a bull as an olah offering and a goat as a chatas offering [for each tribe]; in the other, only a bull is required [for each tribe], as a chatas offering (*Leviticus* 4:13 ff.). The Gemara explains (*Horayos* 8a) that when the erroneous ruling pertained to idolatry, both olah and chatas offerings are required. Where the error of beis din pertained to one of the other prohibitions that bear the penalty of kares, only a bull is brought as a chatas offering.

As noted above (note 12), the obligation to bring a communal-error bull applies if the members of a majority of the tribes of Israel followed the ruling of beis din, even if the other tribes have not sinned (and even if the tribes that have sinned do not comprise a majority of the Jews residing in Eretz Yisrael). Nevertheless, in all cases, *all* the tribes — even those that have not sinned — are obligated to bring these offerings (*Rambam* ibid. 12:1, 13:2; see *Horayos* 4b-5a).

22. This refers to the standard chatas offering, outlined in Mitzvah 121. [See there for why it is called a "fixed" chatas offering.]

23. When all the conditions detailed above are present (e.g., there are seventy-one members who are all eligible and the Head of the Academy is present), beis din is considered "whole."

שֶׁיִּשְׁגּוּ רָאשֵׁיהֶם וְהֵם בִּשְׁלֵמוּתָם.[24]

וְיֶתֶר רֻבֵּי הַצְּדָדִין שֶׁהַיָּחִיד חַיָּב וְהֵם פְּטוּרִין, אוֹ הֵם חַיָּבִין וְהוּא פָּטוּר, וְחִלּוּק הַקָּרְבָּנוֹת שֶׁבֵּינֵיהֶם, כְּגוֹן מַה שֶּׁאָמְרוּ זִכְרוֹנָם לִבְרָכָה (שם ט' ע"א) כָּל הַמִּצְוֹת שֶׁבַּתּוֹרָה שֶׁחַיָּבִין עַל זְדוֹנָן כָּרֵת וְעַל שִׁגְגָתָן חַטָּאת, הַיָּחִיד מֵבִיא כִּשְׂבָּה אוֹ שְׂעִירָה,[25] וְהַנָּשִׂיא[26] שָׂעִיר, וְכֹהֵן מָשִׁיחַ וּבֵית דִּין מְבִיאִין פַּר, וְהוּא הַכֹּהֵן הַגָּדוֹל שֶׁנִּמְשַׁח בְּשֶׁמֶן הַמִּשְׁחָה.[27] וְיֶתֶר פְּרָטֶיהָ, מְבֹאָרִין בְּמַסֶּכֶת הוֹרָיוֹת, וּבִמְקוֹמוֹת מִזְבָּחִים.[28]

---

the only time **there is an indication that** the transgression by the majority of the Jewish people is truly **a "national transgression,"** and not merely a transgression by a large number of individuals, is שֶׁיִּשְׁגּוּ רָאשֵׁיהֶם וְהֵם בִּשְׁלֵמוּתָם — **when their leaders err while they are "whole."**[24]

Chinuch concludes the laws of the mitzvah:

וְיֶתֶר רֻבֵּי הַצְּדָדִין — There are **many additional possibilities** of situations שֶׁהַיָּחִיד חַיָּב וְהֵם פְּטוּרִין — in **which** each **individual** who transgressed **is liable** to bring a *chatas* offering **and they** (i.e., *beis din*) **are absolved** of liability, אוֹ הֵם חַיָּבִין וְהוּא פָּטוּר — **or** where **they are liable** to bring an offering **and [each individual] is absolved** of liability; וְחִלּוּק הַקָּרְבָּנוֹת שֶׁבֵּינֵיהֶם — there **also** are **variations between their** different *chatas* **offerings**, i.e., that of an individual as opposed to that of the *beis din*, כְּגוֹן מַה שֶּׁאָמְרוּ זִכְרוֹנָם לִבְרָכָה — **such as that which [the Sages], of blessed memory, said** (*Horayos* 9a): כָּל הַמִּצְוֹת שֶׁבַּתּוֹרָה — **Regarding all mitzvos of the Torah** שֶׁחַיָּבִין וְעַל זְדוֹנָן כָּרֵת — **for which there is a liability of *kares*** when transgressed **deliberately** שִׁגְגָתָן חַטָּאת — **and** an obligation to bring **a *chatas* offering** when transgressed **in error,** הַיָּחִיד מֵבִיא כִּשְׂבָּה אוֹ שְׂעִירָה — if **an individual** transgressed, he **brings** either **a female sheep or a she-goat;**[25] וְהַנָּשִׂיא שָׂעִיר — if **the *Nasi*[26]** transgressed, he brings **a he-goat;** וְכֹהֵן מָשִׁיחַ וּבֵית דִּין מְבִיאִין פַּר — **and the anointed Kohen or *beis din* brings a bull.** וְהוּא הַכֹּהֵן הַגָּדוֹל שֶׁנִּמְשַׁח בְּשֶׁמֶן הַמִּשְׁחָה — **[The "anointed Kohen"] is the Kohen Gadol who was elevated** to his position by being **anointed with the anointment oil** (Mitzvah 108).[27] וְיֶתֶר פְּרָטֶיהָ — **All these laws, and the additional details of [this mitzvah],** מְבֹאָרִין בְּמַסֶּכֶת הוֹרָיוֹת — **are set forth in Tractate *Horayos*** וּבִמְקוֹמוֹת מִזְבָּחִים — **and in places in** Tractate *Zevachim* (Chs. 4-5).[28]

---

### NOTES

24. When the highest Sanhedrin, which is the "eyes of the assembly," errs in a manner that leads to widespread sin, it is an indication of an underlying spiritual weakness of the nation. Chinuch explains that it is apparent that the error was due to a general weakness of the nation only when the Sanhedrin is functioning at its optimal level, with all members and the Head of the Academy present, and they nevertheless erred with no dissent voiced.

25. The *chatas* obligation on an individual who sinned is set forth in the next mitzvah.

26. Here, *Nasi* (literally, *prince*) refers to the one who holds the highest position of power in the kingdom, i.e., the king (see *Rambam* ibid. 15:6). [As set forth in *Leviticus* 4:1-35 and *Numbers* 15:22-31, there are distinct specifications that apply to the *chatas* offerings of the individual, the Kohen Gadol (see further in Chinuch), the *Nasi*, and *beis din*, which also depend on the exact sin that had been transgressed.]

27. As we have seen in Mitzvah 107, the Torah mandates that a Kohen Gadol be anointed with the unique anointing oil (שֶׁמֶן הַמִּשְׁחָה). This oil was available during the First Temple Era, but not during the Second Temple Era. In the latter era, the Kohen Gadol was installed by "the addition of clothing" — i.e., donning the eight articles of clothing worn by the Kohen Gadol, rather than the four worn by other Kohanim (see Mitzvah 107 note 2). The special *chatas* offering of a Kohen Gadol was brought only by one who was anointed. A Kohen Gadol installed by "the addition of clothing" brought the same offering as a common individual (*Rambam* ibid. 15:6; see *Leviticus* 4:3).

[The requirement for the anointed Kohen to bring a bull for having transgressed a prohibition is not considered a separate mitzvah in the count of the 613 mitzvos. *Minchas Chinuch* (§18) asserts that this requirement is included in our mitzvah, the mitzvah of the bull-offering brought by a *beis din* that erred. R' Y. F. Perla, however, in his glosses to *Minchas Chinuch*, citing *Rambam*, *Sefer HaMitzvos*, *Shoresh* 7, writes that the requirement of the Kohen Gadol to bring a bull is included in Mitzvah 121, the mitzvah of an individual to bring a *chatas* for his transgression.]

28. The laws of this mitzvah are codified in *Rambam*, *Hil. Shegagos*, Chs. 12-14.

## וְנוֹהֶגֶת בִּזְמַן הַבַּיִת שֶׁיֵּשׁ לָנוּ סַנְהֶדְרֵי גְדוֹלָה.

### ⌒ Applicability of the Mitzvah ⌐

**שֶׁיֵּשׁ לָנוּ סַנְהֶדְרֵי גְדוֹלָה — וְנוֹהֶגֶת בִּזְמַן הַבַּיִת** — This mitzvah applies in the time of the Temple when we have the Great Sanhedrin.

---

**❧§ Insight: The Offering for an Erroneous Ruling — Whose Responsibility?**

The פַּר הֶעְלֵם דָּבָר שֶׁל צִבּוּר, *bull for a communal error*, has the distinction of being one of two communal offerings that require *semichah* (leaning), which calls for the owner of the offering to place his hands on its head and lean on it with all of his weight. [The other offering is the he-goat dispatched to *Azazel* as part of the Yom Kippur service.] This procedure is otherwise reserved for private offerings (Mishnah, *Menachos* 92a; *Rambam, Hil. Maaseh HaKorbanos* 3:10).

Since *semichah* is normally performed by the owner of the offering, who performs *semichah* on this bull? Who is considered its "owner"? *Bavli* (*Sanhedrin* 13b) expounds a verse (*Leviticus* 4:15) as teaching that *semichah* is performed by three members of the Great Sanhedrin, and this is the ruling set forth by *Rambam* (ibid.). It is noteworthy, however, that the offering is actually not brought by the judges of the Sanhedrin themselves. Rather, as Chinuch states (at note 20), when the majority of the community transgresses as a result of an error by the Great Sanhedrin, each of the twelve tribes of Israel must bring a *chatas* bull. [The Mishnah (*Horayos* 4b-5a) cites a dissenting view that assigns responsibility to the Great Sanhedrin, but the halachah follows the view that each tribe is liable (see *Rambam, Hil. Shegagos* 12:1 with *Kesef Mishneh*).] *Yerushalmi* (*Horayos* 1:8) asserts that, according to this view, three people from each tribe — not three members of the Sanhedrin — perform *semichah* on the individual bull of that tribe. R' Yechezkel Abramsky (*Chazon Yechezkel, Menachos* 10:3) identifies the fundamental point of contention between *Bavli* and *Yerushalmi* as follows: *Yerushalmi* maintains that the *chatas* offering is a חוֹבַת צִבּוּר, *a public obligation*, brought to atone for the community's collective inadvertent transgression. Hence, the tribes are the "owners" of the offerings, and it is they who perform *semichah*, each through three representatives. *Bavli*, on the other hand, maintains that it is the members of the Sanhedrin who are liable to bring this *chatas* offering, to atone for their erroneous ruling. They fulfill their obligation and achieve atonement by having each of the twelve tribes brings one bull on *their* behalf. Accordingly, the Sanhedrin alone is considered the "owner" of the offerings, and its members perform *semichah* (cf. *Mikdash David, Kodashim* 23:5).

*Bavli's* view concerning the *semichah* procedure is reflected in Chinuch's statement (at note 2) that this mitzvah is incumbent upon the Great Sanhedrin. The fact that representatives of the Sanhedrin, rather than the representatives of the people, perform *semichah* demonstrates that it is the Sanhedrin's liability to bring this *chatas* offering, to atone for its erroneous ruling. Nevertheless, the Sanhedrin fulfills its obligation through having each of the twelve tribes bring a bull offering on its behalf (*Chazon Yechezkel* ibid.; *Simchas HaChag* §1, based on *Kesef Mishneh's* understanding of *Rambam, Hil. Shegagos* 12:1; see also *Minchas Chinuch* §12 and *Tos. Yom Tov, Horayos* 2:2 ד"ה שאין ב״ד).

The fundamental question of whether this offering is a *public obligation* or a *court obligation* relates to another aspect concerning the offering: Are all twelve bulls (brought by the twelve tribes) essential for the effectiveness of the offering? That is, if, for some reason, one of the tribes does not bring the offering [even though it is required to do so], do the other tribes nevertheless fulfill *their* obligation by bringing their offerings? According to the view that the offering is a *public obligation*, with each tribe obligated to bring its own offering, it would seem that each bull — and the atonement it effects — is independent of the others. Thus, any tribe that brings the offering achieves atonement, even though other tribes did not bring an offering. But, according to the view that the offering is a *court obligation*, it stands to reason that the court's offering consists of a total of twelve bulls, and while each of the bulls is brought by a separate tribe, no atonement is achieved unless all twelve are brought. Moreover, since all twelve offerings are required in order to effect atonement, it would follow that no tribe can initially bring an offering unless the other eleven tribes also are bringing their offerings. For discussion, see *Sifrei* to *Numbers* 15:25, with *Sifra DeVei Rav*; *Minchas Chinuch* §11-12; *R' Y. F. Perla*, in his glosses to *Minchas Chinuch* loc. cit. and to *Sefer HaMitzvos* of Rav Saadiah Gaon, *Asei* 136-137 [Vol. I, pp. 766-768].

## מִצְוָה קכא:
## מִצְוַת קָרְבַּן חַטָּאת לְיָחִיד שֶׁשָּׁגַג
## בְּמִצְוֹת לֹא תַעֲשֶׂה שֶׁחַיָּבִין עָלֶיהָ כָּרֵת[1]

שֶׁיַּקְרִיב כָּל שׁוֹגֵג בְּחֵטְא[2] מֵהַחֲטָאִים הַגְּדוֹלִים הַיְדוּעִים קָרְבַּן חַטָּאת,[3]

# Mitzvah 121

## The Obligation Upon an Individual Who Inadvertently Committed a Kares-Bearing Prohibition to Bring a Chatas Offering

וְאִם נֶפֶשׁ אַחַת תֶּחֱטָא בִשְׁגָגָה מֵעַם הָאָרֶץ בַּעֲשׂתָהּ אַחַת מִמִּצְוֹת ה' אֲשֶׁר לֹא תֵעָשֶׂינָה וְאָשֵׁם. אוֹ הוֹדַע אֵלָיו חַטָּאתוֹ אֲשֶׁר חָטָא וְהֵבִיא קָרְבָּנוֹ שְׂעִירַת עִזִּים תְּמִימָה נְקֵבָה עַל חַטָּאתוֹ אֲשֶׁר חָטָא.

*If an individual person from among the people of the land shall sin inadvertently, by committing one of the commandments of HASHEM that may not be done, and he becomes guilty. If his sin that he committed becomes known to him, he shall bring as his offering a she-goat, unblemished, for the sin that he committed* (Leviticus 4:27-28).

וְאִם כֶּבֶשׂ יָבִיא קָרְבָּנוֹ לְחַטָּאת נְקֵבָה תְמִימָה יְבִיאֶנָּה.

*If he shall bring a sheep as his offering for a chatas offering, he shall bring a female, unblemished* (ibid. v. 32).

This mitzvah addresses the *chatas* (sin) offering brought by an *individual* who sinned inadvertently, in contrast to the previous mitzvah, which dealt with the offering for a communal sin. The cited verses deal with the *chatas* offering brought by a common person. Other verses (*Leviticus* 4:1-12; 22-26) deal with the *chatas* offering of a Kohen Gadol and a *Nasi* (king). While there are distinct specifications that apply to the various *chatas* offerings — a commoner brings a female sheep or goat, the Kohen Gadol brings a bull, and the *Nasi* brings a male goat (Chinuch, Mitzvah 120, at note 26) — they are all included in our mitzvah, the mitzvah of the *chatas* offerings brought by an *individual* who sinned inadvertently.[1] שֶׁיַּקְרִיב כָּל שׁוֹגֵג בְּחֵטְא מֵהַחֲטָאִים הַגְּדוֹלִים הַיְדוּעִים קָרְבַּן חַטָּאת — We are commanded **that anyone who sins inadvertently**[2] **by committing one of the grave, known sins must bring a *chatas* offering,**[3]

---

NOTES

1. In other words, all types of personal *chatas* offerings are included in this mitzvah (see *Rambam, Sefer Ha-Mitzvos, Shoresh* 7, and above, Mitzvah 120 note 27). [Interestingly, R' Saadiah Gaon (*Asei* 140,141,143) counts each individual *chatas* offering as a separate mitzvah.]

2. An "inadvertent" transgressor is one who performs the sinful act with intent, but is under the impression that the act is permitted, or that it is not punishable by *kares* (excision); e.g., he intentionally picks figs on the Sabbath in the belief that picking fruit is permitted on the Sabbath or not punishable by *kares*, or, alternatively, he knows that picking fruit is forbidden, but is under the impression that the day is not the Sabbath. In either case, he is liable to a *chatas* offering (*Rambam, Hil. Shegagos* 2:2, with *Mishneh LaMelech*).

On the other hand, one who had no intention to perform the sinful act at all, but was actually intending to perform another act, is not liable to a *chatas*. [This is known as a מִתְעַסֵּק (*misaseik*), *preoccupied transgressor*, rather than a שׁוֹגֵג (*shogeig*), *inadvertent transgressor*.] Thus, for example, one who intended to take a fig that he thought to be detached, but afterward discovered that it was actually an attached fig that he pulled off the tree, is not liable to a *chatas* (*Kereisos* 19a-b, with *Tosafos* 19b ד"ה דהא).

3. Below (at note 13), Chinuch notes that there are forty-three sins for which one incurs *chatas* liability. He refers to these as "grave" sins, because all of them carry the penalty of *kares* if committed intentionally.

## 431 ◻ VAYIKRA / MITZVAH 121: THE OBLIGATION TO BRING A CHATAS OFFERING

שֶׁנֶּאֱמַר (ויקרא ד׳, כ״ז) "וְאִם נֶפֶשׁ אַחַת תֶּחֱטָא בִשְׁגָגָה מֵעַם הָאָרֶץ וְגו׳. וְזֹאת הִיא הַנִּקְרֵאת חַטָּאת קְבוּעָה, כְּלוֹמַר שֶׁהִיא לְעוֹלָם קָרְבָּן בִּבְהֵמָה וְלֹא יַעֲלֶה וְיֵרֵד לְפִי עֹשֶׁר הַמַּקְרִיב וְעָנְיוֹ.[4] וְהַחֲטָאִים שֶׁיִּתְחַיְּבוּ עֲלֵיהֶם חַטָּאת הֵם לְעוֹלָם אוֹתָן שֶׁחַיָּבִין עַל זְדוֹנָן כָּרֵת,[5] וּבִתְנַאי שֶׁתִּהְיֶה מִצְוַת לֹא תַעֲשֶׂה[6] וְיִהְיֶה בָּהּ מַעֲשֶׂה.[7]

כְּבָר אָמַרְנוּ כִּי מִשָּׁרְשֵׁי הַקָּרְבָּן לְהַשְׁפִּיל הַנֶּפֶשׁ הַחוֹטֵאת[8], כַּחַטָּאת כָּאָשָׁם תּוֹרָה אַחַת לָהֶם[9], אֵינֶנִּי צָרִיךְ לְהַחֲזִירוֹ עַל כָּל אֶחָד וְאֶחָד.

---

שֶׁנֶּאֱמַר — **as it is stated** (*Leviticus* 4:27): "וְאִם נֶפֶשׁ אַחַת תֶּחֱטָא בִשְׁגָגָה מֵעַם הָאָרֶץ וְגו׳" — **If an individual person from among the people of the land shall sin unintentionally** ... *he shall bring as his offering, etc.* וְזֹאת הִיא הַנִּקְרֵאת חַטָּאת קְבוּעָה — **This [offering] is the one that is called a "fixed"** *chatas* **offering.** כְּלוֹמַר שֶׁהִיא לְעוֹלָם קָרְבָּן בִּבְהֵמָה — **That is to say, it is always an animal offering,** וְלֹא יַעֲלֶה וְיֵרֵד לְפִי עֹשֶׁר הַמַּקְרִיב וְעָנְיוֹ — **and does not vary** (literally, *rise and fall*), **according to the wealth or poverty of the one who offers it.**[4]

Chinuch now describes the category of sins for which a person brings a fixed *chatas* offering:

וְהַחֲטָאִים שֶׁיִּתְחַיְּבוּ עֲלֵיהֶם חַטָּאת — **The sins for which one is liable on their account to bring a** *chatas* **offering** הֵם לְעוֹלָם אוֹתָן שֶׁחַיָּבִין עַל זְדוֹנָן כָּרֵת — **are always those** very sins **for whose intentional commission one incurs** *kares* **(excision),**[5] וּבִתְנַאי שֶׁתִּהְיֶה מִצְוַת לֹא תַעֲשֶׂה — **provided that it is a mitzvah-prohibition** that is transgressed,[6] וְיִהְיֶה בָּהּ מַעֲשֶׂה — **and that [the violation] involves a** physical **action.**[7]

### ⸺ Underlying Purpose of the Mitzvah ⸺

כְּבָר אָמַרְנוּ — **We have already stated** (in Mitzvos 95 and 120) כִּי מִשָּׁרְשֵׁי הַקָּרְבָּן לְהַשְׁפִּיל הַנֶּפֶשׁ הַחוֹטֵאת — **that among the underlying purposes of** bringing **an offering is for the** desirous **spirit of the sinner to be subdued.**[8] כַּחַטָּאת כָּאָשָׁם תּוֹרָה אַחַת לָהֶם — **This reasoning is true for all** offerings, for "**like the** *chatas* **offering is the** *asham* (guilt) **offering; there is one law for them.**"[9] אֵינֶנִּי צָרִיךְ לְהַחֲזִירוֹ עַל כָּל אֶחָד וְאֶחָד — I, thus, **need not repeat [this reason]** in its entirety **for each and every one** of the offerings.

---

### NOTES

And they are "known," because the *kares*-bearing prohibitions are all mentioned explicitly in the Torah and listed in the Mishnah, *Kereisos* 2a.

4. Mitzvah 123 discusses the קָרְבָּן עוֹלֶה וְיוֹרֵד, *variable [chatas] offering*, i.e., the *chatas* offering brought for certain transgressions that is adjusted in accord with the financial circumstances of the violator. In contrast to the "variable" *chatas*, the *chatas* addressed here is called a "fixed" *chatas*, because the offering is the same, regardless of the violator's financial status. [See *Minchas Chinuch* §16 for whether the animal brought as a "fixed" *chatas* must have a minimal value.]

5. Mishnah, *Kereisos* 2a; Rambam, *Sefer HaMitzvos*, Asei 69, and *Hil. Shegagos* 1:1.

6. All 43 cases of *chatas* liability involve the transgression of mitzvah-prohibitions that carry the *kares* penalty when violated intentionally. There are, additionally, two mitzvah-obligations whose intentional violation carries the penalty of *kares*. The unintentional transgression of these mitzvah-obligations does *not* carry *chatas* liability (Mishnah ibid. and Gemara there, 3a; see also *Makkos* 13b). These mitzvah-obligations are described by Chinuch below. See note 10.

7. With respect to the requirement of bringing a *chatas* offering, the Torah uses the phrase (*Numbers* 15:29): תּוֹרָה אַחַת יִהְיֶה לָכֶם לָעֹשֶׂה בִּשְׁגָגָה, *There shall be a single teaching for one who "acts" inadvertently*, indicating that the liability to bring a *chatas* offering is only for one who sins by performing an action (*Kereisos* 2a, 3a; Rambam ibid.). [*Kares*, however, can be incurred even for a violation that does not involve physical action (see *Kereisos* ibid.).]

8. This, as explained by Chinuch in Mitzvah 95, is one purpose of bringing an offering. Through offering an animal, one will take to heart his animalistic tendencies and internalize the importance of elevating his spirituality over his physicality, so that he not continue to stumble in sin.

9. Stylistic citation of *Leviticus* 7:7. The point is that the suggested underlying purpose for offerings applies to *all* offerings.

**432** □ ויקרא / מצוה קכא: קרבן חטאת ליחיד ששגג במצות לא תעשה שחיבין עליה כרת

מִדִּינֵי הַמִּצְוָה, כְּגוֹן מַה שֶׁאָמְרוּ זִכְרוֹנָם לִבְרָכָה (הוריות ט׳ ע״א) שֶׁאֵין חִיּוּב הַשּׁוֹגֵג לְהָבִיא חַטָּאת אֶלָּא עַל עֲבֵרָה שֶׁחַיָּבִין עַל זְדוֹנָהּ כָּרֵת. וְיֵשׁ בַּתּוֹרָה שְׁלֹשָׁה חֲטָאִים שֶׁאַף עַל פִּי שֶׁיֵּשׁ בִּזְדוֹנָן כָּרֵת אֵין בְּשִׁגְגָתָן חַטָּאת, וְאֵלוּ הֵן, מְגַדֵּף וּמְבַטֵּל מִילָה וְחָדַל מֵעֲשׂוֹת הַפֶּסַח, וְנָתְנוּ טַעַם בְּכָל אֶחָד, וּמְפֹרָשׁ בִּמְקוֹמוֹ[10]. כָּל שְׁאָר הָעֲבֵרוֹת שֶׁזְּדוֹנָן כָּרֵת, שִׁגְגָתָן חַטָּאת קְבוּעָה, חוּץ מִטָּמֵא שֶׁאָכַל אֶת הַקֹּדֶשׁ, וְטָמֵא שֶׁנִּכְנַס לַמִּקְדָּשׁ, שֶׁאַף עַל פִּי שֶׁזְּדוֹנָן כָּרֵת[11] אֵין מְבִיאִין חַטָּאת קְבוּעָה אֶלָּא קָרְבָּן עוֹלֶה וְיוֹרֵד, שֶׁהוּא עוֹף אוֹ קֶמַח, כְּמוֹ שֶׁמְּפֹרָשׁ בַּכָּתוּב (ויקרא ה׳, ו׳-י״ג)[12].

---

### ⁃ Laws of the Mitzvah ⁃

מִדִּינֵי הַמִּצְוָה — **Among the laws of the mitzvah is,** כְּגוֹן מַה שֶׁאָמְרוּ זִכְרוֹנָם לִבְרָכָה — **for example, that which [the Sages], of blessed memory, stated** (*Horayos* 9a, *Kereisos* 2a), שֶׁאֵין חִיּוּב הַשּׁוֹגֵג לְהָבִיא חַטָּאת — **that there is no obligation for the inadvertent sinner to bring a *chatas* offering,** אֶלָּא עַל עֲבֵרָה שֶׁחַיָּבִין עַל זְדוֹנָהּ כָּרֵת — **except for a sin for whose intentional commission one incurs *kares*.**

Chinuch notes:

שֶׁאַף עַל פִּי שֶׁיֵּשׁ בִּזְדוֹנָן וְיֵשׁ בַּתּוֹרָה שְׁלֹשָׁה חֲטָאִים — **There are, however, three sins in the Torah** כָּרֵת — **which, though they bear** the penalty of *kares* **when committed intentionally,** אֵין בְּשִׁגְגָתָן חַטָּאת — **do not carry *chatas* liability when committed inadvertently.** וְאֵלוּ הֵן — **These are [the three sins]:** מְגַדֵּף וּמְבַטֵּל מִילָה וְחָדַל מֵעֲשׂוֹת הַפֶּסַח — **a blasphemer** (Mitzvah 70), **one who neglects** the mitzvah of **circumcision** (Mitzvah 2), **and one who refrains from bringing the *pesach* offering** (Mitzvah 5). וְנָתְנוּ טַעַם בְּכָל אֶחָד — **And [the Sages] have provided the reason for each one,** וּמְפֹרָשׁ בִּמְקוֹמוֹ — **as is explained in its proper place** (*Kerisos* 2a, 3a).[10]

Chinuch notes that there are two sins that meet the conditions for *chatas* liability, yet one does not bring a fixed *chatas* offering on their account:

כָּל שְׁאָר הָעֲבֵרוֹת שֶׁזְּדוֹנָן כָּרֵת — **All other sins that bear** the penalty of *kares* **when committed intentionally** שִׁגְגָתָן חַטָּאת קְבוּעָה — **bear liability to a fixed *chatas* offering when committed inadvertently,** חוּץ מִטָּמֵא שֶׁאָכַל אֶת הַקֹּדֶשׁ — **except for** the sin of **a *tamei*** (one who is ritually impure) **who** inadvertently **eats sacrificial food,** וְטָמֵא שֶׁנִּכְנַס לַמִּקְדָּשׁ — **and** the sin of **a *tamei* who** inadvertently **enters the Holy Temple** (*Beis HaMikdash*). שֶׁאַף עַל פִּי שֶׁזְּדוֹנָן כָּרֵת — **For although [these transgressions] bear** the penalty **of *kares* when committed intentionally,**[11] אֵין מְבִיאִין חַטָּאת קְבוּעָה — **one** who commits them inadvertently **does not bring a fixed *chatas* offering.** אֶלָּא קָרְבָּן עוֹלֶה וְיוֹרֵד — **Rather, he brings a variable *chatas* offering,** שֶׁהוּא עוֹף — **which consists of** an animal, if the sinner is wealthy, or **a pair of birds** for the less prosperous, אוֹ קֶמַח — **or flour,** for a *minchah offering*, in cases of extreme poverty, כְּמוֹ שֶׁמְּפֹרָשׁ בַּכָּתוּב — **as expressed in Scripture** (*Leviticus* 5:6-13).[12]

---

#### NOTES

10. Chinuch (at notes 5-7) set forth the conditions under which liability to a *chatas* offering is incurred: One must *actively* violate a *kares*-bearing mitzvah-prohibition. Accordingly, a *chatas* liability is not incurred for failure to bring a *pesach* offering or to perform the mitzvah of circumcision, for these are *kares*-bearing mitzvah-*obligations*, rather than mitzvah-*prohibitions*. Likewise, a *chatas* liability is not incurred for blasphemy, since it is violated passively (i.e., with speech, which is not considered an action), rather than actively. [Note that the second reason applies also to the failure to bring a *pesach* offering or to perform the mitzvah of circumcision, for these, too, are passive transgressions.]

11. In Mitzvah 123 (at note 12), Chinuch cites the verses that prescribe *kares* for a *tamei* person who intentionally enters the *Beis HaMikdash* or eats sacrificial food.

12. These laws are set out in detail in Mitzvah 123. There are additional sins (listed in Mitzvah 123), for which one brings a variable *chatas* offering. Chinuch mentions specifically these two, for they are the only ones that bear the penalty of *kares* when committed intentionally, so they represent exceptions to the general rule that obligates one to bring a "fixed" *chatas* offering for inadvertently violating a *kares*-bearing prohibition.

## 433 ☐ VAYIKRA / MITZVAH 121: THE OBLIGATION TO BRING A CHATAS OFFERING

נִמְצֵאתָ לָמֵד שֶׁכָּל הָעֲבֵרוֹת שֶׁבַּתּוֹרָה שֶׁהַיָּחִיד מֵבִיא עַל שִׁגְגָתָן חַטָּאת קְבוּעָה, שָׁלֹשׁ וְאַרְבָּעִים הֵם, צֵא וַחֲשֹׁב, כִּי כֵן תִּמְצָאֵם, וְרֻבָּם בַּעֲרָיוֹת.[13] וְכֵן מֵעִנְיָן זֶה מַה שֶׁאָמְרוּ זִכְרוֹנָם לִבְרָכָה (שבת קי״ב ע״א) שֶׁאֵין חִיּוּב הַקָּרְבָּן עַד שֶׁיְּהֵא שׁוֹגֵג מִתְּחִלָּה וְעַד סוֹף.[14] וְחִלּוּקֵי הַיְדִיעוֹת שֶׁאֶפְשָׁר שֶׁיִּהְיוּ לַשּׁוֹגֵג בְּשִׁגְגָתוֹ רַבּוֹת.[15] וְיֶתֶר רַבֵּי פְּרָטֶיהָ

---

Chinuch continues:

נִמְצֵאתָ לָמֵד שֶׁכָּל הָעֲבֵרוֹת שֶׁבַּתּוֹרָה — **It emerges** from this discussion **that you** can **learn** שֶׁהַיָּחִיד מֵבִיא עַל שִׁגְגָתָן חַטָּאת קְבוּעָה — **that the total** number **of sins in the Torah for which an individual is obligated to bring a fixed** *chatas* **offering for committing them unintentionally** שָׁלֹשׁ וְאַרְבָּעִים הֵם — **is forty-three;** צֵא וַחֲשֹׁב כִּי כֵן תִּמְצָאֵם — **you** may **go and reckon** them, **and you will find them to be so,** וְרֻבָּם בַּעֲרָיוֹת — **with most of them** relating to prohibitions of **illicit relations** (*arayos*).[13]

Chinuch discusses the degree of inadvertence necessary for *chatas* liability:

וְכֵן מֵעִנְיָן זֶה — **And, also pertinent to this subject** is מַה שֶׁאָמְרוּ זִכְרוֹנָם לִבְרָכָה — **that which [our Sages], of blessed memory, said** (*Shabbos* 102a), שֶׁאֵין חִיּוּב הַקָּרְבָּן — **that there is no liability to a** *chatas* **offering** עַד שֶׁיְּהֵא שׁוֹגֵג מִתְּחִלָּה וְעַד סוֹף — **unless [the act] is inadvertent from the commencement** of the transgression **until the end.**[14]

One who transgresses the same prohibition repeatedly will, at times, incur only one *chatas* offering and, in other instances, incur a *chatas* for each transgression. Chinuch presents the determining factor:

וְחִלּוּקֵי הַיְדִיעוֹת — Another law relevant to this mitzvah is **the** principle of **"division** of liability **through awareness,"** meaning that when a transgression is repeated numerous times and the perpetrator becomes aware of each transgression separately, each separate awareness of having sinned generates a separate liability to a *chatas* offering; שֶׁאֶפְשָׁר שֶׁיִּהְיוּ לַשּׁוֹגֵג בְּשִׁגְגָתוֹ רַבּוֹת — **for it is possible for the inadvertent sinner to experience [awareness] numerous times regarding his inadvertence** that led him to commit the transgression repeatedly.[15]

Chinuch concludes:

וְיֶתֶר רַבֵּי פְּרָטֶיהָ — These laws, **as well as the many additional details of [this mitzvah],**

---

### NOTES

13. *Rambam* (*Hil. Shegagos* 1:4) enumerates the forty-three transgressions, which consist of twenty-six sins related to *arayos* (illicit relations) and seventeen sins related to other prohibitions. The Mishnah in *Kereisos* (2a) enumerates only thirty-six violations for which one incurs *kares*, thirty-three of which bear a *chatas* obligation. See *Mahari Korkos*, *Mishneh LaMelech*, and *Lechem Mishneh* (to *Rambam* ibid.), who reconcile *Rambam's* (and *Chinuch's*) count with the Mishnah's count.

14. For example, one who desecrates the Sabbath by carrying an item from a private domain to a public domain, must do so "inadvertently" from beginning to end. I.e., from the time he lifts the item in the private domain until the time he sets it down in the public domain, he must be either unaware that this day is the Sabbath, or unaware that this act is prohibited on the Sabbath under pain of *kares*. If, however, he began the act inadvertently and before completing it realized that it was forbidden, or vice versa, he does not bring a *chatas* offering (*Rambam, Hil. Shegagos* 2:1; see further, *Lechem Mishneh* ad loc. and *Minchas Chinuch* §2).

15. This principle has several applications:

(1) Awareness *between* transgressions serves to divide the transgressions into distinct liabilities. Thus, for example, if one inadvertently eats a number of *kezayis* (olive's volume) portions of *cheilev* (forbidden fats) and afterward becomes aware of his numerous transgressions at once, he brings a single *chatas* for all the transgressions. If, however, he becomes aware of his first transgression and then eats another *kezayis* of *cheilev* in another lapse of awareness, he brings two *chatas* offerings, for the awareness between transgressions divides them into distinct liabilities (*Kereisos* 11b; *Rambam, Hil. Shegagos* 5:1 and 6:1).

(2) *Separate* awarenesses of the transgressions can divide them into distinct liabilities, even if no period of awareness intervened *between* the transgressions. Thus, if one ate several portions of "meat" and later discovered that one of them contained *cheilev*, and then — before bringing an offering for his inadvertent consumption of *cheilev* — he further discovered that a *second* one of those portions contained *cheilev*, and so forth, he must bring a separate *chatas* for each and every consumption of *cheilev* that he became aware of separately (*Rambam* ibid. 6:9, 11, as understood by *Kesef Mishneh*; see *Minchas Chinuch* §11).

The basis of these rules is that the actual obligation

מְבֹאָרִים בְּהוֹרָיוֹת (ח׳ ע״א) וּכְרִיתוֹת (ב׳ ע״א), וּבִמְקוֹמוֹת מְשֻׁבָּת (ע׳ ע״ב) וּשְׁבוּעוֹת (י״ט ע״א) וּזְבָחִים.[16]

וְנוֹהֶגֶת בִּזְמַן הַבַּיִת בִּזְכָרִים וּנְקֵבוֹת.[17] וְעוֹבֵר עָלֶיהָ וְלֹא הִקְרִיב חַטָּאת עַל שִׁגְגָתוֹ, בִּטֵּל עֲשֵׂה.[18]

---

מְבֹאָרִים בְּהוֹרָיוֹת וּכְרִיתוֹת וּבִמְקוֹמוֹת מְשֻׁבָּת וּשְׁבוּעוֹת וּזְבָחִים — are set forth in Tractates *Horayos* (8a-9b) and *Kereisos* (2a-4b,15a,19a-20b), as well as in certain places in Tractates *Shabbos* (67b-73a), *Shevuos* (19a-b), and *Zevachim*.[16]

### ~ Applicability of the Mitzvah ~

וְנוֹהֶגֶת בִּזְמַן הַבַּיִת — [This mitzvah] applies in the time of the Temple, when offerings are brought, בִּזְכָרִים וּנְקֵבוֹת — to both men and women.[17] וְעוֹבֵר עָלֶיהָ — One who transgresses [this mitzvah] וְלֹא הִקְרִיב חַטָּאת עַל שִׁגְגָתוֹ — and does not bring a *chatas* offering for his inadvertent sin בִּטֵּל עֲשֵׂה — has violated a mitzvah-obligation.[18]

---

### NOTES

to bring a *chatas* is not incurred at the time of the transgression, but at the time that one becomes *aware* of his transgression. This is derived from *Leviticus* 4:28, which states: אוֹ הוֹדַע אֵלָיו חַטָּאתוֹ אֲשֶׁר חָטָא וְהֵבִיא קָרְבָּנוֹ וגו׳, *If the sin that he committed becomes known to him, he shall bring his offering*, etc. Consequently, if one repeats a transgression and only then becomes aware of both transgressions, he is liable to only one *chatas* offering, but if he first becomes aware of his initial transgression and then repeats it in a new lapse of awareness, he is liable to a separate *chatas* for the second transgression, since it took place after he had already incurred the *chatas* obligation for his first transgression (see *Kereisos* 4a, with *Rashi*). By the same token, if he repeated the transgression in one lapse of awareness but then became aware of each transgression, thus gaining *awareness* of the second transgression after he had already incurred liability for the first, he incurs a separate *chatas* obligation for the second (see *Shabbos* 71b).

Two other matters serve to divide transgressions into distinct liabilities:

(1) שֵׁמוֹת מוּחְלָקִין, *separate designations* (i.e., prohibitions): If one inadvertently transgresses two different *kares*-bearing prohibitions (e.g., he eats *cheilev* and *nossar* [leftover sacrificial meat]), he is liable to two *chatas* offerings even if he committed both transgressions in one lapse of awareness, i.e., he committed the second sin before becoming aware of the first (*Kereisos* 2b; *Rambam* ibid. 4:1; 6:4).

(2) גּוּפִין מוּחְלָקִין, *separate bodies*: If one repeats the *same* transgression with separate bodies, he incurs multiple *chatas* obligations, even if the transgressions were committed in one lapse of awareness. For example, a married woman was notified that her husband died overseas and she proceeded to remarry, and later she was divorced from the new husband and married yet another man. Afterward, her original husband returned alive, so it emerged that she had inadvertently committed adultery with two different men. Although both transgressions occurred in a single lapse of awareness (i.e., while she was unaware that she was still married to the first man), she is liable to a separate *chatas* for each new "husband" (*Rambam* ibid. 5:5; see *Kereisos* 15a). See *Minchas Chinuch* §11-12 for elaboration of these concepts.

16. These laws are codified in *Rambam, Hil. Shegagos*.

17. In accordance with the general rule pertaining to mitzvah-obligations that are not time-specific. See Insight for discussion.

18. That is, aside from the fact that he has failed to achieve atonement for the original transgression, he has additionally violated his *obligation* to bring a *chatas* offering, and thus, has added a new transgression.

---

> **◆§ Insight: A Sinner Below the Age of Twenty**
>
> Various Midrashic sources relate the idea that although one becomes obligated in all mitzvos upon reaching maturity (age 13 for males and age 12 for females), and from that age on is liable to punishment in *beis din* for one's transgressions, with respect to Heavenly punishment there is no culpability for sins committed before the age of 20 (*Bamidbar Rabbah* 18:4; *Shabbos* 89b; *Yerushalmi Bikkurim* 2:1; see *Rashi* to *Genesis* 23:1 and *Numbers* 16:27; see also *Rambam* to Mishnah, *Sanhedrin* 7:4). Based on this principle, some pose an interesting question related to our mitzvah. As Chinuch

stated (at note 6), one brings a *chatas* offering specifically for unintentionally violating *kares*-bearing prohibitions. *Kares*, however, is a Heavenly inflicted punishment, and accordingly, one who is under 20 years of age would never be subject to it. What, then, would be the law of such a sinner with respect to bringing a *chatas* offering? Would his age-based exemption from *kares* free him from liability to the *chatas* offering as well, or would he be liable to bring the offering despite his lack of culpability for the *kares* aspect of the prohibition? (*Maharal*, quoted in *Teshuvos Chacham Tzvi* §49).

*Chacham Tzvi* (loc. cit.) argues emphatically that even young adults below the age of 20 must bring a *chatas* offering. He explains that the prototypical case of *chatas* liability is the unintentional violation of idolatry (see *Numbers* 15:22-31), from which we derive that only those sins that are of a similar category to idolatry — i.e., ones that bear *kares* liability when done intentionally — carry a *chatas* offering obligation when committed inadvertently (*Horayos* 8a). This derivation, explains *Chacham Tzvi*, is simply one of helping to define the parameters of *chatas* liability: One must bring a *chatas* for inadvertently violating the *type* of sin that carries the punishment of *kares* (when done intentionally). The derivation does not state that one must bring a *chatas* for inadvertently committing a sin *because* he would have been liable to *kares* had he done the sin intentionally. That is, the *chatas* offering is not meant to take the place of the *kares* penalty. Rather the *kares* penalty is simply a criterion for defining the type of sin that bears the mitzvah obligation to bring a *chatas* offering. Once one inadvertently violates such a sin, the Torah obligates him to bring a *chatas*, irrespective of whether he personally would have been liable to the *kares* penalty. Thus, a person who has reached bar or bas mitzvah and is therefore obligated in all mitzvos, is clearly obligated to fulfill this mitzvah as well.

Furthermore, in a position shared by a number of other authorities, *Chacham Tzvi* questions the very premise that one who has not yet reached 20 years of age cannot be liable to the *kares* penalty. How can it be, he asks, that the Torah would set forth a prohibition, and hold all those who have reached maturity culpable for court-imposed punishments, including execution when warranted, yet limit liability for the *kares* consequence of the same prohibition? *Chasam Sofer* (*Yoreh Deah*, *Responsa* §155) makes a similar argument, and unequivocally states that once a child reaches adulthood he becomes obligated in all the mitzvos, and also in all of their associated penalties — be they court imposed or Heavenly. *Noda BiYehudah* (II, *Yoreh Deah* §164), too, shares this opinion and argues that the alternative is unfathomable, for if those under age 20 were truly clear of all Heavenly retribution, they could literally get away with murder (so long as there are no witnesses), and the result would be a situation of lawlessness and unbridled depravity among these young adults.

These authorities therefore qualify the Midrashic teaching quoted earlier that exempts those under 20 years of age from all Heavenly culpability. One explanation is that the Midrashic teaching addresses only specific cases (such as the sins of the Generation of the Wilderness), and does not constitute a general rule to be applied to all Torah violations (see *Chacham Tzvi* ibid. and *Chasam Sofer* ibid.). Alternatively, some explain that although the Heavenly Court may withhold punishment from those under age 20 for all mitzvah infractions, once such individuals reach 20 [if they do not repent their deeds] they are indeed punished for those earlier sins (*Chacham Tzvi* ibid.). Finally, some posit that the limit of Heavenly punishment for those below age 20 is only with regard to inflicting such punishment upon the person while he is alive. After his passing, though, he will be held culpable for any and all sins committed upon reaching maturity, including those committed before age 20 (ibid.; *Noda BiYehudah* ibid.).

## מִצְוָה קכב: מִצְוַת עֵדוּת

לְהַגִּיד הָעֵדוּת בִּפְנֵי הַדַּיָּנִין בְּכָל מַה שֶׁנֵּדָעֵהוּ, בֵּין שֶׁיִּתְחַיֵּב בָּעֵדוּת מִיתָה אוֹ מָמוֹן הַמּוּעָד עָלָיו, אוֹ שֶׁיִּהְיֶה הַצָּלָתוֹ בְּמָמוֹנוֹ אוֹ בְּנַפְשׁוֹ, שֶׁנֶּאֱמַר (ויקרא ה׳, א׳) "וְהוּא עֵד אוֹ רָאָה אוֹ יָדָע אִם לוֹא יַגִּיד וְנָשָׂא עֲוֹנוֹ". בְּכָל עִנְיָן חוֹבָה עָלֵינוּ לְהַגִּיד הָעֵדוּת לִפְנֵי הַבֵּית דִּין.

## Mitzvah 122
## The Obligation Regarding Testimony

וְנֶפֶשׁ כִּי תֶחֱטָא וְשָׁמְעָה קוֹל אָלָה וְהוּא עֵד אוֹ רָאָה אוֹ יָדָע אִם לוֹא יַגִּיד וְנָשָׂא עֲוֹנוֹ

*If a person will sin: If he accepted a demand for an oath, and he is a witness, either he saw or he knew, if he does not testify he shall bear his iniquity* (Leviticus 5:1).

In order to resolve a monetary dispute or to determine whether one is guilty of violating a Biblical or Rabbinic commandment, *beis din* will rely upon the testimony of eyewitnesses to the transaction or transgression. The mitzvah of testifying, which is derived from the latter part of this verse,[1] obligates one who observes his fellow violate a transgression or who witnesses a transaction that is the subject of a dispute in *beis din* to testify before *beis din*, thus enabling the judges to ensure that people abide by the Torah and that monetary cases are rightfully adjudicated.

לְהַגִּיד הָעֵדוּת בִּפְנֵי הַדַּיָּנִין בְּכָל מַה שֶׁנֵּדָעֵהוּ — We are commanded **to relate whatever testimony we know before the judges** of a *beis din*. בֵּין שֶׁיִּתְחַיֵּב בָּעֵדוּת מִיתָה אוֹ מָמוֹן הַמּוּעָד עָלָיו — This obligation applies regardless of **whether, due to the testimony, the one regarding whom the testimony is related would become liable to capital punishment or** to pay **money,** אוֹ שֶׁיִּהְיֶה הַצָּלָתוֹ בְּמָמוֹנוֹ אוֹ בְּנַפְשׁוֹ — **or if it would be** the basis **for preserving** either **his money or his life** by proving his innocence. שֶׁנֶּאֱמַר — This obligation is contained in the verse, **as it is stated** (Leviticus 5:1): "וְהוּא עֵד אוֹ רָאָה אוֹ יָדָע אִם לוֹא יַגִּיד וְנָשָׂא עֲוֹנוֹ" — **and he is a witness, either he saw or he knew, if he does not testify he shall bear his iniquity.**[2]

Chinuch discusses the scope of the obligation:

בְּכָל עִנְיָן חוֹבָה עָלֵינוּ לְהַגִּיד הָעֵדוּת לִפְנֵי הַבֵּית דִּין — **In all situations, it is an obligation upon**

---

### NOTES

1. The verse begins by speaking of one who swore falsely that he had no knowledge of testimony on behalf of his fellow, for which he is obligated to bring an offering (see end of this mitzvah and Mitzvah 123). Nevertheless, the Gemara (*Bava Kamma* 56a) explains that the latter part of the verse expresses a mitzvah to testify even when no oath is taken. For discussion, see *Tosafos* to *Bava Kamma* 56a ד״ה פשיטא, *Rashba* there ד״ה אי בתרי, and *Kesef Mishneh* to Rambam, *Hil. Eidus* 1:1.

2. While the verse states that one who does *not* testify has sinned, it does not seem to contain an explicit *commandment* to testify. On what basis, then, is this considered a mitzvah-obligation? *Rambam* (*Sefer HaMitzvos, Asei* 178) indicates that the phrase *and he is a witness, either he saw or he knew,* is understood as meaning that one who has knowledge of an event is obligated to come forward and serve as a witness (see *Radvaz* to Hil. *Eidus* 1:1).

One whose testimony will not be accepted for any reason [such as if the testimony is regarding a member of his family; see below, note 26] is not included in this mitzvah (*Sma, Choshen Mishpat* 28:3; see *Ketzos HaChoshen* there §3 and *Minchas Chinuch* §4). A lone witness, too, in situations where his testimony is not accepted (for example, with regard to capital cases), is not subject to this mitzvah. Where the testimony of a lone witness is effective, however (as in certain cases pertaining to prohibited matters), he would be subject to this obligation. Now, with regard to monetary matters, two witnesses are needed in order to extract money from the defendant. Nevertheless, the testimony of a single witness is effective to require the defendant to take an oath (see Mitzvah 523). While a lone witness is also required to testify in such a case (see *Bava Kamma* 56a and *Rashba* there ד״ה אלא בחר), nevertheless, the specific obligation of this mitzvah (to relate testimony) does not apply [see, however Chinuch below at note 3] (see *Minchas Chinuch* §2; see also *Glosses of R' Chaim Heller* to Rambam, *Sefer HaMitzvos, Asei* 178).

**437** ☐ **VAYIKRA / MITZVAH 122: THE OBLIGATION REGARDING TESTIMONY**

וְאוּלָם חִלּוּק יֵשׁ בֵּין דִּינֵי מָמוֹנוֹת לְדִינֵי נְפָשׁוֹת וּשְׁאָר אִסּוּרִין שֶׁבַּתּוֹרָה, שֶׁבְּדִינֵי מָמוֹנוֹת אֵין אָדָם חַיָּב לְהָעִיד עֲלֵיהֶם מֵעַצְמוֹ אֶלָּא אִם כֵּן יִתְבָּעֶנּוּ בַּעַל הַדָּבָר אוֹ בֵּית דִּין[3], וּבְדִינֵי נְפָשׁוֹת וּבְעֵדוּת שְׁאָר אִסּוּרִין שֶׁבַּתּוֹרָה כְּגוֹן שֶׁרָאָה אֶחָד שֶׁעָבַר עַל אִסּוּר, וְכֵן בְּעֵדוּת נְפָשׁוֹת כְּגוֹן שֶׁרָאָה מִי שֶׁהֲרַג חֲבֵרוֹ, אוֹ בְּעֵדוּת מַכּוֹת שֶׁהִכָּה הָאֶחָד אֶת חֲבֵרוֹ[4], בְּכָל זֶה חַיָּב אָדָם לָבוֹא מֵעַצְמוֹ וּלְהַגִּיד הָעֵדוּת לִפְנֵי הַבֵּית דִּין, כְּדֵי לְבַעֵר הָרָע וּלְהַפְרִישׁ בְּנֵי אָדָם מֵאִסּוּר.[5]

מִשָּׁרְשֵׁי הַמִּצְוָה, לְפִי שֶׁיֵּשׁ בְּמִצְוָה זוֹ תּוֹעֶלֶת גְּדוֹלָה לִבְנֵי אָדָם, אֵין צָרִיךְ לְהַאֲרִיךְ בָּהֶם,

---

**us to relate the testimony before** *beis din*. וְאוּלָם חִלּוּק יֵשׁ בֵּין דִּינֵי מָמוֹנוֹת לְדִינֵי נְפָשׁוֹת וּשְׁאָר אִסּוּרִין שֶׁבַּתּוֹרָה — **However, there is a distinction between** how this obligation applies in **cases of monetary matters** on the one hand, **and how** it applies in **cases of capital punishment or** where **other prohibitions of the Torah** were violated, on the other hand. שֶׁבְּדִינֵי מָמוֹנוֹת — **For in cases of monetary matters,** אֵין אָדָם חַיָּב לְהָעִיד עֲלֵיהֶם מֵעַצְמוֹ — **a person is not obligated to testify regarding them on his own;** אֶלָּא אִם כֵּן יִתְבָּעֶנּוּ בַּעַל הַדָּבָר אוֹ בֵּית דִּין — **he becomes obligated only if the litigant or** *beis din* **demands of him** to testify.[3] וּבְדִינֵי נְפָשׁוֹת — **But in cases of capital law,** וּבְעֵדוּת שְׁאָר אִסּוּרִין שֶׁבַּתּוֹרָה — **and in** the situation of **testimony regarding other Torah prohibitions,** כְּגוֹן שֶׁרָאָה אֶחָד שֶׁעָבַר עַל אִסּוּר — **such as if one saw someone violate a prohibition,** וְכֵן בְּעֵדוּת נְפָשׁוֹת — **and similarly with regard to testimony pertaining to capital offenses,** כְּגוֹן שֶׁרָאָה מִי שֶׁהֲרַג חֲבֵרוֹ — **such as if one saw someone kill his fellow,** אוֹ בְּעֵדוּת מַכּוֹת — **or, in** a situation of **testimony regarding** *malkus* (lashes), שֶׁהִכָּה הָאֶחָד אֶת חֲבֵרוֹ — such as if one saw **that someone struck his fellow,**[4] בְּכָל זֶה חַיָּב אָדָם לָבוֹא מֵעַצְמוֹ — **in all these [situations] a person is obligated to come forth on his own** וּלְהַגִּיד הָעֵדוּת לִפְנֵי הַבֵּית דִּין — **and to relate the testimony before** *beis din*, כְּדֵי לְבַעֵר הָרָע — **in order to purge evil** וּלְהַפְרִישׁ בְּנֵי אָדָם מֵאִסּוּר — **and to distance people from sin,** even if he was not asked to testify.[5]

### ☞ Underlying Purpose of the Mitzvah ☜

לְפִי שֶׁיֵּשׁ בְּמִצְוָה זוֹ תּוֹעֶלֶת — מִשָּׁרְשֵׁי הַמִּצְוָה — **Among the underlying purposes of the mitzvah is** גְּדוֹלָה לִבְנֵי אָדָם — that the obligation to testify is critical **because this mitzvah contains great benefit to mankind;** אֵין צָרִיךְ לְהַאֲרִיךְ בָּהֶם — **there is no need to elaborate on [the benefits],**

---

**NOTES**

3. The Gemara (*Shavuos* 35a) derives from the wording of our verse that the mitzvah to testify does not apply unless the testimony was personally solicited by the litigant. [Acharonim, however, question Chinuch's assertion that *beis din* can also solicit the testimony and thus obligate the witness to testify. For discussion, see *Minchas Chinuch* §5, *Minchas Yitzchak* §22, and *Shaar Mishpat* 28:2.]

4. One who strikes his fellow and does not cause at least a *perutah* (a small denomination) in damages is liable to *malkus* (as opposed to one who causes a *perutah* in damages, in which case he pays for the damages and does not receive *malkus*; see end of Mitzvah 595). See *Minchas Chinuch* §11.

[In the first part of this sentence, Chinuch states that one is required to testify in capital cases and cases of other transgressions even if he is not asked to testify. He then repeats that same law with regard to testimony of capital cases and testimony pertaining to *malkus*, giving specific examples of each one. It would appear that he first addresses general transgressions, and then addresses those cases in which there is a victim (or next-of-kin) who has an interest in the case (see, however, *Minchas Chinuch* ibid.). See also *Rambam, Hil. Eidus* 1:2.]

5. There is a general obligation upon *beis din* to destroy evil and to deter transgression, which includes punishing sinners (see *Deuteronomy* 13:6, 12). One who witnesses a transgression is included in this obligation, and is thus required to notify *beis din* of what he has seen (see also *Rosh, Makkos* 1:11).

[This, however, applies only in a situation where *beis din* will be able to act upon his testimony and punish the offender. In a situation where his testimony will not accomplish anything (e.g., a single witness, whose testimony is insufficient in corporal cases, saw someone commit a transgression), one is actually *prohibited* to relate it before *beis din*, for by doing so he would transgress the prohibition of *lashon hara* [disparaging speech] (*Pesachim* 113b; *Chafetz Chaim, Hil. Lashon Hara* 4:4-5, and *Pesichah, Lavin* 10).]

כִּי יְדוּעִים הַדְּבָרִים לְכָל רוֹאֵי הַשָּׁמֶשׁ.[6]

דִּינֵי הַמִּצְוָה, כְּגוֹן הַחִלּוּקִים שֶׁגִּלּוּ לָנוּ חֲכָמִים זִכְרוֹנָם לִבְרָכָה שֶׁהֵם בְּמִצְוָה זוֹ בֵּין אִישׁ לְאִישׁ, שֶׁלֹּא כָּל אָדָם חַיָּב לָבוֹא לִפְנֵי בֵּית דִּין לְהָעִיד לָהֶם, שֶׁאִם הָיָה הָעֵד חָכָם גָּדוֹל וְהַבֵּית דִּין פָּחוֹת מִמֶּנּוּ, שֶׁיֵּשׁ לוֹ לְהִמָּנַע אִם יִרְצֶה מִלְּהָעִיד לִפְנֵיהֶם, שֶׁמַּעֲשֶׂה שֶׁל כְּבוֹד תּוֹרָה דּוֹחֶה עֲשֵׂה דְעֵדוּת.[7] וְכֵן כֹּהֵן גָּדוֹל גַּם כֵּן אֵינוֹ חַיָּב לְהָעִיד אֶלָּא עֵדוּת שֶׁהִיא לַמֶּלֶךְ בִּלְבַד.[8] וּמַלְכֵי יִשְׂרָאֵל לֹא מְעִידִין עַל אֲחֵרִים וְלֹא אֲחֵרִים עֲלֵיהֶם, מִשּׁוּם מַעֲשֶׂה שֶׁהָיָה, כְּמוֹ שֶׁבָּא בְּסַנְהֶדְרִין פֶּרֶק כֹּהֵן גָּדוֹל[9] (י״ט ע״א),

---

כִּי יְדוּעִים הַדְּבָרִים לְכָל רוֹאֵי הַשָּׁמֶשׁ — as the matter is obvious to all who can see the sun.[6]

## ~ Laws of the Mitzvah ~

הַחִלּוּקִים שֶׁגִּלּוּ לָנוּ חֲכָמִים — The laws of this mitzvah include, כְּגוֹן — for example, דִּינֵי הַמִּצְוָה — the distinctions that the Sages, of blessed memory, revealed to us pertaining to this mitzvah, זִכְרוֹנָם לִבְרָכָה שֶׁהֵם בְּמִצְוָה זוֹ — between one person and another person. That is, the requirement to testify does not apply equally to all people, שֶׁלֹּא כָּל אָדָם חַיָּב לָבוֹא לִפְנֵי בֵּית דִּין לְהָעִיד לָהֶם — as not every person is obligated to come before beis din to testify before [the judges], as follows: שֶׁאִם הָיָה הָעֵד חָכָם גָּדוֹל וְהַבֵּית דִּין פָּחוֹת מִמֶּנּוּ — If the witness was a great Torah scholar and the judges of the beis din were of lesser stature than he, שֶׁיֵּשׁ לוֹ לְהִמָּנַע אִם יִרְצֶה מִלְּהָעִיד לִפְנֵיהֶם — if he wishes, he may refrain from testifying before them, שֶׁמַּעֲשֶׂה שֶׁל כְּבוֹד תּוֹרָה דּוֹחֶה עֲשֵׂה דְעֵדוּת — as the mitzvah-obligation to honor the Torah overrides the mitzvah-obligation of testifying.[7] וְכֵן כֹּהֵן גָּדוֹל גַּם כֵּן אֵינוֹ חַיָּב לְהָעִיד — Similarly, a Kohen Gadol is also not obligated to testify, אֶלָּא עֵדוּת שֶׁהִיא לַמֶּלֶךְ בִּלְבַד — aside from the specific case of testimony pertaining to the king.[8] וּמַלְכֵי יִשְׂרָאֵל לֹא מְעִידִין עַל אֲחֵרִים — Furthermore, Israelite kings (i.e., Jewish kings from any tribe, other than from the House of David) do not testify regarding others, וְלֹא אֲחֵרִים עֲלֵיהֶם — nor do others testify regarding them, מִשּׁוּם מַעֲשֶׂה שֶׁהָיָה — because of an incident that occurred, כְּמוֹ שֶׁבָּא בְּסַנְהֶדְרִין — as is related in Tractate Sanhedrin (19a), in Chapter Kohen Gadol (Ch. 2).[9]

---

### NOTES

6. Matters of dispute are brought to a conclusion through the testimony of witnesses who report what had transpired between the litigants, thus allowing peaceful society to flourish (see Mitzvah 37). Similarly, the laws of the Torah are enforced through the testimony of witnesses, ensuring the continuance of a successful law-abiding society. See also Chinuch's words below, at note 39.

7. [It is a mitzvah-obligation to accord honor to a Torah scholar; see Mitzvah 257.] A Torah scholar is, however, required to testify before a beis din that is of greater stature than he. Similarly, if the judges of a beis din [of even lesser stature] approach him to hear his testimony, in a manner that would not require him to appear in beis din, he is required to testify (Rama, Choshen Mishpat 28:5).

Chinuch stated earlier that, with regard to cases other than monetary disputes (e.g., capital cases and malkus cases), there is a requirement to testify even if one was not asked to do so, due to the requirement to purge evil and to distance people from sin. Similarly, in such cases, a Torah scholar must testify even before a beis din of lesser stature (Rambam, Hil. Eidus 1:2; see Minchas Chinuch §6).

8. That is, testimony pertaining to a king from the House of David, who, as Chinuch will presently explain, is subject to the judgment of beis din (Rambam, Hil. Eidus 1:3, as explained by Lechem Mishneh). The Kohen Gadol is not required to testify regarding cases that involve others, as that is beneath his dignity.

9. The Gemara records an incident in which an Israelite king was summoned to judgment before beis din, and, in accordance with the halachah, was instructed to stand while the witnesses testified against him. He demanded to be allowed to sit, and some of the judges were intimidated by his request. The Gemara relates that because they allowed themselves to be intimidated they were punished by God, and they died instantly. To prevent the recurrence of such an incident, the Sages instituted that Israelite kings not stand in judgment. Accordingly, any testimony regarding them is not accepted.

Similarly, with regard to testifying about others, since witnesses must also stand as they testify, the Sages instituted that an Israelite king not offer testimony (Tos. Yom Tov, Sanhedrin 2:2, based on Rambam, Hil. Eidus 11:9; see, however, Yad Ramah, Sanhedrin 19b;

## 439 □ VAYIKRA / MITZVAH 122: THE OBLIGATION REGARDING TESTIMONY

אֲבָל מַלְכֵי בֵית דָּוִד מְעִידִין[10], וּמְעִידִין עֲלֵיהֶם, וְדָנִין אוֹתָם[11].
וְאֵין נִמְנָעִין מִלְּקַבֵּל עֵדוּת בִּשְׁבִיל אַהֲבָה וְשִׂנְאָה, כִּי שְׁאֵרִית יִשְׂרָאֵל לֹא יַעֲשׂוּ עַוְלָה בְּעֵדוּתָם[12]. אֲבָל לְעִנְיַן הַדִּין אֵינוֹ כֵן, שֶׁאֵין דָּנִין הָאוֹהֵב וְהַשּׂוֹנֵא, מִפְּנֵי שֶׁהַשּׂוֹנֵא אֵין רוֹאֶה זְכוּת וְלֹא הָאוֹהֵב חוֹבָה[13].
וְכָתַב הָרַמְבַּ"ם זִכְרוֹנוֹ לִבְרָכָה שֶׁעִקַּר עֵדוּת שֶׁל תּוֹרָה הוּא מִפִּי הָעֵדִים וְלֹא מִפִּי כְתָבָם, שֶׁנֶּאֱמַר (דברים י"ז, ו') עַל פִּי וְגוֹ'[14], אֶלָּא שֶׁחֲכָמִים, מִפְּנֵי תִּקּוּן הָעוֹלָם שֶׁיִּמְצְאוּ בְּנֵי אָדָם

---

אֲבָל מַלְכֵי בֵית דָּוִד מְעִידִין – **However, kings of the House of David testify** regarding others,[10] וּמְעִידִין עֲלֵיהֶם – others **testify regarding them,** וְדָנִין אוֹתָם – **and they are judged.**[11]
וְאֵין נִמְנָעִין מִלְּקַבֵּל עֵדוּת בִּשְׁבִיל אַהֲבָה וְשִׂנְאָה – **We do not refrain from accepting testimony on the basis of friendship or enmity,** that is, testimony may be accepted even from a witness who has an especially close or adversarial relationship with the plaintiff or defendant, כִּי שְׁאֵרִית יִשְׂרָאֵל לֹא יַעֲשׂוּ עַוְלָה בְּעֵדוּתָם – as **"the remnant of Israel will not commit corruption"** with their testimony.[12] אֲבָל לְעִנְיַן הַדִּין אֵינוֹ כֵן – **However, with regard to judging this is not so,** שֶׁאֵין דָּנִין הָאוֹהֵב וְהַשּׂוֹנֵא – **as one may not judge a friend or enemy,** מִפְּנֵי שֶׁהַשּׂוֹנֵא אֵין רוֹאֶה זְכוּת וְלֹא הָאוֹהֵב חוֹבָה – **for** human nature is that **an enemy does not see merit, nor** does **a friend** see **fault.**[13]

Testimony must generally be submitted orally, and is not valid when submitted in written form. Chinuch discusses the basis for relying on legal documents:

וְכָתַב הָרַמְבַּ"ם זִכְרוֹנוֹ לִבְרָכָה – **Now, Rambam, of blessed memory, writes** (Hil. Eidus 3:4) שֶׁעִקַּר עֵדוּת שֶׁל תּוֹרָה הוּא מִפִּי הָעֵדִים – **that the basic** form of **testimony that is accepted by the Torah is** that which is **delivered orally by the witnesses,** וְלֹא מִפִּי כְתָבָם – **but not** that which is **expressed by their writing,** שֶׁנֶּאֱמַר "עַל פִּי וְגוֹ'" – **for it is stated** (Deuteronomy 19:15): **On the basis of** two witnesses etc., which literally can be translated as *By the mouths of two witnesses,* etc.[14] אֶלָּא שֶׁחֲכָמִים – **However, the Sages,** מִפְּנֵי תִּקּוּן הָעוֹלָם שֶׁיִּמְצְאוּ בְּנֵי אָדָם לִלְוֹות – **for the benefit of society,** that is, **so that people should find** opportunities **to borrow** money,

---

## NOTES

*Rashi, Shavuos* 31a ד"ה כ"ש מלך and *Ri Migash* there).

[Apparently, Chinuch maintains that it is not considered beneath the dignity of a king to testify regarding others, as the only reason why an Israelite king does not testify is because of the tragic incident just mentioned. This is also clear from Chinuch's next words, that kings from the House of David testify regarding others (see next note). See, however, *Yad Ramah* et al. cited above, and *Toras Chaim* and *Aruch LaNer* to *Sanhedrin* 19b.]

10. This is consistent with a manuscript text of *Rambam, Hil. Melachim* 3:7 (see *Shinuyei Nuschaos* in Frankel ed.). In our texts of *Rambam*, however, the word מְעִידִין, *testify,* does not appear, apparently indicating that a king from the House of David also does not testify regarding others (see *Kesef Mishneh* there). See *Minchas Chinuch* §8.

11. The Gemara (*Sanhedrin* 18a) derives from a Scriptural source that only one who is subject to judgment by others is eligible to serve as a judge. Now, since Scripture clearly instructs kings from the House of David to engage in judging others (*Jeremiah* 21:12), it must be that they themselves can also be judged. The Sages were unwilling to enact a law that directly contravenes a Torah law; thus, when they declared that Israelite kings may not be judged or testify, they excluded kings of the House of David (*Kesef Mishneh, Hil. Melachim* 3:7; cf. *Lechem Mishneh* ad loc.).

12. Stylistic paraphrase of *Zephaniah* 3:13. ["The remnant of Israel" is a reference to the Jewish people, who have survived oppression and persecution throughout the generations.]

13. We assume that a Jew will not deliberately attempt to aid his friend by testifying falsely on his behalf, nor will he attempt to harm a foe by testifying falsely against him. Accordingly, both a friend and a foe can serve as a witness. With regard to serving as a judge, however, this is not the case. We are concerned that one will subconsciously assume the innocence of a friend or the guilt of an enemy, and that this will affect his impartiality. Accordingly, one who has a decidedly close or unfriendly relationship with a litigant may not serve as a judge in his case. [See also *Sma, Choshen Mishpat* 33:1.]

14. The verse reads: עַל פִּי שְׁנֵי עֵדִים אוֹ עַל פִּי שְׁלֹשָׁה עֵדִים יָקוּם דָּבָר, *On the basis of two witnesses or on the basis of three witnesses shall a matter be confirmed.* The repetition of the term עַל פִּי (which literally translates as, *By the mouth of*), comes to teach the principle of מִפִּיהֶם וְלֹא מִפִּי כְתָבָם, *from their mouths but not from their script,* which indicates that testimony is valid only when submitted orally; see *Yevamos* 31b (see *Sifsei Chachamim* and *Emek HaNetziv* to the verse).

לִלְווֹת, תִּקְּנוּ שֶׁנַּחְתֹּךְ הַדִּין בְּמָמוֹן עַל פִּי עֵדִים שֶׁבִּשְׁטָר כְּמוֹ מִפִּיהֶם.[15]

וְהָרַמְבַּ"ן זִכְרוֹנוֹ לִבְרָכָה הִקְשָׁה עָלָיו בְּסֵפֶר הַמִּצְוֹת הַרְבֵּה עַל זֶה, וְיֶאֱרַךְ הָעִנְיָן אִם בָּאתִי לִכְתֹּב כֻּלּוֹ. וּכְלַל הַדָּבָר, כִּי הָרַמְבַּ"ן זִכְרוֹנוֹ לִבְרָכָה סוֹבֵר שֶׁעֵדוּת שְׁטָר דְּאוֹרַיְתָא הוּא, דִּכְתִיב (ירמיה ל"ב, מ"ד) וְכָתוֹב בַּסֵּפֶר וְחָתוֹם.[16]

וּמִדִּינֵי הַמִּצְוָה גַּם כֵּן מַה שֶּׁאָמְרוּ זִכְרוֹנָם לִבְרָכָה (כתובות י״ח ע״ב) שֶׁכָּל אָדָם שֶׁהִגִּיד עֵדוּתוֹ בִּפְנֵי בֵית דִּין וַחֲקָרוּהוּ כִּרְצוֹנָם אֵין יָכוֹל לַחֲזֹר וְלִסְתֹּר דָּבָר מִכָּל מַה שֶּׁהִגִּיד בִּפְנֵיהֶם וְלוֹמַר שֶׁמֻּטְעֶה אוֹ שׁוֹגֵג הָיָה, אוֹ שֶׁנִּזְכַּר אַחַר כָּךְ שֶׁאֵין הַדָּבָר כְּמוֹ שֶׁהֵעִיד, וַאֲפִלּוּ נָתַן טַעַם לִדְבָרָיו אֵין שׁוֹמְעִין לוֹ.[17] וְכָל עֵדוּת שֶׁבִּשְׁטָר הֲרֵי הוּא כְּעֵדוּת שֶׁחֲקָרוּהוּ

---

תִּקְּנוּ שֶׁנַּחְתֹּךְ הַדִּין בְּמָמוֹן עַל פִּי עֵדִים שֶׁבִּשְׁטָר — instituted that we decide the law in monetary cases on the basis of witnesses signed on a legal document כְּמוֹ מִפִּיהֶם — just as on the basis of their oral testimony.[15] וְהָרַמְבַּ"ן זִכְרוֹנוֹ לִבְרָכָה הִקְשָׁה עָלָיו בְּסֵפֶר הַמִּצְוֹת הַרְבֵּה עַל זֶה — But Ramban, of blessed memory, in his glosses to Sefer HaMitzvos (end of Shoresh 2) challenged [Rambam] strongly regarding this position. וְיֶאֱרַךְ הָעִנְיָן אִם בָּאתִי לִכְתֹּב כֻּלּוֹ — The discussion of this topic would become lengthy if I undertook to write it in its entirety, וּכְלַל הַדָּבָר — but the general point of the matter is כִּי הָרַמְבַּ"ן זִכְרוֹנוֹ לִבְרָכָה סוֹבֵר שֶׁעֵדוּת שְׁטָר דְּאוֹרַיְתָא הוּא — that Ramban, of blessed memory, maintains that testimony recorded in a legal document is Biblically acceptable, דִּכְתִיב "וְכָתוֹב בַּסֵּפֶר וְחָתוֹם" — as it is stated (Jeremiah 32:44): They will buy fields with money and write it in a document, and seal [it] and designate witnesses.[16]

Chinuch discusses the law of a witness who wishes to rescind his testimony:

וּמִדִּינֵי הַמִּצְוָה גַּם כֵּן מַה שֶּׁאָמְרוּ זִכְרוֹנָם לִבְרָכָה — Also included among the laws of the mitzvah is that which [the Sages], of blessed memory, said (Kesubos 18b): שֶׁכָּל אָדָם שֶׁהִגִּיד עֵדוּתוֹ בִּפְנֵי בֵית דִּין — that once any person related his testimony before beis din וַחֲקָרוּהוּ כִּרְצוֹנָם — and [beis din] investigated it to their satisfaction, אֵין יָכוֹל לַחֲזֹר — [the witness] may not reverse himself וְלִסְתֹּר דָּבָר מִכָּל מַה שֶּׁהִגִּיד בִּפְנֵיהֶם — and contradict anything from all that he had related before them, וְלוֹמַר שֶׁמֻּטְעֶה אוֹ שׁוֹגֵג הָיָה — and say that he had been misled or was mistaken, אוֹ שֶׁנִּזְכַּר אַחַר כָּךְ שֶׁאֵין הַדָּבָר כְּמוֹ שֶׁהֵעִיד — or that he recalled later that the matter was not as he had testified. וַאֲפִלּוּ נָתַן טַעַם לִדְבָרָיו — And even if he gives an explanation for why he said his earlier words, אֵין שׁוֹמְעִין לוֹ — [beis din] does not listen to him.[17] וְכָל הֲרֵי הוּא כְּעֵדוּת שֶׁחֲקָרוּהוּ עֵדוּת שֶׁבִּשְׁטָר — In addition, all testimony contained in a document

---

NOTES

15. The Sages recognized that prospective lenders would be reluctant to lend money if beis din would accept only the testimony of witnesses who come to beis din in person. What recourse would they then have if the borrower denies having taken the loan, and the witnesses left town or are otherwise unable to appear? The Sages therefore instituted that if the loan was recorded in a document that was signed by witnesses, the document would be accepted as valid testimony (see Gittin 36a with Rashi ד"ה מפני תיקון העולם; see also Tosafos, Gittin 2a ד"ה המביא).

16. Ramban argues that the verse cited by Rambam, which indicates that all testimony must be presented orally, needs to be reconciled with the verse that indicates that there is Biblical validity to a document that has witnesses signed upon it. He therefore draws a distinction between testimony that witnesses submit to beis din in writing on their own in lieu of appearing personally in beis din, and a document that is drawn up by the party involved and signed by witnesses. The verse that teaches that testimony presented in writing is not valid refers to a case where the witnesses simply recorded their testimony in document form for the sake of submitting it to beis din. Regarding this case, we have been taught, from their mouths, but not from their script. On the other hand, the verse that indicates that a document is valid refers to a case where a transaction was committed to writing in the form of a document drawn up by the party involved — such as a bill of sale drawn up by the seller, or a promissory note drawn up by the borrower. When the affected party drafts a document and witnesses affix their signatures to it, the document is acceptable as testimony in beis din.

17. Although, in certain limited instances, one who makes a claim and later provides a plausible explanation for why he made that claim may retract the initial statement (for an example, see Kesubos 22a), this is not the law regarding testimony submitted in beis din. Once the testimony was accepted, it cannot be retracted.

## VAYIKRA / MITZVAH 122: THE OBLIGATION REGARDING TESTIMONY

בֵּית דִּין כִּרְצוֹנָם, וְשׁוּב אֵין הָעֵדִים יְכוֹלִים לַחֲזֹר בָּהֶם בְּשׁוּם דָּבָר שֶׁבַּשְּׁטָר.[18] וְדָנִין עַל פִּי הַחֲתוּמִין בְּכָל דְּבַר הַכָּתוּב בַּשְּׁטָר, וְהוּא שֶׁנִּהְיֶה בְּרִיאִים שֶׁאוֹתָם הַחֲתוּמִים הֵם שֶׁחֲתָמוּהוּ אוֹתוֹ שְׁטָר וְלֹא זִיְּפָם מְזַיֵּף.[19] וְזֹאת הַחֲקִירָה יֶשׁ לָנוּ לַעֲשׂוֹתָהּ עַל פִּי אֲנָשִׁים שֶׁיַּכִּירוּ אוֹתָן חֲתִימוֹת שֶׁהֵן כְּתִיבַת אוֹתָם הָאֲנָשִׁים הַחֲתוּמִים, וּצְרִיכִין אָנוּ שְׁנֵי עֵדִים שֶׁיַּכִּירוּ שְׁתֵּי הַחֲתִימוֹת, כָּל אֶחָד מֵהֶם יַכִּירוּ שְׁנֵי הָעֵדִים.[20] וְכֵן אִם שְׁנַיִם מִן הַדַּיָּנִים בְּעַצְמָם מַכִּירִין אוֹתָם, דַּי לָנוּ בְּכָךְ,[21] אוֹ אִם הַחֲתוּמִים בְּעַצְמָם לְפָנֵינוּ וְיָעִיד כָּל אֶחָד עַל חֲתִימָתוֹ דַּי בְּכָךְ,[22] אֲבָל הָאֶחָד אֵינוֹ יָכוֹל לְהָעִיד עַל כְּתִיבָתוֹ וְעַל כְּתִיבַת חֲבֵרוֹ.

---

בֵּית דִּין כִּרְצוֹנָם — **is considered as testimony that** *beis din* **had investigated to their satisfaction,** וְשׁוּב אֵין הָעֵדִים יְכוֹלִים לַחֲזֹר בָּהֶם בְּשׁוּם דָּבָר שֶׁבַּשְּׁטָר — **and the witnesses can no longer reverse themselves regarding any detail of the document.**[18]

The Sages instituted that a document whose authenticity is contested has no validity unless its authenticity is confirmed by verifying the signatures of the witnesses. This is known as קִיּוּם שְׁטָרוֹת, *certification of documents*:

וְדָנִין עַל פִּי הַחֲתוּמִין בְּכָל דְּבַר הַכָּתוּב בַּשְּׁטָר — **[***Beis din***] judges on the basis of the witnesses whose names are signed with regard to all that is written in the document,** וְהוּא שֶׁנִּהְיֶה בְּרִיאִים שֶׁאוֹתָם הַחֲתוּמִים הֵם שֶׁחֲתָמוּהוּ אוֹתוֹ שְׁטָר — **but that is only if we are certain that [the witnesses] whose names are signed are the ones who actually signed the document** וְלֹא זִיְּפָם מְזַיֵּף — **and that [the signatures] were not forged by a forger.**[19]

Chinuch details how *beis din* authenticates the validity of a document:

וְזֹאת הַחֲקִירָה יֶשׁ לָנוּ לַעֲשׂוֹתָהּ — **We** (i.e., *beis din*) **are to perform this determination** עַל פִּי אֲנָשִׁים שֶׁיַּכִּירוּ אוֹתָן חֲתִימוֹת שֶׁהֵן כְּתִיבַת אוֹתָם הָאֲנָשִׁים הַחֲתוּמִים — **through the testimony of people who recognize those signatures as the handwriting of the people who are signed** on the document. וּצְרִיכִין אָנוּ שְׁנֵי עֵדִים שֶׁיַּכִּירוּ שְׁתֵּי הַחֲתִימוֹת — **For this we need two witnesses who recognize the two signatures,** כָּל אֶחָד מֵהֶם יַכִּירוּ שְׁנֵי הָעֵדִים — that is, **each of [the signatures] is recognized by both witnesses.**[20] וְכֵן אִם שְׁנַיִם מִן הַדַּיָּנִים בְּעַצְמָם מַכִּירִין אוֹתָם — **Similarly, if two of the judges themselves recognize [the signatures]** דַּי לָנוּ בְּכָךְ — **that is sufficient for us,**[21] אוֹ וְיָעִיד כָּל אֶחָד אִם הַחֲתוּמִים בְּעַצְמָם לְפָנֵינוּ — **or if the signers themselves are present before us** עַל חֲתִימָתוֹ — **and each one testifies on his own signature,** דַּי בְּכָךְ — **that is sufficient.**[22] אֲבָל הָאֶחָד אֵינוֹ יָכוֹל לְהָעִיד עַל כְּתִיבָתוֹ וְעַל כְּתִיבַת חֲבֵרוֹ — **However, a single** witness **may not testify regarding** both **his own handwriting and the handwriting of his fellow** witness.

---

### NOTES

18. Since a document cannot be executed without the consent of the one who stands to incur a loss through the document, once it has been written and signed it is equivalent to testimony that has been accepted in *beis din*. [Nevertheless, as we shall see immediately, if the authenticity of the document has not yet been established, and can be established only through the testimony of the witnesses who verify their signatures, the witnesses may, under certain circumstances, qualify its contents or even retract their testimony (*Rambam, Hil. Eidus* 3:6). See next note.]

19. As long as the signatures have not been verified, however, the defendant may claim that it is a forgery. He may, in fact, make other claims as well, such as, in the case of a loan document, that he had already repaid it in full. Once the authenticity of the document has been confirmed, however, it is considered as though witnesses testified to the transaction that is recorded within it, and the defendant must prove any counterclaim that he wishes to make (*Rambam, Hil. Malveh VeLoveh* 14:5).

20. When verifying the signatures through the testimony of witnesses other than those who actually signed the document, it is necessary to have two witnesses attest to each of the signatures. The same pair of witnesses can attest to both signatures, or two separate sets of witnesses can attest to each signature, or one witness who recognizes both signatures can join together with two other witnesses who each recognize one of the signatures (*Rambam, Hil. Eidus* 7:3).

21. This is an exception to the general law that the witnesses to a transaction cannot also serve as the judges of the case; see *Kesubos* 21b.

22. In this case, it is viewed as if the testimony is with regard to the loan itself, with each one of the witnesses testifying on the actual loan, rather than on his signature. Therefore, one witness suffices for each signature; see *Kesubos* 21a.

## 442 ◻ ויקרא / מצוה קכב: מצות עדות

וְכֵן אִם כְּתַב יָדָם יוֹצֵא מִמָּקוֹם אַחֵר לְפָנֵינוּ, מְקַיְּמִין מִמֶּנּוּ. וּמְפֹרָשׁ בַּגְּמָרָא (שם כ׳
ע״א) שֶׁאֵין מְקַיְּמִין שְׁטָר מִשְּׁטָר אֶלָּא מִשְּׁנֵי שְׁטָרוֹת שֶׁל שְׁתֵּי שָׂדוֹת שֶׁאֲכָלוּם בַּעֲלֵיהֶן
שָׁלֹשׁ שָׁנִים אֲכִילָה גְלוּיָה בְּלֹא שׁוּם יִרְאָה וָפַחַד מִן תְּבִיעַת בְּעָלִים, אוֹ מִשְּׁנֵי שְׁטָרוֹת שֶׁל
כְּתֻבּוֹת[23], וְהוּא שֶׁיֵּצְאוּ מִתַּחַת יְדֵי אַחֵר לֹא מִתַּחַת יְדֵי זֶה הָרוֹצֶה בַּקִּיּוּם, דְּחַיְישִׁינַן שֶׁמָּא
הַכֹּל זִיֵּף[24], וְכֵן מִשְּׁטָר אַחֵר שֶׁקָּרָא עָלָיו עַרְעַר וְהֻחְזַק בְּבֵית דִּין[25].
וּמַה שֶּׁאָמְרוּ זִכְרוֹנָם לִבְרָכָה גַּם כֵּן שֶׁבְּעֵדוּת שֶׁל חֲתִימָה נֶאֱמָן קָרוֹב לְהָעִיד עַל כְּתִיבַת

---

Chinuch discusses another way that the signatures of a document can be verified: וְכֵן אִם כְּתַב יָדָם יוֹצֵא מִמָּקוֹם אַחֵר לְפָנֵינוּ — **Similarly, if** a document containing **[the witnesses']** **handwriting** (i.e., signatures) **regarding some other matter is produced before us,** מְקַיְּמִין מִמֶּנּוּ — **we can certify** their validity **through it,** by comparing the signatures appearing in the document in question to the signatures appearing in that document.

One might wonder how we can use another document to verify the document in question. Why, even if the signatures of the document in question match the signatures of the other document, perhaps both documents are forgeries! Chinuch addresses this question:

וּמְפֹרָשׁ בַּגְּמָרָא — **It is explained in the Gemara** (Kesubos 20a) שֶׁאֵין מְקַיְּמִין שְׁטָר מִשְּׁטָר — **that we do not certify a document on the basis of another document** that was not verified by beis din, אֶלָּא מִשְּׁנֵי שְׁטָרוֹת שֶׁל שְׁתֵּי שָׂדוֹת — **unless the certification can be done on the basis of two documents,** regarding the purchase **of two** separate **fields,** שֶׁאֲכָלוּם בַּעֲלֵיהֶן שָׁלֹשׁ שָׁנִים — **whose** produce **has been consumed by the** new **owners for three years,** אֲכִילָה גְלוּיָה בְּלֹא שׁוּם יִרְאָה — **consuming** it **openly, without fear** or apprehension **for the claims of** a previous **owner;** וָפַחַד מִן תְּבִיעַת בְּעָלִים אוֹ מִשְּׁנֵי שְׁטָרוֹת שֶׁל כְּתֻבּוֹת — **or on the basis of two kesubah documents.**[23] וְהוּא שֶׁיֵּצְאוּ מִתַּחַת יְדֵי אַחֵר — **And** even **this is only when they are produced from the possession of some other** person, לֹא מִתַּחַת יְדֵי זֶה הָרוֹצֶה בַּקִּיּוּם — **not from the possession of the one who desires confirmation** of the document in question, דְּחַיְישִׁינַן שֶׁמָּא הַכֹּל זִיֵּף — **as we are concerned that perhaps he forged all** the documents.[24] וְכֵן — **Similarly,** we can confirm the validity of a document מִשְּׁטָר אַחֵר שֶׁקָּרָא עָלָיו עַרְעַר וְהֻחְזַק בְּבֵית דִּין — **through** comparing it to **another document that had been contested and was** later **certified in beis din.**[25]

Under Biblical law, a legal document that is presented in beis din is assumed to be authentic, and no certification is required. It is the Sages who imposed the requirement of certification (Kesubos 28a). They therefore allowed certain leniencies in regard to the certification of documents:

וּמַה שֶּׁאָמְרוּ זִכְרוֹנָם לִבְרָכָה גַּם כֵּן — **Additionally** included in the laws of the mitzvah is **what the [Sages], of blessed memory, said,** שֶׁבְּעֵדוּת שֶׁל חֲתִימָה — **that in** the situation of **testimony regarding the signatures** of a document, נֶאֱמָן קָרוֹב לְהָעִיד עַל כְּתִיבַת קְרוֹבוֹ — **one who is related**

---

### NOTES

23. If the document being used to verify the signatures is a record of the sale of real property, and the one identified in the document as the buyer of the property has been openly deriving benefit for at least three years, the document is presumed to be authentic, for otherwise the true owner would not have allowed him to remain there undisturbed (see *Bava Basra* 28a ff.). Although even this is not an absolute proof, as perhaps this document is indeed a forgery but the owner neglected to challenge him, nevertheless, if there are *two* such documents, the overwhelming probability is that they are authentic (*Sma* 46:18). Similarly, if the documents being used to verify the signatures are *kesubah* documents (which a husband gives his wife upon their marriage, confirming his obligations toward

her), it can also be assumed that they are authentic.

24. Even though such documents are normally presumed to be authentic (as explained in the previous note), nevertheless, when we were unable to verify the signatures of the document in question through other means, this raises our suspicions with regard to its validity. Hence, if all the documents are in the hands of one person, we must consider the possibility that he forged all of them. It is only when other people are in possession of the confirming documents that we rely upon them (see *Rambam, Hil. Eidus* 6:3 with *Lechem Mishneh*).

25. For the particulars of these laws, as well as other opinions regarding this matter, see *Choshen Mishpat* 46:7 with commentaries.

קְרוֹבוֹ שֶׁהוּא מַכִּירָהּ, וּמִצְטָרֵף עִם אַחֵר לְקַיֵּם הַשְּׁטָר,[26] וְשֶׁבְּעֵדוּת זוֹ נֶאֱמָן אָדָם בְּגָדְלוֹ לְהָעִיד וְלוֹמַר כְּשֶׁהָיִיתִי קָטָן רָאִיתִי כְּתַב אָבִי אוֹ אָחִי וּמַכִּירָהּ אֲנִי עַכְשָׁו שֶׁהִיא אוֹתָהּ שֶׁרְאִיתִיהָ.[27]

וּמַה שֶּׁאָמְרוּ שֶׁעֲשָׂרָה בְּרִיּוֹת פְּסוּלוֹת לְעֵדוּת מִן הַתּוֹרָה, וּכְמוֹ שֶׁכָּתַבְנוּ לְמַעְלָה בְּמִצְוַת אַל תָּשֶׁת רָשָׁע עֵד.[28] וְכֵן מִי שֶׁאֵינוֹ בְּמִקְרָא וְלֹא בְּמִשְׁנָה וְלֹא בְּדֶרֶךְ אֶרֶץ שֶׁהוּא פָּסוּל מִדִּבְרֵיהֶם, שֶׁחֲזָקָה עָלָיו שֶׁהוּא רָשָׁע, וַהֲרֵי כְּתִיב (שמות כ״ג, א׳) אַל תָּשֶׁת רָשָׁע עֵד.[29] אֲבָל אִם יֶשׁ בּוֹ דֶּרֶךְ אֶרֶץ וְעוֹסֵק בְּקְצָת מִצְוֹת, מְקַבְּלִין עֵדוּתוֹ אַף עַל פִּי שֶׁהוּא עַם הָאָרֶץ.[30] נִמְצֵאתָ אוֹמֵר, כָּל תַּלְמִיד חָכָם בְּחֶזְקַת כָּשֵׁר עַד שֶׁיִּפָּסֵל,

---

to a witness signed on the document **is trusted to testify regarding the handwriting of his relative** — **and he** שֶׁהוּא מַכִּירָהּ — **and to say that he recognizes it,** וּמִצְטָרֵף עִם אַחֵר לְקַיֵּם הַשְּׁטָר **may** thus **join with another** person **to confirm the** authenticity of **the document.**[26] וְשֶׁבְּעֵדוּת זוֹ — **Also,** the Sages said **that for this testimony** נֶאֱמָן אָדָם בְּגָדְלוֹ לְהָעִיד וְלוֹמַר — **a person is trusted, when he is an adult, to testify and say,** כְּשֶׁהָיִיתִי קָטָן רָאִיתִי כְּתַב אָבִי אוֹ אָחִי — **"When I was a minor I saw the handwriting of my father ...,"** or **"... I saw the handwriting of my brother ...,"** וּמַכִּירָהּ אֲנִי עַכְשָׁו — **"... and I recognize [the handwriting]** that is before me **now** שֶׁהִיא אוֹתָהּ שֶׁרְאִיתִיהָ — **that it is** the same as **that which I had seen** then."[27]

Chinuch completes his presentation of the laws of the mitzvah with a discussion of who is disqualified from testifying:

וּמַה שֶּׁאָמְרוּ — Also among the laws pertaining to this mitzvah is **what [the Sages] said,** שֶׁעֲשָׂרָה בְּרִיּוֹת פְּסוּלוֹת לְעֵדוּת מִן הַתּוֹרָה — **that ten** categories of **people are disqualified from testifying, under Biblical law,** וּכְמוֹ שֶׁכָּתַבְנוּ לְמַעְלָה בְּמִצְוַת אַל תָּשֶׁת רָשָׁע עֵד — **as we have written above** in connection with **the mitzvah not to designate a wicked person** to be **a witness** (Mitzvah 75).[28] וְכֵן מִי שֶׁאֵינוֹ בְּמִקְרָא וְלֹא בְּמִשְׁנָה וְלֹא בְּדֶרֶךְ אֶרֶץ שֶׁהוּא פָּסוּל מִדִּבְרֵיהֶם — **Similarly, that one who is not knowledgeable in Scripture or Mishnah, and** who also does **not** behave **in an ethical manner is disqualified by decree of [the Sages],** שֶׁחֲזָקָה עָלָיו שֶׁהוּא רָשָׁע — **for there is a presumption about him that he is a sinner** (literally, *wicked*), וַהֲרֵי כְּתִיב אַל תָּשֶׁת רָשָׁע עֵד — **and, indeed, it is stated** (*Exodus* 23:1, as interpreted by *Mechilta*): **"Do not place a wicked person as a witness."**[29] אֲבָל אִם יֶשׁ בּוֹ דֶּרֶךְ אֶרֶץ וְעוֹסֵק בְּקְצָת מִצְוֹת — **However, if he** conducts himself **in an ethical manner and engages in** the performance of **some mitzvos,** מְקַבְּלִין עֵדוּתוֹ אַף עַל פִּי שֶׁהוּא עַם הָאָרֶץ — [*beis din*] **accepts his testimony even though he is unlearned.**[30] נִמְצֵאתָ אוֹמֵר — **One can thus say** the following rule: כָּל תַּלְמִיד חָכָם בְּחֶזְקַת כָּשֵׁר עַד שֶׁיִּפָּסֵל — **Every Torah scholar is presumed** to be **qualified** to serve as a witness **unless** it becomes known that **he is**

---

### NOTES

26. As Chinuch will state in Mitzvah 589, ordinarily *beis din* may not accept the testimony of a defendant's family member, regardless of whether the testimony will be to his benefit or his detriment. Nevertheless, a family member of a witness whose signature appears on a document may attest to his signature, and thus confirm the document.

27. Generally, testimony regarding something one has witnessed as a minor is not accepted. However, where the need for the testimony is only of Rabbinic origin, such testimony is valid (*Kesubos* 28a). [Nevertheless, *Rambam* (*Hil. Eidus* 7:2) asserts that such testimony is accepted from only *one* of the witnesses who are confirming the document; if *both* witnesses recognize the signature only from the time they were minors, their testimony is not valid.]

There is disagreement among the authorities whether such testimony may be accepted from all people or only from family members or other close acquaintances. See *Choshen Mishpat* 35:4 with *Sma* §10 and *Shach* §4.

28. See Mitzvah 75 with notes, beginning at note 6.

29. [See above, Mitzvah 75, at note 2.] A person who is not only unlearned but also fails to observe mitzvos and to conduct himself in an ethical manner is generally unable to withstand temptations that confront him. He is therefore considered a sinner, and his testimony is disqualified (*Rambam, Hil. Eidus* 11:1).

30. Literally, *people of the land*. [For discussion of this rule, see *Ran* and *Meiri* to *Pesachim* 49a.]

וְעַם הָאָרֶץ בְּחֶזְקַת פָּסוּל עַד שֶׁיְחֻזַּק עִמָּנוּ לְטוֹב.[31] וְכֵן הָאֲנָשִׁים הַבְּזוּיִים בְּיוֹתֵר פְּסוּלִין מִדִּבְרֵיהֶם,[32] כְּגוֹן הָאוֹכְלִים בַּשּׁוּק בִּפְנֵי הַכֹּל[33] וְהַהוֹלְכִים עֲרֻמִּים בַּשּׁוּק,[34] וּמִכְּלַל הַבְּזוּיִים הָאוֹכְלִים צְדָקָה שֶׁל גּוֹיִם בְּפַרְהֶסְיָא,[35] וְיֶתֶר פְּרָטֶיהָ מְבֹאָרִים בְּסַנְהֶדְרִין וּשְׁבוּעוֹת.[36]

וְנוֹהֶגֶת בְּכָל מָקוֹם וּבְכָל זְמָן[37] בִּזְכָרִים אֲבָל לֹא בְנָשִׁים, שֶׁאֵין הַנָּשִׁים בְּתוֹרַת עֵדוּת לְקַלּוּת דַּעְתָּן.[38] וְהָעוֹבֵר עָלֶיהָ וְלֹא הֵעִיד בְּדִינֵי מָמוֹנוֹת כְּשֶׁהִשְׁבִּיעוּהוּ לְעֵדוּת בַּעַל דָּבָר אוֹ בֵּית דִּין,

וְעַם הָאָרֶץ בְּחֶזְקַת פָּסוּל עַד שֶׁיְחֻזַּק עִמָּנוּ לְטוֹב — **but one who is unlearned is** in fact **disqualified, presumed to be disqualified until it is established with us that he is of good repute.**[31] וְכֵן הָאֲנָשִׁים הַבְּזוּיִים בְּיוֹתֵר פְּסוּלִין מִדִּבְרֵיהֶם — **Similarly, exceedingly lowly people are** also **disqualified by decree of [the Sages].**[32] כְּגוֹן הָאוֹכְלִים בַּשּׁוּק בִּפְנֵי הַכֹּל — **This includes, for example, those who eat in the marketplace, in the presence of the entire public,**[33] וְהַהוֹלְכִים עֲרֻמִּים בַּשּׁוּק — **and those who go about unclothed in the marketplace.**[34] וּמִכְּלַל הַבְּזוּיִים — **Also in the category of lowly [individuals]** הָאוֹכְלִים צְדָקָה שֶׁל גּוֹיִם בְּפַרְהֶסְיָא — **are those who partake of the charity of idolaters in public.**[35] וְיֶתֶר פְּרָטֶיהָ מְבֹאָרִים בְּסַנְהֶדְרִין וּשְׁבוּעוֹת — **These laws, and the additional details of [this mitzvah], are set forth in** Tractates *Sanhedrin* **and** *Shevuos*.[36]

### ⁓ Applicability of the Mitzvah ⁓

וְנוֹהֶגֶת בְּכָל מָקוֹם וּבְכָל זְמָן — **[This mitzvah] applies in every location and in all times,**[37] בִּזְכָרִים אֲבָל לֹא בְנָשִׁים — **and is incumbent upon men but not upon women,** שֶׁאֵין הַנָּשִׁים בְּתוֹרַת עֵדוּת — **for women are not subject to the laws of testifying,** לְקַלּוּת דַּעְתָּן — **as their minds are** susceptible to being **swayed.**[38] וְהָעוֹבֵר עָלֶיהָ וְלֹא הֵעִיד — **One who transgresses this [mitzvah] and does not testify,** בְּדִינֵי מָמוֹנוֹת כְּשֶׁהִשְׁבִּיעוּהוּ לְעֵדוּת בַּעַל דָּבָר אוֹ בֵּית דִּין — either **in monetary cases when the litigant or** *beis*

---

### NOTES

31. A Torah scholar is assumed to be an upstanding individual, even if it is unknown whether he maintains a high standard of ethics. Similarly, one who conducts himself in an ethical manner may certainly testify, even if he is not knowledgeable in Torah. However, one who is not a Torah scholar and is also not known to conduct himself ethically is not qualified (see *Radvaz* to *Rambam, Hil. Eidus* 11:3, and *Lechem Mishneh, Hil. Kiddush HaChodesh* 2:2).

32. These people cannot be relied upon to give honest testimony, as they lack the sense of shame and self-respect that provide the natural barriers against testifying falsely (*Rashi, Kiddushin* 40b ד"ה ופסול לעדות).

33. For discussion of this disqualification, see *Tur* and *Beis Yosef, Choshen Mishpat* 34:18.

34. This refers to those who toil in filth, who remove their clothing while engaged in their labor. This indicates an excessive lack of shame, which is the reason for their disqualification (*Rambam, Hil. Eidus* 11:5).

35. One who publicly accepts charity from idolaters displays a lack of dignity and gives the false impression that Jews are not merciful enough to provide for one another. For this reason his word cannot be relied upon (see *Yad Ramah, Sanhedrin* 26b).

36. Primarily, this refers to the third chapter of *Sanhedrin* and the fourth chapter of *Shevuos*. The laws of this mitzvah are codified in *Rambam, Hil. Eidus*, and in *Shulchan Aruch, Choshen Mishpat* §28-38. [For other mitzvos that pertain to the testimony of witnesses, see Mitzvos 37, 75, and 589; see also Mitzvah 579, where Chinuch sets forth many of the laws that pertain to legal documents.]

37. I.e., both in Eretz Yisrael and in the Diaspora, whether the *Beis HaMikdash* is standing or not.

38. The testimony of women is accepted regarding even the gravest matters of אִסּוּרִים (ritual law), such as the kosher or nonkosher status of a food, the laws of *niddah*, and that a woman's husband has died so she may remarry. However, because there may be some instances where they might succumb to the intense pressure of interrogation in a courtroom setting or be intimidated by the challenges of aggressive litigants, the Torah excluded them from the obligation to testify in monetary or criminal cases (see also *Yam Shel Shlomo, Chullin* 1:1).

[Chinuch's position, that women are not included in this mitzvah, is difficult to understand. As indicated, there are instances in which their testimony is accepted. Why should they not be obligated to testify in those instances? For discussion, see *Minchas Chinuch* §4 and §10.]

# 445 ❑ VAYIKRA / MITZVAH 122: THE OBLIGATION REGARDING TESTIMONY

אוֹ בְּדִינֵי נְפָשׁוֹת וּמַכּוֹת וּבָאִסּוּרִין וּבְאִסּוּרִין שֶׁל תּוֹרָה מֵעַצְמוֹ, בִּטֵּל עֲשֵׂה וְעָנְשׁוֹ גָּדוֹל מְאֹד, כִּי בְּכֹחַ הָעֵדוּת יִתְקַיְּמוּ הַיִּשּׁוּבִים, עַל כֵּן נִכְתַּב בּוֹ (ויקרא ה׳, א׳): "אִם לוֹא יַגִּיד וְנָשָׂא עֲוֹנוֹ"[39]. וְאִם תִּהְיֶה הָעֵדוּת אֲשֶׁר כָּבַשׁ עֵדוּת מָמוֹן וְכִחֵשׁ בָּהּ הָעֵד וְנִשְׁבַּע עָלֶיהָ, כְּלוֹמַר שֶׁנִּשְׁבַּע שֶׁאֵינוֹ יוֹדֵעַ לוֹ עֵדוּת, חַיָּב לְהָבִיא קָרְבָּן עוֹלֶה וְיוֹרֵד[40], וּבִתְנָאִים הַיְּדוּעִים בָּעִנְיָן, כְּמוֹ שֶׁמְּפֹרָשׁ בִּמְקוֹמוֹ בִּשְׁבוּעוֹת (ל׳ ע״א), וְהוּא אֶחָד מִשְּׁלֹשָׁה קָרְבָּנוֹת הַבָּאִין בֵּין עַל שׁוֹגֵג בֵּין עַל מֵזִיד[41].

---

*din* summoned him to provide **testimony,** אוֹ בְּדִינֵי נְפָשׁוֹת וּמַכּוֹת וּבָאִסּוּרִין שֶׁל תּוֹרָה מֵעַצְמוֹ – or, **in cases of capital punishment,** *malkus*, **or other Torah prohibitions,** where he is required to come forth **on his own,** בִּטֵּל עֲשֵׂה – **has violated a mitzvah-obligation.** וְעָנְשׁוֹ גָּדוֹל מְאֹד – **Indeed, his punishment will be very great,** כִּי בְּכֹחַ הָעֵדוּת יִתְקַיְּמוּ הַיִּשּׁוּבִים – **because through the power of testimony,** which leads to the correction of wrongs, **society can endure.** עַל כֵּן נִכְתַּב בּוֹ "אִם לוֹא יַגִּיד וְנָשָׂא עֲוֹנוֹ" – **For this** reason, i.e., due to the severity of this transgression, **it is written** in connection with this [mitzvah]: *if he does not testify he shall bear his iniquity*.[39]

Chinuch notes that there is a situation where violating this mitzvah would lead to additional liability: וְאִם תִּהְיֶה הָעֵדוּת אֲשֶׁר כָּבַשׁ עֵדוּת מָמוֹן – **Moreover, if the testimony that he withholds is testimony regarding a monetary issue,** וְכִחֵשׁ בָּהּ הָעֵד וְנִשְׁבַּע עָלֶיהָ – **and the witness** falsely **denies** that he has knowledge of **it and swears to that effect,** כְּלוֹמַר שֶׁנִּשְׁבַּע שֶׁאֵינוֹ יוֹדֵעַ לוֹ עֵדוּת – **that** is to say, he swears that he does not have knowledge of testimony on behalf of [the litigant], חַיָּב לְהָבִיא קָרְבָּן עוֹלֶה וְיוֹרֵד – **he is obligated to bring an** *oleh v'yoreid* **offering,**[40] וּבִתְנָאִים הַיְּדוּעִים בָּעִנְיָן – **provided that the well-known,** required, **conditions are present in the situation,** כְּמוֹ שֶׁמְּפֹרָשׁ בִּמְקוֹמוֹ בִּשְׁבוּעוֹת – **as is set forth in its** appropriate **place in** Tractate *Shevuos* (30a ff.). וְהוּא אֶחָד מִשְּׁלֹשָׁה קָרְבָּנוֹת הַבָּאִין בֵּין עַל שׁוֹגֵג בֵּין עַל מֵזִיד – **This is one of** the **three** instances of **offerings that are brought** regardless of **whether** the transgression **was inadvertent or was intentional.**[41]

---

### NOTES

39. A number of Acharonim note that aside from this mitzvah-obligation, one who withholds testimony on behalf of others may transgress other mitzvos as well; see Mitzvos 237, 243, and 538 (see *Nesivos HaMishpat, Beurim* 28:1; *Shaar Mishpat* 28:2; *Mishkenos Yaakov, Choshen Mishpat* §12). In fact, those mitzvos may apply even in certain situations where our mitzvah does not apply (see the sources cited above for examples). See also above, notes 2 and 3.

40. I.e., a variable *chatas* (sin) offering. This offering is so named because its requirements are not fixed, but rather depend on the financial situation of the one who is liable to it. The laws of this offering are set forth in the next mitzvah.

41. As Chinuch indicated in the previous mitzvah, liability to a *chatas* offering is generally incurred only for the transgression of a sin that was committed inadvertently. However, as the Mishnah (*Kereisos* 9a) explains, there are some instances in which this liability is incurred even for a deliberate sin, one of which is where one swore falsely that he did not have any knowledge with which to testify on behalf of his fellow.

[The Mishnah actually enumerates *four* instances in which one becomes liable to bring an offering even not in the situation of an error. For discussion, see *Minchas Yitzchak*.]

---

> ⋅§ **Insight: Written Testimony**
>
> The Gemara (*Yevamos* 31b) derives from the phrase (*Deuteronomy* 19:15): עַל פִּי שְׁנֵי עֵדִים, which literally translates as *By the mouths of two witnesses,* that in order for testimony to be valid, the *beis din* must receive it מִפִּיהֶם וְלֹא מִפִּי כְתָבָם, *from [the witnesses'] mouths, but not from their script*. Chinuch (at notes 14-16) cites a dispute between *Rambam* and *Ramban* with regard to why legal documents, such as loan documents, are acceptable in *beis din*. *Rambam* maintains that, under Biblical law, even documents are disqualified on account of constituting written testimony, and they are valid only on the basis of a Rabbinic enactment instituted for the benefit of society. *Ramban*, however, maintains that the Biblical disqualification of written testimony applies only to a simple letter or written recollection that the witnesses write of their own accord, but not to a legal contract

drawn up between two parties. Accordingly, such documents are Biblically acceptable as testimony.

Now, while both *Rambam* and *Ramban* agree that a witness cannot submit his testimony to *beis din* in writing, there is another opinion in Rishonim that accepts even written testimony. This view is that of *Rabbeinu Tam* (cited in *Tosafos, Yevamos* 31b ד"ה דחזו בכתבא), who maintains that the principle of מִפִּיהֶם וְלֹא מִפִּי כְתָבָם, *from their mouths, but not from their script,* requires only that the witnesses be *capable* of submitting the testimony orally. A witness who is incapable of testifying orally (i.e., a mute person) is disqualified by the verse, and cannot submit testimony in writing. A witness who is capable of testifying orally, however, may submit his testimony in writing, provided that he remembers the incident at the time he submits his testimony.

Now, in common practice, this position is not followed, and written testimony is generally rejected by *beis din*. Nevertheless, some authorities maintain that this is merely a stringency, and that the basic halachah follows *Rabbeinu Tam*. Based on this, *Sma* (*Choshen Mishpat* 28:42) rules that it is permitted for Torah scholars to submit their testimony to *beis din* in writing, in order that they not be disturbed from their studies (cf. *Nesivos HaMishpat, Chidushim* ad loc. §24).

*Urim VeTumim* (*Tumim* 28:15), however, raises a difficulty with this ruling: As Chinuch stated among the laws of the mitzvah (at note 7), a Torah scholar is not required to testify before a *beis din* that is of lesser stature than he, because the obligation to honor a Torah scholar overrides the obligation to provide testimony. Now, the Gemara (*Shevuos* 30b) explains that this exemption is due to the irreconcilable conflict between the mitzvah to testify and the mitzvah to accord honor to a Torah scholar, which results in a waiving of the obligation to testify. However, asks *Urim VeTumim*, according to *Rabbeinu Tam* this should not be the case. Since a witness who is capable of testifying orally may submit his testimony in writing, there is in fact no conflict between the obligation to honor a Torah scholar and the mitzvah to testify. The Torah scholar can submit his testimony in writing, without appearing before *beis din*, and his honor will not be compromised at all! Why, then, is he exempt from testifying?

It must be, says *Urim VeTumim*, that even *Rabbeinu Tam* concedes that, due to other considerations, written testimony is generally not acceptable. He explains as follows:

The Gemara (*Bava Kamma* 112b) states that, as a general rule, witnesses must testify only in the presence of the defendant. How, then, can we use their written testimony, when it was not written in the presence of the defendant? Perforce, when *Rabbeinu Tam* permits written testimony, he is speaking only about extenuating circumstances, where the Sages relaxed the requirement that the testimony be submitted in the presence of the defendant, such as cases where the witnesses were in poor health or were traveling abroad (see *Choshen Mishpat* 28:16). In these cases, *Rabbeinu Tam* maintains that since the witnesses may testify without the defendant present, they may even testify in writing. Otherwise, if there is no compelling reason to do so, *Rabbeinu Tam* agrees that the witnesses may not submit their testimony in writing.

For this reason, the Gemara finds the obligation to testify before a *beis din* of lesser stature to be irreconcilable with the mitzvah to accord honor to the Torah. Although there are unique situations where their testimony may be submitted in writing, in most cases even Torah scholars must testify orally, which would be compromising to their dignity.

Based on this interpretation of *Rabbeinu Tam's* position, *Urim VeTumim* concludes that, unless the situation requires that testimony be delivered without the defendant present, such as a case of illness, even a Torah scholar must testify (when applicable) in person, despite the fact that this causes an interruption in his studies.

## 447 ❑ VAYIKRA / MITZVAH 123: THE OBLIGATION OF THE OLEH V'YOREID OFFERING

### מִצְוָה קכג: מִצְוַת קָרְבָּן עוֹלֶה וְיוֹרֵד[1]

לְהַקְרִיב קָרְבָּן עוֹלֶה וְיוֹרֵד עַל חֲטָאִים מְיֻחָדִים, וְהֵם טֻמְאַת מִקְדָּשׁ, כְּלוֹמַר אָדָם שֶׁהוּא טָמֵא בְּאַב הַטֻּמְאָה[2] וְנִכְנַס לַמִּקְדָּשׁ בִּשְׁגָגָה[3], וְטֻמְאַת קָדָשָׁיו גַּם כֵּן

## ⤳ Mitzvah 123 ⤴

## The Obligation of the Oleh V'Yoreid Offering

וְנֶפֶשׁ כִּי תֶחֱטָא וְשָׁמְעָה קוֹל אָלָה וְהוּא עֵד ... אוֹ נֶפֶשׁ אֲשֶׁר תִּגַּע בְּכָל דָּבָר טָמֵא ...
אוֹ נֶפֶשׁ כִּי תִשָּׁבַע ... וְהֵבִיא אֶת אֲשָׁמוֹ לַה' ... נְקֵבָה מִן הַצֹּאן ... וְאִם לֹא תַגִּיעַ יָדוֹ דֵּי
שֶׂה וְהֵבִיא ... שְׁתֵּי תֹרִים אוֹ שְׁנֵי בְנֵי יוֹנָה ... וְאִם לֹא תַשִּׂיג יָדוֹ לִשְׁתֵּי תֹרִים אוֹ לִשְׁנֵי
בְנֵי יוֹנָה וְהֵבִיא ... עֲשִׂירִת הָאֵפָה סֹלֶת

*If a person will sin: If he accepted a demand for an oath, and he is a witness ... or if a person will have touched any impure object ...or if a person will swear... He shall bring as his guilt-offering to* HASHEM *... a female from the flock ... But if his means are insufficient for a sheep or goat, then he shall bring ... two turtledoves or two young doves ... But if his means are insufficient for two turtledoves or two young doves, then he shall bring ... a tenth-ephah of fine flour for a chatas offering (Leviticus 5:1-11).*

The subject of the above passage is the mitzvah of the "variable" *chatas* (sin) offering, or *korban oleh v'yoreid*, literally, *the rising and descending offering*. Unlike the "fixed" *chatas* offering (Mitzvah 121), which is incurred for the inadvertent transgression of any *kares*-bearing prohibition, and which always consists of an animal, the *oleh v'yoreid* offering is prescribed for four specific sins, and the type of offering that must be brought depends on the financial ability of the sinner. One who has the means must bring an animal as his offering; one who cannot afford that brings bird offerings; and one whose means are insufficient for even bird offerings brings instead the inexpensive *minchah* (meal) offering.

The four sins for which one incurs liability to bring this offering are: (1) Entering the Temple while *tamei* (ritually impure); (2) eating *kodashim* (sacrificial meat or other foods) while *tamei*; (3) violating an oath; (4) denying under oath that one knows testimony for his fellow.[1] Chinuch begins by defining these prohibitions and explaining the source verses for each obligation:

לְהַקְרִיב קָרְבָּן עוֹלֶה וְיוֹרֵד עַל חֲטָאִים מְיֻחָדִים וְהֵם — We are commanded **to bring an** *oleh v'yoreid* **offering for** transgressing certain **specific sins, which are:** טֻמְאַת מִקְדָּשׁ — (1) *Tumah* (ritual impurity) violations **of the Temple,** כְּלוֹמַר אָדָם שֶׁהוּא טָמֵא בְּאַב הַטֻּמְאָה — that is **to say, if a person is** *tamei* (ritually impure) **by** contact with **an** *av hatumah*, i.e., an original source of *tumah*,[2] וְנִכְנַס לַמִּקְדָּשׁ בִּשְׁגָגָה — **and he enters the Holy Temple** (*Beis HaMikdash*) **inadvertently** while in this state;[3] וְטֻמְאַת קָדָשָׁיו גַּם כֵּן — **as well as (2)** *tumah* violations **of the holy things [of**

---

### NOTES

1. [One who denies a financial obligation under oath is subject to a different offering; see below, Mitzvah 129.]

2. In general, any source from which *tumah* emanates is known as אַב הַטֻּמְאָה, *av hatumah* (literally, *father of tumah*). [*Tumah* is a physically indiscernible ritual impurity that affects persons, articles, foods, and beverages. *Tumah* stems from organic bodies — dead animals and humans, or live humans who experience certain bodily irregularities (*Rambam*, Introduction to *Tohoros*).]

3. It is a violation of a mitzvah-prohibition to enter the *Beis HaMikdash* while *tamei*; see below, Mitzvah 363, for the parameters of this prohibition. With regard to this prohibition, the "*Beis HaMikdash*" includes the Sanctuary and the Inner Courtyard (known as the Israelites' Courtyard), where the Outer Altar was situated (see *Rambam*, *Hil. Bi'as HaMikdash* Ch. 3).

שֶׁהוּא טָמֵא וְאָכַל בְּשַׂר קֹדֶשׁ בִּשְׁגָגָה⁴, וּשְׁבוּעַת בִּטּוּי, כְּלוֹמַר שֶׁנִּשְׁבַּע לַשֶּׁקֶר עַל דָּבָר לַעֲשׂוֹת אוֹ שֶׁלֹּא לַעֲשׂוֹת⁵, וּשְׁאָר צִדְדֵי שְׁבוּעַת בִּטּוּי הַיְדוּעִים⁶ וְעוֹבֵר עָלֶיהָ בִּשְׁגָגָה, וְכֵן שְׁבוּעַת הָעֵדוּת, כְּלוֹמַר שֶׁנִּשְׁבַּע לַחֲבֵרוֹ שֶׁאֵינוֹ יוֹדֵעַ לוֹ עֵדוּת⁷, בֵּין בְּשׁוֹגֵג בֵּין בְּמֵזִיד⁸. עַל אֵלּוּ הַחֲטָאִים חַיָּב אָדָם לְהָבִיא קָרְבָּן עוֹלֶה וְיוֹרֵד, כְּלוֹמַר לְפִי עָשְׁרוֹ וְעָנְיוֹ שֶׁל אָדָם, כְּמוֹ שֶׁמְּפֹרָשׁ בַּכָּתוּב שֶׁנֶּאֱמַר (ויקרא ה, א) וְנֶפֶשׁ כִּי תֶחֱטָא וְשָׁמְעָה קוֹל אָלָה, כְּלוֹמַר קוֹל שְׁבוּעָה שֶׁהִשְׁבִּיעוּהוּ אִם יוֹדֵעַ עֵדוּת, אִם לוֹא יַגִּיד וְנָשָׂא עֲוֹנוֹ (שם)⁹, וְסוֹף הָעִנְיָן וְהֵבִיא אֶת אֲשָׁמוֹ (שם, שם ו).

---

**the Temple**] (i.e., *kodashim*, sacrificial food), שֶׁהוּא טָמֵא וְאָכַל בְּשַׂר קֹדֶשׁ בִּשְׁגָגָה — **that** is, **when one is *tamei* and he inadvertently eats consecrated meat.**[4] וּשְׁבוּעַת בִּטּוּי (3) — **An oath of "utterance,"** כְּלוֹמַר שֶׁנִּשְׁבַּע לַשֶּׁקֶר עַל דָּבָר לַעֲשׂוֹת אוֹ שֶׁלֹּא לַעֲשׂוֹת — that is **to say, that he swears falsely to do or not to do something,**[5] וּשְׁאָר צִדְדֵי שְׁבוּעַת בִּטּוּי הַיְדוּעִים — **or** he swore in any of **the other known ways** that **an oath of utterance** can be made,[6] וְעוֹבֵר עָלֶיהָ בִּשְׁגָגָה — **and he violates [his oath] inadvertently.** וְכֵן שְׁבוּעַת הָעֵדוּת — **Likewise,** (4) **an oath of testimony,** כְּלוֹמַר שֶׁנִּשְׁבַּע לַחֲבֵרוֹ שֶׁאֵינוֹ יוֹדֵעַ לוֹ עֵדוּת — that is **to say, that he swears** falsely **to his fellow that he does not know** anything about which he can give **testimony** in court **for him,**[7] בֵּין בְּשׁוֹגֵג בֵּין בְּמֵזִיד — **whether** he takes this false oath **inadvertently or deliberately.**[8] עַל אֵלּוּ הַחֲטָאִים חַיָּב אָדָם לְהָבִיא קָרְבָּן עוֹלֶה וְיוֹרֵד — **For** any of **these** four **sins, a person is obligated to bring an *oleh v'yoreid* (variable) offering,** כְּלוֹמַר לְפִי עָשְׁרוֹ וְעָנְיוֹ שֶׁל אָדָם — **meaning to say,** the offering that he is obligated to bring varies **commensurate with the wealth or poverty of the individual,** כְּמוֹ שֶׁמְּפֹרָשׁ בַּכָּתוּב — **as it is set forth in Scripture.**

Chinuch explains how each of the four sins listed above are derived from their Scriptural source. He begins with the "oath of testimony."

The full verse regarding the oath of testimony reads: וְנֶפֶשׁ כִּי תֶחֱטָא וְשָׁמְעָה קוֹל אָלָה וְהוּא עֵד אוֹ רָאָה אוֹ יָדָע אִם לוֹא יַגִּיד וְנָשָׂא עֲוֹנוֹ, *If a person will sin: If he accepted a demand for an oath, and he is a witness — either he saw or he knew [testimony] — if he does not testify, he shall bear his iniquity.* Chinuch begins by explaining the term קוֹל אָלָה, which literally means "the voice of an adjuration."

שֶׁנֶּאֱמַר "וְנֶפֶשׁ כִּי תֶחֱטָא וְשָׁמְעָה קוֹל אָלָה" — **We are so commanded, as it is stated** (*Leviticus* 5:1): *If a person will sin: If he accepted the voice of an adjuration,* כְּלוֹמַר קוֹל שְׁבוּעָה שֶׁהִשְׁבִּיעוּהוּ אִם יוֹדֵעַ עֵדוּת — the phrase "the voice of an adjuration," means **to say, the sound of an oath,** i.e., [the litigants] **adjure him** to declare under oath **whether he knows** some **testimony** regarding their case. "אִם לוֹא יַגִּיד וְנָשָׂא עֲוֹנוֹ" — *If he does not testify, he shall bear his iniquity;* that is, if even after being adjured with an oath, he denies knowledge of any testimony that he actually could give, he bears a sin for which he must atone.[9] וְסוֹף הָעִנְיָן "וְהֵבִיא אֶת אֲשָׁמוֹ" — **At the end of the matter** (i.e., at the end of

---

NOTES

4. That is, meat of an offering. Eating *kodashim* while *tamei* violates Mitzvah 167.

5. He swears that he will do a specific action, and then neglects to do it, or he swears that he will not do a specific action and then he does it.

6. This refers to an oath relating to a past event, for example, if one swears falsely that he did or did not do something. See below, Mitzvah 227, for a discussion of the various kinds of oaths that are included in the prohibition.

7. The previous mitzvah discussed the obligation of a person to testify on another's behalf when asked to do so by that litigant. Here, we refer to a situation where a litigant approaches another and asks if he has any information pertaining to the litigant's monetary case that he can present as testimony. If one falsely denies knowledge of any testimony and then takes an oath attesting to his ignorance, he is obligated to bring this offering. [For the various conditions required for this obligation, see *Rambam, Hil. Shevuos*, Chapter 9.]

8. Chinuch below derives this from the wording of the verse. The liability for a *chatas* offering is generally only for inadvertent violations (see above, Mitzvah 121). Taking a false "oath of testimony" is one of the few instances in which one offers a *chatas* even for a deliberate violation.

9. The term "adjured oath" refers to when the litigant asks for one's testimony and, upon receiving a denial of any knowledge, the litigant says, מַשְׁבִּיעַ אֲנִי עָלֶיךָ, *I place*

# 449 □ VAYIKRA / MITZVAH 123: THE OBLIGATION OF THE OLEH V'YOREID OFFERING

וְלֹא נֶאֱמַר שָׁם וְנֶעְלַם מִמֶּנּוּ,[10] לְלַמֵּד שֶׁחַיָּב בְּקָרְבָּן בֵּין שׁוֹגֵג בֵּין מֵזִיד.
וּכְתִיב בְּטֻמְאַת מִקְדָּשׁ וְקָדָשָׁיו (שם, שם ב׳) אוֹ נֶפֶשׁ אֲשֶׁר תִּגַּע בְּכָל דָּבָר טָמֵא וְגוֹ׳,
וְנֶעְלַם מִמֶּנּוּ וְגוֹ׳, וְנֶאֱמַר עַל הַכֹּל בְּסוֹף הָעִנְיָן (שם ו׳) וְהֵבִיא אֶת אֲשָׁמוֹ. וְלֹא בָא בַּכָּתוּב
מְפֹרָשׁ שֶׁחִיּוּב הַטָּמֵא שֶׁנֶּאֱמַר שָׁם יִהְיֶה בְּהִכָּנְסוֹ בַּמִּקְדָּשׁ אוֹ בְּאָכְלוֹ בְּשַׂר קֹדֶשׁ,
אֶלָּא מִפִּי הַשְּׁמוּעָה שָׁמַעְנוּ שֶׁהוּא מְדַבֵּר עַל זֶה,[11] וְאַף עַל פִּי שֶׁהַדָּבָר מִפִּי הַקַּבָּלָה,

the passage that lists all four sins), the verse states the offering that is required (vs. 6-13), beginning **He shall bring as his guilt offering** to HASHEM, and concludes with the three levels of offerings depending on the financial ability of the violator.

Chinuch points out an aspect of this violation that does not apply to the other three sins for which one incurs the *oleh v'yoreid* offering:

וְלֹא נֶאֱמַר שָׁם "וְנֶעְלַם מִמֶּנּוּ" — **It is not stated** in the verse **there** (v. 1), as it is with regard to the other sins, "*it was concealed from him,*" a phrase that indicates an inadvertent violation; לְלַמֵּד שֶׁחַיָּב בְּקָרְבָּן בֵּין שׁוֹגֵג בֵּין מֵזִיד — this is **to teach** that when one takes a false oath of testimony, one is obligated **to bring the offering whether** his violation was **inadvertent or deliberate.**[10]

Chinuch now explains how the violations regarding entering the Temple or eating *kodashim* in an impure state are derived from the verses in this passage. The pertinent verses (v. 2-3) read: אוֹ נֶפֶשׁ אֲשֶׁר תִּגַּע בְּכָל דָּבָר טָמֵא אוֹ בְנִבְלַת חַיָּה טְמֵאָה אוֹ בְּנִבְלַת בְּהֵמָה טְמֵאָה אוֹ בְנִבְלַת שֶׁרֶץ טָמֵא וְנֶעְלַם מִמֶּנּוּ וְהוּא טָמֵא וְאָשֵׁם. אוֹ כִי יִגַּע בְּטֻמְאַת אָדָם לְכֹל טֻמְאָתוֹ אֲשֶׁר יִטְמָא בָּהּ וְנֶעְלַם מִמֶּנּוּ וְהוּא יָדַע וְאָשֵׁם, *Or if a person will have touched any impure object — whether the carcass of an impure beast, the carcass of an impure animal, or the carcass of a creeping animal that is impure — but it was concealed from him, and he is impure and becomes guilty; or if he will touch a human impurity in any manner of its impurity through which he can become impure but it was concealed from him — and he knew and he became guilty.* [These verses refer to contact with various sources of impurity such as *neveilah* (i.e., the carcass of an animal that died by some means other than a valid ritual slaughter); a *sheretz* (i.e., the carcass of one of the eight species of creeping creatures listed in *Leviticus* 11:29-30); a corpse or a person who had contact with a corpse; or a person who is *tamei* with certain forms of *tumah*.]

Chinuch notes that the verses explicitly mention only the fact that the person became *tamei*, not the actual violation of entering the Temple or eating *kodashim* in that state:

וּכְתִיב בְּטֻמְאַת מִקְדָּשׁ וְקָדָשָׁיו — **And it is written regarding** *tumah* **violations of the Temple and of its consecrated [foods]:** "אוֹ נֶפֶשׁ אֲשֶׁר תִּגַּע בְּכָל דָּבָר טָמֵא וְנֶעְלַם מִמֶּנּוּ וְגוֹ׳" — "*or if a person will have touched any impure object, etc., but it was concealed from him, etc.,*" וְנֶאֱמַר עַל הַכֹּל בְּסוֹף הָעִנְיָן — **and it is stated regarding all** the listed sins in the passage, **at the end of the matter,** "וְהֵבִיא אֶת אֲשָׁמוֹ" — "*He shall bring as his guilt offering* to HASHEM, *etc.* [the appropriate offering commensurate with his financial means]. וְלֹא בָא בַּכָּתוּב מְפֹרָשׁ שֶׁחִיּוּב הַטָּמֵא שֶׁנֶּאֱמַר שָׁם — **Now, the verse does not state explicitly that the obligation for** *tumah* **stated there** יִהְיֶה בְּהִכָּנְסוֹ בַּמִּקְדָּשׁ אוֹ בְּאָכְלוֹ בְּשַׂר קֹדֶשׁ — **applies when he enters the Temple or eats consecrated meat;** אֶלָּא מִפִּי הַשְּׁמוּעָה שָׁמַעְנוּ שֶׁהוּא מְדַבֵּר עַל זֶה — **rather, it is from the Oral Tradition that we received** the interpretation of these verses **that [the passage] is speaking of this** manner of violation.[11]

וְאַף עַל פִּי שֶׁהַדָּבָר מִפִּי הַקַּבָּלָה — However, **although the matter is** primarily **known to us by Oral**

---

NOTES

*you under oath.* If the "witness" repeats his denial, he has accepted an adjured oath and is liable. Although the verse speaks only of the case of an adjured oath, the Gemara (*Shevuos* 31a-b) derives that he is equally liable if he takes an oath on his own.

10. Below, Chinuch defines the parameters of deliberate and inadvertent violations of this prohibition.

11. See *Shevuos* 6b-7b, and *Rambam, Hil. Shegagos* 10:5 with *Lechem Mishneh*.

מָצָאנוּ בְּפֵרוּשׁ בְּמָקוֹם אַחֵר חִיּוּב כָּרֵת לְטָמֵא שֶׁאוֹכֵל קֹדֶשׁ אוֹ נִכְנָס לַמִּקְדָּשׁ, שֶׁנֶּאֱמַר (שם ז, כ) "וְהַנֶּפֶשׁ אֲשֶׁר תֹּאכַל בָּשָׂר מִזֶּבַח הַשְּׁלָמִים אֲשֶׁר לַה' וְטֻמְאָתוֹ עָלָיו וְנִכְרְתָה וְגוֹ'", וְכָתוּב אַחֵר אוֹמֵר בְּטָמֵא הַנִּכְנָס לַמִּקְדָּשׁ (במדבר י״ט, כ) "כִּי אֶת מִקְדַּשׁ ה' טִמֵּא וְנִכְרְתָה, וְאַחַר שֶׁנִּכְתַּב כָּרֵת בִּזְדוֹנָן, יֵשׁ קָרְבָּן בְּשִׁגְגָתָן, עִם הַכְּלָל שֶׁלָּנוּ שֶׁכָּל שֶׁזְּדוֹנוֹ כָּרֵת יֵשׁ בְּשִׁגְגָתוֹ חַטָּאת[12]. וּכְתִיב בִּשְׁבוּעַת בִּטּוּי (ויקרא ה׳, ד׳) "אוֹ נֶפֶשׁ כִּי תִשָּׁבַע לְבַטֵּא בִשְׂפָתַיִם וְגוֹ', וְנֶעְלַם מִמֶּנּוּ וְגוֹ', וְהֵבִיא אֶת אֲשָׁמוֹ. וּמִנַּיִן שֶׁהַחִיּוּב בָּהּ בְּקָרְבָּן עוֹלֶה וְיוֹרֵד, שֶׁכָּתוּב שָׁם בַּפָּרָשָׁה (שם ה׳, י״א) "וְאִם לֹא תַשִּׂיג יָדוֹ וְגוֹ'.

מִשָּׁרְשֵׁי הַמִּצְוָה, כְּבָר אָמַרְנוּ כִּי עִנְיַן הַקָּרְבָּן לְהַזְכִּיר וּלְהָשִׁיב הַחוֹטֵא אֶל לִבּוֹ בְּכֹחַ

**Tradition,** מָצָאנוּ בְּפֵרוּשׁ בְּמָקוֹם אַחֵר — the fact that the offerings of the verse apply to these violations can be inferred from the fact that **we find explicitly elsewhere in Scripture** חִיּוּב כָּרֵת לְטָמֵא שֶׁאוֹכֵל קֹדֶשׁ אוֹ נִכְנָס לַמִּקְדָּשׁ — a *kares* (excision) **penalty for a** *tamei* **[person] who eats** *kodashim* **or enters the Temple,** שֶׁנֶּאֱמַר "וְהַנֶּפֶשׁ אֲשֶׁר תֹּאכַל בָּשָׂר מִזֶּבַח הַשְּׁלָמִים אֲשֶׁר לַה' וְטֻמְאָתוֹ עָלָיו וְנִכְרְתָה וְגוֹ'" — **as it is stated** (ibid. 7:20): *A person who eats flesh from the shelamim offering that is Hashem's while his tumah is upon him,* that soul will be cut off *from its people* etc. (thus, *kares* for a *tamei* person who eats *kodashim*); וְכָתוּב אַחֵר אוֹמֵר בְּטָמֵא הַנִּכְנָס לַמִּקְדָּשׁ — **and another verse states, regarding a** *tamei* **[person] who enters the Temple** (Numbers 19:20): "כִּי אֶת מִקְדַּשׁ ה' טִמֵּא וְנִכְרְתָה" — *if he shall have made the Sanctuary of* HASHEM *impure, that person shall be cut off from the midst of the congregation* (thus, *kares* for a *tamei* person who enters the Temple). וְאַחַר שֶׁנִּכְתַּב כָּרֵת בִּזְדוֹנָן יֵשׁ קָרְבָּן בְּשִׁגְגָתָן — **Now, since** *kares* **is written regarding** the **deliberate violation of these** sins, it follows that **there is** an **obligation to bring an offering for their inadvertent** violation, עִם הַכְּלָל שֶׁלָּנוּ שֶׁכָּל שֶׁזְּדוֹנוֹ כָּרֵת יֵשׁ בְּשִׁגְגָתוֹ חַטָּאת — in keeping with **our rule** (set forth in Mitzvah 121) **that any** transgression **whose deliberate violation incurs** *kares***, its inadvertent violation incurs a** *chatas* **offering.** It therefore follows that when the Torah speaks of a variable *chatas* offering pertaining to a sin of *tumah*, it refers specifically to those violations that we know carry the *kares* penalty if they are done deliberately, whose inadvertent violations therefore require an offering as atonement.[12]

Chinuch cites the source for the fourth violation:

וּכְתִיב בִּשְׁבוּעַת בִּטּוּי — **It is written regarding** the sin of **an oath of utterance** (Leviticus 5:4-6): "אוֹ נֶפֶשׁ כִּי תִשָּׁבַע לְבַטֵּא בִשְׂפָתַיִם וְגוֹ' וְנֶעְלַם מִמֶּנּוּ וְגוֹ'" — *or if a person will swear, expressing with his lips* etc. *[to do harm or to do good, anything that a person will express in an oath]*, **but it was concealed from him,** and then he knew, etc., "וְהֵבִיא אֶת אֲשָׁמוֹ" — **He shall bring as his guilt offering** to HASHEM, etc. וּמִנַּיִן שֶׁהַחִיּוּב בָּהּ בְּקָרְבָּן עוֹלֶה וְיוֹרֵד — **And how do we know that the obligation for [any of these** **sins] is an** *oleh v'yoreid* (variable) **offering?** שֶׁכָּתוּב שָׁם בַּפָּרָשָׁה — **Because it is written there in the** same **passage** (vs. 11-13): "וְאִם לֹא תַשִּׂיג יָדוֹ וְגוֹ'" — **But if his means are insufficient** for a sheep or goat, then he shall bring ... two turtledoves or two young doves... But if his means are insufficient for two turtledoves or two young doves, then he shall bring ... a tenth-ephah of fine flour for a chatas offering, **etc.**

### ✦ Underlying Purpose of the Mitzvah ✦

מִשָּׁרְשֵׁי הַמִּצְוָה כְּבָר אָמַרְנוּ — **Among the underlying purposes of the mitzvah is that which we have already stated** (Mitzvah 95), כִּי עִנְיַן הַקָּרְבָּן לְהַזְכִּיר וּלְהָשִׁיב הַחוֹטֵא אֶל לִבּוֹ בְּכֹחַ

---

NOTES

12. The verse certainly cannot be understood to mean that one must bring the offering for the very act of contracting the *tumah*, for there is no prohibition against contracting this kind of *tumah* (see Ramban, Leviticus 5:2). [Even a Kohen is prohibited only from becoming *tamei* through a corpse (Mitzvah 263), but not through other forms of *tumah*.]

הַפְּעֻלָּה כִּי הֵרַע מַעֲשָׂיו, וִישַׁבֵּקֶשׁ מְחִילָה לָאֵל עַל הֶעָשׂוּי, וְיִזָּהֵר עַל הֶעָתִיד.[13] וּמֵחָכְמָתוֹ בָּרוּךְ הוּא וּבִידִיעָתוֹ קַלּוּת שֵׂכֶל בְּנֵי אִישׁ וּמִעוּט הֲבָנָתָם וְדַלּוּת כֹּחָם הֵקֵל עֲלֵיהֶם הַכַּפָּרָה בַּחֲטָאִים הָאֵלֶּה הַנִּזְכָּרִים לִהְיוֹתָם כְּפִי עֹשֶׁר בְּנֵי אָדָם וְעָנְיָם, לְפִי שֶׁכִּשְׁלוֹנָם קָרוֹב אֵצֶל בְּנֵי אָדָם, שֶׁאֵין סָפֵק כִּי חֵטְא הַלָּשׁוֹן קָרוֹב וּתְמִידִי יוֹתֵר מֵחֵטְא הַמַּעֲשֶׂה, וְזֶה יַסְפִּיק לְךָ עַל הַשְּׁבוּעוֹת.

גַּם עַל עִנְיַן טֻמְאַת מִקְדָּשׁ וְקָדָשָׁיו יָדוּעַ שֶׁהַכִּשָּׁלוֹן מָצוּי בּוֹ, שֶׁעִנְיַן הַטָּהֳרָה קָשֶׁה מְאֹד עַל כָּל אָדָם לְשָׁמְרוֹ, עַד שֶׁיֵּשׁ לוֹ לָאָדָם הַטָּהוֹר לְהִזָּהֵר מֵהִתְקָרֵב אֵצֶל בְּנֵי אָדָם מֵחֲשַׁשׁ הַטֻּמְאָה,[14] וְיֶאֱרַךְ הָעִנְיָן אִם בָּאתִי לִכְתֹּב מִכַּמָּה צְדָדִין הַכִּשְׁלוֹנוֹת הַמְּצוּיִין בּוֹ, וְאוּלָם יָדוּעַ הוּא לְכָל מֵבִין.[15]

---

הַפְּעֻלָּה — **that the purpose of an offering is to make the sinner aware and have him take to heart, through the power of this action,** כִּי הֵרַע מַעֲשָׂיו — **that he has acted wickedly,** וִישַׁבֵּקֶשׁ מְחִילָה לָאֵל עַל הֶעָשׂוּי — **and that he should ask forgiveness from the Almighty for what was done,** וְיִזָּהֵר עַל הֶעָתִיד — **and to beware regarding** his actions in **the future.**[13]

Chinuch turns to the specific offering of this mitzvah, which, in its descending order of obligations based on financial ability, is more lenient an atonement than the standard *chatas* offering. Chinuch explains why these specific sins are singled out for leniency, starting with the sin of swearing falsely: וּמֵחָכְמָתוֹ בָּרוּךְ הוּא וּבִידִיעָתוֹ קַלּוּת שֵׂכֶל בְּנֵי אִישׁ — **In [God's] wisdom, blessed is He, and in His knowledge of the shallowness of human intelligence** וּמִעוּט הֲבָנָתָם וְדַלּוּת כֹּחָם — **and the meagerness of their comprehension and the deficiency of their fortitude,** הֵקֵל עֲלֵיהֶם הַכַּפָּרָה בַּחֲטָאִים הָאֵלֶּה הַנִּזְכָּרִים — **He eased for them** the ability to achieve **atonement for these** aforementioned **sins,** לִהְיוֹתָם כְּפִי עֹשֶׁר בְּנֵי אָדָם וְעָנְיָם — **allowing [the offerings] to be brought commensurate with man's wealth or poverty,** לְפִי שֶׁכִּשְׁלוֹנָם קָרוֹב אֵצֶל בְּנֵי אָדָם — **since the potential for stumbling in [these sins] is commonplace to people,** שֶׁאֵין סָפֵק כִּי חֵטְא הַלָּשׁוֹן קָרוֹב וּתְמִידִי יוֹתֵר מֵחֵטְא הַמַּעֲשֶׂה — **as there is no doubt that a sin of the tongue** (such as swearing falsely) **is a more likely and regular** occurrence **than a sin of action.** וְזֶה יַסְפִּיק לְךָ עַל הַשְּׁבוּעוֹת — **This is sufficient** reason **for you** to understand the leniency of the *oleh v'yoreid* offering **for** the sins regarding **oaths.**

Chinuch explains the reason for leniency with regard to *tumah* violations: גַּם עַל עִנְיַן טֻמְאַת מִקְדָּשׁ וְקָדָשָׁיו — **So too, regarding the matter of *tumah* violations of the Temple and its consecrated [foods],** יָדוּעַ שֶׁהַכִּשָּׁלוֹן מָצוּי בּוֹ — **it is known that failure is commonplace,** שֶׁעִנְיַן הַטָּהֳרָה קָשֶׁה מְאֹד עַל כָּל אָדָם לְשָׁמְרוֹ — **for it is very difficult for any person to be vigilant in the matter of** ritual **purity,** עַד שֶׁיֵּשׁ לוֹ לָאָדָם הַטָּהוֹר לְהִזָּהֵר מֵהִתְקָרֵב אֵצֶל בְּנֵי אָדָם — **to the extent that it is proper for a** ritually **pure person to beware of coming in contact with** any other **people out of fear of *tumah*.**[14] וְיֶאֱרַךְ הָעִנְיָן — **The** discussion of this **matter would become** unduly **long** אִם בָּאתִי לִכְתֹּב מִכַּמָּה צְדָדִין הַכִּשְׁלוֹנוֹת הַמְּצוּיִין בּוֹ — **if I were to write the many ways that failure commonly occurs in this** matter; וְאוּלָם יָדוּעַ הוּא לְכָל מֵבִין — **nevertheless, [this matter] is familiar to every understanding person.**[15]

---

## NOTES

13. See Mitzvah 95, where Chinuch explains this concept at length.

14. See, for example, *Rambam, Hil. Metam'ei Mishkav U'Moshav* 10:1. One who is ritually pure must avoid certain kinds of contact not only with people who are certainly impure, but even with those who are generally lax with the laws of purity.

15. There are many ways for a person to become *tamei*, many of which do not involve any violation on the part of the person who contracted the *tumah* (such as touching a carcass), and are part of the regular routines of life. Nevertheless, when any of these occurs, those people are forbidden from entering the Temple or eating *kodashim*.

[*Ramban* (*Leviticus* 5:3) suggests that leniency is provided for this sin because the violations occurred in conjunction with performing a mitzvah, either eating sacrificial meat, or entering the Temple to worship or bring an offering. For this reason, although there was a lapse of awareness of *tumah*, the Torah afforded a person an easier means of atonement.]

## 452 □ ויקרא / מצוה קכג: מצות קרבן עולה ויורד

וּמִן הַשֹּׁרֶשׁ הַזֶּה שֶׁאָמַרְנוּ שֶׁהַכִּשָּׁלוֹן קָרוֹב בְּעִנְיָנִים אֵלֶּה, הֵקֵל לָהֶם עוֹד בִּשְׁבוּעַת הָעֵדוּת לִהְיוֹתָם מְבִיאִים כַּפָּרָה בֵּין עַל שׁוֹגֵג אוֹ מֵזִיד, לְפִי שֶׁעִנְיַן הָעֵדוּת הוּא תְּמִידִי בְּיוֹתֵר וְיֵצֶר לֵב הָאָדָם רַע[16], וְתוֹלִין הַשֶּׁקֶר בְּשִׁכְחָה וְלֹא יְכַוְּנוּ עֵדוּתָם. גַּם יֵשׁ מִן הַבְּרִיּוֹת שֶׁאֵין מַשְׁגִּיחִין כָּל כָּךְ בְּרָעָה הַגְּדוֹלָה שֶׁעוֹשִׂין בְּהַטָּיַת כִּוּוּן הָעֵדוּת, אַחַר שֶׁבִּידֵיהֶם לֹא יִגְזְלוּ וְלֹא יַחְמְסוּ, אַף עַל פִּי שֶׁבְּסִבָּתָם אָדָם עָשׁוּק וְרָצוּץ, לֹא יִתְּנוּ לֵב עַל זֶה. וְעַל כֵּן מֵהִתְמַדַּת הָעִנְיָן וְקַלּוּתוֹ בְּעֵינֵי הֲמוֹן הָעָם הָיָה מֵחֲסָדָיו בָּרוּךְ הוּא לִהְיוֹת בּוֹ כַּפָּרָה בֵּין עַל שׁוֹגֵג בֵּין מֵזִיד.

וְאוּלָם הַמֵּבִין בִּבְנֵי אָדָם יוֹדֵעַ כִּי כָל אֲשֶׁר יַרְחִיקֵנוּ הָאֵל מִמֶּנּוּ, אַף עַל פִּי שֶׁנָּתַן הַדָּבָר לְכַפָּרָה, רָאוּי לָנוּ לְהַרְחִיקוֹ תַּכְלִית הָרִחוּק. וְהָעִנְיָן הוּא כְּאִלּוּ יוֹדִיעַ הָאֵל בָּרוּךְ הוּא אֶל

---

With regard to the sin of denying knowledge of testimony under oath, there is an additional leniency — one can atone with an offering even for a deliberate violation, something generally not possible with other deliberate sins. Chinuch explains why this extra leniency is appropriate:

וּמִן הַשֹּׁרֶשׁ הַזֶּה שֶׁאָמַרְנוּ שֶׁהַכִּשָּׁלוֹן קָרוֹב — **For this underlying purpose that we have stated,** הֵקֵל לָהֶם עוֹד בִּשְׁבוּעַת — namely, **that failure is common in these matters,** בְּעִנְיָנִים אֵלֶּה הָעֵדוּת — [Hashem] added another leniency for the matter of the oath of testimony, לִהְיוֹתָם מְבִיאִים כַּפָּרָה בֵּין עַל שׁוֹגֵג אוֹ מֵזִיד — namely, **that [the transgressors] bring** an offering **for atonement whether** the sin **was inadvertent or deliberate;** לְפִי שֶׁעִנְיַן הָעֵדוּת הוּא תְּמִידִי בְּיוֹתֵר — **because the matter of testimony** occurs **with great regularity,** i.e., it is very common for one to possess knowledge of testimony for another, וְיֵצֶר לֵב הָאָדָם רַע — **but the inclination of man's heart is evil**[16] וְתוֹלִין הַשֶּׁקֶר בְּשִׁכְחָה — **and [potential witnesses]** are able to **attribute the false** claim of ignorance **to having forgotten** what they saw, knowing that the lie can never be proven וְלֹא יְכַוְּנוּ עֵדוּתָם — **so they are not precise** and honest in acknowledging **what they witnessed.**

In addition to the regularity of occurrence and the ease of denial, Chinuch adds another reason for the frequency of failure in this matter:

גַּם יֵשׁ מִן הַבְּרִיּוֹת שֶׁאֵין מַשְׁגִּיחִין כָּל כָּךְ — **Furthermore, there are people who do not fully appreciate** בְּרָעָה הַגְּדוֹלָה שֶׁעוֹשִׂין בְּהַטָּיַת כִּוּוּן הָעֵדוּת — **the tremendous harm that they do when they veer away from** acknowledging **the precise testimony** that they can give, אַחַר שֶׁבִּידֵיהֶם לֹא יִגְזְלוּ וְלֹא יַחְמְסוּ — **since they are not actively stealing** from or extorting others; אַף עַל פִּי שֶׁבְּסִבָּתָם אָדָם עָשׁוּק וְרָצוּץ — **and although it is because of them,** i.e., their withholding of testimony, **that a person is being** unlawfully **oppressed and persecuted,** לֹא יִתְּנוּ לֵב עַל זֶה — **they pay no attention to this.** וְעַל כֵּן מֵהִתְמַדַּת הָעִנְיָן — **Therefore, due to the frequency of the matter** of the obligation to testify, וְקַלּוּתוֹ בְּעֵינֵי הֲמוֹן הָעָם — **and the leniency of [its violation] in the eyes of the common people,** הָיָה מֵחֲסָדָיו בָּרוּךְ הוּא — **it was** ordained, as **one of [Hashem's] acts of kindness, blessed is He,** לִהְיוֹת בּוֹ כַּפָּרָה בֵּין עַל שׁוֹגֵג בֵּין מֵזִיד — **that there should be atonement for [this sin]** by bringing an offering **whether it was inadvertent or deliberate.**

Chinuch concludes this section by warning that one should not think that since Hashem gave people means to atone even for a deliberate violation, one can commit this sin and rely on the atonement of the offering:

וְאוּלָם הַמֵּבִין בִּבְנֵי אָדָם יוֹדֵעַ כִּי כָל אֲשֶׁר יַרְחִיקֵנוּ — **Nevertheless, the wise among people knows** הָאֵל מִמֶּנּוּ — **that whatever** action **the Almighty distanced us from** by prohibiting it in the Torah, אַף עַל פִּי שֶׁנָּתַן הַדָּבָר לְכַפָּרָה — **even though He has provided** a means of **atonement for the matter,** רָאוּי לָנוּ לְהַרְחִיקוֹ תַּכְלִית הָרִחוּק — **it is fitting for us to distance ourselves from it with the greatest possible distance.** וְהָעִנְיָן הוּא כְּאִלּוּ יוֹדִיעַ הָאֵל בָּרוּךְ הוּא אֶל בְּנֵי אָדָם — The essence of **the matter** should be viewed **as though the Almighty, blessed is He, informed people**

---

NOTES

16. Stylistic citation of *Genesis* 8:21.

# 453 □ VAYIKRA / MITZVAH 123: THE OBLIGATION OF THE OLEH V'YOREID OFFERING

בְּנֵי אָדָם, דָּבָר פְּלוֹנִי אֵין רְצוֹנִי שֶׁתַּעֲשׂוּ אוֹתוֹ בְּשׁוּם פָּנִים, וְאוּלָם הַנִּכְשָׁל מִכֶּם וְיַעֲבֹר עָלֶיהָ יַעֲשֶׂה תְּשׁוּבָה בְּכָל כֹּחוֹ וְיִגְדֹּר עַצְמוֹ בְּהַרְבֵּה גְדָרִים[17] וְיָבִיא קָרְבָּן לִקְבֹּעַ הַדָּבָר בְּלִבּוֹ שֶׁלֹּא יִכָּשֵׁל בּוֹ עוֹד. וּמִכָּל מָקוֹם לֹא נִצַּל הָאִישׁ הַהוּא שֶׁלֹּא עָבַר עַל מִצְוַת בּוֹרְאוֹ[18].

מִדִּינֵי הַמִּצְוָה, שֶׁכָּל אֶחָד מֵאַרְבָּעָה חֲטָאִים אֵלֶּה מְחֻיָּב עוֹשֵׂהוּ לְהָבִיא כִּשְׂבָּה אוֹ שְׂעִירָה כְּדִין חַטָּאת קְבוּעָה הַיָּדוּעַ[19], וְאֵינוֹ נִפְטָר בְּעוֹף אוֹ בְּקֶמַח אֶלָּא אִם כֵּן הוּא עָנִי. וְאִם הוּא עָנִי וְהֵבִיא כִּשְׂבָּה אוֹ שְׂעִירָה, לֹא יָצָא יְדֵי חוֹבָתוֹ[20], וְהַטַּעַם לְפִי שֶׁאַחַר שֶׁרִחֵם הָאֵל בָּרוּךְ הוּא עָלָיו וּפְטָרוֹ בְּכָךְ, אֵינוֹ בְּדִין שֶׁיִּדְחֹק עַצְמוֹ לְהָבִיא בְּיוֹתֵר [מִ]מַּה שֶׁתַּשִּׂיג יָדוֹ.

---

as follows: דָּבָר פְּלוֹנִי אֵין רְצוֹנִי שֶׁתַּעֲשׂוּ אוֹתוֹ בְּשׁוּם פָּנִים – "I do not desire that you should do this thing (e.g., the sin of refusing testimony) at all; וְאוּלָם הַנִּכְשָׁל מִכֶּם וְיַעֲבֹר עָלֶיהָ – nevertheless, anyone among you who stumbles and violates [this commandment], יַעֲשֶׂה תְּשׁוּבָה בְּכָל כֹּחוֹ – should repent with all his might, וְיִגְדֹּר עַצְמוֹ בְּהַרְבֵּה גְדָרִים – and safeguard himself from sin with many safeguards,[17] וְיָבִיא קָרְבָּן לִקְבֹּעַ הַדָּבָר בְּלִבּוֹ – and he should bring an offering to establish the matter (i.e., his remorse) firmly in his heart שֶׁלֹּא יִכָּשֵׁל בּוֹ עוֹד – so that he will not stumble in [that sin] again." וּמִכָּל מָקוֹם לֹא נִצַּל הָאִישׁ הַהוּא שֶׁלֹּא עָבַר עַל מִצְוַת בּוֹרְאוֹ – Nevertheless, even after he has brought his offering, that person is not cleared of all wrongdoing as though he had not disobeyed the commandment of his Creator.[18]

## ～ Laws of the Mitzvah ～

מִדִּינֵי הַמִּצְוָה – The laws of the mitzvah include שֶׁכָּל אֶחָד מֵאַרְבָּעָה חֲטָאִים אֵלֶּה מְחֻיָּב עוֹשֵׂהוּ – that each of these four sins obligate the one who committed it לְהָבִיא כִּשְׂבָּה אוֹ שְׂעִירָה כְּדִין – to bring a female sheep or female goat as his offering, in consonance with the known law of the fixed chatas offering (Mitzvah 121),[19] וְאֵינוֹ נִפְטָר בְּעוֹף אוֹ בְּקֶמַח אֶלָּא אִם כֵּן הוּא עָנִי – and he cannot exempt his obligation by bringing the other offerings described in this passage, a bird offering or a flour offering, unless he is a pauper. וְאִם הוּא עָנִי וְהֵבִיא כִּשְׂבָּה אוֹ שְׂעִירָה – And if he is a pauper and he brings a female sheep or female goat as his offering, לֹא יָצָא יְדֵי חוֹבָתוֹ – he also has not fulfilled his obligation.[20] וְהַטַּעַם לְפִי שֶׁאַחַר – The reason for this is that since the Almighty, blessed is He, had pity on [the pauper], exempting him by means of this bird or flour offering from any further obligation, אֵינוֹ בְּדִין שֶׁיִּדְחֹק עַצְמוֹ לְהָבִיא בְּיוֹתֵר [מִ]מַּה שֶׁתַּשִּׂיג יָדוֹ – it is not proper for him to press himself to bring an offering that is more expensive than what he can afford.

---

### NOTES

17. When a person repents, he must examine the causes of his sin, and accept upon himself "safeguards" to avoid the circumstances that brought about the sin, and accept upon himself to refrain from any action, even permitted ones, that could again bring him to sin (see *Shaarei Teshuvah* 1:30, 36).

18. That is, one should not imagine that after he has brought the prescribed offering, it is as if he has never committed the sin, for the punishment or specific acts of atonement do not completely erase the injury a person does to himself by violating the commandment of his creator (see above, Mitzvah 61 and below, Mitzvah 129). [While a full repentance does erase the sin completely (see below, Mitzvah 364), the act of bringing the offering alone does not erase his deed, and one should therefore not sin with the intention that he can simply erase his iniquity by bringing the prescribed offering in atonement. In addition, one who sins with the intention that he will later rectify his sin with repentance is not assisted by Heaven to repent (see *Yoma* 85b; *Rambam, Hil. Teshuvah* 4:1,6).]

[Some manuscripts read: וּמִכָּל מָקוֹם לֹא נִצַּל הָאִישׁ הַהוּא שֶׁעָבַר עַל מִצְוַת בּוֹרְאוֹ, Nevertheless, even after he has brought his offering, that person is not cleared of all wrongdoing, **since he disobeyed** the commandment of his Creator. See similarly, below, Mitzvah 129 note 48.]

19. I.e., the animal offering brought by a person of means under the *oleh v'yoreid* obligation is of the very same species as the animal brought by one who committed a sin for which he incurs a fixed-*chatas* offering.

20. *Rambam* (*Hil. Shegagos* 10:13), however, rules that the pauper has fulfilled his obligation in this case. Commentators find great difficulty with Chinuch's ruling as it seems to be in opposition to an explicit Mishnah (*Negaim* 14:12) regarding the similar case of the offerings of the *metzora* (Glosses of *Mishneh LeMelech, Tzava Rav,* and *Minchas Chinuch* §11). See Insight for further discussion.

454 ❑ ויקרא / מצוה קכג: מצות קרבן עולה ויורד

וּבָזֶה יִקְנֶה כָּל מֵבִין עֵצָה לְבִלְתִּי עֲשׂוֹת הוֹצָאוֹת בְּיוֹתֵר מִן הָרָאוּי לוֹ לְפִי מָמוֹנוֹ, לְמַעַן כִּי בּוֹ סִבָּה לִגְזֹל אֶת הַבְּרִיּוֹת כְּשֶׁמְּבַקֵּשׁ לְמוּדוֹ וְאֵינוֹ מוֹצֵא.

וְאָמְרוּ (כריתות כ״ז ע״ב) גַּם כֵּן שֶׁמִּי שֶׁהָיָה עָשִׁיר וְהִפְרִישׁ מָעוֹת לִקַּח בָּהֶם כִּשְׂבָּה אוֹ שְׂעִירָה וְהֶעֱנִי וְצָרִיךְ לַמָּעוֹת, יִקַּח שְׁנֵי תוֹרִים אוֹ שְׁנֵי בְנֵי יוֹנָה וְיֹאמַר הֲרֵי הַמָּעוֹת הַלָּלוּ מְחֻלָּלִין עַל עוֹפוֹת אֵלּוּ, וְאַחַר כָּךְ יֵהָנֶה בְּכָל הַמָּעוֹת[21]. וְכֵן אִם הִפְרִישׁ מָעוֹת לְעוֹפוֹת וְהֶעֱנִי וְצָרִיךְ לָהֶם, מְחַלְּלָן עַל עֲשִׂירִית הָאֵיפָה קֶמַח[22], וְנֶהֱנֶה בָּהֶן.

וְכֵן עָנִי שֶׁהִפְרִישׁ מָעוֹת לַעֲשִׂירִית הָאֵיפָה וְהֶעֱשִׁיר, מוֹסִיף עֲלֵיהֶן וּמֵבִיא כִּשְׂבָּה אוֹ שְׂעִירָה[23]. וְעָשִׁיר נִקְרָא לְעִנְיָן זֶה כָּל זְמַן שֶׁיֵּשׁ לוֹ.

לְבִלְתִּי וּבָזֶה יִקְנֶה כָּל מֵבִין עֵצָה – **From this** ruling, **every perceptive person should take counsel** עֲשׂוֹת הוֹצָאוֹת בְּיוֹתֵר מִן הָרָאוּי לוֹ לְפִי מָמוֹנוֹ – **not to incur expenses that exceed what is appropriate according to his finances,** לְמַעַן כִּי בּוֹ סִבָּה לִגְזֹל אֶת הַבְּרִיּוֹת – **for [excessive spending] is a cause for one to steal from other people,** כְּשֶׁמְּבַקֵּשׁ לְמוּדוֹ וְאֵינוֹ מוֹצֵא – **when he seeks that which he is accustomed to and does not find it,** i.e., lacks the finances to obtain it.

Chinuch records laws pertaining to one whose financial status changed (as regard to this offering) after he had already designated money for his offering.

Generally, funds that were designated for an offering have the status of "monetary sanctity," and money so designated may not be used for mundane purposes. When the money is used to purchase the offering for which it was designated, the sanctity leaves the money (it is מְחֻלָּל, *deconsecrated*); the offering becomes sanctified in its place and the money may then be used for mundane purposes. Chinuch explains what is done with the money if the level of offering for which it had been designated changed:

וְאָמְרוּ גַּם כֵּן שֶׁמִּי שֶׁהָיָה עָשִׁיר – **[The Sages] have also stated** (*Kereisos* 27b) **that if one was wealthy** when he incurred an *oleh v'yoreid* obligation, וְהִפְרִישׁ מָעוֹת לִקַּח בָּהֶם כִּשְׂבָּה אוֹ שְׂעִירָה – **and he designated money to purchase a female sheep or female goat** for his offering, as is appropriate, וְהֶעֱנִי וְצָרִיךְ לַמָּעוֹת – **and he then became poor and requires the money** for his basic needs, יִקַּח שְׁנֵי תוֹרִים אוֹ שְׁנֵי בְנֵי יוֹנָה וְיֹאמַר – **he should** use some of the money to **buy two turtledoves or two young doves, and declare:** הֲרֵי הַמָּעוֹת הַלָּלוּ מְחֻלָּלִין עַל עוֹפוֹת אֵלּוּ – **"These funds have been deconsecrated,** with their sanctity being transferred **onto these birds,"** וְאַחַר כָּךְ יֵהָנֶה בְּכָל הַמָּעוֹת – **after which he may derive** personal **benefit from all the money** that remains.[21] וְכֵן אִם הִפְרִישׁ מָעוֹת לְעוֹפוֹת – **Similarly, if** a moderately poor sinner **designated money for birds** for his offering, וְהֶעֱנִי וְצָרִיךְ לָהֶם – **and he** then **becomes** even **poorer and requires [the money]** for his basic needs, מְחַלְּלָן עַל עֲשִׂירִית הָאֵיפָה קֶמַח וְנֶהֱנֶה בָּהֶן – **he should deconsecrate [the money] onto a tenth-*ephah* of flour for his offering,**[22] and he may then **derive** personal **benefit from [the money].** וְכֵן עָנִי שֶׁהִפְרִישׁ מָעוֹת לַעֲשִׂירִית הָאֵיפָה וְהֶעֱשִׁיר – **Similarly, if a** very **poor** person **designated money for** the purchase of **a tenth-*ephah* of flour for his offering, and he** then **became wealthy,** מוֹסִיף עֲלֵיהֶן – **he should add** funds **to [the designated money]** וּמֵבִיא כִּשְׂבָּה אוֹ שְׂעִירָה – **and he should bring a female sheep or female goat** offering.[23] וְעָשִׁיר נִקְרָא לְעִנְיָן זֶה כָּל זְמַן שֶׁיֵּשׁ לוֹ – **One is considered "wealthy," in regard to this matter, as long as he has** the means to buy the more expensive offering.

---

NOTES

21. Although only part of the money is used for the offering (as an animal offering is more expensive than a bird offering), all the money is considered deconsecrated in this way. Deconsecrating money upon an offering whose value is less than that amount of money is ordinarily not allowed (although if one does it the transaction is valid after the fact; see *Arachin* 29a). In this case, however, the Gemara (*Kereisos* 27b) cites a special Scriptural verse that allows it even initially (see *Sfas Emes* and *Yad Binyamin* there).

22. This is the prescribed measure of flour for the *minchah* offering of the *oleh v'yoreid* (*Leviticus* 5:11). It is equal to 43.2 egg-volumes.

23. Likewise, if his means increased so that he can now afford bird offerings, but not the animal offering, he should add funds to those designated for the *minchah* and buy the bird offerings (*Rambam, Hil. Shegagos* 10:10).

# 455 ❏ VAYIKRA / MITZVAH 123: THE OBLIGATION OF THE OLEH V'YOREID OFFERING

וְחִיּוּב קָרְבָּנוֹת אֵלֶּה דַּוְקָא בְּשׁוֹגֵג,[24] וּבִשְׁבוּעַת הָעֵדוּת אֲפִלּוּ בְּמֵזִיד,[25] אֲבָל בְּאֹנֶס אֵין בּוֹ חִיּוּב קָרְבָּן בְּאֶחָד מֵהֶם, שֶׁכָּל אֹנֶס הַתּוֹרָה פְּטָרַתּוּ מִכָּל חִיּוּב.[26] וְהַצְּדָדִין שֶׁהֵן בִּשְׁבוּעוֹת שֶׁהָאָדָם נִקְרָא אָנוּס בָּהֶן וּפָטוּר, אוֹ שׁוֹגֵג וְחַיָּב,[27]

---

Actions that violate Torah law can be divided into three general levels of intent: (1) deliberate violation (מֵזִיד, *meizid*), where the person does an action with the knowledge that it violates Torah law; (2) inadvertent transgressions (שׁוֹגֵג, *shogeig*), where there is some level of intent to perform the action but not a deliberate intent to violate the law; and (3) actions completely beyond one's control (אֹנֶס, *oneis*). Chinuch defines the obligation of the *oleh v'yoreid* offering within the context of these levels of intent: וְחִיּוּב קָרְבָּנוֹת אֵלֶּה דַּוְקָא בְּשׁוֹגֵג — **The obligation** to bring **these offerings is specifically for inadvertent** transgressions,[24] וּבִשְׁבוּעַת הָעֵדוּת אֲפִלּוּ בְּמֵזִיד — **and in** the case of **a false oath of testimony,** the obligation is incurred **even for a deliberate violation,** as was stated above.[25] אֲבָל בְּאֹנֶס אֵין בּוֹ חִיּוּב קָרְבָּן בְּאֶחָד מֵהֶם — **But if** the violation is **beyond one's control, he has no obligation to bring an offering for any of [these violations],** שֶׁכָּל אֹנֶס הַתּוֹרָה פְּטָרַתּוּ מִכָּל חִיּוּב — for in the event of **anything beyond one's control, the Torah** always **exempts one from any obligation.**[26]

The parameters of what is considered "beyond one's control" with regard to oaths — including both oaths of testimony and other oaths — are different than they are for other violations:

וְהַצְּדָדִין שֶׁהֵן בִּשְׁבוּעוֹת שֶׁהָאָדָם נִקְרָא אָנוּס בָּהֶן וּפָטוּר — **There are various cases** specifically **with regard to oaths where a person may be considered "forced," and** thus exempt from obligation, אוֹ שׁוֹגֵג וְחַיָּב — **or,** depending on the circumstances, he may be considered to have acted **inadvertently, and** thus **liable** to the offering.[27]

---

NOTES

24. For example, if one entered the *Beis HaMikdash* and ate *kodashim* while *tamei*, it is considered an inadvertent violation if he did not remember at the time that he was *tamei*, or, he knew he was *tamei* but did not realize that the place he was entering was the *Beis HaMikdash* or that the food he was eating was *kodashim* (Chinuch, below). Like other inadvertent violations, the transgressor requires atonement, for although he did not deliberately sin, he also did not take sufficient care to avoid the possibility of sinning. With regard to the definition of *shogeig* and *oneis* as pertaining to oaths of testimony and other oaths, see below.

25. See above, at note 10, where Chinuch derives this from the wording of the verse pertaining to this violation (*Leviticus* 5:1). It is considered a deliberately false "oath of testimony" if, at the time the witnesses took the oath, they remembered the testimony itself and they were also aware that swearing to the contrary was forbidden and carries the penalty of an offering (*Rambam, Hil. Shevuos* 10:1); see further below, note 27.

26. Thus, for example, one who was forced to eat *kodashim* while *tamei*, or was brought into the *Beis HaMikdash* against his will while he was *tamei*, is not liable to bring the offering.

27. Through Scriptural derivation, the Gemara (*Shevuos* 26a) learns that the parameters of *oneis* ("forced") with regard to oaths include cases where the person did not realize that he was swearing falsely. Thus, if one swore that he did not do something, when in fact he had done that thing, if at the time of the oath he had forgotten that he did it and thought he was swearing truthfully, he is not liable for punishment at all, and does not bring an offering. This pertains to all oaths, including oaths of testimony (*Shevuos* 31b; *Rambam, Hil. Shevuos* 1:10,13).

The Gemara (ibid. 26a-b) wonders: If the sin of deliberately swearing falsely cannot be atoned for with an offering (except with regard to oaths of testimony, as above), and mistakenly swearing falsely is considered *oneis* and does not obligate an offering, what then is the case of an "inadvertent" violation of an oath for which one brings the *oleh v'yoreid* offering? The Gemara answers that it is considered an inadvertent transgression if one knowingly swore falsely but did not know that such action carries the obligation to bring an offering. In this case, whether he swore about any past event or, in the case of the oath of testimony, he swore that he knew of no testimony for his fellow, it is considered a *shogeig*, and he is obligated to bring the *oleh v'yoreid* offering.

The above discussion pertains only to one who swore about a past event. With regard to one who swears regarding the future (for example, one swears that he will not eat a certain item), if one violated his oath deliberately (*meizid*), he is not liable to bring an offering, as is the case with other deliberate violations of Torah law (see below, Mitzvah 227, that in this case he incurs *malkus*). If he is forced by circumstances beyond his control to violate his oath (*oneis*), he is also not liable. Based on the particular definitions of *oneis* that relate to oaths, the Gemara (ibid.) details various levels of knowledge and ignorance of the oath at the time of the violation, explaining which would be considered *oneis* ("forced") and which would be considered *shogeig* (inadvertent); see there, and *Rambam* ibid. 3:8-11.

וְהַצְּדָדִין שֶׁאֵין מִתְחַיֵּב אֶלָּא קָרְבָּן אֶחָד אֲפִלּוּ עַל כַּמָּה שְׁבוּעוֹת אוֹ קָרְבָּן אֶחָד עַל כָּל שְׁבוּעָה וּשְׁבוּעָה.[28]

וְכֵן בְּעִנְיַן קָרְבַּן טֻמְאַת מִקְדָּשׁ וְטֻמְאַת קָדָשָׁיו, הַצְּדָדִין שֶׁיֵּשׁ בָּהֶן לְחִיּוּב וְלִפְטוּר, צַד הַחִיּוּב יִהְיֶה כְּשֶׁיֵּשׁ לוֹ לַחוֹטֵא יְדִיעַת הַטֻּמְאָה וְהַקֹּדֶשׁ אוֹ מִקְדָּשׁ תְּחִלָּה וְכֵן בַּסּוֹף וְהֶעְלֵם בֵּינְתַיִם. כֵּיצַד, נִטְמָא וְיָדַע שֶׁנִּטְמָא וּבָא לְיָדוֹ בְּשַׂר קֹדֶשׁ וְיוֹדֵעַ שֶׁהוּא בְּשַׂר קֹדֶשׁ, אוֹ בָּא לִכָּנֵס לַמִּקְדָּשׁ וְיוֹדֵעַ שֶׁהוּא מִקְדָּשׁ, שֶׁעַכְשָׁו יֵשׁ לוֹ יְדִיעָה מִן הַטֻּמְאָה וּמִן הַקֹּדֶשׁ בַּתְּחִלָּה,

---

וְהַצְּדָדִין שֶׁאֵין מִתְחַיֵּב אֶלָּא קָרְבָּן אֶחָד אֲפִלּוּ עַל כַּמָּה שְׁבוּעוֹת — The law further defines **the cases where a person is obligated to bring only one offering, despite** having violated **multiple oaths,** אוֹ קָרְבָּן אֶחָד עַל כָּל שְׁבוּעָה וּשְׁבוּעָה — **or,** conversely, where he is obligated to bring **a separate offering for each and every oath** that he has violated.[28]

Chinuch turns to the laws of *tumah* violations of the Temple or of *kodashim*, explaining that there is a condition for liability regarding these violations that does not exist with regard to other violations. In all cases of inadvertent violation, there is some information that the person does not know or does not remember at the time of the violation. With regard to these *tumah* violations, however, there is an additional condition: the person must have *once known* all the information pertaining to the violation, and only have forgotten it at the time of his violation:

וְכֵן בְּעִנְיַן קָרְבַּן טֻמְאַת מִקְדָּשׁ וְטֻמְאַת קָדָשָׁיו — **So too,** do the laws of the mitzvah include, **regarding the matter of *tumah* violations of the Temple and its consecrated [foods],** הַצְּדָדִין שֶׁיֵּשׁ בָּהֶן — the circumstances in which one becomes **liable** to bring the *oleh v'yoreid* offering, **and** those in which he is exempt. צַד הַחִיּוּב יִהְיֶה — **The circumstance of liability would be** וְהַקֹּדֶשׁ אוֹ — **where the sinner was aware** of his state of *tumah* מִקְדָּשׁ — **and** of **the consecrated** status of the food **or** of the sanctified status of **the Temple,** תְּחִלָּה — **before** the violation **and also afterward,** וְהֶעְלֵם בֵּינְתַיִם — **but between** these two periods of awareness, there **was** a period of **"unawareness,"** i.e., he became temporarily unaware of the circumstances of the violation.

Thus, in order for one to incur liability to an *oleh v'yoreid* for one of these transgressions, a three-step progression is required. The person must have: (1) an awareness of both his *tamei* status and the consecrated status of the food or the place; (2) an "unawareness," or forgetting, of one of those circumstances at the time of the violation; (3) a subsequent realization of the circumstances of the violation. Chinuch proceeds to explain these three steps in detail:

כֵּיצַד — **How so?** נִטְמָא וְיָדַע שֶׁנִּטְמָא — [1] If **one became** *tamei* **and knows that he has become** *tamei***,** וּבָא לְיָדוֹ בְּשַׂר קֹדֶשׁ וְיוֹדֵעַ שֶׁהוּא בְּשַׂר קֹדֶשׁ — **and sacrificial meat comes into his possession, and he knows that it is sacrificial meat,** אוֹ בָּא לִכָּנֵס לַמִּקְדָּשׁ וְיוֹדֵעַ שֶׁהוּא מִקְדָּשׁ — **or he approaches to enter the Temple, and he knows that it is the Temple,** שֶׁעַכְשָׁו יֵשׁ לוֹ יְדִיעָה — **so that now,** before he ate or entered, **he had knowledge of his** מִן הַטֻּמְאָה וּמִן הַקֹּדֶשׁ בַּתְּחִלָּה

---

NOTES

28. One who took an oath of testimony is not liable to bring the offering unless he denies knowledge of the testimony in *beis din* (court). [The oath itself, however, need not be taken in court.] The case where one would be liable for an offering for each oath that he took is as follows: A litigant adjured the witness multiple times out of court, and each time the witness accepts the oath that he knows no testimony. Afterward, in court, he denies knowledge of any testimony. In this case he is liable to bring an *oleh v'yoreid* offering for each oath that he accepted out of court.

On the other hand, if the litigant adjured him multiple times *in court*, he is liable to only one offering despite having accepted many oaths. The reason for this is based upon a law regarding testimony in court: When a person denies knowledge of a certain testimony in court, he may not subsequently change his story and submit testimony regarding that subject, since that would contradict his earlier statement made in court (above, Mitzvah 122). He is therefore no longer considered a valid witness for this testimony. It emerges that at the time of the first oath and denial, he was a valid witness and is therefore liable for falsely claiming ignorance and not testifying for his fellow. After his denial, however, he is no longer a valid witness for this subject, and therefore cannot be liable for refusing to testify (*Shevuos* 31b).

## VAYIKRA / MITZVAH 123: THE OBLIGATION OF THE OLEH V'YOREID OFFERING

וְאַחַר כָּךְ יֵשׁ לוֹ הַעְלָמָה שֶׁשָּׁכַח טֻמְאָתוֹ וְחָשַׁב שֶׁהוּא טָהוֹר, וְכֵן נַמִּי שֶׁנֶּעְלְמוּ מִמֶּנּוּ הַקֹּדֶשׁ אוֹ הַמִּקְדָּשׁ וַחֲשָׁבָם לְחֻלִּין וְאָכַל מִן הַקֹּדֶשׁ אוֹ נִכְנַס לַמִּקְדָּשׁ שֶׁזֶּהוּ הָעְלֵם בֵּינְתַיִם,[29] וְאַחַר כָּךְ נוֹדַע לוֹ שֶׁטָּמֵא הָיָה אוֹ שֶׁבָּשָׂר קֹדֶשׁ אוֹ מִקְדָּשׁ הָיוּ שֶׁזֶּהוּ יְדִיעָה בַּסּוֹף, בְּעִנְיָן זֶה מֵבִיא קָרְבָּן, וְעַל זֶה אָמְרוּ רַבּוֹתֵינוּ זִכְרוֹנָם לִבְרָכָה (שבועות ב׳ ע״א) יְדִיעָה בַּתְּחִלָּה וּבַסּוֹף וְהֶעְלֵם בֵּינְתַיִם.

וְצַד הַפְּטוּר הוּא כְּשֶׁנִּטְמָא וְלֹא יָדַע שֶׁנִּטְמָא, וְנִכְנַס לַמִּקְדָּשׁ אוֹ אָכַל בְּשַׂר קֹדֶשׁ וְאַחַר כָּךְ נוֹדַע לוֹ שֶׁנִּטְמָא וְנִכְנַס לַמִּקְדָּשׁ אוֹ אָכַל בְּשַׂר קֹדֶשׁ, בְּעִנְיָן זֶה הוּא פָּטוּר מִקָּרְבָּן.[30]

וְדִין זֶה אֵינוֹ בִּשְׁאָר חַיָּבֵי כְרֵתוֹת[31] שֶׁבַּתּוֹרָה, שֶׁבִּשְׁאָר הַכְּרֵתוֹת מִכֵּיוָן שֶׁיָּדַע בַּסּוֹף

---

וְאַחַר כָּךְ יֵשׁ לוֹ — *tumah* or of the sacred food or place **at the beginning**, i.e., before any violation. שֶׁשָּׁכַח טֻמְאָתוֹ וְחָשַׁב שֶׁהוּא הָעְלָמָה — [2] **After this, he experiences** a period of **"unawareness,"** טָהוֹר — **that** is, either **he forgot about his *tamei* state and thought he was ritually pure,** וְכֵן — נַמִּי שֶׁנֶּעְלְמוּ מִמֶּנּוּ הַקֹּדֶשׁ אוֹ הַמִּקְדָּשׁ — **or, alternatively, he became unaware of the consecrated status of the food or of the Temple,** i.e., he forgot that the food was *kodashim* or that the place he was approaching was the Temple, וַחֲשָׁבָם לְחֻלִּין — **and he thought them to be** of **non-sacred** status. וְאָכַל מִן הַקֹּדֶשׁ אוֹ נִכְנַס לַמִּקְדָּשׁ — **And,** while not cognizant of these circumstances, **he eats of the *kodashim* or enters the Temple;** שֶׁזֶּהוּ הָעְלֵם בֵּינְתַיִם — **this being** the period of **"unawareness" between** the two periods of awareness.[29] וְאַחַר כָּךְ נוֹדַע לוֹ שֶׁטָּמֵא הָיָה — [3] **After that, it became known to him that,** at the time of the violation, **he was *tamei*,** אוֹ שֶׁבָּשָׂר קֹדֶשׁ אוֹ מִקְדָּשׁ הָיוּ — **or** it became known to him **that [the meat he ate] was sacrificial meat, or [the place he entered] was the Temple;** שֶׁזֶּהוּ יְדִיעָה בַּסּוֹף — **this being** the period of **awareness** of the circumstances **at the end.** בְּעִנְיָן זֶה מֵבִיא קָרְבָּן — **In this situation,** he is liable to **bring an** *oleh v'yoreid* **offering.** וְעַל זֶה אָמְרוּ רַבּוֹתֵינוּ זִכְרוֹנָם לִבְרָכָה — **It is regarding this** series of steps that **our Sages, of blessed memory, stated** in the Mishnah (*Shevuos* 2a): יְדִיעָה בַּתְּחִלָּה וּבַסּוֹף וְהֶעְלֵם בֵּינְתַיִם — *[One is obligated to bring the* oleh v'yoreid *offering only if there is]* **awareness at the beginning and at the end, and an "unawareness" in between.**

וְצַד הַפְּטוּר הוּא כְּשֶׁנִּטְמָא — **The circumstance in which one is exempt** from bringing an offering וְלֹא יָדַע שֶׁנִּטְמָא — **is where he became *tamei*, but did not know that he became *tamei*,** וְנִכְנַס לַמִּקְדָּשׁ אוֹ אָכַל בְּשַׂר קֹדֶשׁ — **and he then entered the Temple or ate sacrificial meat,** וְאַחַר כָּךְ נוֹדַע לוֹ שֶׁנִּטְמָא וְנִכְנַס לַמִּקְדָּשׁ אוֹ אָכַל בְּשַׂר קֹדֶשׁ — **and afterward he became aware that he had been *tamei* and had entered the Temple or eaten sacrificial meat** while *tamei*; בְּעִנְיָן זֶה הוּא פָּטוּר מִקָּרְבָּן — **in this case, he is exempt** from bringing **an offering,** for there was no "knowledge in the beginning," i.e., he did not know of his impure state before the violation.[30]

Chinuch contrasts this with the law governing the standard *chatas* liability for other violations, and provides the Scriptural source for this difference:

וְדִין זֶה אֵינוֹ בִּשְׁאָר חַיָּבֵי כְרֵתוֹת שֶׁבַּתּוֹרָה — **This law does not exist regarding other *kares*-bearing transgressions**[31] **in the Torah,** שֶׁבִּשְׁאָר הַכְּרֵתוֹת מִכֵּיוָן שֶׁיָּדַע בַּסּוֹף — **for with regard to other *kares*-bearing [transgressions], as long as one knew** the circumstances of the transgression at

---

### NOTES

29. The "unawareness" may consist of either forgetting that he is *tamei*, or forgetting that the food or the place is holy, or both.

30. Alternatively, he knew that he was *tamei*, but he found out that the food was consecrated only after he ate it, or he found out that the place was the *Beis HaMikdash* only after he entered it. [Chinuch discusses below how one attains atonement when the transgression was committed in this way.]

31. That is, other prohibitions whose deliberate violation incur the *kares* (excision) penalty. As Chinuch mentioned above, inadvertent violation of such prohibitions obligates one to bring a *chatas* offering. *Tumah* violations of *kodashim* or of the Temple are also sins whose deliberate violation bears liability to *kares*.

אַף עַל פִּי שֶׁבַּתְּחִלָּה לֹא יָדַע חַיָּב בְּקָרְבָּן,[32] וְהַכָּתוּב מַכְרִיעַ בְּכָאן לָדוּן כֵּן דִּכְתִיב בְּטֻמְאַת מִקְדָּשׁ וְקָדָשָׁיו (שם ה׳, ב׳) וְנֶעְלַם מִמֶּנּוּ, מִכְּלָל שֶׁהָיְתָה לוֹ שְׁעַת יְדִיעָה בַּתְּחִלָּה,[33] וְנֶאֱמַר אַחֲרֵי כֵן (שם, שם ג׳) וְהוּא יָדַע, הָא לָמַדְתָּ שֶׁצָּרִיךְ יְדִיעָה בַּתְּחִלָּה וִידִיעָה בַּסּוֹף וְהֶעְלֵם בֵּינְתַיִם. אֲבָל בִּשְׁאָר חַיָּבֵי כְרֵתוֹת כְּתִיב (שם ד׳, כ״ז — כ״ח) בַּעֲשֹׂתָהּ אַחַת מִמִּצְוֹת ה׳ אֲשֶׁר לֹא תֵעָשֶׂינָה וְאָשֵׁם אוֹ הוֹדַע אֵלָיו חַטָּאתוֹ, כְּלוֹמַר מִכֵּיוָן שֶׁיָּדַע בַּסּוֹף אַף עַל פִּי שֶׁלֹּא יָדַע בַּתְּחִלָּה, שֶׁהֲרֵי אֵין כָּתוּב שָׁם וְנֶעְלַם שֶׁנִּלְמַד מִמֶּנּוּ יְדִיעָה בַּתְּחִלָּה.[34]

---

**the end,** i.e., after he committed it, אַף עַל פִּי שֶׁבַּתְּחִלָּה לֹא יָדַע — **even if he did not know** these circumstances **originally,** before he committed the sin, חַיָּב בְּקָרְבָּן — **he is liable to** bring **a** fixed *chatas* offering.[32] וְהַכָּתוּב מַכְרִיעַ בְּכָאן לָדוּן כֵּן — **Scripture mandates to rule this way here,** with regard to *tumah* violations, דִּכְתִיב בְּטֻמְאַת מִקְדָּשׁ וְקָדָשָׁיו — **for it is written regarding** the *tumah* violations of **the Temple and its consecrated [foods]** (*Leviticus* 5:2,3): "וְנֶעְלַם מִמֶּנּוּ" — "**but it became concealed from him,**" מִכְּלָל שֶׁהָיְתָה לוֹ שְׁעַת יְדִיעָה בַּתְּחִלָּה — which **indicates that there was a period at the beginning,** before his transgression, **when he did know,** and after he had known it, the matter became concealed from him, meaning that he experienced a period of unawareness;[33] thus, the verse indicates that there was an initial period of awareness followed by a period of unawareness, וְנֶאֱמַר אַחֲרֵי כֵן "וְהוּא יָדַע" — **and it is stated afterward** (ibid. vs. 3,4): — **and then he became aware,** indicating a final period of awareness. הָא לָמַדְתָּ שֶׁצָּרִיךְ יְדִיעָה בַּתְּחִלָּה וִידִיעָה בַּסּוֹף וְהֶעְלֵם בֵּינְתַיִם — **You thus learn that,** in order for liability to be incurred, **there must be awareness at the beginning and awareness at the end, with a** period of **unawareness in between.** אֲבָל בִּשְׁאָר חַיָּבֵי כְרֵתוֹת כְּתִיב — **However, regarding other** *kares*-**bearing transgressions,** for which one must bring a *chatas* when he commits the transgression inadvertently, **it is written** (ibid. 4:27-28): "בַּעֲשֹׂתָהּ אַחַת מִמִּצְוֹת ה׳ אֲשֶׁר לֹא תֵעָשֶׂינָה וְאָשֵׁם — *If an individual person from among the people of the land shall sin inadvertently,* **by committing one of the commandments of** HASHEM **that may not be done, and he becomes guilty:** "אוֹ הוֹדַע אֵלָיו חַטָּאתוֹ" — *If his sin that he committed becomes known to him,* he shall bring as his offering etc. כְּלוֹמַר מִכֵּיוָן שֶׁיָּדַע בַּסּוֹף אַף עַל פִּי שֶׁלֹּא יָדַע בַּתְּחִלָּה — **That** is **to say,** he is liable to bring a *chatas* offering **as long as he knew** the circumstances of the sin **at the end,** after he committed it, **even if he was not aware** of those circumstances **originally, before the transgression,** שֶׁהֲרֵי אֵין כָּתוּב שָׁם "וְנֶעְלַם" שֶׁנִּלְמַד מִמֶּנּוּ יְדִיעָה בַּתְּחִלָּה — **for it does not state there** "*and it was concealed* from him," **from which we would derive that there had been awareness originally.**[34]

As explained, the *oleh v'yoreid* offering for *tumah* violations is brought only when one had a specific order of awareness and unawareness (first awareness, then forgetting, and then becoming aware again). One who committed an inadvertent *tumah* violation, but without these specific steps, can gain atonement through certain communal offerings, primarily those of Yom Kippur:

---

### NOTES

32. In regard to standard *chatas* liability (for the applicable transgressions), prior knowledge of the prohibited situation is not necessary. For example, if a person inadvertently ate a food that is forbidden under pain of *kares* (such as *cheilev*, forbidden fats), even if he had no prior knowledge of the forbidden nature of the food, he must bring a *chatas* offering when he finds out that the food he ate was forbidden. He need not have known that it was forbidden food before his violation and then have forgotten it, in order to be liable to a *chatas*.

33. The grammatical form of the word וְנֶעְלַם indicates an event that occurred at a certain time. Thus, the word does not merely mean "*it was concealed*" (which could be understood as something that was always unknown) but rather, "*it had become concealed,*" indicating that at a previous time that knowledge was not concealed from him (see *Malbim, Leviticus* 5:3, to *Sifra* §309).

34. The verse mentions only that *after* he committed the sin it "became known to him." It does not mention that at the time he committed the sin it was "concealed" from him. Thus, there is no indication of the necessity for any prior knowledge.

# 459 ☐ VAYIKRA / MITZVAH 123: THE OBLIGATION OF THE OLEH V'YOREID OFFERING

וּמֵעִנְיַן הַמִּצְוָה גַּם כֵּן מַה שֶּׁאָמְרוּ זִכְרוֹנָם לִבְרָכָה (שבועות שם) שֶׁמִּי שֶׁיֵּשׁ לוֹ יְדִיעָה בַּתְּחִלָּה וְלֹא בַּסּוֹף שֶׁאֵין יָכוֹל לְהָבִיא כַּפָּרָה, כְּמוֹ שֶׁאָמְרוּ (שם) שֶׁשְּׂעִיר שֶׁל יוֹם הַכִּפּוּרִים הַנַּעֲשֶׂה בִּפְנִים[35] וְיוֹם הַכִּפּוּרִים בְּעַצְמוֹ[36] תּוֹלִין עַד שֶׁיִּוָּדַע לוֹ וְיָבִיא קָרְבָּן כַּפָּרָתוֹ[37]. וְשֶׁאֵין לוֹ יְדִיעָה בַּתְּחִלָּה אֲבָל יֵשׁ לוֹ יְדִיעָה בַּסּוֹף שֶׁאָמַרְנוּ שֶׁאֵינוֹ מֵבִיא קָרְבָּן לְעוֹלָם, שָׂעִיר הַנַּעֲשֶׂה בַּחוּץ וְיוֹם הַכִּפּוּרִים מְכַפְּרִין עָלָיו[38]. וְעַל שֶׁאֵין בּוֹ יְדִיעָה לֹא תְּחִלָּה וְלֹא סוֹף, שְׂעִירֵי הָרְגָלִים וּשְׂעִירֵי רָאשֵׁי חֳדָשִׁים מְכַפְּרִין עָלָיו[39].

---

מַה שֶּׁאָמְרוּ זִכְרוֹנָם לִבְרָכָה – וּמֵעִנְיַן הַמִּצְוָה גַּם כֵּן – **Also related to the subject of the mitzvah is** that which [our Sages,] of blessed memory, have said (Shevuos 2a), שֶׁמִּי שֶׁיֵּשׁ לוֹ יְדִיעָה בַּתְּחִלָּה וְלֹא בַּסּוֹף – **that one who had awareness**, either of his *tamei* state or of the consecrated status of the food or place, **in the beginning** (before the transgression), **but not at the end** (after the transgression), שֶׁאֵין יָכוֹל לְהָבִיא כַּפָּרָה – **so that he cannot bring an** offering for **atonement,** since he is as yet unaware of any transgression, can nevertheless attain a degree of rectification. כְּמוֹ שֶׁאָמְרוּ – **As** [the Sages], of blessed memory, **have stated** (Shevuos ibid.): שֶׁשְּׂעִיר שֶׁל יוֹם הַכִּפּוּרִים הַנַּעֲשֶׂה בִּפְנִים וְיוֹם הַכִּפּוּרִים בְּעַצְמוֹ – **The he-goat** offering **of Yom Kippur** whose blood procedures **are performed inside** the Sanctuary,[35] **and** the holy nature of the day of **Yom Kippur itself,** תּוֹלִין עַד שֶׁיִּוָּדַע לוֹ – **suspend** punishment **until** the time when **it becomes known to him** that he has sinned.[36] וְיָבִיא קָרְבָּן כַּפָּרָתוֹ – **And** at such time that he does discover his transgression, **he will** then be obligated to **bring the** *oleh v'yoreid* **offering for his atonement.**[37]

וְשֶׁאֵין לוֹ יְדִיעָה בַּתְּחִלָּה אֲבָל יֵשׁ לוֹ יְדִיעָה בַּסּוֹף – **With regard to one who has no awareness at the beginning** (he did not know before the transgression that he was *tamei* or that the food or place was consecrated), **but has awareness at the end,** i.e., he later found out that he had transgressed, שֶׁאָמַרְנוּ שֶׁאֵינוֹ מֵבִיא קָרְבָּן לְעוֹלָם – **regarding whom we have stated** above **that he can never bring an offering** (since he lacked awareness before the transgression), שָׂעִיר הַנַּעֲשֶׂה בַּחוּץ וְיוֹם הַכִּפּוּרִים מְכַפְּרִין עָלָיו – **the he-goat** offering of Yom Kippur whose blood procedures are **performed outside** the Sanctuary, **and Yom Kippur** itself **atone** for his sin.[38]

וְעַל שֶׁאֵין בּוֹ יְדִיעָה לֹא תְּחִלָּה וְלֹא סוֹף – **With regard to one who had no awareness** at all, **neither in the beginning nor at the end,** i.e., he entered the Temple or ate *kodashim* while *tamei* but never knew the circumstances before the transgression and did not find out afterward, שְׂעִירֵי הָרְגָלִים וּשְׂעִירֵי רָאשֵׁי חֳדָשִׁים מְכַפְּרִין עָלָיו – **the he-goat offerings of the festivals and the he-goat** offerings of **Rosh Chodesh atone for him.**[39]

---

## NOTES

35. As part of the Yom Kippur service, two identical goats were brought to the *Beis HaMikdash*; one of them was sent to *Azazel* and the other was slaughtered as a communal *chatas* offering and its blood sprinkled inside the Sanctuary (see below, Mitzvah 185). This *chatas* is referred to as the *he-goat whose procedures were performed inside*, that is, inside the Sanctuary (in contrast to other blood services of that day that were performed on the Outer Altar; see below, note 38).

36. The Gemara (*Shavuos* 8a) derives from Scripture that this "inner" Yom Kippur offering provides atonement specifically to protect the unknowing person from punishment for this sin (see following note). The day of Yom Kippur itself has the capacity to atone and to deflect punishment in conjunction with the prescribed offerings, as stated (*Leviticus* 23:28): כִּי יוֹם כִּפֻּרִים הוּא, *for it is a day of atonement* (Rashi to Shevuos 2a ד"ה שעיר הנעשה בחוץ).

37. The above offerings do not completely expiate his sin; rather, they atone for him enough to suspend punishment until he discovers his transgression. At the time that he does discover it, even if it is after many years, he will finally have met all the conditions for liability — namely, (1) initial awareness, (2) unawareness, and (3) final awareness — and he will be liable to bring the *oleh v'yoreid* offering.

38. Another he-goat offering is brought on Yom Kippur as one of the *mussaf* offerings of the day; its blood is applied to the Altar outside the Sanctuary and it is referred to as the "he-goat [whose blood procedure is] *performed outside*." The Sages derive (*Shevuos* 2a) that it, together with the holy nature of Yom Kippur, effects [full] atonement for this sin, which has no other form of atonement.

39. That these offerings effect atonement for such a circumstance is derived in the Gemara (*Shevuos* 9a) from Scripture.

## 460 ❏ ויקרא / מצוה קכג: מצוות קרבן עולה ויורד

וְעַל זְדוֹן טֻמְאַת מִקְדָּשׁ וְקָדָשָׁיו, פַּר כֹּהֵן גָּדוֹל שֶׁל יוֹם הַכִּפּוּרִים מְכַפֵּר אִם הַמֵּזִיד מִן הַכֹּהֲנִים,[40] וְאִם הָיָה מִיִּשְׂרָאֵל, דַּם שָׂעִיר הַנַּעֲשֶׂה בִּפְנִים וְיוֹם הַכִּפּוּרִים מְכַפְּרִין, שֶׁנֶּאֱמַר (שם ט״ז, ט״ז) "וְכִפֶּר עַל הַקֹּדֶשׁ מִטֻּמְאֹת בְּנֵי יִשְׂרָאֵל".[41]

וּמַה שֶּׁאָמְרוּ זִכְרוֹנָם לִבְרָכָה (הוריות ט' ע״א) כִּי בְּאַרְבָּעָה חֲטָאִים אֵלֶּה הַכֹּל שָׁוִין בָּהֶן בְּקָרְבָּן, מֶלֶךְ וְכֹהֵן מָשִׁיחַ וְהֶדְיוֹט, שֶׁאֵין חִלּוּק בֵּינֵיהֶם בְּקָרְבָּנָם אֶלָּא בְּמִצְוֹת שֶׁחַיָּבִין עַל שִׁגְגָתָן חַטָּאת קְבוּעָה, אֲבָל בְּאֵלּוּ שֶׁחִיּוּבָן עוֹלֶה וְיוֹרֵד, הַכֹּל שָׁוִין בָּהֶן.[42]

וְיֶתֶר פְּרָטֶיהָ, מְבֹאָרִים בִּכְרֵיתוֹת וּשְׁבוּעוֹת.[43]

---

וְעַל זְדוֹן טֻמְאַת מִקְדָּשׁ וְקָדָשָׁיו — **As for deliberate *tumah* violations of the Temple and its consecrated [foods],** for which no personal offerings are brought, פַּר כֹּהֵן גָּדוֹל שֶׁל יוֹם הַכִּפּוּרִים מְכַפֵּר אִם הַמֵּזִיד מִן הַכֹּהֲנִים — **the Yom Kippur bull offering of the Kohen Gadol atones, if the deliberate sinner was a Kohen;**[40] וְאִם הָיָה מִיִּשְׂרָאֵל — **and if the [deliberate sinner] was an Israelite** (i.e., a non-Kohen), דַּם שָׂעִיר הַנַּעֲשֶׂה בִּפְנִים וְיוֹם הַכִּפּוּרִים מְכַפְּרִין — **the blood** service **of the he-goat** of Yom Kippur **performed inside** the Sanctuary **and Yom Kippur** itself **atones,** שֶׁנֶּאֱמַר — **as it is stated** regarding the aforementioned offering (ibid. 16:16): "וְכִפֶּר עַל הַקֹּדֶשׁ מִטֻּמְאֹת בְּנֵי יִשְׂרָאֵל" — ***Thus shall he provide atonement upon the Sanctuary for the tumah [violations] of the Children of Israel*** *even for their rebellious sins,* etc.[41]

At the end of Mitzvah 120, Chinuch cites the Mishnah (*Horayos* 9a) that teaches that for all violations for which a commoner is liable to bring a standard (fixed) *chatas* offering of a female goat or sheep, the *Nasi* (i.e., king), must bring a he-goat as his offering. If it was the "anointed Kohen" (i.e., the Kohen Gadol) who transgressed, he must bring a special bull offering (see there for further discussion). Here, Chinuch discusses the status of the *Nasi* and Kohen Gadol with regard to the four sins for which one is liable to bring the *oleh v'yoreid* offering:

וּמַה שֶּׁאָמְרוּ זִכְרוֹנָם לִבְרָכָה — **Another law concerns that which [the Sages], of blessed memory, have stated** (*Horayos* 9a), כִּי בְּאַרְבָּעָה חֲטָאִים אֵלֶּה הַכֹּל שָׁוִין בָּהֶן בְּקָרְבָּן — **that regarding these four sins** for which one brings an *oleh v'yoreid* offering, **all are equal with** respect to their obligation to bring **the offering:** מֶלֶךְ וְכֹהֵן מָשִׁיחַ וְהֶדְיוֹט — **whether a king** (*Nasi*), **an anointed Kohen** (Kohen Gadol), **or a commoner;** שֶׁאֵין חִלּוּק בֵּינֵיהֶם בְּקָרְבָּנָם אֶלָּא בְּמִצְוֹת שֶׁחַיָּבִין עַל שִׁגְגָתָן חַטָּאת קְבוּעָה — **for there is no distinction between them with respect to their offerings, except with** regard to **commandments for which one incurs liability to a** *fixed chatas* **offering for an inadvertent transgression,** אֲבָל בְּאֵלּוּ שֶׁחִיּוּבָן עוֹלֶה וְיוֹרֵד הַכֹּל שָׁוִין בָּהֶן — **but for these** violations, **whose liability is to an** *oleh v'yoreid* **offering, all are equal.**[42]

וְיֶתֶר פְּרָטֶיהָ — **These laws, and the additional details of [this mitzvah],** מְבֹאָרִים בִּכְרֵיתוֹת וּשְׁבוּעוֹת — **are set forth in** Tractates ***Kereisos*** **and** ***Shevuos***.[43]

---

### NOTES

40. On Yom Kippur, the Kohen Gadol offered a personal bull offering, which effected atonement for himself and his household (*Leviticus* 16:11), and also for the other Kohanim, who are all considered "his household" (*Shevuos* 13b). This atonement was specifically for deliberate *tumah* violations by a Kohen of the Temple and its *kodashim*, as derived in the Mishnah and Gemara (*Shevuos* 2b, 13b).

41. The verse states that the offering provides atonement even for rebellious, i.e., deliberate, sins pertaining to *tumah* violations of the Temple (*Shevuos* 12b).

[If the sinner was warned by witnesses prior to his deliberate violation, he is liable to *malkus* for his sin, and achieves atonement only through the administration of that penalty (*Tiferes Yisrael*, *Shevuos* 1:6).]

Atonement for all other sins is provided by the he-goat sent to Azazel as part of the Yom Kippur service (*Shevuos* 2b).

42. See *Horayos* 8b-9b.

43. The laws of the *oleh v'yoreid* offering are codified in *Rambam, Hil. Shegagos*, Chs. 10-11.

וְנוֹהֶגֶת בִּזְמַן הַבַּיִת בִּזְכָרִים וּנְקֵבוֹת, חוּץ מִקָּרְבַּן שְׁבוּעַת הָעֵדוּת שֶׁאֵינוֹ נוֹהֵג בִּנְקֵבוֹת שֶׁאֵינָן בְּתוֹרַת עֵדוּת כְּמוֹ שֶׁכְּתַבְנוּ לְמַעְלָה. וְעוֹבֵר עָלֶיהָ וְלֹא הִקְרִיב קָרְבָּנוֹ עַל אַחַת מֵאֵלֶּה, בִּטֵּל עֲשֵׂה.[44]

---

## ☙ Applicability of the Mitzvah ☙

וְנוֹהֶגֶת בִּזְמַן הַבַּיִת — [This mitzvah] applies in the times of the Temple, בִּזְכָרִים וּנְקֵבוֹת — to both men and women, חוּץ מִקָּרְבַּן שְׁבוּעַת הָעֵדוּת שֶׁאֵינוֹ נוֹהֵג בִּנְקֵבוֹת — except for the offering brought for an oath of testimony, which does not apply to women, שֶׁאֵינָן בְּתוֹרַת עֵדוּת כְּמוֹ שֶׁכְּתַבְנוּ לְמַעְלָה — since they are not subject to the laws of testifying, as we have written above (Mitzvah 122).

וְעוֹבֵר עָלֶיהָ וְלֹא הִקְרִיב קָרְבָּנוֹ עַל אַחַת מֵאֵלֶּה — One who transgresses [this commandment] and does not bring his required oleh v'yoreid offering for his violation of any one of these sins בִּטֵּל עֲשֵׂה — has violated a mitzvah-obligation.[44]

---

### NOTES

44. See Mitzvah 121, note 18.

---

### ❧ Insight: The Two Bird Offerings of the Poor

Chinuch maintains (at note 20) that if a poor person, whose prescribed offering is a bird or flour, extends himself and offers the animal offering of the wealthy, he does not fulfill his obligation. As noted there, commentators (see *Mishnah LaMelech* and *Tzava Rav*) find great difficulty with this ruling, as it seems to contradict an explicit Mishnah (*Negaim* 14:12). The Mishnah discusses the case of a *metzora* who recovers from *tzaraas*, whose required offerings also vary based on his financial ability: If he can afford to, he must bring two animal offerings: a *chatas* and an *olah*. If he cannot, he brings two birds — a *chatas* and an *olah*. The Mishnah rules that if a *metzora* who is poor brings animal offerings instead of bird offerings, he *does* fulfill his obligation. The parallel to the case of the *oleh v'yoreid* offering of our mitzvah is clear. Why, then, does Chinuch rule that in our case he does not fulfill his obligation?

*Sfas Emes* (*Yoma* 41b ד"ה גופא) points out that there is a great difference between the variable offerings of the *metzora* and the variable offerings discussed in our mitzvah. The *metzora* always brings two offerings, a *chatas* and an *olah*; what is "variable" is only the *kind* of offerings — two animals or two birds. With regard to the four sins in this mitzvah, however, the person of means brings only a single animal offering: a *chatas*. If one cannot afford the animal, he brings *two* bird offerings, one as a *chatas* and one as an *olah*. In this sense, the offering of the poor is broader than the offering of the rich, for the poor person brings an additional offering, albeit a small one. In contrast, the offering of the poor with regard to the *metzora's* obligation is merely a less expensive form of the same two offerings that he would be required to bring if he had the means.

*Sfas Emes* therefore maintains that the ruling of the Mishnah in *Negaim* cannot be brought to bear upon our case. The *metzora* who is permitted to bring two bird offerings may instead spend more and bring two animal offerings, since he has only upgraded his offerings to a more substantial form. In our mitzvah, however, if one's circumstances prescribe that he bring the two offerings of the poor, he may not instead bring only a single offering of the rich, for he will have thereby decreased the number of offerings that he brings. [For other resolutions to this difficulty see *Chidushei Chasam Sofer*, *Shabbos* 132a, and *Minchas Yitzchak*.]

This solution, however, raises a more basic question: Why, indeed, is the poor person required to bring an "extra" *olah* offering in the case of our mitzvah, where the person of means brings only one *chatas* offering?

*Ibn Ezra* (*Leviticus* 5:7) offers two reasons for this difference between the offerings of the rich and the poor, the first of which is as follows: The primary offering for a sin is the *chatas*. When one brings an animal *chatas*, there are parts of the animal that are eaten by the Kohanim and parts that are

burned on the Altar (see *Leviticus* 4:31). In the case of a poor person who sinned, his primary offering is also the *chatas* — though it is a bird. The procedure of a bird *chatas*, however, dictates that its flesh is given entirely to the Kohanim, with only the blood brought to the Altar (*Rambam, Hil. Maaseh HaKorbanos* 7:7). Thus, when the poor person brings a bird instead of an animal as his *chatas*, he must bring an additional offering to be burned on the Altar (the bird *olah*) to "compensate" for the parts of the animal *chatas* that would have been offered on the Altar if he had had the means.

*Ibn Ezra*'s second explanation is that the poor person, who cannot afford the "standard" *chatas* in this case, is likely to be resentful of his lot at this time, when the difference between his abilities and those of the more affluent are brought to the fore. He may therefore harbor thoughts of complaint against God for his diminished financial status in comparison to those who can afford the animal offering. The Torah therefore obligates him to bring an *olah* offering together with his *chatas*, since the *olah* atones for sinful thoughts (see Insight to Mitzvah 115).

[For discussion of how the explanation of *Sfas Emes* cited above (for why the poor person cannot bring the rich man's offering) fits with *Ibn Ezra*'s two reasons for the additional offering, see *Pardes Yosef* to *Leviticus* 5:7.]

### מִצְוָה קכד: שֶׁלֹּא לְהַבְדִּיל הָרֹאשׁ בְּחַטַּאת הָעוֹף[1]

שֶׁלֹּא יַפְרִיד הַכֹּהֵן מִן הָעוֹף הַבָּא לְקָרְבָּן, וְהוּא הַנִּקְרָא חַטַּאת הָעוֹף, הָרֹאשׁ מִן הַגּוּף כְּשֶׁיִּמְלֹק אוֹתוֹ, שֶׁנֶּאֱמַר (ויקרא ה׳, ח׳) וּמָלַק אֶת רֹאשׁוֹ מִמּוּל עָרְפּוֹ וְלֹא יַבְדִּיל[2]. וּפֵרוּשׁ מְלִיקָה הוּא שֶׁנּוֹעֵץ הַכֹּהֵן צִפָּרְנָיו מִמּוּל עָרְפּוֹ[3] דְּהַיְנוּ הָעֶצֶם הַנִּקְרָא עֶצֶם הַמַּפְרֶקֶת, וְחוֹתֵךְ הָעֶצֶם בְּצִפָּרְנָיו עַד שֶׁמַּגִּיעַ לַסִּימָנִין וְחוֹתֵךְ גַּם הַסִּימָנִין בְּצִפָּרְנוֹ,

---

## ≈ Mitzvah 124 ≈
## The Prohibition to Sever the Head of a Bird Chatas Offering

וְהֵבִיא אֹתָם אֶל הַכֹּהֵן וְהִקְרִיב אֶת אֲשֶׁר לַחַטָּאת רִאשׁוֹנָה וּמָלַק אֶת רֹאשׁוֹ מִמּוּל עָרְפּוֹ וְלֹא יַבְדִּיל

*He shall bring them to the Kohen, who shall offer first the one that is for a sin offering; he shall nip its head at its nape, but not separate it* (Leviticus 5:8).

As Chinuch indicated in the previous mitzvah, there are certain instances where one is required to bring a bird *chatas* offering to atone for his sins.[1] Unlike the case of animal offerings, which are slaughtered in the same manner as animals that are used for mundane consumption (i.e., through *shechitah*, described in Mitzvah 451), bird offerings are assigned a special form of slaughter, known as *melikah* (nipping).

A bird can be offered either as a *chatas* or as an *olah,* and the *melikah* procedure of a *chatas* is somewhat different from that of an *olah*. This mitzvah pertains to the procedure in which *melikah* is performed on the bird *chatas* offering.

שֶׁלֹּא יַפְרִיד הַכֹּהֵן — We are commanded **that the Kohen shall not separate** the head מִן הָעוֹף הַבָּא לְקָרְבָּן וְהוּא הַנִּקְרָא חַטַּאת הָעוֹף — **from the bird offering that is known as the bird** *chatas*; הָרֹאשׁ מִן הַגּוּף — that is, he shall not sever **the head from the body** כְּשֶׁיִּמְלֹק אוֹתוֹ — **when he performs** *melikah* **upon it,** שֶׁנֶּאֱמַר — **as is stated** (Leviticus 5:8): "וּמָלַק אֶת רֹאשׁוֹ מִמּוּל עָרְפּוֹ וְלֹא יַבְדִּיל" — **he shall nip its head at its nape, but not separate it.**[2]

Before explaining the mitzvah, Chinuch describes the *melikah* procedure:

וּפֵרוּשׁ מְלִיקָה הוּא — **The definition of** *melikah* **is** שֶׁנּוֹעֵץ הַכֹּהֵן צִפָּרְנָיו מִמּוּל עָרְפּוֹ — that the Kohen **penetrates** with **his fingernail into the [the bird's] nape,**[3] דְּהַיְנוּ הָעֶצֶם הַנִּקְרָא עֶצֶם הַמַּפְרֶקֶת — **that is,** into **the bone known as the** *mifrekes* (i.e., the neck bone), וְחוֹתֵךְ הָעֶצֶם בְּצִפָּרְנָיו עַד שֶׁמַּגִּיעַ לַסִּימָנִין — **and cuts** through **that bone with his fingernail until he reaches the** *simanim* (i.e., the trachea and esophagus). וְחוֹתֵךְ גַּם הַסִּימָנִין בְּצִפָּרְנוֹ — **He then** continues and **also**

---

NOTES

1. In addition to the situations set forth in the previous mitzvah, see Mitzvos 168, 176, 179, 183; see also *Minchas Chinuch* 377:8.

2. As Chinuch will explain below (at note 23), this prohibition does not apply specifically to a Kohen, but actually pertains to all Jews. Although *melikah* must be performed by a Kohen, it is prohibited to sever the head of the bird even *after* the *melikah* is completed, until the application of the bird's blood to the Altar has been performed (see *Tosafos, Zevachim* 65b, ד"ה ורבי אלעזר; *Minchas Chinuch* §2). Nevertheless, since the Torah expresses the prohibition in the context of how the *melikah* should be done, and the actual *melikah* must be performed by a Kohen, Chinuch presents this mitzvah as though it pertains specifically to the Kohen.

3. The primary distinctions between *shechitah* and *melikah* are as follows: (1) *Shechitah* requires the use of a specially sharpened blade, whereas *melikah* is performed specifically with the Kohen's thumbnail. (2) *Shechitah* is performed at the animal's throat, whereas *melikah* must be done at the back of the neck. [*Melikah* done at the front or sides of the neck is not valid] (see *Rambam, Hil. Shechitah* 1:9; *Hil. Maasei HaKorbanos* 6:23).

# 464 ויקרא / מצוה קכד: שלא להבדיל הראש בחטאת העוף

אוֹ רֻבּוֹ שֶׁל אֶחָד מֵהֶן[4], וְזֹאת הִיא שְׁחִיטָתוֹ שֶׁל חַטַּאת הָעוֹף[5], וְצָרִיךְ שֶׁיְּכַוֵּן הַכֹּהֵן שֶׁלֹּא יַחְתֹּךְ הַכֹּל לְגַמְרֵי עַד שֶׁיְּהֵא נִפְרָד הָרֹאשׁ מִן הַגּוּף, וְעַל זֶה נֶאֱמַר וְלֹא יַבְדִּיל[6].

כְּבָר אָמַרְנוּ בְּמִצְוַת בִּנְיַן הַבַּיִת שֶׁאֵין בָּנוּ יְכֹלֶת וְגַם לֹא לַאֲשֶׁר קָטְנוֹ עָבָה מִמָּתְנֵינוּ[7],

---

**cuts** through **the *simanim* with his fingernail, or at least through the greater part of one of them.**[4] אוֹ רֻבּוֹ שֶׁל אֶחָד מֵהֶן — וְזֹאת הִיא שְׁחִיטָתוֹ שֶׁל חַטַּאת הָעוֹף — **This is** the form of **slaughter** that the Torah sets forth **for a bird *chatas* offering.**[5]

Chinuch proceeds to explain the prohibition of our mitzvah:

וְצָרִיךְ שֶׁיְּכַוֵּן הַכֹּהֵן — When performing *melikah*, the **Kohen must use precision** שֶׁלֹּא יַחְתֹּךְ הַכֹּל לְגַמְרֵי — **not to cut [the neck] entirely** through, עַד שֶׁיְּהֵא נִפְרָד הָרֹאשׁ מִן הַגּוּף — **to the extent that the head** of the bird **is separated from** its **body.** וְעַל זֶה נֶאֱמַר "וְלֹא יַבְדִּיל" — **With regard to this, it is stated** (*Leviticus* 5:8): [*the Kohen*] *shall nip its head at the nape,* **but he shall not separate it.**[6]

## ~ Underlying Purpose of the Mitzvah ~

כְּבָר אָמַרְנוּ בְּמִצְוַת בִּנְיַן הַבַּיִת — **We have already stated, in the mitzvah** regarding **building the** Holy **Temple** (Mitzvah 95), שֶׁאֵין בָּנוּ יְכֹלֶת — **that we have no ability,** וְגַם לֹא לַאֲשֶׁר קָטְנוֹ עָבָה מִמָּתְנֵינוּ — **and nor do** those great Sages **whose "little finger is thicker than our waists,"**[7]

---

### NOTES

4. Essentially, *shechitah* entails cutting through the *simanim*, the two life-sustaining pipes that run through the neck. In the case of fowl, although it is preferable to cut through the entirety of both *simanim*, if one cut through the greater part of one of them, the *shechitah* is valid (*Rambam, Hil. Shechitah* 1:9). In the case of *melikah* of a bird *chatas*, as well, if only the greater part of one of the *simanim* was cut, the *melikah* is valid (*Rambam, Hil. Maasei HaKorbanos* 7:6; see, however, note 6).

5. *Melikah*, however, is not a valid form of slaughter for fowl that are not bird offerings. An unconsecrated bird that was slaughtered by *melikah* is considered *neveilah* (unslaughtered carcass), just as any bird that has been killed through means other than *shechitah*, and is prohibited for consumption (Mitzvah 472). Moreover, even a bird *chatas* itself is considered *neveilah* to non-Kohanim, and may be eaten only by a Kohen, upon whom there is a mitzvah to partake of the sacrificial offerings (Mitzvah 102). A non-Kohen who partakes of a bird *chatas* violates the prohibition against eating *neveilah* (see above, Mitzvah 73, at note 63; *Rambam, Hil. Maaseh HaKorbanos* 11:9; see *Yevamos* 32b and *Asvan DeOraisa* §1). [In addition, since during the process of *melikah* the bird's neck is broken before the *simanim* are cut, an unconsecrated bird is also prohibited as a *tereifah* (see Mitzvah 73 note 66).]

6. The Torah stipulates in this verse that when performing *melikah* the Kohen must avoid separating the head of the bird from its body. That is, he must cut through the neck bone and the two *simanim*, but avoid entirely cutting through the flesh and skin of the bird. Indeed, if he did sever the head, the offering is invalid (*Rambam* ibid. 7:6; see also *Sefer HaMitzvos, Shoresh* 8).

It should be noted that although the procedure of *melikah* that is described in this verse applies to both a bird *chatas* and a bird *olah*, the prohibition against severing the head from the body applies only to the bird *chatas*. With regard to a bird *olah*, however, one is actually *required* to separate the head from the body during *melikah* (see *Chullin* 21b, where this is derived from Scripture).

[Chinuch's presentation of this mitzvah follows the opinion of *Rambam* (ibid.), and is consistent with *Rambam's* general position (see *Hil. Shechitah* 1:9) that when performing *shechitah* on a bird, one must ideally cut through both *simanim*. Since the requirement to cut through both *simanim* presumably applies to *melikah* as well, our mitzvah must be interpreted as a prohibition against entirely severing the head from the body (see *Kesef Mishneh* and *Lechem Mishneh*; *Smag, Lo Saaseh* 327).

*Rashi* (*Chullin* 21b ד"ה ואינו מבדיל בסימן אחד), however, has a different opinion with regard to the laws of *shechitah* pertaining to fowl, and in accordance with that opinion, he also explains our prohibition differently. According to *Rashi*, the *shechitah* of a bird even initially requires only the cutting of one of the *simanim*. Thus, when the Torah states "*you shall not separate it*," that is not merely to say that you shall not sever the head from the body, but rather that you shall not sever the *siman* itself. That is, you shall not sever the second *siman*, whose separation is not required for the *melikah*. Similarly, *Rashi* explains that the *obligation* to "separate" that the Gemara (ibid.) speaks of with regard to the *melikah* of the bird *olah* does not require that one sever the head from the body, but that one cut through both *simanim* when performing *melikah* (see *Rashi* to *Zevachim* 64b ד"ה ומבדיל).]

7. [Stylistic paraphrase of *I Kings* 12:10.] I.e., whose ability to fathom the profound underpinnings of the mitzvos greatly surpasses our own.

# VAYIKRA / MITZVAH 124: NOT TO SEVER THE HEAD OF A BIRD CHATAS OFFERING

לִמְצֹא טַעֲנָה גַּם עַל צַד הַפְּשָׁט בְּפִרְטֵי הַקָּרְבָּנוֹת, וְדַי לָנוּ לִמְלַאכְתֵּנוּ זֹאת לְהוֹדִיעַ בְּעִנְיַן הַקָּרְבָּנוֹת דֶּרֶךְ כְּלָל קְצָת טַעַם עַל צַד הַפְּשָׁט, וּכְבָר כָּתַבְתִּי לְמַעְלָה מַה שֶּׁיָּדַעְתִּי וְשָׁמַעְתִּי.[8] וְעִנְיַן הַמְּלִיקָה וְהָאַזְהָרָה שֶׁלֹּא יַבְדִּיל, גַּם זֶה מִפִּרְטֵי הַקָּרְבָּן הוּא. וְאַךְ אָמְנָה, אֲשֶׁר לֹא יָחוּשׁ לְהוֹצִיא כָּל רוּחוֹ[9] יוּכַל לְהָשִׁיב כִּי אוּלַי בִּדְבַר הַמְּלִיקָה הַנַּעֲשֵׂית בְּיַד הַכֹּהֵן בְּחַטַּאת הָעוֹף, שֶׁהוּא קָרְבָּן שֶׁל עָנִי,[10] רֶמֶז שֶׁיְּמַהֵר כָּל אָדָם בְּתַכְלִית הַמְּהִירוּת עֶרְכּוֹ שֶׁל עָנִי, וְעַל כֵּן אֵינוֹ צָרִיךְ קָרְבָּנוֹ שְׁחִיטָה, שֶׁלֹּא יִצְטָרֵךְ הַכֹּהֵן לַחֲזֹר אַחַר הַסַּכִּין וּלְבָדְקוֹ[11], וְיִתְבַּטֵּל שָׁם הֶעָנִי מִמְּלַאכְתּוֹ בֵּינְתַיִם. גַּם לְהַפְלִיג הַמְּהִירוּת אָמַר שֶׁיַּתְחִיל מִמּוּל עָרְפּוֹ, כִּי הוּא הַמּוּכָן אֶל יָדוֹ,

---

**לִמְצֹא טַעֲנָה גַּם עַל צַד הַפְּשָׁט בְּפִרְטֵי הַקָּרְבָּנוֹת** — to find a rationale, even on a basic level, for the **particular** requirements **of the sacrificial offerings.** **וְדַי לָנוּ לִמְלַאכְתֵּנוּ זֹאת** — Thus, it is sufficient for our objective in **this work** **לְהוֹדִיעַ בְּעִנְיַן הַקָּרְבָּנוֹת דֶּרֶךְ כְּלָל קְצָת טַעַם עַל צַד הַפְּשָׁט** — to suggest, for the subject of the sacrificial offerings as a whole, some reason on a basic level. **וּכְבָר כָּתַבְתִּי לְמַעְלָה מַה שֶּׁיָּדַעְתִּי וְשָׁמַעְתִּי** — I have already written above that which I have come to **know and understand** in this regard.[8]

**וְעִנְיַן הַמְּלִיקָה וְהָאַזְהָרָה שֶׁלֹּא יַבְדִּיל גַּם זֶה מִפִּרְטֵי הַקָּרְבָּן הוּא** — Now, the *melikah* procedure and the injunction against separating the head of the bird *chatas* from its body are also among the details of the offerings, and in truth we cannot provide an authoritative reason for them. **וְאַךְ אָמְנָה, אֲשֶׁר לֹא יָחוּשׁ לְהוֹצִיא כָּל רוּחוֹ יוּכַל לְהָשִׁיב** — However, one who is not concerned about "expending all his breath"[9] could argue **כִּי אוּלַי בִּדְבַר הַמְּלִיקָה הַנַּעֲשֵׂית בְּיַד הַכֹּהֵן בְּחַטַּאת הָעוֹף** — that perhaps, in the matter of the *melikah* that is done by the hand of the Kohen on the bird *chatas*, **שֶׁהוּא קָרְבָּן שֶׁל עָנִי** — which is a poor man's offering,[10] **רֶמֶז** — there lies a symbolic lesson: **שֶׁיְּמַהֵר כָּל אָדָם בְּתַכְלִית הַמְּהִירוּת עֶרְכּוֹ שֶׁל עָנִי** — that every man must act with utmost speed to fulfill a poor person's needs. **וְעַל כֵּן אֵינוֹ צָרִיךְ קָרְבָּנוֹ שְׁחִיטָה** — Therefore, [the poor man's] offering does not require *shechitah*, **שֶׁלֹּא יִצְטָרֵךְ הַכֹּהֵן לַחֲזֹר אַחַר הַסַּכִּין וּלְבָדְקוֹ** — in order that the Kohen should not be required to seek a knife and to inspect it,[11] **וְיִתְבַּטֵּל שָׁם הֶעָנִי מִמְּלַאכְתּוֹ בֵּינְתַיִם** — and the poor man would thus be forced to be idle from his work during the interim. **גַּם לְהַפְלִיג הַמְּהִירוּת** — Also, in order to accelerate the speed of the poor man's offering, **אָמַר שֶׁיַּתְחִיל מִמּוּל עָרְפּוֹ** — [the Torah] stated that [the Kohen] shall begin the *melikah* procedure from the nape, **כִּי הוּא הַמּוּכָן אֶל יָדוֹ** — for when holding a bird [the nape] is most accessible to [the Kohen's] hand,

---

## NOTES

8. Chinuch explained in Mitzvah 95 that man cannot fathom the actual reasons for the mitzvos pertaining to the Temple (*Beis HaMikdash*) and the sacrificial offerings, and that he therefore explains them only on what he calls a "basic level." Chinuch adds, though (there, at notes 56-57), that this simple level of explanation will not suffice for the many detailed laws of these mitzvos, and that he is undertaking to explain them only on a general level. [See also Mitzvah 104, and the Insight there.]

[Chinuch nevertheless proceeds to set forth a lesson that can be learned from the *melikah* process, as well as from the prohibition against severing the head of the bird. As he explains in Mitzvah 95 (at notes 58-63), one may present an insight he has into a mitzvah even though it does not capture the full depth of the mitzvah.]

9. In a stylistic paraphrase of *Proverbs* 29:11, Chinuch humbly refers to himself as one who exhausts all his breath in attempting to explain a concept of which he himself has only a limited grasp. See similarly above, Mitzvah 95 (ibid.).

10. In the passage commanding this mitzvah, the Torah specifies that the bird *chatas* is brought by one who cannot afford the more expensive animal offering, as outlined in the previous mitzvah (see also Mitzvah 176). Thus, although there are instances in which a bird *chatas* is required regardless of financial standing (see, for example, Mitzvah 168), it is viewed primarily as an offering of the poor.

11. Unlike *melikah*, which the Kohen performs with his fingernail, *shechitah* requires the use of a knife that was inspected and determined to be free of nicks (see Mitzvah 451). The Torah instituted a more expeditious form of slaughter for the offering of the poor, to convey that one must tend to the needs of the poor with alacrity. [See Insight.]

## ויקרא / מצוה קכד: שלא להבדיל הראש בחטאת העוף

וְלֹא יִצְטָרֵךְ לַהֲפֹךְ הַצַּוָּאר אֶל צַד הַסִּימָנִין.[12] וְעוֹד יֵשׁ רֶמֶז בְּעִנְיַן הַמְּלִיקָה שֶׁהִיא מִמּוּל הָעֹרֶף בְּתוֹרִים וּבְנֵי יוֹנָה, שֶׁנִּמְשְׁלוּ יִשְׂרָאֵל בָּהֶם,[13] שֶׁלֹּא נִהְיֶה קְשֵׁי עֹרֶף.

וְעִנְיַן אִסּוּר הַבְדָּלַת הָרֹאשׁ מִן הַגּוּף דָּבָר רָאוּי הוּא לְהִדּוּר הַקָּרְבָּן, כִּי בֶּאֱמֶת כְּשֶׁרֹאשׁ הָעוֹף דָּבֵק עִמּוֹ הוּא יוֹתֵר מְהֻדָּר, וְרָאוּי לָנוּ לְהַדֵּר קָרְבָּנוֹ שֶׁל עָנִי בְּכָל כֹּחֵנוּ, דַּי לוֹ בַּעֲנִיּוּתוֹ, אֵין לָנוּ לְהוֹסִיף בְּדַלּוּתוֹ לִפְחֹת תֹּאַר קָרְבָּנוֹ.[14] וְכָל זֶה מִן הַיְסוֹד אֲשֶׁר בָּנִינוּ תְּחִלָּה, כִּי מִשָּׁרְשֵׁי הַקָּרְבָּנוֹת לִקְנוֹת בְּנַפְשֵׁנוּ מִדּוֹת טוֹבוֹת וּמַעֲלוֹת, וּלְהַכְשִׁיר פְּעֻלּוֹתֵינוּ בְּכֹחַ הַדִּמְיוֹנוֹת שֶׁאֲנַחְנוּ עֲסוּקִים בָּהֶן,[15] כִּי מִהְיוֹת הָאָדָם בַּעַל חֹמֶר לֹא יְצַיֵּר וִיקַבַּע הַדְּבָרִים צִיּוּר חָזָק בְּנַפְשׁוֹ

---

וְלֹא יִצְטָרֵךְ לַהֲפֹךְ הַצַּוָּאר אֶל צַד הַסִּימָנִין — and thus, **he will not need to turn over the neck to the side of the** *simanim*.[12] שֶׁהִיא מִמּוּל הַמְּלִיקָה וְעוֹד יֵשׁ רֶמֶז בְּעִנְיַן — **There is further symbolism in the law of** *melikah*, הָעֹרֶף בְּתוֹרִים וּבְנֵי יוֹנָה — as it is effected **at the nape of the neck of turtledoves or pigeons,** שֶׁנִּמְשְׁלוּ יִשְׂרָאֵל בָּהֶם — **to which the Jewish people are metaphorically compared.**[13] שֶׁלֹּא נִהְיֶה קְשֵׁי עֹרֶף — Cutting the nape symbolizes **that we must not be stiff-necked** (i.e., stubborn) in our relationship with God.

Having suggested lessons that can be derived from the *melikah* procedure in general, Chinuch proceeds to discuss a reason for the actual prohibition of this mitzvah:

וְעִנְיַן אִסּוּר הַבְדָּלַת הָרֹאשׁ מִן הַגּוּף — As for **the matter of the prohibition against separating the head** of the bird *chatas* **from [its] body,** דָּבָר רָאוּי הוּא לְהִדּוּר הַקָּרְבָּן — **it is an appropriate thing, to enhance the appearance of the offering.** כִּי בֶּאֱמֶת — **For in truth,** כְּשֶׁרֹאשׁ הָעוֹף דָּבֵק עִמּוֹ הוּא יוֹתֵר מְהֻדָּר — **when the bird's head is attached to its body its appearance is enhanced,** וְרָאוּי לָנוּ לְהַדֵּר קָרְבָּנוֹ שֶׁל עָנִי בְּכָל כֹּחֵנוּ — **and it is fitting that we enhance the appearance of the poor man's offering to the extent of our ability.** דַּי לוֹ בַּעֲנִיּוּתוֹ — **It is enough for him** that he must endure his **poverty,** אֵין לָנוּ לְהוֹסִיף בְּדַלּוּתוֹ לִפְחֹת תֹּאַר קָרְבָּנוֹ — **we should not add to his** sense of **indigence by diminishing the appearance of his offering.**[14] וְכָל זֶה מִן הַיְסוֹד אֲשֶׁר בָּנִינוּ תְּחִלָּה — **All this** that we have said here **is based upon the fundamental principle that we initially established** (in Mitzvah 95), regarding offerings in general, כִּי מִשָּׁרְשֵׁי הַקָּרְבָּנוֹת לִקְנוֹת בְּנַפְשֵׁנוּ מִדּוֹת טוֹבוֹת וּמַעֲלוֹת — **that among the underlying purposes of the sacrificial offerings is so that our souls acquire virtuous and elevated character traits,** וּלְהַכְשִׁיר פְּעֻלּוֹתֵינוּ בְּכֹחַ הַדִּמְיוֹנוֹת שֶׁאֲנַחְנוּ עֲסוּקִים בָּהֶן — **and so that we perfect our actions through the power of the symbolism in which we engage.**[15] כִּי מִהְיוֹת הָאָדָם בַּעַל חֹמֶר — **For, since man is comprised of** a **physical** body, לֹא יְצַיֵּר וִיקַבַּע הַדְּבָרִים צִיּוּר חָזָק בְּנַפְשׁוֹ — **he cannot conceive and establish in his soul an abiding concept of these matters** (i.e., refined character traits),

---

### NOTES

12. Chinuch below (at note 17) explains that when preparing to do *melikah,* the Kohen grasps the bird's legs and wings between his fingers. Thus, the back of its neck is naturally exposed. Since *shechitah* would require the additional step of pulling back the bird's head to expose its throat, the Torah instituted the procedure of *melikah.*

13. Scripture often uses pigeons or turtledoves as a metaphor for the Jewish people (for example, see *Song of Songs* 1:15 and *Psalms* 74:19). The Midrash (*Shir HaShirim Rabbah* to cited verse) explains this metaphor in a number of ways; for example, as an allusion to their loyalty, devotion, and willingness to sacrifice for God and His commandments.

14. Similarly, in the case of the bird *olah* offering, the Torah requires that one place the offering upon the Altar in its entirety, without first plucking its feathers. Although the burning feathers will emit an unpleasant odor, the Torah wished to enhance the dignity of a poor person, so it ensured that his offering will have an ample appearance upon the Altar (*Rashi, Leviticus* 1:17 ד״ה בכנפיו).

15. See Mitzvah 95, where Chinuch develops this principle at length. The experience of bringing an offering contains powerful lessons like those Chinuch explains here, which can profoundly elevate a person's thoughts and actions.

ись עַל יְדֵי הַפְּעֻלּוֹת.[16] וְעַד [שֶׁ]שָּׁמַעְנוּ טַעַם אַחֵר, נַחֲזִיק בָּזֶה.

דִּינֵי הַמִּצְוָה כְּגוֹן מַה שֶׁאָמְרוּ זִכְרוֹנָם לִבְרָכָה (זבחים ס״ד ע״ב) כֵּיצַד אוֹחֵז הַכֹּהֵן חַטַּאת הָעוֹף בִּשְׁעַת מְלִיקָה, אוֹחֵז שְׁתֵּי רַגְלֵי הָעוֹף בֵּין שְׁתֵּי אֶצְבְּעוֹתָיו וּשְׁתֵּי גַפֶּיהָ בֵּין שְׁתֵּי אֶצְבְּעוֹתָיו, וּמוֹתֵחַ צַוָּארָהּ אֶל רֹחַב שְׁתֵּי אֶצְבְּעוֹתָיו וּמוֹלֵק[17], וְזוֹ מֵעֲבוֹדוֹת קָשׁוֹת שֶׁבַּמִּקְדָּשׁ.[18] וְאִם שִׁנָּה וְאָחַז, מִכָּל מָקוֹם כְּשֵׁרָה.[19]

וְכָל הַמָּקוֹם מִן הַמִּזְבֵּחַ כָּשֵׁר לִמְלִיקָה[20], פֵּרוּשׁ גַּם זֶה נֹאמַר שֶׁהוּא לְמַהֵר עִנְיָנֵנוּ שֶׁל עֹנִי,

---

**כִּי אִם עַל יְדֵי הַפְּעֻלּוֹת** — except through engaging in physical **activities** that encourage refinement.[16]

**וְעַד [שֶׁ]שָּׁמַעְנוּ טַעַם אַחֵר נַחֲזִיק בָּזֶה** — Although this explanation certainly does not express the entire essence of the mitzvah, **until we hear another reason let us embrace this one.**

### ⁌ Laws of the Mitzvah ⁌

Chinuch explains some of the laws of the *melikah* procedure in general:

**דִּינֵי הַמִּצְוָה** — **The laws of this mitzvah** include, **כְּגוֹן מַה שֶׁאָמְרוּ זִכְרוֹנָם לִבְרָכָה** — **for example,** that which [the Sages], of blessed memory, stated (Zevachim 64b): **כֵּיצַד אוֹחֵז הַכֹּהֵן חַטַּאת הָעוֹף** **בִּשְׁעַת מְלִיקָה** — **How does the Kohen grasp the bird** *chatas* during *melikah*? **אוֹחֵז שְׁתֵּי רַגְלֵי הָעוֹף בֵּין שְׁתֵּי אֶצְבְּעוֹתָיו וּשְׁתֵּי גַפֶּיהָ בֵּין שְׁתֵּי אֶצְבְּעוֹתָיו** — **He grasps the two feet of the bird between his two fingers and its two wings between his next two fingers,** **וּמוֹתֵחַ צַוָּארָהּ אֶל רֹחַב** **שְׁתֵּי אֶצְבְּעוֹתָיו** — **and stretches its neck** into his palm **alongside the width of his two fingers,** **וּמוֹלֵק** — **and** in this manner **he performs** *melikah*.[17] **וְזוֹ מֵעֲבוֹדוֹת קָשׁוֹת שֶׁבַּמִּקְדָּשׁ** — **And,** the Gemara concludes, [the *melikah* procedure] is one of the **most difficult** forms of *avodah* (service) **performed in the Holy Temple.**[18] **וְאִם שִׁנָּה וְאָחַז מִכָּל מָקוֹם כְּשֵׁרָה** — **However,** although this is the preferred manner in which to hold the bird during *melikah*, **if he varied** from it **and grasped** the bird in a different manner, [the *melikah*] is nevertheless valid.[19]

**וְכָל הַמָּקוֹם מִן הַמִּזְבֵּחַ כָּשֵׁר לִמְלִיקָה** — **Any area of the Altar is valid for** *melikah*.[20] **פֵּרוּשׁ גַּם זֶה** **נֹאמַר שֶׁהוּא לְמַהֵר עִנְיָנֵנוּ שֶׁל עֹנִי** — **For the explanation of [this law], as well, we can say that it is**

---

### NOTES

16. Due to the corporeal nature of man, it is not sufficient for him to merely contemplate the refinement of his character, as such contemplation will not have lasting results. Rather, he must translate his thoughts into actions. As Chinuch explained in Mitzvah 95 (at notes 24-25), actions performed within the spiritual purity of the *Beis HaMikdash* will have the most far-reaching and permanent effect on a person's character.

17. The bird is placed face-down upon the back of the Kohen's hand. Its feet are secured between the little finger and the ring finger, and its outstretched wings are held between the middle finger and the index finger. He then uses his thumb to pull its head around his index finger into the palm of his hand, and holds it against his index finger and middle finger. With the back of its neck thus exposed, the Kohen performs *melikah* by piercing the neck with his thumbnail, as Chinuch described above (see Rashi to Zevachim 64b).

According to *Shitah Mekubetzes* (Zevachim 64b, §14), the Kohen must grasp the bird in his right hand and perform the *melikah* with the same hand. Rambam (Commentary to the Mishnah, Zevachim 6:4), however, explains that the bird is held in the left hand while *melikah* is performed with the right hand.

18. According to *Shitah Mekubetzes* cited in the previous note, the difficulty lies in performing *melikah* while grasping the bird in the same hand. Others explain that the difficulty lies in piercing the neck-bone of the bird manually without the aid of a utensil (*Tosafos, Yoma* 49b ד״ה והאיכא קמיצה). For yet another explanation, see *Meiri, Yoma* 47b ד״ה המליקה.

19. *Rambam, Hil. Maaseh HaKorbanos* 7:8.

20. In contrast to the bird *olah*, whose *melikah* should ideally be performed at the southeast corner of the Altar (Rambam ibid. 6:20; see, however, ibid. 7:10), the Torah does not specify a location for the *melikah* of a bird *chatas*.

Although there is no specific location for the *melikah* of a bird *chatas*, Chinuch maintains that it must be performed upon the Altar. While this rule seems to emerge from the Gemara (Zevachim 63b), the Scriptural basis for this requirement is unclear. Thus, although some Rishonim share the position of Chinuch (see *Rambam, Hil. Maasei HaKorbanos* 7:9; Raavad, Commentary to Kinnim 1:1), others maintain that the *melikah* of a bird *chatas* may be performed anywhere in the Courtyard of the *Beis HaMikdash* (see Commentary of R' Zerachyah HaLevi to Kinnim loc. cit.).

## 468 □ ויקרא / מצוה קכד: שלא להבדיל הראש בחטאת העוף

וּלְפִיכָךְ אֵין לוֹ מָקוֹם מְיֻחָד[21], וְיֶתֶר פְּרָטֶיהָ מְבֹאָרִים בִּזְבָחִים (ס״ג ע״א — ע׳ ע״ב)[22]. וְנוֹהֶגֶת בִּזְמַן הַבַּיִת בַּכֹּהֲנִים וּבְכָל אָדָם, שֶׁכָּל מִי שֶׁהִבְדִּיל בְּחַטַּאת הָעוֹף לוֹקֶה[23].

---

**in order to expedite the poor man's affairs;** וּלְפִיכָךְ אֵין לוֹ מָקוֹם מְיֻחָד — namely, **that for this reason** melikah **of a bird** chatas **does not have a designated area,** as that might lead to a delay in its performance.[21]

וְיֶתֶר פְּרָטֶיהָ מְבֹאָרִים בִּזְבָחִים — These laws **and the remaining details of [the** melikah **of the bird** chatas**] are elaborated in** Tractate Zevachim **(63a-66a).**[22]

### ⁓ Applicability of the Mitzvah ⁓

וְנוֹהֶגֶת בִּזְמַן הַבַּיִת בַּכֹּהֲנִים וּבְכָל אָדָם — **This mitzvah applies during the times of the Temple, and applies both to Kohanim and to all people;** שֶׁכָּל מִי שֶׁהִבְדִּיל בְּחַטַּאת הָעוֹף לוֹקֶה — **for anyone who separates** the head of the **bird** chatas from its body **incurs** malkus (lashes).[23]

---

### NOTES

21. If the *melikah* would be confined to a specific area, it would need to be delayed if the *melikah* of another offering was being done at that time. To prevent this, and to teach the need to accelerate tending to the needs of the poor, the Torah allowed that it be performed in any location upon the Altar. [Presumably, this applies to the poor man's *chatas* as opposed to his *olah*, to spare him additional embarrassment when he brings his sin offering.]

22. *Rambam* codifies the laws of the bird *chatas* and bird *olah* in *Hil. Maasei HaKorbanos* 6:20-23 and 7:6-10; the laws of this mitzvah are found there, 7:6.

23. The verse of this mitzvah is addressed to a Kohen, for it is a Kohen who performs *melikah*. Nevertheless, *Chinuch* explains, the prohibition applies even to those who are not Kohanim; see above, note 2.

---

### ◆§ Insight: Tending to Others' Needs in an Expeditious Manner

Chinuch states that the manner in which the Kohen slaughters the bird *chatas*, which is typically brought by the indigent, teaches that one must attend to the affairs of a poor person in an expeditious manner. The bird *chatas* is therefore slaughtered through *melikah*, for *melikah* does not require procurement of a knife and can be performed by the Kohen immediately. Similarly, the place for *melikah* is at the nape, which Chinuch states is the most readily accessible part of the bird's neck. Also to prevent delay, the bird *chatas* may be offered at any convenient location on the Altar. Chinuch explains that the reason one must act expeditiously when tending to the affairs of one who is poor is to avoid needlessly taking up time he could use for earning a livelihood.

According to the reason offered by Chinuch, acting speedily when tending to the poor is a virtuous habit that one should seek to adopt, but is not an actual requirement. There are, however, instances where tending to the needs of the poor with alacrity is indeed required by law.

As Chinuch will set forth in Mitzvah 575 (see also Mitzvos 574 and 438), one who pledges a sacrificial offering or a gift to the poor is required to redeem his pledge in a timely fashion. If he neglects to do so, even if he fulfills his obligation at a later time, he violates both a mitzvah-obligation and a mitzvah-prohibition. Based on Scriptural exegesis, the Gemara (*Rosh Hashanah* 4a-4b) determines that the time for redemption of a pledge for a sacrificial offering is before the passing of the three festivals — Pesach, Shavuos, and Succos. With regard to a pledge of a gift to the poor, however, the Gemara (ibid. 6a) explains that one is required to redeem his pledge immediately. Since poor people can always be found, it is possible to redeem a pledge to the poor at any time. Accordingly, one who fails to redeem such a pledge at the first opportunity violates the obligation to avoid procrastination with regard to pledges.

Based on this, *Mishnah Berurah* (639:35, *Shaar HaTziyun* §67) suggests that one who invites a poor person to his home for a Sabbath meal may be required to begin the meal promptly. Issuing the invitation might be the equivalent of a charitable pledge, and, once the poor person has entered his home, any delay would be a violation of the requirement to fulfill a pledge promptly! Accordingly, *Mishnah Berurah* argues, although there is a requirement to eat a portion of bread in the *succah* on

the first night of Succos, and in the event of rain one is required to wait for the rain to stop in order to fulfill this requirement in its most proper form, one who has invited a poor person to eat with him should begin his meal promptly. Since postponing the meal would cause him to violate the prohibition against delaying his pledge, he must provide the meal without delay.

There is further reason to avoid delay when assisting others, which applies even when helping one who is not poor.

In Mitzvah 64, Chinuch set forth the prohibition against causing distress to an orphan or widow. As was indicated in the Insight to that mitzvah, *Mechilta* (to *Exodus* 22:21) cites the opinion of R' Yishmael that this prohibition is not limited to orphans or widows, but actually applies to any person who is particularly vulnerable due to an emotional, physical, or situational disadvantage. Furthermore, based on a careful reading of the verse of that mitzvah, R' Yishmael points out that the prohibition does not merely require that one refrain from causing serious pain or anguish to one who is vulnerable, but that one avoid causing him even slight distress.

*Mechilta* illustrates this with the following anecdote:

When R' Yishmael and Rabban Shimon ben Gamliel, who were both among the Ten Martyrs, were being led to their execution on the orders of the Roman dictator, Rabban Shimon ben Gamliel expressed his distress to R' Yishmael. He was upset because he was unable to identify the transgression for which Heaven was holding him liable to death. In response, R' Yishmael asked: "Did it ever occur, when a person came to you because he was in need of judgment or the resolution of a halachic query, that you asked him to wait while you finished your drink, or donned your shoes, or wrapped yourself in your cloak? Such a situation is included in the prohibition against causing distress to one who is vulnerable, and incurs the Heavenly wrath that is described as the penalty for one who violates it." Rabban Shimon ben Gamliel accepted this explanation, and proclaimed "My teacher, you have consoled me" (*Mechilta* to *Exodus* 22:21-22 with *Malbim* and *Netziv*).

Anyone who needs assistance is vulnerable to some degree, and, as R' Yishmael explained, unnecessary delay in responding to his need is on some level a violation of the prohibition against causing distress to one who is vulnerable. Thus, for the very great, whose every word and action is in total consonance with the Torah, even keeping a person waiting without adequate cause is considered a transgression.

## מִצְוָה קכה: שֶׁלֹּא לִתֵּן שֶׁמֶן זַיִת בְּמִנְחַת חוֹטֵא[1]

שֶׁלֹּא יָשִׂים הַכֹּהֵן שֶׁמֶן בְּמִנְחַת חוֹטֵא עָנִי, שֶׁנֶּאֱמַר (ויקרא ה׳, י״א) לֹא יָשִׂים עָלֶיהָ שֶׁמֶן, וְאַף עַל פִּי שֶׁבִּשְׁאָר מְנָחוֹת הָיוּ נוֹתְנִין שֶׁמֶן. וּמִפְּנֵי כֵן אָמַרְתִּי חוֹטֵא עָנִי,

## Mitzvah 125
## The Prohibition to Place Olive Oil Upon a Sinner's Minchah Offering

וְאִם לֹא תַשִּׂיג יָדוֹ לִשְׁתֵּי תֹרִים אוֹ לִשְׁנֵי בְנֵי יוֹנָה וְהֵבִיא אֶת קָרְבָּנוֹ אֲשֶׁר חָטָא עֲשִׂירִת הָאֵפָה סֹלֶת לְחַטָּאת לֹא יָשִׂים עָלֶיהָ שֶׁמֶן וְלֹא יִתֵּן עָלֶיהָ לְבֹנָה כִּי חַטָּאת הִוא

*But if his means are insufficient for two turtledoves or two young doves, then he shall bring, as his guilt-offering for that which he sinned, a tenth-ephah of fine flour for a chatas offering; he shall not place oil on it nor shall he put levonah on it, for it is a chatas offering (Leviticus 5:11).*

In Mitzvah 123, Chinuch describes the קָרְבָּן עוֹלֶה וְיוֹרֵד, *the variable offering*, an obligatory *chatas* (sin) offering for one who violated one of a specific list of prohibitions. It is *variable* in that the specific nature of the offering varies depending on the penitent's financial situation. One who can afford an animal must bring an animal offering; one who cannot, brings a less expensive bird offering; one who cannot afford even that is obligated to bring a *minchah* (meal) offering. This is unique, for a *chatas* offering does not take the form of a *minchah* except in this case. [See Mitzvah 116 for discussion of the various obligatory and donated *minchah* offerings.] It is the procedure of this particular *minchah* that is the subject of this mitzvah.

The מִנְחַת חוֹטֵא, *sinner's minchah,* takes the basic form of the *fine-flour minchah* (see above, Mitzvah 116), with two significant omissions. The standard procedure for the fine-flour *minchah* includes an application of oil to the flour (subsequently mixed together), and the placing of *levonah*[1] on top of it. After this, the Kohen would perform the *kemitzah* (i.e., the removal of a fistful of the *minchah*) to be burned with the *levonah* upon the Altar. When the service was complete, the remainder of the *minchah* was given to the Kohanim to eat after it was baked (see Mitzvah 116, note 17). The service and laws of the sinner's *minchah* follow this procedure, except that no oil or *levonah* are added (*Minchas Chinuch* §2).

As Chinuch explains in this mitzvah and in the following one, the Torah's instructions to omit the oil and *levonah* are not merely a description of this particular *minchah*, but actually constitute two specific prohibitions against adding these items into the *minchah* of the sinner. Mitzvah 125 forbids adding the oil, and Mitzvah 126 forbids adding the *levonah*.

שֶׁלֹּא יָשִׂים הַכֹּהֵן שֶׁמֶן בְּמִנְחַת חוֹטֵא עָנִי — **We are commanded that the Kohen shall not put oil in the *minchah* offering of the indigent sinner,** שֶׁנֶּאֱמַר "לֹא יָשִׂים עָלֶיהָ שֶׁמֶן" — **as it is stated** (Leviticus 5:11): **he shall not place oil on it,** וְאַף עַל פִּי שֶׁבִּשְׁאָר מְנָחוֹת הָיוּ נוֹתְנִין שֶׁמֶן — **even though they would put oil on other *minchah* offerings.**

Chinuch explains his use of the term "the indigent sinner":

וּמִפְּנֵי כֵן אָמַרְתִּי חוֹטֵא עָנִי — **For the** following **reason I stated that** this applies to **the indigent sinner:**

---

NOTES

1. The Scriptural term לְבוֹנָה, *levonah*, is generally translated as frankincense — a resinous substance deriving from the sap of certain trees, which hardens into granules that are burned as incense. [Whether the trees identified as the sources of frankincense are indeed identical to the ones from which *levonah* was taken is difficult to determine. However, *Aruch HaShulchan HeAsid* 19:8 cites from the *Siddur* of the *Shelah* that *levonah* indeed comes from the sap of a tree. See also *Tiferes Yisrael* in his *Chomer BaKodesh* (Introduction to *Seder Kodashim*) 2:67. We will refer to this simply as *levonah*.]

# VAYIKRA / MITZVAH 125: NOT TO PLACE OLIVE OIL ON A SINNER'S MINCHAH OFFERING

כִּי חוֹטֵא עָשִׁיר אֵינוֹ מֵבִיא מִנְחַת קֶמַח לְעוֹלָם כִּי אִם קָרְבָּן בְּהֵמָה כְּמוֹ שֶׁמְפֹרָשׁ בַּתּוֹרָה[2].

מִשָּׁרְשֵׁי הַמִּצְוָה, לְפִי שֶׁהַשֶּׁמֶן רֶמֶז לְמַעֲלָה וְלִגְדֻלָּה, שֶׁאִם אַתָּה מְעָרְבוֹ בְּכָל מַשְׁקִין, הוּא צָף עַל כֻּלָּן, וְהוּא דָּבָר חָשׁוּב מְאֹד, וְיָדוּעַ הוּא חֲשִׁיבוּת שֶׁמֶן הַטּוֹב, וְלָכֵן יִמְשְׁחוּ בּוֹ הַמִּתְחַנְּכִים לְמַעֲלַת מַלְכוּת אוֹ כְּהֻנָּה[3], עַל כֵּן אֵין רָאוּי לָתֵת מִמֶּנּוּ בְּמִנְחַת הַחוֹטֵא הַצָּרִיךְ לְהַרְאוֹת בְּעַצְמוֹ דַּאֲגָה וְשִׁפְלוּת עַל שֶׁבָּא דְּבַר עֲבֵרָה לְיָדוֹ[4].

וְעוֹד נֹאמַר שֶׁהוּא לְחֶמְלַת הֶעָנִי שֶׁלֹּא לְהַטְרִיחוֹ יוֹתֵר מִדַּי לְהָבִיא שֶׁמֶן, כִּי הַשֵּׁם בָּרוּךְ הוּא לֹא יַטְרִיחַ בְּרִיָּה. וּמִפְּנֵי זֶה גַּם כֵּן לֹא חִיְּבוֹ רַק בִּמְעַט קֶמַח, שֶׁאִי אֶפְשָׁר לְשׁוּם אָדָם אֲפִלּוּ בְּדַלֵּי דַלּוּת בְּלֹא מְעַט קֶמַח[5]. וְזֶה יַסְפִּיק לָנוּ גַּם עַל הַלְּבוֹנָה.

---

כִּי חוֹטֵא עָשִׁיר אֵינוֹ מֵבִיא מִנְחַת קֶמַח לְעוֹלָם — It is **because a wealthy person who sins never brings a flour** *minchah* **as his sin offering;** כִּי אִם קָרְבָּן בְּהֵמָה כְּמוֹ שֶׁמְפֹרָשׁ בַּתּוֹרָה — he brings **only an animal offering, as set forth in the Torah.**[2]

### ~ Underlying Purpose of the Mitzvah ~

מִשָּׁרְשֵׁי הַמִּצְוָה — **Among the underlying purposes of this mitzvah** לְפִי שֶׁהַשֶּׁמֶן רֶמֶז לְמַעֲלָה וְלִגְדֻלָּה — **is that oil symbolizes an elevated status and grandeur,** שֶׁאִם אַתָּה מְעָרְבוֹ בְּכָל מַשְׁקִין — **for when you mix [oil] with any other liquid,** הוּא צָף עַל כֻּלָּן — **[the oil] floats above all of them.** וְהוּא דָּבָר חָשׁוּב מְאֹד — **In addition, [oil] is a very valuable item,** וְיָדוּעַ הוּא חֲשִׁיבוּת שֶׁמֶן הַטּוֹב — **and the value of fine oil is well-known;** וְלָכֵן יִמְשְׁחוּ בּוֹ הַמִּתְחַנְּכִים לְמַעֲלַת מַלְכוּת אוֹ כְּהֻנָּה — **because of its great value those who are initiated into the elevated status of kingship or priestly service are anointed with it.**[3] עַל כֵּן אֵין רָאוּי לָתֵת מִמֶּנּוּ בְּמִנְחַת הַחוֹטֵא — **Therefore, due to these elevated qualities of oil, it is inappropriate to apply it to the** *minchah* **of the sinner,** הַצָּרִיךְ לְהַרְאוֹת בְּעַצְמוֹ דַּאֲגָה וְשִׁפְלוּת — **who is required to exhibit his concern and lowliness** עַל שֶׁבָּא דְּבַר עֲבֵרָה לְיָדוֹ — **for the fact that a sin occurred through him.**[4]

Chinuch suggests an additional reason for this mitzvah:

וְעוֹד נֹאמַר שֶׁהוּא לְחֶמְלַת הֶעָנִי — **We may also say that the purpose of [this prohibition] is out of compassion for the pauper,** שֶׁלֹּא לְהַטְרִיחוֹ יוֹתֵר מִדַּי לְהָבִיא שֶׁמֶן — **in order not to burden him excessively** by requiring him **to bring oil,** which may be too expensive for him, כִּי הַשֵּׁם בָּרוּךְ הוּא לֹא יַטְרִיחַ בְּרִיָּה — **for Hashem, Blessed is He, does not overburden any person.** וּמִפְּנֵי זֶה גַּם כֵּן לֹא חִיְּבוֹ רַק בִּמְעַט קֶמַח — **And it is for this reason, too, that [Hashem] did not obligate [the pauper]** to bring any offering **other than a small amount of flour,** שֶׁאִי אֶפְשָׁר לְשׁוּם אָדָם אֲפִלּוּ בְּדַלֵּי דַלּוּת בְּלֹא מְעַט קֶמַח — **for it is not possible for any person, even the most impoverished, not to have a little bit of flour.**[5] וְזֶה יַסְפִּיק לָנוּ גַּם עַל הַלְּבוֹנָה — **This** approach to the underlying purpose of the mitzvah **suffices for us** as an explanation of the reason **for the** prohibition to put *levonah* on this offering (Mitzvah 126), **as well.**

---

### NOTES

2. The *minchah* offering as a *chatas* exists as an option only for an impoverished person who committed certain sins (listed above, Mitzvah 123). If he was not completely destitute, he would be obligated to bring a fowl or animal offering as his *chatas* (see introduction to this mitzvah).

3. Fine oil is an item used by royalty and is therefore fitting for use as initiation to royalty or priesthood. See above, Mitzvah 107, regarding the mitzvah to anoint kings and Kohanim Gedolim (High Priests) with the special anointing oil.

4. A similar sentiment regarding the reason for this mitzvah is expressed in *Menachos* 6a; see *Minchas Chinuch* §1.

5. That is, it is out of compassion for the pauper that the Torah allowed him to gain atonement through a flour offering and did not require him to bring an animal offering (see Mitzvah 123, where Chinuch elaborates on this reason). Chinuch here extends this idea to the oil that is usually applied to the flour offering as well: While a poor person can get along without oil, he must always have in his possession some flour from which to live. The Torah prescribed an atonement for the pauper from that which he certainly has available.

## 472 / ויקרא / מצוה קכה: שלא לתן שמן זית במנחת חוטא

מִדִּינֵי הַמִּצְוָה, מַה שֶּׁפֵּרְשׁוּ זִכְרוֹנָם לִבְרָכָה (מנחות ע״ו ע״ב) שֶׁמִּנְחַת חוֹטֵא הָיְתָה עִשָּׂרוֹן אֶחָד,[6] לֹא פָחוֹת וְלֹא יוֹתֵר.[7] וְכָל הַמְּנָחוֹת הַקְּרֵבוֹת לְגַבֵּי מִזְבֵּחַ טְעוּנוֹת שֶׁמֶן וּלְבוֹנָה,[8] וְלֹג[9] שֶׁמֶן לְכָל עִשָּׂרוֹן, וְקֹמֶץ[10] לְבוֹנָה לְכָל מִנְחָה בֵּין שֶׁהָיְתָה עִשָּׂרוֹן אֶחָד אוֹ אֲפִלּוּ שִׁשִּׁים עִשָּׂרוֹן. אֲבָל יוֹתֵר מִשִּׁשִּׁים אֵין מְבִיאִין בְּמִנְחָה אַחַת,[11] חוּץ מִמִּנְחַת קְנָאוֹת[12] וּמִנְחַת חוֹטֵא שֶׁאֵין בָּהֶן שֶׁמֶן וּלְבוֹנָה,[13] שֶׁנֶּאֱמַר (שם) לֹא יָשִׂים עָלֶיהָ שֶׁמֶן וְלֹא יִתֵּן עָלֶיהָ לְבֹנָה. וְיֶתֶר פְּרָטֶיהָ מְבֹאָרִין בִּמְנָחוֹת.[14]

---

### ⇜ Laws of the Mitzvah ⇝

In the following laws, Chinuch contrasts the procedure of the sinner's *minchah* offering with the procedures that apply to all other *minchah* offerings:

מִדִּינֵי הַמִּצְוָה — **Among the laws of the mitzvah is** מַה שֶּׁפֵּרְשׁוּ זִכְרוֹנָם לִבְרָכָה — **that which [the Sages], of blessed memory, have set forth** (*Menachos* 76b): שֶׁמִּנְחַת חוֹטֵא הָיְתָה עִשָּׂרוֹן אֶחָד — **that the sinner's *minchah* offering consists of** exactly **one *issaron*** (one-tenth of an *ephah*) of flour,[6] לֹא פָחוֹת וְלֹא יוֹתֵר — **not less and not more.**[7] וְכָל הַמְּנָחוֹת הַקְּרֵבוֹת לְגַבֵּי מִזְבֵּחַ טְעוּנוֹת שֶׁמֶן וּלְבוֹנָה — **Also,** as a general rule, **all *minchah* offerings that are offered on the Altar require** the application of **oil and *levonah*;**[8] וְלֹג שֶׁמֶן לְכָל עִשָּׂרוֹן — the amount of oil required is **one *log***[9] of oil **for each *issaron*** of flour, וְקֹמֶץ לְבוֹנָה לְכָל מִנְחָה — **and** the amount of *levonah* required is **one *kometz*** (fistful)[10] **of *levonah* for each** entire ***minchah*** offering, בֵּין שֶׁהָיְתָה עִשָּׂרוֹן אֶחָד אוֹ אֲפִלּוּ שִׁשִּׁים עִשָּׂרוֹן — **whether the [*minchah* offering] consists of one *issaron*** of flour **or even sixty *issaron*.** אֲבָל יוֹתֵר מִשִּׁשִּׁים אֵין מְבִיאִין בְּמִנְחָה אַחַת — **However, we do not bring more than sixty *issaron*** of flour **in one *minchah* offering.**[11] חוּץ מִמִּנְחַת קְנָאוֹת — These applications are obligatory to all *minchah* offerings, **except for the *minchah* of jealousies,** i.e., the *minchah* of a *sotah* (a woman suspected of adultery),[12] וּמִנְחַת חוֹטֵא — **and** the sinner's *minchah* offering (the subject of this mitzvah), שֶׁאֵין בָּהֶן שֶׁמֶן וּלְבוֹנָה — **which do not contain oil or *levonah*,** שֶׁנֶּאֱמַר ״לֹא יָשִׂים עָלֶיהָ שֶׁמֶן וְלֹא יִתֵּן עָלֶיהָ לְבֹנָה״ — **as it is stated** (*Leviticus* ibid.): **he shall not place oil on it nor shall he put *levonah* on it.**[13] וְיֶתֶר פְּרָטֶיהָ מְבֹאָרִין בִּמְנָחוֹת — These, **and the additional details of [the mitzvah], are set forth** in Tractate ***Menachos*.**[14]

---

### NOTES

6. An *issaron* is equal to 43.2 egg volumes. [This is between 2.5 and 4.3 liters, depending on the various opinions as to converting Rabbinic measures into contemporary ones; it comes to between 10.5 and 18 cups of flour. This is the same amount of flour that obligates the separation of *challah* (see Mitzvah 385).]

7. Although all *minchah* offerings must contain at least an *issaron* of flour, voluntary *minchah* offerings may contain more than an *issaron* (see Rambam, Hil. Maaseh HaKorbanos 12:5).

8. There are in fact certain other *minchah* offerings that do *not* receive the regular oil and *levonah* applications, aside from the sinner's *minchah*. These include the *Lechem HaPanim* [Mitzvah 97] and the Two Loaves brought on Shavuos [Mitzvah 307]. Chinuch's use of the words, הַקְּרֵבוֹת לְגַבֵּי מִזְבֵּחַ, *that are offered on the Altar*, alludes to these exceptions, as these *minchah* offerings are not offered on the Altar in the classic sense (see Radvaz to Rambam, Hil. Maaseh HaKorbanos 12:7).

9. A *log* is six egg volumes, or between 0.35 liter and 0.6 liter.

10. See Mitzvah 137 for a discussion of how this fistful is measured.

11. The oil and flour of the *minchah* offerings must be able to be blended together properly, and the Sages established that when there is more than sixty *issaron* of flour in one vessel, the oil would not blend properly with the flour (*Menachos* 103b). One who vows to bring more than sixty *issaron* of flour must divide the flour into two separate offerings, one containing sixty *issaron* and the second containing the remainder of the flour (ibid.).

12. The *sotah's minchah* is brought by the husband of a woman who is suspected of an adulterous relationship; see above, Mitzvah 116, at note 13 (and below, Mitzvah 365) for a description of that *minchah*, which differs in many other respects from the sinner's *minchah*.

13. This verse pertains to the sinner's *minchah*. Regarding the *minchah* of the *sotah*, the Torah writes: (*Numbers* 5:15): לֹא יִצֹק עָלָיו שֶׁמֶן וְלֹא יִתֵּן עָלָיו לְבֹנָה, *he shall not pour oil over it and shall not put levonah upon it*. Chinuch discusses the prohibitions of that verse in Mitzvos 366-367.

14. The general laws of *minchah* offerings are set out

# 473 □ VAYIKRA / MITZVAH 125: NOT TO PLACE OLIVE OIL ON A SINNER'S MINCHAH OFFERING

וְנוֹהֶגֶת בִּזְמַן הַבַּיִת בְּזִכְרֵי כְהֻנָּה, כִּי לָהֶם הָעֲבוֹדָה.[15] וְכֹהֵן הָעוֹבֵר וְנָתַן שֶׁמֶן בְּמִנְחָה זוֹ שֶׁל חוֹטֵא עָנִי, לוֹקֶה.

## ☞ Applicability of the Mitzvah ☜

וְנוֹהֶגֶת בִּזְמַן הַבַּיִת — This mitzvah **applies in the time of the Temple** (i.e., when the *Beis HaMikdash* is standing), בְּזִכְרֵי כְהֻנָּה כִּי לָהֶם הָעֲבוֹדָה — **to male Kohanim, for it is to** [the male Kohanim] that **the** Temple **service is** entrusted.[15]

וְנָתַן שֶׁמֶן בְּמִנְחָה זוֹ שֶׁל חוֹטֵא וְכֹהֵן הָעוֹבֵר עָלֶיהָ — **A Kohen who transgresses** [this prohibition] **and applies oil to this** *minchah* **offering of the indigent sinner incurs** the penalty of עָנִי לוֹקֶה — *malkus* (lashes).

### NOTES

in Tractate *Menachos* and codified in *Rambam, Hil. Maaseh HaKorbanos*, Chapters 12, 13, and 17. The laws that apply to the prohibitions regarding the application of the oil and *levonah* can be found in *Menachos* 59b-60a and *Rambam* ibid. 12:7-8.

15. Chinuch's position, that the prohibitions discussed in this mitzvah apply only to Kohanim, is a source of much discussion among the commentators; see Insight.

---

**◆§ Insight: Why Only Kohanim?**

Both in his introduction to the prohibition and when delineating the application of the mitzvah, Chinuch writes that the prohibition against applying oil to the *minchah* of a sinner applies to the Kohanim who perform the *avodah*. Many commentators take note of the fact that there seems to be no source in the Gemara for limiting the application of these prohibitions to Kohanim only. *Minchas Chinuch* (§9) further notes that the point at which the oil is added to other *minchah* offerings is at a preparatory stage of the offering, and there is some question whether it is necessary for the application of oil in those *minchah* offerings to be performed by a Kohen. Why, then, should the prohibition against putting oil in this *minchah* be limited to Kohanim only?

This question may be answered by an examination of the different opinions regarding the specific action that is prohibited by this verse. In the view of most Rishonim, the specific prohibited action is the actual placing of the oil into the *minchah*. This characterization of the prohibition also seems to be the plain meaning of the words of the Mishnah and Gemara that discuss the matter (see *Menachos* 59b-60a with *Keren Orah, Sfas Emes,* and *Zevach Todah;* and *Ohr Same'ach* and *Even HaAzel* to *Rambam, Hil. Maaseh HaKorbanos* 12:8). According to this view, there is in fact no reason to limit the prohibition to Kohanim only.

*Rambam*, however, seems to widen the scope of this prohibition. In describing the independent liability for each application of oil and *levonah* into the *minchah*, *Rambam* writes as follows (*Hil. Maaseh HaKorbanos* 12:8): *If he placed [oil and levonah] and he offered [the minchah upon the Altar], he is liable to malkus for the oil independently and for the levonah independently.* It is clear from *Rambam's* words that, in order to incur liability to *malkus*, it is insufficient for one to simply put oil or *levonah* into the *minchah*. Rather, one is liable only if the enriched *minchah* is also offered upon the Altar. This added criterion is the subject of much discussion among the later commentators, who differ in their understanding of *Rambam's* position.

According to *Even HaAzel*, *Rambam* agrees that the primary forbidden action is the placing of the oil or *levonah* into the *minchah*. *Rambam* maintains, however, that violating the prohibition is conditional upon the *minchah* subsequently being offered upon the Altar. If, after one improperly added the oil, the *minchah* is never offered upon the Altar, he is not liable. If one person added the oil, and then he or another offered the *minchah* upon the Altar, it is the person who added the oil who is considered to be in violation of the prohibition for the act of adding the oil to the *minchah* (see there, however, regarding the *malkus* liability).

According to other Acharonim, however, *Rambam's* position is that the prohibition is *not* the act of adding the oil or *levonah* to the *minchah* at all. As the Gemara (*Menachos* 6a) indicates, the intention of this prohibition is that the *minchah* of a sinner not be adorned as are other *minchah* offerings (see

Mitzvah 125 at note 3). When the Torah writes that one should not add oil to the *minchah*, it actually means only to forbid one to perform the act of *offering upon the Altar* this offering of a sinner to which oil has been added (see *Radvaz* ad loc.; *Ohr Same'ach* ad loc.; *Chazon Yechezkel, Sotah* 1:7; *R' Y. F. Perla, Sefer HaMitzvos* of *Rav Saadiah Gaon, Asei* 77, Vol. I, p. 597).

If we accept that Chinuch, too, understands the prohibition as pertaining only to the act of offering this *minchah* with oil or *levonah* upon the Altar, it becomes clear why Chinuch maintains that the prohibition applies only to Kohanim. The offering of a *minchah* upon the Altar is the actual *avodah* of the *minchah*, not a mere prerequisite, and surely must be performed by a Kohen. When the Torah forbids *offering* a sinner's *minchah* that has been adorned with oil or *levonah*, it must be addressing those who are appointed to perform the *avodah* in the *Beis HaMikdash*. As Chinuch writes, וְנוֹהֶגֶת... בְּזִכְרֵי כְהוּנָה כִּי לָהֶם הָעֲבוֹדָה, *[The mitzvah] applies to the male Kohanim, for it is to them that the Temple service is entrusted* (see *Minchas Yitzchak, Ohr Same'ach* ibid., and *Chazon Yechezkel* ibid.; cf. *Chidushei HaGriz, Menachos* 59b ד"ה במשנה).

## 475 ❏ VAYIKRA / MITZVAH 126: NOT TO PLACE LEVONAH UPON A SINNER'S MINCHAH

### מִצְוָה קכו: שֶׁלֹּא לִתֵּן לְבוֹנָה בְּמִנְחַת חוֹטֵא

שֶׁלֹּא לָתֵת לְבוֹנָה בְּמִנְחָה זוֹ שֶׁאָמַרְנוּ, שֶׁל חוֹטֵא עָנִי, שֶׁנֶּאֱמַר (ויקרא ה׳, י״א) וְלֹא יִתֵּן עָלֶיהָ לְבֹנָה. וּלְשׁוֹן הַמִּשְׁנָה וְחַיָּב עַל הַשֶּׁמֶן בִּפְנֵי עַצְמוֹ וְעַל הַלְּבוֹנָה בִּפְנֵי עַצְמָהּ, לְפִי שֶׁהֵן שְׁנֵי לָאוִין בְּלִי סָפֵק¹. כָּל עִנְיַן הַלְּבוֹנָה בְּעִנְיַן הַשֶּׁמֶן שֶׁכָּתַבְנוּ, אֵין לְהַאֲרִיךְ בּוֹ².

---

## ∽ Mitzvah 126 ∽
### ∽ The Prohibition to Place Levonah Upon a Sinner's Minchah Offering ∽

לֹא יָשִׂים עָלֶיהָ שֶׁמֶן וְלֹא יִתֵּן עָלֶיהָ לְבֹנָה כִּי חַטָּאת הִוא

*He shall not place oil on it, nor shall he put levonah on it, for it is a chatas offering* (Leviticus 5:11).

This mitzvah is a direct continuation of the previous mitzvah, as Chinuch explains.

**שֶׁלֹּא לָתֵת לְבוֹנָה בְּמִנְחָה זוֹ שֶׁאָמַרְנוּ שֶׁל חוֹטֵא עָנִי** — We are commanded **not to place** *levonah* **on this minchah offering of which we have spoken** (Mitzvah 125), that is, the *minchah* **of the indigent sinner,** **שֶׁנֶּאֱמַר "וְלֹא יִתֵּן עָלֶיהָ לְבֹנָה"** — **as it is stated** (Leviticus 5:11): ***nor shall he put levonah on it.*** **וְחַיָּב עַל הַשֶּׁמֶן וּלְשׁוֹן הַמִּשְׁנָה** — **In the language of the Mishnah** (Menachos 59b): **בִּפְנֵי עַצְמוֹ וְעַל הַלְּבוֹנָה בִּפְנֵי עַצְמָהּ** — **One** who applies both oil and levonah to the sinner's minchah **is liable for the oil by itself, and for the levonah by itself.** **לְפִי שֶׁהֵן שְׁנֵי לָאוִין בְּלִי סָפֵק** — One is liable to *malkus* (lashes) for each action, **because they are, without doubt, two** separate mitzvah-**prohibitions.**[1]

**כָּל עִנְיַן הַלְּבוֹנָה בְּעִנְיַן הַשֶּׁמֶן שֶׁכָּתַבְנוּ** — **The entire matter of the** prohibition to put *levonah* on this offering **is like the matter of the** similar prohibition to place **oil upon it, as I have written** in the previous mitzvah; **אֵין לְהַאֲרִיךְ בּוֹ** — **it is** therefore **not** necessary **to expand** further **upon it.**[2]

---

### NOTES

1. Since the verse delineates two separate statements in the form of Biblical prohibitions (*He shall not place oil on it, he shall not put levonah on it*), each is counted as a separate mitzvah in the reckoning of the 613 Mitzvos, and each carries its own penalty.

2. I.e., the definition of the prohibition, the underlying purposes, and the basic laws of the mitzvah are the same. It should be pointed out, however, that there are significant differences in the laws that pertain to the oil and those that pertain to the *levonah* regarding how the application of each would invalidate the offering; see *Menachos* 59b-60a, and *Minchas Chinuch* to the previous mitzvah, §10.

## ויקרא / מִצְוָה קכז: מצוַת תּוֹסֶפֶת חמֵשׁ לָאוֹכֵל מִן הַהֶקְדֵּשׁ אוֹ מוֹעֵל בּוֹ לְשַׁלֵּם

### מִצְוָה קכז

### מִצְוַת תּוֹסֶפֶת חֹמֶשׁ לָאוֹכֵל מִן הַהֶקְדֵּשׁ[1] אוֹ מוֹעֵל בּוֹ[2,3]

לְשַׁלֵּם כָּל הַנֶּהֱנֶה מִן הַהֶקְדֵּשׁ אֶחָד קָדְשֵׁי מִזְבֵּחַ וְאֶחָד קָדְשֵׁי הַבַּיִת[4] וְאַף בְּחֶרְמֵי

## Mitzvah 127

## The Obligation to Add a Fifth [to the Payment] for [Improper] Consumption of Temple Property[1] or Its Misappropriation

נֶפֶשׁ כִּי תִמְעֹל מַעַל וְחָטְאָה בִּשְׁגָגָה מִקָּדְשֵׁי ה' וְהֵבִיא אֶת אֲשָׁמוֹ לַה' אַיִל תָּמִים מִן הַצֹּאן בְּעֶרְכְּךָ כֶּסֶף שְׁקָלִים בְּשֶׁקֶל הַקֹּדֶשׁ לְאָשָׁם. וְאֵת אֲשֶׁר חָטָא מִן הַקֹּדֶשׁ יְשַׁלֵּם וְאֶת חֲמִישִׁתוֹ יוֹסֵף עָלָיו וְנָתַן אֹתוֹ לַכֹּהֵן וְהַכֹּהֵן יְכַפֵּר עָלָיו בְּאֵיל הָאָשָׁם וְנִסְלַח לוֹ

*If a person commits treachery and sins unintentionally against HASHEM's holies, he shall bring his asham (guilt) offering to HASHEM, an unblemished ram from the flock, with a value of silver shekels, according to the sacred shekel, for an asham offering. For what he has deprived the Holy he shall make restitution, and add a fifth to it, and give it to the Kohen; then the Kohen shall provide him atonement with the ram of the asham offering and it shall be forgiven him* (Leviticus 5:15-16).

It is prohibited to derive unauthorized benefit from *hekdesh* (items consecrated to the *Beis HaMikdash* [Holy Temple]), or to appropriate such items from the domain of *hekdesh* (see Mitzvah 447). The misappropriation of *hekdesh* is known as *me'ilah* (literally, *treachery*). One who transgresses this prohibition must make restitution for any benefit he received. As Chinuch shall explain, if one committed the *me'ilah* intentionally, he repays only the principal and also incurs *malkus*. If one committed the *me'ilah* unintentionally, he does not incur *malkus*, but in addition to repaying the principal, he must add a "fifth" (*chomesh*) to his payment,[2] and also must bring an *asham* (guilt) offering. The *asham* offering is discussed in Mitzvah 129. In this mitzvah, Chinuch addresses the requirement of paying the *chomesh*, and other laws pertaining to *me'ilah*.[3]

לְשַׁלֵּם כָּל הַנֶּהֱנֶה מִן הַהֶקְדֵּשׁ — It is an obligation upon **anyone who derived** unlawful **benefit from hekdesh** (property of the *Beis HaMikdash*) **to make restitution.** אֶחָד קָדְשֵׁי מִזְבֵּחַ וְאֶחָד קָדְשֵׁי הַבַּיִת — This applies **whether** the benefit was derived from **items consecrated to** be brought as offerings upon **the Altar, or from items consecrated for** upkeep of **the Temple;**[4] וְאַף בְּחֶרְמֵי

---

NOTES

1. Some editions read הַתְּרוּמָה, *terumah,* but that is problematic, since *terumah* is subject to a penalty of "a fifth" only for its consumption, but not for its misappropriation. We have followed the reading of the Mechon Yerushalayim edition. R' Mordechai Gifter (in *Pitei Minchah — Moriah,* Year 24, 3-4) suggests emending the title of this mitzvah to מִצְוַת תּוֹסֶפֶת חוֹמֶשׁ לָאוֹכֵל מִן הַתְּרוּמָה אוֹ מוֹעֵל בְּהֶקְדֵּשׁ, *The Obligation to add a fifth for consumption of terumah or misappropriation of Temple property.* For further discussion of whether this mitzvah applies to both *terumah* and Temple property or only the latter, see note 7.

2. Chinuch details below (after note 24) how the amount of the *chomesh* is calculated.

3. Whether the primary focus of this mitzvah is on the general requirements pertaining to one who commits *me'ilah,* or on the specific requirement to make restitution for the benefit received and to add a *chomesh,* is a matter of dispute. See note 7 for discussion.

4. *Hekdesh* is divided into two general categories. One category is קָדְשֵׁי מִזְבֵּחַ, *items consecrated for the Altar,* and a second, lower, category is קָדְשֵׁי בֶּדֶק הַבַּיִת, *items consecrated for the upkeep of the Temple* (*bedek habayis*). While items consecrated for the Altar have קְדֻשַּׁת הַגּוּף, *physical sanctity,* inasmuch as they are used as offerings, items consecrated for *bedek habayis* have only קְדֻשַּׁת דָּמִים, *monetary sanctity,* meaning that they are consecrated for their value. They are either used for the repair of the *Beis HaMikdash* or are sold by the Temple treasurer, with the money obtained from the sale then used to

# 477 ❑ VAYIKRA / MITZVAH 127: ADDING A FIFTH FOR MISAPPROPRIATION OF TEMPLE PROPERTY

כֹּהֲנִים,[5] וְכֵן בְּקָדָשִׁים קַלִּים,[6] אוֹ אוֹכֵל קֹדֶשׁ בִּשְׁגָגָה, כְּלוֹמַר הַתְּרוּמָה,[7] כָּל מַה שֶּׁאוֹכֵל אוֹ נֶהֱנֶה מִמֶּנּוּ, בְּתוֹסֶפֶת חֹמֶשׁ,[8] וְיָבִיא קָרְבָּן עַל שִׁגְגָתוֹ[9] אַיִל בִּשְׁנֵי סְלָעִים

---

כֹּהֲנִים — this rule further applies **even to** an item that is the subject of **a** *cherem* that is designated **for the** Kohanim.[5] **וְכֵן בְּקָדָשִׁים קַלִּים** — **Similarly,** this applies **to** one who derives illegal benefit from *kodashim kalim* (offerings of lesser sanctity),[6] **אוֹ אוֹכֵל קֹדֶשׁ בִּשְׁגָגָה** — **or who "eats of the holy in error," כְּלוֹמַר הַתְּרוּמָה** — **that is to say,** a non-Kohen who unwittingly partakes **of** *terumah*.[7] **כָּל מַה שֶּׁאוֹכֵל אוֹ נֶהֱנֶה מִמֶּנּוּ** — One must pay the value of **all that he ate** of the *terumah* **or benefited from [the consecrated items], בְּתוֹסֶפֶת חֹמֶשׁ** — **with the addition of a "fifth"** (*chomesh*).[8] **וְיָבִיא קָרְבָּן עַל שִׁגְגָתוֹ** — **He must also bring an offering** to atone **for his error** (see Mitzvah 129).[9]

---

## NOTES

pay for the repair and upkeep of the *Beis HaMikdash*.

The items consecrated for the Altar themselves can be subdivided into two main groups, each one having a different level of sanctity. The group with greater sanctity is known as *kodshei kodashim* (*most-holy offerings*). This group includes the *olah*, *chatas*, *asham*, and communal *shelamim* offerings. These are subject to the laws of *me'ilah* discussed by Chinuch in this mitzvah. The group with lesser sanctity is known as *kodashim kalim* (*offerings of lesser holiness*). This group includes the *todah* and personal *shelamim* offerings, among others. The law of these offerings with respect to *me'ilah* will be discussed below, in note 6. [See introduction to Mitzvah 102 for some of the differences between these two levels of offerings.]

5. *Cherem* is a form of consecration, in which the consecrated matter is designated to be given to the Kohanim, at which point it no longer retains sanctity. One who derives benefit from such an item *before* it was given to the Kohanim is required to pay for the benefit, and to add a *chomesh*. [There is an additional form of *cherem*, which takes effect when the owner of the object stipulates that the *cherem* be given to the *Beis HaMikdash* rather than to the Kohanim. Unlike the *cherem* of Kohanim, such a *cherem* is of a permanent nature, and is certainly subject to the laws of *me'ilah*.]

6. *Kodashim kalim* were described in note 4. Certain parts of these offerings (known as *emurin*; see Mitzvah 138) are burned on the Altar, and the remaining meat is eaten by their owners. In most cases, the meat may also be eaten by any other Jew. Since the owner partakes of these offerings himself, they are considered his property even after they are consecrated. At that time, they are not subject to the laws of *me'ilah* (though they are initially prohibited for benefit; see *Minchas Chinuch* §1). However, once their blood was applied to the Altar, their *emurin* must be burned upon the Altar. At that time, the *emurin* are considered as *kodshei kodashim* (see *Minchas Chinuch* ibid.), and one who partakes of them has committed *me'ilah* and is subject to the laws stated in this mitzvah (*Rambam, Hil. Me'ilah* 2:1).

7. The phrase *who eats of the holy in error* is used in *Leviticus* 22:14 in reference to a non-Kohen partaking of *terumah*, which may be eaten only by Kohanim (see *Toras Kohanim* ad loc.).

*Minchas Chinuch* (§11) is puzzled by Chinuch's inclusion of one who eats *terumah* in this mitzvah. True, for the wrongful consumption of *terumah*, the Torah prescribes a payment of the principal plus a *chomesh* ("fifth"), but that law is stated in *Parashas Emor* (*Leviticus* ibid.), whereas here we are dealing with the laws of *me'ilah*, i.e., misappropriation of *hekdesh*, which are stated in *Parashas Vayikra* (ibid. 5:15-16). The passage here in *Vayikra*, aside from requiring restitution and payment of a *chomesh*, imposes an obligation to bring an *asham* offering on the one who committed *me'ilah*; this does not apply to a non-Kohen who eats *terumah* (cf. *Meiri* to *Berachos* 35b, *Yevamos* 34a, *Gittin* 54a). Moreover, the *chomesh* payment for *terumah* is imposed only for *eating terumah* (as stated in *Leviticus* 22:14, cited above), whereas the *chomesh* payment for *me'ilah* is imposed for any form of benefit from *hekdesh* or its misappropriation. There also are other differences between *hekdesh* and *terumah* in regard to how liability is incurred (see below, note 31). *Minchas Chinuch* therefore suggests that Chinuch merely mentioned the case of *terumah* here in passing, since the *chomesh* payment applies there as well, but that payment is not included in this mitzvah (see also *Kedushas Yom Tov* [*Maharit Algazi*], end of §43, and *Me'il HaEphod*).

*Minchas Yitzchak* (§1), however, explains that the focus of this mitzvah is the *chomesh* payment, not the general obligations associated with *me'ilah*, and in fact, *all* payments of a *chomesh* for misuse of sacred property — whether *hekdesh* or *terumah* — are included in this mitzvah. See also *Rambam, Sefer HaMitzvos, Asei* 118, who clearly sets forth the mitzvah in this way. [See, however, *Rambam's* enumeration of mitzvos at the beginning of *Hilchos Me'ilah*.]

8. As mentioned in the previous note, with regard to *hekdesh*, one must pay an additional fifth regardless of how he benefited from it. With regard to *terumah*, however, one pays the additional fifth only for *eating* it.

With regard to benefit from something that had been consecrated for the Altar, payment of the principal and *chomesh* is made in the form of an offering to the Altar (see *Rambam, Hil. Me'ilah* 4:7 for the particulars). With regard to something that had been consecrated for Temple upkeep, payment is made to the Temple treasury. In the case of one who eats *terumah*, the principal is paid to the Kohen who owned the *terumah*, while the *chomesh* may be paid to any Kohen (*Rambam, Hil. Terumos* 10:16).

9. As mentioned in note 7, this offering is brought for

# 478 ויקרא / מצוה קכז: מצות תוספת חמש לאוכל מן ההקדש או מועל בו לשלם

אוֹ יוֹתֵר.[10] וְהוּא הַנִּקְרָא אָשָׁם מְעִילוֹת, וְהוּא אֶחָד מֵחָמֵשׁ אֲשָׁמוֹת וַדָּאוֹת הַיְדוּעִים,[11] שֶׁנֶּאֱמַר (ויקרא ה׳, ט״ו) נֶפֶשׁ כִּי תִמְעֹל מַעַל וְגוֹ׳, וְהֵבִיא אֶת אֲשָׁמוֹ וְגוֹ׳, וְנֶאֱמַר (שם, שם ט״ז) וְאֵת אֲשֶׁר חָטָא מִן הַקֹּדֶשׁ יְשַׁלֵּם וְאֶת חֲמִישִׁתוֹ יוֹסֵף עָלָיו.[12]

מִשָּׁרְשֵׁי הַמִּצְוָה, לָתֵת אֵימָה וְיִרְאָה עַל כָּל אָדָם מֵהִתְקָרֵב בְּעִנְיְנֵי הַקֹּדֶשׁ, וּכְבָר כָּתַבְנוּ לְמַעְלָה תּוֹעֶלֶת הַיִּרְאָה וְהַהַגְדָּלָה בַּקֹּדֶשׁ אֶל בְּנֵי אָדָם.[13]

מִדִּינֵי הַמִּצְוָה, מַה שֶּׁאָמְרוּ רַבּוֹתֵינוּ זִכְרוֹנָם לִבְרָכָה (קידושין נ״ד ע״ב) שֶׁהַשּׁוֹמֵעַ אַחַר הַמּוֹעֵל,

---

וְהוּא הַנִּקְרָא — **which must be a ram worth two *sela'im* or more;**[10] וְהוּא — **this offering is the one referred to as the *asham* offering of *me'ilah*,** אֶחָד מֵחָמֵשׁ אֲשָׁמוֹת וַדָּאוֹת הַיְדוּעִים — **and it is one of the five well-known "definite" *asham* offerings.**[11] שֶׁנֶּאֱמַר — **We are so commanded, as it is stated** (*Leviticus* 5:15): וְהֵבִיא "נֶפֶשׁ כִּי תִמְעֹל מַעַל וְגוֹ׳ אֶת אֲשָׁמוֹ וְגוֹ׳" — **If a person commits treachery,** etc. [*and sins unintentionally against* HASHEM'*s holies*]*, he shall bring his asham offering to* HASHEM, *an unblemished ram from the flock, with a value of silver shekels,* etc. וְנֶאֱמַר — **And it is stated** further (ibid. v. 16): "וְאֵת אֲשֶׁר חָטָא מִן הַקֹּדֶשׁ יְשַׁלֵּם וְאֶת חֲמִישִׁתוֹ יוֹסֵף עָלָיו" — *For what he has deprived the holy he shall make restitution, and add a fifth to it.*[12]

### ✺ Underlying Purpose of the Mitzvah ✺

מִשָּׁרְשֵׁי הַמִּצְוָה — **Among the underlying purposes of the mitzvah is** לָתֵת אֵימָה וְיִרְאָה עַל כָּל אָדָם — **to impose awe and fear upon all people** מֵהִתְקָרֵב בְּעִנְיְנֵי הַקֹּדֶשׁ — **to deter them from approaching holy objects.** וּכְבָר כָּתַבְנוּ לְמַעְלָה — **We have already written above** (Mitzvah 98) תּוֹעֶלֶת הַיִּרְאָה וְהַהַגְדָּלָה בַּקֹּדֶשׁ אֶל בְּנֵי אָדָם — **the benefit to mankind that emerges from awe and grandeur of the Temple.**[13]

### ✺ Laws of the Mitzvah ✺

מִדִּינֵי הַמִּצְוָה — **Among the laws of the mitzvah** are the following laws pertaining to *me'ilah*:

The Gemara (*Me'ilah* 18a; see *Rashi, Arachin* 21a ד״ה נפיק) teaches that when a consecrated article is unintentionally misappropriated for non-sacred use, it is removed from its consecrated state. Chinuch discusses ramifications of that law:

מַה שֶּׁאָמְרוּ רַבּוֹתֵינוּ זִכְרוֹנָם לִבְרָכָה — **One of the laws is what our Sages, of blessed memory, said** (*Kiddushin* 54b), שֶׁהַשּׁוֹמֵעַ אַחַר הַמּוֹעֵל — **that** in the case of **one who commits *me'ilah*** on an object

---

### NOTES

unauthorized benefit from the consecrated items enumerated above, not for consumption of *terumah* (but see *Meiri* cited there).

10. A *sela* (pl. *sela'im*) is the Aramaic term for a *shekel*, which is mentioned in the verse of our mitzvah. [Chinuch identifies the specific amount of silver that is included in a *shekel* above, in Mitzvah 105 (at note 27).]

11. That is, it is one of the instances in which an *asham* offering is brought to atone for a definite transgression (see *Rambam, Hil. Shegagos* 9:1). [The other such instances are set forth in Mitzvah 129.] This is in contrast to the *asham talui*, "pending" *asham* offering, which, as Chinuch explains in Mitzvah 128, is brought in a case of uncertain transgression, and after it is brought the person is "pending," so to speak, for if he finds out that he definitely did sin he requires another offering.]

12. As is indicated in the first verse that Chinuch cites, this passage is referring only to one who derives benefit from *hekdesh* unintentionally. At the end of this mitzvah Chinuch will address the law pertaining to one who *intentionally* misappropriates *hekdesh*.

13. Chinuch explained in Mitzvah 98 that enhancing the grandeur of the *Beis HaMikdash* causes people who visit there to be filled with awe and humility, and their souls thus become refined. Earlier, in Mitzvah 95, Chinuch explained that the purpose of the *Beis HaMikdash* service as a whole is to elevate man and refine him. The penalty imposed on one who misappropriates property of the *Beis HaMikdash* for non-sacred use advances this purpose of instilling in people awe for the *Beis HaMikdash* and its items. [See also Mitzvah 129, where Chinuch discusses the severity of the sin of *me'ilah*.]

# 479 □ VAYIKRA / MITZVAH 127: ADDING A FIFTH FOR MISAPPROPRIATION OF TEMPLE PROPERTY

אִם הָרִאשׁוֹן בִּשְׁגָגָה הָאַחֲרוֹן פָּטוּר, לְפִי שֶׁכְּבָר נִתְחַלֵּל הַהֶקְדֵּשׁ אַחַר שֶׁהָרִאשׁוֹן נִתְחַיֵּב בְּתַשְׁלוּמִין וּבְקָרְבָּן, וְאִם הָרִאשׁוֹן בְּמֵזִיד שֶׁאֵינוֹ בְּתוֹרַת קָרְבָּן, הָאַחֲרוֹן בְּתוֹרַת מְעִילָה. וְאֵין מוֹעֵל אַחַר מוֹעֵל בְּמֻקְדָּשִׁין אֶלָּא בִּבְהֵמָה וּכְלֵי שָׁרֵת בִּלְבַד.[14] וְהַנּוֹטֵל פְּרוּטָה[15] מִן הַהֶקְדֵּשׁ עַל מְנָת שֶׁהִיא שֶׁלּוֹ לֹא מָעַל עַד שֶׁיּוֹצִיאֶנָּה בַּחֲפָצָיו,[16] נְתָנָהּ לַחֲבֵרוֹ הוּא מָעַל וַחֲבֵרוֹ לֹא מָעַל, שֶׁאֵין מוֹעֵל אַחַר מוֹעֵל אֶלָּא בִּבְהֵמָה וְכֵלִים כְּמוֹ שֶׁאָמַרְנוּ.

---

**אִם הָרִאשׁוֹן בִּשְׁגָגָה** — **after** another **one had committed *me'ilah*** on that same object, the law is **הָאַחֲרוֹן פָּטוּר** — that **if the first one** who misappropriated the object did so **unintentionally,** then the **second one** who misappropriated it **is exempt** from liability, **לְפִי שֶׁכְּבָר נִתְחַלֵּל הַהֶקְדֵּשׁ** — because **the consecrated** object **had already become deconsecrated** **אַחַר שֶׁהָרִאשׁוֹן נִתְחַיֵּב בְּתַשְׁלוּמִין וּבְקָרְבָּן** — once the first user **became obligated to pay** for it **and to bring an *asham* offering;** therefore, the second one does not incur liability. **וְאִם הָרִאשׁוֹן בְּמֵזִיד** — **If, however, the first violator transgressed intentionally,** **שֶׁאֵינוֹ בְּתוֹרַת קָרְבָּן** — **in which case he is not subject to the law of *asham* offering,** the item was not deconsecrated. **הָאַחֲרוֹן בְּתוֹרַת מְעִילָה** — Thus, **the latter violator is subject to the law of *me'ilah*.** **וְאֵין מוֹעֵל אַחַר מוֹעֵל בְּמֻקְדָּשִׁין** — **And,** as a rule, **in** the case of *hekdesh* **articles, there is no** liability for *me'ilah* on an object **after *me'ilah*** has been committed on it, **אֶלָּא בִּבְהֵמָה וּכְלֵי שָׁרֵת בִּלְבַד** — **except** with regard to **animals** that had been consecrated for offerings **and holy utensils alone.**[14] **וְהַנּוֹטֵל פְּרוּטָה מִן הַהֶקְדֵּשׁ עַל מְנָת שֶׁהִיא שֶׁלּוֹ** — **Also** among the laws of *me'ilah* is **that one who takes a *perutah*[15] from *hekdesh* with the assumption that it is his own** **לֹא מָעַל** — **does not commit *me'ilah*,** **עַד שֶׁיּוֹצִיאֶנָּה בַּחֲפָצָיו** — **unless he spends it on his own purposes.**[16] **נְתָנָהּ לַחֲבֵרוֹ** — **If he gave it to his fellow** as a gift, **הוּא מָעַל וַחֲבֵרוֹ לֹא מָעַל** — **he committed *me'ilah*** by unlawfully transferring the item from the domain of *hekdesh* to a different domain, **but his fellow** who received the item as a gift **did not commit *me'ilah*,** even if he subsequently benefited from the item, **שֶׁאֵין מוֹעֵל אַחַר מוֹעֵל** — **for there is no** liability for *me'ilah* on an object **after *me'ilah*** has been committed once on it, **אֶלָּא בִּבְהֵמָה וְכֵלִים** — **except** with regard to **animals** that had been consecrated for an offering **and holy utensils,** **כְּמוֹ שֶׁאָמַרְנוּ** — **as we have stated.**

---

### NOTES

14. Articles that are "physically sanctified" (see note 4), such as unblemished animals consecrated as offerings, or sacred service vessels, do not become deconsecrated even if they are used for other purposes. They are therefore subject to *me'ilah* even on repeated occasions. [I.e., these items are excluded from the above rule that once one person committed unintentional *me'ilah*, another person cannot be liable for *me'ilah* on the same article] (*Rashi, Kiddushin* 55a ד"ה אין מועל and ד"ה אלא בהמה; cf. *Rambam, Hil. Me'ilah* 6:4).

15. The *perutah*, a small copper coin, was the smallest denomination that had significant value in the time of the Gemara (see *Rashi* and *Meiri* to Mishnah, *Kiddushin* 2a).

16. This law, which is set forth in the Mishnah (*Me'ilah* 20a), is difficult to understand, as *me'ilah* applies if one simply removed a consecrated item from the domain of *hekdesh* by taking possession of it, even if he did not spend it. The Gemara (ad loc.) therefore explains that the Mishnah is referring to the treasurer of *hekdesh*. Since he has jurisdiction over *hekdesh* funds, it is considered as though the money is in the domain of *hekdesh* even when it is physically situated in his domain, provided that he does not intentionally misappropriate it. Only when he removes the funds from his own possession, such as by using them to make a purchase or by giving them as a gift to others, does he commit *me'ilah*.

It is important to note, however, that the law pertaining to the treasurer of *hekdesh* is not reserved for the person officially appointed to that position. *Every individual* who consecrates an article is considered a "treasurer of *hekdesh*" until he delivers it to the *Beis HaMikdash*. As long as the article remains in his physical possession, he has jurisdiction over it, and if he mistakenly takes it as his own property it is not considered as though he removed it from the domain of *hekdesh* unless he spends it or derives actual benefit from it (*Raavad, Hil. Me'ilah* 6:8).

וְדִינֵי הַמְעִילָה, בֵּין בְּקָדְשֵׁי מִזְבֵּחַ בֵּין בְּקָדְשֵׁי בֶּדֶק הַבַּיִת[17], וְשִׁעוּר מְעִילָה בְּשָׁוֶה פְּרוּטָה[18]. דְּבָרִים שֶׁהֻתְּרוּ בַּאֲכִילָה מִן הַקָּרְבָּנוֹת, כְּגוֹן בְּשַׂר חַטָּאת וְאָשָׁם אַחַר זְרִיקַת דָּמָן אוֹ שְׁתֵּי הַלֶּחֶם אַחַר זְרִיקַת דַּם שְׁנֵי הַכְּבָשִׂים[19], אֵין בָּהֶן מְעִילָה[20], אֲפִלּוּ אָכַל הַזָּר מֵאֵלּוּ וְכַיּוֹצֵא בְּאֵלּוּ, הוֹאִיל וְהֵן מֻתָּרִין לְמִקְצָת בְּנֵי אָדָם לֵהָנוֹת בָּהֶן, כָּל הַנֶּהֱנֶה מֵהֶן לֹא מָעַל.

בֵּין בְּקָדְשֵׁי מִזְבֵּחַ בֵּין בְּקָדְשֵׁי בֶּדֶק — וְדִינֵי הַמְעִילָה — **The laws of** *me'ilah* apply to all consecrated items, הַבַּיִת — **whether** benefit was derived from **items consecrated to** be brought as offerings upon **the Altar** or from **items consecrated for upkeep of the Temple.**[17] וְשִׁעוּר מְעִילָה בְּשָׁוֶה פְּרוּטָה — **The amount** of benefit one must derive from *hekdesh* property in order for the *me'ilah* liability to apply **is the value of a** *perutah*.[18]

In the verse of this mitzvah, the Torah states that *me'ilah* applies when a person derives benefit מִקָּדְשֵׁי ה׳, *from the holies of HASHEM.* The Sages explain (*Toras Kohanim* ad loc.) that only consecrated items reserved exclusively for holy purposes are subject to *me'ilah*. Items that have permissible use are not subject to *me'ilah*. Chinuch outlines some applications of this rule: דְּבָרִים שֶׁהֻתְּרוּ בַּאֲכִילָה מִן הַקָּרְבָּנוֹת — **Parts of the offerings** whose service was completed, **that became permitted to be eaten** by the Kohanim, כְּגוֹן בְּשַׂר חַטָּאת וְאָשָׁם אַחַר זְרִיקַת דָּמָן — **such as the meat of** *chatas* **or** *asham* **offerings after the throwing of their blood** upon the Altar, אוֹ שְׁתֵּי הַלֶּחֶם אַחַר זְרִיקַת דַּם שְׁנֵי הַכְּבָשִׂים — **or the Two Loaves** of Shavuos **after the throwing of the blood of the Two Lambs** that are brought with them,[19] אֵין בָּהֶן מְעִילָה — **are not subject to** *me'ilah*.[20] אֲפִלּוּ אָכַל הַזָּר מֵאֵלּוּ — **Even if a non-Kohen partook of these** offerings, וְכַיּוֹצֵא בְּאֵלּוּ — **or of offerings similar to these,** which are permitted only to Kohanim, הוֹאִיל וְהֵן מֻתָּרִין לְמִקְצָת בְּנֵי אָדָם לֵהָנוֹת בָּהֶן — **since it is permitted for some people** (i.e., Kohanim) **to derive benefit from them,** כָּל הַנֶּהֱנֶה מֵהֶן לֹא מָעַל — **therefore, any person** (i.e., even a non-Kohen) **who**

---

NOTES

17. See above, note 4.

18. This halachah applies to the liability to pay an additional *chomesh* and to the requirement to bring an *asham* (as well as to the *malkus* liability for one who transgressed intentionally; see below, at note 31). As with all other obligations that pertain to monetary matters, these penalties do not apply unless one has derived at least the worth of a *perutah* of benefit from *hekdesh*. However, with regard to repayment of the principal, the liability for deriving benefit from *hekdesh* is more stringent than other monetary obligations of the Torah, and one who derives even the smallest benefit from *hekdesh* is obligated to pay for it, even if it is less than the value of a *perutah* (see *Rambam, Hil. Me'ilah* 7:8).

With regard to determining the minimum amount subject to the laws of *me'ilah,* there is a difference between articles that are subject to deterioration through normal use (e.g., a garment, which tends to wear out) and those that are not subject to such deterioration (e.g., a golden goblet, which rarely shows signs of wear). One who derives a *perutah's* worth of benefit from an article that ordinarily deteriorates through use is not liable unless he also diminishes its value by a *perutah* in the course of using it. By contrast, one who derives benefit from an article that does not ordinarily deteriorate is liable as soon as he derives a *perutah's* worth of benefit, even without causing any depreciation in its value (*Rambam, Hil. Me'ilah* 6:1).

19. On Shavuos, two leavened wheat loaves are brought (שְׁתֵּי הַלֶּחֶם), along with two lambs brought as communal *shelamim* offerings (Mitzvah 307). When the lambs are slaughtered, the loaves become established as a part of the lamb offerings, and just as the throwing of the blood renders the meat of the lambs permitted for consumption by Kohanim, so too, it renders the Two Loaves permitted for consumption.

20. The offerings Chinuch mentions here are *kodshei kodashim*, whose *emurin* are burned on the Altar and whose meat is eaten by the Kohanim. Once their blood is thrown upon the Altar, rendering their meat fit for consumption by the Kohanim, they are no longer considered קָדְשֵׁי ה׳, *the holies of HASHEM,* and are not subject to *me'ilah* (*Rambam, Hil. Me'ilah* 2:2). [The *emurin*, however, which never become fit for consumption, remain subject to *me'ilah* until the relevant mitzvos are completed (*Rambam* ibid.).]

As we have seen earlier (note 6), animals consecrated as *kodashim kalim* offerings remain the property of their owners, and their *emurin* alone are subject to *me'ilah* — but only from the time their blood is thrown upon the Altar. It emerges that with regard to *kodshei kodashim*, which had been subject to *me'ilah* from the time they were consecrated, the throwing of the blood *releases* the meat from *me'ilah*. On the other hand, in the case of *kodashim kalim*, which are not subject to *me'ilah* from when they were consecrated, throwing the blood has the effect of *subjecting* the *emurin* to *me'ilah* (*Me'ilah* 7b).

# 481 □ VAYIKRA / MITZVAH 127: ADDING A FIFTH FOR MISAPPROPRIATION OF TEMPLE PROPERTY

וַאֲפִלּוּ נִפְסְלוּ²¹ וְנֶאֶסְרוּ בַּאֲכִילָה, הוֹאִיל וְהָיְתָה לָהֶם שְׁעַת הֶתֵּר אֵין חַיָּבִין עֲלֵיהֶן מְעִילָה. נִסְתַּפֵּק לוֹ אִם מָעַל אוֹ לֹא מָעַל, פָּטוּר מִתַּשְׁלוּמִין וְקָרְבָּן²². וְתַשְׁלוּמֵי הַקֶּרֶן וַהֲבָאַת הַקָּרְבָּן מְעַכְּבִין הַכַּפָּרָה וְלֹא הַחֹמֶשׁ, שֶׁנֶּאֱמַר (שם, שם) בְּאֵיל הָאָשָׁם וְנִסְלַח לוֹ, אַיִל וְאָשָׁם מְעַכְּבִין וְאֵין הַחֹמֶשׁ מְעַכֵּב²³. וְאַחַר שֶׁהוֹסִיף הַמּוֹסִיף הַחֹמֶשׁ, אִם נֶהֱנָה בַּחֹמֶשׁ אַחַר כָּךְ מוֹסִיף חֹמֶשׁ עַל חֹמֶשׁ, דִּכְתְחִלַּת הַקֹּדֶשׁ הוּא חָשׁוּב²⁴.

---

**derives benefit from them does not commit *me'ilah*.** Since a Kohen is permitted to partake of these offerings, they are not considered *the holies of HASHEM* exclusively. Thus, although the non-Kohen is prohibited from partaking of them, the laws of *me'ilah* do not apply.

וַאֲפִלּוּ נִפְסְלוּ – **Furthermore, even if [these offerings] were disqualified** after their service was completed,[21] וְנֶאֶסְרוּ בַּאֲכִילָה – **and they** thus **became prohibited to be eaten** even by Kohanim, הוֹאִיל וְהָיְתָה לָהֶם שְׁעַת הֶתֵּר – nevertheless, **since they had a period of permissibility,** being that it was permissible for Kohanim to partake of them before they became prohibited, אֵין חַיָּבִין עֲלֵיהֶן מְעִילָה – **there is no liability of *me'ilah*** for deriving benefit from **them.** That is, since at one point they were permitted, even though they subsequently became prohibited due to a different prohibition, they are not subject to *me'ilah*.

נִסְתַּפֵּק לוֹ אִם מָעַל אוֹ לֹא מָעַל – Another law pertaining to *me'ilah* is that **one who is uncertain whether or not he committed *me'ilah*** פָּטוּר מִתַּשְׁלוּמִין וְקָרְבָּן – **is exempt from making restitution and from bringing an offering.**[22]

וְתַשְׁלוּמֵי הַקֶּרֶן וַהֲבָאַת הַקָּרְבָּן מְעַכְּבִין הַכַּפָּרָה – Another law pertaining to *me'ilah* is that both **the payment of the principal and the bringing of an offering are essential to the atonement,** וְלֹא הַחֹמֶשׁ – **but the** additional *chomesh* penalty **is not.** שֶׁנֶּאֱמַר – **For** in the verse of the mitzvah **it is stated, *with the ram of the asham offering*** (literally, *guilt*), ***and it shall be forgiven him,*** אַיִל וְאָשָׁם מְעַכְּבִין וְאֵין הַחֹמֶשׁ מְעַכֵּב – which teaches that offering **the ram and** paying **the** amount of his **guilt** (i.e., the principal) **are essential** to the atonement, **but the *chomesh* is not essential** to it.[23]

The following laws pertain to the *chomesh* payment:

וְאַחַר שֶׁהוֹסִיף הַמּוֹסִיף הַחֹמֶשׁ – **After one** who was liable to **add** a *chomesh* **has added the** required *chomesh,* אִם נֶהֱנָה בַּחֹמֶשׁ אַחַר כָּךְ – **if one later derived benefit from that *chomesh*** מוֹסִיף חֹמֶשׁ עַל חֹמֶשׁ – **he must** make restitution for the amount of the original *chomesh* from which he benefited and **add an** additional *chomesh* **to** that *chomesh,* דִּכְתְחִלַּת הַקֹּדֶשׁ הוּא חָשׁוּב – **for [the *chomesh*] is considered to be like an initial *hekdesh* entity.**[24]

---

### NOTES

21. This refers to the Kohanim's portions of an offering that became disqualified after having been rendered permitted by the throwing of the blood; for example, the portions were carried out of the *Beis HaMikdash* or became *tamei.* In such cases, it could be thought that they are considered *the holies of HASHEM,* as they are indeed prohibited for consumption.

22. Thus, no *asham talui* (pending *asham* offering; Mitzvah 128) is brought when one is uncertain whether or not he committed *me'ilah,* nor is he required to repay *hekdesh* (see *Kereisos* 22a and *Rambam, Hil. Me'ilah* 1:5). [See *Kedushas Yom Tov* §67 and *Rashash, Kereisos* (loc. cit.), who discuss why we do not apply the general rule that, with regard to a Biblical obligation, one is obligated in a case of doubt.]

23. In its simple meaning, the verse is referring to the ram that is the offering. However, it seems unnecessary for the Torah to mention that the ram is an *asham* offering. Therefore, the Gemara (*Bava Kamma* 111a) expounds the verse to be teaching that, rather than referring to an offering, the term הָאָשָׁם, which literally means "the guilt," is referring to the value of the benefit derived from the *hekdesh* property unlawfully, for which the person is guilty. Thus, the verse teaches that only the ram (אַיִל) and the amount of the principal (אָשָׁם) are essential to the atonement. Although there is a requirement upon one who committed *me'ilah* to add a *chomesh,* his atonement does not depend on its payment.

24. Once the *chomesh* payment is made to *hekdesh,* that money attains the status of genuine *hekdesh* and is itself subject to the law of *me'ilah.* Thus, if one subsequently derives benefit from the *chomesh* money that was paid, he must compensate *hekdesh* for the value of the benefit [which in this case equals the original *chomesh*], and add a *chomesh* to that [which in this case equals a fourth (see below) of the original *chomesh*]

וְהַחֹמֶשׁ הוּא אֶחָד מֵאַרְבָּעָה עַל הַקֶּרֶן, עַד שֶׁיְּהֵא הוּא וְחֻמְּשׁוֹ חֲמִשָּׁה. וְיֶתֶר פְּרָטֶיהָ מְבֹאָרִין בִּמְעִילָה וּבִתְמוּרָה.[25]

וְנוֹהֶגֶת בִּזְמַן הַבַּיִת[26] בִּזְכָרִים וּנְקֵבוֹת.[27] וְעוֹבֵר עָלֶיהָ[28] וְאָכַל אוֹ נֶהֱנָה בַּעֲשִׂיַּת מַעֲשֶׂה מִן הַהֶקְדֵּשׁ[30,29] בְּשָׁוֶה פְּרוּטָה בְּמֵזִיד, לוֹקֶה,[31] וּמְשַׁלֵּם מַה שֶּׁחִסֵּר מִן הַהֶקְדֵּשׁ[32] הַקֶּרֶן לְבַד,

---

וְהַחֹמֶשׁ הוּא אֶחָד מֵאַרְבָּעָה עַל הַקֶּרֶן — **As for** the amount of **the** *chomesh*, **it is one-fourth of the principal,** עַד שֶׁיְּהֵא הוּא וְחֻמְּשׁוֹ חֲמִשָּׁה — **so that [the principal], combined with the** *chomesh*, **would be five** equal portions. That is, by adding one-fourth of the original to the principal, the *chomesh* amounts to one-fifth of the *entire* sum of his payment to *hekdesh*. For example, if the benefit that one derived was worth $100, he must add $25 to his $100 payment, thus paying *hekdesh* $125. The $25 *chomesh* portion is one-fifth of the total.

וְיֶתֶר פְּרָטֶיהָ מְבֹאָרִין בִּמְעִילָה וּבִתְמוּרָה — These laws, **and the additional details of this mitzvah, are set forth in** Tractates *Me'ilah* **and** *Temurah*.[25]

### ⌦ Applicability of the Mitzvah ⌫

וְנוֹהֶגֶת בִּזְמַן הַבַּיִת — **This** mitzvah **applies during the time of the Temple,**[26] בִּזְכָרִים וּנְקֵבוֹת — and is incumbent **upon both men and women.**[27] וְעוֹבֵר עָלֶיהָ — **One who transgresses [the mitzvah],** i.e., the prohibition of *me'ilah*,[28] וְאָכַל אוֹ נֶהֱנָה בַּעֲשִׂיַּת מַעֲשֶׂה מִן הַהֶקְדֵּשׁ — that is, **he eats or derives benefit from** *hekdesh*[29] **through performing an action,**[30] בְּשָׁוֶה פְּרוּטָה — and the benefit had **the value of** at least **a** *perutah*, בְּמֵזִיד — **if he did so deliberately,** לוֹקֶה — **he incurs** *malkus* (lashes)[31] וּמְשַׁלֵּם מַה שֶּׁחִסֵּר מִן הַהֶקְדֵּשׁ — **and** also **pays for what he depleted of** *hekdesh*.[32] הַקֶּרֶן לְבַד — However, in this case he

---

**NOTES**

(see *Bava Metzia* 54b; see also *Kedushas Yom Tov* §67; *Ohr Same'ach, Hil. Me'ilah* 1:5; *Even HaAzel* ad loc.).

25. Tractate *Me'ilah* is dedicated to the laws of this mitzvah, and some laws are found in Chapter 7 of Tractate *Temurah* (31a ff.). The laws of *me'ilah* are codified in *Rambam, Hil. Me'ilah*. [The laws of paying *chomesh* for eating *terumah* can be found in the Mishnah, *Terumos*, Chs. 6-7, and are codified in *Rambam, Hil. Terumos*, Ch. 10.]

26. See Mitzvah 447, where Chinuch discusses whether the prohibition of *me'ilah* applies even in our times (since if one consecrates an object in our times the consecration takes effect). Nevertheless, the requirement of restitution and adding a *chomesh* addressed in *this* mitzvah [as well as the requirement to bring an offering] is not applicable in our time.

27. As with all mitzvah-obligations that are not time-specific, this mitzvah, which requires one to make restitution and add an additional *chomesh* [as well as to bring an offering], applies to women as well. The prohibition of *me'ilah* (see Mitzvah 447) also applies to both men and women, in accordance with the general rule pertaining to mitzvah-prohibitions.

28. As is evident from the continuation of his words, Chinuch is not referring to this specific mitzvah, which is a mitzvah-*obligation* and does not subject one who transgresses it to *malkus*. Rather, he is addressing the prohibition of *me'ilah*.

29. As noted above (see note 16), *me'ilah* also applies when one removes a consecrated item from the domain of *hekdesh* by taking possession of it, even if he did not spend it or derive benefit from it.

30. As a general rule, *malkus* is administered only when a mitzvah-prohibition was transgressed through an action; if it was transgressed without an action (לָאו שֶׁאֵין בּוֹ מַעֲשֶׂה), no *malkus* penalty applies.

[Chinuch implies that it is possible to commit *me'ilah* without an action, by passively benefiting from an item of *hekdesh*, and if one derives the benefit through an action he incurs *malkus*. However, this would seem to contradict Chinuch's well-known position that a prohibition that *can* be violated without an action never carries the penalty of *malkus*, even when it is violated through an action (see for example, Mitzvah 113, at note 40). See *Minchas Chinuch* §16, who resolves this difficulty on the basis of *Shaar HaMelech's* clarification of Chinuch's view, cited in the Insights to Mitzvah 11 and Mitzvah 68.]

31. Unlike most eating prohibitions, for which the minimum amount that carries the penalty of *malkus* is a *kezayis* (olive's volume), with regard to *me'ilah*, even if one *eats* food of *hekdesh*, the minimum amount for liability is the value of a *perutah*. [For discussion, see *Mishneh LaMelech, Hil. Me'ilah* 1:3.]

[The amount of a *perutah* is applicable only to *hekdesh*. A non-Kohen who eats *terumah* is subject to the requirement of a *chomesh* only upon eating a *kezayis*. See *Minchas Chinuch* §11.]

32. As was explained in note 18, one who derives any benefit from *hekdesh* is liable to pay for it, even if its

## 483 ◻ VAYIKRA / MITZVAH 127: ADDING A FIFTH FOR MISAPPROPRIATION OF TEMPLE PROPERTY

כִּי הַמֵּזִיד אֵינוֹ בְּתוֹסֶפֶת חֹמֶשׁ. וְאַזְהָרָה שֶׁל מְעִילָה לְהַלְקוֹתוֹ מִדִּכְתִיב (דברים י״ב, י״ז) לֹא תוּכַל לֶאֱכֹל בִּשְׁעָרֶיךָ[33], וּכְמוֹ שֶׁנִּכְתֹּב בְּעֶזְרַת הַשֵּׁם בְּסֵדֶר רְאֵה בְּסִימָן (ת״ס) [תמ״ז]. מָעַל בִּשְׁגָגָה, מְשַׁלֵּם מַה שֶּׁנֶּהֱנָה וּמוֹסִיף חֹמֶשׁ וּמֵבִיא קָרְבָּן כְּמוֹ שֶׁכָּתַבְנוּ.

---

pays **only the principal,** כִּי הַמֵּזִיד אֵינוֹ בְּתוֹסֶפֶת חֹמֶשׁ — **as the deliberate** violator **is not subject to adding a** *chomesh.*
וְאַזְהָרָה שֶׁל מְעִילָה לְהַלְקוֹתוֹ — **The Scriptural injunction of** *me'ilah,* **for which one incurs** *malkus,* מִדִּכְתִיב — **is from that which is written** (Deuteronomy 12:17): לֹא תוּכַל לֶאֱכֹל בִּשְׁעָרֶיךָ — **In your cities, you shall not eat** the tithe of your grain and your wine and your oil, the firstborn of your cattle and your flocks, all your vow-offerings that you vow and your free-will offerings, and what you raise up with your hand,[33] וּכְמוֹ שֶׁנִּכְתֹּב בְּעֶזְרַת הַשֵּׁם בְּסֵדֶר רְאֵה בְּסִימָן (ת״ס) [תמ״ז] — as we shall write, with the help of Hashem, in *Parashas Re'eh,* in Mitzvah 447.
מָעַל בִּשְׁגָגָה — **If one committed** *me'ilah* **inadvertently,** מְשַׁלֵּם מַה שֶּׁנֶּהֱנָה וּמוֹסִיף חֹמֶשׁ וּמֵבִיא קָרְבָּן — **he must pay for the benefit he derived and add a** *chomesh,* **and must** also **bring an** *asham* **offering,** כְּמוֹ שֶׁכָּתַבְנוּ — **as we have written.**

---

### NOTES

value was less than a *perutah.* Chinuch's stipulation that the *hekdesh* must be worth a *perutah* refers to *malkus,* which applies only if the benefit had a minimum value of a *perutah* (see *Rambam, Hil. Me'ilah* 7:8).

[As set forth in Mitzvah 48, as a rule, a person does not incur both liability to *malkus* and monetary liability for a single action. For discussion of why this rule does not apply to *me'ilah,* see Insight.]

33. See *Makkos* (17a), where the Gemara explains that the prohibition contained in this verse refers to all types of consecrated items. See also *Raavad, Hil. Me'ilah* 1:3 and *Mishneh LaMelech* ad loc.

Although this verse mentions only eating, there is an established rule (see *Pesachim* 25a; see also above,

Mitzvah 113, at note 7) that whenever the Torah expresses a prohibition with the term "you shall not eat," it is actually also intended as a prohibition against deriving benefit. In addition, Acharonim point out that this verse must comprise a prohibition against deriving all forms of benefit from *hekdesh,* for the words וְכָל נְדָרֶיךָ, *and all your vow offerings,* includes even inedible objects. Since such items cannot be the subject of an eating prohibition, it must be that all other forms of benefit are also prohibited (*Lechem Mishneh, Hil. Maasei HaKorbanos* 11:1; *Maayan HaChochmah, Lo Saaseh* 265-266 and *Beis Yischak* to *Rambam, Hil. Me'ilah* 1:3; see also *Ohr Chadash, Pesachim* 95a ד״ה ויש).

---

> ◆§ **Insight – Malkus and Payment**
>
> Chinuch (based on *Rambam, Hil. Me'ilah* 1:3) states that one who intentionally derives benefit from *hekdesh* is required to pay *hekdesh* for the loss and is also liable to *malkus.* A basic question, however, must be addressed: A fundamental principle regarding the penalties of the Torah is that one can never incur two liabilities, such as a payment obligation and *malkus,* for a single action; in most cases, one found guilty will receive *malkus* and be exempt from payment (see *Rambam, Hil. Geneivah* 3:1 and Chinuch, *Mitzvos* 586 and 591; see also Mitzvah 48). Why, then, with regard to one who intentionally derives benefit from *hekdesh* is there monetary liability in addition to *malkus?*
>
> *Maharit Algazi* (*Kedushas Yom Tov* §65) suggests that the principle that a single action cannot cause two liabilities applies only where the offense that would trigger these liabilities was committed to another person. *Me'ilah,* however, is an offense against Divine property; thus, its liabilities are not subject to the limitations of this principle. He supports this assertion by pointing to another area where *me'ilah* is not subject to the general laws that pertain to monetary liability. We have learned (see note 18) that the smallest value that is subject to the monetary obligations of the Torah is the *perutah,* which was the smallest meaningful denomination in the time of the Talmud. Nevertheless, the liability for deriving benefit from *hekdesh* is more stringent than other monetary obligations, and one who derives benefit from *hekdesh* that is worth even less than this amount incurs an obligation to make restitution to *hekdesh.* Thus, argues *Maharit Algazi,* just as the Torah was stringent with regard to the amount that triggers the *me'ilah* liability, so too it was stringent with regard to the liability itself. Although in other situations one is not liable to both monetary

payment and *malkus* for a single act, in the situation of *me'ilah* both liabilities do indeed apply.

ד"ה ר' נחוניה היא — Another resolution to this issue is offered by *Tzlach* (*Pesachim* 29a, to *Tosafos* cited by *Minchas Chinuch* §16), whose approach is also based on the difference between liability to one's fellow man and an offense against Divine property. *Tzlach* points out that while, indeed, *beis din* does not normally impose monetary liability when there is a liability of *malkus*, that is not to say that the monetary liability is eliminated entirely. The Gemara (*Bava Metzia* 91a; see *Rashi* ad loc. ד"ה רבא אמר) states that even in a situation where *beis din* does not enforce payment of a monetary liability because the person receives *malkus*, in order to fulfill his Heavenly obligation the one who was found liable must make good on his monetary liability — in addition to receiving *malkus*. This is due to the fact that aside from the civil obligation that one has toward another, which is the subject of *beis din's* jurisdiction, one who owes money to another is also subject to a Heavenly obligation. And while *beis din* cannot enforce the monetary liability when it administers *malkus*, the Heavenly obligation remains. In the case of *me'ilah*, however, the entire obligation is to Heaven. Thus, unlike other cases where *beis din* governs only the personal liability, in a *me'ilah* situation *beis din* has clearly been given specific jurisdiction over the Heavenly liability. Therefore, with regard to *me'ilah*, *beis din* will enforce the monetary obligation just as they do the *malkus* obligation.

## מִצְוָה קכח: מִצְוַת קָרְבַּן אָשָׁם תָּלוּי

לְהַקְרִיב קָרְבָּן מִי שֶׁנִּסְתַּפֵּק לוֹ אִם חָטָא בְּחֵטְא מֵהַחֲטָאִים הַגְּדוֹלִים שֶׁאָדָם מִתְחַיֵּב בַּעֲשׂוֹתוֹ אוֹתָם בְּזָדוֹן כָּרֵת וּבִשְׁגָגָה חַטָּאת קְבוּעָה¹, וְיִתְחַדֵּשׁ עָלָיו הַסָּפֵק בְּעִנְיָן זֶה, כְּגוֹן שֶׁתֹּאמַר עַל דֶּרֶךְ מָשָׁל שֶׁהָיוּ לְפָנָיו שְׁתֵּי חֲתִיכוֹת, אַחַת חֵלֶב וְאַחַת שֶׁמֶן כָּשֵׁר, וְאָכַל אַחַת מֵהֶן וְנֶאֶבְדָה הָאַחֶרֶת², וְדוֹאֵג בְּנַפְשׁוֹ שֶׁאֵינוֹ יוֹדֵעַ אִם שֶׁל חֵלֶב אָכַל אוֹ שֶׁל שֶׁמֶן³, זֶה הַקָּרְבָּן הַבָּא עַל הַסָּפֵק הַזֶּה נִקְרָא אָשָׁם תָּלוּי⁴.

# Mitzvah 128
## The Obligation of the Pending-Asham Offering

וְאִם נֶפֶשׁ כִּי תֶחֱטָא וְעָשְׂתָה אַחַת מִכָּל מִצְוֹת ה' אֲשֶׁר לֹא תֵעָשֶׂינָה וְלֹא יָדַע וְאָשֵׁם וְנָשָׂא עֲוֹנוֹ. וְהֵבִיא אַיִל תָּמִים מִן הַצֹּאן בְּעֶרְכְּךָ לְאָשָׁם אֶל הַכֹּהֵן וְכִפֶּר עָלָיו הַכֹּהֵן עַל שִׁגְגָתוֹ אֲשֶׁר שָׁגָג וְהוּא לֹא יָדַע וְנִסְלַח לוֹ.

*If a person will sin and will commit one of all the commandments of HASHEM that may not be done, but he did not know and became guilty, he shall bear his iniquity. He shall bring an unblemished ram from the flock, of the proper value, as an asham (guilt) offering, to the Kohen; the Kohen shall provide him atonement for the inadvertence that he committed unintentionally and he did not know, and it shall be forgiven for him (Leviticus 5:17-18).*

מִי שֶׁנִּסְתַּפֵּק לוֹ אִם חָטָא בְּחֵטְא — לְהַקְרִיב קָרְבָּן — **There is an obligation to bring an** *asham* **offering** מֵהַחֲטָאִים הַגְּדוֹלִים — upon **one who is uncertain whether he committed one of the grave sins** שֶׁאָדָם מִתְחַיֵּב בַּעֲשׂוֹתוֹ אוֹתָם בְּזָדוֹן כָּרֵת וּבִשְׁגָגָה חַטָּאת קְבוּעָה — **for which a person incurs *kares* for committing them intentionally, and a "fixed" *chatas* offering** for committing them **inadvertently.**[1] וְיִתְחַדֵּשׁ עָלָיו הַסָּפֵק בְּעִנְיָן זֶה — **The uncertainty regarding this matter can arise,** כְּגוֹן שֶׁתֹּאמַר עַל דֶּרֶךְ מָשָׁל — **if, say, for example,** שֶׁהָיוּ לְפָנָיו שְׁתֵּי חֲתִיכוֹת — **there were two pieces** of fat **before [a person],** אַחַת חֵלֶב וְאַחַת שֶׁמֶן כָּשֵׁר — **one of *cheilev*** (forbidden fat) **and one of** permissible **kosher fat,** וְאָכַל אַחַת מֵהֶן וְנֶאֶבְדָה הָאַחֶרֶת — **and he ate one and the other was lost,**[2] וְדוֹאֵג בְּנַפְשׁוֹ — **and his conscience now troubles him** שֶׁאֵינוֹ יוֹדֵעַ אִם שֶׁל חֵלֶב אָכַל אוֹ שֶׁל שֶׁמֶן — **for he does not know if he partook of the** prohibited ***cheilev*** **or of the** permissible kosher **fat.** In this case, and cases similar to it, one is obligated to bring an offering.[3]

Chinuch discusses the name of the offering:

זֶה הַקָּרְבָּן — **This offering,** הַבָּא עַל הַסָּפֵק הַזֶּה — **which comes for this** situation of **uncertainty,** נִקְרָא אָשָׁם תָּלוּי — **is called a "pending"** *asham* **offering** (*asham talui*).[4]

---

### NOTES

1. There are 43 sins for which a "fixed" *chatas* is brought when committed inadvertently (Chinuch, Mitzvah 121). When one is unsure whether he committed one of these sins, he brings the "pending" *asham* offering described in this mitzvah. If, however, one is unsure whether he committed one of the sins for which a "variable" *chatas* (Mitzvah 123) or a definite *asham* (Mitzvah 129) is brought, he is not liable to the "pending" *asham* offering (*Kereisos* 25a; *Minchas Chinuch* §1).

2. Or was eaten by another person (*Rambam, Sefer HaMitzvos, Asei* 70, R' Chaim Heller and Frankel ed.).

3. One is obligated to bring this offering only if the uncertainty is not clarified. If, before bringing the "pending" *asham* offering he learns that he did not sin, he brings no offering at all; and if he learns that he did, in fact, sin, he brings a standard "fixed" *chatas* (*Kereisos* 23b, 25a; *Rambam, Hil. Pesulei HaMukdashin* 4:19 and *Hil. Shegagos* 8:1).

4. The specifications of this *asham* offering are the same as those of the definite *asham*, discussed in Mitzvah 129.

## 486 □ ויקרא / מצוה קכח: מצוות קרבן אשם תלוי

וּמִלַּת תָּלוּי נֶאֶמְרָה עַל כָּל דָּבָר שֶׁרָאוּי לָבוֹא אַחֲרָיו עִנְיָן שֶׁיְּגַלֶּה בּוֹ מַה שֶּׁלֹּא נוֹדַע בּוֹ מִקֹּדֶם, כְּגוֹן שֶׁאִם יִוָּדַע אֶל הַחוֹטֵא שֶׁהַחֵלֶב אָכַל, הֲרֵי נִגְלָה לוֹ שֶׁהָרִאשׁוֹן לֹא הִסְפִּיק לוֹ וְצָרִיךְ לְהָבִיא עוֹד קָרְבָּן אַחֵר הַנִּקְרָא חַטָּאת קְבוּעָה לְתַשְׁלוּם כַּפָּרָתוֹ.[5] וְאִם נוֹדַע אֵלָיו שֶׁהַהֶתֵּר אָכַל, הֲרֵי עָלָה לוֹ שֶׁהָרִאשׁוֹן הִסְפִּיק לוֹ[6] וְאֵינוֹ צָרִיךְ עוֹד לְקָרְבָּן אַחֵר אַחֲרָיו, זֶהוּ פֵּרוּשׁ תְּלִיָּתוֹ[7].

וְצִוּוּי קָרְבָּן זֶה מִדִּכְתִיב (ויקרא ה׳, י״ז-י״ח) וְאִם נֶפֶשׁ כִּי תֶחֱטָא וְעָשְׂתָה אַחַת מִכָּל מִצְוֹת ה׳ אֲשֶׁר לֹא תֵעָשֶׂינָה וְלֹא יָדַע וְאָשֵׁם וְנָשָׂא עֲוֹנוֹ, וְהֵבִיא אַיִל תָּמִים מִן הַצֹּאן בְּעֶרְכְּךָ לְאָשָׁם אֶל הַכֹּהֵן וְכִפֶּר עָלָיו הַכֹּהֵן עַל שִׁגְגָתוֹ אֲשֶׁר שָׁגַג וְהוּא לֹא יָדַע, כְּלוֹמַר עַל הֱיוֹתוֹ לֹא יָדַע אִם שָׁגַג אוֹ לֹא שָׁגַג[8], וְזֶה הָעִנְיָן יִקְרָאוּ אוֹתוֹ חֲכָמִים לֹא הוֹדַע.

שֶׁרָאוּי לָבוֹא – וּמִלַּת תָּלוּי נֶאֶמְרָה עַל כָּל דָּבָר – The term "pending" is said regarding any matter אַחֲרָיו עִנְיָן שֶׁיְּגַלֶּה בּוֹ מַה שֶּׁלֹּא נוֹדַע בּוֹ מִקֹּדֶם – where it is anticipated that something may follow it – that will reveal something that was not known previously regarding that matter. כְּגוֹן – For example, in the case described above, שֶׁאִם יִוָּדַע אֶל הַחוֹטֵא שֶׁהַחֵלֶב אָכַל – if it becomes known to the one who might have sinned that, in fact, he ate the *cheilev*, הֲרֵי נִגְלָה לוֹ שֶׁהָרִאשׁוֹן לֹא הִסְפִּיק לוֹ – it would become apparent to him that the first offering, i.e., the pending-*asham*, was not sufficient to atone for him, וְצָרִיךְ לְהָבִיא עוֹד קָרְבָּן אַחֵר – and that, consequently, he must bring an additional offering, הַנִּקְרָא חַטָּאת קְבוּעָה – which is called a "fixed" *chatas* offering, לְתַשְׁלוּם כַּפָּרָתוֹ – to complete his atonement.[5] וְאִם נוֹדַע אֵלָיו שֶׁהַהֶתֵּר אָכַל – And, if, on the other hand, it becomes known to him that he ate the permitted piece, הֲרֵי עָלָה לוֹ שֶׁהָרִאשׁוֹן הִסְפִּיק לוֹ – then it is confirmed for him that the first offering was sufficient to atone for him,[6] וְאֵינוֹ צָרִיךְ עוֹד לְקָרְבָּן אַחֵר אַחֲרָיו – and that he therefore has no need for an additional offering subsequent to it. זֶהוּ פֵּרוּשׁ תְּלִיָּתוֹ – This is the explanation of how [this offering] is pending.[7]

Chinuch now provides the source for this mitzvah:

וְצִוּוּי קָרְבָּן זֶה – The commandment regarding this offering מִדִּכְתִיב – is from that which is written (*Leviticus* 5:17-18): וְאִם נֶפֶשׁ כִּי תֶחֱטָא וְעָשְׂתָה אַחַת מִכָּל מִצְוֹת ה׳ אֲשֶׁר לֹא תֵעָשֶׂינָה וְלֹא יָדַע וְאָשֵׁם וְנָשָׂא עֲוֹנוֹ – *If a person will sin and will commit one of all the commandments of* HASHEM *that may not be done, but he did not know and became guilty, he shall bear his iniquity.* וְהֵבִיא אַיִל תָּמִים מִן הַצֹּאן בְּעֶרְכְּךָ לְאָשָׁם אֶל הַכֹּהֵן – *He shall bring an unblemished ram from the flock, of the proper value, as an asham* (guilt) *offering to the Kohen*; וְכִפֶּר עָלָיו הַכֹּהֵן עַל שִׁגְגָתוֹ אֲשֶׁר שָׁגַג וְהוּא לֹא יָדַע – *the Kohen shall provide him atonement for the inadvertence that he committed unintentionally and he did not know, and it shall be forgiven for him.* כְּלוֹמַר עַל הֱיוֹתוֹ לֹא יָדַע אִם שָׁגַג אוֹ לֹא שָׁגַג – That is to say, the offering is brought on account of his being unaware whether he sinned inadvertently or not.[8] וְזֶה הָעִנְיָן יִקְרָאוּ אוֹתוֹ חֲכָמִים לֹא הוֹדַע – This situation is referred to by the Sages (*Kereisos* 2a) as one in which "it is not known" for certain" whether a transgression occurred.

---

### NOTES

5. The *asham talui* does not *complete* his atonement, but protects the person from Heavenly retribution until his sin becomes known and he brings a standard *chatas* offering (*Kereisos* 25a, 26b; *Rabbeinu Gershom* there 25a; *Yoma* 85b, with *Rashi*; *Rambam, Hil. Shegagos* 8:1).

6. While the *asham talui* does not atone for the actual sin, it does atone for his carelessness that allowed him to fall into a state of uncertainty. Indeed, as Chinuch explains below (at note 9), the entire purpose of the *ashum talui* is to provide atonement for his lack of caution in a matter that could very well have been a sin (see also *Sforno* to *Leviticus* 5-17-19; *Rambam, Hil. Shegagos* 8:1 and in *Sefer HaMitzvos, Asei* 70).

7. The status of the offering is pending in that if it becomes known that he sinned, the offering is insufficient and another offering must be brought, whereas, if it becomes known that he did not sin, it is sufficient to atone for his carelessness. Others render *asham talui* as the "suspended" guilt offering, for it "suspends" punishment until his sin is known and a *chatas* is brought (see *Rashi, Yoma* 85b; *Rambam, Hil. Shegagos* 8:1).

8. The verse describes the person obligated to bring this offering as one who sinned *inadvertently* and also *did not know*. In other words, at most, he sinned inadvertently, but, at this point, "he does not know" whether he sinned at all (see *Malbim* to the verse).

מִשָּׁרְשֵׁי הַמִּצְוָה, שֶׁיִּהְיֶה הָאָדָם זָהִיר וְיָרֵא חֵטְא וִיעַיֵּן בְּכָל מַעֲשָׂיו עִיּוּן טוֹב לְבַל יִכָּשֵׁל בִּדְבַר עֲבֵרָה, וְעַל כֵּן הִצְרִיכַתּוּ הַתּוֹרָה לְהָבִיא קָרְבָּן כְּשֶׁלֹּא נִזְהַר יָפֶה בְּמַעֲשָׂיו עַד כְּדֵי שֶׁלֹּא יוָּלַד עָלָיו סָפֵק זֶה[9]. וְהָרְאָיָה שֶׁאֵינֶנּוּ בָּא רַק לְכַפֵּר עַל עַצְלוּתוֹ בְּכָךְ, שֶׁהֲרֵי אֵינוֹ מִשְׁתָּרֵשׁ אֵלָיו לְכַפֵּר עַל הַחֵטְא כְּלָל, שֶׁכְּשֶׁיִּוָּדַע אֵלָיו הַחֵטְא מִיָּד צָרִיךְ לְקָרְבָּן שָׁלֵם כְּמוֹ שֶׁהָיָה חַיָּב אִם לֹא הִקְרִיב הָרִאשׁוֹן[10].

מִדִּינֵי הַמִּצְוָה, מַה שֶּׁאָמְרוּ זִכְרוֹנָם לִבְרָכָה (כריתות י״ח ע״א) שֶׁאֵין חִיּוּב קָרְבָּן זֶה לְעוֹלָם עַד שֶׁיְּהֵא שָׁם אִסּוּר קָבוּעַ, כְּגוֹן שֶׁהָיוּ לְפָנָיו שְׁתֵּי חֲתִיכוֹת וּבְוַדַּאי אַחַת מֵהֶן חֵלֶב, שֶׁהֲרֵי יֵשׁ כָּאן אִסּוּר קָבוּעַ, וְאָכַל אַחַת מֵהֶן[11], וְכֵן נַמִי אִם אָכַל בְּוַדַּאי חֵלֶב

---

### ⸙ Underlying Purpose of the Mitzvah ⸙

שֶׁיִּהְיֶה הָאָדָם זָהִיר וְיָרֵא **מִשָּׁרְשֵׁי הַמִּצְוָה** — Among the underlying purposes of this mitzvah is חֵטְא — so that a person should be cautious and fearful of sin, וִיעַיֵּן בְּכָל מַעֲשָׂיו עִיּוּן טוֹב and before acting, should analyze all his proposed actions with a thorough analysis, לְבַל יִכָּשֵׁל בִּדְבַר עֲבֵרָה — lest he stumble upon a matter of sin. וְעַל כֵּן הִצְרִיכַתּוּ הַתּוֹרָה לְהָבִיא קָרְבָּן — The Torah therefore required him to bring an offering כְּשֶׁלֹּא נִזְהַר יָפֶה בְּמַעֲשָׂיו עַד כְּדֵי שֶׁלֹּא יוָּלַד עָלָיו סָפֵק זֶה — when he was not sufficiently cautious in his actions so as to prevent such a situation of uncertainty from occurring with him.[9]

Chinuch demonstrates that the purpose of this offering is *not* to atone for the actual sin he may have committed:

וְהָרְאָיָה שֶׁאֵינֶנּוּ בָּא רַק לְכַפֵּר עַל עַצְלוּתוֹ בְּכָךְ — The proof that [this offering] comes only to atone for his laxity in this regard is שֶׁהֲרֵי אֵינוֹ מִשְׁתָּרֵשׁ אֵלָיו לְכַפֵּר עַל הַחֵטְא כְּלָל — from the fact that [the offering] does not at all benefit him with respect to atoning for the sin, in the event that it actually occurred, שֶׁכְּשֶׁיִּוָּדַע אֵלָיו הַחֵטְא — for, even after he has brought the *asham talui*, once the sin becomes known to him, מִיָּד צָרִיךְ לְקָרְבָּן שָׁלֵם — he must immediately bring another whole offering as a fixed *chatas*, כְּמוֹ שֶׁהָיָה חַיָּב אִם לֹא הִקְרִיב הָרִאשׁוֹן — just as he would be obligated to do had he not yet brought [the pending-*asham* offering].[10]

### ⸙ Laws of the Mitzvah ⸙

מִדִּינֵי הַמִּצְוָה — Among the laws of the mitzvah is, for example, מַה שֶּׁאָמְרוּ זִכְרוֹנָם לִבְרָכָה — that which [the Sages], of blessed memory, stated (*Kereisos* 18a), שֶׁאֵין חִיּוּב קָרְבָּן זֶה לְעוֹלָם — that liability for this offering never occurs עַד שֶׁיְּהֵא שָׁם אִסּוּר קָבוּעַ — except with regard to an uncertainty in which an "established prohibition" was present. כְּגוֹן שֶׁהָיוּ לְפָנָיו שְׁתֵּי חֲתִיכוֹת — This means, for example, that there were two pieces of fat before [a person], וּבְוַדַּאי אַחַת מֵהֶן חֵלֶב — one of which was certainly *cheilev*, שֶׁהֲרֵי יֵשׁ כָּאן אִסּוּר קָבוּעַ — such that the presence of a prohibited item has been established here, וְאָכַל אַחַת מֵהֶן — and he ate one of them and is now uncertain whether he ate the prohibited piece or the permitted one.[11] וְכֵן נַמִי אִם אָכַל בְּוַדַּאי חֵלֶב — And

---

### NOTES

9. Man's fear of sin should motivate him to take the utmost precautions against sinning, so that he not even stumble and perform a deed that *might* be a sin. The *asham talui* offering is thus brought not to atone for the transgression he may have committed, but to atone for the deficiency in his fear of sin and consequent lack of caution that allowed him to fall into his current state of uncertainty (see *Sforno*, *Leviticus* 5:17-19; above, note 6).

10. If the *ashum talui* would atone, even somewhat, for the sin that might have been committed, why must a standard *chatas* be brought upon discovering that a sin was in fact committed? The fact that a standard *chatas* must still be brought, even after the *asham talui* was offered, demonstrates that the *asham talui* does not atone for the actual sin, but only for stumbling into a situation in which a sin *might* have been committed. Since it does not atone for the actual sin, a standard *chatas* must still be brought upon discovering that one actually sinned.

11. Some maintain that one brings an *asham-talui* even if one was aware that an "established prohibition"

אֲבָל הוּא מְסֻפָּק אִם הָיָה כַּזַּיִת שָׁלֵם אוֹ לֹא, גַּם זֶה הוּא אָסוּר קָבוּעַ.[12] אֲבָל הָיְתָה לְפָנָיו חֲתִיכָה אַחַת וְסָפֵק אִם הָיָה חֵלֶב אוֹ שֻׁמָּן וַאֲכָלָהּ, פָּטוּר מִן הַקָּרְבָּן, שֶׁאֵין כָּאן אָסוּר קָבוּעַ דְּשֶׁמָּא אֵין כָּאן אָסוּר כְּלָל. וּמִן הַטַּעַם הַזֶּה אָמְרוּ שֶׁהַבָּא עַל סְפֵק מְגֹרֶשֶׁת[13] חַיָּב בְּקָרְבָּן, שֶׁהֲרֵי יֵשׁ כָּאן אָסוּר קָבוּעַ שֶׁנַּעֲמִידֶנָּה בִּקְבִיעוּתָהּ שֶׁהָיְתָה נְשׂוּאָה,[14]

---

the same is also true, if it is known to a person that **he certainly ate** a piece of prohibited **cheilev**, אֲבָל הוּא מְסֻפָּק אִם הָיָה כַּזַּיִת שָׁלֵם אוֹ לֹא — **but he is uncertain whether or not it comprised a complete *kezayis*** (olive's volume), which is the amount required for liability; גַּם זֶה הוּא אָסוּר קָבוּעַ — this, too, is an uncertainty that involves **an "established prohibition."**[12]

Chinuch now contrasts the above with a case that does not involve an "established prohibition":

וְסָפֵק אִם הָיָה חֵלֶב אֲבָל הָיְתָה לְפָנָיו חֲתִיכָה אַחַת — **But, if he had before him** only **one piece** of fat, אוֹ שֻׁמָּן — **and** it is uncertain whether it was *cheilev* or permissible kosher fat, וַאֲכָלָהּ — **and he ate it,** פָּטוּר מִן הַקָּרְבָּן — **he is exempt from** liability to bring **the** pending-*asham* **offering,** דְּשֶׁמָּא אֵין כָּאן אָסוּר — **since an "established prohibition" is not present,** קָבוּעַ כְּלָל — as there might not be a prohibited item here at all!

Chinuch extends this rule to other cases:

וּמִן הַטַּעַם הַזֶּה אָמְרוּ — **And, for this reason, [the Sages] said** (*Kesubos* 22b) שֶׁהַבָּא עַל סְפֵק מְגֹרֶשֶׁת — **that one who cohabits with [a woman]** who was once married, **whose** status as **divorced is doubtful,**[13] חַיָּב בְּקָרְבָּן — **is liable to** bring **a** pending-*asham* **offering,** שֶׁהֲרֵי יֵשׁ כָּאן אָסוּר קָבוּעַ — **since an "established prohibition" is involved** in this uncertainty, שֶׁנַּעֲמִידֶנָּה בִּקְבִיעוּתָהּ — **for we place her in her** previously **established** status, שֶׁהָיְתָה נְשׂוּאָה — namely, **that she was married.**[14]

---

### NOTES

was present, and he still ate one of the pieces. Although he was reckless in eating something that he knows may be prohibited, since in the final analysis he did not intend to violate the prohibition, and afterward he does not know whether he actually sinned by eating the prohibited piece, he brings an *asham talui*. This view is held by *Talmidei Rabbeinu Yonah*, cited by *Shitah Mekubetzes, Kesubos* 22b; see also, *Teshuvos Chasam Sofer, Choshen Mishpat* §29.

Others maintain that if one knew at the outset that there was a prohibited piece present and he ate one of them nonetheless, he is to some extent a deliberate transgressor and does not bring an *asham talui* offering. Rather, the offering is incurred where he ate one piece while thinking that both of them were permitted, and afterward it was ascertained that one of them had been definite *cheilev* (*Rashi* to *Leviticus* 5:17, and *Kereisos* 17b ד"ה אכל אחד; see *Tosafos* there 17a ד"ה ספק). [For further discussion, see *Aruch LaNer* to *Rashi, Kereisos* ibid. and *Chidushei Zera Avraham* §9.]

12. Mishnah, *Kereisos* 17a-b, as understood by *Rashi* 17a and *Rambam, Hil. Shegagos* 8:2 (cf. *Tosafos, Kereisos* 17b ד"ה מדסיפא). [Some suggest that this is considered a situation of an "established prohibition" only if the piece of *cheilev* definitely contained a *kezayis*, and what is unknown is how much the person ingested. Since there was an amount of *cheilev* here that can render one liable to an offering by eating its entirety, it is deemed an "established prohibition." If, however, it is unknown whether the piece contained a *kezayis* in the first place, this is not considered an "established prohibition," since the presence of a prohibited item *with respect to liability* has not been established. Chinuch's language, however, does not seem to support this view. For discussion, see *Mahari Korkos* and *Mirkeves HaMishneh, Hil. Shegagos* 8:2. See also, *Har HaMoriah* ad loc. §4; *Chasam Sofer, Sugyos* (Jerusalem 5707) §13; *Aruch LaNer* to *Kereisos* 18a ד"ה מאי איכא.]

13. E.g., two sets of witnesses offer conflicting testimonies regarding whether she was divorced or not (*Kesubos* 22b).

14. In this case, the woman in question (if she was truly divorced) was permitted to the one who cohabited with her. An established prohibition is, nevertheless, present, because although we are unsure of her current marital status, there is no question that she was *once* married. Her previously established status (*chazakah*) causes us to view the case as one involving an "established prohibition," so that the person who cohabited with her is liable to an *asham talui* (*Kesubos* ibid.; *Rambam, Hil. Shegagos* 8:3, with *Lechem Mishneh*; *Tosafos, Kesubos* 22b ד"ה באשם, in first explanation; cf. second explanation of *Tosafos*).

[Some argue that based on her previously established status, we consider her a *definite* married woman, and one who cohabits with her is liable to a *chatas*, not an *asham talui* (see *Tosafos* ibid. ד"ה הבא; see also Schottenstein ed. of *Bavli Kesubos,* 22b note 7).]

# 489 ❑ VAYIKRA / MITZVAH 128: THE OBLIGATION OF THE PENDING-ASHAM OFFERING

אֲבָל הַבָּא עַל סְפֵק מְקֻדֶּשֶׁת פָּטוּר מִן הַקָּרְבָּן, שֶׁאֵין כָּאן אִסּוּר קָבוּעַ, וַהֲרֵי זֶה כַּחֲתִיכָה אַחַת וְסָפֵק אִם הִיא חֵלֶב אוֹ שֻׁמָּן שֶׁפָּטוּר מִקָּרְבָּן כְּמוֹ שֶׁאָמַרְנוּ, וְיֶתֶר פְּרָטֶיהָ מְבֹאָרִין בִּכְרִיתוֹת.

וְנוֹהֶגֶת בִּזְמַן הַבַּיִת בִּזְכָרִים וּנְקֵבוֹת. וְעוֹבֵר עָלֶיהָ וְלֹא הִקְרִיב קָרְבָּן זֶה אִם אֵרַע לוֹ סְפֵק הַמְחַיֵּב בּוֹ, בִּטֵּל עֲשֵׂה.

---

אֲבָל הַבָּא עַל סְפֵק מְקֻדֶּשֶׁת — **However, one who cohabits with [a woman] who** had the status of an unmarried woman but **might** currently **be married**[15] פָּטוּר מִן הַקָּרְבָּן — **is exempt from** liability to bring **an offering.** שֶׁאֵין כָּאן אִסּוּר קָבוּעַ — The reason for this is **that an established prohibition is not present** in this case, וַהֲרֵי זֶה כַּחֲתִיכָה אַחַת וְסָפֵק אִם הִיא חֵלֶב אוֹ שֻׁמָּן — **and it is, thus, like** the situation of **a single piece of fat** regarding which there is **uncertainty whether it is** *cheilev* **or permitted fat,** שֶׁפָּטוּר מִקָּרְבָּן כְּמוֹ שֶׁאָמַרְנוּ — **where** the law concerning one who eats it is **that he is exempt from** liability to **an offering, as we have already stated.**[16]

Chinuch concludes:

מְבֹאָרִין בִּכְרִיתוֹת וְיֶתֶר פְּרָטֶיהָ — These laws, **as well as the additional details of [this mitzvah], are set forth in** Tractate ***Kereisos.***[17]

## ☞ Applicability of the Mitzvah ☜

וְנוֹהֶגֶת בִּזְמַן הַבַּיִת — **[This mitzvah] applies in the time of the Temple,** when offerings are brought, בִּזְכָרִים וּנְקֵבוֹת — **to** both **men and women.**

וְעוֹבֵר עָלֶיהָ וְלֹא הִקְרִיב קָרְבָּן זֶה אִם אֵרַע לוֹ סְפֵק הַמְחַיֵּב בּוֹ — **One who transgresses this [mitzvah], and does not bring this offering when an uncertainty that obligates him to** bring it **occurs with him,** בִּטֵּל עֲשֵׂה — **has violated a** mitzvah-obligation.[18]

---

### NOTES

15. E.g., two sets of witnesses offer conflicting testimonies regarding whether she accepted *kiddushin* (marriage) from another person prior to this (see *Kesubos* 22b).

16. In this case, it is questionable whether the woman was ever married. Since she might be permitted to the one who cohabited with her, and she does not have a previously established status as a married woman, the law is no different from a case involving a single piece of meat whose status is unknown — in both cases, the violator is not liable to an *asham talui*.

17. These laws are discussed mainly in the fourth and sixth chapters of *Kereisos*, and are codified in *Rambam, Hil. Shegagos* Ch. 8.

18. However, once Yom Kippur passes, he is no longer obligated to bring an *asham talui*, because Yom Kippur effects the necessary atonement (for his lack of caution) (*Kereisos* 25a; *Rambam, Hil. Shegagos* 3:9-10; *Minchas Chinuch* §7). See further above, Mitzvah 121, note 18.

---

**⋙ Insight: The Asham Talui Offering and General Situations of Doubt in Biblical Matters**

As Chinuch explained, the underlying theme of our mitzvah is that one must take precautions to avoid any possibility of sin, and that even one who *might* have violated a Torah prohibition is in need of atonement. The Rishonim cite this mitzvah in connection with a fundamental question that pertains to all situations of uncertainty in halachah.

Chinuch notes elsewhere (see Mitzvah 246) that, generally speaking, one must rule stringently with regard to any situation of uncertainty that pertains to a Biblical obligation or prohibition. This rule is classically known as סְפֵיקָא דְּאוֹרָיְיתָא לְחוּמְרָא, *[With regard to] doubts in Biblical matters [we rule] stringently*. For example, if one is unsure whether or not he fulfilled his Biblical obligation to recite *Bircas HaMazon* after his meal (Mitzvah 430), the above rule would require that one be stringent and (for what may be a second time) recite *Bircas HaMazon* (*Rambam, Hil. Berachos* 2:14; see *Shulchan Aruch, Orach Chaim* 184:4 with *Mishnah Berurah* §15 for the halachah). Similarly, it is Biblically prohibited to wear *shaatnez*, i.e., a garment made of a combination of wool and linen (see Mitzvah 551).

Often, when these materials are not fully processed, wearing such a garment may be only a Rabbinic prohibition (see ibid.). As such, in the case of Biblical *shaatnez*, where one has reason to believe that he may have woven a fully processed linen thread into a wool garment, the garment would be forbidden to be worn until such time as one could be certain that the garment is free of linen. However, in the case of Rabbinically forbidden *shaatnez*, when the existence of prohibited fiber is in doubt, the garment may be worn, for in situations of doubt pertaining to Rabbinic prohibitions the law allows leniency (see *Niddah* 61b; *Shulchan Aruch, Yoreh Deah* §302).

Although the principle of סְפֵיקָא דְאוֹרַיְיתָא לְחוּמְרָא, *[With regard to] doubts in Biblical matters [we rule] stringently*, is universally agreed upon, there is a well-known disagreement among the Rishonim regarding the nature of this principle. *Rambam* maintains that this is a Rabbinic enactment (*Hil. Tumas Meis* 9:12; see also *Hil. Isurei Biah* 15:29 where *Rambam* offers proof for his position). [See *Minchas Chinuch* 210:10, who notes that Chinuch shares *Rambam's* view.] That is, according to *Rambam*, Biblical law itself does not obligate us to be stringent in cases of uncertainty; it is the Sages who decreed that such cases be treated stringently. Thus, in the examples cited above, with regard to the obligation to recite *Bircas HaMazon* when in doubt and with regard to the prohibition against wearing a garment that may still have a Biblical issue of *shaatnez*, the requirement of stringency stems from Rabbinic law.

Other Rishonim disagree with *Rambam* and maintain that the requirement to be stringent in situations of uncertainty regarding Biblical law is itself a Biblical requirement (*Rashba, Toras HaBayis* 4:1; *Ran* to *Rif, Kiddushin* fol. 15b ד"ה גרסי'). These authorities do not actually cite any verse for this requirement; however, they do point out that the very premise of our mitzvah supports their position. That is, if there is no Biblical requirement to refrain from prohibitions in situations of doubt, then on a Biblical level, one who is faced with such a doubt is fully in the right to proceed to do the action in question without any qualms whatsoever. Thus, if one has before him both permitted fat and forbidden *cheilev* and is uncertain which is the *cheilev*, according to *Rambam*, such a person should, by Biblical law, be allowed to eat one of the pieces. How can the Torah obligate him to then bring an *asham* offering?

*Kesef Mishneh* (to *Hil. Tumas Meis* loc. cit.) explains that *Rambam* himself addressed this question. He cites an ancient text of *Rambam's* work [which has since been incorporated into many later editions], in which *Rambam* clearly states that his position applies only to standard prohibitions. However, with regard to prohibitions that bear the penalty of *kares*, the requirement to be stringent is indeed of Biblical origin; for by virtue of the fact that the Torah imposes an obligation of an *asham talui* for such questionable violations, the Torah thereby indicates that one must be additionally careful in those instances and avoid them, even in situations of uncertainty.

*MaHarit* (*She'ilos U'Teshuvos MaHarit, Yoreh Deah* §1) finds a number of difficulties with *Kesef Mishneh's* text, as it seems inconsistent with the words of *Rambam* himself as well as the Talmud. He therefore rejects the emendation, and asserts that it is the work of a scholar who was overzealous to defend *Rambam's* position. Nevertheless, he explains that there is no valid challenge to *Rambam's* position from the Torah's requirement to bring an *asham talui* offering in situations of uncertainty. We have learned that the obligation to bring an *asham talui* applies only in cases where an "established prohibition" (אִסּוּר קָבוּעַ) was present as part of the doubt, such as in the above-quoted example of the two pieces of fat, where one was definitely prohibited and the question is simply which one the person ate. Such cases, argues *MaHarit*, are not included in *Rambam's* position that Biblical law allows one to be lenient in situations of uncertainty. Only in standard cases of doubt, where the presence of a prohibited item has not been established, does *Rambam* maintain that there is no Biblical obligation to avoid the uncertainty (even in situations involving *kares*-bearing prohibitions). However, in cases of doubt where a violation would warrant the bringing of an *asham talui*, i.e., where an "established prohibition" is present, *Rambam* agrees that the need to avoid the doubt and rule stringently is in fact Biblical in origin.

[For further discussion and other views on this topic, see *Pri Chadash* to *Yoreh Deah* 110, *Klalei Sfeik Sfeika* §1; *Chavos Daas, Yoreh Deah* 110 in *Beis HaSafeik; Shev Shmaatsa* 1:1-5; *Shaar HaMelech, Hilchos Tumas Meis* loc. cit.; *Aruch HaShulchan, Yoreh Deah* 110:89-95; *Teshuvos Maharam Schik, Yoreh Deah* §126.]

## מִצְוָה קכט: מִצְוַת קָרְבַּן אָשָׁם וַדַּאי

לְהַקְרִיב קָרְבָּן עַל חֲטָאִים יְדוּעִים כְּמוֹ שֶׁנְּפָרֵשׁ אוֹתָם, וְזֶה הַקָּרְבָּן נִקְרָא אָשָׁם וַדַּאי, וְהוּא קָרְבַּן שֶׁל אַיִל שֶׁצָּרִיךְ לִהְיוֹת שָׁוֶה שְׁתֵּי סְלָעִים.[3,2]

## ⸻ Mitzvah 129 ⸻
## The Obligation of the Definite-Asham Offering

נֶפֶשׁ כִּי תֶחֱטָא וּמָעֲלָה מַעַל בַּה׳ וְכִחֵשׁ בַּעֲמִיתוֹ בְּפִקָּדוֹן אוֹ בִתְשׂוּמֶת יָד אוֹ בְגָזֵל אוֹ עָשַׁק אֶת־עֲמִיתוֹ. אוֹ־מָצָא אֲבֵדָה וְכִחֶשׁ בָּהּ וְנִשְׁבַּע עַל־שָׁקֶר ... וְהָיָה כִּי־יֶחֱטָא וְאָשֵׁם וְהֵשִׁיב אֶת הַגְּזֵלָה אֲשֶׁר גָּזָל ... וְאֶת אֲשָׁמוֹ יָבִיא לַה׳ אַיִל תָּמִים מִן הַצֹּאן בְּעֶרְכְּךָ לְאָשָׁם אֶל הַכֹּהֵן

*If a person will sin and commit a treachery against* HASHEM *and be deceitful to his fellow regarding a deposit or about a putting of a hand or about a robbery; or he defrauded his fellow; or he found a lost item and denied it — and he swore falsely [to that effect] ... It shall be that when he will sin and become guilty, he shall return the robbed item that he robbed ... and he shall bring his asham (guilt) offering to* HASHEM *— an unblemished ram from the flock, of the proper value, as an asham offering — to the Kohen (Leviticus 5:21-25).*

In contrast to the "pending" *asham* of the previous mitzvah, which is brought for a *doubtful* transgression, the *asham* that is the subject of this mitzvah comes to atone for a *definite* transgression. Hence its name — אָשָׁם וַדַּאי, the "definite" *asham* — to distinguish it from אָשָׁם תָּלוּי, the "pending" *asham* (*Rashi* to *Chullin* 41b ד"ה אשם ודאי; see also *Rambam, Hil. Shegagos* 9:1,11).

There are five people who must bring a definite *asham*: (1) one who falsely denies a monetary obligation under oath; (2) one who misappropriates Temple property (i.e., *me'ilah*; see Mitzvah 127); (3) one who cohabits with a betrothed maidservant (see *Leviticus* 19:20-22); (4) a *nazir* who contracts corpse-*tumah* (see Mitzvos 375-376); and (5) a *metzora,* upon his purification from his affliction of *tzaraas* (see Mitzvah 169). Although Scripture expresses the obligation to bring an *asham* with regard to each of these situations separately, Chinuch maintains that they are all reckoned as one mitzvah, i.e., the obligation to bring the definite-*asham* whenever indicated so by the Torah.[1]

לְהַקְרִיב קָרְבָּן עַל חֲטָאִים יְדוּעִים — **We are commanded to bring an offering** to atone **for certain known sins,** כְּמוֹ שֶׁנְּפָרֵשׁ אוֹתָם — **as we will** shortly **specify.** וְזֶה הַקָּרְבָּן נִקְרָא אָשָׁם וַדַּאי — **This offering is referred to** by the Sages (Mishnah, *Chullin* 41b, et al.) as the **definite** *asham*, וְהוּא קָרְבָּן שֶׁל אַיִל שֶׁצָּרִיךְ לִהְיוֹת שָׁוֶה שְׁתֵּי סְלָעִים — **and it is an offering** consisting **of a ram,**[2] **which must be worth** at least **two** *selaim*.[3]

---

NOTES

1. This follows *Rambam's* opinion (*Sefer HaMitzvos, Shoresh* 14) that we reckon all the definite-*asham* liabilities as one mitzvah, in keeping with his principle (ibid.) pertaining to *all* penalties, that the obligation to comply with a given penalty counts as one mitzvah only — even if it applies to several sins (however, see *Zohar HaRakia, Asei* 66; for discussion, see *R' Y. F. Perla, Sefer HaMitzvos of Rav Saadiah Gaon, Asei* 147-148, Vol. I, p. 388b).

2. The requirement for the definite *asham* offering to be of a ram is expressed by Scripture with regard to the *asham* of robbery, the *asham* of *me'ilah* (*Leviticus* 5:15), and the *asham of the betrothed maidservant* (ibid.

19:21). [In regard to the *nazir's asham* (*Numbers* 6:12) and the *metzora's asham* (*Leviticus* 14:12), however, the Torah states explicitly that they are to be *lambs*. Chinuch's implication that *all* the definite *ashamos* are ram offerings requires further study (see also note 20).]

[A "ram" in Biblical terms is a male sheep that is at least 31 days into its second year, i.e., a year and 31 days old, while a "lamb" is a male sheep before its first birthday. During the thirty intermediate days, the sheep is considered neither a lamb nor a ram (*Rambam, Hil. Maaseh HaKorbanos* 1:14 with *Radvaz*).]

3. A *sela* [the term used by the Sages for the Biblical *shekel*, as Chinuch writes in Mitzvah 355] was a silver

וְיֵשׁ מִן הַחֲטָאִים אֵלּוּ שֶׁקָּרְבָּן זֶה בָּא עֲלֵיהֶן בֵּין חָטָא בָּהֶן בְּשׁוֹגֵג בֵּין בְּמֵזִיד, וְיֵשׁ שֶׁאֵינוֹ בָּא אֶלָּא בְּשׁוֹגֵג דַּוְקָא וְלֹא בְּמֵזִיד.[4]

וְאֶחָד מֵחֲטָאִים אֵלֶּה הוּא מִי שֶׁיֵּשׁ בְּיָדוֹ מָמוֹן יִשְׂרָאֵל מִשְׁוֶה פְּרוּטָה וָמַעְלָה שֶׁלֹּא כַּדִּין,[5,6] כְּגוֹן שֶׁגְּזָלוֹ אוֹ גְּנָבוֹ, אוֹ נִשְׁאַר בְּיָדוֹ מִפִּקָּדוֹן שֶׁהֻפְקַד לוֹ,[7] אוֹ נִשְׁאַר בְּיָדוֹ מֵחֲמַת הַלְוָאָה אוֹ שֻׁתָּפוּת. כְּלָלוֹ שֶׁל דָּבָר, כָּל שֶׁאִלּוּ הוֹדָה לוֹ יִהְיֶה חַיָּב לְשַׁלֵּם בַּדִּין, וּתְבָעוֹ מִמֶּנּוּ הַנִּגְזָל אוֹ הֶעָשׁוּק אוֹ יוֹרְשׁוֹ אוֹ הַבָּא מִכֹּחָם וְכָפַר בּוֹ וְנִשְׁבַּע עָלָיו לַשֶּׁקֶר,[8]

---

שֶׁקָּרְבָּן זֶה ... וְיֵשׁ מִן הַחֲטָאִים אֵלּוּ — Now, there are some among these above-referenced sins בָּא עֲלֵיהֶן בֵּין חָטָא בָּהֶן בְּשׁוֹגֵג בֵּין בְּמֵזִיד — for which [the definite-*asham*] offering is brought whether one violated them inadvertently or deliberately, וְיֵשׁ שֶׁאֵינוֹ בָּא אֶלָּא בְּשׁוֹגֵג דַּוְקָא וְלֹא בְּמֵזִיד — while there are others for which [this offering] is brought only when one violated them inadvertently, but not if he violated them deliberately.[4]

The first definite *asham* that Chinuch discusses is the *asham* incurred for taking a false oath to deny a monetary claim, as described in the Scriptural passage above. Chinuch will later identify this as the "*asham of robbery*":

הוּא וְאֶחָד מֵחֲטָאִים אֵלֶּה — One of these sins for which one incurs the obligation to bring a definite-*asham* is מִי שֶׁיֵּשׁ בְּיָדוֹ מָמוֹן יִשְׂרָאֵל מִשְׁוֶה פְּרוּטָה וָמַעְלָה שֶׁלֹּא כַּדִּין — the sin committed by one who unlawfully has in his possession money of his fellow Jew,[5] either actual property or an outstanding debt, worth a *perutah* or more,[6] כְּגוֹן שֶׁגְּזָלוֹ אוֹ גְּנָבוֹ — for example, he had robbed or stolen [the money], אוֹ נִשְׁאַר בְּיָדוֹ מִפִּקָּדוֹן שֶׁהֻפְקַד לוֹ — or it had remained with him from a deposit entrusted to him for safekeeping,[7] אוֹ נִשְׁאַר בְּיָדוֹ מֵחֲמַת הַלְוָאָה אוֹ שֻׁתָּפוּת — or it had remained with him as a result of either an unpaid loan or a partnership — כְּלָלוֹ שֶׁל דָּבָר כָּל שֶׁאִלּוּ הוֹדָה לוֹ יִהְיֶה חַיָּב לְשַׁלֵּם בַּדִּין — the sum of the matter being that he has the money through any means by which, if he would admit the truth to [the fellow], he would be legally obligated to pay it back — וּתְבָעוֹ מִמֶּנּוּ הַנִּגְזָל אוֹ הֶעָשׁוּק אוֹ יוֹרְשׁוֹ אוֹ הַבָּא מִכֹּחָם — and the fellow who had been robbed or cheated, or his heir, or his legal representative, demanded [the money] of him, וְכָפַר בּוֹ וְנִשְׁבַּע עָלָיו לַשֶּׁקֶר — and he denied [the claim] and swore falsely regarding it, i.e., he denied the claim under oath.[8]

---

NOTES

coin that weighed about a half ounce (or approximately .5-.6 troy ounces).

As Chinuch writes in Mitzvah 127 and later in our mitzvah, the ram may be worth *more* than two *selaim*. However, it must not be worth less; if the price of rams depreciated and the choicest ram is now sold in the marketplace for less than two *selaim*, one must wait until the price rebounds (*Rambam, Hil. Pesulei HaMukdashin* 4:23).

4. Most sin offerings (i.e., *chatas* or *asham* offerings) are brought only for inadvertent transgressions. However, the Mishnah in *Kereisos* (9a) lists four cases that require an offering for intentional transgressions as well. Among them are three definite *asham* offerings, which Chinuch will identify below.

5. Although it is categorically prohibited to steal from *any* person, and one who does so must return the stolen item to its rightful owner (see *Rambam, Hil. Gezeilah VaAveidah* 1:2), the *asham* offering for denying the theft under oath pertains only to theft of money from a fellow Jew, as indicated by the phrase (in the passage above), *and be deceitful to "his fellow."* In fact, theft of

sacred property is also not included [though in certain instances one is liable to the *asham of me'ilah*] (*Sifra* to *Leviticus* 5:21).

6. A *perutah* is the smallest coin used in the time of the Gemara, and its value is the minimum that is legally significant. [For discussion of this minimum in regard to the *asham of robbery*, see *R' Akiva Eiger*, Frankel ed. of *Rambam, Hil. Shevuos* 7:16; *Haamek Davar* to *Leviticus* 5:26).]

7. That is, one had deposited money or an item of value with a custodian, who later claimed that it was lost in a manner for which he was not responsible (see Mitzvos 57, 59, and 60, for details of a custodian's liability), but in reality the article of deposit was still in his possession.

8. Thus, his oath falsely absolved him of an obligation to make restitution, i.e., of an *indemnity*.

The reference here is to any kind of oath, whether it was mandated by law in that particular case (see Mitzvah 58 for examples), or it was informally initiated by one of the parties in the course of a monetary dispute (see *Tiferes Yisrael, Shevuos* 5:1). In Talmudic

# VAYIKRA / MITZVAH 129: THE OBLIGATION OF THE DEFINITE-ASHAM OFFERING

וְהָיָה כִּי יָשׁוּב וְנִחַם עַל חֶטְאוֹ וְיָשִׁיב הֶחָמָס אֲשֶׁר בְּכַפָּיו, חַיָּב לְהָבִיא קָרְבָּן זֶה שֶׁאָמַרְנוּ עַל חַטָאתוֹ[9], מִלְּבַד הַחֹמֶשׁ שֶׁחַיָּב לְהוֹסִיף עַל הַקֶּרֶן וּלְתִתּוֹ לַנִּגְזָל[10], שֶׁנֶּאֱמַר (ויקרא ה׳, כ״א) נֶפֶשׁ כִּי תֶחֱטָא וּמָעֲלָה מַעַל בַּיי וְכִחֵשׁ בַּעֲמִיתוֹ וְגוֹ׳, וְאָמַר רַבִּי עֲקִיבָא מַה תַּלְמוּד לוֹמַר מַעַל בַּיי, לְפִי שֶׁכָּל הַלֹּוֶה וְהַמַּלְוֶה אֵינוֹ עוֹשֶׂה אֶלָּא בְּעֵדִים, וּכְשֶׁהוּא מְכַחֵשׁ אֵינוֹ מְכַחֵשׁ אֶלָּא בְּעֵדִים, אֲבָל הַמַּלְוֶה שֶׁלֹּא בְּעֵדִים וּמְכַחֵשׁ בּוֹ [מְכַחֵשׁ בַּ]שְׁלִישִׁי שֶׁבֵּינֵיהֶם, שְׁכִינָה[11],

---

וְהָיָה כִּי יָשׁוּב וְנִחַם עַל חֶטְאוֹ — **If** [the defendant] **now repents and regrets his sin,** וְיָשִׁיב הֶחָמָס אֲשֶׁר בְּכַפָּיו — **and he returns the ill-gotten property that is in his hands,** חַיָּב לְהָבִיא קָרְבָּן זֶה שֶׁאָמַרְנוּ — **he is obligated to bring this offering that we mentioned,** i.e., the definite *asham,* עַל חַטָאתוֹ — **to atone for his sin** of denying the theft under oath.[9] מִלְּבַד הַחֹמֶשׁ שֶׁחַיָּב לְהוֹסִיף עַל הַקֶּרֶן וּלְתִתּוֹ לַנִּגְזָל — **The liability to bring an** *asham* **is in addition to the** surcharge of **"a fifth" that** [the defendant] **must add to the principal and give to the person** whom he had **robbed.**[10] שֶׁנֶּאֱמַר — All this is indicated by Scripture with regard to this sin, **as it is stated** (*Leviticus* 5:21): "נֶפֶשׁ כִּי תֶחֱטָא וּמָעֲלָה מַעַל בַּהּ׳ וְכִחֵשׁ בַּעֲמִיתוֹ וְגוֹ׳" — *If a person will sin and commit a treachery against HASHEM and be deceitful to his fellow,* **etc.** [by denying one of the various monetary obligations delineated above].

Chinuch pauses to cite R' Akiva's homiletic comment on this verse:

וְאָמַר רַבִּי עֲקִיבָא — On this verse, **R' Akiva said** (*Sifra* to *Leviticus* ibid.): מַה תַּלְמוּד לוֹמַר — **What does Scripture** intend to **teach when it says,** "מַעַל בַּהּ׳" — *and commit a treachery "against HASHEM,"* when immediately afterward it describes the sin as that of being deceitful *"to his fellow"*? לְפִי שֶׁכָּל הַלֹּוֶה וְהַמַּלְוֶה — **For whoever borrows or lends** אֵינוֹ עוֹשֶׂה אֶלָּא בְּעֵדִים — generally **does so only with witnesses,** so that the obligation can be upheld in court; וּכְשֶׁהוּא מְכַחֵשׁ — **thus, if** [the borrower] subsequently **denies** the debt אֵינוֹ מְכַחֵשׁ אֶלָּא בְּעֵדִים — **he is denying only the** credibility of the **witnesses.** אֲבָל הַמַּלְוֶה שֶׁלֹּא בְּעֵדִים — **But if one loaned money without witnesses,** וּמְכַחֵשׁ בּוֹ — **and** [the borrower] **now denies** [the lender's] claim to the money, [מְכַחֵשׁ בַּ]שְׁלִישִׁי שֶׁבֵּינֵיהֶם — **he is,** in effect, **denying the existence of the third party Who is between them —** שְׁכִינָה — namely, **the Divine Presence.**[11]

---

## NOTES

parlance, this false oath in denial of a claim is called שְׁבוּעַת הַפִּקָּדוֹן, *an oath regarding a deposit* (see Mishnah *Shevuos* 36b).

[The law that follows, regarding the atonement offering, pertains only to a case where the claim and the oath of denial involved מִטַלְטְלִין, *movable property.* An oath taken in denial of real property (as well as Canaanite slaves or legal documents) does not carry liability to the atonement offering, even though it absolved the defendant of liability to pay (ibid. 37b).]

9. The false denial and oath are prohibited under Mitzvos 225-226; the offering is obligatory under this mitzvah.

[The defendant must repent before he brings an *asham,* because the *asham* comes to atone, and if he has not repented there is no place for atonement (see *Rambam, Hil. Gezeilah* 7:8). For the same reason, he must also first cleanse his hands of the theft and make restitution. In fact, if the *asham* was offered before he returns the stolen goods or repays the debt, it is invalid (*Rambam* ibid. 8:13, and *Hil. Shegagos* 9:7). Even if he makes restitution because the court holds him liable on account of eyewitnesses' testimony, if he persists in his denial he does not bring the *asham* [i.e., he is not eligible for the *asham's* atonement] (*Rambam, Hil. Gezeilah* ibid.).]

10. The manner in which this "fifth" is calculated is explained by Chinuch above, Mitzvah 127, after note 24.

[There is a debate among the authorities as to which mitzvah this obligation of the one-fifth surcharge falls under, and Chinuch's position is unclear. As indicated in the introduction above, the current mitzvah is the obligation to bring the definite-*asham*; paying the one-fifth surcharge, while a component of the Torah's prescribed rectification for falsely denying a debt under oath, is independent of the *asham* obligation (though they generally share the same guidelines with regard to their applicability — see *Minchas Chinuch* §9). For discussion of the various opinions, see *R' Y. F. Perla, Sefer HaMitzvos of Rav Saadiah Gaon, Asei* 147-148, Vol. I, p. 776.]

11. Generally, loans are administered in the presence of witnesses, in order to guarantee repayment. Since the loan is not based on the lender's trust of the borrower, if the borrower ultimately denies the loan, it is not perceived as an inherent breach of faith, but rather

לְכָךְ נֶאֱמַר (שם) וּמָעֲלָה מַעַל בַּה׳ וְכִחֵשׁ בַּעֲמִיתוֹ וְגוֹ׳.[12]

וּכְתִיב בַּתְרֵיהּ (שם, שם כ״ג – כ״ה) וְהָיָה כִּי יֶחֱטָא וְאָשֵׁם, כְּלוֹמַר שֶׁיַּעֲשֶׂה תְּשׁוּבָה שֶׁיַּחֲזִיק עַצְמוֹ בְּאָשֵׁם,[13] וְהֵשִׁיב אֶת הַגְּזֵלָה וְגוֹ׳, וְשִׁלַּם אוֹתוֹ בְּרֹאשׁוֹ וַחֲמִשִׁתָיו יֹסֵף עָלָיו וְגוֹ׳, וְאֶת אֲשָׁמוֹ יָבִיא לַה׳ אַיִל וְגוֹ׳, וְזֶהוּ הַנִּקְרָא אֲשַׁם גְּזֵלוֹת,[14] וְזֶהוּ מִן הַבָּאִים בֵּין עַל שׁוֹגֵג בֵּין עַל מֵזִיד.[15]

לְכָךְ נֶאֱמַר – **It is therefore stated** (ibid.): "וּמָעֲלָה מַעַל בַּה׳ וְכִחֵשׁ בַּעֲמִיתוֹ וְגוֹ׳" – *If a person will sin and commit a treachery against HASHEM and be deceitful to his fellow, etc.*, to teach that deceiving one's fellow in these circumstances constitutes treachery against the Presence of Hashem.[12]

Chinuch resumes his citation of the verses setting forth liability to the *asham of robbery*:

וּכְתִיב בַּתְרֵיהּ – **And it is written after this** (ibid. vs. 23-25): "וְהָיָה כִּי יֶחֱטָא וְאָשֵׁם" – *It shall be that when he will sin and become guilty* – כְּלוֹמַר שֶׁיַּעֲשֶׂה תְּשׁוּבָה שֶׁיַּחֲזִיק עַצְמוֹ בְּאָשֵׁם – **that is to say, that he repents and holds himself guilty**[13] – "וְהֵשִׁיב אֶת הַגְּזֵלָה וְגוֹ׳, וְשִׁלַּם אוֹתוֹ בְּרֹאשׁוֹ וַחֲמִשִׁתָיו יֹסֵף עָלָיו וְגוֹ׳, וְאֶת אֲשָׁמוֹ יָבִיא לַה׳ אַיִל וְגוֹ׳" – *he shall return the robbed item, etc., he shall repay its principal and add its fifth to it, etc. And he shall bring his asham offering to HASHEM – a ram,* **etc.**

וְזֶהוּ הַנִּקְרָא אֲשַׁם גְּזֵלוֹת – **This** *asham* offering, which Scripture requires of one who denied his theft under oath, **is what is referred to** in the Mishnah (*Zevachim* 54b) **as the "asham of robbery,"**[14] וְזֶהוּ מִן הַבָּאִים בֵּין עַל שׁוֹגֵג בֵּין עַל מֵזִיד – **and it is among those [***asham*** offerings] mentioned above that are brought for both an inadvertent** violation **and a deliberate** violation.[15]

Having discussed the *asham of robbery*, Chinuch turns to the next of the five definite-*asham* offerings, the *asham of me'ilah*:

---

## NOTES

as an attempt to circumvent the witnesses' testimony and undermine their credibility. In the event, however, that a loan is administered without the guarantee provided by witnesses, it is based on trust; i.e., the lender trusts the borrower to repay the loan, because of what he perceives as the borrower's integrity and fear of Heaven. If the borrower subsequently denies the loan, he not only breaches that trust but also demonstrates a lack of fear of Heaven (*Raavad* to *Sifra* there; *Gur Aryeh* to *Rashi, Leviticus* 5:21; see also *Malbim* there, cited in footnote to Mechon Yerushalayim edition of *Minchas Chinuch*).

12. To be sure, the laws of one who falsely denies a debt under oath apply also to loans and deposits that were administered in the presence of witnesses (see *Rambam, Hil. Shevuos* 8:14). However, the more common scenario for this oath is when there were no witnesses at all, which allows the borrower to deny at will. It is therefore appropriate that the Torah refers to the transgression as a *"treachery against HASHEM."*

[Our text of *Sifra* reads differently than the text presented here by Chinuch. It makes a distinction between a loan, which is generally administered with witnesses, and a deposit, which is often administered in a more discreet manner (see also *Rashi* to *Leviticus* 5:21).]

13. The verse continues (as Chinuch cites immediately): *he shall return the robbed item,* etc. Thus, the literal understanding of the verse – *It shall be that when he shall sin ... he shall return the robbed item* – implies that the thief is enjoined to return the stolen item at the time of the theft, which is difficult, because it seems useless to instruct a thief to return the item he has just stolen (when he had openly violated the prohibition to steal). Rather, the verse should be read as follows: *It shall be that when he will [acknowledge his] sin and become guilty [in his own eyes], he shall return the robbed item,* etc. (*Mizrachi* to *Rashi,* ibid. v. 23; see *Kli Yakar* there for an explanation of why the thief's repentance is referred to in this manner).

14. The name *"asham of robbery"* refers to the *asham* brought for the denial under oath of *any* of the monetary obligations delineated above by Chinuch.

15. Mishnah, *Kereisos* 9a. The term "inadvertent" does not mean that the person was unaware that the money was in his possession; in that case, since the person thought he was swearing truthfully, he is exempt from an offering. Rather, it means that he was unaware that swearing falsely would render him liable to the *asham* offering (Mishnah, *Shevuos* 36b; *Rambam, Hil. Shevuos* 1:9-11). For elaboration, see above, Mitzvah 123 note 27.

[This is a unique law pertaining to false oaths. In regard to other transgressions, merely being unaware of the liability to an offering would *not* render the transgression "inadvertent." In those cases, inadvertence means that one does not realize that the act is a forbidden one (*Minchas Chinuch* 127:25; see above, Mitzvah 121 note 2).]

# 495 ❑ VAYIKRA / MITZVAH 129: THE OBLIGATION OF THE DEFINITE-ASHAM OFFERING

וּבְזֹאת הַפָּרָשָׁה לֹא נִזְכַּר מִן הָאֲשָׁמוֹת כִּי אִם זֶה שֶׁאָמַרְנוּ, אֲבָל בְּפָרָשָׁה שֶׁל מַעְלָה (שם, שם ט״ו-ט״ז) הֻזְכַּר אָשָׁם אַחֵר שֶׁהוּא מִמִּין זֶה שֶׁנִּקְרָא גַּם כֵּן אָשָׁם וַדַּאי וְהוּא אֲשַׁם מְעִילוֹת, כְּלוֹמַר מִי שֶׁמָּעַל וְנֶהֱנָה מִן הַהֶקְדֵּשׁוֹת[16]. וּלְפִיכָךְ נוֹפֵל בּוֹ לְשׁוֹן מְעִילָה לְפִי שֶׁהוּא דָּבָר רַע מְאֹד, וּכְעֵין מְסִירָה[17], מִי שֶׁפּוֹשֵׁט יָדוֹ לֵהָנוֹת בְּמָמוֹן שָׁמַיִם[18]. וְזֶה הָאָשָׁם אֵינוֹ בָּא כִּי אִם עַל הַשּׁוֹגֵג[19], וּכְמוֹ שֶׁכָּתַבְנוּ לְמַעְלָה בִּמְקוֹמוֹ.

וְעוֹד חִיְּבָה הַתּוֹרָה גַּם כֵּן קָרְבָּן זֶה שֶׁל אָשָׁם וַדַּאי, וְהוּא אַיִל מִשְׁתֵּי סְלָעִים[20], לְנָזִיר שֶׁנִּטְמָא[21], וּכְמוֹ שֶׁנִּכְתֹּב בְּעֶזְרַת הַשֵּׁם בְּסֵדֶר נָשֹׂא[22], וְזֶה גַּם כֵּן יִהְיֶה

---

וּבְזֹאת הַפָּרָשָׁה לֹא נִזְכַּר מִן הָאֲשָׁמוֹת כִּי אִם זֶה שֶׁאָמַרְנוּ — **Now, in this Scriptural passage, no other** *asham* **is mentioned but the one that we just discussed** (the *asham of robbery*). אֲבָל בְּפָרָשָׁה שֶׁל מַעְלָה הֻזְכַּר אָשָׁם אַחֵר שֶׁהוּא מִמִּין זֶה — **However, in a previous passage** (vs. 15-16) **there is mention of another** *asham* **of this kind,** i.e., one that is incurred for a *definite* violation, שֶׁנִּקְרָא גַּם כֵּן אָשָׁם וַדַּאי — **which also goes by the name "definite** *asham*." וְהוּא אֲשַׁם מְעִילוֹת — **This is the** *asham of me'ilah,* כְּלוֹמַר מִי שֶׁמָּעַל וְנֶהֱנָה מִן הַהֶקְדֵּשׁוֹת — **that is to say,** an *asham* incurred **by one who committed a misappropriation and derived benefit from Temple properties.**[16] וּלְפִיכָךְ נוֹפֵל בּוֹ לְשׁוֹן מְעִילָה — **The term** *me'ilah* (treachery) **is indeed fitting to describe [this act],** לְפִי שֶׁהוּא דָּבָר רַע מְאֹד וּכְעֵין מְסִירָה — **because it is a most despicable act** — **akin to the treacherous act of informing against a fellow Jew**[17] — מִי שֶׁפּוֹשֵׁט יָדוֹ לֵהָנוֹת בְּמָמוֹן שָׁמַיִם — **for one to extend his hand and derive benefit from the property of Heaven.**[18]

וְזֶה הָאָשָׁם אֵינוֹ בָּא כִּי אִם עַל הַשּׁוֹגֵג — **In contrast to the** *asham of robbery,* which is brought also for a deliberate violation, **this** particular *asham,* the *asham of me'ilah,* **is brought only for an inadvertent** misappropriation of sacred property,[19] but not for a deliberate misappropriation, וּכְמוֹ שֶׁכָּתַבְנוּ לְמַעְלָה בִּמְקוֹמוֹ — **as we have written above** (Mitzvah 127), **where it is** discussed.

Chinuch now discusses the third instance of a definite *asham,* the *nazir's asham*:

וְעוֹד חִיְּבָה הַתּוֹרָה גַּם כֵּן קָרְבָּן זֶה שֶׁל אָשָׁם וַדַּאי — **The Torah** (Numbers 6:12) **also imposed this obligation of a definite-***asham* **offering,** וְהוּא אַיִל מִשְׁתֵּי סְלָעִים — **which is a ram worth** at least **two** *selaim,*[20] לְנָזִיר שֶׁנִּטְמָא — **on a** *nazir* **who had become impure** by contact with a corpse,[21] וּכְמוֹ שֶׁנִּכְתֹּב בְּעֶזְרַת הַשֵּׁם בְּסֵדֶר נָשֹׂא — **as we will write, with the help of Hashem, in Parashas Naso.**[22] וְזֶה גַּם כֵּן יִהְיֶה — **This** *asham* **obligation, too, applies**

---

## NOTES

16. This sin was discussed at length in Mitzvah 127, which sets forth the obligation upon one who committed *me'ilah* to make restitution and pay an additional penalty of a fifth. His additional obligation to bring an *asham* offering is included in the current mitzvah.

17. The laws of מְסִירָה (literally, *giving over*), a term that depicts the delivery of Jewish persons or property into the hands of idolaters, are discussed by Chinuch in Mitzvah 236.

18. One who engages in מְסִירָה commits the ultimate treason; his own selfish motives drive him to violate the sense of trust and allegiance shared by people of one nation. Chinuch explains that this level of treachery is similarly exhibited when one violates the sanctity of consecrated property — as it were, a crown jewel of Hashem's Kingship — for his own selfish purposes.

19. I.e., the transgressor was unaware that the object was sacred property. See *Pesachim* 32b.

20. *Minchas Chinuch* (§25) states emphatically that this phrase is a copyist's error since Scripture (*Numbers* 6:12) explicitly states that a *nazir's asham* consists of a *lamb* (see note 2).

21. A *nazir* is a person who takes the vow of *nezirus*, which prohibits him to drink wine, eat grapes or grape products, cut his hair, or contaminate himself with the *tumah* (ritual impurity) of a corpse. Should he become *tamei* (ritually impure), he must purify himself, shave the hair of his head at the conclusion of the purification period, and bring a group of offerings on the following day, one of which is an *asham* (see Mitzvos 368-377).

22. This reference is unclear since Chinuch makes no mention there (in Mitzvos 368-377) of the obligation of the *nazir's asham* at all, aside from alluding to it in context of an incident that he cites from the Gemara (see Mitzvah 374). *Minchas Yitzchak* (§5) therefore maintains that the copyist's error inferred by *Minchas Chinuch* (see note 20) extends to this phrase, as well. The text of this paragraph should thus read: וְעוֹד חִיְּבָה הַתּוֹרָה גַּם כֵּן קָרְבָּן זֶה שֶׁל אָשָׁם וַדַּאי לְנָזִיר שֶׁנִּטְמָא, וְזֶה גַּם כֵּן יִהְיֶה בֵּין נִטְמָא בְּמֵזִיד אוֹ בְשׁוֹגֵג, *The Torah* (Numbers 6:12) *also*

בֵּין נִטְמָא בְּמֵזִיד אוֹ בְּשׁוֹגֵג.[23]

וְעוֹד חִיְּבָה הַתּוֹרָה גַּם כֵּן בְּקָרְבָּן זֶה לַמְצֹרָע כְּשֶׁיִּטָּהֵר מִצָּרַעְתּוֹ, וּכְמוֹ שֶׁנִּכְתַּב בְּעֶזְרַת הַשֵּׁם בְּסֵדֶר זֹאת תִּהְיֶה תּוֹרַת הַמְצֹרָע.[24] וְאֵין לְפָרֵשׁ בָּזֶה שׁוֹגֵג וּמֵזִיד, שֶׁאֵין נוֹפֵל כָּאן עִנְיָן שְׁגָגָה וְזָדוֹן.[25]

וְעוֹד חִיְּבָה תּוֹרָה גַּם כֵּן בְּקָרְבָּן זֶה מִי שֶׁבָּא עַל שִׁפְחָה חֲרוּפָה,[26] וּכְמוֹ שֶׁכָּתוּב בְּסֵדֶר קְדֹשִׁים תִּהְיוּ, שֶׁנֶּאֱמַר (שם י״ט, כ״-כ״א) וְאִישׁ כִּי יִשְׁכַּב אֶת אִשָּׁה וְהִוא שִׁפְחָה נֶחֱרֶפֶת לְאִישׁ וְהָפְדֵּה לֹא נִפְדָּתָה וְגוֹ׳, בִּקֹּרֶת תִּהְיֶה וְגוֹ׳, וְהֵבִיא אֶת אֲשָׁמוֹ וְגוֹ׳, אֵיל אָשָׁם, וְזֶה מִן הַבָּאִים בֵּין עַל שׁוֹגֵג בֵּין עַל מֵזִיד.[27] נִמְצְאוּ בֵּין כֻּלָּן הָאֲשָׁמוֹת וַדָּאוֹת חֲמִשָּׁה, וְכֵן מָנוּ אוֹתָן חֲכָמִים זִכְרוֹנָם לִבְרָכָה בַּמִּשְׁנָה (זבחים נ״ד ע״ב), שֶׁאָמְרוּ אֵלּוּ הֵן אֲשָׁמוֹת,

---

בֵּין נִטְמָא בְּמֵזִיד אוֹ בְּשׁוֹגֵג — **whether he became impure deliberately or inadvertently.**[23]

Chinuch goes on to discuss the fourth instance of a definite *asham*, the *metzora's asham*:

וְעוֹד חִיְּבָה הַתּוֹרָה גַּם כֵּן בְּקָרְבָּן זֶה — **The Torah** (*Leviticus* 14:12) **also made liable to this offering** לַמְצֹרָע כְּשֶׁיִּטָּהֵר מִצָּרַעְתּוֹ — a *metzora* — **when** it is time for him to be **purified of his** *tzaraas* — וּכְמוֹ שֶׁנִּכְתַּב בְּעֶזְרַת הַשֵּׁם בְּסֵדֶר זֹאת תִּהְיֶה תּוֹרַת הַמְצֹרָע — **as we shall write, with the help of Hashem, in** *Parashas Metzora* (Mitzvah 176).[24] וְאֵין לְפָרֵשׁ בָּזֶה שׁוֹגֵג וּמֵזִיד — **With regard to [the** *metzora's asham*], we cannot discuss the subject of whether one was **inadvertent or deliberate**, שֶׁאֵין נוֹפֵל כָּאן עִנְיָן שְׁגָגָה וְזָדוֹן — **since the matter of inadvertence or deliberateness does not apply here.**[25]

Chinuch now discusses the fifth case of a definite *asham*, the *asham of the betrothed maidservant*:

וְעוֹד חִיְּבָה תּוֹרָה גַּם כֵּן בְּקָרְבָּן זֶה מִי שֶׁבָּא — **The Torah also imposed** the obligation of **this offering** עַל שִׁפְחָה חֲרוּפָה — **on one who cohabited with a betrothed maidservant,**[26] וּכְמוֹ שֶׁכָּתוּב בְּסֵדֶר קְדֹשִׁים תִּהְיוּ — **as is written in** *Parashas Kedoshim*, שֶׁנֶּאֱמַר — **for it is stated** there (*Leviticus* 19:20-21): וְאִישׁ כִּי יִשְׁכַּב אֶת אִשָּׁה וְגוֹ׳ וְהִוא שִׁפְחָה נֶחֱרֶפֶת לְאִישׁ וְהָפְדֵּה לֹא נִפְדָּתָה וְגוֹ׳ בִּקֹּרֶת תִּהְיֶה וְגוֹ׳ — *If a man lies with a woman, etc., and she is a maidservant who has been designated for another man, and redeemed she was not redeemed, etc., there shall be an investigation, etc.* וְהֵבִיא מִן — אֶת אֲשָׁמוֹ וְגוֹ׳ אֵיל אָשָׁם — **He shall bring his asham offering, etc., a ram asham offering.** וְזֶה מִן הַבָּאִים בֵּין עַל שׁוֹגֵג בֵּין עַל מֵזִיד — **This** *asham* **is among those** *asham* **offerings that are brought for both an inadvertent and a deliberate violation.**[27]

Chinuch sums up the definite-*asham* offerings:

נִמְצְאוּ בֵּין כֻּלָּן הָאֲשָׁמוֹת וַדָּאוֹת חֲמִשָּׁה — **It emerges,** then, that **there are five definite** *ashamos* **in total,** וְכֵן מָנוּ אוֹתָן חֲכָמִים זִכְרוֹנָם לִבְרָכָה בַּמִּשְׁנָה — **and the Sages, of blessed memory, reckoned them as such in the Mishnah** (*Zevachim* 54b), שֶׁאָמְרוּ — **for they stated:** אֵלּוּ הֵן אֲשָׁמוֹת —

---

### NOTES

imposed this obligation of a definite-asham offering on a nazir who had become impure by contact with a corpse. This asham obligation, too, applies whether he became impure deliberately or inadvertently.

23. Mishnah, *Kereisos* 9a. The Gemara there adds that, in fact, he is liable to an *asham* even if the *tumah* was *unavoidable* (אונס), for example, the *nazir* was contaminated with corpse-*tumah* against his will by an idolater (see *Rambam, Hil. Nezirus* 6:3).

24. A *metzora* is a person who has contracted *tzaraas* (see Mitzvah 169), which renders him *tamei*. Once he is cured, he must undergo a purification process lasting seven days, as described in *Leviticus* 14:2-9. On the eighth day, he brings a group of offerings, the first of which is an *asham*. (ibid. 14:10-20).

25. *Tzaraas*, for which the *metzora's asham* is brought, afflicts the person involuntarily. [To be sure, the *tzaraas* afflicted the *metzora* due to his misconduct and lack of restraint with regard various sins, e.g., *lashon hara*, disparaging speech (see *Arachin* 16a; see also Mitzvah 169 and 171), which is the reason he requires atonement with an *asham* (see Mitzvah 176). Nevertheless, it is the *state* of *tzaraas* that actually makes the *metzora* liable to the *asham*, and that is beyond his control.]

26. Chinuch will later discuss the matter of the betrothed maidservant at length.

27. Mishnah, *Kereisos* 9a. As regards this *asham*, an inadvertent transgression means that the man did not know she was a betrothed maidservant.

## VAYIKRA / MITZVAH 129: THE OBLIGATION OF THE DEFINITE-ASHAM OFFERING

א. אֲשַׁם גְּזֵלוֹת ב. אֲשַׁם מְעִילוֹת ג. אֲשַׁם שִׁפְחָה חֲרוּפָה ד. אֲשַׁם נָזִיר ה. אֲשַׁם מְצֹרָע. וְאָשָׁם תָּלוּי הַנִּמְנֶה שָׁם, שְׁמוֹ עָלָיו שֶׁאֵינוֹ מִמִּין הָאֲשָׁמוֹת וַדָּאוֹת.[28]

וּמֵאֵלּוּ הַחֲמִשָּׁה, שְׁלֹשָׁה מֵהֶן בָּאִין בֵּין עַל שׁוֹגֵג בֵּין עַל מֵזִיד, וְהֵן אֲשַׁם גְּזֵלוֹת, אֲשַׁם שִׁפְחָה חֲרוּפָה, אֲשַׁם נָזִיר, וְאֶחָד מֵהֶן אֵינוֹ בָא אֶלָּא עַל שׁוֹגֵג וְלֹא עַל מֵזִיד וְהוּא אֲשַׁם מְעִילוֹת, וְהַחֲמִישִׁי שֶׁהוּא אֲשַׁם מְצֹרָע אֵין נוֹפֵל בּוֹ לְשׁוֹן שְׁגָגָה וְזָדוֹן כְּמוֹ שֶׁאָמַרְנוּ.

וְשִׁפְחָה חֲרוּפָה, הוֹאִיל וַאֲתָא לְיָדָן נֵימָא בַּהּ מִלְּתָא, וְאַף עַל פִּי שֶׁאֵינוֹ בַּסֵּדֶר הַזֶּה, לְפִי שֶׁאֵינָהּ מֵחֶשְׁבּוֹן הַמִּצְוֹת אֵין לִי מָקוֹם לְדַבֵּר בָּהּ כִּי אִם כָּאן.[29]

פֵּרוּשׁ חֲרוּפָה, מְיֻעֶדֶת, כְּלוֹמַר מְקֻדֶּשֶׁת.[30] וְאָמְרוּ בַּגְּמָרָא בְּרֵישׁ פֶּרֶק רִאשׁוֹן בְּקִדּוּשִׁין

---

**These are the *asham* offerings:** א. אֲשַׁם גְּזֵלוֹת ב. אֲשַׁם מְעִילוֹת ג. אֲשַׁם שִׁפְחָה חֲרוּפָה ד. אֲשַׁם נָזִיר ה. אֲשַׁם מְצֹרָע — (1) the *asham* of robbery, (2) the *asham* of *me'ilah*, (3) the *asham* of the betrothed maidservant, (4) the *nazir's asham*, (5) the *metzora's asham*. וְאָשָׁם תָּלוּי הַנִּמְנֶה שָׁם — With respect to **the "pending *asham*"** listed in the Mishnah **there** among the *ashamos*, שְׁמוֹ עָלָיו שֶׁאֵינוֹ מִמִּין הָאֲשָׁמוֹת וַדָּאוֹת — it is not included in this mitzvah, as **its name** (the "pending" *asham*) attests **to it that** while it is an *asham* offering, **it is not in the category of "definite" *ashamos*;**[28] it is, rather, reckoned as a separate mitzvah (Mitzvah 128). Thus, we remain with five definite *ashamos* in total. וּמֵאֵלּוּ הַחֲמִשָּׁה — **Of these five,** שְׁלֹשָׁה מֵהֶן בָּאִין בֵּין עַל שׁוֹגֵג בֵּין עַל מֵזִיד — **three are brought whether** the violation was **inadvertent or deliberate;** וְהֵן אֲשַׁם גְּזֵלוֹת אֲשַׁם שִׁפְחָה חֲרוּפָה אֲשַׁם נָזִיר — namely, the *asham* of robbery, the *asham* of the betrothed maidservant, and the *nazir's asham*; וְאֶחָד מֵהֶן אֵינוֹ בָא אֶלָּא עַל שׁוֹגֵג וְלֹא עַל מֵזִיד — **one of them is brought only for** an **inadvertent** violation **but not for** a **deliberate** violation, וְהוּא אֲשַׁם מְעִילוֹת — namely, **the *asham* of *me'ilah*;** וְהַחֲמִישִׁי שֶׁהוּא אֲשַׁם מְצֹרָע — and as for **the fifth, which is the *metzora's asham*,** אֵין נוֹפֵל בּוֹ לְשׁוֹן שְׁגָגָה וְזָדוֹן — the concept expressed by the terms inadvertent and deliberate does not apply to it, כְּמוֹ שֶׁאָמַרְנוּ — as we have stated above.

Having set forth the mitzvah and its applications, Chinuch digresses to discuss the subject of the betrothed maidservant:

וְשִׁפְחָה חֲרוּפָה — With regard to the matter of **the betrothed maidservant,** הוֹאִיל וַאֲתָא לְיָדָן נֵימָא בַּהּ מִלְּתָא — since it has come our way, let us say something about it. וְאַף עַל פִּי שֶׁאֵינוֹ בַּסֵּדֶר הַזֶּה — **Although it is not** discussed by Scripture **in this *Sidra*** (*Parashas Vayikra*), but rather in *Parashas Kedoshim* (*Leviticus* 19:20-22), לְפִי שֶׁאֵינָהּ מֵחֶשְׁבּוֹן הַמִּצְוֹת — **since [the prohibition to cohabit with a betrothed maidservant] is not** independently reckoned **in the count of the mitzvos,** אֵין לִי מָקוֹם לְדַבֵּר בָּהּ כִּי אִם כָּאן — **I have no** other **place to discuss it but here.**[29]

Chinuch begins by explaining the term חֲרוּפָה, *charufah* (as in "שִׁפְחָה חֲרוּפָה", *betrothed maidservant*): פֵּרוּשׁ חֲרוּפָה מְיֻעֶדֶת — **The meaning of *charufah* is "designated";** כְּלוֹמַר מְקֻדֶּשֶׁת — **that is to say, "betrothed."**[30] וְאָמְרוּ בַּגְּמָרָא בְּרֵישׁ פֶּרֶק רִאשׁוֹן בְּקִדּוּשִׁין — Indeed, **[the Sages] stated in the**

---

### NOTES

28. After listing the five *ashamos* enumerated by Chinuch, the Mishnah (there) adds a sixth *asham*, namely, אָשָׁם תָּלוּי, the "pending" *asham*. Chinuch explains that while it belongs in the Mishnah's list [under the Mishnah's general heading, *these are the "asham offerings"*] it is not included in this mitzvah (see also introduction).

29. Cohabiting with a betrothed maidservant obviously involves a transgression of a mitzvah-prohibition, since the Torah prescribes penalties to both the man and the woman, and "the Torah does not punish without providing a prohibition" (see Mitzvah 69). However, there is no *specific* prohibition against having relations with a betrothed maidservant; rather it falls under the province of a more general mitzvah-prohibition. [Some identify this as the prohibition (*Deuteronomy* 23:18): וְלֹא יִהְיֶה קָדֵשׁ מִבְּנֵי יִשְׂרָאֵל, *and there shall not be a promiscuous man among the Children of Israel* (*Onkelos* ad loc.; *Rashi* to *Yevamos* 55a ד"ה שפחה חייבי לאוין היא; cf. Chinuch, Mitzvah 570; see further, *Rambam*, *Hil. Isurei Biah* 12:11-13 with *Tzafnas Pane'ach*, *Tinyana* p. 95; *Ramban* to *Leviticus* 18:20).] Since there is no mitzvah that specifically pertains to the betrothed maidservant, Chinuch chooses to discuss it here.

30. We have translated the term מְקֻדֶּשֶׁת, *mekudeshes*, as "betrothed" for lack of a better equivalent English term. In truth, *kiddushin* (the noun form of

(ו' ע"א), שֶׁכֵּן בִּיהוּדָה קוֹרִין לַאֲרוּסָה חֲרוּפָה. וּבְשִׁפְחָה כְּנַעֲנִית הַכָּתוּב מְדַבֵּר[31] שֶׁהִיא חֶצְיָהּ שִׁפְחָה וְחֶצְיָהּ בַּת חוֹרִין[32], וְזֶהוּ שֶׁכָּתוּב בָּהּ וְהָפְדֵּה לֹא נִפְדָּתָה, כְּלוֹמַר פְּדוּיָה וְאֵינָהּ פְּדוּיָה[33], וּכְגוֹן שֶׁפָּרְעָה לַאֲדוֹנֶיהָ חֲצִי דָמֶיהָ וְנִתְקַדְּשָׁה לְעֶבֶד עִבְרִי אוֹ לְיִשְׂרָאֵל אַחֵר[34], בְּזוֹ נֶאֱמַר שֶׁאִם בָּא עָלֶיהָ אָדָם אַחֵר בֵּין בְּשׁוֹגֵג בֵּין בְּמֵזִיד[35] שֶׁחַיָּב לְהָבִיא קָרְבָּן זֶה שֶׁהוּא נִקְרָא אָשָׁם, וְהוּא אַיִל שָׁוֶה מִשְׁתֵּי סְלָעִים וּלְמַעְלָה.

---

**Gemara at the beginning of the first chapter of** Tractate ***Kiddushin*** (6a) that if a man said to a woman, "Behold, you are my *charufah*," she is thereby betrothed to him, שֶׁכֵּן בִּיהוּדָה קוֹרִין לַאֲרוּסָה חֲרוּפָה — ***for in*** the land of ***Judea they refer to the betrothed woman as a "charufah"*** — an indication that the term "*charufah*" denotes betrothed. וּבְשִׁפְחָה כְּנַעֲנִית הַכָּתוּב מְדַבֵּר — Now, in the passage of the שִׁפְחָה חֲרוּפָה, **Scripture is speaking of a Canaanite maidservant**[31] שֶׁהִיא חֶצְיָהּ שִׁפְחָה וְחֶצְיָהּ בַּת חוֹרִין — **who has become half-maidservant and half-free.**[32] וְזֶהוּ שֶׁכָּתוּב בָּהּ "וְהָפְדֵּה לֹא נִפְדָּתָה" — **This is** the meaning of what is written regarding her (*Leviticus* 19:20): **and redeemed, she was not redeemed,** כְּלוֹמַר פְּדוּיָה וְאֵינָהּ פְּדוּיָה — **that is to say,** that she is **both redeemed and not redeemed;**[33] וּכְגוֹן שֶׁפָּרְעָה לַאֲדוֹנֶיהָ חֲצִי דָמֶיהָ — **and** this can be the case where **for example, she paid her master half of her value** toward redemption from bondage, which renders half of her a free woman, while the other half remains enslaved. וְנִתְקַדְּשָׁה לְעֶבֶד עִבְרִי אוֹ לְיִשְׂרָאֵל אַחֵר — **[This half-maidservant] became betrothed to a Hebrew bondservant or to any free Jew.**[34] בְּזוֹ נֶאֱמַר — **Regarding this woman, it is stated** in the Torah (ibid vs. 20-22) שֶׁאִם בָּא עָלֶיהָ אָדָם אַחֵר — **that if another man cohabits with her** — בֵּין בְּשׁוֹגֵג בֵּין בְּמֵזִיד — **whether inadvertently or deliberately**[35] — שֶׁחַיָּב לְהָבִיא קָרְבָּן זֶה שֶׁהוּא נִקְרָא אָשָׁם — **he is obligated to bring this offering, namely, an *asham*,** וְהוּא אַיִל שָׁוֶה מִשְׁתֵּי סְלָעִים וּלְמַעְלָה — **which is a ram worth two *selaim* or more.**

---

## NOTES

*mekudeshes*) refers to a stage where — in most respects — the couple is considered legally married. The wife may not have intimate relations with any other man, and the bond can be dissolved only by a *get*, Jewish divorce (see General Introduction to Schottenstein ed. of Tractate *Kiddushin*).

31. A "Canaanite maidservant" refers to a slavewoman who was purchased by a Jew. In order to ensure that she will conform to the lifestyle of a Jewish home, she must give up idol worship and undergo a quasi-conversion (see Mitzvah 347), on the basis of which she is obligated to keep the mitzvos of the Torah, but may not marry or have relations with a Jew. However, her master may arrange for his Hebrew bondservant [עֶבֶד עִבְרִי; see Mitzvah 42] to live with her, though the Hebrew servant may not legally marry her, as her status as Canaanite maidservant precludes legal matrimony.

32. Chinuch will shortly explain how it is possible for a woman to be "half free." In any event, she is partly owned by a master, and partly in her own jurisdiction. Monetarily, the partnership of the half-maidservant and master is administered by dividing the rights to her labor according to time; thus, she serves the master one day and works for herself the next (*Rambam, Hil. Avadim* 7:7; see further, *Shulchan Aruch, Yoreh Deah* 267:62; *Minchas Chinuch* 347:3 ד"ה ובעבד זה).

The partial emancipation affects her status with regard to matrimony. Ordinarily, when a Canaanite maidservant is emancipated, she automatically becomes a full-fledged Jewess and can be married to a Jew. In the case of partial emancipation, the woman takes on a unique status where, legally speaking, she is "half-maidservant and half-freewoman." In this state, too, she can effectively be acquired in matrimony on account of her free half (see *Gittin* 43a).

33. The verse seems to be a contradiction in terms; it states that the maidservant was redeemed and then states that she was not. Chinuch explains that both are true: she was redeemed, but not fully redeemed. [This interpretation of the verse follows the opinion of R' Akiva cited by the Gemara, *Kereisos* 11a. Another interpretation is cited there as well. Chinuch follows *Rambam* (*Hil. Ishus* 4:17 and *Isurei Biah* 3:13) in accepting R' Akiva's opinion.]

34. R' Akiva, in *Kereisos* 11a, specifies that she was betrothed to a Hebrew bondservant, but *Rashi* (*Gittin* 43a ד"ה ואם לחשך) comments that, in fact, betrothal to any Jew effectively renders her "betrothed" (cf. *Rambam, Commentary to the Mishnah, Kereisos* 2:5; for discussion, see note 16 to *Minchas Chinuch*, Mechon Yerushalayim edition).

35. See above, note 27.

## 499 □ VAYIKRA / MITZVAH 129: THE OBLIGATION OF THE DEFINITE-ASHAM OFFERING

וּמִפְּנֵי זֶה מַסְפִּיק קָרְבָּן כַּפָּרָה לְמִי שֶׁבָּא עָלֶיהָ, לְפִי שֶׁאֵין קִדּוּשֶׁיהָ קְדוּשִׁין גְּמוּרִים כְּמוֹ אִם הָיְתָה בַּת חוֹרִין, שֶׁאֵלּוּ בְּבַת חוֹרִין מְקֻדֶּשֶׁת חִיּוּב מִיתָה יֵשׁ לְמִי שֶׁבָּא עָלֶיהָ, אֲבָל בָּזוֹ אֵין קִדּוּשֶׁיהָ גְּמוּרִין מֵחֲמַת חֲצִי שִׁפְחוּת שֶׁבָּהּ עֲדַיִן, וּלְפִיכָךְ מַסְפִּיק קָרְבָּן לְכַפָּרָה אֶל הַנִּכְשָׁל בָּהּ.[36]

גַּם הֵקֵלָּה הַתּוֹרָה בְּבִיאָתָהּ לִפְטֹר בְּקָרְבָּן גַּם הַמֵּזִיד, מַה שֶּׁאֵין דֶּרֶךְ בִּשְׁאָר זְדוֹנוֹת לְפָטְרָן בְּקָרְבָּן, לְפִי שֶׁהָאִשָּׁה הַשִּׁפְחָה אַף עַל פִּי שֶׁחֶצְיָהּ פְּדוּיָה, קַלָּה הִיא בְּעֵינֵי כָּל אָדָם, וְהַכִּשָּׁלוֹן קָרוֹב מְאֹד עָלֶיהָ לְפִי שֶׁאֵין לֵב הֶהָמוֹן חוֹשֵׁב בִּיאָתָהּ לְחֵטְא גָּדוֹל.[37] וְעַל כֵּן יוּסַר עֲוֹנָם וְחַטָּאתָם יְכֻפָּר עִם הַקָּרְבָּן,[38] וּכְעֵין מַה שֶּׁאָמְרוּ זִכְרוֹנָם לִבְרָכָה בְּעִנְיָנִים אֲחֵרִים אֶפְשָׁר לָנוּ לוֹמַר בָּזֶה, רַחֲמָנָא לִבָּא בָּעֵי.[39]

---

Chinuch explains why one does not incur the death penalty for deliberately cohabiting with the betrothed Canaanite maidservant, as he would if he cohabited with a betrothed free woman: וּמִפְּנֵי זֶה מַסְפִּיק קָרְבָּן כַּפָּרָה לְמִי שֶׁבָּא עָלֶיהָ — **The reason that an atonement offering is sufficient to atone for one who cohabits with her** לְפִי שֶׁאֵין קִדּוּשֶׁיהָ קְדוּשִׁין גְּמוּרִים כְּמוֹ אִם הָיְתָה בַּת חוֹרִין — **is because her betrothal is not as complete as it would be if she were free.** שֶׁאֵלּוּ בְּבַת חוֹרִין מְקֻדֶּשֶׁת — **For with regard to a betrothed free woman,** חִיּוּב מִיתָה יֵשׁ לְמִי שֶׁבָּא עָלֶיהָ — **one who cohabits with her** (other than the man to whom she is betrothed) **is liable to death.** אֲבָל בָּזוֹ אֵין קִדּוּשֶׁיהָ גְּמוּרִין — **But with regard to this [woman], her betrothal is not** a **complete** one, מֵחֲמַת חֲצִי שִׁפְחוּת שֶׁבָּהּ עֲדַיִן — **on account of her still-enslaved half,** וּלְפִיכָךְ מַסְפִּיק קָרְבָּן לְכַפָּרָה אֶל הַנִּכְשָׁל בָּהּ — **and an offering is therefore sufficient to atone for one who stumbles** and sins **with her.**[36]

Generally, a deliberate transgression of a mitzvah-prohibition that is not punishable by death carries the punishment of *malkus* (lashes) instead. Chinuch explains why one who deliberately sins with a betrothed Canaanite maidservant incurs only liability to an *asham*: גַּם הֵקֵלָּה הַתּוֹרָה בְּבִיאָתָהּ — **The Torah was further lenient with regard to cohabiting with [the betrothed maidservant]** לִפְטֹר בְּקָרְבָּן גַּם הַמֵּזִיד — **to discharge even a deliberate sinner with an offering,** מַה שֶּׁאֵין דֶּרֶךְ בִּשְׁאָר זְדוֹנוֹת לְפָטְרָן בְּקָרְבָּן — **which is not the norm in** the case of **other deliberate violations** that are not punishable by death, **to discharge [the violators] with** merely **an offering.** לְפִי שֶׁהָאִשָּׁה הַשִּׁפְחָה — **This is because the maidservant,** אַף עַל פִּי שֶׁחֶצְיָהּ פְּדוּיָה — **although she is half-redeemed,** קַלָּה הִיא בְּעֵינֵי כָּל אָדָם — **is regarded lightly in people's eyes,** וְהַכִּשָּׁלוֹן קָרוֹב מְאֹד עָלֶיהָ — **and** people are **very prone to stumble** and sin **with her,** לְפִי שֶׁאֵין לֵב הֶהָמוֹן חוֹשֵׁב בִּיאָתָהּ לְחֵטְא גָּדוֹל — **because the masses do not consider cohabitation with her to be a great sin.**[37] וְעַל כֵּן יוּסַר עֲוֹנָם וְחַטָּאתָם יְכֻפָּר עִם הַקָּרְבָּן — **For this** reason **their iniquity will be taken away and their sin shall be atoned for**[38] **with the offering.** וּכְעֵין מַה שֶּׁאָמְרוּ זִכְרוֹנָם לִבְרָכָה בְּעִנְיָנִים אֲחֵרִים — **Similar to that which [the Sages], of blessed memory, said regarding other matters,** אֶפְשָׁר לָנוּ לוֹמַר בָּזֶה — **we can perhaps say about this** matter: "רַחֲמָנָא לִבָּא בָּעֵי" — **The Merciful One seeks the heart.**[39]

---

### NOTES

36. This leniency, which is due to the incomplete nature of the betrothal, applies to the maidservant as well as the man, for she, too, is not liable to death (though she does not achieve atonement through an offering, as Chinuch will explain).

37. Since a Canaanite maidservant cannot be legally married, the unlearned masses have a mistaken perception of her as someone who is not bound by matrimony — even after she has become half free.

38. Stylistic paraphrase of *Isaiah* 6:7.

39. *Sanhedrin* 106b. [The text in that Gemara actually reads הַקָּדוֹשׁ בָּרוּךְ הוּא לִבָּא בָּעֵי, *the Holy One, blessed is He, seeks the heart*; the term רַחֲמָנָא, *the Merciful One*, appears in *Rashi* ad loc. [ד"ה רבותא]. Hashem evaluates people's actions based on their thoughts and intentions. So, for instance, a small act that is done with utmost sincerity is superior in His eyes to a very impressive act that is done with ulterior motives. Although this idea is generally expressed with regard to good deeds and their reward, Chinuch suggests that it may apply

וּמִכָּל מָקוֹם הַשִּׁפְחָה חַיֶּבֶת מַלְקוּת, שֶׁאֵין לוֹמַר בָּהּ שֶׁתִּהְיֶה קַלָּה בְּעֵינֶיהָ וְשֶׁמִּפְּנֵי כֵן לֹא הִשְׁגִּיחָה בְּעַצְמָהּ לִזְנוֹת. וּמִיהוּ גַּם הִיא לֹא תִּתְחַיֵּב מַלְקוּת אֶלָּא כְּשֶׁנִּבְעֲלָה כְּדַרְכָּהּ[40], וְהִיא גְּדוֹלָה וּמְזִידָה[41]. וְעָלֶיהָ נֶאֱמַר (שם) בִּקֹּרֶת תִּהְיֶה[42], כְּמוֹ שֶׁדָּרְשׁוּ רַבּוֹתֵינוּ זִכְרוֹנָם לִבְרָכָה, בְּקִרְאֵי תְּהֵא, כְּלוֹמַר בְּמַלְקוּת. וְאָמְרוּ רַבּוֹתֵינוּ זִכְרוֹנָם לִבְרָכָה (כריתות י"א ע"א), הִיא לוֹקָה וְלֹא הוּא. וּמִפְּנֵי כֵן הוֹצִיא הַכָּתוּב הַמַּלְקוּת בְּלָשׁוֹן זֶה שֶׁל קְרִיָּה, לְפִי שֶׁהָיוּ קוֹרְאִים עַל הַלּוֹקֶה פְּסוּקִים שֶׁל תּוֹכַחַת בְּעוֹד שֶׁהָיוּ מַלְקִין אוֹתוֹ, כְּדֵי שֶׁיִּשְׁמַע וְיִקַּח מוּסָר, וְהֵם "וְהִפְלָא ה' וְגוֹ'" (דברים כ"ח, נ"ט)[43].

---

This degree of leniency does not apply to the maidservant herself: וּמִכָּל מָקוֹם הַשִּׁפְחָה חַיֶּבֶת מַלְקוּת — **The maidservant herself, though, is liable to** *malkus* (lashes), and cannot discharge herself with an offering alone, שֶׁאֵין לוֹמַר בָּהּ שֶׁתִּהְיֶה קַלָּה בְּעֵינֶיהָ — **because it cannot be said of her that she would regard herself lightly,** וְשֶׁמִּפְּנֵי כֵן לֹא הִשְׁגִּיחָה בְּעַצְמָהּ לִזְנוֹת — **and that, as a result, she was not careful with herself** with regard **to committing adultery.** וּמִיהוּ גַּם הִיא לֹא תִּתְחַיֵּב מַלְקוּת אֶלָּא כְּשֶׁנִּבְעֲלָה כְּדַרְכָּהּ — **However, she, too, becomes liable to** *malkus* **only if she had regular relations** with this man,[40] וְהִיא גְּדוֹלָה וּמְזִידָה — **and** provided that **she is an adult and** that she commits the sin **deliberately.**[41]

Chinuch explains the source for the maidservant's liability to *malkus*, as well as the man's exemption from it: וְעָלֶיהָ נֶאֱמַר — We know that the maidservant is liable to *malkus* [while the man is not] since **regarding her it is stated** (*Leviticus* 19:20): בִּקֹּרֶת תִּהְיֶה — **she shall be "bikkores,"**[42] כְּמוֹ שֶׁדָּרְשׁוּ רַבּוֹתֵינוּ זִכְרוֹנָם לִבְרָכָה — **in accordance with the exposition of our Sages, of blessed memory,** to interpret this phrase as (*Kereisos* 11a): בְּקִרְאֵי תְּהֵא — **she shall be subject to the** reading of Scriptural verses, כְּלוֹמַר בְּמַלְקוּת — which, as shall be explained, means **to say,** she shall be punished **with** *malkus*. וְאָמְרוּ רַבּוֹתֵינוּ זִכְרוֹנָם לִבְרָכָה — **And our Sages, of blessed memory,** further **stated** (ibid.) הִיא לוֹקָה וְלֹא הוּא — that **only [the maidservant] incurs** *malkus*, **but not [the man who cohabits with her],** for the verse states *"she" shall be subject,* etc., indicating that only the maidservant is liable to *malkus* and not the man.

Chinuch explains how the expression "the reading of Scriptural verses" denotes *malkus*: וּמִפְּנֵי כֵן הוֹצִיא הַכָּתוּב הַמַּלְקוּת בְּלָשׁוֹן זֶה שֶׁל קְרִיָּה — **And the reason that Scripture expressed the punishment of** *malkus* **in this language of "reading" is** לְפִי שֶׁהָיוּ קוֹרְאִים עַל הַלּוֹקֶה פְּסוּקִים שֶׁל תּוֹכַחַת בְּעוֹד שֶׁהָיוּ מַלְקִין אוֹתוֹ — **because** whenever *malkus* were administered **[the judges] would read verses of rebuke to the one receiving the** *malkus* **while they were lashing him,** כְּדֵי שֶׁיִּשְׁמַע וְיִקַּח מוּסָר — **so that he should listen and accept discipline.** וְהֵם "וְהִפְלָא ה' וְגוֹ'" — **[These verses] are** (*Deuteronomy* 28:58-59): *If you will not be careful to perform all the words of this Torah ... Then* **HASHEM will make extraordinary** *your blows, etc.*[43]

---

## NOTES

to wrongdoings, as well. That is, the severity of the punishment partially depends on the measure of defiance in man's heart in committing the sin.

Chinuch expresses this idea at length in Mitzvah 123 (after note 13), where he explains that Hashem, in His infinite mercy, considers the nature of the particular sin and man's predisposition to it when deciding the extent of the punishment.

40. In contrast to "irregular relations" (i.e., sodomy) for which she would not incur *malkus* (see *Kereisos* 11a-b).

41. In accordance with all *malkus* liabilities, which are imposed only on adults and for deliberate violations (*Kesef Mishneh* to Rambam, *Hil. Shegagos* 9:1).

[Whenever the maidservant is exempt from *malkus* (e.g., she was a minor), the man also does not incur an *asham* (*Rambam* ibid. 9:2).]

42. We translated this phrase earlier (at notes 26-27) as *there shall be an investigation,* in accordance with its simple meaning. According to the current exposition, however, it is rendered *she shall be bikkores* [with תִּהְיֶה meaning *she shall be*]. See *Malbim* to the verse for the basis of this exposition.

43. Mishnah, *Makkos* 22b. [Our edition of this Mishnah mentions two additional verses, but *Rambam* (ibid.; *Commentary to the Mishnah, Makkos* 3:14) omits them, suggesting that he had a different edition (*Tos. Yom Tov* to *Makkos* 3:14; *Maharsha* to *Makkos* 22b).]

מִשָּׁרְשֵׁי הַמִּצְוָה, לְבַל יַחֲשֹׁב אָדָם שֶׁאַף עַל פִּי שֶׁעִנְיַן אִסּוּר גְּזֵלַת הַמָּמוֹן נִתָּק לַעֲשֵׂה[44], שֶׁנֶּאֱמַר (ויקרא ה׳, כ״ג) "וְהֵשִׁיב אֶת הַגְּזֵלָה"[45], שֶׁיֵּלֵךְ כָּל אֶחָד וְיִגְזֹל מֵחֲבֵרוֹ מַה שֶּׁיִּרְצֶה וִידַמֶּה בִּלְבָבוֹ לֵאמֹר לִכְשֶׁיִּהְיֶה לוֹ וְיָשִׁיב גְּזֵלָתוֹ יְכֻפַּר עֲוֹנוֹ וְיִטְהַר מִמֶּנּוּ, וַהֲרֵי הוּא כְּאִלּוּ לֹא עָשָׂאוּ מֵעוֹלָם וְיִהְיֶה זֶה פֶּתַח לְעוֹבְרֵי עֲבֵרָה[46], לָכֵן הוֹדִיעָה הַתּוֹרָה שֶׁאַף עִם הַהֲשָׁבָה בְּתוֹסֶפֶת חֹמֶשׁ צָרִיךְ הַקָּרְבָּן לְכַפָּרָה עַל שֶׁחָטָא[47]. וּכְבָר כָּתַבְתִּי לְמַעְלָה בְּעִנְיָן זֶה כִּי מִכָּל מָקוֹם לֹא נִצַּל זֶה שֶׁלֹּא עָבַר עַל רְצוֹן בּוֹרְאוֹ[48],

---

### ⸙ Underlying Purpose of the Mitzvah ⸙

Chinuch now returns to the subject of the mitzvah, namely, the obligation of the definite-*asham* offering. For the remainder of the mitzvah, Chinuch focuses the discussion on the *asham of robbery*, which is the one discussed in this Scriptural passage. [The other definite *ashamos* will obviously differ in some respects]:

מִשָּׁרְשֵׁי הַמִּצְוָה — **Among the underlying purposes of this mitzvah,** specifically with regard to the *asham of robbery,* is לְבַל יַחֲשֹׁב אָדָם — **so that a man should not think,** שֶׁאַף עַל פִּי שֶׁעִנְיַן אִסּוּר גְּזֵלַת הַמָּמוֹן נִתָּק לַעֲשֵׂה — **that since**[44] **the matter of the prohibition against stealing property is remedied by a** mitzvah-**obligation,** שֶׁנֶּאֱמַר "וְהֵשִׁיב אֶת הַגְּזֵלָה" — **as it is stated** (*Leviticus* 5:23): *he shall return the robbed item that he robbed* (Mitzvah 130),[45] שֶׁיֵּלֵךְ כָּל אֶחָד וְיִגְזֹל מֵחֲבֵרוֹ מַה שֶּׁיִּרְצֶה — **anyone can go and steal anything he desires from his fellow man,** וִידַמֶּה בִּלְבָבוֹ לֵאמֹר — **while rationalizing in his heart** לִכְשֶׁיִּהְיֶה לוֹ וְיָשִׁיב גְּזֵלָתוֹ — **that when he will have the means and return that which he had stolen,** יְכֻפַּר עֲוֹנוֹ וְיִטְהַר מִמֶּנּוּ — **his sin will be atoned and he will be absolved of it,** וַהֲרֵי הוּא כְּאִלּוּ לֹא עָשָׂאוּ מֵעוֹלָם — **and it will be as if he had never committed [this sin];** וְיִהְיֶה זֶה פֶּתַח לְעוֹבְרֵי עֲבֵרָה — **this would be a pretext for wrongdoers** to follow their desire to take other people's property.[46] לָכֵן הוֹדִיעָה הַתּוֹרָה — **The Torah therefore let it be known,** שֶׁאַף עִם הַהֲשָׁבָה בְּתוֹסֶפֶת חֹמֶשׁ — **that even with the return** of the stolen object — **including a one-fifth surcharge —** צָרִיךְ הַקָּרְבָּן לְכַפָּרָה עַל שֶׁחָטָא — **one still needs the offering to atone for his having sinned.**[47]

Chinuch emphasizes that even the *asham* goes only so far in atoning for the sin:

וּכְבָר כָּתַבְתִּי לְמַעְלָה בְּעִנְיָן זֶה — **Furthermore, I have written above** (Mitzvah 123) **regarding this matter,** כִּי מִכָּל מָקוֹם לֹא נִצַּל זֶה שֶׁלֹּא עָבַר עַל רְצוֹן בּוֹרְאוֹ — **that** even after the thief brings a sin offering **he is still not cleared** of all wrongdoing, as though **he had not disobeyed the Will of his Creator.**[48]

---

#### NOTES

44. The term שֶׁאַף עַל פִּי literally means, *that "although,"* but this is difficult to understand in the context of Chinuch's words. Our translation, *that "since,"* is under presumption that this was Chinuch's intention. [Possibly, שֶׁאַף עַל פִּי is a copyist's error and the correct text is rather שֶׁלְּפִי.]

45. The mitzvah to return the stolen object described in this verse serves as the remedy for violating the prohibition of stealing (*Makkos* 16a). A prohibition of this type is known as לַאו הַנִּיתָּק לַעֲשֵׂה, *a prohibition that can be remedied through [fulfillment of] an obligation* (see General Introduction, note 14). One does not incur *malkus* for violating a prohibition for which the Torah prescribes a mitzvah as a remedy, because it is as if the Torah stated, "Do not commit this sin, but if you do, then perform this remedy and you will be exempt from punishment" (Rashi to *Makkos* 14b ד"ה כל לא תעשה).

46. A person might come to misconstrue the leniency associated with stealing (see previous note) to mean that as long as he complies with the subsequent mitzvah-obligation and returns what he stole, he will have done nothing wrong.

47. By obligating a thief to bring a sin offering, the Torah makes clear that restitution — even when supplemented with an extra punitive payment — will not excuse the thief's actions. Although the victim has been duly reimbursed, the *sin* of stealing was nonetheless committed, and it requires repentance and atonement.

*Minchas Chinuch* (§26) finds this explanation by Chinuch difficult, because the liability to an *asham* is not incurred for stealing, but rather for *swearing falsely* to deny the theft. If one has not taken an oath to deny his theft, restitution [of the principal alone] *would* indeed be sufficient. Thus, one might still reason that as long as he refrains from an oath, he may steal and return. For defense of Chinuch's explanation, see *Minchas Yitzchak* §14.

48. Some editions read, כִּי מִכָּל מָקוֹם לֹא נִצַּל זֶה שֶׁעָבַר עַל רְצוֹן בּוֹרְאוֹ, *that ... he is still not cleared of all wrongdoing,* **since he disobeyed** *the Will of his Creator.* See also above, Mitzvah 123 note 18.

וַחֲבָל עַל רֵישֵׁיהּ דַּעֲבַר עַל רַעֲוָא דְּמָרֵיהּ שְׁמַיָּא וְלוּ יַקְרִיב כַּמָּה אִימְרִין שַׁמְנִין לַעֲלָתָא[49].

וְשָׁם כָּתַבְתִּי גַּם כֵּן שֶׁהַקָּרְבָּן וְהַקֶּרֶן מְעַכְּבִין אֶת הַכַּפָּרָה וְאֵין הַחֹמֶשׁ מְעַכֵּב. דִּינֵי הַמִּצְוָה, כְּגוֹן בְּאֵי זֶה עִנְיָן יִתְחַיֵּב בִּשְׁבוּעָה זוֹ שֶׁיִּהְיֶה חַיָּב עָלֶיהָ אָשָׁם זֶה וּבְאֵי זֶה עִנְיָן יִהְיֶה פָּטוּר מִמֶּנּוּ. וְעַל אֵי זֶה דֶּרֶךְ יִתְחַיֵּב אֲשָׁמוֹת הַרְבֵּה כְּמִנְיָן חִיּוּב הַשְּׁבוּעוֹת

---

וַחֲבָל עַל רֵישֵׁיהּ — Indeed, **woe on his head**, דַּעֲבַר עַל רַעֲוָא דְּמָרֵיהּ שְׁמַיָּא — **for he disobeyed the Will of the Master of the Heavens**, וְלוּ יַקְרִיב כַּמָּה אִימְרִין שַׁמְנִין לַעֲלָתָא — **and even if he would bring many fat sheep for *olah* offerings,** he would still fall short of rectifying his sin.[49]

Since Chinuch has indicated that the *asham* comes to atone, he points out that this is not the case with the one-fifth surcharge:

וְשָׁם כָּתַבְתִּי גַּם כֵּן — **I have also written there,** i.e., previously (Mitzvah 127), regarding the sin of misappropriating sacred property, and the same would apply here, regarding the sin of denying a monetary obligation under oath, שֶׁהַקָּרְבָּן וְהַקֶּרֶן מְעַכְּבִין אֶת הַכַּפָּרָה — **that the offering and the principal are essential to atonement,** וְאֵין הַחֹמֶשׁ מְעַכֵּב — **but the one-fifth** surcharge, though it must ultimately be paid, **is not essential** to atonement.[50]

## ~ Laws of the Mitzvah ~

דִּינֵי הַמִּצְוָה — **The laws of the mitzvah,** with regard to the *asham of robbery*, **include,** כְּגוֹן בְּאֵי זֶה עִנְיָן יִתְחַיֵּב בִּשְׁבוּעָה זוֹ — **for example,** the guidelines that determine **in which case one would be liable for** taking **this** false **oath** (to deny a monetary obligation); שֶׁיִּהְיֶה חַיָּב עָלֶיהָ אָשָׁם זֶה — that is, in which case **he would be liable to this *asham* on account of [the oath],** וּבְאֵי זֶה עִנְיָן יִהְיֶה פָּטוּר מִמֶּנּוּ — **and in which case** of taking the oath **he would be exempt from [this *asham*].**[51] וְעַל אֵי זֶה דֶּרֶךְ יִתְחַיֵּב אֲשָׁמוֹת הַרְבֵּה — **Also** included in the laws are the guidelines that determine **in what circumstances one incurs liability to many *asham of robbery* offerings,** כְּמִנְיָן חִיּוּב הַשְּׁבוּעוֹת — **commensurate with the number of breaches of oaths** (i.e., false denials under oath)

---

NOTES

49. Although the relevant offering is the *asham*, Chinuch refers to the *olah* offering because one may not bring extra *ashamos* (since mandated offerings may not be brought voluntarily), but one may bring as many *olah* offerings as he wishes, as an *olah* may be brought voluntarily (see Mitzvah 115). As explained in the insight to Mitzvah 115, the *olah*, though not a sin offering per se, has a certain capacity to atone, and was often brought to atone for sins that do not have any other prescribed atonement. It would thus be appropriate for one who already brought an *asham of robbery* to bring an *olah* offering — or a number of such offerings — if he seeks further atonement.

50. Mishnah, *Bava Kamma* 110a; Rambam, *Hil. Gezeilah VaAveidah* 8:13. See Mitzvah 127 note 23.

Returning the stolen object or debt is clearly a prerequisite for atonement (see above, note 9), and the *asham* is the means through which atonement is achieved if the oath was taken. The one-fifth surcharge, however, is merely a penalty that the Torah imposed on the sinner — not as a means of atonement, but as an additional monetary obligation (see *Tos. Yom Tov* to *Bava Kamma* 9:12 ד"ה אין החומש; for discussion, see R' Y. F. Perla, *Sefer HaMitzvos of Rav Saadiah Gaon*, Asei 147-148, Vol. I, pp. 388b-389a; *Kovetz Shiurim* to *Pesachim* §133-134).

51. Briefly, the guidelines are: any false oath (in denial of a claim) that *releases* one from a monetary obligation makes him liable to the *asham*, except for denial of obligations with regard to real property, slaves, or legal documents (see above, note 8). Also, the oath must be one that denies a monetary *obligation* to one's fellow, not a punitive fine. Finally, if the false oath was taken in response to a monetary claim but it does not effectively release the swearer from the monetary obligation, it does not make him liable to an *asham* offering (see *Rambam, Hil. Shevuos* 7:1-3). [For numerous examples of oaths in this latter category, see Mishnah, *Shevuos* 49a-b.]

[Even if one is exempt from the theft *asham*, he may still be liable to the variable-*chatas* offering for taking a false *oath of utterance* [Mitzvah 123] (*Rambam* ibid. 7:2-3,15 and 8:5-6).]

# 503 ☐ VAYIKRA / MITZVAH 129: THE OBLIGATION OF THE DEFINITE-ASHAM OFFERING

וְעַל אֵי זֶה לֹא יִתְחַיֵּב אֶלָּא אָשָׁם אֶחָד. וְיֶתֶר פְּרָטֶיהָ, מְבֹאָרִים בִּכְרֵיתוֹת וּבִשְׁבוּעוֹת.

וְנוֹהֶגֶת מִצְוַת חִיּוּב קָרְבָּן זֶה בִּזְמַן הַבַּיִת בִּזְכָרִים וּנְקֵבוֹת. וְעוֹבֵר עָלֶיהָ וְלֹא הִקְרִיבוֹ, אַף עַל פִּי שֶׁהֵשִׁיב גְּזֵלוֹ לֹא נִתְכַּפֵּר חֶטְאוֹ, וְאוּלָם יֵשׁ לְהַאֲמִין שֶׁאֵין עָנְשׁוֹ חָזָק כְּמוֹ שֶׁהָיָה אִלּוּ לֹא הֵשִׁיב הַמָּמוֹן. וְהַמָּשָׁל עַל זֶה, מִי שֶׁהִכָּה חֲבֵרוֹ וְנִתְחַיֵּב קְנָס לַמֶּלֶךְ, וְנִתְפַּיֵּס עִם הַמֻּכֶּה, וְלֹא נִשְׁאֲרָה עָלָיו רַק תְּבִיעַת הַמֶּלֶךְ.

he had committed, וְעַל אֵי זֶה לֹא יִתְחַיֵּב אֶלָּא אָשָׁם אֶחָד — and in what circumstances **he incurs liability to only one** *asham*.[52]

וְיֶתֶר פְּרָטֶיהָ — These, **and the other details of [this mitzvah]**, מְבֹאָרִים בִּכְרֵיתוֹת וּבִשְׁבוּעוֹת — are **set forth in** Tractate *Kereisos* (9a-b, 10b-11b) **and** Tractate *Shevuos* (36b-38b, 49a-b).[53]

## ☞ Applicability of the Mitzvah ☜

וְנוֹהֶגֶת מִצְוַת חִיּוּב קָרְבָּן זֶה — **The mitzvah constituting the obligation to bring this offering** of the definite *asham*, including the *asham of robbery*, **applies** בִּזְמַן הַבַּיִת — **in the time of the Temple**,[54] בִּזְכָרִים וּנְקֵבוֹת — and is applicable **to both men and women**.[55]

וְעוֹבֵר עָלֶיהָ וְלֹא הִקְרִיבוֹ — **With respect to one who transgresses [this mitzvah] and does not bring [the** *asham***]** when he is required to do so, אַף עַל פִּי שֶׁהֵשִׁיב גְּזֵלוֹ — **even if he returned that which he had stolen,** לֹא נִתְכַּפֵּר חֶטְאוֹ — **his sin** of swearing falsely **is not atoned for**.[56] וְאוּלָם יֵשׁ לְהַאֲמִין שֶׁאֵין עָנְשׁוֹ חָזָק כְּמוֹ שֶׁהָיָה אִלּוּ לֹא הֵשִׁיב — **However, there is** reason **to believe** הַמָּמוֹן — **that his punishment** at the hands of Heaven for the unexpiated sin **will not be** as **severe as it would be if he had not returned the** stolen **property.** וְהַמָּשָׁל עַל זֶה — **An analogy for this** would be מִי שֶׁהִכָּה חֲבֵרוֹ וְנִתְחַיֵּב קְנָס לַמֶּלֶךְ — a case of **one who struck his fellow man and was ordered to pay a fine to the king,** וְנִתְפַּיֵּס עִם הַמֻּכֶּה — **but** subsequently **he reconciled with the person who was hit,** וְלֹא נִשְׁאֲרָה עָלָיו רַק תְּבִיעַת הַמֶּלֶךְ — **and all that remained for him** to settle **was the king's claim** to the fine.[57]

---

### NOTES

52. See *Rambam* ibid. 7:9-14, where this is explained at length.

53. See also *Bava Kamma* 103a-111a. The laws of the definite-*asham* are codified in *Rambam, Hil. Shegagos* Ch. 9. [The specific laws of the *asham of robbery* are codified in *Hil. Gezeilah VaAveidah* Chs. 7-8 and *Hil. Shevuos* Chs. 7-8; of the *asham of me'ilah* in *Hil. Me'ilah* 1:3-6; of the *asham of the betrothed maidservant* in *Hil. Isurei Biah* 3:13-17; of the *nazir's asham* in *Hil. Nezirus* 6:11-12 and 10:8; and of the *metzora's asham* in *Hil. Mechusrei Kapparah* 4:2.]

54. For discussion on the applicability of the "one-fifth" surcharge nowadays, see Insight.

55. This is in accordance with the general rule pertaining to mitzvah-obligations that are not time-specific. [In contrast to the *chatas* offering, which varies for a king (*Nasi*) and an anointed Kohen (see end of mitzvah 120), the laws of the definite-*asham* apply to everyone equally (*Rambam, Hil. Shegagos* 9:10).]

56. He has also violated a mitzvah-obligation to bring the *asham* (similar to Mitzvos 121, 123, and 127; see Mitzvah 121 note 18).

57. The purpose of the king's fine was not to compensate the victim (as the fine was to be paid to the king), but to punish the attacker for breaking the law; reconciling with the victim, therefore, does not release the attacker from the fine. Nevertheless, it does rectify the crime to some degree, since civil harmony has been restored. The same is true for one who has made restitution to the person he had robbed, but has not brought an *asham* to atone for the sin. Since the *act* of stealing and its denial under oath are a defiance of Hashem's authority, as Chinuch has stated above, the sin is not expiated by restitution alone and requires atonement. However, some rectification has been made by returning the theft, and the punishment will thus be mitigated.

---

☙ **Insight: Contemporary Application of the Chomesh Payment**

Chinuch writes that the *asham* obligation of one who falsely denies a monetary claim under oath is accompanied by an obligation upon the penitent to return the principal to the claimant, along with an additional payment of one-fifth, i.e., a *chomesh*. At the end of the mitzvah, Chinuch writes

that the *asham* obligation applies only when the *Beis HaMikdash* is standing, but he does not address whether the other monetary obligations also apply only when the *Beis HaMikdash* is standing or whether they are applicable even today. With regard to the principal, there is no question, since that money was genuinely owed to the claimant from the outset, regardless of any false oath or denial. The question arises, however, with regard to the *chomesh* obligation: Today, in the absence of the *Beis HaMikdash*, if one would falsely deny a monetary claim under oath, would it suffice for him to simply pay back the principal, or would he be required to also pay the additional *chomesh* payment?

*Minchas Chinuch* (§9) cites *Rosh* (Bava Kamma 9:24), who writes simply that neither the *asham* offering nor the *chomesh* are applicable nowadays. *Minchas Chinuch*, however, is at a loss to explain this ruling. Today's penitent, *Minchas Chinuch* argues, is not actually exempt from *any* part of the obligation, whether the *asham* or the money. It is just that for lack of a *Beis HaMikdash* he is unable to fulfill his obligation to bring the *asham* offering. Why should the fact that he is prevented from carrying out one obligation (the *asham* offering) exempt him from the other obligation (the *chomesh*), which he *can* carry out? [Indeed, *She'iltos, Parashas Nasso* §119, as understood by *Haamek Davar*, maintains that the *chomesh* obligation is fully in force even nowadays. See also *Yeshuos Yisrael* in *Ein Mishpat, Choshen Mishpat* 1:3.]

Nevertheless, many authorities share the view of *Rosh* that there is no obligation to pay the *chomesh* nowadays (*Rashi, Bava Kamma* 63b ד"ה הודה מעצמו as per *Avnei Nezer, Choshen Mishpat* 84; *Yam Shel Shlomo, Bava Kamma* 9:34; *Sma, Choshen Mishpat* 367:11). *Avnei Nezer* (ibid.) explains the reason for the exemption according to these authorities as follows: The *asham* offering and the *chomesh* each form one part of the overall atonement that the penitent is obligated to obtain for his sin. If the penitent cannot achieve atonement for whatever reason, an obligation for either of these actions does not exist. Since, in point of fact, a penitent cannot today obtain his atonement for lack of ability to bring his offering, there is no obligation to give the *chomesh* either. One part of the atonement without the other does not fulfill the general obligation of achieving atonement, and a half-atonement is simply not required. [See *Avnei Nezer* there for a lengthy discussion of this point. *Minchas Chinuch*, however, disagrees with the characterization of the *chomesh* as a part of the atonement process; see there.]

Another approach to this issue is offered by *Avi Ezri* (Hil. Gezeilah VaAveidah 7:1). In his view, one who falsely denies a monetary obligation under oath nowadays is *inherently* exempt from either obligation, not merely for lack of means to fulfill them. The reason for this is based upon the legal definition of a monetary "denial," and the authority of today's *beis din* in collecting monetary obligations.

The authority of our *batei din* (courts) is limited by the fact that the judges are not *semuchin*, i.e., they did not receive the special *semichah* ordination that completely authorizes them as judges. As Chinuch explains in Mitzvah 491, the original *semichah* was transmitted from one generation to the next in an unbroken chain from the time of Moses. By Biblical law, judgment may be imposed only by a court composed of judges who have received this *semichah*. Since the chain of *semichah* has been broken, the *beis din* of today lacks this authority. Nevertheless, in certain areas of law, the Sages granted, by Rabbinic authority, an allowance for *batei din* to adjudicate despite the lack of *semichah* (see, for example, Chinuch above, Mitzvah 49).

Now, we have learned (see Chinuch at notes 7-8) that the obligation of an *asham* is incurred only for a false denial under oath that exonerates the defendant from paying, meaning that if he had admitted the truth of the claim he would have been obligated to pay. The same holds true regarding the *chomesh* obligation. *Avi Ezri* suggests that, according to *Rosh* and those who share his view, there is another criterion: It must be a denial that exonerates the defendant from having payment *enforced* by the court. In a situation where if he had admitted to the claim he would have been legally liable but could not be *forced* to pay, his denial under oath does not obligate him to bring an *asham* or to pay a *chomesh*. The reason is simple: In such a case, the denial accomplishes nothing at all. The actual debt existed before the claim was advanced and remains afterward despite the false denial, and both the claimant and denier know it. *Beis din*, for its part, could not have enforced payment in any event, so *legally* the denial does not make any difference. If, however, the denial involves a potentially *enforceable* claim, it can trigger the *asham* and *chomesh* obligations, because

it does have an impact: had the defendant admitted the truth, *beis din* could have collected the money from him against his will, and now that he denied it — causing *beis din* to view the debt as questionable — they are unable to do so. Hence, it is only a false denial of an enforceable claim that brings on these obligations.

Nowadays, *beis din* does not have Biblical authority to forcibly impose payment. From a Biblical standpoint, then, what has one accomplished when he falsely denies such obligations? The denial has no impact on the actual debt, which exists regardless of the defendant's lie, nor does it preclude *beis din* from enforcing payment, since they could not have done so even if he had admitted the truth. Since the denial has no legal ramification on the Biblical level, it is not a denial for which the Torah imposes the *asham* and *chomesh* obligations.

Now, on the practical level, the denial does have an impact, for since the Sages authorized *beis din* to enforce basic monetary obligations, a false denial prevents them from forcibly collecting payment. But since the denial has no impact on the *Biblical* level, it will not trigger a Biblical *chomesh* obligation. The Sages, for their part, did not impose a Rabbinic obligation of *chomesh*. When they authorized *beis din* to adjudicate monetary matters, it was merely for the purpose of ensuring that basic obligations would be honored so people would not be reluctant to extend loans. They had no purpose in extending that authority to include the imposition of *chomesh* obligations.

It emerges, according to *Avi Ezri's* explanation, that the reasoning of those who maintain that there is no *asham* or *chomesh* obligation nowadays is not, as suggested above, that we lack the ability to fulfill such obligations. Rather, it is because a denial that occurs today does not trigger such obligations in the first place.

## מִצְוָה קל: מִצְוַת הָשֵׁבַת גָּזֵל [2,1]

שֶׁנִּצְטַוֵּינוּ לְהָשִׁיב אֶת הַגְּזֵלָה בְּעֵין, כְּלוֹמַר שֶׁאִם הַדָּבָר מַמָּשׁ שֶׁגָּזַל הוּא אֶצְלוֹ וְלֹא נִשְׁתַּנָּה בִּרְשׁוּתוֹ, שֶׁחַיָּב לַהֲשִׁיבוֹ אֶל הַנִּגְזָל כְּמוֹת שֶׁהוּא[3] וְלֹא שֶׁיְּקַחֶנּוּ לְעַצְמוֹ וְיִתֵּן דָּמָיו לַנִּגְזָל, שֶׁנֶּאֱמַר (ויקרא ה׳, כ״ג) ״וְהֵשִׁיב אֶת הַגְּזֵלָה אֲשֶׁר גָּזָל״, וְאָמְרִינָן בְּקַמָּא בְּפֶרֶק הַגּוֹזֵל בַּתְרָא[4]

---

# Mitzvah 130
# The Obligation to Return a Stolen Item

וְהָיָה כִּי יֶחֱטָא וְאָשֵׁם וְהֵשִׁיב אֶת הַגְּזֵלָה אֲשֶׁר גָּזָל אוֹ אֶת הָעֹשֶׁק אֲשֶׁר עָשָׁק אוֹ אֶת הַפִּקָּדוֹן אֲשֶׁר הָפְקַד אִתּוֹ אוֹ אֶת הָאֲבֵדָה אֲשֶׁר מָצָא

*It shall be that when he will sin and become guilty, he shall return the stolen item that he stole, or the proceeds of his fraud, or the pledge that was left with him, or the lost item that he found (Leviticus 5:23).*

---

The above verse refers to one who denied under oath goods or money that he owed another. The atonement process for such a sin begins with his returning of the ill-gotten gain, as the verse details.[1] However, the mitzvah to return those items is not limited to a case of one who swore falsely, and is explained by our Sages to apply more broadly to all stolen goods, whether or not an oath was taken (*Minchas Chinuch* §1). This mitzvah — to return stolen goods — is the rectification for one who has violated the prohibition of robbery (Mitzvah 229).[2]

שֶׁנִּצְטַוֵּינוּ לְהָשִׁיב אֶת הַגְּזֵלָה בְּעֵין — **We are commanded that** if we have committed an act of robbery, **we shall return the stolen item itself.** כְּלוֹמַר שֶׁאִם הַדָּבָר מַמָּשׁ שֶׁגָּזַל הוּא אֶצְלוֹ — **That is to say, if the actual item that was stolen is** still **in [the thief's] possession,** וְלֹא נִשְׁתַּנָּה בִּרְשׁוּתוֹ — **and has not undergone a** fundamental **transformation while in his domain,** שֶׁחַיָּב לַהֲשִׁיבוֹ אֶל הַנִּגְזָל כְּמוֹת שֶׁהוּא — **he is liable to return it as is, to the one who was robbed.**[3] וְלֹא שֶׁיְּקַחֶנּוּ לְעַצְמוֹ וְיִתֵּן דָּמָיו לַנִּגְזָל — **He may not keep it for himself and** simply **give its monetary value to the one who was robbed.** שֶׁנֶּאֱמַר ״וְהֵשִׁיב אֶת הַגְּזֵלָה אֲשֶׁר גָּזָל״ — Rather, the thief is obligated to return the item itself, **as it is stated** (Leviticus 5:23): **he shall return the stolen item that he stole.** וְאָמְרִינָן בְּקַמָּא בְּפֶרֶק הַגּוֹזֵל בַּתְרָא — **In explanation of this verse, it has been stated, in** Tractate *Bava Kamma,* **in Chapter** *HaGozeil Basra*[4] (112a):

---

NOTES

1. Additionally, in this case of one who swore falsely, he is to add a fifth to the payment and bring an *asham* offering, as Chinuch discussed in the previous mitzvah, and as delineated in the verses that follow the above quoted verse (vs. 24-25).

2. [See Mitzvah 129 note 45.] In certain respects, the Torah treats the גַּנָּב, *ganav* (a "thief" who steals the item stealthily; see Mitzvah 224), differently from the גַּזְלָן, *gazlan* (a "robber" who takes the item from its owner by force and in the open; see Mitzvah 229). Nevertheless, according to many, although the verse pertaining to our mitzvah states וְהֵשִׁיב אֶת הַגְּזֵלָה אֲשֶׁר גָּזָל, which literally means "he shall return the robbed item that he robbed," the verse is addressing not only the גַּזְלָן, *robber,* but the גַּנָּב, *thief,* as well. Thus, both thieves and robbers are obligated to return the ill-gotten goods to their rightful owner by virtue of this mitzvah (see *Chavos Yair* §193 [p. 104b], *Shaagas Aryeh* §81; cf. *Oneg Yom Tov, Responsa* 118 בהג״ה ד״ה ולכאורה; see also *Achiezer* 1:21). As such, throughout this mitzvah we shall use the terms "robber" and "thief," as well as "rob" and "steal," interchangeably.

[Note that even if a thief is not included in this mitzvah, and, in fact, had this mitzvah not been commanded by the Torah at all, one would certainly be forbidden to retain another person's belongings; this mitzvah is expressing an additional *mitzvah-obligation* to return a stolen item (see *Minchas Chinuch* §5; see also *Ketzos HaChoshen* 351:3).]

3. If, however, the item was irreversibly transformed while in the possession of the thief, he does not return that altered item, but rather the value of the original item that he took, as Chinuch explains below.

4. [*HaGozeil Basra* (the final *HaGozeil*), also known as

# 507 ❑ VAYIKRA / MITZVAH 130: THE OBLIGATION TO RETURN A STOLEN ITEM

(ב״ק קי״ב ע״א) תָּנוּ רַבָּנָן וְהֵשִׁיב אֶת הַגְּזֵלָה אֲשֶׁר גָּזָל, מַה תַּלְמוּד לוֹמַר אֲשֶׁר גָּזָל, יַחֲזִיר בְּעֵין שֶׁגָּזַל.

וְאִם נִשְׁתַּנֵּית הַגְּזֵלָה בִּרְשׁוּתוֹ שֶׁל גּוֹזֵל חַיָּב לְהָשִׁיב דָּמֶיהָ וּפָטוּר בְּכָךְ[5], אַף עַל פִּי שֶׁלֹּא נִתְיָאֲשׁוּ הַבְּעָלִים מִמֶּנָּה[6].

וְאֵי זֶהוּ שִׁנּוּי הַפּוֹטֵר מֵהָשִׁיב אֶת הַגְּזֵלָה בְּעֵין, זֶה הַשִּׁנּוּי שֶׁאֵינוֹ יָכוֹל לַחֲזֹר אַחַר כָּךְ הַדָּבָר לִבְרִיָּתוֹ, כְּגוֹן הַגּוֹזֵל עֵצִים וּשְׂרָפָן[7] אוֹ קָצַץ מֵהֶן קְצָתָן אוֹ שֶׁחָפַר בְּתוֹכָן חֲפִירוֹת,

---

תָּנוּ רַבָּנָן — **Our Sages taught:** "וְהֵשִׁיב אֶת הַגְּזֵלָה אֲשֶׁר גָּזָל" — The verse states, **he shall return the stolen item that he stole.** Now, once the verse has described the item as a "stolen item," it would seem unnecessary to state "that he stole." מַה תַּלְמוּד לוֹמַר אֲשֶׁר גָּזָל — **What,** then, **does** the phrase **that he stole teach** us? יַחֲזִיר בְּעֵין שֶׁגָּזַל — It teaches that, under the obligation to return stolen property, **he must return** the item itself, as long as it is **in the state** that it was when **he stole it.** That is, as long as the item is in its original state, the thief is obligated to return it as is; otherwise he pays the owner the value of the item.

Chinuch now discusses the corollary of this rule — namely, that if the item was transformed, it is not returned as is:

וְאִם נִשְׁתַּנֵּית הַגְּזֵלָה בִּרְשׁוּתוֹ שֶׁל גּוֹזֵל — **If the stolen item was transformed while in the domain of the thief,** חַיָּב לְהָשִׁיב דָּמֶיהָ וּפָטוּר בְּכָךְ — **he is liable to return its monetary value, and is thereby exempt** from any further obligation, and is not required to return the item itself.[5] אַף עַל פִּי שֶׁלֹּא נִתְיָאֲשׁוּ הַבְּעָלִים מִמֶּנָּה — This holds true **even if the owner has not despaired** of recovering it.[6]

Chinuch sets forth which types of transformations of a stolen item constitute a change, making the thief liable to return its monetary value, and exempting him from any further obligation:

וְאֵי זֶהוּ שִׁנּוּי הַפּוֹטֵר מֵהָשִׁיב אֶת הַגְּזֵלָה בְּעֵין — **What** type of **transformation is one that exempts** the thief **from returning the stolen item itself?** זֶה הַשִּׁנּוּי שֶׁאֵינוֹ יָכוֹל לַחֲזֹר אַחַר כָּךְ הַדָּבָר לִבְרִיָּתוֹ — **It is** the type of **transformation wherein the item cannot afterward return to its original state,** כְּגוֹן הַגּוֹזֵל עֵצִים וּשְׂרָפָן — **such as** the case of **one who steals** pieces of **wood and burns them,**[7] אוֹ קָצַץ מֵהֶן קְצָתָן אוֹ שֶׁחָפַר בְּתוֹכָן חֲפִירוֹת — **or cuts off parts of them, or bores holes in them.**

---

## NOTES

*HaGozeil U'Maachil*, is the tenth chapter of *Bava Kamma*. It is called *HaGozeil Basra* to distinguish it from the ninth chapter of the tractate, *HaGozeil Kamma* (the first *HaGozeil*), *HaGozeil Eitzim*.]

5. If the stolen item has undergone a fundamental transformation (Chinuch will provide examples of such transformations shortly), he need not return the item itself, for the phrase אֲשֶׁר גָּזָל, *that he stole,* which teaches that the thief must return the unchanged stolen item as is, also implies that if it *has* changed, he need only make monetary restitution, and is not required to return the item itself (*Bava Kamma* 66a; *Rambam, Hil. Gezeilah* 2:1-2).

There is some question, regarding a case in which the stolen item has changed and the thief makes monetary restitution, whether such monetary restitution is a fulfillment of this mitzvah. Some authorities maintain that monetary restitution is also a fulfillment of this mitzvah (*Ritva, Makkos* 16a ד״ה כיון; *Minchas Chinuch* §1 quoting *Tosafos* ibid. ד״ה התם; *Rosh, Bava Metzia* 2:9 ד״ה אמר רבא). Others, however, argue that one fulfills this mitzvah only when he returns the original item itself. Thus, while the thief is required to repay the victim, his reimbursement of its monetary value is not a fulfillment of this mitzvah (*Rambam* ibid 1:1 according to *Noda BiYehudah* II, *Yoreh Deah* §77; *Chidushei Rabbeinu Chaim HaLevi, Hil. Gezeilah* 9:1 ד״ה והנה ברמב״ם; *Achiezer* 21:2; *Ramah*, quoted in *Ritva* ibid.). See also *Kovetz Shiurim, Bava Kamma* §27.

6. We will see below that a "change of domain" (*shinui reshus*) can bring about a stolen item's acquisition, but only in a situation where the owner also despairs of recovering the item (*ye'ush*); see Chinuch below and notes 26-28 for the particulars of this law. Chinuch here explains that when it comes to a fundamental transformation to the stolen item, that factor alone is enough to effect a stolen item's acquisition and exempt the thief from returning the item itself; there is no need for the additional contributing factor of the owner's *ye'ush*.

7. The reading in the Gemara (*Bava Kamma* 93b) and *Rambam* (*Hil. Gezeilah* 2:12) is וְשִׁיפָּן, *and planes them.* This is also the reading in the earliest manuscript of Chinuch (Parma, 5087/1327, cited by C. Wengrow in *Sefer haHinnuch*, Feldheim 5744/1984).

וְכֵן הַגּוֹזֵל צֶמֶר וּצְבָעוֹ אוֹ הַגּוֹזֵל מַטְוֶה וְעָשָׂה מִמֶּנּוּ בֶּגֶד וְכָל כַּיּוֹצֵא בָּזֶה[8], אֲבָל הַגּוֹזֵל לוּחוֹת עֵץ, אַף עַל פִּי שֶׁבָּנָה מֵהֶן תֵּבָה אֵין זֶה שִׁנּוּי שֶׁאֵינוֹ חוֹזֵר לִבְרִיָּתוֹ, שֶׁהֲרֵי אֶפְשָׁר לְפָרֵק אוֹתָן וְהֵן חוֹזְרִין לוּחוֹת כְּמוֹ שֶׁהָיוּ, וּלְפִיכָךְ חַיָּב לְהַחֲזִיר אוֹתָן בְּעַיִן, וְכֵן כָּל כַּיּוֹצֵא בָּזֶה[9].

שֹׁרֶשׁ הַמִּצְוָה יָדוּעַ[10].

דִּינֶיהָ, כְּגוֹן מַה שֶּׁאָמְרוּ רַבּוֹתֵינוּ זִכְרוֹנָם לִבְרָכָה (ב״מ נ״ה ע״ב), כַּמָּה תִּהְיֶה הַגְּזֵלָה שֶׁיִּתְחַיֵּב הַגּוֹזֵל לַהֲשִׁיבָהּ, כָּל גְּזֵלָה הַשָּׁוָה פְּרוּטָה[11], אֲבָל פָּחוֹת מִכָּאן, אַף עַל פִּי שֶׁעָבַר עַל אִסּוּר תּוֹרָה אֵינָהּ בְּתוֹרַת הַשָּׁבוֹן, וּכְמוֹ שֶׁנִּכְתֹּב בְּאָרְכָּה עַל לָאו דְּלֹא תִגְזֹל[12],

---

אוֹ הַגּוֹזֵל מַטְוֶה וְעָשָׂה מִמֶּנּוּ — **Similarly, one who steals wool and dyes it,** וְכֵן הַגּוֹזֵל צֶמֶר וּצְבָעוֹ — **or who steals spun** thread **and makes fabric from it,** וְכָל כַּיּוֹצֵא בָּזֶה — **or** who steals **any other** item and effects a change **that is similar to these,**[8] he need not return the actual stolen item, but rather returns the item's original value. אַף עַל פִּי שֶׁבָּנָה מֵהֶן תֵּבָה — **However, one who steals boards of wood,** אֲבָל הַגּוֹזֵל לוּחוֹת עֵץ — **even though he built a chest from them,** אֵין זֶה שִׁנּוּי שֶׁאֵינוֹ חוֹזֵר לִבְרִיָּתוֹ — **such** a change **does not constitute an irreversible transformation,** שֶׁהֲרֵי אֶפְשָׁר לְפָרֵק אוֹתָן וְהֵן חוֹזְרִין לוּחוֹת כְּמוֹ שֶׁהָיוּ — **for it is possible to dismantle [the boards]** of the chest, **and they revert to their original state as boards.** וּלְפִיכָךְ חַיָּב לְהַחֲזִיר אוֹתָן בְּעַיִן — **Therefore, he must return [the boards]** themselves (i.e., the chest), and not simply their value. וְכֵן כָּל כַּיּוֹצֵא בָּזֶה — **This same** ruling **applies to anything that is similar to this** type of reversible change.[9]

### ~ Underlying Purpose of the Mitzvah ~

שֹׁרֶשׁ הַמִּצְוָה יָדוּעַ — **The underlying purpose of this mitzvah is well-known.**[10]

### ~ Laws of the Mitzvah ~

דִּינֶיהָ כְּגוֹן מַה שֶּׁאָמְרוּ רַבּוֹתֵינוּ זִכְרוֹנָם לִבְרָכָה — **The laws of [this mitzvah] include, for example, that which our Sages, of blessed memory, stated** (Bava Metzia 55b) כַּמָּה תִּהְיֶה הַגְּזֵלָה שֶׁיִּתְחַיֵּב הַגּוֹזֵל לַהֲשִׁיבָהּ — **with regard to how much the stolen item must be** worth **to obligate the thief to return it,** as follows: כָּל גְּזֵלָה הַשָּׁוָה פְּרוּטָה — **Any stolen item that is worth** at least **a *perutah* must be returned.**[11] אֲבָל פָּחוֹת מִכָּאן — **However,** if the item is worth less than that, אַף עַל פִּי שֶׁעָבַר עַל אִסּוּר תּוֹרָה — **even though [the thief] violated a Biblical prohibition** by stealing it, אֵינָהּ בְּתוֹרַת הַשָּׁבוֹן — **nevertheless, [the stolen item] is not subject to the requirement of returning,** וּכְמוֹ שֶׁנִּכְתֹּב בְּאָרְכָּה עַל לָאו דְּלֹא תִגְזֹל — as we shall write at length with regard to the prohibition of *"you shall not rob"* (Mitzvah 229).[12]

---

### NOTES

8. Such as where one steals stones and chisels them, or where one steals a tree trunk and turns it into beams (*Rambam, Hil. Gezeilah* 2:12-13). In all these cases, the item cannot revert to its original state, and therefore the thief pays its original value to the one from whom he took it.

With regard to the case of spun thread made into fabric, some argue that it is in fact reversible, as the material can be pulled apart back into its original threads (*Kesef Mishneh, Hil. Gezeilah* 2:11; *Beis Yosef, Choshen Mishpat* 360:5 ד״ה ומ״ש טווי, based on *Bava Kamma* 93b and 96a). Others, however, concur with Chinuch's assertion that this is an irreversible change, and note that the threads will never truly revert to their original state after having been woven into fabric (*Bach* ad loc.).

9. Such as where the thief steals dirt and makes mudbricks, which may be ground back into dirt. Similarly,

if he steals metal and produces coins from it, he must return the coins even though the metal is not in its original state, since the coins can be melted down and returned to their original state (*Rambam* ibid. 2:10). [Chinuch below (at notes 20-24) discusses to whom the appreciation in value belongs.]

10. Just as the ethical wrong of stealing and robbing is obvious, and the prohibition of performing such acts is necessary for both moral and social reasons (see Mitzvos 224 and 229), so, too, is the requirement to return a stolen object obvious to all.

11. A *perutah* (pl. *perutos*) is a small copper coin whose value is considered the lowest possible amount to be viewed as having monetary value (see *Tur, Choshen Mishpat* 360:1-2).

12. Chinuch there explains that although, technically,

לְפִי שֶׁיִּשְׂרָאֵל בְּנֵי אַבְרָהָם יִצְחָק וְיַעֲקֹב נְדִיבִים בְּנֵי נְדִיבִים הֵם, וְיָדוּעַ הַדָּבָר שֶׁכָּל שֶׁהוּא פָּחוֹת מִשָּׁוֶה פְּרוּטָה אֲפִלּוּ עָנִי שֶׁבְּיִשְׂרָאֵל, מִכֵּיוָן שֶׁנִּגְזַל מִמֶּנּוּ מוֹחֵל אוֹתוֹ וְאֵין חֶפְצוֹ אַחֲרָיו כְּלָל.[13]

וּלְפִיכָךְ אָמְרוּ זִכְרוֹנָם לִבְרָכָה (ב״ק ק״ה ע״א) שֶׁהַגּוֹזֵל שָׁלֹשׁ אֲגֻדּוֹת[14] שֶׁשָּׁווֹת בִּשְׁעַת גְּזֵלָה שָׁלֹשׁ פְּרוּטוֹת וְהוּזְלוּ בְּיַד הַגַּזְלָן וְעָמְדוּ עַל שְׁתֵּי פְרוּטוֹת, אַף עַל פִּי שֶׁהֶחֱזִיר הַשְׁתַּיִם חַיָּב לְהַחֲזִיר הַשְּׁלִישִׁית, שֶׁאַחַר שְׁעַת גְּזֵלָה אָנוּ דָּנִין, וּכְבָר הָיְתָה שָׁוָה פְּרוּטָה בְּאוֹתָהּ שָׁעָה.[15] גָּזַל שְׁתַּיִם שֶׁשָּׁווֹת פְּרוּטָה וְהֵשִׁיב אַחַת, גְּזֵלָה יֵשׁ כָּאן, הָשֵׁב גְּזֵלָה אֵין כָּאן.[16]

---

**לְפִי שֶׁיִּשְׂרָאֵל בְּנֵי אַבְרָהָם יִצְחָק וְיַעֲקֹב נְדִיבִים בְּנֵי נְדִיבִים הֵם** — The reason for this exemption of returning items that are worth less than a *perutah* is **because Jews,** who are **descendents of Abraham, Isaac, and Jacob, are benevolent ones, the children of benevolent ones, וְיָדוּעַ הַדָּבָר שֶׁכָּל שֶׁהוּא פָּחוֹת מִשָּׁוֶה פְּרוּטָה** — and **it is** thus **known that** with regard to **anything that is worth less than a *perutah*, אֲפִלּוּ עָנִי שֶׁבְּיִשְׂרָאֵל מִכֵּיוָן שֶׁנִּגְזַל מִמֶּנּוּ מוֹחֵל אוֹתוֹ** — **even the poorest among the Jews forgives** the obligation to repay [the stolen item] once it has already been stolen, **וְאֵין חֶפְצוֹ אַחֲרָיו כְּלָל** — and **has no desire** to go **after it whatsoever.**[13]

Chinuch addresses some scenarios related to the rule that any theft of a *perutah* or more must be returned:

**וּלְפִיכָךְ אָמְרוּ זִכְרוֹנָם לִבְרָכָה** — [Our Sages], of blessed memory, **have therefore stated** (Bava Kamma 105a) **שֶׁהַגּוֹזֵל שָׁלֹשׁ אֲגֻדּוֹת שֶׁשָּׁווֹת בִּשְׁעַת גְּזֵלָה שָׁלֹשׁ פְּרוּטוֹת** — **that if one steals three bundles**[14] that together **were worth** a total of **three *perutos* at the time of the theft, וְהוּזְלוּ בְּיַד הַגַּזְלָן וְעָמְדוּ עַל שְׁתֵּי פְרוּטוֹת** — **but** subsequently **they decreased in value in the possession of the thief, so that they were** then **worth** a total of **two *perutos*, אַף עַל פִּי שֶׁהֶחֱזִיר הַשְׁתַּיִם חַיָּב לְהַחֲזִיר הַשְּׁלִישִׁית** — **even though he returned two of** [the bundles], and is therefore left with only a single bundle that is *now* worth less than a *perutah*, **he is** still **liable to return the third** [bundle]. **שֶׁאַחַר שְׁעַת גְּזֵלָה אָנוּ דָּנִין** — This is **because we judge** the value of the item **based on the time of the theft, וּכְבָר הָיְתָה שָׁוָה פְּרוּטָה בְּאוֹתָהּ שָׁעָה** — **and at that time** [each bundle] **was worth a *perutah*.**[15]

**גָּזַל שְׁתַּיִם שֶׁשָּׁווֹת פְּרוּטָה וְהֵשִׁיב אַחַת** — **If one stole two** bundles that together **were worth a *perutah*, but returned** only **one** of them, **גְּזֵלָה יֵשׁ כָּאן** — the prohibition of **theft is** still **extant** and has not been rectified, **הָשֵׁב גְּזֵלָה אֵין כָּאן** — for **he has not** fulfilled the obligation to **return the stolen item.**[16]

---

### NOTES

the prohibition against robbery is violated only when one robs an item of at least a *perutah* in value, it is still Biblically prohibited to rob any amount, for as a rule, one may not engage in prohibited acts even when doing so below the minimum threshold. Nevertheless, if one does steal such minute amounts, he is not required to return the stolen item, for as Chinuch goes on to note, the one who was robbed has surely relinquished any claim (see *Sanhedrin* 57a with *Rashi* ד״ה צערא).

13. See Insight. [It should be noted that some authorities maintain that it is appropriate for the thief to make restitution in all cases (*Meiri, Bava Kamma* 105a ד״ה גזל שתי).]

14. E.g., of vegetables or the like (*Maggid Mishneh* ibid. 1:6).

15. Based on this reasoning, the same would be true in a case where he steals one bundle that was worth a *perutah* and that subsequently depreciated to less than a *perutah*. Since we focus on its value at the time of the theft, the thief would be required to return it. The novelty of the three bundles having been worth three *perutos* and depreciating to two is that even though the thief has fulfilled a mitzvah of returning a stolen item by returning two of the bundles (for he has returned a *perutah*'s worth of stolen goods), he nevertheless remains bound to return the rest, insofar as it was worth a *perutah* at the time of the theft (*Tosafos, Bava Kamma* 105a ד״ה אמר רבא; *Sma, Choshen Mishpat* 360:8).

16. In this case, the value of the two bundles remained constant at one *perutah* (half a *perutah* each). The thief who stole them, and violated the prohibition of robbery by having stolen a *perutah*'s worth of goods, returned only one of the two bundles. In so doing, he has not fulfilled the mitzvah to return stolen property,

וְדִינֵי יֵאוּשׁ וְשִׁנּוּי רְשׁוּת, רַבִּים. וּכְלַל הַדָּבָר כֵּן לְפִי הַנִּרְאֶה מִן הַגְּמָרָא, שֶׁכָּל זְמַן שֶׁהַגְּזֵלָה בְּיַד הַגַּזְלָן אוֹ אֲפִלּוּ בְּיַד בָּנָיו[17] וְלֹא נִשְׁתַּנֵּית, אַף עַל פִּי שֶׁיָּדַעְנוּ בְּוַדַּאי שֶׁהַנִּגְזָל נִתְיָאֵשׁ מִמֶּנָּה, וְהוּא כְּמוֹ שֶׁאָמְרוּ בַּגְּמָרָא (ב״מ כ״ג ע״א) כְּגוֹן דְּשַׁמְעוּהָ בְּנֵי אָדָם שֶׁהָיָה אוֹמֵר וַי לֵיהּ לְחֶסְרוֹנֵיהּ[18], כְּלוֹמַר שֶׁמַּסְכִּים בְּדַעְתּוֹ עַל אוֹתוֹ דָּבָר שֶׁכְּבָר נֶאֱבַד מִמֶּנּוּ וְאֵין דַּעְתּוֹ סוֹמֶכֶת שֶׁיִּרְאֶנּוּ עוֹד, אַף עַל פִּי כֵן דִּין תּוֹרָה שֶׁחַיָּבִין לְהַחֲזִירָהּ לַנִּגְזָל כְּמוֹת שֶׁהִיא,[19]

---

Chinuch now discusses how the law regarding returning a stolen item is impacted when the original owner has despaired of retrieving it (יֵאוּשׁ, *ye'ush*), or when the thief has sold or given the item as a gift to a third party, which constitutes a "change in domain" (שִׁנּוּי רְשׁוּת, *shinui reshus*). He begins by delving into the laws pertaining to *ye'ush,* and will later return to discuss the law regarding items that were subject to a change in domain:

וְדִינֵי יֵאוּשׁ וְשִׁנּוּי רְשׁוּת רַבִּים — **The laws with regard to** the obligation to return a stolen item when either there has been **ye'ush** on the part of the original owner, **or** the item undergoes **a change of domain** (*shinui reshus*) by being transferred to a third party, **are many.** וּכְלַל הַדָּבָר כֵּן לְפִי הַנִּרְאֶה מִן הַגְּמָרָא — **The general rule regarding this matter, as it would appear from the Gemara** (*Bava Kamma* 68a, et al.), **is as follows:** שֶׁכָּל זְמַן שֶׁהַגְּזֵלָה בְּיַד הַגַּזְלָן — **As long as the stolen item is in the possession of the thief,** אוֹ אֲפִלּוּ בְּיַד בָּנָיו וְלֹא נִשְׁתַּנֵּית — **or even in the possession of his children** after his death,[17] **and it has not been** irreversibly **transformed,** it must be returned as is. אַף עַל פִּי שֶׁיָּדַעְנוּ בְּוַדַּאי שֶׁהַנִּגְזָל נִתְיָאֵשׁ מִמֶּנָּה — This holds true **even if we know with certainty that the one who was robbed has despaired of** recovering it. וְהוּא כְּמוֹ שֶׁאָמְרוּ בַּגְּמָרָא — **The** definition of **this** "despair" is, **as stated in the Gemara** (*Bava Metzia* 23a), כְּגוֹן דְּשַׁמְעוּהָ בְּנֵי אָדָם שֶׁהָיָה אוֹמֵר וַי לֵיהּ לְחֶסְרוֹנֵיהּ — **for example, where people heard [the original owner] say, "Woe to him for his loss."**[18] כְּלוֹמַר שֶׁמַּסְכִּים בְּדַעְתּוֹ עַל אוֹתוֹ דָּבָר שֶׁכְּבָר נֶאֱבַד מִמֶּנּוּ — **That is to say,** by virtue of his statement, it is clear that **he has come to terms with** the fact **that that item is already lost to him,** וְאֵין דַּעְתּוֹ סוֹמֶכֶת שֶׁיִּרְאֶנּוּ עוֹד — **and he does not expect to see it again.** אַף עַל פִּי כֵן דִּין תּוֹרָה שֶׁחַיָּבִין לְהַחֲזִירָהּ לַנִּגְזָל כְּמוֹת שֶׁהִיא — **Notwithstanding this** clear expression of despair, as long as the item is still in the thief's possession and has not been irreversibly transformed, **he is Biblically obligated to return it in its current state to the one who was robbed.**[19]

---

### NOTES

for returning less than a *perutah's* value is not viewed as an act of returning. He therefore has not rectified the prohibition at all and remains obligated to do so and thereby fulfill the mitzvah (see *Tur, Choshen Mishpat* 360:4, and *Knesses HaGedolah, Hagahos Beis Yosef, Choshen Mishpat* 360:1 — quoted in *Hagahos VeHe'aros* to *Tur,* Shiras Devorah/Mechon Yerushalayim ed., note 17).

[Our version of the Gemara (*Bava Kamma* 105a) reads: גְּזֵלָה אֵין כָּאן הֲשָׁבָה אֵין כָּאן, **there is no** theft [but nevertheless] he has not fulfilled [the mitzvah of] returning [the stolen item]. That is, even though the item that is retained by the thief is not significant enough for us to say that he still has stolen goods in his possession, nevertheless he has not fulfilled the mitzvah to return the stolen item, since the theft totaled a *perutah,* and he did not return the value of a *perutah* (see *Maggid Mishneh, Hil. Gezeilah* 1:6; see also *Kesef Mishneh* and *Lechem Mishneh* ad loc. and *Bach, Choshen Mishpat* 360:4).]

17. The domain of the thief's heirs is considered an extension of his own domain, so any leniency associated with a "change of domain" (see *Chinuch* below, at notes 27-28) does not apply if he died and the stolen goods fell to his heirs (*Rambam, Hil. Gezeilah* 2:1; *Tur, Choshen Mishpat* 361:7; see *Bava Kamma* 111b, where this is a matter of debate).

18. I.e., woe to *me* for *my* loss. [It was a common euphemism for one to phrase a negative personal occurrence in the third person, trying to distance it from oneself (see *Rashi, Exodus* 1:10, et al.).]

19. That is, *ye'ush* of the original owner alone is insufficient to allow the thief to keep the item and return only its value. Rather, it remains the original owner's throughout, and the thief must return the item itself (*Rambam* ibid.; *Tur* ibid. 361:1; see *Bava Kamma* 66a, where this is a matter of debate). [The reason why *ye'ush* alone does not serve to transfer the item to the thief is because the item entered his domain illegally (see *Tos. Rabbeinu Peretz, Bava Kamma* 68a ד״ה ולא; *Ramban, Milchamos Hashem* to *Rif* ibid. fol. 41a, end of ד״ה ומה; see also *Ketzos HaChoshen, Choshen Mishpat* 353:1).]

# VAYIKRA / MITZVAH 130: THE OBLIGATION TO RETURN A STOLEN ITEM

אֲפִלּוּ הִשְׁבִּיחָהּ בְּיַד הַגַּזְלָן [20] הַשֶּׁבַח לַנִּגְזָל. וְהוּא שֶׁכָּתוּב בַּתּוֹרָה (שם) וְהֵשִׁיב אֶת הַגְּזֵלָה אֲשֶׁר גָּזָל, וּבָא הַפֵּרוּשׁ אִם הִיא כְּמוֹ שֶׁגְּזָלָהּ, כְּלוֹמַר שֶׁלֹּא נִשְׁתַּנֵּית, יַחֲזִירֶנָּה כְּמוֹת שֶׁהִיא, וַאֲפִלּוּ הִשְׁבִּיחָהּ כַּמָּה.[21]

אֲבָל[22] חֲכָמִים תִּקְּנוּ מִפְּנֵי תַּקָּנַת הַשָּׁבִים שֶׁכָּל מַה שֶּׁהִשְׁבִּיחָהּ בְּיַד הַגַּזְלָן אַחַר יֵאוּשׁ הַבְּעָלִים יִהְיֶה שֶׁלּוֹ,[23] וּכְשֶׁיָּבוֹא לְהַחֲזִירָהּ יַחְשֹׁב עִם הַנִּגְזָל כַּמָּה הָיְתָה שָׁוָה בִּשְׁעַת הַגְּזֵלָה

---

אֲפִלּוּ הִשְׁבִּיחָהּ בְּיַד הַגַּזְלָן — In fact, **even if there has been an improvement to [the stolen item] in the domain of the thief,**[20] הַשֶּׁבַח לַנִּגְזָל — **that improvement** belongs **to the one who was robbed,** for it remained his throughout. וְהוּא שֶׁכָּתוּב בַּתּוֹרָה — **It is** in reference to **this** law **that it is written in the Torah,** "וְהֵשִׁיב אֶת הַגְּזֵלָה אֲשֶׁר גָּזָל" — *he shall return the stolen item that he stole.* וּבָא הַפֵּרוּשׁ — **The explanation that has been transmitted** to us regarding this verse (as was stated at the beginning of this mitzvah) is אִם הִיא כְּמוֹ שֶׁגְּזָלָהּ — **that if [the item] is** in the same state **as it was when he stole it,** כְּלוֹמַר שֶׁלֹּא נִשְׁתַּנֵּית — **that is to say, it has not been** irreversibly **transformed,** יַחֲזִירֶנָּה כְּמוֹת שֶׁהִיא — **he must return it as is,** וַאֲפִלּוּ הִשְׁבִּיחָהּ כַּמָּה — **even if there has been a considerable improvement to [the stolen item].**[21]

The above represents the Biblical law. However, based on a Rabbinic legislation known as תַּקָּנַת הַשָּׁבִים, *the enactment to [assist] those who [wish to] repent,* the thief will often be given a certain amount of reprieve to encourage his penitence, as follows:[22]

אֲבָל חֲכָמִים תִּקְּנוּ מִפְּנֵי תַּקָּנַת הַשָּׁבִים — **However, the Sages established an enactment for the sake of those who** wish to **repent,** שֶׁכָּל מַה שֶּׁהִשְׁבִּיחָהּ בְּיַד הַגַּזְלָן אַחַר יֵאוּשׁ הַבְּעָלִים יִהְיֶה שֶׁלּוֹ — **that any improvement to [the stolen item]** that occurs **in the domain of the thief after the owner had** already **despaired** of getting the item back (*ye'ush*) **belongs to [the thief].**[23] וּכְשֶׁיָּבוֹא לְהַחֲזִירָהּ יַחְשֹׁב עִם הַנִּגְזָל כַּמָּה הָיְתָה שָׁוָה בִּשְׁעַת הַגְּזֵלָה — **When [the thief] comes to return [the item], he computes with the one** whom he had **robbed how much it was worth at the time of the theft.**

---

### NOTES

20. For example, one stole a cow that later became pregnant while in the domain of the thief.

21. On the Biblical level, any improvement in the stolen object must be returned to the owner along with the object, since nothing has occurred to effect a transfer of this item into the thief's domain. Thus, if one stole a cow that later became pregnant, the increase in value of the cow due to the pregnancy would belong to the owner (see *Rambam* ibid. 2:2). Nevertheless, as *Chinuch* will proceed to explain, the Sages instituted an enactment allowing the thief to retain the increase in value under certain circumstances.

22. Wishing to make it easier for a thief to repent and become rehabilitated from his past criminal activities, the Sages enacted certain leniencies for his benefit. Collectively, these rules are known as *takanas hashavim* (see *Bava Kamma* 95b; Mishnah, *Gittin* 55a). *Chinuch* now addresses one such manifestation of this enactment, which is that the thief will at times keep the increase in value that occurs to the stolen item while it is in his domain. [Further on in this mitzvah, *Chinuch* will address other manifestations of this enactment (see notes 32-33 below).]

23. Thus, in the above example of one who stole a cow that later became pregnant, the increase in value of the cow due to the pregnancy will belong to the thief, if the original owner had despaired of recovering his animal. Therefore, the thief will return the cow, and be paid by the owner for the difference between the cow's current value and what it was worth at the time of the theft (*Rambam* ibid. 2:6). If, however, the owner did not despair of recovering his cow, the increase in value remains the owner's, for [according to *Chinuch*, following *Rambam* ibid. 2:7] the enactment to assist those who wish to repent does not apply in such cases. Others, however, argue that the enactment applies even if the owner did not despair of recovering his animal, and rule that the thief keeps the value increase in all cases (*Maggid Mishneh* ibid. 2:2; *Tur* ibid. 362:2 and *Sma* §3; cf. *Shach* ibid. 354:4).

[Even according to the first opinion, if the increase in value is due to the investment of the thief (e.g., he fattened it), the thief will be paid for that increase — irrespective of whether or not the owner had despaired of recovering the item (*Rambam* ibid. 2:9). The need for the owner's *ye'ush* is only in cases where the increase in value is associated with a natural process (such as birth, the growth of new wool, etc.), but not when it is due to the thief's investment. As for increases in value due to market forces, see *Chinuch* below.]

וְיָשִׁיב לוֹ הַנִּגְזָל דְּמֵי מַה שֶּׁהִשְׁבִּיחָהּ וְיִקָּחֶנָּה. וְדָבָר זֶה יֵשׁ כֹּחַ בְּיַד חֲכָמִים לַעֲשׂוֹתוֹ, לְפִי שֶׁבְּכָל דָּבָר שֶׁבְּמָמוֹן הֵם יְכוֹלִים לַעֲשׂוֹת בּוֹ כְּחֶפְצָם וַאֲפִלּוּ כְּנֶגֶד צִוּוּי הַתּוֹרָה, כְּמוֹ שֶׁיָּדוּעַ שֶׁהֶפְקֵר בֵּית דִּין הֶפְקֵר.[24]

וּלְפִיכָךְ גּוֹי שֶׁגָּזַל וְהִשְׁבִּיחַ בֵּין קֹדֶם יֵאוּשׁ בֵּין לְאַחַר יֵאוּשׁ, אוֹ יִשְׂרָאֵל גַּזְלָן שֶׁמָּכַר לְגוֹי וְהִשְׁבִּיחַ הַגּוֹי [הַשֶּׁבַח לַנִּגְזָל].[25] מְכָרָהּ לִפְנֵי יֵאוּשׁ, הַדִּין עִם הַשֵּׁנִי כְּמוֹ עִם הָרִאשׁוֹן בְּשָׁוֶה,[26]

וְיָשִׁיב לוֹ הַנִּגְזָל דְּמֵי מַה שֶּׁהִשְׁבִּיחָהּ וְיִקָּחֶנָּה — **The one who was robbed must** then **repay [the thief]** the worth of increase in value from the time of theft, **and he** then **takes [his item]** back. וְדָבָר זֶה יֵשׁ כֹּחַ בְּיַד חֲכָמִים לַעֲשׂוֹתוֹ — **The Sages have the authority to enact this matter,** despite the fact that on a Biblical level the thief has no right to claim this increase in value, לְפִי שֶׁבְּכָל דָּבָר שֶׁבְּמָמוֹן הֵם יְכוֹלִים לַעֲשׂוֹת בּוֹ כְּחֶפְצָם — since with regard to any monetary issue, **they may act as per their discretion,** וַאֲפִלּוּ כְּנֶגֶד צִוּוּי הַתּוֹרָה — **even** where the resulting ruling is **contrary to the dictates of the Torah** for that particular situation, כְּמוֹ שֶׁיָּדוּעַ שֶׁהֶפְקֵר בֵּית דִּין הֶפְקֵר — **for, as it is known,** whatever is **declared ownerless by** *beis din* is indeed **ownerless.**[24]

Chinuch notes exclusions to the above enactment:

וּלְפִיכָךְ גּוֹי שֶׁגָּזַל וְהִשְׁבִּיחַ בֵּין קֹדֶם יֵאוּשׁ בֵּין לְאַחַר יֵאוּשׁ — **Therefore,** in the case of **an idolater who stole** an item **and improved** it in his domain — **whether** the improvement occurred **before** *ye'ush* **or after** *ye'ush* — אוֹ יִשְׂרָאֵל גַּזְלָן שֶׁמָּכַר לְגוֹי וְהִשְׁבִּיחַ הַגּוֹי — **or,** in the case of **a Jewish thief who sold** an item that he had stolen **to an idolater and the idolater improved** it, הַשֶּׁבַח לַנִּגְזָל — **the increase in value belongs to the one who was robbed.**[25]

Chinuch discusses the law with respect to a stolen item that was transferred to a third party (שִׁנּוּי רְשׁוּת):

מְכָרָהּ לִפְנֵי יֵאוּשׁ — **If [the thief] sold [the stolen item]** to a third party] **before** the owner had **despaired** of recovering it, הַדִּין עִם הַשֵּׁנִי כְּמוֹ עִם הָרִאשׁוֹן בְּשָׁוֶה — **the** owner's **claim against the latter** (i.e., the buyer) **is exactly the same as** it was **against the former** (i.e., the thief). That is, just as the original owner was entitled to receive the item itself back from the thief while he had it, so too is he now entitled to receive the item itself back from the buyer.[26]

---

NOTES

24. That is, although the Torah may dictate a particular ruling regarding monetary law, it grants the authority to the courts to legislate liabilities and exemptions based on the power of הֶפְקֵר בֵּית דִּין, *whatever is [declared] ownerless by beis din is [indeed] ownerless.* By virtue of this authority, *beis din* may take money from one party and give it to another when they deem it necessary for the purposes of a particular enactment or safeguard (*Rashi, Gittin* 36a ד״ה מוסרני). [For a discussion of which type of *beis din* is given this authority, see *Rambam, Hil. Shemittah VeYovel* 9:17 with *Kesef Mishneh*; and *Shulchan Aruch, Choshen Mishpat* 2:1.]

25. In these cases, where the increase occurred in the domain of an idolater, he does not keep that increase. Since, according to Biblical law, the item and its increased value belong to the original owner, they will both revert to him, for the Sages did not apply their enactment to idolaters (*Bava Kamma* 96a; *Rambam* ibid. 2:5; *Sma* ibid. 362:11).

26. Since the owner had not despaired of recovering his item, it remains his throughout, even though it was sold and a change of domain (*shinui reshus*) was effected. As Chinuch goes on to explain, a change of domain without the owner's despair does not serve to remove the item from his ownership (see *Rambam, Hil. Geneivah* 5:2). Nevertheless, the buyer may demand compensation from the owner (who in turn will seek reimbursement from the thief) for whatever the buyer had paid for the item, due to a Rabbinic enactment known as תַּקָּנַת הַשּׁוּק, *the remedy of the marketplace.*

תַּקָּנַת הַשּׁוּק, **The remedy of the marketplace:** It is forbidden to buy stolen goods (*Rambam, Hil. Gezeilah* 5:1), or, for that matter, any goods that can be assumed to be stolen (see Mitzvah 224; *Tur, Choshen Mishpat* 369:1). The Sages were concerned, however, that one might innocently buy an item in the marketplace, not realizing that it was stolen property. When the owner comes to retrieve his item, which he may do as long as he did not yet despair of getting it back, the buyer will then experience a complete loss. The Sages therefore enacted the "remedy of the marketplace" (*takanas hashuk*), which allows the buyer to receive compensation from the original owner for the money that he had innocently paid for this item. The owner can then in turn sue the thief for that amount (see *Bava Kamma* 115a with *Rashi* ד״ה תקנת השוק; *Rambam, Hil. Geneivah* 5:2). Furthermore, in a case where the original owner *had* despaired, *takanas hashuk* provides that

# VAYIKRA / MITZVAH 130: THE OBLIGATION TO RETURN A STOLEN ITEM

שֶׁאֵין שִׁנּוּי רְשׁוּת עוֹשֶׂה קִנְיָן אֶלָּא אַחַר יֵאוּשׁ.[27] אֲבָל אַחַר יֵאוּשׁ, בֵּין שֶׁהָיָה אוֹתוֹ יֵאוּשׁ אַחַר שֶׁבָּאַתָה הַגְּזֵלָה לְיַד לוֹקֵחַ אוֹ בְּעוֹד שֶׁהָיְתָה בְּיַד גַּזְלָן, כֵּיוָן שֶׁיֵּשׁ בַּגְּזֵלָה זוֹ יֵאוּשׁ וְשִׁנּוּי רְשׁוּת, קָנְאָה הַלּוֹקֵחַ לְגוּפָהּ שֶׁל גְּזֵלָה.[28] וְאִם אוֹתוֹ גַזְלָן שֶׁמְּכָרָהּ לוֹ הוּא גַזְלָן שֶׁאֵינוֹ מְפֻרְסָם, תִּהְיֶה שֶׁלּוֹ לְגַמְרֵי וְאֵין חַיָּב לְהָשִׁיב כְּלוּם לַנִּגְזָל,[29] אֶלָּא יֵלֵךְ לוֹ הַנִּגְזָל וְיַעֲשֶׂה דִין עִם הַגַּזְלָן. וְאִם הוּא גַזְלָן מְפֻרְסָם, חַיָּב לְהָשִׁיב דְּמֵי הַגְּזֵלָה לַנִּגְזָל וְהוּא יַעֲשֶׂה דִין עִם הַגַּזְלָן.[30]

---

שֶׁאֵין שִׁנּוּי רְשׁוּת עוֹשֶׂה קִנְיָן אֶלָּא אַחַר יֵאוּשׁ — **The buyer may not retain the item, because a change of domain** (such as in this case, where the item goes from the thief's domain to the buyer's domain) **does not bring about** the item's **acquisition** by the third party (i.e., the buyer), **unless there is** the additional factor of *ye'ush* (i.e., the owner's despair of recovering the item).[27] אֲבָל אַחַר יֵאוּשׁ — **However, after** *ye'ush* on the part of the owner, בֵּין שֶׁהָיָה אוֹתוֹ יֵאוּשׁ אַחַר שֶׁבָּאַתָה הַגְּזֵלָה לְיַד לוֹקֵחַ — **whether that** *ye'ush* **occurred after the stolen item came into the buyer's hand,** אוֹ בְּעוֹד שֶׁהָיְתָה בְּיַד גַּזְלָן — **or before the buyer received it, when the [stolen item] was still in the possession of the thief,** כֵּיוָן שֶׁיֵּשׁ בַּגְּזֵלָה זוֹ יֵאוּשׁ וְשִׁנּוּי רְשׁוּת — **since this stolen item has** undergone **both** *ye'ush* of recovering the item **and a change in domain,** קָנְאָה הַלּוֹקֵחַ לְגוּפָהּ שֶׁל גְּזֵלָה — **the buyer acquires the stolen item itself,** for *ye'ush* and change of domain together are able to effect a change of ownership.[28]

While *ye'ush* allows the buyer to retain the item itself, it does not free him from liability to compensate the original owner. Nevertheless, the Sages enacted *takanas hashuk*, "the remedy of the marketplace," which protects a buyer who innocently purchased an item, with no reason to suspect that it was stolen. Chinuch elaborates:

וְאִם אוֹתוֹ גַזְלָן שֶׁמְּכָרָהּ לוֹ הוּא גַזְלָן שֶׁאֵינוֹ מְפֻרְסָם — **If the thief who sold [the stolen item] to him is not a known thief,** תִּהְיֶה שֶׁלּוֹ לְגַמְרֵי — **then [the stolen item] is [the buyer's] to keep outright,** וְאֵין חַיָּב לְהָשִׁיב כְּלוּם לַנִּגְזָל — **and [the buyer] is not liable to compensate the one who was robbed at all.**[29] אֶלָּא יֵלֵךְ לוֹ הַנִּגְזָל וְיַעֲשֶׂה דִין עִם הַגַּזְלָן — **Rather, the one who was robbed should go and litigate** directly **with the thief,** whom *beis din* will then obligate to reimburse him for the theft. וְאִם הוּא גַזְלָן מְפֻרְסָם — **However, if [the thief] was a known thief,** חַיָּב לְהָשִׁיב הַלּוֹקֵחַ דְּמֵי הַגְּזֵלָה לַנִּגְזָל — **the buyer must return the value of the stolen item to the one who was robbed,** וְהוּא יַעֲשֶׂה דִין עִם הַגַּזְלָן — **and [the buyer] must then** go and **litigate with the thief** from whom he bought the item, to get his money back.[30]

---

## NOTES

the original owner may not collect anything from the buyer (who has acquired the item by way of *ye'ush* with *shinui reshus*, as explained below), but rather, must sue the thief alone for his loss (*Rambam* ibid. 5:3).

27. The fact that the item went from the thief's domain to the buyer's (*shinui reshus*) is not enough to bring about the item's legal transfer to the buyer. The owner retains ownership of that item until such time as he despairs of its recovery. If he were to despair, then that *ye'ush* along with the change of domain would together create a legal transfer to the third party, who would then be allowed to retain the item, as Chinuch proceeds to explain.

28. See Mishnah, *Bava Kamma* 114a with *Rashi* ד"ה הרי and *Tos. Rid* ד"ה פסיקא. Chinuch's ruling that it does not matter whether the *ye'ush* occurred before the sale or after the sale follows *Rambam, Hil. Gezeilah* 2:3 (see also *Shulchan Aruch, Choshen Mishpat* 353:3). Others, however, disagree, and rule that unless *ye'ush* occurs before the sale, it will not serve to effect a transfer of ownership to the third party (*Rosh, Bava Kamma* 10:18; *Tur, Choshen Mishpat* 353:3; *Rama* ad loc. 356:3).

[It should be noted that the above represents the original Talmudic law. However, the custom in many communities, based on the local law of the land (*dina d'malchusa*), was that the buyer is required to return the item to the original owner, even where the owner had despaired of his item's recovery (*Rama, Choshen Mishpat* 356:7, 368:1; *Shulchan Aruch HaRav, Hil. Gezeilah U'Geneivah* §11; see also *Tzemach Tzedek, Choshen Mishpat* §46).]

29. He need not return the item itself, for he has acquired it, since there was *ye'ush* and *shinui reshus*. And since the thief is not well-known and the purchase can be assumed to have been done in innocence, *takanas hashuk* will exempt him from having to pay for the item's value. In such cases, the buyer is given complete immunity (*Rambam, Hil. Geneivah* 5:3).

30. [The buyer is not obligated to return the item itself, for since we are discussing a case where the owner has

514 □ ויקרא / מצוה קל: מצוות השבת גזל

וְדִינֵי הַגְזֵלָה, עַד הֵיכָן הוּא חַיָּב לִטְרֹחַ לַהֲשִׁיבָהּ אֶל בְּעָלֶיהָ, כְּמוֹ שֶׁאָמְרוּ רַבּוֹתֵינוּ זִכְרוֹנָם לִבְרָכָה (ב״ק ק״ג ע״א), הַגּוֹזֵל מֵחֲבֵרוֹ שָׁוֶה פְּרוּטָה שֶׁחַיָּב לְהוֹלִיכָהּ אַחֲרָיו אֲפִלּוּ לְמָדַי, כְּלוֹמַר לְמָקוֹם רָחוֹק.[31] וּכְדֵי לְהָקֵל טָרְחוֹ אִם הַהוֹצָאָה מְרֻבָּה, אָמְרוּ רַבּוֹתֵינוּ זִכְרוֹנָם לִבְרָכָה (שם) שֶׁיַּנִּיחֶנָּה בְּיַד בֵּית דִּין וִיוֹדִיעֵם שֶׁאוֹתוֹ מָמוֹן הוּא שֶׁל פְּלוֹנִי וְהֵם יִתְּנוּהוּ לוֹ לִכְשֶׁיִּזְדַּמֵּן[32].

וְדִין גָּזַל קוֹרָה וּבְנָאָהּ בְּבִירָה מַה יְּהֵא עָלֶיהָ[33], וְדִין גָּזַל בְּיִשּׁוּב וְרָצָה לְהַחֲזִיר בַּמִּדְבָּר[34],

---

Chinuch addresses to what extent one must go to return an item that he stole:

וְדִינֵי הַגְזֵלָה עַד הֵיכָן הוּא חַיָּב לִטְרֹחַ — This mitzvah includes **the law regarding** returning **a stolen item** לַהֲשִׁיבָהּ אֶל בְּעָלֶיהָ — with respect to **what extent he is obligated to exert himself to return it to its owner.** כְּמוֹ שֶׁאָמְרוּ רַבּוֹתֵינוּ זִכְרוֹנָם לִבְרָכָה — The law with regard to this is **as our Sages, of blessed memory, stated** (Bava Kamma 103a), הַגּוֹזֵל מֵחֲבֵרוֹ שָׁוֶה פְּרוּטָה שֶׁחַיָּב לְהוֹלִיכָהּ אַחֲרָיו אֲפִלּוּ לְמָדַי — **that one who steals from his fellow** something **worth** at least **a perutah, is obligated to bring it to him** wherever he may have gone, **even to Media,** כְּלוֹמַר לְמָקוֹם רָחוֹק — **that is to say, to a faraway place.**[31] וּכְדֵי לְהָקֵל טָרְחוֹ אִם הַהוֹצָאָה מְרֻבָּה — However, **so as to lessen his efforts if the expense** in doing so **is great,** אָמְרוּ רַבּוֹתֵינוּ זִכְרוֹנָם לִבְרָכָה שֶׁיַּנִּיחֶנָּה בְּיַד בֵּית דִּין — **our Sages, of blessed memory, have stated** (ibid.) **that [the thief] may leave it with** the local **beis din,** וִיוֹדִיעֵם שֶׁאוֹתוֹ מָמוֹן הוּא שֶׁל פְּלוֹנִי — **and inform them that that money belongs to So-and-so** (i.e., the robbed individual), וְהֵם יִתְּנוּהוּ לוֹ לִכְשֶׁיִּזְדַּמֵּן — **and they will give it to him when he presents himself** to beis din.[32]

Chinuch addresses other complications that can arise with respect to fulfilling the mitzvah to return the stolen item:

וְדִין גָּזַל קוֹרָה וּבְנָאָהּ בְּבִירָה מַה יְּהֵא עָלֶיהָ — Also included in this mitzvah is **the law regarding one who stole a beam and built it in a mansion,** namely, **what must be done with it.**[33]

וְדִין גָּזַל בְּיִשּׁוּב וְרָצָה לְהַחֲזִיר בַּמִּדְבָּר — **Also** included is **the law of one who stole** an object from

---

NOTES

despaired of recovering his item, the buyer has acquired it by way of *ye'ush* and *shinui reshus*. He must, however, reimburse the original owner the value of his item that remains in the buyer's possession, just as the thief himself — in a case where he acquired the item through an irreversible change — would have to reimburse the original owner its value.] The buyer is not entitled to relief under *takanas hashuk*, because the Sages only apply *takanas hashuk* to cases where the buyer can be said to be innocent; when buying from a known thief, however, the buyer loses his immunity, and the original owner can therefore demand compensation from him, forcing him to then go and demand reimbursement from the thief (*Rambam, Hil. Gezeilah* 5:7; *Tosafos, Bava Kamma* 115a ד״ה והלכתא; cf. *Tur* and *Rama, Choshen Mishpat* 353:3 quoting *Ri*; see, however, *Shach* ad loc. §6).

Others, however, take a different position, and apply *takanas hashuk* even to one who buys from a well-known thief, as long as he does not know that *this* particular item that he buys is a stolen one. In their opinion, the only time *takanas hashuk* does not apply (and the owner can seek remuneration from the buyer) is when the buyer knows that the item itself that he is buying is stolen property (*Rosh, Bava Kamma* 10:18; *Tur, Choshen Mishpat* 356:8, quoting *Ri*; see *Shulchan Aruch* and *Rama* ibid. 356:2).

31. Media, the northwest region of modern-day Iran, is simply an example of a faraway land. The obligation to travel so far to return the stolen item applies only in a case where the thief had sworn falsely, denying the theft and his monetary obligation to the one whom he had robbed (*Bava Kamma* 103a-b; *Rambam, Hil. Gezeilah* 7:9). If no such oath was made, the thief need not follow the owner to return the item, but merely informs him that he has his article (*Choshen Mishpat* 367:1; see *Pischei Choshen, Hil. Geneivah* 4:4 with notes for further discussion).

[When seeking atonement for a false oath such as this, the thief is required to return the principal about which he had lied, plus an additional fifth, and then bring an *asham* offering (see Mitzvah 129). This atonement process cannot begin without the thief first returning the stolen item (*Rashi, Bava Kamma* 103a ד״ה יוליכנו; see Mitzvah 129 note 9).]

Chinuch's failure to note this caveat of the false oath here is troubling, as noted by the commentators (*Hagahos Mishneh LaMelech*; *Minchas Chinuch* §9), as he seemingly applies this requirement to travel afar to all cases of theft.

32. This is another example of *takanas hashavim* (see note 22), wherein the Sages sought to make it easier for a thief to mend his ways (*Rashi* ibid. ד״ה לשליח ב״ד; *Rosh* ibid. 9:21; cf. *Tosafos* ד״ה אבל), for if he were forced to spend an exorbitant amount to return the item, he would likely be discouraged from doing so.

33. Although the beam has not undergone an irreversible transformation, and should by right be taken out

## VAYIKRA / MITZVAH 130: THE OBLIGATION TO RETURN A STOLEN ITEM

וְדִין גָּזַל וְהִקְדִּישׁ[35], וְגָזַל טָלֶה וְנַעֲשָׂה אַיִל מַה דִּינוֹ[36], וְדִין שֶׁבַח הַבָּא מֵחֲמַת יֹקֶר, שֶׁאֵינוֹ מִן הַתַּקָּנָה אֶלָּא חוֹזֵר לַנִּגְזָל[37], שֶׁלֹּא תִקְּנוּ לַגַּזְלָן אֶת הַשֶּׁבַח אַחַר יֵאוּשׁ אֶלָּא כְּגוֹן שֶׁבַח גִּזּוֹת וּוְלָדוֹת, אֲבָל שֶׁבַח הַיֹּקֶר לֹא.

וְדִין גָּזַל — its owner **in an inhabited place, but wishes to return it** to him **in the wilderness.**[34] וְהִקְדִּישׁ — **Also, the law regarding one who stole** an item and then **consecrated it to the Temple,**[35] וְגָזַל טָלֶה וְנַעֲשָׂה אַיִל מַה דִּינוֹ — **as well as what the law would be if one stole a lamb and it grew into a ram.**[36]

Chinuch returns to the subject of *takanas hashavim*, the enactment for those who wish to repent, and notes another exception to the laws of returning a stolen item:

וְדִין שֶׁבַח הַבָּא מֵחֲמַת יֹקֶר — This mitzvah includes **also the law of increases in valuation that are due to** market-value **appreciation,** שֶׁאֵינוֹ מִן הַתַּקָּנָה אֶלָּא חוֹזֵר לַנִּגְזָל — namely, **that [such increases] are not included in the enactment** to assist those who wish to repent, **but rather, [such increases] are returned to the robbed individual.**[37] שֶׁלֹּא תִקְּנוּ לַגַּזְלָן אֶת הַשֶּׁבַח אַחַר — יֵאוּשׁ אֶלָּא כְּגוֹן שֶׁבַח גִּזּוֹת וּוְלָדוֹת — This is **because [the Sages] enacted that the increase in value that occurs after** *ye'ush* is awarded to **the thief only** in situations of increases **that are similar to the increased value of shearings and offspring,** i.e., where a change in the stolen item itself caused the increased valuation. אֲבָל שֶׁבַח הַיֹּקֶר לֹא — **However, increased value due to** market-value **appreciation** is **not** included in the enactment.

---

### NOTES

of the structure and returned to its owner, the Sages exempted the thief from doing so. They allowed him to simply pay the beam's original value to the owner and leave it in place (Mishnah, *Gittin* 55a; *Rambam* ibid. 1:5). This, too, is part of the *takanas hashavim* (Mishnah ibid.), for if we required him to dismantle the building to return the beam, the thief would likely not do so and would never achieve atonement (*Rashi* ad loc. ד"ה מפני).

34. One who stole an object from its owner in an inhabited area may not force him to accept its repayment upon meeting him in an uninhabited area, such as a desert (Mishnah, *Bava Kamma* 118a). The nature of such uninhabited areas is such that it is difficult to safeguard the item (e.g., from loss or theft); therefore the owner may refuse to accept the repayment until they return to a safer environment (*Rashi* ad loc. ד"ה לא יחזיר; *Rambam* ibid. 1:7), even if that environment is not where the theft had occurred (*Tur* ibid. 366:4). Nevertheless, if the owner accepted repayment in the wilderness, he then becomes responsible for the item, and the thief is exempt from any further liability (*Beis Yosef* ad loc.).

35. If the thief consecrated the stolen item to the Temple (either as a sacrificial offering or as a donation to the Temple treasury) before the owner's *ye'ush*, the consecration is invalid, since one cannot consecrate something that is not his. If, however, the thief consecrated it after the owner's *ye'ush*, the consecration does take effect, for the act of declaring it consecrated effectively places the item under the auspices of the Temple — resulting in a *shinui reshus* (see *Bava Metzia* 6a). As we have seen above, *ye'ush* and *shinui reshus* work in tandem to effect a transfer of ownership, and hence the consecration takes effect (*Bava Kamma* 68b and *Rashi* to 76a ד"ה כי קא טבח; *Rambam, Hil. Geneivah* 2:6-7).

In all cases, the one from whom the item was stolen cannot consecrate the item, as it is not under his control, but rather is in the thief's domain (ibid.). It is derived from Scripture that in order to be able to consecrate an item, one must have both *control* and *ownership* over it (see *Bava Kamma* 68b and 69b).

36. In such a case, the thief acquires the animal, and need not return it, due to the fundamental change it has undergone. He simply returns its original monetary value as of the time of the theft (*Rambam, Hil. Gezeilah* 2:14; cf. *Rashi, Bava Kamma* 65b ד"ה נעשה שינוי with *Pnei Yehoshua*).

Some explain that this is yet another example of an irreversible physical change, much like wood into which holes were bored or wool that was dyed, which Chinuch discussed above (see note 8). Here too, the animal has undergone a significant physical change by growing into a ram (*Yam Shel Shlomo, Bava Kamma* 7:5; *Beur HaGra, Choshen Mishpat* 353:1). Others, however, maintain that this is an example of a new type of change — an irreversible "change in name" [שִׁנּוּי הַשֵּׁם], since the animal is no longer called a lamb but rather a ram. Such irreversible name changes have the same effect as an irreversible physical change (*Rosh, Bava Kamma*, end of 7:2; *Tur* ibid. 353:1; *Shach* ad loc. §1). According to either approach, the thief will acquire the item irrespective of whether *ye'ush* has occurred (see above, note 6).

37. Even if the increase occurs after the owner's *ye'ush*, the item must be returned as is — with its higher valuation. As Chinuch will explain, it is not subject to the *takanas hashavim* that at times allows a thief to keep the increase in value (*Rambam, Hil. Gezeilah* 2:16; *Tur* and *Shulchan Aruch* ibid. 362:10; cf. *Yam Shel Shlomo* 7:7 and *Shach*).

וְדִין תּוֹקֵף עֶבֶד חֲבֵרוֹ וְעָשָׂה בּוֹ מְלָאכָה,[38] וְדִין תּוֹקֵף סְפִינָתוֹ,[39] וְדִין הַדָּר בַּחֲצַר חֲבֵרוֹ שֶׁלֹּא מִדַּעְתּוֹ.[40] וְיֶתֶר פְּרָטֶיהָ מְבֹאָרִין בַּפְּרָקִים הָאַחֲרוֹנִים מִן קַמָּא.[41]

וְנוֹהֶגֶת בְּכָל מָקוֹם וּבְכָל זְמַן בִּזְכָרִים וּבִנְקֵבוֹת.[42] וְעוֹבֵר עָלֶיהָ וְגָזַל וְלֹא הֵשִׁיב בִּטֵּל עֲשֵׂה זֶה, מִלְּבַד הַלָּאו שֶׁעָבַר בִּשְׁעַת גְּזֵלָה. וְאוֹי לוֹ לְמִי שֶׁבְּיָדוֹ לְתַקֵּן הַמְּעֻוָּת וְאֵינוֹ מְתַקְּנוֹ טֶרֶם מוֹתוֹ.[43]

---

Chinuch references laws regarding theft of usage — i.e., stealing the use of another's property, and what the obligation to return that which was stolen demands in such situations: וְדִין תּוֹקֵף עֶבֶד חֲבֵרוֹ וְעָשָׂה בּוֹ מְלָאכָה — Included, **as well, is the law of one who seizes the Canaanite slave of his fellow and has [the slave] perform work** for him,[38] וְדִין תּוֹקֵף סְפִינָתוֹ — **and the law of one who seizes [his fellow's] boat**,[39] וְדִין הַדָּר בַּחֲצַר חֲבֵרוֹ שֶׁלֹּא מִדַּעְתּוֹ — **and the law of one who lives in his fellow's** house in his **courtyard without his knowledge.**[40] וְיֶתֶר פְּרָטֶיהָ מְבֹאָרִין בַּפְּרָקִים הָאַחֲרוֹנִים מִן קַמָּא — These laws **and the additional details of [this mitzvah] are set forth in the final chapters of** Tractate **Bava Kamma.**[41]

### ~ Applicability of the Mitzvah ~

וְנוֹהֶגֶת בְּכָל מָקוֹם וּבְכָל זְמַן בִּזְכָרִים וּבִנְקֵבוֹת — **[This mitzvah] applies in every location and in all times to** both men and women.[42]
וְעוֹבֵר עָלֶיהָ וְגָזַל וְלֹא הֵשִׁיב בִּטֵּל עֲשֵׂה זֶה — **One who transgresses [this mitzvah] by stealing and not** subsequently **returning** the stolen item **has violated this** mitzvah-**obligation.** מִלְּבַד הַלָּאו שֶׁעָבַר בִּשְׁעַת גְּזֵלָה — **This is aside from the prohibition that he violated at the time of the theft.** וְאוֹי לוֹ לְמִי שֶׁבְּיָדוֹ לְתַקֵּן הַמְּעֻוָּת וְאֵינוֹ מְתַקְּנוֹ טֶרֶם מוֹתוֹ — **Woe is to he who had the ability to correct the wrong** that he had committed, **but did not correct it before his death!**[43]

---

NOTES

38. Someone who takes another person's slave to do work for him without the owner's permission has violated the prohibition of robbery (*Rambam, Hil. Gezeilah* 1:3). Nevertheless, if the slave had no work to do for his master at that time, the thief need not pay anything for the work — for the owner is content that his slave not become accustomed to being idle (*Bava Kamma* 97a with *Rashi* ד"ה דלא נסתרי). If, however, the slave would have been working for his master during that time, the thief must pay the owner as per the going rate of a laborer (*Rambam* ibid. 3:7).

39. As in the previous case, making use of someone's property without the owner's permission is an act of robbery. The amount the thief will have to pay the owner depends on, among other considerations, whether this boat was meant to be rented out or not. For details, see *Bava Kamma* 97a; *Rambam* ibid 3:8; *Sma, Choshen Mishpat* 363:12.

40. One who dwells in the home of his fellow without having received permission to do so is liable to pay for the rental value of that home, if the home is normally rented out. If, however, the home is not generally rented out, then the squatter need not pay. This is an example of זֶה נֶהֱנֶה וְזֶה לֹא חָסֵר, *this one* (i.e., the squatter) *gains and that one* (i.e., the owner) *does not lose*, where there is no liability (*Bava Kamma* 21a; *Rambam* ibid. 3:9). Even in such situations, though, if the squatter caused even minimal damage to the home, it cannot be said that the owner has not incurred a loss, and the squatter will have to pay the rental value of the home (*Maggid Mishneh* ad loc.; *Tur* ibid. 363:7). Furthermore, if the owner initially objected to the squatter's presence, then even if the home is not a rental property, the squatter is liable to pay its rental value (*Tur* ibid. 363:6).

41. I.e., Chapters 7-10. Other laws pertaining to stealing and returning stolen items are cited by Chinuch in Mitzvos 224 and 229. These laws are codified in *Rambam, Hilchos Gezeilah* Chs. 1-5, 7-8, and in *Shulchan Aruch, Choshen Mishpat* 353-356, 360-367.

42. I.e., in Eretz Yisrael and the Diaspora, and whether the Beis HaMikdash is standing or not. It applies to women, as well, in accordance with the general rule regarding mitzvah-obligations that are not time-specific.

43. Moreover, neither Yom Kippur nor repentance will provide atonement for sins that one committed against his fellow, until he appeases him (Mishnah, *Yoma* 85b). Therefore, one who has committed a sin that requires him to make restitution to the victim (e.g., stealing, damaging his property or person, etc.) will not attain forgiveness vis-à-vis Heaven until he makes restitution and seeks the forgiveness of the person whom he had wronged (*Rambam, Hil. Teshuvah* 2:9).

### ◈§ Insight: The Exemption From Returning Stolen Goods Worth Less Than a Perutah

While it is prohibited to steal any amount of money or an object of any value, the mitzvah to return a stolen item applies only to goods that are worth at least a *perutah* at the time of the theft (see above, note 11). Chinuch explains that when the stolen object is worth less than a *perutah*, its value is so insignificant that the owner is assumed to have forgiven its repayment. He effectively releases the thief from having to return it.

*Minchas Chinuch* (§4) notes that although this explanation seems to be borne out by the Gemara (see *Sanhedrin* 57a with *Rashi* ד"ה צערא), *Rambam* makes no mention of it. Rather, *Rambam* (*Hilchos Gezeilah* 2:6) states simply that such small amounts are not subject to the mitzvah of returning stolen items. *Rambam* (as explained by *Minchas Chinuch*; see also *Machaneh Ephraim, Hil. Gezeilah* §1, and his son's comment there) seemingly views this as a standard exemption related to *shiurim* (measurements), wherein stolen goods that are worth less than a *perutah* — the minimal threshold vis-à-vis value — are simply below the minimal threshold of the mitzvah. That is, the mitzvah to return stolen property presupposes that there is value in the property that is to be returned, and if there is no such value, the mitzvah simply does not take effect. In short, then, Chinuch exempts repayment of less than a *perutah* because the owner has forgiven the debt, while *Rambam* exempts repayment because the amount is too low for it to be considered a debt altogether, as less than a *perutah* is simply not viewed as having value.

*Minchas Chinuch* notes many practical differences between these two approaches: If the exemption from returning items worth less than a *perutah* is based on the owner forgiving its repayment, as Chinuch states, then in cases where such forgiveness is lacking — such as where the owner explicitly states that he has not relinquished his rights — the thief would indeed be obligated to return the stolen item (see, however, *Levush, Choshen Mishpat* 6:1). The same would apply where forgiveness is simply not possible, such as where the owner is a minor who does not have the legal maturity to forgive money that he is owed. If, on the other hand, money less than a *perutah* is simply below the threshold of value, then even in these cases, the thief would be exempt from having to return the stolen item.

Another fundamental distinction between the two approaches is with regard to whether the thief gains ownership of the stolen item. If the exemption regarding less than a *perutah's* worth is based on the owner having forgiven repayment, it emerges that the owner has effectively granted the thief ownership of the stolen item, and it becomes his. If, however, the stolen goods have simply not reached the minimal threshold of value to be subject to this mitzvah, then although the thief need not return the item, it cannot be said to have become his, for there is no mechanism by which he would have legally acquired it from the owner.

This distinction of whether or not the item now belongs to the thief opens up a number of other practical differences between the two approaches. Consider a case where the stolen item was worth less than a *perutah* but subsequently increases in value and is now worth a *perutah*. According to Chinuch's approach that the owner relinquished his rights to the thief, since it was already considered the thief's it will remain his — even though it is now worth more than a *perutah*. But according to *Rambam's* approach that the owner retains ownership throughout, when it goes up in value to a *perutah* or more, the thief may well be obligated to return it (see *Machaneh Ephraim, Hil. Gezeilah* §1 ד"ה הן אמת).

Another practical difference would be if the stolen item is one of the four species taken on Succos (e.g., a willow branch), where the halachah is that on the first day of Yom Tov [as well as the second day in the Diaspora] the items must belong to the one taking them (*Shulchan Aruch, Orach Chaim* 658:3; a stolen item may actually be invalid throughout Succos — see ibid. 641:1 for the particulars). Now, if the original owner has relinquished his rights, the thief would fulfill his mitzvah of taking the four species. If, however, the thief is merely discharged from his obligation to return it, he cannot fulfill the mitzvah with this item, even though it is worth less than a *perutah*. [See *Tos. Rid, Succah* 41b, who states that one does not fulfill his mitzvah with such stolen items; see also *Sma, Choshen Mishpat* 367:7 and *Derishah* ad loc.] For further discussion of these issues, see *Pischei Choshen, Hil. Geneivah* 1:1 and 4:28 with footnotes.

Until this point, we have been discussing the exemption from returning stolen goods worth less than a *perutah*, but as Chinuch noted above, while one is not liable to return less than a *perutah*, the

original act of taking such goods from their owner is unquestionably forbidden. This is reminiscent of the type of behavior that was characteristic of the generation of the Great Flood, among whom such minimal acts of taking were rampant. *Midrash Rabbah* (*Noach* 31:5) relates how in that era a vendor would bring his basket full of vegetables to market and each person would take one small vegetable worth less than a *perutah*. In no time at all, the vendor's inventory was depleted, with no recourse to collect from the myriad of thieves, for each had taken less than a *perutah*.

[There is, however, an exception of note: If one takes a very small item that no person cares about, it is not considered theft (*Rashba, Bava Kamma* 105a ד"ה אע"פ; *Maggid Mishnah, Hil. Gezeilah* 1:2). Thus, for example, one who takes a splinter from someone else's wooden fence, to use as a toothpick or the like, has not violated the prohibition of theft. Nevertheless, *Yerushalmi* (*Demai* 3:2) states that pious individuals would avoid such behavior (see *Shulchan Aruch, Choshen Mishpat* 359:1), for if everyone who walked by the fence were to do the same, there would eventually be no fence left at all.]